Paul's Second Epistle to the Corinthians

Other books in the BYU New Testament Commentary series

The Gospel according to Mark by Julie M. Smith

The Testimony of Luke by S. Kent Brown

The Epistle to the Ephesians by S. Kent Brown

Epistle to the Hebrews by Richard D. Draper and Michael D. Rhodes

Paul's First Epistle to the Corinthians
by Richard D. Draper and Michael D. Rhodes

The Revelation of John the Apostle
by Richard D. Draper and Michael D. Rhodes

Paul's Second Epistle to the Corinthians

Brigham Young University
New Testament Commentary

Richard D. Draper
and
Michael D. Rhodes

BYU Studies
Provo, Utah

This Commentary Series is made possible by a generous gift from John S. and Unita W. Welch.

Published by BYU Studies. To contact any member of the board of editors or BYU Studies, write to 1063 JFSB, Brigham Young University, Provo, Utah, 84602, or visit https://byustudies.byu.edu or http://www.byunewtestamentcommentary.com.

Cover images courtesy John W. Welch

First time in print. Substantive corrections, additions, questions, or comments may be sent to byu_studies@byu.edu.

Library of Congress Cataloging-in-Publication Data

Names: Draper, Richard D., author. | Rhodes, Michael D., 1946- author.
Title: Paul's Second Epistle to the Corinthians / Richard D. Draper and Michael D. Rhodes.
Other titles: Bible. Corinthians, 2nd. English. Draper and Rhodes. 2023. | New Testament commentary (Brigham Young University)
Description: Provo, Utah : BYU Studies, [2023] | Series: Brigham Young University New Testament commentary series | Includes bibliographical references and index. | Summary: "A verse-by-verse commentary on the New Testament book of Second Corinthians. Provides a modern English version of the text. Cites scriptures of The Church of Jesus Christ of Latter-day Saints (Mormons). Paul's letter to fellow Christians centers on Jesus Christ and the need for Christians to be united in His gospel. It also contains Paul's defense of his ministry"-- Provided by publisher.
Identifiers: LCCN 2023028217 | ISBN 9781958854013 (hardcover) | ISBN 9781958854020 (ebook)
Subjects: LCSH: Bible. Corinthians, 2nd--Commentaries.
Classification: LCC BS2675.3 .D73 2023 | DDC 227/.207--dc23/eng/20230722
LC record available at https://lccn.loc.gov/2023028217

Printed in the United States of America
10 9 8 7 6 5 4 3 2 1

About the Brigham Young University New Testament Commentary Series

Welcome to the BYU New Testament Commentary, a project by a group of Latter-day Saint specialists offering to readers a careful, new look at the biblical records that witness the life and ministry of Jesus Christ and the first generation of his church. The commentary series seeks to make the New Testament more accessible to Latter-day Saint general readers and scholars by employing much of current biblical scholarship while reflecting important LDS insights. At the same time, this effort may also be helpful to interested readers of other faiths who want to learn how a group of Latter-day Saint scholars understands the Bible. A fundamental article of faith for Latter-day Saints (Mormons) affirms the Bible "to be the word of God" while adding, understandably, that it needs to be "translated correctly" in order for it to be accurately comprehendible to modern language speakers.

These objectives have helped shape the purposes and parameters of this commentary series. Serious LDS readers of the Bible search the scriptures, looking for depth and breadth in passages whose meanings and mandates may ultimately be plain but not shallow. Such readers and interpreters are served by treatments that unite faith and research, reason and revelation, in prayerfully confronting profound and difficult issues that arise in the texts and affect one's path of progression. The New Testament has served as an influential guide to western civilization for centuries. As such, its records have long been studied by lay people and scholars alike, resulting in a rich reservoir of information that illuminates the New Testament era culturally, historically, and linguistically. Selectively, the BYUNTC builds upon this vast body of knowledge, resting on the Greek texts of the New Testament and connecting helpful elements of linguistic, literary, historical, and cultural research and traditional scholarship together with LDS scriptures and doctrinal perspectives. The combination of all these features distinguishes the BYUNTC from other commentaries, which are readily available elsewhere and which readers may also want to consult for more encyclopedic or specialized discussions.

The tone of the BYUNTC aims to be informative rather than hortatory, and suggestive rather than definitive in its interpretation. The opinions expressed in this series are the views of its contributors and should not necessarily be attributed to The Church of Jesus Christ of Latter-day Saints; Brigham Young University, where many of those involved here are headquartered; or anyone else, though these works have benefitted from input and guidance from a number of colleagues, advisors, editors, and peer reviewers.

Each volume in this series sets in two parallel columns the King James Version (KJV) and a new working translation of the New Testament. Calling this a new "rendition" clarifies that it does not seek to replace the authorized KJV adopted by the Church of Jesus Christ as its official English text. Rather, it aims to enhance readers' understanding conceptually and spiritually by rendering the Greek texts into modern English with LDS sensitivities in mind. Comparing and explaining the New Rendition in light of the KJV then serves as one important purpose for each volume's notes, comments, analyses, and summaries. This effort responds in modest ways to the desire President J. Reuben Clark Jr. expressed in his diary in 1956 that someday "qualified scholars [would provide] . . . a translation of the New Testament that will give us an accurate translation that shall be pregnant with the great principles of the Restored Gospel."

Depending on their personal skills and interests, the authors of these volumes approach their scholarly sources and LDS materials differently but always with careful exposition and engaging perspectives. In several ways, they employ various interpretive tools, including semantic considerations of Greek vocabulary; cultural, historical, critical, literary, and structural analyses; and intertextual comparisons with other biblical passages, the Book of Mormon, and other scriptural works including the Joseph Smith Translation of the Bible. Observations are also proffered about the doctrinal and spiritual reception of New Testament teachings and practices in the broad LDS religious tradition.

The format also varies moderately from volume to volume regarding introductory materials and the style of commentary. Throughout, Greek and Hebrew terms appear in transliterated form in conformity with standards adopted by the Society of Biblical Literature. In some cases, a volume reproduces the Greek New Testament text based on the Greek text published by the Society of Biblical Literature (2010) or draws upon the twenty-eighth edition of the Nestle-Aland text in *Novum Testamentum Graece* (2012).

Contents

Abbreviations

For ancient works, the footnotes follow the style of Patrick H. Alexander and others, *The SBL Handbook of Style for Ancient Near Eastern Biblical and Early Christian Studies* (Peabody, Mass.: Hendrickson Publishers, 1999).

ABD Freedman, David Noel, ed. *The Anchor Bible Dictionary.* 6 vols. New York: Doubleday, 1992.

BAGD Arndt, William F., and F. Wilbur Gingrich, ed. *A Greek-English Lexicon of the New Testament and Other Early Christian Literature.* 2d ed. Chicago: University of Chicago Press, 1957.

BDAG Danker, Frederick William, ed. *A Greek-English Lexicon of the New Testament and Other Early Christian Literature.* 3rd ed. Chicago: University of Chicago Press, 2000.

BDB Brown, Francis, S. R. Driver, and Charles A. Briggs. *A Hebrew and English Lexicon of the Old Testament.* Corrected ed. Oxford: Clarendon Press, 1976.

BDF Blass, F., and A. Debrunner. *A Greek Grammar of the New Testament and Other Early Christian Literature.* Trans. and ed. Robert W. Funk. Chicago, University of Chicago Press, 1961.

D&C Doctrine and Covenants. Salt Lake City: Church of Jesus Christ of Latter-day Saints, 1981.

DAG Montanari, Franco. *The Brill Dictionary of Ancient Greek.* Ed. Madeleine Goh and Chad Schroeder. Leiden: Brill, 2015.

DNTC McConkie, Bruce R. *Doctrinal New Testament Commentary.* 3 vols. Salt Lake City: Bookcraft, 1965–73.

EM Ludlow, Daniel H., ed. *Encyclopedia of Mormonism.* 4 vols. New York: Macmillan, 1992.

HAL Köhler, L., W. Baumgartner, and J. J. Stamm. *The Hebrew and Aramaic Lexicon of the Old Testament.* Trans. and ed. M. E. J. Richardson. 5 vols. Leiden: E. J. Brill, 1994–2000.

JD *Journal of Discourses.* 26 vols. London: Latter-day Saints Book Depot, 1854–86.

JST Joseph Smith Translation of the Bible.

KJV King James Version of the Bible.

LSJ Liddell, Henry G., and Robert Scott, comp. *Greek English Lexicon.* Rev. and aug. Henry Stuart Jones. Oxford: Clarendon Press, 1968.

LXX Septuagint version of the Old Testament.

MM Moulton, James H., and George Milligan. *The Vocabulary of the Greek Testament: Illustrations from the Papyri and Other Non-literary Sources.* 1930. Rpt., Grand Rapids, Mich.: William B. Eerdmans, 1985.

NID Silva, Moisés. *New International Dictionary of New Testament Theology and Exegesis.* 5 vols. Grand Rapids, Mich.: Zondervan, 2014.

NIV New International Version.

NR New Rendition.

NRSV New Revised Standard Version.

SCI Liddle, Stephen W., and Richard C. Galbraith. Scripture Citation Index. Version 3.5.0. https://scriptures.byu.edu.

TDNT Kittel, Gerhard, and Gerhard Freidrich, eds. *Theological Dictionary of the New Testament.* Trans. Geoffery W. Bromiley. 10 vols. Grand Rapids, Mich.: Wm. B. Eerdmans, 1964–76.

TDOT Botterweck, G. Johannes, Helmer Ringgren, and Heinz-Josef Fabry, eds. *Theological Dictionary of the Old Testament.* Trans. David E. Green. 17 vols. Grand Rapids: William B. Eerdmans, 1974–2021.

Preface

The nascent Christian community did not develop in a vacuum. It matured in a specific historical and multicultural sphere, one interestingly not particularly favorable for its growth and advancement. The Christian movement developed around neither philosophical nor theological constructs but through events that took place between 6 BC and AD 100 that affected the first through third generations of converts. During that period, they came to understand who they worshiped, including both how and why. In the process, they discovered who they were as a people, what their belief system consisted of, and how they were to apply those beliefs in the world they lived in. The foundation of their faith was Jesus Christ, and the structure of that faith was his teachings. However, the doctrines that grew out of his teachings developed line by line, here a little and there a little, as inspiration and revelation came and understanding increased. The Savior gave the responsibility for the doctrinal development and its practical application to the apostles and prophets. In so doing, he kept the responsibility within the bounds of those who had his personal authority to declare his word and perform his ordinances. These authorized followers met with many challenges and worked diligently to overcome them. One of the ways they did so was through the power of the epistle.

Written texts could do what the individual could not, namely reach across distances and bring instruction to disparate congregations. Admittedly, personal visits were imperative, but written communications conveyed teachings and instructions in a way that could be shared broadly and lay the groundwork that made the visits even more productive. Further, at least initially, on these letters rested the institutional memory the Christian community. One of the major responsibilities of these leaders, then, was to teach the doctrine of the kingdom. Paramount among the teachings was detailing the importance of the life, ministry, work, and identity of the Savior. Among those who took up this remarkable if somewhat overwhelming task was the Apostle Paul.

Our primary audience, as we explore his works, is the educated Latter-day Saint who wishes to distill more from the text than one can usually get from more popular and less extensive works. Though we are aware of the many scholarly debates and issues that abound in New Testament studies, because of who our primary audience is, we have chosen not to become mired in the technical issues. Thus, we have not directed our efforts to the advanced student or those seeking a graduate level of study, but we have placed, in the footnotes, references not only to the authorities we use but also to discussions and arguments that some readers may be interested in exploring but that go beyond the reach of this study.

Having noted that, we must say that the Translation Notes and Comments are of necessity more technical than the Analysis and Summary Sections. This is because we wish both the Latter-day Saint and non–Latter-day Saint reader to understand both how and why we rendered a word, phrase, or verse the way we have. Even here, we are careful not to overly use specialized technical grammatical terms unless these are necessary in interpreting and understanding the meaning of a word or phrase.

Some words and phrases are loaded theological implications, nuances, and ramifications. Many have both denotative and connotative properties that both deserve and demand exploration and the plumbing of their depths. Though rendering the Greek into English demands that a specific word be used, the value of this (as well as any) commentary is that it allows the full range of a word or phrase's meaning to be noted and explored, thus allowing the reader to get a feel for a range of meanings and better understand the depth or breadth of importance that the word or phrase carries.

In this, the preserved second epistle to the Corinthians, Paul wrote again to a certain body of Christians who continued to face specific problems. Every word, phrase, and sentence that he wrote had both a historical and a social context. He wrote to his fellow Saints in a language that they could understand, and he did so with force, insight, power, and love.

Paul's purpose is the starting point of our work. We have tried diligently and to the highest degree possible to capture the thrust and trajectory of his ideas so the modern reader can understand the writings of this deeply spiritual and profoundly insightful leader in their context. We spend little time addressing the relevance of the Apostle's writings to the modern reader. That is not to say we believe any relevance is absent. It is there! The author's writings contain insights, instructions, and admonitions that are grounded in revelation and testimony that transcends time and culture and therefore can meaningfully address similar conditions and situations met by the modern Saint.

Our focus, however, as noted above, is on understanding the text as the author and his readers understood it. We fully believe that one of the most important purposes of scripture is for the application of those who read it. But we also feel that when a text is understood in its context, it can then be better applied to conditions today. Otherwise, it is possible to give a passage a greater significance or make it have a different application than the original text warranted or the author intended.

The Book of Mormon does encourage its readers to "liken all scriptures" unto themselves that these timeless teachings might be for their "profit and learning" (1 Ne. 19:23), but it also warns that it is possible for people to "wrest [the scriptures] to [their] own destruction" (Alma 13:9). Likewise, as the Doctrine and Covenants points out, many err because "they do wrest the scriptures and do not understand them" (D&C 10:63). Placing a scripture in its context mitigates this problem. It is our hope that by placing the scriptures in their theological, historical, social, and cultural settings, modern readers can readily see their relevance and desire to apply the principles and doctrines in their lives. Believing that to be the case, we leave it up to the readers to make the proper application. When that happens, the underlying intent and primary motivation behind our writing of this commentary will be realized.

All in all, our work is designed neither to be all inclusive nor definitive but tentative and suggestive. We expect and hope that others will come along who will improve our work. In the meantime, we hope we have laid a firm foundation and put up a solid scaffolding that they can use to continue to build an ever better understanding of God's word as revealed through his New Testament apostles and prophets.

Due to the complexity of this work, we have called upon many to assist us, and to them we give our heartfelt thanks. Our praises go out to a bevy of Brigham Young University research assistants, particularly Hanna Searic, who not only helped the project move along but supplied much needed material and assistance. We also appreciate the source checkers, Lane Welch, Tina Hawley, Susanna Bergeson Dimig, Taylor Crofts, Julia Harrison, Sydney Gee, and Marny K. Parkin, who made this volume as accurate as possible. Our thanks also go out to Julianne Nelson, who read the full text for clarity, cohesion, and comprehension. To Professor Brent J. Schmidt, we are particularly indebted for his insights and helpful suggestions on both our rendering of the Greek passages and presentation of the Greco-Roman and Second Temple Jewish cultures in which the epistle was written. Finally, we give thanks to our wives, whose enthusiasm and support for our work has been most gratifying and encouraging.

Throughout this study, we have sought to faithfully interpret the Greek into English, to be in harmony with the doctrines of The Church of Jesus Christ of Latter-day Saints, to follow teachings found in the standard works of the Restoration, and to accurately represent to all readers the powerful testimony of Paul's Second Epistle to the Corinthians. Even so, the assertions, conclusions, and the overall work represent our own thinking and not that of the Church, BYU Studies, Brigham Young University, or any of those associated with this work.

Richard D. Draper
Michael D. Rhodes

Introduction

The Relevance of Paul's Writing for the Modern Disciple

This epistle commends itself to all who take Paul seriously and see in his writings the inspiration of the Holy Spirit. The Apostle promotes a practical religion that translates into everyday actions and conduct both in his time and in ours. He stresses the importance of forgiving others (2:10), being hopeful and encouraging in trying circumstances (4:8–10), recognizing that affliction for the kingdom's sake is the Church's true glory (4:8–10, 16–18; 6:3–10), and being glad to suffer for God's cause (12:8–10). He notes the need to walk by faith and not by sight while the Christians suffer through mortality (5:7). He also encourages the Saints to be anxiously engaged in pleasing God (5:9) and warns them against being mismatched with unyielding and hardened unbelievers, even insisting that they separate themselves from such (6:14–17). He admonishes them to do what they can to take care of the poor in the kingdom (chaps. 8, 9). He cautions Church members about being overly eager to defend themselves against those who attack them but also insists that there are times when a strong defense is called for, especially when the integrity of the gospel has been challenged (chaps. 10, 11). Thus, the Apostle preaches a practical religion that is still applicable here and now.

Furthermore, he never loses sight of the eternal consequences of gospel living that modern disciples must also keep in mind. God designed such living to buoy them up and strengthen them during this time of trial and preparation. Paul's primary push is one of reconciliation between God and the sinner such that the sinner is transformed into a Saint (5:18–21). He witnesses that all will eventually appear before the judgment seat of Christ to receive full compensation for their actions, whether good or ill (5:10). Thus, he stresses the need for his readers to cleanse themselves from every defilement of the body and to make holiness complete through their fear of God (7:1). Indeed, he insists that the gospel is the fragrance of life leading to life (2:16) and notes that it is through Christ that the Saint is changed from one degree of glory (the earthly) to another degree of glory (the heavenly) (3:18). He explains that this little moment of affliction God has designed to prepare his people for an eternal weight of glory that is beyond comparison (4:17). And what makes eternal life possible? It is the ability of the Saints to see through the eye of faith beyond the transient moment to the unseen reality of the celestial world (4:18). Thus, they are to live so that what is mortal may be swallowed up in eternal life (5:4). These principles, along with the admonition that grows out of them, are as true today as they were in Paul's day.

The Integrity of the Work

Due to its internal evidence and wide circulation, from the earliest period the Christian community has accepted 2 Corinthians as an authentic epistle of the Apostle Paul. Among modern scholars, however, it is unique in that it is the only one that some have suggested is actually a composition of pieces of at least two if not more different letters. Because the flow of the epistle seems to break at 6:14 through 7:1, not only from Paul's usual rhetorical style but also introducing strong tones of early Jewish polemic, some scholars have argued that, at some point, someone inserted this material into a copy of the epistle. Many of these same scholars see an abrupt break in the flow between Paul's account of his delightful and informative meeting with Titus (8:16–24) and the epistle's discussion of the collection being made to benefit the Jerusalem Saints (8:1–15; 9:1–15). Some break this section down even further, noting that there seem to be two discrete arguments presented here, and suggest wrongly that, again, at some later point, someone inserted these two independent pieces into the text. Finally, they argue that the strident tone by which Paul defends himself in 2 Corinthians 10–13 is inconsistent with the character and language of the former portion of the epistle. They note particularly that in these chapters the harshness of his tone clashes with the conciliatory language in 7:5–16 that suggests a full reconciliation between the Apostle and the Corinthian Saints. Further, the last section seems to be a reversal of Paul's double insistence that he will not commend himself to his readers (3:1; 5:12), which he does to a very great extent in the last three chapters. In all, some insist that at some point in the past, someone joined as many as five discrete letter fragments together, thus making up the epistle as we have it today.[1]

That the current document may be a composition of several fragments pieced together at some point in the past is not beyond question. It is possible that, out of respect for Paul, certain Saints preserved fragments of his work which someone (at a later date) compiled into this rather short letter. However, such a scenario seems tenuous at best, especially when one takes Paul's rather clamorous relationship with the Corinthians into account. Indeed, a stark piece of evidence against the notion of compilation is that, as it stands, the letter has one major theme—Paul's defense of his authority and doctrine—that runs from beginning to end, uniting all the pieces. Given the tension between Paul and the Corinthian Saints and the pall it casts over them, it is a wonder anyone decided to preserve the epistle at all, let alone fragments. "The notion that a letter that was instrumental in cementing the bond between the church and apostle would be subject to a scissors-and-and paste operation, even at a later time, is difficult to imagine. The burden of proof surely lies upon any theory of a composite letter."[2] From the beginning of the Restoration to the present, Latter-day Saint leaders have assumed the integrity of this epistle; none of them, therefore, have addressed this question.

---

1. Richard Neitzel Holzapfel and Thomas A. Wayment, *Making Sense of the New Testament: Timely Insights and Timeless Messages* (Salt Lake City: Deseret Book, 2010), 368–69; Thomas A. Wayment, *From Persecutor to Apostle: A Biography of Paul* (Salt Lake City: Deseret Book, 2006), 177; Mark A. Seifrid, *The Second Letter to the Corinthians* (Grand Rapids, Mich.: William B. Eerdmans; Cambridge, UK: Apollos, 2014), xxix–xxxi. For overviews of the various studies dealing with this subject, see B. K. Peterson, *Eloquence and the Proclamation of the Gospel in Corinth* (Atlanta: Scholars Press, 1998), 39–51; and particularly the extensive work by Murray J. Harris, *The Second Epistle to the Corinthians: A Commentary on the Greek Text* (Grand Rapids, Mich.: William B. Eerdmans, 2005), 8–51.

2. Seifrid, *Second Letter,* xxx. For a good overview dealing with the integrity of the work see Hans Dieter Betz, *2 Corinthians 8 and 9: A Commentary on Two Administrative Letters of the Apostle Paul,* ed. George W. MacRae, Hermenia (Philadelphia: Fortress Press, 1985), 27–35. Gert J. C. Jordaan, "A Hypothesis for the Composition History of Paul's Second Letter to the Corinthians," *In die Skriflig* 48, no. 2 (2014): 1–9, argues that instead of 2 Corinthians being an amalgamation of different Pauline letters, it was actually written by Paul over an extended period of time as he traveled from Ephesus to Corinth during his third missionary journey. Tackling the arguments preferred by various scholars suggesting that the epistle is a compilation, Jordaan insists on the letter's overall coherence and that its awkward transitions can be easily satisfied by understanding that Paul's composing the letter over the course of his journey.

Reading the letter in its context suggests that any ostensible inconsistency or incoherence is based more on appearance than reality. Given the circumstances in which this letter was dashed off (see below), the coherent rhetoric that one finds throughout the epistle is quite remarkable. The material in each of the apparent interruptions actually fits within the whole given the thrust of Paul's argument. That argument, as he develops it in 6:14–7:1, follows both the language and form of Jewish polemics and not only anticipates but prepares his readers for the pointed, even heated, language of 10–13. One trained, as Paul had been, would have found that kind of argument not only easy to produce but also fully effective for his purposes.[3]

As will be developed more fully below, the section dealing with Titus's role in the collection for the Jewish Saints in Jerusalem, rather than being an interruption, pushes the theme of the epistle.[4] Paul's aim is first to cement his position as an authentic Apostle of the Lord among the Corinthians. Secondarily, he seeks to bind these branches to the larger Christian community, especially those found in Jerusalem and the surrounding area. This is exactly what the collection would do. Thus, to reinforce the success of Titus's visit, Paul's admonition for these Saints to complete their promised contribution seems perfectly natural. That being the case, the unusual inverted form of the admonition found in 8–9 (wherein the exhortation to give is followed by the theology of giving) actually reflects the current situation. Paul's readers have, under his direction, for a number of months, been enthusiastically gathering materials and goods for the poverty-stricken Jewish Saints. Thus, he can say in 9:1, "For now indeed it is unnecessary for me to write to you concerning this ministering to the saints" (NR). That he now gives them further instructions on how to prepare the offering for his coming, though

3. Seifrid, *Second Letter,* xxx; Richard Lloyd Anderson, *Understanding Paul* (Salt Lake City: Deseret Book, 1983), 131–32.

4. See Troels Engberg-Pedersen, "The Unity of 2 Corinthians as Reflected in the Account of Paul's and Titus' Travels between Ephesus, Macedonia and Corinth and the Theology of 2:14–7:4" (paper presented at the Society of Biblical Literature Annual Meeting, San Francisco, California, November 19, 2011), who argues that the references to Paul's and Titus's journeys through 2 Corinthians demonstrates its unity. He shows how chapters 1:1–7:16 form a coherent story surrounding Paul's travels to Macedonia and search for Titus that argues for this section's integrity. Then chapters 8–9 show Titus's journey to Corinth. And finally, chapters 10–13 then show Paul's preparation to go to Corinth that is connected with the journey he discusses in 8–9. In sum, Paul's scheme of using his and Titus's travels in relation to Corinthians binds the whole document together.

delayed in its development, is fully in keeping with his intent and therefore does not evidence a break in the flow of his argument.[5]

Admittedly, the break in style and tone between 1–7 and 10–13 is obvious even to the casual reader. But this too is more apparent than real because the trajectory of the argument remains the same. The calm feeling found in 8–9 is more like a pause in the storm that so marks the relationship between Paul and his readers and should not be given undue weight. Throughout the letter we find clues that, despite Titus's success, there remains some discord between the Apostle and these Saints (3:1; 5:12; 6:1–2, 11–13; 6:14–7:1). It is true that the whole of the last section is laced with barbed sarcasm not found earlier in the letter. But its effect lays heavily on the success of chapters 1–7, where the Apostle describes and defends in some detail his apostolic mission. His thrust, as in 1 Corinthians, is the paradox of strength growing out of weakness, a theme his readers would understand but not relish. In a community enamored with prestige and power, Paul's argument would not have found easy footing. But the Apostle never backs off from his thesis. He readily admits the "paradoxical nature of God's work in Christ and Christ's apostle, in which life is given in death, light in darkness, comfort in affliction,"[6] all of which Paul develops in the forepart of his letter. Chapters 10–13 articulate with force and conviction the Apostle's theme that God's "power is made perfect in weakness" (12:9, NR). "This word of Christ to Paul constitutes his defense of the apostolic mission—not merely that mission in general, but the mission in Corinth. The defense of that mission constitutes the thematic unity of the letter."[7]

Structure and Organization

If we hypothesize that the letter as it stands today closely reflects the original as dictated by Paul, we can address its themes and unity. Admittedly, the approach can be daunting, since there are various ways of attacking

5. George H. Guthrie, *2 Corinthians* (Grand Rapids, Mich.: Baker Academic, 2015), 29.

6. Seifrid, *Second Letter,* xxxi.

7. Seifrid, *Second Letter,* xxxi. Today many scholars are returning to the view that 2 Corinthians, as is it stands today, is how it was when initially dictated by Paul. For other defenses of the integrity of epistle, see Guthrie, *2 Corinthians,* 23–38; and Thomas Schmeller, "No Bridge over Troubled Water? The Gap between 2 Corinthians 1–9 and 10–13 Revisited," *Journal for the Study of the New Testament* 36 (2013): 73–84.

the makeup of the text.[8] Given, however, that the letter was written to the Corinthian Saints, who would have highly valued a rhetorical approach and been more easily persuaded to yield to Paul's appeal by this method, this seems the best way to examine the epistle and see Paul's development.[9] As such, it breaks down as follows:

I. Epistolary prescript (1:1–2)
II. Primary apologetic: Paul's explanation of his conduct and apostolic ministry (chaps. 1–7)
    a. The Apostle's past experience, including his gratitude for divine comfort in past afflictions (1:3–11)
    b. Transition to and development of his first theme: Paul's self-defense
        i. The integrity of his motives and conduct (1:12–2:4)
        ii. The need to treat an offender with forgiveness (2:5–11)
        iii. The sweet fragrance of the ministers' work (2:12–17)
    c. The Apostle's second and main theme: Paul's ministry
        i. The Apostle's competence through God's help (3:1–6)
        ii. The greater splendor of the present dispensation of light over that of Moses (3:7–4:6)
        iii. Treasure in earthen jars and the affliction of the righteous (4:7–16a)
        iv. The specter of death and Christian fearlessness (4:16b–5:10)

---

8. For development dealing with literary structure, see David E. Garland, *2 Corinthians,* vol. 29 of New American Commentary (Nashville: Broadman and Holman, 1999), 33–38; and Craig Blomberg, "The Structure of 2 Corinthians 1–7," *Criswell Theological Review* 4, no. 1 (1989): 3–20, both of whom see a chiastic structure to chap. 1–7. For development dealing with thematic elements, see Scott J. Hafemann, *2 Corinthians* (Grand Rapids, Mich.: Zondervan, 2000), 37–39; Frank J. Matera, *II Corinthians: A Commentary* (Louisville: Westminster John Knox Press, 2003), 8–9. For studies dealing with rhetorical forms, see Harris, *Second Epistle,* 105–10; David R. Hall, *The Unity of the Corinthian Correspondence* (London: T&T Clark, 2003), 89–91; and especially Ben Witherington III, *Conflict and Community in Corinth: A Socio-rhetorical Commentary on 1 and 2 Corinthians* (Grand Rapids, Mich.: William B. Eerdmans; Carlisle, U.K.: Paternoster Press, 1995) 39–61.

9. Though the art of rhetoric was highly abused during the period of the Second Sophistic (see Hugh Nibley, *The Ancient State: The Rulers and the Ruled,* ed. Donald W. Parry and Stephen D. Ricks [Salt Lake City: Deseret Book; Provo, Utah: Foundation for Ancient Research and Mormon Studies, 1991], 243–44), that did not dissuade Paul from being aware of its rudiments and using them to his advantage. See Gary Layne Hatch, "Paul among the Rhetoricians: A Model for Proclaiming Christ," in *The Apostle Paul, His Life and His Testimony: The 1994 Sperry Symposium on the New Testament,* ed. Paul Y. Hoskisson (Salt Lake City: Deseret Book, 1994), 65–79; Peter Marshall, *Enmity in Corinth: Social Conventions in Paul's Relations with the Corinthians* (Tübingen, Ger.: Mohr Siebeck, 1987).

v. The need to be reconciled to God (5:11–6:10)
vi. An appeal to separate from unrighteousness and to live Christian ideals (6:11–7:4)

III. The meeting with Titus (7:5–16)

IV. The Apostle's third theme: Collection for the afflicted in Jerusalem (chaps. 8–9)
a. The need for generosity (8:1–15)
b. Titus and his companions sent to Corinth to assist in the collection (8:16–9:5)
c. The promise for generous giving (9:6–15)

V. The Apostle's fourth theme: A polemic against his detractors and a vindication of his authority (chaps. 10–13)
a. His defense of apostolic authority (chap. 10)
b. His foolish boasting (chaps. 11–12)
c. His final warning (13:1–10)

VI. Final admonition and closing (13:11–14)

There are three golden strands that run through the epistle binding it together. The first, briefly noted here but developed more fully below, is that of the authenticity of Paul's apostolic office. Certain individuals had come to Corinth, apparently from congregations in the east, and had joined with Paul's Corinthian detractors in denying the Apostle's authority, denigrating his works, and spurning his doctrine. From beginning to end, Paul makes an excellent defense of his quality of life, the authenticity of his teachings, and the legitimacy of his apostolic office.

The second thread is that of Paul's theology. When Paul's antagonists arrived in Corinth, they brought with them what the Apostle calls the preaching of "another Jesus" along with doctrine contrary to that taught by the Lord. The result was the introduction of a different "spirit" than that which the community already enjoyed (11:4). Though the exact content of these antagonists' teaching is blurred, certain elements do stand out. They seem to have proclaimed Jesus as a lordly figure using Moses as an example (chap. 3) of how Christians should behave and be perceived by people. They seem to have set the example of superiority themselves. Such a position flew in the face of Paul's proclamation of strength through (apparent) weakness and a faith-filled submission to the will of Christ and authentic apostolic authority.[10]

10. Ralph P. Martin, *2 Corinthians,* 2nd ed., vol. 40 of *Word Biblical Commentary* (Grand Rapids, Mich.: Zondervan, 2014), 121–22.

Right from the beginning of the epistle, Paul proclaims that he is "an Apostle of Jesus Christ by the will of God" and that it is from the Father and Jesus Christ, and them alone, that all grace, peace, mercy, and spiritual comfort flow (1:1–3). Further, Christ knew suffering and could therefore lift those who also suffered. Indeed, he had already so lifted Paul during one of the most frightening periods of his life (1:5–10). Further, the work of the Apostle and his associates was not to boast of themselves but to proclaim "Christ Jesus the Lord" and themselves as the Corinthians' faithful servants for the Savior's sake (4:5). These Saints, however, must never forget that it was God who brought forth the true light of godly knowledge and glory as manifested in the "face of Christ" (4:6). Paul and his associates were driven by love, convinced that Christ died for all "so that the living might no longer live for themselves but live for him who died and was raised up again for their salvation" (5:14–15, NR). They were also driven by another fact: "All must appear before the judgment seat of Christ so that each person may receive a recompense for the things that he or she has done by means of the body, whether good or bad" (5:10, NR). The righteous, however, have nothing to fear, for those who become one with Christ also become "a new creature" and are reconciled by Christ to God (5:17–19, NR). For those who have sinned, "godly sorrow produces repentance that leads to salvation that is without regret" (7:10, NR). He assures them that "God can provide you with every grace in abundance, so that you will always have enough of everything and have an ample means for every good work" (9:8, NR). All in all, it was the Lord who gave Paul and his companions authority to build the Corinthians up (10:8). But the one lesson Paul knew intimately came from a difficult personal experience, one he called "a thorn in the flesh." Whatever it was (discussed below), it made him less effective in preaching the gospel, and he prayed fervently for it to be removed. In the end, it was not. The Lord's explanation? "My power is made perfect in weakness" (12:8–9). By that means—that is, the success of the weak things of the earth—God manifests that his power and wisdom is far beyond what humankind can comprehend and that, when all is said and done, what he has determined will be done. Finally, though Christ was "crucified because of weakness," he now lives "because of the power of God," and those who follow him shall also "live together with him because of the power of God" (13:4, NR).[11]

The third thread is Paul's eschatology—that is, his view of the nature and purpose of mortality in light of his understanding of death, judgment, and the

11. Compare Paul Barnett, *The Second Epistle to the Corinthians* (Grand Rapids, Mich.: William B. Eerdmans, 1997), 221–22.

final destiny of the soul. He states his core belief in 4:18–5:10. In his view, the life of the Christian in mortality is little more than a burden on the soul coupled with anxiety and fear, while life in immortality is coupled with light and power (5:2–3; see also 1:4–5). Indeed, God's plan is for mortality to be swallowed in immortality, the promise of which has now been made certain to these Saints by the witness of the Holy Ghost (5:5; compare 1:22). But being able to see the future reward requires the Saints to walk "by faith, not by sight" (5:7). In doing so, they will please God (5:9), knowing that Christ will judge all according to their deeds (5:10). Therefore, in the present, faith, expressed in living as Christ has shown that the Christian must, is all important. The Apostle points out that it is critical that the Saints continue to yield to the "letter written in our hearts," one "written not with ink, but with the Spirit of the Living God, not on stone tablets but on the tablets of human hearts" (3:2–3, NR; compare Jer. 31:33). He admonishes his readers not to enter into the grace of God in vain, for now is the day of their salvation (6:1–2). Behind his statement stands a tacit reminder that the day may pass and leave them behind. Indeed, the present objective is for the Saints to cleanse themselves "from every defilement of the flesh and spirit, and thereby complete our sanctification through reverence for God" (7:1, NR). One way to do so, he shows, is in generous giving to those in desperate need (chap. 8–9).

In sum, gentleness, meekness, and humility are the way of the Christian. Given this, it is easy to see that Paul would be greatly concerned with those who proclaimed "another Jesus" and brought in a "another gospel" that resulted in "another spirit" (11:4), one that placed high value on one's station in mortality, promoted pride of position, and sought to preempt the true doctrine of Christ with one that was self-serving and spiritually destructive. In chapters 10–12, Paul challenged the views of these people and showed the true way to eternal life.

Paul's Understanding and Use of the Old Testament

To bolster his arguments, Paul appeals to scripture directly eleven times in 2 Corinthians with more oblique refernces to others.[12] The text that he used, however, was not that preserved in Hebrew but one translated into Greek.

12. These are: 2 Cor. 3:7–18 references Ex. 34:29–35; 4:6 references Gen. 1:3 and reflects Ps. 18:28; 4:13 references Ps. 116:10; 6:2 references Isa. 48:8 and echoes Isa. 55:6 and Ps. 69:13; 6:16–17 references Isa. 52:11 and echoes Ezek. 20:34, 41; 6:18 references 2 Sam. 7:14 and echoes 2 Sam. 7:8 along with Ex. 4:22 and Isa. 43:6; 9:6 references Prov.

Known today as the Septuagint (often denoted by the Roman numerals LXX), this work was a translation of Old Testament documents completed sometime between 300 and 100 BC. Being from Tarsus, a city in the province of Cilicia (today a portion of southeast Turkey), Paul spoke Greek and was well acquainted with the LXX. His knowledge and use of this work may have helped him during his ministry since proselytes, God-fearers, and Jews living in what is called the "diaspora" all spoke Greek and, therefore, would have preferred this version of the Old Testament.[13] Further, both Jewish and Gentile converts would have seen the Old Testament writings as both authentic and binding. Thus, Paul often appealed to them in his teachings and directions.[14]

Paul was trained within the rabbinic circle (Acts 23:6; 26:5) and was thus very familiar with their way of understanding and interpreting the biblical texts. His commitment to the scriptures clearly parallels theirs. To both, the Old Testament books preserved the word and will of Jehovah. Both showed their deep reverence by quoting specific verses as accurately as possible. They also saw a coherence of the whole to the parts as demonstrated by their combining various passages to make a single point. Their reverence for the scripture, however, did not prevent them from using passages in a new context. Nonetheless, both show that they had an understanding of the larger context in which the various scriptures were found.[15]

But there was a point at which Paul broke from the rabbinic circle. Through the stunning incident that triggered his conversion, he realized the Old Testament was more than a catalogue of divinely inspired performances, ordinances, laws, statutes, and commandments. It was a primary source that revealed the nature, work, and ministry of Jesus Christ. He came to understand what the Book of Mormon makes very clear: God gave the Mosaic law to Israel, which demanded performances "from day to day, to keep them in remembrance of God" (Mosiah 13:30). But he designed

11:24–25 and 22:9; 9:9 references Ps. 112:9; 10:17 references Jer. 9:24 and echoes Ps. 34:2 and 44:8; 11:3 references Gen. 3:1–6, 13; and 13:1 references Deut. 19:15. This entire section follows Richard D. Draper and Michael D. Rhodes, *Paul's First Epistle to the Corinthians* (Provo, Utah: BYU Studies, 2017), 8–10.

13. Proselytes were converts to Judaism while God-fearers were Gentile men drawn to Judaism but who would not go through the ordeal of circumcision. Paul F. Stuehrenberg, "Proselyte," in *ABD,* 5:503–5.

14. For a study, see E. Earle Ellis, *Paul's Use of the Old Testament* (Grand Rapids, Mich.: Wm. B. Eerdmans, 1957; rpt., Eugene, Ore.: Wipf and Stock Publishers, 2003).

15. Gareth Lee Cockerill, *The Epistle to the Hebrews* (Grand Rapids, Mich.: Eerdmans, 2012), 54–56.

the law to do more. Through its "many signs, and wonders, and types, and shadows," it showed to them "concerning [the Savior's] coming." In addition, the "holy prophets [also] spake unto [Israel] concerning his coming" (Mosiah 3:15). Though the law was full of performances and ordinances, the Book of Mormon notes, "all these things were types of things to come" (Mosiah 13:30–31). Paul's writings show he understood the Old Testament in much the same way (see, for example, 10:6; Rom. 4:23–24).[16]

Paul's use and interpretation of these texts clearly reveal his ever-deepening understanding of the revelation of Christ that he found there. Paul had made it clear that much of his understanding of gospel truths came not from human sources. He told his readers that "the gospel which was preached of me is not after man. For I neither received it of man, neither was I taught it, but by the revelation of Jesus Christ" (Gal. 1:11–12). That portion of his understanding, however, seems limited to the mission and Atonement of the Lord. But this was not his only contact with the Divine that brought him understanding. He notes that "he was caught up into paradise, and heard unspeakable words, which it is not lawful for a man to utter" (2 Cor. 12:4). These experiences would certainly have established an expanded and divine basis for his doctrines. He told the Corinthians he had "delivered unto you first of all that which I also received, how that Christ died for our sins according to the scriptures; And that he was buried, and that he rose again the third day according to the scriptures" (1 Cor. 15:3–4). This witness could describe in part what came from his theophany. But he goes on to say that Jesus "was seen of Cephas, then of the twelve: After that, he was seen of above five hundred brethren at once; of whom the greater part remain unto this present, but some are fallen asleep. After that, he was seen of James; then of all the apostles. And last of all he was seen of me also, as of one born out of due time" (1 Cor. 15:3–8). His words show that he is passing down material he received from others. It would seem, therefore, that only part of Paul's gospel understanding came via revelation. Other sources included the scriptures and Church conventions and practices as taught and preserved by his follow Apostles, other Church leaders, and Jewish traditions.[17]

Nonetheless, there was tension, because (as broad as these sources were) none covered all the situations the Church was encountering in different areas. Jesus had clearly stated that, though he had fulfilled some of

---

16. Moisés Silva, *New International Dictionary of New Testament Theology and Exegesis, 5 vols.* (Grand Rapids, Mich.: Zondervan, 2014), 4:507 (hereafter cited as *NID*).

17. Peter J. Tomson, *Paul and the Jewish Law: Halakha in the Letters of the Apostle to the Gentiles* (Assen/Maastricht, Neth: Van Gorcum; Minneapolis: Fortress Press, 1990), 82–85.

the law, "till heaven and earth pass, one jot or one tittle shall in no wise pass from the law, till all be fulfilled" (Matt. 5:18). These words suggest the need for continued adherence to some aspects of the teachings of the Old Testament, but which ones? The Apostle clearly understood and taught that there was no salvific power in the law. Nonetheless, its moral teachings and admonitions as well as its guidelines for social behavior, whenever they applied to conditions met by the expanding Church, seemed in order. The decision made by the Jerusalem Council in AD 49 was helpful with a few of the major problems, but it dealt mostly with issues concerning pagan cultic practices and immorality (Acts 15:23–29). As a result, even that official declaration left much to be resolved. We see in Paul's writings a man who cherished the word of God and used it to the best of his ability as a guide to determine doctrine and establish practices within the congregations of the Church for which he was responsible.

The proper understanding of the Old Testament, however, demanded it be read in a certain way. If it were not, then it could bring death and not life (2 Cor. 3:6).[18] Paul realized that the coming of Jesus gave the Hebrew writings new importance as a window into who and what the Messiah Jesus was for the Christian community. The Apostle, with others, saw that events of both the Savior's life and station were mapped out in the old record. Therefore, Paul freely appealed to that record as an authoritative witness to the gospel message. However, in doctrine and practice, there was a definite break between the old covenant and the new. This opened the way for the scriptures to be used as a polemical weapon, and Paul mastered the technique. In dealing with his antagonists, Paul quite deliberately painted their position as negatively as possible and then demolished it by showing that they simply did not understand the true meaning of the sacred text.[19] The same was true, but to a greater extent, of the Jews themselves. Because they refused to interpret the law through the lens of Christianity, they would never come to the truth (3:14–15). Thus, Paul's writings present a continual tension between the old and new covenants. On the one hand, he appeals to the authority of the Hebrew Bible, while on the other he insists it is a poor second if not an actually dangerous source of doctrine.[20]

The historical situation in which the Apostle operated generated the acute tension between the two covenants. Paul, however, met that tension head-on by developing an understanding of the relationship between the

---

18. See Translation Notes and Comments for 3:6 below.
19. *NID,* 1:607.
20. *NID,* 1:607.

two and then articulating his position. His writings show that he developed a synthesis that relied on types, such as Moses, the veil, or Eve, to provide the necessary historical value. In doing so, he showed that it was not necessary to dissolve the old covenant just because it was overshadowed by Christ.[21] As a result, the Apostle gave proper place to both covenants.

Conclusion

The epistle as a whole shows Paul's attempt to bring the Corinthians more closely to the Father and Son. To do this, he had to vindicate his teachings and way of life among them. That demanded that they understand his apostolic authority, for on it lay the very ground of the doctrine he taught. He therefore had to not just undercut but destroy the claims and teachings of his antagonists because their teachings were spiritually deadly. The Apostle emphasized that the life he lived while among the Corinthians evidenced that his purpose in writing was not for self-glorification, but for the glory of God and his Christ. His motivation, as he so clearly expressed, was inspired by a deep love for them.

The Historical, Geographical, and Cultural Background to the Epistle

The Geographical, Political, Social, and Economic Setting of Corinth

The Corinth that Paul came to know in AD 50–56 was a bustling but relatively new city under Roman rule. In the past, Corinth had been a wealthy maritime power allied with Sparta (sixth to fourth centuries BC) and during the third and second centuries had been part of the powerful Achaean league, a confederation of cities in the northern Peloponnesus formed as a defense against forces threatening these city-states. The Latin writer Cicero described the city during that period as "the light of all Greece."[22] In the second century, the league stood against Roman expansion into the area. However, their combined strength helped neither the Corinthians nor the rest of the Peloponnesian organization. City after city fell to Roman might.

---

21. *NID,* 1:208.

22. Cicero, *Pro Lege manilia (De imperio Cn. Pompeii)* 5. For background, see Draper and Rhodes, *Paul's First Epistle to the Corinthians,* 11–25.

But trade was not the only source of wealth for the city. Every two years it sponsored the Isthmian Games, which brought in great crowds with their money.[35] These popular religious and athletic festivals involved such things as "musical and literary competitions, contests in public speaking, contests involving horses (e.g. chariot races, skills in chariot driving, men leaping on and off both horses and chariots), various kinds of footraces, the pentathlon, and boxing. The festival was a boon to the Corinthian economy and image as a major tourist destination."[36]

Further, as Corinth was the provincial headquarters of Achaia, ambassadors and other officials came to meet with the proconsul, bringing added recognition as well as income into the city. Also contributing greatly to the city's affluence were its artists and their excellent works, many made of the uniquely blended and much-sought-after bronze, a product for which the city was renowned.[37] The result was that Corinth became the biggest and most powerful city in the entire region, eclipsing even Athens. All this wealth contributed to the production of splendid buildings and other facilities, including shopping areas, administrative buildings, a senate house, a library, a theater, numerous temples, gymnasiums and athletics fields, parks, fountains, and monuments.[38]

There was also another social factor that played heavily in the development of the Church in Corinth. As noted, the widespread decadence left its mark on the soul of the city. Wealth and ease did not bring comfort and security but rather a continual and unremitting restlessness that contributed to self-promotion, glory seeking, and one-upmanship. Success and applause took on disproportionate importance.[39] The whole culture also put pressure on people to get ahead, and some, especially among the less scrupulous, as noted, slipped into shady if not outright dishonest dealings. Appearance was

---

35. Strabo, *Geographica* 8.6.20.

36. Guthrie, *2 Corinthians,* 13.

37. Strabo, *Geographica* 8.6.23; Pliny the Elder, *Natural History* 34.1, notes that Corinthian bronze was valued above silver and sometimes even gold.

38. Strabo, *Geographica* 8.6.21a; Pausanias, *Description of Greece,* 2.1–3.1. See also Victor Paul Furnish, "Corinth in Paul's Time: What Can Archeology Tell Us?," *Biblical Archeological Review* 14, no. 3 (May–June 1988): 14–27.

39. See Quintilian, *Institutio oratoria* 2.2.9–12; Seneca, *Controversiae* 9.1. For more background material, see Jennifer C. Lane, "Jews and Greeks: The Broader Context for the Writing of the New Testament," in *How the New Testament Came to Be: The Thirty-fifth Annual Sidney B. Sperry Symposium,* ed. Kent P. Jackson and Frank F. Judd Jr. (Provo, Utah: Religious Studies Center, Brigham Young University; Salt Lake City: Deseret Book, 2006), 62–77.

all-important. It was a society in which shame and honor, values that already were significant to most Gentiles, were of the highest importance. To bring shame upon oneself or upon one's house was considered a grievous offense, one that extended to one's fraternal, social, and civic relationships. Honor (which was sometimes not associated with honesty) meant everything, and many used whatever means they could to capture as much power as possible.[40] Thus, fame and glory were in high demand, and those who wanted them were willing to do whatever it took to gain them.

Advantages of Corinth to the Spread of the Gospel

All these forces and conditions drew people from all over the Mediterranean to Corinth. Thus, it was an ideal place for Paul to set up the headquarters of his missionary activities. Though the city, unfortunately, had its seamy elements, there were people who ached for a higher stratum of life. Some of these were draw to the highly moral lifestyle of the Jewish population that had grown from the time of the founding of the city. Among these, as well as others, were those who were attracted to the gospel Paul preached, one of a God who sent his divine Son to save the world. As a result, missionary work thrived.

Challenges the Social Conditions Made for the Church

In such an atmosphere, Christianity offered a radical departure from the norm. Paul preached a weakness-to-strength motif that did not sit well with the majority of the city's inhabitants, and resistance to the idea kept creeping into the Church's assemblies. Thus, the theme of "Christ, and him crucified" (1 Cor. 2:2)—that is, the paradox of strength though weakness—played a major part in both the preaching and writings of Paul. He knew that though power, authority, and glory ever remained important principles and carried heavy weight, they had to be harnessed to loving service that sought to build up each person singly and the Church collectively (2 Cor. 10:8; 13:10).

---

40. For a short study, see Halvor Moxnes, "Honor, Shame, and the Outside World in Paul's letter to the Romans," in *The Social World of Formative Christianity and Judaism: Essays in Tribute to Howard Clarke Kee,* ed. Jacob Neusner and others (Philadelphia: Fortress Press, 1988), 207–18. For an extended study, see Ramsay MacMullen, *Roman Social Relations, 50 BC to AD 284* (New Haven, Conn.: Yale University Press, 1974), 62–106; and for a general study, see Wayne A. Meeks, *The First Urban Christians: The Social World of the Apostle Paul,* 2nd ed. (New Haven, Conn.: Yale University Press, 2003).

Some Gentile converts to the Church (likely because they did not fully understand the gospel message and had grown up valuing competitive and glory-seeking behaviors) resisted certain teachings and thereby forfeited the ability of the gospel to reshape their lives. Thus, among other challenges, and largely due to the influence of the pagan culture and secular mores that dominated the city, a number of converts appear to have been partially blinded to the requirements of the gospel.[41] In sum, "they were Hellenists through and through, and this eschatological, cross-centered, body-affirming Jewish sect called Christianity demanded that they enter another theological ethical world. It is no surprise that these residents of Corinth would seek rhetorical wisdom, be unconcerned with immorality and preservation of the body, be infatuated with asceticism and spiritual empowerment, and preserve the distinctions between rich and poor. The Corinthians were simply trying to be Christian with a minimal amount of social and theological disturbance."[42] To make matters worse, during this same period, a delegation arrived apparently from the eastern branches of the Church who also questioned Paul's doctrine and authority. They preached, according to Paul, "another Jesus" (11:4), and taught for doctrines items that meshed with those of the Apostle's other detractors.

These preachers all seem to have played on a misconstrued understanding of the nature and force of leadership. For the Corinthians in general, leadership meant being able to use power and authority, and even coercion when necessary, to get what one wanted. Much of this ability was tied to one's status and wealth. Indeed, many citizens expected the powerful to fund all kinds of showy civic projects and public events. Those who did so found popular support in the patron-client relationship. By this means the leading citizens increased their popularity and prestige, helping them to move farther along the *cursus honorum*.[43] Paul not only refused to play this game but also condemned it. The Apostle's rejection of financial assistance for himself and insistence that the rank-and-file members contribute money to

---

41. Bruce W. Winter, *After Paul Left Corinth: The Influence of Secular Ethics and Social Change*, 2nd ed. (Grand Rapids, Mich.: William B. Eerdmans, 2001), 43.

42. Lyle D. Vander Broek, *Breaking Barriers: The Possibilities of Christian Community in a Lonely World* (Grand Rapids, Mich.: Brazos, 2002), 27–28.

43. The *cursus honorum* denotes those military and civil stations those of aspiring senatorial status had to go through in order to keep or achieve recognition and honor. For a list, see N. S. Gill, "Hierarchy of Roman Offices in the Cursus Honorum," ThoughtCo, February 28, 2018, accessed January 8, 2019, https://www.thoughtco.com/cursus-honorum-roman-offices-120107.

help those hit hard by the misfortunes that engulfed the Holy Land (chapters 8–9) cut hard against the grain. "In short, in the apostle's seeming humility (even humiliation, 12:21), his taking on the role of a servant, his rejection of patronage and the concomitant rejection of financial gain, and his refusal to advance his status by use of rhetorical skills, he stood in violation of key leadership values and principles embedded in the Corinthian culture. The apostle, on the other hand, presents to the Corinthians an alternative: a theocentric and biblical vision of authentic leadership."[44] Paul understood that the gospel's push had to help its recipients become mature in faith through adherence to Christ, his teachings, and the way of life that he demanded.[45] Only in this way could they both lead and follow as taught by the gospel and find the change of soul it resulted in.

Paul's Relationship with the Corinthian Church

Background to the Epistle

Through a divine manifestation, Paul entered into Europe and began his preaching in the cities of Macedonia and Greece, slowly moving to the south (Acts 16–18). Though Luke's historical work, the Acts of the Apostles, provides a general outline and does preserve important events, from statements and hints in Paul's writings, it is obvious that Luke did not include all that happened. The result is that an exact chronology of events can only be conjectured. Below is our attempt to put Luke's account of this period together with material from Paul's letters and come up with a possible working model of how events played out.

On his arrival at the Achaean Capitol, Paul realized the value the city could have for extending the word of God not just in the East but in the West as well. He settled into the city, taking a job at the business of some newly found Church members, Aquila and Priscilla. He worked as a σκηνοποιός (*skēnopoios*), translated as "tentmaker" in the KJV (Acts 18:3). The word actually denotes those who work with leathers and fabrics.[46] During his

44. Guthrie, *2 Corinthians,* 16–17.

45. Martin, *2 Corinthians,* 125.

46. Though translated as "tent maker" in the KJV, the Greek term *skēnopoios* is found only here in the New Testament, and therefore its exact definition is uncertain. It definitely applied to some kind of manual labor. The province of Cilicia, in which Paul grew up, was known for tents made from a coarse fabric consisting of goat's hair that the

stay with them, he preached the gospel every Sabbath day to Jews and was successful in converting both Greeks and Jews, and that included Crispus, a leader of the local synagogue, with all his household (Acts 18:8). The Apostle was joined later that year by both Silas and Timothy, who apparently brought donations with them that allowed Paul to quit working for a season and devote himself full time to the ministry (Acts 18:5). During that period, he had a revelation in which the Lord told him to preach without fear, for there were many in the city who would respond to the gospel message (Acts 18:9–10).

Under his supervision, the membership of the Church greatly increased, but not without opposition. Some of the Jewish leaders seem to have realized that Christianity threatened their religion, and they stirred up opposition against Paul and refused to have him preach any longer in their synagogue. Not to be deterred, Paul set up headquarters in the home of Justus, a new convert, whose house shared a common wall with a Jewish house of worship (Acts 18:6–7). So agitated were the Jews that they took Paul to task before the proconsul of the city, L. Junius Gallo. Much to the Jews' chagrin, Gallo would have nothing to do with the problem and thereby assured, if tacitly, that the Christians would be protected by the government (Acts 18:12–15).

After a year and a half, Paul felt the need to return to Jerusalem and report on his activities. On the way, he stopped for an extended period at Ephesus and found the area ripe for further missionary work.[47] Based on these findings, he determined to return to that city in the near future (Acts 18:18–21). After about a year's absence, he did return and labored there for over two years. During that time, he learned of troubles in Corinth. He

---

Roman called *cilicium.* Paul could have learned the technique of weaving tenting material in his youth, but this is doubtful on three accounts: first, *cilicium* had a much wider range of uses than just for tent making, second, most tents were made of leather, and third, weaving was considered a disgraceful occupation that a young scholar like Paul would have carefully avoided. Much more respectful was the work of a "saddler," the word meaning broadly anyone who works in leather. Wilhelm Michaelis, "σκηνοποιός," in Gerhard Kittel and Gerhard Freidrich, eds., *Theological Dictionary of the New Testament,* trans. Geoffery W. Bromiley, 10 vols. (Grand Rapids, Mich.: Wm. B. Eerdmans, 1964–76), 7:393–94 (hereafter cited as *TDNT*); F. F. Bruce, *The Acts of the Apostles: Greek Text with Introduction and Commentary,* 3rd rev. ed. (Grand Rapids, Mich.: William B. Eerdmans, 1990), 392.

47. It may be that the Apostle John had been working successfully in that area for some time. See Wayment, *From Persecutor to Apostle,* 147–48. If that were the case, Paul would have found a fond reception among these early Christians.

wrote them a letter, now lost, but from what we can tell, it addressed at least Paul's concern with those who were being pulled away from the Church due to association with those who were immoral. His counsel was that the Christians should break off all relationships with the licentious (1 Cor. 5:9).

Sometime thereafter, Paul received word from Stephanas, a prominent Church member, and his traveling associates, as well as from the servants of Chloe, another prominent member, that factions were developing in the various house churches and that a number of theological principles were under attack. Paul responded by writing what is now known as the first letter to the Corinthians.

Because there are a number of items in that epistle that bear on our understanding of 2 Corinthians, we need to review them at this point. Denunciation of factionalism takes high priority in the first part of that letter (1 Cor. 1:10–4:20) and stands as one of Paul's major motivations in revisiting the branch (4:16–21). Also at issue among some of the Corinthians was Paul's apostolic office and his right to give counsel and direction to the Church. For this reason, among others, he had to defend his position and office in order for the members to yield to the way of life he promoted (9:1–7). Indeed, he himself was the test case of Christian living and asked the members to follow his example "as I myself follow Christ's example" (4:6; 11:1, NR). They would not do so unless they believed he truly represented the Christian way of life. Thus, we see that his major concern was with the form of apostolic life and practice. For Paul it was critical that these Christians see that strength grows out of weakness and suffering. These represented the form and very nature of Christian existence in this world. The problem was that after Paul had written to these Saints, certain individuals came among them proclaiming apostolic authority and proffering a "gospel" that held much greater appeal by offering more glory and reward in the here and now. That "gospel" threatened to replaced Paul's doctrine that hinged on "Christ, and him crucified" (1 Cor. 2:2) and the kind of life that demanded in the present.[48] Paul's authority to preach this gospel and the authenticity of his doctrine, therefore, had to become the focal point in 2 Corinthians.

Unfortunately, though the thrust of 1 Corinthians may have done some good, further troubles developed. At least one member of prominence in the Christian community continued to take exception to Paul's authority and some aspects of his doctrine. Likely due to the threatening nature of this challenge, the Apostle took a quick trip to visit the branches and settle

48. Seifrid, *Second Letter,* xxiv–xxv.

the affair. In 2 Corinthians 2:1, he indicates that he came to them "with sorrow" (NR) to make his case. However, this Church member, apparently in high social standing, openly opposed him. The members, unfortunately, did not openly support Paul's cause and by their inactivity tacitly supported the rebellious person.[49] Paul left the city, as he says, in "great tribulation and anguish of heart" (2:4, NR).

Thus, he returned to Ephesus very downhearted and greatly concerned (2:4). Conditions did not improve for him in Ephesus. This was, ironically, due to the success of Christianity in the area. Because so many people gave up idolatry, the craft of the idol makers was hurt. Under the direction of a particularly outspoken and angry member of their guild, Demetrius, they stirred up a riot against Paul, who seems to have been the face of Christianity in the area. Fortunately, the rulers of the city succeeded in getting conditions settled (Acts 19:21–41).

It may be, however, that Paul was arrested for a brief period.[50] It was probably during his incarceration that he had time to yield to his hurt and frustration by writing to these less-than-supportive souls a pointed and rather harsh letter using Titus as its bearer.[51] It was not easy for the Apostle to write such a biting epistle. Indeed, as he later tells them, he wrote it in tears (2:3–4; 7:8). His purpose, he stressed, was not to cause them pain but to show his abundant concern and love for them (2:4). It is likely Titus read the epistle to the membership and then waited to see what their response would be (7:5–16). This harsh letter (Paul's third) has since been lost.

About this time, Paul, with some other Church members, decided it was best that he leave Ephesus (Acts 20:1–2). In response to that decision, he moved on to Macedonia. He was met there by Titus, who informed him that the members had been humbled to tears by Paul's letter and were greatly sorrowful for their lack of support when the Apostle had visited them. They now openly expressed their fervent love for him (7:6–7). They had even gone so far as to rebuke and perhaps even further punish the

49. Wayment, *From Persecutor to Apostle,* 163. Some have suggested he was the immoral man Paul condemned in 1 Cor. 5:1–5. See, for example, J. H. Bernard, "The Second Epistle to the Corinthians," in *The Expositor's Greek Testament,* ed. W. Robertson Nicoll, vol. 3 (1897; rpt., Grand Rapids, Mich.: William B. Eerdmans, 1980), 10. But that Paul does not reiterate the instructions he had already given Church leadership concerning how to deal with him suggests the two are different. Seifrid, *Second Letter,* xxv–vi.

50. Wayment, *From Persecutor to Apostle,* 167.

51. From his cell, he may have written Philippians and Philemon. Wayment, *From Persecutor to Apostle,* 172–74.

offending party (2:6). This report prompted Paul to immediately write them again. This letter (his fourth) has been preserved as 2 Corinthians.

This epistle, like his harsh letter, was entrusted to Titus. In it the Apostle could say that, though he was deeply sorry he had to write the harsh letter, he rejoiced that it had brought them to repentance and back to unity with him (7:9–10). Paul's writings hint at the warm depth of feelings he had for them and his joy at their renewed eagerness and zeal toward him. These writings also show his concern with the indignation the members expressed toward the offending person and more especially the overambitious punishment they afflicted on him. The Apostle made sure his readers understood that he was not motivated to write as a means of taking vengeance on the person who offended him but for the good of the community as a whole (7:12). Paul asked that they treat the offender, if he was willing to receive it, with love and fellowship (2:6–8).

With some relief, the Apostle then proceeded to Corinth, where he stayed for a few weeks strengthening the Church before returning to Jerusalem. He may have had to depart sooner than he wished due to a plot against his life by a rabid segment of the Jewish population (Acts 20:1–3).

The surviving historical documents do not indicate that Paul had any further dealings with the Corinthian Saints, although they suggest that the divisive character of the branches did not fully dissipate over time. Around the turn of the first century, the Roman Bishop Clement wrote to the Corinthian Christians. The occasion was that a group of Church members had banded together and dismissed some of their leading officers. Clement viewed this as an act of sedition[52] and wrote pleading with them for unity in love and fellowship,[53] stressing the importance of Church officers for the smooth running of the Church.[54]

Why Paul Wrote 2 Corinthians

In reading any of the works of Paul, four forces that greatly shaped his doctrine and drove his preaching should be kept in mind. The first was the nature of his conversion to Christ. As an aggressive prosecutor of what he saw as a dangerous heresy, namely Christianity, he had moved effectively against the Church. But in doing so, he was also fighting against the will of his God and thereby committing a very grave sin. That he moved in

52. *1 Clem.* 1.2; 47.5–7; 44.5; 57.1.

53. *1 Clem.* 7.2–5; 14.1–3; 50.2.

54. *1 Clem.* 44.1–4.

ignorance did not make the gravity of his actions any less serious. Thus, in an act of pure grace, Christ reached out to him at the height of his sin, forgave him, and brought him into God's fold.

The second force was his experience with divine revelation in the form not only of inspiration but also of visions from the Lord. In these he learned much. Indeed, at one time he was caught up into celestial glory and there learned pure doctrine from the divine source (12:1–2). As a result, he confidently stated, "I want you to know, brothers and sisters, that the gospel that was taught by me, was not of human origin, for I neither received it nor was I taught it from any human being, but received it through revelation from Jesus Christ" (Gal. 1:11–12, our translation). Even so, Paul was respectful of the Church authorities, and years before he began his apostolic ministry, he visited with Peter and James, the Lord's brother, to secure his doctrinal position. Even after he began his ministry, he met with Peter, John, and James and explained to them the gospel he preached among the Gentiles to make certain he was not "running or had run in vain" (Gal. 2:2, our translation). The result was a vindication and verification not only of his teachings (Gal. 2:7–9) but also of his authority as one commissioned and sent by God.

The third force was Paul's awareness of the coming apostasy. Before he ever wrote to the Corinthian Saints, he warned the Thessalonians of the coming revolution (2 Thes. 2:3–12), and that revolution was one of his major teachings while he labored at Ephesus, one delivered, he states, "with tears" over a three-year period (Acts 20:28–31). Knowing of the inevitability of the coming apostasy of the Church seems to have driven him with an intense urgency that heightened his zeal and pushed him in the work. The heat the reader feels in Paul's writings was fanned largely by this flame.

The epistle reveals that the Apostle's paramount fear is that his work in Corinth will come to naught if his critics win the battle for the loyalty of the Saints. The risk was not just Paul's apostolic credibility but his missionary work in the entire Aegean region, headquartered as it was in Corinth. Losing this segment of the Church would mean the loss of his entire efforts and thus put in jeopardy his intended mission to Rome and eventually Spain.[55]

The fourth force was his belief, at least up through the midpoint of his apostolic career, that the Second Coming, with its accompanying judgment, would follow fast upon the heels of the apostasy.[56] Thus, in his

---

55. Martin, *2 Corinthians,* 492.

56. That the leadership of the primitive Church held this idea has been confirmed by Brigham Young, who noted, "There can be no doubt but they were mistaken with regard

earliest preserved letter, he could assure the Thessalonians that, when Christ returned, "the dead in Christ shall first rise; then we who are alive, who are left, shall be caught up together with them" (1 Thes. 4:16–17, our translation). The statement suggests that Paul planned to be a part of that group. This feeling carried over into 1 Corinthians. He told his readers, "Not all of us will fall asleep [that is, die], but we will all be changed in a moment" (1 Cor. 15:51–52, NR). That being the case, he was most anxious that his readers prepare for this event by putting their lives in order and staying true to the faith during what the Apostle understood would be very difficult times ahead. He assured them, however, that their faith would result in their full vindication by God and a place in his eternal world.[57]

Between writing that epistle to the Corinthians and writing his next one, he experienced a terrible ordeal that brought death's door very near. From that point on, he seems convinced that it was death, not the Parousia, that he must prepare for. When he wrote to the Philippians before leaving Ephesus, he revealed his new position: "For to me to live is Christ, and to die is gain. If it is to be life in the flesh, that means productive labor for me. Yet which I shall choose I cannot tell. I am hard pressed between the two" (Philip. 1:21–23, our translation). From this point on, Paul never uses "we" when speaking of the coming Parousia. On the contrary, he could tell the Corinthian Saints that "we know that the one who raised the Lord Jesus will also raise us together with Jesus and bring us together with you into his presence" (4:14, NR). There is no hint here that he feels the Second Coming is near.

The Apostle was filled with the necessity for all to work to please God, "for we all must appear before the judgment seat of Christ so that each person may receive a recompense for the things that he or she has done by means of the body, whether good or bad" (5:10, NR). No longer is his major aim preparing for the Second Coming, but for divine judgment.[58]

In addition to these forces, there is another factor that stands out clearly in Paul's teachings that the modern disciple should ever keep in mind: that he knew he was, in the fullest sense, an Apostle of Christ Jesus. The Greek word ἀπόστολος (*apostolos*) designated a person who was dispatched for a

---

to the time of the winding up scene, thinking it was much nearer than it really was, and they might have made mistakes in other respects." *Journal of Discourses,* 26 vols. (London: Latter-day Saints Book Depot, 1854–86), 12:65 (hereafter cited as *JD*).

57. Wayment, *From Persecutor to Apostle,* 170.

58. Wayment, *From Persecutor to Apostle,* 170.

specific purpose with authority to carry out that purpose. In the New Testament sense, it denoted primarily one who acted as God's envoy and functioned under his power and authority.[59] The designation could, therefore, refer to persons in addition to those that formed the original Quorum of Apostles or those who were later made members of it.[60] Even so, within the New Testament, it is used "predominately [for] a group of highly honored believers with a special function as God's envoys."[61] These made up the one Quorum. Though certainty cannot be achieved, Paul's writings suggest he was a member of that Quorum. He begins each of his epistles with "Paul, an apostle," thus consistently showing claim to the office. His statement in 1 Corinthians 1:1–7 shows that he had no doubt he held full apostolic authority. He insists that he had the same rights and privileges as Peter, James (the brother of the Lord), and the other apostles. In Galatians 2:7–9, he convincingly shows that he was directly called by Christ to preside over the work of taking the gospel to the gentile world. In Galatians 1:17, he refers to the other apostles as "οἱ πρὸ ἐμοῦ ἀπόστολοι" (*hoi pro emou apostoloi*), those "who were called before me," which suggests he was now one of them.[62] In sum, there is no evidence in the New Testament that ἀπόστολος

59. Walter Bauer, *A Greek-English Lexicon of the New Testament and Other Early Christian Literature,* ed. Frederick W. Danker, 3rd English ed. (Chicago: University of Chicago Press, 2000), 122 (hereafter cited as BDAG). For a fuller discussion, see *NID,* 1:365–76. For an exploration of the term and its nuances, see Bo Young Kang, *Heralds and Community: An Enquiry into Paul's Concept of Mission and Its Indebtedness to the Jesus-Tradition* (Carlisle, U.K.: Langham Monographs, 2012), 301–9.

60. Because individuals have been called to that office without also being members of the high Quorum in this dispensation, it is possible the same occurred in the meridian of time. These include Joseph Smith; Oliver Cowdery; Joseph F. Smith, an Apostle for a year before being added to the Quorum; and Joseph Angell Young (https://www.mormonwiki.com/Joseph_Angell_Young), Brigham Young Jr. (https://www.mormonwiki.com/Brigham_Young,_Jr.), Alvin R. Dyer (https://www.mormonwiki.com/Alvin_R._Dyer), and Thorp B. Isaacson (https://www.mormonwiki.com/Thorpe_B._Isaacson), who never became members of the Quorum of the Twelve. The latter two served as members of the First Presidency but upon their release became assistants to the Twelve.

61. BDAG, 122.

62. The only other men in the New Testament besides the original Twelve who are called Apostles are Matthias (Acts 1:25–26)—who was definitely a member of the Twelve, Barnabas (Acts 14:14), and James, the Lord's brother (Gal. 1:19). Based on Rom. 16:7, some want to include Andronicus and Junia/Junias (possibly a woman's name), because it states οἵτινές εἰσιν ἐπίσημοι ἐν τοῖς ἀποστόλοις (*hoitines eisin episēmoi en tois apostolois*), "who are well-known among the apostles." However, the Greek is ambiguous and could also be understood to mean they were well-known *to* the apostles rather than

(*apostolos*) was used for anyone other than a "special witness of the name of Christ"—that is, an apostle and member of the Quorum as we understand the term in this dispensation (D&C 107:23; see also D&C 27:12).

Whatever the case, Paul did not rest his defense on whether or not he was a member of the leadership quorum, but on his authority as one called and commissioned by Jesus and under the direction of the Church's authorities. "When Paul mentions 'Apostle of Christ' it means a delegate appointed *by Christ in person,* given with his authority as opposed to a delegate appointed by man to men."[63] It was this authority that his detractors attacked in order to undercut not only his station but also his doctrine so that they might replace it with their own.

Though this is the most personal and self-revealing of all Paul's letters, the way the Apostle binds the gospel to his defense must not be overlooked or underplayed. He fully understood that what was at stake in Corinth was the essence of the gospel message expressed in the Atonement of Christ that enabled God to put his seal upon them and give them his Spirit in their hearts as a guarantee of their salvation (1:21–22).

Paul's objective is primarily to bring the Church to a unity under Christ. A major way he attempts to do this is by changing the primary socializing agent in many of the converts' lives, specifically the greater Corinthian culture with its values and mores. His means of doing so is to bind them more closely to one another in the context of the gospel (his emphasis in 1 Corinthians) and to himself (his emphasis in this epistle). To do the latter, he works to convince these Christian converts that his apostolic position is that of establishing "a sort of patronal-kinship relationship, by which Christ becomes the Corinthians' benefactor through Paul."[64] His success in bringing about such unity would radically change and diverge the Christian's world from the world around these Saints. It would do so by changing the aim of life from retaining or increasing personal honor and prestige through successful competition to gaining the glory of God through service and love. The result for the Church would be greater "knowledge of the Son of God" and a maturing "in every way unto him who is the head, into Christ" by which every part of the body of the Church would work properly and each person grow in greater love (Eph. 4:13, 15, our translation).

known to *be* apostles. The NET translates this phrase as "They are well known to the apostles."

63. Kang, *Heralds and Community,* 308, emphasis in original.

64. Witherington, *Conflict and Community,* 456–57.

Paul's Critics at Corinth

As noted above, not long after the Apostle left Corinth for the first time, at least one member of the Christian community called into question Paul's apostolic authority. Before long, other individuals came into Corinth, likely from an eastern branch of the Church, and rekindled the issue. In analyzing their impact, it is important to neither overestimate nor underestimate it or them. We should keep in mind that congregations met in various house churches, not, as yet, in large congregations attending a single chapel. That being the case, the disaffection from Paul may have been localized to some house churches, while Saints belonging to other congregations in the city and in the greater province of Achaia (of which, for example, Cenchrea was one [see Rom. 16:1]) would have remained either lightly affected or untouched by the controversy.[65]

It may be that the interlopers who arrived in Corinth merely exacerbated conditions and tendencies that already existed in Corinth, such as pride, factiousness, fascination with Sophistic rhetoric and gifts of the spirit, which were coupled with a critical view of Paul, his authority, and his teachings.[66] But it is also likely that they were adding something new to the preexisting conditions, such as accusing Paul of laboring for monetary profit. Based on 1 Corinthians, it seems most likely that they were doing both but especially magnifying existing conditions for their own prestige and place in the Christian community.[67] Paul called these men "false apostles, deceitful workers, [who transformed] themselves into the apostles of Christ" (11:13). These men, he noted, came to Corinth preaching "another Jesus" and "another gospel" (11:4). They worsened the situation by not only preaching false doctrine but also attacking Paul's reputation and denigrating his credentials as an Apostle of Christ. The danger in their attack centered on the practical application of the gospel in the lives of the Corinthian Saints. In this way, they introduced a different "spirit" than that shared when Paul was with the community.[68] False doctrine leads to improper comportment

---

65. Martin, *2 Corinthians,* 463.

66. For a study arguing that the apostasy arose quite early due to, among other forces, the conflict between disciples and the planting of false doctrines by those influenced by Satan, see John W. Welch, "Modern Revelation: A Guide to Research about Apostasy," in *Early Christians in Disarray: Contemporary LDS Perspectives on the Christian Apostasy,* ed. Noel R. Reynolds (Provo, Utah: Brigham Young University Press, 2005), 101–32.

67. Witherington, *Conflict and Community,* 345.

68. Context suggests that Paul was not referring to the Holy Ghost when he castigated his detractors for bringing in a different "spirit," but was rather referring to the feelings—

and behavior. As such it not only interferes with correctly translating the gospel into everyday life but also with pleasing God. Thus, such doctrine can destroy one spiritually with the consequent loss of eternal life.

Paul's antagonists based their authority and its legitimization on three factors: the credentials they brought with them from another segment of the Christian Church, their charismatic powers, and their claim of divine revelation and direction.[69] They pushed the idea that the Apostle's ministry was ineffectual (10:10; 11:6) and lacked the gifts that they boldly prided themselves in having. Further, they accused Paul of "vacillation (1:17–18, 23), pride and boasting (3:1, 12; 5:12), lack of success in preaching (4:3), physical weakness (10:10), 'rudeness' of speech, defective[ness] in rhetorical skills (11:6), being an ungifted person (4:7–10; 10:10; 12:7–10; 13:9), dishonesty (12:16–19), posing as a 'fool' (5:13; 11:16–19; 12:6), and lacking of apostolic standing (11:5; 12:12)." Above all, they accused him of being "a deceiver (4:8) and a charlatan (10:1), [who pushed] a blatant denial of the power of the Christian message (13:2–9)."[70] In order to retain his position and spiritually save the congregation, Paul had to undercut each of these accusations.

Though the text reveals the number of the charges brought against Paul by his detractors, it does not reveal his antagonists' exact nature nor the content of the "other gospel" they were preaching. We know, based on the Apostle's writings to both the Galatian and Roman Churches, that he had to deal with a strong Judaizing force. This push was promulgated by Jewish Christians who believed the Mosaic law was still in effect but needed to be translated, understood, and lived through the lens of the Rabbi Jesus' teachings. A central tenant of their doctrine was that Gentiles who became Christians had to be circumcised (Acts 15:1). For Paul, the issue was not in the act itself for he felt that being circumcised or uncircumcised made no difference to one's standing with the Lord (Rom. 2:25–29). The problem was that the Judaizers viewed circumcision as a covenantal act through which persons took upon themselves the full weight of the law of Moses with all its requirements. Salvation, these men insisted, still came by obedience to that law. Thus, they did not see the Savior as fulfilling the law, but as giving it a proper interpretation. They therefore attacked Paul on the basis that he subverted the law and had abandoned the decree sent out to all the churches (see Acts 15:19–21).

---

both the emotion and mood—that attended the preaching of these people when compared with that which accompanied the initial preaching of the gospel.

69. Martin, *2 Corinthians,* 80.

70. Martin, *2 Corinthians,* 80.

The problem with the view that Paul's detractors, in this case, were Judaizers is that Paul uses none of the defenses against them that we find in Galatians or Romans. It may be that this particular group were not so bent on making circumcision of Gentiles the central point of their platform and also softened other points, but given the Judaizing insistence on the importance of the Mosaic law, it seems improbable that Paul's antagonists belonged to that group. Even if the idea of Judaizing forces is ruled out, that still allows from some of Paul's main detractors being Jewish Christians.[71]

But these antagonists could also have arisen from Christian Sophistry. Indeed, that Paul confronts his adversaries on essentially Hellenistic grounds gives force to this idea.[72] They appealed to their charismatic powers and the claim that they were the mouthpieces of divine revelation and had credentials that authenticated them.[73] These men would have easily attacked Paul on the basis that he neither understood nor clearly presented the gospel because he was unskilled in both their depth of thought and their precise way of teaching.

Some of these may have proclaimed an advance on Paul's teachings of grace through faith *alone* as the means of salvation by pushing his ideas to an antinomian extreme.[74] If that is the case, then these men were proclaiming that the Christians were under no obligation to obey the laws of ethics or morality, having been freed from all constraints by the power of Christ's Atonement. Such an idea Paul would have found absolutely abhorrent. If they preached such, their false doctrine could place them in the camp of "Gnostic

---

71. Jerry L. Sumney, *Identifying Paul's Opponents: The Question of Method in 2 Corinthians* (Sheffield, Eng.: JSOT Press, 1990), 181–84; compare Ralph P. Martin, "The Opponents of Paul in 2 Corinthians: An Old Issue Revisited," in *Traditions and Interpretations in the New Testament: Essays in Honor of E. Earle Ellis for His 60th Birthday,* ed. Gerald F. Hawthorne and Otto Betz (Grand Rapids, Mich.: William B. Eerdmans Publishers, 1987), 279–89.

72. C. K. Barrett, "Paul's Opponents in 2 Corinthians," in *Essays on Paul* (Philadelphia: Westminster Press, 1982), 80.

73. Martin, *2 Corinthians,* 120. C. K. Barrett, "Cephas and Corinth," in Barrett, *Essays on Paul,* 35–36, suggests that these men represented Peter and the Jerusalem branch of Christianity. According to his theory, their assignment was to disrupt Paul's work at Corinth. The problem with his thesis is that Paul, in his defense so clearly expressed in this epistle, never mentions Peter but does address Paul's opponents in the most virulent of terms (11:13–15). If these people did come from Jerusalem, it is more likely that they were going beyond their actual authority by claiming to represent the apostolic leadership.

74. The adjective "antinomian" describes the view that Christians are released by grace from the obligation of observing the moral law. For a study, see Robert H. Wall, "Antinomianism," in *The Anchor Bible Dictionary,* ed. David Noel Freedman, 6 vols. (New York: Doubleday, 1992), 1:263–64 (hereafter cited as *ABD*).

pneumatics."[75] It is clear that they paraded their supposed superior authority before the Christian community at Corinth and took pride in their status, resulting in an overbearing attitude toward lesser members of the Church.[76] But what is more likely is that they were Jewish Christian pneumatics. That is, they were men who, converting from Judaism, paraded their supposedly high devotion to God and deep spiritual nature before the Corinthian Saints and insisted that they had apostolic authority to minister in the affairs of the Church. Their attack on Paul made apostolic legitimation the central issue and the possession of the Spirit the main point of contention.[77]

Two of their main charges against the Apostle come clear from the text. The first had to do with Paul's refusal to use the Sophists' rhetorical tricks, smooth words, and attention-grabbing ways as a means of persuasion in his effort to promote the gospel. They berated what they considered his amateurish and unprofessional presentations (10:10; 11:6). Paul countered by parading his weaknesses and boasting "as a fool" (11:21–29) and by that means undercut the force of their efforts. The second was Paul's refusal to accept patronage and monetary support from the wealthier members of the branches. Given the culture, this act was tantamount to not only declining their friendship but also repudiating any value they may have had to him. But given the reconstruction of social values that Paul was promoting, he simply could not be beholden to anyone other than the Lord. To do otherwise was nothing less than validating the social condition he was fighting against.[78]

---

75. The term "Gnosticism" (γνωστικός [*gnostikos*], "having knowledge," from γνῶσις [*gnosis*], "knowledge") is a modern name for a variety of ancient religious ideas and systems somewhat influenced by Middle Platonism that made their way into both Jewish and Christian theological circles during first and second centuries AD. Based on a rather curious misreading of the Genesis, Gnostics believed that the material world was created by a jealous, inferior emanation of the highest God. This emanation, the Demiurge, trapped a portion of the high god's divine spark in fallen man. This spark could be liberated and return home by "gnosis," esoteric knowledge passed on through sacred rituals. The "Pneumatics" ("spiritualists," from πνεῦμα, "spirit") were, according to the gnostic system, the highest order of humans (the other two orders being psychics, "naturalistic," and hylics, "materialistic"). Pneumatics saw themselves as escaping the doom of the material world via transcendent knowledge. Paul was very concerned about the influence such ideas were having on some branches of the Church and instructed Timothy saying, "Avoid the godless chatter and contradictions of what is falsely called knowledge" (1 Tim. 6:20, our translation). For a study, see Kurt Rudolph, "Gnosticism," in *ABD,* 2:1033–40.

76. For discussion, see Rudolf Bultmann, *The Second Letter to the Corinthians,* ed. Erich Dinkler, trans. Roy A. Harrisville (Minneapolis: Augsburg, 1985), 203; and Walter Schmithals, *Gnosticism in Corinth* (Nashville: Abingdon Press, 1971), 124–35.

77. Witherington, *Conflict and Community,* 344–45.

78. Martin, *2 Corinthians,* 125.

The letter now under consideration—the fourth Paul wrote to Corinth—was the Apostle's response to Titus's positive if not glowing report concerning the attitude of the Saints toward Paul. Primarily due to this condition, albeit there were others, Paul wrote this epistle as both an apology and defense.

Summary. What was at stake and what Paul needed to pin down while the majority of members were still filled with godly zeal toward him was his apostolic authority. The total epistle, from the opening section (1:1–2, 17; 3:1–7:16) through the section dealing with the Jerusalem contribution (8:1–9:15), and especially in his closing defense (10:1–13:10), underscored but one theme—the legitimate nature of Paul's authority. Therefore, what constitutes the proof of a true Apostle and the range of his authority was the question at issue (13:1–6). In short, the question was what could be authentic evidence that a claimant had authority.[79] The antagonists rejected Paul's position as an "apostle of Christ Jesus by the will of God" (1:1). Paul, with urgency and a bit of vitriol, defended the authenticity of his authority brilliantly, taking his antagonist head-on in the last three chapters of his work. The question "And who is qualified for these things?" (2:16, NR; see also 3:4–6) is answered, albeit obliquely, in 13:5–6, where Paul shows that his competence comes directly from God, who made him a minister of the new covenant.

Also at stake was the crucial question of the source of doctrine. Paul's adversaries insisted that they had approved authority for their teachings—they came with letters of recommendation (3:1)—but their "gospel" ran diametrically opposed to that taught by Paul not only in content but also in application. Paul insisted that his doctrine was based on his apostolic call, authority, and conformance with Church practice. In doing so, he set the authority for directing Church affairs on the foundation of apostolic supremacy and divine revelation.[80]

Theirs appears to have been a theology based on acquisition of glory and superior position. They presented a Christianity that asserted a dominance and superiority of station. Though this played well in the status-conscious Corinth, it was not the Christianity of strength through meekness, kindness, service, and love that Paul preached. His was the theology of the cross.

---

79. Martin, *2 Corinthians,* 111.

80. Where Paul's antagonists insisted that authenticity must be decided on appearance, Paul insisted that apostolic authority is not subject to human judgment, but on its effect on the hearer. Seifrid, *Second Letter,* 104–5.

Indeed, for him strength, including his own, grew out of apparent but not actual weakness as understood in the death of the Lord. This weakness-to-strength motif, emphasized in the symbol of the cross, dominated both of Paul's existing writings to the Corinthians. Power and authority remain very important principles and carry heavy weight (10:8; 13:10), but, Paul stressed, they must be harnessed to loving service that seeks to build up each person singly and the Church collectively. Its push must be to help its recipients become mature in faith through ever greater faithfulness.[81]

Thus, the very foundation of what was truly Christian behavior and conduct—how the Christian translated the gospel into everyday life—was at stake here. Proper and godly behavior, based on faith and strengthened by grace, was the key to eternal life. Strip those away, and the resultant path was not to heaven but to hell. Little wonder then that Paul called his adversaries the ministers of Satan (11:13–14).[82] He clearly understood that the very salvation of his readers stood on their acceptance of the Apostle's divine authority. Paul's self-legitimization was "not carried out in the abstract. The question is whether Paul, who lives in weakness, bears the power and authority of Christ as the apostle to the Corinthians. Does the risen Lord speak in Paul, the weakling (13:3)?"[83]

In sum, whoever his detractors were, Paul blasted them as "false" or "fake apostles" (ψευδαπόστολοι, *pseudapostoloi*) who will be exposed to divine judgment for their falsity and arrogance (11:13–15). Indeed, the Apostle would not so much as dignify them with the sacred title of "apostle" but called them, rather, low-level servants (διάκονοι, *diakonoi*) of the devil (11:15) and sat himself apart from them by asking, "Are they servants of Christ?" and then saying, "I am more" (11:23, NIV) and then outlining all that he had done for the kingdom (11:23–29).

Given all the above, let us stress that Paul's aim was not to destroy the opposition as much as it was to unite the Corinthians once more with him. Paul's purpose in writing was to build on the reconciliation between and newly founded zeal of the Apostle and the Church generated by the "tearful letter" and the visit by Titus. Paul insisted that reconciliation was possible because God had already reconciled the world to himself. The process of reconciliation, however, must advance in the Christian community by being applied to concrete human situations and conditions. Here it was the

81. Martin, *2 Corinthians,* 125.

82. Martin, *2 Corinthians,* 115.

83. Seifrid, *Second Letter,* xxvii.

Apostle's relationship with the Corinthians. Because he felt his cause was just, he could call upon God as his ally in his effort to reproduce the close and enduring relationship he had had with them (6:11). He held no hard feelings toward them (6:11), and they, he insisted, should not toward him (6:12; 7:2–4).[84]

In sum, the situation that drove Paul to write 2 Corinthians was not the same as that for 1 Corinthians. The first instance was motivated by the development of internal factions leading to divisions among the Corinthian Saints (1 Cor. 1:10–16; 3:21–22). These factions promoted various false doctrines. Among them was an insistence that Christ was already reigning, that they were now kings being enriched by his power (1 Cor. 4:8), and, by extension, that there would be no bodily resurrection (1 Cor. 15:12). Among the factions were those who insisted that the Saints arose in a newness of life through baptism, which bestowed upon them an exalted status in the present world. By downplaying or denying any future judgment, these overly zealous souls opened the door to overly fervent practices and aberrations in worship that allowed for a very libertine and immoral lifestyle among the members. These and many more issues Paul had to address. But the point is that all these seem to have developed in-house.

In 2 Corinthians, the situation was much different. The conditions that Paul addressed came not exclusively from within the congregations but were largely brought in from outside. In this epistle, as noted above, we see Paul clearly on the defense for his own apostolic position and doctrinal teachings because of those who came from outside the Corinthian sphere. The evidence suggests, however, that Paul faced not one foe but multiple. Even so, whether Paul's detractors were Judaizers, Gnostics, Christian Sophists, or some combination of other theological systems, their core charge was directed at his authority and doctrine.

One problem Paul faced in making his defense was that, so far as the record shows, he was out of touch with the two eastern centers of Christian worship, Jerusalem and Antioch. Though he had made peace at least with Church leaders at Jerusalem, suspicion among many of the Jewish Saints still hung over him (Acts 21:19–25). This made him vulnerable to the attackers as noted above.

---

84. Martin, *2 Corinthians,* 120. See also Laurie Brink, "From Wrongdoer to New Creation: Reconciliation in 2 Corinthians," *Interpretation: A Journal of Bible and Theology* 71, no. 3 (2017): 298–309, who argues that God is the initiator of reconciliation and for the Corinthian Saints; Paul is the proof that it works.

Because the challenge was immediate, Paul did not have time to appeal to Church authority. Instead, he turned to an even more impressive and immediate proof of his apostolic power. This proof was in his bequeathing of the power of the Holy Spirit.[85] His appeal to this glorious gift suggests that not only for him but also for many of the Saints, it was the singular and most important sign that a new era had commenced, and though not yet fully realized, its sanctifying power was already manifest in the lives of his readers. The challenge was that it would continue to remain so only if they continued in faithfulness (3:17–18). Further, its reception was the guarantee that they had a share in the present reality of the new Christian age and that they would receive a full share of glory in the world to come (5:17–6:2). Thus, he used the undeniable presence of the Spirit to validate his authority as an Apostle of the Lord and thereby the authenticity of his teachings.

The question naturally arises whether this letter actually worked or, in other words, whether reconciliation was ever accomplished. From evidence within the epistle itself, it would appear that Paul thought so. He speaks of returning to Corinth for a third visit (13:1). But was he right? From the present vantage point, there is no certainty, but based on Romans 15:25–26; 16:1, 23–24, it appears that Paul did actually return to Corinth and stayed with members there where he wrote to the Roman Saints. In that epistle, he sends greetings from leading members of the Corinthian branch. Further, the collection for the Jerusalem poor was completed throughout Achaea, and that would include Corinth. Thus, it would appear that the Apostle succeeded in his efforts. That being the case, this epistle is "a shining example of how message, method, and ministry may come together to accomplish a theologically grounded social aim. It reflects Paul at his most powerful and poignant. If reconciliation is a sign of greatness, then 2 Corinthians is the clearest evidence of his stature."[86]

Paul's Methodology

Paul's objectives drove his methodology. These were to reset and anchor the gospel of Jesus Christ on its foundation such that God and Christ remained center stage and the Christian way of life was promoted and lived. In order to do this, as noted above, Paul had to work to overcome not only

85. Paul had already made his point in his first epistle to establish his authority. See 1 Cor. 9:1–2.

86. Witherington, *Conflict and Community*, 351.

the false teachings of his antagonists but also many of the social values and particular cultural orientation that his readers had acquired over their lifetimes. He had to "further his converts' resocialization by deinculturating them from some of their former primary values, chiefly by invoking certain eschatological ideas and the ethical implication of those ideas."[87] To do so he had to "clarify what the church's social relations with the world as it existed in Roman Corinth could and should be."[88]

Using his ample skills as a writer (and as one who understood the basics of rhetorical argument), he carefully laid out his motives and doctrine while defending his actions. He stressed his love for the Corinthian Church members as the driving force behind all that he did (2:4; 5:14), emphasized what he had already endured in their behalf because of that love (1:8–11; 4:1–3, 8–10; 6:4–6; 11:24–29), and asked them to reciprocate (7:2–4). In this way he attempted to unite them to him. He appealed to scriptural authority to bolster his positions (3:7–18; 4:5, 13; 6:15–17; 8:15; 9:7–10; 11:2–3, 24; 13:1). He emphasized and defended his apostolic authority (1:1, 21–22; 2:14–17; 4:1; 5:11–15) and warned his readers against those who sought to undermine that authority and the teachings that rested upon it (chaps. 11–13). To validate his authority, he appealed to the deeply beautiful and spiritual conversion experience of the Christians themselves and reminded them that this happened due to his preaching and under his administration (3:1–6, 18; 5:16–21; 10:7). He stressed the need to live the Christian lifestyle in the way he and his associates did (1:12–14; 4:1–2, 5–6, 16–18; 5:6–9, 11–13; 6:4–10; 7:1; 12:6–10) and noted the rewards that such a lifestyle brought (3:18; 4:11–15; 5:1–5, 10, 15, 17–19; 6:17–18; 9:6–15).

Paul used metaphor, irony, parody, diatribe, comparison, invective, and paradox to get his point across to his primary audience, the Corinthian Saints. He never addresses his antagonists directly, and thus they ever remain in the background, but we feel their menace behind what Paul writes. All the means he used reveal the intensity of the Apostle's feelings as he writes his defense, all to the end of reinforcing the Christians' faithfulness and devotion to the Lord and the divine reconciliation made possible by the loving act of their Savior.

---

87. Witherington, *Conflict and Community*, 8.

88. Witherington, *Conflict and Community*, 29.

A Note on the Greek Manuscripts, Translation Methods, and Use of Secondary Scholarship

Important Greek Manuscripts and Variants

The earliest lists of undisputed books always list 2 Corinthians among Paul's writings. From patristic evidence, it was circulating as early as the late first and early second centuries of the Christian era.[89] The earliest-known text containing virtually all of 2 Corinthians is the papyrus codex 𝔓[46] dated between AD 175 and 225,[90] which means it was copied (likely from another copy that itself was a copy) 120 to 180 years after Paul wrote the letter. The epistle is also found in the important codices Sinaiticus and Vaticanus as well as other early codices and in various fragments.[91] There are a number of variant readings in the existing manuscripts of 2 Corinthians, but few of them are of any theological importance. Those variants that do have such value are discussed in this commentary where appropriate.

89. Two of the earliest Church Fathers either quote or paraphrase passages from it. Polycarp, Bishop of Smyrna (d. 155) quoted 2 Cor. 5:10 in *Poly.* 6:2 and Clement, Bishop of Rome, quoted both 2 Cor. 9:12 and 11:9 in *1 Clem.* 38.2. Both, along with the Epistle of Barnabas, also paraphrase passages from it. For a study, see Richard D. Draper, "The Earliest New Testament," in *How the New Testament Came to Be,* ed. Kent P. Jackson and Frank F. Judd Jr. (Provo, Utah: Religious Studies Center, Brigham Young University; Salt Lake City: Deseret Book, 2006), 279.

90. Bruce W. Griffin, "The Paleographical Dating of P-46" (paper, Society of Biblical Literature conference, New Orleans, November 1996, http://biblical-data.org/P-46%20Oct%201997.pdf).

91. These two codices are the oldest ones that contain a near complete set of the New Testament books. Codex Vaticanus is housed in the Vatican in Rome. The Codex Sinaiticus was originally housed in St. Catherine's Monastery at the base of the traditional Mount Sinai. Thus, its name. The British library holds a majority of Sinaiticus; the Monastery of Saint Catherine, the University Library in Leipzig, and the National Library of Russia in Saint Petersburg all possess portions. See particularly https://codexsinaiticus.org/en/codex/history.aspx and https://codexsinaiticus.org/en/codex/date.aspx and codexsinaiticus.org. Both appear to be mid-fourth-century documents. See Kurt Aland and Barbara Aland, *The Text of the New Testament: An Introduction to the Critical Editions and to the Theory and Practice of Modern Textual Criticism,* 2nd ed., trans. Erroll F. Rhodes (Grand Rapids, Mich.: William B. Eerdmans; Leiden, Neth.: E. J. Brill, 1995), 107, 109.

The Nature of Paul's Greek

Paul used standard Koine Greek in his epistles, but in a way that revealed his education and skill as a writer and dictator. He was completely fluent and comfortable in Greek and was, therefore, able to utilize the full capacity of that remarkably flexible language to clarify and explain his messages to his audience. The general fluency of his Greek, in addition, allowed him to see and understand the implications and nuances of the Septuagint, his primary Old Testament text, which he skillfully put to full use. However, compared to his use of the Greek in some of his other epistles, especially Romans and 1 Corinthians, that in 2 Corinthians is rougher, thus supporting that idea that the letter was dashed off and therefore did not receive the polish that Paul's other epistles did. As a result, it contains "some of the most difficult Greek in the New Testament" to translate.[92]

Translation Philosophy

Due to our deep respect for the care and time that the various highly trained scholars took in translating the King James Version of the Bible, it has been with some trepidation and humility that we have undertaken the task of the rendering of the ancient Greek text into English. However, we do feel that such was necessary in order to present a script that reflects insights that come through the Restoration and also to overcome some of the weaknesses found in the KJV. The King James translators never overcame three challenges. The first was the late medieval Greek manuscript, the Textus Receptus, from which the translators worked. It was the product of Erasmus, the fifteenth-century Dutch theologian, whose manuscripts reached only back to the twelfth century. Though Theodore Beza, a French theologian, published an edition of the Greek New Testament based on more ancient and less corrupt manuscripts in 1565, the King James Translators were not provided with it. The second challenge they faced was their unfamiliarity with Koine Greek. These men were classists and knew well the power and beauty of the Attic prose of Plato and Aristotle. Unfortunately, "the rubbed down and difficult Greek" of the New Testament era held a number of mysteries they were unable to solve because Bible scholarship was still in its infancy. This has left a number of

92. Seifrid, *Second Letter,* ix.

passages, especially in the dense and difficult writings of Paul, virtually unintelligible in their translation (see, for example, 6:11–13, KJV).[93]

The third problem these translators faced was their biased understanding of certain Greek words and ideas. That bias rested on theologically "orthodox" views that were derived from middle platonic and Neoplatonic assumptions about the nature of salvation and the Godhead. As a result, the KJV translation sometimes reflects Augustinian and other early "orthodox" writings instead of a first-century context. Fortunately, the Book of Mormon and other Restoration scriptures have corrected these.

Exacerbating the problem were less-than-careful printers of the first editions. These copies were filled with errors, including misprints, wrong references, and spelling mistakes,[94] and various ones of these made their way into other editions. It was not until the nineteenth century that a scholar made a full collation of all the changes in the various editions. He found over twenty-four thousand variants.[95] The point is that, even to date, "no one such thing as 'The King James Bible'—agreed, consistent and whole—has ever existed," only various editions of the same.[96] For these reasons, we have felt justified in proceeding with a new rendering of the ancient Greek texts.

All in all, our work is designed to be neither all inclusive nor definitive, but tentative and suggestive. We expect and hope that others will come along who will improve our work. In the meantime, we hope what we have laid a firm foundation and put up a solid scaffolding which they can use to continue to build an ever-better understanding of God's word as revealed through his New Testament Apostles and prophets as viewed through the lens of the Restoration.

In our translation, we have attempted to present the original meaning of Paul's writings as faithfully and clearly as possible in modern English. We have constantly felt the need to balance the esoteric details of a text with the importance of communicating the breadth of its meaning as clearly as

---

93. Adam Nicolson, *God's Secretaries: The Making of the King James Bible* (New York: HarperCollins, 2003), 224.

94. A most notable and alarming mistake was replacing "Jesus" with "Judas" in one of the Gospels. Nicolson, *God's Secretaries,* 225–26.

95. Frederick H. A. Scrivener and Edward Miller, *A Plain Introduction of the New Testament for Use of Biblical Students* (Cambridge, Eng.: George Bell and Sons, 1894), https://archive.org/details/aplainintroductiooscriuoft.

96. Nicolson, *God's Secretaries,* 226.

possible to English readers. Fortunately, because this is a commentary and not a stand-alone translation, the Notes and Comments section allows us to further elucidate and expand the range of meanings of a word or phrase and, thereby, render it to a greater extent. We are ever aware that individual words have both denotations and connotations and are best understood within their semantic fields. Further, meaning does not reside in individual words alone but in collections of words found in clauses, phrases, sentences, and ultimately whole discourses. Our task was to first determine the meaning of any given cluster of words in the biblical text and then convey that meaning as accurately as possible into natural English.

Sometimes grammatical and syntactical forms that make good sense in Greek seem stilted, odd, and even weird when translated word for word into English. Our purpose has been to render the Greek in such a way that an educated reader could readily understand its meaning. And so, because of the marked difference between English and Greek grammar and syntax, we have especially tried to avoid an overly "literal" translation, which we feel could often obscure Paul's intent. We have, therefore, followed Bruce Metzger's dictum to be "as literal as possible, but as free as necessary" in order to communicate to the modern English reader the meaning of the text.[97]

Still, individual words do count, and therefore, we have labored carefully to determine how each word contributes to the clause, phrase, or sentence in which it is found. Our intent has been to convey, to the best of our ability, the meaning of the whole. Therefore, our Rendition should not be seen as prescriptive but as descriptive. It is in no way intended to be the ultimate Latter-day Saint translation but, rather, a rendering of the Greek to assist the modern reader in understanding the power and beauty of Paul's message. Where textual variants in the ancient manuscripts have significant impact on the meaning of the text, we have tried to select the one that is the most likely to have been the original, but when the variants do not affect the understanding of the text, we have ignored them. There are times when the words in our Rendition will be exactly the same as those in other translations. This is because that is the best and, in some cases, the only way a Greek text can be brought into English.

97. The dictum is found in the NRSV introduction, "To the Reader." For discussion on the challenges of translation, see Douglas J. Moo, *We Still Don't Get It: Evangelicals and Biblical Translation Fifty Years after James Barr* (Grand Rapids, Mich.: Zondervan, 2014).

Guidelines in This Volume on the Use of Material from Scholars and General Authorities

With sincere respect to those scholars, both within and without the Church, whose works have contributed so heavily to this volume, we have chosen not to refer to them by name in the body of the text. The major reason is to give greater emphasis to a teaching or thought rather than to the person who said it. The exceptions are quotes from General Authorities of the Church. Since this is a work that focuses on how Latter-day Saints view Paul's teachings, we thought it helpful to note which Church authorities said what. We have been very careful, however, to recognize and give credit in the footnotes to all the contributors.

The criteria we have used to determine which statements of both scholars and Church authorities to use—either to clarify, emphasize, or to expand on various teachings—is their harmony with the Standard Works. Early in this dispensation, the Lord revealed the means by which his doctrine would be established. To Oliver Cowdery he said, "And now, behold, I give unto you, and also unto my servant Joseph, the keys of this gift [of translation], which shall bring to light this ministry; and in the mouth of two or three witnesses shall every word be established" (D&C 6:28; see also D&C 128:3).[98] It is this principle we have tried to constantly apply. Because any number of line segments can be drawn through a single point, but only one can be drawn between two points, at least two anchors are needed. With the scriptures, we have four: the Bible, the Book of Mormon, the Doctrine and Covenants, and the Pearl of Great Price.

The reason we have adopted this criterion is based on a statement by President Joseph Fielding Smith, who wrote, "you cannot accept the books written by the authorities of the Church as standards of doctrine, only in so far as they accord with the revealed word in the standard works. Every man who writes is responsible, not the Church, for what he writes." He went on to say that if anyone "writes something which is out of harmony with the revelations, then every member of the Church is duty bound to reject it. If he writes that which is in perfect harmony with the revealed word of the Lord, then it should be accepted."[99] In this volume, we have tried to

98. On the divine law of witnesses, see Joseph Fielding Smith, *Answers to Gospel Questions,* 5 vols. (Salt Lake City: Deseret Book, 1957), 1:205.

99. Joseph Fielding Smith, quoted in *Doctrines of Salvation: Sermons and Writings of Joseph Fielding Smith,* ed. Bruce R. McConkie, 3 vols. in one (1954–56; rpt., Salt Lake City: Bookcraft, 1999), 3:203–4.

follow this dictum for quotes from both LDS and non-LDS scholars and authorities, including within the section "LDS Leaders' Use of 2 Corinthians." There we have not quoted everyone who has spoken on a specific scripture, but rather we have chosen a few statements that give the general feel for how General Authorities understand the scripture.

The Use of 2 Corinthians among the Latter-day Saints

LDS Leaders' Use of 2 Corinthians

Only one General Authority has commented on the full text of 2 Corinthians—Elder Bruce R. McConkie in his three-volume work *Doctrinal New Testament Commentary.* As the study below shows, other Church leaders have quoted from and commented on various verses or phrases within this epistle. However, unlike its sister epistle, 1 Corinthians, Church leaders have appealed to it to a far lesser degree. While 2 Corinthians thus ranks rather low as a source of doctrine, LDS leaders have used it to provide important insights, but more often to confirm a position or push an admonition. We have used the Scripture Citation Index (hereafter cited as SCI)[100] as the primary source to determine which scriptures have received the most attention and what Church leaders have said out them. Because scriptures cited fewer than nine times likely had little to contribute to Church doctrine or teachings, they have not been analyzed in this study.

Verse 5:10

According to the SCI, LDS Church leaders have referenced 2 Corinthians 5:10 more often than any other verse in this epistle, but most refer specifically to the version found in the JST. Only a few have cited it as it appears in the KJV.[101] The latter reads, "For we must all appear before the judgment seat of Christ; that every one may receive the things done in his body, according to that he hath done, whether it be good or bad." The JST version changes this to read, "For we must all appear before the judgment

100. Stephen W. Liddle and Richard C. Galbraith, Scripture Citation Index, version 3.5.0, https://scriptures.byu.edu.

101. SCI shows eighty citations with eight coming from the KJV text and seventy-two from the JST.

seat of Christ; that every one may receive *a reward of the deeds done in the* body, *things* according to what he hath done, whether good or bad" (italics show changes). The modification in the JST clarifies the ambiguity in the scriptures' use of the noun "things." It is the idea that judgment is based in large part on a person's deeds that general authorities most often reference.

In studying the citations listed, however, it becomes unclear if the General Authorities who used the phrase actually had this verse in mind. The reason is because this same thought is found in Alma 5:15. In the most recent citation, that of Spencer W. Kimball in 1964, the reference is clearly to the biblical source.[102] That, however, is not the case in most of the references to the *Journal of Discourses* listed in the SCI. For instance, Brigham Young stated, "I will now refer you to the scripture where it reads that we shall be judged according to the deeds done in the body."[103] The word "deeds" is not found in the KJV but, as noted above, only in the JST version and in Alma. It is because the phrase can be found in the Book of Mormon that we cannot be sure that those who used it were expressly thinking of 2 Corinthians.

In fact, it is most likely they did not, because, at that point in Church history, few would have been acquainted with Joseph Smith's changes.[104] Unfortunately, before the 1890s, few General Authorities specifically stated in their talks what scripture they were using. In 1899, however, the Church began publishing the official conference reports, in which scripture citations were given. These show that after that year, in using the phrase "deeds done in the body," only four General Authorities consciously referred to the verse in the KJV or the JST. Thus, it is doubtful that the SCI, in this case,

---

102. Spencer W. Kimball, *One Hundred Thirty-Fourth Semi-annual Conference of The Church of Jesus Christ of Latter-day Saints* (Salt Lake City: The Church of Jesus Christ of Latter-day Saints, 1964), 27.

103. Brigham Young, in *JD,* 3:205.

104. The documents containing the changes became the property of the Reorganized Church of Jesus Christ of Latter Day Saints and were not published until 1867. This publication is often referred to as the "Inspirited Version." It had little influence on the LDS Church, often being held suspect because it was published by a rival. Only after the work begun in the 1960s by Robert J. Matthews and Richard P. Howard did the Church come to accept the Inspired Version as a correct edition of Joseph Smith's original work and begin using it in earnest. For a study, see Robert J. Matthews, *"A Plainer Translation": Joseph Smith's Translation of the Bible—a History and Commentary* (Provo, Utah: Brigham Young University Press, 1975); and Scott H. Faulring, Kent P. Jackson, and Robert J. Matthews, eds., *Joseph Smith's New Translation of the Bible: Original Manuscripts* (Provo, Utah: Religious Studies Center, Brigham Young University, 2004).

accurately reflects the actual number of times LDS leaders referred to this verse and is, therefore, not a good indicator of its actual theological weight. Even so, the verse does substantiate the doctrine that the final judgment does focus, in large part, on deeds that a person does here in mortality.

Verse 5:17

Given the above, it is most likely that the scripture that General Authorities have referred to the most in conference addresses is 2 Corinthians 5:17.[105] The sources listed in the SCI appear to be a good indicator of the scripture's use, and thus it has actual theological weight. The verse states: "Therefore if any man be in Christ, he is a new creature: old things are passed away; behold, all things are become new." Commonly, this scripture is used in connection with others to support the doctrine of spiritual rebirth. For instance, President Spencer W. Kimball stated that "the Lord is not primarily interested in having His children only convinced of His work. He would like them to be converted to the gospel. Truly converted persons change their old sinful ways and turn to a new life in Christ; there is truly a 'converting' or a changing in their lives." He then quoted this verse to emphasize his point.[106]

Twice in general conferences, Elder David A. Bednar quoted this verse, along with Mosiah 5:2 and Mosiah 27:25, to provide a scriptural foundation for the need of spiritual rebirth.[107] He said, "As we honor the ordinances and covenants of salvation and exaltation (see D&C 20:25), 'press forward with a steadfastness in Christ' (2 Nephi 31:20), and endure in faith to the end (see D&C 14:7), we become new creatures in Christ (see 2 Corinthians 5:17)."[108] Elder Bednar explained what that change entails: "Please note that the conversion described in these verses is mighty, not minor—a spiritual rebirth and fundamental change of what we feel and desire, what we think and do, and what we are. Indeed, the essence of the gospel of Jesus Christ entails a fundamental and permanent change in our very nature made possible through our reliance upon the merits, and mercy, and grace of the Holy Messiah (2 Nephi 2:8)." Elder Bednar further explained that

---

105. SCI shows twenty-eight conference address citations and twenty-five JD citations.

106. Spencer W. Kimball, "It Becometh Every Man," *Ensign* 7, no. 10 (October 1977): 5.

107. David A. Bednar, "Converted unto the Lord," *Ensign* 42, no. 11 (November 2012): 107; "Exceeding Great and Precious Promises," *Ensign* 47, no. 11 (November 2017): 93.

108. Bednar, "Converted unto the Lord," 107. While not every General Authority uses 2 Cor. 5:17 along with other scriptures, most do so.

becoming a new creature is not overexaggerating the change conversion brings. Feelings, thoughts, and actions are all changed, fully meriting the description of a "new creature" for the one who truly converts.[109]

Earlier General Authorities have also used the verse to describe spiritual rebirth. For instance, President John Taylor observed of those who believed in Christ that "they were born of the water and of the Spirit and were made new creatures in Christ Jesus."[110] Elder Orson Pratt explained what it meant to be born of the Spirit. He asked, "What do we understand by the birth of the spirit? I answer, that there is a birth of the spirit, in other words, those persons who receive the Holy Ghost are filled with it, are immersed within it, they are clothed upon therewith, and consequently are born anew of it, and they are without desires to do evil, their desires to do that which is wrong are taken away, and they become new creatures in Christ Jesus."[111]

However, not every General Authority has used this verse exclusively to support the idea of spiritual rebirth. Elder Pratt also used it to convey the idea of old things becoming new in the context of the Second Coming. He said, "And then, after all things are made new, and old things have passed away, the two Jerusalems will come down from God out of heaven, and will rest upon the new earth."[112] It is of note that he applies the complete spiritual change usually associated with personal spiritual rebirth to the physical changes the earth and humanity will undergo during the Second Coming. Just as a person is completely changed through the influence of the Spirit, so too the earth and all on it will experience a similar degree of change.

Verses 12:7–10

The number of citations or allusions by LDS leaders in their conference addresses to 12:7–10 makes it the second or third most quoted section from this epistle depending on how 5:10 is taken.[113] It states, "And lest I should be exalted above measure through the abundance of the revelations, there was given to me a thorn in the flesh, the messenger of Satan to buffet me, lest I should be exalted above measure. For this thing I besought the Lord

---

109. David A. Bednar, "Ye Must Be Born Again," *Ensign* 37, no. 5 (May 2007): 20.

110. John Taylor, in *JD,* 25:262.

111. Orson Pratt, in *JD,* 17:150.

112. Orson Pratt, in *JD,* 16:323.

113. SCI shows that either a verse or a set of verses have been cited thirty-nine times in total.

thrice, that it might depart from me. And he said unto me, My grace is sufficient for thee: for my strength is made perfect in weakness. Most gladly therefore will I rather glory in my infirmities, that the power of Christ may rest upon me. Therefore I take pleasure in infirmities, in reproaches, in necessities, in persecutions, in distresses for Christ's sake: for when I am weak, then am I strong."

Though scholars have speculated heavily on the nature of Paul's thorn, Church leaders have been unconcerned about its exact nature. Instead they have used the Apostle's experience as a model for how modern Saints can overcome the "thorns" in their own lives, whatever those may be. For example, President Lee observed, speaking to Church leaders, "So it is with you who in Zion preside in the various places. Sometimes there is given infirmity, difficulty, hardship upon you to try your souls; and the powers of Satan seem to be enrolled against you, watching and trying to break down your powers of resistance; but your weakness, through those infirmities, will give you the power of God that shall rest upon you even as the Apostle Paul was reconciled and comforted by the thought that through his trials the power of God might rest upon him."[114]

Picking up on this same theme, Elder Gary B. Sabin stated that "we stand up inside when we wait patiently upon the Lord to remove or give us strength to endure our thorns in the flesh. Such thorns may be disease, disability, mental illness, death of a loved one, and so many other issues."[115] His statement shows that "thorns" can refer to a wide variety of afflictions.

General Authorities have also cited this section to help explain why God does not remove trials in our lives. Elder Richard G. Scott, after citing from this passage, said, "[God] gave Paul strength to compensate so he could live a most meaningful life. He wants you to learn how to be cured when that is His will and how to obtain strength to live with your challenge when He intends it to be an instrument for growth. In either case the Redeemer will support you."[116] It is noteworthy that Elder Scott acknowledged that sometimes it is God's will that one be released from a trial, but in many cases it is not. An important part of mortality is enduring what life presents. However, Elder Scott does note that Christ is there to support his people at all times.

---

114. Harold B. Lee, in *One Hundred Twentieth Semi-annual Conference of The Church of Jesus Christ of Latter-day Saints* (Salt Lake City: The Church of Jesus Christ of Latter-day Saints, 1949), 57.

115. Gary B. Sabin, "Stand Up Inside and Be All In," *Ensign* 47, no. 5 (May 2017): 53.

116. Richard G. Scott, "To Be Healed," *Ensign* 24, no. 5 (May 1994): 7.

General authorities have also used this scripture in another way—namely, to encourage members to trust in the Lord. For example, Elder D. Todd Christofferson, before quoting this scripture, stated that "the Apostle Paul understood that one who has entered into a covenant with God is both given the faith to face trials and gains even greater faith through those trials."[117] While Paul does not specifically mention faith in these verses, Elder Christofferson points out that Paul's actions show his deep trust and faith in God. In sum, Paul's willingness to endure the ongoing trial of his thorn necessitated a faith and allowed him to develop an even greater faith in the Lord.

Verse 13:1

The verse that LDS leaders cite the next most is found at 13:1.[118] This verse states, "This is the third time I am coming to you. In the mouth of two or three witnesses shall every word be established." It is the second sentence that General Authorities find the most pertinent. Paul's rendering is a close paraphrase of Deuteronomy 19:15, but most General Authorities who cite the idea use the New Testament passage as a proof text for a point they are making. For example, Elder Tad R. Callister referred to it to explain why the Lord brought forth the Book of Mormon. He stated, "To help bring this oneness about, the Lord established a divine law of witnesses. Paul taught, 'In the mouth of two or three witnesses shall every word be established.' The Bible is one witness of Jesus Christ; the Book of Mormon is another."[119] Elder Callister's use of the scripture shows that he took the idea of witnesses as a general principle. It is obvious that he did not believe that Paul was using it to help support the need for the Book of Mormon.

Indeed, the General Authorities who cite this verse never use it to make the same point Paul did.[120] Rather they emphasize the general principle and its benefit. For example, Elder Joseph B. Wirthlin explained, "Many of our assignments in the Church are shared with companions. Ever since the Lord sent out His disciples two by two, companionships have advanced the work of the Kingdom. The Lord's law of witnesses requires that 'in the mouth of two or three witnesses shall every word be

117. D. Todd Christofferson, "The Power of Covenants," *Ensign* 39, no. 5 (May 2009): 21.

118. SCI shows thirty-three citations.

119. Tad R. Callister, "The Book of Mormon–a Book from God," *Ensign* 41, no. 11 (November 2011): 75.

120. For discussion of Paul's use of this phrase, see the Analysis of 13:1.

established.'"[121] President Henry B. Eyring qualifies the "law of witnesses" by noting that the witnesses have to be "authorized."[122] Elder Pratt also used the verse to stress the benefits the application of the principle has given to the Lord's work. In discussing the founding of the Church, he stated that the Lord "did not raise up this Church, he did not commence the organization thereof until he had given sufficient evidence to a sufficient number of witnesses to commence the establishment of this work."[123] He went on to observe that the number of witnesses included the eleven witnesses of the Book of Mormon, which is well above the required two or three mentioned in 2 Corinthians. The witnesses were necessary, he noted, to give sufficient credibility to the latter-day work. President Joseph F. Smith also showed how the "law of witnesses" was operating as Joseph Smith and Oliver Cowdery received the priesthood. He said, "It is significant that the Prophet Joseph Smith did not receive the priesthood by himself, but he, together with Oliver Cowdery, received the priesthood, and it was Oliver Cowdery's calling to bear witness to these things."[124] In sum, while none of the General Authorities have examined the "law of witnesses" from a legal, theological, or contextual perspective, they exclusively used it to give credibility to the Church's practice and its scriptural base.

Verses 12:2–4

Tying with 2 Corinthians 13:1 in the number of citations listed in the SCI, LDS leaders have frequently appealed to 12:2–4 to substantiate certain doctrines.[125] It states, "I knew a man in Christ above fourteen years ago, (whether in the body, I cannot tell; or whether out of the body, I cannot tell: God knoweth;) such an one caught up to the third heaven. And I knew such a man, (whether in the body, or out of the body, I cannot tell: God knoweth;) How that he was caught up into paradise, and heard unspeakable words, which it is not lawful for a man to utter." Paul's statement is important in LDS theology, supporting as it does the doctrine of three kingdoms of glory.

---

121. Joseph B. Wirthlin, "Valued Companions," *Ensign* 27, no. 11 (November 1997): 34.

122. Henry B. Eyring, "Finding Safety in Counsel," *Ensign* 27, no. 5 (May 1997): 25.

123. Orson Pratt, in *JD*, 19:355.

124. Joseph F. Smith, in *One Hundred Fifteenth Semi-annual Conference of The Church of Jesus Christ of Latter-day Saints* (Salt Lake City: The Church of Jesus Christ of Latter-day Saints, 1944), 109.

125. SCI shows thirty-two citations.

The connection between the third heaven and the celestial sphere traces back to the Prophet Joseph Smith, who noted that "Saint Paul informs us of three glories and three heavens, he knew a man that was caught up to the third heaven, now if the doctrine of the sectarian world, that there is but one heaven, is true, Paul, what do you tell that lie for, and say there are three?"[126] While the Prophet did not say specifically that heaven is divided up into the celestial, terrestrial, and telestial kingdoms, other general authorities have tied what Paul said to material in the seventy-sixth section of the Doctrine and Covenants and come to that conclusion. For instance, Elder LeGrand Richards said, referring to the heavenly condition, "Paul was privileged to see it, for he was caught up into the third heaven and the paradise of God, but he was not permitted to write the things that he beheld."[127]

Elder Dallin H. Oaks tied these verses to 1 Corinthians 15:40, where Paul writes of celestial and terrestrial bodies. Elder Oaks noted, "In his letters to the Corinthians, the Apostle Paul described these places. He told of a vision in which he was 'caught up to the third heaven' and 'heard unspeakable words, which it is not lawful for a man to utter.' Speaking of the resurrection of the dead, he described 'celestial bodies,' 'bodies terrestrial,' and 'bodies telestial,' each pertaining to a different degree of glory. He likened these different glories to the sun, to the moon, and to different stars."[128] By joining 1 Corinthians 15:40 and 2 Corinthians 12:2–4, Elder Oaks provides the New Testament evidence for the doctrine of three degrees of glory further detailed in Doctrine and Covenants 76. While Paul's words have provided ample disagreement and discussion among other Christians and scholars, Latter-day Saints have seen Paul's words as clear evidence for the three degrees of glory.

Verse 7:10

The verse LDS leaders cited most frequently next to those listed above is found in 7:10.[129] It reads, "For godly sorrow worketh repentance to salvation

---

126. "History, 1838–1856, Volume D-1 [1 August 1842–1 July 1843]," 1574, Joseph Smith Papers, accessed November 17, 2022, https://www.josephsmithpapers.org/paper-summary/history-1838-1856-volume-d-1-1-august-1842-1-july-1843/219, capitalization modernized.

127. LeGrand Richards, in *One Hundred Sixteenth Annual Conference of The Church of Jesus Christ of Latter-day Saints* (Salt Lake City: The Church of Jesus Christ of Latter-day Saints, 1946), 83.

128. Dallin H. Oaks, "Apostasy and Restoration," *Ensign* 25, no. 5 (May 1995): 86. The phrase "bodies telestial" is not found in the KJV but it is in the JST.

129. SCI shows twenty-nine citations.

not to be repented of: but the sorrow of the world worketh death." The major General Authorities have focused on the phase "godly sorrow" and the role it plays in the repentance process. President Dieter F. Uchtdorf, for example, stated, "Godly sorrow inspires change and hope through the Atonement of Jesus Christ. Worldly sorrow pulls us down, extinguishes hope, and persuades us to give in to further temptation. Godly sorrow leads to conversion and a change of heart."[130]

Elder Royden G. Derrick connected this verse with Matthew 5:4, which states, "Blessed are they that mourn: for they shall be comforted." He equated "godly sorrow" with mourning for past sins and noted that it "is necessary to repent of our sins if we are to be forgiven and if the atonement of Jesus Christ is to be effective in our lives. Oh! how joyous it is to work with a person as he goes through the process of repentance, enters the water of baptism, and comes into the kingdom of God."[131] While Elder Derrick did not use the verse in Matthew as normally understood, his connecting it with 2 Corinthians does emphasize the need for deep sorrow as a means of reestablishing a close relationship with God.

Of note is that General Authorities in the nineteenth century included in their quotes of this verse the phrase "which needeth not to be repented of." As it stands in the KJV, it is rather ambiguous, but President Joseph F. Smith defined it. He said, "But first having repented of our sins with that repentance which needeth not to be repented of, [or] in other words, putting away from us every evil, and shunning even the appearance of sin."[132] Thus the phrase points to righteous actions for which there will never be a call for repentance. During the twentieth century, however, General Authorities have usually elided that phrase. For example, President Uchtdorf quoted the verse as saying, "'*godly sorrow* worketh repentance to salvation . . . but the *sorrow of the world* worketh death.'"[133] Note that he deliberately excluded the ambiguous phrase, probably so it would not add any confusion to or detract from his point. Other General Authorities have followed this same pattern.[134]

---

130. Dieter F. Uchtdorf, "You Can Do It Now!," *Ensign* 43, no. 11 (November 2016): 56, italics removed.

131. Royden G. Derrick, "The Beatitudes and Our Perfection," *Ensign* 7, no. 5 (May 1977): 58.

132. Joseph F. Smith, in *JD,* 18:272.

133. Uchtdorf, "You Can Do It Now!," 56, italics in original.

134. For examples, see Steven L. Richards, in *One Hundred Twenty-fourth Annual Conference of The Church of Jesus Christ of Latter-day Saints* (Salt Lake City: The Church of

Verse 3:6

The next most cited verse is found at 3:6.[135] It states, "Who also hath made us able ministers of the new testament; not of the letter, but of the spirit: for the letter killeth, but the spirit giveth life." LDS leaders have appealed to the last two phrases. For instance, Elder James E. Faust referenced this verse to encourage the Saints to seek more from their temple worship. He stated, "In our desire to create in our people more commitment to the holy work of the temples, we must urge them to look deeper to the profound spiritual meaning to be found there. As Paul reminded us, 'For the letter killeth, but the spirit giveth life.'"[136] Though Elder Faust used this verse, in this instance, to emphasize the importance of seeking deeper, more spiritual meaning in temple worship, he also used it in other contexts. For example, after quoting this verse, he noted, "We are not only to avoid evil, not only to do good but, most importantly, to do the things of greatest worth. We are to focus on the inward things of the heart, which we know and value intuitively but often neglect for that which is trivial, superficial, or prideful. . . . I have some fear, however, that some members consider guidelines and procedures to be as important as the timeless, immutable laws of the gospel."[137] In using the phrase in this setting, he demonstrates that, like most other General Authorities, he viewed Paul's words as a good aphorism that could be applied to a number of situations. Noteworthy is that he delineated what constitutes "the letter" and "the spirit." The inward things of greatest worth—the "timeless, immutable laws of the gospel"—he connects to "the spirit," whereas undue devotion to the "trivial, superficial, or prideful" and some "guidelines and procedures" he connects to "the letter."

Even though the General Authorities have tended not to specify exactly what constitutes the "letter," like Elder Faust, some have reached for a definition. For instance, Elder Pratt said, in relation to various Christian sects, that "they may have the word, but the Bible itself says that the letter killeth."[138] In contrast, Elder Pratt noted that the Latter-day Saints have

---

Jesus Christ of Latter-day Saints, 1954), 11; and Victor L. Brown, in *One Hundred Thirty-Sixth Annual Conference of The Church of Jesus Christ of Latter-day Saints* (Salt Lake City: The Church of Jesus Christ of Latter-day Saints, 1966), 22.

135. SCI shows twenty-six citations.

136. James E. Faust, "Standing in Holy Places," *Ensign* 35, no. 5 (May 2005): 63.

137. James E. Faust, "The Weightier Matters of the Law: Judgment, Mercy, and Faith," *Ensign* 27, no. 10 (October 1997): 53.

138. Orson Pratt, in *JD,* 16:348.

the spirit since they have living prophets and not just the written word. It appears that, from his point of view, sole reliance on the Bible qualifies as "the letter" that kills. This position, however, few other General Authorities have taken. President Thomas S. Monson discussed how the New Testament brought "a spirit of awakening to the human soul" and thereby placed the New Testament in the category of "the spirit" rather than "the letter."[139] Even though LDS leaders have not precisely defined what constitutes "the letter" and "the spirit" of the law, they have used Paul's words to encourage Latter-day Saints to hold to that which is of greatest worth.

Verse 4:4

General Authorities have cited 2 Corinthians 4:4 the next most.[140] It states, "In whom the god of this world hath blinded the minds of them which believe not, lest the light of the glorious gospel of Christ, who is the image of God, should shine unto them." During the nineteenth century, LDS leaders most frequently appealed to the phrase "god of this world" to make their point. President John Taylor, for example, talked about some Saints who "have become blinded by the God of this world."[141] Brigham Young tied gold or money to the "god of this world," noting that "a little gold dust was found near Pike's Peak; the golden god—the god of this world," and warned that those who follow after this god "will learn that they have been cheating themselves for the golden god—the Mammon of this world."[142]

LDS leaders have not appealed to this scripture much since the turn of the last century (only four citations are listed after 1899), although in 2014, President Uchtdorf cited phrases from the verse and then asked the rhetorical question "Have you allowed 'the god of this world' to darken your minds to 'the light of the glorious gospel of Christ'?"[143] He then admonished the Saints to let Christ's light shine in their lives. It is of note that the General Authorities have not cited the whole verse but have used this phrase to provide a distinction between those who kept to the true faith and those who were seduced away by the things of the world.

To a lesser extent, some Church authorities have used this verse to show that the Savior looks like his Father. For instance, Delbert L. Stapley said that the Apostle "Paul declared to the Corinthian saints that Christ is

139. Thomas S. Monson, "'The Spirit Giveth Life,'" *Ensign* 15, no. 5 (May 1985): 68.
140. SCI index shows twenty-three citations.
141. John Taylor, in *JD*, 10:260.
142. Brigham Young, in *JD*, 8:168, 171–72.
143. Dieter F. Uchtdorf, "'Lord, Is It I?,'" *Ensign* 44, no. 11 (November 2014): 57.

'the image of God' and to the Hebrews that Christ is 'the express image of [God's] person.'"[144]

Verse 5:7

Because of the appeal of an important doctrine taught in 5:7, LDS leaders have used it the next most.[145] It states: "For we walk by faith, not by sight." Leaders' focus has been on the Saints' need to rely on faith as they progress through life. Elder Bruce R. McConkie noted some of the implications of this need when he stated that "it is not the Lord's program to appear personally to every man [and woman] and tell [them] what to believe and how to act to be saved. In this, our second estate, we are to walk by faith, not by sight."[146] The purpose of this mortal existence, the leaders have insisted, is to have all God's children exercise moral agency. If God were to always tell everyone exactly what to do, their agency would be limited. Walking by faith allows people to fully take advantage of their second estate by giving them the freedom to choose exactly what they wish to be. Brigham Young pointed out that the leaders of the Church are not exempt from this condition. He explained that God will "let His servants gaze upon eternal things for a moment, but straightway the vision is closed, and they are left as they were, that they may learn to act by faith, or as the Apostle has it, not walking by sight, but by faith."[147] Thus, even God's servants are required to walk by faith even though they may have visions and revelation others may not have had. All men and women must ultimately rely on faith, no matter what their position in the Church is.

Elder Neal A. Maxwell, discussing how walking by faith is actually safer than walking by sight, explained, "When unaided spiritually, natural sight often shrinks from the odds. It is immobilized by improbabilities. Mauled by his moods and intimidated by his fears, the natural man overreacts to, while hope [with the faith it engenders] overrides, the disappointments of the day."[148] Rather than faith being a poor substitute for sight, Elder Maxwell shows that Paul's words are a reminder of the strength and assistance faith gives to the Saints.

---

144. Delbert L. Stapley, "Easter Thoughts," *Ensign* 6, no. 5 (May 1976): 76.

145. SCI shows eighteen citations.

146. Bruce R. McConkie, in *One Hundred Thirty-Fourth Semi-annual Conference of The Church of Jesus Christ of Latter-day Saints* (Salt Lake City, The Church of Jesus Christ of Latter-day Saints, 1964), 37.

147. Brigham Young, in *JD,* 1:264.

148. Neal A. Maxwell, "Brightness of Hope," *Ensign* 24, no. 11 (November 1994): 36.

Verse 5:20

Next to the scriptures studied above, LDS leaders have cited portions of 5:20 the most.[149] It states, "Now then we are ambassadors for Christ, as though God did beseech you by us: we pray you in Christ's stead, be ye reconciled to God." It is of note that none of the General Authorities have cited the whole verse in their talks. Instead, like most of the other scriptures noted above, they have taken phrases from it to give force to points in their talks. For instance, President Lorenzo Snow and Elder Charles W. Penrose both referred to the ancient Apostles as "ambassadors of the Lord Jesus Christ."[150] Lorenzo Snow gave a definition of the phrase, observing that "you may only be a hod-carrier [someone who supplies a brick layer with mortar], but remember you are an Elder in Israel, you are an ambassador of the Lord Jesus Christ, and if you are in the line of your duty you are in possession of that which the world cannot give nor take away; and you are held accountable to God for the honest use of the talent over which he has made you steward, whether it be large or small."[151] Though the Prophet directed this statement toward men, the title "ambassador" holds true for all, both men and women, who hold callings and positions of trust in the kingdom. Indeed, President Gordon B. Hinkley referred to missionaries as "ambassadors of the Lord Jesus Christ."[152]

In his admonitions to the Saints, following the practice of other General Authorities at the time,[153] President Young frequently used the phrase "be ye reconciled to God" to stress the need for the Saints to do so.[154] For example, he admonished "all who hear me, be ye reconciled to God, and ask for the things that you want. If you want life and salvation, ask for it in faith, humility and meekness."[155] The prophet's words tacitly point to what grows out of reconciliation—namely, a desire for eternal life. He further stated, "I will say to my friends—those who believe in the Lord Jesus

149. SCI shows seventeen citations.

150. Lorenzo Snow, in *JD,* 18:298; Charles W. Penrose, in *JD,* 22:157.

151. Lorenzo Snow, in *JD,* 18:299.

152. Gordon B. Hinckley, "To Men of the Priesthood," *Ensign* 32, no. 11 (November 2002): 58.

153. For example, see Orson Pratt, in *JD,* 7:85; Heber C. Kimball, in *JD,* 4:335.

154. For example, see Brigham Young, in *JD,* 12:32. The SCI shows that President Young referred to this verse nine times. In six of them, he explicitly used this phrase. Though the phrase is also found in Rom. 5:10 and 2 Ne. 25:23, the context of Presidents Young's use shows he had 2 Cor. in mind.

155. Brigham Young, in *JD,* 14:136.

Christ—'I beseech you in Christ's stead, be ye reconciled to God.' Treasure up every truth that you hear, practice it in your lives, for this will lead you to Jesus."[156] It is of note that the SCI shows no listing for the use of this verse by Church leaders in conferences after 1900. Just why this is the case is unknown, but it does suggest that this verse has not played a significant role in LDS theology.

Verse 4:7

Though the SCI shows no twentieth-century Church leaders referencing the material in 4:7, those of the nineteenth did.[157] It states: "But we have this treasure in earthen vessels, that the excellency of the power may be of God, and not of us." Once again it was not the whole verse but only a phrase that caught their attention. The phrase was "treasures in earthen vessels." President John Taylor was particularly fond this imagery. For instance, to stress the need for members to be more forgiving, he asked, "Have I got a treasure?" and then answered, "Yes, but we are told that it is held in 'earthen vessels,' which are subject to all the weaknesses, infirmities and follies, incident to humanity."[158] His point was that, even though people may possess heavenly gifts, they are still weak and need tolerance. In another discourse he asked, "Are the Saints perfect? I wish you were. We are all surrounded by weaknesses and infirmities. I acknowledge I am, and I think I could so speak for some of my brethren, but I do not propose to confess their weaknesses. Notwithstanding all the blessings conferred upon us through the Gospel we have received, we, all of us, have 'the treasures in earthen vessels.' I suppose that God has given us these infirmities that no flesh might glory in his presence, but that we might all feel our littleness and weakness, realizing every day that we need to pray just as the Lord taught his disciples to pray."[159] His point was that because human weakness is so ubiquitous, all should, of necessity, be more forgiving.

In another address, he gave a slightly different nuance to the phrase. Speaking of the gospel, he noted that, "This light and intelligence was communicated to men in the dark ages. This treasure, says the Apostle, we have in earthen vessels. This was what Jesus referred to when he said to the woman of Samaria—'If thou hadst asked of me I would have given thee

156. Brigham Young, in *JD,* 13:56.

157. SCI shows seventeen citations, including one in 2020.

158. John Taylor, in *JD,* 20:160.

159. John Taylor, in *JD,* 18:283–84.

water which would have been in thee a well springing up to everlasting life.'"[160] In this case, President Taylor referred to the "treasure in earthen vessels" as the possession of Christ's power by which one can obtain eternal life.

Elder Orson Hyde connected the "treasure in earthen vessels" to living Church leaders. After noting that the Lord had set up the Church under the direction of specific officers, he noted that God put these in position to "to guide his people;—the oracles (or in other words, the Holy Ghost,) not on paper, bound in calf, sheep, or any other manufactured article, but in the hearts of his chosen servants. Paul says—'We have this treasure (not in a book, but) in earthen vessels, that the excellency of the power may be of God, and not of us.'"[161] His point was that, through the power of the Holy Ghost, God's "earthen vessels," meaning Church authorities, have godly power to do his will.

Verse 11:14

The next most frequently referenced scripture by LDS leaders is found in 11:14.[162] It states: "And no marvel; for Satan himself is transformed into an angel of light." General Authorities have used this verse to show that Satan can disguise himself and his teachings and thus beguile unwitting souls to do his will. Elder Faust noted that "as the great deceiver, Lucifer has marvelous powers of deception." Elder Faust then quoted this verse to stress the point.[163] Elder Jedediah M. Grant discussed the means whereby Satan is able to push forward his work. He said, "Now Lucifer has philosophy enough and religion enough to suffer his agents to run along with the truth hand in hand, and make himself appear like an angel of light, and teach hundreds of true principles, if he can only thereby get you to swallow one item of false doctrine."[164] Though this is true, as President Harold B. Lee taught, God has provided a way for the Saints to detect the evil one. "Because of Satan's ability thus to cleverly deceive, the Lord has given us a key in the scriptures by which we may be able to detect him when he comes presenting himself as that angel of light." President Lee was here referring to instructions given in Doctrine and Covenants 129:8. He goes on to say, "And so we are told to be constantly on guard against these things."[165]

---

160. John Taylor, in *JD,* 16:194.
161. Orson Hyde, in *JD,* 7:151.
162. SCI shows fifteen citations.
163. James E. Faust, "The Great Imitator," *Ensign* 17, no. 11 (November 1987): 34.
164. Jedediah M. Grant, in *JD,* 2:15.
165. Harold B. Lee, in *One Hundred Twentieth Semi-annual Conference,* 57.

President Lee's point is that there is no reason for the Saints to be deceived because the Father has provided a way for the adversary's detection.

Verse 5:1

Next, Church leaders cited the material in 5:1 the most.[166] It states: "For we know that if our earthly house of this tabernacle were dissolved, we have a building of God, an house not made with hands, eternal in the heavens." Like nearly every other scripture studied here, General Authorities have used only a phrase or two from this verse to make their point. They have used these primarily to give encouragement to the Saints to continual faithfulness by showing what blessings await in the future. For instance, President Taylor, speaking of faithful members, said: "They know that if the earthly house of this tabernacle dissolves they have a building of God, a house not made with hands, eternal in the heavens. Knowing this they feel that all is right."[167] Here the Prophet highlighted the value of this doctrine in providing a basis for enduring the threat of death. President Young expanded that value by noting that "to a person who has such a glorious hope everything is bright and beautiful."[168] For example, President Young prefaced this idea with an observation that "the faithful Latter-day Saint knows that the dissolution of this mortal house will introduce his immortal spirit to freedom from death and punishment, and to the enjoyment of the society of the spirits of just men made perfect."[169] Thus, it is not just the threat of death that this hope helps the Saints to handle, but all the vicissitudes of life.

Verse 2:16

Once again, as with the scriptures studied above, certain ideas contained in 2:16 have caught LDS leaders' attention.[170] It states, "To the one we are the savour of death unto death; and to the other the savour of life unto life. And who is sufficient for these things?" General Authorities have used the phrases "death unto death" and "life unto life" to help show the consequences of people's acceptance or rejection of the gospel. Elder Franklin D. Richards, for example, stated that "you do a vast deal of good you cannot see. Your testimonies to the world are a savor of life unto life or of death unto death—life unto life to those who receive and render obedience to the

166. SCI shows fifteen citations.
167. John Taylor, in *JD,* 15:349.
168. Brigham Young, in *JD,* 11:16.
169. Brigham Young, in *JD,* 11:16.
170. SCI shows fourteen citations.

America began and lives as a result of faith in God. The Bible has been and is the foundation for this faith."[183] Presidents Benson's words indicate that true freedom and liberty are dependent on the Spirit. This liberty includes that in the political realm as well as the spiritual.

Analysis

When compared to the number of times LDS leaders have appealed to 1 Corinthians, those appealing to 2 Corinthians seem paltry indeed. But there is a reason for this. First, the most salient doctrines General Authorities refer to in this epistle (that God's final judgment upon his children will be largely based on the deeds they did in the flesh, that the Saints must yield to the converting power of the gospel and face the vicissitudes of life with faith knowing that the Savior will sustain them, and that there are three degrees of glory in the eternities) can be found in other scriptures and usually in more detail; thus there is little that is unique in this epistle. Second, Paul did not design this work as a statement on certain doctrines or a clarification of important gospel principles, as he did with 1 Corinthians, but as a defense against his detractors. What gospel principles we do find in the epistle are of secondary importance to the Apostle's purpose and used primarily to bolster his station. Even so, the epistle is rich in Paul's faith in the Lord and his strong desire to have his readers attain that same depth of faith. This alone makes the epistle a necessary read.

As the study above shows, it is rare for General Authorities to use any critical analysis on a given text from this epistle. Their common practice is to simply quote a scripture to bolster a point that they wish to make and then move on without giving the scriptural text any further treatment.[184] It is very common for them to take a given scripture out of context in order to make it fit their purpose. Thus, their primary use of the scriptures is as prooftexts for the doctrine or principle they are making or the admonition they are giving. It is still important, however, to see which scriptures the General Authorities have used to support their positions, for it reveals specific interests in certain teachings, doctrines, principles, or practices that became important during periods of LDS Church history.

---

183. Ezra Taft Benson, in *One Hundred Thirty-Third Annual Conference of The Church of Jesus Christ of Latter-day Saints* (Salt Lake City: The Church of Jesus Christ of Latter-day Saints, 1963), 109.

184. Interestingly, in doing so, they follow the practice not only of Paul but that of ancient General Authorities as well.

LDS Scholars' Work on 2 Corinthians

Though 2 Corinthians has not been neglected by LDS scholars, neither has any, before the present, sought to do a commentary on just this book. The epistle, therefore, has received, at best, coverage that is limited and generally targeted to a popular audience. For examples, see Sidney B. Sperry, *Paul's Life and Letters* (Salt Lake City: Bookcraft, 1955), 118–36; Richard Lloyd Anderson, *Understanding Paul* (Salt Lake City: Deseret Book, 1983), 130–47; D. Kelly Ogden and Andrew C. Skinner, *Verse by Verse: Acts through Revelation* (Salt Lake City: Deseret Book, 1998), 149–57; Thomas A. Wayment, *From Persecutor to Apostle: A Biography of Paul* (Salt Lake City: Deseret Book, 2006), 161–74; Richard Neitzel Holzapfel and Thomas A. Wayment, *Making Sense of the New Testament: Timely Insights and Timeless Messages* (Salt Lake City: Deseret Book, 2010), 368–79. Some scholars have analyzed specific issues in this epistle in various symposia proceedings, but again, none of these have focused exclusively and comprehensively on the epistle as a whole.

Chapter 1

Paul's Outreach to the Corinthian Saints

Introduction

Paul's relationship with the members of the Church at Corinth was fragile at best. Even though he was the founder of Christianity in the area and had labored in the city for months, some members simply could not abide him. In his absence, one in particular had made some pretty hard jabs at his character and authority, and others responded in kind. Even so, the Apostle continued to love them as well as the other members of the Church and worked for their spiritual and temporal welfare. His love, unfortunately, did not lessen the underlying antagonism some felt toward him. As a result, it took little for antagonists (likely coming from an eastern branch of the Church) to once again incite these Corinthian Church members, and perhaps others, against the Apostle. Due to this, he had written a very harsh letter to the branch.[1] The reason for this is explained in what we call 2 Corinthians. "For I wrote to you out of great tribulation and anguish of heart with many tears, not that you would be made sorrowful, but rather that you would recognize the greater love I have for you" (2:4, NR).

Fortunately, many stood with him, and it was to these that he directed the epistle under study. In it, he defended his way of life, doctrine, and authority against his attackers. He was clear in giving them a reason for his writing this epistle: it was to prepare them for his arrival that would soon take place. He assured them that his coming was "not that we would lord it over your faith,

1. Although some scholars feel that 1 Cor. was that letter—and it has harsh elements—that is unlikely. From what 2 Cor. states, the harsh letter was exactly that and nothing more. Anderson, *Understanding Paul*, 131; Harris, *Second Epistle*, 54–58.

but rather we are workers with you for your joy, because you stand firm in the faith" (1:24, NR). Even so, he was coming to straighten out affairs.

His detractors seem to have questioned his authority to direct affairs in the branch and insisted that he was interfering where he should not. It is therefore not surprising that right from his salutation he stressed his God-given authority as an Apostle of Christ Jesus. But he did more. Using that authority, he wrote not just to the Corinthian Saints but also to all those "in the whole province of Achaia." His initial act was to pronounce a heartfelt blessing upon the branches that they would enjoy God's grace (1:1, NR). That blessing was important because it would be only through the impartation of divine grace that his readers would hear, accept, and act on his counsel. He also desperately yearned that they would feel godly peace, a spiritual condition the divisive congregation desperately needed. Thus, by means of the salutation, he asserted his right to lead the branches and direct affairs there.

Salutation (1:1–2)

As with many of his other epistles, Paul somewhat follows the conventions governing prescripts specifically designed to separate an epistle from an informal letter and mark it as an official communication sent to a specific body of people by one in authority. These prescripts contain the name of the person (in this case, persons) sending the letter, his position, the audience he addresses, and an appropriate greeting. Paul, however, as shown below, is also careful to nuance his greetings such that they fit his purpose and bolster his theology.[2]

Greek Text

1 Παῦλος ἀπόστολος Χριστοῦ Ἰησοῦ διὰ θελήματος θεοῦ καὶ Τιμόθεος ὁ ἀδελφὸς τῇ ἐκκλησίᾳ τοῦ θεοῦ τῇ οὔσῃ ἐν Κορίνθῳ, σὺν τοῖς ἁγίοις πᾶσιν τοῖς οὖσιν ἐν ὅλῃ τῇ Ἀχαΐᾳ· 2 χάρις ὑμῖν καὶ εἰρήνη ἀπὸ θεοῦ πατρὸς ἡμῶν καὶ κυρίου Ἰησοῦ Χριστοῦ. [SBLGNT]

---

2. Guthrie, *2 Corinthians,* 55. For a study on the subject of letter writing in New Testament times, see Hans-Josef Klauck, *Ancient Letters and the New Testament: A Guide to Context and Exegesis,* trans., Daniel P. Bailey (Waco, Tex.: Baylor University Press, 2006).

King James Version

1 Paul, an apostle of Jesus Christ by the will of God, and Timothy our brother, unto the church of God which is at Corinth, with all the saints which are in all Achaia: 2 Grace be to you and peace from God our Father, and from the Lord Jesus Christ.

New Rendition

1 Paul, an apostle of Christ Jesus by the will of God, and our brother Timothy to the church of God that is in Corinth, together with all the saints who are in the whole province of Achaia. 2 Grace to you and peace from God our Father and from the Lord Jesus Christ.

Translation Notes and Comments

1:1 *an Apostle . . . by the will of God:* With his very first phrase, Paul reminds his readers of his rank, that of Apostle. This follows Paul's pattern in each of his epistles where he also emphasizes that his apostolic calling is based on divine mandate, making him a special witness of Jesus Christ with the same authority and privileges as the original Twelve.[3] The title ἀπόστολος (*apostolos*), "apostle," was chosen by the Lord to designate those he selected as his leaders (Luke 6:13; John 15:16). The term denoted persons set apart with extraordinary power to carry out specific responsibilities.[4] Indeed, the Greek word, literally meaning "sent out," carried the force of a legitimate and authorized person who fully represented the one who commissioned him.[5] The Twelve were the Lord's chosen ministers specifically ordained to bear witness of him and to carry out his work (see Matt. 28:19–20; compare D&C 107:23–24). It is in the sense of Jesus being God's fully authorized minister that, in Hebrews 3:1–2, the Lord is given this same designation.

The noun θέλημα (*thelēma*), "will," denotes a person's determination to make something happen either through his or her own actions or by delegating the responsibility to another. In the instance of Paul's call to the Apostleship, the initiator was Deity.[6] The participial phrase δία . . . θεοῦ (*dia . . . theou*), "by . . . God," stresses the idea that the acting agent is God,

---

3. *NID,* 1:371.

4. An exact parallel to the noun's meaning in the New Testament is hard to find, but ancient documents do attest the idea of "envoy" and "messenger." James H. Moulton and George Milligan, *The Vocabulary of the Greek Testament: Illustrations from the Papyri and Other Non-literary Sources* (1930; rpt., Grand Rapids, Mich.: William B. Eerdmans, 1985), 70 (hereafter cited as MM); BDAG, 122.

5. *NID,* 1:366–67.

6. BDAG, 447; Otto Schrenk, "θέλμα," in *TDNT,* 3:52–62.

and thus, his authority undergirds Paul's call.[7] Taken together, the whole phrase stresses the fact that the Apostle's call and standing is divine. He is, therefore, on the Lord's errand and working under his authority.

Jesus Christ / Christ Jesus: The KJV follows the Textus Receptus, which reads Ἰησοῦ Χριστοῦ (*Iēsou Christou*), "Jesus Christ," whereas the earliest manuscripts reverse the order, Χριστοῦ Ἰησοῦ (*Christou Iēsou*), "Christ Jesus."[8] In our Rendition, we have followed the earlier texts, but we have also based our choice on Paul's frequent use of this phrase (for example, see 4:5; Acts 19:4; Rom. 3:24; 8:1, 2, 39; 15:5; 16:3; and 1 Cor. 1:30; 15:31).

Through his often-reversed order in referring to the Lord, Paul stresses the Lord's office. The Greek χριστός (*christos*) is used as a translation for the Aramaic מָשִׁיחַ (*māšîaḥ*), denoting one who has been anointed under God's authority.[9] In the Old Testament, only priests and kings were anointed and thereby became "anointed ones." Because, as many believed, the prophesied Deliverer would hold both offices through God's power, it was an easy step to apply the term to him as *the* Messiah. The Lord's disciples recognized him as that deliverer and stressed his station as the "Anointed One," thus promoting the title with his person.

The non-Aramaic-speaking inhabitants of Syrian Antioch, not recognizing the title, assumed it was a name and began calling the Lord's disciples by that term, and thus the (likely pejorative at the time) designation Χριστιανός *(Christianos)*, "Christian," was born (Acts 11:26).[10] Paul, however, kept the focus on the title and tacitly on its significance and by

7. Though the preposition δία (*dia*) is translated as "by" in the NRSV, NIV, and REB, the translation as "through" better catches the nuance of the Greek because it shows agent, mode, means, and efficient cause. See BDAG, 223–26.

8. Bruce M. Metzger, *A Textual Commentary on the Greek New Testament, Second Edition: A Companion Volume to the United Bible Societies' Greek New Testament (Fourth Revised Edition)* (Stuttgart, Ger.: Deutsche Bibelgesellschaft/United Bible Societies, 1994), 505. The change may show a changing Christological emphasis where the very Jewish Paul highlights Jesus as the expected Messiah while later scribes emphasize Jesus as a person.

9. BDAG, 1091. In the New Testament, מָשִׁיחַ (*māšîaḥ*) is consistently translated as Χριστός (*Christos*). There are, however, two places where a transliterated form appears. See John 1:41; 4:25.

10. BDAG, 1090; MM, 693. Members of the LDS Church should relate, having been given the initially pejorative nickname "Mormon." Early detractors of the Church said the name derived from the Greek Μορμώ (*Mormō*), referring to a she-monster or bogeyman. Henry G. Liddell and Robert Scott, comps., *Greek English Lexicon,* rev. and aug. Henry Stuart Jones (Oxford: Clarendon Press, 1968), 1147 (hereafter cited as LSJ). For Joseph Smith's response insisting the name means "more good," see *Times and Seasons* 4 (May 15, 1843): 194, and for its general acceptance today, see Gordon B. Hinkley, "Mormon Should Mean 'More Good,'" *Ensign* 20, no. 11 (November 1990): 51–54.

that means emphasized his own legitimate position as the envoy of the "Anointed One."

Timothy: The name is also transliterated as Timotheus in the KJV (for example, see 1:19; Acts 18:5; 19:22; 20:4; Rom. 16:21; 1 Cor. 4:17). The name means "honored of God." He was a citizen of Lystra and the son of a Greek father and a Jewish mother, Eunice. She, along with her mother, Lois, and son, was converted to Christianity. Timothy gained a solid reputation not only in Lystra but also in Iconium. Paul was so impressed with the young man that he called him to be his missionary companion during a portion of both his second and third missionary journeys. His willingness to submit to the ordeal of circumcision in order to better fit the mission's needs stands as an excellent indicator of the young man's faith. His endorsement by Church leaders is also confirmed by their willingness to give him authority through the laying on of hands (1 Tim. 1:18; 4:14; 2 Tim. 1:6). Paul's referring to him as "my beloved son" (1 Cor. 4:17; compare Philip. 2:22) shows his enduring affection, and Timothy's title as "brother" suggests he functioned in a quasi-official capacity (as in 8:22).[11] On more than one occasion, he acted as the Apostle's trusted emissary. He also joined Paul as cosender not only of this epistle but also the epistles to the Philippians, Colossians, 1 and 2 Thessalonians, and Philemon. Paul also wrote two instructive letters to him. According to tradition, he became the first bishop in Ephesus.[12]

the church of God: The phrase τοῦ θεοῦ (*tou theou*), "of God," is a genitive of possession, and by using it, Paul stresses that the Church belongs neither to any individual (no matter how rich or well positioned) nor to some inner circle of elite (no matter how spiritual or holy), but to God alone. It is of note that Paul is well aware of the social stratification that existed in the branches where freedmen and slaves, rich and poor all met together. He in no way tries to change this social condition, but he does believe that such stratification should not stand in the way of spiritual equality and oneness.[13]

The word ἐκκλησία (*ekklēsia*), translated "church" in the KJV, did not have an exclusively religious connotation in Paul's day. Rather, it denoted any assembly to which the townspeople were called together by a herald's trumpet or cry.[14] On this basis, it is easy to see why the Saints referred to

---

11. Martin, *2 Corinthians,* 136.

12. John Gillman, "Timothy," in *ABD,* 6:558–60.

13. Joseph A. Fitzmyer, *First Corinthians: A New Translation with Introduction and Commentary* (New Haven, Conn.: Yale University Press, 2008), 125.

14. They are literally "the called out group." Witherington, *Conflict and Community,* 355; see also Thiselton, *First Epistle,* 75.

their meetings as *ekklēsia,* for they were called of God to meet regularly and do his will. Identifying the *ekklēsia* with God did give the term a spiritual dignity and authority. Here the term applies not to a single congregation but the whole of those in the province.

with all the saints: The adjectival noun ἅγιος (*hagios*), "sacred, holy," is often used in the New Testament to designate those who have been converted to the gospel, been baptized, and received the Holy Ghost. In such cases, it is translated as "Saint." It is directly related to the noun ἁγιωσύνη (*hagiōsynē*), "holiness," an attribute that is the very essence of God (Lev. 11:44–45).[15] Indeed, the word, whether applied to mortals or gods, has no secular nuance. The LXX uses it as the translation of the Hebrew קָדוֹשׁ (*qādôš*), "holy," which carries the idea of separation, specifically that which is outside the sphere of the mundane and profane and therefore bears the attribute of purity.[16]

When applied to mortals in the New Testament, it does not carry the popular meaning denoting a super spiritual or ultra-hallowed person, but rather one who, through covenantal commitment to the Lord, has been set apart for his purpose.[17] Specifically, it connotes one who has responded to God's call to service. "In all these cases holiness implies a relationship with God that is expressed primarily not thought the cult but through the fact that the believers are 'led' by the Holy Spirit (Rom. 1:4)" that "demands behavior that rightly responds to" that Spirit.[18] The end result is being "sanctified"—that is, entering into a new state where one receives the qualities and characteristics of the divine.[19]

in all Achaia / in the whole province of Achaia: Achaia (also spelled Achaea) was a Roman senatorial province that included much of central and southern Greece. Its administrative seat was at Corinth.[20] The phrase "province of" is not found in the Greek text but is strongly implied and therefore added in our Rendition.

---

15. BDAG, 11. Ancient pagan religious texts show that it was a title given to various gods and, therefore, it held a very sacred meaning. MM, 4.

16. *NID*, 1:124–25.

17. Guthrie, *2 Corinthians,* 58; Victor Paul Furnish, *II Corinthians: A New Translation with Introduction and Commentary,* Anchor Bible Series (Garden City, N.Y.: Doubleday, 1984), 100.

18. *NID,* 1:130.

19. For a study, see Otto Procksch, "ἅγιος in the New Testament," in *TDNT,* 1:100–110.

20. Jerry A. Pattengale, "Achaia," in *ABD,* 1:53.

1:2 ***Grace be to you and peace / Grace to you and peace:*** Though part of Paul's greeting, the phrase also serves as an apostolic prayer in behalf of these people. The phrase also shows how Paul strays from the usual construction for an epistle's prescript to support his theological purposes. It was common for letters to include the salutation χαίρειν (*chairein*), "greetings."[21] The idea behind the word in such use expressed a desire for favor or good will to follow the recipient.[22]

Paul, however, uses instead the noun χάρις (*charis*), the word carrying a broad range of meanings, including "grace, favor, mercy, kindness, and good will."[23] It points to the idea of generously and graciously giving some beneficence to another. The bestowal, however, does imply some kind of obligation on the part of the receiver.[24] Therefore, the word "grace," as opposed to "mercy, kindness, or goodwill," is the better translation here because the word does imply that the beneficiary of God's grace is under obligation to carry out the divine will.[25]

But there is another dimension of grace that must not be overlooked. This is as a designation for divine transforming power. Indeed, all perfecting attributes are ultimately "'bestowed upon all who are true followers of . . . Jesus Christ' (Moro. 7:48) by grace through his atonement."[26] Through faithful obedience to the Lord, individuals can receive strength that assists them to do God's work that they may not otherwise be able to do. In sum, this bestowal of grace—as an enabling power—assists faithful people in gaining eternal life and exaltation.[27]

---

21. For a discussion on the use of the infinitive form of the verb in greetings, see Klauck, *Ancient Letters*, 18–19.

22. BDAG, 1075.

23. BDAG, 1079–81; Johannes P. Louw and Eugene A. Nida, *Greek-English Lexicon of the New Testament Based on Semantic Domains,* 2nd ed., 2 vols. (New York: United Bible Societies, 1989), §§25.89; 33.350; 88.66 (hereafter cited as Louw-Nida).

24. Louw-Nida, §57.103.

25. For studies of grace from an LDS perspective, see Draper and Rhodes, *Paul's First Epistle to the Corinthians,* 76–100; and Brent J. Schmidt, *Relational Grace: The Reciprocal and Binding Covenant of* Charis (Provo, Utah: BYU Studies, 2015), who concludes, "The meaning commonly understood by a broad range of cultures up until the fifth century was that grace was the essence of a two-way, unequal, reciprocal, binding agreement between two parties in which both were obligated to each other" (201).

26. Bruce C. Hafen, "Grace," in *Encyclopedia of Mormonism,* ed. Daniel H. Ludlow, 4 vols. (New York: Macmillan, 1992), 2:562 (hereafter cited as *EM*).

27. Robert L. Millet, *What Happened to the Cross?: Distinctive LDS Teachings* (Salt Lake City: Deseret Book, 2007), 120. One of the effects the Holy Ghost has on the Saints is that of strengthening not only their desires to act righteously, but also strengthening

Paul adds to his salutation the word εἰρήνη (*eirēnē*), "peace." Though often interpreted in the modern sense of "tranquility, rest, and harmony," which does conform largely to its meaning in *Koine* Greek, the noun, in a religious sense, refers to a state of harmony between a god and his followers. For the Christian community, it certainly connoted a warm and personal relationship between the Saint and the Father and the Son that ensured a bright future. Indeed, such peace was "nearly synonymous with messianic salvation."[28]

***from God our Father and from the Lord Jesus Christ*:** Paul's emphasis, however, is not so much on grace and peace themselves as on their source and results. It is God, through his loving kindness (expressed in his giving to his Saints such things as the gospel, the Spirit, its witness of the truth, and ultimately, his Son), from whom these gifts ultimately come. Paul tacitly noted the impetus of these gifts—namely, God's love for each Saint borne out of his fatherhood.

But such grace and peace come not as gifts from God alone. Indeed, the Savior has also given much for the Saints, including his whole mortal life. And it is through communion with him that these gifts are obtained and maintained (John 16:33; Philip. 4:7; 1 Pet. 5:14). "The whole process of believers' sanctification, preservation, and perfecting (1 Thes. 5:23; Heb. 13:20) serves to deepen their participation in the peace of God"[29] and their appreciation of the divine grace that makes the whole process possible.

The title which Paul gives to the Son is of importance. The noun κύριος (*kyrios*), "lord, master," refers to one who acts in a capacity of authority due to possession or oversight.[30] In many uses, it carries the strong nuances of both "master"—that is, a person to whom service is due on any basis—and Deity. It is the latter that comes strongly into play in the writings of the New Testament. The title consistently refers to Jehovah in the LXX. Jesus did not hesitate to take upon himself this title (see, for example, Matt. 7:21–22; 9:38; 22:41–45; and Mark 5:19). With two exceptions (Acts 2:47; Rev. 7:14), there is no evidence in any of the works between Acts and Jude that the term was ever again used by believers for anyone other than Jesus.[31] Its use by Paul continues to tie Christ to the Old Testament God and explains why

---

the ability to act. Furthermore, as they act upon this grace by serving others, they move from one level of grace to a higher level just as the Savior did. See D&C 93:12–20.

28. BDAG, 287–88.

29. *NID*, 2:116.

30. BDAG, 576–78.

31. For a study, see Werner Foester, "κύριος," in *TDNT*, 3:1039–96.

Jesus, as well as the Father, can be the source of grace and peace—that is, because Christ is God in his own right.[32]

Analysis and Summary

Paul was careful and consistent in calling himself an Apostle commissioned by God. The term "apostle" (ἀπόστολος, *apostolos*) carried no religious nuance in secular Greek. It simply denoted anyone acting in the capacity of a messenger from a simple courier to a fully invested governmental envoy. Even so, the word always carried the idea of one being sent out to do something and often connoted the authority and accompanying power of the individual or body that did the sending. Its most frequent use in the first century AD referred to a delegate or envoy.[33]

It was the philosophical school of Cynics that gave the term a theological turn. They saw themselves as invested representatives of the divine sent forth to do the god's bidding.[34] Though the term "apostle" may never have become so technical that it denoted exclusive divine authorization, it was nonetheless often associated in such contexts.[35] That is the case with its use in the New Testament, where it designates those whom Jesus singled out and empowered to carry out his mission (Matt. 10:1–2; Mark 6:30; Luke 6:13).[36] Paul's use of the title in reference to himself shows he fell into this category.

---

32. Richard Bauckham, *God Crucified: Monotheism and Christology in the New Testament* (Grand Rapids, Mich.: William B. Eerdmans, 1999), 45–77; and Larry W. Hurtado, *One God, One Lord: Early Christian Devotion and Ancient Jewish Monotheism,* 2nd ed. (Edinburgh: T&T Clark, 1998), 93–128, have both shown the strong identity between Jesus and God as viewed in earliest Christianity. Much of this is based on the Church's appropriation of the Old Testament title to apply it to Jesus.

33. LSJ, 220.

34. For example, see Epictetus, *Discourses* 3.22, where the philosopher states that a genuine Cynic must see himself as an envoy of Zeus. For a discussion, see Karl Heinrich Rengstorf, "ἀπόσολος" in *TDNT,* 1:409–13.

35. *NID,* 1:365–66.

36. Given the Gentile influence that permeated the Galilee, it is not beyond question that the Lord knew Greek and may have actually used this term. It is more likely, however, that he appealed to Jewish ideas. Some have argued that the same idea is carried by the Hebrew term שָׁלִיחַ (*šālîaḥ*) and the Aramaic שְׁלִיחַ (*šĕlîaḥ*) that is, the divine giving of authority and responsibility to someone to carry out a task. See Francis Brown, S. R. Driver, and Charles A. Briggs, *A Hebrew and English Lexicon of the Old Testament,* corrected ed. (Oxford: Clarendon Press, 1976), 1018–19 (hereafter cited as BDB). This idea, however, has not gone unchallenged, but the idea of a divine commissioning cannot be discounted. For discussion, see F. Hossfeld-van der Velden, *TDOT,* 15:49–55.

In his greetings he also adds Timothy as a co-sender of the epistle (1:1), and this likely indicates why there are a number of times Paul used the plural pronoun "we" in the text. There has been a good deal of speculation as to why Paul mentioned his companion. These include Paul's effort to give the young man more honor and respect in the Christian community at Corinth or to follow the Old Testament mandate that confirmations must be made by two witnesses (Deut. 19:15).[37] That Timothy was the co-sender of five other of Paul's epistles suggests that Paul simply wanted to recognize him as his companion who stood with him in ministering to the Saints.

He refers to those whom he writes as belonging to "the assembly of God" (*tē ekklisia tou theou*). His words are evidence that he sees no difference between Gentile and Jewish congregants. He apparently sees the whole as the true successors of the people of God, whom Jehovah himself designated as Israel.[38] This betrays Paul's view that the Church is not a human creation. God is responsible for the gathering of his people, and whether in individual house churches or in smaller groups, the whole comprises "the assembly of God."[39]

Paul addresses the letter not just to the Corinthian congregations but also to all those throughout central and southern Greece (1:1). He may have done so because he designed his epistle as a circular letter to be read in the branches throughout the whole area. It may also be that they saw themselves as associated with and under the direction of the Corinthian base, and he therefore wanted them to feel included.[40] The epistle's broad reach does suggest that he did see the problems he focuses on as not just affecting the central place but endemic to the region.[41]

Paul addresses his epistle to the "Saints" in the whole area. In the broader Greek culture, the adjective ἅγιος (*hagios*) referred to that which was devoted to the gods and, when applied to people, designated those who dedicated themselves to the service of the divine.[42] They, therefore, belong

37. Witherington, *Conflict and Community,* 354; for discussion, see Guthrie, 2 *Corinthians,* 57.

38. Judges 20:2 notes that the Israelites met "in an assembly of the people of God" (בִּקְהַל עַם הָאֱלֹהִים, *biqĕhal ʿam hāʾĕlōhîm*). The LXX translates this as ἐν ἐκκλησίᾳ τοῦ λαοῦ τοῦ θεοῦ (*en ekklēsia tou laou tou theou*).

39. Witherington, *Conflict and Community,* 355.

40. Guthrie, 2 *Corinthians,* 58.

41. This was the opinion of the early Christian theologian John Chrysostom (d. AD 407). See *The Homilies on Second Epistle of St. Paul, the Apostle, to the Corinthians* 1:2.

42. LSJ, 9.

to the ἐκκλησία (*ekklesia*), or "called out group,"[43] because they are set apart for God's work. This emphasizes the idea that "what Christians are as individuals and what they are as a group are interrelated. The character of the individual is dependent on and affected by the group, and vice versa."[44]

Paul seems to have used the term in the sense of being devoted to the Savior and thereby at work in his service. At that time, the adjective did not carry the force of one who was especially pure or unusually holy, but was more closely associated to one being called to the service and showing fidelity toward the Lord. The term also suggests being elected by him to duties in the Church. Though it did not carry the full weight of ethical behavior gained over time, it did carry the idea of behavior that responded fully to the will of the Holy Spirit.[45]

Of the significance of this title, Elder Mark E. Petersen stated, "The members of the true church anciently did not call themselves Christians, for that was but a nickname applied to them in derision by those who hated Christ. The members of the Church called themselves *saints,* as may be seen from various New Testament references (see 1:1; Rom. 16:2), which are confirmed by Webster's dictionary and by the Bible scholars. This, then, is one of the identification marks of the true Church. The members are called *saints.*"[46]

The word carries the idea of holiness—that is, of separation from the worldly through yielding to the influence of the Holy Ghost. Paul notes that his target audience has been "sanctified in Christ Jesus" (1 Cor. 1:2). The phrase carries the idea that the Savior used his power to separate them from the world and make them his people. The application of the word does not, however, describe what they presently were (indeed, the divisive attitude of some members in Corinth suggests they stood in need of more saintliness) but stood as a reminder of what they were chosen to

---

43. See note 38.

44. Witherington, *Conflict and Community,* 355.

45. *NID,* 1:130. Over the centuries, Christian thinkers began to associate the word more and more with persons of unusual holiness who possessed unusual grace that manifested itself in miracles. Due to such qualities, they came to be viewed as persons who, after death, had influence with the Divine. As a result, some Christians began to worship them such that even their relics became a source of power. For a study, see Lawrence S. Cunningham, *The Meaning of Saints* (San Francisco: Harper and Row, 1980).

46. Mark E. Petersen, "Signs of the True Church," *Ensign* 9, no. 5 (May 1979): 22; italics in original. See also D. Kelly Ogden and Andrew C. Skinner, *Verse by Verse: Acts through Revelation* (Salt Lake City: Deseret Book, 1998), 130.

become.[47] Baptism, the first step in a long development leading to full saintliness, ideally began a transformation process by cleansing and, thus, sanctifying them, but only to a degree.[48] The process goes well beyond being sin free. Through the power of the Redeemer, the person slowly and eventually changes such that he or she becomes a new creature, even a son or daughter of Christ. Along the path they eventually lose every desire for sin and become "submissive, meek, humble, patient, full of love, willing to submit to all things which the Lord seeth fit to inflict upon him, even as a child doth submit to his father" (Mosiah 3:19; see also 2 Cor. 5:17; Gal. 6:15; Mosiah 5:2, 7; 27:25–27; Ether 3:14; and D&C 20:31).

The Apostle, as he does in many of his other epistles, includes in the prescript his heartfelt blessing of grace and peace (for example, see Rom. 1:7; 1 Cor. 1:3; Gal. 1:3; Eph. 1:2; and Philip. 1:2).[49] The two words are loaded with meaning (see Translation Notes for 1:2 above). Essentially, he blesses his readers that they might have divine empowerment and a feeling of unity with the Father and Son.

47. Nelson Mandela is quoted as saying, "A saint is a sinner who keeps on trying" to become spiritually better. Dale G. Renlund, "Latter-day Saints Keep On Trying," *Ensign* 45, no. 5 (May 2015): 56.

48. See C. Eric Ott, "Sanctification," in *EM*, 4:1259–60.

49. Paul was not the only one to use the phrase. See also 1 Pet. 1:2; 2 Pet. 1:2, and Rev. 1:4.

Excursus on Paul's Relationship with the Twelve Apostles

Answering the question about Paul's possible instatement as one with the original Twelve Apostles, through the use of ancient sources, is influenced by bias. On the one hand, the general Christian belief is that Jesus never intended the Apostolate to become either an office or the ruling council of the Church. This position is necessary because none have the apostolic office. Based on Acts 1, supporters of this view insist, the qualifications for apostolic membership were that the person had to have "accompanied" the disciples "during all the time that the Lord Jesus went in and out among [them], beginning from the baptism of John until the day when he was taken up from [them]" and to have been an eyewitness of the Resurrection (Acts 1:21–22, our translation). Thus, only persons living in the first generation could qualify as members of the Twelve.[50] Paul, being converted after Jesus' death, did not meet the criteria and therefore could never have been a part of this circle. Thus, anything that suggests otherwise these people discount.

On the other hand, two chief qualifications for membership in the august body were a personal witness to the Lord's Resurrection and the reception of his authority with its attendant commission. The original Twelve were all called by him and charged under his direction. Suggesting that the office was not meant to exist for only a short time is that, after the Resurrection, Jesus again personally commissioned the Twelve and gave them their assignments (Matt. 28:16–20; Acts 1:4–9). Thus, they took his place as earthly leaders of his "kingdom" and pushed forward his work. It is clear from Acts that the Lord's intent was not for the Twelve to minister for a brief span of time but for the whole period until his coming.[51] Thus, the Lord cemented the calling's place into his Church.[52] This requirement demanded the filling of the vacancy left by Judas (Acts 1:21–26) and, by extension, others.

---

50. For a discussion, see *NID,* 1:365–376; Karl Heinrich Rengstorf, "Ἀπόστολος," in *TDNT,* 1:424–43.

51. Rengstorf, "Ἀπόστολος," in *TDNT,* 1:432.

52. The Lord's placing twelve men as the senior authorities in his church in America also demonstrates this. See 3 Ne. 11:18–12:1 and compare 3 Ne. 13:25–34; 15:11–16:20; 18:36–37; 27:13–21.

Further evidencing that the office was meant to stay is the "Teachings of the Twelve Apostles," also known as the *Didachē*. This treatise was composed anonymously with at least portions of it written as early as the late first century AD. A section gives instructions on how the people should treat the Apostles.[53] Given its title, the work suggests that, at that time, the office was still functioning and that Church members viewed the Twelve as authoritative leaders who could give direction to the various congregations.[54]

But did Paul have membership in this body? Luke uses the term "apostle" consistently in his gospel and Acts to designate members of the Twelve. Twice in Acts 14 he uses the term "apostle" in connection with Paul, suggesting that he viewed him as a member of the Twelve. The problem is that the earliest reference (Acts 14:4) is vague. It states that, during a confrontation in which Paul and Barnabas were involved, some of the people sided with the Jews, and others with the Apostles. The way the text reads leaves the door open to the idea that the Apostles referred to were the Twelve and that Paul and Barnabas sided with them. However, the sense of the text suggests that Luke had Paul and Barnabas in mind and viewed them as members of the body. Evidencing this is Acts 14:14, where Luke definitely identifies them as Apostles. Unfortunately, textual evidence does not solve the problem because ancient texts vary on the reading of this verse. Some leave out the word "apostle," while others exclude Paul from the title.[55] Such changes, however, could be due to a bias on the part of ancient copyists who had a desire to lessen the importance of the office. Given that, it is possible that Luke does view Paul as a member of the Twelve. Whatever the case, there is no doubt that Paul put his office on parity with the Twelve whom, he notes, were "apostles before me" (Gal. 1:17) and even admits, after mentioning the Twelve, that he was "least of the apostles" (1 Cor. 15:9). Though "least," as he points out, he had received a divine witness of the Resurrection and, at some point, had been commissioned to the work under the Lord's authority.[56] This leaves open the door to his membership among the Twelve.

---

53. *Didache* 11:1–3.

54. Robert A. Kraft, "Didache," in *ABD*, 2:197–98.

55. Metzger, *Textual Commentary*, 370–71, 74; Wayment, *From Persecutor to Apostle*, 90–91.

56. For discussion, see Anderson, *Understanding Paul*, 36–37.

With the Restoration, the early Church leaders consistently viewed the New Testament apostolate as the major ruling council of Christ's Church and the foundation upon which it stood. They never questioned that it was an official office within the Lord's kingdom and acted as the quorum of leadership. They appealed to Ephesians 2:20 and 4:11–13 to support their view.[57] The reason it ceased to function, they taught, was not because it became unnecessary but because the rapid onset of the apostasy precluded its membership being kept up.[58] Because of its position as a ruling council, it had to be restored again as a body within the priesthood. The Quorum, with its keys, powers, and mission, was reintroduced on the earth in February 1835[59] and has functioned according to divine instruction and mandate since that time. When, due to death, a position opens, it is quickly filled.

Based on modern practices of the Quorum, it is easy to read the same as occurring in New Testament times, but that may not be the case. Exactly how this body operated after the death of the Lord is unknown, though there is no doubt that it functioned as the core of Church leadership and held undisputed authority among faithful Christians. If membership in the Quorum followed today's procedures and replacements entered its ranks only when a vacancy due to death occurred, there is a problem with Paul entering its ranks. Only two of the body's original members are known to have suffered death before Paul in AD 65. These were Judas, who committed suicide at the time of the crucifixion, and James, the son of Zebedee, who died a martyr about AD 44. Since Matthias replaced Judas, so far as the text allows, only the place held by James became open during Paul's ministry. Textual evidence suggests that it was James, the Lord's brother, who took John's position among the Twelve (1 Cor. 15:7; Gal. 1:19). However, in addition to Paul and James, there are four others associated with the position. These are Barnabas, Andronicus, and Junias (Rom. 16:7).[60] Paul's writings themselves evidence that there were people who had a recognized claim to the title but who were not among the Twelve (in addition to Rom. 16:7, see 1 Cor. 15:5–7). All this suggests that Paul did not have to have membership in the Quorum in order to use the title.

---

57. See John Taylor, in *JD,* 11:341; 16:373; George A. Smith, in *JD,* 13:293.

58. Orson F. Whitney in *JD,* 26:262–64.

59. S. Kent Brown, "Apostle," in *EM,* 1:61.

60. The latter is of particular interest since ancient manuscripts differ on the gender of the person, thus some allowance for a woman to be numbered among the apostles, albeit not as a member of the Twelve, must be given. Metzger, *Textual Commentary,* 475–76.

On the other hand, using modern practice as a guide, if the Quorum of the First Presidency were formed, then an opening for at least three new Apostles in the Quorum of the Twelve would be possible. Unfortunately, the text gives no indication that such happened. Even so, by the Restoration definition of the word "apostle," there can be no question that Paul held that office. He was in very deed an "especial witness[] of the name of Christ in all the world" (D&C 27:12) who differed "from other officers in the church in the duties of [his] calling" (D&C 107:23). Because of his unique experiences and the authority he exercised, his membership in the Quorum of the Twelve cannot be ruled out.[61]

61. For discussion, see Anderson, *Understanding Paul,* 36–37.

Thanksgiving for Godly Comfort in Suffering (1:3–7)

Having delivered his salutation, Paul now develops his prologue and in doing so lays the foundation on which he will build the rest of his epistle. His subject is suffering for God's sake, something his audience was very well acquainted with. Events over the past few years had caused a great deal of spiritual and emotional bruising and even opened wounds, some not yet healed. Such suffering can not only cause bitterness but also break down the relationship between the sufferer and the Father. Here the Apostle shows that suffering, properly seen, can be redemptive. He therefore refuses to give into bitterness and regret but "offers one of the most beautiful and beloved passages in the [New Testament], turning his suffering into a song of thanks to God and an appeal for continued partnership with the Corinthian church."[62]

This pericope breaks down into two units. The first comprises 1:3–7 and is investigated here; the next will be investigated below. At this point in his epistle, the Apostle praises the sustaining power of God and strikes a theme of encouragement during times of affliction (1:3). He then explains God's purpose in allowing for such suffering and persecution (1:4–6) and points out—and this is the mean purpose of this pericope—how mutual suffering has forged a stronger bond between him and his fellow Saints at Corinth (1:7).

Greek Text

3 Εὐλογητὸς ὁ θεὸς καὶ πατὴρ τοῦ κυρίου ἡμῶν Ἰησοῦ Χριστοῦ, ὁ πατὴρ τῶν
οἰκτιρμῶν καὶ θεὸς πάσης παρακλήσεως, 4 ὁ παρακαλῶν ἡμᾶς ἐπὶ πάσῃ τῇ θλίψει
ἡμῶν, εἰς τὸ δύνασθαι ἡμᾶς παρακαλεῖν τοὺς ἐν πάσῃ θλίψει διὰ τῆς παρακλήσεως
ἧς παρακαλούμεθα αὐτοὶ ὑπὸ τοῦ θεοῦ. 5 ὅτι καθὼς περισσεύει τὰ παθήματα τοῦ
Χριστοῦ εἰς ἡμᾶς, οὕτως διὰ τοῦ Χριστοῦ περισσεύει καὶ ἡ παράκλησις ἡμῶν. 6 εἴτε
δὲ θλιβόμεθα, ὑπὲρ τῆς ὑμῶν παρακλήσεως καὶ σωτηρίας· εἴτε παρακαλούμεθα,
ὑπὲρ τῆς ὑμῶν παρακλήσεως τῆς ἐνεργουμένης ἐν ὑπομονῇ τῶν αὐτῶν παθημάτων ὧν καὶ ἡμεῖς πάσχομεν, 7 καὶ ἡ ἐλπὶς ἡμῶν βεβαία ὑπὲρ ὑμῶν· εἰδότες ὅτι ὡς
κοινωνοί ἐστε τῶν παθημάτων, οὕτως καὶ τῆς παρακλήσεως. [SBLGNT]

62. Guthrie, *2 Corinthians,* 62.

King James Version	New Rendition
3 Blessed be God, even the Father of our Lord Jesus Christ, the Father of mercies, and the God of all comfort; 4 Who comforteth us in all our tribulation, that we may be able to comfort them which are in any trouble, by the comfort wherewith we ourselves are comforted of God. 5 For as the sufferings of Christ abound in us, so our consolation also aboundeth by Christ. 6 And whether we be afflicted, it is for your consolation and salvation, which is effectual in the enduring of the same sufferings which we also suffer: or whether we be comforted, it is for your consolation and salvation. 7 And our hope of you is steadfast, knowing, that as ye are partakers of the sufferings, so shall ye be also of the consolation.	3 Blessed be the God and Father of our Lord Jesus Christ, the Father of mercy and God of all comfort, 4 who comforts us in all our affliction so that we can comfort those in any affliction of theirs with the same comfort by which we ourselves are comforted by God. 5 For just as Christ's sufferings abound to our advantage, so also does our comfort abound through Christ. 6 And if we are afflicted, it is for your comfort and salvation, and if we are comforted, it is for your comfort, which produces patient endurance in the same sufferings that we ourselves endure. 7 And our hope for you is firm, knowing that just as you share in our sufferings, so also you share in our comfort.

Translation Notes and Comments

1:3 ***Blessed be God / Blessed be the God:*** Paul begins the formal portion of his letter with a doxology—that is, a praise of God.[63] The adjective εὐλογητός (*eulogētos*), "blessed," is related to the verb εὐλογέω (*eulogeō*), "to speak well of someone," and, when pertaining to God, carries the force of admiration evidenced in acclaim.[64] This feeling is based on a deeply felt recognition that he is the source of life and all that is good.[65]

Father of our Lord Jesus Christ: The noun πατήρ (*patēr*), "father," in this instance, stresses the literal relationship between God and Christ. It rests

63. A doxology is not a prayer per se, but a heartfelt exclamation of adoration and love for the Divine expressed by the word εὐλογητός (*eulogētos*), "blessed." Bernard, "Second Epistle," 38.

64. Hermann W. Beyer, "εὐλογέω, εὐλογητός, εὐλογία, ἐνευλογέω," in *TDNT,* 2:754–66.

65. Beyer, "εὐλογέω," in *TDNT,* 2:761–65. The expression exposes Paul's pharisaical background as it echoes Jewish prayers of the day, especially that of the *bĕrākâ,*"blessing," particularly in the Eighteen Benedictions also known as the *Shemoneh Esreh.* See David Instone-Brewer, "The Eighteen Benedictions and the *Minim* before 70 CE," *Journal of Theological Studies* 54 (April 2003): 41–42.

upon the recognition of God as *the* life-giving principle in the universe.[66] By noting the fatherhood of God, Paul tacitly highlights the divine power and office that rests with his Son. Further highlighting that power is Paul's use of the title "Lord" for Jesus. On this, see Translation Notes on 1:2 above.

the Father of mercies / the Father of mercy: The noun οἰκτιρμός (*oiktirmos*), "mercy," denotes strong compassion and sympathy for the suffering of another.[67] By making the Divine the figurative "Father" of this virtue, Paul reveals both its source and godlike nature. The noun amplifies the idea carried by the verb οἰκτίρω (*oiktirō*), "to have compassion, pity for the ills of another," and therefore connotes God's visceral reaction to such suffering.[68] The strength of his reaction leads to his reaching out to lessen if not alleviate it. Here Paul uses the plural and in so doing suggests not only the depth but also the breadth of God's heartfelt compassion, laying the foundation for discussing its result—namely, godly comfort.

God of all comfort: The noun παράκλησις (*paraklēsis*) denotes "the lifting of another's spirit" and thereby carries the primary meaning of "comfort and consolation."[69] The intimate and warm English word "comfort" carries the idea of bringing relief from suffering or sorrow through the impartation of strength or hope.[70] The biblical word retains the idea of relief but stresses hope as its foundation. Therefore, a fullness of comfort must come through God and be based on the Atonement of Jesus Christ and the hope of salvation he promises. That godly comfort, however, does not come as an end in itself (as acceptable as that might be). Rather, its major purpose is to encourage and assist the Saints to remain true to the faith no matter what condition they face.[71] Comfort does not come from God as a

---

66. BDAG, 786–88; Louw-Nida, §10.14.

67. BDAG, 700.

68. BDAG, 700.

69. This nuance is very strong in both the Masoretic and Septuagintal texts. The Hebrew root נחם (*nḥm*) in the *niphal* generally means "*be sorry, rue, suffer grief, repent,* of one's own doings" and is most often translated as "repent" in the KJV, but in the *piel,* it means "comfort, console." L. Köhler, W. Baumgartner, and J. J. Stamm, *The Hebrew and English Lexicon,* trans. and ed. M. E. J. Richardson, 5 vols. (Leiden, Neth.: E. J. Brill, 1994–2000), 636–37 (hereafter cited as *HAL*). See also BDB, 636–37.

70. *Merriam-Webster's Dictionary of Synonyms* (Springfield, Mass.: Merriam-Webster, 1984), s.v. "comfort."

71. BDAG, 766. The verb form includes such nuances as "to strengthen, cheer, enliven, and reassure," but the heaviest weight is on "to comfort" and "to encourage." Otto Schmitz, "παρακαλέω, παράκλησις," in *TDNT,* 5:774–79.

promise to the righteous that he will ward off sorrow and pain. It comes as he assists them thorough it. Thus, comfort is God's response to pain and suffering. Further, its major purpose is to encourage the beleaguered Saints to endure. Indeed, the idea of comfort is so tied to encouragement in the noun *paraklēsis* that the two cannot be fully separated.[72]

The word also carries a heavy eschatological overtone. As noted above, the basis of both God's comfort and encouragement is ultimately tied to a witness of the Spirit to the truthfulness not only of the gospel message but also of the promise of salvation and eternal felicity. Though God gives compassionate comfort and strength in temporal situations, comfort's solace comes from knowing that, no matter what the current circumstances are, eternal joy awaits the faithful.[73]

Paul's use of the adjective πᾶς (*pas*), "all,"[74] suggests the breadth of the Father's compassion and his response thereto by giving all possible comfort and therewith every encouragement to those in need.[75] This twofold nuance—comfort and encouragement—should color our understanding in all the places where Paul uses the word.[76] Admittedly, there are phrases in this section where "encouragement" could be the better translation of *paraklēsis,* but we have chosen to use only "comfort" for two reasons: first, because Paul uses the same word throughout this section, and second, because the idea of comfort stands behind all other nuances.

1:4 ***Who comforteth us in all our tribulation / who comforts us in all our affliction:*** With these words, Paul notes the breadth of God's response to suffering. There is nothing he considers too small. The noun θλίψις (*thlipsis*) denotes a particularly distressing kind of trouble afflicting one either inwardly or outwardly.[77] Behind the noun stands the idea of being squeezed, pressed down, and even crushed.[78] Out of this grows three

72. Martin, *2 Corinthians,* 142–43; Guthrie, *2 Corinthians,* 67.

73. Otto Schmitz, "παρακαλέω, παράκλησις," in *TDNT,* 5:794–99.

74. BDAG, 782–85.

75. Harris, *Second Epistle,* 142–43.

76. The breadth of the meanings of both the verb and noun should be kept in mind in reading the word and the best nuance dictated by the context should be applied. See C. K. Barrett, *A Commentary on the Second Epistle to the Corinthians* (London: Adam and Charles Black, 1973), 60.

77. BDAG, 457.

78. Heinrich Schlier, "θλίβω θλῖψις," in *TDNT,* 3:139–40. Because the noun "tribulation" is derived from the Latin *tribulum,* which denotes the drag used in threshing grain, it reflects the idea behind θλίψις (*thlipsis*) very well.

nuances: "oppression," denoting being weighed down in body or mind, usually brought on by an external force's misuse of power or authority;[79] "tribulation," denoting suffering from any source that tries one's courage and patience to the core; and "affliction," denoting suffering imposed by others such that it challenges one's ability to endure. It is the latter that best fits the context here and is used in our Rendition. That Paul uses the possessive pronoun ἡμῶν (*hēmōn*) with *thlipsis*, "*our* affliction," points to trials that he and Timothy are currently enduring and, by extension, also to the comfort they are currently receiving. The result is continual divine encouragement.

that we may be able to comfort them which are in any trouble / so that we can comfort those in any affliction of theirs: With the phrase εἰς τὸ δύνασθαι (*eis to dynasthai*), literally "with the view that we are able," Paul explains, at least in part, why he and Timothy are being tried. It is enabling them to have the necessary compassion to give needed comfort to their readers.[80] The phrase ἐν πάσῃ θλίψει (*en pasē thlipsei*), literally "in every affliction," suggests that the distress that Timothy and Paul are enduring and have endured has enabled them to bring comfort no matter what the nature of their readers' afflictions might be.

by the comfort wherewith we ourselves are comforted of God / with the same comfort by which we ourselves are comforted by God. Here Paul notes the quality of the comfort that he and Timothy are receiving. It is divine. And with it has come commensurate encouragement. Because they have received that quality of comfort and encouragement, they can give it. The present tense of the verb παρακαλέω (*parakaleō*), "to comfort,"[81] is important here because it shows the hand of the Father currently lifting and comforting the two missionaries. The dynamic and current nature of divine comfort stands as these missionaries' witness that God will also comfort and encourage their readers if they too will stand fast in the Lord.

1:5 *For as the sufferings of Christ abound in us / For just as Christ's sufferings abound to our advantage:* The conjunction ὅτι (*hoti*), "for," is causal and is important here because it explains that experiencing Christ-like suffering enables Paul and Timothy to give comfort to others.[82]

---

79. *Merriam-Webster's Collegiate Dictionary* (Springfield, Mass.: Merriam-Webster, 2008), s.v. "oppression."

80. Barnett, *Second Epistle,* 73.

81. BDAG, 764–65.

82. Barnett, *Second Epistle,* 74; Guthrie, *2 Corinthians,* 70.

The noun πάθημα (*pathēma*) refers to what a person suffers or endures.[83] When associated with Jesus, though the idea often points more specifically to his atoning suffering (Heb. 2:10; 1 Pet. 4:13; 5:1), it generally refers to the suffering he had to endure through faithlessness, disappointment, and betrayal during his ministry, a suffering Paul and others could not only identify with but actually experience.[84]

The verb περισσεύω (*perisseuō*) has the sense of being "more than enough" and, therefore, "to abound," with the idea of overflowing.[85] The concept the word carries is important to Paul, for it expresses the unbounded nature of Deity's giving (see 3:9; 4:15; 8:2, 7; 9:8).

The preposition εἰς (*eis*) is here used to express advantage.[86] Paul's point is that Christ's sufferings in Gethsemane and on the cross have resulted in great benefits to all those who believe in him.

so our consolation also aboundeth by Christ / so also does our comfort abound through Christ: Here Paul makes a point of comparison: to the same degree that the Savior's Atonement overflows to the believer's advantage, to that same degree, the Lord's comfort overflows and, thereby, encourages the Christian. The preposition διά (*dia*) is important, acting as it does as a marker of instrumentality.[87] All godly comfort comes *through* the Lord Jesus. He is the instrument God uses to bequeath his comfort to his children.

1:6 ***And whether we be afflicted, it is for your consolation and salvation / And if we are afflicted, it is for your comfort and salvation:*** This verse is somewhat enigmatic and therefore hard to translate. We have constructed our Rendering based on what Paul said above.

The conditional particle εἴτε (*eite*), "if," is not a marker for a hypothetical condition but emphasizes the reality of the assumption.[88] Paul and

---

83. BDAG, 747.

84. Guthrie, *2 Corinthians,* 71. Paul understood that Christians were fellow-sufferers with the Savior (Rom. 8:17; Philip. 3:10; Col. 1:22; and specifically in 2 Cor. 4:10–11). However, there was another dimension that was likely playing in the background. Jewish doctrine held the idea of "the afflictions of the Messiah" (חֶבְלֵי הַמָּשִׁיחַ, *ḥablê hammašiaḥ*). The concept pointed not to the suffering he would endure but rather to that associated with the messianic age and that which his followers would endure until the coming age of joy. It was a small step for the Christians to identify with this idea. Martin, *2 Corinthians,* 143.

85. BDAG, 805; Bernard, "Second Epistle," 38.

86. BDAG, 290.

87. BDAG, 224.

88. F. Blass and A. Debrunner, *A Greek Grammar of the New Testament and Other Early Christian Literature,* trans. and ed. Robert W. Funk (Chicago, University of Chicago

Timothy really do feel the heavy weight of their responsibilities and, thus, know full well its cost. The Apostle seems to be giving a reason why he and Timothy are afflicted. It is so that they are in a position to give encouraging comfort.[89] However, that relief does not come as an end in itself. Its objective is to bring the comforted one to salvation. The noun σωτηρία (*sōtēria*), "salvation,"[90] could have a transcendent nuance, thus referring to exaltation in God's kingdom, but given the context, it more likely refers to deliverance from the distress and worry the Saints are currently feeling through the promises contained in the gospel.[91]

or whether we be comforted, it is for your consolation and salvation / and if we are comforted, it is for your comfort: As in the phrase above, the conditional particle εἴτε (*eite*), "if," does not indicate a hypothetical but an actual situation. Paul and Timothy truly experience godly comfort. Paul's use of *eite* twice (if . . . if . . .) does not denote mutually exclusive situations (either suffering or encouragement) but rather two events that occur in succession (first suffering and then encouragement).[92] With this phrase Paul explains why, at least in part, he and Timothy have received that comfort. It is so that they can impart comfort to their fellow Saints.

which is effectual in the enduring of the same sufferings which we also suffer / which produces patient endurance in the same sufferings that we ourselves endure: The present, middle participle ἐνεργουμένης (*energoumenēs*) of the verb ἐνεργέω (*energeō*) in this context means "to produce, effect."[93] The effect it produces is ὑπομονή (*hypomonē*), translated here as "patient endurance." The word denotes the ability "to hold out or bear up in the face of difficulties"[94] but carries the nuance of standing fast, or holding one's ground, thus patiently but actively not yielding place to an adversary.[95]

1:7 ***our hope of you is steadfast / our hope for you is firm:*** The noun ἔλπις (*elpis*), "hope," denotes an anticipated positive outcome based on

Press, 1961), §371 (hereafter cited as BDF).

89. Barnett, *Second Epistle,* 71.

90. BDAG, 985–86. According to MM, 622, the noun "came to denote Messianic and spiritual salvation, either as a present possession, . . . or as to be realized fully hereafter."

91. Louw-Nida, §21.18.

92. Harris, *Second Epistle,* 147.

93. BDAG, 335.

94. BDAG, 1039–40.

95. *NID,* 4:564–71.

a confident expectation in realizing the object.[96] The predicate adjective βέβαιος (*bebaios*), "firm, unwavering, persistent,"[97] strengthens the confidence found in the "hope."

knowing, that as ye are partakers of the sufferings, so shall ye be also of the consolation / knowing that just as you share in our sufferings, so also you share in our comfort: Here the circumstantial participle εἰδότες (*eidotes*), "knowing," from the verb οἶδα (*oida*), "to know,"[98] is causal and therefore carries the nuance of "since we know" or "because we know."[99] The phrase looks at what the Apostle and the Saint experience together—that is, both Christlike suffering and godly comfort.

Paul's use of the noun κοινωνός (*koinōnos*), "companion, partner, sharer," is important because it marks those who share together in a deeply religious experience that acts to bind them together.[100] It is this mutual sharing that is the ground of Paul's unflinching hope in the Saints. Behind his statement is his full confidence that the Father will come through for them.

Analysis and Summary

Paul's major thrust in this section deals with divine comfort, but he sets it against "our afflictions," and "our suffering" (1:4–7). He identifies his suffering with that of the Lord to emphasize the depth of the comfort he has received from the Divine source. It is of note that Paul does not say that faithfulness either prevents suffering or takes suffering away, but that because of it the Saint receives comfort and, through it, encouragement from the Father and the Son to stay faithful.

Paul begins this pericope with a beautiful, effusive blessing toward God that emphasizes particularly his position as Father (1:3). The Apostle focuses on the aspect of fatherhood that expresses itself in two ways: as the literal Father of the Savior and as the figurative Father of all mercies (οἰκτιρμός, *oiktirmos*), the word denoting a deep sense of compassion, even empathy, for the suffering of another.[101] It is his fatherhood of the first that opens the door to his fatherhood of the second. Indeed, it is because

96. BDAG, 319.
97. BDAG, 172.
98. BDAG, 693–94.
99. Guthrie, *2 Corinthians,* 74.
100. BDAG, 553; *NID,* 2:711–12.
101. BDAG, 700.

of the saving work of Christ that God's full mercies can flow to his children. On this stands his role as the "God of all comfort" (1:3), the Atonement opening the way for the Father to exercise his mercy by touching, consoling, and encouraging his tormented child.

By placing mercy and comfort in the genitive mood, Paul does not simply identify two of God's attributes; he actually discloses God himself. Mercy and comfort not only belong to God, but they define him—that is, they reveal not only what he is but who he is. He feels for his children. In response he extends *himself* though his mercy in giving comfort in the here and now. What the Apostle is emphasizing is that God is nothing short of a merciful and comforting Father.[102]

However, the immediate agent through whom he administers these divine attributes is his Son (1:19). He can do this because the Son, too, possesses these qualities. That this is the case can be seen even in Old Testament times when Jesus, in his capacity as Jehovah, revealed himself to Moses, saying that he is "merciful and compassionate, slow to anger, abounding in loving kindness and truth" (Ex. 34:6, our translation).[103] Thus, the Godhead shares in these attributes to the good of the faithful.

The Apostle nuances the word "mercies" so that it emphasizes the depth of God's feelings. So deep are they that the suffering of his righteous children brings a strong visceral response.[104] The Father's answer is to reach out through his Son in merciful comfort. Behind the word "comfort" (παράκλησις, *parakēsis*) stands the idea of help that is felt as a lifting of the spirit and an endowment of strength. Strongly connected to the word is its result, encouragement though knowing one does not stand alone. Such comfort *speaks* to the soul. "It brings not only outward relief but the knowledge that there is One who loves and cares, a God who sees distress and answers lament. Those who are in the midst of distress need something more than the external assistance than a mere technician might deliver. They need the warmth of compassion and concern and they need it from the One who has power over all things, the ability to bring true help and deliverance."[105]

---

102. God's temporal orientation is revealed in the Psalmists recognition of him as "God of my righteousness" (Ps. 18:46), and "God of our salvation" (Ps. 85:4), both statements pertaining to a mortal situation. Seifrid, *Second Letter,* 18 and n. 94.

103. Seifrid, *Second Letter,* 18–19.

104. BDAG, 700.

105. Seifrid, *Second Letter,* 21.

God's objective in giving such encouragement is to motivate the recipient to move forward in obedient faith. The basis of that encouragement is Spirit derived. It is the witness of the Holy Ghost to the soul concerning not only the truthfulness of the gospel message but also the promise of salvation and eternal felicity that awaits the faithful.[106] The current feeling of strength and comfort that the Saints receive is also the assurance that faithfulness will be rewarded. The end result provides the energy to endure life's trials.

At the time Paul wrote, the Corinthian Saints were experiencing such trials. Paul does not soft-pedal their feelings of distress. Indeed, his use of the noun "affliction" (θλίψις, *thlipsis*) emphasizes the great difficulty of their ordeal.[107] But, being a realist, he does put their difficulties in perspective. He understands that such pressure comes from being in a hostile world. For that reason, suffering should be no surprise. Jesus himself had warned his disciples that in this world they would have tribulation, but he assured them that he had overcome the world (John 16:33). Whether or not Paul knew of this teaching, he and Barnabas were well aware that only though many afflictions could the Saints enter the kingdom of God (Acts 14:22). The Savior himself was not free of tribulation, and in such each Christian joined him (compare Philip. 3:10 and 1 Pet. 4:13). It was this solidarity with the Lord that not only explained why troubles came but also witnessed that they could be endured. By this means there was a bond formed between the Savior and the saved.[108]

The suffering Son is central to this section. It is *from* him that Paul's suffering overflows because he has called Paul to a very painful ministry, but it is also *through* him that comfort overflows from God.[109] Therefore, Paul could say that the Savior's suffering abounds (περισσεύω, *perisseuō*) to their advantage (1:5) because it shows that, with divine help, deep suffering can be endured and eventually overcome. Thus, does their "comfort abound through Christ" (1:5, NR).

Paul gives a reason why he and Timothy have and are enduring Christ-like suffering. It is to enable them to strengthen the Christians in theirs by showing that they need not yield to it.[110] And how is that possible? It

106. Otto Schmitz, "παρακαλέω, παράκλησις," in *TDNT*, 5:793–99.
107. BDAG, 457.
108. NID, 2:463–64.
109. Barnett, *Second Epistle*, 74–75.
110. Bernard, "Second Epistle," 38–39.

is due to divine comfort that "abound[s] through Christ" (1:5, NR). Thus, Paul declares, "if we are comforted, it is for your comfort," for it "produces [your] patient endurance in the same suffering that we ourselves endure" (1:6–7, NR). Thus, the Apostle can declare the utter confidence he has in his hope for their success because he knows that "just as you share in our sufferings, so also you share in our comfort" (1:7, NR), and with the strength that comes from that comfort, they will endure all that their antagonists place upon them.[111] The key word here is "fellow-sharers" (κοινωνοί, *koinōnoi*), which, for Paul, implies a joint participation in a uniquely deep spiritual experience. That shared experience, in this case, is the uplift and strength that come through mutually experiencing divine, encouraging comfort that sustains one in trials and afflictions.[112]

But what is the basis for Paul's hope? It is ultimately his experience with God and what the Father has already done for the Church. Paul reminds the Saints that it is God who continually strengthens them in their relationship with Christ (1:21). Through such godly encouraging comfort, they have endured and can endure affliction and in doing so boldly manifest that they are authentic Christ-followers. Indeed, it is Christlike suffering for his cause and the comfort that comes as a result that serve as the validating marks of a true Christian.[113]

By beginning this pericope with a doxology (1:3), Paul "not only expresses his own heartfelt praise but also mentors the Corinthians in proper Christian response to suffering" by showing them his personal response to his own situation and having them "consider their own response to the circumstances in which they find themselves." His purpose is "challenging them to bless God in the midst of suffering."[114]

111. His strong statement of hope for the Saints here stands in contradistinction to the fear he voices in 5:20 and 6:1 that they might fall into apostasy. He here might build up support so that when he turns to chastise them they will be willing to heed his word. B. J. Oropeza, *Exploring Second Corinthians: Death and Life, Hardship and Rivalry* (Atlanta: SBL Press, 2016), 72–73.

112. Martin, *2 Corinthians*, 145.

113. Guthrie, *2 Corinthians*, 74.

114. Guthrie, *2 Corinthians*, 65.

The Harrowing Experience in the Province of Asia (1:8–11)

What follows is an analysis of the second unit into which this pericope breaks down 1:8–2:16. Here the Apostle continues to build on his theme by illustrating his point that suffering, properly seen, can be redemptive. He uses his harrowing brush with death as a case in point. His purpose is to have his readers relate to and appreciate what he has all too recently gone through (1:8) and to show them how the experience altered his attitude and that of his companions. It forced them to change perspective from relying on themselves to trusting fully in God even should they have suffered death (1:9). His deliverance, however, as he explains, has resulted in the hope that such will continue (1:10), and he gives much credit for his future success to the prayers of these Saints (1:11).

It is noteworthy that both the salutation and the prologue begin and end with the Apostle's celebration of the Father's comforting power (1:3, 11) and trumpet his redemption of Paul and his company from affliction (1:4, 6, 9). Also, both halves close by focusing on the Apostle's partnership with his target audience, the Corinthian Saints (1:7, 11).[115]

Greek Text

8 Οὐ γὰρ θέλομεν ὑμᾶς ἀγνοεῖν, ἀδελφοί, ὑπὲρ τῆς θλίψεως ἡμῶν τῆς γενομένης ἐν τῇ Ἀσίᾳ, ὅτι καθ' ὑπερβολὴν ὑπὲρ δύναμιν ἐβαρήθημεν, ὥστε ἐξαπορηθῆναι ἡμᾶς καὶ τοῦ ζῆν· 9 ἀλλὰ αὐτοὶ ἐν ἑαυτοῖς τὸ ἀπόκριμα τοῦ θανάτου ἐσχήκαμεν, ἵνα μὴ πεποιθότες ὦμεν ἐφ' ἑαυτοῖς ἀλλ' ἐπὶ τῷ θεῷ τῷ ἐγείροντι τοὺς νεκρούς· 10 ὃς ἐκ τηλικούτου θανάτου ἐρρύσατο ἡμᾶς καὶ ῥύσεται, εἰς ὃν ἠλπίκαμεν ὅτι καὶ ἔτι ῥύσεται, 11 συνυπουργούντων καὶ ὑμῶν ὑπὲρ ἡμῶν τῇ δεήσει, ἵνα ἐκ πολλῶν προσώπων τὸ εἰς ἡμᾶς χάρισμα διὰ πολλῶν εὐχαριστηθῇ ὑπὲρ ἡμῶν. [SBLGNT]

King James Version

8 For we would not, brethren, have you ignorant of our trouble which came to us in Asia, that we were pressed out of measure, above strength, insomuch that we despaired even of life: 9 But we had the sentence of death in ourselves,

New Rendition

8 For we do not want you to be unaware, brothers and sisters, of the affliction that we suffered in the province of Asia—that we were oppressed utterly beyond our strength so that we even despaired of life itself. 9 Indeed, we felt

115. Guthrie, *2 Corinthians*, 62.

that we should not trust in ourselves, but in God which raiseth the dead:
10 Who delivered us from so great a death, and doth deliver: in whom we trust that he will yet deliver us;
11 Ye also helping together by prayer for us, that for the gift bestowed upon us by the means of many persons thanks may be given by many on our behalf.

that we had received a verdict of death so that we would not trust in ourselves but rather in God, who raises the dead.
10 He who rescued us from so great a peril of death will continue to rescue us. We have set our hope on him that he will also rescue us again,
11 as you join in helping us by your prayers so that many might give thanks on our behalf for the gift of many people to us.

Translation Notes and Comments

1:8 The KJV translates this verse quite literally. In our Rendition we have tried to better express the sense of the passage in contemporary English.

For we would not, brethren, have you ignorant of our trouble / For we do not want you to be unaware, brothers and sisters: The causal conjunction γάρ (*gar*), "for," ties, if somewhat loosely, the following to what Paul has said before and thus explains why he praises God. The verb ἀγνοέω (*agnoeō*), "to be unaware, ignorant of," carries the nuance of not recognizing or not paying attention to the significance of something.[116] In this instance, it is likely the latter meaning that is at play. If that is the case, then the Apostle is asking them not just to recall but to take very seriously what he now reminds them of.[117]

The plural noun ἀδελφοί (*adelphoi*), literally "brethren," is regularly translated as "brothers and sisters" in our Rendition because it was often used in ancient religious literature to include both men and women.[118]

---

116. BDAG, 12–13, but it can also denote willful ignorance. MM, 4.

117. Guthrie, *2 Corinthians,* 78. David Starling, "'We Do Not Want You to Be Unaware . . .': Disclosure, Concealment and Suffering in 2 Cor 1–7," *New Testament Studies* 60, no. 2 (2014): 276, looks at the grammar in 1:8 and how it differs from standard disclosure language. This double negative, instead of standard disclosure language, works "both to introduce the topic of Paul's afflictions in Asia and to express a disavowal of any attempt on his part to conceal them from the Corinthians."

118. BDAG, 18; *NID,* 1:149. The term ἀδελφός (*adelphos*) carries the idea of family relationship. Jesus taught that, figuratively and also spiritually, those who do God's will by obeying the Son's word are his brothers and sisters as well as his mother. In short, they are members of his spiritual but nonetheless real family (Matt. 3:31–35). The Qumran literature uses the term אָח (*aḥ*) in the figurative sense of communal family membership (see, for example, 1QS 6.22; 1QSa 1.18) that reflects the idea found in Pauline literature where it bears a strong sense of "siblings." Guthrie, *2 Corinthians,* 391 n. 2.

our trouble which came to us in Asia / the affliction that we suffered in the province of Asia: As is always the case in the New Testament, "Asia" does not refer to the far eastern continent, but to the Roman province that was located in the western part of present-day Turkey; hence, for clarification, we refer to it as "the province of Asia."

With the phrase τῆς θλίψεως ἡμῶν (*tēs thlipseōs hēmōn*), literally "the affliction of us," the Apostle points to a specific harrowing event and broadly locates it. Unfortunately, he identifies neither exactly where it took place nor what it was. It is likely, however, that his readers were aware of his reference, and that is the reason he didn't need to give any details.[119]

were pressed out of measure, above strength, insomuch that we despaired even of life / we were oppressed utterly beyond our strength so that we even despaired of life itself: With this phrase, Paul describes his feelings while experiencing the harrowing event. The key thought here is expressed by the phrase καθ' ὑπερβολὴν (*kath' hyperbolē*). It denotes such excessive force that it is irresistible, thus beyond one's strength to resist.[120] To even better communicate the dire feelings he had at the time, he chose the passive of the verb βαρέω (*bareō*), "to be oppressed, burdened, weighted down."[121] The imagery is like that of an overloaded ship foundering with no hope of salvation.[122] To put the final touch on trying to communicate the depth of his feeling and reveal his mental state, he uses the verb ἐξαπορέομαι (*exaporeomai*), "to be in utmost despair," a condition that results from a total lack of hope.[123]

1:9 ***But we had the sentence of death in ourselves / Indeed, we felt that we had received a verdict of death:*** This phrase translated literally as "But

---

119. Barrett, *Second Epistle,* 63–64. He may have alluded to this event in Philip. 1:12–26. Compare Acts 19:23; 1 Cor. 15:32.

120. BDAG, 1032. The basic idea behind the word is "throwing beyond" others and therefore denotes, on the positive side, the idea of excellence, super abundance, supereminence. On the negative side it denotes what is out of measure or beyond measure. See Gerhard Delling, "ὑπερβάλλω, ὑπερβαλλόντως, ὑπερβολή," in in *TDNT,* 8:520–22.

121. BDAG, 166.

122. Martin, *2 Corinthians,* 149. See G. Adolf Deissmann, *Bible Studies: Contributions Chiefly from Papyri and Inscriptions to the History of the Language, the Literature, and the Religion of Hellenistic Judaism and Primitive Christianity,* trans. Alexander Grieve (Peabody, Mass.: Hendrickson, 1988), 257, who examines the technical language found here and suggests it carries the modern idea of a "death-warrant."

123. In the New Testament, the word is found only as the passive deponent ἐξαπορέομαι (*exaporeomai*), meaning "to be utterly at a loss." See BDAG, 345. It expresses "a state of excess to an extraordinary degree." Guthrie, *2 Corinthians,* 82.

in ourselves had received the sentence of death." The noun ἀπόκριμα (*apokrima*) denotes an official report or decision,[124] but in proconsular Asia Minor it did not refer to a death sentence per se, but rather to a negative verdict in answer to a petition.[125] Thus, the phrase does not refer to an actual sentence of death but to the negative result of an appeal for protection or release from prison. The idea conveyed by the Greek word is that, while no actual sentence of death had been formally decreed against them, the situation was such that they felt as if one had been and therefore feared death's inevitability. We wrote the Rendition to catch that nuance.[126]

that we should not trust in ourselves / so that we would not trust in ourselves: In this phrase Paul explains why he and his companions suffered so. It centers on the issue of what or who to trust. The verb πείθω (*peithō*) denotes a situation so strong that it convinces a person to put her or his full confidence in something or someone.[127] In this case, the horrible experience forcefully redirected the missionaries' trust away from themselves and toward a higher power.

but in God which raiseth the dead / but rather in God, who raises the dead: Here Paul states not only the object of their trust but also the reason. The conjunction ἀλλά (*alla*) can be translated as "indeed," and in that case it would reinforce the extent of the despair Paul has described.[128] It can also be translated as "yet" or "but rather"[129] and thus provide a sharp contrast between the missionaries' feeling of deep despair due to the imminent and hopeless promise of death and their feeling of purposefulness once God had provided perspective on the situation.[130] Because it better fits the context, we have chosen the latter for our Rendition.

The phrase τῷ ἐγείροντι τοὺς νεκρούς (*tō egeironti tous nekrous*), "who raises the dead," could be taken to refer to the Father's ability to resuscitate those who have died, such as in the case of Jairus' daughter (Matt. 9:23–26; Mark 5:35–43) or Lazarus (John 11:43–44). Such a view could have supported the missionaries during this ordeal. Through faith, they could easily believe that though their lives might be taken, God would resuscitate them

124. BDAG, 113; Friedrich Büchsel, "ἀπόκριμα," in *TDNT,* 3:945–46.
125. C. J. Hemer, "A Note on 2 Corinthians 1:9," *Tyndale Bulletin* 23 (1972): 103–7.
126. Martin, *2 Corinthians,* 149.
127. BDAG, 7921–92.
128. See Furnish, *II Corinthians,* 113; Harris, *Second Epistle,* 155.
129. BDAG, 44–45; Louw-Nida, §§89.125; 91.2; Guthrie, *2 Corinthians,* 82.
130. Barrett, *Second Epistle,* 64.

so that they could continue their mission. However, since the Christian message, proclaimed by Paul and the other missionaries, centered on the Lord's Resurrection (for example, see 5:1–10, 15, and 1 Cor. 15), it seems far more likely that the strength the missionaries received was due to their belief in the promise of being resurrected into a state of glory.

1:10 ***Who delivered us from so great a death, and doth deliver / He who rescued us from so great a peril of death will continue to rescue us:*** The verb ῥύομαι (*rhyomai*) denotes being delivered or rescued from death. It does not here carry the nuance of being "preserved from death" in general, but of being rescued from a situation in which actual death is threatened.[131] That Paul uses the demonstrative pronoun τηλικοῦτος (*tēlikoutos*), "so great," or by extension, "so excessive,"[132] with the noun θάνατος (*thanatos*), "death,"[133] underscores just how great a peril the missionaries felt they were in.

in whom we trust that he will yet deliver us / We have set our hope on him that he will also rescue us again: On "hope," see Translation Notes for 1:7. The reality and severity of the threat of death now becomes the basis that the Apostle uses to show why the missionaries hope that God can and will deliver them from any and all threats when he so chooses.

1:11 The Greek of this phrase is extremely complicated. It translates literally as "so that from many people the gift to us through many thanks might be given in our behalf." In our Rendition we have made several changes to make the meaning clearer in contemporary English. These include changing the word order; using an active voice rather than the passive of the Greek verb εὐχαριστέω (*eucharisteō*), "to thank";[134] and translating the nominal phrase τὸ εἰς ἡμᾶς χάρισμα (*to eis hēmas charisma*), "the gift to us," into the verbal relative clause "the gift that many people gave us."

Ye also helping together by prayer for us / as you join in helping us by your prayers: Here Paul notes the conditional nature of future rescues. The verb συνυπουργέω (*synypourgeō*) denotes people cooperatively joining

---

131. BDAG, 907–8. Although both "rescue" and "deliver" denote freeing one from confinement, danger, or even death, "rescue" is the better translation here because the English word denotes delivering a person from imminent danger. *Dictionary of Synonyms,* s.v. "rescue." See also Martin, *2 Corinthians,* 148.

132. BDAG, 1001–2.

133. BDAG, 442–43.

134. BDAG, 415–16.

together with others to meet a specific goal or purpose.[135] In this case it is the Corinthian Saints joining with God to help Paul and his companions overcome the trials of missionary work.[136] With these words, the Apostle acknowledges his dependence on the Corinthian Saints and in that way attempts to bind them to him. He identifies how they can help—namely, through heartfelt prayers.

that for the gift bestowed upon us by the means of many persons thanks may be given by many on our behalf / so that many might give thanks on our behalf for the gift that many people gave us: Here he gives the reason why his readers should pray for the missionaries. The phrase πολλῶν προσώπων (*pollōn prosōpōn*), "many people," translates literally as "many faces." The noun πρόσωπον (*prosōpon*) can also refer to "appearance" and "countenance"[137] and therefore connote the personality or emotional state of a person. Paul may have in mind many people raising their faces to God in sincere thanksgiving.[138]

His use of the plural adjective πολλῶν (*pollōn*), "many,"[139] is vague both times he uses it. The "many" who give the gift of prayer appear to be different from the "many" who give thanks for the missionaries. It may be that those giving the gift are Paul's supporters in Corinth who are willing to pray for him and his companions, and those giving thanks are those nonmembers who will be blessed as the missionaries bring the gospel into their lives.[140]

---

135. BDAG, 977.

136. Seifrid, *Second Letter,* 44.

137. BDAG, 887–88. When the prophet Alma asked "Have ye received [Christ's] image in your countenances?" (Alma 5:14), the context is that of the whole person.

138. Paul often uses noun πρόσωπον (*prosōpon*), but with various nuances such as the actual face (3:7, 12, 18; 4:6; 11:20), one's appearance (5:12; 10:7), and one's presence (2:10; 8:24; 10:1). Guthrie, *2 Corinthians,* 87.

139. The word can denote a large number of people. BDAG, 847.

140. Guthrie, *2 Corinthians,* 86. There may be a play on the idea of brokerage going on there. The idea is that there is an intermediary in the patron-client system that facilitates the relationship between the two. David Briones, "Mutual Brokers of Grace: A Study in 2 Corinthians 1.3–11," *New Testament Studies* 56, no. 4 (October 2010): 536–56, states that in 2 Cor 1:3–11, Paul shows a "mutual brokerage" relationship. On the one hand, God is the patron and Paul is the broker with the Corinthians as clients. On the other hand, since the Corinthians also help Paul receive God's grace (1:11), Paul is also a client and the Corinthians are brokers. This relationship ensures, Briones notes on page 554, "that each participant in this economy depends upon the other to receive grace from God."

Analysis and Summary

To illustrate his point that suffering, properly seen, can be redemptive, Paul calls his readers' attention to a most harrowing experience that he and his missionary companions had in the province of Asia. He also explains why he is so thankful to God for its outcome. His description of the depth of his and his companions' fear betrays how terrifying the ordeal really was. Indeed, he states they were "oppressed utterly beyond [their] strength so that [they] even despaired of life itself" (1:8). His words suggest that they felt a sentence of death had been passed against them (1:9).

Just where they were when this happened is unclear from the text, and there has been much speculation about not only this but also the exact circumstances they were under.[141] A place of possible intersection is the riot that took place in Ephesus against the Christians (Acts 19:21–41). The problem is, however, that the account in Acts, though showing how intense the near riot was, does not give the impression that Paul's life, or anyone else's, was in danger, and thus the door is left open to other possibilities. It may be that, for missionary purposes, Luke underplayed the event. It is likely that Paul was arrested, albeit briefly, after this event, but Acts is silent on this point. One thing is clear: due to the strength of the hostility generated against Paul, for his safety the local Church leaders had Paul leave the city. Further, wherever the place was, what is sure is that Paul and his companions despaired of life; that is, they viewed their situation as so desperate that they really thought they were going to die.

The result of their experience brought a new understanding of this kind of suffering. In this section, Paul revealed their new insight, one that focused on suffering *with Christ.* The incident is important to Paul because it was during that trying time that he and his companions were forced to turn away from their own means and rely totally on God (1:9). In fact, his own suffering for the gospel's sake seems to have caused him to relate to the Lord's own suffering for that cause. Paul saw the implications—if the Christians shared in Christ's suffering, and particularly in his death, then they would also share "in his resurrection and his glory." As a result, "not

---

141. Oropeza, *Exploring Second Corinthians,* 186–89; Guthrie, *2 Corinthians,* 79–81. Both explore the various opinions on this subject. These sources include the suggestion that Paul was referring to his strained relationship with the Corinthians, to a serious, even life threating illness (possibly referred to in 2 Cor. 12:7), to an imprisonment in which he and others felt they were on death row.

only [would] the Saints receive comfort from God, but they [would] also be victorious with Christ in the future (1:5–7, 9–10)."[142]

It is of note that their trust did not initially rest on being rescued from death. Rather, it rested on God's power over death. Thus, these missionaries could have had in mind God's power to resuscitate them so that they could carry on their mission or, more likely, to eventually resurrect them through the power of the Atonement into eternal life and glory. Apparently, in some miraculous way God did not allow them to suffer death but rescued them from that terrifying and hopeless situation (1:10). By doing so, God turned their condition inside out. Fear and perplexity gave way to a new understanding and perspective that Paul felt compelled to communicate to his readers.[143] Paul and his companion came to understand that even when conditions seemed hopeless, God had the power to rescue his people.

In 1:11, Paul does three important things that further assist him in laying down the foundation on which he will build the rest of his epistle. First, he acknowledges the help his readers can give him and his companions as they lift their voices to God in fervent prayer. As they do so, he tacitly reminds them, they actually join with God in supporting the missionaries. Second, he enlists their help in the ministry as they join together in thankful prayers to God for what he has done for Paul and others and, by inference, can and will do for all. Such would have a sanctifying effect on them (as it had on the missionaries) as they relied on and glorified God rather than themselves. And finally, he reinforces their alignment with him in his role as an Apostle. Indeed, their response to his request publicly reveals and reinforces that they stand with him.[144]

---

142. Holzapfel and Wayment, *Making Sense,* 370.

143. Guthrie, *2 Corinthians,* 82.

144. Guthrie, *2 Corinthians,* 86. Furnish, *II Corinthians,* 125, and Witherington, *Conflict and Community,* 360, suggests that the Apostle's primary objective in his outreach to the branch was "to build up goodwill and compassion" between him and his readers and to get them to unite with him.

Paul Explains the Reason for His Confidence in the Correctness of His Dealing with the Corinthian Saints (1:12–14)

With this pericope, Paul begins his letter in earnest. His harrowing experience in the province of Asia, culminating in his rescue by God, has illustrated his initial theme that the Father comforts the afflicted. The Apostle has shown that the source of his comfort has been through God's intercession, which has now brought the Apostle's heartfelt thanksgiving. Because of God's intervention, Paul has declared his intent to bless the Father and rely upon him for further deliverance. He also has acknowledged the help his loyal supporters in Corinth have and continue to give him and his fellow missionaries by enjoining God through prayer in their behalf. In doing so, Paul has carefully laid the groundwork such that he can now turn to the delicate matter of answering his detractors' continual and intense criticism of his person, doctrine, and authority.[145]

This section (1:12–14) contains the thesis of the whole work, as the Apostle to the Gentiles attests to the purity of his motives, the clearness of his writings to these people, and his pride in them.[146] This section constitutes a rather lengthy *apologia* or "defense," wherein Paul explains why he was unable to fulfill his plans to visit these Saints, but behind that is his attempt to disarm those who criticized him due to the harsh tone of his letter.[147]

Greek Text

12 Ἡ γὰρ καύχησις ἡμῶν αὕτη ἐστίν, τὸ μαρτύριον τῆς συνειδήσεως ἡμῶν, ὅτι
ἐν ἁγιότητι καὶ εἰλικρινείᾳ τοῦ θεοῦ, οὐκ ἐν σοφίᾳ σαρκικῇ ἀλλ' ἐν χάριτι θεοῦ,
ἀνεστράφημεν ἐν τῷ κόσμῳ, περισσοτέρως δὲ πρὸς ὑμᾶς· 13 οὐ γὰρ ἄλλα γρά-
φομεν ὑμῖν ἀλλ' ἢ ἃ ἀναγινώσκετε ἢ καὶ ἐπιγινώσκετε, ἐλπίζω δὲ ὅτι ἕως τέλους
ἐπιγνώσεσθε, 14 καθὼς καὶ ἐπέγνωτε ἡμᾶς ἀπὸ μέρους, ὅτι καύχημα ὑμῶν ἐσμεν
καθάπερ καὶ ὑμεῖς ἡμῶν ἐν τῇ ἡμέρᾳ τοῦ κυρίου ἡμῶν Ἰησοῦ. [SBLGNT]

145. Barnett, *Second Epistle,* 90–91.

146. Matera, *II Corinthians,* 47.

147. Ivor H. Jones, *The Contemporary Cross: The Study for Passiontide—a Theme and Four Biblical Variations* (London: Epworth, 1973), 36.

King James Version

12 For our rejoicing is this, the testimony of our conscience, that in simplicity and godly sincerity, not with fleshly wisdom, but by the grace of God, we have had our conversation in the world, and more abundantly to you-ward. 13 For we write none other things unto you, than what ye read or acknowledge; and I trust ye shall acknowledge even to the end; 14 As also ye have acknowledged us in part, that we are your rejoicing, even as ye also are ours in the day of the Lord Jesus.

New Rendition

12 Now the reason for our pride is this: the testimony of our conscience, that with godly holiness and sincerity, not with human wisdom but with the grace of God, we have conducted ourselves in the world and especially in regard to you. 13 For we do not write anything to you except what you can read and also understand. And I hope you will completely understand, 14 as you have also partially understood us, that we are your source of pride, just as you will also be ours in the day of our Lord Jesus.

Translation Notes and Comments

1:12 ***For our rejoicing is this / Now the reason for our pride is this:*** The conjunction γάρ (*gar*) usually carries causal force and is therefore often translated as "for" or "because." Here, however, it functions to denote a new division or set of ideas and is, thus, translated as "now."

The noun καύχησις (*kauchēsis*), "pride, praise, boasting," refers to what constitutes the result of Paul's sureness about his correctness of his dealings with the Corinthian Saints.[148] The root of the word means "to boast," but in the present context it should be understood to denote the "reason for boasting"—that is, what he can claim with proper and justifiable pride.[149] The Greek noun carries the same tension as does the English word "pride." It can connote that which is good (thus, self-respect and delight in others)[150] or that which is bad (thus, self-conceit and competition with others).[151] To guard against the latter, the Bible stresses that all praise should be directed toward God in recognition of his goodness (see, for example, Jer. 9:23–24 and 1 Cor. 1:31). Such insight excludes self-boasting (see the warnings in 1 Cor. 5:6 and James 4:16).

148. BDAG, 537.

149. Paul boasts only "to remind his enemies of his credentials on knowing Judaism, suffering, and the visions of the Lord." Anderson, *Understanding Paul,* 135.

150. For example, see Prov. 16:31; 17:6, where a form of the noun in the LXX is translated as "glory" in the KJV.

151. Compare Judg. 7:2; 1 Sam. 2:3; Jer. 12:13; and Ezek. 24:25. Witherington, *Conflict and Community,* 362.

Paul stresses the theme of proper boasting in many of his letters. Looking at how the Apostle does it shows his insistence that it must be directed toward others and more especially toward the Father and the Son. He puts special emphasis on the cross—that is, the Atonement of the Savior (Gal. 6:14; see also 1 Cor. 1:29; 2 Cor. 10:17). By doing that, he eliminates all aspects of self-conceit and self-praise, the centers of "evil boasting."[152]

the testimony of our conscience: This phrase reveals what Paul takes pride in. The noun συνείδησις (*syneidēsis*), "conscience," denotes the capacity to know right from wrong.[153] In its theological sense, the word nuances "the faculty by which we apprehend the will of God, as that which is designed to govern our lives," and by yielding to this, we follow our consciences and avoid guilt.[154]

The noun μαρτύριον (*martyrion*), "testimony," denotes that which acts as proof for a belief or position.[155] Here Paul uses it to refer to his personal witness borne by a clear conscience as to the correctness of his dealings with the Corinthian Saints.

that in simplicity and godly sincerity / that with godly holiness and sincerity: Though the KJV follows the Western and Byzantine reading of ἁπλότητι (*haplotēti*), "simplicity," the alternate reading, ἁγιότητι (*hagiotēti*), "holiness," has both earlier and stronger support, and we, therefore, use it in our Rendition.[156]

The conjunction ὅτι (*hoti*), "that," plays an important role here as it introduces the phrase that gives the content or substance behind Paul's clear conscience. His guiltlessness is expressed by the main verb in the clause, ἀναστρέφω (*anastrephō*), "to act, behave, conduct" (see below), which points to a life governed by the two virtues mentioned next.[157]

The noun ἁγιότης (*hagiotēs*), "holiness," denotes that which is free from worldliness. It nuances *the* primary characteristic or attribute of God. When used with people, it carries the idea of moral purity and having a godlike nature.[158]

---

152. *NID,* 2:651–55; Guthrie, *2 Corinthians,* 93.

153. BDAG, 967–68.

154. For extended discussion, see Christian Maurer, "σύνοιδα, σμνείδησις," in *TDNT,* 7:898–919; *NID,* 4:402–6.

155. BDAG, 619.

156. Metzger, *Textual Commentary,* 507; Bernard, "Second Epistle," 42.

157. BDAG, 72; Harris, *Second Epistle,* 186; Guthrie, *2 Corinthians,* 95.

158. BDAG, 11; Otto Procksch, "ἁγιότης," in *TDNT,* 1:114.

The noun εἰλικρίνεια (*eilikineia*), "sincerity," denotes "a state of being free from dissimulation" and thereby stresses the idea of "purity of motive." It connotes the idea of integrity and honesty.[159]

To these Paul adds the phrase τοῦ θεοῦ (*tou theou*), "of God," translated adverbially as "godly" in our Rendition. By using this phrase, he puts even more stress on the quality of his actions toward the Corinthian Saints that underscore his guiltless feelings.

not with fleshly wisdom / not with human wisdom: The adjective σαρκικός (*sarkikos*) refers to that which is human and therefore fleshly but on a level that is natural, weak, and disappointing.[160] Behind it stands the connotation of something that cannot be trusted. The noun σοφία (*sophia*), "wisdom," denotes "the capacity to understand and function accordingly."[161] Wisdom can be divided into two broad categories: one human and the other divine.

The σοφίᾳ σαρκικῇ (*sophia sarkikē*), "wisdom of the flesh," denotes that which pertains to mortals. Though it does have many connotations that are not pejorative (intelligence, skill, common sense, applied knowledge), they are all linked to that which is uninspired and of human derivation—therefore, that which is earthly, vulnerable, transitory, and perishable. In our literature, the pejorative nuance dominates. Human wisdom stands behind their rejection of God's ways.[162]

The σοφία θεοῦ (*sophia theou*), "wisdom of God," stands in contrast to human wisdom. It is based on people's acceptance of God and willingness to learn and implement what God decrees. Thus, godly wisdom is rooted in the fear (reverence) of the Divine (Job 28:28; Ps. 111:10; Prov. 1:7; 9:10; 15:33).[163] As such, it is a gift from God.[164] Paul builds on this theme.

---

159. BDAG, 282; Guthrie, *2 Corinthians,* 95. For a study of Paul's self-depiction in 1:12–14, see John T. Fitzgerald, *Cracks in an Earthen Vessel: An Examination of the Catalogues of Hardships in the Corinthian Correspondence* (Atlanta: Scholars Press, 1988), 166–80.

160. BDAG, 914. For an extended study of the idea of "flesh" in biblical times, see Eduard Schweizer, "σάρξ, σαρκικός, σάρκινος," in *TDNT,* 7:98–151.

161. BDAG, 934–35.

162. This is particularly true of the rejection of the central tenet of Paul's theology, "Christ crucified" (1 Cor. 1:23; 2:2). The wisdom of the cross is all-important to him (1 Cor. 1:17–18; Gal. 6:12–16; Col. 1:20).

163. The verb יָרֵא (*yārēʾ*), though primarily meaning "to fear" or "be full of dread," in its positive nuances, as used here, carries the notion of reverential awe and deep respect. *HAL,* 433; BDB, 431.

164. See Isa. 50:4. Compare Matt. 10:16–20; Acts 6:10; D&C 11:21; *NID,* 4:330–39.

but by the grace of God / but with the grace of God: Here Paul shows the source of his clear conscience when it comes to his dealings with the Corinthian Saints. It did not come via human wisdom but rather came ἐν χάριτι θεοῦ (*en chariti theou*), "by means of God's grace." The dative phrase shows instrumentality or means and thus points to God's enabling power. The noun χάρις (*charis*) has a breadth of meanings,[165] but here it denotes a heavenly enabling power given as a gift that assisted Paul and his companions in living as they did.[166]

we have had our conversation in the world and more abundantly to you-ward / we have conducted ourselves in the world and especially in regard to you: The verb ἀναστρέφω (*anastrephō*) denotes conduct that is based on high ethical or moral principles.[167] The word is translated consistently as "conversation" in the KJV because that noun, in that era, denoted such conduct.[168] Here it refers to a kind of grace-filled life made possible through the power of God (see above).

The noun κόσμος (*kosmos*), "world,"[169] does not carry, in this instance, a pejorative nuance of evil or depravity[170] but rather that of the geographical area in which Paul labors. His work, as he states, was that of reconciling the world to God (5:19).

The adverb περισσοτέρως (*perissoterōs*), "especially," expresses a degree well beyond the standard.[171] Paul uses it to stress the care with which he and his companions conducted themselves while at Corinth.

1:13 ***For we write none other things unto you, than what ye read or acknowledge / For we do not write anything to you except what you can read and also understand:*** The conjunction γάρ (gar), "for," unlike its use in 1:12, has explanatory force here.[172] It signals that Paul will now explain

165. BDAG, 1079–81; Louw-Nida, §§25.89; 33.350; 88.66.

166. Louw-Nida, §57.103. Once given, the recipient of such grace was obligated to give unselfish service to others in turn. Thus, they would move from one level of grace or ability to a higher level. See D&C 93:19–20.

167. The verb has a wide range of meanings (see BDAG, 72) but, in the broader Greek culture, it referred to a life lived according to patterns of high social and ethical conduct. Guthrie, *2 Corinthians*, 95.

168. *Collegiate Dictionary*, s.v. "Conversation."

169. BDAG, 561–63.

170. Note JS–M 1:4. Both Platonic and Gnostic systems saw the κόσμος (*kosmos*) as the seat of evil. For discussion, see *NID*, 2:730–39.

171. BDAG, 806.

172. BDAG, 189; Guthrie, *2 Corinthians*, 97.

the nature of his written communications to the Corinthian Saints. It is based on Paul's intent. First, his writings are done with care so that they be easily read. The verb ἀναγινώσκω (*anaginōskō*), "to read," includes not just personal reading but more especially reading something in public for the benefit of others, a trademark of the activity of the synagogue.[173] It must be kept in mind that the vast majority of the people were illiterate and were therefore dependent on others to read to them in order to understand written communications.

Paul states his second intent. His writings are done with care so that his readers can understand. The ἐπιγινώσκω (*epiginōskō*), "understand," means "to know" but carries the nuance of knowing something fully or exactly and, therefore, understanding it.[174] Essentially Paul is saying that he is careful to write only what they can grasp. He thus qualifies what he writes with the phrase ἀλλ' ἢ (*all' ē*), "other than, except." The phrase denotes that there is nothing in his writings except what is obvious. In short, his writings contain no hidden agenda, no coded messages. What the Saints read and understand is all there is. That he has to explain the nature of his writings suggests there were those who were reading between the lines and by that means twisting his words to say things he never meant.

and I trust ye shall acknowledge even to the end / And I hope you will completely understand: On the verb ἐλπίζω (*elpizō*), "to hope," see Translation Notes on 1:7 above. The noun τέλος (*telos*), though it can denote the end of an era and nuance specifically the Parousia or Second Coming,[175] in this case, carries the idea of a high degree of completeness.[176] Thus, the phrase ἕως τέλους ἐπιγνώσεσθε (*heōs telous epignōsesthe*) means to "completely understand." The key to what Paul hopes his readers will understand lies in his switching from the first-person-plural verb "we" to the

173. BDAG, 60.

174. BDAG, 369. There is no doubt that Paul did weave allusions and echoes of Christian history into his writings. Laurence L. Welborn, "Paul and Pain: Paul's Emotional Therapy in 2 Corinthians 1.1–2.13; 7.5–16 in the Context of Ancient Psychagogic Literature," *New Testament Studies* 57, no. 4 (2011): 547–70, shows that, although some scholars discredit the idea because his audience would not have understood such, in actuality all knew the single narrative in which Jesus' death and resurrection were decisive moments and which Paul believed himself to carry forward in its new phase, and thereby they were able to follow him. See also N. T. Wright, "Israel's Scriptures in Paul's Narrative Theology," *Theology* 115, no. 5 (2012): 323–29.

175. BDAG, 998; Louw-Nida, §67.66.

176. Louw-Nida, §78.47; Furnish, *II Corinthians,* 128.

first-person-singular "I." His hope is that they will come to fully understand him and his motives. It was this desire empowered by that hope that drove him to write this epistle.

1:14 ***As also ye have acknowledged us in part / as you have also partially understood us:*** These words reveal the root of the problem. The genitive phrase ἀπὸ μέρους (*apo merous*), "in part,"[177] describes the incomplete nature of their understanding of Paul and his message. Though there are some things about him they seem to have readily grasped, there are others that have eluded them.

that we are your rejoicing / that we are your source of pride: In this phrase, the Apostle points out a very important matter in his relationship to them that they have missed. He uses the noun καύχημα (*kauchēma*), "the source of pride" or "cause of boasting."[178] The source of the Saints' pride was having a knowledge of the gospel and the work of the Father and the Son. The source of that pride, which some of these people seem to have missed, was Paul and his companions who first introduced the gospel to the area.

even as ye also are ours in the day of the Lord Jesus / just as you will also be ours in the day of our Lord Jesus: This phrase reveals the positive result of their fully comprehending Paul. Just as it is with his present pride in them, so they will have the same toward him. That he appeals to τῇ ἡμέρᾳ τοῦ κυρίου ἡμῶν Ἰησοῦ (*tē hēmera tou kyrou hēmōn Iēsou*), "the day of the Lord Jesus," suggests that he has full confidence in the Savior's future vindication of all he has done. This is because, in the day of the Lord, all things will be disclosed.[179] At that point, the missionaries will be able to take pride in their Corinthian brothers and sisters because they have united with the missionaries and their message.

---

177. BDAG, 633–34.

178. BDAG, 536–37.

179. A number of Old Testament prophets looked to this day. For example, see Isa. 2:2–21; Joel 1–3; Amos 8:9–11; 9:9–12. It is a day when all things shall be made known. For example, see Isa. 57:17–21; Luke 8:17; 12:3; 2 Ne. 27:11; D&C 88:108–10. For discussions from an LDS point of view, see James E. Talmage, *Vitality of Mormonism* (Salt Lake City: Deseret Book, 1919), 173–75; Ezra Taft Benson, "Prepare Yourselves for the Great Day of the Lord," devotional, Brigham Young University, April 14, 1981, Provo, Utah, audio recording and transcript, https://speeches.byu.edu/talks/ezra-taft-benson/prepare-great-day-lord/; and Bruce R. McConkie, *The Millennial Messiah* (Salt Lake City: Deseret Book, 1982), 24–29.

Analysis and Summary

Paul begins this pericope (1:12–2:13) by bearing a strong witness as to how guilt free his conscience is when it comes to his dealings with the Saints at Corinth. Indeed, he states that his clear conscience is a source of pride with him. It is grounded on his conduct (ἀναστρέφω, *anastrephō*)—that is, his actions following the highest order of ethical behavior.[180] He testifies that these actions were grounded in that kind of holiness and sincerity that is enabled by God and is not based on fallible worldly wisdom.[181]

Indeed, his former (and by extension, present) conduct is filled with the grace of God that authenticates all he did and now does. Paul feels assured that he can stand on his integrity. Though acting according to conscience is his and his companions' general comportment, they exercised it more especially during the times spent at Corinth. The Apostle's not-so-hidden message is, then, that he and his companions stand blameless before God. On this condition—his total feelings of guiltlessness—Paul builds the rest of his defense that continues through chapter 7. In doing so, it is likely he is very deliberately laying the groundwork for his forceful defense against those who had impugned his character and apostolic office.[182]

Based on his integrity, Paul declares to his readers that he has been straightforward in all his correspondence with them. He has never, he assures them, used his writings to hide an agenda or veil a teaching. Because some have read his letters supposing that they contained some veiled material, they have understood neither his intentions, his doctrine, nor his use of authority. As a result, the congregation has had, at best, only a partial understanding of him. He therefore stresses the transparency of his epistles to assure them that they can take at face value what he has written and will write to them, and through that means they can come to understand him more fully.

Because of the propensity of some to misread his material, it appears that the congregation's positive response to his harsh letter may have been more superficial than he desired. They still did not understand his humility

180. Guthrie, *2 Corinthians*, 95.

181. It is, unfortunately, possible for people to be misled by their conscience believing desperately that they are doing what is right. Paul, however, assures his readers that his conscience is clear due to divine manifestation. Indeed, it is this heavenly reassurance on which the Apostle's confidence is based. Garland, *2 Corinthians*, 89.

182. Martin, *2 Corinthians*, 155.

and meekness and as a result were vulnerable to the blandishments of the opposition party. Misunderstanding him likely opened the doors for his detractors to misrepresent and thereby twist his intentions, thus gaining disciples to their cause and his hurt.[183] Paul's supporters apparently resisted the attacks. This varied condition would account for his mixed signals (of both joy and anxiety), with which the epistle is loaded concerning these people.[184] His desire, as he states, is to have the Saints, through means of this letter, more accurately understand him, his motives, and his message. As this happens, hopefully by understanding the content of the present letter, they will come to feel a sense of pride in him just as he expects that he will take pride in them "in the day of the Lord." (1:14).[185] The reason for this mutual pride will likely be because they can stand up in the judgment "and testify on each other's behalf to the Lord about how good each has been to and for the other."[186]

---

183. This problem was well-known, for 2 Pet. 3:15–16 states that Paul wrote according to the wisdom given him but "there are some things in them that are hard to understand, which the unlearned and unstable twist to their own destruction" (our translation).

184. Matera, *II Corinthians,* 49–50.

185. Guthrie, *2 Corinthians,* 98–99.

186. Witherington, *Conflict and Community,* 362.

Excursus on Pride and Boasting in the Writings of Paul

In this epistle, the theme of pride and boasting (which includes both their good and bad aspects) plays a major role. Because of that, we felt that an expanded exploration would help the reader more fully understand and appreciate the points Paul makes.[187]

The Greek words that Paul uses are the verb καυχάομαι (*kauchaomai*), meaning "to take pride in something" to the point of boasting about it;[188] the noun καύχημα (*kauchēma*), referencing "the act of taking pride in something" and again boasting about it;[189] and the noun καύχησις (*kauchēsis*), denoting "that which constitutes the source of pride" and therefore the reason for boasting.[190] Boasting can also be understood as glorifying, praising, or exalting in something or someone. Note that the words themselves are neutral when it comes to having a moral quality. Only the context in which they are used can reveal whether the act is to be taken as a good or bad thing.

According to the writers of the Old Testament, as viewed through the lens of the LXX, wrongful pride centers in a person's determination to make his or her own way fully independent of God. At its core, it expresses distrust in the Divine. Indeed, "the true sin of self-glorying is man's failure to acknowledge God as the Author and Lord of all being and the Giver of all good things"[191] (for example, see Lev. 26:15–19; Deut. 8:11–14; 1 Sam. 2:3; Neh. 9:12–16; Ps. 10:4; 40:4; 119:21; and Prov. 6:16–17; 16:18; 28:25).

True pride is Godward, and as such it carries the sense of rejoicing, glorying, or exalting in the Divine. The reason for giving glory and praise is often based in a personal recognition of what God has done for the individual. Such people recognize their dependence upon the Father as the God of creation and all that is good. All they have is the result of the trust placed in them by the Creator. Through their humble submission to the will of the Father, they attain God's grace and a feeling that they properly glory in what the Father and Son have done for their ultimate salvation (1 Chr. 16:33; Ps. 31:23; 149:5; Zech. 10:12).

---

187. This study follows Rudolf Bultmann, "καυχάομαι, καύχημα, καύχησις," in *TDNT,* 3:645–54.

188. BDAG, 536.

189. BDAG, 536–37.

190. BDAG, 537.

191. Bultmann, "καυχάομαι," in *TDNT,* 3:648.

The rabbis took the idea of boasting a step further, insisting that the faithful should also rejoice in suffering since it often acts as Godly chastisement divinely designed to bring the sinner back to God. As such, affliction should be seen as an expression of God's love (for example, see Prov. 3:11–12).

Paul builds on the Old Testament foundation. The Apostle sees false pride as the basic problem that hinders the Jews from accepting the Lord. Their self-defeating attitude is actually one of being overly self-confident in seeking glory *before* God through self-righteousness rather than *from* him through faith in Christ. Faith in the Lord guards against pride. It is of note that the first question Paul askes after his major treatise on faith (Rom. 3:21–26) is "Where then is boasting (καύχησις, *kauchēsis*)?" (Rom. 3:27). He rests his case on the scriptural point that with Abraham, who exercised complete faith in Jehovah and thereby became the beneficiary of his covenant, there was no pride (καύχημα, *kauchēma*) before God (Rom. 4:1–2).

Paul sees that a major problem with the Jews results from a perversion of the law. The scriptural requirement of boasting in God had been changed to "rest[ing] on the law" rather than on Christ (Rom. 2:17, 23). Indeed, the result of their pride is actually "confidence in the flesh" (meaning circumcision as representing taking upon oneself the weight of the Mosaic law; Philip. 3:3). Paul sides with the Old Testament understanding of the issue in that proper pride stands primarily in fully trusting in God. That means that pride in God (καυχώμενοι ἐν τῷ θεῷ, *kauchōmenoi tō theō*) forcefully disallows any exclusive kind of self-confidence. Further, true boasting in God must come through the Lord Jesus Christ (Rom. 5:11), who has brought to a full end all the greatness of both the Jews and Gentiles (1 Cor. 1:25–31 in light of Jer. 9:21–24; compare 2 Cor. 10:17). Proper understanding and worship of God eliminates all self-boasting (Philip. 3:3) so that Paul can say, "Be it far from me to take pride (καυχᾶσθαι, *kauchasthai*) except in the cross of our Lord Jesus, through which the world has been crucified unto me, and I to the world" (Gal. 6:14, our translation).

Faith in Christ actually opens the way to true boasting because self-glorification has been done away. It has been replaced with another kind of boasting centered in personal achievements made possible through the Lord, especially in the propagation of the faith (Gal. 6:13). A good example can be seen in Ammon's boasting in God (Alma 26:1–10). His exaltation seemed so excessive that his brother, Aaron, rebuked him, but Ammon explained, "I do not boast in my own strength, nor in my own wisdom; but behold, my joy is full, yea, my heart is brim with joy, and I will rejoice in my God" (Alma 26:11). The faith-filled see their work as growing out of the grace of God that attended them in his service (1 Cor. 3:5–7; 15:10).

Because their success is a divine gift, Paul can ask, "What do you have that you have not received?" The implied answer is "Nothing." He goes on to ask, "if you have received it, why do you boast as if you had not received it?" (1 Cor. 4:7, NR). His implication is that accomplishments that were dependent on grace disannul any personal credit. Thus, as he says, "let no one boast in mankind" (1 Cor. 3:21, NR) because the divine endowment lifts the grace-filled above any dependence or obligation to humankind.[192] Paul explains the reason why. It is because they "belong to Christ, and Christ belongs to God" (1 Cor. 3:23, NR). Thus, all judgment must be based not on "those who take pride in outward appearance" but rather "what is in the heart" (2 Cor. 5:12, NR).

Paul pushes hard not only on the Old Testament theme that persons can truly boast only when they look beyond themselves to God and the goodness that flows from him but also on the rabbinical view that the true believer also boasts in his afflictions and weaknesses (Rom. 5:3). In Second Corinthians the Apostle clearly illustrates this point and shows how the transcendent power of God sustains the believer in all of his or her trials (4:7–11; compare 11:23–29). On that basis, Paul can say, "If I must boast, I will boast about the things that show weakness" (11:30, our translation), for in his overcoming his weakness the enabling and sustaining power of God is clearly revealed.

His position maintains a very realistic view of earth life and especially the added challenges it heaps upon a believer. The commitment to follow Christ does not relieve the disciple of life's challenges or vicissitudes. Indeed, it may exacerbate them. The Savior made this point clear when he said, "Blessed are you when men revile you and persecute you and utter all kinds of evil against you falsely on my account. Rejoice and be glad, for your reward is great in heaven, for so they persecuted the prophets who came before you" (Matt. 5:11–12, our translation). Jesus was clear that the gospel would not be a unifying force. He asked his disciples, "Do you think I have come to give peace on earth?" and then answered, "No, I tell you, but rather division; from henceforth in one house there will be five divided against two and two against three," and as a result the family will be torn apart (Luke 12:49–53, our translation). Certainly, the Corinthian branch of the Church experienced division over what the gospel was and who had authority to interpret and administer it.

---

192. Although a person is not obligated to anyone except God for the enjoyment of heavenly gifts, the person, by accepting the Father's grace, becomes obligated to serve humankind. See D&C 93:19–20.

It must be noted that for Paul suffering never bears meaning in and of itself. In short, it is not an end in itself. His glorying in affliction is not self-grounded as it is in the case with ascetic achievement where humiliation of the flesh is the endgame. For the Apostle, it is rather a means of accessing divine power, often through the humility and dependency on God that suffering brings (12:9).[193] Paul ever keeps the suffering of the Savior before his readers as marking the path that they themselves should expect to follow (4:10–12).

In this perspective, boasting looks away from oneself toward a future where one, through Christ, escapes the weaknesses, pains, sorrows, and persecutions of this world. Thus, boasting in trials is also boasting in the "hope of sharing in the glory of God" (Rom. 5:2, our translation). These words show that Paul sees suffering as something more than the Jewish belief that it is merely a means of godly correction and discipline. He understands that God's power, granted by the grace of Christ, though only fully realized in the future, is presently at work in the life of the disciple. Therefore, he can say, "We do not lose heart, but even if our physical body is being destroyed, our soul is being renewed day by day. For our present, insignificant affliction is producing for us an eternal fullness of glory beyond all measure and proportion" (2 Cor. 4:16–17, NR).

The question naturally arises, What about Paul's references to boasting in himself and in others? In reality, the way he boasts does not violate his theology because it is always directed toward something higher than the immediate source. For example, when the Apostle boasts of the strength of certain portions of the Corinthian congregation in relationship to others (7:4, 14; 8:24; 9:2–3), he is simply expressing his confidence in them. His glorying in them does not stand in contradiction to his glorying in Christ. This is because the pride he has in them is grounded in what the Savior has done through him for the branches and their response to that effort (Rom. 15:17–18; 1 Cor. 15:10). He is very aware that his efforts in no way earn God's favor—because it is always there—but rather the success of his efforts contributes to his personal favor toward God. Thus, he is careful to emphasize that the pride he has in the Saints is through "Jesus Christ our Lord" (Rom. 5:21). In sum, his words reveal his keen awareness that the pride he has in his work is grounded in what Christ has done through him (Rom. 15:17–18; 1 Cor. 15:10). Thus, he states that he "will not boast beyond proper limits but will keep to the limits of the assigned area that God has given us, to reach even to you" (2 Cor. 10:13, NR).

---

193. For further study, see Translation Notes and the Analysis on 12:9 below.

Further, Paul's self-confidence or sense of pride does not arise from comparing himself with others. In fact, he decries those who "commend [them]selves" and by that means come off very well (3:1; compare 10:7). His self-praise has no hint of arrogance or personal self-superiority over others. He feels no need to boast in himself, he insists, because his sole commendation is the work Christ does through him, which work becomes bona fide in the hearts of his converts (3:1–2; 4:2). By this means he sets up the sole basis by which true apostolic authority, with its accompanying work, may properly be judged. Indeed, when all is said and done, the full measure of authenticity is in the effective power that works through the apostle and blesses the disciple (6:7; 13:4). That in turn leads to the praise of the power of God (4:7).

The final chapters of 2 Corinthians contain the paradoxical situation, not only recognized but also set up by the Apostle, in which boasting in God's grace and power is anchored in Paul's self-boasting. The Apostle stresses that he has been forced into this position by those who have contested his authority. He justifies his action because his authority does not promote his own cause but that of the Lord from whom his authority comes. Therefore, he must boast of what he has done. He admits that there is some danger in doing so, but he maintains that he has been driven to it (10:8; 12:11). He, however, shows his recognition of its paradoxical nature by insisting that what he is doing is acting the part of a fool (11:16–19) and admits that "what I say, I say not according to the Lord, but as a fool, in undertaking this boasting" (11:17, NR).

He then lists his qualifications for service and by that means shows that his detractors cannot even begin to measure up (11:22–29). He then hints at a number of great spiritual events that demonstrate his favor with God (12:1–4). These deep and powerful experiences should set him well above all others, but he will not have it. Instead, he says, "If I must glory [and this not as a fool], I will glory in my weaknesses" (11:30, NR). By this means he shifts his praising from his deeds to that of the power and grace of God (12:8–10 in light of 4:7). He can therefore testify that "we do not proclaim ourselves, but Christ Jesus as Lord, and ourselves as your servants for Jesus' sake" (4:5, NR).

Here then is the center of Paul's boasting and epicenter of his pride, that he is privileged to continually experience the power and grace of God in his personal life and to be the servant of Christ in bearing the gospel to the world.

Why He Defends His Actions (1:15–20)

In this pericope, Paul appears to be addressing one of the attacks against his authority and personal commitment to the Corinthian Saints. The point of attack appears to have focused on Paul's not visiting the congregations when he said he would. In the section above, he set up his explanation and defense by noting the purity of both his motives and actions toward the Corinthians in the past (1:12) and assuring them that when they fully understood him, he would be a source of pride with them (1:13–14). He now explains that his inability to come when promised was not an act of caprice on his part but necessitated by divine action (1:15–20).

Greek Text

15 Καὶ ταύτῃ τῇ πεποιθήσει ἐβουλόμην πρότερον πρὸς ὑμᾶς ἐλθεῖν, ἵνα δευτέραν
χάριν σχῆτε, 16 καὶ δι' ὑμῶν διελθεῖν εἰς Μακεδονίαν, καὶ πάλιν ἀπὸ Μακεδονίας
ἐλθεῖν πρὸς ὑμᾶς καὶ ὑφ' ὑμῶν προπεμφθῆναι εἰς τὴν Ἰουδαίαν. 17 τοῦτο οὖν βου-
λόμενος μήτι ἄρα τῇ ἐλαφρίᾳ ἐχρησάμην; ἢ ἃ βουλεύομαι κατὰ σάρκα βουλεύομαι,
ἵνα ᾖ παρ' ἐμοὶ τὸ Ναὶ ναὶ καὶ τὸ Οὒ οὔ; 18 πιστὸς δὲ ὁ θεὸς ὅτι ὁ λόγος ἡμῶν ὁ
πρὸς ὑμᾶς οὐκ ἔστιν Ναὶ καὶ Οὔ. 19 ὁ τοῦ θεοῦ γὰρ υἱὸς Ἰησοῦς Χριστὸς ὁ ἐν ὑμῖν
δι' ἡμῶν κηρυχθείς, δι' ἐμοῦ καὶ Σιλουανοῦ καὶ Τιμοθέου, οὐκ ἐγένετο Ναὶ καὶ Οὔ,
ἀλλὰ Ναὶ ἐν αὐτῷ γέγονεν· 20 ὅσαι γὰρ ἐπαγγελίαι θεοῦ, ἐν αὐτῷ τὸ Ναί· διὸ καὶ
δι' αὐτοῦ τὸ Ἀμὴν τῷ θεῷ πρὸς δόξαν δι' ἡμῶν. [SBLGNT]

King James Version

15 And in this confidence I was minded
to come unto you before, that ye might
have a second benefit; 16 And to pass by
you into Macedonia, and to come again
out of Macedonia unto you, and of you
to be brought on my way toward Judæa.
17 When I therefore was thus minded,
did I use lightness? or the things that
I purpose, do I purpose according to
the flesh, that with me there should be
yea yea, and nay nay? 18 But as God is
true, our word toward you was not yea
and nay. 19 For the Son of God, Jesus
Christ, who was preached among you
by us, even by me and Silvanus and

New Rendition

15 And with this confidence, I intended
to come to you first so that you would
have a second proof of my goodwill.
16 I planned on visiting you on my way
to Macedonia, and on my return from
Macedonia to come to you and then be
sent by you on my way to Judea. 17 Now
because I intended to do this, was I
being fickle? Or do I make my plans
based on human standards, indecisively
saying both "yes, yes!" and "no, no!"?
18 On the contrary, as God is faithful, our
word to you is not both "yes" and "no."
19 For God's Son, Jesus Christ, who was
preached to you by us, by me and Silas

Timotheus, was not yea and nay, but in him was yea. 20 For all the promises of God in him are yea, and in him Amen, unto the glory of God by us.

and Timothy, was not "yes" and "no" but it has always been "yes." 20 For all God's promises are "yes" in him. Therefore, also through him "Amen" is said by us to God's glory.

Translation Notes and Comments

1:15 ***And in this confidence I was minded to come unto you before / And with this confidence, I intended to come to you first:*** The noun πεποίθησις (*pepoithēsis*), "confidence," denotes such a strong state of certainty that it allows for full trust or assurance in the object. Here it refers to Paul's sureness of his comportment among the Corinthians.[194] The translation of the adverb πρότερον (*proteron*), "formerly, earlier, first,"[195] presents a problem because it could modify the verb βούλομαι (*boulomai*), "wish, desire, intent,"[196] or the aorist infinitive ἐλθεῖν (*elthein*), "to come."[197] Given the context, it seems best to see it as modifying the infinitive and thus meaning that Paul desired to visit them first and then move to other areas in Greece and Macedonia.[198]

that ye might have a second benefit / so that you would have a second proof of my goodwill: The conjunction ἵνα (*hina*), "so that," introduces the reason why Paul intended to visit these people before moving on. His reason is revealed in his use of the noun χάρις (*charis*), usually translated as "grace, favor, or benefit," but in this case, it looks more at "the practical application of goodwill."[199] Had he been able to follow his initial itinerary, Paul would have given the Corinthians double proof of his goodwill toward them by visiting them right after he left Ephesus and before moving on to see other branches of the Church in Greece and Macedonia and then returning to Corinth before sailing to Jerusalem.[200]

---

194. BDAG, 796; Guthrie, *2 Corinthians,* 104.

195. BDAG, 888–89; Louw-Nida, §60.47.

196. BDAG, 182. According to MM, 115, the verb connotes an intent that comes through premeditation.

197. BDAG, 393–95.

198. Furnish, *II Corinthians,* 133.

199. BDAG, 1079–80.

200. Guthrie, *2 Corinthians,* 105. Seifrid, *Second Letter,* 56, notes that the grace of God had been given to Paul and that determined his earlier conduct among the Saints (1:12). When putting his initial itinerary together, he hoped to fully share that grace with them through the two visits.

1:16 ***And to pass by you into Macedonia, and to come again out of Macedonia unto you / I planned on visiting you on my way to Macedonia, and on my return from Macedonia to come to you:*** The senatorial province of Macedonia lay to the immediate north of Greece. Paul brought the gospel to three of its principle cites: Philippi, Thessalonica, and Berea (Acts 16:11–26; 17:1–13). Given Corinth's location, it is easy to see why Paul made the plans as he did. As he traveled by ship from the province of Asia to Greece, Corinth would have been a natural disembarking point. Likewise, it would be a natural embarking point when leaving Greece for Jerusalem.

and of you to be brought on my way toward Judæa / and then be sent by you on my way to Judea: The verb προπέμπω (*propempō*), "to send," can mean to accompany a person to his or her destination (as in Acts 20:38),[201] but it is more likely that, in this case, it refers to assisting another with goods, supplies, and funds for a trip.[202]

1:17 ***When I therefore was thus minded, did I use lightness? / Now because I intended to do this, was I being fickle?:*** Paul again uses the verb βούλομαι (*boulomai*), "wish, want or desire" (here in the participial form), to express his intention to come visit Corinth first.[203] The noun ἐλαφρία (*elaphria*), "fickleness, lightmindedness, or frivolous," denotes the condition of treating an important matter frivolously, revealing an irresponsible state of mind given to caprice.[204] Paul's use of the definite article with the phrase suggests that he had a specific charge against him in mind.[205]

In both Jewish and Greco-Roman cultures, to be accused of fickleness, lightmindedness, indecisiveness, and especially capriciousness carried heavy negative weight. This flaw could hardly be tolerated and was severely condemned when found in anyone who held a leadership position. Keeping one's word was all important. The oversensitive nature of the Corinthians to the mores of the time exacerbated such a charge, and since keeping covenant was especially important to both Jews and Christians, to break one's word only heightened the feelings of outrage. The result was often hot censure.[206] Apparently, Paul's antagonists insisted that his change of plans proved he had an unstable character and thus his words were not worth listening to.

---

201. BDAG, 873; Martin, *2 Corinthians,* 161.
202. BDAG, 873; Guthrie, *2 Corinthians,* 106.
203. BDAG, 182.
204. BDAG, 314; Louw-Nida, §88.99.
205. Martin, *2 Corinthians,* 161.
206. Guthrie, *2 Corinthians,* 107 with n. 13.

or the things that I purpose, do I purpose according to the flesh / Or do I make my plans based on human standards?: Again Paul uses the verb βούλομαι (*boulomai*), "intend," in the sense of making plans. The noun σάρξ (*sarx*), literally "flesh," denotes, in this case, the outward expression of life and, therefore, the act of basing one's actions according to human standards.[207] It connotes "the psychological aspect of human nature which contrasts with the spiritual nature; in other words, that aspect of human nature which is characterized by or reflects typical human reasoning and desires in contrast with those aspects of human thought and behavior which relate to God and the spiritual life."[208]

that with me there should be yea yea, and nay nay? / indecisively saying both "yes, yes!" and "no, no!"?: The particle ναί (*nai*), "yes," denotes affirmation,[209] while οὐ (*ou*), "no," indicates negation.[210] In the phrase ναὶ ναὶ καὶ τὸ ου οὔ (*nai nai kai to ou ou*), Paul is again emphasizing that he was not being fickle and unable to make up his mind, saying both "yes" and "no" at the same time (compare Matt. 5:37 and James 5:12).

1:18 ***But as God is true, our word toward you was not yea and nay / On the contrary, as God is faithful, our word to you is not both "yes" and "no":*** So important is Paul's reputation to him that he here continues his defense with a mild oath.[211] The particle δέ (*de*), "but," is grammatically positioned in this phrase potentially as an adversative, carries a very contrastive force, and therefore means "on the contrary,"[212] helping push Paul's point. The oath centers on one aspect of God's character: he is πιστός (*pistos*), "trustworthy, dependable, faithful."[213] By appealing to this godly trait, the Apostle substantiates his own witness as to his personal trustworthiness. His words reveal his full assurance that God would stand behind his claim. Therefore, his word (λόγος, *logos*) has never been and is not now capricious.[214]

---

207. BDAG, 914–16.

208. Louw-Nida, §27.6.

209. BDAG, 665.

210. BDAG, 733–34. Paul's words echo the teaching of the Savior in Matt. 5:37 and the warning in James 5:12. Seifrid, *Second Letter,* 57. See also David Wenham, "2 Corinthians 1:17, 18: Echo of the Dominical Legion," *Novum Testamentum* 28, no. 3 (1986), 271–79.

211. Harris, *Second Epistle,* 199.

212. Daniel B. Wallace, *Greek Grammar beyond the Basics: An Exegetical Syntax of the New Testament* (Grand Rapids, Mich.: Zondervan, 1996), 671; Guthrie, *2 Corinthians,* 109 n. 18.

213. BDAG, 818–20.

214. Martin, *2 Corinthians,* 163. With the use of the noun λόγος (*logos*), "word," the Apostle could be echoing John 1:1–3, thus, associating his actions to those of the Lord who was "the Word" that was made flesh. John 1:14. Barnett, *Second Epistle,* 103.

1:19 ***For the Son of God, Jesus Christ, who was preached among you by us / For God's Son, Jesus Christ, who was preached to you by us:*** It is important that the conjunction γάρ (*gar*), "for," in the present context, is given its full weight as marking why something is said or done. This is because Paul rests much of his case on the clause it introduces.[215] It acts to heighten the self-evident conclusion that Paul pronounces at the end of the sentence.[216]

The word order is important in this phrase. In the Greek text, the noun θεός (*theos*), "God," comes before the conjunction and in doing so brings the Father into prominence, thus assisting us in seeing the sequence of Paul's thoughts.[217]

The verb κηρύσσω (*kēryssō*), "to preach," designates a public pronouncement. The word, however, was loaded with religious significance, nuancing a decree that was of divine origin—in this case, the proclamation of the trustworthiness of the Lord.[218]

even by me and Silvanus and Timotheus / by me and Silas and Timothy: Paul lists his two companions who assisted him in bringing the gospel to Corinth. The first is identified by two names in the KJV. In Acts he is referred to as Σιλᾶς (*Silas*), while in the Pauline letters he is called Σιλουανός (*Silouanos*), transliterated as "*Silvanus*" in the KJV. "Either he had two names (like Paul), one [Semitic], and one [Latin], or *Silouanos* is the [Latin] form of the same name as that is Grecized in *Silas*."[219] He was one of the "chief men," indeed, a prophet, among the Saints at Jerusalem (Acts 15:22, 32). He was one of the delegates sent to Antioch to confirm the apostolic decree concerning Christian Jew/Gentile relations (see Acts 15:6–23). He remained in Antioch assisting in the work there and, at some point, risked his life for the sake of the gospel (Acts 15:26). His diligence as well as his apparent acceptance of those Gentiles who were converted to the Lord endeared him to Paul. It is therefore not surprising that Paul chose him as his companion for his second missionary journey (Acts 15:40–18:21).[220]

Paul's second companion is also identified by two names in the KJV, "Timotheus" and "Timothy"; however, in this case they are both transliterations of the Greek name Τιμόθεος (*Timotheos*). He lived in the province

---

215. Martin, *2 Corinthians*, 162.

216. BDAG, 189–90.

217. Bernard, "Second Epistle," 44.

218. BDAG, 543–44.

219. BDAG, 923.

220. John Gillman, "Silas," in *ABD*, 6:22–23.

of Lycaonia and likely in the city of Lystra. His father was a Greek married to "a Jewess" (Acts 16:1). His name is unknown but Paul's letters do preserve the names of Timothy's grandmother, Lois, and mother, Eunice, both of whom converted to Christianity, as did Timothy, likely as a child (2 Tim. 1:5). It may be that, because of their conversion, Eunice never had her son circumcised (Acts 16:3). In any case, it is clear that Timothy's family did not observe Jewish norms, but mother and son were highly religious. Indeed, even at a young age Timothy distinguished himself not only in Lystra but also in nearby Iconium (Acts 16:2). It may have been his devotion to the Christian cause that brought him to the attention of Paul and Silas during the Apostle's second missionary journey. When invited, he readily accepted their offer to accompany them on the rest of their mission. That, however, did require an act of tremendous faith on his part. Since his mother was Jewish and because of the matrilineal principle of descent, he would have been considered a Jew. Therefore, Paul insisted Timothy go through the ordeal of circumcision in order to be acceptable to both Jews and Gentiles (Acts 16:3). Thereafter, he became not only a companion to Paul but also a trusted emissary and full associate (συνεργός, *synergos*, Rom. 16:21)—not only on this mission but throughout their lives.[221]

was not yea and nay, but in him was yea / was not "yes" and "no" but it has always been "yes": Here Paul uses the perfect tense of the verb γέγονεν (*gegonen*), "to be." That tense denotes a past action whose result continues into the present. By using it, Paul makes a strong statement about the continual integrity of God—he always has and always will keep his word, and that is corroborated through the ministry of his Son.

1:20 ***For all the promises of God in him are yea / For all God's promises are "yes" in him:*** The noun ἐπαγγελία (*epangelia*), "promise," carries with it an emphasis on obligation. When associated with God, it denotes a "divine assurance for good."[222] The third-person masculine pronoun *auto*, "him," refers to the Son of God through whom the blessings and promises of God come to fulfillment, the divine "Yes."

and in him Amen, unto the glory of God by us / Therefore also through him "Amen" is said by us to God's glory: The Greek phrase is both convoluted and compact. It translates literally as "therefore also through him the Amen to God for glory through us." The third-person singular pronoun

---

221. John Gillman, "Timothy," in *ABD*, 6:558–60.

222. BDAG, 355; Julius Schniewind and Friedrich Gerhard, "ἐπαγγέλλω, ἐπαγγελλία, ἐπάγγελμα, προεπαγγέλλομαι," in *TDNT*, 2:576–86.

autou, "him," refers to Christ. The particle ἀμήν (*amen*) is a transliteration of the Hebrew אָמֵן (*'āmên*).[223] The basis of the word means "trustworthy" and carries the sense of "truly," meaning that which is correct and therefore reliable. Over time it became a solemn spoken affirmation, meaning "May it be so." Thus, it expressed more than a wish but rather an approval and confirmation. It became very important in covenant making, for therewith the person bound him- or herself to its terms, conditions, curses, and blessings.[224] This verse reveals Paul's position that all God's promises are both fulfilled and guaranteed in Christ. When the congregation recognizes what the Father has done through the Son, they give glory to God though their heartfelt "amen."[225]

Analysis and Summary

In this section, Paul address one of the attacks that has been made on his character. He had indicated in an earlier epistle (1 Cor. 16:2–9) that he planned to spend some time with the Corinthian Saints before heading back to Jerusalem. Apparently, his change in itinerary became known to the people and opened the door for his detractors to accuse him of incompetence, caprice, or a lack of care.[226] He begins his defense by confirming that his initial plans were to come to them before proceeding to Macedonia and then, once his work was done there, to return to them before proceeding to Jerusalem (1:15–18). Unfortunately, he explains, through no fault of his own, his plans had been interrupted. His point is that, due to circumstances beyond his control, he does not have a shred of a guilty conscience for not being able to follow through with his intent.

He assures his readers that he does not base his intentions according to mere human standards. The phrase he uses (κατὰ σάρκα, *kata sarka*) refers to human dynamics totally devoid of any spiritual quality.[227] Paul refuses

223. In 1 Cor. 14:16, "amen" also carries the definite article. The Hebrew root אמן (*'mn*) nuances the idea of solidarity or agreement with what the preachment, confession, or prayer had to say. Martin, *2 Corinthians,* 163 n. 25.

224. BDB, 53. For a study, see J. L. Wu, "Liturgical Elements," in *Dictionary of Paul and His Letters,* ed. Gerald F. Hawthorne, Ralph P. Martin, and Daniel G. Reid (Downers Grove, Ill.: InterVarsity Press, 1993), 558–59.

225. Guthrie, *2 Corinthians,* 111–12.

226. On what the Corinthians may or may not have known about Paul's travel plans, see Harris, *Second Epistle,* 196.

227. The phrase κατὰ σάρκα (*kata sarka*) is a uniquely Pauline expression. He uses it to denote a person's heritage (for example, see Rom. 1:3; 4:1; 9:3), but also to refer to what is limited to a human perspective (for example, see 5:16; 1 Cor. 1:26; Eph. 6:5; and

to have his readers believe he leads a godless life, and thus, he categorically denies that the change in his plans shows any fickleness, flaw of character, or lack of inspiration on his part (1:17).

The charge leveled against him was a heavy one. In that culture, vacillation and indecision were condemned, and not keeping one's word was especially so. Since integrity carried a highly moral component, to default on it denigrated everything else a person did or said. Thus, the attack on Paul was likely designed to make all his teachings suspect. Therefore, it was especially important that he reassure his readers that, despite what his antagonists claimed, he did not follow the bad behavior of some saying "absolutely" in one breath and "no way" in the next (1:17).[228]

To bolster his point, Paul swears an oath that looks to the faithfulness of God. In doing so, the Apostle aligns his own integrity with that of the Father (1:18) and by this means assures his readers of his own faithfulness. Thus, he is able to shift the responsibility of actions from himself to God and thereby emphasize the lack of capriciousness in them.

To further his case, Paul appeals to the preachment of Christ as proclaimed by Silas, Timothy, and himself. They all acted in concert witnessing the truthfulness that was centered in but one unified message—the integrity of God.[229] With him there is never vacillation, never a "yes" and "no," but always a "yes" as seen in the ministry and life of his Son. Indeed, the Savior was "God's unambiguous and unretracted 'Yes'" (1:19).[230]

With this verse, Paul launches a rather clever justification for the change in his travel plans. His point is that as God's word is consistent and not capricious, so too is and has been his word right from the beginning of his ministry among the Corinthians. The work and testimony of Timothy and Silas confirm this is so. No one could contest that these missionaries had brought the gospel to the Corinthians in saving power. Thus, they acted as God's tools, and therefore their word was his word. The tacit message was that as the Father had been active in Paul's life before, he remained active even now. Thus, any and all of Paul's travel plans, including any changes in his itinerary, had come according to divine direction.[231]

Col. 3:22), and specifically to identify a worldly pattern of life that stands opposite to one filled and directed by the Spirit (for example, see 10:2–3; 11:18; and Rom. 8:4–5, 12–13).

228. Guthrie, *2 Corinthians,* 107–8 with n. 13. A modern idiom would be to speak out of both sides of one's mouth.

229. Their combined word would fulfill the law of witness. See Deut. 19:15; compare Deut. 17:6; Num. 35:30; and Martin, *2 Corinthians,* 162.

230. Barnett, *Second Epistle,* 105.

231. Witherington, *Conflict and Community,* 363; Barnett, *Second Epistle,* 105–6.

The Apostle continues to stress his point concerning the centrality of Christ's making God's promises sure. As the Apostle says, the promises all find "yes" in Christ, meaning that he fulfills them. When the congregation recognizes this and give a heartfelt "amen," by which they affirm the truth of the doctrine, it expresses their praise and glorification of God for what he has done (1:20).

The fulfillment of divine promises plays an important role in the theology of Paul. He sees the realization of them as a gift given through God's grace. He alone has the power to fulfill his word (Rom. 4:21) and will do so because he is the "God who does not lie" (Titus 1:2, NIV). Therefore, God's promises stand in contradistinction from the law of Moses. That law demanded perfect obedience for salvation, which no one could give (Rom. 3:19–20, 23). God's promises of salvation, on the other hand, rested fully on the Son and demanded a person's faith in him (Rom. 3:21–22). Paul saw that a person's trust and reliance on Jesus, while striving to keep his commandments, opened a portal to the Father's grace, and with its reception justification came (Rom. 3:24, 28; 4:16). By thus standing sin free through faith, the person's salvation was assured (Rom. 5:1–3). For the Apostle, it was essential for his readers to understand that God's promises, fulfilled in salvation, have been given an exclusive "yes" through Christ (2 Cor. 1:20). In sum, "the sending of Jesus, with all that he did, is God's active ratification of all his promises of salvation."[232]

The Saving Work of God, Christ, and the Holy Ghost (1:21–22)

The role that Paul intended for this particular piece to play is unclear. It is likely a heartfelt witness inspired by his articulation of the Father's saving work. Whatever the case, it does contain one of the most remarkable, if brief, enunciations of the saving work of the Godhead.

Greek Text

21 ὁ δὲ βεβαιῶν ἡμᾶς σὺν ὑμῖν εἰς Χριστὸν καὶ χρίσας ἡμᾶς θεός, 22 ὁ καὶ σφραγισάμενος ἡμᾶς καὶ δοὺς τὸν ἀρραβῶνα τοῦ πνεύματος ἐν ταῖς καρδίαις ἡμῶν. [SBLGNT]

232. *NID*, 2:234.

King James Version

21 Now he which stablisheth us with
you in Christ, and hath anointed us, is
God; 22 Who hath also sealed us, and
given the earnest of the Spirit in our
hearts.

New Rendition

21 Now it is God who strengthens us
together with you in Christ and has
anointed us. 22 He has also sealed us
and placed the pledge of the Spirit in
our hearts.

Translation Notes and Comments

1:21 ***Now he which stablisheth us with you in Christ, . . . is God / Now it is God who strengthens us together with you in Christ:*** In this phrase, Paul uses the present participial form of the verb βεβαιόω (*bebaioō*), "establish, strengthen." In the present context, it expresses the act that makes a person firm in commitment to something or someone.[233] Paul is likely alluding to the shared testimony held by both the Apostle and his readers that makes them mutually committed to the Son. The present tense of the participle suggests that the current and ongoing reality of the God-given bond the Christian community shares is due to their mutual witness of who Christ was and is.[234]

In this verse, by exclusively using the title "Christ," Paul focuses on Jesus as the Anointed One. The author of Hebrews states that the Father anointed the Son with "the oil of joy more than [all his] companions" (Heb. 1:9, Lexham English Bible). That anointing gave him the title of the "Anointed One" (Χριστός [*Christos*], "Christ," in Greek, or מָשִׁיחַ [*māšîaḥ*], "the Messiah," in Hebrew).[235] Due to the anointing act being used almost exclusively as a means of delegating the authority that made its recipient king, prophet, or priest, the title bore much weight.

The preposition εἰς (*eis*), "in, into," could be a marker of reference, and therefore the phrase could be translated as "in reference to Christ." However, it seems better to see it as a marker of instrumentality meaning "through, or by means of Christ," indicating that the Father uses the Son as the means of making the believer firm in the faith.[236]

---

233. BDAG, 172–73.

234. Although the tense is present, it carries an imperfect aspect suggesting an ongoing movement. Guthrie, *2 Corinthians,* 114 n. 34.

235. The scripture highlights his anointing through which he gained royal status. For a study, see Sungho Choi, *The Messianic Kingship of Jesus: A Study of Christology and Redemptive History in Matthew's Gospel with Special Reference to the Royal-Enthronement Psalms* (Eugene, Ore.: Wipf and Stock Publishers, 2011).

236. BDAG, 288–91; Louw-Nida, §89.76.

It is noteworthy that Paul separates himself from the Corinthian Saints by use of the plural pronouns ἡμᾶς (*hēmas*), "us," and ὑμῖν (*hymin*), "you." Besides Paul, it is difficult to know who else he had in mind. He could be thinking of his missionary companions. Given, however, that the issue in Second Corinthians is that of apostolic authority, Paul may have been thinking of all those who held apostolic authority. The phrase does make it clear that whoever "us" and "you" are, both share together the strength of Christ that holds them firm to the faith.

and hath anointed us / and has anointed us: The verb χρίω (*chriō*), "to anoint," denotes rubbing, smearing, or dabbing olive oil on an individual, through which he or she receives special powers or is invested with certain authority necessary in the performance of a duty.[237] The practice in the Old Testament was limited to the setting apart of kings, prophets, and priests. The word stands in distinction to ἀλείφω (*aleiphō*), the verb used generally in the Bible to indicate an anointing with oil. This kind of anointing, however, did not bequeath power or authority but was used for the purpose of healing, refreshing, honoring a person, or preparing a body for burial.[238]

Because Paul's statement referring to God's anointing lacks context, it is hard to know exactly who and what he is referring to. The problem is exacerbated by the ambiguity of the plural pronoun ἡμᾶς (*hēmas*), "us," which could refer to a group which the Corinthian Saints were either included in or excluded from.

If it includes them, then Paul appears to be using the phrase figuratively, as did Peter when he testified that "God anointed Jesus of Nazareth with the Holy Ghost and with power" (Acts 10:38; compare 1 John 2:20, 27). If that is the case, then the Apostle is referring to the bequeathing of the gift of the Holy Ghost after baptism. If so, it refers neither to "an outpouring of the Holy Spirit" nor to "a flash of spiritual insight, as may be the case in the life of any sincere investigator of the truth," but to the receiving of "a manifold outpouring of this greatest of all gifts, to actually receive the companionship of this member of the Godhead."[239]

If the phrase excludes the Saints, then Paul is likely referring to an apostolic endowment of power and authority held by all those who share this office.

---

237. BDAG, 1091.

238. BDAG, 41; Franco Montanari, *The Brill Dictionary of Ancient Greek,* ed. Madeleine Goh and Chad Schroeder (Leiden: Brill, 2015), s.v. ἀλείφω (hereafter cited as *DAG*).

239. Bruce R. McConkie, *Doctrinal New Testament Commentary,* 3 vols. (Salt Lake City: Bookcraft, 1973), 3:383.

1:22 *Who hath also sealed us / He has also sealed us:* The verb σφραγίζω (*sphragizō*), "to seal," denotes the act of providing something with a seal as a security measure. The major purpose of the seal is to guarantee that the contents of the thing sealed are not tampered with. The act marks the object's permanence and purity. Further, the seal indicates the owner; what he seals belongs to him. There is an important additional dimension in its use here that points to the endowing of the object with divine power.[240]

Paul uses the term in a metaphorical sense to designate a major work of the Father in relation to those he has chosen—namely, sealing them as his own and as a result into eternal life (compare Eph. 1:13). That Paul uses the middle voice of the participle (σφραγισάμενος, *sphragisamenos*) is important because that voice shows that God has a vested interest in the act of sealing and empowering the person.[241] In short, the performance is not only for the good of the Saints but also for that of the Father himself.[242]

The question remains as to whom Paul has in mind. Definitely the circle of the sealed ones includes those, like Paul, who have been called to apostolic authority. But based on his declaration in Ephesians 1:13–14, righteous Saints are not excluded. Yet, due to his rocky relationship with the some of the Corinthian Saints, he may have excluded them.

and given the earnest of the Spirit in our hearts / and placed the pledge of the Spirit in our hearts: The noun ἀρραβών (*arrabōn*), "pledge, earnest, deposit,"[243] is a technical term that denotes a down payment or initial installment that guarantees the full amount of a contract will be paid. It prohibits the seller from disposing of the item and assures the buyer that it will be hers or his, whatever the duration, as long as she or he meets the conditions of the contract.[244] In a theological sense, the item is ultimately

---

240. BDAG, 980; compare John 6:27. For a study, see G. W. H. Lampe, *The Seal of the Spirit: A Study in the Doctrine of Baptism and Confirmation in the New Testament and the Fathers,* 2nd ed. (London: SPCK, 1976). Paul speaks metaphorically of sealing Rom. 4:11; 15:28; 1 Cor. 9:2.

241. Wallace, *Greek Grammar,* 414–15.

242. See Moses 1:39, which states that God's work and glory is for the exaltation of his children. According to D&C 132:6, God instituted the new and everlasting covenant not only for the Saint's salvation but for his own glory. Furthermore, the promises he gave to Abraham were designed to continue the "works of [the] Father, wherein he glorifieth himself" (D&C 132:31).

243. BDAG, 134; Yon-Gyong Kwon, "Ἀρραβών as Pledge in Second Corinthians," *New Testament Studies* 54, no. 4 (2008): 525–41.

244. *NID,* 1:404–5; Harris, *Second Epistle,* 207–8. The word is related to the Hebrew עֵרָבוֹן (*ʿērābôn*) that denotes a "security, pledge." *HAL,* 881.

eternal life. The assurance or guarantee that a person will receive it is the gift of the Holy Ghost. It acts as the deposit or first installment and, thus, the guarantee that the person will actually achieve what is for now but a wonderous prospect. In the short term, however, the pledge of the Spirit shows that a person is, at present, God's own, his son or his daughter.[245]

The noun καρδία (*kardia*), "heart," used here metaphorically, connotes the entire spectrum of mental and emotional activities, including all rational elements.[246] It comprises the "hidden springs of the personal life."[247] What is placed there cannot be denied or gainsaid. Thus, the most sure place God can put his assurance that a person will have eternal life is in the heart.

Again, just who Paul has in mind remains ambiguous, but nothing here excludes faithful members of Christ's kingdom.

There is one more important point that these verses teach. The words "anointed" and "given" (in connection with the seal) are aorist participles. This aspect suggests that the bedrock of the testimony shared by this group is the work that God has simply completed already in anointing and sealing them. The Holy Spirit they have received may be a token of their filial relationship with the Father and also act as the assurance of their eternal life (compare Eph. 4:30).

Analysis and Summary

Just what Paul's intent is in this tangential but very informative piece remains ambiguous. The problem lies in his separation of himself from the community of the Corinthian Saints by the use of "us" (ἡμᾶς, *hēmas*) and "you" (ὑμῖν, *hymin*) in 1:21 and then referring just to "us" throughout the rest of 1:21–22. His language does not reveal if he intended to keep the

---

245. Ogden and Skinner, *Verse by Verse,* 150. This teaching is congruent with the doctrine of being "born again." (John 3:1–7). The necessity arose due to sin through which the person lost his or her place in the family of God (Moses 6:55–60; Mosiah 16:4–9). Thus, the person must be born again to regain that position (John 3:1–7; Alma 5:49; 7:14). The process is twofold: a person must first be reborn into the family of Christ (Ether 3:14; Mosiah 5:7) who then brings them into the family of the Father (D&C 76:24). The process begins when a person yields to the preaching of the gospel (1 Pet. 1:23). It is having the Holy Ghost active in one's life that is the sign that one has been born again.

246. In modern culture the heart is tied more directly to the emotional side of a person while the brain or head is tied to the conscious or rational side. Such was not the case in a New Testament context. See Johannes Behm, "καρδία," in *TDNT,* 3:605–14.

247. BDAG, 508–9; *NID,* 2:622–26.

separation going. If he were following his original flow of thought, and thereby following up on his word play of "amen" (a strong affirmation of agreement), then his use of "us" would include the whole community. In that case, he would be extracting the maximum value he could from the point he made and thus emphasizing all that the Father had done through the apostolic ministry for the Christian community. It would also reference all that they shared in.

On the other hand, if he were keeping the separation going, then his purpose was defensive, thus stressing the difference between him and the Saints. His purpose in these verses was to build up the basis of his own trustworthiness by showing all that the Father had done for him and, by inclusion, all those with apostolic authority. If that is the case, then these verses act as a rebuttal to the innuendoes of Paul's detractors. He is, thus, testifying that he and his companions in the ministry are men of probity and trustworthiness since the Father has given them his spirit-based seal.[248]

What can be said for sure is that, given Paul's teachings in other places (5:5; Eph. 1:13–14), he believes that all the faithful can enjoy the strengthening, anointing, and sealing by God and thereby receive the deposit of the Spirit. This pericope is, thus, a beautiful climax listing the affirmations of what the Father has done for those who have joined together in their oneness with the Son. It is God who has made the Saints firm in their commitment through the Savior, given them the anointing or gift of the Holy Ghost, sealed them into eternal life through that power (and their continued faithfulness), and then guaranteed them eternal life (1:21).

God does not keep the faithful Saints in doubt as to their standing with him and his promises. He gives them the assurance that they will have eternal life as they follow his ways. That assurance is the Gift of the Holy Ghost. Having the power of the Spirit in their lives is, then, more than a promise of eternal life; it is the guarantee that they will receive it as they continue faithful. In another place, Paul referred to this as being sealed by "the holy Spirit of promise" (Eph. 1:14). The phrase looks specifically at the role of the Holy Ghost as the sealing and ratifying agent of the Godhead. He has been given the power "to ratify and approve the righteous acts of men [and women] so that those acts are binding on earth and in heaven" (see D&C 132:7). "An act which is sealed by the Holy Spirit of Promise is one which is ratified by the Holy Ghost; it is one which is approved by the Lord; and the

248. Martin, *2 Corinthians,* 165.

person who has taken the obligation upon himself is justified by the Spirit in the thing he has done."[249]

Paul states that God places this assurance or guarantee in a person's heart (1:21). While in modern usage, the heart is the seat of emotion; in the Apostle's world it connoted the whole spectrum of mental and emotional activities that includes all rational elements.[250] Therefore, this assurance was more than a mere emotional tug, but a declaration that touches both the emotional and intellectual levels of the soul.

The essence of what Paul is saying in 1:20–22 centers on his use of the verb "to seal" (σφραγίζω, *sphragizō*). The term denotes the act of placing one's signet or monogram on something. Doing so secures for that person the property thus marked. Though the religious and eschatological element (referring to the assurance of eternal life) lies behind the idea and therefore cannot be ignored, it does not stand in center place in this case. Paul's point is that "by the Spirit, who is the foretaste and down payment of what God has promised to give believers, the Corinthian Christians have been claimed as God's property. They belong to God."[251]

Also noteworthy is that in 1:21 Paul's words suggest a tripartite division of labor among the members of the Godhead. The Father is the initiator of all aspects of the salvation process, but his specific work is to anoint the Saints by giving them the Holy Spirit and setting his seal upon them. The work of Christ is to make the people firm in their gospel commitments, and the work of the Holy Ghost is to act as the down payment on and therefore the assurance of eternal life.[252]

---

249. Bruce R. McConkie, *Doctrinal New Testament Commentary,* 3 vols. (Salt Lake City: Bookcraft, 1973), 2:494 (hereafter cited as *DNTC*). In connection with Ephesians 1:13–14, Joseph Smith taught that the sealing of the Holy Spirit of Promise acts to make a person's calling and election sure. See "History, 1838–1856, Volume C-1 [2 November 1838–31 July 1842]," 1141, Joseph Smith Papers, accessed November 17, 2022, https://www.josephsmithpapers.org/paper-summary/history-1838-1856-volume-c-1-2-november-1838-31-july-1842/313. This Holy Spirit of Promise acts as a "comforter" giving as it does the recipient the promise of eternal life, "even the glory of the celestial kingdom" (D&C 88:3–5).

250. Behm, "καρδία," in *TDNT,* 3:605–14.

251. Witherington, *Conflict and Community,* 364. See also Barnett, *Second Epistle,* 112–13.

252. Martin, *2 Corinthians,* 165.

Why Paul Postponed His Visit (1:23–24)

In these last two verses of this chapter, Paul clearly picks up his defense and explains precisely why he did not come directly to Corinth from Ephesus. His argument continues through 2:4.

Greek Text

23 Ἐγὼ δὲ μάρτυρα τὸν θεὸν ἐπικαλοῦμαι ἐπὶ τὴν ἐμὴν ψυχήν, ὅτι φειδόμενος ὑμῶν οὐκέτι ἦλθον εἰς Κόρινθον. 24 οὐχ ὅτι κυριεύομεν ὑμῶν τῆς πίστεως, ἀλλὰ συνεργοί ἐσμεν τῆς χαρᾶς ὑμῶν, τῇ γὰρ πίστει ἑστήκατε. [SBLGNT]

King James Version

23 Moreover I call God for a record upon my soul, that to spare you I came not as yet unto Corinth. 24 Not for that we have dominion over your faith, but are helpers of your joy: for by faith ye stand.

New Rendition

23 Now I call upon God as a witness upon my soul that it was to spare you that I did not come again to Corinth. 24 Not that we would lord it over your faith, but rather we are workers with you for your joy, because you stand firm in the faith.

Translation Notes and Comments

1:23 ***Moreover I call God for a record upon my soul / Now I call upon God as a witness upon my soul:*** Having illustrated his rightness with God as one whom the Father has established for, sealed upon, and guaranteed eternal life, Paul returns to his defense. The verb ἐπικαλέω (*epikaleō*), "to call upon," carries the nuance of appealing to a higher power to settle an issue (see Acts 25:11–12, 21). Since the ultimate power is that of the Divine, the word carries heavy religious overtones and is thus often found, as here, as a means of invoking an oath.[253] Paul's invocation shows just how serious he is. The noun μάρτυς (*martys*), "witness," carries legal connotations referring to one who testifies to or affirms the truth of something.[254] Since God is all knowing, he is the ultimate witness.

253. BDAG, 373; Paul uses the same language in Rom. 1:9; Philip. 1:8; and 1 Thes. 2:5, 10.
254. BDAG, 619–20.

The pronoun ἐπί (*epi*), "for," has a wide range of meanings, including making reference in behalf of or against something.[255] The noun ψυσχή (*psychē*), "soul," in the present context refers to the very center or essence of a person, the seat of his or her emotions, desires, affections, and aversions.[256] Thus, the whole phrase, τὴν ἐμὴν ψυχήν (*tēn emēn psychēn*), could be rendered as "upon my life" or "against my life." The nuance is that Paul is willing to put his life on the line to show that he is not lying.[257]

that to spare you I came not as yet unto Corinth / that it was to spare you that I did not come again to Corinth: The noun φείδομαι (*pheidomai*), "to spare," means to save someone from pain or hurt.[258] Paul gives this as the main reason why he did not stop at Corinth after leaving Ephesus.

1:24 ***Not for that we have dominion over your faith, / Not that we would lord it over your faith:*** The verb κυριεύω (*kyrieuō*), "rule, have dominion, lord over," denotes the act of exercising authority,[259] and though it often refers to rulership and governance, it carries a strong negative nuance that includes ruling harshly as well as exercising unrighteous dominion by the unjust use of power. In this context, it carries the tinge of a showy displaying of airs and the oppressive use of authority, specifically dominance over the faith of the Corinthian Saints.[260]

but are helpers of your joy / but rather we are workers with you for your joy: The noun συνεργός (*synergos*) pertains to two or more parties working together for a common goal. In that context, it denotes a helper or fellow worker.[261] The noun χαρά (*chara*), "joy," refers to what brings sustained pleasure and more specifically rejoicing.[262] It suggests a deep-rooted, even rapturous, emotion.

for by faith ye stand / because you stand firm in the faith: The conjunction γάρ (*gar*), "for, because," in the present context points to the reason why Paul and his companions act toward the Saints the way they do. The verb ἵστημι (*histēmi*), "to stand," carries the nuance of being firm in one's

---

255. BDAG, 366.

256. BDAG, 1098–1100. The word has a wide range of meanings including life itself as well as the immortal portion of a person. In some respects, it is that portion of a person that can be most attuned to the Divine. For a study, see *NID*, 4:725–34.

257. Guthrie, *2 Corinthians*, 121.

258. BDAG, 1051.

259. BDAG, 576; Louw-Nida, §37.50.

260. Barnett, *Second Epistle*, 114–16; Guthrie, *2 Corinthians*, 122–23.

261. BDAG, 969; Louw-Nida, §42.44.

262. BDAG, 1077; *NID*, 4:644–49.

faith.[263] It is found here in the perfect tense, suggesting that these people were and still are firm in their trust in the Savior. It is for this reason that Paul and his associates can work with them toward the same end—namely, joy. The noun πίστις (*pistis*), in the present context, refers to the whole of the gospel in both principle and doctrine.[264]

Analysis and Summary

Working to drive home the reason why he changed his travel plans, Paul makes what amounts to a solemn oath invoking God as his witness (1:23). The verb he uses, "to call" (ἐπικαλέω, *epikaleō*), carries strong civil and religious overtones. It connotes calling upon a higher authority to verify a fact or position. Paul's calling upon God to do so shows his absolute sureness of his position, for as the scriptures make clear, God knows the "reins and the heart" (Jer. 20:12; see also Jer. 17:10 and Rev. 2:13)—that is, everything about the person, including his or her most inner secrets. So certain is Paul of his position that, in taking the oath, he also puts his own life on the line. By means of such a solemn declaration, the Apostle assures his readers of the truthfulness of what he is about to say.[265] He likely designed this rather bold act to have a considerable sobering effect upon his target audience.

Having made his declaration, Paul gives the major reason why he adjusted his travel plans (1:23). He had already caused some of these people quite a bit of grief due to both his harsh letter and their initial support of one of his major antagonists. Further, whenever he came, he would have to confront and likely discipline any he felt were out of the correct way.[266] He was hoping that by biding his time, he would give them a chance to repent if necessary and determine where they stood in relationship to him. The

---

263. BDAG, 482–83. The imagery Paul uses looks to both court and the battlefield where both testing and trial take place. Standing means victory while falling means defeat. The verb therefore carries a reminder that the Christians are at war with this world and must not only endure through faith but push forward the cause of Christ. Seifrid, *Second Letter,* 72.

264. Louw-Nida, §§31, 43, 102, 104.

265. Martin, *Second Corinthians,* 171.

266. A mandate set upon the Apostles was to keep the Church in order through Church discipline. For a study, see G. W. H. Lampe, "Church Discipline and the Interpretation of the Epistles to the Corinthians," in *Christian History and Interpretation: Studies Presented to John Knox,* ed. W. R. Farmer, C. F. D. Moule, and R. R. Niebuhr (Cambridge: Cambridge University Press, 1967), 337–61.

question was, then, not one of the purpose or appropriateness of his visit, but of its timing.[267] In the next verse he explains further why he changed his itinerary.

Paul's words do raise a question: How can he say that he wants to spare the Saints pain but deny any intent to lord it over them? The answer is likely because what he wants to spare them from is specifically the need for apostolic reproof and correction (13:2), albeit even here he would use "the meekness and gentleness of Christ" (10:1–2). His objective is not, however, to dictate, demand, or impose faithfulness and trust in Christ.[268] Indeed, Paul fully understands that true faith in the Lord can be neither coerced nor result from fear. "Instead, it has right relationship as its source and 'joy' as its outcome."[269] It is the latter to which the Apostle joins with the Saints to produce, for it is the ultimate aim of Christian living.[270]

In sum, the Apostle wants his readers to encourage and gladden his heart, but that could not happen if Paul's actions among them only resulted in further hurt and alienation. By waiting, he believes they will get their house fully in order such that when he does come, they will all share in a common joy because they now stand firm in the covenant (1:24). In sum, his choice to not visit them "was not an act of refraining from love," of which some may have accused him, "but an act of love."[271]

---

267. Guthrie, *2 Corinthians,* 121.

268. Barnett, *Second Epistle,* 115–16.

269. Guthrie, *2 Corinthians,* 123.

270. As 2 Ne. 2:25 teaches, the purpose of life is that people might obtain joy. This is a major thrust of the gospel. See Matt. 25:21, 23; John 15:11; 16:24; 17:13; Rom. 14:17; 15:13; 1 Pet. 1:8; 4:13; 1 John 1:4; 2 Ne. 27:30; Alma 33:23; 3 Ne. 28:10; and D&C 11:13; 42:61; 51:19; 70:18.

271. Witherington, *Conflict and Community,* 364 with n. 13.

Chapter 2

Ministers of the New and Glorious Covenant

Introduction

The first four verses of this chapter conclude the explanation that Paul was making in the last portion of chapter 1, focusing on why he did not visit the Corinthian Saints immediately after leaving Ephesus. In the next seven verses, he turns to the matter of dealing appropriately with an unnamed person who had behaved unseemly toward him. Though Paul is vague on the subject, it would appear that the person was the primary mover in stirring up resistance against the Apostle. Some type of action, of which Paul had been informed, had already been taken against the offender. Paul, at this point, writes to instruct his readers that he feels that the punishment has been sufficient and therefore asks that the brother not only be forgiven but also be treated with love (2:5–11).

He next recounts the success of the missionary movement in Troas and Macedonia, noting that the work has been going so well that he feels to praise God in thanksgiving (2:12–14). He does make an aside that, despite all the success, he was very troubled because his expectation of meeting up with Titus had not been realized. Because he feared for Titus's welfare, he relates, he left Troas for Macedonia in search of him (2:13).

He breaks his narrative at this point and, using an analogy, notes why the work is going so well: it is due to the sweet and attractive fragrance of the gospel that attracts many who are spiritually sensitive to it. Unfortunately, he admits, not all feel the aroma is sweet. In fact, there are some among the spiritually weak who insisted that the smell was more like the stench of death (2:15–16).

He concludes by assuring the Saints that, unlike many (specifically his detractors), he and his companions do not peddle the word of God but do preach out of sincerity as demanded by the commission from God they carry (2:17).

Why Paul Postponed His Visit *(continued)* (2:1–4)

Greek Text

1 ἔκρινα γὰρ ἐμαυτῷ τοῦτο, τὸ μὴ πάλιν ἐν λύπῃ πρὸς ὑμᾶς ἐλθεῖν· 2 εἰ γὰρ ἐγὼ
λυπῶ ὑμᾶς, καὶ τίς ὁ εὐφραίνων με εἰ μὴ ὁ λυπούμενος ἐξ ἐμοῦ; 3 καὶ ἔγραψα τοῦτο
αὐτὸ ἵνα μὴ ἐλθὼν λύπην σχῶ ἀφ᾽ ὧν ἔδει με χαίρειν, πεποιθὼς ἐπὶ πάντας ὑμᾶς
ὅτι ἡ ἐμὴ χαρὰ πάντων ὑμῶν ἐστιν. 4 ἐκ γὰρ πολλῆς θλίψεως καὶ συνοχῆς καρδίας
ἔγραψα ὑμῖν διὰ πολλῶν δακρύων, οὐχ ἵνα λυπηθῆτε, ἀλλὰ τὴν ἀγάπην ἵνα γνῶτε
ἣν ἔχω περισσοτέρως εἰς ὑμᾶς. [SBLGNT]

King James Version

1 But I determined this with myself, that I would not come again to you in heaviness. 2 For if I make you sorry, who is he then that maketh me glad, but the same which is made sorry by me? 3 And I wrote this same unto you, lest, when I came, I should have sorrow from them of whom I ought to rejoice; having confidence in you all, that my joy is the joy of you all. 4 For out of much affliction and anguish of heart I wrote unto you with many tears; not that ye should be grieved, but that ye might know the love which I have more abundantly unto you.

New Rendition

1 So I made up my mind to never again come to you with sorrow. 2 For if I cause you sorrow, who would make me happy except someone who has been made sorrowful by me? 3 And I wrote this very thing so that when I came, I would not feel sorrow for those who ought to make me happy since I have confidence in all of you that my happiness would also be yours. 4 For I wrote to you out of great tribulation and anguish of heart with many tears, not that you would be made sorrowful but rather that you would recognize the exceedingly great love I have for you.

Translation Notes and Comments

2:1 ***But I determined this with myself / So I made up my mind:*** The KJV translation of the phrase ἔκρινα γὰρ ἐμαυτῷ τοῦτο (*ekrina gar emautō touto*) is very literal and therefore rather awkward, because it literally says, "I judged in reference to myself." In our Rendition we have given a less literal translation but one that idiomatically renders the sense of the Greek meaning to decide or make up one's mind.

The conjunction γαρ (*gar*), "so," as used here, is a marker of inference signaling to Paul's readers that he is drawing a self-evident conclusion as to why he did what he did.[1] The verb κρίνω (*krinō*), in the present context, means to come to a conclusion after careful deliberation and thus to judiciously make up one's mind to do something.[2]

that I would not come again to you in heaviness / to never again come to you with sorrow: The adverb πάλιν (*palin*), "again," plays a very important role here in that it provides the basis for the belief that Paul took a quick, albeit unproductive, trip to Corinth while staying in Ephesus. The aorist infinitive's aspect probably refers to a onetime, simple action. There is, however, some controversy as to its use in the present context.[3] The adverb can be taken to indicate a statement added to the course of an argument. Taken thus it can be translated as "moreover," or "further." However, because its most common use is that of repeated action, the weight of scholarly opinion is on the first translation, which we have chosen to follow.[4]

The noun λύπη (*lypē*), "sorrow, grief," carries a range of meanings that denote emotional or spiritual pain, including grief, anguish, and affliction. The Greek Old Testament uses the term to refer to the agony of childbirth (LXX Gen. 3:16) as well as emotional turmoil (Bar. 2:18; Sir. 30:21; compare Matt. 26:37). The prepositional phrase ἐν λύπῃ (*en lypē*), "in sorrow," in this context is ambiguous in that Paul does not specify who will be in distress, neither himself nor his readers. In the following sentence, however, Paul makes it clear that he is referring to the suffering the Corinthians would feel if he came before the current situation were resolved.

2:2 ***For if I make you sorry / For if I cause you sorrow:*** Paul again uses the conjunction γαρ (*gar*), "for," but in this case as a marker of clarification.[5]

---

1. BDAG, 189–90.

2. BDAG, 567–69; Louw-Nida, §30.75.

3. See Stephen C. Carlson, "On Paul's Second Visit to Corinth: Πάλιν, Parsing, and Presupposition in 2 Corinthians 2:1," *Journal of Biblical Literature* 135, no. 3 (2016): 597–615, who argues that too much exegetical weight has been placed on this adverb and argues that more evidence is needed to confirm Paul's quick visit to Corinth. Most scholars, however, are convinced that the Apostle did make a quick trip to Corinth. For example, see Bernard, "Second Epistle," 46; Barnett, *Second Epistle,* 116–17; Seifrid, *Second Letter,* 72; Ogden and Skinner, *Verse by Verse,* 150.

4. BDAG, 752–53; Louw-Nida, §§67.55; 89.97, 129; MM, 475–76.

5. BDAG, 189–90.

By repeating this word, he indicates that he is now elaborating on the point he made earlier. On λύπη (*lypē*), "sorrow," see above.

who is he then that maketh me glad, but the same which is made sorry by me? / who would make me happy except someone who has been made sorrowful by me?: The verb εὐφραίνω (*euphrainō*) means to make glad, happy, or cheerful.[6] Paul's words show that his personal happiness is anchored in the happiness he brings to the Corinthian congregations. On λύπη (*lypē*), "sorrow," see 2:1 above. Paul's point is that, had circumstances not changed, the only people who could cheer him up were the very ones he had grieved. The likelihood of that happening was nil.

2:3 ***And I wrote this same unto you, / And I wrote this very thing:*** The reference is to the "harsh letter" Paul had written after his unsuccessful trip to Corinth. The antecedent of the phrase τοῦτο αὐτό (*touto auto*), "this very thing," was his informing his readers why he had changed his mind about visiting them directly after leaving Ephesus.[7]

lest, when I came, I should have sorrow from them of whom I ought to rejoice / so that when I came, I would not feel sorrow for those who ought to make me happy: The phrase ἵνα μή (*hina mē*), "lest, so that," informs Paul's readers that he is about to explain his reasoning for changing his itinerary. The verb ἔρχομαι (*erchomai*) is found here as an aorist participle, means "to come," and Paul uses it in a temporal sense, showing that he is looking toward a simple, positive future visit.[8] The clause, as we render it, refers to the outcome he desires for this future visit.[9] On λύπη (*lypē*), "sorrow," and εὐφραίνω (*euphrainō*), "cause to rejoice," see 2:1–2 above.

having confidence in you all / since I have confidence in all of you: The verb πείθω (*peithō*), "to have confidence in," found here as a perfect participle, looks to a conviction so strong that one puts one's full confidence in it.[10] The perfect tense suggests that Paul sees the positive change by the Saints in the recent past as still continuing. The phrase ἐπὶ πάντας ὑμᾶς (*epi pantas hymas*), "in all of you," is inclusive and counts even those who were once Paul's local antagonists.[11]

---

6. BDAG, 414–15; Louw-Nida, §25.131.
7. Guthrie, 2 *Corinthians,* 124.
8. Guthrie, 2 *Corinthians,* 125.
9. BDAG, 393–95; Seifrid, *Second Letter,* 73 n. 273.
10. BDAG, 791–92.
11. His defense found in chapters 11–12 suggests he does not include those who came from outside the Corinthian branches.

that my joy is the joy of you all / that my happiness would also be yours: The conjunction ὅτι (*hoti*), "that," likely marks the reason for Paul's trust—that is, he and his readers all enjoy a shared happiness.[12] On εὐφραίνω (*euphrainō*), "cause to rejoice," see 2:2 above. The construction in this phrase is emphatic, showing that happiness or joy, in order to be full, must be shared by both Paul and his readers; otherwise it would not be achieved.[13]

2:4 ***For out of much affliction and anguish of heart I wrote unto you with many tears / For I wrote to you out of great tribulation and anguish of heart with many tears:*** Again, the reference is to the "harsh letter." Once more Paul introduces the clause with the conjunction γάρ (*gar*), "for," this time marking an explanation of he wrote as he did.[14]

The noun θλίψις (*thlipsis*), "tribulation," denotes a particularly distressing suffering, whether internal or external.[15] The English word "tribulation" translates the sense well since it means the extreme trying of one's patience, endurance, or self-control due to a very difficult situation.[16] The noun συνοχή (*synochē*), "anguish," denotes a high state of distress.[17] The noun καρδία (*kardia*), "heart," used here metaphorically, connotes the entire spectrum of mental and emotional activities.[18] In linking *thlipsis* and *synochē* with *kardia*, Paul stresses the depth of his personal pain in having to write his "harsh letter." Indeed, it brought him to tears.

not that ye should be grieved / not that you would be made sorrowful: The verb λυπέω (*lypeō*) means "to cause mental or emotional distress" and points to the source of the grief, sorrow, or pain.[19] This phrase, introduced by the particle οὐχ (*ouch*), "not," stresses that Paul's intent in writing his "harsh letter" was not to bring further distress to his readers.

but that ye might know the love which I have more abundantly unto you / but rather that you would recognize the exceedingly great love I have

---

12. Guthrie, *2 Corinthians,* 125.

13. Seifrid, *Second Letter,* 73–74.

14. It is possible that he could have used it to substantiate the reason for his writing rather than personally coming to Corinth. If that is the case, then he is saying, "If my letter caused grief, how much more a personal visit!" Barnett, *Second Epistle,* 121 with n. 16.

15. BDAG, 457.

16. *Dictionary of Synonyms,* s.v. "trial."

17. BDAG, 974.

18. In modern culture the heart is tied more directly to the emotional side of a person while the brain or head is tied to the conscious or rational side. Such was not the case the world of the Bible. Johannes Behm, "καρδία," in *TDNT,* 3:605–14.

19. BDAG, 604. In the vast majority of New Testament occurrences, the word denotes a distinctive Christian virtue. *NID,* 3:177–78.

for you: By using the conjunction ἀλλά (*alla*), "but, rather,"[20] Paul reveals his real intent in writing. The verb, γινώσκω (*ginōskō*), "to know, recognize," suggests grasping the meaning and importance of something[21]—in this case, why Paul wrote what he did.

The noun *agape*, "love," denotes a very deep, warm, and accepting affection.[22] That Paul introduces the last clause with this noun, placing it even before the conjunction ἵνα (*hina*), "that," heightens its emphasis.[23] The comparative adverb περισσοτέρως (*parissoterōs*), "far greater, even more," denotes a high degree of something.[24] Its use here is somewhat ambiguous and thus leaves open three possibilities: First, it could add intensity to the noun ἀγάπη (*agape*), thus referring to the great abundance of the love Paul has for the people. Second, it could delimit the verb γινώσκω (*ginōskō*), thus referring to the special importance of recognizing Paul's position. Or third, it could delimit the verb ἔχω (*echō*), "to have,"[25] thus denoting the love the Apostle has especially for these Saints.[26] Given the context, we felt the first option was the best.[27]

Analysis and Summary

Attacks against Paul's character and conduct seem to have suggested that his actions were based on capriciousness. These occurrences pushed Paul to explain, as fully as possible, why he made changes to his travel plans that no longer included Corinth as his first stopping point (1:15–18). In these verses, he explains that his major reason was to avoid exacerbating the tension and suffering that had been running high in the branches. He assures his readers that he had carefully thought through his decision and determined that his delay in visiting them would be the best for all. The reason was his fear that a premature visit would once again produce sorrow or mental distress (λύπη, *lypē*).[28] Paul states that he simply did not want to stir up those raw feelings again. Rather, he stresses, his desire was to wait until

20. BDAG, 44–45.
21. BDAG, 199–201.
22. BDAG, 6–7.
23. Bernard, "Second Epistle," 47.
24. BDAG, 806.
25. BDAG, 420–22.
26. Guthrie, *2 Corinthians*, 127.
27. Martin, *2 Corinthians*, 173–74; Barnett, *Second Epistle*, 121–22.
28. His concern over the grief either he or the others would suffer is evidenced by his use of this idea (as either a noun or verb) in 2:1–7 and again in 7:8–19 seventeen times but only five times in the rest of his epistles combined. Barnett, *Second Epistle*, 120.

he heard how the congregations reacted toward his harsh letter. Once he knew that, he would decide what to do next. He was well aware that some of his readers could have viewed the harshness of his letter as indicating malice toward them.[29] (As he wrote these words, as he notes in 7:10, he already knew that his readers' grief had turned into godly sorrow leading to repentance, but in order to keep his narrative going, he does not mention that at this point in his letter.) To drive that point home, Paul asks, to paraphrase, "Who would cheer me up?" and concludes, "Certainly not the person who was grieved on my account" (2:2).[30] In doing so he reveals that his joy is dependent on how they feel toward him.

He notes that he wrote the former letter, though harsh, in the hopes of bringing about a reconciliation. Indeed, their grief was his grief, and conversely, their joy would be his joy.[31] The word Paul uses (εὐφραίνω, *euphrainō*) to express his feelings denotes happiness and joy that are made all the stronger by being shared by a community of believers.[32] In sum, Paul is telling the Corinthians that his relationship with them "can only go forward on a common set of values, common commitments, and therefore, a common source of joy."[33] At the time he is writing this epistle, he feels this condition has indeed been realized. For that reason, he assures them, he can write in full confidence (πείθω, *peithō*) that they all share the same feelings (2:3), and as a result, they will accept what he now tells them.

Paul feels the necessity of letting his readers know the depth of the agony he felt as he wrote the "harsh letter." To do so he uses three very graphic expressions: the experience was gut-wrenching (θλίψις, *thlipsis*), heartbreaking (συνοχῆς καρδίας, *synochēs kardias*), and executed with a flood of tears (2:4).[34] His purpose, he insists, was not to cause further sorrow (λυπέω, *lypeō*) but rather in the hope that they would recognize that, despite their harshness, his words would expose the exceeding (περισσοτέρως, *perissoterōs*) love he had for them. Tacitly, he is noting that, like God, he rebukes those whom he loves.[35]

---

29. Barnett, *Second Epistle,* 122 n. 19.

30. Martin, *2 Corinthians,* 172.

31. Seifrid, *Second Letter,* 74.

32. BDAG, 414–15; Louw-Nida, §25.131. *NID,* 2:331–33, notes that the word was used in connection with the united and often ecstatic joy felt by pagans in their celebrations. Among Christians, the word continued to have a religious connotation.

33. Guthrie, *2 Corinthians,* 125.

34. Guthrie, *2 Corinthians,* 124.

35. Witherington, *Conflict and Community,* 364–65; Seifrid, *Second Letter,* 74.

Forgiveness for the Sinner (2:5–11)

Greek Text

5 Εἰ δέ τις λελύπηκεν, οὐκ ἐμὲ λελύπηκεν, ἀλλὰ ἀπὸ μέρους ἵνα μὴ ἐπιβαρῶ πάντας ὑμᾶς. 6 ἱκανὸν τῷ τοιούτῳ ἡ ἐπιτιμία αὕτη ἡ ὑπὸ τῶν πλειόνων, 7 ὥστε τοὐναντίον μᾶλλον ὑμᾶς χαρίσασθαι καὶ παρακαλέσαι, μή πως τῇ περισσοτέρᾳ λύπῃ καταποθῇ ὁ τοιοῦτος. 8 διὸ παρακαλῶ ὑμᾶς κυρῶσαι εἰς αὐτὸν ἀγάπην· 9 εἰς τοῦτο γὰρ καὶ ἔγραψα ἵνα γνῶ τὴν δοκιμὴν ὑμῶν, εἰ εἰς πάντα ὑπήκοοί ἐστε. 10 ᾧ δέ τι χαρίζεσθε, κἀγώ· καὶ γὰρ ἐγὼ ὃ κεχάρισμαι, εἴ τι κεχάρισμαι, δι᾽ ὑμᾶς ἐν προσώπῳ Χριστοῦ, 11 ἵνα μὴ πλεονεκτηθῶμεν ὑπὸ τοῦ Σατανᾶ, οὐ γὰρ αὐτοῦ τὰ νοήματα ἀγνοοῦμεν. [SBLGNT]

King James Version

5 But if any have caused grief, he hath not grieved me, but in part: that I may not overcharge you all. 6 Sufficient to such a man is this punishment, which was inflicted of many. 7 So that contrariwise ye ought rather to forgive him, and comfort him, lest perhaps such a one should be swallowed up with overmuch sorrow. 8 Wherefore I beseech you that ye would confirm your love toward him. 9 For to this end also did I write, that I might know the proof of you, whether ye be obedient in all things. 10 To whom ye forgive any thing, I forgive also: for if I forgave any thing, to whom I forgave it, for your sakes forgave I it in the person of Christ; 11 Lest Satan should get an advantage of us: for we are not ignorant of his devices.

New Rendition

5 But if anyone has caused sorrow, he has caused not only me sorrow, but to some extent (not to exaggerate) he has also caused all of you sorrow. 6 This punishment imposed by the majority is sufficient for such a person, 7 and so instead you should forgive and encourage him so that this person will not be overwhelmed by excessive sorrow. 8 Therefore, I urge you to affirm your love for him. 9 For this purpose I wrote to ascertain if you would be obedient in all things. 10 Now whomever you forgive for anything, I also will forgive, for indeed what I have forgiven (if I have forgiven anything), I have done so for you in Christ's presence 11 so that we may not be outwitted by Satan, for we are not ignorant of his designs.

Translation Notes and Comments

2:5 *But if any have caused grief, he hath not grieved me / But if anyone has caused sorrow, he has caused not only me sorrow:* With the use of the conjunction "but" (δέ, *de*), Paul indicates he is making a slight shift in his argument. The masculine indefinite pronoun τις (*tis*), "someone," hints that it was but one particular individual who led the opposition against Paul. On λύπη (*lypē*), "sorrow," see 2:1 above.

but in part, that I may not overcharge you all / but to some extent (not to exaggerate) he has also caused all of you sorrow: The noun μέρος (*meros*), "part, extent," denotes that which is done partially, to a certain degree or extent.[36] The noun ἐπιβαρέω (*epibareō*), "to overcharge, exaggerate," carries the idea of weighing down or putting a burden on something. In the present context it means "to heap up a great burden of words," or in short, "to say too much"—that is, "to exaggerate."[37] This, Paul explains, he will not do. That the form of the verb is present active subjunctive and used with the negative in a preventive sense shows that "Paul wants to stop short of pressing the issue and burdening the Corinthians more than is necessary."[38] We have taken the phrase ἵνα μὴ ἐπιβαρῶ (*hina mē epibarō*), "not to exaggerate," as parenthetical.[39]

2:6 ***Sufficient to such a man is this punishment / This punishment . . . is sufficient for such a person:*** Again, Paul does not mention the name of the individual but refers to him using only the adjective τοιοῦτος (*toioutos*), "this person."[40] The noun ἐπιτιμία (*epitimia*) primarily denotes a punishment or penalty but can also refer to a public censure.[41] On the whole, the term bears the sense of an action taken by an authorized body due to the reprehensible nature of the deeds of one of its members. Such punishment can range from a strong rebuke to an excommunication. The adjective ἱκανός (*hikanos*) denotes that which is adequate or sufficient to meet a necessary objective.[42] Taking the phrase as a whole, it would appear that the punishment consisted of a strong censure against or disfellowship of the person rather than an expulsion from the community.

which was inflicted of many / imposed by the majority: The verb "afflicted," found in the KJV, or "imposed" in our Rendition, is not in the Greek text but has been added for clarification. Paul uses the plural nominalized adjective πλειόνων (*pleionōn*) to denote the large size of the group who punished the wayward person.[43] In this case, it likely refers to the majority of those in the branch.[44]

---

36. BDAG, 633–34; Louw-Nida, §63.14; Guthrie, *2 Corinthians,* 132.
37. BDAG, 368.
38. Guthrie, *2 Corinthians,* 133.
39. Bernard, "Second Epistle," 48.
40. BDAG, 1009–10.
41. BDAG, 384; *NID,* 2:258–60; Barnett, *Second Epistle,* 126.
42. BDAG, 472.
43. BDAG, 847–50; *NID,* 4:97–100.
44. It is possible that the phrase ὑπὸ τῶν πλειόνων (*hypo tōn pleionōn*), "the majority," may actually be all inclusive as is the case with the Hebrew הָרַבִּים (*hārabbim*) "used in Dan

2:7 ***So that contrariwise ye ought rather to forgive him, and comfort him / and so instead you should forgive and encourage him:*** The adverb with article τοὐναντίον (*tounantion*), "instead, otherwise," sets up these actions in contrast with what they had done before. The verb χαρίζομαι (*charizomai*), "to forgive," used here, stands in contrast to the verb ἀφίημι (*aphiēmi*) that is most commonly used to denote the simple pardoning of another.[45] *Charizomai* gives warmth to the idea, suggesting not just pardoning but also forgiving given as a favor.[46] In the present context it refers to forgiving the sins of Paul's former antagonist. The verb παρακαλέω (*parakaleō*), "to comfort, encourage, urge," carries the nuance of encouraging and sustaining another who stands in need.[47]

lest perhaps such a one should be swallowed up with overmuch sorrow / so that this person will not be overwhelmed by excessive sorrow: The phrase μή πως (*mē pōs*), "lest, so that not," expresses the reason for an action to be discontinued. The verb καταπίνω (*katapinō*) means "to be swallowed up, devoured," and by extension, "to be overwhelmed, overcome, or consumed by something."[48] On the noun λύπη (*lypē*), "sorrow, grief," see Translation Notes for 2:1 above. That the noun is modified by the comparative adjective περιςότερος (*perissoteros*), "even more, far more," suggests a profuse amount of grief or sorrow.[49]

2:8 ***Wherefore I beseech you that ye would confirm your love toward him / Therefore, I urge you to affirm your love for him:*** The coordinating conjunction διό (*dio*), "therefore," signals the reason for an action to be taken and refers back to Paul's fear of losing the repentant soul.[50] The verb κυρόω (*kyroō*), "confirm, affirm," means to decide in favor of someone, even going so far as to make the position legally binding.[51] The verb suggests an authorized action and could be pointing to a formal acceptance by a disciplinary body. Paul described the depth of that acceptance with

---

9:27; 11:33. 39; 12:3 (citing Isa 53:11) and at Qumran for the community as a whole." Martin, *2 Corinthians,* 37. If that is the case, then the entire branch joined in the censure of the man. The context, however, suggests that there was a minority who did not participate in the censure but who were brought in line because of it. Barnett, *Second Epistle,* 125 n. 17.

45. Guthrie, *2 Corinthians,* 134.

46. BDAG, 1078.

47. The basic meaning is "to call to one's side," usually for assistance, consolation, or encouragement. BDAG, 764–65.

48. BDAG, 524; Louw-Nida, §25.285; Barnett, *Second Epistle,* 127.

49. BDAG, 806.

50. BDAG, 250.

51. BDAG, 579.

the warm noun ἀγάπη (*agape*), "love," often translated as "charity." The word denotes a heartfelt regard for another and carries with it a touch of the divine.[52]

2:9 ***For to this end also did I write / For this purpose I wrote:*** The prepositional phrase ἐις τοῦτο (*eis touto*), literally "for this" in the present context, points to the reason for an act.[53] The verb γράφω (*graphō*), "to write," found here in the aorist tense, can be taken two ways. As a preterit aorist, it would refer to an act of writing that was done in the past. In that case, its antecedent would be the "harsh letter" Paul had previously written. As an epistolary aorist, it would refer to the act of writing taking place in the present but which would be in the past when it was actually read. In that case it would be this letter. The context (see discussion on the next phrase below) suggests that the latter is intended here.[54]

that I might know the proof of you, whether ye be obedient in all things / to ascertain if you would be obedient in all things: The noun δοκιμή (*dokimē*), "proof, test," refers to a process by which the value or truth of an object can be ascertained.[55] The nuance of the word is generally positive in that the process is usually designed to bring out the best of something.[56] The Apostle's use of the conditional particle εἰ (*ei*), "if," suggests, however, that in this case, the outcome is not certain. His request in this letter, therefore, is a test to see how genuine his readers are in their willingness to accept and follow him. Indeed, they must actually demonstrate their position.[57] To prove this, he must be not only ὑπήκοος (*hypēkoos*), "obedient,"[58] but more particularly εἰς πάντα (*eis panta*), in "all things."[59] The phrase extends the proving beyond the immediate need to forgive and love the repentant person but also includes all that Paul has asked and will ask them to do. What this is he explains in the next verse.

---

52. BDAG, 6–7.

53. BDAG, 740–41.

54. Thomas D. Stegman, "Reading ἔγραψα in 2 Corinthians 2:9 as an Epistolary Aorist," *Novum Testamentum* 54, no. 1 (2012): 50–67, correctly argues that taking ἔγραψα (*egrapsa*) in this way makes 2:5–11 more coherent.

55. It does carry the idea of testing or putting something through an ordeal. BDAG, 256; Louw-Nida, §27.45. Paul is the only New Testament writer to use this noun (2:9; Rom. 5:4; 8:2; 9:13; 13:3; Philip. 2:22), and he does so in reference in determining a person's or community's character. Guthrie, *2 Corinthians,* 135.

56. Louw-Nida, §65.12; 72.7; BDAG, 740–41.

57. Louw-Nida, §72.7.

58. BDAG, 1035.

59. BDAG, 288, 783; TDNT, 5:888–89.

2:10 ***To whom ye forgive any thing, I forgive also / Now whoemver you forgive for anything, I also will forgive:*** The conjunction δέ (*de*), "now,"[60] returns the focus to the present situation. On χαρίζομαι (*charizomai*), "to forgive, bestow favor on,"[61] see 2:7 above. Here Paul reverses the order of events, putting the Christians' response first, and by so doing shows he is as willing to follow them in the act of forgiveness as he expects them to follow him in doing so. By this means he reinforces the solidarity between him and the branch members.[62]

for if I forgave any thing, to whom I forgave it / for indeed what I have forgiven (if I have forgiven anything): Paul is likely using the vague indefinite pronoun τι (*ti*), "anything," so as not to overstate his case. Even so, the oblique antecedent is the sin of the offender. Both uses of the verb χαρίζομαι (*charizomai*), "to forgive, bestow favor on," are in the perfect tense, indicating that Paul forgave the individual in the past and that his forgiveness continues into the present.[63]

The parenthetical expression, at first reading, seems rather dismissive considering the seriousness of the event. Given the context, however, it is unlikely that Paul is expressing any kind of uncertainty but rather deliberately understating his role in the whole affair for the sake of unity with his readers.[64]

for your sakes forgave I it in the person of Christ / I have done so for you in Christ's presence: The preposition διά (*dia*), in the present context, acts as a marker of a cause or reason for an act.[65] With the phrase δι' ὑμᾶς (*di' hymas*), "for your sake, for you," Paul explains why he acts as he does. It is for their good or advantage. The noun πρόσωπον (*prosopon*) refers literally to the face, but here it is used figuratively, suggesting an action taken as if the Lord himself were present as witness.[66]

---

60. The conjunction acts as a marker linking the former segment with the present but with additive force. BDAG, 213; Guthrie, *2 Corinthians,* 136.

61. BDAG, 1078.

62. Barnett, *Second Epistle,* 130.

63. There is no doubt that Paul, at some previous point, forgave the man and thus, as his audience reads his letter, his forgiveness has been fully realized. That being the case, then both uses of χαρίζομαι (*charizomai*) are "epistolary perfects." Barnett, *Second Epistle,* 130 n. 43.

64. Harris, *Second Epistle,* 232.

65. BDAG, 223–26.

66. BDAG, 887–8; Martin, *2 Corinthians,* 176; Barnett, *Second Epistle,* 131 n. 48. To say, as does the KJV, that Paul did what he did "in the person of Christ," would mean that he did what he did as the Savior's delegate. The use of πρόσωπον (*prosopon*) here argues against that interpretation. Bernard, "Second Epistle," 49.

2:11 ***Lest Satan should get an advantage of us / so that we may not be outwitted by Satan:*** With these words, Paul reveals a major reason why he is pushing for forgiveness all the way around. The phrase that introduces this clause, ἵνα μὴ (*hina mē*), "lest, so that not," signals fear or apprehension that something bad could happen unless preventative measures are taken.

The noun σατάν (*satan*) acts as both a name and a title. It denotes literally an adversary, but here it refers to the enemy of God and of those who belong to him—that is, the Devil. The special emphasis in this verse is on his work to incite people to do evil.[67]

The verb πλεονεκτέω (*pleonekteō*) denotes the act of taking advantage of another and thus, "to exploit, outwit, defraud, or cheat."[68] Because "outwit" carries the idea of using craft, superior cleverness, or cunning (all a part of Satan's tool chest) to get the better of another,[69] we use it in our Rendition.

for we are not ignorant of his devices / for we are not ignorant of his designs: The verb ἀγνοέω (*agnoeō*), "to be ignorant," in the present context, does not denote a failure to understand but rather the absence of the knowledge of something.[70] The negative particle οὐ (*ou*), "not," modifying *agnoeō*, shows that something is actually fully known (in this case Satan's desires) and recognized for what it is. The noun νόημα (*noema*) refers to the activities of the mind and often means "purpose."[71] It carries a reference to Satan's evil schemes, notably that which he intends to bring about by stratagem in an effort to reach his objective. Thus, we translated the word as "designs" in our Rendition.[72] Paul could be using wordplay here between the verb and the noun such that the phrase could be read as "We are not unmindful of his mind."[73]

Analysis and Summary

For the first time, if obliquely, Paul reveals the seat of the problem he faced before and during his quick trip to Corinth. That problem centered on the activities of a certain "someone" (τις, *tis*) whom Paul does not name but

67. BDAG, 916–17.

68. BDAG, 824.

69. *Collegiate Dictionary,* s.v. "outwit"; *Dictionary of Synonyms,* s.v. "frustrate."

70. BDAG, 12–13.

71. BDAG, 675.

72. BDAG, 675. Only Paul uses the word and, apart from Philip. 4:7, it always refers to the corrupt thoughts of men and particularly the devices of Satan. J. Behm, "νόημα," in *TDNT,* 4:960–61.

73. Barnett, *Second Epistle,* 132 n. 53.

who generated all the grief that went around.[74] It seems likely that this person was the one who headed the local opposition challenging the Apostle's authority and doctrine.[75]

Paul assures his readers that he recognizes that not only has he been hurt by this person's attack but so has the whole branch (2:5). Indeed, the discord that the offender sowed hurt nearly everyone. It brought sincere sorrow and even grief to some once they realized how deeply this person had driven the wedge between the people and the Apostle.

The passage, however, illustrates Paul's magnanimity. He does not name the individual and through this act of kindness shows his desire to continue not only the individual's but also the branch's healing process. The censure imposed on the individual by the majority of the branch has done what it was intended for, either in intensity or duration. Thus, Paul insists not only that no more punishment is needed but also that the person should be fully taken care of and encouraged to keep the commandments (2:6).[76]

In addition to the one above, Paul likely intends to send another message, this one to the minority who had originally sided with the individual. The more tacit message is that Paul's chief interest is not that of punishment but of unity and oneness. His major desire is that of unity within the Christian community under apostolic leadership.[77]

To help the community heal, Paul admonishes his readers to care for the individual (2:7). The verb he uses (χαρίζομαι, *charizomai*) means to bestow favors or gifts and carries the idea of a gracious and caring attitude given freely.[78]

But Paul askes for even more. He wants the Saints to reach out and encourage (παρακαλέω, *parakaleō*) the individual. The idea behind the word is to give that which heals, lifts, and inspires him to repent. Thus, the forgiven one would be fortified "in heart, mind, and soul."[79] By extending such sincere

---

74. In 2:6 he uses the nominalized adjective τοιοῦτος (*toioutos*), "that person," to refer to the individual. Ogden and Skinner, *Verse by Verse,* 150.

75. Some scholars believe that this person was the incestuous man Paul condemned in 1 Cor. 5:1–5. For example, see Bernard, "Second Epistle," 48; and Garland, *2 Corinthians,* 121–22. The context, however, especially in light of 2:10, suggest this man is not in view. Barnett, *Second Epistle,* 125 n. 13. For further study, see Guthrie, *2 Corinthians,* 139–40.

76. Guthrie, *2 Corinthians,* 133. Paul's words suggest that there was a disciplinary council held following a known procedure "whose outlines are only dimly and incompletely visible from this historical distance." Barnett, *Second Epistle,* 130.

77. Martin, *2 Corinthians,* 174.

78. BDAG, 1078.

79. Garland, *2 Corinthians,* 60. Paul's counsel lines up with Luke 17:3, which states if a brother sins he should be rebuked and, upon repentance, forgiven, and also with the

kindness to him, any residual resistance on his part would likely be overcome and full fellowship established. This is exactly the condition Paul wants. The Apostle, however, wants even more. Because the demands of repentance have been met, to continue the punishment might cause the person to end up drowning (καταπίνω, *katapinō*) in a sea of grief, an act that would be both unfortunate and inappropriate. Once repentance has done its work, further discipline would be nothing less than punitive, "leading to a sort of grief that is worldly and finds no relief in God's redemptive approach to sin" (compare 7:9–11).[80] Thus, modern revelation states, "Reproving betimes with sharpness, when moved upon by the Holy Ghost; and then showing forth afterwards an increase of love toward him whom thou hast reproved, lest he esteem thee to be his enemy" (D&C 121:43).

Paul askes his readers to respond in love (2:8). "For Paul, [love] is not an ethereal concept but is a concrete reality fully expressed in the teachings and actions of the Master. It is neither a sweet sentiment nor even some motivational power behind certain actions. For him, it is action; nothing less will do. Where inaction resides, love does not. As such *agapē* [ἀγάπη, "love"] is neither a human virtue inherent within the soul nor a talent developed by discipline and hard work. It is *the* touch of the divine."[81] It is this kind of love Paul wants his readers to extend to the once-offender. And there is good reason. He must be not only forgiven but also raised to his former position of respect. The reason is that to punish the person without healing him would make all losers.[82]

The Apostle admits that he writes in order to test them to see if they will do as he requests (2:9). Since many had been hurt by the offender (2:5), the Apostle's request is a good test to see if they will accept Paul and follow his example in forgiving the man. But the test goes further, for they must show a willingness to follow apostolic authority "in all things" (εἰς πάντα, *eis panta*). The reason is that "partial obedience is disobedience. Church discipline cannot be conducted halfway, since its effectiveness depends in part on a clearly defined and united stand in relation to the offender."[83]

---

instructions given in D&C 121:43 that an offender should be rebuked with sharpness but, when repentance is complete, shown an increase of love.

80. Guthrie, *2 Corinthians,* 135.

81. Draper and Rhodes, *Paul's First Epistle to the Corinthians,* 624, italics in the original; for further analysis, see pp. 649–65. See also Ceslaus Spicq, *Agape in the New Testament,* 3 vols. (Eugene, Ore.: Wipf and Stock Publishers, 2006). The second volume of this work, with the exception of 1 Peter, is devoted to the study of love in the Pauline corpus.

82. Guthrie, *2 Corinthians,* 135.

83. Guthrie, *2 Corinthians,* 136.

On the other hand, Paul's insistence on full fellowship reveals he is not a bit interested in demonstrating any kind of victory, and thus dominance, over the man but rather in the well-being of the Church as a whole. No lingering bitterness is to canker the soul of the congregation. His request maintains his position as "*both* a servant-figure *and* an appointed leader."[84]

Paul has already enjoined forgiveness for the sake of the offender to prevent him from becoming overwhelmed by excessive sorrow (2:7). Now he does so for the sake of δι' ὑμᾶς (*di hymas*)—that is, the wellbeing of the branch members (2:10). He constructs this sentence thus so as to downplay his own role in the forgiving process and elevate that of his readers. What they forgive, he says, he will also forgive. He assures them that any forgiveness on his part has been for their sake and emphasizes the sincerity of his position by stating he has done so as if the Savior himself were present as witness (ἐν προσώπῳ Χριστοῦ, *en prosōpō Christou*).

The passage shows that Paul views Church discipline as based on a sincere expression of both love and grace. It demands accountability and change, leading to a more Christ-centered life. Those who mistakenly see grace as only forgiveness miss its real substance and purpose. It is not an escape from confronting an injured soul guilty of blatant and public sin. It is rather the means by which that soul can be healed and transformed. Paul clearly shows that grace demands not only forgiveness on the part of the offended but also reformation on the part of the offender.[85] Seeking revenge on one who has truly repented of his sins and seeks for forgiveness betrays an unmerciful and hardened character itself very much in danger of judgment.[86]

The Apostle states that he has forgiven everyone of everything; albeit the repentant offender stands in the foreground. Paul stresses that he has done so as a necessary foil against Satan's designs and purposes (νόημα, *noēma*) that are aimed at outwitting (πλεονεκτέω, *pleonekteō*) the Saints and bringing them under his spell (2:11). Paul is well aware of the adversary's tactics, especially his desire to destroy the Church (2 Thes. 2:9–10). Through the power of forgiveness, Paul works to guard against a number of possible attacks by Satan. If all had a forgiving heart, he understands, it would hinder the minority (those who had sided with the offender) from

84. Martin, *2 Corinthians,* 176, italics in the original.

85. Guthrie, *2 Corinthians,* 137–38; compare *DNTC,* 2:412.

86. Stephen E. Robinson and H. Dean Garrett, *A Commentary on the Doctrine and Covenants,* 4 vols. (Salt Lake City: Deseret Book, 2000–2005), 2:212.

retaining hard feelings and thus open the way to full unity with the majority as well as with Paul himself.[87] It would also help individuals, as the Apostle notes elsewhere, remain reconciled to one another and thus protect them from returning to "the dominion of darkness" from which they had been rescued and brought "into the kingdom of [God's] beloved Son through whom [they] have redemption and the forgiveness of sin" (Col. 1:13–14, our translation).

An unwillingness to fellowship others by being forgiving and bestowing kindness and encouragement works well to bring them under Satan's power. This is because the lack of acceptance can eat at their souls, igniting the desire for recompense and often revenge. Unfortunately, an unforgiving attitude did handicap these early Saints. Indeed, as the Lord revealed, "My disciples, in days of old, sought occasion against one another and forgave not one another in their hearts; and for this evil they were afflicted and sorely chastened. Wherefore, I say unto you, that ye ought to forgive one another; for he that forgiveth not his brother his trespasses standeth condemned before the Lord; for there remaineth in him the greater sin. I, the Lord, will forgive whom I will forgive, but of you it is required to forgive all men" (D&C 64:8–10). Here we see Paul fighting against this very outcome. In this section, Paul teaches the gospel principle of loving and fellowshipping others, even those who are difficult to love.

Paul's Anxiety in Troas (2:12–13)

At this point in his narrative, Paul returns to reporting on his activities. Instead of going by sea, which he likely would have done had he headed straight for Corinth, he has taken the land route going through the province of Mysia along what is now the western coast of Turkey. His objective is to eventually reach Corinth, but he has determined to visit the churches in Macedonia along the way and collect their offerings for the Jerusalem poor.

87. For various views on what Paul could have been addressing here, see Barnett, *Second Epistle,* 132 with n. 54.

Greek Text

12 Ἐλθὼν δὲ εἰς τὴν Τρῳάδα εἰς τὸ εὐαγγέλιον τοῦ Χριστοῦ καὶ θύρας μοι ἀνεῳγμένης ἐν κυρίῳ, 13 οὐκ ἔσχηκα ἄνεσιν τῷ πνεύματί μου τῷ μὴ εὑρεῖν με Τίτον τὸν ἀδελφόν μου, ἀλλὰ ἀποταξάμενος αὐτοῖς ἐξῆλθον εἰς Μακεδονίαν. [SBLGNT]

King James Version

12 Furthermore, when I came to Troas to preach Christ's gospel, and a door was opened unto me of the Lord, 13 I had no rest in my spirit, because I found not Titus my brother: but taking my leave of them, I went from thence into Macedonia.

New Rendition

12 Now when I came to Troas to preach the gospel of Christ and a door was opened for me by the Lord, 13 I had no rest for my spirit because I did not find my brother Titus there. So I said farewell to them and departed for Macedonia.

Translation Notes and Comments

2:12 *Furthermore, when I came to Troas / Now, when I came to Troas:* The conjunction δέ (*de*), "now," indicates that Paul is opening a new unit of discussion. It will focus on his feelings about the ministry and God's work. The noun Τρῳάς (*Trōas*), "Troas," refers to the capital of the Roman province of Mysia. Though populated at the height of Macedonian power in the fourth century, the Macedonian general Lysimachus renamed it Alexandria Troas in 301 BC in honor of the famous Alexander the Great. Caesar Augustus (Octavian) made it a Roman colony with all the privileges of cities of that legal distinction. From that time on it was known simply as "Troas." Its excellent harbor, opening as it did into the Aegean Sea, made it a strategic location for any wanting to cross to Neapolis in Macedonia, where the main Roman highway Via Egnatia began and stretched all the way to Rome itself. As the major port connecting Anatolia and Europe, the city thrived. In Paul's day it had a stable population of about forty thousand.[88] It was from here that Paul and Luke sailed in response to the Apostle's vision in which he saw a Macedonian man beseeching him to come and preach the gospel to the people (Acts 16:1–13). Though the city would have been an excellent location for missionary work, it appears that, due to the urgency of the vision, the Apostle did not stop to preach the gospel at that time. Now, having been forced out of Ephesus,[89] he returned to the city in order

---

88. The geographer Strabo, *Geography* 13.1.26, called it "one of the notable cities of the world." For more information, see Edwin M. Yamauchi, "Troas," in *ABD,* 6:666–67.

89. Harris, *Second Epistle,* 236.

to catch a ship to Greece. His letter indicates that missionary work had been going on and quite a number of people had been converted.

Paul, however, may have been referring to more than the city itself. This is because the phrase he used contains a definite article, τὴν Τρῳάδα (*tēn Trōada*), which could be interpreted as "the Troad," thus referring to the region in which the city sits. Since the Apostle most often does not use a definite article when he refers to a city,[90] its use here suggests he likely had the region in mind. If that is the case, then the gospel had spread throughout the area.

to preach Christ's gospel / to preach the gospel of Christ: The noun εὐαγγέλιον (*euangelion*), literally "good news," is usually translated as "gospel," and in the New Testament it has two main meanings. It can describe the act of proclaiming the gospel or refer to the content or principles of the gospel.[91] We have followed the KJV in assuming it is used in the first sense so that we have translated the phrase εἰς τὸ εὐαγγέλιον τοῦ Χριστοῦ (*eis to euangelion tou Christou*), literally "for the preaching of gospel of Christ," as "to preach the gospel of Christ," where the preposition εἰς (*eis*) expresses "purpose."[92]

and a door was opened unto me of the Lord / and a door was opened for me by the Lord: The noun θύρα (*thyra*), "door," is used figuratively here, denoting something that has been made possible.[93] In this case the possibility comes from direct divine intervention. The verb ἀνοίγω (*anoigō*), "to open,"[94] found here in the form of a perfect passive participle, suggests that the Lord had made something possible for the Apostle at one point in the recent past and that he took advantage of it as soon as he could. Paul does not explain what that opportunity was.

2:13 ***I had no rest in my spirit / I had no rest for my spirit:*** The perfect tense of the verb ἔχω (*echō*), "to have," is one of the few examples of a dramatic or historical perfect found in the New Testament. Like the related historical present, historical perfect is a rhetorical device used to "describe an event in a highly vivid way."[95] The noun πνεῦμα (*pneuma*), "spirit," denotes both feelings and emotions and points to how deeply Paul was affected.[96]

---

90. Note Acts 16:8, 11; 20:5; and 2 Tim. 4:13. Even so, Harris, *Second Epistle,* 236; and Barrett, *Second Epistle,* 93–94, argue that, from the Corinthian point of view, Paul would have designated a place rather than a region for his rendezvous with Titus. For discussion, see Guthrie, *2 Corinthians,* 148–49.

91. Gerhard Friedrich, "εὐαγγέλιον," in *TDNT,* 2:730; BDAG, 402–3.

92. BDAG, 288–91.

93. BDAG, 462.

94. BDAG, 84–85.

95. Wallace, *Greek Grammar,* 578.

96. BDAG, 833–36.

because I found not Titus my brother / because I did not find my brother Titus there: This phrase, τῷ μὴ εὑρεῖν με Τίτον (*tō mē heurein me Titon*), is difficult to translate, largely because it is the only example in the entire New Testament of an infinitive with a dative definite article. It reads literally, "for me not to find Titus." Given the context, we have followed the KJV and taken the infinitive in a causative sense in our Rendition.[97]

Titus was from Antioch and apparently a convert of Paul's. He, like his fellow worker Timothy, was a companion of Paul. Unlike Timothy, however, both Titus's parents were Gentiles. In AD 49, he accompanied Paul to the Jerusalem Council and became the test case to determine whether or not Gentiles needed to be circumcised and follow the Mosaic law (Acts 15). For the sake of the ministry, Paul had insisted that Timothy be circumcised because his mother was Jewish.[98] The Apostle, however, refused to have Titus do the same since he had no Jewish connection. Paul's position was that the Mosaic law, being fulfilled in Christ, was done away for Gentiles. The Council decided in favor of Paul's position (Gal. 2:1–10). Titus later accompanied Paul on his third missionary journey and acted as his spokesperson. The Apostle sent him to Corinth with the "harsh letter" with the hope he could remedy the fallout caused by both Paul's antagonist and the Apostle's painful visit.[99] He was successful in doing so, but the Apostle did not know that until they finally met each other in Macedonia. In the meantime, Paul was very concerned about how the Christians responded to his letter.

Due to Titus's success as troubleshooter and peacemaker, Paul used him as courier for this letter, 2 Corinthians, and also enlisted his support in gathering the collection for the poor in Jerusalem. Some eight years later, after Paul's first Roman imprisonment, he had Titus again join him at Ephesus, where they journeyed to Crete. There Titus remained to act as its chief minister. While he was there, he received a letter from Paul instructing him on items for the ministry. Sometime thereafter he was sent on a mission to Dalmatia, and from there he has been lost to history.[100]

but taking my leave of them / So I said farewell to them: The contrasting connective conjunction ἀλλά (*alla*), "but," can be taken in two ways. First, it sets this phrase in contrast to the "open door" that Paul mentioned earlier, and taken in this way it suggests that even though he received a

---

97. BDF, §401.

98. Jewish descent was counted through the matriarchal line. Had Timothy not been circumcised, he would have been viewed as apostate among the Jewish community and therefore impeded Paul's work of proselyting among them.

99. See the introduction under the heading "Background to the Epistle."

100. For more information, see John Gillman, "Titus," in *ABD,* 6:581–82.

spirit-inspired opportunity to preach the gospel, Paul decided to move on. However, after a negative (such as we find introducing this verse), *alla* can mean "on the contrary, so that," or simply "so."[101] In that case, the Apostle is referring not to his preaching of the gospel but to his restless spirit that was driving him forward. Given the context, this is the likely nuance.

The plural pronoun αὐτοῖς (*autois*), "to them," refers to specific people, but Paul does not indicate who they are. The context suggests, however, that the Corinthian Saints would have been familiar with the referents, and therefore they were likely fellow Christians (see Acts 18:18, 21).

I went from thence into Macedonia / and departed for Macedonia: The noun Μακεδονία (*Makedonia*), "Macedonia," refers to the Roman province directly north of Achaia. Originally it had been a kingdom, and both Philip and Alexander the Great (fourth century BC) expanded its power and area. In 148 BC, its self-styled king, Andriscus of Macedon, opposed Roman advances into the area and was roundly defeated. The Roman Senate then organized the whole region into the new and rather large province that took up the whole of the northern Greek peninsula.[102]

Analysis and Summary

Some feel that Paul headed for Troas in fear that Titus had been hindered from meeting him earlier due to sickness, accident, or being waylaid by bandits. Perhaps fear drove the Apostle's anxiety and desire to find and help him.[103] The text, however, is clear that whatever was driving Paul, it was for the purpose of preaching the gospel of Christ (2:12). The effect of not heading directly to Corinth by ship added a great deal of time and effort to the journey, nearly tripling the miles Paul had to travel. He was, however, not his own man. He was an Apostle of the Lord working under his command and was determined to do whatever his Savior demanded. That meant flexibility, "a willingness to move in unexpected ways under the Lord's leadership. The call to go north for the sake of the gospel preempted the apostle sticking to a previously communicated itinerary, and this insight forms the capstone of his defense of his changed itinerary."[104]

Paul is clear that the hand of the Lord was involved in his movements. It was God who opened a door for the Apostle to accomplish a certain mission,

101. Wallace, *Greek Grammar,* 672; Guthrie, *2 Corinthians,* 147.

102. The new province included the areas of Epirus, Thessaly, and parts of Illyria, Paeonia, and Thrace. For a study, see F. F. Bruce, "Macedonia," in *ABD,* 4:454–57.

103. For example, see Barrett, *Second Epistle,* 94–95.

104. Guthrie, *2 Corinthians,* 145–46.

and he responded to it. Unfortunately, Paul does not say what that mission was. His focus is more on his anxiety over the absence of his companion Titus, and therefore, he is vague in exactly what happened before he met Titus in Macedonia. He states simply that he came for the sake of the gospel of Christ and that "a door had been opened for me by the Lord" (2:12, NR). His words can be taken in at least two ways depending on how one takes the connective καί (*kai*), "and." Most scholars take it simply as connecting two ideas, that Paul came to Troas *and*—that is, *because*—the Lord opened the door for him to proclaim the gospel. Taken thus, the Apostle came, under inspiration, to Troas for the purpose of preaching the gospel and found a very warm reception among several people living in the area.[105] In this view, though the labor was moving with success, Paul was so anxious due to Titus's failure to meet him that he forsook the work in order to find his companion.

It is not difficult to read the text this way, but the idea that he came to Troas because the Lord had opened the way for him to preach the gospel in the area is reading words into the text that are not there. It is possible that the connective *kai*, "and," could be used in the continuative sense connecting the two events in a consecutive way. Read in this way, Paul was at Troas already, *and then* the Lord provided an opportunity for him to move on to Macedonia. Thus, the Apostle was not shirking his duty as a missionary but following the Lord's lead.

The frustration he faced in not meeting with Titus may have been due to climate. During the winter, sea passage was very dangerous. Between October and March, few ships would venture out under the treacherous conditions stirred by the Mediterranean winds and waters. It may be that Paul found a way of getting to Macedonia much earlier than he had anticipated.[106] Thus, the "open door" he refers to was a way of crossing the Aegean Sea to Macedonia and hunting for Titus while engaging in the work there. In that case, his anxiety was due both to the opportunity to further the work and his need to find his companion. Certainly, the glowing report he records concerning the churches in that area (8:1–4) suggests that the ministry there was proving fruitful.[107] Whatever the case, Paul said goodbye to his fellow Saints in Troas and headed for Macedonia.

---

105. Barnett, *Second Epistle,* 135. Some suggest that *kai* could be read concussively, thus making the passage read "although a door stood open." See Harris, *Second Epistle,* 235; and Barrett, *Second Epistle,* 94. Both translations, however, come to the same conclusion: Paul found a wide-open opportunity to preach the gospel in Troas.

106. Barnett, *Second Epistle,* 136–37.

107. Guthrie, *2 Corinthians,* 146–47.

Paul's Reflections on the Effects of the Gospel (2:14–17)

At this point, the Apostle stops his narrative and does not return to it until 7:5. Rather, he takes time to rhapsodize on the effects of the gospel on its hearers and to explain his own ministry in light of the power of the word. This rather abrupt break has led some commentators to posit that this portion of the epistle is an insertion added by a later redactor.[108] However, a close reading shows how this examination of the power and purpose of gospel and Paul's faithful ministering therein integrates purposefully into the Apostle's overall theme and self-defense.[109]

In this section (2:14–7:4) Paul first lays down the foundation for his defense and then builds upon it. In it he gives his readers a number of compelling reasons why they should be delighted that they received the gospel through him—indeed, that he is their Apostle. For these reasons, as he tacitly implies, they should be neither criticizing him nor comparing him with those interloping false Apostles who were challenging Paul's authority and preaching a false gospel.[110]

This section contains the very heart of the letter's message. Here we find a theological richness unparalleled in the whole of the New Testament gained through the depth of Paul's reflections on the nature of true ministering. It could easily be seen as a digression from the narrative flow, since the Apostle leaves his account of seeking Titus only to return to it later.[111] Yet it is not a digression in the sense of being off topic. It is, rather, the ground on which the epistle stands and which gives the whole "its theological center of gravity."[112] It is based on Paul's thoughtful reflections and his sincere testimony, which focuses on three aspects of his devout Christ-centered ministry: the first, found in 2:14–4:6, treats the dynamics of such a ministry; the second, found in 4:7–5:10, reflects on the suffering too often associated with that ministry; and the third, found in 5:11–7:4, contains Paul's appeal to his readers to accept him and his companions as true representatives of the authentic gospel. The whole brings together "a poignant treatment of the theological, ethical, and spiritual superiority

108. See the section "The Integrity of the Work" in the introduction.
109. Guthrie, *2 Corinthians,* 150.
110. Matera, *II Corinthians,* 66.
111. Harris, *Second Epistle,* 240.
112. Guthrie, *2 Corinthians,* 150.

of true Christian ministry, which exhibits a posture of submission to God," lived with integrity before the Saints with the objective of full reconciliation with the Father.[113]

Greek Text

14 Τῷ δὲ θεῷ χάρις τῷ πάντοτε θριαμβεύοντι ἡμᾶς ἐν τῷ Χριστῷ καὶ τὴν ὀσμὴν
τῆς γνώσεως αὐτοῦ φανεροῦντι δι᾽ ἡμῶν ἐν παντὶ τόπῳ· 15 ὅτι Χριστοῦ εὐωδία
ἐσμὲν τῷ θεῷ ἐν τοῖς σῳζομένοις καὶ ἐν τοῖς ἀπολλυμένοις, 16 οἷς μὲν ὀσμὴ ἐκ
θανάτου εἰς θάνατον, οἷς δὲ ὀσμὴ ἐκ ζωῆς εἰς ζωήν. καὶ πρὸς ταῦτα τίς ἱκανός; 17 οὐ
γάρ ἐσμεν ὡς οἱ πολλοὶ καπηλεύοντες τὸν λόγον τοῦ θεοῦ, ἀλλ᾽ ὡς ἐξ εἰλικρινείας,
ἀλλ᾽ ὡς ἐκ θεοῦ κατέναντι θεοῦ ἐν Χριστῷ λαλοῦμεν. [SBLGNT]

King James Version

14 Now thanks be unto God, which
always causeth us to triumph in Christ,
and maketh manifest the savour of his
knowledge by us in every place. 15 For
we are unto God a sweet savour of
Christ, in them that are saved, and in
them that perish: 16 To the one we are
the savour of death unto death; and
to the other the savour of life unto life.
And who is sufficient for these things?
17 For we are not as many, which corrupt the word of God: but as of sincerity, but as of God, in the sight of God
speak we in Christ.

New Rendition

14 But thanks be to God who always
leads us in a triumphal procession with
Christ and makes known the fragrance
of the knowledge of him through us in
every place. 15 For we are to God the
pleasant odor of Christ among those who
are saved and among those who are perishing. 16 To the latter an odor of death
unto death but to the former of life unto
life. And who is qualified for these things?
17 For we are not like so many others who
peddle the word of God for profit. On the contrary, we speak in Christ before God
as men of pure motive, as men of God.

Translation Notes and Comments

2:14 *Now thanks be unto God, which always causeth us to triumph in Christ / But thanks be to God who always leads us in a triumphal procession with Christ:* With the adversative connective δέ (*de*), "now, but," Paul contrasts his anxiety over his temporal concerns that have been his major focus in this section with his delight in the success of the spiritual, which he now turns to. He gives God full credit for the achievement he has seen in the spreading of the gospel. The noun he uses, χάρις (*charis*), "thanks," indicates "a gift to God," but idiomatically it denotes a deeply felt expression of thanks for

113. Guthrie, *2 Corinthians,* 150–51.

divine favor or assistance. Though often translated as "grace," in this context, it carries the sense of deeply felt gratitude as an "appropriate response to the Deity for benefits conferred."[114] That Paul often uses this expression (see 8:16; 9:15; Rom. 6:17; 7:25; and 1 Cor. 15:57) shows how conscious he is that the Father stands behind all the success that has gone on.

To push his point, Paul appeals to the imagery of a grand parade. The verb θριαμβεύω (*thriambeuō*), found here in the form of a present active participle, refers to a celebratory procession, but of what kind exactly is debated.[115] This is because the word can refer to any public celebration of victory, and Paul, the only New Testament writer to use the term (here and in Col. 2:15), does not specify what he means. Given, however, the widespread use of the verb to describe the elaborate parade called a triumph, given to celebrate the victory of a Roman general,[116] most scholars feel that this is what the Apostle had in mind, and we agree.[117] The force of the participle is important here. Though in the present tense, it carries an imperfective aspect that emphasizes the ongoing nature of the Christians' triumph in Christ.[118]

and maketh manifest the savour of his knowledge by us in every place / and makes known the fragrance of the knowledge of him through us in every place: In addition to leading his missionaries in triumph, God does more.[119] The verb φανερόω (*phaneroō*) refers to making something publicly known.[120] The noun γνῶσις (*gnosis*) denotes comprehending or

---

114. BDAG, 1079–81.

115. Note the various definitions given in BDAG, 459. The general meaning of the verb is "to cause to triumph" or "to triumph over." Louw-Nida, §§39.59, 60. Paul Brooks Duff, "Metaphor, Motif, and Meaning: The Rhetorical Strategy behind the Image 'Led in Triumph' in 2 Corinthians 2:14," *Catholic Biblical Quarterly,* 53 no. 1 (1991): 79–92, argues that Paul was deliberately ambiguous so that his readers could see either a reference to a Roman triumph or a Hellenistic royal epiphany procession depending on their position concerning Paul.

116. For example, see Plutarch, *Aemilius Paullus* 5.8; 35.2; Plutarch, *Tiberius et Caius Gracchus* 2.17.6; Plutarch, *Marius* 24.1; 27.6; and Appian, *Bella civilia* 2.13.93; 4.6.38. MM, 293, notes that the basic meaning is "to make a show of" and sees Paul's use of the word as a military metaphor.

117. See particularly Guthrie, *2 Corinthians,* 157–63. He notes in 158 n. 6 that the Roman triumphal parades were so well-known that it was "woven into the public consciousness of the Greco-Roman world of Paul's time."

118. Guthrie, *2 Corinthians,* 164.

119. Though the participle could be taken as adverbial and thus showing the circumstances surrounding God's triumph, we have taken it as substantival and thus showing the Father as both the leader of the triumph and also the source of the wonderful aroma.

120. BDAG, 1048.

intellectually grasping an idea or fact[121] and in this case, it is an understanding of the nature of Christ. The noun ὀσμή *(osmē)* denotes a scent or odor.[122] In general Greek literature, it most often referred to a rather unpleasant order, but among the writings of the Jews and Christians, it denoted a pleasant fragrance.[123] In the Roman triumphal parade, a large group of men bearing censures in which burned frankincense and other aromatic spices immediately preceded the general (thus holding pride of place).[124] Among some Greek thinkers, smell was viewed as having "life-giving force,"[125] infusing a divine quality in existence. Paul's imagery picks up this idea and pictures the witness of Christ, due to the work of the disciples, as a pleasant aroma wafting everywhere and changing lives.

2:15 ***For we are unto God a sweet savour of Christ / For we are to God the pleasant odor of Christ:*** The noun εὐωδία (*euōdia*) denotes a pleasing smell,[126] but it is used here metaphorically for that which pleases God. In this case, it represents Paul and his companions because they are doing the work of the Savior and thus carry, as it were, his delightful fragrance.

in them that are saved / among those who are saved: The verb σῴζω (*sōzō*), "to save," found here as a present passive participle with a theological nuance, denotes being preserved from death and hell. The means of doing so includes both human and divine agents; albeit the Father is the ultimate source, but he works primarily through the Son. Those who are "the saved" accept him as their Lord and in faith follow his ways.[127]

and in them that perish /and among those who are perishing: The verb ἀπόλλυμι (*apollymi*), "to destroy," found here as a present passive participle, carries the idea of moving to destruction.[128] The use of the participle suggests that the referents have not yet spiritually died but are moving toward that end.

---

121. BDAG, 203–4.

122. Louw-Nida, §79.45.

123. The LXX uses the term to refer to the scent arising from temple sacrifices (Ex. 29:18; Lev. 1:9; Num. 15:3). In that work, the noun is sometimes paired with εὐωδία (*euōdia*), "fragrance" (for example, see Gen. 8:21 and Ex. 29:18, where it is the translation of the Hebrew רֵיחַ נִיחוֹחַ [*rēaḥ nîḥôaḥ*] and is found in the KJV as "a sweet savour"), indicating a very satisfying aroma.

124. Appian, *Punic Wars* 9.66; Dionysius, *Roman Antiquities* 7.72.13.

125. *NID,* 3:559–61.

126. BDAG, 417.

127. *NID,* 4:420–35.

128. BDAG, 115–16.

2:16 ***To the one we are the savour of death unto death / To the latter an odor of death unto death:*** Paul again uses the noun ὀσμή (*osmē*), "smell" (see 2:14 above), to get his point across. In the case of those who reject the gospel, God's word not only carries a stench but acts as an actual poison leading to death.

and to the other the savour of life unto life / but to the former of life unto life: For the believing, the gospel not only carries a sweet fragrance but actually brings with it a strengthening and invigorating power advancing a higher quality of spiritual life.

And who is sufficient for these things? / And who is qualified for these things?: The adjective ἱκανός (*hikanos*) denotes that which is fit, adequate, appropriate, or qualified but connotes what is worthy or good enough.[129] The demonstrative adjective ταῦτα (*tauta*), "these things," refers to the overwhelming power held within the gospel and its preaching. The word of God deals with life and death but not on a mere mortal scale. Its ramifications are eternal.[130] Therefore, Paul's question is a good one: Who is qualified to preach the word and explain the works of God?

2:17 ***For we are not as many, which corrupt the word of God / For we are not like so many others who peddle the word of God for profit:*** The verb καπηλεύω (*kapēleuō*) denotes the peddling, trading, or hawking of wares and other products. The word, however, carries the very negative nuance of deceptiveness and being motivated by greed and profit. It also suggests adulteration.[131] That Paul attributes this trait to οἱ πολλοί (*hoi polloi*), "the many," suggests that a number of parties were guilty of trying to profit from the word of God and were anything but careful to keep it pure.

but as of sincerity, but as of God, in the sight of God speak we in Christ / On the contrary, we speak in Christ before God as men of pure motive, as men of God: The conjunction ἀλλα (*alla*), "but, rather," sets up a contrast and is thus translated as "on the contrary" in our Rendition.[132] Doing so emphasizes the distance Paul puts between himself with his coworkers and

---

129. Louw-Nida, §§75.2; 78.50; BDAG, 472.

130. Guthrie, *2 Corinthians*, 178.

131. Louw-Nida, §57.202; BDAG, 508. Initially the word denoted any small shopkeeper or retailer, but in the general literature of Paul's day, it carried the pejorative sense of the conscienceless hustler who sets up an illicit business to cheat the innocent and gullible for his personal gain. See Scott J. Hafemann, *Suffering and Ministry in the Spirit: Paul's Defense of His Ministry in II Corinthians 2:14–3:3* (Grand Rapids, Mich.: William B. Eerdmans, 1990), 115–17.

132. BDAG, 44–45.

those who preach for gain. The phrase "in Christ" (ἐν Χριστῷ, *en Christō*) suggests that Paul speaks or proclaims the Savior's words. In the phrase "before God" (κατέναντι θεοῦ, *katenanti theou*), the preposition κατέναντι (*katenanti*), "before," carries the nuance "in the sight of" or "in the judgment of"[133] and suggests that Paul insists that God himself stands as judge over what the Apostle and his coworkers are doing. The noun εἰλικρινεία (*eilikrineia*) denotes that which is free of dissimulation and, therefore, emphasizes the purity of motives.[134] The phrase "as men of God" (ὡς ἐκ θεοῦ, *hōs ek theou*) denotes those in whom God finds favor.

Analysis and Summary

At this point, Paul breaks into his narrative with a joyful praise to God, expressed in a metaphorical description of his work (2:14). The Apostle unites three images—a triumphal parade, a sweet aroma, and a pungent odor—to show his understanding of God and how he works. Understanding how Paul integrates the three images reveals what he had in mind.[135]

The Apostle draws his readers' attention away from the anxiety-filled account of his travels and toward the success of the gospel by appealing to the imagery of the *pompa triumphalis*,[136] a very elaborate parade that celebrated the success of a Roman general and drew crowds of thousands. Among the items exhibited in the parade were the more spectacular spoils of war and important captives. Before the proud general came a large number of men holding censers burning sweet-smelling spices and frankincense,[137] while the victorious troops brought up the rear of the parade.[138] These herded the defeated captives before them, some on their way to execution.

Paul shows God as the triumphator but not apart from Jesus.[139] They are victorious together. This is an important point, for though God leads the

133. Louw-Nida, §90.20; BDAG, 530–31.

134. BDAG, 282.

135. Guthrie, *2 Corinthians, 159*.

136. Though some scholars object to his exact understanding, the widespread reports of these parades shows that knowledge of them was a cultural artifact and broad part of the public consciousness. See Guthrie, *2 Corinthians*, 157. For a study, see Hafemann, *Suffering and Ministry*, 19–34.

137. Barrett, *Second Epistle*, 98.

138. For a study, see H. S. Versnel, *Triumphus: An Inquiry into the Origin, Development, and Meaning of the Roman Triumph* (Leiden, Neth.: E. J. Brill, 1970).

139. J. M. Scott, "The Triumph of God in 2 Corinthians 2:14: Additional Evidence of Merkabah Mysticism in Paul," *New Testament Studies* 42 (1996): 260–81, parallels

procession, he does so with Christ. It is this image of co-victors that constitutes the special knowledge of Christ Paul wishes to present. But God does more than enjoy praise with his Son; he manifests the gospel—meaning victory through Jesus—as a sweet aroma that wafts everywhere. Here is where the missionaries come in; they act as his agents.

But what role do they play in the imagery of the grand parade? It could be that the Apostle sees himself and companions as captives being led in God's triumphal procession, carrying the embarrassment of being public spectacles, and bearing the full brunt of social shame.[140] Because he frequently applies the label of "slave" (δοῦλος, *doulos*) to himself (for example, see Rom. 1:1; 1 Cor. 9:19; and Gal. 1:10) as well as that of a prisoner of war (see Rom. 16:7; Col. 4:10; and Philem. 1:23), this view seems well taken.

However, the feel of the whole section suggests the Apostle sees neither himself nor his fellow missionaries as defeated and disgraced but rather as fellow triumphators sharing fully in God's victory.[141] Indeed, God uses them in the role of the incense bearers that spread the aroma of victory everywhere.[142] The Apostle notes that, from God's point of view, the missionaries themselves are the ones who bear the sweet fragrance of Christ (2:15) and carry it to others.

The odor, though the same for all, has several very different effects on those who smell it (2:16). In the imagery of the parade, to the prisoners of war on their way to execution, it would dramatize not only their defeat but

---

the Roman general's chariot with that of God's throne chariot in Jewish tradition. See particularly Ezek. 1:4–25. In Christian tradition, Christ shares this throne with his Father. See Richard Bauckham, *Jesus and the God of Israel:* God Crucified *and Other Studies on the New Testament's Christology of Divine Identity* (Grand Rapids, Mich.: William B. Eerdmans, 2009), 172–81.

140. Furnish, *II Corinthians,* 173.

141. As Barnett, *Second Epistle,* 150, notes, given Paul's love for paradoxes, it may be that he wishes to bring both the image of the captured and disgraced prisoner/slave and that of the triumphant celebrant to the mind of his readers for he certainly saw himself in both roles. Thus, the metaphor could be "triumphal and antitriumphal. It is as God leads his servants as *prisoners of war* in a victory parade that God spreads the knowledge of Christ everywhere through them. Whereas in such victory processions the prisoners would be dejected and embittered from this captive's lips [that is, Paul's] comes only thanks giving to God his captor. Here is restated the power-in-weakness theme (cf. 1:1–3) that pervades the letter." Italics in the original.

142. Barrett, *Second Epistle,* 98; for a study, see George H. Guthrie, "Paul's Triumphal Procession Imagery (2 Cor 2.14–16a): Neglected Points of Background," *New Testament Studies* 61, no. 1 (2015): 79–91.

also their death. To them the scent would be awful.[143] For the victorious on their way to great reward and renown, it would indicate not only their success but also their triumph. To them the aroma would be the sweetest of fragrances.

In a less metaphorical sense, to the intractably unbelieving and resolute apostate, the word of Christ not only carries the stench of death but acts as a poison to bring death about. To the faithful and believing, it is the fragrance that not only bespeaks of an ever-increasing abundance of life but also acts as a life-giving force. The Apostle's imagery shows vividly not only how the gospel divides people, demanding as it does some kind of response, but also its inherent power to bring life or death.[144]

Given the gospel's awful power, it is little wonder that Paul asks who is actually qualified to preach the word and declare the works of God (2:16). The Apostle looks to "a profoundly staggering, deeply sobering reality. Those who proclaim the gospel participate in cosmic-sized matters, spiritual life and death, liberation and destruction. Who can be considered adequate for such a role? This maybe *the* key question in the whole book, for Paul seeks to establish the fundamental difference between his gospel ministry and the misguided 'ministries' of those who seek to lead the Corinthians in his absence."[145] He will answer the question in 3:5.

Staying with the metaphor of aromas, Paul uses the analogy of peddlers hawking spices (καπηλεύω, *kapēleuō*) to move to his next point. Some peddlers of his day carried all kinds of spices and aromatic herbs in their wares. Rabbinic literature used stories of such peddlers to teach important lessons. One had to be careful of these men, some stories warn, for their products could be beneficial or harmful depending on what they were and how people used them.[146]

Paul compares himself to a peddler but not of the mundane sort. He is, indeed, no mere merchant of worldly items, for his wares have spiritual consequences and, as he has already pointed out, can be either harmful or beneficial depending on the spiritual state of those who hear him.[147] He castigates those who "peddle the word of God for profit" (2:17, NR). There

---

143. Likely conjuring up images of fellow soldiers, friends, and perhaps even family members who had perished in the battles.

144. *NID,* 3:560; *DNTC,* 2:413.

145. Guthrie, *2 Corinthians,* 178, italics in original.

146. Tzvi Novick, "Peddling Scents: Merchandise and Meaning in 2 Corinthians 2:14–17," *Journal of Biblical Studies* 130, no. 2 (2011): 543–49.

147. For a study, Novick, "Peddling Scents," 543–49.

were, as the Apostle notes, "many" (οἱ πολλοί, *hoi polloi*) who were guilty of doing so. This practice would likely open the door to, in LDS parlance, the practice of priestcraft. This enterprise carries a very grave danger, for "priestcrafts are that men preach and set themselves up for a light unto the world, that they get gain and praise of the world" (2 Ne. 26:29). These people care nothing for the truth and are therefore willing to say whatever is necessary, thereby adulterating the word of God in order to get profit from the lazy, sinful, or gullible people.

The Book of Mormon gives a very clear picture of how they work. A good example is Nehor. He insisted that his teachings were based on "the word of God" and likely used passages from the Old Testament to support his views. He "testified unto the people that all mankind should be saved at the last day, and that they need not fear nor tremble, but that they might lift up their heads and rejoice; for the Lord had created all men, and had also redeemed all men; and, in the end, all men should have eternal life." He further insisted that those in the ministry should be paid. By teaching the latter, he introduced priestcraft among the Nephites (Alma 1:2–4, 12).[148] That those who followed this false theology built their man-made doctrine on the scriptures is suggested by the work of Sherem. He stoutly defended the Pentateuch, insisting on the importance of keeping the Mosaic law. He, however, stressed that because no one could know the future, any teaching about the coming of Christ was not only bogus but blasphemous (Jacob 7:1–20).[149] By implication, he was also objecting to the higher morality that Christian worship, as preached by Jacob, demanded. Sherem anchored his teachings on the value of the law as the only means of salvation. The result would have likely been what we see among certain Jews in New Testament times, who insisted on works of righteousness as the means of salvation and therefore rejected the Savior.[150]

Paul concludes this section by tacitly addressing one of the main charges his antagonists have brought against him. Their claim is that he is no Apostle

---

148. See Chauncey C. Riddle, "Nehor," in *Book of Mormon Reference Companion,* ed. Dennis R. Largey (Salt Lake City: Deseret Book, 2003), 582–83.

149. See Robert James Norman, "Sherem," in Largey, *Book of Mormon Reference Companion,* 720; John W. Welch, "Sherem's Accusation against Jacob," *FARMS Update,* no. 74 (January 1991).

150. For example, the Pharisees developed a rather large body of traditions based on the law of Moses that they considered binding in order to receive eternal life. See Frederick J. Murphy, *Early Judaism: The Exile to the Time of Jesus* (Peabody, Mass.: Hendrickson Publishers, 2002), 218–20.

because he refuses to accept patronage. His primary motive, they apparently insist, was to secretly bilk the Saints out of money through his appeal for assistance to the Jerusalem poor. As such, they claimed, he was a dishonest schemer, unlike themselves—they were perfectly willing to accept support, and further, they had letters to authenticate their authority.[151]

The Apostle sets himself and his coworkers apart from these men who are most willing to preach the gospel for hire. Paul insists that he and the other missionaries work from a "pure motive," as they are "men of God" (2:17, NR). To stress the point of the purity of their motives, he uses the very strong phrase "according to God's judgment" (κατέναντι, *katenanti theou*). By this means, the Apostle sets the foundation for his defense, on which he will build starting in chapter 3.

151. Witherington, *Conflict and Community,* 371.

Chapter 3

Components of an Authentic Ministry

Introduction

This chapter, as well as the next, presents especially knotty problems for interpreters. In it we see the reality of the comment made by Peter concerning Paul's writings. The Church president said that "there are things in them hard to understand, which the ignorant and unsteady twist to their own destruction, as they do other scriptures" (2 Pet. 3:16, our translation). As one scholar noted, "Understanding chs. 3–4 requires a considerable amount of reading between the lines and a willingness to go with the flow of ever-developing and mixed metaphors."[1] Even so, as is shown in this introduction and that for the next chapter, Paul's overall themes can be easily grasped. It is with some of the particulars that the problems lie.

This chapter picks up where the last one left off. There Paul makes reference to his detractors, noting that they have begun the shameful process of peddling the word of God for profit (2:17). Here he notes that they carry letters of recommendation as a means of establishing their authority. His credentials and what has established his authority, he insists, are his converts. These, as letters, reside in his and his fellow workers' hearts, written there by the power of the Spirit (3:1–3). His personal competence in gospel matters, he relays, comes directly from God. By this means, he and his associates minister a "new covenant" that follows not the letter of the old law but the spirit of it (3:4–6).

This new ministry, he says, eclipses the old one. He uses three examples to highlight how much more glorious the new covenant is over the old one: First, though the old one came with so much glory that the Israelites could not even look upon Moses while the Spirit of God was upon him, the new one came

1. Witherington, *Conflict and Community*, 377.

with such power that the Spirit could act directly upon the Saints, bringing even greater glory. Second, the old ministry with all its glory resulted in nothing more than condemnation, while the new one, because of its increased glory, brings righteousness. Finally, even though the old ministry had its glory, it is now becoming inoperative and, on that account, Paul stresses the importance of the new ministry that will operate forever. In sum, compared to the glory of the new ministry, the old had hardly any at all (3:7–11).

He next contrasts himself and his companions with Moses. Where the Old Testament prophet had to put a veil over his face to hide the divinely radiant glory from the people, Paul and his companions boldly and with open faces display the glory of the new ministry. He does castigate the Jews, noting that, figuratively, the veil as yet covers their hearts. This is because they deny Christ, whose power alone can take off the veil and reveal the glory of the new covenant. Any, however, who yield to the power of God's Spirit will have the veil lifted and be able to not only see, as in a mirror, the glory of Christ but also be transformed into his likeness through ever-increasing glory (3:12–18).

Ministers of the New Covenant (3:1–3)

Greek Text

1 Ἀρχόμεθα πάλιν ἑαυτοὺς συνιστάνειν; ἢ μὴ χρῄζομεν ὥς τινες συστατικῶν ἐπιστολῶν πρὸς ὑμᾶς ἢ ἐξ ὑμῶν; 2 ἡ ἐπιστολὴ ἡμῶν ὑμεῖς ἐστε, ἐγγεγραμμένη ἐν ταῖς καρδίαις ἡμῶν, γινωσκομένη καὶ ἀναγινωσκομένη ὑπὸ πάντων ἀνθρώπων·
3 φανερούμενοι ὅτι ἐστὲ ἐπιστολὴ Χριστοῦ διακονηθεῖσα ὑφ' ἡμῶν, ἐγγεγραμμένη οὐ μέλανι ἀλλὰ πνεύματι θεοῦ ζῶντος, οὐκ ἐν πλαξὶν λιθίναις ἀλλ' ἐν πλαξὶν καρδίαις σαρκίναις. [SBLGNT]

King James Version

1 Do we begin again to commend ourselves? or need we, as some others, epistles of commendation to you, or letters of commendation from you?
2 Ye are our epistle written in our hearts, known and read of all men: 3 Forasmuch as ye are manifestly declared to

New Rendition

1 Are we starting again to commend ourselves? We certainly do not need, as some do, letters of commendation to or from you, do we? 2 You are our letter, written in our hearts, understood and read by everyone. 3 You clearly show that you are Christ's letter, delivered

be the epistle of Christ ministered by us, written not with ink, but with the Spirit of the living God; not in tables of stone, but in fleshy tables of the heart.

by us, written not with ink but by the Spirit of the Living God, not on stone tablets but on tablets of human hearts.

Translation Notes and Comments

3:1 ***Do we begin again to commend ourselves? / Are we starting again to commend ourselves?:*** The verb συνίστημι (*synistēmi*), "commend," together with the reflexive pronoun ἑαυτούς (*heautous*), carries the idea of self-commendation.[2] That Paul uses the adverb πάλιν (*palin*), "again," shows that he has already used this means before, likely when he first began preaching the gospel in the city. Self-commendation served the same purpose as letters of recommendation but without the involvement of a third party. It was done either by the presentation of credentials or by personal testimony of one's position for the purpose of establishing "a reciprocal, trust-based relationship."[3] It was also used in cases where strained relationships needed to be repaired, such as Paul now faces.[4]

or need we, as some others, epistles of commendation to you, or letters of commendation from you? / We certainly do not need, as some do, letters of commendation to or from you, do we?: The phrase ὥς τινες (*hōs tines*), "as some," refers to Paul's enemies. For a discussion of who these were, see "Paul's Enemies at Corinth" in the introduction.

The συστατικαὶ ἐπιστολαί (*systatikai epistolai*), "letters of recommendation," were used widely in the Greco-Roman world, and there were even manuals that gave instructions on the most effective way to compose them.[5] Such shows that to the Mediterranean people, credentialing was very important, and that they gave considerable weight to the opinions of relatives or people of prominence.[6] Such letters were generally used by a person moving to a new location to validate status and to gain support or

2. BDAG, 972–73. The verb is found sixteen times in the New Testament with thirteen found in Paul's letters, six of them in this epistle (3:1, two times; 4:2; 5:12; 10:12; 12:11).

3. Guthrie, *2 Corinthians,* 183.

4. For a study, see Marshall, *Enmity in Corinth,* 266–73.

5. Furnish, *II Corinthians,* 180.

6. See the section in the introduction entitled "The Geographical, Political, Social, and Economic Setting of Corinth" for insights into the importance of the patron-client relationships that existed in the Greco-Roman empire.

assistance from those in the area.[7] The New Testament documents also show they were used by the early disciples (see Acts 9:2; 15:25–27; 18:27; 22:5; Rom. 16:1–2; Philem. 1:1–25; and 3 John 1:7–8). Clearly Paul is not opposed to such letters, but he forcefully rejects the idea that they are needed to establish his credentials in the Church, even if they would demonstrate his respectful pedigree.[8]

3:2 ***Ye are our epistle, / You are our letter:*** The noun ἐπιστολή (*epistlolē*), "epistle, letter,"[9] is sometimes used in our source as a synonym for γράμμα (*gramma*), a letter.[10] In a more specific sense, however, each connotes a different type of written communication. A *gramma,* "letter," afforded the writer more latitude in development, subject matter, and expression than did a formal epistle. "A letter is usually occasional; that is, it is written in consequence of some circumstance which requires it to be dealt with promptly. The style of a letter depends largely on the occasion that calls it forth. It expresses the writer's views, sympathies, and interests. On the other hand, an epistle carries more authority, has a general aim, and targets a specific group of people. It is more formal like a public speech and lends itself to publication with the intent of more broad dissemination."[11] Paul's writings carry both elements but fall lightly into the category of an epistle, addressing as they do, by authority, specific issues with the intent that the instructions be published for others.[12]

---

7. Witherington, *Conflict and Community,* 377; William Baird, "Letters of Recommendation: A Study of II Cor 3:1–3," *Journal of Biblical Literature* 80 (1961): 166–72.

8. Martin, *2 Corinthians,* 191; Guthrie, *2 Corinthians,* 187. Though some have suggested that the bearers of this letter were such notables as Peter, James, or Apollos, this is clearly wrong given that they were known to the Corinthians and would, therefore, have needed no introduction. Witherington, *Conflict and Community,* 377. See also David I. Yoon, "Ancient Letters of Recommendation and 2 Corinthians 3.1–3: A Literary Analysis," *Journal of Greco-Roman Christianity and Judaism* 12 (2016): 45–72, who argues that Paul's associating himself with letters of recommendation does more than commend his ability and validity as an Apostle. Yoon shows that letters of recommendation in ancient times communicated a personal, vested commitment by *the recommender* in the one recommended. In this case, the recommender was Jesus and Paul's inference is that the Lord represents Paul and takes responsibility for him. By using this understanding, the Apostle cleverly bolstered his position and authority.

9. BDAG, 381.

10. BDAG, 205–6.

11. Ulrich Wilckens, "ἐπιστολὴ," in *TDNT,* 7:593.

12. Though Adolf Deissmann, *Light from the Ancient East: The New Testament Illustrated by Recently Discovered Texts of the Graeco-Roman World,* trans. Lionel R. M.

Paul's metaphorical use of the phrase ἡ ἐπιστολὴ ἡμῶν (*hē epistolē hymōn*), "our letter," emphasizes his recognition that the greatest proof of his authority and position as a trustworthy Apostle is the conversion of his readers.

written in our hearts: The verb ἐνγράφω (*engraphō*), found here as a perfect passive participle, means "to write down, inscribe,"[13] while the noun καρδία (*kardia*), "heart," shows the location of the writing. The imagery is important, for the term "heart" connotes the inner life of the person that directs thinking, volition, and emotion.[14] It is where the Spirit works (1:22) and spiritual illumination takes place (3:15–16; 4:6). In sum, what is there defines what the individual is.[15]

There is some debate as to whose heart Paul has in mind. Some ancient manuscripts have ὑμῶν (*hymōn*), "your," while others have ἡμῶν (*hēmōn*), "our."[16] It makes sense that Paul would say that the letter was written on his readers' hearts where it could be seen in their witness to the world. However, the context (and better manuscript tradition) argues for the letter to be in Paul and his companions' hearts such that "all men" could see the converting power that was in *them*.[17] With his use of the perfect tense of the participle, Paul shows that the letter written earlier clearly still remains to be read and known by all who will look.

known and read of all men / understood and read by everyone: The nature of the lives of the converts is public and bears witness to the power that Paul and his companions carry. The verb γινώσκω (*ginōskō*) means not only "to know" but also "to comprehend"[18] and suggests that others can see the power that Paul and his companions carry in the effect it has on the lives of the Saints. The verb ἀναγινώσκω (*anaginōskō*) means "to read" but carries the nuance of reading aloud,[19] and again, it highlights the public nature

---

Strachan (Grand Rapids, Mich.: Baker Book House, 1978), 233–45, insisted Paul's communications were by letters, MM, 246, notes that more recent studies of the term *epistolē* "serve as a needed corrective on the over-emphasis of Deissmann."

13. BDAG, 270–71.

14. BDAG, 508. That Paul uses the imagery of the heart eleven times (1:22; 2:4; 3:2–4, 15; 4:6; 5:12; 6:11; 7:3; 8:16; 9:7) shows how important this symbol was to him.

15. For studies, see *NID*, 2:622–27; and Johannes Behm, "καρδία," in *TDNT*, 3:605–14.

16. Metzger, *Textual Commentary*, 509.

17. Baird, "Letters of Recommendation," 169–70, shows that such letters were about the bearer. In that light, "our" makes the best sense.

18. BDAG, 199–201.

19. BDAG, 60.

of the power the Apostle and his colleagues carry. Both verbs, as found here, are in the form of present passive participles and are cognates, but the aspect of the tense is continuous into the present, suggesting the ongoing nature of the power of the gospel as preached by Paul and the others. The force of the grammar is important here. The perfect participle of ἐνγράφω (*engraphō*) has as its subject the noun ἐπιστολή (*epistolē*), and the construction emphasizes the ongoing openness of the Apostle's ministry played out on the Corinthian stage for all to see.[20]

3:3 ***Forasmuch as ye are manifestly declared to be the epistle of Christ / You clearly show that you are Christ's letter:*** The conjunction ὅτι (*hoti*), "that," signals to the reader that what Paul says in this verse explains or clarifies what he said in the former one. The verb φανερόω (*phaneroō*), "to show, disclose, be manifest," is found here as a present passive participle but carries an intransitive sense of showing something. It carries the nuance of doing so clearly, with some detail, and publicly.[21] It further suggests that what is made known is the external but nevertheless true revelation of the thing, in this case the recommending force of the disciples' lives.[22] The present tense of the participle shows that the process of revelation is continuing to happen at this very moment.

In the phrase ἐπιστολὴ Χριστοῦ (*epistolē Christou*), "epistle of Christ," the genitive case of the noun can be taken as objective and thereby denote a letter about the Savior. However, given the context, it is more likely a genitive of production, showing that Jesus is the one who wrote the letter.[23] It, therefore, belongs to him. Paul does not say just how these Saints "clearly show" that they are Christ's letter, but it is likely because of the kind of lives they are living as converts.

ministered by us / delivered by us: The verb διακονέω (*diakoneō*) denotes the performance of a service very often performed by a go-between or

---

20. Guthrie, *Second Corinthians,* 189 with n. 16. Baird, "Letters of Recommendation," 166–72, has shown that it was customary for the authors of the recommendation to spend considerable time referring to themselves.

21. BDAG, 1048; Louw-Nida, §28:36.

22. The word stands in contrast to ἀποκαλύπτω (*apokalyptō*), "revelation," which is an internal disclosure to the believing individual. Its focus is on the information revealed. This unveiling precedes and produces the *φανερόω* (*phaneroō*), "public manifestation," and focuses on the persons to whom the information comes. Rudolph Bultmann and Dieter Lührmann, "φανερόω," in *TDNT,* 9:3–6.

23. Wallace: *Greek Grammar,* 104–5.

agent.[24] When a person is acting in an official capacity, the best understanding of the word is "to minister," but in keeping with the metaphor of a letter, the Apostle acts in the capacity of a postman whose task is to deliver the letter composed and sent by the Savior.[25] Without the service of the Apostle and the other missionaries, the letter would remain ever undelivered and therefore unknown.

written not with ink: The verb ἐνγράφω (*engraphō*), found here again (as in 2:3) as a perfect passive participle, means "to write down, inscribe."[26] Paul uses it as a metaphor to represent the Saints who are the written letter that he so dearly loves and serves. The noun μέλαν (*melan*), "ink," refers to a product made of soot and gum that, when applied with a reed pen, left readable pigment on a surface.[27] By the use of the negative particle οὐ (*ou*), "not," Paul shows he is referring to conventional writing that is transitory and temporal.[28]

but with the Spirit of the living God / but by the Spirit of the Living God: With this phrase, Paul brings the final element, namely the one he serves, into play. It is because of the living and therefore active Spirit of the Father that Paul feels such a deep commitment to and love for these people. It is the Spirit that the Father uses as his primary means or instrument in producing results.[29]

not in tables of stone / not on stone tablets: The phrase πλαξὶν λιθίναις (*plaxin lithinais*), "stone tablets," echoes the material on which God

---

24. BDAG, 229–30. It also carries the nuance of acts "of a humble or menial nature." See Louw-Nida, §35.19, 37.

25. On the translation of διακονέω (*diakoneō*) as "to deliver a message," see Josephus, *Antiquities of the Jews* 6.13.6 §298. For a study, see John N. Collins, *Diakonia: Reinterpreting the Ancient Sources* (New York: Oxford University Press, 1990), who shows that the word connotes primarily doing the bidding of another and more specifically performing an errand or conveying a message.

26. BDAG, 270–71. For a study of the writing process and material used in the first century AD, see Hans-Josef Klauck, *Ancient Letters and the New Testament: A Guide to Context and Exegesis,* trans. Daniel P. Bailey (Waco, Tex.: Baylor University Press, 2006), 44–54.

27. Louw-Nida, §6:57.

28. The particle οὐ (*ou*), "not," negates the noun, not the participle; thus, the wrong translation would be "not written with ink." See Nigel Turner, *A Grammar of New Testament Greek,* vol. 3, *Syntax,* ed. James Hope Moulton (Edinburgh: T. & T. Clark, 1963), 285–87.

29. The workings of the Spirit are important in Paul's theology. He uses the term πνεῦμα (*peneuma*) seventeen times in this letter alone. In this verse, it is the living or life-producing nature of the Spirit that he emphasizes, paralleling the imagery of the "living" God he uses in 6:16.

inscribed the law of Moses (see LXX Ex. 31:18). Paul seems to be using the imagery to compare or contrast what he is saying with the old covenant.

but in fleshy tables of the heart / but on tablets of human hearts: The adjective σάρκινος (*sarkinos*), "fleshly, material, human," though sometimes associated with that which is worldly and even sinful, in this context denotes that which belongs to the physical world or human sphere.[30] On the meaning of καρδία (*kardia*), "heart," see 3:2 above. That God writes on the human heart suggests that this mortal and even fallen organ can be transformed into the continuous bearer of God's laws (compare Jer. 31:31–33 and Ezek. 11:19; 36:26–27).

Analysis and Summary

The question at issue here is what constitutes a legitimate Christian ministry. What does it mean to "speak in Christ before God as men of pure motive, as men of God" (2:17, NR)? What is at stake is Paul's legitimacy as an Apostle but, more broadly, that of apostolic authority in general. Who has the right to preside over the Church? In his defense, what Paul does here is reestablish the rules of presidency and thereby show who is able to govern with presiding and thereby legitimate authority. Paul insists on a divine, not human, criterion that is dependent not on the judgment of the branches but on the authority of the risen Lord, the power of the Spirit, and the discernment it brings.[31] To push his point, at places throughout the rest of the epistle, he admits to the physical weaknesses his adversaries accuse him of but then shows that such weaknesses do not disqualify his apostolic authority. Rather that authority is confirmed by the profound spiritual change in the hearts of his converts (3:2). Not backing away from this point, Paul is not a bit afraid of either commending himself and his companions or boasting about what he, through divine help, has been able to do.[32] The text clearly shows that Paul "does not regard his own person as anything special."[33]

He unabashedly admits that he is once again commending himself but seems to be asking why he has to go through the whole process once more

---

30. Louw-Nida, §§26.8; 41.42; 79.4; BDAG, 914.

31. Scott Hafemann, "'Self-Commendation' and Apostolic Legitimacy in 2 Corinthians: A Pauline Dialectic?," *New Testament Studies* 36, no. 1 (January 1990): 66.

32. Guthrie, *2 Corinthians,* 180–81; see also Linda L. Belleville, "A Letter of Apologetic Self-Commendation: 2 Corinthians 1:8–7:16," *Novum Testamentum* 31, no. 2 (1989): 142–63.

33. Seifrid, *Second Letter,* 111.

since he had already cleared that hurdle without the need for letters of reference (3:1). It is little wonder that he felt put out. He was, after all, their spiritual father—God's appointed Apostle—who brought them the word of salvation (1 Cor. 4:14–15). His magnanimity is shown by his willingness to re-present his case in order to reestablish their mutual trust. As he will show, his appeal to them is that of an Apostle who can commend himself "by his conscience and transparency of life and heart (4:1–2; 5:11–13; 6:4). Paul's 'self-commendation' is paradoxical . . . because it is not a *self*-commendation but the commendation of the Gospel and of the work of God that takes place in him. He thus will commend himself in everything that the Corinthians do not expect or seek: in perseverance, in afflictions, in experiences of need and the suffering of distress (6:4–10)."[34]

Part of what drives him is his detractors' castigation of his authority and teachings. They apparently do so on the basis of their own supposed authority bolstered by letters of recommendation. Just who produced these letters is unknown, but they seem to have been derived from a branch or branches that the Corinthian Saints held in respect. It would have been easy for short-time members to give deference to those who were long-time ones. Since the oldest branches of the Church were in the eastern Mediterranean, persons coming from those branches would have been met with great respect. Since it was these very branches that were having the most difficulty in transitioning from the old covenant to the new, it is not surprising that the issue was transplanted to the west. Thus, the place of the law of Moses within Christianity was central to many of the theological difficulties the western Church faced.[35]

A problem with these letters of endorsement is that one branch might unknowingly perpetuate false doctrine innocent of any deception. "One community could easily perpetuate a problem by endorsing a missionary who in turn passed on peculiar doctrinal teachings."[36] As Elder McConkie noted, "It is much the same today where congregations of new converts are concerned. These new church members come from the sects of Christendom into the living kingdom of power and glory. Their baptism does not automatically cause them to forget all they have known and believed and perhaps taught. In the very nature of things and almost without being aware of it, some of them still retain fragments of those sectarian vagaries

34. Seifrid, *Second Letter,* 100.
35. Wayment, *From Persecutor to Apostle,* 178–80.
36. Wayment, *From Persecutor to Apostle,* 179.

inherited from their fathers."[37] If Church authorities were unable to correct such doctrines, as seems to have been the case with the early Church, then false teachings could become the norm, forcing out the true. Paul fought hard against this possibility.

In this portion of his epistle, he produces his own letter of recommendation (3:2). It is his converts who he feels are the best evidence of his power and truthfulness as an Apostle of Christ. His words express his high admiration for and also the importance of the truly converted. Their love and good works not only demonstrate the power of the gospel but also validate the integrity of the Apostle. Thus, the lives of the disciples commend the Apostle more than any mere letter, no matter by what authority it may have been written. By noting that the letter is inscribed (ἐνγράφω, *engraphō*) on "our hearts," Paul expresses the closeness, even intimacy, that he and his companions feel toward these Saints.[38] The imagery infers that he carries his love for these people everywhere he goes.[39]

Paul further notes that, though the letter is written on his heart, it is not hidden there. He demonstrates it so that it is known and read by everyone who is willing to give it a glance. The apostolic power of the ministry is both ongoing and transparent for all not only to see but also to enjoy if they will. Since letters were commonly read aloud, the imagery suggests the public nature of Paul's ministry. Nothing is hidden and all is made known, and thus the gospel can be understood for what it truly is.[40]

Paul is certain that, for those who will see, the lives of his converts are the only letters of recommendation that he needs. The living God has written, as it were, their names on Paul's heart by the power of his Spirit (3:3). However, "given the disloyalty, fickleness, and waywardness evident within the messianic community in Corinth," his assertion is quite remarkable.[41] Nonetheless, it seems fully genuine. God's Spirit has moved upon him to such an extent that he has a deep-felt love for these people and wants only the best for them even if it means they must endure a sound scolding.[42]

---

37. *DNTC,* 2:414.

38. Guthrie, *2 Corinthians,* 188.

39. Matera, *II Corinthians,* 77.

40. Guthrie, *Second Corinthians,* 189.

41. Barnett, *Second Epistle,* 164.

42. The author of Hebrews was well aware that it was a godlike attribute, for even God rebukes his children when necessary (Heb. 12:5). We are reminded of the sermons recorded

This medium stands in contrast to the law of Moses, which was written on tablets of stone and unfortunately brought no life to those who would not internalize it. The new law is at its seat internal and life changing. Paul's imagery echoes that of Jeremiah 31:31–33, in which the prophet looked to a day when the Lord would "make a new covenant with the house of Israel, and with the house of Judah: Not according to the covenant that I made with their fathers. . . . But this *shall be* the covenant that I will make with the house of Israel; After those days, saith the Lord, I will put my law in their inward parts, and write it in their hearts; and will be their God, and they shall be my people." In Paul's case, it is not God's laws but the names of the converts that are written on the hearts of the missionaries. "Christ has done an authentic, spiritual work in the Corinthians, yet in Paul as well. For, as the Spirit has worked through him to minister to the Corinthians, the Spirit has also worked on Paul, fostering a ministry of concern, compassion, and commitment toward them. Paul is not an opportunist ministering for his own profit (2:17), nor a hireling merely fulfilling an assigned drudgery. He is a called, deeply committed minister of Jesus Christ, who loves Christ's church."[43]

The Saints are the product of the work of Christ, who alone has made them a fit and authentic letter of recommendation. Even so, the missionaries have played a part for they are the ones who prepared the letter.[44] The words Paul uses, "having been prepared by us" (διακονηθεῖσα ὑφ' ἡμῶν, *diakonētheisa hyph' hēmōn*), keep the image of a letter before his readers and suggest that the missionaries' role is that of an amanuensis, or secretary.

God is the author of the human letter. The instrument he uses to write it is his living Holy Spirit.[45] Through the work of the Spirit, the heart is changed—one might even say, exchanged. According to Ezekiel 11:19, God will give to believers a heart that is undivided. Indeed, as he promises, he "will put a new spirit in them, and will remove the heart of stone from their bodies and give them a heart of flesh" (our translation; compare Ezek.

---

in Jacob 2–3 and Alma 5, which contain very strong condemnations of the actions of quite a number of individuals but were delivered out of love and concern for them.

43. Guthrie, *Second Corinthians,* 189.

44. For Paul, the service (διακονία, *diakonia*) of the missionaries expressed the whole of the salvation process, that is, God's salvific service through Christ to all humankind. *NID,* 1:704.

45. The imagery does not suggest that Paul has the operation of the Holy Ghost directly in mind here, but rather the influence of God's holy spirit. See D&C 88:14–16.

36:26–27). This spiritual transplantation produces the true Saint, whose changed life then becomes the letter of recommendation *sine qui non* for apostolic authority.

God Made Us Capable (3:4–6)

Greek Text

4 Πεποίθησιν δὲ τοιαύτην ἔχομεν διὰ τοῦ Χριστοῦ πρὸς τὸν θεόν. 5 οὐχ ὅτι ἀφ'
ἑαυτῶν ἱκανοί ἐσμεν λογίσασθαί τι ὡς ἐξ αὐτῶν, ἀλλ' ἡ ἱκανότης ἡμῶν ἐκ τοῦ θεοῦ,
6 ὃς καὶ ἱκάνωσεν ἡμᾶς διακόνους καινῆς διαθήκης, οὐ γράμματος ἀλλὰ πνεύματος, τὸ γὰρ γράμμα ἀποκτέννει, τὸ δὲ πνεῦμα ζῳοποιεῖ. [SBLGNT]

King James Version

4 And such trust have we through Christ to God-ward: 5 Not that we are sufficient of ourselves to think any thing as of ourselves; but our sufficiency is of God; 6 Who also hath made us able ministers of the new testament; not of the letter, but of the spirit: for the letter killeth, but the spirit giveth life.

New Rendition

4 Now we have such confidence through Christ toward God. 5 Not that we of ourselves are capable of thinking that anything came from ourselves. On the contrary, our competence comes from God, 6 who indeed made us capable ministers of a new covenant, not of the letter but of the Spirit, because the letter kills, but the Spirit gives life.

Translation Notes and Comments

3:4 ***And such trust have we through Christ to God-ward / Now we have such confidence through Christ toward God:*** The noun πεποίθησις (*pepoithēsis*), "confidence," denotes a state of certainty about a thing so as to rely on it fully and completely. Here it carries the nuance of the assurance of an expected positive outcome.[46] With the demonstrative adjective τοιοῦτος (*toioutos*), "such," the phrase "such confidence" points back to the trust Paul has in both the authority with and the purity in which he and his companions preached the gospel to the Corinthian Saints (2:17). He assures his readers that his confidence comes διὰ Χριστοῦ (*dia Christou*), "through

46. BDAG, 796; Louw-Nida, §31.82.

Christ," who is the active agent.[47] The implication is that his authority and ministry are divinely anchored. But he goes a step further. His confidence is also πρὸς τὸν θεόν (*pros ton theon*), "toward God," where the preposition πρός (*pros*) marks an action directed to or done with reference to or with regard to someone, in this case, God.[48]

The JST changes the verse to read, "such trust we have through Christ toward God," thus emphasizing that it is only through Christ that one comes to God (John 14:6; D&C 132:12).

3:5 ***Not that we are sufficient of ourselves to think any thing as of ourselves / Not that we of ourselves are capable of thinking that anything came from ourselves:*** This verse stresses and expands the point Paul made in the one above. The adjective ἱκανός (*hikanos*), "capable," denotes that which is proficient in meeting a standard, thus "competent, sufficient, capable, qualified."[49] The verb λογίζομαι (*logizomai*) means to think about or believe in something but carries the nuance of thinking carefully about the thing believed in.[50] The phrase ἀφ' ἑαυτῶν (*aph' heautōn*), "of ourselves," stands parallel to the phrase ἐξ ἑαυτῶν (*ex heautōn*), "from ourselves," and together they stress Paul's point. The first phrase negates any idea that Paul and his companions see themselves as the *cause* of their competence in the gospel.[51] The second phrase negates any idea that they see themselves as the ultimate source of "anything" (τι, *ti*)[52] that has made their mission successful.[53] The whole phrase stresses the idea that Paul and his companions do not have even a shadow of belief that they are the cause of all the good that has come about.

but our sufficiency is of God / On the contrary, our competence comes from God: Again, Paul uses the noun ἱκανότης (*hikanotēs*), "competence," to express his understanding of the source of his power or ability. The noun denotes a "state of being qualified or adequate for something," meaning that the thing is in need of nothing more.[54] By using the adjective, the Apostle bears his heartfelt understanding that the source of his abilities is

---

47. In the present context, διά (*dia*) plus the genitive communicates agency—that is, "by" or "through." BDAG, 225; Guthrie, *2 Corinthians,* 194 n. 26.

48. Guthrie, *2 Corinthians,* 194; BDAG, 875.

49. BDAG, 472.

50. BDAG, 597–98.

51. One nuance of the preposition ἀπό (*apo*) is "cause, means, or outcome." BDAG, 106.

52. Some nuances of the preposition ἐκ (*ek*) denote "origin, cause, motive, reason." BDAG, 296.

53. Guthrie, *2 Corinthians,* 196.

54. BDAG, 473; Karl Heinrich Rengstorf, "ἱκανος, ἱκανότης, ἱκανόω," in *TDNT,* 3:293–96.

God given. Underlying it stands another message—the source of his apostolic authority and doctrine is also divinely derived. His words express his heartfelt understanding that he could never, on his own, have come up with anything so wonderful and beautiful as the gospel message or, for that matter, even have understood it. Further, it was God who revealed Christ to the Apostle and from whom Paul derived his authority.[55]

3:6 ***Who also hath made us able ministers of the new testament / who indeed made us capable ministers of a new covenant:*** The verb ἱκανόω (*hikanoō*) means "to cause to be capable or adequate" and suggests the idea of the empowerment of a person or the authorization of an action.[56] The noun διάκονος (*diakonos*), "minister, servant,"[57] in Paul's thought, refers specifically to a Christian minister, a person, whether male or female, empowered to do God's saving work through direct service. The idea came from Christ himself, who insisted that he and those who followed his way were to serve others in their quest for eternal life (Mark 9:35; 10:45; Luke 22:26–27). The idea behind the word is one of direct involvement. Such personal action broke with Jewish norms, where one's social responsibility rested on giving alms that others ministered (compare Luke 10:30–35). In the general society, lowly service was viewed as too menial and well below the dignity of a free person (compare Luke 7:44–46). Paul's teachings counter this idea and show Christian service as involving the entire community in the whole of the salvation process but under the direction of apostolic authority.[58]

The phrase καινῆς διαθήκης (*kainēs diathēkēs*), "new covenant," circumscribes the whole process. The noun διαθήκη (*diathēkē*), "covenant," refers to an agreement that is made by one person's initiative and not a compact derived from the work of two or more persons.[59] In this case, it is God alone who sets the conditions. The recipients have the right to choose whether or not to enter into the covenant, but they have no authority to negotiate terms or to modify the agreement in any way. It is an all-or-nothing deal.

---

55. R. V. G. Tasker, *The Second Epistle of Paul to the Corinthians: An Introduction and Commentary* (Grand Rapids, Mich.: Wm. B. Eerdmans, 1958), 60.

56. BDAG, 473; Louw-Nida, §75.3; Karl Heinrich Rengstorf, "ἱκανός, ἱκαντόης, ἱκανόω," in *TDNT,* 3:293–96.

57. BDAG, 230–31.

58. *NID,* 1:701–5.

59. It can also refer to "testament or will," that is, a document that transfers the property of a deceased person to a living one. Louw-Nida, §57.124. Context shows that this nuance does not work here. Neither does the idea that Paul is referring to the New Testament since such did not exist in Paul's day.

The adjective καινός (*kainos*), "new," refers not just to what has been in existence for a relatively short time but, more especially in the present context, to "that which is recent in contrast" to that which has existed for a long time and, due to its age, is both obsolete and inferior in its nature. Thus, "the new is superior in kind" and established for the purpose of replacing the old.[60] The restored and fully implemented gospel is so superior to the law of Moses. Though designed to bring people to Christ, the law of Moses served only as a type or shadow of things to come with no power in and of itself to actually save anyone (Col. 2:16–17; Heb. 8:5; 10:1; 2 Ne. 11:4; Mosiah 3:15; 13:27–28). The new covenant, based on the Savior's Atonement, not only fulfilled the old covenant but brought the life it could not.[61]

not of the letter, but of the spirit / not of the letter but of the Spirit: The noun γράμμα (*gramma*), "letter," can refer to a single unit in an alphabet, a correspondence or document, or even an entire book.[62] The word does not carry, as is often supposed, the nuance of reading something too literally or narrowly. In the present context, it most likely refers to the whole of the Mosaic law. The noun πνεῦμα (*pneuma*), "spirit," can refer to the spirit of an individual, to an unembodied being, or as is the case here, to the Holy Spirit of God (see 3:3).[63] Paul's statement shows that the "Spirit" stands in contrast to the "letter" of the law.[64] Thus, the term γραμμα (*gramma*), "letter," summarizes the whole of the old covenant while πνεῦμα (*spirit*) does the same for the new. That being the case, the term "letter" refers to that which is obsolete, stagnant, and lifeless, while "the Spirit" refers to that which is new, necessary, and life giving.

for the letter killeth, but the spirit giveth life / because the letter kills, but the Spirit gives life: With the conjunction γάρ (*gar*), "for, because," Paul

60. BDAG, 496–97. For an in-depth study, see Matthew Barrett, "What Is So New about the New Covenant? Exploring the Contours of Paul's New Covenant Theology in 2 Corinthians 3," *Southern Baptist Journal of Theology* 19, no. 3 (Fall 2015): 61–96, http://equip.sbts.edu/publications/journals/journal-of-theology/what-is-so-new-about-the-new-covenant-exploring-the-contours-of-pauls-new-covenant-theology-in-2-corinthians-3/.

61. Robert J. Matthews, *A Bible! A Bible!* (Salt Lake City: Bookcraft, 1990), 52–53.

62. BDAG, 205–6.

63. BDAG, 832–36.

64. LSJ, 358 notes that, in singular, γράμμα (*gramma*) refers to the law of Moses, which stands in opposition to the Spirit of God. A number of early Christians interpreted the term "letter" as referring to a too-literalist reading of any scriptural text while "the Spirit" referred to discerning its true intent. To miss the intent could be deadly. Such an interpretation, however, does not square with what Paul is teaching here. Gottlob Schenk, "γράμμα," in *TDNT,* 1:764–69.

signals he is going to explain why he ministers the new covenant and forsakes the old. The verb ἀποκτείνω (*apokteinō*), "to kill," denotes depriving something of life either by killing or eliminating it.[65] In this case the reference is to spiritual life. The verb ζωοποιέω (*zōopoieō*) means "to make alive" and, when associated with God, carries the transcendent sense of having a higher quality of spiritual life or enlivening.[66]

Because it is vague, this phrase has generated three main schools of thought. For many in the early Christian movement, the term "letter" pointed to a too-literal reading of a scriptural text, while "the spirit" referred to a discernment of the true meaning that stood behind it. By the time of the Reformation, theologians interpreted the phrase as showing that a radical dualism existed between the old and new covenants. The former produced condemnation and death while the latter brought justification and life. This view saw the old law as abrogated and completely replaced by the new as the means of salvation. Between these two views were those who saw the old and new covenants not as in radical opposition but as belonging to a continuum. This school viewed the tension set up in 3:6 as "a contrast between those who attempted to keep the law apart from the work the Spirit" and those who accepted and relied upon it. These theologians insisted that the law could be fulfilled only with the help of the Spirit.[67]

Analysis and Summary

To counter any suggestion that what the Apostle has said in this section of his letter (2:14–3:3) shows an arrogance on his part (after all, he is claiming a partnership with God), the Apostle explains the source and basis of his confidence (πεποίθησις, *pepoithēsis*) and competence (ἱκανότης, *ikanotēs*). He gives an unflinching testimony that the whole of his ministry relies on and is derived from Christ (3:4). Christ is the very basis of Paul's confidence in all that the Apostle does and says. Further, the Lord gives the enabling power that Paul uses to push forward the work. However, though the Savior is the immediate agent working with the Apostle, there is one greater who stands behind the Lord and of whom Paul is constantly aware. This is the Father. That Paul's affirmation that everything he does is directed "toward God" (πρὸς τὸν θεόν, *pros ton theon*) stresses his acute

65. BDAG, 114.

66. BDAG, 431–32. For a detailed study of the spirit/letter antithesis, see James D. G. Dunn, "'The Letter Kills, but the Spirit Gives Life' (2 Cor. 3:6)," *Pneuma* 35, no. 2 (2013): 163–79.

67. Guthrie, *2 Corinthians,* 198; for a study, see Guthrie, *2 Corinthians,* 198–99.

awareness that he must act according to the Father's will. There is also here a tacit message to his detractors concerning the source and authenticity of his ministry.[68]

In 3:5, Paul answers the rhetorical question he asked in 2:16, "And who is qualified for these things?" As stated in the Translation Notes there, the question is a good one, and the Apostle's reflections captured in 3:1–3 have only served to accentuate its importance. Paul's answer to the question given in 3:3–4 is emphatic: only those whom God qualifies.[69] Paul's point is that, being aware of this qualification, neither he nor his companions would or could even think that they were somehow responsible for their successes. Further, his statement that all he does is directed "toward God" (πρὸς τὸν θεόν, *pros ton theon,* 3:4) reveals his awareness of his own lack of sufficiency in carrying out the work of the all-sufficient Father. The effect on Paul is a deeply felt humility.[70] This attitude placed him in direct contrast with the self-aggrandizing and self-competent detractors that were making a show among the Corinthian Saints.[71] His heartfelt attitude, however, does not leave him dubious about his ministry and the authority that stands behind it. Due to his call and station as an Apostle of the Savior, he has full confidence (πεποίθησις, *pepoithēsis*) that his qualifications (ἱκανότης, *hikanotēs*) are God derived, and from this he will not back down even in the face of strong opposition.

Paul and his party, unlike his detractors, are "new-covenant ministers." In 3:6, he confesses to his readers that of himself he is not adequate for such a ministry, but he and his companions have been made so (ἱκανόω, *hikanoō*) by God. Thus, despite their inadequacy, they have both a God-given assignment and the necessary authority to perform that task. Paul's continual use of the word "minister" (διάκονος, *diakonos*), or its cognates, throughout the epistle helps him stress this point.[72] The word in its present context carries the idea of official service performed by a representative

68. Guthrie, *2 Corinthians,* 194–95.

69. Furnish, *II Corinthians,* 196–97.

70. Jehovah's title אֵל שַׁדַּי (*'el šadday*) focuses attention on his full self-sufficiency. In this regard, see the use of ἱκανός (*hikanos*) in LXX Ruth 1:20; LXX Job 21:15; 31:2; 40:2; and LXX Ezek. 1:24. Martin, *2 Corinthians,* 193. Paul's Jewish Christian readers would have likely resonated with his point since many in Judaism confessed God to be the only truly sufficient One. For example, see Philo, *Allegorical Interpretation* 1.44.

71. Guthrie, *2 Corinthians,* 195.

72. In 2 Cor., Paul uses the noun διάκονος (*diakonos*) five times (3:6; 6:4; 11:15 [twice], 23), the term διακονία (*diakonia*) twelve times (3:7–9 [four times]; 4:1; 5:18; 6:3; 8:4; 9:1, 12–13; 11:8), and the verb διακονέω (*diakoneō*) three times (3:3; 8:19–20).

of the Lord. This service is based on the new, not the old, covenant.[73] The focus of the word is on the service performed, not on the social relationship between the person being served and the one doing the service.[74] Paul seems to have used it to define the entire work encapsulated in the new covenant. It carries "the special quality of indicating very personally the service rendered to another" that is often generated by love.[75]

By stressing the need for service, Paul is pushing, if not breaking, social norms. Among the Greeks, service carried little dignity. Many of the leisure class felt that happiness could not be found in any kind of menial work, no matter whom or how one served.[76] Thus, in that culture, any concrete obligation to one's neighbor hardly existed. Even among many of the Jews at the time, the unconditional command to love and serve others had dissolved into meaninglessness. "Service was less and less understood as sacrifice for others and more and more as a work of merit before God. Finally, there arose in Judaism the idea . . . not to accord [even] service at table, to the unworthy."[77] Such an exclusivist and unloving attitude ran contrary to the tenets of the new covenant. The doctrine of the Savior reached back to the Old Testament command that God's people love and serve one another, and Jesus, the undisputed master of all, set the example by being the servant of all (Luke 22:24–27). This was the very heart of the new covenant.

This new covenant, as Paul knew (see 1 Cor. 11:23–28), had as its backdrop the Last Supper. There the Savior held up a cup of wine and said, "This cup is the new covenant established by my blood, which is shed for you" (Luke 22:20, our translation; compare 1 Cor. 11:25).[78] His words echo those of Jeremiah, who prophesied of the day when Jehovah would establish a "new covenant" with the house of Israel. At that time, the Lord promised he would "put [his] laws into their mind, and write them upon their hearts; and [he would] be to them a God and they [would be his] people" (LXX Jer. 38:31–33; Jer. 31:33, KJV). Both scriptures combine to define the nature of the Christian ministry. Its objective is bringing people under the transforming

73. Guthrie, *2 Corinthians,* 197.

74. The term δοῦλος (*doulos*), "slave," focuses on the interpersonal relationship between the person served and serving. For an extended study, see Karl Heinrich Rengstorf, "δοῦλος, σύνδουλος, δοῦλη, δουλεύω, δουλεία," in *TDNT,* 2:261–80.

75. Hermann W. Beyer, "διάκονος," in *TDNT,* 2:81.

76. Plato, *Gorgias* 491e.

77. Beyer, "διάκονς," in *TDNT,* 1:83.

78. The Greek phrase ἐν τῷ αἵματί μου (*en tō haimati mou*), literally "in [or though] the blood of me," points to the means by which the new covenant was established.

power of the new covenant established and empowered by the death and Resurrection of the Lord.

Paul's major concern is how God's will comes to be fulfilled in the life of the Saint. He sees no value in the "letter" (γράμμα, *gramma*) of the law. In the Apostle's context, the noun "letter" refers exclusively to that which had been written. In its most strict definition, it denotes the Decalogue, but Paul apparently uses it to include the whole of the Mosaic writings along with the traditions that developed out of them.

In 3:6, Paul sets up an antithesis between the old "letter" and the "Spirit" as revealed through the new covenant. This covenant, unlike the old, is not bound by what is merely written or has become traditional but by the Spirit. Thus, the Apostle is not comparing a literal or legalistic reading of the Old Testament to a more nuanced spiritual one. His issue is not with the Old Testament itself but with the old *Mosaic covenant,* especially, as 3:7–11 show, with that portion that was written in stone, most notably the Ten Commandments.[79]

In Paul's writings, do the Spirit and the Mosaic law stand in unconditional antithesis? The Apostle's exposition on this subject is not as clear as we would like. He does believe that the law of Moses was given by God and was holy and good (1 Tim. 1:8). The Apostle, however, to make his point, reduces the whole of the law to the single word "letter" (γράμμα, *gramma*), the term referring exclusively to that which had been written of old. From Paul's point of view, because the law was, from the beginning, merely words inscribed on stone, it always lacked the ability to give spiritual life; it simply did not have the power to transform the soul from that of the natural man to that of a Saint (1 Cor. 2:14; compare Mosiah 3:19).[80] This is the Apostle's main point. As a former Pharisee (Acts 26:5), he well knew "the religion of the Synagogue" with its emphasis on the scriptures. He also knew, even more fully, its total futility in bringing one to righteousness and

79. Witherington, *Conflict and Community,* 379.

80. Paul's conversion experience colored everything that he taught. He had lived the law with unusual diligence, but it did not bring him to know God or to greater righteousness (Acts 9:1–5). As the Book of Mormon asks, so far as things of God are concerned, "what natural man is there that knoweth these things?" and then answers, "there is none that knoweth these things, save it be the penitent. Yea, he that repenteth and exerciseth faith, and bringeth forth good works, and prayeth continually without ceasing—unto such it is given to know the mysteries of God" (Alma 26:21–22). Paul initially lacked both penitence and faith. The shock of the theophany generated both, and revelation followed.

into full service to God.[81] The Hebrew scriptures themselves give ample evidence that Israel's history during and after the Mosaic period was one of disaster following disaster. As biblical history clearly showed, the old law was fully ineffective in nature. Its problem was that it had no life, no means in and of itself of transforming the heart. In sum, the Hebrew scriptures themselves presented clear and incontrovertible proof that the words of the law never lifted off the stone tablets on which they had been written, and because of that, they remained ineffective for all.

From the text itself, Paul seems to have drawn his conclusion that "the letter kills," because it lacks any kind of saving power. But how does he justify that statement? He is, admittedly, speaking in hyperbole to make his point. It is important to note that Paul does not ascribe the killing to a false use of the Old Testament or to a too-literal reading of the text. It is the nature of the "letter" itself—the whole law—wherein the problem lies.[82] The law kills in two ways. The first is due to its inability to be nothing more than writing on stone tablets with no power to give help to its recipients.[83] The second is that it reveals what constitutes sin, namely disobedience to any point of the law. In revealing how to sin without any ability to help people resist it, it ends up being the means of their spiritual death. The Book of Mormon concurs. It asks the questions "How could [a person] sin if there was no law? How could there be a law save there was a punishment?" and then answers, "Now, there was a punishment affixed, and a just law given," and the consequence was the "remorse of conscience unto man. . . . [I]f there was no law given against sin men would not be afraid to sin. And if there was no law given, if men sinned what could justice do, or mercy either, for they would have no claim upon the creature?" (Alma 42:17–21). Thus, the law made sin possible, and as Paul knew full well, "the wages of sin is death" (Rom. 6:23), and further, "all have sinned, and come short of the glory of God" (Rom. 3:23). But there is hope, for "the gift

81. Note John 5:39–47, where the pharisaical pursuit of understanding the scriptures brought them neither to love God nor to recognize his Son.

82. Hebrews 7:18–19 also testifies to the ineffectiveness of the law. For a study, see Richard D. Draper and Michael D. Rhodes, *Epistle to the Hebrews* (Provo, Utah: BYU Studies, 2019), 393–95, 403–4.

83. According to JST Ex. 34:1–3, the original covenant between God and Israel did contain the fullness of the gospel and the authority of the higher Priesthood. These, however, were taken away due to Israel's immature and weak spiritual condition and replaced with a preparatory gospel and lesser priesthood. See D&C 84:23–26 and Mosiah 3:14–15; 13:29–30.

of God is eternal life," but it comes only "through Jesus Christ our Lord" (Rom. 6:23), not from the law.

Thus, the ineffectiveness of the old law is, as Paul makes clear, done away in Christ. To countermand the weakness of the old covenant, God established the new one. As a result, the Saints simply do not need that law anymore because they are led by the Spirit which the Savior gives. That is not to say that the Savior did away with law. He did not. Instead he gave a new and living law dictated by the Spirit. This holy power writes the conditions and statutes governing the new covenant on the heart of the Saint. In doing so, it brings with it a transformation of the soul more in keeping with God's holiness. Paul derives his position from his understanding of LXX Jeremiah 38:33 (Jer. 31:33, KJV). The prophet told of the coming day when God would write his law on the hearts of his people, and Paul could see that that promise was now being fulfilled. The agent executing the new covenant is the Spirit. In distinction to the dead "letter," it alone can make a person more alive by three means: first, by revealing the content of the new covenant; second, by transforming the heart to accept the law; and third, by giving assisting power so that the person can live the law. It is this new covenant, not the old one, that Paul and his colleagues minister.

In sum, Paul's "comparison here has more to do with *contrasting approaches to ministry* and the *outcomes of those ministries,* rather than with successive dispensations of the old covenant over against the new covenant. It is the new covenant that makes authentic Christian ministry possible, powerful, and productive (3:3, 6). The contrast in 2 Cor. 3 is not *primarily* with the old covenant per se but with the ongoing attempt to minister apart from the work of the Spirit and through a veil that lies over people's hearts (3:14–15). The 'letter,' then, refers to an attempt to minister or engage the Scriptures apart from the new-covenant work of the Spirit. That form of ministry 'kills' just as it did in the old-covenant era."[84]

84. Guthrie, *2 Corinthians,* 199–200, italics in original.

The Glory of the New Covenant (3:7–11)

Greek Text

7 Εἰ δὲ ἡ διακονία τοῦ θανάτου ἐν γράμμασιν ἐντετυπωμένη λίθοις ἐγενήθη ἐν
δόξῃ, ὥστε μὴ δύνασθαι ἀτενίσαι τοὺς υἱοὺς Ἰσραὴλ εἰς τὸ πρόσωπον Μωϋσέως
διὰ τὴν δόξαν τοῦ προσώπου αὐτοῦ τὴν καταργουμένην, 8 πῶς οὐχὶ μᾶλλον ἡ δια-
κονία τοῦ πνεύματος ἔσται ἐν δόξῃ; 9 εἰ γὰρ τῇ διακονίᾳ τῆς κατακρίσεως δόξα,
πολλῷ μᾶλλον περισσεύει ἡ διακονία τῆς δικαιοσύνης δόξῃ. 10 καὶ γὰρ οὐ δεδόξα-
σται τὸ δεδοξασμένον ἐν τούτῳ τῷ μέρει εἵνεκεν τῆς ὑπερβαλλούσης δόξης· 11 εἰ
γὰρ τὸ καταργούμενον διὰ δόξης, πολλῷ μᾶλλον τὸ μένον ἐν δόξῃ. [SBLGNT]

King James Version

7 But if the ministration of death, writ-
ten and engraven in stones, was glori-
ous, so that the children of Israel could
not steadfastly behold the face of Moses
for the glory of his countenance; which
glory was to be done away: 8 How shall
not the ministration of the spirit be
rather glorious? 9 For if the ministration
of condemnation be glory, much more
doth the ministration of righteousness
exceed in glory. 10 For even that which
was made glorious had no glory in this
respect, by reason of the glory that
excelleth. 11 For if that which is done
away was glorious, much more that
which remaineth is glorious.

New Rendition

7 Now if the ministry of death, which
was carved in letters on stone tablets,
produced such glory that the children
of Israel could not look at the face of
Moses because of the glory of his face,
a glory that was to be abolished, 8 will
the ministry of the Spirit not be much
more glorious? 9 For if there was glory
in the ministry of condemnation, there
is much greater glory in the ministry of
righteousness. 10 Indeed, that which had
been glorious does not now appear glo-
rious because of the surpassingly greater
glory. 11 For if that which was to be abol-
ished seemed glorious, how much more
glorious is that which remains.

Translation Notes and Comments

3:7 ***the ministration of death / the ministry of death:*** The noun διακονία (*diakonia*), "ministry, service," in this phrase, refers specifically to the service that the old covenant rendered.[85] The word generally had a very positive nuance and could, therefore, be used to describe God's service to the Hebrews in giving them the old covenant. Paul, however, gives it a negative spin based on its results. In calling the Decalogue, if not the whole system,

85. BDAG, 230.

"the ministry of death," the Apostle, for the sake of argument, exaggerates its results.[86] There can be no doubt that the old covenant did prove itself to be deadly due to the faithlessness of Israelites who refused to live it and in consequence died both physically and spiritually. Had they lived it in faith, however, it would have brought them to their Messiah and to life (2 Ne. 25:25; Jacob 4:5–6).

written and engraven in stones / carved in letters on stone tablets: The reference is to Exodus 34:27–28, where Moses inscribed the law on the two stone tablets as revealed and dictated by the Lord. The verb ἐντυπόω (*entypoō*), "to carve," means to precisely incise letters, usually by chiseling them into stone.[87] The imagery stands in stark contrast to the law written by the Spirit on the human heart.[88]

The biblical text suggests that what Moses inscribed was only the Decalogue. The scriptures of the Restoration, however, show that the writings on the stone tablets consisted of much more than that. The first set contained the fulness of the gospel law. The second, however, due to Israel's rebellion, contained much less. Indeed, the higher ordinances, along with the priesthood that administered them, Jehovah took away, and unstable Israel was left with the preparatory gospel and the Aaronic Priesthood (Ex. 34:1–2, JST; D&C 84:19–27).[89]

was glorious, so that the children of Israel could not steadfastly behold the face of Moses for the glory of his countenance / produced such glory that the children of Israel could not look at the face of Moses because of the glory of his face: The reference is to Exodus 34:29–35. The verb γίνομαι (*ginomai*), found here as a passive aorist, means "to come into existence, to be produced."[90] The noun δόξα (*doxa*), "splendor, glory,"[91] appears twice in this verse. In the first case it refers to the glory produced by the "ministry of death"—that is, the Mosaic dispensation. In the second case it refers to the divine light that radiated from Moses' countenance after he'd been in

86. He uses a similar conceptualization of the Mosaic law leading to a person's death in Rom. 7:10.

87. BDAG, 342; Louw-Nida, §33.67. The Hebrew text states that Moses "wrote" (כָּתַב, *kātab*; BDB, 507–8) the words, and the LXX agrees, using γράφω (*graphō*) as the translation of *kātab*. BDAG, 207–8.

88. Guthrie, *Second Corinthians,* 207.

89. For an extended analysis, see Robinson and Garrett, *Commentary on the Doctrine and Covenants,* 3:31–33.

90. MM, 126–27; BDAG, 196–99.

91. BDAG, 256–58.

the divine presence for nearly six weeks and remained upon him for a time after he came down.[92] This second "glory" was simply a reflection or result of Moses being in the presence of God as the law was given.

which glory was to be done away / a glory that was to be abolished: This phrase is an aside in which Paul makes a comment about the nature of the glory associated with the old covenant. In it, he transitions to another meaning of the noun δόξα (*doxa*), "glory." Here it carries the idea of "esteem, greatness, honor"[93] and more especially the good reputation or standing of something or someone within a community.[94] In the LXX, the word carries the idea of "heaviness" or "weightiness."[95] Taking all these nuances together, we see the greatness, respect, reputation, and dignity that God intended for the Mosaic ministry to have.

The verb καταργέω (*katargeō*) is often used by Paul, and only two of the twenty-seven occurrences in the New Testament are found outside his writings. It is used four times in this chapter (3:7, 11, 13, and 14). It is a compound of ἀργέω (*argeô*) derived from the adjective ἀργός (*argos*) that carries the sense of being idle.[96] The prefix κατά (*kata*) adds a causative sense, "to make useless, make of no effect," and in the passive, "to be abolished, cease."[97] In Paul's writings, it carries any of three senses: "to make completely inoperative, to put out of action," or "to deprive of power."[98]

Paul's point is, therefore, that through the operation of Christ's Atonement, the ministry of the old covenant with its law, ordinances, and services is being set aside or becoming inoperative. Therefore, any former obligations or commitments that were once associated with it are also

---

92. Joseph Smith experienced this glory and described it not only as being "above the brightness of the sun" but also being able to eclipse the solar body's brilliance at noon-day. JS–H 1:16; "Church History," *Times and Seasons* 3 (March 1, 1842): 706–7.

93. BDAG, 256–58; Louw-Nida, §33.357; 87.4, 23.

94. Jehovah's glory, "*doxa,*" was associated with his reputation among his people as a God of power, might, and mercy. In the honor/shame society of the Greco-Roman world, one's reputation or glory was paramount to almost anything else. Guthrie, *Second Corinthians,* 208. For an extended study, see Gerhard von Rad and Gerhard Kittel, "δόξα," in *TDNT,* 2:233–55.

95. The LXX most frequently uses δόξα (*doxa*) as the translation of the Hebrew כָּבוֹד (*kābôd*), carrying the idea of being weighed down with honor or glory. HAL, 457–58. For a study of the term *doxa,* see James M. Hamilton Jr., *God's Glory in Salvation through Judgment: A Biblical Theology* (Wheaton, Ill.: Crossway, 2010), particularly 56–58.

96. The noun, which is a contraction of *ἀ-εργός* (*a-ergos*), means primarily "not working the ground" but carries the idea of being idle or lazy. LSJ, 28.

97. LSJ, 908; BDAG, 525–26.

98. Gerhard Delling, "καταργέω," in *TDNT,* 6:452–54.

passing away.[99] Paul is using the verb καταργέω (*katargeō*) to describe the present position of the old covenant. As the gospel spreads, the ministry of old is continually losing its force, weight, or glory. In sum, in view of the new covenant, the old one is being made inoperative and therefore can no longer demand allegiance. That the Apostle placed the verb (*katargeō*) last in the sentence gives strong emphasis to the idea of the covenant becoming inoperative.

3:8 ***How shall not the ministration of the spirit be rather glorious? / will the ministry of the Spirit not be much more glorious?:*** The negative particle οὐχί (*ouchi*) introduces a question that expects an affirmative answer.

For the noun "ministry," see 3:7 above.

In the present context, the noun δόξα (*doxa*, "glory") denotes the same idea as it did in 3:7 above—that is, it points to the esteem, honor, and prestige that the new ministry should have among the Christians. It also suggests the obligation and commitment to the restored gospel that it requires.[100] Again, for the sake of flow, we have translated the prepositional phrase ἐν δόξῃ (*en doxa*), literally "in glory," as an adjective, "glorious," in our Rendition.

The noun πνεῦμα (*pneuma*), "spirit," has a wide range of meanings, including "wind, breath, life-spirit," and can refer to a person's personal spirit.[101] In the present context, however, it refers to the divine element that centers in God and emanates from him. It is, in LDS theology, sometimes referred to as "light," "which light proceedeth forth from the presence of God to fill the immensity of space—the light which is in all things, which giveth life to all things, which is the law by which all things are governed, even the power of God who sitteth upon his throne, who is in the bosom of eternity, who is in the midst of all things" (D&C 88:12–13).[102] It is also referred to as "the light of Christ" because it flows from the Father through the Son to humankind.[103] In the present context it is the bearer of

---

99. BDAG, 525–26.

100. BDAG, 256–58.

101. For the full range of meanings, see Louw-Nida, 1:200.

102. In LDS vernacular, it is often referred to as "the light of Christ." See C. Kent Dunford, "Light of Christ," in *EM,* 2:835. For a study, see Richard D. Draper, "Light, Truth, and Grace: Three Themes of Salvation (D&C 93)," in *Sperry Symposium Classics: The Doctrine and Covenants,* ed. Craig K. Manscill (Provo, Utah: Religious Studies Center, Brigham Young University, 2004), 234–47.

103. See Dunford, "Light of Christ," 2:835. It is also referred to as "the Spirit of Jesus Christ" (D&C 84:45) and "the Spirit of Christ" (Moro. 7:16).

the divine will. It can be enhanced in the lives of those who correctly seek it. It has the ability to enhance individuals' righteousness and heighten their relationship with God, making it firm and permanent. Its possession serves to distinguish the Christian from the unbelievers and brings the Saints into fellowship one with another and with God (1 John 1:5–7).[104] With the restoration of this power in the days of the Apostles, the ministry of the Spirit had begun, and the ministry of the law of Moses was being superseded.[105]

3:9 ***For if the ministration of condemnation be glory / For if there was glory in the ministry of condemnation:*** On the noun "ministration," see 3:7 above, and on the noun "glory," see 3:8 above. The noun κατάκρισις (*katakrisis*), "condemnation," refers to "a judicial verdict involving a penalty, and connotes that which is found definitely guilty."[106] Paul's use of it as a reference to the Mosaic ministry shows his deliberate denigration of that system to enhance his point. The old ministration carried with it penalties for those who did not adhere to it, and since Israel did not, its term of service proved to be one of condemnation rather than blessing.

much more doth the ministration of righteousness exceed in glory / there is much greater glory in the ministry of righteousness: On the noun "ministry," see 3:7 above, and on the noun "glory," see 3:8 above. Paul expresses the power of the new age with the verb περισσεύω (*perisseuō*), which means "to be great, to abound, overflow," and also "to be extremely rich,"[107] and carries with it the nuance of being "of great advantage."[108] The Apostle's point is that the new age is extremely rich and even overflows in what is beneficial to the Saints.

The noun δικαιοσύνη (*dikaiosynē*), "righteousness," in the present context denotes the "quality or state of judicial correctness with focus on a redemptive action."[109] The Apostle uses the noun to contrast the ministry of the Christian era with that of the Mosaic law. Where the latter brought only condemnation, the former brings in abundance the glory of righteousness, redemption, and promise.

---

104. BDAG, 832–36.

105. In the present context, the term does not refer to the Holy Ghost, one of the members of the Godhead. Even so, this member of the Godhead, as with the others, does use this force in his ministrations (Acts 8:17–18; 19:2–6; 2 Tim. 1:6; Heb. 6:2.). See Bruce Douglas Porter, "Gift of the Holy Ghost," in *EM,* 2:543–44.

106. BDAG, 519; Louw-Nida, §56.31.

107. BDAG, 805.

108. Louw-Nida, §65.47.

109. BDAG, 247–49.

3:10 *For even that which was made glorious had no glory in this respect, by reason of the glory that excelleth / Indeed, that which had been glorious does not now appear glorious because of the surpassingly greater glory:* The verb δοξάζω (*doxazō*) means "to clothe in splendor, glorify."[110] Here, it is found in the form of a perfect passive participle that emphasizes the glory that had once shone from the face of Moses.[111] Paul uses it as a metaphor to represent the honor which the Mosaic ministry once had but has no more. The reason it has lost its excellence the Apostle expresses with the phrase τῆς ὑπερβαλλούσης δόξης (*tēs hyperballousēs doxēs*)—literally, "the excelling" or "surpassing glory," referring to Christian ministry. The verb ὑπερβάλλω (*hyperballō*), found here in the form of a present active participle, refers to that which has an extraordinary or surpassing degree of glory and in this case refers to the new ministry.[112] On the noun "glory," see 3:7–8 above.

3:11 *For if that which is done away was glorious, much more that which remaineth is glorious / For if that which was to be abolished seemed glorious, how much more glorious is that which remains:* On the verb κατεργέω (*katargeō*), "to abolish," see 3:7 above. It is found here in the form of a present passive participle, denoting "that which was to be abolished."[113] Paul uses the term to refer to the Mosaic ministry. To describe it, he uses the phrase *dia doxēs,* literally "of glory," while the new covenant he describes as *en doxēs,* literally "in glory." The difference between the two phrases may be a case of hairsplitting, but if there is a difference, it is that Moses' dispensation was glorious at its inception, while the new one remains in glory.[114]

The verb μένω (*menō*), found here in the form of a present active participle, refers to that which "remains, lasts, persists and continues to be active."[115] The verb stands in contrast to κατεργέω (*katargeō*), which denotes that which is becoming inoperative. Paul uses *meno* to refer to the ministry of the new covenant in which the Apostles are engaged, which

110. BDAG, 258.

111. In both Ex. 34:29 and 34:35, the LXX, as in this verse, uses the perfect passive participle of the verb δοξάζω (*doxazō*) to refer to Moses' face. Guthrie, *2 Corinthians,* 215.

112. BDAG, 1032.

113. BDAG, 525–26; Louw-Nida, §13.100.

114. Compare C. F. D. Moule, *An Idiom Book of New Testament Greek,* 2nd ed. (London: Cambridge University Press, 1960), 58.

115. BDAG, 630–31.

includes a restoration of the fulness of the gospel advancing under the power of the Spirit of God.

Analysis and Summary

The problem Paul faced is largely due to the continuing tendencies of Jewish converts to cling to Mosaic practices and promulgate the importance of the law of Moses.[116] It is possible that this section contains an implicit polemic that Paul launched against his detractors.[117] These men could have been using Moses and the glory that fell upon him when he received the old covenant as a model of spirituality and proper ministry. The imagery of the splendor that rested on the Mosaic law stood in contradistinction to the supposed inglorious ministry of Paul and his associates.[118] This view, however, is weakened because there is no concrete evidence in the letter itself that the Apostle had his detractors in mind.

Based on the context, rather than indirectly bashing his critics, the Apostle is pushing the abundant adequacy of his ministry (3:5) and the openness with which he proclaims it (3:12). That being the case, his purpose in writing this section is to portray the authentic nature of his ministry through a vigorous defense of his authority and doctrine.[119] His focus is, therefore, less on the contrast between the old and new covenants and more on the differences between their ministrations. He describes the old ministry as that of "the letter" (3:6) and that of the new as the ministry of "the Spirit" (3:6,

116. C. Brian Hardy, "Paul: Personal Disclosures through His Epistles," in *A Symposium on the New Testament: August 14, 15, 16, 1980, Brigham Young University, Provo, Utah* (Salt Lake City: The Church of Jesus Christ of Latter-day Saints, [1980]), 89.

117. The exegetical method he used in 3:7–18 would have been effective to his Jewish audience since it was widely used at the time. For a study, see Michael Cover, *Lifting the Veil: 2 Corinthians 3:7–18 in Light of Jewish Homiletic and Commentary Traditions* (Berlin: Walter de Gruyter, 2015), who posits a link between the methodology used by Philo and other commentators with Paul and suggests that the common source is that of a common exegesis as taught within Judaism.

118. Paul may have been responding to a Midrashic commentary on Ex. 34. See Barnett, *Second Epistle*, 178–79. See also George H. Guthrie, "Καταργέω and the People of the Shining Face (2 Corinthians 3:7–18)," *Southern Baptist Journal of Theology* 19, no. 3 (Fall 2015): 41–60, who argues that in 3:17–18, Paul is looking at competing approaches to ministry in his own day. He uses "glory" as a countercultural alternative that democratizes the attainment of glory as for all people of the new covenant (3:17–18), not just for the "glorified" false leaders.

119. Furnish, *II Corinthians*, 242–45; Garland, *2 Corinthians*, 169–70. Even so, the work of his antagonists must have been playing in the back of his mind. Guthrie, *Second Corinthians*, 203–4.

NR). One is the ministry of "death" (3:7); the other is that of "the Spirit" (3:8, NR). One is the ministry of "condemnation" (3:9); the other the ministry of "righteousness" (3:9). Thus, Paul's contrasts suggest that his focus is on the "superiority of his new-covenant form of ministry, and specifically on the proclamation of the Word of God under the power of the Spirit."[120]

The Apostle forcefully sets up this portion of his argument by using very vivid language. He calls the application of the Mosaic law the "ministry of death" carved in stone. He also describes it as the "ministry of condemnation" (3:7, 9, NR). In doing so, he paints a very low picture of Israel's response to the offices, duties, and functions of the old covenant.

The modern disciple should keep in mind, as Elder McConkie has noted, that

> the law which God gave Moses is not to be taken lightly. True it was a "manifestation of death," in that salvation did not come by the law alone. True it was a "ministration of condemnation," in that those who received it had first rejected the law of God; but it was the most perfect system of religion on earth for a millennium and a half; and it was so designed as to prepare men [and women] for the fulness of that gospel truth which Christ brought. Paul's approach here is to say: "There was glory and honor in the law of Moses, during the time when God reigned through it, but now, through Christ, has come 'the glory that excelleth.' If the law of Moses 'was glorious,' how much more so is the gospel of Christ?[121]

Paul begins his argument by noting that the condemning and deadly ministry came with splendor as evidenced by the glory that radiated from Moses' face. To stress his point, Paul then uses a rhetorical devise known as *qal wāḥômer,* which is basically an *a fortiori* argument that emphasizes an idea by stressing that if a minor point *x* is important, then the major point *y* must be all the more important.[122] In the present context, *x*

---

120. Guthrie, *Second Corinthians,* 206. See also G. Anthony Keddie, "Paul's Freedom and Moses' Veil: Moral Freedom and the Mosaic Law in 2 Corinthians 3.1–4.6 in Light of Philo," *Journal for the Study of the New Testament* 37, no. 3 (Fall 2015): 267–89, who argues that Paul uses Moses' mediation as a foil for the Apostle's own mediation of the gospel, which does not limit revelation but affords freedom apart from the written law. Paul is not castigating the old covenant per se, but rather uses Mosaic mediation as a way to bolster his own authority as a mediator of divine revelation.

121. *DNTC,* 2:415.

122. This formulation, later codified by the rabbis, was designed to draw a conclusion that is inferred to be even more certain than another and to emphasize the distance between the consequences of two actions. Luke Timothy Johnson, *Hebrews* (Louisville: Westminster John Knox Press, 2006), 338. Witherington, *Conflict and Community,* 380,

(a position on which all the Saints likely agreed) was that Moses exhibited a wondrous glory when he came down from Sinai (3:7), while *y* (the point Paul wishes to make) is that the new ministry, attended as it is by the Holy Spirit, has a glory that eclipses into insignificance that which was once upon Moses (3:8).

Paul refers to the restored order with the fulness of the gospel and priesthood as "the ministry of the spirit." The phrase emphasizes a major difference between the old and new covenants—namely, the restored and dynamic work of the Spirit now active among the faithful. It would be wrong, however, to see Paul as contrasting the letter (γράμμα, *gramma*) against the Spirit (πνεῦμα, *pneuma*) such that the letter counts for nothing and the Spirit for all. The Apostle should not be seen as "opposing the basic intent of the Scripture to its specific wording, as in our familiar distinction 'the spirit and the letter of the law.' Nor is he thinking [that there is] some mystical latent sense concealed beneath the text's external form. The Spirit that Paul is talking about is the Holy Spirit, who is palpably present on the community as an experienced reality, manifest in spiritual gifts such as tongues and prophecy . . . [and is] transforming the lives and empowering the work of the ministry."[123] The problem, as Paul views it, is that Israel could not keep the law without the enabling power of the Spirit to attend it. The Ten Commandments with the other statutes and ordinances were clear enough, and the Apostle sees no antagonism between their meaning and that of the intent of the Spirit. But the problem was that the "letter," when separated from the "Spirit," given fallen human nature, resulted not in life-giving obedience but in death-dealing disobedience. The Christian under the new covenant, therefore, must have both the law and the Spirit. This is because the letter without the Spirit leads not only to legalism but, more importantly, to a deadening effect on its adherence. The Spirit without the letter may bring life, but not how such a life ought to be lived. In sum, both are equally needed in the lives of the Saints.[124] As Elder Neal A. Maxwell asked, "Can we not keep the spirit of the law without leaving other things undone? Without such spiritual balance, staying on the straight and narrow path will be a great trial for us."[125]

---

points out that the argument does not look at the idea of bad to good but from the perspective of a lesser good to far greater one.

123. Richard B. Hays, *Echoes of Scripture in the Letters of Paul* (New Haven, Conn.: Yale University Press, 1989), 150.

124. Witherington, *Conflict and Community,* 384 with n. 34.

125. Neal A. Maxwell, "Answer Me," *Ensign* 18, no. 11 (November 1988): 31.

The term "Spirit" (*pneuma*) in the LXX, when speaking theologically, refers to the element that centers in and emanates from God.[126] It is universally present but can come with greater concentration upon a person (see, for example, Judg. 14:6 and 1 Sam. 16:13), bringing with it divine power, ability, and authority. One of its chief effects upon an individual is that of prophesy—that is, the right and power to speak with God's authority.[127] The rabbis taught that this Spirit had been withdrawn from Israel after the ministry of Malachi and would not return until the last days.[128] As a result, when Jesus came in the role of an inspired prophet (Matt. 13:57), it drew their attention (Mark 1:22, 27). His teachings clearly revealed that he was the eschatological Messiah bringing in the foreseen new age (see Deut. 18:15–19; Isa. 61:1–2; and Luke 7:22). One component of that new age was judgment, and Jesus reinforced that aspect (Matt. 10:34–36; Luke 12:49–53). He insisted, however, that the new ministry would deal much more with bringing blessings and life and oneness with God (Matt. 10:8; 11:28–29; Mark 2:17; 3:14–15; Luke 6:31–33; 9:54–56; John 3:16–17, 36; 5:23–24; 17:6–9). His response to the query by John the Baptist as to whether Jesus was the awaited Savior (Matt. 11:2–3; Luke 7:20–22) strongly suggests Jesus brought the promised blessing recorded in Isaiah (see Isa. 29:18–20; 35:3–5; 61:1–2). That the Apostles continued to work under that power motivated the Jewish leadership to continue to fight against them.

A critical aspect of the Lord's ministry was his giving an endowment of the Spirit to others (see, for example, Mark 1:7–8 and John 20:21–22), which action continued into the post-Resurrection ministry (Acts 1:2; 2:4, 38) yet still under his direct supervision (Acts 2:33). The power of the Spirit was most clearly evidenced in prophecy. Indeed, it became the touchstone that the new age had commenced. "The same power that had inspired David and the prophets in the old age (Acts 1:16; 3:18; 4:25; 28:25) was now poured out in eschat[ological] plentitude as Joel had foretold

---

126. The word carries a wide range of meanings including air movement, breathing, a person's life-spirit, and an incorporeal being. See BDAG, 832–36. In a theological sense, the noun refers to God's controlling influence exhibited in its salvific nature in the character, enhanced abilities, and activities of the Saints. For an extended study of its use in the New Testament, see Eduard Schweizer, "πνεῦμα, πνευματικός, πνέω, ἐμπνέω, πνοή, ἐκπνέω, θεόπνευστος," in *TDNT,* 7:332–455.

127. For example, see Sir. 48:12. On "prophecy" as the power to utter and interpret divine will, see BDAG, 889–90.

128. *NID,* 3:810.

([Acts] 2:17–21)."[129] This power was the seat of individual conversion and brought with it the missionaries' boldness in testifying and living the truth (Acts 4:8, 13, 29–31; 7:55; 13:9).

For Paul, this divine power was discernable by its manifest effects shown in speaking in tongues, healings, and, as noted, particularly in prophetic utterance (1 Cor. 12:3–11; 14:3–5). Its endowment brought with it the greatest of spiritual gifts, that of faith, hope, and divine love (1 Cor. 13:1–3, 13). In short, when filled by the Spirit, the Saints walked after the ways of God and manifested his power in their lives. The challenge of the Christians was to allow God to mold their character according to the pattern of life revealed by the Savior. The Apostle viewed such a life not as something the Saints achieved by themselves—that is, by their works alone—but principally as the product of the action of the Spirit upon them—that is, by its fruits (Gal. 5:18–23). It was in this way that they could walk or be led by the Spirit (Rom. 8:4–6, 14; Gal. 5:16, 18, 25).

The point that the Apostle is making here is his clear understanding that the "ministry of the spirit" stands in contrast to that of the old covenant. No longer were the disciples dependent on the "rule book" of the Mosaic law, which they had been expected, before their conversion, to follow blamelessly (Rom. 7:6; 2 Cor. 3:6; Gal. 5:1, 6). Now the Saints were to yield to the force of the new covenant both because it was written on their hearts (Jer. 31:31–33) and because it came with the power of God's spirit. In sum, it brought with it both a true knowledge of God and the ability to discern and implement his will in their lives (Rom. 12:2; 2 Cor. 3:3).[130] The result was the acquisition of glory.

In 3:7–8, the Apostle uses two nuances of the word "glory" (δόξα, *doxa*) to make his point. The noun could refer either to splendor and brilliance or to honor and esteem. Paul uses it initially in a scriptural context (Ex. 34:29–35) to describe Moses' countenance as he came down from Sinai. The splendor radiated from the prophet's countenance with such brilliance that the Israelites could look at him only with discomfort. Paul uses the second nuance in relationship to the ministry of the law to illustrate the preliminary high esteem or honor it was supposed to have had.

In 3:9, Paul skillfully contrasts two words: "condemnation" (κατάκρισις, *katakrisis*) and "righteousness" (δικαιοσύνη, *dikaiosynē*). Both have forensic force, the first denoting an act that demands censure and conviction, while

---

129. *NID*, 3:813.
130. *NID*, 3:816–17.

the latter denotes the positive result of divine judgment.[131] The contrast helps him point out the difference between the old and new ministrations. The new age, he declares, overflows or is extremely rich (περισσεύω, *perisseuō*) in glory. Such glory the old ministry never achieved because, as he notes, it was suppressed by the veil Moses had to wear that, therefore, limited its glory to Moses alone. Not so in the new age. Under the indwelling of the Spirit during this ministration of righteousness, heavenly power involved every person who came actively into the new covenant and infused each with divine access and the rule of righteousness that flowed therefrom (3:17).[132] Paul admits that currently this glory is "inward and unseen" by the spiritually myopic but is expressing itself in the message delivered by the Apostles and in the lives of those who receive the gospel (3:18).[133]

By noting that the glory of the law is becoming "inoperative" (καταργέω, *katargeō*), the Apostle emphasizes the continually growing loss of the esteem, reverence, and honor it once held. Indeed, with the spreading of the new covenant, the old one was losing what little effectiveness it yet held. Paul's analogy does not actually denigrate the old covenant itself but rather shows that, due to the glory or brightness of the ministry of righteousness, what glory the old ministry had is now so fully eclipsed it appears as nothing.[134] Therefore, any obligation, commitment, or allegiance the old covenant once commanded is now also done away.[135]

He next asks, paraphrasing the scripture, "If the dispensation of death came with glory, will not the dispensation of life be attended with a much greater glory?" (3:9). He then testifies that the new ministry, one of righteousness, far outshines the ministry of condemnation. Indeed, in contrast to the immense glory of the new dispensation, the old one actually had no splendor at all (3:10).

His point is that the glory associated with the restored ministry is better than that of the old for two reasons: first, the initial ministry brought condemnation while the latter brings righteousness (3:9); and second, the former had only a glint that vanished away, while the latter has a splendor that will abide forever (3:11).[136]

---

131. Seifrid, *Second Letter,* 157.
132. Guthrie, *2 Corinthians,* 214.
133. Seifrid, *Second Letter,* 151.
134. Guthrie, *2 Corinthians,* 216.
135. BDAG, 525–26.
136. Bernard, "Second Epistle," 54–55.

The Ministry of the New Covenant (3:12–18)

Greek Text

12 Ἔχοντες οὖν τοιαύτην ἐλπίδα πολλῇ παρρησίᾳ χρώμεθα, 13 καὶ οὐ καθάπερ
Μωϋσῆς ἐτίθει κάλυμμα ἐπὶ τὸ πρόσωπον αὐτοῦ, πρὸς τὸ μὴ ἀτενίσαι τοὺς υἱοὺς
Ἰσραὴλ εἰς τὸ τέλος τοῦ καταργουμένου. 14 ἀλλὰ ἐπωρώθη τὰ νοήματα αὐτῶν.
ἄχρι γὰρ τῆς σήμερον ἡμέρας τὸ αὐτὸ κάλυμμα ἐπὶ τῇ ἀναγνώσει τῆς παλαιᾶς δια-
θήκης μένει μὴ ἀνακαλυπτόμενον, ὅτι ἐν Χριστῷ καταργεῖται, 15 ἀλλ᾽ ἕως σήμερον
ἡνίκα ἂν ἀναγινώσκηται Μωϋσῆς κάλυμμα ἐπὶ τὴν καρδίαν αὐτῶν κεῖται· 16 ἡνίκα
δὲ ἐὰν ἐπιστρέψῃ πρὸς κύριον, περιαιρεῖται τὸ κάλυμμα. 17 ὁ δὲ κύριος τὸ πνεῦμά
ἐστιν· οὗ δὲ τὸ πνεῦμα κυρίου, ἐλευθερία. 18 ἡμεῖς δὲ πάντες ἀνακεκαλυμμένῳ
προσώπῳ τὴν δόξαν κυρίου κατοπτριζόμενοι τὴν αὐτὴν εἰκόνα μεταμορφούμεθα
ἀπὸ δόξης εἰς δόξαν, καθάπερ ἀπὸ κυρίου πνεύματος. [SBLGNT]

King James Version

12 Seeing then that we have such hope,
we use great plainness of speech: 13 And
not as Moses, which put a veil over his
face, that the children of Israel could not
steadfastly look to the end of that which
is abolished: 14 But their minds were
blinded: for until this day remaineth the
same veil untaken away in the reading
of the old testament; which veil is done
away in Christ. 15 But even unto this
day, when Moses is read, the veil is upon
their heart. 16 Nevertheless when it shall
turn to the Lord, the veil shall be taken
away. 17 Now the Lord is that Spirit: and
where the Spirit of the Lord is, there
is liberty. 18 But we all, with open face
beholding as in a glass the glory of the
Lord, are changed into the same image
from glory to glory, even as by the Spirit
of the Lord.

New Rendition

12 Therefore, since we have such hope,
we use great plainness of speech,
13 unlike Moses, who would put a veil
over his face so that the children of Israel
would not stare at the end of that which
was to be abolished. 14 On the contrary,
their minds were closed, for even until
this present day, the same veil remains
unlifted during the reading of the old
covenant, because that veil is abolished
in Christ. 15 But until this very day,
whenever Moses is read, a veil remains
over their heart. 16 But whenever their
heart turns to the Lord, the veil is taken
away. 17 Now the Lord is the Spirit, and
where the Spirit of the Lord is, there
is freedom. 18 And all of us who with
unveiled faces contemplate the glory of
the Lord are being transformed into the
same image from glory to glory, just as
from the Spirit of the Lord.

Translation Notes and Comments

3:12 ***Seeing then that we have such hope, we use great plainness of speech / Therefore, since we have such hope, we use great plainness of speech:*** With the phrase ἔχοντες οὖν (*echontes oun*), "seeing then,"[137] Paul shows that he believes his readers have followed his argument and accepted it. The point of that argument explains the basis for the "hope" he and his fellow missionaries have in carrying out the new ministry. On "hope," see Translation Notes on 1:7 above. The hope of the glory that is part of the "ministry of the spirit" compels Paul and those working with him not to hide or diminish the word in any way. The noun παρρησία (*parrēsia*), "boldness, frankness, outspokenness, plainness," refers to a type of speech deliberately designed to neither hide nor conceal anything.[138] The adjective πολύς (*polys*), "much, many, great,"[139] suggests the magnitude of the force the missionaries use in declaring the glory of the blessings available under the new ministration. The verb χράομαι (*chraomai*), "to use" or "to make use of," denotes acting or thinking in a certain way toward others.[140] In this case, it refers to preaching the gospel through frank and open declarations concerning the blessing of living under the power of the Spirit.

3:13 ***And not as Moses, which put a veil over his face / unlike Moses, who would put a veil over his face:*** The reference is to Exodus 34:29–35. Paul contrasts the open declaration by the missionaries of the glory of the new covenant with Moses' veiled declarations of the old covenant, shown by his having to cover his face when he taught the Israelites.

Due to vagueness, the whole phrase presents several translation difficulties. The verb τίθημι (*tithēmi*), "to put or place,"[141] found here in the imperfect tense, suggests that, for some time, Moses had to keep taking off and putting on a veil as he interacted with Jehovah and his people. This was because the Israelites could not long withstand the glory radiating from Moses' face. The verb ἀτενίζω (*atenizō*), found here as an aorist infinitive, means "to look at" but carries the nuance of "looking with an intense fixation on an object" or "to stare."[142] Thus, the idea conveyed in the phrase is not that the Israelites could not look momentarily on the glory streaming from Moses's countenance but that they could not endure a prolonged exposure to it.[143]

that the children of Israel could not steadfastly look to the end of that which is abolished / so that the children of Israel would not stare at the

---

137. The verb ἔχω (*echō*), "to have, hold," is in the form of a present participle and carries the idea of holding a particular view of something (BDAG, 420–22; Louw-Nida, §31.1), and, therefore, "to consider, understand, see."

138. BDAG, 781–82.

139. BDAG, 487–50.

140. Louw-Nida, §41.4; BDAG, 1087–88; *DAG*, s.v. "χράομαι."

141. BDAG, 1003–4.

142. BDAG, 148; Louw-Nida, §24.49.

143. Guthrie, *2 Corinthians*, 219.

end of that which was to be abolished: Paul again uses the verb καταργέω (*katargeō*; see 3:7 above), found here as a present passive participle. It denotes that which is losing its significance, being put to an end, or being rendered inoperative.[144] Here the dominant nuance is the latter. The noun τέλος (*telos*) denotes "an end, outcome, result, or the completion" of something.[145] The text is vague on what *telos* refers to, since it is followed by the articular, genitive participle τοῦ καταργουμένου (*tou katargoumenou*), "of that which was being abolished." But what is being abolished?

The dominant scholarly view concerning this passage is that Moses was hiding his face from the Israelites as a result of (*telos*) its once resplendent glory now beginning to fade (*tou katargoumenou*).[146] The problem with this interpretation is that there is no scriptural evidence that the glory gradually faded. It seems, rather, to have just vanished at some point.

Others interpret the passage by looking at what Moses wanted to accomplish by veiling his face. According to this view, his action was motivated by Israel's hardheartedness. Due to that condition, the prophet wanted to hide from them the ultimate significance of the glory shining from Moses' face: it was a manifestation of the power and might of Jehovah. By veiling his face, the prophet illustrated that the Israelites, due to their recalcitrance, would not be able to share in Jehovah's glory.[147]

Closely related to the above is the interpretation that sees *telos* as referring to the outcome of what Moses did—that is, actually hiding God's reflective glory from the Israelites. In this case, the act symbolized God's judgment against these intractable people. By covering his face, Moses illustrated that

144. The difficulty in determining the correct translation for this verb is evidenced by the KJV's use of ten different word to do it. For a study, see Harris, *Second Epistle,* 299, who identifies the two major categories in which the word can be translated as teleological—"goal, purpose, significance"—or as temporal—"end, termination, cessation" with the idea of being "blocked" or "hindered" work. See also William R. Baker, "Did the Glory of Moses' Face Fade? A Reexamination of Καταργέω in 2 Corinthians 3:7–18," *Bulletin for Biblical Research* 10, no. 1 (2000): 1–15. The best use in this present context is that of being rendered inoperative. *NID,* 2:640–42.

145. BDAG, 998–99. The range of the word also includes such meanings as "'goal' or 'purpose,' or indeed 'ultimate significance.'" Martin, *2 Corinthians,* 210–11.

146. Scott J. Hafemann, *Paul, Moses, and the History of Israel: The Letter/Spirit Contrast and the Argument from Scripture in 2 Corinthians 3* (Eugene, Ore.: Wipf and Stock Publishers, 2008), 347.

147. Anthony Tyrrell Hanson, *Jesus Christ in the Old Testament* (London: SPCK, 1965), 27–29. Because Christ was the Jehovah of the Old Testament, the light was a reflection of the power of Christ and of his gospel.

the full covenant, with its power and ordinances, had been taken away.[148] Taking the phrase *eis to telos* as a whole (literally, "as unto the end") bolsters this idea.[149] It carries the idea of purpose or reason. This nuance suggests that Moses initially had a purpose in mind for the people that could only be realized if a certain condition was met. Just what that condition was is suggested in LXX Exodus 33:16. There Moses pleads with the Lord not to forsake Israel on account of their faithlessness evidenced in their making the golden calf. The prophet asks the Lord not to leave the Israelites but to remain with them, for only in that way could *Moses and his people* be glorified beyond all other nations. We see here the end or goal or purpose (*telos*) of what Moses initially wanted—namely, for Jehovah to remain among his people, thus *glorifying them.* The action with the veil shows that Moses was illustrating that this outcome or end could not be realized. The Israelites' fear of approaching the divinely radiant Moses evidenced more than their yet-poor spiritual condition. It revealed that these people yet refused to live such that they could feel comfortable in God's glory. The prophet's veiling God's reflected glory symbolized that they were cut off from Jehovah and the glory of the greater covenant.[150] In sum, the veil connoted the resultant barrier—produced by the sin of persistent rebellion—between the manifest presence of Jehovah and these people. Thus, Moses' action not only was based on the Israelites' fear of Jehovah but acted as a "judgment on the rebellion that spawned that fear."[151]

---

148. Hafemann, *History of Israel,* 357–58. According to D&C 84:23–26, "Moses plainly taught to the children of Israel in the wilderness, and sought diligently to sanctify his people that they might behold the face of God; but they hardened their hearts and could not endure his presence; therefore, the Lord in his wrath, for his anger was kindled against them, swore that they should not enter into his rest while in the wilderness, which rest is the fulness of his glory. Therefore, he took Moses out of their midst, and the Holy Priesthood also; and the lesser priesthood continued, which priesthood holdeth the key of the ministering of angels and the preparatory gospel."

149. The phrase is found only here in the New Testament. The usual phrase found in the scriptures is εἰς τέλος (*eis telos*), meaning "in the end" or "finally," but that interpretation does not work here. This phrase translates literally as "unto the end." By looking at its use in the LXX and secular literature of the day, it refers to the completion of something. Guthrie, *2 Corinthians,* 220 n. 42.

150. Baker, "Did the Glory of Moses' Face Fade?," 1–15.

151. Seifrid, *Second Letter,* 164; Guthrie, *2 Corinthians,* 220–22. Thus, Paul is not speaking of "what was being brought to an end" during the Israelite period but of the "goal of that which is done away with" due to the present ministry of Christ. Seifrid, *Second Letter,* 164 n. 236.

3:14 ***But their minds were blinded / On the contrary, their minds were closed:*** The noun νόημα (*noema*), "mind," in the present context denotes "the faculty of producing thought."[152] The verb πωρόω (*pōroō*), "to close," in the form of an aorist passive refers to that which causes someone "to have difficulty in understanding or comprehending something."[153] What caused the Israelites' difficulty is obscured by the use of the passive voice, but the context suggests that the culprit was their refusal to come directly before Jehovah.[154]

for until this day remaineth the same veil untaken away in the reading of the old testament / for even until this present day, the same veil remains unlifted during the reading of the old covenant: Because the punctuation for this clause is uncertain, various translations have been offered.[155] Our Rendition follows the broad sense of the passage.

The phrase τῆς σήμερον ἡμέρας (*tēs sēmeron hēmeras*), "unto this very day," shows that the problem faced and the effect realized by the early Israelites yet remain among their unconverted descendants.

The verb ἀνακαλύπτω (*anakalyptō*) means "to uncover or unveil."[156] It is found here as a neuter present passive participle. Due the vagueness of the passage, it is uncertain what the verb's subject is. The KJV and many other translations take κάλυμμα (*kalymma*), "veil," as the subject of the participle.[157] In that case, Paul uses the veil as a metaphor for Moses' judgment against Israel. Because the veil has never been lifted, it still affects the minds of the Jews by prohibiting them from seeing that the old covenant is coming to an end.[158] In short, the barrier that separated them from God because of their closed minds yet remains intact. Some scholars see a problem with this view because the text seems to say that it is not the *veil* that is being uncovered; it is the *face.* However, there is a passage in the LXX where the verb *anakalyptō* is used with a "covering" (συγκάλυμμα, *synkalymma)* as a direct object, rather than the object that is covered, and there

---

152. BDAG, 675. The noun also refers to "a concept, plan, or design." Johannes Behm, "νόημα," in *TDNT,* 4:960–61.

153. Louw-Nida, §27.51; BDAG, 900.

154. Barnett, *Second Epistle,* 192–93.

155. Barnett, *Second Epistle,* 193 n. 21, examines these.

156. BDAG, 65.

157. That both the participle and the noun are neuter in gender, thus allowing for the connection, but it is admittedly not decisive.

158. Witherington, *Conflict and Community,* 381.

are several other examples of *anakalyptō* governing the covering rather than what is being covered.[159] See below for further discussion.

Only here out of all his writing does Paul refer to the Mosaic law as τῆς παλαιᾶς διαθήκης (*tēs palaias diathēkēs*), "the old covenant." The adjective παλαιός (*palaios*), "old," in the present context, carries the pejorative idea of something being antiquated, obsolete, and of no further use.[160] In 3:6, he refers to the restored gospel as καινῆς διαθήκης (*kainēs diathēkēs*), "a new covenant," which he now seems to be contrasting with the Mosaic law. It is the restoration of the new covenant that has made the earlier covenant old and depleted.

which veil is done away in Christ / because that veil is abolished in Christ: Some scholars suggest that this clause is the subject of the participial ἀνακαλυπτόμενον (*anakalyptomenon*), "to be uncovered or unveiled," found in the previous phrase. To be so, this clause must be taken as a kind of accusative absolute not dependent on what precedes it. That being the case, what Paul is saying is that to the Israelites, it was not uncovered or revealed (μὴ ἀνακαλυπτόμενον, *mē anakalyptomenon*) that the old covenant is abolished in Christ.[161] Most commentators, however, regard this reading as less likely since this would be the only example of the use of a participial accusative absolute in the entire New Testament,[162] and therefore, we have followed the more conventional translation in our Rendition.

Paul, again, uses the verb καταργέω (*katargeō*; see 3:7 above) found here as a present passive participle and thus understood to mean "to be abolished, removed, or made inoperative."[163] In doing so, he is saying that only in Christ is the barrier (symbolized by the Mosaic veil that evidenced the separation of Israel from God) being made inoperative because of the power of the Atonement.

---

159. In LXX Deut. 23:1 (Deut. 22:30 in KJV), we find οὐκ ἀποκαλύψει συγκάλυμμα (*ouk apokalypsei synkallyma*), which has a variant reading ἀνακαλύψει (*anakalypsei*), where the Hebrew verb being translated is גִּלָּה (*gilleh*) "to uncover." *HAL*, 486. In the pseudepigraphal Testament of Judah 14:5, *anakalyptō* is also followed by κάλυμμα (*kalymma*) in the accusative case. BDAG also list two other instances of *anakalyptō* followed by an accusative case of a covering rather than the thing being covered.

160. BDAG, 751; Louw-Nida, §58.75. Here Paul parallels the thought in Hebrews 8:13: "By saying 'new,' God has declared the first covenant obsolete and what becomes obsolete and grows old will soon vanish" (our translation).

161. An argument for this position can be found in Seifrid, *Second Letter*, 168–70.

162. *NID*, 2:614–15; compare Margaret E. Thrall, *A Critical and Exegetical Commentary on the Second Epistle to the Corinthians*, 2 vols. (London: T&T Clark International, 1994–2000), 1:263–66; BDF, §424.

163. BDAG, 525–26.

3:15 ***But even unto this day, when Moses is read, the veil is upon their heart / But until this very day, whenever Moses is read, a veil remains over their heart:*** For emphasis, Paul repeats the thought he made in 3:14, which is an allusion to Exodus 34:34. The conjunctive phrase ἥνικα ἂν (*hēnika an*), "whenever," stresses the idea that in their public devotions, the Jews are unable to see either the law's intent or Moses' judgment against them.[164]

With a rather clever switch to a metaphor, the Apostle turns the literal veil worn by Moses into a symbolic one that covers the hearts of the unconverted Jews. The imagery shows that the yet-unlifted veil still keeps them from seeing and thereby understanding the truth.[165]

The noun Μωϋσῆς (*Mōusēs*), "Moses," as used here, refers most narrowly to the Decalogue and most broadly to the first five books of the Hebrew Bible. It is likely, however, that Paul has in mind the whole system of laws and ordinances plus the traditions the Jews built upon them.

The noun καρδία (*kardia*), "heart," connotes the very core of the person in Semitic cultures. It is here where we find both the rational and emotional elements that define all that the person is.[166] That the veil remains over the heart emphasizes the extreme nature of the handicap placed upon the whole of the person.

3:16 ***Nevertheless when it shall turn to the Lord, the veil shall be taken away / But whenever their heart turns to the Lord, the veil is taken away:*** The opening phrase ἡνίκα δὲ ἐὰν (*hēnika de ean*), "but whenever," is important because by its use the Apostle shows that each and every time a condition is met, something good happens. Here it looks to a change of heart.

The verb ἐπιστρέφω (*epistrephō*), "to turn, return," in a religious sense, refers to a positive change of belief with its accompanying elevation in behavior. The force of the verb looks also at the thing to which one turns.[167] In this case, it is "the Lord." In this phrase, the verb does not have an expressed antecedent, but the construction suggests it is τὴν καρδίαν αὐτῶν (*tēn kardian autōn*), "their heart," found in 3:15. Supporting this translation is the JST of the verse, which reads, "when their heart shall turn to the Lord, the veil shall be taken away." The noun acts as a fitting symbol

---

164. Seifrid, *Second Letter,* 167.

165. Witherington, *Conflict and Community,* 381.

166. Fredrich Baumgärtel and Johannes Behm, "καρδία," in *TDNT,* 3:605–13; *NID,* 2:622–27.

167. BDAG, 382. In some passages, it is difficult to determine if the emphasis should be on the belief or the behavior. It would be best to keep both in play even if one nuance predominates. Louw-Nida, §§31.60; 41.51.

for what happens to each individual who, in humility, allows the Lord to do his work. The passive voice of the verb hides the actor that takes away the veil, but Paul shows below that it is through spiritual power that it happens. Through that means, one leaves behind the hardened heart and allows the veil to be lifted. As a result, that barrier can no longer hinder such persons from seeing the beauty and power of the new covenant and the God who stands behind it.

The meaning of the noun κύριος (*kyrios*), "Lord," is vague. It could refer to either God or Christ, or possibly even to the Holy Spirit. How one reads the next phrase determines which of these entities is meant here.

3:17 ***the Lord is that Spirit / the Lord is the Spirit:*** This phrase is yet another example of Paul's ability to be obtuse, and the number of ways it is translated illustrates this point. [168] The noun κύριος (*kyrios*), "lord," can refer to any divine being, but in the Bible, it usually refers to either God or Christ and the latter more especially in the New Testament.[169] However, in the present context it is highly likely that the term refers to the Spirit of God.[170] Indeed, the noun πνεῦμα (*pneuma*), has a wide range of meanings,[171] but the one that best fits in the present context is that of the divine influence or force that acts upon a human recipient.[172] The definite article ὁ (*ho*) would then act as a demonstrative pronoun referring to a specific spirit and therefore need to be translated as "that." The simplest way to take the phase is to see ὁ κύριος (*ho kyrios*) as an epexegetical remark[173] uniting κύριος (*kyrios*), "Lord," and πνεῦμα (*pneuma*), "spirit." By doing so, the phrase

---

168. For a discussion of the many ways this phrase can be taken, see David Greenwood, "The Lord Is the Spirit: Some Considerations of 2 Cor 3: 17," *Catholic Biblical Quarterly* 34, no. 4 (October 1972): 467–72.

169. BDAG, 576–79.

170. The phase does not refer to the Holy Ghost but rather to that which is often called "the light of Christ" in LDS theology. See Dunford, "Light of Christ," 2:835.

171. These include "wind, breath, the personal spirit, as well as ghosts and evil spirits." In a theological sense, it most often refers to God's divine influence or force that acts upon a human recipient. BDAG, 832–36.

172. Louw-Nida, §12.18. As stated in note 149 above, the phrase does not refer to the activities of the Holy Ghost, although this member of the Godhead also uses this divine force to fill its missions. See also Andrés García Serrano, "The Pauline Sense of the Expression 'Now the Lord Is the Spirit' (2 Cor. 3:17a)," *Expository Times* 127, n. 10 (2016): 479–87, whose study explicates the relationship that Paul established between the meaning signified by the nouns "Lord" and "Spirit." In particular, it addresses the issue of how the Lord and the Spirit are interrelated.

173. That is, the process of adding more words to give a clear meaning to one's thought.

would read, "Now when I say 'Lord,' I mean 'the Spirit.'"[174] By translating it this way, the idea aligns nicely with what Paul says next.

where the Spirit of the Lord is, there is liberty / where the Spirit of the Lord is, there is freedom: The phrase τὸ πνευμα κυρίου (*to pneuma kyriou*), "the spirit of the Lord," likely defines what Paul is referring to in the previous phrase. It is neither the Savior nor God but rather their divine influence that he has in mind. The term, therefore, does not refer to the Holy Ghost. It denotes, rather, as noted in 3:8 above, the divine influence that acts upon the recipient that brings to him or her powers not otherwise available. Paul describes what it brings as ἐλευθερία (*eleutheria*), "freedom." In the present context the noun denotes an escape from the slavery of the Mosaic law.[175] This is because the Spirit removes the inhibiting veil and opens its recipients' eyes to the truth of salvation in Christ alone.

3:18 ***But we all, with open face beholding as in a glass the glory of the Lord / And all of us who with unveiled faces contemplate the glory of the Lord:*** The conjunction δέ (*de*), "and, but," here indicates continuation of thought and is, therefore, translated as "and" in our Rendition.[176] The phrase ἡμεῖς . . . πάντες (*hēmeis . . . pantes*), "all of us," shows the universal nature of the phenomenon Paul now describes. The verb ἀνακαλύπτω (*anakalyptō*), "to unveil or uncover,"[177] found here as a perfect passive participle, indicates that an unveiling has taken place in the past and that its effect continues into the present. The verb κατοπτρίζω (*katoptrizō*), "to view through the use of a mirror, or contemplate," found here as a present middle participle, denotes primarily seeing something in a mirror—that is, seeing its reflection only, not the thing itself.[178] Anciently most mirrors were made of polished bronze.[179] Mirrors made in Corinth were highly valued because of the fine workmanship used in their making.[180] Paul picks

---

174. Witherington, *Conflict and Community,* 382. Compare Earl J. Richard, "Polemics, Old Testament, and Theology: A Study of II Cor., III, 1–IV, 6," *Revue Biblique* 88, no. 3 (July 1981): 357, who comes to the same conclusion.

175. BDAG, 316.

176. BDAG, 213.

177. BDAG, 65.

178. BDAG, 535, *DAG,* s.v. "κατοπτρίζω"; Louw-Nida, §24.44.

179. Bronze, a product of adding zinc to copper, was very durable.

180. Henry S. Robinson, *Corinth: A Brief History of the City and a Guide to the Excavations* (Athens: The American School of Classical Studies in Athens, 1972), 5. By the first century, glass mirrors began to be introduced, but because these were generally inferior in giving an accurate reflection, metal mirrors remained popular for quite some time. See J. D. Douglas, ed., *The Illustrated Bible Dictionary,* part 2 (Leicester, Eng.: Inter-Varsity

up on this item of pride (see also 1 Cor. 13:12) to illustrate that no matter the quality of the mirror, it does not reproduce the genuine article but only an indirect nonreality of it.[181] Even so, his metaphorical mirror can do something no real mirror can. Through the power of the spirit, it can make the invisible visible to the believer.[182] But it only works if a certain condition is met—namely, having the obscuring veil of hardheartedness and unbelief removed. With uncovered faces the Saints can see the glory of the Lord. That glory, however, is only a reflection seen as it were through a mirror. Even so, it shows the potential of what the believer may achieve.

are changed into the same image from glory to glory / are being transformed into the same image from glory to glory: The verb μεταμορφόω (*metamorphoō*), found here as a present passive, in its spiritual sense means "to change inwardly in fundamental character" and, given the force of the passive voice, "to be transformed."[183] In LDS parlance, it denotes being changed from a "natural man" with his tendencies toward selfishness, egotism, and self-aggrandizement into a Saint who is "submissive, meek, humble, patient, [and] full of love" toward others (Mosiah 3:19).

The noun εἰκών (*eikōn*), "image," denotes both something that is "made or drawn to conform to the likeness of the original" and "that which has the same form as the original."[184] In this case, it refers not to the actual physical image of the Savior. Rather, it refers to the Christlike perfection, powers, and station that the Saints can achieve.

On δόξα (*doxa*), "glory," see 3:7–8 above. In the present context, it refers to that ever-increasing power through which the Saints take upon themselves the power, majesty, and station of Christ by moving from a lesser level of glory to an ever-greater one until they receive a fulness of all that the Savior has (Rom. 8:17; compare Luke 12:42–44).

even as by the Spirit of the Lord / just as from the Spirit of the Lord: The adverb καθάπερ (*kathaper*), "just as, exactly as," acts as "an emphatic

---

Press; Wheaton, Ill.: Tyndale House; Sydney: Hodder and Stoughton, 1980), 1011–12, s.v. "mirror."

181. Gordon D. Fee, *The First Epistle to the Corinthians,* The New International Commentary on the New Testament (Grand Rapids, Mich.: Wm. B. Eerdmans, 1987), 647–48; Joseph A. Fitzmyer, *First Corinthians: A New Translation with Introduction and Commentary* (New Haven, Conn.: Yale University Press, 2008), 499–500; Thiselton, *First Epistle,* 1068–70.

182. Gerhard Kittle, "κατοπτρίζομαι," in *TDNT,* 2:696–67.

183. BDAG, 639–40; Louw-Nida, §13.53.

184. BDAG, 281–82.

marker of comparison between events."[185] Here it points to the ongoing, dynamic power by which the Saints are transformed from a lower level of glory to a higher one. Paul is careful to identify that power. The preposition ἀπὸ (*apo*), "from," acts here as a marker identifying the source.[186] The phrase ἀπὸ κυρίου πνεύματος *(kyriou pneumatos)*, "from the Lord's spirit," identifies that source. Again, it does not appear that Paul has the Holy Ghost in mind, but rather the enabling power that flows through Christ to assist in the transformation of the willing and reaching soul.

Analysis and Summary

The major thrust of Paul's intent in 3:12–18 is to explain both his and the other missionaries' audacious and open-faced proclamation of the gospel to all who will listen (3:12), in contrast to Moses' veiled face when he spoke with the congregation of Israel (3:13; Ex. 34:33).

To further his point, the Apostle turns from his focus on the great difference between the glories of the Mosaic and current ministries to an examination of the implications in the story of Moses' interaction with the children of Israel (Ex. 34:29–35). According to the Exodus account, when the people saw him, they were consternated because his countenance radiated with divine glory. Due to their discomfort at having to endure that radiance, Moses hid the glory by putting a veil over his face when working with the people. However, he took it off when he went into the tabernacle and stood before Jehovah. From Paul's perspective, these acts had important theological significance. The first prevented the Israelites from seeing, due to their continuous rebellion, the completion of what was even then becoming inoperative—namely, the power of the old covenant (3:13). In short, the veil represented Moses' judgment against hardhearted Israel. His act symbolized his refusing or cutting this recalcitrant people off from direct access to their God and the fulness of his covenant. They would no longer experience God's manifest presence.[187] The second act, removing the veil, showed that Moses could still personally commune directly with God and receive his word (Ex. 33:9, 11), thus showing that such a close and personal relationship was possible for any who would be as the prophet.

---

185. Louw-Nida, §64.15; BDAG, 488.

186. BDAG, 105–7.

187. W. J. Dumbrell, "The Newness of the New Covenant: The Logic of the Argument in 2 Corinthians 3," *Reformed Theological Review* 61, no. 2 (August 2002): 61–64; Baker, "Did the Glory of Moses' Face Fade?," 1–15.

Unfortunately, as the Apostle laments in 3:14–15, the problem of the veil's affects yet remained upon the hardhearted among the Jews even though the gospel was now being preached. The veil metaphorically continued to cover the Jews' hearts as they read Moses' words. The stubborn persistence of the problem was due to their refusal to accept Christ. Therefore, they could not see that the ministry of the old covenant was being annulled and replaced by the new. In sum, the totality of the old system was coming to an end (τέλος, *telos*), but the Jews were blind to the fact that the old law had had its day and was being discontinued.[188] The glory of the old covenant as a means of procuring a more holy life had become inoperative and would remain so. The only way to lift the veil was to accept the Savior and the new covenant.[189]

In 3:16, the Apostle insists that whenever a person accepts Jesus as the divine Son of God, the separating barrier, symbolized by the veil, is taken away. When he states that "we all . . . behold in a mirror the glory of the Lord" (3:18), he is emphasizing the effect of the veil's removal. Each convert can see and enjoy a reflected and beautiful glory like that revealed in the countenance of Moses. As a result, the Saints all share the common salvation brought by the force of the new covenant. Of this fact, Paul is the unapologetic and almost brazen bearer. Three spiritually powerful events stand at the heart of the Apostle's boldness: first, the Spirit's lifting the veil from off the hearts of the converts; second, the ability of the converts to see the new covenant with its attending ministry for what it is; and finally, their experiencing the transforming effects in their lives.[190]

The result is, as Paul notes in 3:17, freedom (ἐλευθερία, *elytheria*). For Paul, such freedom does not refer to some psychological or intellectual state that detaches one from sin, suffering, and death. The Apostle is well aware that he and his fellow Saints are, due to Christ, suffering in abundance. No, freedom does not mean being autonomous or unfettered from all bounds. It consists, rather, of being freed of the Mosaic law and the heavy restrictions it placed upon the observant.

---

188. Witherington, *Conflict and Community,* 380–81.

189. Hardy, "Paul: Personal Disclosures," 89.

190. Seifrid, *Second Letter,* 162. Paul's shows that by taking a stand on Moses and all he stood for as the basis of their authority, his antagonists expose a self-delusion that prohibits them, like a veil, from seeing that truth. On the impact of their Moses typology, see John Howard Schütz, *Paul and the Anatomy of Apostolic Authority* (Cambridge: Cambridge University Press, 1975, repr., Louisville: Westminster John Knox Press, 2007), 173–74, 185, pagination refers to the Westminster printing.

But there is more to it than that. "Freedom from" carries with it the force of "freedom to." The new "freedom to" is one of communion. It is freedom to hear and act directly with the Savior through the ministration of the Spirit conveyed via the new covenant. That includes not only praise to the Divine but also laments and petitions arising from suffering and need. Further, Paul sees this freedom as expanding beyond service to God to include service to neighbors and friends, whom the Christian can now freely serve.[191]

One aspect of that freedom Paul details in 3:18. Through the transforming power of the "spirit of the Lord" that is now operating upon the believers, the person is changed (μεταμορφόω, *metamorphoō*), by degrees, into Christlike glory. In his writings to the Romans, the Apostle makes a similar point. He admonishes his readers to not "conform to the pattern of this world but be transformed (*metamorphoō*) by the renewal of your mind, that you may prove what is the will of God, what is good, acceptable, and perfect" (Rom. 12:2, our translation). The renewal "in mind" that he refers to certainly involved a change in his readers' mental or cognitive processes, including reasoning and perception, but reaches far beyond that. "Paul is not merely encouraging the Roman Christians to adopt a new moral outlook—he is impressing on them, the need for a profound transformation of the whole person."[192] Though long in process, this transformation is real and comes with ever-increasing glory until its recipients fully take upon themselves the nature of the Lord and obtain a celestial glory.[193] Paul's theology shows that he fully accepted the idea of theosis (that a person really can become as God).[194]

As Paul noted elsewhere, it is through the power of Christ that the Saints' imperfect and weak bodies become "transformed in likeness to his glorious body, by the power which enables him to subject all things to himself" (Philip. 3:21, our translation). Only at the resurrection will the action become complete (Col. 3:4).[195] This transformation into the image

---

191. Seifrid, *Second Letter*, 177.

192. *NID*, 3:340–41.

193. *NID*, 3:340.

194. On this idea in LDS theology, see Keith E. Norman, "Deification, Early Christian," in *EM*, 1:369–70; Ernst W. Benz, "Imago Dei: Man in the Image of God," in *Reflections on Mormonism: Judaeo-Christian Parallels*, ed. Truman G. Madsen (Provo, Utah: Religious Studies Center, Brigham Young University, 1978), 201–21.

195. Harris, *Second Corinthians*, 317.

of Christ, we need to stress, does not come by an act of will alone. It takes far more than that; it takes divine power given through the Spirit of Christ.

The Apostle skillfully reveals the ramifications arising from the ministration of the new dispensation. God's people can now operate under the influence of the Holy Spirit. Therefore, all the believers have access to Christ's spirit and his power, making it possible for them to come before the Father "with unveiled faces" (3:18, NR). This alone shows how much greater the new covenant is than the old. It is based on the ongoing nature of the ministry now being executed under the hands of the Apostles and their fellow missionaries. Through their means, God's work in carrying out the "ministry of righteousness" is moving in the world, assisted and verified by the power of the Spirit itself that is being continually made manifest in the lives of the Saints (3:17–18).[196]

---

196. Thus, in this section, Paul fully develops the *qal wāhômer* argument (from lesser to greater) he began in 3:7–11 and forcefully illustrates the overpowering glory of the new ministration compared to the slight glint of the old one. On the nature and use of this type of argument, see Analysis and Summary for the section above.

Chapter 4

Components of an Authentic Ministry, Continued

Introduction

In the first portion of this chapter (4:1–6), Paul continues to answer the question he asked in 2:16 about who is qualified to preach the word and explain the works of God. At this point, however, he adds elements to his argument to answer charges made by his antagonists, especially their insistence that he has insincere motives in preaching the gospel. To make a defense of his integrity and to push his main argument further, the Apostle has his readers consider elements in the epistle that rest upon the solid foundation he has been laying since 2:14. In doing so, he forces them to focus on the striking pieces that showcase authentic ministry and illustrate his personal integrity in preaching the gospel.[1] This allows him to describe afresh the mission that Christ has given him. Before (3:4–18), he presented his labors in light of "the communication of the Spirit," but now he emphasizes God's saving work as he moves through the Apostle and his missionary companions to effect the broader mission to the world.[2]

In 4:1–6, Paul gives punch to the point he is making by employing an ancient literary technique known as "ring-composition," in which "his closing thoughts revert to his earlier statements and complete the circle of ideas."[3] In

1. For example, the text recalls such themes as ministry (3:6; 4:1), "the Word of God" (2:17; 4:2), proper preaching of the word (2:17; 4:2), the manifestation of truth (2:14; 4:2), abuse of God's word (2:17; 4:2), self-commendation (3:1; 4:2), and the preaching of Christ (2:17; 4:5). For an additional list, see Guthrie, *2 Corinthians,* 233.

2. Seifrid, *Second Letter,* 187.

3. Martin, *2 Corinthians,* 219. These passages do not follow a strict chiastic structure as the term "ring-composition" would usually imply. For a study on this type of structure, see Mary Douglas, *Thinking in Circles: An Essay on Ring Composition* (New Haven, Conn.: Yale University Press, 2007). Although Paul clearly refers to what he has done before, the structure is looser than what ring composition usually requires.

doing so, he signals his readers that he is bringing this portion of his analysis and defense to a close. He does so by showcasing his integrity as a minister of Christ.

The Apostle, however, does more than simply build on the points he made against his adversaries in chapter 2 by adding another line of argument to answer their criticism of his ministry and message. The text suggests that some of his adversaries attacked him on the basis of a growing physical infirmity that manifested itself in increasing bodily weakness of some sort. From their point of view, this condition makes his message ineffectual (see 10:10). Paul's pushback shows his challengers as groping in the darkness because of their insistence that his preaching lacks "the demonstrable signs of power" needed to convince them of its truth.[4] In point of fact, he insists, his preaching cannot help them because they refuse to see it for what it is. As a result, "the god of this world" (4:4) has been able to blind their minds to the truth.[5] He is not bothered by their blindness, for his ministry is ever before God. This knowledge explains his forthrightness in proclaiming the gospel as he does (3:12). With this argument, he concludes the defense he began in 2:14.

With 4:7, Paul opens a new argument in his defense. It does not come to a close in this chapter but runs through 5:10. The text suggests that the Apostle designed this argument in such a way as to gain further trust and acceptance from his readers by showing them the cost he and other missionaries have had to pay for the gospel's sake. He begins by clearly stating the suffering his ministry has cost him (4:7–15) and then describes the perspective he has achieved from this suffering (4:16–18).

His writing in this section reveals Paul's deliberate intent of further winning his readers to his side and away from the self-styled "apostle" (10:12–18) who has attacked both his integrity and doctrine. Quite a number of the Saints, unfortunately, had been won over by this person's self-promotion. Paul must now win them back, but he is walking a tightrope. He "wants his converts neither to adore nor to ignore him, so he will praise himself in a way that is consistent with his own principle that the Christian boaster should boast in the Lord (1 Cor. 1:30–31). This means that he will boast of his own weakness and sufferings in order to show that his triumphs must result from God's work through him."[6]

---

4. Martin, *2 Corinthians,* 220.

5. Martin, *2 Corinthians,* 220.

6. Witherington, *Conflict and Community,* 385.

Their response to his former letters has informed him that his target audience resonates best to both his ἦθος (*ēthos*; an appeal to character and proper past conduct)[7] and πάθος (*pathos*; endured hardships and suffering for a cause).[8] He, therefore, concentrates on both aspects in this chapter.

Paul's Perseverance in the Ministry (4:1–6)

Greek Text

1 Διὰ τοῦτο, ἔχοντες τὴν διακονίαν ταύτην καθὼς ἠλεήθημεν, οὐκ ἐγκακοῦμεν,
2 ἀλλὰ ἀπειπάμεθα τὰ κρυπτὰ τῆς αἰσχύνης, μὴ περιπατοῦντες ἐν πανουργίᾳ μηδὲ
δολοῦντες τὸν λόγον τοῦ θεοῦ, ἀλλὰ τῇ φανερώσει τῆς ἀληθείας συνιστάνοντες
ἑαυτοὺς πρὸς πᾶσαν συνείδησιν ἀνθρώπων ἐνώπιον τοῦ θεοῦ. 3 εἰ δὲ καὶ ἔστιν
κεκαλυμμένον τὸ εὐαγγέλιον ἡμῶν, ἐν τοῖς ἀπολλυμένοις ἐστὶν κεκαλυμμένον,
4 ἐν οἷς ὁ θεὸς τοῦ αἰῶνος τούτου ἐτύφλωσεν τὰ νοήματα τῶν ἀπίστων εἰς τὸ
μὴ αὐγάσαι τὸν φωτισμὸν τοῦ εὐαγγελίου τῆς δόξης τοῦ Χριστοῦ, ὅς ἐστιν εἰκὼν
τοῦ θεοῦ. 5 οὐ γὰρ ἑαυτοὺς κηρύσσομεν ἀλλὰ Χριστὸν Ἰησοῦν κύριον, ἑαυτοὺς
δὲ δούλους ὑμῶν διὰ Ἰησοῦν. 6 ὅτι ὁ θεὸς ὁ εἰπών· Ἐκ σκότους φῶς λάμψει, ὃς
ἔλαμψεν ἐν ταῖς καρδίαις ἡμῶν πρὸς φωτισμὸν τῆς γνώσεως τῆς δόξης τοῦ θεοῦ
ἐν προσώπῳ Χριστοῦ. [SBLGNT]

King James Version

1 Therefore seeing we have this ministry,
as we have received mercy, we faint not;
2 But have renounced the hidden things
of dishonesty, not walking in craftiness,
nor handling the word of God deceitfully; but by manifestation of the truth
commending ourselves to every man's
conscience in the sight of God. 3 But if
our gospel be hid, it is hid to them that
are lost: 4 In whom the god of this world
hath blinded the minds of them which
believe not, lest the light of the glorious
gospel of Christ, who is the image of

New Rendition

1 Therefore, since we have this ministry, because we have been given mercy,
we do not become discouraged. 2 On
the contrary, we have renounced the
shameful hidden things, neither practicing deception nor distorting the
word of God, but by the open proclamation of the truth we commend ourselves to everyone's conscience in the
sight of God. 3 But even if our gospel is
hidden, it is only hidden to those who
are perishing, 4 among whom the god
of this world has blinded the minds of

7. BDAG, 435.

8. BDAG, 748; Witherington, *Conflict and Community*, 353.

God, should shine unto them. 5 For we
preach not ourselves, but Christ Jesus
the Lord; and ourselves your servants
for Jesus' sake. 6 For God, who com-
manded the light to shine out of dark-
ness, hath shined in our hearts, to give
the light of the knowledge of the glory
of God in the face of Jesus Christ.

those who do not believe so that they do
not discern the light of the glorious gos-
pel of Christ, who is the image of God.
5 For we do not proclaim ourselves but
Christ Jesus as Lord and ourselves as
your servants for Jesus' sake. 6 For it is
God who said, "Out of darkness light
will shine" [Gen. 1:3], who shined in our
hearts to bring to light the knowledge
of God's glory in Christ's face.

Translation Notes and Comments

4:1 ***Therefore seeing we have this ministry / Therefore, since we have this ministry:*** The retrospective phrase,[9] διὰ τοῦτο (*dia touto*), "therefore, because of this," refers back to the ministry which Paul has been developing since 2:14, a ministry he has described as a "new covenant" (3:6) with its own glory that also comes with God's liberating spirit. The noun διακονία (*diakonia*), "ministry,"[10] refers to the new covenant that Paul and his companions had been mercifully granted (this is a favorite theme of Paul's; see 1 Cor. 7:25; 1 Tim. 1:13, 16) and were now extending to others. His careful development of the nature and authenticity of his ministry (2:14–3:18) forms the foundation of his current defense against his detractors.[11]

as we have received mercy / because we have been given mercy: The verb ἐλεέω (*eleeō*), "to have compassion, mercy, pity,"[12] is found here in the form of an aorist passive and means "to be given mercy." The subordinate conjunction καθως (*kathōs*) carries a causative force, "because, since"; therefore we have translated καθὼς ἠλεήθημεν (*kathōs ēleēthēmen*) as "because we have been given mercy."[13] This is an example of a "divine passive" where God or Christ is the unnamed agent.[14] The phrase may refer back to the grace-filled mercy Christ bestowed upon Paul at the time when he, as a young man, was fighting against the Church (Acts 9:1–9). Despite

9. The phrase shows a causal relationship between the points Paul has made before and the ones he will now make. Harris, *Second Epistle,* 322.

10. BDAG, 230.

11. Guthrie, *2 Corinthians,* 234.

12. BDAG, 315.

13. Wallace, *Greek Grammar,* 674; BDAG, 493–94.

14. Wallace, *Greek Grammar,* 437.

his misdirected and malicious intent, the Lord forgave him and called him to service in the new covenant.[15]

we faint not / we do not become discouraged: The verb ἐγκακέω (*enkakeō*) means, at best, "to lose enthusiasm, be discouraged, lose heart" and, at worst, "to giving up on something."[16] The verb also carries the nuance of "failing," which includes moral failures such as acting wrongly. With the negative particle οὐκ (*ouk*), "not," the phrase denotes never losing heart or determination for a cause.[17] The nuance of "not failing" also links the idea here with Paul's assertion of his personal integrity (4:2) as well as with his defense of the apostolic mission in the larger arena.[18] He and his companions are determined to not fail. Thus, the missionaries, no matter what the opposition, neither lose enthusiasm nor become discouraged because they recognize that it is God, through his mercy, who has given them the divine ministry.[19] To become discouraged in preaching the gospel would devalue both it and the divine mercy that generated it.

4:2 ***But have renounced the hidden things of dishonesty / On the contrary, we have renounced the shameful hidden things:*** The conjunction ἀλλά (*alla*), "on the contrary, but,"[20] at the beginning of this verse plays an important role by effecting a sharp contrast with what has come before. It emphasizes those items the missionaries have given up.[21] The verb ἀπεῖπον (*apeipon*) means to "disown, forbid, renounce."[22] This is the only occurrence of the word in the New Testament, and that makes it hard to be precise in capturing Paul's intent. In non-canonical papyri fragments where the word is found, it means "to forbid."[23] "The meaning 'to renounce' may therefore carry with it the thought of forbidding the approach of the things disowned. If that idea is at play here, then it suggests the willful distance that the missionaries keep from anything that would be shameful.

The noun αἰσχύνη (*aischynē*), "shame," denotes a discreditable deed but carries the nuance of doing something that, if exposed, could bring upon one

15. Barnett, *Second Epistle*, 212.

16. BDAG, 272–73; Thrall, *Critical and Exegetical Commentary*, 1:299–300, suggests the ideas of "letting up," or "being remiss in one's duties."

17. Bernard, "Second Epistle," 59. The phrase "we faint not" echoes 2 Tim. 1:7, where Paul states that "God hath not given us the spirit of fear."

18. Seifrid, *Second Letter*, 190.

19. Bernard, "Second Epistle," 59–60.

20. BDAG, 44–45.

21. Guthrie, *2 Corinthians*, 235.

22. BDAG, 100.

23. MM, *Vocabulary*, 56.

ignominy with its deep disgrace.[24] The adjective κρυπτός (*kryptos*) denotes what is hidden,[25] but in the plural phrase τὰ κρυπτά (*ta krypta*), it is nominalized as "the hidden things" and refers to all that is deliberately hidden. It describes both actions and intents that Paul feels are shameful or disgraceful[26] and likely refers, at least in part, to the methods of the false teachers who are making their way among the Saints (Philip. 3:18–19). For Paul, the noun can also refer to the condition of the heart that attempts to hide the motives that drive patterns of behavior.[27] All this gives the sense of the phrase not simply as that which is hidden out of a sense of shame[28] but as that which is hidden because of the fear that if the true motives were exposed, the person would suffer disgrace. Such a situation many in the Greco-Roman world would have found most repellent and therefore be very willing to use any means (except, unfortunately, being outright honest) to prevent exposure.

Paul's meaning in his use of the phrase τὰ κρυπτὰ τῆς αἰσχύνης (*ta krypta tēs aischynēs*), "hidden things of shame," is unclear. The problem centers around the genitive noun αἰσχύνης (*aischynēs*), "of shame." The case can be taken in various ways. It can refer to source (the hidden things yielding shame), possession (the hidden things that belong to shame), quality (the hidden things that consist of shame), and even epexegesis.[29] We treated it as a genitive of quality, a common construction in koine Greek that reflects a Hebrew influence, since Hebrew often uses a noun in a construct to compensate for its sparsity of adjectives.[30] Hence our translation, "shameful hidden things."

not walking in craftiness / neither practicing deception: The noun πανουργία (*panourgia*) denotes "cunning, craftiness, trickery."[31] Its components, παν- (*pan-*, "all") and ἐργ- (*erg-*, "work"), carry the idea of being adroit or shrewd due to a very discerning mind. It carries the very negative nuance of deliberate, carefully thought-out, unscrupulous behavior done to achieve one's ends.[32] The preposition ἐν (*en*), usually meaning "in," can

24. BDAG, 29–30.

25. BDAG, 570–71.

26. Thrall, *Critical and Exegetical Commentary,* 1:303. Harris, *Second Epistle,* 324, after examining the various ways in which the phrase can be taken, elects for "underhanded and disgraceful ways."

27. For example, see Rom. 2:29; 1 Cor. 4:5; Guthrie, *2 Corinthians,* 236.

28. BDAG, 570–71.

29. Seifrid, *Second Letter,* 192.

30. BDF, §165.

31. BDAG, 754.

32. *NID,* 3:602–3; Seifrid, *Second Letter,* 192.

also be understood as denoting "means." If that is the case, then the phrase ἐν πανουργίᾳ (*en panourgia*) would mean "by means of deceit or trickery."[33]

The verb περιπατέω (*peripateō*), found here as a present participle, means both "to walk around" and "to comport oneself," the latter connoting a habit of conduct.[34] It is one of Paul's favorite means of describing both immediate conduct and a broad pattern of life.[35] The idea it conveys in this clause is that of continual behavior or deliberate action and is likely meant to characterize the work of the Apostle's adversaries, who, through the deliberate use of cunning and tricky speech, are able to garner a following.[36]

nor handling the word of God deceitfully / nor distorting the word of God: The verb δολόω (*doloō*), found here as a present participle, denotes deliberately falsifying or distorting something.[37] A cognate, the noun δόλος (*dolos*), originally referred to fish bait, then to "any cunning contrivance for deceiving or catching," and in an abstract sense it referred to "craft, cunning, treachery."[38] This nuance gives the verb the force of the intentional adulteration of something as a means of catching someone through a falsehood. In this case, what is being distorted or adulterated is τὸν λόγον τοῦ θεοῦ (*ton logon tou theou*), "the word of the God." Paul's point seems to be that these crafty deceivers mix God's word with wrong models to come up with false doctrines in order to snare their victims. Their intent is likely to bolster their position and influence in the Christian community, not to promote the ways of the Divine.[39]

The phrase *ton legon tou theou,* "the word of the God" or the Father, refers to the gospel, as 4:3–4 make clear.

but by manifestation of the truth / but by the open proclamation of the truth: With this clause, Paul sets his ministry in stark contrast to that of those he calls "false brethren" (11:26). The noun φανέρωσις (*phanerōsis*), "open proclamation, manifestation,"[40] denotes "making something fully known by revealing [it] clearly and in some detail."[41] In the present context

33. Guthrie, *2 Corinthians,* 236.

34. BDAG, 803.

35. Examples can be seen in Rom. 6:4; 8:4; 1 Cor. 3:3; 7:17; 2 Cor. 5:7; 10:2–3; Gal. 5:16; Eph. 2:2, 10; 4:1; Col. 1:10; 1 Thes. 2:12; 4:1.

36. Guthrie, *2 Corinthians,* 236.

37. BDAG, 256.

38. LSJ, 443; BGD, s.v. "δόλος"; Harris, *Second Epistle,* 325.

39. Guthrie, *2 Corinthians,* 236–37.

40. BDAG, 1048–49.

41. Louw-Nida, §28.36.

it likely refers to the gospel, for in Paul's eyes, it contains the ultimate truth. The idea that stands behind the noun "truth" is more than a cognitive process, though it includes that, but it is larger than human cognition, often requiring revelation to both disclose and make it comprehensible.[42]

commending ourselves to every man's conscience / we commend ourselves to everyone's conscience: The verb συνίστημι (*synistēmi*), "commend, recommend," carries the idea of providing evidence of personal character through some kind of action for the purpose of establishing a positive bond between parties.[43] In this case that action is not distorting the truth but setting it forth openly, accurately, and clearly. The noun συνείδησις (*syneidēsis*), "conscience," in the present context, does not carry the usual connotation of the human faculty that distinguishes right from wrong and stings when one fails to do what is right. Rather, it refers to an awareness or consciousness of certain information with the ability to make a moral judgment about it.[44] In this case, the information is the missionaries' clear declaration of truth that permits the willing listeners to understand the mysteries of God (1 Cor. 2:7) and thereby understand the Divine and their relationship thereto. The phrase πᾶσαν συνείδησιν ἀνθρώπων (*pasan syneidēsin anthrōpōn*), "every person's conscience," then refers to every possible variety of human conscience[45]—that is, all levels of awareness, emphasizing the breadth of people the missionaries preach to.

in the sight of God: The preposition ἐνώπιον (*enōpion*), "before," denotes something that is in view of another.[46] This phrase is small but very important, for it discloses Paul's knowledge that God is always aware of what he is doing, and therefore he does it the best that he can.

4:3 ***But if our gospel be hid, it is hid to them that are lost / But even if our gospel is hidden, it is only hidden to those who are perishing:*** The verb καλύπτω (*kalyptō*), found here as a perfect passive participle, means "to be hidden, concealed, covered over," with the intent of actively keeping

---

42. Jerome Murphy-O'Connor, "Truth: Paul and Qumran," in *Paul and Qumran: Studies in New Testament Exegesis,* ed. Jerome Murphy-O'Connor (Chicago: Priory Press, 1968), 179–230, stated that the noun "truth" often acted to designate revealed doctrine which embodied both the law and its interpretation.

43. BDAG, 972–73; Louw-Nida, §§28.49; 33.334, 63.6.

44. Louw-Nida, §28.4; Christian Maurer, "σύνοιδα, συνείδησις," in *TDNT,* 7:898–919, see especially 917.

45. Bernard, "Second Epistle," 59–60.

46. BDAG, 342.

something from being known or found out.[47] The grammatical construction of the phrase εἰ . . . ἔστιν κεκαλυμμένον (*ei . . . estin kekalymmenon*), "if [it] is has been hidden," shows that Paul is referring not to a possibility but to an actual situation.[48] The force of the perfect tense here suggests that the gospel, actively hidden by some in the past, continues to remains so.

The verb ἀπόλλυμι (*apollymi*), found here as a middle present participle, generally means "to be utterly destroyed," but in the middle voice it means "to perish." As such it does not refer to the annihilation of being, but of well-being. The word also carries the nuance of a failure to obtain something of value.[49] In this case it refers to the loss of salvation. The implication of the present tense is that those in this condition have not yet lost their redemption but are currently in the act of doing so.[50]

4:4 *the god of this world:* The noun θεος (*theos*), "god," is the general appellation of deities or divinities in the Greco-Roman world. The term also included anything that seemed to possess a divine quality, nature, or power. The "god of this world" is Satan.[51] Referring to this evil being as a "god" is unique in scripture.[52] Paul is not, however, attributing divine qualities to him, but rather inferring that his influence and power over this fallen world is causing people to yield, if ignorantly, to his ways.[53]

---

47. BDAG, 505; Louw-Nida, §§28.79; 79.114. The related noun κάλλυμα (*kalymma*) refers to a veil that is used to hide the face but also to that which obscures the truth and thereby prevents understanding. BDAG, 505.

48. Guthrie, *2 Corinthians,* 239.

49. Louw-Nida, §§20.31; 57.67.

50. BDAG, 115–16.

51. *DNTC,* 2:417. Several General Authorities view the god of the age as love of gold or love of wealth—that is, materialism. For example, see Brigham Young, in *JD,* 1:335; 10:267; George A. Smith, *JD,* 9:199. John Taylor, in *JD,* 10:260, saw this "god" as both Satan and materialism but also felt it referenced anyone who led the Saints astray. See John Taylor, in *JD,* 6:167; 7:120. For insights on wealth and righteousness, see Hugh Nibley, "Semester 2, Lecture 43: Alma 1–2, Escapes, Wealth," in *Teachings of the Book of Mormon: Semester 2* (Salt Lake City: Deseret Book, 1993), 233–38.

52. Due to its uniqueness, some commentators have suggested that Paul actually has Elohim in mind. See James M. Scott, *2 Corinthians* (Peabody, Mass.: Hendrickson Publishers, 1998), 84, who makes this case. However, the negative context suggests that Satan fits better. See Hafemann, *2 Corinthians,* 177–78; Thrall, *Critical and Exegetical Commentary,* 1:308. For general background concerning Paul's thought in this area, see Ralph P. Martin, *Reconciliation: A Study of Paul's Theology,* 2nd ed. (Grand Rapids, Mich.: Academie Books, 1989; reprint, Eugene, Ore.: Wipf and Stock, 1997), 51–54.

53. Guthrie, *2 Corinthians,* 240 n. 17.

The noun αἰών (*aiōn*), "world," has a number of important nuances. It generally refers to an era or historical period, indicating the aggregate of things contained within that time frame.[54] It also carries the idea of a period of weakness, instability, impiety, and calamity with its resultant misery. More specifically it connotes both the age and the place where the devil rules the thoughts and deeds of people—thus, the current world.[55]

hath blinded the minds of them which believe not / has blinded the minds of those who do not believe: The verb τυφλόω (*typhloō*), "to blind,"[56] is used here figuratively and indicates one of the chief methods Satan uses to seduce people to his ways. The noun νόημα (*noēma*), "mind,"[57] has two nuances. One refers to the intellectual process of thinking, thus denoting "thought," the other to the faculty where such thinking takes place—that is, "the mind."[58] It is the latter nuance that is used here. Both nuances, however, connote the idea of a careful consideration of an idea, action, or position. The point is that deriving a correct understanding takes accurate knowledge. When such is lacking, an outcome can be wrong, even disastrous. In the scriptures, the "mind" always carries a theological usage centered on understanding the divine will, especially in terms of salvation.

Paul refers to those whom Satan has been able to blind as ὁ ἄπιστος (*ho apistos*), "the unbeliever."[59] The nuance the word carries is not that of simple disbelief but of active rejection.[60] It is a thought-out process. Thus, the objective for both Satan and God is capturing people's minds. The noun generally denotes Gentiles but, in this case, could include those Jews who oppose the Christians and even those Christians who oppose Paul.

lest the light . . . should shine unto them / so that they do not discern the light: The phrase εἰς τὸ μή (*eis to mē*), "lest, so that not," used with an infinitive refers to the result of an effort.[61] In this case it describes Satan's objective in spiritually blinding people. The verb αὐγάζω (*augazō*) means "to see, shine."[62] A more expanded definition would be "to cause to see

54. BDAG, 32–33; Louw-Nida, §67.143.

55. LSJ, 45; Louw-Nida, §41.38.

56. BDAG, 1021.

57. BDAG, 675.

58. Louw-Nida, §§26.14; 30.15.

59. This is one of his favorite designations for those who oppose the gospel of Christ. For example, see 1 Cor. 6:6; 7:12–15; 14:22–24; 2 Cor. 6:14–15; compare 1 Tim. 5:8; Titus 1:15.

60. BDAG, 103–4; Rudolf Bultmann, "πιστεύω," in *TDNT*, 6:176–78.

61. Guthrie, *2 Corinthians*, 240.

62. BDAG, 149.

clearly" and, by extension, "to illuminate, discern."[63] The English word "discern," referring as it does to "the power of deeply perceiving and of distinguishing or discriminating what the senses perceive,"[64] seems to best capture Paul's intent.

The masculine noun φωτισμός (*phōtismos*), "light, enlightenment,"[65] refers to what is made fully known through clear and detailed revelation. The word, in a scriptural context, refers to "the illumination of the inner life"[66] and more specifically to the revealed truth concerning the nature and mission—that is, the "good news" (εὐαγγέλλιον, *euangellion*)—of Christ.[67]

The phrase presents a translation challenge, since the grammatical construction makes it unclear whether the verb αὐγάζω (*augazō*) is transitive or intransitive. [68] If it is intransitive, the subject of the verb is φωτισμός (*phōtismos*), "light," and the translation would be "so that the light does not shine."[69] If it is transitive, then the subject would be αὐτούς (*autous*), "they," referring back to τῶν ἀπίστων (*tōn apistōn*), "those who do not believe," which must be suppled since it is not in the text but is easily implied,[70] making the translation "so that they do not see clearly," or "so that they do not discern the light." Following most translators, we have taken the verb as intransitive.[71] One reason we have done so is that disbelief does not stop light from shining, only from being seen or discerned.

the light of the glorious gospel of Christ: The noun εὐαγγέλιον (*euangelion*), "gospel," by New Testament times, denoted "good news."[72] The earliest Christian use of the word encapsulates the whole of the ministry of Christ, including his teachings, activities, death, and Resurrection. But undergirding the noun is the idea of the living power that infuses the message. The

63. *NID*, 1:439; Louw-Nida, §28.37; BDG, s.v. "αὐγάζω"; MM, 90. This is the only place the word is found in the New Testament and therefore the precise meaning Paul intended can only be approximated. The related noun αὐγή (*augē*) refers to the dawn. BDAG, 149–50. The inference in this passage is that Satan works so that the truth about Christ "does not dawn on" the unbelievers. Bernard, "Second Epistle," 60.

64. *Dictionary of Synonyms,* s.v. "see."

65. BDAG, 1074.

66. BDAG, 1074.

67. Louw-Nida, §§28.36; 72.3.

68. Gerhard Kittle, "αὐγάζω," in *TDNT,* 1:507–8; Barnett, *Second Epistle,* 218 n. 41.

69. The KJV follows this construction and, therefore, takes φωτισμόν as the subject of the verb. *NID,* 1:440.

70. Some ancient texts actually have the pronoun but these are generally later versions.

71. Barnett, *Second Epistle,* 218 n. 41. *NID,* 1:440, allows for both readings but prefers the second.

72. BDAG, 402–3.

word connotes salvation history that is derived as a revelation from and of God as manifest in Christ.[73] The noun δόξα (*doxa*), "glory," in the present context, carries the nuances of "splendor, magnificence, prestige."[74]

The noun χριστός (*Christos*), "Christ," is a Greek translation of the Hebrew מָשִׁיחַ (*māšîaḥ*), both meaning "the anointed one." The title is one of importance, for it was associated in Hebrew theology with kingly, prophetic and priestly rights and powers as derived directly from God himself. The anointing gave the individual the right to use his position, authority, and power to do God's bidding and to be *the* administrator over his kingdom. Thus, the title fits the position of Jesus very well, for he was and is God's "anointed one." The term gradually took on the distinction of an actual name. This change was due to certain passages in which the term *christos* did not refer to the idea of a messiah in general but to a very specific Messiah—that is, Jesus himself.[75] Paul's writings show that this transfer, however, had not yet taken place. For him, Jesus was *the* "anointed one" who performed always in that office.

This phrase τὸν φωτισμὸν τοῦ εὐαγγελίου τῆς δόξης τοῦ Χριστοῦ (*tou phōtismon tou euangeliou tēs doxēs tou Christou*) presents a number of translation difficulties. A literal translation reads, "the light of the gospel of the glory of Christ," and, as can be seen, stacks up three genitives. These offer several translation possibilities determined by how each one is construed.

The question is, What does the genitive phrase τῆς δόξης (*tēs doxēs*), "of the glory," refer to? Is it the gospel or Christ? Some commentators see it as modifying Christ. In this case the genitive is one of content, marking the substance of the message preached—namely, Christ in his role as Savior.[76] Taking it that

73. In Attic Greek, it initially denoted the reward for bringing good news. More specifically it denoted the first announcement of victory after a battle that brought the bearer a nice prize. Over time the word came to denote any type of good news. Gerhard Freidrich, "εὐαγγέλιον,"in *TDNT,* 2:721–37. As Anderson, *Understanding Paul,* 133–34, notes, its glorious light dawned at Corinth as the "good news" or "message of happiness." The concept carries the "same positive tones for man as 'the great plan of happiness' referred to in the Book of Mormon (Alma 42:8). Christ's atonement made it so, and Paul was one of the 'ministers of the new covenant; not of the letter, but of the spirit (2 Cor. 3:6)."

74. BDAG, 256–58; Louw-Nida, §§33.357; 87.4, 23.

75. The moving of the title "Christ" to that of a name can be seen in such passages as Matt. 1:16; 27:22; John 4:25. The Gentile Greek speakers, being unfamiliar with the Hebrew term, understood it as a name which to them sounded like χρηστός (*chrēstos*) even in pronunciation. BDAG, 1091; for studies, see *NID,* 4:688–97; Walter Grundmann and others, "χρίω, χρισός," in *TDNT,* 9:493–581.

76. Bernard, "Second Epistle," 60.

way, it would refer to "the display of the glory of Christ."[77] In the same vain, some see the phrase as epexegetical[78] and thus translate it as "the gospel, that is, the light which is Christ's glory."[79] Other commentators see δόξα (*doxa*) as modifying "gospel." In that case, it is either a genitive of source or origin, referring to "the light emanating from the gospel,"[80] or of quality, thus reading "the glorious light of the gospel," referring to the gospel's wonderful nature.[81]

Based on two conditions, the syntax of the phase and the role of the genitive to limit or qualify the meaning of a noun,[82] we see the two genitives, τῆς δόξης (*tēs doxēs*), "of the glory," and τοῦ Χριστοῦ (*tou Christou*), "of the Christ," qualify τοῦ εὐαγγελίου (*tou euangeliou*), "of the gospel." The imagery the phrase creates is that of light streaming from the gospel, whose subject is Christ, and who is himself a being of glory.[83] Since the genitive of quality, also known as an attributive or a Hebrew genitive, is found in a number of places in Paul's writings, we have cautiously accepted that grammatical nuance for our Rendition, and since the best way to translate that into English is as an adjective, we have translated *doxa* as "glorious."[84]

who is the image of God: The noun εἰκών (*eikōn*), "image, likeness, form, appearance,"[85] denotes the object itself but as expressed through some means other than its actual presence. The term suggests an equality with the original as an authentic representation.[86] The wording Paul uses suggests the closeness he sees between the Father and the Son.[87] The Messiah holds the rank of God and acts in that capacity.

4:5 ***For we preach not ourselves, / For we do not proclaim ourselves:*** By introducing the new sentence with the explanatory γάρ (*gar*), "for," Paul clues in his readers that he will now address his role in what he has

---

77. *NID*, 4:642; Louw-Nida, §28.37; Seifrid, *Second Letter*, 196–97.

78. This is a grammatical function where words are added to clarify the meaning of the object.

79. Guthrie, *2 Corinthians*, 241, with n. 19.

80. Barnett, *Second Corinthians*, 218 n. 43.

81. Wallace, *Greek Grammar*, 84–86.

82. Nigel Turner, *Grammatical Insights into the New Testament* (Edinburgh: T&T Clark, 1965), 218, states that when a number of genitives are strung together, the governing genitive is usually placed first.

83. Barnett, *Second Epistle*, 218 n. 43.

84. Wallace, *Greek Grammar*, 86.

85. BDAG, 281–82.

86. Guthrie, *2 Corinthians*, 241.

87. The phrase echoes John 1:1–3 and suggests that Paul may have been acquainted with this gospel. The suggestion is fortified by ideas found in Paul's writings that strongly echo John 8:44–45; 12:31; 14:30; 16:11. Bernard, "Second Epistle," 60.

previously said about the gospel. The verb κηρύσσω (*kēryssō*), "proclaim, preach," denotes what is made public through an open and clear declaration. It carries two important nuances: that of being official and also of being divine.[88] The present tense of the verb, as used here, is important, reflecting as it does an ongoing practice repeated on a regular basis.[89] Its use stresses Paul's point that the missionaries never put themselves before their message.

Though Paul uses the verb in the more general sense of a public declaration, it still holds a religious connotation.[90] Most often he uses it to identify his public work in proclaiming either the gospel or Christ. His proclamation consists of bearing witness, making exhortations, and giving warnings as well as encouragement, but all with the Messiah as center.

Christ Jesus the Lord / Christ Jesus as Lord: On the noun Χριστός (*Christos*), "Christ," see Translation Notes for 4:4 above. Paul often placed this title before the Savior's mortal name and thereby empathized his divine authority as *the* Messiah, or "anointed one" (for examples, see Rom. 8:1; 15:5; 1 Cor. 4:15; 15:31; 16:24; Gal. 3:26; 4:14). For more information, see Translation Notes and Analysis for 1:1. The noun κύριος (*kyrios*), "lord, master," refers to one who acts in a capacity of authority due to possession or oversight.[91] In the LXX, the term consistently refers to Jehovah. Its use by Paul continues to tie Christ to that being and strongly suggests that Jesus is God in his own right.[92]

---

88. BDAG, 543. The verb is derived from the noun κῆρυξ (*kēryx*) that denotes an empowered envoy or herald. The office held importance in the Greek world because it was attached to proclaiming the will of the gods. Over time, it became sacrosanct. Included within the heralds' function was the maintenance of laws both of a political and religious nature. They never acted on their own authority, rather that of the master whom they served. A deepening connection with divinity came with the preaching of the Cynic philosophers who were viewed as messengers of the gods and guardians of the divine word and will. That the noun appears only in the writings of Paul (1 Tim. 2:7; 2 Tim. 1:11) and Peter (2 Pet. 2:5) suggests that the activities and functions of the herald did not play a major role in the Christian understanding of the verb κηρύσσω (*kēryssō*). Still, echoes likely continued to influence people's understanding of the word. For studies, see Gerhard Freidrich, "κῆρυξ," in *TDNT*, 3:683–718; *NID*, 2:674–682.

89. Wallace, *Greek Grammar*, 521.

90. For example, see Rom. 2:21 where he mentions the verb in relationship to the commandment not to steal.

91. BDAG, 576–79.

92. For a study, see Bauckham, *God Crucified*, 45–77; and Hurtado, *One God*, 93–128. Both studies show the strong identity between Jesus and God as viewed in earliest Christianity. Much of this is based on the early Christians' appropriation of the Old Testament title as applied to Jesus.

and ourselves your servants / and ourselves as your servants: The noun δοῦλος (*doulos*), "servant," denotes a "slave."[93] In the Greco-Roman world, the term did not carry the onerous nuance that it does in English.[94] Though it did refer to one who was under another person's total control and considered to be her or his property, the nuance of the word also included those who gave themselves freely and fully to another. In such a case, they were never another's property. The term "servant" best describes those in this condition, and that would include Paul. Thus, we translate it that way in our Rendition. The Apostle often described himself as the servant of God or Christ, showing that he had given himself to them and was theirs, and because of that, he sought to do their will. But there is another positive nuance at play here. In the Near East, to be the *doulos* of a king or an important official often carried with it some prestige due to the responsibility that fell to the person. Thus, the position held both weight and honor.[95] Those who followed the Apostle likely saw him in this light.[96] Those, however, who did not would have recoiled at the idea.

for Jesus' sake: The preposition διά (*dia*) with the accusative acts as a marker of a cause, with varying shades of meaning such as "because of, on account of, by reason of, thanks to, by aid of," etc.[97] A number of manuscripts, including the early 𝔓[46], have 'Ιησοῦ (*Iēsou*), "Jesus," in the genitive case. In that case, *dia* with the genitive can be used as a marker of personal agency; thus διὰ 'Ιησοῦ (*dia Iēsou*) would be translated "through (or by) Jesus." The evidence is fairly balanced between the two readings, but the accusative case seems to be the better reading since the same prepositional

93. BDAG, 259–60.

94. There are a number of differences between early American and ancient slavery. Among them are that no racial factors played a part, education was encouraged, slaves could own their own property including the right to own slaves, some held positions of authority and power, and above all, many earned emancipation by the time they were thirty. S. Scott Bartchy, "Slavery (Greco-Roman)," in *ABD,* 6:65–73.

95. Louw-Nida, §87.76. See also Matthew J. Grey, "'A Slave of Christ Jesus': Ancient Slavery as a Biblical Metaphor for Salvation," in *Selections from the Religious Education Student Symposium 2003* (Provo, Utah: Religious Studies Center, Brigham Young University, 2003), 81–100, https://contentdm.lib.byu.edu/digital/collection/rsc/id/52034/rec/29; Wayne G. Rollins, "Greco-Roman Slave Terminology and Pauline Metaphors," in *Society of Biblical Literature Seminar Papers,* ed. Kent Harold Richards (Atlanta: Scholars Press, 1987), 100–110. For an extended study, see Keith Hopkins, *Conquerors and Slaves,* vol. 1 of Sociological Studies in Roman History (Cambridge: Cambridge University Press, 1978).

96. An idea floating in the background may be that the road to being master begins with that of being the slave. Indeed, Jesus was a "slave" but by his death became *the* minister to the Jews (Mark 10:44; Rom. 15:8; Philip. 2:7–11).

97. BDAG, 223-26; Wallace, *Greek Grammar,* 368–69; LSJ, 388-89; BDF, §222.

phrase with the accusative is also found in 4:11 with no variant reading in the genitive.[98]

4:6 *For God, who commanded the light to shine out of darkness / For it is God who said, "Out of darkness light will shine":* The verb "is" is not in the text, but in Greek the copula is often not written, but understood.[99] The noun σκότος (*skotos*), "darkness,"[100] refers to the absence of light, the condition that reigned during the primordial chaos. The noun φῶς (*phōs*), "light," denotes the power God called forth that pushed away the darkness as part of the creation process.[101] The verb λάμπω (*lampō*), "to shine,"[102] found here is a future indicative.

This phrase acts as a précis combining two scriptures.[103] The first is Genesis 1:3–4, where God commands that there be light and separates the light from the darkness. The other is LXX Isaiah 9:2, which states that those people who walk in darkness will see a great light; indeed, it promises that "a light will shine on [them]." The construction here indicates that Paul cast the words in the form of a quote. In his day, no one would have been bothered by that, since the idea did indeed come from inspired writings, and that was what counted.[104] The difference between the Apostle's statement and the Old Testament scriptures is significant. Though both show that God is the author of the light that shines, the Apostle's statement re-forms the idea as a future event and thereby makes it more prophetic than imperative.

hath shined in our hearts, to give the light of the knowledge of the glory of God / who shined in our hearts to bring to light the knowledge of God's glory: This passage once again illustrates the translation challenge that some of Paul's writing can present.

The verb λάμπω (*lampō*) "to shine,"[105] is in the aorist tense. The subject of the verb cannot be φῶς (*phōs*), "light," because the noun *phōs* is neuter, and the relative pronoun ὅς (*hos*), "who,"[106] found here, is masculine

98. Metzger, *Textual Commentary,* 509–10.

99. Barnett, *Second Epistle,* 223 with n. 67.

100. BDAG, 932.

101. BDAG, 1072.

102. BDAG, 585–86.

103. It is possible that the phrase also alludes to the servant motif found in Isa. 49:6 (compare 42:6, 16; 60:1–2). This servant is described as "a light to the Gentiles," the very role Paul played. Martin, *2 Corinthians,* 224.

104. See in the introduction of this volume the section on "Paul's Understanding and Use of the Old Testament."

105. BDAG, 585–86, translates the phrase as "God, who has shone in our hearts."

106. BDAG, 725–27.

singular; therefore it must refer back to ὁ θεός (*ho theos*), "God," at the beginning of the verse.

The noun καρδία (*kardia*), "heart,"[107] is used here in its figurative capacity that connects the entire spectrum of mental and emotional activities, including all rational elements as well as the "hidden springs of the personal life."[108] On the negative side, it points to "the seat of total depravity, the principle in the center of man's inward life that defiles all he does" (see Matt. 15:19–20).[109] On the positive side, it is "the sphere of Divine influence."[110] As used here, the imagery connotes not simply emotions, as it does in English, but more especially the full spectrum of a person's mental and emotional activities. Further, it points to the very depths of the soul, that which determines who and what a person is.[111]

The noun φωτισμός (*phōtismos*), "light, enlightenment,"[112] generally means "illumination" in the physical sphere, but in the New Testament, it is used only figuratively with the sense of causing something to be fully known through revelation.[113] It refers to an illumination of the inner self that makes clear the revelations about God. It can therefore denote "enlightenment," but in the more active sense it means "bringing to light." The noun refers broadly to God's mastery over light in the Creation but is narrowed in the present context to the specific form of light that he gives in order for the Saints to have a personal comprehension—that is, a sure knowledge—of his glory.[114]

The preposition πρός (*pros*), "for," indicates a conscious striving for a goal or the realization of a purpose.[115] Thus, the phrase πρὸς φωτισμόν (*pros phōtismon*) means "for the purpose of enlightenment" or "toward light" and refers to the method through which God gives knowledge of himself to the righteous.

The noun δόξα (*doxa*), as noted in 4:4 above, has a wide range of meanings,[116] but because it is associated with the light of God in the present

---

107. BDAG, 508-9.

108. *NID,* 2:622–27.

109. *NID,* 2:622–27.

110. BDAG, 508–9; *NID,* 2:622–27; see Acts 15:9; Rom. 2:15.

111. See Johannes Behm, "καρδία," in *TDNT,* 3:605–9.

112. BDAG, 1074.

113. Louw-Nida, §§28.36; 72.3.

114. Guthrie, *2 Corinthians,* 245. We take the genitive τῆς γνώσεως (*tēs gnōseōs*), "the knowledge," as epexegetical or explanatory, thus referring to personal comprehension that includes not only the rational but also the cognitive portion of understanding.

115. BDAG, 873–75.

116. BDAG, 256–258.

context, it seems to carry such nuances as splendor, dignity, magnificence, power, and might. God's glory is that portion of his nature that, at least to some degree, humankind can experience,[117] but Paul's meaning of the term is best understood through the lens of the next phrase.

in the face of Jesus Christ / in Christ's face:[118] The noun πρόσωπον (*prosōpon*), "face," also refers to a person's countenance and carries the nuance of outward appearance. By using the term, Paul moves his imagery from that of an internal conversion to an external reality.[119] The noun Χριστός (*Christos*), "Christ," is in the genitive case and can denote either the source or the subject. If it is taken as source, then Christ is the font of the knowledge of God's glory. If the subject, then Christ is the being in whom God has placed his glory and through whom he makes it known.[120] Either way, a major role of the Savior is to bring to knowledge the glory of God.

Analysis and Summary

Paul has already alluded to the great difficulties his ministry has imposed upon him (1:4), most notably the near-death experience he had in the Roman Province of Asia, now the northwestern end of Turkey (1:8). But trials did not end there. He experienced additional problems evidenced in his strained relationship with various branches of the Church and especially with those in Corinth (2:1–10). These, coupled with his concern for his fellow missionaries (2:12–13), constantly pressed upon him. However, as he states in 4:1, despite all the hardships and suffering, he did not give up. Given all that he had endured, it is amazing that the temptation to ease up, pull back, or leave the mission never seems to have touched him. His forthrightness to Christ's cause, therefore, evidences the powerful effect the shower of the Messiah's mercy has had upon him. Due to the expression of such divine love and grace, he insists he cannot turn his back on his Savior or even slack in his work. Indeed not, for by fearlessly and indefatigably pushing forward, he expresses his thanks to his Lord (4:1). Thus, he gives continual diligence to spreading and defending God's message. His conversion experience may have motivated him in an additional way. Due to the mercy he had received, he could hope that his converts would also receive the same.

---

117. Guthrie, *2 Corinthians,* 246.

118. The noun "Jesus" is not found in the best manuscripts and is therefore left out of our Rendition.

119. Garland, *2 Corinthians,* 217–18.

120. For discussion, see Harris, *Second Epistle,* 335–36.

As clearly shown in 4:2, Paul rests his defense on the openness and candor of his preaching. Based on the textual evidence, it is clear that suspicion has fallen upon him. Based on what he said earlier, the initial opposition rested on at least two factors: his refusal to receive support from certain Corinthians and his failure to visit the congregations when promised (1:15–22; 12:14–18). This section of his epistle suggests that his enemies have now opened up an additional line of attack, one that questions the authenticity of his claim that God is working through him. By taking this tack, his detractors are able to throw doubt on his insistence that he exercises the power of Christ. This line of attack, then, is not so much on Paul's person as it is on his legitimacy as God's spokesman. Paul knows that the question of his divine acceptability cannot be answered through human judgment (1 Cor. 4:1–5). However, his legitimacy stands on his integrity, and therefore he must, at all costs, defend that. Thus, his insistence that he and the other missionaries have "renounced the shameful hidden things" and have practiced neither deception nor distortion of the word of God (2 Cor. 4:2, NR).[121]

Paul's concern is with those who are abusing God's word (2:17). For him the gospel message is the standard of truth. In his view, truth includes not only a cognitive process but also one that is larger than what people are able to determine on their own. It requires revelation to disclose and make it comprehensible.[122] That being the case, the Apostle is neither the originator nor the judge of truth but its proclaimer. It abides in Paul and is exposed not only in his integrity but in both the suffering that he has endured and his deliverance from it. His whole body and life manifest the gospel's power to all who will see. Indeed, God's truth has the power to expose error. Thus, "it is not the Corinthians who assess the truth. It is the truth that assesses them. Their 'hidden things of shame,' their darkness and lies, are exposed by it."[123]

In sum, Paul insists, with the other missionaries, that they carefully avoid the shameful deeds and actions that others use but hide. The Apostle likely has in mind those who, as he noted earlier, "peddle the word of God for profit" (2:17, NR) and, as a result, preach a misleading doctrine that takes people away from the truth. They must hide this tactic, however, lest through the exposure of their shifty dealing they lose their influence and position among the Saints. Paul fully rejects such shameful practices and insists that "authentic ministers (1) do not live by pedagogical tricks, (2) do not twist

---

121. Seifrid, *Second Letter*, 191–92.
122. For discussion, see Murphy-O'Connor, "Truth: Paul and Qumran," 179–230.
123. Seifrid, *Second Letter*, 193.

the word of God, but rather (3) live out a pattern of life and ministry that is commendable."[124]

That Paul uses the verb "commend" (συνίστημι, *synistēmi*) nine times in this epistle suggests its importance for his purpose in writing this letter.[125] The primary denotation of the word is that of building personal relationships through trust.[126] Paul's personal commendation before God to the Saints is his public proclamation of gospel truths (4:2). He does nothing behind closed doors or through hiding the truth by twisting the word of God. In dealing with the idea of commendation, whether through one's own efforts or that of another, Paul exposes his self-awareness of his authentic work as a servant (δοῦλος, *doulos,* literally "slave") of Christ. His knowledge leaves him totally without concern or need for the commendation of others, either for the establishment or the retention of his reputation. Thus, he refuses to compare himself with them.[127]

Even so, he does not shy away from commending himself and the other missionaries before God to the conscience of every person who will listen (4:2). In this instance, the Apostle disconnects the term "conscience" (συνείδησις, *syneidēsis*) from the idea of wounded feelings due to an acute awareness of ill behavior. He redefines it as the central self-consciousness within knowing and acting humankind that allows them to discern the difference between right and wrong and thus to make moral judgments.[128] It is his own conscience that allows him to commend himself and the other missionaries to any who will hear without prejudice. His desire is to continue in, if not increase, a positive relationship with the Corinthian Saints. In order to reach this goal, he spends time on how he and his coworkers have suffered and sacrificed for the sake of God's people (4:8–9).[129]

As noted above, Paul bases the purity and authenticity of his commendation on the way he and his colleagues preach the gospel, through open and clear pronouncements (φανέρωσις, *phanerōsis*)[130] that consist of the truth, declared fully, publicly, and without distortion. The word *phanerōsis* is important because it reveals the means by which the missionaries are able to bring those who will hear to Christ. By the power of the Spirit working

124. Guthrie, *2 Corinthians,* 236.

125. They are 3:1; 4:2; 5:12; 6:4;7:11;10:12, 18 (twice), 12:11.

126. BDAG, 972.

127. Wilhelm Kasch, "συνίστημι," in *TDNT,* 7:896–98.

128. Maurer, "συνοῖδα, συνείδησις," in *TDNT,* 917.

129. Guthrie, *2 Corinthians,* 237.

130. BDAG, 1048–49.

through their open and very public witness, unbelievers become believers. His target audience is anyone who has a discerning conscience, or "the capacity for moral judgment" (συνείδησις, *syneidēsis*).[131] Such people, he feels, can see the tangled false web spun by his adversaries when compared to the harmonious tapestry of light and truth woven by him and the other missionaries. These are the ones who present "a consistent picture of integrity before self, before others—whether a particular community or people in general—and before God."[132] All this he does, as he states, in the sight of God (ἐνώπιον τοῦ θεοῦ, *enōpion tou theou*). The statement not only reveals his deep sense of responsibility before the Divine[133] but also bears witness to his complete confidence in the authority and correctness of what he does and declares.

In 4:3, Paul centers his attention on the inhibiting effects of a spiritual veil that prevents people from seeing that which he calls "our gospel." Paul's reference to "our gospel" suggests he is separating the gospel he and his companions preach from another gospel (Gal. 1:6). It seems likely that his adversaries are claiming that the reason "his gospel" is not understood or more fully accepted can be largely laid at his feet. Their line of attack includes at least two possibilities: first, that his form of the gospel is either too obscure or foreign for anyone to really understand;[134] or second, that his personal bodily weakness and independent lifestyle hindered the message. If either of these is the case, then "his gospel" would certainly have stood in contrast to the "another gospel" his detractors are advocating (11:4).

Paul denies the charge that either his message or his person is responsible for people not understanding the gospel. For one reason, as his use of the phrase "our gospel" shows, he is not alone in preaching a given understanding of Jesus and his message. Thus, he can insist that he has laid and is laying bare before the consciences of the people and before God the truthfulness of the divine message. So why has it not been better received?

Paul supplies the answer in 4:3–4: because it is hidden. This concealment has been made possible by two circumstances: first, the spiritual condition of those who refuse his message and, second, the work of the "god of this world." His point is that if either one of these is the case, he should

131. Barrett, *Second Epistle,* 129.

132. Guthrie, *2 Corinthians,* 328.

133. Guthrie, *2 Corinthians,* 328.

134. The accusation could also have originated with the unbelieving Jewish community for whom Christ's crucifixion was a stumbling block (Acts 18:4–6; 1 Cor. 1:23); Thrall, *Critical and Exegetical Commentary,* 1:305.

not be blamed. The "god of this world," though the primary agent who has the power to keep people blind to the gospel, does not work alone. As the Apostle will show (11:14–15), the evil one's work is proclaimed and intensified by his servants—namely, Paul's detractors.

The phrase reveals Paul's understanding of Satan's work but tacitly points to that of God as well. The evil one works by somehow blocking the light (φῶς, *phōs*) from coming into the unbelievers' minds and by that means keeps them in spiritual darkness. As a result, they are unable to discern (αὐγάζω, *augazō*) the light (φωτισμός, *phōtismos*)—that is, the revealed truths of the gospel that discloses the way to salvation.

Paul's use of the noun "mind" (νόημα, *noēma*) is important. Though the usual nuance of the word is "thought," in the plural it denotes the place where thought takes place—that is, "the mind."[135] In the scriptures, its cognate, "mind" (νοῦς, *nous*), always carries a theological nuance that centers on an understanding of the divine will, especially in terms of salvation. Unfortunately, the mind can be corrupted through blindness. As Paul clearly shows, one of the tools Satan uses to get people to distort, dismiss, or ignore God's word is to blind them to its importance. When that happens, as Paul states, they are unable to perceive the gospel that discloses the glory of Christ.[136] The Apostle is well aware of how Satan works (2:11). This knowledge gives force and direction to Paul's work, which is, as he makes clear, to destroy all satanic arguments and to put down every obstacle that stands in the way of the correct knowledge of God. But there is more to his apostolic work than that. He also desires to take every thought captive in an effort to get it to submit to the will of God (10:4–5). His words suggest that when he speaks of the "mind," he means "the general faculty of judgment itself, which can make decisions and pronounce verdicts right or wrong, depending on the influence to which it is exposed."[137] Thus, the work of both God and Satan is to capture the mind. That being the case, the Apostle works against the adversary by proclaiming publicly the truth of the gospel so that his hearers have the correct information they need to commit to Christ.

When Paul states that, due to the adversary's work, some are unable to "discern the light," he does not use the normal word for "light" (φῶς, *phōs*) but rather one that includes the idea of "enlightenment" or "perspicacity" (φωτισμός, *phōtismos*). His choice of this word is telling. When speaking

135. BDAG, 675.

136. Guthrie, *2 Corinthians,* 240.

137. *NID,* 3:432.

figuratively, the two nouns share an important connection. The noun "light" (φῶς, *phōs*) is directly associated with the Divine. Indeed, God is light and dwells in light (1 John 1:5, 7); Jesus is "the light of the world," and to those who follow him he gives "the light of life" (John 8:12). On the human level, the term connotes what is ethically good and is associated with the illuminating power of scripture. To open one's heart to the light is to experience God's saving power. Receiving light, therefore, has a direct connection to redemption from evil.[138] Thus, an essential component of light is divine power that individuals can receive and that assists them in the salvation process.[139] The noun "enlightenment" (φωτισμός, *phōtismos*) denotes a keen knowledge and understanding of gospel truths that have been revealed in some detail.[140] In Paul's case, it refers to the ability of people to discern the glory of gospel truths and more specifically the glory that belongs to Christ in his role as Savior.

Therefore, the gospel has a glorious aspect. By using the noun "glory" (δόξα, *doxa*), the Apostle "makes a direct relationship between the glory of the Christ and the person of God the Father,"[141] which leads him to proclaim that Christ "is the image of God." By using the noun "image" (εἰκών, *eikōn*), the Apostle reveals his understanding of the relationship between the Father and the Son. The Lord shares the power and glory of the Father, but more importantly, it is through the Messiah that God is made known to mortals (see John 14:7–11). That the Savior is the image of God suggests the perfection with which he is able to disclose God. Furthermore, Christ has become like and looks like the Father. That Paul uses the same imagery in some of his other writings suggests the importance of this idea to him (for example, see Philip. 2:6 and Col. 1:15; compare Heb. 1:3).[142]

Satan, as Paul shows, blinds people to this aspect of Jesus. It is important to note that it is only a certain class of people who cannot see the gospel truths—namely, those who are in the process of perishing. By rejecting the message of Paul and the other missionaries, they have put themselves in a position of divine condemnation (2:15; 1 Cor. 10:10; 2 Thes. 2:10).[143] Paul calls these people "the unfaithful" (οἱ ἄπιστοι, *hoi apistoi*). The noun

---

138. *NID,* 4:637–43; BDAG, 1072–73.

139. For a study, see Draper, "Light, Truth, and Grace," 234–47.

140. Louw-Nida, §28.36; 72.3.

141. Guthrie, *2 Corinthians,* 241.

142. His view agrees with that of Latter-day Saints. For example, see J. Reuben Clark, *Behold the Lamb of God* (Salt Lake City: Deseret Book, 1962), 194–95; Dallin H. Oaks, "Teachings of Jesus," *Ensign* 41, no. 11 (November 2011): 90.

143. Guthrie, *2 Corinthians,* 239.

generally referred to Gentiles, but in Corinth and other places where there was Jewish opposition, it could also include Jews. The word also carries the idea not only of simple disbelief but also of active rejection,[144] so it could also include those antagonistic to Paul and his companions.

In 4:5, Paul briefly but powerfully explained what he and his companions were and were not about. At the heart of his declaration is his assurance to his readers that his purpose has never been to put himself or his fellow missionaries forward. Christ as Lord is the focus of all they do. For that reason, all ministers have to humbly take a back seat. As noted in the introduction of this volume, such a position flew in the face of certain attitudes and mores in the Greco-Roman world. This was a place where self-aggrandizement and self-promotion were all important, especially among those influenced by sophist philosophy. Those converted out of this philosophical environment may have continued to cling to old notions, believing that education and skill in oratory were prerequisites for Church position. The Jews were not exempt. Some pursued teaching positions not for the sake of promoting virtue and the betterment of society but because the position allowed them to either parade their superiority or act as a steppingstone to a higher, often religio-political, office.[145]

Paul's refusal to put himself forward, to hide his imperfections and bodily weaknesses, or to play rhetorical games, along with his insistence on paying his own way, drew the ire of many. His further practice of preaching the gospel in clear simplicity to all who would hear only exacerbated the antagonism of his enemies toward him. Yet Paul would not back down. Instead, he not only gloried in his weaknesses but also paraded them for all to see. The reason? It reinforced his insistence that the success of his work (which is quite remarkable) is not his own doing but belongs to the Divine. As for himself, he sees weakness as the means that God uses to reinforce the Apostle's severe reliance on Christ (12:7–9), one that forces him to put the full brightness of the spotlight where it belongs.[146] Thus, the thrust of his message comes not only through the wholehearted giving of himself but also through his care to make sure the gospel light shines exclusively on the Messiah, specifically revealing his role as the crucified and risen God (1:19; 11:4; 1 Cor. 1:23; 15:12).

---

144. BDAG, 103–4; Rudolf Bultmann, "πιστεύω," in *TDNT,* 6:176–78.

145. Bruce W. Winter, *Philo and Paul among the Sophists: Alexandrian and Corinthians Response to a Julio-Claudian Movement* (Grand Rapids, Mich.: Wm. B. Eerdmans, 2002), 244.

146. Guthrie, *2 Corinthians,* 242–43.

Paul sees himself as the Lord's servant (δοῦλος, *doulos,* literally, "slave"), fully and completely. However, the Apostle's service does not end there. Through Jesus, he is also the willing servant of the Corinthians until he is "spent" in their behalf (12:15). The preposition "through" (διά, *dia*) here has the sense of "because of" or "through the agency of" someone else.[147] In this case, the subject is Jesus, whose purpose is the salvation of humankind. Though Paul does not mention the way the Savior realizes this objective here, he did so in his earlier epistle. He shows that it is through love—the power behind the proper behavior of people, one toward the other (1 Cor. 13:1–8).[148] The Apostle appreciates this divine power because, among other reasons, it leads to "no schism in the body" of the Church. It results rather in members having "the same care one for another" (1 Cor. 12:25). It is to this end that Paul and his companions are willing "servants" to the Corinthian Saints (2 Cor. 4:5).

The phrase "through Jesus" also carries another important nuance. It subtly shows that Paul did not view the Corinthians as his masters. Indeed, he has but one, and that is Jesus.[149] Paul and his companions, thus, do all that they do for one Master, the exalted Lord through whom "they are constantly being transformed (3:17–18)."[150]

Paul designs his teachings not only to give information and declare his formal allegiance to his Master but also to promote a faith in him that involves a trust so deep that it leads to self-surrender (1 Cor. 15:11). Such a proclamation required, as the Apostle fully understood, that its promulgators have legitimate and commissioned priesthood authority (Rom. 10:8–12, 15; compare Acts 13:3 and Isa. 52:7). The requirement is absolutely necessary because Christ has to be not only the message's subject but also its object, having full authority over all its details. This situation is necessary for two reasons: first, because the Messiah had to be part of the conversion process, and second, the gospel hearers had to experience him through yielding to the demands of his word.

Paul's brief statement in 4:5 is full of insight on the nature and manner of the Christian proclamation. As one scholar noted, "It would be hard to

147. The preposition acts as a marker of cause or means, or marker of the agent. BDAG, 225; Louw-Nida, §90.44; Wallace, *Greek Grammar,* 369–70; LSJ, 389; BDF, §222. Barnett, *Second Epistle,* 222 n. 61.

148. Jesus said that the command to love fulfils the biblical requirements for salvation (Matt. 22:40). Paul agrees (Gal. 5:14).

149. Harris, *Second Epistle,* 333.

150. Guthrie, *2 Corinthians,* 243; see 2 Corinthians 3:17–18.

describe the Christian ministry more comprehensibly in so few words."[151] What Paul does is briefly identify the means, content, and manner that he and the other missionaries use to publish their message. The *means* the Apostle describes in terms of proclamation (φανέρωσις, *phanerōsis*)—that is, giving a public and clear declaration of the gospel that is preached in such a way that, for those who will hear, it develops their faith in the Savior. The *content* he summarizes as "Christ Jesus as Lord."[152] This very brief declaration is loaded with nuances. It looks not only at the position of Jesus as the "anointed one" (Christ, Messiah) and therefore the legitimate bearer of God's word and power[153] but also as the one who, as Lord (κύριος, *kyrios*), holds divine power and authority in his own right.[154] Behind the phrase is the understanding of Jesus as the crucified one who, as the suffering servant, worked out the Atonement and, through the Resurrection, became the ruler of the world. The *manner* is that of a "servant (δοῦλος, *doulos,* literally "slave") for Jesus' sake"—that is, one who has voluntarily given himself over to Christ no matter the cost in order to better push the Messiah's cause of salvation.[155] But the manner is also that of a "servant" to the Corinthians who is willing to give himself in full measure in serving them. In this, he follows the Lord's own model, who described himself coming "not . . . to be served but to serve" and insisted that he who would "be first among you will be the slave of all" (Mark 10:45, 44, NR).[156] In this we see the "upside-down orientation of true Christian leadership. Instead of advancing the kingdom by power, true leaders advance God's kingdom by sacrificial service."[157]

---

151. Barrett, *Second Epistle,* 134.

152. Paul uses this phrase elsewhere as a summary of the Christian message. See 1 Cor. 12:3; Philip. 2:10–11.

153. The English word "Christ" is a transliteration of the Greek Χριστός (*Christos*) which means "an anointed one." The Greek-speaking Christians used this word to interpret the Aramaic מְשִׁיחָא (*měšîḥāʾ*), which denoted the same thing.

154. The title "Lord" references one of the translations for the name of Jehovah. A connection between Jesus and Jehovah can be seen in Paul's statement that whosoever calls on the Lord's (Jesus') name shall be saved (Rom. 10:13) with the Old Testament promise that whosoever calls on the Lord's (Jehovah's) name shall be delivered (Joel 2:32).

155. "Slaves were also anciently freed by the hand of the master (*manu-mitted*) as they took upon themselves the master's name and inherit all he had. Most importantly, Jesus freed Paul and all of us from spiritual and physical death," as noted by Brent Schmidt in an email February 12, 2020. For a study of Paul as a servant of Jehovah, see G. K. Beale, "The Old Testament Background of Reconciliation in 2 Corinthians 5–7 and Its Bearing on the Literary Problems of 2 Corinthians 6:14–7:1," *New Testament Studies* 35 (1989): 562–66.

156. Barnett, *Second Epistle,* 221–23.

157. Guthrie, *2 Corinthians,* 243.

In 4:6, Paul shows that God can shine the saving, illuminating light "in our hearts." The state of the heart is what is at issue. Indeed, much of humankind's spiritual ability depends on the condition of the heart. If people are unable to see the light of the gospel, it is because a veil of darkness lies over their hearts (3:15; compare Rom. 1:21, 24; 2:5; and Eph. 4:18). It is here, at the very core of the individual, where "the god of this world" works to create darkness among the unbelievers (2 Cor. 4:4). When the heart is dark, the things of God cannot be discerned. When they are not discerned, God remains unknown,[158] thus the necessity of God enlightening the heart in order to reveal his glory as expressed in the countenance (πρόσωπον, *prosōpon*) of Jesus. Further, it takes divine power to transform their hearts so that they are enabled to move both into and then forward in the new covenant (3:4–6).

Paul refers to this divine transforming power as "light" (φῶς, *phōs,* 4:6). As God allows light to shine in the hearts of the seeking and repentant, it brings them "enlightenment" (φωτισμός, *phōtismos*). The word refers to the ability not only to see and believe but also to accept the new covenant and allow it to become a part of them (Jer. 31:31–33; Heb. 8:7–13). This enlightenment has blessed Paul and his companions and many of his readers. Thus, he can appeal to their witness as to the truth of what he is saying. From Paul's point of view, his detractors have yielded to the influence of the "god of this world" and thus remain in darkness. The inference for his readers is that they should neither follow nor listen to them.

To bolster his point, in 4:6 Paul appeals to scripture. He apparently joined the thoughts contained in two disparate verses, both, however, dealing with light. These are Genesis 1:3–4 (where God brings forth light and separates it from the darkness) and Isaiah 9:2 as found in the Septuagint (that promises that those who walk in darkness will not only see a great light but it will dwell within them).[159] Since both scriptures contain the idea of light shining forth, Paul could easily join them.[160] It may also

158. Thus, the Savior warned that even though there were those who would do good deeds, because these did not bring them to know him, the people were working iniquity. As a result, he would say to them, "Ye never knew me: depart from me" (JST Matt. 7:22–23).

159. Harris, *Second Epistle,* 334.

160. He could be making his case using an ancient Jewish method that is called *gezerah shawah,* which is "an argument by analogy that is based on the presence of an identical term or phrase in two different scriptural texts such that the two texts can be read together." David M. Moffitt, "The Interpretation of Scripture in the Epistle to the Hebrews," *Reading the Epistle to the Hebrews: A Resource for Students,* ed. Eric F. Mason and Patrick B. McCruden (Atlanta: Society of Biblical Literature, 2011), 83. This is based on the idea that

have been the larger context of the Isaiah passage that drew Paul to it.[161] The section in which the idea is located looks to the future of Israel after its captivity and speaks of the coming of a child named Immanuel, meaning "God with us" (Isa. 7:14), who would be a stumbling stone, causing many to fall (Isa. 8:14–15). It also promised the birth of a child who would hold the titles of "Wonderful, Counselor, Almighty God, Everlasting Father, and Prince of Peace," and whose task it would be to bring in a renewed age dominated by the kingdom of God (Isa. 9:6–7).[162] Standing behind these is also another point Isaiah makes that is relevant to Paul's situation. Jehovah states that people can draw near him with their mouths and honor him with their lips while their hearts remain far from him (Isa. 29:13). That seems to have been the case with Paul's enemies. They were proclaiming what appeared to be the things of God but were actually trying to bring glory to themselves. The Apostle understood that the only way to transform them was to get divine light into their lives. But the only way to do that was if they were willing to believe. Only then could they receive the light that enabled them to comprehend the "knowledge of God's glory" (4:6, NR).[163]

The noun "glory" (δόξα, *doxa*) denotes a manifestation of God's nature and character that humankind can comprehend, at least to a degree. The term refers not only to his greatness, power, and majesty but also to his saving work. It is when people discern the latter that they find themselves drawn to him in thankfulness, reverence, and worship. Christians understand that God has revealed his glory perfectly though one person, Jesus

---

"all Scripture is meaningful and indeed has a single author, so that an occurrence of a word in one passage can be used to illuminate the use of a word in another passage. The two passages can [thus] be mutually interpretive." Johnson, *Hebrews,* 175. (For an example, see the juxtaposition of Ps. 2:7 with 2 Sam. 7:14 in Heb. 1:5). Using scriptures in this way does violate traditional post-Enlightenment procedures but it fits easily in to the mind set of Second Temple Judaism and thereby into earliest Christianity. For a study, see David H. Wenkel, "*Gezerah Shawah* as Analogy in Hebrews," *Biblical Theological Bulletin: Journal of Biblical Culture* 37, no. 2 (May 2007): 62–68.

161. Paul's writings reveal that he was well acquainted with Isaiah. See Timothy B. Savage, *Power through Weakness: Paul's Understanding of the Christian Ministry in 2 Corinthians* (Cambridge: Cambridge University Press, 1995), 113, who cites four places where Paul clusters passages from Isaiah as a proof text for the points he wishes to make. These are in Rom. 2–3; 9–11; 1 Cor. 1–2; and 2 Cor. 3–4. See also the discussion in the introduction to this volume, "Paul's Understanding and Use of the Old Testament."

162. Matt. 4:14–16 states that Isa. 9:1–2 was fulfilled in Jesus.

163. Harris, *Second Epistle,* 334.

Christ. Paul uses the image of Christ's "countenance" (πρόσωπον, *prosōpon,* literally "face") as the instrument through which the knowledge of God's glory is made manifest. But the term, as used here, likely refers to the teaching, ministry, and saving work of the Messiah. This idea is confirmed by the Lord himself. His awareness of his responsibility to disclose the glory of God can be seen in his statement that "I do nothing of myself; but as my Father hath taught me, I speak these things" (John 8:28). So careful and complete has he been in this assignment that he can say to Philip, "he that hath seen me hath seen the Father," and assure him that "I am in the Father, and the Father in me" and that "the words that I speak unto you I speak not of myself: but the Father that dwelleth in me, he doeth the works" (John 14:9–10). Thus, as Paul states, it is in the "face of Jesus Christ" that people can see manifest the knowledge of God's glory (4:6).

Treasures in Clay Jars (4:7–12)

At this point, Paul begins a new segment in his epistle which will run through 5:10. The major theme of this section relates to the suffering he and the other missionaries have had to endure for the sake of the ministry. He begins by noting the paradoxical fact that the glory and wonder of the new covenant moves out into the world through people he describes as jars of clay. He admits to their fragility and notes the suffering this condition imposes upon them as they carry out God's work. The Apostle does not demur in describing the difficulties he and others have had to endure. This is because, as he shows, such suffering serves to advance the gospel's spread throughout the entire area.[164] He is fully aware that, in other circumstances, such intense suffering could be devastating to the work at hand. But, as he well knew, "rather than being destroyed by the traumas faced in ministry, true Christian ministers experience renewal (4:16), and the suffering faced in ministry has a personal outcome: the building up of an eternal 'tonnage of glory' [4:17] that makes suffering pale by comparison."[165]

164. Guthrie, 2 *Corinthians,* 249.
165. Guthrie, 2 *Corinthians,* 249.

Greek Text

7 Ἔχομεν δὲ τὸν θησαυρὸν τοῦτον ἐν ὀστρακίνοις σκεύεσιν, ἵνα ἡ ὑπερβολὴ τῆς
δυνάμεως ᾖ τοῦ θεοῦ καὶ μὴ ἐξ ἡμῶν· 8 ἐν παντὶ θλιβόμενοι ἀλλʼ οὐ στενοχωρού-
μενοι, ἀπορούμενοι ἀλλʼ οὐκ ἐξαπορούμενοι, 9 διωκόμενοι ἀλλʼ οὐκ ἐγκαταλει-
πόμενοι, καταβαλλόμενοι ἀλλʼ οὐκ ἀπολλύμενοι, 10 πάντοτε τὴν νέκρωσιν τοῦ
Ἰησοῦ ἐν τῷ σώματι περιφέροντες, ἵνα καὶ ἡ ζωὴ τοῦ Ἰησοῦ ἐν τῷ σώματι ἡμῶν
φανερωθῇ· 11 ἀεὶ γὰρ ἡμεῖς οἱ ζῶντες εἰς θάνατον παραδιδόμεθα διὰ Ἰησοῦν, ἵνα
καὶ ἡ ζωὴ τοῦ Ἰησοῦ φανερωθῇ ἐν τῇ θνητῇ σαρκὶ ἡμῶν. 12 ὥστε ὁ θάνατος ἐν ἡμῖν
ἐνεργεῖται, ἡ δὲ ζωὴ ἐν ὑμῖν. [SBLGNT]

King James Version

7 But we have this treasure in earthen
vessels, that the excellency of the power
may be of God, and not of us. 8 We are
troubled on every side, yet not dis-
tressed; we are perplexed, but not in
despair; 9 Persecuted, but not for-
saken; cast down, but not destroyed;
10 Always bearing about in the body
the dying of the Lord Jesus, that the life
also of Jesus might be made manifest in
our body. 11 For we which live are alway
delivered unto death for Jesus' sake,
that the life also of Jesus might be made
manifest in our mortal flesh. 12 So then
death worketh in us, but life in you.

New Rendition

7 But we have this treasure in clay jars
to show that this extraordinary power
comes from God and not from us. 8 We
are oppressed on every side but not
crushed, perplexed but not driven to
despair, 9 persecuted but not forsaken,
struck down but not destroyed. 10 We
are always carrying around in our bod-
ies the putting to death of Jesus so that
the life of Jesus might also be revealed
in our body. 11 For we who are alive are
always being handed over to death for
Jesus' sake so that the life of Jesus might
also be revealed in our mortal flesh.
12 Therefore death is at work in us, but
life is at work in you.

Translation Notes and Comments

4:7 ***But we have this treasure in earthen vessels / But we have this treasure in clay jars:*** Paul's metaphor draws upon the practices of the day, in which precious items where often placed in various clay vessels to keep them in one place, out of sight, and thus more secure.[166] The noun θησαυρός (*thēsauros*), "treasure," denotes items of exceptional value that need to be safeguarded.[167] The term also carries a figurative nuance connoting spiritual

166. D. Kelly Ogden, *Where Jesus Walked: The Land and Culture of New Testament Times* (Salt Lake City: Deseret Book, 1991), 69; Witherington, *Conflict and Community*, 386–87.

167. Louw-Nida, §65:10.

or transcendent matters of eternal worth. In this context it most likely refers to the knowledge of God's glory as manifest in the work, words, and ministry of Jesus, but it could also refer either to the gospel as a whole[168] or to its ministry.[169]

The adjective ὀστράκινος (*ostrakinos*), "clay," denotes anything made out of earthly materials, but primarily of clay,[170] while the noun σκεῦος (*skeuos*) refers to any type of vessel.[171] The imagery in the phrase ἐν ὀστρακίνοις σκεύεσιν (*en ostrakinois skeusin*), "in clay jars," emphasizes the weak and fragile nature of the human body itself as well as that of the soul. Although pots are fragile, potsherds still can be useful and written upon by anyone, including God, as ancients wrote on fragments of clay pots or plates called *ostraka*. Humankind, in its fallen state, is weak but, like a pot, can physically deliver food, goods, or messages for God to bless others, even in a fragmentary state. Thus, the phrase shows the paradox of great spiritual treasures being housed within it.[172]

that the excellency of the power may be of God, and not of us / to show that this extraordinary power comes from God and not from us: The conjunction ἵνα (*hina*), "to show that," is a marker indicating purpose or aim.[173] It indicates why God places his treasure in mere humans. The noun ὑπερβολή (*hyperbolē*) denotes a state of exceeding excellence or greatness "beyond all measure or proportion."[174] The noun δύναμις (*dynamis*), "power," refers to that which has "might, capability, force," but, within the biblical context, it often connotes the greatness of God's "new and higher forces that have entered and are working in this lower world."[175] These are generated by God working either directly or indirectly with or through humankind. In this case, "power" represents the might of this very personal God, by which he carries out his will, often through the use of an authorized agent.[176]

---

168. Barrett, *Second Epistle,* 137.

169. BDAG, 456; Bultmann, *Second Letter,* 112, notes that the nuance could also be to its glory.

170. BDAG, 730.

171. BDAG, 927.

172. Ogden and Skinner, *Verse by Verse,* 151.

173. BDAG, 475–77.

174. BDAG, 1032.

175. BDAG, 262–63.

176. For a study, see Walter Grundmann, "δύναμαι/δύναμις," in *TDNT,* 2:284–317.

The phrase μὴ ἐξ ἡμῶν (*mē ex hēmōn*), "not from us," explains why God has placed his glory in weak human beings. It is to demonstrate beyond reason that this "exceeding greatness of power" that nothing can withstand is his, not something derived from human will or effort.[177]

4:8–9 With verse 8, Paul begins a list of the trials he and others suffer on account of the gospel and expresses the result due to the hope in Christ. To do so he strings together a series of present passive or middle participles. The tense suggests the ongoing nature of both the trails and the unconquerable spirit that faith in Christ produces. In the notes below, we have given the present active form of the verbs but translated them with the passive voice of the participles.[178]

4:8 ***We are troubled on every side, yet not distressed / We are oppressed on every side but not crushed:*** The verb θλίβω (*thlibō*), "oppress, afflict,"[179] denotes strong discomfort coming from outside, pressing upon the soul.[180] We have followed the KJV in translating the prepositional phrase ἐν παντί (*en panti*), literally "in everything," as "on every side." The verb στενοχωρέω (*stenochōreō*), in the passive as here, denotes a circumstance in which there seems no way out.[181] It carries much the same nuances as *thlibō* but enhanced such that "oppressed" becomes "crushed."

we are perplexed, but not in despair / perplexed but not driven to despair: The verb ἀπορέω (*aporeō*), "to be perplexed, uncertain," denotes being in a confused state of mind to the point of being out of one's wits,[182] the reason often being that the person sees no way out of a painful or dangerous situation.[183] The verb ἐξαπορέομαι (*exaporeomai*) is the previous verb ἀπορέω (*aporeō*) with the prefix ἐξ- (*ex*-), which adds the sense of "thoroughly, completely" to the simple verb.[184] Thus the meaning is "to be in despair," with the idea of being in great difficulty, sometimes even losing hope of life.[185]

---

177. Bernard, "Second Epistle," 61.

178. Lisa M. Bowens, "Investigating the Apocalyptic Texture of Paul's Martial Imagery in 2 Corinthians 4–6," *Journal for the Study of The New Testament* 39, no. 1 (September 2016): 3–15, suggests that Paul is using military imagery demonstrate his point.

179. BDAG, 457.

180. MM, 292.

181. BDAG, 942–43.

182. BDAG, 119.

183. Louw-Nida, §32.9, translates it as "being at a loss."

184. Smyth, *Greek Grammar,* §1688, 2.

185. BDAG, 345.

4:9 ***Persecuted, but not forsaken:*** The verb διώκω (*diōkō*), "to be persecuted," has the strong nuance of being driven out and even pursued because of what one believes. The verb ἐγκαταλείπω (*engkataleipō*), "to be forsaken," means "to be abandoned, deserted," with the idea of being left helpless.[186]

cast down, but not destroyed / struck down but not destroyed: The verb καταβάλλω (*kataballō*), "struck down, thrown down," suggests receiving a blow that not only knocks a person down but also causes actual harm.[187] The verb ἀπόλλυμι (*apollymi*) in the middle voice, as found here, means "to perish, be ruined," and has the nuance of being ruined utterly so far as well-being is concerned.[188]

4:10 ***Always bearing about in the body the dying of the Lord Jesus / We are always carrying around in our bodies the putting to death of Jesus:*** This verse further reveals the continual distress that Paul and his companions are in. The adverb πάντοτε (*pantote*), "always,"[189] coupled with the verb περιφέω (*peripherō*), found here as a present participle, "to carry about, around,"[190] stresses the unrelenting nature of the burden the missionaries carry. The phrase suggests that suffering is "the essential and continuing characteristic of apostolic service."[191]

The noun νέκρωσις (*nekrōsis*), "dying, mortification," does not refer to death itself but rather to the process, thus "dying."[192] It is not the word Paul most often uses for death (θάνατος, *thanatos*).[193] That he chose this one suggests that he wanted to give the imagery he creates here a special stress. The word nuances the idea of mortification[194]—that is, the humiliation and shame caused by the wounding (or worse, the butchery) of a person's reputation. The graphic imagery points to the suffering, perplexity, persecution,

---

186. BDAG, 273; MM, 179.

187. Louw-Nida, §20.21; BDAG, 514.

188. BDAG, 115–16.

189. BDAG, 755.

190. BDAG, 808.

191. Furnish, *II Corinthians,* 283.

192. BDAG, 668.

193. Paul uses θάνατος (*thanatos*) forty-five times in his writing but *νέρωσις* (*nekrōsis*) only twice, here and Rom. 4:19. Barrett, *Second Epistle,* 139–40. Because Paul is the only New Testament writer to use the word and does it so infrequently, his exact meaning is not as clear as we would like. It is possible that he is referring to death itself and even to the death of Jesus. For discussion, see Guthrie, *2 Corinthians,* 259–60. We follow the majority of commentators feeling this interpretation best suits the context.

194. BDAG, 668.

humiliation, and even the threat of death that Paul and the other Christians must endure constantly on account of their loyalty to Christ.[195] For the Lord, that ultimate humiliation and mortification culminated at his scandalous death on the cross. Paul's phrase, "the dying of Jesus," emphasizes the distressing and sometimes intense mortification the Lord experienced while in mortality as felt by the Saints.[196] In sum, "Paul regards the suffering to which he is constantly exposed in his work as the process in which the death of Jesus is effected in him as a continual mortifying or modification."[197]

that the life also of Jesus might be made manifest in our body / so that the life of Jesus might also be revealed in our body: In the phrase ἵνα καί (*hina kai*), *hina* acts as a marker of purpose,[198] while *kai* functions adverbially with the sense "also."[199] Together they give the reason why Paul and his companions must endure the heavy burdens their faith in Christ places upon them.

The phrase καὶ ἡ ζωὴ τοῦ Ἰησοῦ (*hē zōē tou Iēsou*), "the life of Jesus," could refer to his life and ministry, but given the current context, it more likely points to his Resurrection, which not only brought to naught all the shame and humiliation crucifixion was designed to communicate but also held the promise of the quality of life promised to the Saints.[200]

The verb φανερόω (*phaneroō*), "reveal," means "to cause something to be visible."[201] It is found here as a subjunctive passive aorist, with the passive hinting at the work God does behind the scenes, revealed not only in the life of Jesus but also in the lives and actions of his servants.[202]

The noun σῶμα (*sōma*), "body," refers to the physical nature of humankind, including a person's natural desires.[203] Paul appears to be using it to refer to the mortal condition under which he and his colleagues labor.

---

195. Barnett, *Second Epistle,* 234; Harris, *Second Epistle,* 345; Bernard, "Second Epistle," 62.

196. Paul's point is vague enough that the passage may be understood in different ways. Among them are that (1) Paul viewed himself as suffering in some sense the same way Jesus did, (2) through the Apostle's baptism, he suffered a union with Christ's death, and (3) through revelation, Paul understood the meaning of the suffering of the Lord on the cross and bore that "dying" with him continually. For further discussion, see Thrall, *Critical and Exegetical Commentary,* 1:332–34. Given the context of this pericope, the first option seems best.

197. Rudolf Bultmann, "νέκρωσις," in *TDNT,* 4:895.

198. BDAG, 475–77.

199. Smyth, *Greek Grammar,* §2881; Barnett, *Second Epistle,* 235 n. 40.

200. Guthrie, *2 Corinthians,* 260.

201. BDAG, 1048; Louw-Nida, §24.19.

202. Barnett, *Second Epistle,* 235 n. 43.

203. Louw-Nida, §§8.1, 9.8; BDAG, 983–84.

The point this verse makes is that "Paul's sufferings are in keeping with the death of Christ, so that the (resurrection) life of Jesus might be more evident. And all of this is the theological background for the opening statement of [4:7]," dealing with God's power being kept in "clay jars" (NR).[204]

4:11 ***For we which live are alway delivered unto death for Jesus' sake / For we who are alive are always being handed over to death for Jesus' sake:*** This verse parallels the one above, and Paul likely adds it for emphasis and clarity. The introductory conjunction γάρ (*gar*), "for," expresses the reason for an action. That action is in the last phrase of the previous verse. The verb ζάω (*zaō*), "to live,"[205] is found here as a present participle. The tense conveys the idea of continually being in the mortal state.[206] The adverb ἀεί (*aei*), "always," expresses a continuously occurring action.[207] Paul places it at the beginning of the sentence to stress the difficulty he and his companions constantly face.

The verb παραδίδωμι (*paradidōmi*), "to hand over, deliver up," here in passive voice, denotes the delivering up of a person to the control of someone or something. It carries the nuance that this is because undue advantage has been taken of that person.[208] The noun θάνατος (*thanatos*), "death," in the present context, denotes the demise of the human body.[209] On the preposition διά (*dia*), "for the sake of," as a marker of cause,[210] see Translation Notes for 4:5.

The focus of the verse is on the central points of the gospel—namely, the "dying" and "life" of Jesus, the very means of salvation. But for Paul it seems to be more than an analogy. He sees what happened to the Lord as extended in time and evidenced in the missionaries' suffering and then deliverance from those very sufferings. Paul clearly states that the reason he and others suffer both mental and physical stress, if not outright anguish (he refers to this state as "always being handed over to death" [NR]), is because they not only follow but also preach about Christ.

that the life also of Jesus might be made manifest in our mortal flesh / so that the life of Jesus might also be revealed in our mortal flesh: Paul repeats the phrase "so that the life of Jesus might also be revealed" found in

---

204. Barnett, *Second Epistle,* 236 n. 47.

205. BDAG, 424–26.

206. The present tense can convey the continuation of a situation. Smyth, *Greek Grammar,* §1852; Wallace, *Greek Grammar,* 521.

207. BDAG, 22.

208. Louw-Nida, §37.111.

209. Louw-Nida, §23.99.

210. BDAG, 225.

the previous verse, but "in our bodies" is replaced with "in our mortal flesh" (see Translation Notes on 4:10). The noun ζωή (*zōē*), "life," in the present context denotes the quality of transcendent life that the Savior received through the Resurrection.[211] The phrase ἡ ζωὴ τοῦ Ἰησοῦ (*hē zōē tou Iēsou*), "the life of Jesus," refers to more than Jesus' earthly ministry—to the life he now has as a resurrected being and which he promises to those who come under the new covenant with full purpose of heart.[212]

On the verb φανερόω (*phaneroō*), "reveal," meaning "to cause something to be visible,"[213] see comments on 4:10. The noun σάρξ (*sarks*), "flesh," carries the nuance of the physical limitations imposed by mortality.[214] The phrase ἐν τῇ θνητῇ σαρκὶ ἡμῶν (*en tē thnētē sarki hēmōn*), "in our mortal flesh," emphasizes the very human and weak condition under which Paul and the others labor. It is because of, not in spite of, their physical limitations that the glory of Christ's Resurrection and the promise it holds for the believers are promulgated. The reason is that it proves that the great success that the missionaries have had comes from not human but divine strength.

4:12 *So then death worketh in us, but life in you / Therefore death is at work in us, but life is at work in you:* The conjunction ὥστε (*hōste*), "therefore, for this reason,"[215] signals the reader that Paul is now making his point. The noun θάνατος (*thanatos*), "death," refers to all the sufferings the missionaries have endured and do endure that Paul has been referring to. The noun ζωή (*zōē*), "life," refers to the promise of eternal life, which the gospel message has brought to the Corinthian Saints. The verb ἐνεργέω (*energeō*), "to work, operate," refers to the immediate operative force that is functioning.[216] That force is "death" in the missionaries but "life" in the Saints. The sentence is one of contrast, emphasizing the difference between the conditions the missionaries endure and those the Corinthian Saints enjoy.

---

211. BDAG, 430–31.

212. Guthrie, *2 Corinthians,* 260. We translate the noun Ἰησοῦ (*Iēsou*) as a subjective genitive.

213. BDAG, 1048; Louw-Nida, §24.19.

214. BDAG, 914–16. Usually this noun has negative connotations while the noun σόμα (*soma*), "body," is positive. However, Paul seems to be using them interchangeably in 4:10–11 to highlight the weaknesses associated with mortality. See Barnett, *Second Epistle,* 237 n. 53.

215. Translated thus because it prefaces an independent clause. BDAG, 1107.

216. BDAG, 335; Louw-Nida, §42.4.

The JST makes two changes in this verse. It reads, "So then *it worketh death unto us,* but life *unto you*" (the italics show the changes). The addition of the word "it" points back to Jesus' earthly ministry and, on the one hand, suggests that the missionaries are following the same mortal path the Savior did, ever walking in the shadow of an early death. On the other hand, Jesus' mortality ended in the Resurrection with its promise of eternal life for the faithful, and thus he works life unto them.

Analysis and Summary

The Apostle has effectively answered the question he asked in 2:16: Who is qualified to preach the stunning and holy gospel and proclaim the glorious wonders of God? He has shown that his detractors, who peddle the word of God (2:17) for their own profit and remain ever blinded by the god of this world (4:4), are not the ones who are so qualified. On the other hand, Paul and his associates, who have spoken with boldness, integrity, and reverence "in the sight of God," are fully qualified (2:17; 4:1–2).

At this point, Paul takes another tack in his self-defense. This tack highlights the suffering he and his companions have had to endure on account of Jesus. This condition has resulted because they have become his disciples and preach his word. Paul's primary focus is on the heavy, often painful, and sometimes frightening hardships he and his companions have had to endure. He again uses one of his favorite themes, that of equating mortal suffering with the suffering of Jesus in death. Though from a modern perspective this imagery may seem an overreach, given the very difficult and ofttimes life-threatening conditions under which the early missionaries and Apostles labored, the metaphor of dying with Christ on a daily basis really works. Their lives are one continual and grueling experience after another. These demanding and even exhausting episodes bring to the surface the weaknesses of those called to serve. Paul showcases these conditions even though his antagonists appear to have used his (and others') manifest weaknesses against him. Boldly, he neither hides nor diminish them. Instead, he both embraces and magnifies them by referring to himself and others as "clay jars" (4:7, NR).

It was a common practice to store valuables, including gold and silver coins, in fragile and expendable earthen vessels. The Old Testament's equating human beings with vessels of clay emphasizes a powerlessness and littleness in humankind in comparison with God. Vessels were made by potters according to their whim or design and took any shape they chose. These objects could be and were easily destroyed (Job 10:9; Isa. 30:14;

Jer. 19:11; compare Rom. 9:20–22). Many of the earthenware vessels that Corinthian potters turned out were cheap and quite fragile. They made lamps in particular very thin to allow light to pass through the sides as well as the top.[217] This imagery would work well for Paul on two levels: first, the lamp is not the source of the light but its bearer, and such are missionaries, and second, their own fragility and weakness evidences that their success must actually be attributed to God. The problem is that people did not generally store treasure in lamps but in pots and jars.

Paul seems to be using "jar" (σκεῦος, *skeuos*) to denote the human body.[218] There seems to be an echo here to the formation of humankind out of "the dust" of the earth (Gen. 2:7; 3:19). Thus, the imagery is fitting because humans all too often prove themselves to be weak and untrustworthy. Despite this, God continues to entrust his greatest treasures to their safe-keeping. Through this imagery, Paul ably deflects those blows struck at him on the basis of his and others' bodily weaknesses.[219]

Though his earthly jar, as he admits, has been greatly strained due to trials, abuse, and hardship, it is still intact and fully able to hold the treasure. His imagery suggests that the Apostle saw himself as ordinary at best, but more probably as inferior,[220] since an earthen vessel is the storehouse that holds valuables, but of itself it can be quite unseemly.[221] Certainly Paul sees himself not as a piece of art but as something cheap, lowly, and expendable.[222] Even so, the imagery creates a bit of a paradox. While the earthen vessel may appear inferior, it contains something quite precious that gives it an importance beyond its own, at least as long as its contents remain in place. That is the apostolic position. These officers may be weak and lowly, but their message, testimony, and authority make them most valuable. They are without question the receptacle of God's power.[223]

Paul's imagery shows that he is fully aware that what is outside (ἔξω, *exō*) might be expendable and subject to change, but what is inside (ἔσω, *esō*) is a most precious and enduring gift. Paul's very ministry proves that, though

---

217. Martin, *2 Corinthians,* 230.

218. The term has a range of meanings including "thing, object, container, vessel, jar, dish," or of people, "instrument" and "vessel." See BDAG, 927–28.

219. Bernard, "Second Epistle," 61.

220. Garland, *2 Corinthians,* 220.

221. Harris, *Second Epistle,* 340.

222. Garland, *2 Corinthians,* 221.

223. Barnett, *Second Corinthians,* 230–31.

the jar itself may be neither strong nor beautiful, God strengthens it and makes it able to hold its precious treasure.[224]

The treasure, as Paul makes clear in 4:4, is the knowledge of God's glory as revealed through the word, work, and person of Christ.[225] The reason that God places his glory in weak human beings is so that no one can deny that "the exceeding greatness of power" as displayed through the missionaries belongs to God alone. It is derived from neither human will nor human effort.[226]

Paul's words stress his awareness that the knowledge of God's glory that his heart bears manifests itself not at all in his mortal condition. Indeed, his outward life suggests just the contrary, for it is on the surface quite inglorious.[227] Although he and his companions labor to be righteous, ultimately their righteousness is because of the grace, power, and gift of God (4:7).[228]

In 4:8–9, Paul lists four paradoxes that constitute mainly his life but also that of all the faithful. For an analysis of each of these, see the Translation Notes above. Paul well understood that life is full of affliction, and the Apostle does not downplay this. Rather, he not only admits but also emphasizes them to make his point. His suffering, though great, shall not only be overcome but be made up more than fully through the comfort and deliverance that Christ through his power grants (compare Rev. 7:17; 21:4).[229] These verses show God's indominable power as evidenced in Paul's own life. "This is more than just having a positive mental attitude. Faith in God provides mental stability, knowing that he is ultimately in charge."[230] Thus, though suffering, even unfair suffering, is part of the human experience, the faithful find power through Christ to endure and benefit from it.

In 4:10–11, Paul reaches the climax of his antithesis: dying yet living. The idea is that Paul and his companions, and even the Saints, live under the constant threat of being killed like Jesus—that is, by violence.[231] As the Apostle sees it, the nature of the world in which he works demands Christlike suffering

---

224. Harris, *Second Epistle,* 339–40; Garland, *2 Corinthians,* 222, notes that an important part of the imagery is its stress on how wise, powerful, and transformative God is.

225. Witherington, *Conflict and Community,* 386; Harris, *Second Epistle,* 340.

226. Bernard, "Second Epistle," 61.

227. Seifrid, *Second Letter,* 205.

228. Jay A. Parry and Donald W. Parry, *Understanding the Book of Revelation* (Salt Lake City: Deseret Book, 1998), 252.

229. Seifrid, *Second Letter,* 206.

230. Ogden and Skinner, *Verse by Verse,* 151.

231. Louw-Nida, §23.99.

in order to advance the gospel. In short, in order for people to experience Jesus' promised life, Paul and his companions have to experience his "dying"—that is, the continual suffering necessitated by the demands of their mission.[232] Paul seems to be saying that the often-threatened and sometimes abusive condition of his and his companions' lives imitates the slow, painful dying of the Lord. That is, they live in a state of continual mortification (νέρωσις, *nekrōsis*). In saying this, Paul takes nothing away from Christ's Atonement and the intense suffering he went through in order to achieve it (see D&C 19:18). He seems, rather, to be looking not at that portion of the spiritual and physical suffering that the Lord went through in Gethsemane and on Golgotha but rather at the stigma, the ignominy, indeed, the very depth of humiliation that was associated with crucifixion in the Greco-Roman world. To continually, patiently, and faithfully endure mortification for the gospel's sake was, for Paul, the equivalent of dying as did Jesus.

This is one of Paul's favorites themes. He connects being in hourly perils to dying daily (1 Cor. 15:30–31) and states that "for thy sake, we are killed all the day long" (Rom. 8:36). Christian suffering, when done in a Christlike manner, he avers, conforms to the Savior's own death (Philip. 3:10). Paul, thus, sees "dying" (νέρωσις, *nekrōsis*) as the uniting force between Christ and Christian. They become as one in facing the world's humiliating opposition but also in evidencing the hope of the coming triumph and glory of the resurrection (Rom. 8:17; compare Rom. 6:5, 8). In all this we see the paradox of the gospel expressed in the Lord's declaration: "He who finds his life shall lose it: and he who loses his life for my sake shall find it" (Matt. 10:39, our translation).[233] Somehow the Saint, in order to achieve eternal life, must become united with Christ in death—that is, in a willingness to suffer mortification for the truth as he did.

The imagery is admittedly stark and awful, but it expresses well the idea that even in the severe moments of the Saints' lives, they are being conformed to Christ's image.[234] The missionaries' perpetual dying is more than an expression of the weakness and frailty of the "clay jars" (4:7, NR) that they are. The dying are lifted up and transformed according to divine purpose and power such that they becomes a precise vehicle "for the

---

232. Guthrie, *2 Corinthians,* 260, with n. 28.
233. Bernard, "Second Epistle," 62–63.
234. Witherington, *Conflict and Community,* 387.

display of the life of Jesus in that same body which carries about the dying of Jesus."[235]

With the brief sentence in 4:12, Paul summarizes his point. He tells his Corinthian brothers and sisters that he and his companions are dying while the Saints are living. Paul seems to be saying that through the "death" that works in the missionaries—that is, by their absorbing some of the messianic suffering—their converts do not have to endure them, and in doing so, the missionaries bring them life.[236] His point is that the missionaries struggle under the throes of mortal life, including hardships, stresses, and even the threat of death—in Paul's imagery, "dying daily"—so that the Saints may have the hope and power of divine life continually abiding in them.[237]

In sum, 4:10–12 shows that missionary service is the vehicle through which God proclaims the gospel to the world. The proclamation includes both the death and renewed life of Jesus. The suffering that Paul and his coworkers endure—which includes the very real threat of death—is in similitude of the suffering of the Savior himself. It was the Lord's suffering that made the gospel (the good news of salvation in Christ) a reality; it is the missionaries' suffering that spreads the message to all the world. This is the divine method by which the world learns of the death and resurrected life of Christ and what it means for those who accept him and follow his ways. The work, however, forces Paul and his companions to carry about in their mortal bodies the "dying of Jesus." They do this in two ways: first, their labor is in similitude to that of the Lord who lived, suffered, and died for the cause of God, and second, they proclaim his death as the central message of the gospel mediated by weak humans, whom Paul describes as "clay jars" (4:7, NR).[238]

---

235. Philip Edgcumbe Hughes, *Paul's Second Epistle to the Corinthians: The English Text with Introduction and Notes* (Grand Rapids: Wm. B. Eerdmans, 1962), 142.

236. Witherington, *Conflict and Community,* 389.

237. Bernard, "Second Epistle," 62–63; compare Seifrid, *Second Letter,* 207.

238. Guthrie, *2 Corinthians,* 261–62.

An Eternal Weight of Glory (4:13–15)

Paul again takes up his eschatological theme, focusing on the hope believers have in coming to divine glory (3:12). In part, this condition is already being realized in that the Saints are already being transformed into Christ's image, from one degree of glory to a higher one, through the operation of the Lord's divine power (3:18). The transformation, however, will only be fully realized at the time of the resurrection, when all, whether good or bad, will stand to be judged before the bar of Christ (4:14; 5:10).

Between 4:16 and 5:10, Paul describes both his and his readers' future. Within these verses he sets out his overarching eschatological dualism, which contrasts the present transient visible world of suffering and grief with the immortal invisible world of glory, joy, and rest. The tension is between the temporal/transitory and the immortal/never-ending. He also sets out a corresponding anthropological dualism between the outer person (ὁ ἔξω . . . ἄνθρωπος, *ho exō . . . anthrōpos*), who belongs fully to this age and is constantly "wasting away," and the inner person (ὁ ἔσω . . . ἄνθρωπος, *ho esō . . . anthrōpos*), who is striving for the age to come and is, therefore, renewed daily. "The contrast between the two ages, present and coming, and between the outer and inner person, is the source of powerful antitheses that characterize the majority of the verses in this passage. Whereas the eschatological dualism hinges on the general resurrection, the anthropological dualism is created by the eschatological Spirit, whom God gives now as a 'deposit, guaranteeing what is to come' (5:5). It is the Spirit who creates the sense that the 'outer person' is 'wasting away' and the 'inner person' is 'being renewed.'"[239]

Paul declares that his motivation is spirit driven (4:13) but also based on his firm testimony of the reality of the coming resurrection and the reward judgment will bring (4:14). All these things, he witnesses, are to bring God glory.

Greek Text

13 Ἔχοντες δὲ τὸ αὐτὸ πνεῦμα τῆς πίστεως, κατὰ τὸ γεγραμμένον· Ἐπίστευσα, διὸ ἐλάλησα, καὶ ἡμεῖς πιστεύομεν, διὸ καὶ λαλοῦμεν, 14 εἰδότες ὅτι ὁ ἐγείρας τὸν Ἰησοῦν καὶ ἡμᾶς σὺν Ἰησοῦ ἐγερεῖ καὶ παραστήσει σὺν ὑμῖν. 15 τὰ γὰρ πάντα δι'

239. Barnett, *Second Epistle*, 246.

ὑμᾶς, ἵνα ἡ χάρις πλεονάσασα διὰ τῶν πλειόνων τὴν εὐχαριστίαν περισσεύσῃ εἰς τὴν δόξαν τοῦ θεοῦ. [SBLGNT]

King James Version

13 We having the same spirit of faith,
according as it is written, I believed, and
therefore have I spoken; we also believe,
and therefore speak; 14 Knowing that
he which raised up the Lord Jesus shall
raise up us also by Jesus, and shall pres-
ent us with you. 15 For all things are for
your sakes, that the abundant grace
might through the thanksgiving of
many redound to the glory of God.

New Rendition

13 Now we have the same spirit of faith
as written in the scriptures, "I believed,
therefore I spoke" [Ps. 116:10]. We
also believe, therefore we also speak
14 because we know that the one who
raised the Lord Jesus will also raise us
together with Jesus and bring us together
with you into his presence. 15 For all
these things are for your sake so that the
grace as it increases throughout more
and more people may cause thanksgiv-
ing to abound to God's glory.

Translation Notes and Comments

4:13 *We having the same spirit of faith, according as it is written, I believed, and therefore have I spoken; / Now we have the same spirit of faith as written in the scriptures, "I believed, therefore I spoke":* To explain why the missionaries do what they do, Paul quotes from Psalm 116:10, noting that they are driven by the same "spirit of faith" as those of old. The verb ἔχω (*echō*), "to have,"[240] found here as a present participle, plays two roles: first, it introduces the ground or cause for the missionaries' willingness to speak (as Paul notes in the next phrase; see below), and second, taking as its grammatical object "the same spirit of faith," it introduces the forceful role faith plays in the proclamation of the gospel.[241] It is the Apostle's conviction that the Christians possess this divine spirit (πνευμα, *pneuma*) and that this separates them from all other people.[242] In the missionaries, it drives them to preach. The noun πίστις (*pistis*), "faith," in the present context, denotes a belief strong enough to engender complete confidence, trust, and reliance in others, leading to a willingness to follow their example.[243] In this case, it is the psalmist whose faith drove Paul to declare his message.

240. BDAG, 420–22.
241. Guthrie, *2 Corinthians*, 262.
242. BDAG, 833.
243. Louw-Nida, §§31.85, 88, 102.

we also believe, and therefore speak / We also believe, therefore we also speak: The conjunction καί (*kai*), "also," usually translated as "and," in this case acts as a marker of an added relationship and therefore has the meaning of "also" or "likewise."[244] It references both the faith and the action of Paul and his companions that imitate that of the psalmist. The verb πιστεύω (*pisteuō*), "believe," has the same nuance as the noun πίστις (*pistis*), "faith" (see above). The verb λαλέω (*laleō*), "to speak," denotes expressing oneself out loud.[245] In this case, it refers to the public declaration of the gospel message.

4:14 ***Knowing that he which raised up the Lord Jesus shall raise up us also by Jesus / because we know that the one who raised the Lord Jesus will also raise us together with Jesus:*** The verb οἶδα (*oida*), "to know," is perfect in form but present in meaning.[246] It is found here as a circumstantial participle with a causative sense, so we have translated it as "because we know." The verb ἐγείρω (*egeirō*) means basically to rouse from sleep. Since many in the Greco-Roman world viewed death as a kind of sleep, the word came to carry a nuance meaning "to rise from death," thereby connoting the resurrection.[247] In the present context it denotes God raising both his Son and the Saints into eternal life (compare 1:9).

The preposition σύν (*syn*) means "with,"[248] but Paul's statement that God will raise up the faithful "with Christ" seems odd in that Jesus had already been resurrected. Further, Paul has stated already that by this "man [Jesus] came also the resurrection of the dead" and that through him all of humanity will gain victory over death (1 Cor. 15:21, 57). Therefore, *syn* probably does not carry the sense of "at the same time as," or "in the company of," or "in union with." Rather, the phrase *syn Iēsou,* "with Jesus," seems to indicate the idea of "in the wake of Jesus' resurrection," or "by virtue of Jesus' resurrection."[249]

244. BDAG, 495.

245. BDAG, 582–83.

246. BDAG, 693.

247. BDAG, 271–72. The noun that denotes resurrection is ἀνάστασις (*anastasis*), literally, "standing up again," BDAG, 71–72. The reading in the KJV that God "shall raise up us also by Jesus," can be construed to mean that Paul felt he would see the Parousia (that is, the Second Coming). This view, however, comes from misreading the Greek text. Bernard, "Second Epistle," 63; see also A. C. Perrimann, "Paul and the Parousia: 1 Corinthians 15:50–57 and 2 Corinthians 5:1–5," *New Testament Studies* 35, no. 4 (October 1989): 512–21.

248. BDAG, 961–62.

249. Harris, *Second Epistle,* 353.

and shall present us with you / and bring us together with you into his presence: The verb παρίστημι (*paristēmi*) has the root sense "to cause to be present in any way."[250] In a general sense it meant to bring someone into another's presence. It was also used as a legal technical term for bringing someone before a judge, which seems to be its use here.[251] The Greek phrase is rather compact: παραστήσει σὺν ὑμῖν (*parastēsei syn hymin*), "he [God] will cause [us] with you to be present." The subject is ὁ ἐγείρας τὸν κύριον Ἰησοῦν (*ho egeiras ton kyrion Iēsoun*), "the one who raised the Lord Jesus"—that is, God the Father—and is found at the beginning of the verse, and the direct object ἡμᾶς (*hēmas*), "us," is carried over from the previous phrase. Finally, it is into God's own presence where the Saints will be brought. Thus in our Rendition we have expanded this passage into "bring us together with you into his presence."

4:15 ***For all things are for your sakes / For all these things are for your sake:*** The phrase τὰ γὰρ πάντα (*ta gar panta*), "for all these things," refers back to the items Paul has noted from 4:7. This verse, thus, captures and reiterates ideas he has developed up to this point. The preposition διά (*dia*), "for the sake of," in the present context, carries the idea of doing something to benefit another[252] and suggests Paul has his ministry to the Corinthians specifically in mind.[253]

The JST corrects this phrase to read, "*For we bear* all things for your sakes." The change clarifies who is doing what for the good of the Saints. It is the missionaries who are shouldering the major administrative and missionary burdens so that the Saints will not have to.

that the abundant grace might through the thanksgiving of many redound to the glory of God / so that the grace as it increases throughout more and more people may cause thanksgiving to abound to God's glory: This clause is syntactically challenging. The verb πλεονάζω (*pleonazō*) is normally intransitive in the New Testament ("to become more, grow, increase"), the single certain transitive example being 1 Thes. 3:12, where the subject is God.[254] It is found here as a circumstantial, aorist participle, ἡ χάρις πλεονάσασα (*hē charis pleonassa*), "the grace, as it increases." The comparative adjective πλείων (*pleiōn*) is used in an elative sense, "very

250. BDAG, 778.
251. BDAG, 778.
252. Louw-Nida, §90.38.
253. Guthrie, *2 Corinthians*, 264–65.
254. BDAG, 824.

many" or "more and more."[255] It is nominalized with the definite article and thus has the sense "more and more people." The preposition διά (*dia*) used with the genitive case has the sense "through."[256] The verb περισσεύω (*perisseuō*) is here used in the transitive sense, "to cause to abound."[257] The object that is caused to abound is τὴν εὐχαριστίαν (*tēn eucharistian*), "thankfulness, gratitude," or "reciprocity."[258]

The noun δόξα (*doxa*), "glory," in the present context refers to "honor, magnificence, respect, reputation."[259]

Analysis and Summary

In this section of his epistle, Paul continues to explain why he does not lose heart even though the outer part of him, the "clay jar," is wasting away. His faith points him toward the resurrection, which gives him hope even for the old "jar."[260] His words show that, for him, "the source of all comfort is Christ's atonement."[261]

In 4:12, Paul signals his readers with the use of the conjunction "therefore" (ὥστε, *hōste*) that he is bringing his argument to a close. His statement at the end of the verse, however, seems to have redirected his thoughts from the missionaries to the Corinthians and the "life" that they have received due to missionary effort. As a result, he develops one more idea before moving on. Once again, his efforts seem to be directed at relieving any remaining tension over the nature of his apostolic ministry that exists between him and some of the members of the house churches.[262] Therefore, Paul takes a moment to stress again why he and his companions do what they do.[263]

---

255. Wallace, *Greek Grammar,* 300. Moule, *Idiom Book,* 108, takes the phrase as "the increasing numbers," thus implying Paul's desire that the gospel message reach ever-increasing numbers of people.

256. BDAG, 223.

257. BDAG, 805.

258. BDAG, 416.

259. BDAG, 256–58.

260. Witherington, *Conflict and Community,* 389.

261. Ogden and Skinner, *Verse by Verse,* 151.

262. At this period in church history, most if not all the Christian congregations met in the homes of their wealthier members. Such homes could accommodate no more than a few dozen worshippers. As a result, more than on home was need to serve as meeting places. For a study, see Robert Banks, *Paul's Idea of Community: The Early House Churches in Their Historical Setting* (Peabody, Mass.: Hendrickson, 1994).

263. Barnett, *Second Epistle,* 239.

He begins by appealing to the scriptures (Ps. 116:10) and thus shows that the missionaries follow the pattern laid down there. Like the psalmist, they are compelled by faith to declare openly what they know.[264] In their case, this knowledge is the witness to the "life of Christ" that is at work in the Corinthian Saints. The Apostle's insistence that he and his companions are speaking under the same divine influence that motivated the psalmist hearkens back to the first paragraph of his excursus on ministering the new covenant. There he contrasts his efforts to freely give the message with the efforts of those who "peddle the word of God" for profit (2:17). His declaration that, due to his God-given ministry, he refuses to become discouraged even in the face of opposition furthers his argument (4:1). Repeating this idea in 4:13 rounds out his discussion and bring the whole to an interim conclusion.[265]

The psalm Paul chose serves his purpose very well. It reads, "I believed, wherefore I have spoken; but I was greatly disparaged" (our translation).[266] The quote certainly described the Apostle's current condition, but its broader context may have been what drew him to it. It shows that the Lord "delivered [the psalmist's] soul from death" and will also make him walk "in the land of the living" (Ps. 116:8–9, KJV). Further, the psalmist declares that "precious in the sight of the Lord is the death of his saints" (Ps. 116:15, KJV). As one scholar noted, the context of the whole contains rich reflections of the very themes Paul has been addressing: "deliverance from difficulties and death." This scholar went on to state that "this section of the psalms must have been comforting to Paul, and here he also finds a deep resonance with the faith and the expression of faith portrayed by the psalmist."[267]

In 4:14, Paul identifies the basis of his courageous and unflagging preaching—sure knowledge. Of what? The coming resurrection. Likely it is based on Paul's own conversion experience when he met the resurrected Messiah (Acts 9:1–9). His understanding may also have derived from information he received when he was "taken up into paradise and he heard inexpressible words that are not proper for a person to speak" (12:4, NR). Certainly, on the road to Damascus, he learned personally and undeniably the reality

---

264. Bernard, "Second Epistle," 63.

265. Barnett, *Second Epistle,* 239.

266. The verb used in LXX Ps. 115:1 is ταπεινόω (*tapeinoō*) and means "to be brought low, humbled, abased, or disparaged." LSJ, 1757. The latter word, meaning "to be evilly spoken of," is a condition Paul knew well. The verb in the Hebrew Bible, where this passage is Ps. 116:10, is עָנָה (*ʿānāh*), meaning "to be brought down, made low, humbled, or afflicted." BDB, 777.

267. Guthrie, *2 Corinthians,* 263; compare Seifrid, *Second Letter,* 206–7.

of the Lord's Resurrection. Based upon that sure knowledge, it would not have been hard for him to extrapolate that the same would happen to him and to all the faithful. His knowledge, like the psalmist's belief, drove him to speak. But it did more: it also drove him to bear witness to the truth he knew. Though God had already rescued him from "a peril of death" (1:10, NR), continued to lead him in triumph (2:14), and sustains him in the suffering he endures for the ministry (4:7–11),[268] that was not the end; God would also give him victory over physical death in the day of the Lord.

Though he carries the threat of death with him continually, he knows that he will, with the Saints, be raised into eternal life.[269] Paul's words show that he sees the resurrection as consisting of both the restoration of the body to life (but in perfected form; see 1 Cor. 15:20–25) and the presentation of the person before Christ in judgment. His witness is reflected in the Book of Mormon, which states "the atonement bringeth to pass the resurrection of the dead; and the resurrection of the dead bringeth back men into the presence of God; and thus they are restored into his presence, to be judged according to their works, according to the law and justice" (Alma 42:23). But who is that God? The book makes this clear, stating that "the keeper of the gate is the Holy One of Israel; and he employeth no servant there; and there is none other way save it be by the gate; for he cannot be deceived, for the Lord God is his name" (2 Ne. 9:41). The book also is clear that "all [will] stand before the judgment-seat of Christ, yea, every soul who belongs to the whole human family of Adam; and . . . must be judged of [their] works, whether they be good or evil" (Morm. 3:20; see also 3 Ne. 27:14; Ether 12:38; and Moro. 8:21).[270]

The Greek in 4:15, as the Translation Notes show, presents a number of translation difficulties. Even so, Paul's thought does come through. In that verse, he once again briefly outlines the purpose, means, and goal of his work that has been and continues to be so beneficial for the Saints. His purpose is so that grace may increase thankfulness. The means is through more and more people receiving that grace with thanksgiving. The goal is

---

268. Barnett, *Second Epistle,* 214.

269. Witherington, *Conflict and Community,* 389.

270. In LDS theology, there are three judgments, two partial and one final. The first partial judgment takes place at the time of death (Alma 40:11–14) and the second at the time of the resurrection (Alma 11:45). The final and full judgement that consigns individuals to their eternal status takes place about the time when earth is remade into a celestial sphere (Rev. 20:12; D&C 38:5). For a study, see Donald N. Wright, "Judgment Day, Final," in *EM,* 2:774–75.

so that God will receive greater respect and honor (*doxa*). In Paul's formula, it is God's grace itself, as multiplied through many, that causes thanksgiving to overflow, resulting in an increase in appreciation, honor, respect, and reverence—in a word, glory (δόξα, *doxa*)—toward God.[271]

In sum, Paul's witness is that in spite of the hardships he and his fellow missionaries face, they carry out their ministry for the benefit of the Corinthian Saints. They rejoice as they see the gift of God, referring to Christ's Atonement and other gifts, spread among and blessing more and more people as they gain a relationship with the Father by keeping commandments and covenants. As it makes its impact in transforming lives, there is an increase of thanksgiving that overflows to God's glory.[272]

Renewal through Suffering (4:16–18)

Greek Text

16 Διὸ οὐκ ἐγκακοῦμεν, ἀλλ' εἰ καὶ ὁ ἔξω ἡμῶν ἄνθρωπος διαφθείρεται, ἀλλ' ὁ ἔσω ἡμῶν ἀνακαινοῦται ἡμέρᾳ καὶ ἡμέρᾳ. 17 τὸ γὰρ παραυτίκα ἐλαφρὸν τῆς θλίψεως ἡμῶν καθ' ὑπερβολὴν εἰς ὑπερβολὴν αἰώνιον βάρος δόξης κατεργάζεται ἡμῖν, 18 μὴ σκοπούντων ἡμῶν τὰ βλεπόμενα ἀλλὰ τὰ μὴ βλεπόμενα, τὰ γὰρ βλεπόμενα πρόσκαιρα, τὰ δὲ μὴ βλεπόμενα αἰώνια. [SBLGNT]

King James Version

16 For which cause we faint not; but though our outward man perish, yet the inward man is renewed day by day. 17 For our light affliction, which is but for a moment, worketh for us a far more exceeding and eternal weight of glory; 18 While we look not at the things which are seen, but at the things which are not seen: for the things which are seen are temporal; but the things which are not seen are eternal.

New Rendition

16 Therefore, we do not lose heart, but even if our physical body is being destroyed, our soul is being renewed day by day. 17 For our present insignificant affliction is producing for us an eternal fullness of glory beyond all measure and proportion 18 because we do not focus on the things that are visible, but on the things that are not visible because the visible things are transient, but the things that are not visible are eternal.

271. Seifrid, *Second Letter,* 212.
272. Guthrie, *2 Corinthians,* 266.

Translation Notes and Comments

4:16 ***For which cause we faint not / Therefore, we do not lose heart*:** The conjunction διό (*dio*),[273] "therefore" (translated as "for which cause" in the KJV), refers back to 4:15 and explains that the desire to bring God glory evermore drives the missionaries to work. The verb ἐγκακέω (*engkakeō*), "lose heart, become discouraged," denotes "the loss of motivation in continuing desirable conduct or activity."[274]

but though our outward man perish, yet the inward man is renewed day by day / but even if our physical body is being destroyed, our soul is being renewed day by day: The phrase εἰ καί (*ei kai*), "even if," introduces not a mere contingency but the fact that the "clay jar," as Paul calls the body (4:7, NR), is in a state of continual decline. The adverb ἔξω (*exō*), "outside," often acts as an adjective referring to the outer part of something, thus ὁ ἔξω . . . ἄνρωπος (*ho exō . . . anthrōpos*), literally "the outer human being," refers to the human body.[275] The verb διαφθείρω (*diaphtheirō*), found here in passive voice, means "to be destroyed, perish," and carries such nuances as being spoiled, ruined, or disabled.[276] The adverb ἔσω (*esō*), "inside,"[277] is also used adjectivally, so that ὁ ἔσω . . . ἄθρωπος (*ho es exō . . . anthrōpos*), literally "the inner human being," is used figuratively to denote the inner being of a person and can refer to her or his spiritual nature. We translate this as "soul" in our Rendition. The verb ἀνακαινόω (*anakainoō*), found here in passive voice, means "to be renewed" with the sense of reaching a previous, preferable state or, better, becoming superior to what one was before.[278] Since the antonyms for "renew" are "deplete, exhaust, impoverish," these may give a better nuance to Paul's meaning in using *diaphtherō*. Given his penchant for vivid imagery, however, "being destroyed" fits his motif.

4:17 ***For our light affliction, which is but for a moment / For our present insignificant affliction:*** The adverb παραυτίκα (*parautika*), "present, immediate," acts as an adjective in this phrase[279] and usually denotes an

273. BDAG, 250.

274. BDAG, 272.

275. BDAG, 354; *NID*, 2:297–98.

276. LSJ, 418; BDAG, 239. The word has the literal meaning: "to rot thoroughly." See also Bernard, "Second Epistle," 64, who translates it as "to be decaying."

277. BDAG, 398; *NID*, 2:297–98.

278. BDAG, 64; Louw-Nida, §§13.67; 58.72.

279. BDAG, 772, translates the phrase as "slight *momentary* trouble."

immediate circumstance with emphasis on its temporary nature.[280] It could denote a brief temporal affliction, but given the present context, it appears that Paul is comparing the state in which the Saints "now" exist—namely, mortality—to that when they are made immortal.[281] The adjective ἔλαφρον (*elaphron*) refers to something having little weight, thus "light" and by extension "insignificant."[282] It is here converted into a neuter noun by the definite article τό (*to*), "lightweight, insignificant." It is followed by the noun θλίψις (*thlipsis*), "affliction," in the genitive case. This is another attributive genitive that Paul regularly uses, literally "insignificance of affliction," which we translate "insignificant affliction."[283] It looks particularly at the kind of heavy pressure that burdens the spirit and thus can also denote "oppression." Paul's use of this mild adjective to modify the very heavy noun creates a strongly marked contrast that helps highlights his point.

worketh for us a far more exceeding and eternal weight of glory / is producing for us an eternal fullness of glory beyond all measure and proportion: The verb κατεργάζομαι (*katergazomai*), "to bring about, produce, create,"[284] is used here in the present tense. The dative case of the pronoun ὑμῖν (*hymin*) carries the sense of advantage and is therefore translated as "for us." Once again Paul refers to δόξα (*doxa*), "glory," but this time in association with what comes not to God but to the Saints. Even so, it carries more than a hint of the divine and points to the state of eternal well-being that results from becoming Christlike in virtue and power. He uses two words to describe the nature of the glory the Saints will receive. The first is the adjective αἰώνιος (*aiōnios*), "eternal," which speaks to duration. The second is the noun βάρος (*baros*), which has a generic sense of "weight, burden," but it came to indicate "a high point in a scale of evaluation, fullness."[285] In this case, it indicates a hefty weight or fullness of glory.[286]

---

280. Louw-Nida, §67.109.
281. Bernard, "Second Epistle," 64.
282. BDAG, 314.
283. BDAG, 457. See Wallace, *Greek Grammar,* 89–90.
284. BDAG, 531.
285. Louw-Nida, §§22.4; 78.23; BDAG, 167.
286. Guthrie, *2 Corinthians,* 272, translates the word as "tonnage."

The noun ὑπερβολή (*hyperbolē*) refers to something that exceeds expectations to an extraordinarily high degree.[287] For emphasis, Paul repeats the word twice in the phrase καθ' ὑπερβολὴν εἰς ὑπερβολὴν (*kath' hyperbolēn eis hyperbolēn*), literally "excessively to excess," which we have rendered "beyond all measure and proportion."[288] The phrase's reference is to the "eternal fullness of glory" and points to the unimaginable blessed state in which celestial souls shall dwell.[289]

4:18 ***While we look not at the things which are seen / because we do not focus on the things that are visible:*** The verb σκοπέω (*skopeō*) means "pay careful attention to." The phrase μή σκοπούτων ἡμῶν (*mē skopountōn hēmōn*) is a genitive absolute participial phrase and is grammatically unusual, since one would expect the participial phrase to be in the dative to agree with the possessive pronoun ἡμῖν (*hēmin*), "for us," of the preceding verse. However, Paul may have chosen the genitive absolute to make the clause more independent of the previous clause and thus more forceful.[290] He is plausibly giving the cause or explanation as to why he and his associates act the way they do. It is because their eyes are focused on the eternal. To put over this sense we have translated the phrase as "because we do not focus on."[291] The plural, neuter definite article τὰ (*ta*) nominalizes the present passive participle βλεπόμενα (*blepomena*), "what is seen,"[292] and is therefore translated as "the things that are visible" in our Rendition. The context suggests that Paul has in mind the vicissitudes and trials of life faced not just by the missionaries but by the Saints in general.[293] Again, the context suggests that the Apostle has in mind earthly negative experiences.

---

287. Louw-Nida, §§78.33.

288. BDAG, 1032.

289. Those who receive this exalted state of glory will have "ministering angels" to assist them. The latter are persons who did not live up to celestial standards but have become cleansed and purified. Doctrine and Covenants 132:17.

290. Though the genitive absolute would normally give full independence to this verse from what Paul had said before (see Smyth, *Greek Grammar,* §§2070–75; Harris, *Second Epistle,* 363; Furnish, *II Corinthians,* 263), both Guthrie, *2 Corinthians,* 273, and Barnett, *Second Epistle,* 253 n. 20, note that taking New Testament use of the construction in general, it is unnecessary to be overly strict in this instance. See also Harris, *Second Epistle,* 364.

291. Due to the vagueness of the syntax here, the phrase could be translated temporally as "while we do not consider," conditionally as "provided we do not consider," causally as "because we do not consider," or resultantly as "with the result that we do not consider." For comment, see Guthrie, *2 Corinthians,* 273.

292. BDAG, 178–79.

293. Barnett, *Second Epistle,* 253.

but at the things which are not seen / but on the things that are not visible: The invisible things, reaching back to what the Apostle stated earlier, include the resurrection with its promise of a full weight of eternal glory. They are invisible in the present because they have not yet been fully realized.

for the things which are seen are temporal / because the visible things are transient: The introductory conjunction γάρ (*gar*), "because, for,"[294] acts as a marker of clarification identifying the problem, noted here, and the solution, noted in the next phrase. The adjective πρόσκαιρος (*proskairos*), "transient, temporary,"[295] refers to something that passes quickly. In this case, it is the challenges and suffering that mortality presents.

but the things which are not seen are eternal / but the things that are not visible are eternal: The adjective αἰώνιος (*aiōnios*) in the New Testament can describe "a long period of time" or "a period of time without beginning or end, eternal."[296] The second sense is the more common, and that is how we have translated it.

Analysis and Summary

Paul's forthright statement that "we do not lose heart" in discharging the duties of the ministry (4:16) is repeated from 4:1. Here he explains why that is the case: though the body continues to become ever weaker, it is offset by the renewing of the spirit through the power of divine grace. It is the present experience coupled with the hope for full renewal—even of the body—that is the reason Paul and the others "do not lose heart."[297]

Paul's writings in 4:16 reveal his understanding that there is a body/spirit dualism, but his view shows this dualism to be very soft as opposed to some of his contemporaries who saw it as very hard.[298] The Apostle's thoughts clearly reveal his understanding that there is a nonphysical, or spiritual, component of the human being. He expresses his view with the admission that though his outward form, the "clay jar" (4:7, NR) is being depleted day by day, his inner person is being renewed day by day

294. BDAG, 189–90.

295. BDAG, 880–81.

296. BDAG, 33.

297. Bernard, "Second Epistle," 64.

298. Some have suggested that Paul has been influenced by Hellenistic ideas. See Furnish, *II Corinthians*, 261. Paul's statements, however, do not reveal a belief that the body imprisons an immortal soul. Witherington, *Conflict and Community*, 389.

(compare Rom. 7:14–25). In this way the "new creation"—that is, the spiritual being—finds continual strength to push forward. His words show that "the work of the Spirit is not a once-in-a-lifetime event but a daily experience for the apostle. Day after day, according to Paul's need, he is 'made new.' God does not grant him strength in advance—lest, perhaps, he should trust in that strength—but removes him from trouble only as trouble comes to him. Comfort arrives only with the suffering of Christ, not beforehand."[299]

Paul's witness, as he instructs the Corinthians, is based on and determined by the mercy and grace extended to him through the personal appearance of and further instructions by the Messiah himself (Acts 9:1–9; Gal. 1:11–12). By this means, the light of the glory of Christ has been placed in Paul's heart and shared by the other missionaries (2 Cor. 4:6). He and the others have been made new (4:16) due to the power of the Savior as revealed in the message they proclaim and authenticate by the power of the Spirit in their lives. However, for some their newness remains hidden under the afflictions and trials the Christian missionaries are going through. Though his life and teaching are beyond reproach, Paul admits that it is God's will that the Apostle is *not* transformed outwardly. Rather, it is the divine will that he remains in weakness so that God's power might be displayed through the Apostle's work (4:7).[300] The logic of his argument is that since he is admittedly weak, he can accomplish all that he does only and exclusively if God is with him.

Paul assures his readers in 4:17 that the present affliction brings about "for us" (ἡμῖν, *hymin*) a breathtaking and eternal mass (ὑπερβολή, *hyperbolē*) of glory, the same as that associated with the Divine. Perspective is all important. Suffering does not last forever, while glory does (compare D&C 121:7). Paul's symbolic language really makes his point. To restate what he says in modern vernacular, the Saints' few ounces of affliction cannot compare to the tonnage of glory that they will eventually receive (compare D&C 63:66).[301]

Though it may appear that Paul is downplaying the hardship that he, his companions, and many of the Saints are experiencing, we must keep in mind that he is well aware of those hardships—even death threats—that

---

299. Seifrid, *Second Letter,* 217.
300. Seifrid, *Second Letter,* 205.
301. Guthrie, *Second Epistle,* 271–72.

he and others have already suffered (see Translation Notes at 1:8). Though admittedly the outer being suffers, the trials will yield an incomprehensible glory in the world to come. "Furthermore," as Paul makes clear, "his labors and sufferings are not just the unfortunate cost of apostleship or occasions to demonstrate his faith, but they are at the heart of his witness."[302] As one scholar noted, "All distress and affliction suffered by the Christians, which are caused by the pressure of the world on them, must always be understood in the light of their solidarity with Christ's afflictions. Only so can they rightly be explained and endured" (compare Philip. 3:10 and 1 Pet. 4:13).[303] "If persecution and death alone were sufficient to bring about [salvation], then when the wicked slay the wicked, . . . it would take them both to the kingdom of God" (2 Cor. 4:17).[304] No, persecution and suffering are not in themselves sanctifying. Salvation requires enduring life's difficulties and unfairness—and especially when one is persecuted for the gospel's sake—in righteousness (Matt. 5:11–12). Thus, suffering has its purpose.

The reward for persistence in righteousness in face of oppression Paul describes as "glory" (δόξα, *doxa*). Though it is something that can be bestowed on humankind, the nuance of its divine property to empower individuals to move toward godhood remains. In his high priestly prayer, the Savior asked the Father to share with the disciples the same glory he had given the Son (John 17:22). Indeed, as Paul affirms, God has called his Saints to glory (1 Thes. 2:12), even to "obtaining of the glory of our Lord Jesus Christ" (2 Thes. 2:14), and has witnessed that they "are being transformed in the same [divine] image from glory to glory" (2 Cor. 3:18, NR). Peter knows this to be true, for he was, as he says, a sharer in God's glory (1 Pet. 5:1). Thus, John can confirm that when Christ shall appear, "we shall be like him; for we shall see him as he is" (1 John 3:2).

---

302. Witherington, *Conflict and Community,* 390. For a study, see David M. Hay, "The Shaping of Theology in 2 Corinthians: Convictions, Doubts, Warrants," *Society of Biblical Literature 1990 Seminar Papers,* ed. D. J. Lull (Atlanta: Scholars Press, 1990), 257–72.

303. *NID,* 2:463–64. In this light, consider Christ's counsel to Joseph Smith when he said, "If thou art called to pass through tribulation; if thou art in perils among false brethren; if thou art in perils among robbers; if thou art in perils by land or by sea; . . . and all the elements combine to hedge up the way; and above all, if the very jaws of hell shall gape open the mouth wide after thee, know thou, my son, that all these things shall give thee experience, and shall be for thy good. The Son of Man hath descended below them all. Art thou greater than he?" (D&C 122:5, 7–8).

304. William E. Berrett, *Blessed Are They Who Come unto Me* (Provo, Utah: Ensign, 1979), 94–95.

The point Paul strives to make is that such earthly—but divine—glory, even though marvelous and to be sought after, pales almost to nothingness when compared to the eternal weight of glory that God will give to the faithful in the resurrection.[305] Such glory will be both eternal and full beyond all measure and proportion. Paul, at least to a degree, experienced this when he was "caught up into paradise, and heard unspeakable words, which it is not lawful for a man to utter" (2 Cor. 12:4). Thus, Paul can witness to "that which neither eye has seen, nor ear heard, nor entered into a person's heart—all these things God has prepared for those who love him" (1 Cor. 2:9, NR). The Doctrine and Covenants witnesses that "the saints shall be filled with his glory, and receive their inheritance and be made equal with [Christ]" (D&C 88:107). Jesus himself promised that the Saints shall "receive of his fulness, and be glorified in me as I am in the Father" (D&C 93:20).

Elder Bruce R. McConkie has stated in this connection that

> mortal trials, persecution, suffering, even the laying down of one's life for the Cause of Christ, are as nothing compared to the immortal glory reserved for those who endure all things well. All these things are part of the Lord's program for testing his saints to the full. "I will try you and prove you herewith," he says. "And whoso layeth down his life in my cause, for my name's sake, shall find it again, even life eternal. Therefore, be not afraid of your enemies, for I have decreed in my heart, saith the Lord, that I will prove you in all things, whether you will abide in my covenant, even unto death, that you may be found worthy. For if ye will not abide in my covenant ye are not worthy of me." (D. & C. 98:12–15.)[306]

In 4:18, Paul gives the reason why he and his companions focus as they do on the eternal rather than the temporal. In the visible but very temporary world, the Christians experience unhappiness, pain, trials, and even undeserved persecution. In the eternal world, as they are promised, there will be an unimaginable weight of glory with its associated joy, peace, concord, and amity.

---

305. As Paul understands it, the weight of glory is so great that it surpasses even that which surpasses (καθ' ὑπερβολὴν εἰς ὑπερβολήν, *kath' hyperbolēn eis hyperbolēn*) and is thus incomprehensible. "Paul's hope as expressed in these verses shows a fundamental shift from an expectation of immediate triumph to a hope for otherworldly glory. Affliction is momentary whereas resurrection is endless, insinuating that the immediate recognition his opponents are receiving will be nothing compared to the eventual glory that will be shared by the Saints." Holzapfel and Wayment, *Making Sense,* 372.

306. *DNTC,* 2:418–19.

The Apostle's emphasis is on what the people are going through when compared to what they will receive for doing so in faith.[307] One is transitory and therefore should command little attention. The other is eternal and should therefore command a great deal of attention. Paul echoes Hebrews 11:1 (see also Alma 32:21 and Ether 12:6), where faith is described as the power to see as a reality the future glory that one can obtain.

Thus Paul teaches that the present circumstances do have their value, for they prepare the Saint for the reception of an eternal weight of glory. As one scholar noted, "The coming age does not occur by a merely mechanical process through our 'suffering' in this age. Rather two activities of this age—the 'suffering' and 'the [not] looking to things [not] seen'—must be regarded as inseparable."[308] Paul's point seems to be that if the Saints concentrate too intently on their obvious earthly methods or objectives, they all too easily lose sight of their eternal goals (4:18).[309]

As this chapter shows, Paul's description of the Apostolic ministry is one of multiple paradoxes: glory through shame, strength in weakness, riches through poverty, life through death. In creating these paradoxes, the Apostle shows that, in part, there are two opposing powers that operate in this world and struggle to possess the human soul—on the one hand, there is God as revealed in Christ, and on the other, there is the god of this world known as Satan. The latter not only afflicts both Christian and Apostle but also blinds the unfaithful so they are incapable of recognizing the truth.[310]

The greatest of Paul's paradoxes is that the power of God resides in humankind, more especially in Paul, as manifest through humility and weaknesses. From his point of view, where there is inappropriate boasting with its underpinning of arrogance, divine power cannot exist. This is because, as he well knows, the power to change humankind came into the world through the cross and is promulgated and affirmed through the modest, willing life and ministry of his servants. In this section, the Apostle declares his heartfelt belief that only in weakness does he find strength. Only when he is emptied of all but Christ does he become "a true and open vessel, a true conduit of power, light, and life in Christ."[311]

---

307. We see this in his emphatic use of the first person plural pronouns "we" and "us."

308. Barnett, *Second Epistle,* 254.

309. See Dallin H. Oaks, "Weightier Matters," *Ensign* 31, no. 1 (January 2001): 13.

310. Witherington, *Conflict and Community,* 390.

311. Witherington, *Conflict and Community,* 390. See also Nicolas J. Frederick and Frank F. Judd Jr., "The Revelation of Jesus Christ to Paul: Presenting a Deeper, Full Christology," in *Thou Art the Christ, the Son of the Living God: The Person and Work of Jesus in*

Given the above, it is easy to see why some of the Apostle's contemporaries would reject his proclamation. His startling doctrine flies against the demands of the social norms so important in Corinthian society and requires a new conceptual framework as the basis for what it means to be a man or woman "in Christ." Some among the Corinthian Saints simply could not handle such strictures and therefore were unwilling to follow Paul and sought after another easier gospel (Gal. 1:6) that was more compatible with what they wanted to believe.[312]

the New Testament, ed. Eric D. Huntsman, Lincoln H. Blumell, and Tyler J. Griffin (Provo, Utah: Religious Studies Center, Brigham Young University; Salt Lake City: Deseret Book, 2018), 228.

312. Witherington, *Conflict and Community,* 390.

Chapter 5

The Ministry of Hope and Reconciliation

Introduction

This chapter of Paul's epistle breaks down into two disparate components. The first deals with the hope and assurance of the Resurrection (5:1–10), while the second focuses again on the ministry of reconciliation (5:11–21). We will introduce the second section below when we examine verses 11–21. This first section contains "one of the most discussed and debated passages in 2 Corinthians."[1] Once again the thoughtful reader of Paul's words can sympathize with Peter's statement that in Paul's epistles there "are some things hard to understand, which the ignorant and unstable . . . twist to their own destruction" (2 Pet. 3:16, our translation). Peter was not castigating his fellow Apostle, but actually endorsing him while admitting that it took a deeper understanding of the scriptures (namely, the Old Testament) than most people were willing to give in order to understand Paul. Knowing this, Peter admonished his readers to put themselves in a position where they would not be "led astray by the deception of lawless men" (2 Pet. 3:17, our translation). They, like Paul and Peter, needed to be grounded in the scriptures as a precaution against entertaining false doctrine.

In this section, Paul continues his discourse on the hardships attendant to both his own and his companions' authentic ministry (4:7–5:10). He has already noted the steady grind and daily suffering, including the near-constant threat of death, that hang over him and his fellow missionaries as well as the Church in general (4:16–18). He now transitions from that topic to focus on the eternal realities that put all the trials in perspective

1. Guthrie, *2 Corinthians*, 275.

and give both energy and direction to the work of the ministry. "In 5:1–10 the section on suffering arrives at a fitting crescendo: Paul explains how the unseen realm mentioned in 4:18 relates to the ultimate hope of those often caught in the tumultuous mill of ministry."[2] That hope centers on the reality of the resurrection and the blessing that event will bring to the faithful. To make his point, the Apostle uses a series of word pictures, including an "earthly house," "a tent," "a building," and an "outer garment," to describe frail and mortal bodies in comparison to the ones that will be made without mortal hands—that is, by God (5:1).

On Our Heavenly Dwelling (5:1–5)

Greek Text

1 Οἴδαμεν γὰρ ὅτι ἐὰν ἡ ἐπίγειος ἡμῶν οἰκία τοῦ σκήνους καταλυθῇ, οἰκοδομὴν ἐκ θεοῦ ἔχομεν οἰκίαν ἀχειροποίητον αἰώνιον ἐν τοῖς οὐρανοῖς. 2 καὶ γὰρ ἐν τούτῳ στενάζομεν, τὸ οἰκητήριον ἡμῶν τὸ ἐξ οὐρανοῦ ἐπενδύσασθαι ἐπιποθοῦντες, 3 εἴ γε καὶ ἐνδυσάμενοι οὐ γυμνοὶ εὑρεθησόμεθα. 4 καὶ γὰρ οἱ ὄντες ἐν τῷ σκήνει στενάζομεν βαρούμενοι ἐφ' ᾧ οὐ θέλομεν ἐκδύσασθαι ἀλλ' ἐπενδύσασθαι, ἵνα καταποθῇ τὸ θνητὸν ὑπὸ τῆς ζωῆς. 5 ὁ δὲ κατεργασάμενος ἡμᾶς εἰς αὐτὸ τοῦτο θεός, ὁ δοὺς ἡμῖν τὸν ἀρραβῶνα τοῦ πνεύματος. [SBLGNT]

King James Version

1 For we know that if our earthly house of this tabernacle were dissolved, we have a building of God, an house not made with hands, eternal in the heavens. 2 For in this we groan, earnestly desiring to be clothed upon with our house which is from heaven: 3 If so be that being clothed we shall not be found naked. 4 For we that are in this tabernacle do groan, being burdened: not for that we would be unclothed, but clothed upon, that mortality might be swallowed up of life. 5 Now he that

New Rendition

1 For we know that if the earthly house of our body is destroyed, we have a building from God—an eternal house in the heavens not made by hands. 2 For indeed, in this earthly body we groan because we want to put on our heavenly body, 3 provided that when we have put it on, we will not be found naked. 4 For indeed, we who are in this body groan because we are weary since we do not want to be unclothed, but to be further clothed so that the mortal might be swallowed up by life. 5 Now he who

2. Guthrie, *2 Corinthians*, 275.

hath wrought us for the selfsame thing is God, who also hath given unto us the earnest of the Spirit.	prepared us for this very thing is God, who gave us the pledge of the Spirit.

Translation Notes and Comments

5:1 ***For we know that if our earthly house of this tabernacle were dissolved / For we know that if the earthly house of our body is destroyed:*** The verb οἶδα (*oida*), "to know," carries the idea of knowing something either absolutely (as through divine revelation) or from observation. In either case, it nuances what is fully known, perceived, or comprehended.[3] Though Paul had not personally experienced the resurrection, he had seen its reality at the time Jesus appeared to him (Acts 9:1–9). The noun οἰκία (*oikia*), "house," denotes a dwelling place, be it a home or an apartment. Figuratively, it refers to the mortal body as the residence of the spirit.[4] The adjective ἐπίγειος (*epigeios*) denotes that which is earthly rather than heavenly.[5] Here it shows that Paul is referring to the mortal body. The noun σκῆνος (*skēnos*) can denote a "tent" but is also used to denote a "human body" as it does here.[6] Hence, we have translated it as "body." The verb καταλύω (*katalyō*), "to destroy," found here as a subjunctive aorist, means "to take down, dismantle, destroy" and, keeping with Paul's imagery, often refers to the destruction of a house.[7] The conjunction ἐάν (*ean*) "if" used with an aorist subjunctive in the protasis and a present tense in the apodosis (as is the case here) forms a present general condition that denotes what is expected to occur or is normal and accepted.[8]

we have a building of God, an house not made with hands, eternal in the heavens / we have a building from God—an eternal house in the heavens not made by hands: Paul's use of the present active verb ἔχω (*echō*), "to have, possess,"[9] illustrates his sureness of the resurrection and his willingness to verify its reality to his readers. The noun οἰκοδομή (*oikodomē*), "building, edifice,"[10] denotes the result of a building process while the

---

3. *DAG,* s.v. "εἴδω"; Louw-Nida, §§28.1; 32.4.

4. BDAG, 695; Otto Michel, "οἰκία," in *TDNT,* 5:131–34.

5. It can carry the negative nuance of human weakness it but does not do so here. BDAG, 368–69.

6. *DAG,* s.v. "σκῆνος"; Wilhelm Michaelis, "ποοράω, προεῖδον," in *TDNT,* 5:381–82.

7. BDAG, 521–22; Bernard, "Second Epistle," 65.

8. BDAG, 267.

9. BDAG, 420–22.

10. Louw-Nida, §7.1; BDAG, 696.

prepositional phrase ἐκ θεοῦ (*ek theou*), "from God,"[11] shows who that builder is. In this case, the "building" is the resurrected body. On οἰκία (*oikia*), "house," see above. The adjective ἀχειροποίητος (*acheiropoiētos*) means "not made by hands"[12] and carries the nuance of that which is not of human but of divine construction. Our bodies are made by our Heavenly Father. The adjective αἰώνιος (*aiōnios*), "eternal," refers to "a period of unending duration, without end."[13] It connotes not just quantity but also a positive quality, especially when associated with the Divine.[14] The phrase uses the plural of the noun οὐρανός (*ouranos*), "heaven," and although the idea of the celestial sphere containing more than one heaven was known to both Jews and Christians, the idea here is that of the abode of Deity.[15] Scholars have debated on what Paul meant by the term "heavenly house,"[16] but given the context, he is almost certainly referring to the resurrected body.[17] Such a body is one God has made fit for the future when there will be a new heaven and a new earth "wherein dwelleth righteousness" (2 Pet. 3:13; compare Isa. 65:17; Rev. 2:7; 21:1–4; Ether 13:9; and D&C 29:23).[18]

5:2 ***For in this we groan / For indeed, in this earthly body we groan***: The neuter demonstrative adjective τούτῳ (*toutō*), "this," refers back to σκῆνος (*skēnos*), "tent," in 5:1. In our Rendition, we have added "earthly body" for clarification. The verb στενάζω (*stenazō*), "to groan," denotes an involuntary groan, moan, or sigh "in the face of undesirable circumstances."[19] By using the word, Paul stresses how he feels about the weight, feebleness, and limitations of the mortal body.

---

11. The preposition ἐκ (*ek*) acts as a marker denoting origin or derivation of the object. BDAG, 295–98.

12. *DAG,* s.v. "ἀχειροποίητος"; BDAG, 159–60.

13. *DAG,* s.v. "αἰώνιος"; BDAG, 33.

14. Louw-Nida, §67.96.

15. BDAG, 737–38; *NID,* 3:565–72.

16. The "house in heaven" some argue could refer to the body of Christ, the new temple, a celestial dwelling place, or celestial glory. For discussion, see Harris, *Second Epistle,* 371–78.

17. Garland, *2 Corinthians,* 248–53; Guthrie, *2 Corinthians,* 278. Since human hands do not precisely construct the human body, the idea is a bit vague. It is more clearly expressed in Heb. 9:11. Bernard, "Second Epistle," 65. For a study, see Oscar Cullman, *Immortality of the Soul or Resurrection of the Dead? A Witness of the New Testament* (London: Epworth Press, 1964; rpt., Eugene, Oreg.: Wipf and Stock, 2000).

18. N. T. Wright, *The Resurrection of the Son of God* (Philadelphia: Fortress Press, 2003), 366–67.

19. BDAG, 942.

earnestly desiring to be clothed upon with our house which is from heaven / because we want to put on our heavenly body: The verb ἐπιποθέω (*epipotheō*), "to yearn, desire, long for," not only denotes an unusually strong longing for something but also implies a need for it.[20] Paul uses it to describe a yearning for the kind of immortality that comes by possessing a celestial body. The noun οἰκητήριον (*oikētērion*) refers to a "dwelling, habitation,"[21] but like σκῆνος (*skēnos*) in 5:1, it denotes a physical body,[22] and so we have translated it as such. The verb ἐπενδύομαι (*ependyomai*) is found only here and in 5:4 in the New Testament. It carries the idea of putting one garment over the top of another.[23] Though the word could imply that Paul is expressing his desire for a spiritual or heavenly body or power to be put on over his mortal one,[24] the context suggests he is referring to his immortal spirit being clothed with a heavenly, celestial, resurrected body.

5:3 ***If so be that being clothed we shall not be found naked / provided that when we have put it on, we will not be found naked:*** This verse has been the subject of much debate. The problem is that ἐνδυσάμενοι (*endysamenoi*), which is the aorist middle passive participle of ἐνδύω (*endyō*) with the meaning "to clothe oneself in, put on,"[25] has a variant reading in some manuscripts of ἐκδυσάμενοι (*ekdysamenoi*), which means "to undress oneself."[26] The reading "put on" has the oldest and best external attestation by far,[27] although some scholars maintain that, as the verse stands, what it says is so obvious that it seems "banal and even tautologous."[28] However, internal evidence also favors this reading. It may seem that "provided that when we have put it on, we will not be found naked" is an obvious statement, and some scribe may have thought so and changed the participle. But in fact, 5:3 appears to be parenthetical, and the idea that "we do not want to be unclothed, but . . . clothed" (NR) is found again in 5:4. This concept also

20. BDAG, 377.

21. BDAG, 695.

22. Michel, *TDNT,* 5:155.

23. BDAG, 361; Louw-Nida, §49.2.

24. Bernard, "Second Epistle," 65.

25. BDAG, 333.

26. BDAG, 301.

27. The manuscripts supporting ἐνδυσάμενοι (*endysamenoi*) are 𝔓[46] ℵ B C D2 K L P Ψ 0243, 33, 81, 104, 365, 630, 1175, 1241, 1505, 1739, 1881, 2464 𝔐 lat sy co; Cl, whereas those supporting ἐκδυσάμενοι (*ekdysamenoi*) are *txt* D*.c F G ar fc; Mcion Tert Spec. See the textual apparatus for 5:3 in Eberhard Nestle and others, eds., *Novum Testamentum Graece: Nestle-Aland,* 28th ed. (Stuttgart, Ger.: German Bible Society, 2012).

28. Metzger, *Textual Commentary,* 511.

shows up in 5:2 with the phrase "we want to put on" (NR). Thus, the context argues for "put on" as the original reading, and we have so translated it in our Rendition.

The adjective γυμνός (*gymnos*), "naked," carries a range of meaning from being completely undressed to being either immodestly or inappropriately dressed.[29]Among the Jews, the word carried the figurative nuances of embarrassment, helplessness, and vulnerability.[30] With the resurrection, the soul escapes all these conditions. That being the case, Paul seems to be emphasizing the idea that being clothed with a divine, physical, resurrected, celestial body protects the eternal soul from ever being vulnerable or helpless again.

5:4 ***For we that are in this tabernacle do groan, being burdened / For indeed, we who are in this body groan because we are weary:*** The beginning phrase, καὶ γάρ (*kai gar*), "for indeed," emphasizes the point that being in the "tent" causes groaning. On the verb στενάζω (*stenazō*), "to groan," see 5:2 above. The verb βαρέω (*bareō*), found here as a passive participle, denotes being weighed down or burdened under a heavy load, whether physical or mental.[31] Though Paul may be exaggerating for effect, this phrase does show that he and others genuinely feel the stress that adherence to their religion has called them to suffer.

not for that we would be unclothed, but clothed upon /since we do not want to be unclothed, but to be further clothed: With this phrase, Paul makes it clear that it is not the physical body itself that is the problem but its mortal condition. The verb ἐκδύω (*ekduō*), found here as aorist middle infinitive, means to strip or undress oneself.[32] The verb ἐνδύω (*enduō*), also found here as an aorist middle infinitive, means either to clothe or to have clothing put on oneself.[33] This figure of speech views the body as something the spirit wears and that can therefore be stripped or taken off and put back on. It works well in this instance in that a different set of clothing can be exchanged for the one taken off. In this case, it is the mortal body that is taken off and the immortal, glorious, resurrected body that is put on.

that mortality might be swallowed up of life / so that the mortal might be swallowed up by life: The verb καταπίνω (*katapinō*), "to be swallowed up," found here as a passive aorist subjunctive, also carries the additional

---

29. BDAG, 208; Louw-Nida, §49.22. One of the conditions of prison life and poverty was being inadequately dressed. See Matt. 25:36, 38, 43–44; James 2:15.

30. *NID*, 1:610–12.

31. BDAG, 166–67.

32. BDAG, 301.

33. BDAG, 333–34. See also ἐπενδύομαι, BDAG, 361.

nuance of being destroyed.[34] The noun ζωή (*zōē*), "life," though often referring to physical life, carries the strong nuance of the transcendent life shared by the Father and Son with all those who are faithful.[35] That seems to be the case here. Paul's point is that mortality—that is, death—is swallowed up or destroyed by the power of eternal life that comes through the resurrection.

5:5 ***Now he that hath wrought us for the selfsame thing is God / Now he who prepared us for this very thing is God:*** The verb κατεργάζομαι (*katergazomai*), "to prepare," found here as an aorist middle participle, denotes the preparation of someone for something but nuances the thoroughness of that preparation.[36] The phrase εἰς αὐτὸ τοῦτο (*eis auto touto*), "for this very thing," refers back to τῆς ζωῆς (*tēs zōēs*), "the life," found in 5:4, and refers not just to the resurrection but to the quality of life that the righteous will achieve at the time of their resurrection. Paul is emphatic that the one who thoroughly prepares the Saints for this celestial blessing is God himself. Given Paul's deep faith in and appreciation for the work of the Messiah, it may seem strange that he does not give at least partial credit to the Lord. The Apostle's focus, however, is not on the intermediary, as essential as his work is, but on the Father, who is the actual author of and power behind the resurrection.

who also hath given unto us the earnest of the Spirit / who gave us the pledge of the Spirit: This phrase shows that God has done something in addition to—that is, related to—preparing a person for eternal life. The verb δίδωμι (*didōmi*), "to give," is found here as an aorist participle, which expresses simple occurrence, generally antecedent to the main verb.[37] The noun ἀρραβών (*arrabōn*), "pledge, earnest, deposit,"[38] is a technical term that denotes a down payment or initial installment guaranteeing that the full amount of a contract will be paid and assuring that the object will be realized. The phrase τοῦ πνεύματος (*tou pneumatos*), "of the Spirit," is epexegetical,[39] making clear that what God gave and is still giving is the Spirit. Paul's point is that the reception of the Spirit is God's pledge or assurance to the individual that he or she will have eternal life (see Translation Notes for 1:22).

---

34. BDAG, 524.
35. BDAG, 430–31.
36. BDAG, 531; Louw-Nida, §77.6.
37. Smyth, *Greek Grammar,* §1872.c.
38. BDAG, 134.
39. This describes a condition when, to make a statement clear, additional words are used.

Analysis and Summary

The present section (5:1–5) continues Paul's exposition that he began in 4:7 dealing with the apostolic ministry. He starts this section with his heartfelt testimony. His words "we know" (οἴδαμεν, *oidamen*) denote more than a fundamental or theological conviction of his faith. They connote a sure knowledge, in Paul's case one that is based on his personal experience in seeing the resurrected Lord and what he learned from the other eyewitnesses (Acts 9:1–9; 1 Cor. 15:3–8). The knowledge from these sources was bolstered by material he learned during visions, material he was not to directly share (2 Cor. 12:1–4) but that highly influenced his knowledge and understanding of divine ways. What he absolutely knows is that when a person is unclothed from his or her mortal body, he or she will be reclothed with a heavenly and eternal one like Heavenly Father has. Here Paul more fully contrasts the temporary with the permanent, the mortal with the eternal, and the seen with the unseen (4:18; compare 1 Cor. 15:51–58). "To keep the contrast before his readers, Paul describes in 5:1 the antithesis of the Christian present body, namely, the future 'spiritual' body."[40] In doing so, he reiterates what he has already explained to his readers in his previous letter, wherein he contrasted the "natural body" with the "spiritual body," the former "sown in corruption" while the latter is "raised in incorruption" when we are resurrected with a celestial body (1 Cor. 15:42–44). The present finite body is subject to pain and suffering, wear and tear, sorrow and grief. But that is not the final destiny of the soul. The present mortal body with its earthly encumbrances and restrictions, Paul teaches, will be replaced with an eternal body freed from the frailties, pains, and corruption imposed by mortal life.

In 5:2–4, he explains why he groans under the limitations and burdens of his earthly body and why he yearns for a heavenly one. His experience, he shows, acts to stoke his desire for "our habitation from heaven." He here changes his imagery from that of the body as a tent to one of it as an outer garment. He has two such garments in mind. One is mortal and physical while the other is immortal and spiritual. The latter provides for the Saint an adequate dress for celestial glory. It is noteworthy that Paul does not desire to be rid of a body but rather to arrive at the time when his earthly body will be changed into a heavenly, celestial, and glorious one of

40. Martin, *2 Corinthians,* 243.

flesh and bone (D&C 130).[41] The sentence found in 5:3 acts as a parenthetical correction designed to head off any misreading of his statement in 5:2. He is looking at the nature of the soul between death and resurrection. He refers to this state of a bodiless spirit as being "naked"—that is, vulnerable and helpless as it must wait on other factors before it can be clothed upon again. Only with the resurrection can it receive the power and honor it desires by once again being clothed by its physical body, howbeit divinely transformed, purified, and glorious. Though Paul does not look forward to this possible period of "nakedness" with its uncomfortable helplessness, his emphasis centers on his expectation of receiving his divinely endowed resurrected body.[42]

In 5:5, Paul witnesses how God is active in the salvation process. First, he fully prepares the individual for eternal life. The Apostle does not elaborate on how the Father has done this but assures his readers it is so. Second, he states that God has given the Saints the Holy Spirit, which acts as a divine assurance or guarantee that they will actually achieve the eternal life that God has promised them. His point is important. The companionship of the Holy Ghost acts as a purifying agent to gradually provide the promise or sealing (ἀρραβών, *arrabōn*) that the recipient, at that point in her or his life, has become cleansed and will receive all that Heavenly Father has in the highest of his kingdoms.

41. Paul shows no inclination to accept the Platonic notion that the body is a burden that must be escaped. For him, the ideal is being fully embodied but a body with heavenly properties. Guthrie, *2 Corinthians,* 279–80. Paul's metaphor is a bit mixed, viewing the body as a kind of "imperishable topcoat" (Linda L. Belleville, *2 Corinthians,* ed. Grant R. Osborne, D. Stuart Briscoe, and Haddon Robinson [Downers Grove, Ill.: InterVarsity Press, 1996], 134) but at the same time as a dwelling. His imagery presents the view of an immortal body as a residence that one wears. Guthrie, *2 Corinthians*, 280.

42. Guthrie, *2 Corinthians,* 282.

Excursus on Paul's Understanding of the Resurrection

There is a good deal of debate focusing on whether Paul, when he wrote to the Corinthians, felt he would be alive to see the Parousia and thereby personally experience the instant change from mortality to immortality.[43] When he wrote to the Thessalonians some years before, he seemed to have fully expected the Second Coming to be in his lifetime. He admitted then that no one knew when it would come because it would be as a thief in the night (1 Thes. 5:2), and therefore all should be prepared for the event, but he expected to see it (1 Thes. 4:4–17). Even so, this epistle shows that the Apostle definitely believed that there was an intermediate state between death and the resurrection inhabited by departed spirits (1 Thes. 4:13–17). That the early Christians had a knowledge of this state of existence is confirmed by Peter's references to the world of spirits (1 Pet. 3:19; 4:6) coupled with John's (see also Rev. 20:12–13; compare Alma 11:43–44; 40:11–26; and D&C 29:13; 88:96–101). Scholars debate the question as to whether Paul's statements to the Corinthians show he was hoping to avoid that state by moving directly from mortality to immortality at the Second Coming.[44] His words, as recorded in the New Testament, do leave the subject open, but the debate must not cloud the point he is making. It rests on his firm testimony that whatever happens, near or far, the resurrection is sure.

Even so, understanding the Apostle's view of the resurrection is key to interpreting his Corinthian correspondences. He addresses the issue twice in his Corinthian epistles (1 Cor. 15:35–58; 2 Cor. 5:1–10),[45] but the theme threads its way through much of Paul's writings. A central point that Paul

43. This essay follows Martin, *2 Corinthians,* 227–71.

44. Martin, *2 Corinthians,* 261–63. The JST changes 1 Thes. 4 to show that Paul did not include himself among those who would be alive at the Parousia. However, Brigham Young, in *JD,* 12:65, stated, "There can be no doubt but they [the early Saints] were mistaken with regard to the time of the winding up scene, thinking it was much nearer than it really was."

45. Debates center on the degree of consistency between these two treatments and the possible influence of ideas coming from Gnosticism, Greek philosophy, and Judaism. For an overview, see John Gillman, "A Thematic Comparison: 1 Corinthians 15:50–57 and 2 Corinthians 5:1–5," *Journal of Biblical Studies* 107 (1988): 439–54. For a thorough study, see Wright, *Resurrection of the Son of God.* Since much in these debates focuses neither on issues directly relevant to Paul's major points nor the purposes of this study, we do not address them here.

addresses in 1 Corinthians 15 is the nature of the resurrection. He refers to what exists after the resurrection as a "spiritual body" (σῶμα πνευματικόν, *sōma pneumatikon*), while that which exists in mortality he labels a "natural" or earthly "body" (σῶμα ψυχικόν, *sōma psychikon*). Though some argue that Paul's reference to a "spiritual body" points to a postresurrection nonphysical body or some transcendent physical essence, his focus is not actually on the nature of the two types of bodies but rather on the very different modes of existence the two types of bodies occupy.[46] The preresurrected body occupies a state of weakness, decay, and humiliation while the postresurrected body occupies a state of strength, honor, and power (1 Cor. 15:42–43), a point that most Christians have historically ignored because they considered matter evil due to Neoplatonic Greek influences. However, these verses emphasize the physical nature and beauty of having a celestial, resurrected body like Heavenly Father has. As Greek grammar bears out, the -ικον (*-ikon*) ending of the adjective πνευματικόν (*pneumatikon*), "spiritual," does not refer to the composition of the body but rather denotes "modes of being or characteristics." In Paul's writings, "spiritual" refers most specifically "to being derived from, or being about, the spirit."[47] Paul creates a strong contrast between "fleshly" (σαρκικός, *sarkikos*) and "spiritual" (πνευματικός, *pneumatikos*) bodies. The first body is under the influence of the flesh and is driven thereby while the second body is dominated by the Spirit and led thereby (1 Cor. 15:47). By taking Paul's treatment on the subject as a whole, we see that the resurrected mode of existence is characterized by the reversal of weakness and decay and the gain of splendor and power. Being constituted by and under the direction, control, and character of the Spirit, such a body, we should expect, would not "*be reduced in potential from the physical capacities which biblical traditions value, but* [be] *enhanced above and beyond them in a way that both assimilate and transcend them.*"[48]

Thus, though Paul in 1 Corinthians is not speaking directly of a somatic (that is, a physical) existence, he is speaking of it indirectly and so shows the mode in which the resurrected body will eternally live. In 2 Corinthians 5, he picks up the theme and describes the earthly transitive body as a mobile "tent" (σκῆνος, *skēnos*) in contrast to the permanent one that he

46. This position is strengthened by Paul's use of ἐν (*en*, "in") in the modal sense of state or condition. BDAG, 326–330; Martin, *2 Corinthians*, 251.

47. Thiselton, *First Epistle*, 1276; Louw-Nida, §12.20, 21.

48. Thiselton, *First Epistle*, 1279, italics in original.

describes as the "home" (οἰκία, *oikia*) of the eternal spirit. Paul views being without any kind of physical body as being "naked" (γυμνός, *gymnos*). We are naked without a physical body because, we learn in D&C 138:50, the dead in the spirit world look "upon the long absence from their bodies as a bondage," and, according to Restoration material, "the spirit and the body are the soul of man" (D&C 88:15). Among the Jews, the word carried the nuance of extreme helplessness (Job 24:7; Ezek. 16:22) and the inability to hide oneself from God (Gen. 3:7–10; Moses 4:12–17). Under his piercing glance, everything not repented of is laid bare, no matter how uncomfortable one might find that exposure to be (Heb. 4:12; compare D&C 33:1). The Apostle is, thus, emphasizing "the Jewish hope, that it is not good for a person to be without a body, that is, 'naked,' rejecting any Greco-Roman notion of death," which was that the essence of the self would be either gone or in a bodiless, dark, foreboding, and mirthless state.[49]

Paul makes it clear that, speaking of the future reward of the Saints, "we have [ἔχομεν, *echomen*] a building [οἰκοδομή, *oikodomē*] from God" (5:1, NR). Because the verb is in the present tense, some scholars have argued either that believers receive a "new" body at baptism, because it is now under the influence of the Holy Ghost, or that they have become members of the "body" of the Church at that time.[50] The present tense, however, does not always have temporal force and is sometimes used to make a general statement of truth.[51] That is likely the case here. The tense, therefore, suggests Paul's certainty of an actual resurrection with a physical body and his hope that his will be one of glory.[52]

The question remains, did Paul expect to live to the Parousia and at that time be changed in the "twinkling of an eye" from mortality to immortality (1 Cor. 15:52)? In other words, do his statements here betray a fear he would die before the Second Coming?[53] The context again suggests that Paul fully understood that he would receive an immortal body only at the

49. Martin, *2 Corinthians,* 254. For a study, see Jeremiah Mutie, *Death in Second-Century Christian Thought: The Meaning of Death in Earliest Christianity* (Eugene, Ore.: Pickwick, 2015).

50. Martin, *2 Corinthians,* 254.

51. Smyth, *Greek Grammar,* §1877.

52. Matera, *II* Corinthians, 120–21. There is more than one resurrection. See 1 Cor. 15:20–23. For a discussion in the context of the Corinthian correspondences, see Draper and Rhodes, *Paul's First Epistle to the Corinthians,* 775–78.

53. This position is explored in Thrall, *Critical and Exegetical Commentary,* 1:370.

Parousia, *whenever* that would be. Paul's description of the body being "destroyed" or "dismantled" (καταλύω, *katalyō*) and the soul being left "naked" suggests he was well aware that that the Saints would exist in a temporary interim bodiless state (2 Cor. 5:1). Due to the weight of the present distress, Paul notes that he longs for a future existence when body and spirit would be united, making a dwelling (οἰκητήριον, *oikētēpιον*) that would be strong, everlasting, and holy. Therefore, in the present, as he so graphically states, he faces death but with hope, knowing that whenever the Parousia happens, it will bring the blessing of eternal life with Christ (5:8; Philip. 1:23). The message Paul wants to leave with his readers focuses on the importance and joy of the Parousia. This event, not the death that might precede it, is the climax of the Christian hope and the apex of its theology. Only when that time comes will the Saints be fully transformed and enabled to live in the presence of the Divine. In this way, Paul gives the Saints a hope that transcends their present distress and brings anticipation to both the living and the dead. All this, Paul assures his readers, is based not on speculation or desire but on a sure witness. He knows (οἶδα, *oida*) of what he speaks.

In sum, Paul's resurrection theology is consistent in both 1 Corinthians 15 and 2 Corinthians 5. Both look to the same type of resurrection that centers on the Jewish hope of an embodied salvation. "Language of body/spirit (soul) dualism may arise at points as Paul addresses the views of the Corinthians and his opponents. However, Paul's arguments always end with embodiment."[54] His language shows that he is well aware of a period of disembodiment before the Parousia and that he may well face it. He does not yearn to do so, for he feels it will be a time of uncomfortable "nakedness." Modern revelation confirms his view that time in the spirit world, even for the righteous, is not fully comfortable. The Doctrine and Covenants reports that, at the time of the Savior's death, a "vast multitude waited and conversed, rejoicing in the hour of their deliverance from the chains of death." When the Lord appeared, he proclaimed "liberty to the captives who had been faithful" (D&C 138:18). Note that even the righteous feel they are captives bound by death's chains and yearn for release. Therefore, with the immanent resurrection in sight, the Saints "rejoiced in their redemption, and bowed the knee and acknowledged the

54. Martin, *2 Corinthians,* 255.

Son of God as their Redeemer and Deliverer from death and the chains of hell" (D&C 138:23).

But it must be kept in mind that Paul's purpose in bringing up this subject is likely polemical. His purpose is to discuss neither the timing of the Second Coming nor the nature of bodies either mortal or immortal but to stress the transforming power for both that can only be found in Christ Jesus. Even so, Paul does speak of his hope for the resurrection in a very personal manner. His desire is likely augmented by the constant threat of death that he and others face. In addressing the subject, he tacitly answers charges about his personal weaknesses, which he readily admits having, by showing that he succeeds only because of the power of God in his life. This is what not only allows but also enables him to suffer as he does in behalf of his Christian brothers and sisters. It is, however, his sure witness of the resurrection that assists in fueling the fire of his testimony and driving him ever forward in the cause of the Messiah, even in the face of death. Whatever happens in mortality, he tells his readers, he and they are assured by the presence of the Spirit (5:5) that they will be raised up at the Second Coming and receive transformed bodies enabled to dwell eternally in the fire of celestial glory. "Paul's hope as expressed in these verses shows a fundamental shift from an expectation of immediate triumph to a hope for otherworldly glory. Affliction is momentary whereas resurrection is endless, insinuating that the immediate recognition his opponents are receiving will be nothing compared to the eventual glory that will be shared by the Saints."[55]

55. Holzapfel and Wayment, *Making Sense,* 372.

We Labor That We May Be Accepted of Him (5:6–10)

Greek Text

6 Θαρροῦντες οὖν πάντοτε καὶ εἰδότες ὅτι ἐνδημοῦντες ἐν τῷ σώματι ἐκδημοῦμεν ἀπὸ τοῦ κυρίου, 7 διὰ πίστεως γὰρ περιπατοῦμεν, οὐ διὰ εἴδους— 8 θαρροῦμεν δὲ καὶ εὐδοκοῦμεν μᾶλλον ἐκδημῆσαι ἐκ τοῦ σώματος καὶ ἐνδημῆσαι πρὸς τὸν κύριον· 9 διὸ καὶ φιλοτιμούμεθα, εἴτε ἐνδημοῦντες εἴτε ἐκδημοῦντες, εὐάρεστοι αὐτῷ εἶναι. 10 τοὺς γὰρ πάντας ἡμᾶς φανερωθῆναι δεῖ ἔμπροσθεν τοῦ βήματος τοῦ Χριστοῦ, ἵνα κομίσηται ἕκαστος τὰ διὰ τοῦ σώματος πρὸς ἃ ἔπραξεν, εἴτε ἀγαθὸν εἴτε φαῦλον. [SBLGNT]

King James Version

6 Therefore we are always confident, knowing that, whilst we are at home in the body, we are absent from the Lord:
7 (For we walk by faith, not by sight:)
8 We are confident, I say, and willing rather to be absent from the body, and to be present with the Lord. 9 Wherefore we labour, that, whether present or absent, we may be accepted of him.
10 For we must all appear before the judgment seat of Christ; that every one may receive the things done in his body, according to that he hath done, whether it be good or bad.

New Rendition

6 Therefore, we are always confident and recognize that while we are at home in the body, we are away from the Lord. 7 For we walk by faith not by sight. 8 And we are confident, I repeat, and prefer to depart from this body and be at home with the Lord. 9 Therefore, we also eagerly strive to please him, whether in this body or absent from it.
10 For we all must appear before the judgment seat of Christ so that each person may receive a recompense for the things that he or she has done by means of the body, whether good or bad.

Translation Notes and Comments

5:6–8 Paul continues his treatment of mortal life and its resultant death and communicates the importance and nature of both to his readers by breaking from the thought he began in verse 6 to convey the information in verse 7 and then coming back to the original thought in verse 8. Thus verse 7 is a break in the flow of the argument for the purpose of clarification. After this interjection, the Apostle resumes his statement but alters his grammar slightly, making verse 8 an anacoluthon that picks up and finishes his thought. Thus what he says in verse 6 anticipates his statement in verse 8 that he would prefer to be absent from this mortal life, with its encumbering and weak body, in order to be present with the Lord.[56]

5:6 *Therefore, we are always confident:* The conjunction οὖν (*oun*), "consequently, therefore," refers back to the hope Paul expressed in 5:5 and links it to the confidence the Apostle has in what he now shares. It also affirms that, no matter what state, mortal or postmortal, one is in, "there is no room for despondency."[57] The verb θαρρέω (*tharreō*) means both "to be courageous" and "to be confident."[58] The word connotes a certainty that broaches no doubt and thereby leads to courage even during periods of testing or danger.[59] In the present context, it is the aspect of confidence that seems to dominate. By adding the adverb πάντοτε (*pantote*), "always," Paul emphasizes that there is, at least for him, never a point of uncertainty.

knowing that, whilst we are at home in the body, we are absent from the Lord / recognize that while we are at home in the body, we are away from the Lord: This phrase creates a non sequitur with the one above. Though Paul expresses his confidence there, being away from God while at home in the body is hardly a condition that generates such assurance. On the contrary, as he has shown, mortality presents nothing but one trouble after another, exacerbated by the absence of Divine association.[60] Paul does pick up his theme of confidence in 5:8 by repeating the verb θαρρέω (*tharreō*), "be confident." Given that, 5:6–7 appears to be a short digression that he is using to counter what may have been a false belief among some of the Corinthian Saints. It is possible that, sensing the Spirit in their lives (see 1 Cor. 14:36), some were teaching that they were already "with the Lord."[61] Paul denies this idea, insisting that the very nature of mortal existence proves this not the case.[62]

---

56. Seifrid, *Second Epistle*, 230.

57. Martin, *2 Corinthians*, 265.

58. BDAG, 444.

59. Louw-Nida, §25.156.

60. Since in 4:16, 18; 5:1, 3, 4, Paul has denigrated the mortal body, he is likely doing the same here. His feelings are, however, not based on the body being sinful but due to its weak and inferior state. For a study, see Fredrik Lindgård, *Paul's Line of Thought in 2 Corinthians 4:16–5:10* (Tübingen, Ger.: Mohr Siebeck, 2005).

61. Jerome Murphy-O'Connor, "Being at Home in the Body We are in Exile from the Lord (2 Cor. 5:6b)," *Revue Biblique* 93, no. 2 (1986): 214–21, posits that the phrase "at home with the Lord" was a slogan stemming from the spiritualists Paul addressed in 1 Cor. 14.

62. Barnett, *Second Epistle*, 269–70.

The verb ἐνδημέω (*endēmeō*), "to be at home," denotes being among one's own people, but here it is used metaphorically to refer to mortality.[63] The verb ἐκδημέω (*ekdēmeō*) means "to leave an area"[64] but carries the nuance of being "absent from a place where one rightfully and normally belongs."[65] Though that would generally refer to one's home, in this case it is being with the Lord. However, Paul is not suggesting that mortality is void of communion with God. His point is, rather, that in comparison with what will come when the Saints see the Father "face to face" (1 Cor. 13:12), their experience here is comparatively weak. Thus, to be in the body is to be separated from the fulness of the association that the gospel promises.

5:7 ***For we walk by faith not by sight:*** With this short interjection, Paul describes the very nature of mortality as designed by God. The verb περιπατέω (*peripateō*), "to walk," also denotes comportment or behavior.[66] That the verb is in the present tense suggests that the Apostle has the whole of the mortal experience in mind.[67] The preposition διά (*dia*), "by means of," acts, in this case, as a "marker of instrumentality or circumstance whereby something is made possible."[68] It modifies the noun πίστις (*pistis*), "faith," stressing that it is this virtue that makes walking in a godly way possible.

As with the English noun "faith," the Greek noun (*pistis*) has a wide range of meanings ranging from active belief to absolute sureness.[69] The degree of a person's faith expresses itself in the amount of trust and adherence that the person gives to the idea, teaching, cause, or person that she or he is attracted to and to which the person acts accordingly.

As Christian history shows, it was the theologian Augustine, writing in the fifth century, who transformed the understanding of the term "faith" (Latin, *fides*) to refer to either of two conditions. The first referenced "that which is believed," specifically "The Rule of Faith" (*fides qua creditor* in his words). This rule made the condition of salvation simply a matter of

---

63. BDAG, 332.

64. BDAG, 300.

65. Louw-Nida, §85.21.

66. Louw-Nida, §§15.227; 41.11; BDAG, 803.

67. Martin, *2 Corinthians*, 266.

68. BDAG, 223–26. This nuance is stressed when the object is in the genitive case as "faith" is here.

69. Louw-Nida, §§31.43, 85, 88, 102, 104; 33.289. In contrast to πίστις (*pistis*), which is belief expressed through action, Platonic Greek used δόξα (*doxa*) to denote a passive belief that rested on expectations or opinions and required no action. *BGD*, s.v. "δόξα," 584.

accepting credal statements. The second referenced emotional, mystical, and passive born-again experiences (*fides quā creditor* in his words). It defined faith as but an experience by which something comes to be believed.[70] His understanding has guided both Catholic and Protestant thinking on the subject to this day.

Unfortunately, both of his definitions stand in sharp contrast to the understanding of faith among the earliest Christians. To these Saints, faith was both personal and dynamic. Within the nascent Church, it referred to a commitment to Christ based on understanding his teaching, mission, and nature as the divine, resurrected Son of God. The scriptures do show, however, that there are degrees of faithfulness. Little faith expresses itself in adherence only when it is convenient or of little cost. Conversely, great faith expresses itself in adherence not only when such is inconvenient but also when it demands self-control and sacrifice.

The noun "faith" as used by Paul connotes the high degree of confidence the Saints should have in the reliability of Jesus. The word also carries the strong nuance of conformity to the exactions the Lord demands of his people, including keeping commandments and making and keeping covenants.[71] Faith in him is expressed in one's love for him as manifest in active, purposeful obedience to his will (John 14:15; compare Deut. 30:20 and Eccl. 12:13). This is the quintessence of faith.[72]

The disturbing transformation of the meaning of faith during the apostasy undermined the importance of expressing faith in Christ through service in his new covenant community. It replaced active allegiance with passive, mystical, born-again experiences that bestowed upon the believer a "grant of faith" and by so doing assured that the sacrifice required to obtain true faith would never be met.

---

70. For a study, see Brent J. Schmidt, *Relational Faith: The Transformation and Restoration of* Pistis *as Knowledge, Trust, Confidence, and Covenantal Faithfulness* (Provo, Utah: BYU Studies, 2022).

71. For a study see *NID,* 3:759–72.

72. For studies from an LDS perspective, see Douglas E. Brinley, "Faith in Jesus Christ," in *EM,* 2:483–85; Schmidt, *Relational Faith.* In the *Lectures on Faith* (study material for the School of the Elders held in Kirtland, Ohio and published in the 1835 edition of the Doctrine and Covenants), faith is defined on the basis of Heb. 11:1–3 as "the principle of action in all intelligent beings" and as "the principle of power" by which God formed the world and life upon it as well as giving to humankind the plan of salvation. The study also affirms that God should be the center of one's faith and that salvation depends on one's faithfulness to the ways of God. For a study, see Larry E. Dahl and Charles D. Tate Jr., eds., *The Lectures on Faith in Historical Perspective* (Salt Lake City: Deseret Book, 1990; rpt. 2014).

The noun εἶδος (*eidos*), "appearance, sight," denotes both the outward form of something (its "appearance") and the act of looking or seeing something (that is, "sight").[73] It is this latter sense that we have used in our Rendition. Paul is saying that a true disciple of Christ conducts his or her life based on knowledge gained through faith rather than through the physical senses. This is the "assurance of things not seen" referred to in the definition of faith found in Hebrews 11:1 (JST).

5:8 ***We are confident, I say, and willing rather to be absent from the body, and to be present with the Lord / And we are confident, I repeat, and prefer to depart from this body and be at home with the Lord:*** With the repetition of the verb θαρρέω (*tharreō*), "confident," Paul picks up the train of thought he began in 5:6. He again uses the verbs ἐκδημέω (*ekdēmeō*), "to be away from a place" (in this case, the mortal body), and ἐνδημέω (*endēmeō*), "to be at home" (in this case, with God).[74] He appears to be referring to the state of the spirit between death and resurrection.[75] Being in such a bodiless state, he is saying, does not bother him for two reasons. The first is obvious: he will be with the Lord. The other is more oblique but suggests that he understands that this bodiless state is only temporary and will end with the resurrection. His thought here strongly echoes his statement in Philippians 1:21, "For me to live is Christ, and to die is gain" (compare Rom. 14:8).

5:9 ***Wherefore we labour, that, whether present or absent, we may be accepted of him / Therefore, we also eagerly strive to please him, whether in this body or absent from it:*** The referential conjunction διό (*dio*), "wherefore, for this reason," is important, pointing back as it does to Paul's ever-abiding confidence. Its use emphasizes the staying force behind his labors but also transitions to the reason he labors so hard. It alerts Paul's readers that he is now going to make the logical conclusion to his argument.[76] The verb φιλοτιμέομαι (*philotimeomai*) has the root meaning of "to love or seek after honor," emphasizing the effort put into obtaining it and

---

73. BDAG, 280. The phrase is vague, thus allowing for some debate on Paul's exact meaning. For discussion, see Martin, *2 Corinthians,* 266–67. Context suggests that "sight" is the better choice and, therefore, we have used it in our Rendition.

74. Harris, *Second Epistle,* 404–5, reads the phrase as "whether resident in the body or absent from it" because it keeps the condition in order and reiterates the thoughts found in Rom. 14:8 and Philip. 1:20, and anticipates the prepositional phrase in 5:10 "while in the body."

75. Barnett, *Second Epistle*, 272–73.

76. BDAG, 250.

focusing on the idea of rendering service.[77] Because the word does emphasize the intense effort needed to obtain that objective, we translate it as "eagerly strive" in our Rendition. The adjective εὐάρεστος (*euarestos*) means "pleasing, acceptable," and in the New Testament it is generally used with reference to God.[78] Paul's use of the word "comprises both the goal and the motive of the Christian life" that he is admonishing his readers to pursue.[79]

Paul again uses the verbs ἐνδημέω (*endēmeō*)and ἐκδημέω (*ekdēmeō*; see 5:6), but this time in the participial phrase ἐνδημοῦντες εἴτε ἐκδημοῦντες (*endēmonuntes eite ekdēmountes*). Translated literally, the phrase reads "being at home or being away from home,"[80] but the context in which Paul uses it shows that he is referring to earthly and post-earthly existence and, therefore, uses the words metaphorically. Thus we have translated the phrase as "in this body or absent from it" in our Rendition.[81]

5:10 ***For we must all appear before the judgment seat of Christ / For we all must appear before the judgment seat of Christ:*** The conjunction γάρ (*gar*), "for," is causal and explains why the Saint should eagerly strive to please God. The verb φανερόω (*phaneroō*), "to cause to become visible," in the passive voice, as found here, has an intransitive sense, "to appear."[82] The impersonal verb δεῖ (*dei*) denotes what is necessary or must happen and carries the notion of compulsion.[83] The adjective πάντας (*pantas*), "all," is inclusive, showing that there will be no exceptions to judgment.[84] The noun βῆμα (*bēma*), "judgment seat," refers both to a raised platform on which a judge sits and to the tribunal itself.[85] Paul makes it clear in his other writings that Christ himself is the judge (see also Rom. 14:10; 2 Ne. 9:44; Moro. 10; etc.).

that every one may receive the things done in his body, according to that he hath done, whether it be good or bad / so that each person may receive a recompense for the things that he or she has done by means of the body, whether good or bad: The conjunction ἵνα (*hina*), "so that," points to the purpose of an act—that is, in this case, judgment. The adjective ἕκαστος (*hekastos*), "each one," emphasizes the individual nature of that judgment.

---

77. LSJ, 1941; BDAG, 1059.

78. BDAG, 403.

79. Werner Foerster, "εὐάρεστος" in *TDNT,* 1:456–57.

80. Bernard, "Second Epistle," 67.

81. See note 75 above.

82. BDAG, 1048.

83. BDAG, 213–14; Guthrie, *2 Corinthians*, 288.

84. BDAG, 782–84.

85. BDAG, 175. 2 Ne. 9:15 uses this same imagery. Compare 3 Ne. 28:31.

The verb πράσσω (*prassō*) denotes "to bring about or accomplish something through activity."[86] The verb κομίζω (*komizō*), in the middle voice, as here, means "to get (for oneself), receive recompense" for something that is deserved or owed.[87]

The noun σῶμα (*sōma*) refers to the mortal "body." [88] In the phrase διὰ τοῦ σώματος (*dia tou sōmatos*), the preposition *dia* with the genitive case is used instrumentally, "by/through/by means of the body."[89] Our physical bodies are controlled *by* our spirits. The recompense is based on one of two types of acts: ἀγαθός (*agathos*) or φαῦλος (*phaulos*), "good or bad." The former has a wide range of meanings, including acts that are useful, valuable, excellent, and distinguished. It denotes especially those of high moral quality.[90] The latter also has a wide range of meanings, including acts that are ordinary, useless, or valueless, and generally refers to what is of an inferior quality or morally substandard.[91] Because it is likely that Paul is using both terms more colloquially than technically, the general English notion within the words "good" and "bad" works (compare John 5:29). Though both words are adverbs in the Greek text, we have rendered them as neuter singular. The nuance of the change is that "though each individual is judged on the basis of his or her behavior, the person's habitual action, and not his [or her] individual acts, is the basis for judgment. . . . God's judgment is also impartial, for what is due to a person is what is given that person."[92]

The JST clarifies the KJV here, changing the phrase "may receive the things done in the body" to "may receive a reward of the deeds done in the body." The use of the word "reward," however, does not negate the idea of punishment if such is demanded. "Recompense" would probably give a better understanding of the blessings and consequences of making choices in mortality.

Analysis and Summary

In 5:6–7, Paul gives witness to his continued confidence even in the face of difficulties and the adversity he experiences on an almost-daily basis. But his claim is not to some personal heroic faith. His is God-given based

86. BDAG, 860–61; Christian Maurer, "πράσσω," in *TDNT,* 6:632–38.
87. Guthrie, *2 Corinthians*, 289; Louw-Nida, §90.92; BDAG, 557.
88. BDAG, 983–84.
89. BDAG, 224.
90. Louw-Nida, §88.1; Walter Grundmann, "ἀγαθός," in *TDNT,* 1:15; BDAG, 3–4.
91. BDAG, 1050–51.
92. Martin, *2 Corinthians,* 271–72.

on the Apostle's assurance of the resurrection as certified and guaranteed by the continual operation of the Spirit in his life. This "down payment" (ἀρραβών, *arrabōn*) on his future celestial abode makes it sure. It is this sureness that is the source and power behind his constant and sustaining confidence. This confidence reaches into the future, in which the Apostle anticipates his final judgment before Christ, where his works will be fully manifested and approved.[93] His confidence acts as a foil against his Corinthian antagonists, for it stresses the feeling he has as to the correctness of his teachings and lifestyle before God.

In 5:6, Paul insists that he is not simply *being* confident but that he *has* continual and overflowing confidence through the principle of faith. This spiritual condition is not something he musters from within but is a gift given to him from above based on this testimony of the reality of the resurrection. That he uses the plural pronoun "we" shows that such confidence does not belong to him alone but to all who move forward in life through faith.[94]

In this section, Paul's thoughts have moved from his concern with the possible period of "nakedness" in the spirit world where the soul feels the full weight of an uncomfortable helpless existence. Instead, he looks confidently to the glorious future beyond that period.

The thought expressed in 5:7 (though but an interjection) that mortality consists of walking by faith, not by sight, identifies the quintessence of the mortal condition as viewed by the Christian. It also expresses the central argument of the whole of this epistle.[95] As Elder Bruce R. McConkie noted, "In the pre-mortal life we were in the presence of God; we saw him and knew the course he had charted for us. Now we are out of his personal presence, no longer remember our association in his household, and are being tested under circumstances where we must accept him and his laws on faith."[96]

Paul uses the phrase to amend his point that being in mortality demands not being with the Lord. His words show that being mortal does not mean that a person is cut off completely from the Divine. It is the invisibility of God to the natural man, not his absence, that Paul is stressing.[97]

---

93. Seifrid, *Second Epistle,* 230.
94. Seifrid, *Second Epistle,* 230.
95. Seifrid, *Second Letter,* 232.
96. *DNTC,* 2:420.
97. Martin, *2 Corinthians,* 266.

His words explain the very nature of mortality for the faithful by stating what it is and what it is not. It is a walk, a movement along a path toward an objective. The path is defined by faith in Christ. In this instance, πίστις (*pistis*) encapsulates the idea of a confidence in the Savior so strong that one is willing to acknowledge, follow, and obey him at all cost. What mortality isn't is a walk by sight with the end clearly visible and assured. The Saints can have hope, though temporarily away from the Lord, because of their testimony of the reality of the Messiah, even though, for the present, he is unseen (compare 1 Pet. 1:8–9).[98]

In the modern world, faith is often described as a "a blind leap into the dark." For Paul and Christians in the New Testament world generally, such an idea would not ring true. As one scholar noted, "The modern misconception comes from a naturalistic view of the world that suggests God does not intervene, indeed cannot intervene in the cause-and-effect system of the physical order. Thus a person must take a leap against or in face of, what modern science tells us is true. Biblical faith, on the other hand, constitutes a 'step into the light,' holding that bold steps are in order because God has revealed what is true about himself, the world, and life in the world (Heb. 11:12)." Further, when Paul describes the Christian as one who walks by means of faith, he is referring to God's revelation of what is true about reality and life in particular and acting accordingly. For in-depth analysis, see Translation Notes on 5:7 above. In sum, his trust in God is anchored in revelation and covenants.[99] This means that there is no darkness to leap into.

Paul is very concerned with the value the Corinthian Saints put on mere appearance. The Apostle insisted that, in respect to God's saving purposes, it is the "things that are not visible" that trump "things that are visible" (4:18, NR). The latter consists of simple appearance (εἶδος, *eidos*), while the former represents reality, both mortal and eternal. This reality, as Paul testifies, deals with "that which neither eye has seen, nor ear heard, nor entered into a person's heart—all these things God has prepared for those who love him." But "to us God has revealed them by the Spirit, for the Spirit fathoms all things, even the deep things of God" (1 Cor. 2:9–10, NR).[100] For the Christian faithful, due to the action of the Spirit, the promised blessings have been heard, felt, and to a degree received, but the fulness waits to be "seen," and the ability to see rests on faith.

98. Martin, *2 Corinthians,* 266.

99. Guthrie, *2 Corinthians,* 286.

100. Seifrid, *Second Letter,* 233.

Unfortunately, for too many of the Corinthian Saints, appearance is what is important and therefore the means by which they judge all things. This malady has allowed Paul's detractors to disparage his character and teachings, making him suspect among those who follow them. His purpose in this section is to provide a doctrinal basis for his actions, teachings, and character by showing the Saints the true basis by which proper judgment can be made.[101]

In 5:8–9, Paul returns to the theme of the confidence he has in the Lord due to the life that the Apostle has lived before the Divine. He clarifies his feelings about escaping the vicissitudes of mortality and the constant grind he is under. Death holds no fear for him, he assures his readers. Rather, he sees it as a real boon, for he will be with the Lord. That he states he will be "at home" (ἐνδημέω, *endēmeō*) shows the positive nature of the relationship he expects to have with the Divine during the time he will spend in the spirit world. It is knowing that he will someday be with the Lord that drives him to do what is pleasing before his Master. The very thought forces him to "eagerly strive" (φιλοτιμέομαι, *philotimeomai*) to please him. Paul's point is that it does not matter where a person's spirit is when the Second Coming happens. Whether on earth or in paradise, each Saint should be anxiously engaged in doing what will please God (compare John 8:29 and 1 John 3:22).[102] Though Paul does not state the specifics of how the Saints are to please God, he does indicate the degree of energy each one should put into it, specifically "zealous effort."[103]

In Paul's admonition, there is no hint that his efforts are to accumulate favor or merit with God. He already has the assurance of the Spirit that his life is acceptable. Rather, his efforts are due to the prospect of being with the Lord, whom he is driven to please due to the deep love he has for him.[104] This love is generated by the pure act of grace Christ extended to this man while he was committing grave sin. The Savior reached out to him, saved him, forgave him, and gave him new purpose and direction. Further, he gave him the pledge of the Spirit (ἀρραβῶνα τοῦ πνεύματος, *arrabōna tou pneumatos*), which confirmed his place with God (1:21–22; Eph. 1:13–14). This pledge, however, was not given to him alone but to the faithful Saints at Corinth. Therefore, he could ask them, "Have I not seen Jesus our Lord?

101. Seifrid, *Second Letter,* 233–34.
102. Martin, *2 Corinthians,* 269–70.
103. Hughes, *Second Epistle,* 178 n. 54.
104. Barnett, *Second Epistle,* 272–73.

Are you not the evidence of my work in the Lord?" (1 Cor. 9:1, NR). He had been the means by which they, too, had received divine grace and favor by and through the Lord. However, such did not relieve them of striving to please him, as grace and divine favors were expected to be reciprocated at this time. Indeed, given the mores of the day, having received such a high degree of grace placed upon them great responsibility, indeed a heavy obligation, to give grace to others in return. Thus, their labor was not to gain merit but to gracefully express their acceptance and recognition of what God had done for them and meet the obligation by passing it onto others in the spirit of first-century χάρις (*charis*) or reciprocal and relational grace.[105] In doing so, they please God. Such, as Paul understands it, should be both motive and goal of the Christian's life.[106]

In 5:10, Paul explains clearly why he and others should be anxiously engaged in pleasing the Lord. The trial will be a pleasant experience because of the *charis* relationship with the Father, with Jesus as the mediator and gift-broker. This verse also has judicial overtones, reflecting the practice of the day when a judge sat on a raised platform, or "bema," to hear cases and give his verdict. Paul had personally experienced this very action (see Acts 18:12–17). It is Christ who will be the sole judge at the Final Judgment (2 Ne. 9:41), and his judgment will be based on each person's faith or faithlessness equally (compare Alma 5:15; 11:41; and 3 Ne. 26:4).[107]

Paul is clear that all *must* appear (φανερωθῆναι δεῖ, *phanerōthēnai dei*) before the judgment seat of Christ. Though the scriptures do state that God is the judge of the world (Eccl. 3:17; 12:14; Rom. 3:6; Heb. 12:23), they also make it clear that he does so through Christ (for example, see Rom. 2:16; 14:10).[108]

Paul's words show that this personal appearance consists of more than just showing up. Rather, it refers to the moment when the soul is laid bare such that all will see the true nature of the person's character based on faithfulness according to one's understanding.[109] Judgment will be rendered according to what has been revealed. Paul's point seems to be that even though a person is a Christian, more is necessary. The solemnity demanded

105. In Greco-Roman society, the giving of grace always carried with it an obligatory dimension. For a study of grace in its historical context, see Brent L. Schmidt, *Relational Grace: The Reciprocal and Binding Covenant of* Charis (Provo, Utah: BYU Studies, 2015).

106. Werner Foerster, "εὐαρεστός," in *TDNT,* 1:456–57.

107. Harris, *Second Epistle,* 405, 409.

108. See also 2 Ne. 28:23; Mosiah 16:10; and Alma 12:12, which speak of judgment before the bar of God.

109. Martin, *2 Corinthians,* 270.

by the coming judgment must be kept in mind, since "the life of faith does not free the Christian from the life of obedience."[110]

Paul points to some specifics about the Final Judgment. First, mortal actions have immortal consequences that one cannot escape, and second, a person's entire future life is determined by the decision of the divine tribunal.[111] The Apostle shows us that "Christ's judgment will be universal and dispassionate, including, in the first instance, the totality of his own people ('we all . . . each'). It is not, however, a judgment '*en masse,* or in classes, but one by one, in accordance with individual merit.'"[112] According to Joseph Smith, the Lord "holds the reins of judgment in his hands. He is a wise lawgiver and will judge all men, not according to the narrow contracted notions of men, but 'according to the deeds done in the body, whether they be good or evil,' or whether the deeds are done in England, America, Spain, Turkey, [or] India."[113]

The question is, Who does Paul have in mind as coming before the judgment seat of Christ? Is it exclusively the Christian community, or does the Apostle include all people? Again, the context is helpful. Based on 5:4–5, where Paul looks to the resurrection of the Saints, along with Paul's statement here that "all of *us*" (πάντας ἥμᾶς, *pantas hēmas*) must appear before the judgement seat, it is most likely he has his fellow Christians in mind.[114] That point should not be taken to mean that Paul believes there is no resurrection for others; he clearly sees the resurrection as universal (1 Cor. 15:22, 52; 2 Cor. 1:9). Here, however, his focus is on the community of Christians and on the positive or adverse effect the Judgment will have on *them.*[115]

110. Martin, *2 Corinthians,* 271.

111. Garland, *2 Corinthians,* 266.

112. Barnett, *Second Epistle,* 275.

113. *Times and Seasons* 3 (April 15, 1842): 759.

114. Guthrie, *2 Corinthians,* 288–89. In Rom. 2:7–10, Paul looks at the comprehensive judgment and clearly refers to two sets of people, both believers and unbelievers, while here he refers to two kinds of deed, good or bad. Based on this, Harris, *Second Epistle,* 406, also concludes Paul has only Christians in mind.

115. Paul's statement that the Final Judgment will be based on the Christians' good or bad behavior has caused a good deal of scholarly debate due to those who see Christ's grace accepted through faith devoid of works as the sole means of salvation that does not take a "saved" Christian's behavior into account. Due to the clear force of Paul's statement, some have concluded that a person's bad behavior could mean forfeiture of eternal blessings. For examples, see E. P. Sanders, *Paul and Palestinian Judaism: A Comparison of Patters of Religion* (London: SCM, 1977; rpt. 40th anniversary ed., Minneapolis: Fortress Press, 2017), 543; Thrall, *Critical and Exegetical Commentary,* 1:395; and Harris, *Second Epistle,* 408.

The purpose of the appearance is to receive a recompense (κομίζω, *komizō*) for what one has done (πράσσω, *prassō*). Paul's wording shows that the recompense will be based on consistent and constant types of behavior that define the quality of a person's life. Thus, though the grace of Christ through the Saint's faith and partaking of sacred covenants and ordinances has brought him or her into a personal relationship with Deity, his or her behavior thereafter determines the degree to which that grace will be applied at the time of judgment. Those who have kept the faith and lived such that the redeeming blood of the Savior has continually worked in their lives will find the Lord's grace fully efficacious. Their lives, though maybe not perfect, yet showing a consistent pattern of goodness, service, and love, become the final measure of their eternal reward. Those, however, who have broken the covenants and lived outside gospel standards will find no grace nor the gift of mercy from Christ's Atonement and face the judgment bar without it. This class, however, will be saved because, though they refused to receive the testimony of Jesus or the prophets, they did not deny the Holy Ghost.[116] Even so, they will be thrust down to hell, but only for a time, being yet heirs of salvation (D&C 76:84–101). Therefore, even in their case, the infinite gift of Christ's grace will eventually catch up with them and in the end save them in a kingdom of glory. This will not happen, however, until after their full and sincere repentance, leading to a change in their nature for good and acceptance of the Lord as their Savior. Even so, their recompense, a telestial salvation, will still be far less than what the faithful will enjoy.

But is there an intermediary group—that is, some whose sins Christ has forgiven but who do not, at the time of judgment, come under the full measure of his grace or gift of his Atonement and whose recompense will be less than full reward? The answer seems to be yes. In this case, "recompense" carries more the idea of evaluation than one of condemnation (Rom. 5:16, 18; 8:1; 1 Cor. 3:10–15; 4:5). The scriptures are clear that, though there is only one level of condemnation, there are multiple levels of commendation (Matt. 25:14–30; Luke 12:42–44; 19:12–27). In Paul's understanding, the recompense or reward for full devotion to God brings "all the blessings that are in Christ and the future tangible recognition of

116. The fate for those who deny the Holy Ghost, a condition passible only to rebellious members of the LDS Church, is eternal damnation. These become sons of perdition and suffer the full wrath of God with the devil and his angels. See D&C 76:30–38 and Rodney Turner, "Sons of Perdition," in *EM,* 3:1391–92.

service in the furtherance of the gospel."[117] It is possible, however, that a person may have been lackluster in her or his devotion to Christ. In such a case, the recompense would be some degree of loss but not the loss of forgiveness of sin. They would forfeit some degree of privilege or reward but maintain Christ's forgiveness.[118] In sum, "these are they who [were] not valiant in the testimony of Jesus" as well as the "honorable men of the earth, who were blinded by the craftiness of men." These "obtain not the crown over the kingdom of our God" (D&C 76:75, 79). Nonetheless, they find place in the first resurrection and are "Christ's at his coming" (1 Cor. 15:23; D&C 88:99) and "receive of his glory, but not of his fulness." Theirs is a terrestrial reward.[119]

Workers Together with Christ (5:11–7:4)

At this point, Paul begins a new development that will run through 7:4. Up to this point, he has carefully laid down the strong theological foundation that he now builds upon. He designed the explication and defense of the authenticity of his ministry (2:14–4:6) and his enumeration of the suffering that ministry has demanded (4:7–5:10) to resonate with his readers and undercut the efforts of his detractors. Certainly, those who know him could gainsay neither his efforts nor his successes. Based on these, he now gives a series of strong exhortations to those attending the various Corinthian house churches. He forces them to start thinking personally about how they are going to respond to his words. In doing so, he creates "one of the most pregnant, difficult, and important [sections] in the whole of Pauline literature."[120] Despite its difficulty, this unit is filled with powerful, poignant, and beautiful expressions of the gospel and highlights Paul's role as God's personal

117. R. M. Fuller, "Rewards," in Hawthorne, Martin, and Reid, *Dictionary of Paul and His Letters,* 819.

118. Guthrie, *2 Corinthians,* 289–90.

119. The terrestrial kingdom will also be inhabited by those who died without law, those who received a testimony of Jesus as spirits, and those who were honorable and good but blinded by the craftiness of others. See D&C 76:71–80. For studies dealing with the resurrection and afterlife, see Douglas L. Callister, "Resurrection," in *EM,* 3:1222–23; Larry E. Dahl, "Degrees of Glory," in *EM,* 1:367–69; Susan Easton Black, "Celestial Kingdom," in *EM,* 1:259–60; Susan Easton Black, "Terrestrial Kingdom," in *EM,* 4:1470; and Clyde J. Williams, "Telestial Kingdom," in *EM,* 4:1443.

120. Barrett, *Second Epistle,* 163.

representative (5:20) sent to testify to the work of the Son of God (1:19). It extends, as noted, to 7:4. Its unity can be seen in its logical progression:

A self-defense (5:11–13)
  B emissary of Christ (5:14–6:2)
A′ self-defense (6:3–10)

The unit closes with a series of admonitions (6:11–7:4) based on points Paul has and will lay down.[121]

Paul develops his theme in four sets. In the first, he describes his position concerning God, then his relationship to people generally, and finally his attitude toward the Corinthian Saints in particular (5:11–13). He assures them that due to his "fear of God," he lives a life open to the Divine (5:11, NR). His "fear" is the basis for his reaching out to people to come to Christ. The purpose of his outreach is, in part, to challenge his readers to evaluate and properly respond to his ministry (5:12–13).

In the second, he sets forth the basis for a correct evaluation of the leadership of the Church. His response is directed to his antagonists—those false teachers who have called his Apostolic leadership into question. Paul therefore details the force and implications of a Christocentric ministry as the proper means of dealing with others and approaching life in general (5:12–13). His point is that the death and resurrection of Christ have drastically changed the understanding of life and how it should be lived (5:14–15) and that judgments made solely on mortal terms are inadequate and obsolete. Indeed, embracing the power of the gospel changes a person into a new creation that allows her or him to see in a more exalted way (5:16–17).

In the third, based on the above, the Apostle begins a series of admonitions that define what the Saints are now to do in light of what he has taught them. In this hortatory section, he again reiterates his major purpose in writing—to reconcile the Corinthian Saints to God and, as a subset, to Paul and his mission. Previously, the Apostle quite deliberately and carefully defended his actions, motives, and objectives. In the process, he has provided his readers with a powerful summary showing that, at its heart, the gospel message is one of reconciliation. He makes it clear that the Savior made it possible for transgressions to no longer separate the person from God and, thus, for reconciliation to be fully made (5:18–6:2).

---

121. Some scholars state there is no contextual relationship between this unit and those that come before and after it. Others, especially Witherington, *Conflict and Community,* 403–4, see it as a whole. For discussion, see Guthrie, *2 Corinthians,* 293 n. 1. The above schematic supports the idea that the unit is a whole and follows Reimund Bieringer and Jan Lambrecht, *Studies on 2 Corinthians* (Brussels: Louven University Press, 1994), 364–65, with modifications suggested by Guthrie, *2 Corinthians,* 293 n. 1.

In the final set, he turns to exhortation. This we can divide into four subsets where he pleads for his readers to accept the grace that God offers, defends his own integrity, lists the various stresses he and others have been under, and finally admonishes the Saints not to associate with those who would lead them astray (6:3–7:4).[122] By this means, the Apostle eloquently and powerfully defends himself, all the while persuading his readers to join once more with him for the sake of the ministry and the unity that being one in the body of Christ demands.

Knowing the Fear of God (5:11–15)

Greek Text

11 Εἰδότες οὖν τὸν φόβον τοῦ κυρίου ἀνθρώπους πείθομεν, θεῷ δὲ πεφανερώμεθα·
ἐλπίζω δὲ καὶ ἐν ταῖς συνειδήσεσιν ὑμῶν πεφανερῶσθαι. 12 οὐ πάλιν ἑαυτοὺς συνι-
στάνομεν ὑμῖν, ἀλλὰ ἀφορμὴν διδόντες ὑμῖν καυχήματος ὑπὲρ ἡμῶν, ἵνα ἔχητε
πρὸς τοὺς ἐν προσώπῳ καυχωμένους καὶ μὴ ἐν καρδίᾳ. 13 εἴτε γὰρ ἐξέστημεν, θεῷ·
εἴτε σωφρονοῦμεν, ὑμῖν. 14 ἡ γὰρ ἀγάπη τοῦ Χριστοῦ συνέχει ἡμᾶς, κρίναντας
τοῦτο ὅτι εἷς ὑπὲρ πάντων ἀπέθανεν· ἄρα οἱ πάντες ἀπέθανον· 15 καὶ ὑπὲρ πάντων
ἀπέθανεν ἵνα οἱ ζῶντες μηκέτι ἑαυτοῖς ζῶσιν ἀλλὰ τῷ ὑπὲρ αὐτῶν ἀποθανόντι καὶ
ἐγερθέντι. [SBLGNT]

King James Version

11 Knowing therefore the terror of the
Lord, we persuade men; but we are
made manifest unto God; and I trust
also are made manifest in your con-
sciences. 12 For we commend not our-
selves again unto you, but give you
occasion to glory on our behalf, that
ye may have somewhat to answer them
which glory in appearance, and not
in heart. 13 For whether we be beside
ourselves, it is to God: or whether we
be sober, it is for your cause. 14 For the
love of Christ constraineth us; because

New Rendition

11 Therefore, since we know the fear of
the Lord, we keep trying to persuade
people, but we are well-known to God,
and I hope we are also well-known in
your consciences. 12 We are not trying
to commend ourselves to you again;
on the contrary, we are giving you an
opportunity to be proud of us so that
you can have an answer for those who
take pride in outward appearance rather
than what is in the heart. 13 For if we
were out of our minds, it would be for
God to decide; if we are of sound mind,

122. Guthrie, *2 Corinthians,* 293–94.

we thus judge, that if one died for all, then were all dead: 15 And that he died for all, that they which live should not henceforth live unto themselves, but unto him which died for them, and rose again.

it is for your benefit. 14 For Christ's love urges us on because we have come to this conclusion: that one man died for all humankind, thus, in a manner of speaking, all humankind have died. 15 And he died for the salvation of all humankind so that the living might no longer live for themselves but live for him who died and was raised up again for their salvation.

Translation Notes and Comments

5:11 ***Knowing therefore the terror of the Lord / Therefore, since we know the fear of the Lord:*** The conjunction οὖν (*oun*), "therefore,"[123] plays both an inferential and a transitional role in this phrase. Inferentially it refers back to the inevitable judgement to which Paul has testified. The fear of the coming judgment drives Paul and other Christians in their work. Transitionally it moves the discussion away from the authenticity of Paul's mission with its associated suffering to the series of direct appeals to the Corinthian Saints that the Apostle is now preparing to make.[124]

On the verb οἶδα (*oida*), "to know," see Translation Notes for 5:1. The word is found here as an active participle; though perfect in form, it is present in meaning, and carries a range of meanings from possessing information about something to having actually experienced it.[125] The context suggests the latter nuance. The noun φόβος (*phobos*) carries the disparate nuances of both "terror" and "awe." The word stresses the high degree of the emotion felt, whether negative or positive, when one is confronted with overwhelming power. On the one hand, *phobos* denotes "a state of severe distress, aroused by intense concern for impending pain, danger, evil," and so on.[126] On the other, it denotes profound respect, reverence, and awe for Deity.[127] What makes the emotion either positive or negative is

123. BDAG, 736–37.

124. Guthrie, *2 Corinthians,* 296.

125. Louw-Nida, §§28.1; 32.4; BDAG, 693–94.

126. Louw-Nida, §25.251.

127. Louw-Nida, §53.59. The New Testament consistently uses this term to denote a deep respect and awe based on God's mighty acts. Horst Balz and Gerhard Schneider, ed., *Exegetical Dictionary of the New Testament,* vol. 3 (Grand Rapids, Mich.: Wm. B. Eerdmans, 1993), 433–34.

the person's feelings toward the power, majesty, and might of the object. In this case, it is "the Lord," likely referring to Jesus.[128] Due to the overwhelming purity, magnificence, power, and splendor of the Divine (whether Jesus, God, or angels), it is little wonder that they can and often do generate terror in anyone who meets them. That is not, however, their objective. Rather, their appearances, and more specifically that of the Father, are generally to instill within people respect and awe not only for God's power but also for his mercy, grace, and love. Often the theophany is to assure them of their divine acceptance. In the scriptures, this "godly fear" (Heb. 12:28) "is equivalent to reverence, awe, worship, and is therefore an essential part of the attitude of mind in which we ought to stand toward the All-holy God."[129]

The purpose of φόβος (*phobos*) is not to frighten people to death, unlike in Calvinistic theological interpretations. Therefore, a continual refrain in the scriptures is for the faithful to "fear not" (for example, see Gen. 15:1; 26:24; and Luke 1:13, 30). Paul certainly gives the Saints solid ground for confidence as they prepare to meet God. Indeed, the Apostle witnesses that those who have received the Holy Spirit need not fear, for they can call, "Abba, Father" (Rom. 8:15; compare Gal. 4:6 and 2 Tim. 1:7). Paul's colleague in the ministry, John, testifies that "there is no fear in love, but perfect love casts out fear, because fear has to do with punishment, and he who fears is not made perfect in love" (1 John 4:18, our translation). In sum, "it is this love, not fear of punishment, that provides the motive and power to keep God's commands."[130]

In the present context, both the negative and positive aspects of the word work. Paul and his companions know what it is that causes the fear of God—namely, divine judgment (5:10). For the righteous, their φόβος (*phobos*) will manifest itself positively in awe and reverence for God's mercy and grace. For the wicked, their *phobos* will manifest itself in dreadful torment. Concerning each non-repentant person, the Book of Mormon states that "the demands of divine justice [will] awaken his immortal soul to a lively sense of his own guilt, which [will] cause him to shrink from the presence of the Lord, and [will] fill his breast with guilt, and pain, and

---

128. The term κύριος (*kyrios*) is ambiguous and could refer to the Father (see Furnish, *II Corinthians,* 306), but the conjunction οὐν (*oun*), "therefore," at the beginning of 5:11 suggests that the fear is associated with the judgment bar of Christ. Barnett, *Second Epistle,* 279 n. 3.

129. "Bible Dictionary," in the Holy Bible published by The Church of Jesus Christ of Latter-day Saints (1976), s.v. "fear."

130. *NID,* 4:614.

anguish, which is like an unquenchable fire, whose flame ascendeth up forever and ever" (Mosiah 2:38). If the experience of one rebellious soul is any indication, "the very thought of coming into the presence of . . . God [will] rack [their souls] with inexpressible horror." They will wish that they "could be banished and become extinct both soul and body, that [they] might not be brought to stand in the presence of [their] God, to be judged of [their] deeds" (Alma 36:12–15).

we persuade men / we keep trying to persuade people: With this phrase, Paul identifies what, at least in part, motivates him and his companions in preaching the gospel. His use of the verb πείθω (*peithō*), "to persuade," here combines both the iterative and connotative senses of the present tense,[131] yielding "we keep trying to persuade" as in our Rendition. As such, it shows that the missionaries, and especially Paul, are not always successful in persuading people to their cause. But which people? In the broad context of Paul's work, it could refer to non-Christians. "Gentiles" are certainly the focus of his mission. In the present context, however, it could refer more to the Corinthian Saints, whom Paul wants to draw back to his cause.[132] Whichever the case, the phrase does show that Paul and his companions are indefatigable in their efforts. The noun ἄνθρωπος (*anthrōpos*), though masculine in gender, can also include women and is therefore translated as "people" in our Rendition.[133]

we are made manifest unto God / we are well-known to God: The verb φανερόω (*phaneroō*) means "to expose something publicly," but in the passive voice, as here, it has intransitive force, denoting "being well known."[134] Even so, the nuance of full exposure or openness remains. By using the word, Paul could be tacitly telling his readers that he and his companions have nothing to hide or be ashamed of.[135] His more direct point seems to be that whether or not the missionaries are successful in their endeavors, God is well aware of them and approves of their efforts.

131. Wallace, *Greek Grammar*, 534.

132. Martin, *2 Corinthians*, 278. Based on Paul's infrequent use of the verb *πείθω* (*peithō*), Hughes, *Second Epistle*, 186, argues that Paul defends himself against his detractors by using their term when they say "he is good at persuading people but cannot deceive God." Thrall, *Critical and Exegetical Commentary*, 1:402–3, suggests that Paul's detractors say that since he lacks the splendor associated with Moses, he must have "cajoled them in some devious fashion."

133. BDAG, 81–82.

134. BDAG, 1048.

135. Martin, *2 Corinthians*, 279.

I trust also are made manifest in your consciences / I hope we are also well-known in your consciences: That Paul begins this phrase with "I hope" (ἐλπίζω, *elpizō*) rather than "we hope" emphasizes his personal stake in this particular matter. It suggests that he is taking a stand and pleading his case.[136] The verb he uses, "to hope" or "trust," denotes a positive outlook allowing a person to move forward with confidence.[137] Paul again uses the verb φανερόω (*phaneroō*) in the passive voice, thus meaning "to know something or someone well." Its use here suggests that Paul is hopeful that, in the eyes of his readers, his actions are viewed as open and genuine.[138] The noun συνείδησις (*syneidēsis*), "conscience," found here in the plural, often denotes the human faculty that distinguishes right from wrong, including the sting when one fails to do what is right. In the present case, however, it refers to an awareness or consciousness of certain information with the ability to make a moral judgment about it.[139] Paul's use of the plural is inclusive and therefore refers to the conscience of the entire body of the Saints.[140] His words express his expectation that his character and work, as well as that of his companions, have proved them to be men of moral worth.

5:12 ***For we commend not ourselves again unto you / We are not trying to commend ourselves to you again:*** The verb συνίστημι (*synistēmi*), "to commend," carries the idea of self-recommendation or promotion. Such an act was generally viewed negatively,[141] and Paul seems to be trying to avoid any appearance of doing so (see Translation Notes and Analysis for 3:1). The present tense of the verb is used here in the connotative sense, yielding the translation "trying to commend."[142] The Greek sentence begins with the particle οὐ (*ou*), "not," making the negation emphatic and thus emphasizing Paul's insistence that he is not commending himself or others.

but give you occasion to glory on our behalf / on the contrary, we are giving you an opportunity to be proud of us: The conjunction ἀλλά (*alla*), "instead, but, on the contrary," serves as a marker introducing Paul's real intent.[143] The verb δίδωμι (*didōmi*), "to give," is found here as a present

136. Martin, *2 Corinthians,* 280.
137. Louw-Nida, §25.59; BDAG, 319.
138. Martin, *2 Corinthians,* 279.
139. Louw-Nida, §28.4; BDAG, 967–68.
140. Barnett, *Second Epistle,* 281 n. 13.
141. BDAG, 972–73.
142. Smyth, *Greek Grammar,* §1878; Wallace, *Greek Grammar,* 534; BDF, §319.
143. Louw-Nida, §89.125; BDAG, 44–45.

participle used circumstantially. We have, for the sake of flow, translated it as a finite present. The noun ἀφορμή (*aphormē*), literally means "a base or circumstance from which other action becomes possible" or generally "occasion, opportunity."[144] Paul's point is that the blameless conduct of both himself and his coworkers should give the Corinthian Saints evidence to use against the missionaries' detractors. The noun καύχημα (*kauchēma*) denotes a cause of pride or of boasting.[145] Its nuance can be either positive or negative depending on context. In this case, it is positive.

that ye may have somewhat to answer them which glory in appearance / so that you can have an answer for those who take pride in outward appearance: The conjunction ἵνα (*hina*), "so that," acts as a marker denoting a purpose, aim, or goal.[146] Here it indicates the reason why Paul is making such a strong defense. The phrase ἵνα ἔχητε πρὸς τοὺς (*hina echēte pros tous*), literally "so that you can have for those," lacks an expressed direct object.[147] In our Rendition, we follow the KJV and add "an answer" for clarity. Paul uses the verb καυχάομαι (*kauchaomai*), "to take pride in, boast, glory," which is derived from the above-mentioned noun καύχημα (*kauchēma*), but here it has a negative sense with preposition ἐν (*en*), "in," indicating the thing one takes pride in.[148] The noun πρόσωπον (*prosōpon*), "external things, appearance,"[149] refers literally to the face but figuratively to what is viewed externally. It carries the inference of what is peripheral, superficial, or illusionary rather than what is essential, vital, or real.[150]

and not in heart / rather than what is in the heart: The noun καρδία (*kardia*) refers to the human heart, but metaphorically it connotes the person's inner life that directs thinking, volition, and emotion.[151] In the present context, however, it likely refers to sincere intents, desires, or purposes.

5:13 ***For whether we be beside ourselves, it is to God / For if we were out of our minds, it would be for God to decide:*** The conjunction, γάρ (*gar*), "for," suggests that Paul is addressing some kind of accusation made against him. The verb ἐξίστημι (*existēmi*), "to be out of one's mind," may define what that

144. BDAG, 158; LSJ, 292.

145. BDAG, 536–37.

146. BDAG, 475–77.

147. Such an anacoluthon is not unknown in this epistle. See 7:5; 8:18.

148. BDAG, 536.

149. BDAG, 888; Louw-Nida, §8.18.

150. BDAG, 887–88; Louw-Nida, §§24.24; 30.120.

151. BDAG, 508–9. That Paul uses the imagery of the heart eleven times (1:22; 2:4; 3:2–3, 15; 4:6; 5:12; 6:11; 7:3; 8:16; 9:7), shows how important this symbol was to him.

accusation was. The verb generally denotes experiencing something that makes little or no sense, resulting in being amazed or astounded.[152] It can, however, carry the more negative nuance of being out of one's senses.[153] The verb is in the aorist tense and forms the protasis of a contrary-to-fact conditional clause,[154] so we have translated it with an English subjunctive. The protasis of a contrary-to-fact condition usually has the particle ἄν (*an*) following the verb, but since here the protasis is the single word θεῷ (*theō*), "for God," with an understood verb "to be," the particle is missing.

The noun θεῷ (*theō*), "God," is in the dative case. Though it could be seen as a dative of advantage, indicating that what happens is meant to benefit God, it probably is a dative of reference, indicating that the matter is between Paul and God, and only God is able to decide whether Paul is crazy or not.[155]

or whether we be sober, it is for your cause / if we are of sound mind, it is for your benefit: The verb σωφρονέω (*sōphroneō*), "to have a sound mind," denotes thinking clearly, being reasonable, or being sane.[156] It is in the present tense and forms the protasis of a simple present condition, implying that something is assumed true for argument's sake.[157] This stands in contrast to the contrary-to-fact condition in the preceding conditional clause. The pronoun ὑμῖν (*hymin*), "you," is in the dative case, likely one of advantage, inferring that what Paul is doing is for the benefit of his readers.

5:14 Once again, we have come to a verse that presents several translation challenges. The problems arise from the imprecision of the verse as a whole, exacerbated by the vagueness of some of its parts. We have

---

152. Louw-Nida, §25.220. The word is often found describing the reaction of people to miracles. For example, see Matt. 12:23; Mark 2:12; 5:42; Luke 8:56; 24:22; Acts 2:7; 10:45. Paul's words suggest that his antagonists could have seen him as exhibiting erratic behavior that led to an outrageous lifestyle, but it seems more likely that they saw his sole-minded concentration on God and Christ as indicating he was out of his mind. Paul admits his behavior and means of addressing the people could be seen as unusual, but he could be offering theological justification for what they see as his nonsensical way of speaking because he avoided eloquence in preaching Christ crucified. For him, however, his true witness was more important than impressing people with flowery language. For a study, see Moyer V. Hubbard, "Was Paul Out of His Mind? Re-reading 2 Corinthians 5:13," *Journal for the Study of the New Testament* 70 (1998): 39–64.

153. BDAG, 350.

154. Wallace, *Greek Grammar,* 694–95.

155. Smyth, *Greek Grammar,* §§1481; 1496; F. F. Bruce, *1 and 2 Corinthians* (Grand Rapids, Mich.: Wm. B. Eerdmans, 1971), 207; Guthrie, *2 Corinthians,* 299 n. 7.

156. BDAG, 986.

157. Wallace, *Greek Grammar,* 690.

attempted to clearly and carefully show the process we used so that the reader may follow our attempt to parse out Paul's meaning.

For the love of Christ constraineth us / For Christ's love urges us on: The meaning of the phrase ἡ γὰρ ἀγάπη τοῦ Χριστοῦ (*hē agape tou Xristou*), "the love of Christ," is ambiguous. Is Paul referring to the love people have for Christ (an objective genitive) or to Christ's love for the people (a subjective genitive)? Either one is possible, but, given the context, it is the latter that seems to be the Apostle's intent.[158] Therefore, we have translated it as "Christ's love," which, in English, clearly denotes a subjective genitive. This reasoning works with what Paul states next about the redeeming work of the Lord (a work that he did because of his love for others; see John 15:13) that has so impressed and propelled the Apostle.[159]

The verb συνέχω (*synechō*), "to urge," has a wide range of meanings. Its root sense is "to hold or keep together."[160] Out of this grew the negative idea of oppressing or overpowering another and also the positive idea of providing an "impulse for some activity, urge on, impel" and holding "within bounds so as to manage or guide, direct, control."[161] Context implies the positive sense, and we have translated it as "urges us on." In this case, it is the love of Christ that Paul continually feels and that binds him to his Savior, directs his actions, and urges him onward in all that he does.

because we thus judge / because we have come to this conclusion: The verb κρίνω (*krinō*), "consider, judge," found here as a circumstantial aorist participle, has at its root the idea of separating or distinguishing.[162] The context carries no forensic force, and therefore the idea of judgment does not seem to work. On the other hand, the phrase "come to a conclusion," denoting the process of making "a judgment based on taking various factors into account," seems to give the best understanding.[163] Given what Paul is doing here, this small clause acts as an important springboard to the point he will make in 5:14–15 concerning the all-consuming power that the love for Christ has upon him. The demonstrative pronoun, τοῦτο (*touto*), "this," points to what he had considered at some time in the past and infers the conclusion he drew from it—namely, what Christ has done for humankind (as Paul states in the next phrase).

---

158. Harris, *2 Corinthians,* 418–19.

159. This view has the consensus. See Martin, *2 Corinthians,* 285.

160. LSJ, 1714.

161. BDAG, 970–71.

162. LSJ, 996.

163. BDAG, 567–69.

that if one died for all / that one man died for all humankind: This brief phrase summarizes the heart of Paul's appreciation for what Jesus did and the seat of the Apostle's love for his Lord. The conjunction ὅτι (*hoti*), "that," signals that what follows is a summary of Paul's carefully considered conclusion.[164] The Greek uses the masculine form of the cardinal number εἷς (*heis*), "one," nominally; thus, we have supplied "humankind" for clarity. The verb ἀποθνήσκω (*apothnēskō*), "to die,"[165] found here in the aorist tense, refers to the Savior's crucifixion in its historical context. The conditional particle εἰ (*ei*), "if," though found in the Textus Receptus that the KJV is based on, is not found in the earliest manuscripts and is, therefore, not used in our Rendition.

The meaning of the preposition ὑπέρ (*hyper*), "for," is ambiguous here. From a grammatical standpoint, it can be understood in three different ways. First, it can be taken in a representative sense, meaning that Jesus acted "for the sake of all [humankind]"; that is, in dying, he "identified himself with their humanity and plight" such that "his death to sin can be regarded as an act of obedience and surrender that benefitted them,"[166] and they can thereby partake of the positive result—namely, resurrection for all humankind. Or second, it can be taken in a beneficiary sense, carrying the force of "in behalf of" to indicate that his death was done for his disciples' good. Finally, it can be taken in a substitutionary sense meaning "in place of, instead of," indicating he acted as proxy for the people, explicitly expressing the doctrine of vicarious atonement.[167] Context gives the first nuance the better weight,[168] and we have chosen the translation "for the salvation of" as best catching the intended sense.[169]

then were all dead / thus, in a manner of speaking, all humankind have died: What Paul means by this phrase is, to say the least, unclear. It translates literally as "so all died." The particle ἄρα (*ara*) can carry the force of an informal inference, "so, thus, as it seems."[170] However, it can also express something tentative, "perhaps, conceivably, as it seems."[171] Finally,

---

164. Here the conjunction marks an explanatory clause. BDAG, 731–32.

165. BDAG, 111.

166. Martin, *2 Corinthians,* 302.

167. The beneficiary nuance, "for the sake of," is the more common (Louw-Nida, §90.36), but the substitutionary nuance, "instead of" or "in place of," is also used (BDAG, 1030–31).

168. Hughes, *Second Epistle,* 193.

169. *BGD,* s.v. "ὑπερ," lists "for the salvation of" as one of the nuances of this preposition.

170. BDAG, 127, LSJ, 232–33.

171. BDAG, 127.

it can be used epexegetically, "that is to say, so to speak."[172] Hence, in our Rendition, we have translated it as "in a figurative sense."

But is there a direct connection between the death of Jesus and that of all humankind? Paul stated, in the previous clause, that "Christ died,"[173] meaning that he shared the same demise as all other mortals. But, as Paul noted above, he did more. The verb ἀποθνήσκω (*apothnēskō*), "to die," is in the aorist tense, expressing the simple occurrence of an action in the past,[174] thus suggesting that Paul has the Lord's death through crucifixion in mind. Based on his other writings, Paul is likely not saying that everyone's mortal demise is due to or a result of Christ's death. The Apostle clearly expressed his belief that universal death resulted from Adam's transgression (1 Cor. 15:22).

Taking the Apostle's use of the adjective πᾶς (*pas*), "all," as fully inclusive, then it may be that, based on his judgment, *if* one died (namely, Jesus) in behalf of all, *then* all died. This suggests that he may have had the idea of substitution in mind. If that is the case, then he is thinking in terms of the exclusive place-taking that seems to be implied here and that yields an inclusive place-taking. "Christ was not merely a representative. In his self-giving death, he also incorporated 'all,' so that all humanity was [somehow] present in him. His death was their death. In Christ, all died."[175]

On the other hand, taking Paul's use of the adjective *pas,* "all," in a less inclusive sense, it could refer only to those to whom certain conditions apply. If that is the case, then the Apostle had a more figurative kind of death in mind. What this may be becomes clearer in Paul's epistle to the Romans. To them, he noted that believers become tied to the Savior "in the likeness of his death [that is, in the same death that he died]" but also become "united with him in his resurrection." The Apostle went on to state that "we understand that our old self was crucified with him, so that the sinful body might be done away with, so that we might no longer be enslaved by sin" and he concludes that "whoever has died is freed from sin" and insists that "one who dies, dies once and for all with respect to sin, but one who lives, lives with respect to God. So, we also consider ourselves to

172. *DAG,* s.v. "ἄρα."

173. This phrase disallows the idea of a limited atonement for the genitive pronoun "all" rules out the idea of Christ dying either for a few or even many. Seifrid, *Second Letter,* 244 n. 495.

174. Smyth, *Greek Grammar,* §1923.

175. Seifrid, *Second Letter,* 244; compare Bernard, "Second Epistle," 70. Harris, *Second Epistle,* 950, interprets the sentence thus: "That one person died for all, and therefore in one sense all died—his death was their death."

be dead with respect to sin, but alive with respect to God in Christ Jesus" (Rom. 6:5–11, our translation). What dies, using Book of Mormon symbolism, is the natural man. This enemy to God must be "put off" so that the Saint can come to be (Mosiah 3:19; see also 1 Cor. 2:14 and Mosiah 16:3–4). The death of the natural man makes being resurrected into a newness of life necessary, for only therein does the Saint receive the power to walk in God's way.[176]

5:15 ***And that he died for all, that they which live should not henceforth live unto themselves / And he died for the salvation of all humankind so that the living might no longer live for themselves:*** The conjunction καί (*kai*), "and," plus the repetition of the verb ἀπέθανεν (*apethanen*), "he died," connects what Paul says here to the statement he made above, thus allowing him to build on it. This verse reveals both the universal and individual aspects of the Atonement. Concerning the universal aspect, Christ died ὑπὲρ πάντων (*hyper pantōn*), "for the salvation of all," referring to his death and Resurrection. Concerning the individual aspect, Christ died ἵνα (*hina*), "so that," each person could overcome a selfish lifestyle. The conjunction ἵνα (*hina*) serves as a marker pointing to Christ's purpose, aim, or goal in dying.[177] His atoning sacrifice provides the opportunity for people to live a higher quality of life. The verb ζάω (*zaō*), "to live," in the present context, refers to "the manner in which a person behaves or conducts himself [or herself] in relationship to other persons and God."[178] Here the context is adverse, referring to a lifestyle that is self-centered, egotistical, and selfish. With this phrase, Paul emphasizes that Christ died to break the bonds of such an egocentric existence.

but unto him which died for them, and rose again / but live for him who died and was raised up again for their salvation: The conjunction ἀλλά (*alla*), "but, instead," serves here to mark a strong alternative.[179] The verb "live" is not found in the Greek of this phrase, but it is implied, and we have supplied it for the sake of flow. It refers to a pattern of life that is other-centered, humble, and selfless. The verb ἐγείρω (*egeirō*),[180] "to raise

---

176. Both the Savior and his prophets have used the symbolism of being born again as the consequence of putting off the natural man. See Mosiah 27:25–28; Alma 5:49; and Moses 6:59.

177. BDAG, 475–77.

178. Louw-Nida, §41.2. See also BDAG, 424–25. The verb, as in English, has a wide range of meanings.

179. BDAG, 44–45.

180. BDAG, 271–72.

up," found here as a passive aorist participle, in the present context, refers to the Resurrection. The tense suggests the singularity of the past act, while the voice tacitly gives God credit for the deed. With the phrase, Paul points out that the reason Christ died and was resurrected was for the salvation of all humankind, so that they might live "for him," a lifestyle that begins in mortality and is perfected in the world to come.[181]

Analysis and Summary

Paul begins this section with the witness of the missionaries' personal knowledge of the "fear" (φόβος, *phobos*) of God (5:11). What experiences the other missionaries may have had with God and Christ have not been preserved. Fortunately, at the least, some of Paul's have. His first was with the resurrected Lord on the road to Damascus (Acts 9:1–9). That experience, though terrifying in the moment, did not leave him with a sense of dread and debilitation but with an appropriate respect and sincere awe for his Savior. Further, it left him with a desire to serve Christ for the rest of his life. It sits at the very center of his appeal to others on Christ's behalf.[182] But that was not his only encounter. In vision, he was privileged to see "the third heaven" and "paradise," at which time he was given personal instruction concerning heavenly matters, some of which were so sacred that he could not relate them (2 Cor. 12:1–4). But the aftermath was an abiding "fear" or deep-seated "awe" for God. As Paul now writes to the Corinthians, that motivating fire not only drives him to the work but also enhances his desire to be united with the Lord.

Paul's writings reveal that "fear," or better, "awe," in this case, promotes reliance on God, along with the power of his Spirit in both preaching and living the gospel (1 Cor. 2:4). Indeed, salvation is worked out "with fear and trembling" (Philip. 2:12; compare 2 Cor. 7:15). The phrase should not be construed to mean that terror should be the motivating power that dictates a person's life. Rather, it depicts an attitude that each Saint should have toward the Divine. Indeed, "the attitude here recommended has nothing to do with slavish terror: as Paul assures the Christians in Rome, 'you did not receive a spirit that makes you a slave again to fear' (Rom. 8:15). It is rather an attitude of due reverence and awe in the presence of God, a sensitivity to his will, an awareness of responsibility in view of the account to be

181. The appeal to a newness of life is a frequent exhortation of Paul's writings. See Rom. 6:11; 14:7–8; see also 1 Pet. 3:18. Bernard, "Second Epistle," 70.

182. Guthrie, *2 Corinthians*, 296.

rendered before the tribunal of Christ."[183] In Paul, faith and fear are united, but for him fear has no anxiety. Instead, it brings hope and anticipation. The attitude expressed in the phrase "trembling and fear" brings "out the radical and total dependence of the believer on the saving work of God."[184] Thus, fear does not determine the life of the Saint but that, even after conversion, he or she must be conscious of and respect God and Christ's places as judge (Rom. 11:20). By living according to such consciousness, the Saint can enjoy the hope of finding her or his recompense in the Savior's words "Well done, thou good and faithful servant" (Matt. 25:21).[185]

The points made above should be kept in mind as one reads Paul's appeal in 5:11–13, for therein is the heart of the defense of his work, teachings, and integrity. He has shown his readers that it is his sense of fear that stands behind his desire to please God (5:6–10) and that it is also the basis of his service to the Saints. His life is marked by both his dependence on and faith in Christ and his continual striving to do as Christ commands. Based on that, Paul assures the Corinthians that he has been honest, transparent, and sincerely loving toward them. "He has done nothing out of motives of selfish ambition but has served them with their best interest in mind. As Paul will suggest, his credentials consist not of external 'honors' but of a life marked by dedication to God and to the people to whom he is sent." Such, he insists, should be the only standard for evaluating his ministry.[186]

Through his clear and truthful reasoning, he undercut his opponents' apparent accusations that he worked out of impure motives for his own benefit. His logic is compelling. He has already shown his readers that God has given his ministry the "seal of mine apostleship" (1 Cor. 9:1–2) and thus stands behind it. Even at this writing, Paul can assure his readers that he is "well-known to God" (2 Cor. 5:11, NR). Since Paul can stand before God with a clear conscience, he certainly can do so before the Christian house churches at Corinth. Furthermore, since the "fear of God" motivates his every effort, he certainly would not jeopardize his standing with the Divine by preaching falsehoods or being deceitful, and in this, he is willing to let God be the judge.[187] Paul admits that he has to "keep trying to persuade people" (5:11, NR) to his cause but can do so because it is just. He expresses his personal hope

183. F. F. Bruce, *New International Biblical Commentary: Philippians* (Peabody, Mass.: Hendrickson, 1989), 82.

184. Horst Balz, "φόβος," in *TDNT*, 9:13–14.

185. Martin, *2 Corinthians*, 276–77.

186. Martin, *2 Corinthians*, 278.

187. Barrett, *Second Corinthians*, 164; Bruce, *1 and 2 Corinthians*, 206.

that as he is well-known to God, so also he is to his readers.[188] He appeals to their conscience (συνείδησις, *syneidēsis*), a noun that, in this case, refers to a consciousness or awareness on their part concerning the character and good works of the missionaries and more especially those of Paul himself.

In 5:12, Paul addresses the issue of self-commendation.[189] Here he stresses, once again, that he is not seeking any kind of self-glory. His assurance is likely necessary because his self-justification in the previous verses could easily be viewed as self-commendation, a state his detractors could easily twist in a negative way. His frustration that his beloved converts could be persuaded by these interlopers drives him to make sure these Saints fully understand his motivation. Paul had found himself on the horns of a dilemma. On the one side, any self-commendation that the Apostle offered would take credit for all that he was and did away from God. On the other side, he had to do something to protect himself from the accusations of his accusers that he neither had authority nor presented the gospel as God intended but worked for his own ends. As the examination that follows shows, Paul successfully escaped the dilemma.[190]

In order to deflect the inevitable attack that he and his companions are once again commending themselves (an accusation Paul denied in 3:1), the Apostle asserts that he and his companions "are well-known to God"[191] and are therefore innocent of any self-congratulations. Though he denies commending himself, the context, both here and throughout the epistle, clearly shows that he is doing so and with force. His denial, however, as seen through his eyes, is genuine for two reasons. First, the source of a true recommendation is those who know the individual, even though by making the recommend, the person is recommending him- or herself as a judge of character. Second, all too often, self-commendation is both self-centered and self-promoting. What Paul is doing meets neither of these conditions. His commendation is centered in God and Christ and promotes their will and way. Further, it is based on the exemplary life he has lived among the Corinthian Saints. That puts them, not some outsider, in the position of being the ones who can recommend him, and as they do so, he has no need to recommend himself.[192]

---

188. Martin, *2 Corinthians,* 279.

189. This thread flows throughout the epistle. See 3:1; 4:2; 5:12; 6:4; 7:11; 10:12, 18.

190. Martin, *2 Corinthians,* 281.

191. Barnett, *Second Epistle,* 282.

192. Guthrie, *2 Corinthians,* 298–99. Witherington, *Conflict and Community,* 393, notes that Paul is, despite his statement to the contrary, recommending himself, but "in

Paul's purpose in telling them his intent, as he states, is to give them "an opportunity" (ἀφορμή, *aphormē*) or base from which they can successfully repel the attack that his adversaries are making against him and his companions. It is less likely that Paul is giving his readers new information than it is that he is calling their attention to what they already know[193]—namely that his fidelity to the gospel as he received and taught it (2:17; 4:3) is the proof of his genuineness.[194] Further, the example of the life he lived among them for months should provide them with a solid base on which not only to judge him but also to recommend him to others. Their ability to endorse him should totally undermine anything his antagonists are saying against him.[195]

Further, he is getting his readers to see that an attack on him is an attack on the gospel message that he has brought them. The proof of its value and truth is the newness of life that they are now enjoying. It is on this basis that he can appeal to their "conscience" (συνείδησις, *syneidēsis*, 5:11)—that is, their ability to discern not only between right and wrong but also between correct and incorrect. On the basis of this ability, he insists, they should have the resources to be proud of him and his companions and to defend them against the brazen interlopers.[196]

The problem with his antagonists, as he notes, is that they take pride in wrong things. For them, it is only the outward appearance (πρόσωπον, *prosōpon*) that they take into account and promote. On that basis, he admits, they could insist that Paul did not measure up to expectations. Their charges, as he presents them, include his supposed poor relationship with the Jerusalem Church (Gal. 2:11–16), his unwillingness to keep his word (2 Cor. 1:18–20), his lack of a forceful personality (10:10), his inferior oratory skills (11:6), and his bodily infirmities (12:5–10).

Paul castigates them for seeing only the "outward appearance" and being impressed by mere external qualifications. Because they refuse to see what is in the heart, they are guilty of gross misjudgments and boasting about credentials that do not really count while rejecting those that do. Paul's words seem to be a tacit appeal to 1 Samuel 16:7, which states that God looks on the heart, not the outward appearance. Since it is only

---

an inoffensive and rhetorically non-Sophistic way" that allows his friends not only to be proud of him but also able to boast about his ministry.

193. Martin, *2 Corinthians,* 282.

194. Barnett, *Second Epistle,* 282.

195. Hughes, *Second Epistle,* 188–89.

196. Martin, *2 Corinthians,* 282.

concerning the heart where proper judgment can be made, Paul notes, it is the only basis of accurate perception and understanding. If boasting is to be done, the Apostle states, it should be based on what is within a person, not what is without.

In sum, Paul's argument undercuts his detractors' position because they rely on outward appearance to determine what is true. Because they refuse to look deeper—that is, at the heart of the matter—they have come to wrong conclusions and should be ignored.[197] In contrast, Paul opines that his readers should know the life he lived among them and the power of his teachings. Remembering these should supply them with the ammunition they need to launch an effective defense in his behalf. He seems to be willing to demand such a defense because it is proper, being centered not on Paul but on the gospel that he preaches and the authority that stands behind it (see 2 Thes. 2:4–8 and Acts 20:24; 26:19). Remembering Paul's example and integrity while he lived among them meets two important conditions. First, they should be able to see, as he does, that God stands behind his work. Second, they should be able to successfully defend both his work and doctrine. As these conditions are met, the Apostle will successfully escape the dilemma noted above.[198]

In 5:13, Paul seems to be rebuffing additional charges that were made against him by his detractors. Due to his perceived self-commendation, these interlopers could have raised the charge that he was not being rational. Though the verb he used to counter the possible charge can denote being in a state of insanity (ἐξίστημι, *existēmi*), its main nuance is that of being out of one's mind. This state could derive from an ecstatic experience or a very powerful spiritual one. The related noun he uses (ἔστασις, *ekstasis*) can mean either "ecstasy" or "amazement" and connotes the condition where a person is out of his or her usual mental state due to the effects of a trance or other deeply spiritual event. The vagueness of the word as used here could indicate that Paul was tacitly referring to such an event. He was certainly familiar with them (see Acts 10:10; 11:5; 22:17).

Had Paul used the common word of "insanity" (μανία, *mania*), which he did during his defense before Festus (Acts 26:24–25), it would be clear that he was referring to a state of mental illness. Though that may not be the case here, there is little doubt but that his detractors did see his spiritual

197. Bernard, "Second Epistle," 68–69; Martin, *2 Corinthians*, 282.

198. Martin, *2 Corinthians,* 283.

zeal as a kind of religious mania (2 Cor. 11:1, 16–33). That he did not use the common term, however, opens the door to viewing his words as referring to exceptional spiritual experiences. That he had spoken in tongues (1 Cor. 14:18), had visions (2 Cor. 12:7), and experienced a theophany (Acts 9:1–9) certainly gave him experiences that could be described as being out of one's ordinary mind. His report that, during such times, he did not know whether he was in or out of the body and that he learned material beyond comprehension suggests such a state (12:1–2; 1 Cor. 15:44; compare 3 Ne. 28:13–15 and D&C 137:1). Further, that he says this state served to God's advantage also points to something besides madness, since being crazy would not seem to serve God's purposes very well. Though he contrasts that state with being of sound mind (σωφρονέω, *sōphroneō*), the Greek verb, in this context, could refer not just to sanity but also to rational behavior.[199] If that is the case, then "Paul is dividing into categories his behavior toward God, namely ecstatic, and toward the Corinthians, namely rational and controlled. The people could then boast of having an apostle who does both well."[200]

Paul's defense is two-pronged. First, if he is either crazy or ecstatic, it is to God's advantage. That statement stresses yet again the Godward orientation that marks the pattern of the Apostle's efforts. All that he does is for the glory of God and to promote God's will and way. Second, if he has a sound mind or is being very rational (*sōphroneō*), it is to the Saints' advantage, for they can then take him at his word.[201] In sum, Paul is assuring his readers that however they read him—as acting insanely, ecstatically, or rationally—he is doing what he does for the good of the Saints and their God.[202]

Paul's statement in 5:14 brings to an end his explicit proof that he has not engaged in self-commendation as he stresses that the love of Christ is the compelling force that completely dominates and urges him forward (συνέχω, *synechō*). This love is deeper and more gripping than mere "moral influence,"

---

199. See Hubbard, "Was Paul Out of His Mind?," 39–63, who presents an investigation of the wide implications of both ἐξίστημι (*existēmi*) and σωφρονέω (*sōphroneō*).

200. Martin, *2 Corinthians,* 285.

201. Harris, *Second Epistle,* 418 n. 44, notes that the terms ἐξίστημι (*existēmi*) and σωφρονέω (*sōphroneō*) were found in rhetorical handbooks of the day to differentiate between good and bad oratorical styles. That Paul used these terms may indicate that, at least in part, he was defending himself against those who accused him of lacking skill in public speaking.

202. Guthrie, *2 Corinthians,* 299–300.

even though that would constrain a person from boasting in her- or himself. In the missionaries' case, and especially for Paul, however, such love is a positive force that both allows and urges them to move forward in the proclamation of Christ and his gospel.[203] Certainly it is what dominates Paul's willingness to suffer the loss of all material things and even to die for the cause if necessary (Philip. 1:21; 3:7–11). It is the overmastering force that drives him in all his missionary efforts to bring people to know the Lord, in the hopes that they will come to that same depth of love.[204] It is by revealing the motivational force that envelops and drives him that he "defends his conduct before the Corinthians here; Christ's love claims him in such a way that in relation to others he can no longer live for himself—in contrast to his opponents, who boast to the Corinthians that they are religious and spiritual, that they are something in themselves."[205]

Paul's purpose in 5:14–15 is to shore up his reason for preaching. These verses speak of the representation and renewal that grows out of the implications of an aspect of the Savior's mission as Paul came to understand it. The Apostle draws his readers' attention to what Jesus did: he shared what all humans share—namely, death—the universal condition brought about due to Adam's transgression (Rom. 5:12, 14). But Jesus did more; he died for the salvation of all humanity (ὑπὲρ πάντων ἀπέθανεν, *hyper pantōn apethanen*). The preposition ὑπέρ (*hyper*) has numerous possible translations, but among those that could apply to the three instances in these two verses are the following: "on behalf of," "in place of," "in the name of," "for the sake of," and, most notably in the present context, "for the salvation of."[206] It is reasonable to assume that all three instances in these two verses have the same sense and thus show that Jesus benefitted all humankind in the death that he suffered. Thus, according to Paul's theological argument, "just as the condemnation of all mankind came through a single transgression, so also justification leading to [eternal] life was made available to all mankind through a single righteous act" (Rom. 5:18, our translation).

---

203. George S. Hendry, "ἡ γὰρ ἀγάπη τοῦ Χριστοῦ συνέχει ἡμᾶς—2 Corinthians v. 14," *Expository Times* 59, no. 3 (December 1947): 82, suggests that the love of Christ "allows" one into Christ's service.

204. Hughes, *Second Epistle,* 193; Martin, *2 Corinthians,* 285–86.

205. Helmut Köster, "συνέχω," in *TDNT,* 7:882–85.

206. BDAG, 1030–31; LSJ, 1857–58. *DAG,* s.v. "ὕπερ," gives twenty-five possible translations.

Paul's point is that the Savior's death does not automatically give a high quality of spiritual life to all as they move through their mortal existence. Indeed, those who refuse to walk his path remain morally condemned and spiritually dead, not having been adopted as God's sons and daughters (Rom. 8:15; Gal. 4:6), and are therefore shut out from his presence. Thus, they move in a living death headed for physical death and eventually judgment and punishment. The only way "all" can benefit from Christ's death and Atonement is through repentance and gospel living; otherwise, they find condemnation.[207] Even so, he has paid the debt. If they choose not to accept what he has done, then for the punishment they suffer they have only themselves to blame.

The Savior died, in part, to free people from a "fatal bondage to themselves" that expressed itself in the deadly but all-too-pervasive Corinthian narcissism.[208] This spiritual disease seems to have affected a rather large percentage of those who made up the various house churches in Corinth as well as Paul's antagonists. It appears to have been a driving factor in the feelings of the Apostle's detractors that allowed them not only to judge him but also to insist that they were competent to replace him.[209] These interlopers were steeped in the Corinthian norm "of self-aggrandizement and one-upmanship politics," and they brought it into the Church. The Apostle insists that such a posture is diametrically opposed to what it means to be a Christian.[210] Christ must be the center of true worship if one is to be free. In short, Paul is not speaking of being indebted *to Christ* but of being liberated *by Christ.* He personally knows that the love of the Messiah can emancipate a person from the weight of self and urge (*synechō*) that person on to do unselfishly the work of the ministry.[211] Thus, Paul's words here are autobiographical. Even though, before his conversion, he was zealous in his supposed cause for Jehovah that led to his persecution of the Christians (Philip. 3:6; compare Acts 22:3–4 and Gal. 1:13–14), he now realizes he was actually "putting confidence in the flesh."[212]

---

207. Guthrie, *2 Corinthians,* 305–6.
208. Seifrid, *Second Letter,* 244–45.
209. Seifrid, *Second Letter,* 244–45.
210. Guthrie, *2 Corinthians,* 306.
211. Seifrid, *Second Letter,* 245.
212. Barnett, *Second Epistle,* 292 n. 22.

In 5:15, Paul states clearly and succinctly what Christ has done for his readers. If the Saints can just see it, "they have been liberated from their being-turned-in-upon-themselves and have been given the freedom of abiding communication with 'the One who died and rose again on their behalf.' Their death is conquered in his death. Their life is found in his life. Christ remains to them an unqualified Giver."[213] But that giving came not just with the expectation that they would give in return but also with the empowerment to do so. It is this emancipation from self that brings joy and direction to those who, having died with Christ, now live in a newness of life (Rom. 6:1–11; 1 Cor. 15:47–49). Such a life is filled with the Spirit that empowers the person to serve in a Christlike, selfless way willingly (1 Cor. 15:10).

The Messiah not only died but also rose again, in part, to make this happen. This is an important point in Paul's theology. He does not speak of Christ's death without reference to his Resurrection. The Lord's saving power rests neither on mere "faithfulness" nor on mere "obedience" to the Father. Christ's act of submission to God's will by being crucified "is an act of power by which he comes to his saving Lordship and possesses humanity: he is the one who died and was raised again *on our behalf.*"[214]

This verse declares in no uncertain terms the centrality of Christ in the salvation process both universally and personally. Universally, he died for *all*; personally, he died so that those who are spiritually alive in him "might no longer live for themselves" but live for him and for the benefit of promoting his gospel. Thus, he died and was resurrected more especially for them.[215] The phrase "no longer" signals the point of conversion. At that point they are miles away from where they were before they were adopted into the divine family and could cry "Abba, Father" (Rom. 8:15). Through their conversion, selfishness has been done away, allowing them to live for others. In the present context, those converted are Paul and his companions and those others in their audience who live unselfishly for the good of the Corinthian Saints.[216]

---

213. Seifrid, *Second Letter,* 245.

214. Seifrid, *Second Letter,* 245, emphasis in original.

215. The Book of Mormon notes that, when Jesus suffered for sin, he saw "his seed." It declares that "his seed" are all those who have "hearkened unto [the words of the prophets], and believed that the Lord would redeem his people, and have looked forward to that day for a remission of their sins, [indeed] these are his seed, or [in other words] they are the heirs of the kingdom of God" (Mosiah 15:10–11).

216. Barnett, *Second Epistle,* 292–93.

The New Creature in Christ (5:16–17)

Greek Text

16 Ὥστε ἡμεῖς ἀπὸ τοῦ νῦν οὐδένα οἴδαμεν κατὰ σάρκα· εἰ καὶ ἐγνώκαμεν κατὰ
σάρκα Χριστόν, ἀλλὰ νῦν οὐκέτι γινώσκομεν. 17 ὥστε εἴ τις ἐν Χριστῷ, καινὴ κτί-
σις· τὰ ἀρχαῖα παρῆλθεν, ἰδοὺ γέγονεν καινά· [SBLGNT]

King James Version

16 Wherefore henceforth know we no man after the flesh: yea, though we have known Christ after the flesh, yet now henceforth know we him no more.
17 Therefore if any man be in Christ, he is a new creature: old things are passed away; behold, all things are become new.

New Rendition

16 And so from now on, we do not know anyone from a human point of view; even though we once came to know Christ from a human point of view, now we no longer know him in that way.
17 Therefore, if anyone is in Christ, he or she becomes a new creature. Former things have passed away; now they have become new.

Translation Notes and Comments

5:16 *Wherefore henceforth know we no man after the flesh / And so from now on, we do not know anyone from a human point of view:* The conjunction ὥστε (*hōste*), "and so, wherefore," refers to the result of a previous experience.[217] In this case, it points to the change of heart that Christ, through the Atonement, has performed on those "who are alive" such that they live for Christ and others. The phrase, ἀπὸ τοῦ νῦν (*apo tou nyn*), "from now on," refers to the continuing effect of that change of heart.[218] The verb οἶδα (*oida*), "to know," has a range of meanings, from being superficially acquainted with something to having a close, even intimate, understanding of it.[219] Here it is the former nuance that is in mind.[220] The adjective οὐδεῖς (*oudeis*) acts here as a substantive, meaning "no one" or

217. Louw-Nida, §89.52; BDAG, 1107.

218. The adverb νῦν (*nyn*), "now," focuses on the present moment. BDAG, 681–82. Given the context in 6:2, its emphasis is on the importance of the moment so far as salvation is concerned.

219. BDAG, 693–94.

220. Guthrie, *2 Corinthians,* 307.

"not anyone."[221] The prepositional phrase κατὰ σάρκα (*kata sarka*), literally "according to the flesh," is used here figuratively to express "from a human point of view."[222] Paul's argument is that, due to the change conversion brings, the missionaries can no longer view people from a mere human perspective but see them within the context of their divine potential.

yea, though we have known Christ after the flesh, / even though we once came to know Christ from a human point of view: The phrase εἰ καί (*ei kai*), "even though," points back to Paul's earliest view of Jesus as a disruptive and dangerous mortal.[223] The verb γινώσκω (*ginōskō*), found here in the perfect tense, means "to know" and carries nearly the same range of meanings as οἶδα (*oida*) used in the phrase above.[224] The nuance here is also one of a more superficial understanding. The verb's tense refers to a process begun in the past but consummated in the present, thus pointing to what was once but is no longer done or believed.[225] That Paul uses the title Χριστός (*Christos*), "Christ," rather than the name Ἰησοῦς (*Iēsous*), "Jesus," suggests he is viewing the Lord from the standpoint of his office as the Messiah rather than as a person.

The phrase "to know Christ" is vague and, therefore, can be taken three ways. The first is to evaluate his station "from a purely human point of view." This was the perspective of many of the Jews who insisted that he was a messianic imposter because he did not free them from Roman oppression and make them rulers over the earth. The second is to understand his work in view of worldly standards, in which case, as both Jew and Gentile saw it, he failed miserably, evidenced in his suffering the ignominy of the cross. The third is to view his station from an outward point of view—that is, strictly by appearance. Again, in this he fell short, for he was but a peasant, not the commanding, even royal, figure many expected the Messiah to be. Each of these nuances work, but the latter is the most likely, for Paul is castigating those who see and promote only how things appear outwardly.[226]

yet now henceforth know we him no more / now we no longer know him in that way: The phrase ἀλλὰ νῦν οὐκέτι γινώσκομεν (*alla nyn ouketi gnōskomen*) translates literally as "but now we no longer know." It lacks a

---

221. BDAG, 735.

222. BDAG, 916; Martin, *2 Corinthians,* 311.

223. We have construed the phrase as reflecting a real condition as opposed to an unreal condition. Martin, *2 Corinthians,* 311.

224. BDAG, 199–201.

225. Wallace, *Greek Grammar,* 577.

226. Witherington, *Conflict and Community,* 394–95.

direct object, but "Christ" is understood, and therefore we have supplied the pronoun "him." Further, for clarity, we have also supplied the words "in that way," showing that Paul's conversion changed his perception so that he now correctly understands what messiahship is all about. The temporal adverb νῦν (*nyn*), "now," denotes the present moment, but with salvific implications (compare 6:2). The nuance of γινώσκω (*ginōskō*), "to know," in this phrase shifts from what is superficial and distant to what is intimate and personal.

5:17 ***Therefore if any man be in Christ, he is a new creature / Therefore if anyone is in Christ, he or she becomes a new creature:*** The Greek in this phrase, ὥστε εἴ τις ἐν Χριστῷ, καινὴ κτίσις (*hōste ei tis en Christō, kainē ktisis*), is very compact. It translates literally as "Therefore if anyone in Christ, new creation/creature." As with the previous verse, this one also begins with ὥστε (*hōste*) and thus ties together the thought that "those who are alive in Christ no longer live for themselves."[227] The verb "to be" is missing from both units of the above phrase, but because it is understood, we have added it to our translation.

In the phrase ἐν Χριστῷ (*en Christō*), "in Christ," the preposition ἐν (*en*) marks a close relationship to Christ. Paul often uses the phrase to denote the theological idea of corporate status—that is, of being in a covenantal union with the Lord. It is this close relationship that both triggers God's creation of the new creature and provides the foundation of the Christian life (see, for example, Rom. 8:1–2; 16:3; Gal. 2:4; 3:28; 6:15; and Eph. 1:1; 2:6, 10, 13; 3:11).[228]

The conditional conjunction εἰ (*ei*), "if,"[229] shows that establishing a saving relationship with Christ is not universal but contingent on the action of each individual. It also stresses the need for the gospel to be proclaimed and thereby the importance of the work of Paul and the other missionaries (see 1 Cor. 1:26–31).[230]

The noun κτίσις (*ktisis*) can refer to either "the act of creation" or what is created—namely "a creature."[231] On the basis of context, we have taken

---

227. Guthrie, *2 Corinthians,* 307.

228. Thiselton, *First Epistle,* 76. The preposition ἐν (*en*) with a dative of person expresses a relationship broader than instrumentality or agent. It can connote, at the very least, a personal presence if not a very close personal relationship. See BAGD, 326–30; Guthrie, *2 Corinthians,* 308.

229. BDAG, 277–78.

230. Seifrid, *Second Letter,* 251.

231. BDAG, 572.

it in the second sense, denoting someone who "is the creation of some power or influence and that, usually, is subject to it or obedient to its will."[232] In this case, the creator is God, and the Saint is the new creature willingly subject to him.

The phrase καινὴ κτίσις (*kainē ktisis*), "a new creature," is ambiguous because, as is often the case with Greek, the verb "to be" is not expressed but understood. The subject is also unexpressed. As a result, it could be understood in either of two ways. The first way is to take it broadly, thus translating it as "there is a new creation." Taken in this way, the phrase refers "to the whole new world that Christ's death created."[233] His Atonement brought into being a newly created order in which the Saints can now participate by living according to its principles and mandates. In it the love of others impels (5:14) the converted to live for Christ. They do this by putting away the old order of self-centeredness that viewed others "from a human point of view." They now view people in light of the gospel of Christ or the new order that he has set up that makes everyone brothers and sisters and therefore equals within God's kingdom.

The second way is to take it narrowly, referring to the change that Christ's death and Resurrection make on all those who enter into an association with him. In this case, it is the individual who becomes "a new creature." This interpretation has a slight edge over the one above as being Paul's intent for the following reasons:

- The pronominal adjective τις (*tis*), "anyone," found in the first phrase, should likely be understood as the subject for the second phrase.
- Paul's discourse centers on how the convert's worldview makes a subjective change in the person who follows this view.
- In Judaism of the time, proselytes were often referred to as new creatures.
- Also pointing in this direction is Paul's reference to the believers' consciences and judgment.
- Finally, Ephesians 4:24, where Paul admonishes his readers to "put on the new man"—that is, God's creation—strongly echoes the thoughts here.[234]

old things are passed away / Former things have passed away: The plural adjective ἀρχαῖα (*archaia*), here used nominally, thus, "former things," denotes the earlier state of existence in which the Christians lived before their conversion. This existence included its own worldview and

232. *Dictionary of Synonyms,* s.v. "entity."
233. Witherington, *Conflict and Community,* 395.
234. Witherington, *Conflict and Community,* 395.

lifestyle.[235] The verb παρέρχομαι (*parerchomai*), "to pass away," found here in the aorist tense, refers to something that has, in the past, come to lose all force and validity.[236] Taken as a whole, the phrase refers primarily to the former worldly existence with its narrow, mundane viewpoint in which Paul's readers were trapped before their conversion.

behold, all things are become new / now they have become new: Paul begins this phrase with the particle ἰδού (*idou*), "behold."[237] Its purpose is to draw attention to and emphasize what he says next, and we have translated it as "now." The adjective καινός (*kainos*) denotes what is "new" in the sense of that which replaces what has become obsolete and valueless.[238] The verb γίνομαι (*ginomai*), "to become," found here in the perfect tense, refers to the new order the Savior's Atonement brought into existence and in which his newly made creature can now exist.[239]

Analysis and Summary

With 5:16–17, Paul makes very clear his intentions in writing this unit of his letter. He states that, due to the effects of the Atonement, those who have been converted, as he has, can no longer see people from a limited mortal point of view (κατὰ σάρκα, *kata sarka*). They have become quite indifferent to the mere external qualifications of others. Their heightened viewpoint stands in marked contrast to Paul's antagonists, who put full confidence in such things.[240] Paul's point is that conversion prohibits a person from seeing and judging others based on superficial criteria. That being the case, the Apostle's words suggest many among the Corinthian Saints "were inadequately socialized converts. They still evaluated things by the criteria they had imbibed from the rhetoric-infatuated culture in Roman Corinth."[241]

Paul admits that there was a point in his own life when he viewed Jesus, as did many of his colleagues among the rulers of the Jews, as but a mere mortal.[242] Based on their very limited human viewpoint, Jesus did not

235. BDAG, 137.

236. BDAG, 775–76.

237. BDAG, 468.

238. Louw-Nida, §58.71; BDAG, 496–97.

239. The Doctrine and Covenants uses much of the same language but applies it to the end time when heaven, earth, and all things shall become new. See D&C 29:24; 63:49.

240. Bernard, "Second Epistle," 70.

241. Witherington, *Conflict and Community,* 395.

242. Bultmann, *Second Letter,* 156. The view held by Saul of Tarsus conforms to the Book of Mormon prophecy that despite Jesus' many miracles, the Jewish leadership

meet their expectations for messiahship. He also threatened the very foundations of their traditions, station, and religion. These facts Saul, the Pharisee, knew well and, as a consequence, moved against those who followed Christ's way. But the Apostle Paul now knew that this flawed historical viewpoint had to yield to the insights gained by the power of the Spirit that not only transcended but also corrected the very limited human perspective.[243] As a result, he could no longer view the Lord's office as Messiah ("Christ") as he did before.

Paul's wording in 5:17, though very brief, "marks the unqualified and undiminished entrance of the [new Christian age] into the present world" but carries an implicate reserve that the entrance is localized to being found "in Christ, the crucified and risen Lord alone."[244] Paul describes the effects that the Atonement can have not only upon all those who enter into a relationship with the Messiah (ἐν Χριστῷ, *en Christō*) but also upon their worldview. The Savior's death, as Paul understands it, brought to pass a new epoch in history and with it a new understanding of existence itself. All that came before this period, for both Jewish and Gentile converts, had now passed away because it had become obsolete and valueless in the salvation process.[245] In their place a new social order, theological system, moral code, and sacred literature were growing as the missionaries pushed God's word and the people accepted it.[246]

Paul fully and completely knew the results of being "in Christ," for he himself had become a "new creature." His experience confirms the statement made by Elder David A. Bednar that being in Christ marks a "fundamental change of what we feel and desire, what we think and do, and what we are. Indeed, the essence of the gospel of Jesus Christ entails a fundamental and permanent change in our very nature made possible through our reliance upon 'the merits, and mercy, and grace of the Holy Messiah' (2 Nephi 2:8)."[247] Paul understood that the change "marks the outward life of Christians. It marks all their judgments concerning others, plus all their decisions about life." Indeed, the new creature has "a new relation with God. The idols of the human heart have been stripped away," and

---

would "consider him a man, and say that he hath a devil, and shall scourge him and shall crucify him" (Mosiah 3:9).

243. Bernard, "Second Epistle," 70–71.

244. Seifrid, *Second Letter,* 252.

245. Isaiah 42:9; 43:18–19; 48:6 carries the same imagery.

246. Bernard, "Second Epistle," 72.

247. David A. Bednar, "Ye Must Be Born Again," *Ensign* 37, no. 5 (May 2007): 20.

a new covenant with God inaugurated "of which Paul has been made an emissary."[248] This idea is central in Paul's battle with the Corinthian interlopers. If he can get the Corinthian Saints to partake fully of the transforming power of the Atonement, he will win his case.

Message of Reconciliation (5:18–21)

Greek Text

18 τὰ δὲ πάντα ἐκ τοῦ θεοῦ τοῦ καταλλάξαντος ἡμᾶς ἑαυτῷ διὰ Χριστοῦ καὶ δόντος
ἡμῖν τὴν διακονίαν τῆς καταλλαγῆς, 19 ὡς ὅτι θεὸς ἦν ἐν Χριστῷ κόσμον καταλ-
λάσσων ἑαυτῷ, μὴ λογιζόμενος αὐτοῖς τὰ παραπτώματα αὐτῶν, καὶ θέμενος ἐν
ἡμῖν τὸν λόγον τῆς καταλλαγῆς. 20 ὑπὲρ Χριστοῦ οὖν πρεσβεύομεν ὡς τοῦ θεοῦ
παρακαλοῦντος δι᾽ ἡμῶν· δεόμεθα ὑπὲρ Χριστοῦ, καταλλάγητε τῷ θεῷ. 21 τὸν μὴ
γνόντα ἁμαρτίαν ὑπὲρ ἡμῶν ἁμαρτίαν ἐποίησεν, ἵνα ἡμεῖς γενώμεθα δικαιοσύνη
θεοῦ ἐν αὐτῷ. [SBLGNT]

King James Version

18 And all things are of God, who hath
reconciled us to himself by Jesus Christ,
and hath given to us the ministry of
reconciliation; 19 To wit, that God was
in Christ, reconciling the world unto
himself, not imputing their trespasses
unto them; and hath committed unto
us the word of reconciliation. 20 Now
then we are ambassadors for Christ, as
though God did beseech you by us: we
pray you in Christ's stead, be ye reconciled to God. 21 For he hath made him
to be sin for us, who knew no sin; that
we might be made the righteousness of
God in him.

New Rendition

18 Now all these things are from God,
who reconciled us to himself through
Christ and gave us the ministry of reconciliation; 19 that is, God was reconciling the world to himself in Christ,
not counting their transgressions
against them and entrusting us with the
message of reconciliation. 20 Therefore, we are representatives of Christ
as if God himself were encouraging
you through us. We plead with you on
behalf of Christ, be reconciled to God.
21 God made Christ, who knew no sin,
become sin for our sakes so that we
might become the righteousness of
God in Christ.

248. Seifrid, *Second Letter,* 255.

Translation Notes and Comments

5:18 ***And all things are of God, / Now all these things are from God:*** The phrase τὰ πάντα (*ta panta*), "all these things," points back to those items Paul has addressed—namely, the future final judgment all will face, the love of Christ that spurs the missionaries to action, and the power of his sacrifice that has made it possible for his readers to become new creatures with their new and inclusive worldview. Behind all these things, Paul declares, stands God.

who hath reconciled us to himself by Jesus Christ / who reconciled us to himself through Christ: The verb καταλλάσσω (*katallassō*), "to reconcile," found here and in the following two verses, is used in the New Testament to describe "the exchange of hostility for a friendly relationship."[249] Paul's witness is that God is the one who made this exchange possible through the Atonement of the Savior.

and hath given to us the ministry of reconciliation / and gave us the ministry of reconciliation: The verb δίδωμι (*didōmi*), "to give," found here as an aorist participle, denotes both bestowing something on and entrusting something to another.[250] It carries a heavy theological nuance in the New Testament, being tied to God's giving to others eternal life through his Son and the Son's giving himself for all.[251] Since the context of the word often associates it with what both God and Christ have given, it points to the salvific process.

The noun διακονία (*diakonia*), "ministry," denotes the discharge of certain obligations within a community but carries the nuance of doing such service through genuine love.[252] It refers especially to the duty of those who execute the commands of others, and in a religious sense, those who by the command of God proclaim and promote his message among the people.[253] Here the aorist tense of the participle shows that God had previously given this specific duty to Paul and the others (see 4:1). Thus, this specific work had long been a part of the apostolic commission.

The noun καταλλαγή (*katallagē*), "reconciliation," denotes the reestablishment of "proper friendly interpersonal relations after these have been

---

249. BDAG, 521.
250. BDAG, 242–43.
251. Friedrich Büchsel, "δίδωμι," in *TDNT,* 2:166.
252. Hermann W. Beyer, "διακονία," in *TDNT,* 2:87–88.
253. BDAG, 230.

disrupted or broken."[254] The word presumes that a former state of opposition and even hostility once existed between two parties, which the process of reconciliation reverses and eliminates. Thus, the word is translated in Romans 5:11 (KJV) as "atonement." The translation as "reconciliation" stresses the process, while that of "atonement" stresses the result. In the present context, the word denotes the restoration of a once-estranged person to complete favor with God and, thus, carries here the nuance of "reconciliation."[255]

Due to the noun *katallagē* being in the genitive case, the phrase "ministry of reconciliation" can be taken in four ways: First, it could mean that this type of ministry has its origin and base in the grace that precedes and attends reconciliation (genitive of origin); second, it could mean that Paul's ministry is "characterized by reconciliation" (qualitative genitive); third, that "his ministry proclaims, offers, or brings about reconciliation (objective genitive)"; or fourth, that reconciliation is the content of his ministry (genitive of content).[256] Though the first option has some draw, all have a measure of truth behind them and therefore could carry Paul's intent.[257]

5:19 ***To wit, that God was in Christ reconciling the world unto himself / that is, God was reconciling the world to himself in Christ:*** What Paul meant by the opening words ὡς ὅτι (*hōs hoti*), "that is," is unclear. The context suggests that Paul used them to introduce either a quote or a clarifying statement. Because there is nothing to indicate the Apostle is quoting from some known source, the words most likely signal his clarification of the point he just made.[258] As such it refers back to the statement that God reconciled the world to himself by means of his Son.

The whole phrase is vague, allowing it to be construed in at least two ways.[259] The first would be translated as "God was in Christ reconciling the world to himself." This translation focuses on the indwelling relationship between the Father and the Son (see John 14:9–11).[260] Translated this

254. Louw-Nida, §40.1.

255. BDAG, 521.

256. Garland, *2 Corinthians,* 291.

257. Witherington, *Conflict and Community,* 395–96.

258. Barnett, *Second Epistle,* 305–6. For a study, see Takamitsu Muraoka, "The Use of ΩΣ in the Greek Bible," *Novum Testamentum* 7 (1964): 51–72, particularly 65.

259. Martin, *2 Corinthians,* 313, lists four but only two are really plausible.

260. According to Hyrum L. Andrus, *God, Man, and the Universe* (Salt Lake City: Bookcraft, 1968), 208–9, the Father and Son's "relationship in glory bears some analogy to a powerful electrical circuit, with the electricity passing without restriction from one pole or center of power to another and back again. But in the case of these two glorified

way, the message would be that reconciliation became possible because God spiritually dwelt in power in the Son (Col. 1:19; D&C 93:3–4). The emphasis of this translation is on the work of the Father. The second would translate the phrase as "God was reconciling the world to himself in (that is, through) Christ." This translation would emphasize the work of Christ as Savior. Since this view parallels Paul's thought in 5:18, it is preferred in our translation.[261]

The object of the reconciliation is ὁ κόσμος (*ho kosmos*), "the world." The noun has a wide range of meanings, but the context suggests Paul is referring to all the inhabitants of the earth,[262] thus making God's outreach universal.

not imputing their trespasses unto them / not counting their transgressions against them: The verb λογίζομαι (*logizomai*), "to account, impute, reckon," denotes the act of taking an account or reckoning of a report or record, including both debts and credits.[263] Here the context is negative in the sense of counting something against a person in order to punish him or her.[264] The noun παράπτωμα (*paraptōma*) is literally "a false step, slip,"[265] and can describe "a violation of moral standards, offense, wrongdoing, sin."[266] Paul's words show that, by divine law, even a simple misstep must be accounted for and payment made. No infraction, no matter how small, gets a pass.

and hath committed unto us the word of reconciliation / entrusting us with the message of reconciliation: The verb τίθημι (*tithēmi*), has the root sense of "to lay, put, place"; in the middle voice, as it is found here, it can have the sense of "to establish, give," with the nuance "to entrust"

---

beings, the indwelling substance consists of the Holy Spirit which centers initially in the Father. . . . The Holy Spirit is developed in the Son to quicken and endow the Son with the 'mind, glory, and power' of the Father, and to give the Son all power in heaven and on earth. Thereby, the two glorified beings are united in one, each possessing the same indwelling Spirit or divine mind as the other."

261. Barnett, *Second Epistle,* 305–6; Martin, *2 Corinthians,* 301. The verbal form could be used as a predicate, which would dictate the translation found in the KJV, or as periphrasis, which would dictate the translation used in the Rendition. Because of Paul's periphrastic use of participle καταλάξαντος (*katalaxantos*) in connection with God just before this clause and the coordinate, periphrastic use of the participle θέμενος (*themenos*) just after it, we feel our translation is best. See Seifrid, *Second Letter,* 255 n. 526.

262. BDAG, 561–63.

263. Louw-Nida, §57.227.

264. BDAG, 597–98.

265. LSJ, 1322.

266. BDAG, 770.

someone.[267] The noun λόγος (*logos*), "message, word," has a wide range of meanings but in the present context, it carries the idea of communicating something both orally and in writing. Thus, we translate it as "message."[268] For the noun καταλλαγή (*katallagē*), "reconciliation," see 5:18.

5:20 ***Now then we are ambassadors for Christ / Therefore, we are representatives of Christ:*** The Greek sentence begins with ὑπὲρ Χριστοῦ (*hyper Christou*), literally "In behalf of Christ." The preposition indicates authorized activity in the interest or in behalf of another—namely, the Messiah.[269] By placing these words first, Paul emphasizes their importance, but for the sake of flow, like the KJV we have shortened the phrase and placed it last. The verb πρεσβεύω (*presbeuō*), with the root meaning of "being either older or oldest,"[270] is here used in a technical sense, denoting an ambassador, envoy, or representative.[271] Because the title "ambassador" commonly refers to an envoy of a political entity, we have chosen the translation of "representative." The understanding that such an individual has the official authorization to act for the sponsoring agent or party (common to both words) should, however, be kept in mind. Through the implicit use of the language, Paul makes clear his authority. It is not humanly derived but comes directly from the Messiah, whose endorsement he carries especially in what he says.[272]

as though God did beseech you by us / as if God himself were encouraging you through us: The comparative particle ὡς (*hōs*) often has the meaning of "as" or "like,"[273] but when construed with a genitive absolute, as here, it means "as if,"[274] carries the nuance of certainty, and can be understood as introducing an actual fact.[275] It denotes an action done by one person that carries the same weight and authority as if done by the originating person. To emphasize this nuance, we have added the pronoun "himself" to the translation. The verb παρακαλέω (*parakaleō*) means "to make a

267. BDAG, 1003–4.

268. BDAG, 599.

269. BDAG, 1030–31; Louw-Nida, §90.36.

270. LSJ, 1462.

271. LSJ, 1462; BDAG, 861.

272. Witherington, *Conflict and Community,* 396.

273. Louw-Nida, §64.12; but for other nuances, see BDAG, 1103–6.

274. Bernard, "Second Epistle," 73. BGD, s.v. "ὡς"; See also Smyth, *Greek Grammar,* §2086.

275. Guthrie, *2 Corinthians,* 311.

strong request" or "to urge or encourage another to action."[276] The phrase δι' ἡμῶν (*di' hēmōn*), "through us," identifies Paul and his fellow workers as the means God is using to speak to the Corinthian Saints.

we pray you in Christ's stead, be ye reconciled to God / We plead with you on behalf of Christ, be reconciled to God: The verb δέομαι (*deomai*), "to ask for something pleadingly," carries the nuance of an urgent beseeching or pleading.[277] The preposition ὑπέρ (*hyper*), in this context, denotes speaking in behalf of or in the name of another and carries the nuance of doing so with their authority.[278] The verb καταλλάσσω (*katalassō*), in the passive voice as here, means "to be reconciled."[279] The passive form of this verb contains the nuances of atonement and suggests that one need to become faithful in a covenant relationship to gain the full benefits of the Atonement of Jesus Christ.[280] For discussion, see 5:18 above.

5:21 ***For he hath made him to be sin for us, who knew no sin / God made Christ, who knew no sin, become sin for our sakes:*** In our rendition, we have replaced "he" with "God" and "him" with "Christ" for clarity's sake. The noun ἁμαρτία (*hamartia*), "sin," denotes a range of meanings, from an involuntary mistake, missing the mark, or a character flaw to serious offenses against a deity.[281] The verb ποιέω (*poieō*), "to make," in the present context, means to do something that brings about a specific object, result, or state.[282] In this case, it is God treating Christ, who was absolutely sin-free, as a sinner to the fullest degree. The preposition ὑπέρ (*hyper*), "for our sakes," is very important here as it carries the nuance of benefaction.[283] God did what he did for the benefit of all his children.

that we might be made the righteousness of God in him / so that we might become the righteousness of God in Christ: The conjunction ἵνα (*hina*), "so that," is important here as it shows the reason for or the objective of an action.[284] The noun δικαιοσύνη (*dikaiosynē*), "righteousness," carries the sense of acting in accordance with divine, moral law and, thus, being

---

276. BDAG, 764–65.
277. Louw-Nida, §33.170; BDAG, 218.
278. BDAG, 1030–31; Louw-Nida, §90.36.
279. BDAG, 521.
280. LSJ, 889; BGD, s.v. "καταλλάσσω."
281. BDAG, 50–51, Louw-Nida, §88.118.
282. BDAG, 839–42.
283. BDAG, 1030.
284. BDAG, 475–77.

acceptable to God.[285] Paul's understanding of the term is complicated. On the one hand, it refers to God's pardoning action through which he forgives sin, and on the other refers to the way or means by which the Father shares his divine nature with those who willingly subject themselves to him and who, in turn, exhibit that same righteousness. That may be the case here if we view *dikaiosynē* as an abstract stand-in for something concrete. It is also possible that Paul is viewing God's righteousness as a function of his power (δύναμις, *dynamis*, see 6:7) operating within the Christian, thus connoting "the way God acts in justifying or restoring people to a relationship with [himself that then] serves as a model for Christian interaction."[286] In the last phrase, ἐν αὐτῷ (*en autō*), literally "in him," we have replaced the pronoun with "Christ," for clarity. The phrase stresses that it is only through Christ, or because of his Atonement, that God can justifiably act in favor of the Christian.

Analysis and Summary

At this point, Paul has come to the end of his rather lengthy discourse on his apostolic ministry that he began in 4:7. He will now turn his focus to his apostolic labor. To be as effective as possible, he takes great care to explain his position, for he is dealing "in matters of ultimate significance. Through him, God works death and life itself in the world,"[287] but his desire is life through reconciliation. The Greek noun translated "reconciliation" (καταλλαγή, *katallagē*) is exclusively Pauline and with its verbal cognate appears five times in this brief treatise, suggesting the importance of the idea that the word carries to the Apostle's point.[288] The need for reconciliation is the outgrowth of a person's willful rebellion (sin). Reconciliation is the personal restoration, or at-one-ment, that shifts the covenant relationship between God and the person from being adversarial to being consonant.[289] Paul uses the term to emphasize that a person can be restored to a proper relationship with God despite sinful tendencies, delineating the effects of Jesus' Atonement.

---

285. BDAG, 247-49.
286. BDAG, 247.
287. Seifrid, *Second Letter,* 255.
288. Harris, *Second Epistle,* 435.
289. Garland, *2 Corinthians,* 290.

In 5:18, the Apostle teaches that God, and he alone, initiates the act of reconciliation. The single objective of this act is to restore a person's good relationship with him.[290] To stress the point, Paul shows that the action is unilateral; it is the person who is reconciled to God, not God who is reconciled to the person.[291] Deity acts, and he acts first. Thus, Paul reveals God as the Great Benefactor, with Christ as the means of that benefaction and Paul with his companions as the human agents or representatives of the munificence of salvation.

But how is reconciliation even possible? This is what Paul makes clear in 5:19. He has already taught that judgment is coming, in which people will receive recompense for their actions (5:10). Indeed, *all* will face the day of reckoning. Such reckoning takes three steps. The first is the collection of all charges, the second is the totaling of the full debt, and the final is the placing of the full balance to a person's account.[292] What is placed there is moral wrongness. Paul uses a Greek word (παράπτωμα, *paraptōma*) that includes all types of sin. Its nuances range from simple missteps to acts of outright rebellion. The doctrine he teaches is that even the slightest infractions of divine law must be accounted and paid for.

Paul's answer to the question posed above is that Christ's Atonement made it possible for the Father to not reckon or impute sin to the sinner. The point that the Apostle makes in 5:21 "is one of the most critical in this letter and, indeed, within the writings of the apostle Paul, . . . and is the theological foundation . . . for the entire passage."[293] To express how God does what he does, Paul uses the word "imputation" (λογίζομαι, *logizomai*; see also Rom. 4:4–8).[294] The sins of the sinner God imputes to Christ. This is more than an act of substitution. In that case, there would have been an interchange of guilt and righteousness. In this case, what happens becomes much deeper and far more personal, indeed, "(a) becomes (b), so that (b) may become (a)."[295] This idea is borne out in the phrase "for our sake" (ὑπὲρ ἡμῶν, *hyper hēmon*). The phrase connotes more than mere advantage, but that imputation or transference actually takes place. In other words, Christ becomes, as it were, the sinner, and the sinner becomes, as it were, the

290. Harris, *Second Epistle,* 436.

291. Barnett, *Second Epistle,* 304; Harris, *Second Epistle,* 437.

292. BDAG, 596.

293. Barnett, *Second Epistle,* 312.

294. Louw-Nida, §57.227.

295. Martin, *2 Corinthians,* 303.

righteous son. As such, the Father could accept the once-sinner as one fully righteous on Christ's scale and, thereby, be reconciled to him or her. The process is allowed because of the absolute sinlessness of the Messiah in mortality.[296] It was because of this that he could act as a substitutionary sacrifice for sin. Thus, as Paul states, "God made him sin for us,"[297] or in other words, Jesus was made a sinner in our stead.

The Father's action should not in any way discount the seriousness of sin, even small ones. Actually, it is just the opposite. He deals with these and all others, however, not according to human reckoning but according to what Christ's death on the cross allows. It enables God to fully remove sin's consequences from the person by imputing the full weight and responsibility to Christ. It is in this way that God made Christ "sin for us" (5:21). God's application of this option must not be seen as a sign that he does not take sin seriously. It must be kept in mind that his willingness not to impute sin to the sinner cost him dearly in the giving of his Son to suffer hours of spiritual and physical torture, concluded only with his Son's death on the cross.[298]

In sum, the Apostle shows that reconciliation—with its undertone of mercy and grace—is even possible thanks only to Christ's obedience to the Father's will. The Apostle emphasizes this fact by making Christ the subject every time he uses the verb "to reconcile" (καταλλάσσω, *katalassō*) in the active voice.[299] Further, by placing the verb in the aorist tense, he stresses that the power to reconcile by atonement has already been completed through Christ's death.[300] The grammatical structure emphasizes Paul's understanding that God has already acted in Christ and through Christ to make this wonderous relationship between the Father and each of his children possible.[301] Thus, Paul stresses that God made Jesus the source

296. The gospel record is replete with this concept. See John 7:18; 8:46; 14:30; Heb. 4:15; 7:26–28; 9:14; 1 Pet. 1:19; 2:22; 3:18; and 1 John 3:5, 7. See also Gerald N. Lund, "Plan of Salvation, Plan of Redemption," in *EM,* 3:1088–91.

297. That Christ died as a sacrifice due to sin a constant theme in Paul's writings. See Rom. 3:22–25; 5:6–8; 14:15; 2 Cor. 5:14–15; Gal. 1:4; 2:20; 3:13; 1 Thes. 5:9–10; and 1 Tim. 2:6.

298. *NID,* 3:123–126, especially 126.

299. Margaret E. Thrall, "Salvation Proclaimed, V. 2 Corinthians 5:18–21: Reconciliation with God," *Expository Times* 93 (1981–82): 227–32.

300. Barnett *Second Epistle,* 302.

301. Garland, *2 Corinthians,* 289, 291. Martin, *2 Corinthians,* 300, views this material as Paul's rephrasing of accepted material dealing with the theme of reconciliation. The structure, he notes, gives all the "appearance of a creedal statement."

of reconciliation so that the Father could discount the sins of those who accept his Son.[302]

Paul states in 5:18 that God had entrusted or put into the care (τίθημι, *tithēmi*)[303] of the Apostle and his associates this wonderful doctrine as the seat of the message of their ministry. This divine act of delegating responsibility for proclaiming the message emphasizes that those who have been reconciled "have the privilege and responsibility to share in this great divine enterprise and are to call others to be reconciled to God."[304] This task Paul and his associates have gladly taken up as their God-assigned mission (διακονία, *diakonia*), one that also bears his authority.

When Paul talks about how "the world" (ὁ κόσμος, *ho kosmos*) can be reconciled to God in Christ (5:19), he seems to be referring to a universal event as opposed to something that affects only the Saints. That being the case, *no one* is barred from being reconciled with the Father and finding association with him. However, the Father never forces others to be reconciled to him. His children have to choose whether or not they want this to happen.[305] And there is a cost. Full reconciliation is only possible when sinners acknowledge their sins, repent, and allow reconciliation to take place.[306]

The scriptures are replete with references to *all* returning to God. According to the Book of Mormon, "concerning the state of the soul between death and resurrection . . . the spirits of all [people], as soon as they depart from this mortal body, yea, the spirits of all [people], whether they be good or evil, are taken home to that God who gave them life," where they are judged (Alma 40:11). Eventually, "every knee shall bow, and every tongue confess before [God]. Yea, even at the last day, when all men shall stand to be judged of him, then shall they confess that he is God" (Mosiah 27:31). As part of that confession, all will say, "Fear God, and give glory to him who sitteth upon the throne, forever and ever; for the hour of his judgment is come" (D&C 88:104). This does not mean, however, that every person will initially bow the knee happily but that nearly everyone will *eventually* be reconciled to God in that all hostility between them and him will be gone. But hostility's passing, for many, will come through pain, for "they [shall] confess, who

302. Barnett, *Second Epistle,* 301.

303. BDAG, 1003–4.

304. Garland, *2 Corinthians,* 289.

305. Harris, *Second Epistle,* 438.

306. Garland, *2 Corinthians,* 292.

live without God in the world, that the judgment of an everlasting punishment is just upon them; and they shall quake, and tremble, and shrink beneath the glance of his all-searching eye" (Mosiah 27:31). With the exception of a very few,[307] however, all the rest will be forgiven. "For they shall be judged according to their works, and every man shall receive according to his own works, his own dominion, in the mansions which are prepared." But for these formally wicked souls, "they shall be servants of the Most High; but where God and Christ dwell they cannot come, worlds without end" (D&C 76:111–12). Even so, there will be no hostility and, thus, God will have reconciled even these, at least to a degree, to himself, but only after they have repented and accepted Christ as their Savior.

In 5:20, Paul identifies the authority by which he and his companions work and which undergirds their message. They "are representatives" (πρεσβεύομεν, *presbeuomen*) of Christ. The Greek verb carries the idea of having an official authorization, and, in this case, an authorization that is divine in origin and purpose. As concerning Paul and his companions, that authority expresses itself in what these emissaries proclaim. They speak the word and will of God, and therefore there should be no debate. On that basis, the Apostle could insist that "God makes his plea through us," meaning that what Paul says "is nothing less than the voice of God."[308]

The usual work of such civil representatives was ambassadorial—that is, to represent their government before a superior power or authority. During the Christian era, both provinces and nations sent their ambassadors to present their cases before the various Caesars. In striking contrast, the New Testament shows God, the supreme authority, sending his representatives to present his case to the people. Paul's witness is that he and his fellow representatives function to proclaim that the Father is seeking reconciliation with those who lacked, due to their choice, association with him and that the Father has opened the way for unity to once again occur through Christ.[309]

Paul is here emphasizing that Jesus' oneness with the race of humankind allowed him to act in their name by being made a sin offering in their behalf. As such, he was their proxy, making "an oblation of filial obedience and

---

307. These are the "sons of perdition." On these, see D&C 76:30–37 and Rodney Turner, "Sons of Perdition," in *EM,* 3:1391–92.

308. For a study of Paul's view of his authority to preach, see Jerome Murphy-O'Connor, *Paul on Preaching* (New York: Sheed and Ward, 1963), 72–76. Compare D&C 21:5–6.

309. Guthrie, *2 Corinthians,* 311.

allegiance that God accepted and because of which he acted forgivingly to restore" them to himself.[310] Paul is here saying more than that Jesus died for others acting representatively in their behalf. His action had "the profound effect of changing [their] personal attitudes and dispositions" in that they could now live for others. The Apostle's overarching point, as seen in 5:18–21, is that the Messiah did something for them that they could not do for themselves.[311] In this way, Paul emphasizes the vicarious nature of the Atonement and the empowerment it brings.[312]

But why does he urge the Corinthian Saints to be reconciled to God when this should have already happened? Paul is encouraging the Corinthians to take full advantage of the Atonement of Jesus Christ by keeping his commandments and adhering to his new covenant in a reciprocal relationship. We do this conditionally by obedience to the laws and ordinances of His gospel (A of F 1:3). Given the context of the epistle as a whole, it is certain that Paul is defending himself against antagonists who have called into question his apostolic authority and his teachings. In listening to and in some cases following these alternate voices (2:17; 11:4), many of the Saints had inadvertently stepped out of harmony with God and were no longer following correct principles. By alienating themselves from Paul, they had also alienated themselves from the gospel he preached and the power of union with God it brought. Therefore, Paul beseeches them, in the strongest terms—even proclaiming to speak God's very words—to be reconciled once more to the Father.[313]

But what does Paul mean in 5:21 by saying that God did what he did so that "we might be made the righteousness of God in him," meaning Christ? The answer is found in the phrase "in him" (ἐν αὐτῷ, *en autō*)—that is, through the Messiah. Due to strong echoes between Paul's statement here and Isaiah 53, some commentators have argued that this Old Testament passage is the tacit source of Paul's doctrine.[314] That passage does stress the absolute sinless state of the "suffering servant" who bore the sins of and suffered for others in order to justify (that is, to make righteous) many. "That

310. Martin, *2 Corinthians,* 303.

311. Martin, *2 Corinthians,* 303. Compare Alma 42:9–15.

312. For a study, see Jeffrey R. Holland, "Atonement of Jesus Christ," in *EM,* 1:82–86.

313. Guthrie, *2 Corinthians,* 311–12. For a study, see Seyoon Kim, "2 Cor. 5:11–21 and the Origin of Paul's Concept of 'Reconciliation,'" *Novum Testamentum* 39 (1997): 360–84.

314. See John Hoad, "Some New Testament References to Isaiah 53," *Expository Times* 68, no. 8 (May 1957): 254–55; Barnett, *Second Epistle,* 313; Harris, *Second Epistle,* 456; Guthrie, *2 Corinthians,* 314–15.

passage expresses the idea[s] of identification, substitution, and transformational interchange, which also lie at the heart of 2 Cor. 5:21."[315]

It is noteworthy that Paul does not, in this instance, mention the Savior's willing obedience to the task he alone could do (as he stresses in Philip. 2:6–8). Instead, he focuses on the act of God who "made" (ποιέω, *poieō*) Christ a sinner for all.[316] The Apostle likely meant the word to be taken in the sense of being appointed or designated. The reason he gives credit to the Father may be that the Apostle felt the need to spotlight the Father as the one who worked to save humankind. Nonetheless, he concludes that it is due to Christ that we are able to take on that high degree of righteousness that reconciliation demands. In sum, it was "the Father's initiative [that assigned] Christ the role of sin-bearer" and the Son's love (5:14) that gave him the daring to perform his sacrificial death. Thus, "the Father and the Son are one mind and purpose in the act that reconciles humans to [God]."[317]

315. Guthrie, *2 Corinthians,* 314.
316. Martin, *2 Corinthians,* 304.
317. Guthrie, *2 Corinthians,* 314.

Chapter 6

"I Will Be a Father to You"

Introduction

Much of the opposition against Paul arose, as noted previously, due to two forces: first, the harsh letter that he had sent to the Corinthian Saints, and second, the perceived breaking of his promise to visit the various branches in the near future. To ascertain the Saints' current feelings about the Apostle, he sent Titus ahead. He was thrilled when his coworker returned with positive news (7:1–9). That news, however, did not mean that everything was settled and that everyone was anxious for Paul's return. Thus in this section, he once again appeals to the Saints to receive him in good faith so that he can further clear up any misunderstandings (6:11–13). His posture at this point is, therefore, as if nothing had been resolved and that opposition still remains high. We see this in his rather critical language toward his detractors in this chapter even though these people do not yet take center stage (6:14–7:1).

To gain a hearing, the Apostle does praise his readers for their positive response to Titus's visit. Paul's motivation in doing so, though somewhat manipulative, is derived from his genuine love and interest in their physical and spiritual well-being. Indeed, he goes out of his way to communicate this fact (7:2–16). He knows that much still needs to be resolved, and so he holds in reserve his most pointed and direct language against his adversaries until the close of his letter (chaps. 10–13).[1] By this means he is able to effectively defend himself while putting down his detractors.

The basis of his appeal is on the wonder of reconciliation that can take place between God and each Christian. This reconciliation can take place only if Paul's audience accepts the witness of his testimony and the truthfulness

1. Seifrid, *Second Letter*, 268–69.

of his doctrine. In sum, his readers must first be reconciled to the Apostle before they can be reconciled to God, because apostolic authority provides the means, and his doctrine necessarily shows the way. For this reason, he commends himself at length (6:3–10). He couches his self-commendation in such a manner that it is subordinate to God and his work. Paul stresses that he is but the messenger—a very committed and self-sacrificing messenger, but a messenger nonetheless—who has been true to his charge to deliver God's word fully, truthfully, and plainly.[2]

Four discreet units comprise this chapter. The first unit (6:1–2) contains the applied conclusion that results from the Apostle's theological reflections on the wonder of reconciliation that he began in 5:18. The application, in the form of an admonition, is for his readers to make that reconciliation a reality in their lives. To give his admonition additional punch, he quotes scripture to stress the idea that "now" is "a day of salvation" and thus the time to act, for that day will come to an end, and with it the opportunity will be lost.

In the second unit, with marked abruptness, Paul lists the condition and character of his ministry (6:3–10), focusing on the fact that though he and his fellow workers give no intentional offense to anyone, they still suffer greatly for the cause of Christ. The Apostle uses a highly crafted and carefully structured writing style that includes rhythmic repetition to capture his readers' attention and draw them along. In this way, he likely gave them a sense for the depth of the hardships these early missionaries had suffered for Christ's sake.[3] In doing so, he places his readers in a position to yield to the appeal he makes in the ensuing portion.

The third unit (6:11–13) consists of Paul's sincere, emotional, and powerful appeal (which also acts as a defense) to the members of the Corinthian house churches. He stresses that he and his companions have been transparent in their work with and affection for these people and expresses his desire that they reciprocate. There is good reason for his desire. The tension between Paul and one of the subgroups of Christians who have yielded to Paul's detractors apparently lies in a low moral posture from which some of these have no desire to repent (12:21). Their adamant stance has resulted in a roadblock to the reconciliation now open to all who will be faithful. The spiritual reunion, however, demands conversion from a mundane and immoral past to a moral and spiritual present and future. Thus, what he

2. Seifrid, *Second Letter,* 268–69.

3. Guthrie, *2 Corinthians,* 321.

says here anticipates the issues he will address in chapters 10–13.[4] In sum, "the material in this section is the climax of Paul's exposition of his apostolic ministry, inasmuch as it calls the Corinthians to be reconciled with Christ's ambassador."[5]

The final unit (6:14–7:1) begins with another abrupt break in the flow of Paul's discourse. It consists of a strong warning against having too familiar association with unbelievers who would both hurt the Saints' spirituality and hinder the work. Apparently, such a condition is a major source of the problems that afflict the Corinthian church. Therefore, Paul demands total separation from these people. Using scripture, he lists God's promises for those willing to do so. Among these is the Father's readiness to accept these people in a filial relationship through which they become his sons and daughters. Based on that possibility, Paul ends this section with a strong appeal that they purify themselves, both soul and body. By using their awe-filled reverence for God, he tells them, they can achieve a state of holiness resulting in oneness with the Divine.

"Now Is the Day of Salvation" (6:1–2)

Greek Text

1 Συνεργοῦντες δὲ καὶ παρακαλοῦμεν μὴ εἰς κενὸν τὴν χάριν τοῦ θεοῦ δέξασθαι ὑμᾶς· 2 λέγει γάρ· Καιρῷ δεκτῷ ἐπήκουσά σου καὶ ἐν ἡμέρᾳ σωτηρίας ἐβοήθησά σοι· ἰδοὺ νῦν καιρὸς εὐπρόσδεκτος, ἰδοὺ νῦν ἡμέρα σωτηρίας. [SBLGNT]

King James Version

1 We then, as workers together with him, beseech you also that ye receive not the grace of God in vain. 2 (For he saith, I have heard thee in a time accepted, and in the day of salvation have I succoured thee: behold, now is the accepted time; behold, now is the day of salvation.)

New Rendition

1 Now since we are coworkers, we also urge you to not receive God's grace in vain. 2 For he says, "At a favorable time I heard you and in a day of salvation I helped you" [Isa. 49:8]. Look, now is "a very favorable time"; now is "a day of salvation"!

4. Guthrie, 2 *Corinthians,* 341.
5. Matera, *II Corinthians,* 160.

Translation Notes and Comments

6:1–2 Though the KJV places this section with what follows, the context itself shows that it is the conclusion of Paul's theological development in 5:18–21.[6]

6:1 ***as workers together with him / Now since we are coworkers:*** The Greek of this phrase is very brief: συνεργοῦντες δὲ (*synergountes de*), literally "now working together." The conjunction δέ (*de*) serves to connect one clause to another and can express contrast, "but," or simple continuation, "now, then, so, that is,"[7] as is the case here, where it connects 6:1 with 5:18–21.

The verb συνέργω (*synergō*) has the basic sense of "to work together with, assist, help."[8] Its form here is a plural present participle used circumstantially with a causative sense. Since the phrase has no pronoun to indicate who Paul and his companions are working together with, it could apply to the Corinthian Saints or to God. The KJV assumes the latter and thus has added the phrase "with him." On the other hand, Paul could have his readers in mind, in which case the translation should be "with all of you." In our translation, we have not added a pronoun, thus preserving the ambiguity. However, because Paul stated in 5:20 that he and his companions were representatives of God, it is most likely that he has the Father in mind here.[9]

We then, . . . beseech you also that ye receive not the grace of God in vain / we also urge you to not receive God's grace in vain: The conjunction καί (*kai*) is often translated as "and," but here it indicates an "additive relation" and is translated "also."[10] The verb παρακαλέω (*parakaleō*), "urge, exhort," carries the idea of making a strong appeal or request.[11]

The noun χάρις (*charis*), "grace," in this instance, denotes the specific favor and care of God for the Saints, through which reconciliation and ultimate salvation can come.[12]

---

6. Some scholars have followed the KJV, but from a pragmatic standpoint, as Guthrie, *2 Corinthians,* 315 n. 23, points out, this exhortation is "based on the theological substance of 5:18–21."

7. BDAG, 213.

8. BDAG, 969.

9. For discussion of this problem, see Martin, *2 Corinthians,* 326–27.

10. BDAG, 494–96.

11. BDAG, 764–65.

12. BDAG, 1079–81; Guthrie, *2 Corinthians,* 316. The noun χάρις (*charis*) denoted in New Testament times the giving of a gift that obligated the recipient to respond with some kind

The prepositional phrase εἰς κένον (*eis kenon*), "in vain," denotes a complete lack of result or effect.[13] The verb δέχομαι (*dechomai*), "to receive," found here as an aorist infinitive, generally denotes receiving something that is offered by another,[14] but in the present context it nuances an approval or conviction indicated by a willingness to receive what is offered.[15] That offering is the "grace of God."

6:2 ***For he saith / For he says:*** The reference here is to God and introduces a quote from LXX Isaiah 49:8. By using it, Paul gives emphasis to the truthfulness and importance of what he says next.

I have heard thee in a time accepted / At a favorable time I heard you: The noun καιρός (*kairos*), "time," refers to a specific period, often with the implication of it being especially fit or appropriate for something.[16] The adjective δεκτός (*dektos*), "favorable," carries the idea of something being pleasing or favorable because it is associated with what God approves.[17] The phrase καιρῷ δεκτῷ (*kairō dektō*) is a dative of time indicating a "time when" and under what conditions something was done.[18] In this case it is when God favors his people. The verb ἐπακούω (*epakouō*), "to hear," denotes listening with "the implication of being responsive"[19] and therefore intimates a willingness to respond to a need. The Masoretic Hebrew of the phrase, בְּעֵת רָצוֹן (*bĕʿēt rāṣôn*), "at a pleasing/favorable time,"[20] indicates the moment when all the necessary pieces come together so that Jehovah can bestow some blessing. As the next phrase shows, that blessing is God's help.

and in the day of salvation have I succoured thee / and in a day of salvation I helped you: The definite article found in the KJV is absent in the Greek text. Therefore, the phrase ἡμέρᾳ σωτηρίας (*hēmera sōtērias*), "a day

---

of token or reciprocal gift; otherwise the purpose of giving was in vain. The *charis* was often given in a covenantal context. For a study, see Schmidt, *Relational Grace,* who lists a number of examples of this practice in the first century.

13. BDAG, 539; Louw-Nida, §89.53. According to Guthrie, *2 Corinthians,* 317, the reference is to a "foolish response that fails to lead to an intended result."

14. BDAG, 221.

15. Louw-Nida, §31.51, notes that the word indicates the reception of information readily because it is regarded as true.

16. BDAG, 497. For a study of the noun καιρός (*kairos*) denoting the realization of salvation made possible by an actual historical event, see Oscar Cullmann, *Christ and Time: The Primitive Christian Conception of Time and History,* trans. Floyd V. Filson (Philadelphia: Westminster Press, 1950), 37–59.

17. BDAG, 217; *NID,* 1:675.

18. Wallace, *Greek Grammar,* 155–57.

19. BDAG, 358.

20. HAL, 899–902, 1282.

of salvation," does not point to the Final Judgment but to any time when God reaches out to his people because of their positive response to his will and their need for aid.

The noun σωτηρία (*sōtēria*), "salvation," denotes both temporal and spiritual deliverance from adversarial forces, be they satanic, physical, mortal, or temporal.[21]

The verb βοηθέω (*boētheō*), "to help, aid," denotes acting in order to relieve a person or people in distress.[22]

behold, now is the accepted time; behold, now is the day of salvation / Look, now is "a very favorable time"; now is "a day of salvation": With the promise of the scripture set before them, Paul makes his appeal using the temporal adverb νῦν (*nyn*), "now," twice. The word carries the nuance of "Pay attention! This is important!"[23] and stresses the urgency to act fast, for "there is no time to lose."[24] His first use of the word stresses that the present is one of the promised moments during which salvation is possible.[25]

He modifies the noun "time" with the adjective εὐπρόσδεκτος (*euprosdektos*), "very favorable." The root of the adjective is δεκτός (*dektos*), "favorable," found in the above phrase but with two prefixes added. The first, εὐ- (*eu-*), carries the sense of "well, thoroughly, fortunately, happily,"[26] and the second, πρός (*pros-*), carries the sense of "besides, over and above."[27] Hence, they combine to give the noun καιρός (*kairos*), "time," the quality of being "very favorable." Noteworthy is that Paul does not use the word σήμερον (*sēmeron*), "today," as does the author of Hebrews 3:7–19, but ἡμέρα (*hēmera*), "a day." In doing so, Paul broadens out the time period to include his dispensation, or the time when the gospel has again been restored to the earth.[28]

---

21. BDAG, 985–86; *NID,* 4:420–35, especially 431–32. The word did not, as some modern understanding suggests, indicate a mystical, passive, and immediate salvation experience.

22. BDAG, 180.

23. Guthrie, *2 Corinthians,* 318.

24. Martin, *2 Corinthians,* 330.

25. The context of the paraphrase is Isaiah 49. Though Isaiah refers to a later day of salvation, Paul does not feel bound by the same temporal constraints, and applies the scripture to the current situation. For a study, see Mark Gignilliat, "2 Corinthians 6:2: Paul's Eschatological 'Now' and Hermeneutical Investigation," *Westminster Theological Journal* 67, no. 1 (2005): 147–61.

26. LSJ, 704.

27. LSJ, 1499.

28. Bernard, "Second Epistle," 74. According to *DNTC,* 1:161, the acceptable day of the Lord is the day when salvation is available to men.

His second use of the adverb νῦν (*nyn*), "now," stresses why the present is so favorable. This is because it is the day in which salvation must be gained. These people live in the new-covenant era (3:6) initiated by the death and Resurrection of the Lord that *now* opens the opportunity for them to be saved.[29] But this opportunity demands an immediate response, or it will be lost, and Paul admonishes them not to let that happen.

Analysis and Summary

Having established the doctrine that reconciliation is possible between each person and God, Paul now makes his point. Since the Saints are living when God's grace is being extended, they must embrace it before it is too late. To bolster his plea, Paul quotes from LXX Isaiah 49:8. The setting of this verse in the Old Testament is the challenging ministry faced by the Servant of the Lord (Isa. 49–54). More specifically, this section (LXX Isa. 49:7–12) looks at both the role and the result of the Servant's ministry. Paul likely uses it to place his teachings in "the broader redemptive drama found in Isaiah 40–66, declaring how the covenant-keeping God draws a wayward people back to himself."[30] The Apostle understands fully how this is accomplished—namely, through the ministry and Atonement of Christ Jesus (2 Cor. 5:14–15).

Here Paul uses the scripture to highlight God's open invitation for the Saints to join him.[31] They, however, have a responsibility; they have to willingly receive that grace with full conviction.[32] There is, however, a message behind the message. It is tacitly implied by the adverb "now." It is that such a period is not indefinite, and therefore, Paul's readers must act immediately. His words show that even though the Divine reaches out in grace, the individual must accept it, otherwise God's effort has, unfortunately, neither result nor effect. The Apostle's words indicate that, though it is God, and he alone, who extends grace, it is up to each individual to receive it. God does not force his grace upon anyone because he is always respectful of their agency. However, "without a concrete human response, this *charis* ["grace"] remains just a theoretical possibility, albeit with dire

29. Guthrie, *2 Corinthians,* 319.

30. Guthrie, *2 Corinthians,* 317.

31. Isa. 49:8 with its companion scripture 61:2 indicate that the "acceptable time" is when God has put into position all that is necessary for him to accept humankind. Martin, *2 Corinthians,* 330.

32. Louw-Nida, §31.51, notes that the verb δέχομαι (*dechomai*) indicates the reception of information readily because it is regarded as true.

consequences for those who reject it, as Paul implies in his paraenetic call to the Corinthians."[33] The result of rejection leaves people in their very weak, mortal condition to follow their own devices and to reap the negative consequences that naturally follow.

Given the broader context in which this section lies, it is likely that Paul is addressing the need for the people not only to not miss the opportunity to be reconciled to God by receiving the outpouring of his grace unto salvation but also to live a life worthy of one who follows Christ (5:9–10, 14–15). He seems to be asking them to rededicate their lives to the Christian ideal that he has not only been preaching but also setting the example of (as he shows in 6:14–7:1).[34] God, working through Paul, is providing the Corinthians with the best possible prospect of accepting and living under his grace at that very moment.[35]

Paul's admonition at the end of 6:2 gives stress to his readers' need to act willingly and with full commitment without delay. The reason is that the present time, the "now," demands immediate action. The present holds the very favorable time to act, for God's grace is being extended, resulting in the present being the time of salvation. The phrase emphasizes Paul's urgency that the moment be not lost, likely due to his awareness of the all-too-rapidly approaching apostasy (2 Thes. 2:1–12; Acts 20:28–31). He is well aware that "a day of salvation" is coming to an end. When that happens, it will leave all who have not responded to his message, at least for the time being, unsaved.

---

33. Stephan J. Joubert, "Χάρις in Paul: An Investigation into the Apostle's 'Performative' Application of the Language of *Grace* within the Framework of His Theological Reflection on the Event/Process of Salvation," in *Salvation in the New Testament: Perspectives on Soteriology,* ed. Jan G. van der Watt (Leiden, Neth.: Brill, 2005), 204. See also Barrett, *Second Epistle,* 183. Accepting the *charis* either established or continued a relationship between giver and recipient, provided that the recipient returned some kind of gift. However, because of the possible asymmetrical status between the giver and recipient, the recipient's gift did not have to be of equal value. As Brent Schmidt's work *Relational Grace* has shown, Christians living in the first-century Mediterranean world understood that coming under God's grace obligated them to keep commandments and enter into covenant ordinances like baptism.

34. Martin, *2 Corinthians,* 331.

35. Martin, *2 Corinthians,* 331.

The Condition and Character of Paul's Mission (6:3–10)

Greek Text

3 μηδεμίαν ἐν μηδενὶ διδόντες προσκοπήν, ἵνα μὴ μωμηθῇ ἡ διακονία, 4 ἀλλ' ἐν
παντὶ συνιστάνοντες ἑαυτοὺς ὡς θεοῦ διάκονοι· ἐν ὑπομονῇ πολλῇ, ἐν θλίψεσιν,
ἐν ἀνάγκαις, ἐν στενοχωρίαις, 5 ἐν πληγαῖς, ἐν φυλακαῖς, ἐν ἀκαταστασίαις, ἐν
κόποις, ἐν ἀγρυπνίαις, ἐν νηστείαις, 6 ἐν ἁγνότητι, ἐν γνώσει, ἐν μακροθυμίᾳ,
ἐν χρηστότητι, ἐν πνεύματι ἁγίῳ, ἐν ἀγάπῃ ἀνυποκρίτῳ, 7 ἐν λόγῳ ἀληθείας, ἐν
δυνάμει θεοῦ· διὰ τῶν ὅπλων τῆς δικαιοσύνης τῶν δεξιῶν καὶ ἀριστερῶν, 8 διὰ
δόξης καὶ ἀτιμίας, διὰ δυσφημίας καὶ εὐφημίας· ὡς πλάνοι καὶ ἀληθεῖς, 9 ὡς ἀγνο-
ούμενοι καὶ ἐπιγινωσκόμενοι, ὡς ἀποθνῄσκοντες καὶ ἰδοὺ ζῶμεν, ὡς παιδευόμε-
νοι καὶ μὴ θανατούμενοι, 10 ὡς λυπούμενοι ἀεὶ δὲ χαίροντες, ὡς πτωχοὶ πολλοὺς
δὲ πλουτίζοντες, ὡς μηδὲν ἔχοντες καὶ πάντα κατέχοντες. [SBLGNT]

King James Version

3 Giving no offence in any thing, that
the ministry be not blamed: 4 But in
all things approving ourselves as the
ministers of God, in much patience,
in afflictions, in necessities, in dis-
tresses, 5 In stripes, in imprisonments,
in tumults, in labours, in watchings, in
fastings; 6 By pureness, by knowledge,
by longsuffering, by kindness, by the
Holy Ghost, by love unfeigned, 7 By
the word of truth, by the power of God,
by the armour of righteousness on the
right hand and on the left, 8 By hon-
our and dishonour, by evil report and
good report: as deceivers, and yet true;
9 As unknown, and yet well known; as
dying, and, behold, we live; as chas-
tened, and not killed; 10 As sorrowful,
yet alway rejoicing; as poor, yet making
many rich; as having nothing, and yet
possessing all things.

New Rendition

3 We do not give any offense to any-
one so that no fault may be found with
our ministry. 4 But in everything we
show ourselves to be God's ministers:
with great endurance, in tribulations,
in troubles, in difficulties, 5 with beat-
ings, with imprisonments, with mob-
bings, with hardships, with lack of sleep,
with hunger; 6 by purity, by knowledge,
by patience, by kindness, by the Holy
Ghost, by genuine love, 7 by truthful
speech, by God's power; by means of
weapons of righteousness in the right
hand and the left; 8 through glory and
dishonor, through slander and praise;
viewed as deceivers yet honest; 9 as
unknown yet well-known, as dying yet
we are alive, as scourged yet not put to
death, 10 as sorrowful yet ever rejoicing,
as poor yet making many rich, as having
nothing yet possessing everything.

Translation Notes and Comments

6:3 *Giving no offence in any thing / We do not give any offense to anyone:* With this verse, Paul begins his defense of the nature of the actions both he and his fellow missionaries have taken. The focus in this clause is on their attempt not to displease or affront anyone. The noun προσκοπή (*proskopē*) refers to "an occasion for taking offense."[36] It is modified by the adjective μηδείς (*mēdeis*), "not one, not even one."[37] Paul gives the adjective emphatic force by placing it first in the sentence, thus indicating that he and his coworkers try not to give even a single offense! The nuance of the noun is not of offenses that the spiritually blind or publicly hostile might take toward the gospel but rather of actions, misjudgments, or missteps that could offend moral or cultural sensibilities. Here Paul insists he has never deliberately given offense in anything that he has done.

The verb δίδωμι (*didōmi*), "to give," found here as a present active participle, we have translated as a finite verb with the understood subject ἡμεῖς (*hēmeis*), "we," for clarity and to better conform to contemporary English usage. The tense of the participle likely acts as a customary present, denoting a current pattern of behavior that is ongoing.[38]

The adjective μηδείς (*mēdeis*), "not any, no," is used twice in this clause. The first instance is μηδεμίαν (*mēdemian*), which modifies the noun προσκοπήν (*proskopēn*), "offense," giving the meaning "no offense." In the second instance is the prepositional phrase ἐν μηδενί (*en mēdeni*), where it is used pronominally in the dative. The meaning is ambiguous since *mēdeni* could be either masculine or neuter, so either "to anyone" or "in anything" could be meant. The KJV takes it as neuter, hence its translation, "in anything." But given the context,[39] it is better to take it as masculine since that is much more likely. Thus we have rendered the phrase as "not . . . anyone."

that the ministry be not blamed / so that no fault may be found with our ministry: Here Paul gives the reason why he has been careful in all his actions. The verb μωμάομαι (*mōmaomai*) means "to find fault, criticize, or

36. BDAG, 882.

37. LSJ, 1125; BDAG, 647.

38. Guthrie, *2 Corinthians,* 325, n. 3. Some note it "durative in nature." Martin, *2 Corinthians,* 331 n. 924.

39. The noun προσκοπήν (*proskopēn*) denotes a cause of stumbling (BDAG, 882) while the related noun πρόσκομμα (*proskomma*) denotes a stone that does so (BDAG, 882). Since the stumbler is a person, the translation of ἐν μηδενί (*en mēdeni*) as "anyone" rather than "anything" seems best.

mock."[40] Paul's use of the word reveals the cloud of suspicion his detractors have been able to raise concerning his authority and legitimacy.[41]

The noun διακονία (*diakonia*), "ministry, service," can denote any service given within a community, but in this case, it references the work of those who, by the command of God, proclaim and promote his message among the people.[42] There is an important variant to this phrase. Some texts add the pronoun ἡμῶν (*hēmōn*), "our,"[43] thus limiting "the ministry" to the work of Paul and his companions. This reading is likely the more correct since the Apostle is defending not himself here but his position and teachings, and thus we use it in our Rendition.[44]

6:4–10 Paul begins, with 6:4, a section of emotive writing that follows its own logic but in doing so creates a uniform whole that packs quite a punch. It does contain an uneven use of two prepositions and an adverb, making precise interpretation more challenging. The Apostle lists difficulty after difficulty that he and his fellow missionaries have faced. The first set of difficulties he introduces with the preposition ἐν (*en*), "in" or "with" (6:4–7a); the second with the preposition διά (*dia*), "by" or "through" (6:7b–8a); and the final set with the adverb ὡς (*hōs*), "as" or "like" (6:8b–10). Making the switches keeps the rhythm and force of his argument moving and allows him to highlight each difficulty. Though we have done our best to express the force of the Greek, its power cannot be fully captured in translation.

6:4 ***But in all things approving ourselves as the ministers of God / But in everything we show ourselves to be God's ministers***: The verb συνίστημι (*synistēmi*), "to show," is here used with the sense "to provide evidence of a personal characteristic or claim through action," thus "to demonstrate, show," with the objective of forming a friendly and trusting relationship.[45] It is found here as a present active participle used circumstantially, indicating a pattern of behavior.[46] We have translated it as a finite present tense in our Rendition and added the understood subject ἡμεῖς (*hēmeis*), "we."

---

40. BDAG, 663.

41. The word appears only one other time in the New Testament (8:20), in which it also indicates Paul's ministry was suspect. Martin, *2 Corinthians,* 332.

42. BDAG, 230.

43. These belong to the Western Text family, D F G it vg sr. The definite article found in the other manuscripts does point to the new covenant that Paul and his companions have been mercifully granted and have been assigned to extend to others. As a result, the possibility that this is the correct reading should be considered. Martin, *2 Corinthians,* 321 n. c.

44. Martin, *2 Corinthians,* 332.

45. BDAG, 972.

46. Guthrie, *2 Corinthians,* 325, n. 3.

For an analysis of the noun διάκονος (*diakonos*), "minister," see Translation Notes for 3:6. Here Paul is referring to persons who have been empowered by God to carry out his work, but the emphasis is on the unimpeachable but very challenging life such empowerment demands. The overall effect of the word is that of a positive self-commendation. The genitive form of the word may be taken in two ways: either these servants belong to God (genitive of possession), or they are sent from God (genitive of source). Either way, the phrase shows that God stands behind his missionaries.[47]

in much patience / with great endurance: The noun ὑπομονή (*hypomonē*), "endurance, patience," denotes "the capacity to hold out or bear up in the face of difficulties" and thereby carries such additional nuances as "fortitude" and "perseverance."[48] The noun "patience" entails calmness and composure in situations that are provocative, stressful, or painful, while the noun "endurance" connotes "stamina and firmness of mind."[49] Because the Apostle seldom exhibited the former qualities but did the latter, "endurance" seems the better rendition.

The adjective πολύς (*polys*), "many, much, great," acts as a marker for the highest degree of something.[50] Here it modifies "endurance," thus stressing the heaviness of the weight the Apostle and his companions continually and unrelentingly bear.

in afflictions / in tribulations: The noun θλίψις (*thlipsis*), "tribulation, affliction," denotes any situation that produces distress.[51] While "affliction" refers to imposed suffering that challenges a person's endurance, "tribulation" refers to a trial of endurance or patience with a heightened sense of suffering and anguish.[52] The latter seems to best carry Paul's intent here.

in necessities / in troubles: The noun ἀνάγκη (*anankē*) denotes a state of distress or trouble, whether imposed by external or internal pressures.[53]

in distresses / in difficulties: The noun στενοχωρία (*stenochōria*), literally "narrowness," denotes "a set of stressful circumstances," thus "distress, difficulty, anguish, trouble."[54]

47. Guthrie, *2 Corinthians*, 326.
48. BDAG, 1039–40.
49. *Dictionary of Synonyms*, s.v. "patience"; "bear," definition 3.
50. BDAG, 847–48.
51. BDAG, 457–58.
52. *Dictionary of Synonyms*, s.v. "trial."
53. BDAG, 60–61.
54. BADG, 943.

6:5 *In stripes / with beatings:* The noun πληγή (*plēgē*) denotes a wound caused by a blow.[55] As 11:24–25 states, Paul was whipped five times, beaten with rods three times, and, according to Acts 14:19, also stoned nearly to death.

imprisonments: The noun φυλακή (*phylakē*), "prison,"[56] denotes a place for guarding people. Such could be pits, caves, or cells. In Roman times, the δεσμωτήριον (*desmōntērion*), "jail," consisted of several compartments, with the central one being the most unpleasant but most secure.

Greco-Roman society did not see imprisonment in and of itself as a means of punishment. Such consisted of, among other actions, death, mutilation, flogging, banishment, ostracism, forfeiture of possessions, or fining. People living during New Testament times did not conceive prison as being a place where persons were reformed before re-entering society but where they were held before and during trials or while they arranged to pay imposed debts and meet other obligations to society or to other persons. Prisoners usually had to supply their own food and bedding, along with other necessities and comforts.[57] Paul was imprisoned in Ephesus, Philippi, Caesarea Maritima, and Rome, but as a citizen he must have received better treatment than most.[58]

tumults / mobbings: The verb ἀκαταστασία (*akatastasia*) denotes "opposition to established authority," thus "disorder, anarchy,"[59] and carries a nuance of unlawful, seditious, or rebellions actions.[60] Due to that nuance, we have translated the word as "mobbings."[61] Paul was attacked by unruly crowds a number of times, some leading to bodily injury (see Acts 13:50; 14:5; 16:22; 17:5; 19:29–30; 21:30–31).

labours / hardships: The noun κόπος (*kopos*), "trouble, difficulty, hardship," denotes "a state of discomfort or distress."[62] Paul had to perform hard manual labor as he hiked from place to place, particularly in Corinth, as he labored to sustain himself so as not to be a burden upon the Saints there (see Acts 18:3 and 1 Cor. 4:12).

---

55. BDAG, 825.

56. BDAG, 1067–68.

57. W. L. Liefield, "Prison, Prisoner," in *Zondervan Pictorial Encyclopedia of the Bible*, ed. Merrill C. Tenney and Steven Barabas, 5 vols. (Grand Rapids: Zondervan, 1975–76), 4:869–70; Karel van der Toorn, "Prison," in *ABD*, 5:468–69.

58. Wayment, *From Persecutor to Apostle*, viii–xi.

59. BDAG, 35; LSJ, 48.

60. Louw-Nida, §§39.34, 36.

61. BDAG, 35, notes that, in this context, it likely refers to mob action.

62. BDAG, 558.

watchings / lack of sleep: The noun ἀγρυπνία (*agrypnia*) denotes "sleeplessness" either from anxiety or external circumstances.[63]

fastings / hunger: The noun νηστεία (*nēsteia*), "hunger," is most often used in the scriptures to refer to voluntary fasting for religious purposes, but given the parallel idea in 11:27, the present context suggests Paul meant going hungry "brought about by necessity" (see also 1 Cor. 4:11).[64]

6:6 ***By pureness / by purity:*** The noun ἁγνότης (*hagnotēs*) carries the sense of "moral purity and blamelessness."[65] The New Testament lists its cognate, the adjective ἁγνός (*hagnos*), "pure, holy,"[66] as an attribute of Jesus (1 John 3:3), a virtue to be carefully considered (Philip. 4:8) and one of the important standards of a Christian life (1 Pet. 3:2). Paul demanded this quality of those who bore office in the Christian community (1 Tim. 5:22).[67]

knowledge: The noun γνῶσις (*gnōsis*), "knowledge," denotes both "the intellectual grasp of something" and "the content" of what is grasped.[68] There are degrees of knowledge determined by the depth of study, observations, investigations, and experiences of the person plus the inferences that the person draws from these. In the present context, it "refers specifically to understanding of the Scriptures."[69]

longsuffering / patience: The noun μακροθυμία (*makrothymia*) here denotes the "state of being able to bear up under provocation," thus "forbearance, patience."[70]

kindness: The noun χρηστότης (*chrēstotēs*) describes usefulness or "the quality of being helpful or beneficial," thus "goodness, kindness, generosity." Together with its cognate adjective χρηστός (*chrēstos*), it is used to describe an attribute of both God and the best of humankind.[71] It was a very common name for slaves. Its pronunciation in Koine Greek was also very similar to Χριστός (*Christos*, Christ) and was thus probably associated with the Savior.

63. BDAG, 16; Louw-Nida, §23.73.

64. BDAG, 671–72.

65. Friedrich Hauck, "ἁγνός, ἁγνότης," in *TDNT*, 1:124; BDAG, 13; Bernard, "Second Epistle," 76.

66. BDAG, 13.

67. Hauck, "ἁγνός, ἁγνότης," in *TDNT*, 1:122–24.

68. BDAG, 203–4.

69. BDAG, 203. The λόγος γνώσεως (*logos gnōseōs*), "word of knowledge," is one of the gifts of the Spirit. See 1 Cor. 12:8.

70. BDAG, 612–13. Paul also ascribes the virtue to God. See Rom. 2:4; 11:22; Eph. 2:7; and Titus 3:4.

71. BDAG, 1090. See also Konard Weiss, "χρηστότης," in *TDNT*, 9:489–92.

Whether to translate it as "kindness" or "goodness" is difficult to decide. The English word "goodness" is quite broad, denoting "an excellence so deeply established that it is often felt as inherent or innate rather than acquired or instilled" and includes such virtues as kindness and generosity.[72] The English word "kindness" is less broad, denoting "a nature that is gentle, considerate, and inclined" to benevolence or beneficence that includes both acts and utterances.[73] In this context, it seemed to us that "kindnesses" had the better feel.

the Holy Spirit / the Holy Ghost: This phrase refers to the influence of the Holy Ghost, the third member of the Godhead. The context of the phrase centers on those internal attributes and virtues of a Christian minister. As such, the phrase denotes the power and gifts that flow through this member of the Godhead to the worthy individual as a result of baptism and confirmation.[74]

love unfeigned / genuine love: The noun ἀγάπη (*agapē*), with its cognate verb ἀγαπάω (*agapaō*), describes "a warm regard for and interest in another" and a deep affection and high regard for others and, within the Christian context, can also describe the love of and for God and Christ.[75]

The adjective ἀνυπόκριτος (*anypokritos*), "genuine, unfeigned," in the present context, denotes a feeling that is without pretense.[76] This emotion is sincere and authentic, being exactly what it purports to be. The whole phrase emphasizes a pureness of love toward another person, motivated by altruistic reasons and devoid of any self-interest.

6:7 ***By the word of truth / by truthful speech:*** The noun λόγος (*logos*), "speech, word," denotes the verbal means by which the mind finds expression.[77] That can include what is false, speculated, or true. The noun ἀλήθεια (*alētheia*) refers to "the quality of being in accord with what is true."[78] The phrase stresses the accuracy, reliability, and inspiration behind what the missionaries speak.

---

72. *Dictionary of Synonyms,* s.v., "goodness."

73. *Dictionary of Synonyms,* s.v., "kind."

74. See Jerry A. Wilson, "Holy Spirit," in *EM,* 2:651; and Joseph Fielding McConkie, "Holy Ghost," in *EM,* 1:649–51. For a study of the Pauline understanding of the nature and work of the Holy Spirit, see F. W. Horn, "Holy Spirit," in *ABD,* 3:271–80.

75. BDAG, 6.

76. BDAG, 91.

77. BDAG, 598–601.

78. BDAG, 42.

the power of God / by God's power: Paul uses this phrase, δυνάμει θεοῦ (*dynamei theou*), in connection with the authority that stands behind the preaching of the gospel and more particularly the Lord's Atonement (Rom. 1:16; 1 Cor. 1:18, 24).

by the armour of righteousness on the right hand and on the left / by means of weapons of righteousness in the right hand and the left: The noun ὅπλον (*hoplon*), "weapon," refers to any defensive or offensive instrument used in a military operation.[79]

The noun δικαιοσύνη (*dikaiosynē*) denotes "the quality or characteristic of upright behavior, uprightness, righteousness."[80] In Romans 6:13, Paul uses a similar phrase, ὅπλων τῆς δικαιοσύνης (*hoplōn tēs dikaiosynēs*), "weapons of righteousness," to denote the power of the disciplined physical body as a means of serving God. In the present context, it seems to describe all the tactics and means used by the missionaries to win souls to God and to protect both themselves and the believing community from detractors and enemies.

The adjective δεξιός (*dexios*) denotes "right,"[81] while ἀριστερός (*aristeros*) denotes "left."[82] The Greek text has no object, but "hand" is implied, which we supply in our Rendition. The Greek idiom denotes weapons that are used for both offense and defense that often consisted of the sword in the right hand and the shield in the left (compare Eph. 6:11–17; 1 Thes. 5:8).[83]

6:8 *By honour and dishonour / through glory and dishonor:* The noun δόξα (*doxa*), "glory," in the present context, denotes the opinion people have of something, or its reputation, "fame, recognition, renown."[84] Many caught up in the honor/fame culture of the day sought for glory above all else, and even the Jews did not escape its effects.[85]

The noun ἀτιμία (*atimia*) denotes conditions ranging from disgrace through ignominy and stands opposite "glory." Many in the honor-conscious society of that day felt that bringing dishonor to self, family, or others was abhorrent. Those who fell under such shame were often maltreated.[86]

---

79. BDAG, 716.
80. BDAG, 248.
81. BDAG, 217.
82. BDAG, 131.
83. Bernard, "Second Epistle," 76; BDAG, 131.
84. BDAG, 256–58; Louw-Nida, §§33.357; 87.4, 23.
85. *NID,* 1:761–767, especially 765–66.
86. BDAG, 149.

by evil report and good report / through slander and praise: The noun δυσφημία (*dysphēmia*), "slander, defamation," denotes "the act of detracting from or damaging another's reputation,"[87] while the noun εὐφημιά (*euphēmia*) denotes the giving of a favorable report about someone.[88]

as deceivers, and yet true / viewed as deceivers yet honest: The verb "viewed," is not in the Greek text but we added it to our Rendition for clarity. Paul replaces the preposition, διά (*dia*), "through," used in the comparisons above with the comparative adverb ὡς (*hos*), "as." The conjunction καί (*kai*), usually translated "and," here emphasizes a fact that is surprising or unexpected, thus we have translated it here as "yet."[89] The adjective πλάνος (*planos*), "deceitful," here acting as a substantive, refers to one considered to be a deceiver or imposter.[90] The adjective ἀληθής (*alēthēs*) denotes what conforms to reality, including what is honest, upright, and truthful.[91]

6:9 ***as unknown yet well known:*** The verb ἀγνοέω (*agnoeō*), "unknown," found here as a present passive participle, can refer to people who are unidentified or obscure. The word also carries the inference of persons "without proper credentials."[92] This was one of the main attacks Paul's antagonists used against him (3:1–2). The verb ἐπιγινώσκω (*epiginōskō*) means "to know completely, recognize,"[93] and thus indicates one who is familiar to many.

as dying, and, behold, we live / as dying yet we are alive: The verb ἀποθνήσκω (*apothnēskō*), to "die," found here in the form of a present participle, carries the idea of facing death with the action in process.[94] The grammar points to the mortal danger (of one kind or another) that the missionaries continually and unrelentingly face.

The phrase καὶ ἰδοὺ ζῶμεν (*kai idou zōmen*), "yet we are alive," carries a sense of irony. Though the threat of death is very real and ever present, it has, almost surprisingly, never been able to take them.

---

87. BDAG, 265.
88. BDAG, 414.
89. BDAG, 494.
90. BDAG, 822.
91. BDAG, 43; Louw-Nida, §§70.3; 72.1.
92. Bernard, "Second Epistle," 76; BDAG, 12–13.
93. BDAG, 369.
94. BDAG, 111; Smyth, *Greek Grammar,* 1872.a.3.

as chastened, and not killed / as scourged yet not put to death: The verb παιδεύω (*paideuō*) has nuances that range from gentle teaching through moderate admonishing and strict chastising to cruel scourging. It primarily refers to those methods used to teach children, including general instruction, reprimand, and punishment. Blows, when necessary, would also be invoked. The most severe nuance would be of the brutal act of scourging.[95]

The verb θανατόω (*thanatoō*), "to die," found here as a present passive participle, means "to be put to death."[96] Due to scourging often being a prelude to death by crucifixion, and following Paul's strong imagery, we have translated παιδέω (*paideuō*) with the verb "scourge." The idea certainly suggests how painful and hard to bear Paul felt his life was. The continual accusations with the mistrust they generated were mentally like being continually scourged. His words echo that of LXX Psalm 117:18 (Ps. 118:18, KJV), where the Psalmist declares, "The Lord has sorely chastened me, but he has not given me over unto death" (our translation).

6:10 ***As sorrowful, yet alway rejoicing / as sorrowful yet ever rejoicing:*** The verb λυπέω (*lypeō*), "to feel sorrow," found here as a present passive participle, means to be placed in a state of sorrow, sadness, or distress.[97]

On the other hand, the verb χαίρω (*chairō*), "to rejoice," found here as a present active participle, denotes being in a state of happiness or gladness that causes one to rejoice.[98] In the New Testament context, this near-euphoric state is grounded in the uplifting aspects of the gospel of Jesus Christ.[99] For Paul, this state takes on the dimension of a Christian duty he gladly performs (see 1:24; 7:4).

as poor, yet making many rich: The adjective πτωχός (*ptōchos*), "poor," denotes not just the lack of material goods but also the dependence one must have on others for one's sustenance. Thus, the word carries the nuance of having to beg.[100]

The verb πλουτίζω (*ploutizō*), "to be rich," found here as a present participle, refers to making someone else rich.[101] In this case it refers to the heavenly riches that Paul and his companions have brought to their converts

---

95. For a study of the range and uses of the word, see Georg Bertram, "παιδεύω," in *TDNT*, 5:596–625.

96. BDAG, 443–44.

97. BDAG, 604.

98. BDAG, 1074–75.

99. Conzelmann, "χαίρω, χαρά, συγχαίρω," in *TDNT*, 9:359–71.

100. BDAG, 896.

101. BDAG, 831.

(see 1 Cor. 1:5; compare Matt. 5:3; Paul's imagery seems to be based on Prov. 13:7). The way Paul juxtaposes the words in this phrase emphasizes the irony of his situation and highlights his point.

having nothing, and yet possessing all things / as having nothing yet possessing everything: The nominalized neuter adjective μηδέν (*mēden*), "nothing,"[102] in the present context, looks to worldly possessions. That Paul often had to work while serving as a missionary as well as receive benefices from the branches suggests his lack of sustained earthly goods.

The verb κατέχω (*katechō*), found here as a present active participle, means "to keep in one's possession, possess."[103] The nuance that the verb carries suggests the value or importance of the thing possessed. Paul describes what he possesses with the adjective πάντα (*panta*), "all things," which emphasizes the wholeness, fullness, or totality of what he has been given.[104] Paul has already witnessed to these people that "everything belongs to you, whether Paul or Apollos or Cephas or the world or life or death, or the present or the future, everything belongs to you, and you belong to Christ, and Christ belongs to God" (1 Cor. 3:21–23, NR).[105]

Analysis and Summary

This section (6:3–10) marks a rather abrupt change in Paul's focus. Just before, he was admonishing the Corinthians to be reconciled to God, and then suddenly he begins a long catalogue of his credentials. Though the transition is abrupt, the content of this section actually continues a theme that he has been developing beginning in 2:14—namely, the nature of an authentic ministry. This section ties directly to the desire he expressed in 5:18 to give the Corinthian Saints a reason to be proud of him and his associates. Thus, the catalogue of his hardships, along with his list of the manner and means of the ministry, all show his excellence as a disciple of the Savior and lay the foundation for his beloved converts to appreciate

102. BDAG, 647.

103. BDAG, 532–33.

104. Louw-Nida, §§59.23; 63.2; 78.44.

105. See David L. Mealand, "'As Having Nothing and yet Possessing Everything': 2 Kor 6:10c," *Zeitschrift für die neutestamentliche Wissenschaft und die Kunde der Alteren Kirche* 67 (1976): 277–79. He concludes that the phrase is Stoic, showing that "Paul uses occasional ideas and sentences of this kind. But he builds them into a theological and ethical framework which is quite different from that of the philosophers," thus showing he "is influenced by the language but not the thought of his Hellenistic contemporaries."

and even be proud of him.[106] Thus, it is not surprising that here we find "a characteristic outburst of impassioned eloquence on a topic in which the Apostle [feels] an intense personal interest. But its [fervor] has not been permitted to interfere with the careful choice of words: the balanced antithesis, the rhythmic cadences and assonances, which abound throughout, betray the literary training of the writer."[107]

That Paul does not list the influence of "the Holy Ghost" until verse 6 seems odd, since this gift is paramount and often a precursor, if not the generator, of the other virtues and would seem best to be named first. Paul does not, however, order these virtues by their importance or other logical considerations but rather by the "sound and rhythm" each produces.[108]

He lists here those characteristics that are the basis of a true and valid commendation (see 3:1) by which authentic ministers can be known. The description breaks into four units: (1) the outward hardships (6:4b–5), (2) the inward and saintly characteristics (6:6–7a), (3) the armor of righteousness whether well or ill spoken of (6:7b–8ab), and (4) the characteristics just the opposite of those Paul's detractors ascribe to him (6:8c–10).[109]

In 5:3, the Apostle stresses that he and the others are striving to behave in such a way that no one should have been able to take cultural or public offense at anything he or his companions have done. The reason they have acted as they did, he emphasizes, is to avoid bringing any justified criticism of the ministry. He then, on the flipside of the argument, states what they *have* done—namely, "in everything we show ourselves to be God's ministers" (6:4a, NR).[110] His point is that he and his companions have both acted appropriately in social and cultural ways and exemplified the laudatory pattern of life expected of the Lord's servants. By providing this imposing list of evidence of the validity of the ministry that he and his coworkers have carried out, Paul picks up a vitally important thread that he has been weaving and continues to weave throughout his epistle (3:1; 4:2; 5:12; 10:12, 18; 12:11), and one that is at the heart of his contentions with the fractious branch of the Corinthian

106. Guthrie, *2 Corinthians,* 321.

107. Bernard, "Second Epistle," 75, who also notes that this section carries the same beautiful compositional style as do Rom. 8:31–39 and 1 Cor. 13:1–13 and suggests Paul's acquaintance with "Stoic paradoxes" associated with the skill and competence of the ideal sage.

108. Bernard, "Second Epistle," 76.

109. Bernard, "Second Epistle," 75. Each unit is marked by both thematic development and a change in introductory prepositions. The first two units use ἐν (*en,* "in"), the third διά (*dia,* "through"), and the fourth ὡς (*hōs,* "as"). Guthrie, *2 Corinthians,* 321–22.

110. The verb translated a "show" is συνίστημι (*synistēmi*), which, in this context, has the sense "to provide evidence of a personal characteristic." BDAG, 972–73.

Christians—namely, whether he really needs to prove the validity of his ministry to these people given all he has given of himself for their sake.[111]

Paul's antagonists may have argued that his ministry did not paint a picture of an effective, successful, and blessed work. All his suffering and sacrificing seems to suggest just the opposite. In presenting his list as credentials of an authentic and faithful ministry, Paul "offers a countercultural picture of 'success' when it comes to carrying out God's work in the world, one that follows in the footsteps of the Suffering Servant, whose authentic ministry led to the cross. Such a ministry makes clear the power of God rather than the prominence of the individual. In carrying around 'the dying of Jesus' in his ministry, Paul points to Jesus's life in a way that marks [Paul's] ministry as an exemplar of true Christian mission (4:7–12)."[112]

It would appear the Apostle is concerned with more than mere finger pointing. His message, after all, was continually inalienably offensive, being based on the ignominy of the cross (1 Cor. 1:23), and for it he took a lot of heat (Gal. 5:11). Rather, his concern may have been that some were trying to make his ministry that of a fool (that is, a senseless or absurd person; see 11:16) because, given his physical weakness and continual state of distress, it did not seem to come with divine sanction. He needed to convince his larger audience that his work did not lead people (whether believers or nonbelievers) away from God. If his detractors could prove his work did so, he should indeed be an object of ridicule. He simply could not let that happen.[113] His defense is, therefore, that he has done nothing by way of self-promotion and has been open and transparent in all his dealings and teachings. Thus, his ministry should stand clear of any disparagement.[114] In sum, this portion of the epistle goes a long way toward affirming the Apostle's work, ministry, and especially teachings.[115] To emphasize what living in such a way has cost, Paul lists, in two sets of phrases, all that he and the others have endured for the sake of the ministry.

The first set (6:4b) looks at what Paul and the others have had to suffer generally—namely, tribulations, distresses, and calamities. Common to all the words in this set is the idea of pressure and confinement, with each one listed becoming ever narrower with the last suggesting no room for movement or escape.[116] It is little wonder, then, that Paul emphasizes that what

111. Guthrie, *2 Corinthians,* 325.
112. Guthrie, *2 Corinthians,* 326.
113. Martin, *2 Corinthians,* 332.
114. Martin, *2 Corinthians,* 333.
115. Guthrie, *2 Corinthians,* 325.
116. Bernard, "Second Epistle," 75.

he and his people had to deal with required "great endurance" (ὑπομονὴ πολλή, *hypomonē pollē*).

The next set (6:5a), beatings, imprisonments, and mobbings, appears to relate to unpleasant, even dangerous, encounters met by Paul and the others as they acted as missionaries. The following set (6:5b), hard unavoidable work, anxious sleeplessness, and hunger, gives a feeling for the bodily hardships they voluntarily endured for the ministry.

Having catalogued the sufferings that he and his companions have endured, the Apostle next presents two sets of traits or qualities he and his companions have striven to emulate. The first set (6:6a) enumerates four of those inward qualities that Christian ministers should display in order to best commend themselves—namely, purity, knowledge, forbearance, and kindness, all of which describe aspects of the inner being. The first denotes an uprightness in a person's life that expresses itself in moral faultlessness. The second suggests a testimony or inborn witness that has a Spirit-derived depth, breadth, and sureness. The third denotes the ability "to bear up against provocation." And the final one refers to a virtue that encompasses the whole nature of the Saint, causing her or him to be mellow, gentle, charming, calm, and agreeable. These virtues become the seed of enduring friendships.

The next set of traits (6:6b–7a) Paul describes with just two words each and in doing so keeps the rhythm of his piece moving. Those traits—the gifts associated with the possession of the Holy Ghost, genuine love, truthfulness, and godly power—go to the heart of what the gospel is all about. Though the "good news" centers on overcoming death and hell, it is how these are accomplished that is the central message that the missionaries proclaim and that touches, draws, and holds both the investigator and member. An indispensable characteristic of the message is its truthfulness. This truthfulness can be authenticated by what it produces. This includes the other three virtues and the supernal traits Paul lists here.

Having finished his list of Christian virtues, the Apostle next responds to the two ways people have treated him (6:7b–9a). He begins each clause with the preposition διά (*dia*), "by" or "through," identifying the means by which the acts were done. Almost from the beginning of his ministry, he has faced opposition, distrust, slander, and misrepresentation. He has not taken these lightly (note his response in 1 Cor. 4:12–13), and though he has defended himself—sometimes with a rather sharp quill—his motives have always been driven by the hope of winning people over through sincere caring. Many have positively responded to his attempts, even defending him. Here he contrasts these two very different responses, one consisting of the attacks made against him by his detractors and the other consisting of the defense made by his friends in his behalf. Nothing stops him. He ministers through dishonor and glory as well as slander and praise. He has been viewed as a deceiver while actually being true to his mission and has been branded a nobody without credentials while actually being well-known and validated by God.

The final section (6:9b–10) looks at the physical conditions under which Paul labored and his attitude concerning them. He faced not only the continual threat of death but also the pain and sorrow attached to an unappreciated ministry along with the lack of temporal resources that can make life easier. Yet he rejoiced that despite the threat of death and the accompanying pain, even anguish, that it caused, he yet lived, possessed the fullness of the gospel, and thereby made others rich in spiritual power and knowledge.

Paul's Appeal to the Corinthian Saints (6:11–13)

Greek Text

11 Τὸ στόμα ἡμῶν ἀνέῳγεν πρὸς ὑμᾶς, Κορίνθιοι, ἡ καρδία ἡμῶν πεπλάτυνται·
12 οὐ στενοχωρεῖσθε ἐν ἡμῖν, στενοχωρεῖσθε δὲ ἐν τοῖς σπλάγχνοις ὑμῶν· 13 τὴν
δὲ αὐτὴν ἀντιμισθίαν, ὡς τέκνοις λέγω, πλατύνθητε καὶ ὑμεῖς. [SBLGNT]

King James Version

11 O ye Corinthians, our mouth is open unto you, our heart is enlarged. 12 Ye are not straitened in us, but ye are straitened in your own bowels. 13 Now for a recompence in the same, (I speak as unto my children,) be ye also enlarged.

New Rendition

11 O Corinthians, our mouth is open to you; our heart is open wide. 12 There is no restraint in our affection for you, but there is restraint in your affection for us. 13 As a fair exchange—I speak as to my own children—open wide your heart also.

Translation Notes and Comments

6:11 ***O Corinthians:*** The phrase introduces a plea.

our mouth is open unto you / our mouth is open to you: The noun στόμα (*stoma*), "mouth,"[117] when used metaphorically, refers to speaking.[118] The

117. BDAG, 946–47.
118. Louw-Nida, §§33.74, 101.

idiom "to speak with an open mouth" denotes being "completely open with, to conceal nothing from, to speak the whole truth" to others.[119]

our heart is enlarged / our heart is open wide: The noun καρδία (*kardia*), "heart," when used metaphorically, as noted in 3:15, connotes the very core of the person. It is here where we find both the rational and emotional elements that define all that the person is.[120]

The verb πλατύνω (*platynō*), found here in the perfect tense, means "to cause something to be broad, to enlarge," and in the passive voice, as here, "to be enlarged, to open wide."[121] With the use of the perfect tense, Paul stresses the continuous nature of his deep affection for the members of his audience.[122]

6:12 ***Ye are not straitened in us, but ye are straitened in your own bowels / There is no restraint in our affection for you, but there is restraint in your affection for us:*** The Greek of this sentence translates literally "You are not restricted in us, rather you are restricted in your own hearts." The verb στενοχωρέω (*stenochōreō*), "restraint," in the passive voice, as found here, means "to be confined, restricted."[123] The noun σπλάγχνον (*splangchnon*), "affection," refers literally to "the inward parts of the body," but it is often used metaphorically, especially in the plural, as here, for "love, affection."[124] In the previous verse, Paul stresses that he and his coworkers had "opened their hearts" to the Corinthians. This affection, Paul states here, has not, however, been reciprocated.

6:13 ***Now for a recompence in the same / As a fair exchange:*** The noun ἀντιμισθία (*antimisthia*), "reciprocal exchange," denotes "a recompense based upon what one deserves, either positive or negative, but with emphasis on the reciprocal nature of the recompense."[125] In the present context, the reference is to the affection Paul and his companions have freely given to the Corinthian Saints. Paul is appealing to the custom at the time that constrained a person upon whom a benefice was given to return the same.

I speak as unto my children / I speak as to my own children: Though the Greek phrase translates literally "I speak as to children," such a strict

119. Louw-Nida, §33.252.

120. *NID*, 2:622–27.

121. BDAG, 823.

122. Garland, *2 Corinthians*, 328–29.

123. BDAG, 942.

124. BDAG, 938.

125. Louw-Nida, §38.15; BDAG, 90.

reading misses the force of Paul's point, suggesting as it does that Paul is speaking down to or castigating his audience. Such is not the case. When the noun was used to describe the near-spiritual relationship of a student to a teacher or honored leader, "child" (τένον, *teknon*) carried an endearing, personal connection.[126] Thus, we translate the plural as "my own children."

be ye also enlarged / open wide your heart also: Paul again uses the passive form of the verb πλατύνω (*platynō*), "to cause something to be broad, . . . enlarge,"[127] as he appeals for his readers to feel and express the same affection toward him and his companions as they have to them.

Analysis and Summary

Having listed both the difficulties he has faced and is facing (to which some of his readers have contributed to a lesser or greater degree) and his own positive attitude toward them, Paul makes a plea to his readers. He bases his plea not only on his outward openness to them, in which he has hidden nothing, but also on his inward openness through which he has fully exposed his feelings to them. He uses the verb "to restrain" (στενοχωρέω, *stenochōreō*) three times to refer to both his attitude and theirs. The verb carries the idea of being "narrow, cramped, or constricted" in one's feelings. He assures his readers that such a condition has not been his, but he fears that it has been theirs and worries that they have closed off their hearts to him. Though Paul assures them of his love for them, he also lets them know that he will not back down from telling them what God wants for them.[128] The restraint can only be overcome, as Paul emphasizes in the next section of his address, through a process of reconciliation between the Corinthian branches, himself, and God. Further, their salvation depends on it. He stresses that he has already done his part by being as open and loving toward them as he wishes them to be toward him and assures them that his paternal feelings for them continue.[129] In sum, "Paul's basic point in vv. 11b and 12a is that his 'heart' for the Corinthians is wide open, not constricted. In medical terms, an enlarged heart is a dangerous liability; in spiritual terms, an enlarged heart is a productive asset."[130]

126. BDAG, 994–95.
127. BDAG, 823.
128. Garland, *2 Corinthians,* 329.
129. Barnett, *Second Epistle,* 336–37.
130. Harris, *Second Epistle,* 490.

A Warning against Too-Familiar Association with Unbelievers (6:14–18)

Greek Text

14 Μὴ γίνεσθε ἑτεροζυγοῦντες ἀπίστοις· τίς γὰρ μετοχὴ δικαιοσύνῃ καὶ ἀνομίᾳ, ἢ
τίς κοινωνία φωτὶ πρὸς σκότος; 15 τίς δὲ συμφώνησις Χριστοῦ πρὸς Βελιάρ, ἢ τίς
μερὶς πιστῷ μετὰ ἀπίστου; 16 τίς δὲ συγκατάθεσις ναῷ θεοῦ μετὰ εἰδώλων; ἡμεῖς
γὰρ ναὸς θεοῦ ἐσμεν ζῶντος· καθὼς εἶπεν ὁ θεὸς ὅτι Ἐνοικήσω ἐν αὐτοῖς καὶ ἐμπε-
ριπατήσω, καὶ ἔσομαι αὐτῶν θεός, καὶ αὐτοὶ ἔσονταί μου λαός. 17 διὸ ἐξέλθατε ἐκ
μέσου αὐτῶν, καὶ ἀφορίσθητε, λέγει κύριος, καὶ ἀκαθάρτου μὴ ἅπτεσθε· κἀγὼ
εἰσδέξομαι ὑμᾶς· 18 καὶ ἔσομαι ὑμῖν εἰς πατέρα, καὶ ὑμεῖς ἔσεσθέ μοι εἰς υἱοὺς καὶ
θυγατέρας, λέγει κύριος παντοκράτωρ. [SBLGNT]

King James Version

14 Be ye not unequally yoked together
with unbelievers: for what fellowship
hath righteousness with unrighteous-
ness? and what communion hath light
with darkness? 15 And what concord
hath Christ with Belial? or what part hath
he that believeth with an infidel? 16 And
what agreement hath the temple of God
with idols? for ye are the temple of the
living God; as God hath said, I will dwell
in them, and walk in them; and I will be
their God, and they shall be my people.
17 Wherefore come out from among
them, and be ye separate, saith the Lord,
and touch not the unclean thing; and I
will receive you, 18 And will be a Father
unto you, and ye shall be my sons and
daughters, saith the Lord Almighty.

New Rendition

14 Do not be yoked in an unequal part-
nership with unbelievers. What do
righteousness and lawlessness have in
common, or what fellowship does light
have with darkness? 15 And what agree-
ment does Christ have with Beliar, or
what does a believer have in common
with an unbeliever? 16 And what agree-
ment is there between God's temple
and idols? For we are a temple of the liv-
ing God, even as God said, "I will dwell
among them and walk with them, and
I will be their God, and they will be my
people" [Lev. 26:11–12; Jer. 32:38; Ezek.
27:37]. 17 Therefore, "Come out from
among them and be separate," says the
Lord, "and do not touch any unclean
thing" [Isa. 52:11], "and I will receive
you" [Ezek. 20:41], 18 "and I will be a
father to you, and you will be my sons
and daughters, says the Lord Almighty"
[compare 2 Sam. 7:14, 8; Isa. 43:6].

Translation Notes and Comments

6:14 ***Be ye not unequally yoked together with unbelievers / Do not be yoked in an unequal partnership with unbelievers:*** This verse begins a rather abrupt change of topic and direction. The noun ζυγός (*zygos*) refers to a wooden collar used to couple two animals together that they might work as a team.[131] The verb ἑτεροζυγέω (*heterzygeō*) denotes the mismatching of animals of different species to a yoke, such as an ox and a donkey, which makes work difficult, if not impossible, because the yoke does not properly fit the pair.[132]

Metaphorically, the verb refers to entering into an unequal partnership where one person does more work than the other. It is found here in the present tense, "indicating the beginning of a state," and thus signifying that Paul's readers should not become entangled with certain people.[133] The adjective ἄπιστος (*apistos*) is formed from the adjective πιστός (*pistos*), "faithful, believing," prefixed by the alpha privative ἀ- (*a*-), which negates the meaning of the word. It refers to a person who is faithless or unbelieving, and in the present context it carries the connotation of evildoing.[134] People of this caliber could easily draw unsuspecting victims into a very bad situation and then abandon them such that they have to bear the full weight of the consequences.

what fellowship hath righteousness with unrighteousness / What do righteousness and lawlessness have in common: The noun δικαιοςύνη (*dikaiosynē*), "righteousness," denotes that which is right with the law and is thus in a state of judicial correctness.[135] The noun ἀνομίᾳ (*anomia*), "lawlessness," is formed from the noun νομία (*nomia*), "lawfulness,"[136] prefixed by the alpha privative ἀ- (*a*-), which negates the meaning of the word, thus yielding the idea of that which is unbound by law.[137] The noun μετοχή

---

131. LSJ, 757. The Old Testament uses the Hebrew עוֹל (*ʿôl*) for such an instrument (HAL, 828) and מוֹטָה (*môṭāh*) for an oxbow or yoke for but one animal (HAL, 555).

132. BDAG, 399.

133. Bernard, "Second Epistle," 78.

134. BDAG, 103–4.

135. BDAG, 247–49. This noun has a wide range of meaning that must be determined by context. Even then, pinning down an exact nuance is frequently difficult because of its use in both concrete and abstract aspects drawn from the mores of Greco-Roman society and Old Testament constructs. For discussion, see *NID*, 1:723–41.

136. LSJ, 1179.

137. BDAG, 85.

(*metochē*) denotes "sharing, participation," or having something in common.[138] The implied answer to Paul's question is "nothing."

and what communion hath light with darkness? / what fellowship does light have with darkness?: The noun κοινωνία (*koinōnia*), "fellowship," denotes a relationship that involves "mutual interest and sharing."[139] The noun φῶς (*phōs*), "light," metaphorically refers to that which is "the element and sphere of the divine,"[140] while σκότος (*skotos*), "darkness," metaphorically refers to "the state of disbelievers and the godless" (compare 4:6; 11:14).[141] The implied answer to Paul's query is "none."

6:15 *what concord hath Christ with Belial / what agreement does Christ have with Beliar:* The noun συμφώνησις (*symphōnēsis*), "agreement," denotes "a state of shared interest."[142] The proper noun Βελιάρ (*Beliar*) comes from the Hebrew בְּלִיַּעַל (*bĕliyaʿal*), meaning "worthlessness."[143] Paul uses it only here and apparently does so to refer to the devil. Its use in Hebrew scriptures, however, shows that it does not point exclusively to Satan, for it is also used to denote the homosexuals at Gibeah as well as people who worked to convince others to worship false gods. "In the Qumran texts, *beliya'al* is the angel of enmity whose domain is darkness and who counsels evil and superintends angels of destruction."[144] These angels are his portion of humankind, and they fight against the sons of light who are God's portion. Broadly, Belial refers to anyone who tempts others towards sin, and in Pseudepigrapha, the term is sometimes identified with the anti-Christ.[145] Even so, the nuance of the term fits Satan very well, and it is not surprising Paul would use it to designate him (compare 1 Cor. 10:21).

or what part hath he that believeth with an infidel? / or what does a believer have in common with an unbeliever? The adjective πιστός (*pistos*), "trusting, believing, faithful," is here used nominally to refer to a Christian believer.[146] For the nominalized adjective ἄπιστος (*apistos*), "unbeliever,"

---

138. BDAG, 643.

139. BDAG, 552–53.

140. BDAG, 1072–73.

141. BDAG, 932. For comparison with the same imagery see Acts 26:18; Rom. 13:12; and 1 Thes. 5:5.

142. BDAG, 961.

143. BDAG, 173. Some manuscripts have Βελιάλ (*Belial*), the interchange of *l* and *r* being common in the Aramaic of the New Testament period. For a study, see Theodore J. Lewis, "Belial," in *ABD*, 1:654–56.

144. Harris, *Second Epistle*, 501–2, also notes that the term refers to both what is worthless and what brings destruction.

145. Garland, *2 Corinthians*, 335.

146. BDAG, 820–21.

see Translation Notes for 6:14. The noun μερίς (*meris*) describes a "share, portion."[147] The entire phrase translated literally is "or what share/portion to believer with unbeliever?" Our translation gives the sense of the Greek in contemporary English.

6:16 *what agreement hath the temple of God with idols? / what agreement is there between God's temple and idols?* The noun συγκατάθεσις (*synkatathesis*), "agreement, union,"[148] carries the idea of two entities coming to a mutual arrangement.[149] In the present context, the phrase ναῷ θεοῦ (*naō theou*), "temple of God," does not refer to an actual sanctuary. In Paul's writings, there is but one authorized and functioning temple, and that one consists of those who belong to the body of believers (see 1 Cor. 3:16–17; 6:19). The noun εἴδωλον (*eidōlon*), "idol,"[150] often refers to the image or statue Gentiles created as an object of worship. However, by the process of metonymy, it gained the nuance not only of the spuriousness of the object worshipped but also of its unreality. Paul previously stressed that idols were nothing—that is, they had no substance or greater reality than the material from which they were made. He did, however, see the likelihood that devils were using them to captivate the people (1 Cor. 8:4; 10:20–21; compare Rom. 1:18–32). Paul makes his point here by contrasting the real with the unreal, the substantial with the unsubstantial.[151]

for ye are the temple of the living God; as God hath said, I will dwell in them, and walk in them; and I will be their God, and they shall be my people. / For we are a temple of the living God, even as God said, "I will dwell among them and walk with them, and I will be their God, and they will be my people": There is a variant reading to this phrase. The reading ἡμεῖς . . . ἐσμεν (*hēmeis . . . esmen*), "we . . . are," is strongly supported by both Alexandrian and Western manuscripts and is preferable to ὑμεῖς . . . ἐστε (*humeis . . . este*), "you . . . are," which the KJV follows.[152]

The conjunction γάρ (*gar*), "for,"[153] acts as a marker of clarification and, thus, signals that Paul is going to elucidate his point. He does so in two ways: identifying who the Christians are and using three scriptures as proof texts to shore up his point. His focus is on an aspect of the nature of God,

147. Louw-Nida, §63.13; BDAG, 632.
148. BDAG, 951.
149. Louw-Nida, §31:18.
150. BDAG, 280–81.
151. For a study, see *NID*, 2:98–102.
152. Metzger, *Textual Commentary*, 512.
153. BDAG, 189–90.

namely, that he is living. The verb ζάω (*zaō*), "living,"[154] found here as a present active participle, denotes that which can act, move, and affect its surroundings. By placing it last in the clause, Paul gives it an emphatic position, thus stressing not only God's reality but also his ability to be with and bless his people.

At this point, Paul conflates three Old Testament scriptures (LXX Lev. 26:12; LXX Jer. 39:38 [Jer. 32:38, KJV], and LXX Ezek. 37:27).[155] He begins his paraphrase with God's word that "I will dwell among them" and then continues echoing the promise found in Leviticus, Jeremiah, and Ezekiel that those with whom God dwells will be his people. Paul uses the verb ἐνοικέω (*enoikeō*), "live, dwell in,"[156] to refer to God's indwelling spiritual presence within his people both as individuals and as a community (see 1 Cor. 3:16–17; 10:20–21; compare Rom. 8:11 and 2 Tim. 1:14). Here the entire community is the focus.

The verb ἐμπεριπατέω (*emperipateō*) has the meaning "to walk about, move."[157] It is because Jehovah will dwell among the people and walk with them that a mutual relationship is formed by which he becomes their God and they become his people. This relationship can happen because they walk as he does (compare Ex. 6:7; Jer. 31:33; Ezek. 11:20; and Zech. 8:8).

6:17 *Wherefore come out from among them, and be ye separate, saith the Lord, and touch not the unclean thing; and I will receive you / Therefore, "Come out from among them and be separate," says the Lord, "and do not touch any unclean thing," "and I will receive you":* The conjunction διό (*dio*), "therefore,"[158] acts inferentially to denote a point arrived at based on a previously established truth. That truth is that God can dwell among

---

154. BDAG, 424–26.

155. These scriptures are LXX Lev. 26:12, καὶ ἐμπεριπατήσω ἐν ὑμῖν καὶ ἔσομαι ὑμῶν θεός, καὶ ὑμεῖς ἔσεσθέ μου λαός (*kai emperipatēsō en hymin kai esomai hymōn theos, kai hymeis esesthe mou laos*), which we render as "and I will walk among you and I will be your God, and you will be my people"; LXX Jer. 39:38 (Jer. 32:38, KJV), ἔσονταί μοι εἰς λαόν, καὶ ἐγὼ ἔσομαι αὐτοῖς εἰς θεόν (*esontai moi eis lao, kai egō esomai autois eis theon*), which we render as "They will be my people, and I will be their God"; and Ezek. 37:27, καὶ ἔσται ἡ κατασκήνωσίς μου ἐν αὐτοῖς, καὶ ἔσομαι αὐτοῖς θεός, καὶ αὐτοί μου ἔσονται λαός (*kai estai hē kataskēnōsis mou en autois, kai esomai autois theo, kai autoi mou esontai laos*), which we render as "and my dwelling will be among them, and I will be their God, and they will be my people."

156. BDAG, 338.

157. BDAG, 323.

158. BDAG, 250.

his people. To indicate how this can happen, the Apostle refers to two more Old Testament scriptures (Isa. 52:11; Ezek. 20:41).

Paul's paraphrases indicate that the Saints must leave behind that which is unclean. The adjective ἀκάθαρτος (*akathartos*), "unclean," denotes what is morally impure, defiled, or ritually unclean.[159] The noun "thing" is not in the Greek text but is implicit since the gender of the adjective is neuter.

The verb ἅπτω (*haptō*), "touch,"[160] carries the nuance of contacting and even clinging to something. Here it refers more specifically to uncritical association with unbelievers.

The verb εἰσδέχομαι (*eisdechomai*), "to receive," denotes the gracious reception of someone into the presence of another. [161]

6:18 ***And will be a Father unto you, and ye shall be my sons and daughters, saith the Lord Almighty / "and I will be a father to you, and you will be my sons and daughters, says the Lord Almighty":*** In this verse, Paul does not quote entire verses from the Bible but rather paraphrases words and ideas found in 2 Samuel 7:8, 14 and Isaiah 43:6. The account in 2 Samuel 7:4–16 retains the words of the prophet Nathan that God commanded him to tell David, but Paul applies them to the Corinthian Saints. Both these passages in the Old Testament are explicitly attributed to God's spoken words,[162] allowing the Apostle to have no compunction in ascribing his reconstruction to the Divine.

Paul's words emphasize the warm and filial relationship the Lord designs to have with his children. This idea is expanded since neither the MT nor the LXX has the phrase "and daughters" in them. Thus, Paul gives a broader reading so that the whole of his audience is included, both men and women.

The phrase κύριος παντοκράτωρ (*kyrios pantokratōr*), literally "Lord Almighty One," comes from 2 Samuel 7:8. The phrase combines two nouns, but we have translated them "Lord Almighty," with the second treated as an adjective modifying the first. In both the LXX and the Greek New Testament, the noun παντοκράτωρ (*pantokratōr*)[163] is used exclusively for the Divine[164] or, as here, to point to a godly attribute—namely, that of "the

159. BDAG, 34; Louw-Nida §53.39.

160. BDAG, 126.

161. BDAG, 293.

162. Isa. 52:5 has λέγει κύριος (*legei kyrios*), "says the Lord," while 2 Sam. 7:8 has λέγει κύριος παντοκράτῶρ (*legei kyrios pantrokratōr*), "says the Lord Almighty."

163. BDAG, 755.

164. The term is found in Rev. 1:8; 4:8; 11:17; 15:3; 16:7, 14; 19:6, 15; 21:22 and refers to either the Father or the Son. In the LXX, κύριος παντοκράτωρ (*kyrios pantokratōr*)

immense greatness of God, whose power prevails over all."[165] Paul uses the phrase to emphasize the supremacy of God, thereby showing that he can accomplish all his will, including dwelling with his people and accepting them as his sons and daughters.

Analysis and Summary

This section presents a translation problem in that it seems to break up the flow of Paul's argument by introducing an irrelevant warning in the middle of his appeal. Indeed, his argument flows better if these verses are dropped and one begins reading again at 7:2. Because of this seeming interjection, some scholars see this section of 2 Corinthians as supporting the position that the epistle is a composite of several Pauline letters.[166] They note further that this section possesses a number of words that do not occur elsewhere in Paul's epistles.[167] Though this assertion cannot be disproved, it is not particularly strong. First, the rare words that the Apostle uses here either derive from Old Testament passages that stand behind his appeal or are synonyms of words he has used and, to avoid repetition while continuing the flow and rhythm of his argument, he picks up. Further, this section contains quite a number of Pauline phrases.

Second, the seemingly abrupt change in flow may have arisen due to information that Titus brought back to Paul and that the Apostle paused to address at this point. It is more likely, however, that Paul may have realized that his admonition for the Saints to "enlarge their hearts" actually

---

translates the Hebrew יהוה צְבָאוֹת (*yhwh ṣĕbāʾôt*). The KJV renders it as "Lord of Hosts." The noun צְבָאוֹת (*ṣĕbāʾôt*) is the plural of צָבָא (*ṣābāʾ*) that can refer to "military men, troops," or "heavenly bodies, stars."

165. *NID*, 2:742.

166. For discussion, see the sections "Integrity of the Work," and "Structure and Organization" in the introduction to this volume. For a study, see David Rensberger, "2 Corinthians 6:14–7:1—a Fresh Examination," *Studia Biblica et Theologica* 8 (1978): 25–49, who concludes that the case of authorship must remain open until more evidence becomes available.

167. These *hapax legomena* (words that appear only once in an author's work) break into two groups. The first consists of ἑτεροζυγέω (*eterozygeō*), "to be unequally yoked," Βελιάρ (*beliar*), "worthlessness," and μολυσμός (*molysmos*), "defilement," while the second consists of μετοχή (*metochē*), "share," συμφώνησις (*symphōnēsis*), "agreement," and συγκατάθεσις (*syngkatathesis*), "union." The first set are all biblical while the second are synonyms of words Paul has already used and that he likely picked up for literary variety. For a study, see Gordon D. Fee, "II Corinthians VI.14–VII.1 and Food Offered to Idols," *New Testament Studies* 23 (1977): 140–61.

had a very negative connotation if viewed through the lens of the Mosaic Law (see Deut. 11:16). Such a view could be seen as allowing for the worship of false gods and participating in pagan practices. If that is the case, the Apostle may have sensed the need to give a warning that his words should not be taken as license to tolerate idolatry or indiscriminate association with gentile neighbors, friends, or associates.[168]

To emphasize his point, Paul uses five sets of images that effectively contrast the marked difference that should exist between the Corinthian Christians and their unredeemed neighbors (6:14a–17a).[169] He uses them to underscore his insistence that his readers guard against being unequally yoked (ἑτεροζυγέω, *heterozygeō*) in partnerships with others (6:14). The term "unequally yoked" designates the teaming of animals so different that they cannot effectively do the necessary work.[170] The various examples given by the Apostle all emphasize the need for the Christian to dissociate him- or herself from the unfaithful. To further push this point, Paul paraphrases certain Old Testament scriptures that all show the need for his readers to separate themselves from any who would harm them or the work. Using symbolism, he stresses the nature of the Corinthian branches. They are, as he states, the temple of God wherein the spirit of the Divine resides (6:16). He clearly points out the result of living in this state: God will not only dwell with his people but also establish a filial relationship in which he will claim them as his sons and daughters (6:18). That Paul adds the phrase "and daughters" to the passage he quotes (2 Sam. 7:14) should not be overlooked. Since the temple God is now building consists of all those who at the time enter the new covenant, then women must be included because they have indispensable standing in God's community. Indeed, they participate in very meaningful ways, giving life to the community as a whole. This addition also reveals Paul's desire to be reconciled to all members of the Corinthian community.[171]

---

168. Bernard, "Second Epistle," 78.

169. Bernard, "Second Epistle," 79.

170. For a study, see J. Duncan and M. Derrett, "2 Cor 6,14ff: A Midrash on Dt 22,10," *Biblica* 59, no. 2 (1978): 231–50, who argues that there is the echo of financial dealings here, but the main point is that God is not only concerned with how people treat people but also how they treat animals, and when two are unequally yoked, the difference for the weaker can be most uncomfortable and even torturous.

171. Lee Magness, "The Significance of Paul's Addition of 'and Daughters' in 2 Corinthians 6:18," *Priscilla Papers* 29, no. 2 (2015): 3–5.

Chapter 7

Godly Sorrow for Sin Leads to Repentance

A Warning against Too Familiar Association with Unbelievers *(continued)* (7:1)

The first verse of this chapter belongs to the former discussion (6:14–18) and should be read as its conclusion. It constitutes both an appeal and an exhortation. Its center is a twofold admonition that the Saints cleanse themselves from both physical defilement and spiritual pollutions and take upon themselves an ever-greater degree of holiness motivated by their reverence for God. We include it here to keep our Rendition parallel with the KJV. The rest of the chapter is introduced below.

Greek Text

1 ταύτας οὖν ἔχοντες τὰς ἐπαγγελίας, ἀγαπητοί, καθαρίσωμεν ἑαυτοὺς ἀπὸ παντὸς μολυσμοῦ σαρκὸς καὶ πνεύματος, ἐπιτελοῦντες ἁγιωσύνην ἐν φόβῳ θεοῦ. [SBLGNT]

King James Version

1 Having therefore these promises, dearly beloved, let us cleanse ourselves from all filthiness of the flesh and spirit, perfecting holiness in the fear of God.

New Rendition

1 Now since we have these promises, dear friends, let us purify ourselves from every defilement of the flesh and spirit and thereby complete our sanctification through reverence for God.

Translation Notes and Comments

7:1 ***Having therefore these promises / Now since we have these promises:*** The verb ἔχω (*echō*), "to have," is found here as a plural present participle and is used circumstantially with a causative sense. We have, therefore, translated it as "since we have." The noun ἐπαγγελία (*epangelia*), "promise," carries the "implication of obligation to carry out what is stated."[1] The promises that God makes to the righteous are the ones that Paul refers to in the last two verses of the preceding chapter (see Translation Notes for 6:16–17). These are that God will favorably receive these people, walk among them, and accept them as his sons and daughters.

dearly beloved / dear friends: The term is one of endearment designed to express the Apostle's care for his readers. The phrase places Paul's following admonition as an act of love and consideration for what is best for both them and him. We have translated the adjective ἀγαπητοί (*agapētoi,* literally "beloved") as "dear friends" to be more in line with current English usage.

let us cleanse ourselves from all filthiness of the flesh and spirit / let us purify ourselves from every defilement of the flesh and spirit: The verb καθαρίζω (*katharizō*), "cleanse, purify,"[2] is found here as an aorist hortatory subjunctive and, because of the aorist aspect, expresses an urgent desire for the results of something that is contingent on an action. Here it is that the Christian becomes morally pure. Paul's use of the first-person plural "let us" shows his willingness to be identified with his readers and emphasizes his loving relationship with them.[3] The verb, in a religious sense, refers to purifying an object, thus making it acceptable to God. In the broader biblical context, it most often refers to ritual cleansing, through which one is prepared for temple worship by being freed from the defilement of sin. Through this act, in the Pauline context, the person makes himself or herself right before God through the sanctification of the heart and soul. This state comes through obedience to the great commandment to love God and neighbor. Though there is a strong connection between this act and baptism, with its total remission of sins,[4] in the present context Paul is referring more to the repentance process after baptism.

1. BDAG, 355–56.
2. BDAG, 488.
3. Hughes, *Second Epistle,* 257.
4. Friedrich Hauck, "καθαρός," in *TDNT,* 3:425–26.

The noun μολυσμός (*molysmos*), "defilement,"[5] in the figurative sense as here strongly implies befoulment of something that should have been kept morally clean, pure, and especially sacred.[6] It can refer to a condition that results from evil acts or intentions and often through heathen associations.[7] The noun σάρξ (*sarx*), "body," figuratively refers to "the outward side of life,"[8] while πνεῦμα (*pneuma*), "spirit," figuratively represents the inner self. Thus, the phrase "body and spirit" refers to "the whole personality, in its inner and outer aspects."[9]

perfecting holiness in the fear of God / and thereby complete our sanctification through reverence for God: The verb ἐπιτελέω (*epiteleō*), found here as a plural present participle, has the root sense of bringing something to an end, but here the nuance is to "complete, accomplish, perform, bring about."[10] It is used as a circumstantial participle of manner; hence we have translated it as "thereby complete." It suggests the cooperative need for the Christian to be engaged in a process that brings about the desired result. For Paul, that result is ἁγιωσύνη (*hagiōsynē*), "holiness."[11] In the present context, the noun denotes that aspect of moral purity that comes not through cultic practices but by being led by the Holy Spirit (Rom. 1:4). Its result is sanctification, wherein one receives the qualities and characteristics of the divine.[12] Paul's admonition should not be taken to suggest an advocation of instant holiness in this life, for that would be contrary to his teachings in other places. Rather, he is advocating an ever-advancing holiness that is derived through repeated acts of self-consecration.[13]

Paul refers to the instrument or means for doing so as ἐν φόβῳ θεοῦ (*en phobō theou*), "through reverence for God."[14] The noun φόβος (*phobos*), "fear," "reverence,"[15] denotes the very strong emotional reaction when one

---

5. BDAG, 657.

6. Friedrich Büschsel, "μολυσμός," in *TDNT,* 4:737–41; *Dictionary of Synonyms,* s.v. "contaminate."

7. Bernard, "Second Epistle," 80.

8. BDAG, 914, 916.

9. BDAG, 832–36.

10. BDAG, 383, noting that the purpose here is to bring about sanctification.

11. For discussion, see Translation Notes for 1:1. Proper character is the object of holiness. In Christ, ἁγιωσύνη (*hagiōsynē*) referred to his perfectly divine character, but in the Christian, it refers to a process through which the Saint's character grows toward ultimate perfection.

12. For a study, see Otto Procksch, "ἅγιος," in *TDNT,* 1:100–110.

13. Martin, *2 Corinthians,* 375.

14. For a study, see Translation Notes and the accompanying Analysis for 5:11.

15. BDAG, 1062.

is confronted by overpowering might.[16] That reaction can be either positive or negative depending on how one sees oneself in relation to that power.[17] If negative, the result would be terror with a desire to flee.[18] If positive, the result would be deep reverence with the desire to worship.[19] Due to the sense of worship that the noun carried, it became exclusively associated with the faithful's reaction toward the Divine. In the New Testament, it describes the motivational factor that drives each Christian to follow God. Though it never fully lost its sense of dread in displeasing God, it came more and more to denote the respect and awe that the believer had toward the Father and Son. That respect was generated by Deity's graciousness and mercy, especially as expressed in the Atonement of Christ.

The phrase ἐν φόβῳ (*en phobō*), "through reverence," in the dative case expresses the instrument or means through which holiness is derived. For Paul, the driving force of his ministry was his deep and abiding awe and feelings of love generated by all that the Savior had done not just for him but for many others. His hope appears to be that, for his followers, it was reverence, awe, or love, not the fear of provoking God, that provided the instrument and power to follow the way of the Father, no matter the cost.[20]

Analysis and Summary

The material in 7:1, though placed with chapter 7 in the KJV, actually concludes Paul's argument begun in 6:14 and should, therefore, be read as part of it. For the sake of keeping our Rendition parallel with the KJV, we analyze it here.

The motivations behind Paul's words are very clear. The Corinthians must be reconciled to the Apostle and to the gospel message he preaches. In order to reach them, he has used a tone that is strident, even severe. Given, however, the force of the opposition against him, sharpness appears to be all the more necessary to prick those he wishes to reach back into

---

16. Horst Balz, "φοβέω," in *TDNT,* 9:189-97.

17. Louw-Nida, §§25.251; 53.59.

18. Initially, the noun denoted flight. Over time it came to refer to what causes one to flee, namely fear, dread, or terror. For a study, see *NID,* 4:609–14.

19. Over time, due to its connection with strong emotion, the noun came to describe the faithful's reaction to Jehovah, namely one of deep reverence and respect that carried with it a willingness to follow his word. For a study, see Horst Balz, "φοβέω," in *TDNT,* 9:208–17.

20. For a study, see *NID,* 4:609–14.

oneness with him. Perhaps sensing that his language could be taken as too impersonal and rigorous, Paul now deftly changes tone as he moves into a short resumption of his plea that the Saints, once again, be united with him.[21]

Based on the scripturally derived promises he has brought to the fore (see Translation Notes for 6:16–17), the Apostle admonished his readers to accomplish two tasks. The first is to cleanse themselves from two destructive forces—namely, the filthiness of the flesh and the filthiness of the spirit. The word for defilement that Paul uses here, μολυσμός (*molysmos*), generally "refers to religious defilement from worshipping other gods" that renders one, from both the Jewish and Christian point of view, both physically and spiritually impure.[22] Associating with nonbelievers in their idolatrous practices was one sure way of contracting deep uncleanliness, especially due to the immoral behavior often associated with their form of worship. When he says to cleanse themselves, contextually Paul asks them to "withdraw . . . from any unholy alliances and association with idolatry."[23] Thus, Paul's admonition does not apply to literal ceremonial washing such as the Jews practiced, but to a spiritual and figurative purity.[24] The idea grew out of Jesus' teachings found in the Sermon on the Mount (Matt. 5–7). There, the Lord gave the higher law, showing that purity was not a matter of outward washings but of being pure of heart and character. By the time Paul wrote, the Christians had adopted this view.[25] It is primarily to maintain such a state of purity that Paul admonishes the Christians to refrain from the practice of any unholy things (6:17; this idea is echoed in D&C 109:20).[26] The Apostle's words show that moral cleanliness consisted of more than the physical or external side of life (the flesh); it also included the internal (the spirit). Thus, Paul is admonishing his readers to purify the whole of their personalities in both the external and internal dimensions.

The second task he wishes his readers to achieve is a state of holiness (ἁγιωσύνη, *hagiōsynē*) motivated by their reverence and awe (φόβος,

21. Martin, *2 Corinthians,* 377.

22. Garland, *2 Corinthians,* 342.

23. Garland, *2 Corinthians,* 343.

24. Harris, *Second Epistle,* 511–12.

25. Colin Brown, *New International Dictionary of New Testament Theology,* 4 vols. (Grand Rapids, Mich.: Zondervan, 1978), 3:106–8.

26. He treated his concern for this challenge to the Christian community in the eighth chapter of 1 Cor.

phobos) for God. Holiness is a specific state associated with the Divine and the objective he assigns his people. Proper character is the object of holiness. In Christ, the noun "holiness" refers to his perfectly divine character, but in the Christian, it refers to a process through which the Saint's character grows toward ultimate perfection. The seat of saintly reverence and awe is love for God inspired by the gospel—that is, the plan of salvation—that he has put into action.

Looking at Paul's wish through a Latter-day Saint lens is helpful. Of himself the Lord declared, "Man of Holiness is my name" (Moses 7:35), thus connoting his very nature. For that reason, he can say that all "must repent, or they can in nowise inherit the kingdom of God" (Moses 6:57). The reason is that, in order to be comfortable with him, adherents must partake of his nature. As the Book of Mormon warns unbelievers, "Do ye suppose that ye shall dwell with him under a consciousness of your guilt? Do ye suppose that ye could be happy to dwell with that holy Being, when your souls are racked with a consciousness of guilt that ye have ever abused his laws? Behold, I say unto you that ye would be more miserable to dwell with a holy and just God, under a consciousness of your filthiness before him, than ye would to dwell with the damned souls in hell" (Morm. 9:3–4). For this reason, God demands that his people be like him. As he says, "be holy, for I am holy" (Lev. 11:45; 1 Pet. 1:15–16).[27]

Paul's writings show he is well aware of this injunction (Rom. 12:1; 1 Cor. 3:16–17; Eph. 1:4; Col. 1:22–23; Titus 1:8). The state of holiness comes by resisting and then overcoming the forces and enticements that hold one to the world. It is tracked by the degree of one's separation from the mundane and profane[28] and expressed by the fact that the Saint is led by the Holy Spirit (Rom. 8:14).[29] The means or instrument for achieving this highly sanctified state, as Paul says, is the awe or reverence that the Saint feels toward the Father and Son. A life generated by these feelings promotes the pursuit of holiness in thought and action.

---

27. For a study, see Robert L. Millet, "A Call to Holiness," in *Selected Writings of Robert L. Millet* (Salt Lake City: Deseret Book, 2000), 348–55.

28. The Hebrew noun קָדוֹשׁ (*qādôš*) contains elements of both separation and purity and connotes a condition that promotes ethical values. Thus, the idea transcended the cultic sphere and included that of both the individual and society as a whole. BDB, 872.

29. For a study, see *NID,* 1:124–33.

The Appeal Based on Titus's Report (7:2–16)

At this point (7:2–4), Paul picks up the plea he began in 6:11–13 that these people accept him as he has accepted them. The rest of the chapter is but an elaboration of the appeal the Apostle makes here. Though, as his words make clear, he and his companions have achieved an important if temporary victory, in which he greatly rejoices, not all the local challenges have been overcome. Indeed, his detractors are yet present and active. He must, therefore, pursue his cause. Even so, this chapter never loses its very positive tone.

Once he has made his plea, he reaches back to where he left off at 2:11–13. There he expressed his heartfelt concerns for both Titus and the Corinthian Saints. The themes and questions he registered there he picks up again in this section and in doing so refreshes his readers' memory concerning the drama that caused him to write this letter.

He reminds them that his great anxiety over not finding Titus where he expected him (2:13) enhanced the agony he suffered due to his concern especially for Corinthian Saints (7:5).[30] His pain centered on the possibility that the Apostle's tearful and very forceful letter delivered by Titus may have further alienated his readers rather than uniting them to him. Thus, as he explains, his reuniting with Titus is now the cause of an overflowing fulness of joy due to his companion's report of the very positive reception both he and Paul's letter received among the house churches in the area (7:5–7). We see in this pericope how Paul again brings up the themes of joy and sorrow his relationship with this segment of the Church has caused (see 1:23–2:4). In doing so, he signals he is now closing that portion of his argument (7:8–13a). He concludes this section by emphasizing the joy both he and Titus felt because of the Saints' positive and humble reaction to Paul's rather harsh letter (7:13b–16).[31]

This pericope reveals that Paul's major concern does not center on his relationship with the branches in the area only. "The fidelity of the Corinthians to the apostle is no private matter, and it does not have to do with

30. Witherington, *Conflict and Community,* 409, notes that, though Paul was no doubt anxious about Titus, his major concern was with the spiritual welfare of the Corinthian branches.

31. Seifrid, *Second Letter,* 302.

Paul's person. It has to do with the fidelity to the Gospel, which binds them to Christ, and thereby to Titus and to all other Christians."[32] To fail to achieve this unity would exacerbate the forces of apostasy already too rampant among many branches of the nascent Church. Therefore, Paul must continue to be forceful, convincing, and uniting. The following study shows his skill in doing so.

"Receive Us": The Plea Resumed (7:2–4)

Greek Text

2 Χωρήσατε ἡμᾶς· οὐδένα ἠδικήσαμεν, οὐδένα ἐφθείραμεν, οὐδένα ἐπλεονεκτήσαμεν. 3 πρὸς κατάκρισιν οὐ λέγω, προείρηκα γὰρ ὅτι ἐν ταῖς καρδίαις ἡμῶν ἐστε εἰς τὸ συναποθανεῖν καὶ συζῆν. 4 πολλή μοι παρρησία πρὸς ὑμᾶς, πολλή μοι καύχησις ὑπὲρ ὑμῶν· πεπλήρωμαι τῇ παρακλήσει, ὑπερπερισσεύομαι τῇ χαρᾷ ἐπὶ πάσῃ τῇ θλίψει ἡμῶν. [SBLGNT]

King James Version

2 Receive us; we have wronged no man, we have corrupted no man, we have defrauded no man. 3 I speak not this to condemn you: for I have said before, that ye are in our hearts to die and live with you. 4 Great is my boldness of speech toward you, great is my glorying of you: I am filled with comfort, I am exceeding joyful in all our tribulation.

New Rendition

2 Make room for us in your hearts. We have treated no one unjustly; we have corrupted no one; we have taken advantage of no one. 3 I am not saying this to condemn you, for as I have already said, you have a place in our hearts such that we would live or die together with you. 4 I have great confidence in you; I have great pride in you. I am filled with comfort. I am overflowing with joy in all our tribulation.

Translation Notes and Comments

7:2 ***Receive us / Make room for us in your hearts:*** With this verse, Paul begins another pericope, in which he seeks to further reconcile himself to his readers and to the Corinthian house churches as a whole. The verb χωρέω (*chōreō*), "to be able to accept, to receive," or "to make room for,

32. Seifrid, *Second Letter,* 302.

hold, contain,"[33] found here as an aorist imperative expressing the aorist aspect of urgency, figuratively refers to making room for someone in one's heart and thus accepting her or him as a friend.[34] The phrase "in your hearts" is not in the Greek but is implied, and so we use it in our Rendition. By using the imperative mood, the Apostle stresses his desire that friendship be, once more, kindled between himself and his readers.

Note Paul's repeated use of the nominalized adjective οὐδείς (*oudeis*), "no one," in each of the following statements. In Greek they give this passage a rhythm and force that would appeal especially to the ears of those who listened to the epistle being read. The threefold declaration would likely help unite them with the Apostle.

we have wronged no man / We have treated no one unjustly: Having asked his readers to renew their friendship with him, Paul now gives three reasons why that should happen. The verb ἀδικέω (*adikeō*), "do wrong," denotes treating someone unjustly with the nuance of causing them injury.[35]

we have corrupted no man / we have corrupted no one: The verb φθείρω (*phtheirō*), "ruin, corrupt," carries the nuance of a deterioration in the inner life leading to moral destruction.[36] This condition was generally brought about by an association with evil persons.[37]

we have defrauded no man / we have taken advantage of no one: The verb πλεονεκτέω (*pleonekteō*), "exploit, outwit, defraud," denotes the act of taking advantage of another, often motivated by greed.[38]

7:3 ***I speak not this to condemn you / I am not saying this to condemn you:*** The noun κατάκριτις (*katakrisis*), "condemnation," denotes judging someone "definitely guilty and thus subject to punishment."[39] The Apostle's negation of the force of the noun assures his readers that he in no way assumes that they are thinking the worst of him.

for I have said before, that ye are in our hearts to die and live with you / for as I have already said, you have a place in our hearts such that we would live or die together with you: The sentiment Paul expresses here

33. Louw-Nida, §31.57; BDAG, 1094.

34. LSJ, 2015; BDAG, 1094; Louw-Nida, §34.13; *DAG*, s.v. "χωρέω."

35. BDAG, 20.

36. BDAG, 1054; Louw-Nida, §88.266.

37. Louw-Nida, §20.23, notes the verb can refer to either financial ruin or an undermining of faith. Paul's antagonists accused him of doing both.

38. BDAG, 824; Louw-Nida, §88.144.

39. Louw-Nida, §56.31. The phrase reads literally, "for the purpose of condemnation, I do not speak."

echoes that found in 3:2 and 6:11 (compare Philip. 1:7). The noun καρδία (*kardia*), "heart," here expresses Paul's deep feelings of love for these people (see Translation Notes for 1:22). The verb συναποθνησκω (*synapothēskō*) denotes dying with someone,[40] while συζάω (*syzaō*) means living together with someone.[41] In the larger Greco-Roman world, the phrase "to live and die with someone" expressed "the abiding nature of real friendship."[42]

7:4 ***Great is my boldness of speech toward you / I have great confidence in you:*** The meaning of the Greek phrase is unclear and, therefore, can be taken in a number of different ways. The adjective πολύς (*polys*), "much," "great," denotes what is "high on a scale of extent" and thus also carries the nuances of "strong" and "profound." The adjective also denotes what is "large in quantity and measure," thus "many, large, great, extensive."[43] The English word "great," expressing as it does a high degree of something, catches the flavor in the present context.

The adjective παρρησία (*parrēsia*), "confidence," has three nuances. It can refer to "boldness" of speech, denoting a form of speech that neither passes over nor conceals anything and is, thus, frank and plain.[44] The KJV follows this nuance. In a related way, the adjective denotes "openness in speaking and acting in public" and can be translated "I have spoken to you with great openness." Taken in this way, and based on 3:12 and 6:11, Paul could be reiterating and thus stressing his open posture and frankness of speech when dealing with these people.[45] Finally, the adjective carries the idea of "confidence, boldness, fearlessness."[46] Taken in this way, Paul could be reassuring these Saints of his absolute sureness in their feelings toward him. Given the context, we follow the majority of translations and take this position in our Rendition.[47] His point seems to be that he has used complete candor when it comes to his relationship with them and that he is fully confident in their willingness to accept him once more.

great is my glorying of you / I have great pride in you: On the adjective πολύς (*polys*), "great," see above. The noun καύχησις (*kauchēsis*), "pride," denotes "the state of being rightfully proud"[48] of someone or something.

---

40. BDAG, 965.

41. BDAG, 954.

42. Guthrie, *2 Corinthians,* 362–63.

43. BDAG, 847–50.

44. BDAG, 781.

45. Guthrie, *2 Corinthians,* 363; Thrall, *Critical and Exegetical Commentary,* 1:485.

46. BDAG 781.

47. As Hughes, *Second Epistle,* 262, notes, translating the term as "confidence" does not preclude boldness of speech since such can reflect confidence of the heart.

48. Louw-Nida, §25.204.

or death.[64] He recognizes that they are all in this struggle together, and for their sake, he is willing to go the distance. Where such affection and sympathy abound, he assures them, there can be no room for condemnation.[65]

In the broader context of the letter itself that speaks so openly of life and death (2:16; 4:10–12; 5:14–15; 6:9), we see the Apostle using the metaphor in a particularly theological way. Indeed, life and death are the way of the Christian, for they were the way of Christ. "For the believer, both death and life are aspects of a true ministry, true community, and a true walk with God. Thus, Paul's expression of friendship, that he is ready to die or live with the Corinthians, is undergirded by a robust theology of relationships with Christ."[66] Those who have entered this relationship and, thus, come under the power of his grace with its reciprocal obligations are to live in a way that is holy. They achieve this by both separating themselves from the world of sin and dedicating themselves to the service of God.[67] They do not, however, cloister themselves away from the world. Instead, they live in a condition of continual outreach to people who can benefit from and are willing to receive their help. Certainly, to effectively discharge the work of their ministry, they must remain ever in the service of those in both God's kingdom and the world.[68]

Paul's statement in 7:4 reveals the great relief caused by the very positive report he has now received from Titus, newly returned from Corinth. He can now not only have full confidence (παρρησία, *parrēsia*) in his readers but also speak of his boasting (καύχησις, *kauchēsis*) about their faithfulness to him. Indeed, Titus's report has brought him such complete comfort (παράκλησις, *paraklēsis*) that he can testify that he is now overflowing (ὑπερπερισσεύω, *hyperperisseuō*) with joy (χαρά, *chara*). Paul's use of the perfect tense, "I am filled," suggests that the Corinthian Saints have been for some time the source of his delight and that his long-past loving feelings for them, with the patience that they allowed, have now been fully and joyfully justified.[69]

---

64. Paul's love for these people forms a consistent theme within his epistle. See 1:7, 14, and 1:23–2:4.

65. Bernard, "Second Epistle," 80.

66. Guthrie, *2 Corinthians,* 363.

67. The adjective ἅγιος (*hagios*), "holy," carries both a negative and positive aspect. On the negative side it denotes separation from the mundane and profane, and on the positive side it denotes full dedication to God and his service. Louw-Nida, §§53.45; 88.24; Otto Procksch and Karl Georg Kuhn, "ἅγιος," in *TDNT,* 1:88–110.

68. Martin, *2 Corinthians,* 376.

69. Martin, *2 Corinthians,* 388.

There is a point, however, that must not be overlooked. Paul and the others, even though they strive for righteousness and are fully engaged in God's employ, still suffer tribulation. Though some may wish this condition otherwise, hoping that righteousness will act as a kind of insurance against life's challenges and sorrows, it will not play out. Mortality demands that most will pass through tribulation, including periods of harsh afflictions, heartfelt distress, and deep sorrow (see, for example, D&C 78:14; 109:5; 112:13; 122:5). Such should not be a surprise, because the Master has clearly warned that "in the world ye shall have tribulation" (John 16:33).[70] Further, John declared that the exalted are those "who have come out of great tribulation; they have washed their robes and made them white in the blood of the Lamb" (Rev. 7:14, our translation).

What Paul shows us is that, even during rough periods, joy is still possible. The object of his joy, however, is surprising. It is not the Saints he joys in but, based on 1:4, the tribulation he and his fellow missionaries have faced. Paul knew of what he spoke, telling the Roman Saints that "we glory in tribulations, knowing that tribulation produces endurance, and endurance produces character, and character produces hope, and hope does not disappoint us, because God's love has been poured into our hearts through the Holy Spirit that has been given to us" (Rom. 5:3–5, our translation). As Paul sees it, it has been on account of the missionaries' faithfulness during tribulation that they have received and continue to receive divine comfort and assurance. Titus's report now amplifies, to a near-overwhelming degree, the divinely derived comfort and joy the missionaries have already received. However, even though Paul and his companions are experiencing such great joy, the context suggests that Paul is acutely aware that these afflictions are not yet over. Clearly no one has yet reached that point. From all appearances, however, Paul senses that it is approaching.[71] This hope could be the ground that allows Paul to counterattack his detractors in chapters 10–13.

Noteworthy is that something quite remarkable happens in this section. Paul's words of praise for his readers show that he and the Church have exchanged roles. As he noted in 1:3–7, it is the Apostle who first received comfort during distress, so he was in a position to give it to the Corinthian Saints. Now, it is the Apostle who is receiving comfort from them. They have become God's tools and agents in bringing comfort and hope to the missionaries. This section shows that, in the Christian way, there are no absolute givers and no absolute receivers. Each Saint is expected to give *and*

70. *DNTC,* 2:429.

71. Martin, *2 Corinthians,* 388.

to receive as demand requires. The object is for the Saints to receive while in need so that they can be in a position to give to others who are in need. "In speaking in this way to the Corinthians, Paul elevates them remarkably. He does not leave them entrapped in a [potentially worldly] relationship of dominance and dependence, which they would have known quite well from Greco-Roman society, and which they experience from the [false] apostolic claimants. Paul allows them to be givers to him" and in so doing puts all on an equal footing. And he does more: "He implicitly draws them into acceptance of him as their suffering apostle."[72] In doing so, they bring to pass the reconciliation he so desires and with it all the attendant blessings.

Joy in the Report of Titus (7:5–7)

Greek Text

5 Καὶ γὰρ ἐλθόντων ἡμῶν εἰς Μακεδονίαν οὐδεμίαν ἔσχηκεν ἄνεσιν ἡ σὰρξ ἡμῶν,
ἀλλʼ ἐν παντὶ θλιβόμενοι—ἔξωθεν μάχαι, ἔσωθεν φόβοι— 6 ἀλλʼ ὁ παρακαλῶν
τοὺς ταπεινοὺς παρεκάλεσεν ἡμᾶς ὁ θεὸς ἐν τῇ παρουσίᾳ Τίτου· 7 οὐ μόνον δὲ ἐν
τῇ παρουσίᾳ αὐτοῦ, ἀλλὰ καὶ ἐν τῇ παρακλήσει ᾗ παρεκλήθη ἐφʼ ὑμῖν, ἀναγγέλλων
ἡμῖν τὴν ὑμῶν ἐπιπόθησιν, τὸν ὑμῶν ὀδυρμόν, τὸν ὑμῶν ζῆλον ὑπὲρ ἐμοῦ, ὥστε με
μᾶλλον χαρῆναι. [SBLGNT]

King James Version

5 For, when we were come into Macedonia, our flesh had no rest, but we were troubled on every side; without were fightings, within were fears. 6 Nevertheless God, that comforteth those that are cast down, comforted us by the coming of Titus; 7 And not by his coming only, but by the consolation wherewith he was comforted in you, when he told us your earnest desire, your mourning, your fervent mind toward me; so that I rejoiced the more.

New Rendition

5 For even when we came to Macedonia, our body found no rest at all; rather, we were afflicted in every way—struggles on the outside, fears within. 6 But God, who encourages those who are discouraged, encouraged us by the arrival of Titus. 7 And not only by his arrival but also by the encouragement he received while among you when he reported to us your longing, your mourning, your earnest concern for me, so that I rejoiced even more.

72. Seifrid, *Second Letter,* 305.

Translation Notes and Comments

7:5 ***For, when we were come into Macedonia / For even when we came to Macedonia:*** The conjunction γάρ (*gar*), "for," forms the connecting link between the foregoing material and what Paul is about to say concerning what it was that brought him the overwhelming joy he noted above.[73] The phrase ἐλθόντων ἡμῶν (*elthontōn hēmōn*), a genitive absolute construction used temporally, "when we came," returns the course of the letter to where Paul broke off at 2:13.[74] That he uses the plural "we" here is a bit surprising since, in his early account (2:1–13), he mentions no one traveling with him. Though it is very likely he did not travel alone, his use of the plural may have been to deflect "attention from Paul's person to his apostolic mission."[75]

The Roman province of Macedonia lay in the middle of what is now the Greek peninsula. In Paul's day, the senatorial province of Thrace was on the north and Achaia on the south.[76] During his second mission, Paul had preached in the Macedonian cities of Philippi, Thessalonica, and Berea (Acts 16:9–17:10).

our flesh had no rest / our body found no rest at all: The noun σάρξ (*sarx*), "body," "flesh," refers literally to the substance that covers the bones of both humans and animals and also to the body itself.[77] By extension, it refers to both people and nations.[78] Metaphorically, however, its nuances range widely. Three of the more prominent are the nature of unregenerate humankind, the externals of one's life, and the physical limitations imposed by mortality.[79] Given the connection between 2:13 and 7:5, the latter seems the best choice, thus indicating the stress felt by Paul's weak, physical body due to the outward pressure he was experiencing at the time.[80] Even so, because he had earlier stressed the weighed-down nature of his spirit, it is

---

73. Guthrie, *2 Corinthians,* 370.

74. Martin, *2 Corinthians,* 389.

75. Seifrid, *Second Letter,* 306.

76. The new province included the areas of Epirus, Thessaly, and parts of Illyria, Paeonia, and Thrace. For a study, see F. F. Bruce, "Macedonia," in *ABD,* 4:454–57.

77. Louw-Nida, §8.4, 63.

78. Louw-Nida, §§9.12; 10.1.

79. BDAG, 914–16. Usually, this noun has negative connotations while the noun σόμα (*soma*), "body," is positive. However, Paul seems to be using them interchangeably in 4:10–11 and 7:1, 5 to highlight the weaknesses associated with mortality. See Barnett, *Second Epistle,* 237 n. 53.

80. Robert Jewett, *Paul's Anthropological Terms: A Study of Their Use in Conflict Settings* (Leiden: Brill, 1971), 134; Martin, *2 Corinthians,* 389; for a study, see *NID,* 4:251–62.

likely that his use of *sarx* should be understood synonymously with both "spirit" and "body," indicating his total distress in not hearing from Titus.[81]

The noun ἄνεσις (*anesis*), "rest, relaxation, relief," denotes escape from anything that is onerous or troubling.[82] The adjective οὐδείς (*oudeis*), "no,"[83] emphasizes that Paul did not have the slightest degree of rest during this period. The verb ἔχω (*echō*), "to experience something, have, hold."[84] found here in the perfect tense, is telling. The worrisome restlessness he describes had begun sometime in the past but continued with him into the present. His wording suggests that, even though Titus had brought him very good news, he still felt, as he wrote these words, the possibility that trouble still remained among the Corinthians' house churches, and this left him yet a bit unsettled.[85]

but we were troubled on every side / rather, we were afflicted in every way: The verb θλίβω (*thlibō*), "to be troubled," found here as a present passive participle, denotes suffering that comes due to the antagonism of persons or to the pressure of circumstances (compare 4:8).[86] Given the historical context, it is likely that Paul has the latter nuance in mind. This phrase is an anacoluthon—that is, its syntax does not correlate with what one would expect.[87] The phrase begins with a finite verb but then interrupts the structure with the participle. For flow, we have translated the participle as a verb. Paul's use of the phrase ἐν παντὶ θλιβόμενοι (*en panti thlibomenoi*), literally "in every way being afflicted," emphasizes the breadth of his mental and emotional torment at the time.

without were fightings, within were fears / struggles on the outside, fears within: The adverb ἔξωθεν (*exōthen*), "outside," denotes what is external to the individual[88] and, therefore, refers to what is going on around him or her. The noun μάχη (*machē*), "fighting, quarrels," denotes generally any kind of strife or fighting.[89] It carries the nuance of "serious conflict, either physical

---

81. Hughes, *Second Epistle,* 265; Seifrid, *Second Letter,* 306. On Titus, see Translation Notes for 2:13 with corresponding Analysis.

82. BDAG, 77–78.

83. BDAG, 735.

84. BDAG, 420–22.

85. Martin, *2 Corinthians,* 390.

86. MM, 292; Louw-Nida, §22.21; BDAG, 457.

87. BDF, §468.1.

88. BDAG, 354–55.

89. In the general literature, the noun denotes an encounter fought with weapons, but in the New Testament it takes on a more metaphorical meaning that thus precludes armed assault. BDAG, 622.

or non-physical, but clearly intensive and bitter."[90] The adverb ἔσωθεν (*esōthen*), "within," in the present context denotes the "inner being,"[91] while the noun φόβος (*phobos*), "fear," designates "a state of severe distress, aroused by intense concern for impending pain, danger, evil, etc."[92] With these two phrases, Paul powerfully communicates the intense state that surrounded and engulfed him as he journeyed toward Corinth.

7:6 ***Nevertheless God, that comforteth those that are cast down, comforted us by the coming of Titus / But God, who encourages those who are discouraged, encouraged us by the arrival of Titus:*** The adversative conjunction ἀλλά (*alla*), "but, yet, rather,"[93] is important here because it acts to shift "the semantic center of gravity to a positive tone."[94] The verb παρακαλέω (*parakaleō*), "comfort, encourage," primarily means to call someone to one's side, generally so they can give aid.[95] By extension, it took on the nuances of both comforting and encouraging another. In Paul's writings, the Apostle "sets consolation over against tribulation, suffering, and death, identifying his own sufferings with those of Christ, and at the same time sharing in Christ's comfort."[96] Paul also uses the word to denote the "act of emboldening another in belief or course of action," thus "encouragement."[97] In his writings, the idea of comfort is so tied to encouragement in the noun παράκησις (*paraklēsis*) that the two cannot be fully separated.[98] For discussion, see Translation Notes for 1:3–5 with associated Analysis.

The noun ταπεινός (*tapeinos*) generally carries the nuance of "humble, lowly," but Paul, at this point, does not communicate any sense of self-humiliation as a means of gaining divine comfort, and therefore, such a nuance is absent here. On the other hand, the feeling carried by the nouns "downcast" and "discouraged" works.[99] Paul's context shows that he has been brought low because of the circumstances that have surrounded him. According to the scriptures, it is those who have been brought down due

90. Louw-Nida, §39.23.

91. Louw-Nida, §§26.2; 83.16; BDAG, 398.

92. Louw-Nida, §25.251; BDAG, 1062.

93. BDAG, 44.

94. Guthrie, *2 Corinthians,* 373.

95. BDAG, 764–65.

96. *NID,* 3:631.

97. BDAG, 766.

98. Martin, *2 Corinthians,* 142–43; Guthrie, *2 Corinthians,* 67.

99. For a study, see *NID,* 4:448–55, which gives, in addition to "humble, lowly," the nuance of "down-hearted." Martin, *2 Corinthians,* 391, opts for "downcast," while Guthrie, *2 Corinthians,* 373, opts for "discouraged."

not to their improper actions but to their suffering for righteousness' sake whom God comforts.[100]

The noun παρουσία (*parousia*), "coming," refers primarily to the personal presence of an individual but also denotes a person's arrival as the first stage of so being.[101] It carries a positive nuance, connoting as it does both the coming and presence of either a god, a ruler, or their envoy. Often its purpose is to give largess to a people.[102] Within the Christian community, its positive nuance was strengthened due to its association with the agreeable side of the Second Coming, with the reward that event promised. Its use here is appropriate, "since Titus was an envoy of Paul who was an envoy of Christ. Titus's coming was in a sense a royal appearance of God's surrogate, and Paul treats it as a special coming indeed."[103] No doubt Titus's personal arrival brought great comfort to Paul, but the more important source of that comfort was, however, Titus's report of both his acceptance by the community and the positive reaction of the Corinthian Saints to Paul's harsh letter.

7:7 ***And not by his coming only, but by the consolation wherewith he was comforted in you / And not only by his arrival, but also by the encouragement he received while among you:*** With this clarification, Paul gives credit where credit is due. The phrase οὐ μόνον (*ou monon*), "not only," reveals that Titus's coming did bring Paul joy, but the major comfort, signaled by the phrase ἀλλὰ καί (*alla kai*), "but also," came due to the envoy's report on the positive reaction of the Saints to the Apostle's epistle. As in the previous verse, Paul uses the idea of "comfort, encouragement" to describe what is going on. The last phrase in this clause is grammatically rather convoluted. It translates literally as "in the encouragement by which he was encouraged among you." We have provided a more understandable contemporary English rendering.

---

100. Seifrid, *Second Letter,* 307. See Matt. 5:10–11 and LXX Isa. 49:13, which note God has mercy on his people and comforts the humble.

101. BDAG, 780–81.

102. LSJ, 1343; *DAG,* s.v. "παρουσία"; Martin, *2 Corinthians,* 391; Witherington, *Conflict and Community,* 409. For a study on Paul's use of the term, see Ben Witherington III, *Jesus, Paul, and the End of the World* (Downers Grove, Ill.: InterVarsity Press, 1992), 152–55. For a broader study, see *NID,* 3:647–57.

103. On Paul acting as God's envoy, see Margaret M. Mitchell, "New Testament Envoys in the Context of Greco-Roman Diplomatic and Epistolary Conventions: An Example of Timothy and Titus," *Journal of Biblical Literature* 111, no. 4 (1992): 641–62, who shows that envoys were or ought to have been accepted with the same dignity and respect as the person they represented.

when he told us your earnest desire, your mourning, your fervent mind toward me / when he reported to us your longing, your mourning, your earnest concern for me: The verb ἀναγγέλλω (*anangellō*), "to carry back information, to report."[104] It is found here as a present active participle in the nominative case and used circumstantially with a temporal connotation, "when he [Titus] reported." From a strict grammatical standpoint, the participle should be in the genitive case rather than the nominative since it refers back to Τίτου (*Titou*) in the previous verse, which is in the genitive case, but the meaning is clear. It is likely that Paul is more concerned about making his point than following grammatical rules when his point can be easily understood.[105]

His triple use of the pronoun ὑμῶν (*hymōn*), "your," is telling because it points to the positive change of heart that Paul's harsh letter had caused among those who listened to it.[106] To give it special emphasis, he places it in each incident between the definite article and the noun.[107]

Here Paul mentions three conditions that contributed to the great comfort that Titus's report brought him. He captures the first with the noun ἐπιπόθησις (*epipothēsis*), "yearning desire for" something.[108] The word emphasizes the strength of the yearning.[109] He captures the second with the noun ὀδυρμός (*odyrmos*), denoting "lamentation, mourning."[110] The word is most often found in the context of funerary anguish, but it can be used for any occasion that engenders genuine grief or deep sorrow.[111] The third condition he captures with the noun ζῆλος (*zēlos*), "zeal, ardor,"[112] which expresses "deep concern for or devotion to someone or something."[113]

so that I rejoiced the more / so that I rejoiced even more: The verb χαίρω (*chairō*), found here as an aorist infinitive, means to "rejoice" and expresses

---

104. BDAG, 59.

105. Martin, *2 Corinthians,* 393.

106. Martin, *2 Corinthians,* 393.

107. Hughes, *Second Epistle,* 267 n. 5.

108. BDAG, 377. The verb form, ἐπιποθέω, denotes "strong desire." BDAG, 377. This noun is rare in the Bible, being found only here and in 7:11 and Ezek. 23:11 Aq.

109. Louw-Nida, §25.18, 47. Paul does use the verb ἐπιποθέω (*epipotheō*), "to strongly desire" or "to have great affection for," quite a number of times. See Rom. 1:11; Philip. 1:8; 2:26; and 1 Thes. 3:6.

110. BDAG, 692.

111. Louw-Nida, §52.3. Neither of these nouns have an expressed object, but given the context, it seems clear that they are connected to Paul. Barrett, *Second Epistle,* 208.

112. BDAG, 427.

113. Louw-Nida, §§25.46; 78.25.

either the great delight a person feels in something or someone or a state of happiness and comfort.[114] The former best fits the context here. The adverb μᾶλλον (*mallon*), "even more," denotes something felt to a higher extent than before.[115]

Analysis and Summary

Beginning with 7:5, Paul returns the course of his letter back to his account left off at 2:13. Paul has used the long interruption that separates the historical narrative introduced in 2:14 and concluded at 7:4 to vindicate his apostolic office and doctrine and to praise God for his place in the ministry. His high acclaim for the Corinthian Saints found in 7:3–4, though not referring directly to his adventures in Macedonia, does pave the way for his return to the story of his meeting with Titus and then, at this point (7:5–7), stresses the relief and joy the latter's very positive report brought him and why that was the case.[116]

The major cause of Paul's anxiety was his fear that the forceful or tearful letter he had sent would further alienate the Corinthian Saints. Whether or not Titus actually carried the harsh letter to the Corinthians, the text does not state. Paul may have sent it ahead so that the local Saints would have time to ruminate on it before Titus arrived. It seems more likely, however, given Titus's role as envoy, that he carried it.[117]

In chapter 2, the Apostle noted that while he was at Troas, he was struck with great anxiety when he was unable to rejoin Titus as he expected. He was hoping that his fellow missionary would meet him there with a report on how the Corinthian Saints had responded to his harsh letter. Even though God had provided an "open door" for his work in Troas (2:12), his anxiety to meet Titus precluded him from taking advantage of it. The fact that Paul would miss a God-given opportunity for furthering the advance of the gospel in the area underscores the seriousness with which the Apostle took the non-appearance of his friend. In the present passage (7:5), we see that his fear continued with him as he crossed into Europe.[118]

In 2:13 and 4:8, Paul alluded to the extreme mental and emotional distress he was under as he traveled toward Corinth, noting that his spirit was in a constant state of agitation. At this point (7:5), he elaborates on

114. BDAG, 1074–75; Louw-Nida, §25.125.
115. BDAG, 613–14.
116. Martin, *2 Corinthians,* 389.
117. Martin, *2 Corinthians,* 393.
118. Bernard, "Second Epistle," 81.

the soul-crushing weight he was carrying at the time. That Titus did not meet him when and where he expected likely exacerbated his fears. To stress his condition at that time, he uses very strong imagery. Surrounding him, he states, were serious, if nonphysical, struggles of an intense and bitter nature,[119] while within him were fears (φόβοι, *phoboi*) arising from "a state of severe distress."[120] Thus, he could testify that in every conceivable way he was suffering due to heavy worry and emotional pain (ἐν παντὶ θλιβόμενοι, *en panti thlibomenoi*).

This junction presents a significant turning point in the epistle. "These descriptions of conflicts and emotional turmoil, which are painted as both external and internal, express that the apostle had a difficult time of it during this period of ministry, and the trouble had taken its toll [compare 1:8–11]. But the experience also served to drive Paul deeper in his experience of God as is underscored in the next verse."[121]

Indeed, in 7:6, Paul's language suggests he experienced near-rapturous relief at the arrival and report of Titus. Truly, as the Apostle states, he received encouragement (παρακαλέω, *parakaleō*) derived from the Divine. As Paul's envoy to the Corinthian Saints, Titus would have both recited and interpreted the letter, then likely answered any questions and attempted to dispel any concerns.[122] This put him in a good position to judge his listeners' reaction to Paul's missive. Titus's account brought the Apostle such cheer and hope that it all but dissipated his emotional distress and pain and greatly strengthened his resolve to visit the Corinthian Saints.

According to 7:7, there were three items in Titus's report that Paul found particularly comforting. The first was the Saints' strong desire (ἐπιπόθησις, *epipothēsis*) to please Paul and yield to his appeal as expressed in his harsh epistle. The second was their mourning (ὀδυρμός, *odyrmos*) because of the irritation, worry, and even misery that they had caused the Apostle, which led to his need to castigate them.[123] The third, and perhaps the most important, was the fervor or ardor (ζῆλος, *zēlos*) they now expressed toward the Apostle. The attitude suggests that they were anxious to put things right with

119. Louw-Nida, §39.23.

120. Louw-Nida, §25.251.

121. Guthrie, *2 Corinthians,* 372.

122. On Titus's task as the letter bearer, see R. F. Ward, "Pauline Voice and Presence as Strategic Communication," *Semeia* 65 (1994): 102–4.

123. It is possible, that the sorrow could have arisen from Paul's inability to visit the branch some time earlier, but the context suggests that it was because of the grief they caused the Apostle. Martin, *2 Corinthians,* 393.

the Apostle and, likely, to defend him against his detractors.[124] The result of this report, as he notes, greatly increased Paul's joy even over that of reuniting with his good friend and companion. Once again, we see that the Apostle's joy is enhanced by the joy of others (compare Philip. 2:27–28) and more especially by the effect of Titus's mission on these beloved people.[125]

The overall thrust of this section centers on the reconciliation that has now occurred between Paul and these treasured Corinthian Saints and the great relief and absolute joy it brought him. Titus's report has made it clear that Paul's love has been reciprocated and his primary audience now stands with him against those who were attacking him. This is an important point. His antagonists have not gone away. Based on what we will read in chapters 10–13, they are still working among the Saints and remain unbowed. Thus, the total unity between the various house churches has not been achieved.[126]

Even so, among Paul's primary audience, reconciliation, to his joy, has been achieved. The result is, as noted above, "a rare reversal of roles [in that] it is the apostle who [has been] a channel of comfort to the Corinthians and others (1:3–7). They now have become God's means of comforting him in the midst of other unnamed troubles to which he refers in v. 5. The relationship between the apostle and his church is not one-way. He will not lord his authority over their faith (1:24). When and where God chooses, they must be the source of comfort to him."[127]

The Positive Effects of Paul's Harsh Letter (7:8–12)

Greek Text

8 ὅτι εἰ καὶ ἐλύπησα ὑμᾶς ἐν τῇ ἐπιστολῇ, οὐ μεταμέλομαι· εἰ καὶ μετεμελόμην
(βλέπω ὅτι ἡ ἐπιστολὴ ἐκείνη εἰ καὶ πρὸς ὥραν ἐλύπησεν ὑμᾶς), 9 νῦν χαίρω, οὐχ
ὅτι ἐλυπήθητε, ἀλλ' ὅτι ἐλυπήθητε εἰς μετάνοιαν, ἐλυπήθητε γὰρ κατὰ θεόν, ἵνα ἐν
μηδενὶ ζημιωθῆτε ἐξ ἡμῶν. 10 ἡ γὰρ κατὰ θεὸν λύπη μετάνοιαν εἰς σωτηρίαν ἀμετα-
μέλητον ἐργάζεται· ἡ δὲ τοῦ κόσμου λύπη θάνατον κατεργάζεται. 11 ἰδοὺ γὰρ αὐτὸ
τοῦτο τὸ κατὰ θεὸν λυπηθῆναι πόσην κατειργάσατο ὑμῖν σπουδήν, ἀλλὰ ἀπολογίαν,

124. Martin, *2 Corinthians*, 393.

125. Hughes, *Second Epistle*, 268.

126. Witherington, *Conflict and Community*, 409.

127. Seifrid, *Second Letter*, 308.

ἀλλὰ ἀγανάκτησιν, ἀλλὰ φόβον, ἀλλὰ ἐπιπόθησιν, ἀλλὰ ζῆλον, ἀλλὰ ἐκδίκησιν· ἐν παντὶ συνεστήσατε ἑαυτοὺς ἁγνοὺς εἶναι τῷ πράγματι. 12 ἄρα εἰ καὶ ἔγραψα ὑμῖν, οὐχ ἕνεκεν τοῦ ἀδικήσαντος, οὐδὲ ἕνεκεν τοῦ ἀδικηθέντος, ἀλλ' ἕνεκεν τοῦ φανερωθῆναι τὴν σπουδὴν ὑμῶν τὴν ὑπὲρ ἡμῶν πρὸς ὑμᾶς ἐνώπιον τοῦ θεοῦ. [SBLGNT]

King James Version

8 For though I made you sorry with a letter, I do not repent, though I did repent: for I perceive that the same epistle hath made you sorry, though it were but for a season. 9 Now I rejoice, not that ye were made sorry, but that ye sorrowed to repentance: for ye were made sorry after a godly manner, that ye might receive damage by us in nothing. 10 For godly sorrow worketh repentance to salvation not to be repented of: but the sorrow of the world worketh death. 11 For behold this selfsame thing, that ye sorrowed after a godly sort, what carefulness it wrought in you, yea, what clearing of yourselves, yea, what indignation, yea, what fear, yea, what vehement desire, yea, what zeal, yea, what revenge! In all things ye have approved yourselves to be clear in this matter. 12 Wherefore, though I wrote unto you, I did it not for his cause that had done the wrong, nor for his cause that suffered wrong, but that our care for you in the sight of God might appear unto you.

New Rendition

8 For even if I caused you sorrow with my letter, I do not regret it (even though I initially regretted it, for I see that the letter made you sorry, although only for a short time). 9 Now I am happy, not because you were made sorry but that your being made sorry led you to repentance. For you were made sorry in a godly manner such that you suffered no loss through us. 10 For godly sorrow produces repentance that leads to salvation that is without regret. But worldly sorrow produces death. 11 For see what this very thing, this being made sorry in a godly manner, has produced in you—what earnestness, indeed what eagerness to defend yourselves, what indignation, what alarm, what longing, what zeal, what desire to see justice done! In every particular you have shown that you were innocent in the matter. 12 And so, even though I wrote to you, it was not because of the one who did the wrong nor on account of the one who was wronged, rather it was in order to demonstrate to you your eagerness on our behalf before God.

Translation Notes and Comments

7:8 This verse presents a number of translation difficulties and, as a result, there are a number of different modern punctuation schemes and various translations. That others saw problems with the verse, as the number of variants found among the ancient manuscripts attest, reaches back at least as far as the third through fifth centuries.[128] Copyists rightly recognized

---

128. For a list of the variants, see Martin, *2 Corinthians,* 378 n. f. For discussion, see Metzger, *Textual Commentary,* 512.

that Paul had begun a new portion of his argument with the phrase εἰ καὶ μετεμελόμην (*ei kai metemelomēn*), "though I regret it," but were not sure just where it went next. Some thought it ended with the phrase beginning βλέπω (*blepō*), "I see,"[129] while others saw it as extending all the way to νῦν χαίρω (*nyn chairō*), "now I rejoice," in 7:9. The KJV has Paul's argument beginning "I see," but in doing so it forces the clause to state wrongly why Paul made the Corinthian Saints sorry. We have followed other copyists who saw all the material from "though I regret it" through "for a short time" as a parenthetical explanation. Though we found that certainty cannot be achieved by placing the words "for I see" as part of the parenthetical expression, it shows why Paul regretted having hurt the Corinthian Saints, and that seems to best fit the overall context.[130]

For though I made you sorry with a letter / For even if I caused you sorrow with my letter: The verb λυπέω (*lypeō*) means to "become sad, sorrowful, distressed."[131] In 7:10, Paul also uses the noun λύπη (*lypē*), "sorrow." Though each word can refer to physical pain (such as hunger or thirst or heat or cold), in the present context their nuance is more to the emotional side of distress. In that vein, they refer to pain that includes anxiety, anger, sorrow, or grief. The noun *lypē* is often translated as "grief." Since, however, the word denotes "an intense emotional suffering or poignant sorrow especially for some real and definite cause," it seems too strong to express the feelings of either Paul or his audience. The noun "sorrow," expressing as it does the idea of distress of mind due to guilt,[132] seems to catch the emotion felt by both parties better, and we use it throughout our Rendition. Paul's words show that deep sorrow can, under certain circumstances, beget further and greater knowledge. His view conforms with that found in both the Greek and Hebrew Old Testaments: sorrow and suffering can have a positive outcome, provided they are met with faith, for the latter is the driving force behind repentance and becoming one with God, out of which comes peace.[133]

The noun ἐπιστολή (*epistolē*), "letter," denotes any written document, but in this case, it refers specifically to the harsh, if sad, missive Paul wrote to the Corinthian Saints shortly after his brief and unsuccessful second visit (2:3–4).[134] The Greek text has ἡ ἐπιστολή (*hē epistolē*), "the letter," but the

129. Even though that translation demanded cutting the conjunction γάρ (*gar*), "for."

130. For a discussion of the entire problem, see Martin, *2 Corinthians,* 378–79 n. f.

131. BDAG, 604; Louw-Nida, §2.275.

132. *Dictionary of Synonyms,* s.v. "grieve."

133. For discussion, see Rudolf Bultmann, "λύπη, λυπέω," in *TDNT,* 4:313–22.

134. Sperry calls it a flying visit to Corinth. See *Life and Letters,* 115–16.

definite article has the sense of a possessive pronoun;[135] hence "my letter" in our Rendition.

I do not repent / I do not regret it: The verb μεταμέλομαι (*metamelomai*), "to have regrets," denotes a wish that something could be undone.[136] The KJV translation of the word as "repent" can easily be misconstrued to suggest that Paul thought he had crossed a moral line.[137] Such is not the case. He simply regretted, for a time, that he wrote the letter, sensing after he sent it that its effect could not only cause sorrow to the people he loved (see 2:3–4) but also hurt his own cause.[138]

though I did repent / even though I initially regretted it: The phrase εἰ καί (*ei kai*), "even though," used here concessively,[139] points to a moment in the past when Paul regretted sending the harsh letter. Thus, we have added the word "initially" to carry this nuance.

for I perceive that the same epistle hath made you sorry / for I see that the letter made you sorry: The conjunction γάρ (*gar*), "for," introduces the reason for the regret, and the rest of the phrase reveals Paul's deep care for these people. The verb βλέπω (*blepō*), "to perceive, . . . see,"[140] in the present context means to become aware of something, in this case Paul's realization of the negative effect his letter could have. On the verb λυπέω (*lypeō*), "to cause sorrow," see above.

though it were but for a season / although only for a short time: The phrase πρὸς ὥραν (*pros hōran*), literally "for an hour,"[141] denotes "a relatively short period of time, with emphasis upon the temporary nature of the event or state,[142] but based on Paul's usage of the term in Galatians 2:5 and 1 Thessalonians 2:17, it connotes a short period of time that nonetheless seems to drag on and on.[143]

---

135. Wallace, *Greek Grammar,* 215–16; Smyth, *Greek Grammar,* §1121.

136. BDAG, 639.

137. There is a semantic difference between μεταμέλομαι (*metamelomai*), "to regret," and μετανοέω (*metanoeō*), "to repent." Though both can carry the idea of changing one's mind, the latter, in the New Testament, carries the nuance of doing so for the better due to remorse for a sinful act. The former nuances the regret even for an act that is not sinful. See Louw-Nida, §§25.270; 31.59; and BDAG, 639, 640. For a study, see John Moncure, "II Corinthians 7:8–10," *Review and Expositor* 16 (1919): 476–77.

138. Martin, *2 Corinthians,* 394.

139. Moule, *Idiom Book,* 167.

140. BDAG, 178–79.

141. Louw-Nida, §67.199. The noun ὥρα (*hora*) can refer to any portion of a day as well as a specific hour within it. BDAG, 1102–3.

142. Louw-Nida, §67.109.

143. Seifrid, *Second Letter,* 308, n. 685.

7:9 ***Now I rejoice, not that ye were made sorry / Now I am happy, not because you were made sorry:*** The adverb νῦν (*nyn*), "now," denotes less the present moment and more the present situation in which Paul finds himself.[144] On the verb χαίρω (*chairō*), "be glad," see Translation Notes for 7:7. Here the context connotes a state of happiness or well-being.[145] Paul is saying that the present situation has brought him happiness. On the verb λυπέω (*lypeō*), "to cause sorrow," see Translation Notes for 7:8.[146] He uses the phrase οὐχ ὅτι (*ouch hoti*), "not because," to assure his readers that it was not their pain that made him happy.

but that ye sorrowed to repentance / but that your being made sorry led you to repentance: The phrase ἀλλ' ὅτι ἐλυπήθητε εἰς μετάνοιαν (*all' hoti elypēthēte eis metanoian*) translates literally "but that you were made sorry to repentance." We rephrased it in our Rendition to better convey the contemporary English sense of the passage. On the verb λυπέω (*lypeō*), "to cause sorrow," found here as an aorist passive, see Translation Notes for 7:8. The noun μετάνοια (*metanoia*), though consistently translated as "repentance" in most biblical versions, does not necessarily carry the idea of spiritual or emotional remorse or contrition due to sin as does the English. In the present context, its focus is on a change of attitude, with its accompanying behavior brought on by sorrow due to a now-recognized inappropriate act.[147]

for ye were made sorry after a godly manner / For you were made sorry in a godly manner: The conjunction γάρ (*gar*), "for," is causal explaining what caused the Apostle to feel the way he currently does. On the verb λυπέω (*lypeō*), "to cause sorrow," found here as an aorist passive, see Translation Notes for 7:8. The preposition κατά (*kata*), literally "according to" or "in conformity with,"[148] denotes doing something according to the will or manner of another. In this case, it is God. As such, the thrust is toward the quality of the sorrow rather than its fact.[149] Paul is saying that

---

144. BDAG, 681. The situation is the state of his feelings as he writes the letter. Barnett, *Second Epistle,* 374.

145. BDAG, 1074–75.

146. Paul uses the verb in the inceptive sense in each of the three times that he uses it in this verse. Thus, the translation "you became sorry." Barnett, *Second Epistle,* 374, n. 11.

147. Louw-Nida, §41.52. The noun combines the prefix μέτα (*meta*), "after," with the verb νοέω (*noeō*), "to perceive," thus, "to perceive afterwards," yielding the idea of reconsidering something or thinking differently about it. For a study, see *NID,* 3:290–93.

148. The preposition κατά (*kata*) acts here as a marker of similarity or homogeneity. BDAG, 511–13.

149. Barnett, *Second Epistle,* 374 n. 12; Louw-Nida, §§89.4, 8, 113.

his readers' response to his harsh letter expressed God's way and will. Specifically, here, it seems that godly sorrow refers to "the sorrow of the man who has become aware of his lostness in the world, and who cries again to God in [repentance] from the world."[150]

that ye might receive damage by us in nothing / such that you suffered no loss through us: The conjunction ἵνα (*hina*), "such that," expresses result.[151] The verb ζημιόω (*zēmioō*), "to suffer damage" or "loss,"[152] found here as an aorist subjunctive passive, refers to experiencing the loss of something "with [the] implication of undergoing hardship or suffering."[153] The prepositional phrase ἐν μηδενί (*en mēdeni*), "in no way," stresses the total lack of something.[154] The whole phrase explains why Paul feels happy with developments. Not only was no one hurt in any way by his harsh letter, but more importantly, good came of it.

7:10 ***For godly sorrow worketh repentance to salvation not to be repented of / For godly sorrow produces repentance that leads to salvation that is without regret:*** The conjunction γάρ (*gar*), "for," is again causal and introduces the reason Paul's readers were not harmed by his harsh letter. He again refers to "godly sorrow" and the "repentance" it engenders. On these, see Translation Notes for 7:9. The verb ἐργάζομαι (*ergazomai*), "work,"[155] in this context denotes that which carries out, brings to pass, or produces something[156]—namely, σωτηρία (*sōtēria*), "salvation." The noun denotes deliverance from harm, and here refers particularly to the deliverance of the soul in immortality that Jesus as Savior provides.[157] Its promise, however, is manifest in the present by the reception of the Spirit (Eph. 1:13–14; 4:30; John 14:16–17). Paul describes this kind of salvation with the adjective ἀμεταμέλητος (*ametamelētos*), "without regret," denoting that which brings neither remorse, sorrow, nor emotional or spiritual suffering of any kind ever.[158]

---

150. Rudolph Bultmann, "λύπη, λυπέω," in *TDNT,* 4:320–21.

151. Louw-Nida, §89.49.

152. BDAG, 428.

153. Louw-Nida, §57.69.

154. BDAG, 647. Hughes, *Second Epistle,* 269–70, argues that the loss they may have suffered was their reward in the next life, a subject of high interest to Paul.

155. Louw-Nida, §42.41.

156. Louw-Nida, §13.9.

157. BDAG, 985–86.

158. Louw-Nida, §25.271; BDAG, 53. The root verb μεταμέλομαι (*metamelomai*) means "to experience remorse" caused when persons see "the bitter end of sin" which drives them to repentance through which they are able to break free of it. The effect is described as ἀμεταμέλητος (*ametamelētos*), that which brings neither regret nor remorse—ever. This

but the sorrow of the world worketh death / But worldly sorrow produces death: On the noun λύπη (*lypē*), "sorrow," see Translation Notes for 7:8. The noun κόσμος (*kosmos*), "world,"[159] though often carrying the positive nuance of order and harmony as produced by God, in the present context takes on a negative color connoting human affairs that are alienated from God and opposed to him.[160] The word is found in the phrase ἡ δὲ τοῦ κόσμου λύπη (*hē de tou kosmou lypē*), literally "but the sorrow of the world." We have translated this as "worldly sorrow" to better catch the sense in contemporary English.[161] The verb κατεργάζομαι (*katergazomai*), "produce," refers to causing a state or condition.[162] In this case, that condition is θάνατος (*thanatos*), "death." Though often referring to physical death, in the present context the noun refers to spiritual death resulting from an unwillingness to repent and accept the saving power of Christ.[163]

7:11 ***For behold this selfsame thing, that ye sorrowed after a godly sort / For see what this very thing, this being made sorry in a godly manner, has produced in you:*** The particle ἰδού (*idou*), "see, look, behold,"[164] acts as a marker of strong emphasis nuancing the complete validation of what Paul has said. In this case, as the phrase αὐτὸ τοῦτο (*auto touto*), "this very thing," shows, *idou* refers back to the effect of Paul's harsh letter on its target audience. To make sure his readers understand exactly to what he is referring, the Apostle explicitly identifies it in a parenthetical expression. On the verb "sorry," see Translation Notes for 7:8; on the phrase κατὰ θεόν (*kata theon*), "in a godly manner," see Translation Notes for 7:9; and on the verb κατεργάζομαι (*katergozomai*), "to produce," see Translation Notes for 7:10.

what carefulness it wrought in you / what earnestness: The noun σπουδή (*spoudē*), "earnestness," "haste," or "diligence," denotes an eager willingness to discharge an obligation.[165] In King James English, the word "careful"

---

verse shows that "what is of God causes no remorse," for a "real change of heart (μετανοία, *metanoia*, 7:9) is a divine operation in spite of and precisely in suffering. In repentance is new salvation (7:10) and new life (7:11)." Otto Michel, "μεταμέλομαι," in *TDNT,* 4:626–29.

159. BDAG, 561–63.

160. Louw-Nida, §41.38.

161. Harris, *Second Epistle,* 540, notes that the phrase acts as adjectival genitive, thus the translation "worldly."

162. BDAG, 531.

163. BDAG, 442–43.

164. BDAG, 468. Ἰδού (*idou*) is most often translated as "but, yet, rather." See Louw-Nida, §91.10.

165. BDAG, 939–40.

denoted an anxiousness to fill a task with care[166] and was, thus, used properly to translate the Greek term. Since the modern English word "careful" has lost that nuance, the archaic meaning no longer works. We have, thus, translated the Greek using the modern English word that best fits.

yea, what clearing of yourselves / indeed what eagerness to defend yourselves: The conjunction ἀλλά (*alla*), "but, yet, rather," usually has an adversative sense,[167] but here it marks a contrastive emphasis,[168] which Paul uses to introduce each new element "in an emphatic manner to denote an idea reaching a climax."[169] The KJV translates this with the English adverb "yea," which introduces an explicit or emphatic phrase,[170] but we have translated it as "indeed" since that better conveys the sense in contemporary English. Though the KJV, following the Greek text, has the adverb at the beginning of each noun, we have chosen, for the sake of flow, to leave it untranslated after its first use. The adjective πόσος (*posos*), "what," denotes a degree of magnitude and is often translated as "how great" or "how much."[171] Since the English adjective "what" acts as an "interrogative expressing inquiry about the identity, nature, or value of an object,"[172] we have followed the KJV in using it to introduce each of the following phrases even though the Greek text has it only here. The noun ἀπολογία (*apologia*), "defense," here expresses the act of eagerly protecting oneself or others, so we have translated it as the phrase "eagerness to defend yourselves" to clarify the sense in contemporary English.[173]

what indignation / what indignation: On πόσος (*posos*), "what," see above. The noun ἀγανάκτησις (*aganaktēsis*), "indignation,"[174] refers to the strong opposition, displeasure, or anger aroused by something judged as wrong or mean.[175]

what fear / what alarm: On πόσος (*posos*), see above. The noun φόβος (*phobos*), "alarm," refers to one's reaction to an intimidating or alarming force.[176]

---

166. *Collegiate Dictionary,* s.v. "careful."

167. Ἀλλά (*alla*) is usually translated as "but"; however, that is not the proper nuance here. See Louw-Nida, §91.2; and BDAG, 44–45.

168. Louw-Nida, §91.11.

169. Martin, *2 Corinthians,* 401. See also BDF, §448.6.

170. *Collegiate Dictionary,* s.v. "yea."

171. BDAG, 855–56.

172. *Collegiate Dictionary,* s.v. "what."

173. Louw-Nida, §33.435. The term often referred to a defense in which one explained the circumstances or reasons for actions. These were done personally or in writing either before an official or in a court of law. Guthrie, *2 Corinthians,* 380.

174. BDAG, 5.

175. Louw-Nida, §88.186.

176. BDAG, 1062.

what vehement desire / what longing: On πόσος (*posos*), see above. The noun ἐπιπόθησις (*epipothēsis*) denotes a yearning or deep desire for something.[177]

what zeal: On πόσος (*posos*), see above. The noun ζῆλος (*zēlos*), "zeal," denotes an intensity of positive involvement and care for something often intimating a dedication to that thing.[178]

what revenge / what desire to see justice done: On πόσος (*posos*), see above. The noun ἐκδίκησις (*ekdikēsis*) expresses the desire to have justice meted out.[179]

In all things ye have approved yourselves to be clear in this matter / In every particular you have shown that you were innocent in the matter: The phrase ἐν παντί (*en panti*), literally "in everything," refers to every respect in which something happened, and here it indicates various ways these Saints have shown they have taken the Apostle's censure seriously.[180] The verb συνίστημι (*synistēmi*), "to show," denotes causing something to be revealed through an action.[181] In this case what is shown is ἁγνός (*hagnos*). The adjective refers to what is pure or innocent.[182] The noun πρᾶγμα (*pragma*), "thing, matter," denotes that which has happened,[183] but the nuances of the word are very broad.[184] In this case, it points to the rebellion against Paul and his companions. But the Apostle's use of this very broad word softens its thrust and thereby reflects his desire to leave behind the whole affair.[185]

7:12 ***Wherefore, though I wrote unto you, I did it not for his cause that had done the wrong / And so, even though I wrote to you, it was not because of the one who did the wrong:*** The conjunction ἄρα (*ara*), "so," "consequently," expresses a result.[186] The preposition, ἕνεκεν (*heneken*), meaning "for the sake of" or "because," marks the cause or reason for an action.[187] By using the

177. Louw-Nida, §25.18; BDAG, 377.

178. Louw-Nida, §78.25; BDAG, 427.

179. BDAG, 301; Louw-Nida, §56.35.

180. Guthrie, *2 Corinthians,* 381. The preposition ἐν (*en*) "in," marks the condition or circumstance in which an action takes place. BDAG, 326–30. The adjective παντί, (*panti*), "all things," shows the extent of the action or circumstance. Louw-Nida, §59.23.

181. Louw-Nida, §28.49.

182. BDAG, 13.

183. BDAG, 858–59. The noun has a quasilegal nuance connoting a legal dispute or judicial question (Louw-Nida, §56.2) suggesting that the affair could have led to church discipline.

184. *DAG,* s.v. "πρᾶγμα."

185. Barnett, *Second Epistle,* 379, n. 33.

186. BDAG, 127.

187. BDAG, 334.

phrase οὐχ ἕνεκεν (*ouch heneken*), "not because of,"[188] Paul makes it clear that his major purpose in writing the harsh letter was not directed at the offending party. The verb ἀδικέω (*adikeō*), "do wrong," found here as an aorist masculine participle, denotes an act that, at its core, is unjust and causes injury.[189] The gender of the participle shows that the offender was a man.

nor for his cause that suffered wrong / nor on account of the one who was wronged: Using the conjunction οὐδέ (*oude*), "nor,"[190] Paul signals another factor that did not motivate him to write the harsh letter. The verb ἀδικέω (*adikeō*), "to do wrong," is found here as an aorist passive masculine participle and means "to be wronged," with the gender showing that the offended party was a man.

The use of the passive voice, "the one who was," keeps the offended person out of direct sight. There is little doubt the phase is an oblique reference to Paul himself, who by this means is able to keep himself in the background and, thus, dampen any remaining antagonism. The verb does, however, suggests the deep hurt that Paul suffered personally and publicly because of what happened.

but that our care for you in the sight of God might appear unto you / rather it was in order to demonstrate to you your eagerness on our behalf before God: On the conjunction ἀλλά (*alla*), "but, yet, rather," see Translation Notes for 7:11. Here it introduces a contrast[191] and points to why Paul wrote his harsh letter. He again used the preposition ἕνεκεν (*heneken*), "in order to" (see above), to indicate his reason for writing. The verb φανερόω (*phaneroō*), "reveal, expose, . . . disclose," found here as an aorist passive infinitive, refers to making something publicly known by disclosing it fully and clearly.[192] Paul expresses the object of the demonstration with the prepositional phrase πρὸς ὑμᾶς (*pros hymas*), "to you."[193] The purpose of the letter was to create a situation in which these Saints could see their error. On the noun σπουδή (*spoudē*), "eagerness," see Translation Notes for 7:11. The preposition ὑπέρ (*hyper*), "in behalf of," denotes what is to the advantage of another.[194] The phrase ὑπὲρ ἡμῶν (*hyper hēmas*), "in our behalf," shows the direction of the advantage. It was directed primarily at Paul but also at his associates. The phrase ἐνώπιον τοῦ θεοῦ (*enōpion tou theou*), "before God,"

188. The preposition ἕνεκεν (*heneken*), "because of" (BDAG, 334), is negated by the negative particle οὐχ (*ouch*) (BDAG, 733–34).

189. BDAG, 20; Louw-Nida, §§20.25; 88.22, 128.

190. BDAG, 734–35.

191. BDAG, 44–45.

192. BDAG, 1048; Louw-Nida, §28.36.

193. Smyth, *Greek Grammar,* §1331; Guthrie, *2 Corinthians,* 382.

194. BDAG, 1030–31.

speaks "of a right posture spiritually, whereby a person or community live in an awareness of their obligation to . . . God."[195] Paul places it last in the sentence to emphasize its importance to all that has happened.

Analysis and Summary

In the subsection 7:8–12, Paul comments on why he wrote the harsh letter and happily notes its positive effect, which he desired it to have, on his target audience. Earlier (2:4) he noted the gut-wrenching emotions that filled him as he wrote that letter. What he did took "risky, tremulous courage,"[196] for, it seems, he realized that his words, rather than bringing reconciliation, could easily result in further alienation. If that happened, it would both embarrass him and hurt his cause.[197] Indeed, his anxiety amounted to near mental and spiritual paralysis, such that he could not conclude his mission the area of Troas (2:12–13)[198] but had to move on, driven by the hope of finding Titus. It must be kept in mind, however, that it was love, not malice, that drove him to write the stinging rebuke.

In 7:8, he readily admits he knew his letter would not just upset many among the Saints but also cause them emotional pain. For that reason, there was a time, he admits, that he regretted having to send it.[199] That period may have lasted up to the moment he heard Titus's positive report.[200] Despite all the agony he suffered, as he now writes, he neither backs away nor tries to dilute his awareness that he caused the Saints a good deal of pain. Thus, his words in 7:9 do not constitute an apology. Indeed, given the present circumstances, he assures his readers that he now has no regrets for writing it. The reason is that their salutary hurt acted as a catalyst to their repentance and their reconciliation with him.[201]

Likely recognizing that his admission in not regretting sending the letter could be interpreted as a callous, if not cruel, sentiment, he explains, parenthetically, that it did, if temporarily, cause him sorrow. But he goes

---

195. Guthrie, *2 Corinthians,* 382.

196. Guthrie, *2 Corinthians,* 378. The Book of Mormon prophet Jacob also experienced anxiety for having to deliver a harsh message. See Jacob 2:6–7.

197. Martin, *2 Corinthians,* 394–95.

198. Seifrid, *Second Letter,* 309.

199. Guthrie, *2 Corinthians,* 376.

200. Barnett, *Second Epistle,* 374. Hughes, *Second Epistle,* 269–70, argues that Paul was actually under moral necessity to write the letter. Not to have done so would have amounted to apostolic neglect and spiritual irresponsibility on his part. Guthrie, *2 Corinthians,* 377–78, notes that one of the most difficult tasks of ministration is having to correct those who have gone astray.

201. Martin, *2 Corinthians,* 394–95.

on to state that at present, in light of Titus's report, he rejoices that he had the courage to send it. Even so, Paul desires now to put that whole matter behind everyone and move on. He hopes they can do this, because the pain he caused them, though sharp, was but only "for a moment" (πρὸς ὥραν, *pros hōran*) and led to healing repentance.[202] That positive outcome being the result, there was no need, he feels, to dwell on the past.[203]

Noteworthy is that Paul refers to repentance only six times in all his writings.[204] At first glance, it seems strange that he would pay seemingly little attention to a primary gospel principle. It is likely that the reason is because the word, as understood at the time, did not sufficiently stress God's action in the salvation process. With its Hebrew equivalent (תְּשׁוּבָה, *tĕšûbāh*), it means simply "turning," a strictly human experience and operation. Paul, based in the few instances he uses the term, fills out what repentance actually requires. It is a process in which one recognizes one's wrongdoing in the sight of God and seeks to make amends. Such wrongdoing includes improper behavior toward God's anointed servants.[205] Indeed, such behavior is actually an affront to God himself. The reason is that his servants proclaim his word and exercise his authority. They do not act for themselves but for the Divine. To reject them is to reject him and his word.[206]

On that basis, as revealed in 7:10, it is not surprising that recognizing what they had done brought the Corinthian Saints not just to feel badly but also to sorrow "in a godly manner" (κατὰ θεόν, *kata theon*).[207] The phrase shows that these people sorrowed according to God's will—that is, in such a way that it was heartfelt and life changing. According to Elder Bruce R. McConkie, godly sorrow "includes an honest, heartfelt contrition of soul, a contrition born of a broken heart and a contrite spirit. It presupposes a frank, personal acknowledgment that one's acts have been evil in the sight

---

202. Paul uses the phrase to denote a short period of time that seems to drag on forever. See Gal. 2:5; 1 Thes. 2:17; and Seifrid, *Second Letter,* 308, n. 685. On healing repentance, see James K. Lyon, "Repentance," in *EM,* 3:1216–18.

203. Martin, *2 Corinthians,* 394–95.

204. It appears in 7:8 twice and in 7:9; 7:10; Rom. 2:4; and 2 Tim. 2:25. The verb μετανοέω (*metanoeō*) occurs in only 2 Cor. 12:21.

205. It is turning to Paul, not God, that is the focus of the repentance process in these verses. Even so, Paul is not trying to replace or upstage Deity. He, however, clearly understands that, in order to be reconciled and made one with God, the Saints must be so reconciled to his emissary because he is the source of both the doctrine and revelation of Christ's will. Barnett, *Second Epistle,* 375, with nn. 15, 16.

206. Martin, *2 Corinthians,* 396–97.

207. The phrase refers to that which is "godly" or done as God would want it to be done. BDAG, 511–13.

of Him who is holy. There is no mental reservation in godly sorrow, no feeling that perhaps one's sins are not so gross or serious after all. It is certainly more than regret either because the sin has been brought to light or because some preferential reward or status has been lost because of it."[208]

The Saints, through the instruments of Paul's harsh letter and Titus's work, seem to have recognized that by rejecting Paul, they had also rejected his message, the true gospel, and had thereby placed themselves in a most precarious spiritual position.[209]

Fortunately, through their repentance, as Paul notes, they "were harmed in no way by us." But what harm did they avoid, and how was it related to Paul and his companions? Certainly, one answer is that the missionaries would not have visited them, and reconciliation with Paul, and by implication with God, would not have occurred. Instead, bitterness and schism in their relationship with Paul would have endured.[210] It is more likely, however, that the Apostle has eternal consequences in mind. As he notes in 7:10, godly sorrow leads to repentance, and repentance leads to eternal life. By realizing what they had done and feeling deeply sorrowful because of it in accordance with God's will, they were once again reconciled to Paul and in the same breath to God, thus again assuring themselves of salvation.[211]

The implication of these verses is largely missed by Catholic and Protestant scholars. Because they have long since devalued the importance of the apostolic office, they do not catch the fact that Paul insists that reconciliation with God is impossible without the authority and direction of these presiding officers. They are his only duly appointed emissaries (πρεσβεύω, *presbeuō*)[212] on the earth. Only they have his authority to pronounce his will, declare his doctrine, and delegate the performance of his ordinances and priesthood to others. Their first and foremost assignment is to bear witness to Christ in all the world (Matt. 28:19–20) and oversee others called to assist them (Acts 1:21–26; 6:1–4; 11:1–18; 1 Cor. 12:28; Eph. 4:11–14).[213] Paul

---

208. *DNTC,* 2:430. See also Brent L. Top, "Repentance," in *Book of Mormon Reference Companion,* ed. Dennis L. Largey (Salt Lake City: Deseret Book, 2003), 676–78.

209. Martin, *2 Corinthians,* 396–97.

210. Thrall, *Critical and Exegetical Commentary,* 1:492.

211. Hughes, *Second Epistle,* 269–70; Martin, *2 Corinthians,* 397.

212. In 2 Cor 5:20, Paul refers to his apostolic work as ὑπὲρ Χριστοῦ οὖν πρεσβεύομεν ὡς τοῦ θεοῦ παρακαλοῦντος δι' ἡμῶν· (*hyper Christou oun presbeuomen hōs tou theou parakaloutos di' hēmōn*), "Therefore, we are representatives of Christ as if God himself were encouraging you through us" (NR).

213. S. Kent Brown, "Apostle," in *EM,* 1:59–61.

clearly understood, as did the Corinthian Saints who followed him, that only through union with him could they be reconciled to God, because he not only preached the correct doctrine but also had authority to implement its teachings and regulations. The Divine authenticated this apostolic power through confirming signs and more especially the gift of the Holy Ghost with its attendant wonders. By this means, testimony was, as it were, written on the hearts of the Saints (1:21–22; 3:3, 6; 4:6; 5:20; 12:12; see also 1 Cor. 9:1–2; 12:28; Eph. 2:20; 4:11–13; 6:20). Without this authority and its transforming power, salvation was impossible.[214]

Paul goes on to note, in 7:10, that there is a difference between worldly and godly sorrow. The latter results in repentance that leads to positive actions that bring spiritual benefit that will never lead to regret because "it rests on true principles and never need[s] to be changed."[215] On the other hand, any remorse of the former is often shallow, full of bitterness, self-pity, and devoid of positive actions.[216] Such sorrow can actually lead to greater harm because its suffering can yield to "a thirst for revenge."[217]

Paul's remarks in 7:11 play a critical role in his outreach to his readers. Though he readily admits that his harsh letter caused sorrow, he is also quick to point out that the effect brought reconciliation, not harm, and more importantly spiritual life, not spiritual death, to the recipients. It was the comforting report of Titus, as Paul's words show, that lifted him from the depth of his former apprehensiveness to the height of the joy he now feels.[218] To emphasize the point, he uses seven nouns, each an attribute of these people, to illustrate the magnitude of the positive effect his letter had on them and the good it brought as the Saints practiced the repentance that led to salvation.[219] The Apostle uses the noun "eagerness," or "earnestness" (σπουδή, *spoudē*), as expressed in the actions of these Saints, to stress the source of his newfound relief and joy. The word reveals that these Saints not only were sincere about

---

214. In the modern Church, along with the Quorum of the Twelve Apostles, the Quorum of the First Presidency is made up exclusively of those who have been ordained to the Apostleship. See J. Lynn England and W. Keith Warner, "First Presidency," in *EM,* 2:512–14. The scriptures do not give a clear picture of the organization of the nascent Church and therefore if there was a quorum akin to today's First Presidency is unknown.

215. Anderson, *Understanding Paul,* 138.

216. Barnett, *Second Epistle,* 376–77; Garland, *2 Corinthians,* 355–56; Harris, *Second Epistle,* 540.

217. Guthrie, *2 Corinthians,* 379.

218. Hughes, *Second Epistle,* 274.

219. Barnett, *Second Epistle,* 378.

being reconciled to the Apostle but also did it with dispatch.[220] That Paul preceded this noun with the indefinite adjective "what" (πόσος, *posos*) stresses the depth of their earnestness (as does the noun's repetition in 7:12). Each of the following attributes continue to be colored by this nuance, and in doing so, Paul creates "an ascending climactic effect from [this] initial word."[221]

Their earnestness was first expressed by their strong desire to defend themselves (ἀπολογία, *apologia*). Though the noun could infer that they were trying to disclaim any association with Paul's detractors, this interpretation seems weak because the text shows that they were at the least complacent in the Apostle's libeling. Better interpretations would be that they either were desirous to defend themselves against any thought that they would condone any such behavior in the future or were defending themselves against Paul's accusations that they had accepted false teachers. Either way, even though their stand was at least tacitly an admission of guilt,[222] "this was an improvement over [their] earlier lethargy" and revealed the correctness of the doctrine "that godly sorrow motivates people to seek correction in the sight of God."[223]

Their earnestness next expressed itself through their "indignation" (ἀγανάκτησις, *aganaktēsis*). Paul does not identify those at whom these Saints' strong displeasure was directed. The term could refer to how they felt about themselves for their former inaction or, more likely, to those perpetrators, including either the man who had caused so much grief (2:6–8) or those who had attacked Paul or both. At any rate, it seems to have been directed at any who caused the distress the branch had suffered.[224]

Going on, the Apostle notes they experienced "alarm" (φόβος, *phobos*). Again, he does not indicate what the source was. It could be their recognition that they had offended God's representative and, in doing so, put themselves in a position to be rebuked by him (in 1 Cor. 4:21, he did threaten, speaking metaphorically, to come against them with a whip unless something was done)[225] or, better, that they had put themselves under divine

220. Martin, *2 Corinthians,* 401.

221. Barnett, *Second Epistle,* 378.

222. Barrett, *Second Epistle,* 211.

223. Martin, *2 Corinthians,* 401.

224. Martin, *2 Corinthians,* 401.

225. A secondary definition of the noun φόβος (*phobos*) is that of deep respect, even awe (BDAG, 1062). Such an emotion may have been engendered as these people, once again, realized that Paul was the apostolic representative of God.

condemnation.[226] This may be the source of the last three qualities Paul attributes to these people—namely, their deep longing (ἐπιπόθησις, *epipothēsis*), likely to be reconciled to Paul and thus to God; their zeal (ζῆλος, *zēlos*) in making that reconciliation happen; and finally, their desire to see justice done (ἐκδίκησις, *ekdikēsis*).[227] The latter could refer to an attempt either to vindicate themselves from direct blame for the offense against Paul or to vindicate him against those who spurned him and rejected his authority.[228]

With a degree of magnanimity, the Apostle states that due to their efforts, these Saints have proven themselves "to be innocent in the matter" (ἁγνοὺς εἶναι τῷ πράγματι, *hagnous einai tō pragmati*). The statement should not be taken to mean that Paul felt they were initially guiltless but that, through the depth and sincerity of their repentance, they had become effectively blameless since they now had their former relationship with Paul restored.[229]

This verse highlights the forgiving spirit that marks the life of this Apostle. Though the actions of certain Corinthian Saints had caused him both high anxiety and great distress, he now declares them guiltless. Thus, he holds nothing against them and in doing so reveals the depth of his forgiveness. Such forgiving "is an expression of the Gospel: the rebellion and failure of the Corinthians are completely overcome, done away with. They no longer exist. Love does not keep an account of evil (1 Cor. 13:5)."[230]

The content of 7:12 clearly shows the central point of the harsh letter that had caused the sorrow Paul's audience had initially experienced. The near-breaking point between him and these Saints had arisen, as the Apostle notes, over a confrontation that had happened sometime before between a person who had done wrong and a person wronged (2:5–7). The context shows that the latter was Paul himself. Someone in the branch had done him a grave injustice (ἀδικέω, *adikeō*). But just who was it? Though it may have been the incestuous person referred to in 1 Cor. 5:1–5, whose actions had been justified by some, this is unlikely because his sinful act would not

---

226. Given that the most frequent definition of the noun φόβος (*phobos*) is "fear" or "terror" (see BDAG, 1062; and *DAG,* s.v. "φόβος"), these people may have sensed how their inaction could have put them under divine interdiction, which realization aroused alarm. Martin, *2 Corinthians,* 402.

227. On these qualities denoting the Corinthians desire to be reconciled to the Apostle, see Hughes, *Second Epistle,* 274–75; and Martin, *2 Corinthians,* 402.

228. Barnett, *Second Epistle,* 379 n. 30.

229. Hughes, *Second Epistle,* 275; Thrall, *Critical and Exegetical Commentary,* 1:495.

230. Seifrid, *Second Letter,* 310.

have been directly injurious to Paul himself.[231] It is more likely that it was the turbulent fellow who confronted Paul face-to-face during his "flying visit" to Corinth.[232]

Just how this individual harmed Paul, the Apostle kindly does not say. Whatever the offense was, clearly it caused Paul the loss of face and credence among a certain number of branch members. The "wrong" the majority of the Saints may have committed was little more than expressing indifference in the matter. This may have been because they did not recognize its very serious implications and consequences until Titus, through the harsh letter, brought it forcefully to their attention.[233] The whole matter, however, Paul now wishes to be swept aside. His harsh letter had accomplished its goal in that the guilty party or parties, and more especially the offender, had been properly chastised. That was enough.[234]

Having made that point, Paul next places his harsh letter in a larger context. Though he had written it to right a wrong, through God's influence (ἐνώπιον τοῦ θεοῦ, *enōpion tou theou*) it had done much more. It had forced the Saints to see (φανερόω, *phaneroō*) that once they knew the truth, they were eager to defend him and his cause.[235]

But it should be kept in mind that, from Paul's point of view at least, the issue is not reconciliation between them and him (as a person), but between them and his apostolic authority, witness, and doctrine. Therefore, he is very willing to overlook the guilt of these Saints, treating it as nonexistent. As such, he puts into practice his own counsel concerning the need to be reconciled to one another and to God.[236] "This was not a mere fiction on his part: he means and believes what he says when he speaks of Christ having become sin, that we might become the righteousness of God in him (5:21)." [237]

---

231. See Translation Notes and associated Analysis for 2:5–8. For a detailed study, see Furnish, *II Corinthians,* 164–66, who rebuts the idea that the offender was the incestuous man.

232. Sperry, *Life and Letters,* 115–16. The references to a single person in 2:5–8, 10 and 7:12 all point to a single offender. Barrett, *Second Epistle,* 212–13; Martin, *2 Corinthians,* 405.

233. Martin, *2 Corinthians,* 404–5. The narrow window the text opens suggests that a minority of members had sided with the offender while the rest did little or nothing about it. For Paul, however, such lethargy was a major offense. The value in such a reconstruction is that it allows chapters 10–13 to stand on their own being a response to developments that happened after the events now in focus and thus helps make sense of the whole epistle. See C. K. Barrett, "'O Αδικησας (2 Cor. 7.12)," in Barrett, *Essays on Paul,* 115.

234. Seifrid, *Second Letter,* 311–12.

235. Barnett, *Second Epistle,* 381.

236. Barnett, *Second Epistle,* 382.

237. Seifrid, *Second Letter,* 311.

"I Have Complete Confidence in You" (7:13–16)

Greek Text

13 διὰ τοῦτο παρακεκλήμεθα.
Ἐπὶ δὲ τῇ παρακλήσει ἡμῶν περισσοτέρως μᾶλλον ἐχάρημεν ἐπὶ τῇ χαρᾷ Τίτου,
ὅτι ἀναπέπαυται τὸ πνεῦμα αὐτοῦ ἀπὸ πάντων ὑμῶν· 14 ὅτι εἴ τι αὐτῷ ὑπὲρ ὑμῶν
κεκαύχημαι, οὐ κατῃσχύνθην, ἀλλ' ὡς πάντα ἐν ἀληθείᾳ ἐλαλήσαμεν ὑμῖν, οὕτως
καὶ ἡ καύχησις ἡμῶν ἡ ἐπὶ Τίτου ἀλήθεια ἐγενήθη. 15 καὶ τὰ σπλάγχνα αὐτοῦ
περισσοτέρως εἰς ὑμᾶς ἐστιν ἀναμιμνῃσκομένου τὴν πάντων ὑμῶν ὑπακοήν, ὡς
μετὰ φόβου καὶ τρόμου ἐδέξασθε αὐτόν. 16 χαίρω ὅτι ἐν παντὶ θαρρῶ ἐν ὑμῖν.
[SBLGNT]

King James Version

13 Therefore we were comforted in
your comfort: yea, and exceedingly
the more joyed we for the joy of Titus,
because his spirit was refreshed by you
all. 14 For if I have boasted any thing
to him of you, I am not ashamed; but
as we spake all things to you in truth,
even so our boasting, which I made
before Titus, is found a truth. 15 And
his inward affection is more abundant
toward you, whilst he remembereth the
obedience of you all, how with fear and
trembling ye received him. 16 I rejoice
therefore that I have confidence in you
in all things.

New Rendition

13 Therefore, we have been encouraged.
And in addition to our own encouragement, we rejoiced even more greatly
at Titus's joy because his spirit has been
refreshed by all of you. 14 For if I have
boasted about anything to him concerning you, I have not been put to shame.
Instead, just as everything we told you in
truth so also our boasting about you to
Titus proved true. 15 And his affection
for you is even greater when he remembers the obedience of all of you—how
you received him with fear and trembling. 16 I rejoice because I have complete confidence in you.

Translation Notes and Comments

7:13 ***Therefore we were comforted in your comfort / Therefore, we have been encouraged:*** This sentence finishes Paul's thought begun in 7:8 explaining the result of Paul's having written "to demonstrate to you your eagerness on our behalf before God" (7:12, NR).

The phrase διὰ τοῦτο (*dia touto*), "therefore, on account of this," refers back to the source of Paul's encouragement, namely the God given comfort through which he has sustained Paul and the other missionaries in all their trials (1:3–4; 7:4). On παρακαλέω (*parakaleō*), "to encourage, exhort, comfort," see Translation Notes and associated Analysis for 7:6–7. Here it is found as a perfect passive participle. The force of the passive voice, like the connective phrase, looks back at the divine encouragement and comfort Paul and his fellow laborers have had and continue to enjoy.[238]

yea, and exceedingly the more joyed we for the joy of Titus / And in addition to our own encouragement, we rejoiced even more greatly at Titus's joy: This clause marks the beginning of a new paragraph and additional information in Paul's explication. It begins with the preposition ἐπί (*epi*), which, with the dative, usually means "at" or "upon"[239] but here carries the idea of "in addition to" or "over and above."[240] On the verb παρακαλέω (*parakaleō*), "to encourage," see Translation Notes and associated Analysis for 7:6–7. On the verb χαίρω (*chairō*), "to rejoice," see Translation Notes for 7:7.

The adverb περισσοτέρως (*perissoterōs*) denotes that which generates "a much greater degree" of something.[241] In this case, it refers to χαρά (*chara*), "joy," "gladness."[242] The noun carries the nuance of "great happiness."[243] To stress the point, Paul adds the adverb μᾶλλον (*mallon*), "even more."[244] Its role here is actually redundant since the adverb *perissoterōs* carries the idea of great abundance, but its use does allow the Apostle to stress the greatness of the joy felt due to Titus's report.[245]

because his spirit was refreshed by you all / because his spirit has been refreshed by all of you: The conjunction ὅτι (*hoti*), "because," marks the reason for or cause of an event.[246] The noun πνεῦμα (*pneuma*), "spirit," in the present context, denotes the inner being of a person.[247] The verb ἀναπαύω (*anapauō*), "refresh,"[248] found here as a perfect passive, denotes the stoppage of physical, mental, or emotional stress and its replacement by

---

238. Barnett, *Second Epistle,* 383, n. 2.

239. BDAG, 363–67.

240. Martin, *2 Corinthians,* 407.

241. BDAG, 806. The comparative noun περισσότερος denotes that which goes "beyond a standard of abundance" (BDAG, 806) or that "which is considerably in excess of some point" (Louw-Nida, §78.31).

242. BDAG, 1077.

243. Louw-Nida, §25;123. By means of metonymy, it can also refer to the cause of joy. BDAG, 1077.

244. BDAG, 613–14. The combination of the two terms gives the sense of "still much more." BDF, §§60.3; 246; Martin, *2 Corinthians,* 407.

245. The feeling of this verse is captured well in the less literal translation, "We were *especially* delighted to see how happy Titus was" (NIV, italics added).

246. BDAG, 732.

247. Louw-Nida, §26.9.

248. BDAG, 69; Louw-Nida, §23.84.

finding respite and renewal.[249] The preposition ἀπό (*apo*), "from," carries the concept of "because of"[250] and gives credit to the Corinthian Saints for Titus's delight. This phrase is quite revealing, for it suggests the strain and worry Titus felt as the bearer of the harsh letter and his great relief once his hearers reacted positively and humbly to it.[251] But, as the verb suggests, it did more. It brought revitalization, a new vigor to the young disciple.[252] Paul's use of the perfect tense shows that Titus's joy did not dissipate even after he met up with the Apostle.

7:14 ***For if I have boasted any thing to him of you / For if I have boasted about anything to him concerning you:*** The conditional particle εἰ (*ei*), "if," suggests Paul's initial concern about how the proceedings would go. The verb καύχαομαι (*kauchaomai*), "boast about,"[253] found here in the perfect tense, expresses a high degree of confidence in someone who has already proved exceptionally noteworthy.[254] The tense highlights Paul's "ongoing pride in them."[255] The preposition ὑπέρ (*hyper*) can have the various meanings "for, in behalf of, concerning, etc." We have selected "concerning" as the best English rendering of the sense here. This was likely necessary because Titus, based on the Corinthian Saints' past treatment of Paul and Timothy, had reservations about how these members would receive him. This concern made the Apostle's assurance all the more important.

I am not ashamed / I have not been put to shame: The verb καταισχύνω (*kataischynō*), "disgrace," "shame," found here as an aorist passive, means "to be put to shame." The nuance points to the disgrace and disappointment that comes "to one whose faith or hope is shown to be vain."[256]

but as we spake all things to you in truth, even so our boasting, which I made before Titus, is found a truth / Instead, just as everything we told you in truth so also our boasting about you to Titus proved true: Paul here reiterates, likely for emphasis, what he has already said. The conjunction ἀλλά (*alla*), usually translated as "but,"[257] here marks a strong contrast.[258] To catch that nuance, we have translated it as "instead."

---

249. Friedrich Baurnfeind, "ἀναπαύω," in *TDNT,* 1:350.
250. Louw-Nida, §89.25; BDF, §210.2.
251. Barnett, *Second Epistle,* 384.
252. Guthrie, *2 Corinthians,* 383.
253. BDAG, 536.
254. Louw-Nida, §33.368.
255. Barnett, *Second Epistle,* 384, n. 14.
256. BDAG, 517.
257. Louw-Nida, §89.125.
258. BDAG, 44–45.

The verb λαλέω (*laleō*), found here in aorist tense, means to "talk, speak" with the idea of expressing oneself.[259] The noun ἀλήθεια (*alētheia*), "truth," denotes both the content of what is true and a state of reality.[260] In using the phrase ἐν ἀληθείᾳ (*en alētheia*), "in truth," Paul could be referring to either his justification for not visiting them as he intended (which his detractors played so heavily) or to the points he made in the harsh letter or to what he has declared in this one.[261] Whatever the case, Paul is using the truthfulness of his boast about these Saints as evidence that everything else he has said in his defense is also true. On the verb καύχαομαι (*kauchaomai*), "to boast about," see above. In the prepositional phrase ἐπὶ Τίτου (*epi Titou*), "to Titus," *epi* denotes "before" or "in the presence of."[262] It shows that, in speaking to Titus, Paul expressed his personal witness to his friend but let Titus determine the case by either accepting or rejecting the assignment.

7:15 ***And his inward affection is more abundant toward you whilst he remembereth the obedience of you all / And his affection for you is even greater when he remembers the obedience of all of you:*** The noun σπλάγχνον (*splangchnon*) literally refers to "the inward parts of the body, especially the viscera," but as with καρδία (*kardia*), "heart," the word was used metaphorically to refer to some aspect of the psychological or emotional side of humankind. [263] In this case, in addition to affection, it connoted compassion, sympathy, and love.[264] On the adverb περισσοτέρως (*perissoterōs*), "even greater," see Translation Notes for 7:13 with associated Analysis. The verb ἀναμιμνήσκω (*anamimnēskō*), found here as a passive participle, means "remind someone of something."[265] The noun ὑπακοή (*hypakoē*), "obedience," denotes, in this context, the fulfilling of apostolic counsel (10:6; Philem. 1:21).[266]

how with fear and trembling ye received him / how you received him with fear and trembling: For the noun φόβος (*phobos*), "fear," "reverence," "respect,"[267] see Translation Notes for 7:1. The word denotes either a positive

259. BDAG, 582–83.

260. BDAG, 42–43.

261. Furnish, *II Corinthians,* 390; Barnett, *Second Epistle,* 384, n. 15. In 1:12–22, Paul defended himself against those who claimed he was unreliable and questioned his character. Guthrie, *2 Corinthians,* 384.

262. BDF, §234.4; Barnett, *Second Epistle,* 384, n. 16.

263. BDAG, 938.

264. Louw-Nida, §§8.58; 25.49; *NID,* 4:351–54.

265. BDAG, 68.

266. BDAG, 1028.

267. Louw-Nida, §§25.251; 53.59.

or a negative reaction to authority depending on how one sees oneself in relation to it.[268] Thus the noun can refer to one's distress or to one's admiration. The noun τρόμος (*tromos*), "trembling,"[269] refers to a physical shaking or quivering, usually due to anxiety or dread but also due to excitement or anticipation. This phrase is unique to Paul, and he uses it three times in his writings (here and in 1 Cor. 2:3 and Philip. 2:12). What Paul means to convey by using it is hard to determine because of the very different nuances possessed by each noun. If they are taken positively, then they show that the Saints welcomed Titus with excitement and respect. If taken negatively, they show that the Saints received him with an anxiety that expressed itself in trembling. The phrase echoes LXX Isaiah 19:16, which describes the reaction of Egypt as Jehovah moves against it, giving Paul's use of the phrase negative force, and it could describe the Corinthians' distress as they realized that by yielding to the accusations of the interlopers, they had put themselves in a position for apostolic and divine censure if not outright condemnation. The context, however, suggests that Paul intended the more positive nuance. A source of Titus's joy grew out of the positive, even enthusiastic, response of these people to his coming. Their response revealed their excited anticipation and respect. It may be that these people did feel some anxiety because they distrusted their own ability to meet all the requirements imposed by Paul and the gospel he taught. But at the same time, because they were religiously striving to do their full duty, they also anticipated Titus's visit with enthusiasm.[270]

7:16 ***I rejoice therefore that I have confidence in you in all things / I rejoice because I have complete confidence in you:*** On the verb χαίρω (*chairō*), "to rejoice," see Translation Notes for 7:7. The verb θαρρέω (*tharreō*), "be confident, courageous,"[271] denotes certainty in a matter and showing firmness, boldness, or courage "in the face of danger or testing."[272] The adjective πᾶς (*pas*), "full," "completeness," "whole,"[273] expressing as it does the highest degree of

268. Louw-Nida, §§25.251; 53.59.

269. BDAG, 1016.

270. Martin, *2 Corinthians,* 411–12. The other scriptures where the phrase is found all suggest it should be taken positively. The passage in 1 Cor. 2:2–4 expresses Paul's humility while he worked among them. In Philip. 2:1, he states that because his readers had continually obeyed, they were to work out their salvation with and in anticipation and excitement of a good reward. In a related phrase, found in Eph. 6:5, he admonishes the servants to treat their masters as they would Christ—that is, with honor and respect rather than anxious dread.

271. BDAG, 444.

272. Louw-Nida, §25.156.

273. BDAG, 783.

something, reveals the depth of Paul's confidence that these Saints will continue to support him.

Analysis and Summary

Prior to this point, Paul's focus has been on his own interaction with the Saints. He now rejoices as he turns to the result of Titus's interaction. His was the significant, yet difficult, even frightening, task of being the interface between the two estranged parties.[274] The text (7:13) suggests that Titus had misgivings about being Paul's agent in delivering the harsh letter, even though the Apostle expressed his faith that the Saints would readily accept Titus.[275] Titus was, therefore, not only very relieved but also delighted to a high degree to find that Paul's encouraging words proved true.[276] We must not, however, take anything away from the role that Titus played. The text suggests that he deftly negotiated the rough, raging sea that was the taxed relationship between these two parties. Through his adroitness, he was able to calm the troubled waters.[277] Due to the positive response to his efforts, the young disciple's mind was quickly set at ease.[278] Out of this grew not only further encouragement but also joy. Titus's encouragement became the basis of Paul's own, and the disciple's joy the source of the Apostle's.[279]

We must keep in mind, however, that the very pleasant picture painted in this pericope did not include everything or everyone. Paul's defense against his detractors in chapters 10–12 shows that there were holdouts within the Corinthian membership. His stress in this section that he had always spoken the truth to them (7:14) may have been a polemical swipe at his antagonists, who impugned his reliability and credibility (1:13–23).[280] Even so, it would appear that he now had the majority behind him. At the very least, Titus had been able to largely dispel the lethargy, if not the outright disunity, that once affected many and bring about the overall harmony that now prevailed. The expression of unity and loyalty to Paul is important to the Apostle as he now turns to the subject of the Jerusalem collection,[281] in which he hopes the Corinthian Saints will play a large part.[282]

---

274. Guthrie, *2 Corinthians,* 383.
275. Barnett, *Second Epistle,* 382.
276. Guthrie, *2 Corinthians,* 383.
277. Guthrie, *2 Corinthians,* 383.
278. Thus, the translation in the NRSV.
279. Martin, *2 Corinthians,* 407.
280. Martin, *2 Corinthians,* 410.
281. On this subject, see Translation Notes for 8:4 with corresponding Analysis.
282. Martin, *2 Corinthians,* 418.

In 7:14, Paul again expresses his great confidence (παρρησία, *parrēsia*) in these members (see Translation Notes for 7:4). This was not, however, the only way he expressed that confidence. He boasted (καύχομαι, *kauchomai*) about these people as he reassured Titus that he would be well received. That Paul felt he could boast about these Saints is doubly noteworthy. First, he generally insists that any boasting should be used in terms of expressing one's feelings toward and witness of God, not other Saints, let alone humankind in general (10:17–18).[283] Secondly, until Titus's return, these members were far more a source of general concern (if not anxiety, frustration, and even sorrow) than a source of vaunting.[284] Boasting in these people carried a great deal of risk. Thus, Paul's boasting to Titus about his faith in these Saints could have proven vapid if the Corinthians rejected or mistreated the carrier of the letter. The result would have brought at best embarrassment to Paul and at worst great shame. Given the culture of honor/shame that existed in Corinth, Paul was taking a very real and potentially costly risk.[285] To his great relief, the risk proved worth the effort.

The context suggests that, in this whole section, Paul praises these Saints as a means of ingratiating himself with them. He does so by generating an emotional effect that he designed to draw them ever closer. His tack is to use honey, not vinegar, as the means of attracting and holding them. The reason seems to be that he senses, even after Titus's success, that his relationship with them has not yet been fully secured and thus needs an extra boost.

Using their kindly reception of Titus as the first step, the Apostle seeks, in this section of his letter, to fully gain their allegiance. Yet, his method—boasting about them—is shaped by the gospel and is thus tied to his belief that boasting should center on God and his work. The evidence that his trust in the gospel informs his boasting is seen in his encouragement to Titus that it took place *before* the young man left on his assignment. The move expresses raw confidence in the power of the word to perform its healing effect in and among the Saints. Paul's usual habit of boasting exclusively in the Lord "does not exclude, but includes boasting in the Corinthians, *precisely in this otherwise unwarranted and unexpected form.* He boasts in them when they least deserve it, and hardly earn it."[286] Thus, we can understand his great relief and heightened joy when these Saints did not let

283. Guthrie, *2 Corinthians,* 384.

284. Seifrid, *Second Letter,* 312.

285. Guthrie, *2 Corinthians,* 384.

286. Seifrid, *Second Letter,* 312, italics in the original.

him down. In their repentance and acceptance of him, God's word through the Spirit had performed its perfect work *in them* and thus drove the full reconciliation of the parties, thus fulfilling the reality of this confidence.[287]

In 7:15, Paul gives credit for the success of Titus's visit and the great amount of encouragement it generated to these Saints. He does so by relating, in some detail, the effect it had not only on the young disciple's emotions but also on those of the Apostle himself. Both felt a deeper affection (σπλάγχνον, *splangchnon*) for these people, which affection Titus demonstrated "very abundantly." Indeed, it left him with "a warm place in his heart for the Corinthians, thereby showing the sincerity of their acceptance of him as Paul's delegate."[288] The basis of his joy was their quick obedience to the demands placed upon them. Whether these demands were in the harsh letter or generated by Titus himself the text does not say. What the text does make clear is that the Saints recognized and accepted Titus "with reverence and respect" (μετὰ φόβου καὶ τρόμου, *meta phobou kai tromou*) as Paul's envoy. The implication is that they also recognized that in doing so, they were, once again, in harmony with God (2:9).[289]

On this basis, Paul concludes this section of his letter (7:16) by repeating the compliment he expressed in 7:4. There he expressed the high degree of trust that he has that they will continue to support him even in the face of opposition, and thus he can proceed without fear.[290]

In sum, this section suggests that the harsh letter, coupled with Titus's explication and defense of it, resulted in an exoneration of Paul that greatly exceeded expectations. The support and love the Saints now express for their Apostle stands as the springboard for the next section of Paul's epistle. Therein he turns to the necessity of the Jerusalem collection and the important role these people can play in it. Thus, this 7:16 acts as a transition between the two sections,[291] the forepart (7:4–16) showing Paul's return to full confidence in these people, and the latter part (chapters 8–9) revealing the opportunity he gives them to confirm their confidence in him through the very practical means of donating funds to meet the desperate needs of the Jerusalem Christians.[292]

287. Seifrid, *Second Letter,* 312; Barnett, *Second Epistle,* 384–85.

288. Martin, *2 Corinthians,* 410–11.

289. Martin, *2 Corinthians,* 411.

290. Hughes, *Second Epistle,* 267.

291. Hughes, *Second Epistle,* 282, calls it a perfect transition.

292. Martin, *2 Corinthians,* 412–13.

Chapter 8

The Gentile Collection

Introduction

At this point, Paul addresses the second major purpose for writing his epistle—namely, the collection of funds. These funds had been and were being specifically donated by various branches of the Church for the benefit of the poor among the Jewish members in and around Jerusalem. The nascent Church already had a working welfare system for taking care of the poor and the needy (Acts 6), and therefore, what Paul and others were doing would not have been new to them. "The giving of alms was an important aspect of first-century Judaism and had become a symbol among Christians of covenant faithfulness."[1] The early Church seems to have accepted the scriptural mandate and enhanced it.[2] The initial efforts of the Twelve and others had brought thousands into the newly established kingdom. The leadership established an order in which "all who believed were together and had all things common; and they sold their possessions and goods and distributed them to all, as they had need" (Acts 2:44–45, our translation). The Gentile segments of the Church "were part of the program that continued from Pentecost, both in Jerusalem and Antioch. Considerable property was laid 'at the apostles' feet,' with distribution continuing on the basis of need (Acts 4:35)."[3]

Unfortunately, circumstances beyond the Church's control overwhelmed this system, thus demanding an infusion of funds from a wider area to sustain all these people. The exact cause is unknown,[4] but Acts reports that around

1. Holzapfel and Wayment, *Making Sense,* 374.

2. The mandate can be found in Ex. 23:10–11 and is pushed by the later prophets as evidenced by Isa. 58:6–7, 9–10 and Amos 2:6–8; 5:11–12; 8:4–6. For the program's inception in the modern Church, see D&C 42:30; 104:14–18.

3. Anderson, *Understanding Paul,* 139.

4. Holzapfel and Wayment, *Making Sense,* 374.

AD 46, the prophet Agabus foretold of a coming famine, and Luke informs us that this famine happened during the reign of Claudius Caesar (AD 41 to 54).[5] Responding to the prophecy, the leadership of the Church began preparing to help the local Saints (Acts 11:27–29). The leading brethren gave Paul, along with other mission assignments, the charge to remember the poor (Gal. 2:10). Thus the Church's welfare policy provides the background for the Apostle's gentile contribution. Though the first mention of this aspect of Paul's work appears in an oblique reference in 1 Corinthians 16:1–4 and in detail here in 2 Corinthians, clearly the actual work had begun some time before. Being yet in contact with the Galatian churches where he had proselyted a few years earlier, the Apostle asked them to also support the collection (1 Cor. 16:1). He was now moving the work toward completion, after which he would convey the funds to the Church leaders in Jerusalem (See 1 Cor. 16:1–4; Rom. 15:27–29).[6] According to Acts 24:17, Paul successfully accomplished this assignment.[7]

From the Apostle's point of view, there were several reasons for the collection. The more obvious reason was to give financial assistance to those Jewish Saints in need. But the underlying and more important reason was to, through this act of caring, unite the mostly gentile branches of the Church with the Jewish branches (8:14). An additional reason was to allow the Saints to follow the example of the Savior and thus demonstrate their Christianity (8:9). By connecting their giving with the downpouring of God's grace (χάρις, *charis*) upon the Macedonians, Paul gives the donations a divine mandate (8:1). However, he does balance giving with the means that the Corinthian Saints currently had (8:11–15). Through Paul's words, we see that the collection is emblematic of what the Corinthians should do to follow Christ. He emphasizes the idea of equality by insisting

5. The reign of Claudius was marked by famines. Suetonius, *Life of Claudius* 18.2. In addition to the one that hit the Holy Land, one hit Rome early in his rule, Egypt five years later, Greece about three or four years after that, and then Rome again two to four years later. The one that hit Judea, likely begun in 46 or 47, seems to have been particularly harsh. Josephus, *Ant.* 3.320–22; 20.51–53, 101. Its effects would have yet been felt in 49 if not later. F. F Bruce, *The Acts of the Apostles: The Greek Text with Introduction and Commentary,* 3rd rev. ed. (Grand Rapids, Mich.: William B. Eerdmans, 1990), 276.

6. For a study, see Dieter Georgi, *Remembering the Poor: The History of Paul's Collection for Jerusalem* (Nashville: Abingdon Press, 1992). See also Deborah Elaine Watson, "Paul's Collection in Light of the Motivations and Mechanisms for Aid to the Poor in the First-Century World" (PhD diss., University of Durham, 2006), who states that this collection reflects normal Jewish/Christian piety concerning charitable giving for the poor living either locally or abroad.

7. Holzapfel and Wayment, *Making Sense,* 374.

that the Corinthians give freely and lovingly according to God's way. Thus Paul makes a Christological point through the collection for Judean Saints by asserting that, as the Corinthians do in fact give freely, they are imitating the Lord, who went so far as to empty himself in behalf of others.[8]

In 8:8, the Apostle clarifies his tone and identifies what motivates his exhortation.[9] He then, in 8:16–17, announces Titus's eager desire to return to Corinth. Paul notes that the missionary will be accompanied by two unnamed brethren acting as envoys from the churches in Macedonia (8:16–24).

In this portion of Paul's letter, the Apostle chooses to downplay his stormy relationship with some members of the Corinthian church. His positive statements about the branches as a whole, though very likely sincere, should not be interpreted as his belief that all are now restored to full fellowship with him. They should, rather, be viewed as a rhetorical devise designed to reduce stress as he moves both to encourage his readers to respond favorably to his request for assisting the Jerusalem Saints (8:6–9:15) and to accept the forceful defense of his actions with which he closes his letter (10:1–13:14).

Paul's words make it clear that he is seeking to bind these people not to himself but to Christ. They must, however, recognize his apostolic authority if he is to have any cachet with them. His great desire is to motivate them to reach for a full fellowship with the Christian Church in general. He understands that it is through unity between all members that there can be a greater outpouring of God's grace upon them all.[10]

The story of the Gentile collection is inspiring on several levels. For one, it shows that, despite long distances, the Church formed "a brotherhood of love in action. . . . [In] 2 Corinthians 8 and 9 . . . Christ's second great commandment is so visible. Paul's encouragement to generous giving recalls other 'golden rules' of the Lord: 'It is more blessed to give than to receive' (Acts 20:35)—'Give, and it shall be given unto you' (Luke 6:38). So Paul stresses the example of the giving Savior, who gave his spiritual riches to raise mankind from spiritual poverty [to heavenly treasures] (2 Cor. 8:9). The principle of sacrifice is clear."[11]

---

8. For a study, see David Horrell, "Paul's Collection: Resources for a Materialist Theology," *Epworth Review* 22, no. 2 (1995): 74–83.

9. Guthrie, *2 Corinthians,* 388.

10. Seifrid, *Second Letter,* 314–15.

11. Anderson, *Understanding Paul,* 140. Paul's letters reveal both conventions on and rules for donating. See 2 Thes. 3 and 1 Tim. 5.

The Macedonian Church's Abundance of Generosity (8:1–7)

Greek Text

1 Γνωρίζομεν δὲ ὑμῖν, ἀδελφοί, τὴν χάριν τοῦ θεοῦ τὴν δεδομένην ἐν ταῖς ἐκκλησίαις τῆς Μακεδονίας, 2 ὅτι ἐν πολλῇ δοκιμῇ θλίψεως ἡ περισσεία τῆς χαρᾶς αὐτῶν καὶ ἡ κατὰ βάθους πτωχεία αὐτῶν ἐπερίσσευσεν εἰς τὸ πλοῦτος τῆς ἁπλότητος αὐτῶν· 3 ὅτι κατὰ δύναμιν, μαρτυρῶ, καὶ παρὰ δύναμιν, αὐθαίρετοι 4 μετὰ πολλῆς παρακλήσεως δεόμενοι ἡμῶν, τὴν χάριν καὶ τὴν κοινωνίαν τῆς διακονίας τῆς εἰς τοὺς ἁγίους— 5 καὶ οὐ καθὼς ἠλπίσαμεν ἀλλ' ἑαυτοὺς ἔδωκαν πρῶτον τῷ κυρίῳ καὶ ἡμῖν διὰ θελήματος θεοῦ, 6 εἰς τὸ παρακαλέσαι ἡμᾶς Τίτον ἵνα καθὼς προενήρξατο οὕτως καὶ ἐπιτελέσῃ εἰς ὑμᾶς καὶ τὴν χάριν ταύτην· 7 ἀλλ' ὥσπερ ἐν παντὶ περισσεύετε, πίστει καὶ λόγῳ καὶ γνώσει καὶ πάσῃ σπουδῇ καὶ τῇ ἐξ ἡμῶν ἐν ὑμῖν ἀγάπῃ, ἵνα καὶ ἐν ταύτῃ τῇ χάριτι περισσεύητε. [SBLGNT]

King James Version

1 Moreover, brethren, we do you to wit of the grace of God bestowed on the churches of Macedonia; 2 How that in a great trial of affliction the abundance of their joy and their deep poverty abounded unto the riches of their liberality. 3 For to their power, I bear record, yea, and beyond their power they were willing of themselves; 4 Praying us with much entreaty that we would receive the gift, and take upon us the fellowship of the ministering to the saints. 5 And this they did, not as we hoped, but first gave their own selves to the Lord, and unto us by the will of God: 6 Insomuch that we desired Titus, that as he had begun, so he would also finish in you the same grace also. 7 Therefore, as ye abound in every thing, in faith, and utterance, and knowledge, and in all diligence, and in your love to us, see that ye abound in this grace also.

New Rendition

1 Now brothers and sisters, we are making you aware of God's grace that has been given to the Macedonian churches, 2 that in the midst of a severe ordeal of affliction, their abundance of joy and their extreme poverty have produced an abundance of their generosity. 3 For I testify that they voluntarily gave according to their means and even beyond their means, 4 urgently pleading with us for the privilege of participating in this ministry to the saints. 5 And not as we expected, but they gave themselves first to the Lord and also to us through God's will. 6 So we encouraged Titus to finish up the collection of this charitable offering with you just as he had already begun. 7 But just as you abound in everything—in faith, in speech, in knowledge, in complete devotion, and in your love for us—see that you also excel in this charitable offering.

Translation Notes and Comment

8:1–7 All the material from 8:1 through 8:6 is one long sentence in the Greek text. For the sake of flow and ease of communicating Paul's thoughts in English, we have broken it into four sentences. After the initial introduction (8:1), Paul uses two subordinate clauses as the framework for developing his thought. These clauses are introduced by the conjunction ὅτι (*hoti*), which acts as a marker of explanation.[12] In the first clause (8:2), Paul explains in some detail the difficult conditions under which the northern Saints had given so liberally to the welfare collection for the Jewish Saints. In the second (8:3–5), he identifies the breadth of their giving. In 8:6, he states the result.

By placing a period at the end of 8:5, a number of translations indicate that Paul's thought ends there, with 8:6 beginning a new idea.[13] Though we have, for the sake of flow, also placed a period at the end of 8:5, grammatically speaking Paul's thought flows from 8:5 through 8:6. The latter is the result clause of the idea Paul began in the former clause. These people had given themselves to the Lord and to the cause of the missionaries, and *as a result,* as the text indicates in 8:6, Paul and others sent Titus to finish the collection for the poor. Thus, following the rules of grammar, the unit should extend through 8:6. That 8:7 begins with ἀλλ' (*all'*), "but," shows correctly that it is a new sentence. Even so, the motifs Paul uses in this verse suggest that 8:7 is actually an integral part of the thoughts contained in the first six verses. These motifs are χάρις (*charis*), "grace" (8:1, 4, 6, 7); δίδωμι (*didōmi*), "to give" (8:1, 5, and understood in 3, 7); and περισσεύω (*perisseuō*), "to abound" (8:2, 7a, 7d).[14] Taken together, they give a high level of lexical cohesion to the whole of 8:1–7 that we follow in our Rendition.[15] However, this verse does act in a transitional capacity to introduce the next subdivision that focuses on the Corinthians' role in the collection process.

---

12. BDAG, 731–32.

13. For example, see KJV, NIV, New English Translation.

14. Though two of these words show up later in the chapter, χάρις (*charis*) is found only in 8:9—but not in connection with giving—and in 8:16, and δίδωμι (*didōmi*) appears only once at 8:10 and not in connection with giving financial aid. The verb περισσεύω (*perisseuō*) does not show up in the rest of the chapter.

15. Guthrie, *2 Corinthians,* 389–90.

8:1 ***Moreover, brethren / Now brothers and sisters:*** The noun ἀδελφοί (*adelphoi*), literally "brothers," in plural form, as here, refers to all members of the community, including women (see Translation Notes for 1:8).[16]

we do you to wit of the grace of God / we are making you aware of God's grace: The KJV translates the Greek verb γνωρίζω (*gnōrizō*), "to make known,"[17] as the now-obsolete verb "wit," which means "to know." We have rendered it as "making you aware." The JST carries the same idea but with different words, stating, "We would have you to know." On the noun χάρις (*charis*), "grace," see Translation Notes for 1:2. Here the word denotes an outpouring of God's beneficence such that it empowered the Macedonian Saints to freely give of their means.

bestowed on the churches of Macedonia / that has been given to the Macedonian churches: The verb δίδωμι (*didōmi*), "to give,"[18] found here as a perfect passive participle, shows that God's gift of grace, given in the past, still abides upon these faithful people. The preposition ἐν (*en*), usually translated as "in, among,"[19] in this instance is equivalent to a simple dative case, "to,"[20] and points to the indwelling nature of the grace residing in the various branches. For Macedonia and Paul's work in that area, see Translation Notes for 1:16.

8:2 ***How that in a great trial of affliction the abundance of their joy and their deep poverty abounded unto the riches of their liberality / that in the midst of a severe ordeal of affliction, their abundance of joy and their extreme poverty have produced an abundance of their generosity:*** Paul explains in detail how God's grace was manifest among these faithful people. He notes three items that contributed to the Macedonian Saints' generous liberality.

The first was the conditions under which they labored. The noun δοκιμή (*dokimē*), "trial, test, ordeal," denotes a testing process that both "promotes and validates the character of the one [or in this case, the ones] undergoing it."[21] The adjective πολύς (*polys*), "great, extensive," stresses the depth of the ordeal these people were going through, and the noun θλίψις (*thlipsis*),

16. BDAG, 18.

17. BDAG, 203.

18. BDAG, 242–43.

19. BDAG, 326–30.

20. BDF, §220.1. Here it acts as a marker showing where the gift has become manifest, namely in the power of the Saints to contribute to the cause. Guthrie, *2 Corinthians,* 392.

21. BDAG, 256. This is the earliest that the noun is found in the whole of Greek literature. It is doubtful that Paul coined the word, but he did use it to his advantage. See MM, 167.

"affliction,"[22] indicates an imposed suffering that could challenge the Saints' endurance in their cause if they were weak in the faith.

The second item was what the gospel brought. The noun περισσεία (*perisseia*), "surplus, abundance," denotes that which is beyond an expected amount but can also imply an excess.[23] That which the Saints held in richness Paul described with the noun χαρά (*chara*), "joy." The word refers to what brings sustained pleasure and, more specifically, rejoicing.[24] Paul does not identify the source of that joy, but it seems to be due to their voluntary response to the request that they partner in giving to the poor Saints in Judea.

The final condition was their state of existence. The noun πτωχεία (*ptōcheia*), "poverty," refers to a state of deficiency of means,[25] while the noun βάθος (*bathos*) usually refers figuratively to the depth of something.[26] In the prepositional phrase κατὰ βάθους (*kata bathous*), as here, it takes on the force of an adjectival phrase connoting "extreme poverty."[27] Paul does not say how this contributed, but it was likely because they could sympathize with the distress of their Judean sisters and brothers.

He is clear on the result. The verb περισσεύω (*perisseuō*) means "to abound," or "to be found in abundance" even beyond what is expected.[28] The noun πλοῦτος (*ploutos*), "wealth, riches," denotes earthly goods.[29] Given that these people were experiencing a high degree of poverty themselves, the noun likely refers not so much to the amount given as to the purity of the motive that stood behind giving anything at all.

The noun ἁπλότης (*haplotēs*), "simplicity, liberality, generosity,"[30] found here in the genitive case, carries with it the nuance of the sincere pureness of the motive that stands behind the giving.[31] Its basic meaning, "simplicity," denotes an absence of pretense or guile and, in its religious sense, describes

22. BDAG, 457. This was a condition well-known to these faithful people. See 1 Thes. 1:6; 2:14; 3:3–4; and 2 Thes. 1:4–7.

23. BDAG, 804–5; Louw-Nida, §§59.53; 78.31. As used in Matt. 25:21, 23, the word reflects the circumstances attending cooperation with in the authority of the Lord, and that may be the nuance here.

24. BDAG, 1077; *NID,* 4:644–49.

25. BDAG, 896.

26. BDAG, 162.

27. The phrase translates literally as "according to depth." Louw-Nida, §78.22.

28. BDAG, 805. This nuance directly relates to the force of the noun περισσεία (*perisseia*).

29. BDAG, 832.

30. BDAG, 104; BAGD, s.v. "ἁπλότης," LSJ, 191; Louw-Nida, §57.106.

31. Louw-Nida, 88.44. BDAG, 104, notes that the sense of "generosity" or "liberality" are in dispute and the reference is likely to the "sincere concern" or "simple goodness," that stood behind the giving.

The KJV adds, "This they did." The JST reads, "And this they did, not as we *required*" (italics ours), thus pointing out that the act went beyond the usual obligation associated with charitable giving.

The verb ἐλπίζω (*elpizō*), "to expect, to hope," in the present context refers to the anticipation of some benefit.[47] Its use suggests that the outpouring of giving from these branches went well beyond what the missionaries expected.

but first gave their own selves to the Lord / but they gave themselves first to the Lord: The verb δίδωμι (*didōmi*), "to give,"[48] here emphasizes the idea of "[dedicating] oneself for some purpose or cause," and carries the nuance of "self-sacrifice."[49] The verb shows that these people had given themselves to the task of bringing about the will of their Lord, Jesus Christ. The adverb πρῶτον (*proton*), "first," like its English counterpart, has various senses, including "first in time, sequence or prominence."[50] In our Rendition, we have preserved this ambiguity, noting that the important point is that these Saints considered dedicating themselves to the Lord their first priority.[51]

and unto us by the will of God / and also to us through God's will: The giving, however, had not been to God alone. These people also gave themselves to the missionaries, or better, to their cause. This act, however, was motivated by the θελήματος θεοῦ (*thelēmatos theou*), "the will of God," implying that the Saints' strong desire to join the cause of the missionaries was divinely inspired and directed.

8:6 *Insomuch that we desired Titus / So we encouraged Titus:* The verb παρακαλέω (*parakaleō*), "to urge, encourage,"[52] here carries the idea of an urgent appeal. It is found here as an aorist infinitive with a neuter definite article. An articular infinitive governed by the preposition εἰς (*eis*), "to, into," can indicate purpose, result, or clarification.[53] In our translation we used the conjunction "so," which can express either purpose or result, thus preserving the ambiguity of the Greek.

that as he had begun, so he would also finish in you the same grace also / to finish up the collection of this charitable offering with you just as he had already begun: The verb ἐπιτελέω (*epiteleō*), "to complete, to

---

47. Louw-Nida, §30.54.

48. Louw-Nida, §57.71.

49. BDAG, 242–43; Louw-Nida, §53.48.

50. Louw-Nida, §60.46; BDAG, 892–94.

51. Guthrie, *2 Corinthians,* 399.

52. BDAG, 764–65.

53. Wallace, *Greek Grammar,* 611.

finish," refers to successfully completing a task already begun,[54] but can also carry the nuance of doing so according to a predesigned plan.[55] The word can also carry the idea of religious obligation.[56] The noun χάρις (*charis*) is most often translated as "grace" in the New Testament, as in verse 8:1 above, but it has a variety of nuances depending on context.[57] In 8:4 above, it has the sense of "favor, privilege." In this verse, however, it refers specifically to the money that Paul was collecting to help the needy Saints in Jerusalem, so in our Rendition we have translated it as a phrase—namely, "collection of this charitable offering"—to best convey the sense of the word in this context.[58] The adverb καθώς (*kathōs*), "just as," with the verb προενάρχομαι (*proenarchomai*), "to begin,"[59] found here as an aorist, refers to a task already set in motion and references the work in which Titus had already been engaged.

8:7 ***Therefore, as ye abound in every thing / But just as you abound in everything:*** The verb περισσεύω (*perisseuō*) refers to having something in great, even overflowing, abundance (see 8:2),[60] but here it carries the nuance of reaching and even surpassing the demands of an accomplishment or achievement.[61] Though Paul uses the phrase ἐν παντί (*en panti*), "in everything,[62] he has in mind the specific characteristics associated with his readers that he lists next.

in faith, and utterance, and knowledge, and in all diligence, and in your love to us / in faith, in speech, in knowledge, in complete devotion, and in your love for us: The noun πίστις (*pistis*), "faith," in the present context, refers to adherence to the whole of the gospel in principle and doctrine.[63] Though the noun λόγος (*logos*), "speech,"[64] again in the present context,

---

54. Louw-Nida, §68.22.

55. BDAG, 383; Louw-Nida, §13.108.

56. See Translation Notes for 8:11 along with the associated Analysis.

57. BDAG, 1079–80.

58. For χάρις (*charis*) referring to the act of charitable giving, see Gordon D. Fee, "ΧΑΡΙΣ in II Corinthians 1:15: Apostolic Parousia and Paul-Corinthian Chronology," *New Testament Studies* 24 (1978): 535–36.

59. BDAG, 868.

60. Louw-Nida, §§59.52; 57.24; 78.31. The noun χάρις (*charis*) in the present context carries the nuance of the graciousness or benevolence that stands behind both the act and the gift. See Witherington, *Conflict and Community,* 419–20.

61. BDAG, 805.

62. BDAG, 782–84.

63. Louw-Nida, §§31.102, 104.

64. Louw-Nida, §33.99.

could refer to such things as speaking in tongues or prophesying (see 1 Cor. 12:10), it more likely refers to speaking well or persuasively and may allude to defending the Church. The noun γνῶσις (*gnosis*), "knowledge,"[65] denotes the comprehension or grasp of ideas and teachings and suggests the depth of understanding of gospel doctrine some of these Saints possessed.[66] The noun σπουδή (*spoudē*), "diligence, eagerness, devotion,"[67] denotes an "earnest commitment in the discharge of an obligation."[68] Paul stresses this particular characteristic by modifying it with the adjective πᾶς (*pas*), "full, complete."[69] We translate the phrase as "complete earnestness" because it connotes a "seriousness of purpose as well as sincerity and, often, zealousness and enthusiasm" for a cause.[70] Given the context, that cause is likely the gospel. The noun ἀγάπη (*agapē*), "love," carries the nuance of deep appreciation, concern for one's well-being, and high regard for the person so loved.[71]

see that ye abound in this grace also / see that you also excel in this charitable offering: Paul again uses the verb περισσεύω (*perisseuō*), "abound" (see above), found here in the subjunctive mood, which with the conjunction ἵνα (*hina*) gives the phrase imperative force, thus "see that you excel."[72] For the translation of χάρις (*charis*) as "charitable offering," see comments to 8:6 above. Paul's use of καί (*kai*), "also," is significant, pointing back as it does to the enviable attributes the Corinthian Saints have already displayed.

---

65. BDAG, 203–4.

66. Paul often uses the noun to denote his readers' grasp of Christian truths. See 1 Cor. 1:5; 8:1, 7, 10–11; 12:8; 13:2, 8; 14:6; and 2 Cor. 2:14; 4:6; 6:6; 8:7; 10:5; 11:16.

67. BDAG, 939–40.

68. In the Greco-Roman world, the noun referred to an "extraordinary commitment to civic and religious responsibilities, which were [frequently] intertwined, and also of concern for personal moral excellence or premium devotion to the interest of others." See BDAG, 939–40.

69. BDAG, 782–84.

70. *Dictionary of Synonyms,* s.v. "serious."

71. Louw-Nida, §25.43. There is a manuscript variant for the last phrase. Some early manuscripts read ἐξ ἡμων ἐν ὑμῖν (*ex hēmōn en hymin agapē*), "our love for you." Although some scholars accept this as original because it is a harder reading (see Metzger, *Textual Commentary,* 512–13), and even though Paul expresses his love for this wayward branch a number of times (6:11–12; 11:11; 12:15), he nowhere gives evidence for any reciprocation on their part (Barnett, *Second Epistle,* 403) with the possible exception here. However, because his love for them is not an attribute that they possess and therefore does not fit in a list of virtues they excel in and on the weight of the majority of Greek text, we have rendered the passage as referring to their love for Paul.

72. BDAG, 475–77; Wallace, *Greek Grammar,* 476–77.

The position of ἐν ταύτῃ τῇ χάριτι (*en tautē tē chariti*), "in this charitable offering," is emphatically helping Paul stress his point. He is very anxious that the Saints do not perceive him as trying to find fault, but he also clearly wants to motivate them to immediate and heartfelt action.[73]

Analysis and Summary

At this point, Paul transitions to the next reason he wrote to the Corinthian Saints. It is his desire to motivate them to contribute generously to the donations he and others are gathering to assist the impoverished and struggling Saints in Judea (Rom. 15:27–29).[74] This verse acts as an introduction to the next seven verses, which make up the first paragraph of this section of his epistle. We must stress here, however, that his major intent is neither to bind these people to himself nor to generate funds for the Jerusalem poor. It is to bind these Saints first to God and then to the rest of the Christian community. The charitable giving is but a means to that end.[75]

In chapters 8 and 9, the Apostle engages in a calculated, daring, but risky move. "He concluded his previous argument by stating that he has complete confidence in the Corinthians. They have passed one test in regard to an isolated offender and he now offers them another chance to prove their genuineness and their confidence in him by following his exhortation to complete the collection for the poor Christians of Judea."[76] To do so, he pushes them to prove themselves by freely and liberally donating to the cause. It is in that push where he takes the risk, for he could alienate some if they misread his intent. Though risky, this move was not inappropriate, for the text clearly shows that the reason he puts his readers on the defensive is because they had earlier committed to the cause but had not given themselves fully to it.[77] Here the Apostle "offers the Macedonians as an example

73. Martin, *2 Corinthians,* 439.

74. Although the Apostolic leadership at Jerusalem had given the general instructions for the missionaries to assist the poor, it seems likely that this specific push was initiated by Paul and included members of the church in Galatia, Asia, and Macedonia as well as Achaia (1 Cor. 16:1). Clearly one of his messages was the need to take care of the poor and the weak (see Acts 20:35). See Barnett, *Second Epistle,* 395–98. For a study of how money was handled in the first century Church, see Charles H. Talbert, "Money Management in Early Mediterranean Christianity: 2 Corinthians 8–9," *Review and Expositor* 86, no. 3 (1989): 359–70.

75. Seifrid, *Second Letter,* 315.

76. Witherington, *Conflict and Community,* 411.

77. Witherington, *Conflict and Community,* 411.

of how God has manifested his grace by doing a great work in, but also through, their church."[78] To do so, he not only emphasizes the overabundant generosity of the Saints in Macedonia but also stresses the hardships they themselves were going through while refusing to let such impede their abundant contribution to the collection.

In 8:2, he points out the condition under which these faithful Saints labored—namely, an extensive and ongoing "affliction" (θλίψις, *thlipsis*) that resulted from their religious observance.[79] This was a condition imposed by a less-than-sympathetic state that readily ostracized them from societal functions, employment, and other associations.[80] This condition, however, was offset due to an outpouring of divine grace or blessings that resulted in an abundance of joy (χαρά, *chara*). The noun refers not only to a state of sustained pleasure, yielding even to rejoicing among some,[81] but also to a "saving gift from God, part of the new creation, and brought on through the Holy Spirit."[82] In this context then, the term "grace" points not just to God's favor but also to "the concrete expression of that favor in the life of the Macedonian Church," as made manifest in the generosity of their giving under very difficult circumstances.[83]

Even so, Paul stresses that, though these people are spiritually rich, their financial status could be described as nothing less than deep poverty (πτωχεία, *ptōcheia*). Even so, they give not of their surplus or even limited means but beyond them.[84] Their station may have caused them to sympathize deeply with their Judean counterparts and, thus, provide a generous donation, one so great that it surprised Paul and his companions. Thus, it was easy for him to use these faith-filled Saints as an example for the better-off Corinthian brothers and sisters.

We must emphasize, however, that it is not the depth of the giving that is at the heart of Paul's example. As we will show below, the Apostle stresses

78. Guthrie, *2 Corinthians,* 392.

79. BDAG, 457.

80. Barnett, *Second Epistle,* 398.

81. BDAG, 1077; *NID,* 4:644–49.

82. Georgi, *Remembering the Poor,* 71.

83. Seifrid, *Second Letter,* 319. An extreme example of giving due to the converting power of God is the story of the Anti-Nephi-Lehies. These righteous people freely gave their very lives for their cause. Though the word "grace" does not appear in the story, the testimony of their king, referring as it does to all that God had done for these people, shows this power operating in their lives, enabling them to take this inordinate action. See Alma 24:5–18.

84. Martin, *2 Corinthians,* 433.

that he does not expect the Corinthian Saints to give as did the Macedonians (8:12–13). The example he sets up is, therefore, not the depth of the sacrifice of the giving but that the giving was a manifestation of the result of the downflow of divine grace upon these people. In doing so, Paul continues to highlight the importance and effect of the power of the Lord upon his people and, thus, keeps him at the center even in this seemingly mundane and temporal matter.[85]

This section of the epistle shows that Paul's understanding of generosity as a means of remembering the poor is not only the heart of his gospel but is also rooted in his understanding of the story of Jesus himself. It was the Master who insisted on a willingness to lower oneself temporally in order to care for the needy and open the gates to heavenly blessings (8:9).[86] For Paul, the poor, as mentioned in Galatians 2:10, are not geographically restricted. They are found both in Judea and in the local congregations that he established in the Mediterranean region. It would appear, however, that those hardest hit were in the Holy Land, and so the Apostle is asking those with more to give to those with less. Paul also expected the wealthier households to give a higher percentage of their means than poorer ones. For him, this was a means by which the confession of the gospel of Jesus Christ is authenticated through love in action.[87]

In 8:2–5, the Apostle details the depth of the Macedonian Saints' faithfulness by emphasizing the surprising amount of funds they raised for the Judean cause. His motive is clearly to encourage the Corinthian branches to also freely give to the collection. Given the shame/honor code at the basis of Greco-Roman society, reputation meant much to these people on both the individual and societal levels.[88] Few would accept being seen as less than others, on either the social or the personal plane. This predicament led, at times, to attempts to outdo others in a show of generosity.[89] In the Jewish world, the pious were expected to give in proportion to their

85. Seifrid, *Second Letter,* 318.

86. For examples, see Matt. 19:27–30; JST Matt. 19:26; and Mark 10:17–22.

87. For a study, see Kar Yong Lim, "Generosity from Pauline Perspective: Insights from Paul's Letters to the Corinthians," *Evangelical Review of Theology* 37, no. 1 (2013): 20–33.

88. For a study, see Stephen Charles Mott, "The Power of Giving and Receiving: Reciprocity in Hellenistic Benevolence," in *Current Issues in Biblical and Patristic Interpretation: Studies in Honor of Merrill C. Tenney Presented by His Former Students,* ed. Gerald F. Hawthorne (Grand Rapids, Mich.: William B. Eerdmans, 1975), 60–72.

89. For a study focusing on the present context, see Witherington, *Conflict and Community,* 414–19.

means, but even this, at times, led to showing off (see Matt. 6:1–2; compare 3 Ne. 13:1–2), which was not helpful.[90]

Given the context of chapter 8, it seems unlikely, however, that Paul is playing on these societal mores. Though there is no doubt he is encouraging the Corinthian members to reach deep into their pockets to assist the poor as had their northern neighbors, his greater desire is that they share in the abundant downflow of grace that made the depth of the giving of the Macedonian Saints possible. Thus he asks that his readers neither match nor outdo the contribution of their northern neighbors. In fact, he emphasizes that their gift is neither to be extraordinary nor to cause them affliction (8:12–13). They were not to play the competitive game so rife in their world.[91]

The idea Paul wanted to get across is that the northern Saints had gone beyond all normal expectation not only in their giving but also in their life orientation. The Macedonians, he insists, reflect God's will in the way they gave both of themselves and of their resources.[92] "In the upside-down world of God's kingdom values, monetary help from the Macedonian churches flowed not from a reservoir of monetary wealth, but from joy-filled, integrity-infused, poverty. They were a 'rich poor' church that despite their impoverished condition refused to turn inward."[93]

Paul's description of the conditions under which they so generously gave highlights the depth of their generosity. First, they gave voluntarily. There was no coercion or even light pressure. The missionaries presented the opportunity, and these grace-filled people immediately responded. Second, they not only gave, but considering the financial distress under which they lived, they gave beyond even what the missionaries expected. Third, the Apostle notes that they even begged for the opportunity to be involved in the grace offering. His words suggest that the missionaries may have tried to limit the amount that they were offering, but they would have

90. Watson, "Paul's Collection," 3–4.

91. For a study, see Peter Marshall, *Enmity in Corinth: Social Conventions in Paul's Relation with the Corinthians* (Tübingen: Mohr-Siebeck, 1987), 1–34.

92. For a study, see Emmanuel Nathan and Thomas A. Vollmer, "Paul's Reference to the Macedonians in 2 Cor 8:1–5: A Test-case to Introduce Reputation Theory," *Australian Biblical Review* 63 (2015): 42–51, who argue that Paul may have been exaggerating in order to instill a higher degree of charitable giving among his readers. If that is the case, then he is really putting the pressure on the Corinthian Saints to measure up. Given what Acts and some of Paul's epistles teach of these people, it is unlikely that Paul is exaggerating their goodness. See 1 Thes. 1:1–3 and 2 Thes. 1:1–5.

93. Guthrie, *2 Corinthians,* 396.

none of it. The irony of this situation is that normally it is the "givers" who are begged for help, but here it is the "givers" who have turned into "beggars" in their desire to participate in the gift.[94] But such is the case when divine grace flows and conversion takes place.

Paul states that they gave of their "earthly goods" (πλοῦτος, *ploutos*). Given the high degree of poverty these people were experiencing, the noun likely refers not just to the amount they gave but also to the purity of the motive that stood behind it. The word Paul uses to describe their simple giving (ἁπλότης, *haplotēs*) can be understood as "generous liberality." The word connotes the depth of their spirituality—a "faultless innocence" and an "uncompromising rectitude" reveling in "a deep-seated purpose, a condition of the soul" that brings the blessing of God by which they became spiritually rich.[95]

This sincere outpouring of charity won a place in Paul's affections. He honored these faith-filled Saints because of their "participation in the gospel from the first day until now" (Philip. 1:5, our translation). Their actions demonstrated that the transforming power of true conversion had become a real and vital force in their lives, their grace reflecting that of the Lord.[96] Paul's goal is to have this same spiritual conversion happen to the Corinthian Saints. For him, it is more important that they open their hearts than their purses. Thus, later in his epistle, he can reveal to them that "I am not seeking [what is] yours, but you" (12:14), for he knew that if their hearts changed, their giving would be full and proper.[97]

Noteworthy is that Paul goes to some length to show that even when authentic Christianity manifests the depth of its care of humankind through selfless service, it very often meets difficulty, suffering, and even persecution. The Apostle nowhere hints that the problems besetting the Macedonian branches were due to some impropriety or wrongdoing on the part of either the Church or individuals therein. He clearly understands that affliction is the mark of authenticity or, at the very least, the common situation in which the Christian cause moves forward.[98]

---

94. Guthrie, *2 Corinthians,* 397–98.

95. In the Wisdom literature, this attribute was "considered the supreme virtue of the patriarchs." Ceslaus Spicq, *Theological Lexicon of the New Testament,* trans. James D. Ernest, 3 vols. (Peabody, Mass.: Hendrickson Publishers, 1994), 1:169–70, as quoted in Guthrie, *2 Corinthians,* 396, n. 16.

96. Garland, *2 Corinthians,* 369–70.

97. Guthrie, *2 Corinthians,* 400.

98. Guthrie, *2 Corinthians,* 394.

Paul's use of religious metaphors suggests that he views the contributions in terms of a sacred offering imitating the acts of the Savior. In doing so, he reframes gift giving as an act of religious devotion in which mutual obligation results not in the praise of human benefactors (the basis of the Greco-Roman practice) but of God as the source of all benefaction, rather than a social obligation. He strengthens his point with metaphors of harvest,[99] thus stressing his position that it is God who is the ultimate benefactor responsible for the workers reaping "bounteously" (9:6, NR). It is on this basis that he teaches that even this seemingly temporal act originates in "the grace of God" (χάρις τοῦ θεου, *charis tou theou*) and results in the "gift to God" (χάρις τῷ θεῷ, *charis tō theō*). Indeed, as the Apostle states in 8:5, these people had given themselves to the Lord and as a result could sense his will that they give to others. As a result, they gave themselves also to the cause of the collection.[100] In making this observation, Paul emphasizes that God, ever active and influential in human affairs, is the source that motivates and empowers these sincere actions of human benefaction.[101]

In 8:6, Paul notes the result of the wonderous giving of the Macedonian Saints. It inspired the leadership to encourage Titus (and it seem to have taken little) to go back to Corinth with the assignment to further the collection. The text suggests that Titus had already renewed the Corinthians' efforts to this task because Paul had encouraged him to finish up the collection of this charitable offering just as he had already begun by returning to Corinth and pushing this ministry there.[102]

In 8:7, Paul skillfully sets up the Corinthians for Titus's success by pointing out that they already possessed many spiritual attributes and that the expression of one more is all that is necessary to accomplish the mission's goal. Paul seems to be building on the pride they took in their spiritual gifts (χαρίσματα, *charismata*, see 1 Cor. 12:4–11; 14:1–9). His exhortation makes the need implicit in 8:6 now explicit. He has it rest on those items in which they excel—faith, speech, knowledge, heartfelt earnestness, and love for Paul and the other missionaries. Because they have excelled in

---

99. In Rom. 15:28, he refers to the offering as "this fruit," and in 2 Cor. 9:6–15, he speaks of sowing and reaping with God giving both the growth and the harvest, but greatly blessing the ones who do the work.

100. Seifrid, *Second Letter,* 324.

101. For a study, see David J. Downs, *The Offering of the Gentiles: Paul's Collection for Jerusalem in Its Chronological, Cultural, and Cultic Contexts* (Tübingen, Ger.: Mohr Siebeck, 2008).

102. Seifrid, *Second Letter,* 325; Guthrie, *2 Corinthians,* 401.

these matters, he asks them to also excel in one more—that is, in the graciousness of giving. Thus he calls the contribution a "charitable offering" (χάρις, *charis*). In this way, he draws a parallel between the excellent qualities he has observed among them and the positive response to the plea he is now making. Paul is tacitly suggesting that by generously responding to the work now being rekindled by Titus, they would both build upon and continue the excellent manifestations of God's grace the Apostle had already observed among them.[103]

Encouragement to Be Generous (8:8–15)

Greek Text

8 Οὐ κατ᾽ ἐπιταγὴν λέγω ἀλλὰ διὰ τῆς ἑτέρων σπουδῆς καὶ τὸ τῆς ὑμετέρας ἀγάπης
γνήσιον δοκιμάζων· 9 γινώσκετε γὰρ τὴν χάριν τοῦ κυρίου ἡμῶν Ἰησοῦ Χριστοῦ,
ὅτι δι᾽ ὑμᾶς ἐπτώχευσεν πλούσιος ὤν, ἵνα ὑμεῖς τῇ ἐκείνου πτωχείᾳ πλουτήσητε.
10 καὶ γνώμην ἐν τούτῳ δίδωμι· τοῦτο γὰρ ὑμῖν συμφέρει, οἵτινες οὐ μόνον τὸ
ποιῆσαι ἀλλὰ καὶ τὸ θέλειν προενήρξασθε ἀπὸ πέρυσι· 11 νυνὶ δὲ καὶ τὸ ποιῆσαι
ἐπιτελέσατε, ὅπως καθάπερ ἡ προθυμία τοῦ θέλειν οὕτως καὶ τὸ ἐπιτελέσαι ἐκ τοῦ
ἔχειν. 12 εἰ γὰρ ἡ προθυμία πρόκειται, καθὸ ἐὰν ἔχῃ εὐπρόσδεκτος, οὐ καθὸ οὐκ
ἔχει. 13 οὐ γὰρ ἵνα ἄλλοις ἄνεσις, ὑμῖν θλῖψις· ἀλλ᾽ ἐξ ἰσότητος. 14 ἐν τῷ νῦν καιρῷ
τὸ ὑμῶν περίσσευμα εἰς τὸ ἐκείνων ὑστέρημα, ἵνα καὶ τὸ ἐκείνων περίσσευμα γένη-
ται εἰς τὸ ὑμῶν ὑστέρημα, ὅπως γένηται ἰσότης· 15 καθὼς γέγραπται· Ὁ τὸ πολὺ
οὐκ ἐπλεόνασεν, καὶ ὁ τὸ ὀλίγον οὐκ ἠλαττόνησεν. [SBLGNT]

King James Version

8 I speak not by commandment, but by
occasion of the forwardness of others,
and to prove the sincerity of your love.
9 For ye know the grace of our Lord
Jesus Christ, that, though he was rich,
yet for your sakes he became poor, that

New Rendition

8 I am not saying this as a command, but
I am testing the genuineness of your love
through the eagerness of others. 9 For
you know the grace of our Lord Jesus
Christ—that although he was rich, he
impoverished himself for your sakes so

103. According to *DNTC,* 2:433, "Those who abound in faith and the attributes of godliness are the ones who impart liberally of their substance for the temporal welfare of their brethren in the kingdom." The three key elements of Paul's address are "grace" (χάρις, *charis*), "sharing" (κοινωνία, *koinōnia*), and "service" (διακονία, *diakonia*). For a detailed study of the importance and interplay of these three words, see Keith F. Nickle, *The Collection: A Study in Paul's Strategy* (London: SCM Press, 1966), 105–11.

Christ's voluntary willingness to leave his exalted position in heaven to enter into a lowly mortal state and suffer a brutal death by crucifixion δι' ὑμᾶς (*di' hymas*), "for your sakes," Paul uses the verb πτωχεύω (*ptōcheuō*), "to become poor."[114] To bring out this emphasis, we translated this as "he impoverished himself" in our Rendition.

that ye through his poverty might be rich / so that you might be enriched by his poverty: The conjunction ἵνα (*hina*), "so that," points to both the reason and result of an act.[115] The verb πλουτέω (*plouteō*), "to be or become rich," is found here as an aorist subjunctive.[116] In the present context, it points to the blessings associated with coming under Christ's grace. The noun πτωχεία (*ptōcheia*) refers to a "state of being deficient in means of support, poverty."[117] In the present context, both the verb and the noun refer to being rich or poor, either in status or in transcendent values.[118] The Savior became poor by leaving his divine glory and taking upon himself full mortality, including suffering death. The Saints can become rich in two possible ways: first, by coming to possess what Paul describes as "the righteousness of God," a condition he notes that comes through divine grace (5:12–16); and second, by sharing in an overflowing of grace as evidence in the gifts of the Spirit they enjoy (8:7). Given the context, the latter is more likely.[119]

8:10–11: These verses present an unusual translation challenge. The main reason is that herein Paul uses a grammatical construction in which a neuter definite article is prefixed to an infinitive. This articular infinitive takes on the character of a noun describing the action of the verb but still retains the functions of a verb.[120] In translating an articular infinitive into English, one can use either a gerund or an infinitive with the preposition "to."[121] We have rendered these with the latter.

---

114. BDAG, 896. The verb is in the aorist tense and is often viewed as an ingressive aorist (see Smyth, *Greek Grammar,* §1865.b) meaning "to begin to be poor"; however, the context suggests he actually was poor due to his incarnation. Hughes, *Second Epistle,* 300 n. 24.

115. Louw-Nida, §§89.59; 90.22.

116. BDAG, 831.

117. BDAG, 896; Louw-Nida, §§57.52, 54; MM, 558.

118. BDAG, 896.

119. Barnett, *Second Epistle,* 408–9.

120. Smyth, *Greek Grammar,* §2025; Wallace, *Greek Grammar,* 234–35.

121. This construction is fairly rare in the New Testament, but Paul uses it six times in these two verses: τὸ ποιῆσαι (*to poiēsai*), "the doing," τὸ θέλειν (*to thelein*), "the desiring," in 8:10, and τὸ ποιῆσαι (*to poiēsai*), "the doing," τοῦ θέλειν (*to thelein*), "of the desiring," τὸ

8:10 ***And herein I give my advice / And I am giving you my opinion on this matter:*** The noun γνώμη (*gnōmē*), "opinion, judgment," here has the sense of "a declaration that expresses formal consideration of a matter,"[122] hence our Rendition.[123] The prepositional phrase ἐν τούτῳ (*en toutō*), literally "in this," we have translated as "on this matter" to better express the sense in contemporary English. But what is the matter Paul refers to? It could be the need to prove their love, or to donate to the collection, or to yield to the Apostles' "considered opinion." The context suggests the latter.[124]

for this is expedient for you / because this is to your advantage: The conjunction γάρ (*gar*), "for, because," in this context expresses the reason for an action.[125] The neuter pronoun τοῦτο (*touto*), "this," refers to the Corinthians yielding to Paul's considered opinion.[126] The verb συμφέρω (*sympherō*), "to be advantageous," denotes not only something that is advantageous to another but also what confers a benefit that is either useful or profitable.[127]

who have begun before, not only to do, but also to be forward a year ago / Last year you began not only to act but also to desire to act: The adverb πέρυσι (*perysi*) means "last year,"[128] not "a year ago" as the KJV translates it. The amount of time it entails depends on when the new year started and when the epistle was written. It could range, therefore, from just a few months up to twenty-three.[129] The verb ποιέω (*poieō*), "to do, make,"[130] and the verb θέλω (*thelō*), "to want, desire,"[131] are both articular infinitives with a prefixed definite article (see the explanation that introduces 8:10–11 above).[132] Both are grammatically direct objects of the verb προενάρχομαι (*proenarchomai*), "to begin previously,"[133] found here as an aorist, which

---

ἐπιτελέσαι (*to epitelesai*), "the finishing," and τοῦ ἔχειν (*tou echein*), "of the having," in 8:11. The actual nouns these replace must be determined by context.

122. BDAG, 202–3; LSJ, 354.

123. Guthrie, *2 Corinthians,* 407.

124. Barnett, *Second Epistle,* 410–11, translates the word as "advise."

125. BDAG, 189–90.

126. Barnett, *Second Epistle,* 410, translates the term as "advise."

127. Louw-Nida, §65.44; BDAG, 960.

128. BDAG, 808.

129. Barnett, *Second Epistle,* 410 n. 35.

130. BDAG, 839–42.

131. BDAG, 447–48.

132. On articular infinitives acting as verbal nouns, see Smyth, *Greek Grammar,* §§2001–7; and Wallace, *Greek Grammar,* 234–35.

133. Louw-Nida, §68.4; BDAG, 868.

denotes a simple past event. A literal translation of the phrase would be "You began last year not only the doing but also the desiring," where both the "doing" and the "desiring" refer to participating in the charitable collection for the Saints in Jerusalem. However, this is a little awkward in English, so for clarity we translated τὸ ποιῆσαι (*to poiēsai*), "to give," and τὸ θελεῖν (*to thelein*), "to desire to give," in our Rendition.

8:11 ***Now therefore perform the doing of it / But now also finish what you started:*** With the opening adverbial phase νυνὶ δὲ καί (*nyni de kai*), "but now also," Paul brings his audience back to the present but does so in such a way as to contrast the Saints' earlier giving, as expressed by "last year," with their current state of inaction. The phrase calls for action "right now,"[134] and the conjunction καί (*kai*), "also," emphasizes the idea "that a present response needs to be added to the past acts and intentions."[135] In this phrase, Paul once again uses an articular infinitive (see the explanation that introduces 8:10–11 above), τὸ ποιῆσαι (*to poiēsai*), "the doing," which he also used in the previous verse. We have translated it as "what you started" to clarify that it is referring to their contribution to the charitable collection. The verb ἐπιτελέω (*epiteleō*), found here as an aorist imperative, means "to complete" or "finish" a task that has an identified end result.[136] Importantly, it can also carry the nuance of discharging a religious duty.[137] The Apostle's use of the word suggests that he conceives of this collection as a moral obligation,[138] and that may be a contributing reason why he is urging them to finish the job.

that as there was a readiness to will, so there may be a performance also out of that which ye have / so that your eager desire to do it is matched by your completion of it according to what you have: The Greek here is very compact, and translating it into English presents a definite challenge. The clause begins with the conjunction ὅπως (*hopōs*), "so that," marking the

134. Barnett, *Second Epistle,* 411, with n. 40.

135. Guthrie, *2 Corinthians,* 409.

136. Louw-Nida, §§68.22; 13.108.

137. Paul uses ἐπιτελέω (*epiteleō*) four other times in ritual observance. In Gal. 3:3, it deals with Christian spiritual formation; in Philip. 1:6, it is tied to Christian duty; in Heb. 8:5; 9:6, it is used in the context of priestly duties and religious service; and in 1 Pet. 5:9, it is used in reference to Christian character formation. The verb ἐπιτελέω (*epiteleō*) also occurs in the performance of sacred rites by classical authors, especially with respect to the rites of Zeus.

138. For a study, see Richard S. Ascough, "The Completion of a Religious Duty: The Background to 2 Corinthians 8.1–15," *New Testament Studies* 42, no. 4 (1996): 584–99.

purpose of an action.[139] The conjunction normally is followed by a finite verb in the subjunctive mood. However, there is no finite verb here. Instead there are three articular infinitives (see the explanation that introduces 8:10–11 above). Following the conjunction are the correlative adverbs καθάπερ . . . οὕτως καί (*kathaper . . . houtōs kai*), "just as . . . so also."[140] The noun προθυμία (*prothymia*) expresses "being eager to be of service,"[141] which is modified by the genitive articular infinitive τοῦ θέλειν (*tou thelein*), "of the desiring."[142] Following the second half of the correlative phrase "so also" is the articular infinitive τὸ ἐπιτελέσαι (*to epitelesai*), "the finishing."[143] The clause closes with a third articular infinitive in τοῦ ἔχειν (*tou echein*), "the having," governed by the preposition ἐκ (*ek*) "from."[144] Putting this all together, we get a very unsatisfying literal translation: "so that just as the eagerness of the doing, so also the completion from the having." In our Rendition, we have supplied the understood but unstated elements of this statement.

8:12 ***For if there be first a willing mind / For if the willingness is present:*** This verse is a conditional sentence that Paul skillfully creates to make his point. This construction imparts the idea that if or since something is true (and the inference is that it is; in this case, it is the willingness of the Saints to give), then what follows is also true (in this case, that their offering will be accepted).[145]

The conjunction γάρ (*gar*), "for," signals the explanation of an action. Many translations use the word "if,"[146] and we have as well in our Rendition. But Paul has clearly shown that, though the Saints' giving has fallen off, their desire has not. The noun προθυμία (*prothymia*), "willingness," denotes "an exceptional interest in being of service."[147] The verb πρόκειμαι (*prokeimai*) means "to be present"[148] and carries the idea of being so with an openness so evident that all can see it.[149]

---

139. BDAG, 718.

140. BDAG, 488, "the formulation contributes a solemn official tone to the text."

141. BDAG, 870.

142. BDAG, 447–48.

143. BDAG, 383.

144. BDAG, 295–98.

145. The conditional particle εἰ (*ei*), "if" with the indicative mood, can refer to a present reality with almost a causal sense, "since." BDF, §372.

146. See, for example, KJV, NIV, and NRSV.

147. BDAG, 870. Both the noun and the verb forms carry the idea of earnestness and enthusiasm toward an objective. MM, 540.

148. BDAG, 871.

149. Louw-Nida, §13.75.

it is accepted according to that a man hath, and not according to that he hath not / the act is acceptable according to whatever one might or might not have: The adjective εὐπρόσδεκτος (*euprodektos*), "acceptable," denotes that which is truly favorable and pleasing[150] and, in this case, refers to the person's willingness to give. But acceptable to whom? Though Paul does not say, his use of the term or its cognates elsewhere ties it to the Divine (Rom. 12:1; Philip. 4:18; compare Heb. 13:16). The adverb καθό (*katho*) refers to the degree to which something can be done or expected.[151] It is followed by the particle ἐάν (*ean*)—that is, a "marker of condition, with probability of activity expressed in the verb left open and thereby suited esp. for generalized statements."[152] That condition is expressed by the verb ἔχω (*echō*), "to have," found here with ἐάν (*ean*) in the subjunctive mood. Together they nuance what one *might* have. Though the phrase has no expressed subject, grammatically the verb implies an impersonal subject, which we have rendered as "one."[153]

In the following clause, the verb ἔχω (*echō*), "to have," is in the present, indicative mood rather than the subjunctive found in the previous clause. There is a subtle nuance here. The subjunctive in the previous clause indicates that the amount a person might possess is indefinite, whereas the indicative found here implies that what she or he does *not* have is definite. With this caveat, Paul assures his audience that he does not expect them to borrow funds in order to contribute to the collection.

8:13 ***For I mean not that other men be eased, and ye burdened / For it is not that others should have relief and you be burdened:*** The conjunction γάρ (*gar*), "for," [154] signals the reason for an action and rests on Paul's assurance that he is not asking them to borrow in order to give. The adjective ἄλλος (*allos*), "other," acts here as a substantive referring to other people—namely, the Jerusalem Saints.[155] The clause has no verb, so we have supplied "should have" for clarity in English. The noun ἄνεσις (*anesis*), "relief," denotes freedom from something "onerous or troublesome."[156] The noun θλῖψις (*thlipsis*), "affliction, distress, burden,"[157] denotes the kind of

150. Louw-Nida, §§22.44; 25.86.

151. Louw-Nida, §78.53.

152. BDAG, 267. The particle is usually written as ἄν (*an*), but becomes ἐάν (*ean*) after relative pronouns.

153. Barnett, *Second Epistle,* 412 n. 51.

154. BDAG, 189; Louw-Nida, §89.23.

155. BDAG, 46–47; Guthrie, *2 Corinthians,* 412.

156. BDAG, 77–78.

157. BDAG, 457; Guthrie, *2 Corinthians,* 412.

trouble or worry that puts a person under a good deal of emotional or spiritual pressure.[158] In the LXX, it denotes the extreme misery or need felt at times for the people of Israel (Ex. 3:9; 4:31),[159] and Paul's use of the term is a reminder of the circumstances of the Macedonian Saints.

8:13–14 ***But by an equality / but it is a matter of fairness:*** The KJV places this phrase at the beginning of 8:14, whereas the Greek text places it at the end of 8:13. The noun ἰσότης (*isotēs*) denotes a sense of "equality," "in the sense of having equal features or characteristics,"[160] but here it has the extended meaning of "fairness."[161] We have rendered the prepositional phrase ἐξ ἰσότητος (*ex isotētos*), literally "out of fairness," as above to better capture its sense in contemporary English.

8:14 ***But by an equality, that now at this time your abundance may be a supply for their want / At the present time, your abundance can meet their need:*** On the KJV phrase "but by an equality," see 8:13–14 above. The prepositional phrase ἐν τῷ νῦν καιρῷ (*en tō nyn kairō*), "at the present time," plays a key role in understanding Paul's point but is a bit vague. On the one hand, it could suggest the need for immediate and full action in contrast to the slowdown that occurred over the previous year.[162] On the other hand, it could carry a developmental nuance referring to the state of affairs that were developing in this "now time" when the kingdom of God had been restored and the new covenant established, with both moving forward.[163] Such an age demands equality and fairness among those who belong to the Christian community as a whole. "This is to be expressed in the first instance in a spiritual fellowship and unity among the ecumenical body of believers, but, where appropriate and necessary, it should issue in material assistance as well," allowing all to prosper.[164] Such a setting lifts the collection from a more commonplace and immediate effort to a general stance that provides the underpinnings for the theology of practical relief, appropriate to those who belong to "the Israel of God" (Gal. 6:16),

158. *NID,* 2:461–64.

159. Guthrie, *2 Corinthians,* 412.

160. Louw-Nida, §58.32. "In the ancient world, the term had to do with a state of being fair or balanced. The noun and its cognate adjective (ἴσος, *isos,* equal) were used in the realms of arithmetic and geometry to refer to equal sums or measurements, equal rights or justice in the political realm, or equal sums of money in accounting." Guthrie, *2 Corinthians,* 412. In the realm of social interactions, the idea of fairness dominated.

161. BDAG, 481.

162. Barnett, *Second Epistle,* 414–15.

163. See Rom. 3:26; 8:18, where the phrase is used in this eschatological sense.

164. Barnett, *Second Epistle,* 415.

genuineness of their love as his children. In doing so, he "brings the integrity of the readers to play as the onus is now placed on them to manifest their love for God and their fellow Christians in a concrete manner."[173] In this, we do hear echoes of patronage in play that invite the Saints to make and keep covenants because of the graceful gifts God the Father bestowed upon them. But this condition "was not just a matter of economic and social power, but also a matter of honor and shame, and it is no accident that chs. 8–9 use the language of honor and shame."[174]

In linking the collection to the value system of his audience, the Apostle Paul skillfully places more pressure on them than any direct command would do.[175] On the other hand, by not commanding them to give, Paul allows their free-will offering to be an actual act of grace that reveals the depth of God's love that abides in them.[176]

In 8:9, Paul does not allow the generousness of the Macedonian Saints to stand as the greatest show of love. Instead, he has his audience look at one of the greatest of all acts of love that makes pale what the Macedonians did. This act is the condescension of Christ, in which he not only gave up his riches but also became poor in order to make the believers rich.[177] In giving them this reminder, the Apostle reaches back to the idea of the effects of divine grace (χάρις, *charis*) by holding Christ up as the exemplar gift-giver, whom we can have a relationship with in the new covenant through service. In doing so, the Apostle connects the kindness in giving back to the kindness of this Son of God in giving of himself. The Redeemer chose poverty by forsaking heavenly glory. It is the Apostle's hope that the Lord's love-filled action will stir his readers to also act out their faith (the center of their being rich; see 6:10; 9:11) by generously giving to the collection.

Paul's example functions here in a rather intriguing way, for he is *not* asking his audience to become poor like Jesus. Rather he wants them to give out of concern for the sake of equity, due to their indebtedness to the Savior's own lavish gift to them.[178] As they consider what Christ has done

173. Joubert, "Behind the Mask," 107.

174. Witherington, *Conflict and Community,* 419.

175. Joubert, "Behind the Mask," 107.

176. Barnett, *Second Epistle,* 406.

177. Gary Webster Griffith, "Abounding in Generosity: A Study of *Charis* in 2 Corinthians 8–9" (PhD diss., Durham University, 2005), 135–39. The ultimate riches that the Lord gives are those of eternal life. See D&C 6:7.

178. Furnish, *II Corinthians,* 418.

for them and how they themselves have come to him, they should respond appropriately to the Apostle's imperative call: "This is what you should do" (8:10)—namely, as he notes in 8:11, "Complete your action."[179]

In 8:10, "Paul moves directly from the unusually powerful imagery—and thus theology—of v. 9 to a direct application of all of this to the Corinthians themselves."[180] Again he does not command the Corinthian Saints to act. Instead, he notes that he has carefully considered the matter and has determined the best course of action *for them*. Even so, there is no doubt that he is giving his request weight by placing it in the form of "serious, apostolic counsel" as directed by the Holy Spirit.[181] Giving him energy to make his appeal is his belief that, though the actual giving to the Jewish Christian cause has slowed or ceased, the desire is still there. He plays on this but adds another reason why his audience should renew their giving: it will be to their advantage in that they themselves will receive some benefit from it. This benefit, as he notes in 8:11, is that their desires and acts will make them fully integrated into the charitable program and any current spiritual dissonance between their strong desire and charitable action will be eliminated.[182]

His reference to how they had initiated the work "last year" (πέρυσι, *perysi*) suggests that they were the first church in the area introduced into the program and that they willingly accepted the opportunity.[183] In 8:11, he encourages them to finish it but adds the caveat "according to what you have." By adding this phrase, he is not putting the Corinthian members in a position where they would need to compete with the overabundance of giving that the Macedonian Saints had exhibited. He is not lowering the bar but telling his audience that what he is asking them to do is immediately attainable.[184]

In 8:12, Paul aligns the Christian understanding of giving with that of the Old Testament. What counts is not how much is given but the state of the giver's heart (Isa. 1:10–15; 43:24–28; Amos 5:25–27; compare D&C 64:34). By this means, he defuses any concerns on the Corinthians' part that he expects them to imitate the copious action of their northern sisters and brothers. Further, he mitigates any suspicions and perhaps actual accusations that he is attempting to gain some moral advantage by

179. Martin, *2 Corinthians,* 441.
180. Barnett, *Second Corinthians,* 409.
181. Furnish, *II Corinthians,* 405.
182. Guthrie, *2 Corinthians,* 408.
183. Guthrie, *2 Corinthians,* 408.
184. Guthrie, *2 Corinthians,* 409.

boasting of the Macedonians' abundant giving. He clearly signals that he is a caregiver and protector, not some manipulator.[185]

Paul references the idea of proportional giving based on what one has on hand through expressing a general truth in a condition (καθὸ ἐὰν ἔχῃ, *katho ean echē*), not on some speculation as to what one might have in the future. He clearly points out that as long as the reciprocal giving is in proportion to one's means—but given with full heart—it is acceptable to the Lord, whatever the amount may be, large or small.[186] Some may have felt a need to compete with the northern Saints, given what they knew of the conditions in which the Macedonians lived. Though members of the upper echelon within the Macedonian cities were thriving at that time, that wealth was slow to reach the bottom levels of society. In Paul's Mediterranean world, many of the very poor relied on a benefactor's patronage to provide for them.[187] On the other hand, the wealth of Corinth, the provincial capital, had grown for decades, and much of the money was reaching the lower ranks. Even so, Paul may have been sensitive to the lower stratum of members. Slaves, particularly, would have had little to give, especially if they were saving toward their *peculium* as established by Roman law, which resulted in manumission.[188]

Paul's use of the idea of grace (χάρις, *charis*) falls within the Hellenistic reciprocity system, with its involvement in patronage and beneficiation, but he does not fully accept patronage as it usually works. In that system, to accept a gift involved one in "an inescapable train of obligations. . . . but to refuse a gift was no easier, for one then incurred the burden of enmity."[189] Having suffered from the latter via the reproach and even slander he received, the Apostle here seeks to transform the system by extricating the Christians from the burdensome demands that this system—with

185. Barnett, *Second Epistle,* 412.

186. Thrall, *Critical and Exegetical Commentary,* 2:538. Note D&C 51:3 and 82:17 address the idea of temporal equality on the basis that all receive according to their needs and wants but not in getting exactly the same proportion of goods as another. Ogden and Skinner, *Verse by Verse,* 154–55. See also D&C 49:19–20.

187. Rainer Riesner, *Paul's Early Period: Chronology, Mission Strategy, Theology,* trans. Doug Stott (Grand Rapids, Mich.: Wm. B. Eerdmans, 1988), 376–77.

188. Garland, *2 Corinthians,* 381–82. On Christian slavery, see John M. G. Barclay, "Paul, Philemon, and the Dilemma of Christian Slave-Ownership," *New Testament Studies* 37, no. 2 (1991): 161–86, particularly 179–80.

189. E. A. Judge, "The Social Identity of the First Christians: A Question of Method in Religious History," *Journal of Religious History* 11, no. 2 (1980): 214. For a study, see Marshall, *Enmity in Corinth,* 35–69.

its tyranny of a commensurate response—imposed. He did this in large part by allowing each Saint to choose how much to give according to her or his individual circumstances. Thus, his efforts worked toward a countercultural model of obligation and reciprocity derived from the teachings and acts of the Redeemer.[190] Here he forces "the Corinthians to rethink social relationships in the light of Christ. [The Apostle's] rejection of personal patronage in Corinth is of a piece with his rejection of other status conventions of Greco-Roman antiquity. For the Corinthians to respond to what Paul says will involve them in seeing God in Christ as their ultimate patron or benefactor."[191]

There is some speculation that Paul was motivated in this work due to some obligation he felt the Gentile Church had toward the Jewish. While it is true that he felt that the Gentiles converts did owe a debt to the Jews (Rom. 15:27), that debt was spiritual. Rather, Paul likely saw this action as an expression of solidarity between the two Christian communities that could act as a witness to non-Christian Jews that Old Testament prophecy was being fulfilled: Gentiles sending gifts to Jerusalem.[192]

There is an important idea housed here that highlights the difference between the thinking of the Gentile world and that of the Christian community. It centers on Paul's understanding of equality or fairness (ἰσότης, *isotēs*). His understanding does not appear to have been scripturally based[193] but rather derived from his reaction to the Greco-Roman world view vis-à-vis his Christian understanding. According to Gentile thinking, the idea of equality developed in three contexts: between friends, in the polis (that is, the community of citizens), and in the cosmos (that is, the world order in general).

---

190. For a study, see James R. Harrison, *Paul's Language of Grace in Its Graeco-Roman Context* (Tübingen, Ger.: Mohr Siebeck, 2003). The Gentile members of Paul's audience would have clearly understood the act of the *charisma* (a gift graciously given). Considering their background, they would have viewed the relationship between a god and a human being as involving reciprocity. "The god gave blessings and the human being responded or petitioned with prayers, sacrifices, verbal or written praise (gratitude), and the like. With such a background, the concept of grace itself must have been quite different for the Gentile Corinthians to grasp, but the idea of God as a benefactor to whom one was obligated to respond would not have been difficult to grasp." Witherington, *Conflict and Community,* 420 n. 28.

191. Witherington, *Conflict and Community,* 418.

192. Garland, *2 Corinthians,* 387–90.

193. The word appears only twice in the LXX, in Job 36:29 and Zach. 4:7, and therefore would contribute little to Paul's understanding.

In the context of friendship, Greek philosophy argued that true friends were equal and alike, while the Romans allowed for an unequal friendship that expressed itself through patronage. Both the Greek and Roman systems included an inverse relationship of equality, meaning that between unequal parties, all will "equally" receive benefits *but* according to their honors and merits. Paul challenges this system by inviting the Corinthians to give of their own means to the Jerusalem Saints, who were, at the time, in no position to reciprocate.

In the second context (that is, that of philosophy), the writings of the day viewed equality as the force that preserved the cosmos. Preserving equality, even a differentiated equality, conserved the civil order of the Greco-Roman world. Paul again challenges this idea through his system of voluntary self-impoverishment, in which the Divine opens a new space for human action that results in the improvement of society as a whole.[194]

In 8:1–5, Paul ascribes this improvement within the Church to the empowering effects of the grace of God upon the Macedonian Saints. In 8:7, he tacitly notes that God's grace is also at work among the Corinthian Saints by listing the spiritual values they continually excel in (compare 1 Cor. 1:4–5). However, he points out there is yet one more area they can shine in—namely, generously giving to the collection.

To emphasize his point, Paul figuratively uses the idea of poverty when he refers to the Savior's actions in behalf of the Corinthian (and as a matter of fact, for all) Saints. The Apostle states that the Lord "impoverished himself" (ἐπτώχευσεν, *eptōcheusen,* 8:9). The Apostle had already addressed this idea in his letter to the Philippians. There he taught that the Savior, having "the very nature of God, . . . made himself nothing," even taking

194. There is another possible context. This one focuses on the polis or politics. Equality was the basic principle of democracy. Even so, in the Greek state, legal equality of persons before the law came to be differentiated from the social inequality of persons by nature (that is, according to their several abilities and social standings). This view sustained and even promoted a very differentiated equality. Because it is uncertain to what degree the idea of democracy yet lingered, it is unknown to what degree Paul's appeal for partnership in the Jerusalem collection would have been seen as a political matter. Even in that context, however, he would have challenged the Gentile system but in an even more radical way, for few would have accepted the idea that the Jews enjoyed equal rights with members of any of the Greek cities of the Roman east. Even so, the idea of inequality between branches of the Church was not one that Paul would tolerate. For a study, see Laurence L. Welborn, "'That There May Be Equality': The Contexts and Consequences of a Pauline Ideal," *New Testament Studies* 59, no. 1 (2013): 73–90.

"the form of a slave." In doing so, he humbled himself. The depth of that humility expressed itself ultimately in his becoming "obedient to death—even death on the cross" (Philip. 2:6–8, our translation).

The Book of Mormon parallels this idea when speaking of "the condescension of God." The term "condescension" denotes "the stooping of one who is actually exalted in power, rank, or dignity so as to accommodate [him- or herself] to intercourse with those who are his [or her] inferiors."[195] In the Book of Mormon, however, it carries the idea of doing so with graciousness and courtesy motivated by love.[196] An angel taught Nephi that Christ condescended to be mortally born, be baptized, do the work of his ministry, be judged by mere mortals, and suffer death through crucifixion (1 Ne. 11:16–33). According to Abinadi, "God himself [would] come down among the children of men" and take upon himself "the form of a man." He would also allow himself to be despised, rejected, "oppressed and afflicted" (Mosiah 13:33–35). In the process of his mortal sojourn, he would be wounded and bruised for other people's transgressions. Further, he would be numbered with lawbreakers yet bear "the sins of many, and [make] intercession for the transgressors," and finally pour "out his soul unto death" (Mosiah 14:3–5, 12; compare Mosiah 3:5–10 and Isa. 53).

This view shows that the condescension of the Savior consisted not only of his becoming mortal but also of his performing the Atonement.[197] Thus, as Paul clearly states, Jesus impoverished himself for a reason: "so that you might be enriched by his poverty" (8:9, NR). As the saying goes, "Christ . . . became what we are, that he might make us as he is himself."[198] By impoverishing himself, he fully identified with humankind. Noteworthy is that Jesus was born and lived in very humble circumstances. The scriptures provide various hints about the family's low financial state. For example, when Mary and Joseph brought Jesus to the temple for his redemption,[199]

195. *Dictionary of Synonyms,* s.v. "stoop."

196. Dennis L. Largey, ed., *Book of Mormon Reference Companion* (Salt Lake City: Deseret Book, 2003), 213.

197. Fred B. Craddock, "The Poverty of Christ: An Investigation of II Corinthians 8:9," *Interpretation* 22, no. 2 (1968): 166–67. Some authorities see the Lord's poverty as consisting only of his incarnation. For discussion, see Griffith, "Abounding in Generosity," 146–49.

198. Irenaeus, *Against Heresies* 5, introduction, in Jacques-Paul Migne, ed. *Patrologia Graeca,* 161 vols. (Paris: Imprimerie Catholique, 1857–66), 17:1120, "Cristum . . . factus est quod sumus nos, uti nos perficeret esse quod est ipse" (our translation).

199. See Ex. 34:19 in light of Ex. 13:2 and Lev. 1:14; 5:7.

they offered the least costly of the acceptable sacrifices, that of "a pair of turtle doves" (Luke 2:22–24). In addition, their circumstances compelled them to live in Nazareth, a village of little regard (John 1:46), where both Jesus and Joseph held the less-than-prestigious position of a "carpenter" (τέκτων, *tektōn*; Matt. 13:55; Mark 6:3).[200] Finally, during his ministry, the Lord himself noted his personal penury, stating that "foxes have holes, and birds of the air have nests, but the Son of man hath not where to lay his head" (Matt. 8:20; Luke 9:58).[201]

Paul's point in using the Savior as an example is that the Lord gives the opportunity for others to be made rich through his act of self-impoverishment. In doing so, Paul interweaves the idea of temporal poverty with spiritual riches.[202] He shows that the riches of the Macedonian Saints did not consist of material wealth but of their sincere generosity (8:2). In sum, God's grace did not alleviate their temporal poverty, but it did make them abound in spiritual richness. That wealth allowed them to make an offering beyond what anyone would have expected of them. In their giving, we hear echoes of the widow's mites (Mark 12:42–44; Luke 21:2–4).[203] Given their circumstances, although what they gave may not have amounted to much, it was inestimable, for they gave beyond their means. Thus they proved that they themselves were the true riches. It is little wonder then that they experienced an abundance of joy manifest in the downflow of God's grace (8:2).

But the Savior's story does not end with his poverty. There was far more to his mission than becoming mortal just to understand the delights,

---

200. The noun τέκτων (*techtōn*), "artificer," refers to craftsmen who worked in wood and stone. BDAG, 995, notes that the profession was not well respected in some circles. See also W. B. Wallis, "Carpenter," in *The Zondervan Pictorial Encyclopedia of the Bible,* ed. Merrill C. Tenney and Steven Barabas, 5 vols. (Grand Rapids, Mich.: Zondervan, 1975–76), 1:757.

201. Witherington, *Conflict and Community,* 420; but see also George Wesley Buchanan, "Jesus and the Upper Class," *Novum Testamentum* 7, no. 3 (1964–65): 195–209, who argues that Jesus may have been wealthy at one point but gave away his riches.

202. For a study, in addition to Griffith, "Abounding in Generosity," see David F. Ford, "The Economy of God: Exploring a Metaphor," in *Meaning and Truth in 2 Corinthians,* ed. Frances Young and David F. Ford (London: SPCK, 1987), 166–85, who argues that Paul contrasts heavenly and earthly economies. Where in earthly economy scarcity is a driving factor, in divine economy it is a superabundance that dominates. That abundance is the grace of God and Christ of which there is never a shortage, but a continual overflowing.

203. Griffith, "Abounding in Generosity," 140–41.

difficulties, challenges, joys, and heartaches of earth life. He came to make others rich. Indeed, his objective is to share with them the richness of the glory he enjoyed before he descended into mortality (John 17:5, 22). Thus, through the power of the Atonement, the true believer will share in his eternal riches. Because these abound, there is no need for competition between the branches.

By noting this, Paul addresses another concern that some of the Corinthian Saints may have had—namely, that he is demanding more than they can really give. His boasting of the abundant, even awe-inspiring, donations given by the Macedonian Saints likely led to this concern. He assures his audience that this is not the case, for they are not to give what they do not have (8:12). Thus the nature of their giving should not produce any real hardship (ὑστέρημα, *hysterēma*) for them. He assures them here that he is asking them to do no more than what they originally agreed to do (see 1 Cor. 16:1–2). That agreement, as he notes in 8:13, assured that fairness (ἰσότης, *isotēs*) would govern all transactions.[204]

In 8:14, Paul states what he means by fairness and how it works.[205] Given the distress the Jewish Saints are presently under, the Corinthians' giving of their abundance (περίσσευμα, *perriseuma*), while placing no great hardship on them, could alleviate the great need (ὑστέρημα, *hysterēma*) of their eastern sisters and brothers. In this act, a kind of fairness was assured.

But what kind of fairness does Paul have in mind? Two possibilities come to mind. He could be thinking of a hypothetical future reversal in economic conditions, in which the Jerusalem Saints would return the benefaction,[206] or he could have in mind a more immediate reciprocation, in that the Jerusalem Saints, by receiving the goods, would generate a loving and prayerful fellowship with these giving western members, as 8:14 implies.[207] He could actually have both ideas in mind, feeling that the loving relationship will definitely occur, while the reversal of economic fortune might occur.[208]

204. Barnett, *Second Epistle,* 414.
205. Guthrie, *2 Corinthians,* 412.
206. Hughes, *Second Epistle,* 306.
207. Harris, *Second Epistle,* 591–92.
208. Barnett, *Second Epistle,* 414.

The Mission of Titus (8:16–24)

Greek Text

16 Χάρις δὲ τῷ θεῷ τῷ διδόντι τὴν αὐτὴν σπουδὴν ὑπὲρ ὑμῶν ἐν τῇ καρδίᾳ Τίτου,
17 ὅτι τὴν μὲν παράκλησιν ἐδέξατο, σπουδαιότερος δὲ ὑπάρχων αὐθαίρετος ἐξῆλθεν
πρὸς ὑμᾶς. 18 συνεπέμψαμεν δὲ μετ' αὐτοῦ τὸν ἀδελφὸν οὗ ὁ ἔπαινος ἐν τῷ εὐαγγε-
λίῳ διὰ πασῶν τῶν ἐκκλησιῶν— 19 οὐ μόνον δὲ ἀλλὰ καὶ χειροτονηθεὶς ὑπὸ τῶν
ἐκκλησιῶν συνέκδημος ἡμῶν σὺν τῇ χάριτι ταύτῃ τῇ διακονουμένῃ ὑφ' ἡμῶν πρὸς
τὴν αὐτοῦ τοῦ κυρίου δόξαν καὶ προθυμίαν ἡμῶν— 20 στελλόμενοι τοῦτο μή τις
ἡμᾶς μωμήσηται ἐν τῇ ἁδρότητι ταύτῃ τῇ διακονουμένῃ ὑφ' ἡμῶν, 21 προνοοῦμεν
γὰρ καλὰ οὐ μόνον ἐνώπιον κυρίου ἀλλὰ καὶ ἐνώπιον ἀνθρώπων. 22 συνεπέμψα-
μεν δὲ αὐτοῖς τὸν ἀδελφὸν ἡμῶν ὃν ἐδοκιμάσαμεν ἐν πολλοῖς πολλάκις σπουδαῖον
ὄντα, νυνὶ δὲ πολὺ σπουδαιότερον πεποιθήσει πολλῇ τῇ εἰς ὑμᾶς. 23 εἴτε ὑπὲρ Τίτου,
κοινωνὸς ἐμὸς καὶ εἰς ὑμᾶς συνεργός· εἴτε ἀδελφοὶ ἡμῶν, ἀπόστολοι ἐκκλησιῶν,
δόξα Χριστοῦ. 24 τὴν οὖν ἔνδειξιν τῆς ἀγάπης ὑμῶν καὶ ἡμῶν καυχήσεως ὑπὲρ
ὑμῶν εἰς αὐτοὺς ἐνδεικνύμενοι εἰς πρόσωπον τῶν ἐκκλησιῶν. [SBLGNT]

King James Version

16 But thanks be to God, which put
the same earnest care into the heart of
Titus for you. 17 For indeed he accepted
the exhortation; but being more for-
ward, of his own accord he went unto
you. 18 And we have sent with him the
brother, whose praise is in the gospel
throughout all the churches; 19 And
not that only, but who was also chosen
of the churches to travel with us with
this grace, which is administered by us
to the glory of the same Lord, and dec-
laration of your ready mind: 20 Avoid-
ing this, that no man should blame us in
this abundance which is administered
by us: 21 Providing for honest things,
not only in the sight of the Lord, but
also in the sight of men. 22 And we have
sent with them our brother, whom we
have oftentimes proved diligent in
many things, but now much more dili-
gent, upon the great confidence which I
have in you. 23 Whether any do inquire

New Rendition

16 But thanks be to God, who put the same
devotion I have for you into the heart of
Titus. 17 Because he not only accepted
my appeal, but also, being even more
eager, he is coming to you on his own
initiative. 18 And we sent with him the
brother whose fame in connection with
the gospel has spread through all the
churches. 19 And not only that, but he
was also chosen by the churches to be
our traveling companion in connec-
tion with this charitable offering that
is administered by us for the glory of
the Lord himself as well to show our
willingness to help. 20 We did this
to prevent anyone from finding fault
with us in this liberal gift that we are
administering. 21 For we are concerned
about doing what is right not only in
the Lord's sight but also in the sight of
men [Prov. 3:4]. 22 And with them we
sent our brother whose diligence we
have often tested and proved in many

of Titus, he is my partner and fellow-helper concerning you: or our brethren be inquired of, they are the messengers of the churches, and the glory of Christ. 24 Wherefore shew ye to them, and before the churches, the proof of your love, and of our boasting on your behalf.

ways but now is even more diligent because of his confidence in you. 23 As for Titus, he is *my* partner and also a fellow worker for you. As for our brothers, they are envoys of the churches, a glory of Christ, 24 so show them proof of your love and of our boasting about you before the churches.

Translation Notes and Comments

8:16 ***But thanks be to God, which put the same earnest care into the heart of Titus for you / But thanks be to God, who put the same devotion I have for you into the heart of Titus:*** With the particle δέ (*de*), "but," Paul signals he is moving to his next point. His first statement, χάρις δὲ τῷ θεῷ (*charis de tō theō*), "thanks be to God," is a formal expression of gratitude that he often uses to denote direct and current divine action (2:14; 9:15; Rom. 6:17; 1 Cor. 15:57). The verb δίδωμι (*didōmi*), literally "to give,"[209] found here as an aorist participle, can carry certain financial overtones, such as depositing funds with the intent of earning interest.[210] The inference is that by the prior action of divine grace, God gave Titus sincere caring as a motivation to finish the charitable work. The aorist tense "reflects Titus's decision in the (recent) past to return to Corinth."[211] For the noun σπουδή (*spoudē*), "earnestness, eagerness, devotion," see 8:7 above. Here, the phrase τὴν αὐτὴν σπουδὴν (*tēn autēn spoudēn*), "the same devotion," captures the idea of gratitude or sincere caring for others, "the proper response to God, who is the ultimate benefactor."[212] It could, however, refer to the zeal the Corinthians had for Paul. It is more likely, given the context, that this refers to his urgent desire for these people's welfare.

The phrase ὑπὲρ ὑμῶν (*hyper hymōn*), "on account of" or "for you," confirms that the eagerness expressed by Titus has nothing to do with the funds being raised but is for the people themselves.[213] There is no profit motive driving either him or Paul. The clause "I have" is not in the Greek text but is implied by Paul's use of the preposition ὑπέρ (*hyper*).[214] The

209. Louw-Nida, §57.71.
210. Louw-Nida, §57.217; BDAG, 242–43.
211. Barnett, *Second Epistle,* 416 n. 1.
212. Witherington, *Conflict and Community,* 421.
213. Hughes, *Second Epistle,* 311.
214. Bernard, "Second Epistle," 88; Guthrie, *2 Corinthians,* 420–21.

prepositional phrase ἐν τῇ καρδίᾳ Τίτου (*en tē kardia Titou*), "into the heart of Titus," evidences the depth of the feelings shared by these two brethren toward the Corinthian Saints. For Titus, see Translation Notes for 2:13 and associated Analysis.

8:17 ***For indeed he accepted the exhortation / Because he not only accepted my appeal:*** The conjunction ὅτι (*hoti*), "for, because," acts here as a marker of causality,[215] thus evidencing the godly grace acting upon Titus to encourage him to take the assignment. The noun παράκλησις (*paraklēsis*), "exhortation, appeal," denotes both the act of emboldening another to a course of action and making a strong request.[216] Since Titus was already disposed to the work, the latter seems the best translation.

but being more forward, of his own accord he went unto you / but also, being even more eager, he is coming to you on his own initiative: The adjective σπουδαῖος (*spoudaios*), "zealous, diligent, eager"—here in the comparative—denotes consciousness in discharging an obligation or duty[217] but can also carry the nuance of being extremely earnest or eager.[218] The verb ἔρχομαι (*exerchomai*), "to come," is found here as an epistolary aorist in which a writer puts himself in the position of his audience who would view a present action as past; thus we have rendered the verb as "is coming."[219] This interpretation makes sense because Titus had not yet left Macedonia. The adjective αὐθαίρετος (*authairetos*), "voluntarily, of one's own accord" denotes more than a willingness to act; the person does so as a personal choice.[220] Thus, we have translated the word as "on his own initiative."[221]

8:18 ***And we have sent with him the brother, whose praise is in the gospel throughout all the churches / And we sent with him the brother whose fame in connection with the gospel has spread through all the churches.*** The verb συμπέμπω (*sympempō*), "to send with or at the same time," is also an epistolary aorist (see the phrase above) and so is translated as "are sending." The noun ἀδελφός (*adelphos*), "brother," denotes a male kinsman and but can also refer to one engaged with others in a common interest or cause;[222]

---

215. BDAG, 731–32.

216. BDAG, 766; Louw-Nida, §33.168.

217. BDAG, 939.

218. The adjective "was employed in the broader culture to describe a heightened sense of civic duty" and zealousness to a cause. Guthrie, *2 Corinthians,* 421, with n. 6.

219. Smyth, *Greek Grammar,* §1942; Wallace, *Beyond the Basics,* 562–63. This translation can also be found in the NIV, the New English Translation, and others.

220. BDAG, 150; Louw-Nida, §25.66.

221. Barnett, *Second Epistle,* 419 n. 20.

222. BDAG, 18.

thus, in this context, the person is a fellow believer. The phrase "the brother" could carry a more technical inference, pointing to a Christian who has been set apart for the ministry. The latter idea is supported by the sense that the person is "sent," suggesting that apostolic authority stands behind him.[223]

The noun ἔπαινος (*epainos*), "praise, fame," denotes "that which is worthy of or deserves praise,"[224] but, in the present context, the word points more to the good reputation of this person and so is translated as "fame" in our Rendition.[225] For the noun εὐαγγέλιον (*euangellion*), "gospel," see Translation Notes for 4:4 with related Analysis.[226] The preposition ἐν (*en*), "in," here acts as a marker by which something shows itself.[227] Hence, we have translated it as "in connection with." In this case, it shows that the brother's fame is tied to either his preaching of the gospel or his devotion to it.[228] The phrase διὰ πασῶν τῶν ἐκκλησιῶν (*dia pasōn tōn ekklēsiōn*), "throughout all the churches," shows the breadth of the person's reputation. That breadth, however, would seem to be limited to the Macedonian Saints, since the brother is unknown to the Corinthian members.[229]

8:19 ***not that only but . . . also / not only that, but . . . also:*** The phrase οὐ μόνον δὲ ἀλλὰ καὶ (*ou monon de alla kai*), "and not only but also," indicates "something important contrasted with something even more important."[230] That more important item Paul identifies in the next phrase.

who was also chosen of the churches to travel with us with this grace, which is administered by us / he was also chosen by the churches to be our traveling companion in connection with this charitable offering that is administered by us: The verb χειροτονέω (*cheirotoneō*), literally "to stretch out the hand," carries two meanings: first for the purpose of giving one's vote and then more generally "to appoint, choose."[231] In at least one passage, the verb refers to ordaining an elder (πρεσβύτερος, *presbyteros*) by the

223. Guthrie, *2 Corinthians,* 422–23.

224. Louw-Nida, §33.355.

225. BDAG, 357.

226. It is unlikely that the reference is to the person's fame coming from being mentioned in a gospel account since none of the Gospels had yet been written. Martin, *2 Corinthians,* 453.

227. BDAG, 326–30.

228. Guthrie, *2 Corinthians,* 423; Thrall, *Critical and Exegetical Commentary,* 2:548; for the former, see also Seifrid, *Second Letter,* 339.

229. That his reputation could be located in such places as Judea or in the Greek provinces of Asia Minor is possible but unlikely. Barnett, *Second Epistle,* 420.

230. Barnett, *Second Epistle,* 421 n. 29.

231. BDAG, 1083; Louw-Nida, §§37.103; 30.101; Furnish, *II Corinthians,* 422; *DAG,* s.v. "χειροτονέω"; LSJ, 1986; see also Eduard Lohse, "χειροτονέω," in *TDNT,* 9:437. The verb

laying on of hands.[232] It seems reasonable that the leadership would have selected the individual, and then the congregations agreed to the appointment. That would mean, in Latter-day Saint parlance, that the person was sustained to perform the task at hand. The noun συνέκδημος (*synekdēmos*) denotes "a traveling companion" and carries the weight of one appointed to an official assignment.[233] On the noun χάρις (*charis*), "grace," translated as "charitable offering," see 8:6 above. The verb διακονέω (*diakoneō*), "to minister, administer," found here as a passive participle, refers "to the function of an intermediary" assigned to a task,[234] in this case collecting the offering for the Jerusalem poor. By use of the participle, Paul clearly indicates that his role and that of the others is strictly that of administrator, with no authority to use the offering for themselves.

to the glory of the same Lord / for the glory of the Lord himself: The preposition πρός (*pros*), "for," indicates the purpose for which something is done;[235] in this case, it shows the contribution is for the Lord's "glory." The noun δόξα (*doxa*), "glory," in the present context denotes "renown, fame, honor."[236] The noun κύριος (*kyrios*), "lord,"[237] is a term of honor that in the present context could refer to either God or Christ.[238] Given, however, that the gracious act is to benefit members of his Church, Jesus seems the more likely candidate.[239]

and declaration of your ready mind / as well to show our willingness to help: This phrase is very short, consisting of but three words: καὶ προθυμίαν ἡμῶν (*kai prothymian hēmon*), literally "and our willingness." The noun προθυμία (*prothymia*), "willingness," denotes "exceptional interest in being of service"[240] and stresses the eagerness that drives the willingness.[241]

The phrase can be taken in three ways depending on how the governing preposition πρός (*pros*; see above) is nuanced. First, it can indicate "in

---

is used only here and in Acts 14:23, in relation to Paul and Barnabas's appointment of church leaders.

232. LSJ, 1986.

233. BDAG, 968.

234. BDAG, 229–30.

235. Louw-Nida, §89.60; BDAG, 873–75; Guthrie, *2 Corinthians,* 424 n. 16.

236. BDAG, 256–58.

237. Louw-Nida, §12.9.

238. Furnish, *II Corinthians,* 423, opts for God while Barnett, *Second Epistle,* 422 n. 39, opts for Christ.

239. For more on κύριος (*kyrios*), see Translation Notes for 1:2.

240. BDAG, 870.

241. BDAG, 870.

accordance with," showing that Paul's willingness is on the same level as that which motivated the appointment of "the brother." Second, it can indicate result. The appointment of the brother resulted in the heightening of Paul's zeal toward the project.[242] Third, it could show purpose. Just as the purpose of the mission is to manifest the glory of the Lord, so too it manifests the Apostle's willingness to show his readiness to help. Although any of these are possible, given that a preposition normally governs both nouns in the same way in such a construction,[243] we feel it would do the same here. Since it clearly refers to "purpose" in the first phrase, it should do so in the second. Thus it shows Paul's purpose—that is, his willingness to help.[244]

8:20 ***Avoiding this, that no man should blame us / We did this to prevent anyone from finding fault with us:*** The verb στέλλω (*stellō*), "to avoid doing,"[245] is found here as a present middle participle used circumstantially with the understood subject being "we."[246] We have rendered it as a finite verb to better express the sense in contemporary English. The verb μωμάομαι (*mōmaomai*), found here as an aorist middle subjunctive, means "to find fault with, to criticize."[247] It is governed by the conjunction μή (*mē*), "lest, so that not." A literal translation of the phrase would be "[We are] avoiding this, lest anyone find fault with us." Our Rendition expresses the same sense in contemporary English. The nuance is that Paul is here buttressing the probity of the cause by detailing how the funds will be looked after and finally delivered to Jerusalem.[248]

in this abundance which is administered by us / in this liberal gift that we are administering: The noun ἁδρότης (*hadrotēs*), "abundance, generous gift," denotes "an abundant amount with the implication of generosity."[249] We have rendered it as an adjective and supplied the word "gift" for clarity. The phrase suggests that the collected amount of funds was considerable. On the verb διακονέω (*diakoneō*), "to administer," see 8:19 above.

---

242. Thrall, *Critical and Exegetical Commentary,* 2:550.

243. Guthrie, *2 Corinthians,* 424 n. 17.

244. Matera, *II Corinthians,* 197; Guthrie, *2 Corinthians,* 425. A number of translations agree. See, for example, NIV and NRSV.

245. Louw-Nida, §13.159; BDAG, 942; Martin, *2 Corinthians,* 455.

246. Smyth, *Greek Grammar,* §2054; Harris, *Second Epistle,* 605.

247. BDAG, 661–62.

248. Barnett, *Second Epistle,* 423 n. 43.

249. Louw-Nida, §59.60. The word appears only here in the New Testament, but even so, its meaning is clear. Its cognate adjective ἁδρός (*hadros*) appears in LXX Jer. 5:5, indicating a rich man.

8:21 ***Providing for honest things, not only in the sight of the Lord, but also in the sight of men. / For we are concerned about doing what is right not only in the Lord's sight but also in the sight of men:*** In writing this phrase, Paul appears have in mind a passage from LXX Proverbs 3:4, which states, "Be concerned about what is morally proper in the eyes of the Lord and the eyes of men."[250]

The verb προνοέω (*pronoeō*), found here as an imperative, means "to take careful thought for."[251] The object of the verb is the nominalized neuter plural adjective καλά (*kala*), here with the sense "morally good things."[252] The preposition ἐνώπιον (*enōpion*), "before, in the sight of," carries the nuance of being in a position so that a person can make an evaluation.[253] Thus we have rendered the phrase as above.

Paul's reconstruction of the scripture differs from the biblical text in that he adds οὐ μόνον (*ou monon*), "not only," and ἀλλά (*alla*), "but also." He uses this construction to emphasize one part of the text over the other,[254] and in doing so he stresses his deeply felt need to be particularly transparent with his fellow Saints.[255] That he repeats the idea in Romans 12:17 and 1 Timothy 5:8 suggests this need is ever on his mind.

8:22 ***And we have sent with them our brother / And with them we sent our brother:*** Here Paul introduces a second church member who will assist in the final arrangements and transport of the collection for the Jewish poor. The plural pronoun αὐτοῖς (*autois*), "them," refers to Titus and the unnamed brother mentioned in 8:18. On the verb συμπέμπω (*sympempō*), "to send," and the noun ἀδελφός (*adelphos*), "brother," see 8:18 above.

whom we have oftentimes proved diligent in many things / whose diligence we have often tested and proved in many ways: The verb δοκιμάζω (*dokimazō*) has the sense of drawing "a conclusion about worth on the basis of testing."[256] When it comes to people, it denotes finding out the worthiness or genuineness of people by proving them in the required position. The word carries a positive overtone of trying someone with the intent

250. The passage reads καὶ προνοοῦ καλὰ ἐνώπιον κυρίου καὶ ἀνθρώπων (*kai pronoou kala enōpion kyriou kai anthrōpōn*).

251. BDAG, 872.

252. BDAG, 505.

253. BDAG, 342.

254. See 8:8, 10, where he also does this. Barnett, *Second Epistle,* 424 n. 51.

255. Guthrie, *2 Corinthians,* 427.

256. BDAG, 255.

of approval.[257] To express the full sense of the verb, we have rendered the phrase with two English verbs, "tested and proved."

On the adjective σπουδαῖος (*spoudaios*), "eager, diligent," see 8:17 above. In the present context, it denotes a "steady, earnest, and energetic effort," thus favoring the translation "diligence."[258] Here it is modified by the participial ὤν (*ōn*), "being," which supplements the action of the verb δοκιμάζω (*dokimazō*). Thus the Greek reads, "being diligent."[259] For flow in English, we have rendered it as "whose diligence" and moved it to the front of the phrase. The adjective πολύς (*polys*) denotes "much, many." It is governed by the preposition ἐν (*en*), "in," and denotes "in many things." However, given that the related adverb πολλάκις (*pollakis*), here modifying *polys*, means "many times, often, frequently," we have rendered the phrase as "in many ways."[260]

but now much more diligent, upon the great confidence which I have in you / but now is even more diligent because of his confidence in you: The adverb νυνί (*nyni*), "now,"[261] references the current mental state of this brother. The adjective σπουδαῖος (*spoudaios*), translated as "diligence" above, is here found as a comparative and therefore rendered as "even more diligent."[262] The phrase points out that something has energized his desire to be involved. The next phrase shows what did it. The noun πεποίθησις (*pepoithēsis*), "confidence, trust," denotes a certainty that allows one to rely fully upon another.[263] Here it is in the form of an instrumental dative, thus denoting "through" or "by whom" something happens. In this case, it is through the way the Corinthian Saints have responded to Titus. In our Rendition, we have tried to capture the sense in English.

---

257. Louw-Nida, §§27.45; 30.114; *NID*, 756–59. There is in 1 Cor. 16:3 an interesting parallel. There Paul tells his audience that after he arrives, he will "send those whom you approve with letters of explanation to carry your charitable offering to Jerusalem" (author's translation). In this context, the verb appears to connote a recommendation. Guthrie, *2 Corinthians,* 428 n. 30.

258. *Collegiate Dictionary,* s.v. "diligent." For "diligence" as a translation, see BDAG, 939; Louw-Nida, §25.75.

259. On the supplementary use of participles, see BDF, §416.

260. Thus, the phrase ὃν ἐδοκιμάσαμεν ἐν πολλοῖς πολλάκις σπουδαῖον ὄντα (*hon edokimasamen en pollois pollakis spoudaion onta*) is translated literally as "whom we have tested and proved often, in many ways, to be diligent."

261. BDAG, 682.

262. Guthrie, *2 Corinthians,* 429. On the comparative, see BDF, §244.

263. Louw-Nida, §31.82; BDAG, 796.

8:23 This verse has several ellipses that require the addition of words in English that are not present but understood in the Greek. For this reason, we provide more information as to why we translate a phrase the way we do. Further, the sentence breaks down into two clauses, both beginning with the coordinating conjunction εἴτε (*eite*).[264] In this construction, the term is usually translated as "if . . . if" and is used to set in contrast two elements,[265] in this case, Titus with the two brothers. Also, the preposition ὑπέρ (*hyper*), usually denoting "for, on behalf of,"[266] in this construction coordinates with περί (*peri*) and means "concerning, about."[267]

Whether any do inquire of Titus, he is my partner and fellowhelper concerning you / As for Titus, he is* my *partner and also a fellow worker for you: The first phrase, εἴτε ὑπὲρ Τίτου (*eite hyper Titou*), literally "if about Titus," means something like "if [there is a question] about Titus."[268] We have translated this as "As for Titus," for better flow in contemporary English. The next phrase, κοινωνὸς ἐμός (*koinōos emos*), literally "partner mine," is missing a form of the verb "to be," which is understood in Greek but must be supplied in English. The noun κοινωνός (*koinōnos*), "companion, partner,"[269] denotes someone who takes part with another in an enterprise or activity.[270] The form of the pronoun, ἐμός (*emos*), "my," is emphatic. By using it rather than the normal form μού (*mou*), Paul emphasizes his personal and close relationship with Titus, thus he "is *my* partner."

The next phrase, καὶ εἰς ὑμᾶς συνεργός (*kai eis hymas synergos*), translates literally as "and also to you[, a] fellow-worker." Here the conjunction καί (*kai*), usually translated as "and," is used in its emphatic sense "and also,"[271] thus stressing the connection between two ideas or objects. Here it connects "partner" with "fellow worker." The noun συνεργός (*synergos*) denotes someone who labors with another. Though it can nuance a state of inequality and thus be translated as "helper," here it nuances a state of equality and is thus

264. BDF, §454.3, translates the conjunction in this construction as "whether it concerns."

265. Martin, *2 Corinthians,* 456.

266. Louw-Nida, §90.36; BDAG, 1030–31.

267. Louw-Nida, §90.24.

268. Here ὑπέρ (*hyper*) functions as a "marker of general content" thus translated as "concerning" or "about." BDAG, 1031.

269. BDAG, 553–54.

270. Louw-Nida, §34.6.

271. BDAG, 494–96.

translated as "fellow worker."[272] The preposition εἰς (*eis*), which has the general sense of "motion into a thing" or "relation to something,"[273] is here used likely to replace a dative of advantage[274] and thus shows that Titus is a fellow worker "for the benefit" of the Corinthian Saints.

or our brethren be inquired of, they are the messengers of the churches, and the glory of Christ / As for our brothers, they are envoys of the churches, a glory of Christ: On the translation of the conjunction εἴτε (*eite*), see above. The phrase εἴτε ἀδελφοὶ ἡμῶν (*eite adelphoi hēmōn*) translates literally as "if the brothers of us." It can be translated as "and if [there is a question about] our brothers." We have rendered it "as for our brothers" for better flow in English. The "brothers" are Titus and his two unnamed companions earlier referred to. Paul calls these men ἀπόστολοι (*apostoloi*), "apostles." The title, in its general meaning, designates one who is sent in behalf of another.[275] In secular Greek, the noun denoted an agent who worked in the full authority of another. The Cynics gave it a religious cast, using it to denote an official representative of the gods. In Judaism, the term carried both financial and religious overtones, being used to denote persons assigned to bring offerings from the Diaspora to the temple in Jerusalem.[276] The primary use of the noun in the New Testament refers to the twelve men Jesus chose as the primary officers in his Church. It is, however, used for others who act in authoritative positions in the work of the ministry.[277] Although the noun often means "messenger," the English term that best translates the context here is "envoy," denoting as it does an office of second rank given to a representative of one party in its dealings with another party.[278] As one scholar has noted, "By using the term

---

272. BDAG, 969; Louw-Nida, §42.44. "Paul regarded these co-workers less as helpers than as sharers in a common enterprise." Martin, *2 Corinthians,* 457. It is of note that already in the nascent Church, titles of ministry were being used. Such designations denoted local, regional, and general authorities.

273. BDAG, 288.

274. BDAG, 290.

275. The term is an amalgamation of the prefix ἀπό (*apo*), "out of, from," and στέλλω (*stellō*), "to be sent."

276. BDAG, 122. For studies, see *NID,* 1:365–76; Karl Heinrich Rengstorf, "Apostolos," *TDNT,* 1:398–447.

277. Among these are Andronicus, Junia (Rom. 16:7), Epaphroditus (Philip. 2:25); Silas, and Timothy (1 Thes. 2:6).

278. The noun "delegate" is also often used. It denotes an agent of first rank who has power to represent an organization or group in matters concerned with the welfare of

ἀπόστολος [apostle] of these two Christian brothers, Paul is not suggesting that they shared his status as ἀπόστολος Χριστοῦ 'Ιησοῦ [Apostle of Jesus Christ] (1:1), someone who, like the Twelve (Matt. 10:2; 1 Cor. 15:5, 7), had seen the risen Lord (1 Cor. 9:1) and had been commissioned directly by Christ to exercise a distinctive leadership role within the church (1 Cor. 15:9–11; Gal. 1:1). Rather than being ἀπόστολοι Χριστοῦ [apostles of Christ] (11:13; cf. 1 Thess. 2:7 [2:6]; Jude 17), these men were ἀπόστολοι ἐκκλησιῶν [apostles of the church,] 'envoys belonging to, sent by, and representing the churches.'"[279]

The phrase δόξα Χριστοῦ (*doxa Christou*), "a glory of Christ," denotes a title of high honor. The object of the phrase is ambiguous. Although it could refer to the Church, the context leans toward the chosen brethren.[280]

The JST makes substantial changes to this section of Paul's letter. It reads, "Therefore we send him unto you, in consequence of the great confidence we have in you, that you will receive the things concerning you to the glory of Christ; whether we send by the hand of Titus, my partner and fellow-laborer, or our brethren, the messengers of the churches." In doing so, it combines and leaves out elements of 8:22 and 23. In its deviation from the KJV, the text properly picks up that the act of sending the brother is current, not past. It leaves out any testing of the individual on the part of Paul and others. Further, it shifts the confidence in the Corinthian Saints from the brother to Paul and his associates. Finally, it defines wherein that confidence lies—namely, in Paul's belief that the Corinthians will do what will bring them divine approbation.

8:24 ***Wherefore shew ye to them, and before the churches, the proof of your love, and of our boasting on your behalf / so show them proof of your love and of our boasting about you before the churches:*** Paul uses the conjunction οὖν (*oun*), "so, then, therefore" to indicate he is clinching the argument he has been making in 8:16–23 and is setting his readers

---

the whole. Its powers are broad, being limited only by the requirement of the assignment. An envoy, on the other hand, is an agent of second rank who still has full power to take independent action but within the bounds of the task at hand. See *Collegiate Dictionary,* s.v. "envoy"; *Dictionary of Synonyms,* s.v. "ambassador" and "delegate." Because the two brothers are definitely of second rank, standing behind both Paul and Titus, yet still invested with delegated power, "envoy" best fits their station.

279. Harris, *Second Epistles,* 611.

280. Although Barnett, *Second Epistle,* 427, takes it as referring to the Church, Hughes, *Second Epistle*, 320; Furnish, *II Corinthians,* 425; and Martin, *2 Corinthians,* 457, take it as referring to the brethren based on context.

up for what he wants them to do in light of what he has said. The pronoun αὐτούς (*autous*), "them," refers to Titus and the unnamed brothers. The verb ἐνδείκνυμι (*endeiknymi*) means "to demonstrate, show, prove,"[281] and although it is found here as a present middle participle, it is used as an imperative.[282] The direct object of this verb is the noun ἔνδειξις (*endeixis*), "demonstration, proof,"[283] and is a cognate of the above verb.

The "proving" involves two activities. The first is expressed by the phrase τῆς ἀγάπης ὑμῶν (*tēs agapēs hymōn*), "your love," the noun ἀγάπη (*agapē*) denoting a very deep, warm, and accepting affection.[284] The second is expressed by the phrase ἡμῶν καυχήσεως ὑπὲρ ὑμῶν (*hēmōn kauchēseōs hyper hymōn*), "our boasting about you." The noun καύχησις (*kauchēsis*), "boasting," denotes "the act of taking pride in something" or someone.[285] Here it refers to the Corinthian Saints' acceptance of Titus and their willingness to reengage in the collection. The phrase εἰς πρόσωπον τῶν ἐκκλησιῶν (*eis prosōpon tōn ekklēsiōn*), literally "in the face of the churches" expresses the reason and nature of the proving. It is to disclose, on a large and conspicuous level, why the Apostle has pride in the entire congregation. We have translated it as "before the churches" to better convey its sense in English.

Analysis and Summary

We have now come to a critical point in this epistle. "Having made his appeal to the Corinthians to complete the collection (vv. 1–7) and, further, having anticipated and responded to their misgivings (vv. 8–15), the apostle now—at last!—commends to the church Titus, his chief delegate (vv. 16–17)."[286] So important is his mission that he is not coming alone. Two other agents will attend with him. One is well-known among the branches of the Macedonian Churches (8:18); the other is less well-known, but still respected (8:22). Both are coming to support Titus. The impetus for getting the work finished on behalf of the suffering Jerusalem Saints is the hopeful and encouraging nature of this letter.

---

281. BDAG, 331.

282. On the participle used in lieu of a finite verb, see BDF, §468. This is one of very few examples in the New Testament where a participle is used as an imperative. Wallace, *Greek Grammar,* 650–51.

283. BDAG, 332.

284. BDAG, 6–7. For a study, see *NID,* 1:103–15.

285. BDAG, 537.

286. Barnett, *Second Epistle,* 417.

18; 4:6, 15). Once again, we see expressed Paul's theology of giving. Its center is in the downflow of the transforming and empowering effect of grace (χάρις, *charis*), God's gift. That gift allows a person to give his or her own gift but from the heart. As Paul sees it, "In giving we receive. Only in this way can it be that the collection is for the Lord's glory, and not that of the human participants."[296]

But there was something else at play here. The phrase stresses that Paul's intentions for and motives behind the collection are pure. He was not working to get anything personally out of it.[297] This brings us to his second expressed reason for the collection: it allows Paul and the other missionaries to indicate their eager willingness (προθυμία, *prothymia*) to assist in the work. Taking the verse altogether, it defuses any idea that Paul's motives were anything more than those of assisting the poor and glorifying the Lord.[298]

In 8:20, what Paul tacitly indicated before he now states openly. Clearly, his detractors have already accused him of being deceitful and motivated by financial gain.[299] Here, he continues to build a case against these accusations by explaining to the Corinthian Saints that he is not going to administer the charitable offering by himself but will be assisted by Titus as well as by a well-respected brother.[300] It is little wonder that some with a suspicious mindset might question the administration of the funds. That Paul refers to collection as a generous even liberal (ἁδότης, *hadotēs*) amount suggests that by this time the collection had grown into a very large sum. Thus, Paul has so arranged the circumstances of the final collection and its transportation to Jerusalem, not only to make sure the donation got to its destination but also to protect his good name and that of the apostolic ministry.[301]

---

296. Seifrid, *Second Letter,* 343.

297. Guthrie, *2 Corinthians,* 424.

298. Hughes, *Second Epistle,* 316 n. 44, suggests that Paul's intent here is apologetic. The clause both anticipates and answers any fractious comments.

299. On Paul's defense against these accusations, see Translation Notes for 2:17; 4:2; 7:2–4.

300. Given the information in Acts 19:29; 20:4, and 27:2, 19, as many as six individuals could have been dispatched to Corinth to assist in finishing the collection and safeguarding the funds' passage to Jerusalem. If the charitable gift included donations from the Galatian and Asian provinces as well, it could have amounted to a very large sum. Given that, there could have been concerns that it would be in danger from malfeasance or robbery and thus needed guarding.

301. Barnett, *Second Epistle,* 424. On the practice of devout persons escorting funds to sacred destinations, see Watson, "Paul's Collection," 142.

The latter point he makes clear in 8:21. He does this by closely paraphrasing scripture (LXX Prov. 3:4) that teaches that a leader's actions "must be open to . . . scrutiny" not only before God but more especially before the people.[302] Every action done, every deed accomplished, every movement attempted must be transparent so that the people can not only judge the leaders' intent but also feel confident in following them. Paul has already appealed to his own transparency in 4:2 (compare 2:17; 5:11). This condition, he stresses here, is especially so when it comes to financial administration, where the greatest temptation lies to violate a trust.[303]

In that light, in 8:22, he introduces yet another assistant who will help gather, guard, and transport the funds. It is also possible that this man servers as a third witness who confirms, according the law of Moses, the propriety and rightness of an action (Deut. 19:15). In that case he would be here "confirming the integrity of the collection."[304]

The Apostle Paul recommends this individual based on three criteria. First, he is "our brother" (ἡμῶν ἀδελφόν, *hēmōn adelphon*)—that is, he is in full fellowship with the Saints. Second, the individual has been tried "often and in many ways" (ἐν πολλοῖς πολλάκις, *en pollois pollakis*) through being assigned to various responsibilities, in which he has proved himself fully diligent (σπουδαῖος, *spoudaios*). Finally, he is now diligent (σπουδαῖος, *spoudaios*) in taking up the task, as displayed by an energetic, even zealous effort for the cause due to the reported goodness of the Corinthians and their own reported enthusiasm for finishing the collection.[305] It is likely that this brother was well aware of the tension that had existed between the members of the Corinthian house churches and the Apostle and this may have made him initially reluctant to get involved. The positive report of Titus energized him to bring his proven talents to assist the cause.

All this leads to the questions "Who are these men?" and "Why does Paul not name them?" On these subjects there has been a great deal of scholarly speculation. Suggestions on whom these men might be range from Luke,[306] through Apollos and Timothy,[307] to Sopater, Aristarchus, Secundus, and

302. Barnett, *Second Epistle,* 424.

303. Financial integrity, though valued in the general Greco-Roman world, was especially so in the Jewish. The religion prized all avoidance of scandal. See Josephus, *Jewish Antiquities* 18.81–84; *m. Šeqalim* 3.2; Guthrie, *2 Corinthians,* 427 n. 27.

304. Seifrid, *Second Letter,* 345.

305. Guthrie, *2 Corinthians,* 428–29.

306. Hughes, *Second Epistle,* 312–13.

307. William O. Walker Jr., "Apollos and Timothy as the Unnamed 'Brothers' in 2 Corinthians 8:18–24," *Catholic Biblical Quarterly* 73, no. 2 (2011): 318–38.

Gaius,[308] all known associates of Paul. The Apostle provides two particular qualifications for the first brother: first, that throughout the churches (at least in Macedonia), people respect him and second, that the churches in the region had appointed him to this task.[309] For the second brother, the Apostle notes but one (albeit a very important) attribute: he has proved himself diligent in all assignments given him. These three qualifications do not narrow the field because all the men mentioned above seem to meet them. That the men were most likely from Macedonia helps narrow the field, only three being from that province. Sopater was from Berea, while Aristarchus and Secundus were from Thessalonica (Acts 20:4). As a result, support for any two of these three seems cautiously warranted.[310]

In setting up this delegation, Paul and the Church are following a long-established Jewish practice. The Diaspora Jews chose men of highest repute to gather the annual temple tax and escort it safely to Jerusalem.[311]

The question still remains why Paul did not name these men, since he is quite liberal in mentioning those who assist him. Speculation ranges widely. Among the suggestions are that these men were totally unknown to any of the Corinthian Saints and, therefore, naming them would have meant nothing to Paul's target audience. Conversely, these men were well-known to the Corinthians and, therefore, mentioning them was superfluous. Going on, since Paul regularly names those whom he appoints, he left the names of these men out because he did not appoint them. And again, naming them would have given them a status Paul did not want them to have, fearing it would dilute Titus's influence. Finally, their names were in the original letter but later removed by an overzealous scribe because he felt they had become associated with heresy.[312] Of these, the idea that they were unknown to the Corinthian members of the Church seems the best choice because it seems the most logical.[313]

---

308. Furnish, *II Corinthians,* 435–36. Acts 19:29 lists Gaius and Aristarchus as Paul's traveling companions, while 27:2 mentions Aristarchus again. Acts 20:4 expands the list to include Sopater, Secundus, and Gaius.

309. Harris, *Second Epistle,* 601.

310. Barnett, *Second Epistle,* 422.

311. Philo, *On the Special Laws* 1.78, notes that the synagogues chose men only of the highest reputation to carry the sacred tribute. Roman law protected the collection and transportation of these funds. See Josephus, *Jewish Antiquities* 16.172.

312. For fuller examinations, see Harris, *Second Epistle,* 601–2; and Garland, *2 Corinthians,* 391–93.

313. Guthrie, *2 Corinthians,* 428 n. 28.

In 8:23, Paul gives the status of the men both he and the Macedonian Churches are sending to assist in the fundraising. He declares Titus to be both his partner (κοινωνός, *koinōnos*) and his "fellow worker" (συνεργός, *synergos*). The way Paul structures his wording emphasizes that Titus is his full partner in this enterprise. Both titles highlight a state of equality between the two men and thus stress Titus's authority to act. However, as Paul notes, he is to use that authority only to benefit the Corinthian Saints. The two accompanying brethren Paul refers to as "envoys" (ἀπόστολοι, *apostoloi*), men having full authority to act but in a secondary position. He enhances their status, however, by stating that they are "reflections of the splendor of Christ" (δόξα Χριστοῦ, *doxa Christou*).[314] This designation bestows upon them a sense of the divine that gives purity to their character and a pure quality to the motive behind their mission. And it does more. The phrase echoes scriptures that state that Jehovah will make his servants a covenant to God's people and a "light of the Gentiles" (Isa. 42:6; 49:6; compare Col. 1:27).[315] Certainly, the faithfulness of these men is setting an example for others that both Jew and Gentile can follow.

By highlighting their authority and character in glowing terms, Paul confirms, if not elevates, their status before his target audience and thereby, hopefully, makes these emissaries men whom the Corinthians would be willing to accept and assist. In 8:24, he exhorts his audience as to how to do so. It is by proving (ἐνδείκνυμι, *endeiknymi*) themselves in two ways. First, they must express a deep, warm, and sincere love (ἀγάπη, *agapē*).[316] Though Paul does not state specifically what the object of that love should be, the tacit implication is that it is Titus and his companions. Based on his statement in 8:8, connecting love with the collection, the Corinthians were to express their love by following the example of the Macedonian Saints in freely giving to the collection. Second, they must confirm the propriety of Paul's bragging (καύχησις, *kauchēsis*) about the virtues of the Corinthian Saints to these men. Paul then exhorts these Saints to express their love and confirming actions so conspicuously that the entire family of Saints in the area will be aware of and hopefully positively influenced by it.

There is little wonder he desires a show of acceptance and support for these agents. Based on the last three chapters of the epistle, it is evident that pockets of opposition continue to linger in Corinth. The terms Paul uses to

---

314. Martin, *2 Corinthians,* 457.

315. Seifrid, *Second Letter,* 346.

316. BDAG, 6–7. For a study, see *NID,* 1:103–15.

to stimulate the giving of their northern sisters and brothers (9:2). He now expresses his concern that his bragging about his current readers would be not only in vain but also of a great personal embarrassment if the delegation from Macedonia, likely bearing with them those Saints' contribution,[3] arrived in Corinth and found the project yet stalled (9:3–4).

He assures his audience that he does not expect that to happen and, thus, moves on to a new topic—namely, whether or not the collection will provide a liberal gift somewhat commensurate with the spirit expressed by the Macedonians (9:5). In this way, he is not so subtly pushing his readers to give a "generous offering" (εὐλογία, *eulogia*). In 9:6–7, he stresses the need to give with the proper attitude.[4] He ends this section with the promise, backed by scripture, that donating generously will result in substantial blessings from God and thankfulness on the part of the recipients (9:8–15).

Further Instructions Concerning the Collection (9:1–5)

Greek Text

1 Περὶ μὲν γὰρ τῆς διακονίας τῆς εἰς τοὺς ἁγίους περισσόν μοί ἐστιν τὸ γράφειν
ὑμῖν, 2 οἶδα γὰρ τὴν προθυμίαν ὑμῶν ἣν ὑπὲρ ὑμῶν καυχῶμαι Μακεδόσιν ὅτι Ἀχαΐα
παρεσκεύασται ἀπὸ πέρυσι, καὶ τὸ ὑμῶν ζῆλος ἠρέθισε τοὺς πλείονας. 3 ἔπεμψα
δὲ τοὺς ἀδελφούς, ἵνα μὴ τὸ καύχημα ἡμῶν τὸ ὑπὲρ ὑμῶν κενωθῇ ἐν τῷ μέρει
τούτῳ, ἵνα καθὼς ἔλεγον παρεσκευασμένοι ἦτε, 4 μή πως ἐὰν ἔλθωσιν σὺν ἐμοὶ
Μακεδόνες καὶ εὕρωσιν ὑμᾶς ἀπαρασκευάστους καταισχυνθῶμεν ἡμεῖς, ἵνα μὴ
λέγωμεν ὑμεῖς, ἐν τῇ ὑποστάσει ταύτῃ. 5 ἀναγκαῖον οὖν ἡγησάμην παρακαλέσαι
τοὺς ἀδελφοὺς ἵνα προέλθωσιν εἰς ὑμᾶς καὶ προκαταρτίσωσι τὴν προεπηγγελμένην εὐλογίαν ὑμῶν, ταύτην ἑτοίμην εἶναι οὕτως ὡς εὐλογίαν καὶ μὴ ὡς πλεονεξίαν. [SBLGNT]

King James Version

1 For as touching the ministering to the saints, it is superfluous for me to write to you: 2 For I know the forwardness of your mind, for which I boast of you to them of Macedonia, that Achaia was

New Rendition

1 For now indeed it is unnecessary for me to write to you concerning this ministering to the saints 2 since I know your willingness concerning which I boast about you to the Macedonians—that

3. Guthrie, *2 Corinthians*, 432–33.
4. Martin, *2 Corinthians*, 461.

ready a year ago; and your zeal hath provoked very many. 3 Yet have I sent the brethren, lest our boasting of you should be in vain in this behalf; that, as I said, ye may be ready: 4 Lest haply if they of Macedonia come with me, and find you unprepared, we (that we say not, ye) should be ashamed in this same confident boasting. 5 Therefore I thought it necessary to exhort the brethren, that they would go before unto you, and make up beforehand your bounty, whereof ye had notice before, that the same might be ready, as a matter of bounty, and not as of covetousness.

Achaia has been ready since last year—and your zeal has roused most of them to action. 3 Nevertheless, I am sending these brothers so that our boasting about you would not prove empty in this matter so that you would be ready, just as I kept telling them, 4 so that even if some Macedonians should come with me and find you unprepared, we (not to mention you) would not be humiliated in this undertaking. 5 Consequently, I considered it necessary to urge the brothers to go on ahead to you and prepare in advance the generous gift that you had previously promised so that this would be ready as a generous gift and not as one given grudgingly.

Translation Notes and Comments

9:1 ***For as touching the ministering to the saints, it is superfluous for me to write to you / For now indeed it is unnecessary for me to write to you concerning this ministering to the saints:*** The conjunction γάρ (*gar*), "for," acts here to turn the discussion from the commissioners (spoken of in the last chapter) back to the collection itself. The adjective περισσός (*perissos*) means "abundantly, superfluous," but carries the nuance of greatly exceeding what is actually needed.[5] Paul's use of the term implies that he does not want the Corinthian Saints to take his action in writing as an indication that he does not have faith in them.

The verb γράφω (*graphō*), "to write,"[6] found here as a present articular infinitive, carries an imperfect aspect, suggesting the sense of "to keep on writing."[7] Its use evidences Paul's awareness that some might feel his continual addressing of the subject a bit tedious. He is willing to take the chance, however, because he needs to explain why he is sending the delegation.[8]

The noun διακονία (*diakonia*), "ministry, task,"[9] denotes "rendering specific assistance" to someone and infers giving funds to those in need. In

5. Louw-Nida, §§59.51; 71.40; BDAG, 805–6.

6. BDAG, 206-7.

7. Wallace, *Greek Grammar,* 519; Guthrie, *2 Corinthians,* 434.

8. Guthrie, *2 Corinthians,* 434.

9. Louw-Nida, §35.21.

this instance, it also carries the added dimension of service performed "in genuine love."[10] Each of these nuances is an aspect of giving that Paul wants to connect to the charitable contribution for the needy Saints in Jerusalem.[11]

Noteworthy is Paul's use of the particle μέν (*men*), "indeed." It signals to his readers that he is in the process of making a contrast that he wishes to emphasize. That particle's effect prepares them to pick up on that contrast, which is noted by his use of the particle δέ (*de*), "nevertheless," at the beginning of 9:3 (NR). Through this grammatical construction, they would have understood him to say, "Indeed [*men*], though there is no need to remind you, . . . nevertheless [*de*] I am sending the brethren."[12]

9:2 *I know the forwardness of your mind / I know your willingness:* The noun προθυμία (*prothymia*), "eagerness, desire,"[13] is "characterized by action as well as willingness," [14] and, based on the force of the related adjective πρόθυμος (*prothymos*), "ready, willing, eager" (see 8:12), stresses the eagerness that drives that willingness.[15]

for which I boast of you to them of Macedonia / concerning which I boast about you to the Macedonians: Because the verb καυχάομαι (*kauchaomai*), "to be proud of, boast," is in the present tense, it suggests that Paul continues to feel the same enthusiasm for and confidence in these people as he did when he was among them.[16] He defines his act of boasting with the phrase ὑπὲρ ὑμῶν (*hyper hymōn*), "about you."[17] The tense also shows that Paul is writing from Macedonia.[18]

that Achaia was ready a year ago / that Achaia has been ready since last year: The verb παρασκευάζω (*paraskeuazō*), "to prepare, be ready,"[19] found here in the perfect tense, translates literally as "has been ready"[20] and suggests that the collection was completed months before Paul's writing. Yet it is obvious from the present context that such is not the case. It seems likely that Paul is using the idea of "being ready" in two ways. The first denotes

---

10. Hermann W. Beyer, "διακονία," in *TDNT,* 2:87.
11. BDAG, 230; Louw-Nida, §57.119; Guthrie, *2 Corinthians,* 398.
12. Smyth, *Greek Grammar,* §2904; compare Martin, *2 Corinthians,* 463.
13. Louw-Nida, §25.68.
14. Karl Heinrich Rengstorf, "προθυμία in the New Testament," in *TDNT*, 6:699–700; LSJ, 1481; Louw-Nida, §25:68.
15. BDAG, 870.
16. Guthrie, *2 Corinthians,* 435.
17. BDAG, 1030; Harris, *Second Epistle,* 619.
18. Bernard, "Second Epistle," 90.
19. BDAG, 771.
20. Louw-Nida, §77.8.

the Corinthians' "readiness of intent," referring to their initial "eagerness" for the project, and the second denotes their "readiness of completion," which they still lack. In sum, "consistently the apostle has [both] celebrated [and bragged about] their readiness in terms of *eagerness*, not in terms of thoroughness in the task itself."[21]

The adverb of time, πέρυσι (*perysi*), that Paul uses denotes both "a year ago" and "last year."[22] Its lack of precision allows for the collection to have begun anytime from just a few months to more than a year earlier.

Paul's reference to the Saints living throughout the province of Achaia rather than just to those in Corinth is arresting because it shows an initial widespread support for the project while bypassing any Corinthian hesitation.

and your zeal hath provoked very many / and your zeal has roused most of them to action: The noun ζῆλος (*zēlos*), "zeal, ardour," denotes "intense positive interest in something,"[23] in this case the challenge accepted by the Achaeans to raise money for the Jerusalem needy. The verb ἐρεθίζω (*erethizō*) means "to cause someone to react in a way that suggests acceptance of a challenge, arouse," and although it often carried a negative connotation, it could also express a positive sense of "giving an encouraging example," which it does here.[24] The KJV's use of the verb "provoke" is based on its archaic meaning "to arouse to a feeling or action."[25] Thus we have translated it as "roused . . . to action." At that time, it carried none of the negative inferences that it has in modern English. The adjective πολύς (*polys*), "much," is found here in a nominalized comparative form, πλείονες (*pleiones*), denoting "the majority, most,"[26] and amplifies the information Paul supplied in 8:1–5 concerning those who gave. Its use suggests that not every Macedonian Saint felt stirred by the Corinthian enthusiasm for the project, yet a great many did.[27]

9:3 ***Yet have I sent the brethren / Nevertheless, I am sending these brothers:*** The conjunction δέ (*de*), "yet, but, nevertheless,"[28] acts as a marker of contrast indicating that despite what Paul has said about his audience, he

21. Guthrie, *2 Corinthians,* 436.
22. Louw-Nida, §67.204; BDAG, 808
23. BDAG, 427.
24. BDAG, 391; *DAG,* s.v. "ἐριθίζω."
25. *Collegiate Dictionary,* s.v. "provoke."
26. See Translation Notes for 2:6; BDAG, 847–50; see also Louw-Nida, §78.28.
27. Barnett, *Second Epistle,* 431 n. 15.
28. BDAG, 213. To make the contrast stand out, Guthrie, *2 Corinthians,* 437, uses "nevertheless."

we (that we say not, ye) should be ashamed in this same confident boasting / we (not to mention you) would not be humiliated in this undertaking: The phrase ἵνα μὴ λέγωμεν ὑμεῖς (*hina mē legōmen hymeis*), literally "that we might not mention you," is parenthetical.[45] It reflects the idea that not just Paul but the Corinthians may also find themselves humiliated, as discussed above.

The noun ὑπόστασις (*hypostasis*), "plan, project, undertaking,"[46] refers to the Gentile collection.

The noun καυχήσεως (*kauchēseōs*), "boasting," found in the KJV, does not appear in the best manuscripts, and therefore we have omitted it from our Rendition.[47]

9:5 *Therefore I thought it necessary to exhort the brethren, that they would go before unto you / Consequently, I considered it necessary to urge the brothers to go on ahead to you:* The conjunction οὖν (*oun*), "consequently,"[48] refers back to Paul's point in the previous verse (his concern that he and these Saints could find themselves in a very embarrassing position) and reveals the motive for the actions he now describes.

The verb ἡγέομαι (*hēgeomai*), "to consider," found here in the aorist tense, denotes the act of thinking carefully about something. The adjective ἀναγκαῖος (*anangkaios*), "necessary," denotes something that meets a need.[49]

That "need" Paul identifies with the verb παρακαλέω (*parakaleō*), "to encourage," found here as an aorist infinitive. The term also carries the nuance of the earnestness by which a request is made.[50] The context suggests that Paul urged not only Titus to the task but the other two brethren as well. He pushed them to do two things. The first he expressed with the

---

45. In some manuscripts the verb is in the first person singular λέγω (*legō*), "I might not mention," which may be the original reading, the plural form being a scribal assimilation to the καταισχυνθῶμεν ἡμεῖς, "we be ashamed." Metzger, *Textual Commentary,* 514.

46. The noun is used only by Paul (here and in 11:17) and the author of Hebrews (in 1:3; 3:14; 11:1). The word has a wide range of meanings including the basis or foundational support of faith, thus, "trust, confidence, assurance." Louw-Nida, §31.84. Here it refers more to a "plan, undertaking," or "purpose." See Helmut Köster, "ὑπόστασις," in *TDNT,* 8:572–89, particularly 584, where he notes that he believes the idea was borrowed from 1 Cor. 11:17.

47. Metzger, *Textual Commentary,* 514.

48. Louw-Nida, §89.50.

49. BDAG, 60.

50. Louw-Nida, §§ 25.150; 33.168.

verb προέρχομαι (*proerchomai*) in the form of an aorist infinitive, meaning "to go on ahead."[51]

And make up beforehand your bounty, whereof ye had notice before / and prepare in advance the generous gift that you had previously promised: The second task that Paul urged the delegation to do he expressed with the verb προκαταρτίζω (*prokatartizō*), "to make arrangements in advance."[52] Their work is specifically to help the Corinthian members in gathering the contributions for the Jerusalem Saints so that all will be ready when he arrives.

The noun εὐλογία (*eulogia*), literally "good language" (thus "praise") has several extended meanings, including "a blessing" and "a generous gift."[53] It is this latter sense that is at play here. The noun is modified with the perfect passive participle of the verb προεπαγγέλλω (*proepangellō*), "to promise beforehand."[54] Thus we have rendered the phrase τὴν προεπηγγελμένην εὐλογίαν ὑμῶν (*tēn proepēngelmenēn eulogian hymōn*), literally "the previously promised gift of yours," as above to better express the sense in English.

that the same might be ready as a matter of bounty, and not as of covetousness / so that this would be ready as a generous gift and not as one given grudgingly: The demonstrative pronoun ταύτην (*tautēn*), "this," refers back to εὐλογία (*eulogia*), the "generous gift," and is modified by the adjective ἕτοιμος (*hetoimos*), "ready, prepared." We have taken the infinitive εἶναι (*einai*), "to be," as expressing purpose,[55] thus "so that this would be." The noun πλεονεξία (*pleonexia*) describes "the state of desiring to have more than one's due," thus "greediness, avarice," but here the context "calls for the pregnant [meaning] 'a gift that is grudgingly granted by avarice.'"[56] Thus we have rendered the phrase as above.

---

51. BDAG, 868–69.

52. BDAG, 871.

53. The word has a wide range of meanings that include "praise," "benefit," "blessing," and "gift." Louw-Nida, §§33.356, 470; 57.105: 88.70. The blending of the ideas of blessing and gift can be seen in the LXX translation of the Hebrew בְּרָכָה (*bĕrākāh*) as the Greek *eulogia.* Blessings of this nature always portended a gift of some kind. Such blessings from Jehovah include the gifts of righteousness (Ps. 24:5), life (Ps. 133:3), prosperity (2 Sam. 7:29), and salvation (Ps. 3:8).

54. BDAG, 868.

55. Smyth, *Greek Grammar,* §2008.

56. BDAG, 824.

Analysis and Summary

In this chapter, Paul continues to express his confidence that the Achaean Saints will finish what remains of the funds gathering for the poor Jewish Christians suffering in the Holy Land. "In many ways this was a radical call to discipleship and a test for the Gentile converts who may have felt marginalized by some Jewish-Christians. It was also unprecedented in its scope—collecting a charitable donation from around the Mediterranean world for a specific group in Judea."[57]

Though he is confident that his readers will respond to his encouragement, he still sends Titus and two associates to push forward the work. That Paul includes the Christians living not just in Corinth but in the whole province of Achaea is telling. The Christian community, so far as we know, had not yet begun to construct and gather in church buildings. Thus they were yet meeting in individual house churches. That being the case, opposition to Paul may have been rather selective, mostly affecting some of those Christians living in the city but not those in the country. If that is the case, then his high praise for the Saints in the general region and his expressed concern for some individuals and congregations in specific areas can be easily understood. By being thus quite inclusive, Paul does protect himself from any tension between him and those less-than-friendly branches of the Church in Corinth.

The central message of this paragraph (9:1–5) deals with Paul's "pride and boasting" in the matter of these Saints' readiness to complete what they had begun some time earlier—namely, the Gentile collection (see 9:12–13). Paul's confidence that they would fulfill their pledge is central to his discussion here. As he notes, he has already boasted about the Corinthians' enthusiasm for the project, and that continues to stand at the heart of the Apostle's concern in 9:3–5.[58] The rub is that their enthusiasm has not produced the results he expected. He reports that his boasting about their initial enthusiasm motivated many among the Macedonians to give, but it is now obvious that the Corinthians do not have the funds ready. If that condition continues, as he notes, he and they will suffer acute humiliation.

A broad look at Paul's confidence in these southern Greeks (and their partnering with him in this and other activities in the Aegean area), as seen

57. Holzapfel and Wayment, *Making Sense,* 374.

58. Hafemann, *2 Corinthians,* 363.

in both chapters 8 and 9, is the key to understanding his primary point.[59] Everything looks to the need for Christian union.

Also linking the two chapters is Paul's use of the phrase "for now indeed" (περὶ μὲν γάρ, *peri men gar*) in 9:1. These words "connote a close connection" between what he has just stated in chapter 8 and the broader discourse that he now further develops.[60] In sum, he previously addressed the "who" he is sending and now (9:1–5) turns to "why" he is sending them.

Paul describes the spirit that drives the enterprise as "eagerness" (προθυμία, *prothymia*), a key term with three aspects. First, it is the foundation of his appeal to his audience as inferred in 8:4. Indeed, any current lack of "eagerness" would cast shame on the Apostle due to his boasting about the Achaeans to the Macedonian Saints. Second, it plays an essential part in the Apostle's determination to see the task completed (8:16). And third, these people had zealously expressed this trait months before (8:10–11), and he now wants them to again exercise it in bringing the offering to a close.

Although in 9:1–2 he assures them that his confidence in their completing the collection makes his writing to them on that subject superfluous, in 9:3 he gives two reasons why he is doing so. The first reason (and his main concern) is the possible negative outcome of his boasting about the Achaeans to the Macedonians in light of Titus's very positive report on how the collection was advancing. If, however, the delegation arrived only to find the work unaccomplished, Paul's confident boasting about these people would become vacuous (κενόω, *kenoō*).[61] Indeed, it would undercut the original enthusiasm for the collection and spoil the Apostle's reputation thereafter. He immediately moves on to the second reason he is writing, "that you might be prepared" with everything ready when the delegation arrives. It is only in this way that Paul's continued boast about the Corinthians will be fully justified.

In 9:4, the Apostle further explains why it is important for him that the Macedonian delegation find the Corinthian Saints well on their way to finishing the collection. It is so that he can avoid being humiliated (καταισχύνω, *kataischynō*). Given the Greco-Roman culture's concern with face, members of all levels of society were highly concerned about their honor and, therefore, went to great measures to avoid shame. In the

59. Jones, *Contemporary Cross,* 33–37.

60. Guthrie, *2 Corinthians,* 433.

61. Barnett, *Second Epistle,* 432.

broader Greek culture, authorities would publish in the Athenian Agora the names of those who defaulted on loans or pledges and thus bring public shame upon them. Given this background, we can see that the verb Paul uses connotes much more than the modern idea of "embarrassment" and looks more at public humiliation.[62] For the Apostle, such a position would be untenable, for it would undercut both his authority and effectiveness. Further, as Paul notes parenthetically and thus kindly, the humiliation would be borne by the Corinthian Saints as well.

In 9:5, Paul states the third reason he is sending the delegation. While doing so, he makes clear three items: the reason for their trip, what he wants the delegates to accomplish, and his hope that the Saints will give what they promised and with the correct attitude.[63] His purpose also appears to prepare his audience for the instructions that he will give in 9:6–15.

Significantly, at this point he gives his message a theological spin. As he has already indicated, though he has encouraged (παρακαλέω, *parakaleō*) Titus and those with him to take up this mission, they have willingly assumed the task and, as a result, acted somewhat as independent agents. Their task is to prepare, in advance of Paul's arrival, "the generous gift" (εὐλογία, *eulogia*; 9:15, NR). The noun nuances the idea of a divine blessing that a righteous person calls down upon someone in need.[64] By using this term, Paul ties the gift to Deity. Thus he puts the Corinthians in the position of acting as God's agents, a task not only heavy with responsibility but also potentially abounding in delight, as they act in a godly way by sharing in the abundance that the Divine has given them.

Hebrew ethics made alms giving an important duty to be done without grudge.[65] As noted in the introduction, the Christians continued to emphasize the practice. The Apostle will teach this same principle to the Roman Saints (Rom. 12:8) in addition to those whom he now addresses.[66] Noteworthy,

---

62. Guthrie, *2 Corinthians,* 439. In the light of Acts 5:1–11, the position of the nascent Christian community concerning the breaking of a pledge can be decerned. Both Ananias and Sapphira lost their lives by claiming to give what they did not. See Betz, *2 Corinthians 8 and 9,* 96; and Garland, *2 Corinthians,* 403.

63. Guthrie, *2 Corinthians,* 440.

64. BDAG, 408–9.

65. Both the Old Testament and Apocrypha insist on generous and ungrudging giving. For example, see Deut. 15:10; Tobit 4:7; and Ecclus. 35:9. For a study, see Kaufmann Kohler, "Alms," in *Jewish Encyclopedia* (1906), accessed August 7, 2020, https://www.jewishencyclopedia.com/articles/1295-alms.

66. Bernard, "Second Epistle," 92. Nathan Eubank, "Justice Endures Forever: Paul's Grammar of Generosity," *Journal for the Study of Paul and His Letters* 5, no. 2 (Fall 2015):

however, is that his insistence on personal action went against the Jewish norm. That norm dictated that one's social obligation ended with the giving. Because administering such funds was considered, in general society, a lowly service, many of the middle and upper class viewed it as too menial and undignified for them to be involved in (note Luke 21:1). Paul's teachings counter this idea by showing that Christian giving must involve the whole community in the temporal salvation process under the direction of apostolic authority.[67]

By asking his audience to act in a godly way, Paul put them in a compromising position if they did not respond. The coming delegation could interpret these Saints' delay as an unwillingness to give due to a stingy or greedy (πλεονεξία, *pleonexia*) determination to hold on to their earthly goods.[68] The Apostle assures his readers that he does not want them to be seen in such a negative and unflattering light and therefore asks them to willingly live up to their promise *before he gets there* so that no one would think that they gave only because Paul wrung the money out of them.[69]

On Sowing Generously (9:6–15)

Greek Text

6 Τοῦτο δέ, ὁ σπείρων φειδομένως φειδομένως καὶ θερίσει, καὶ ὁ σπείρων ἐπ'
εὐλογίαις ἐπ' εὐλογίαις καὶ θερίσει. 7 ἕκαστος καθὼς προῄρηται τῇ καρδίᾳ, μὴ ἐκ
λύπης ἢ ἐξ ἀνάγκης· ἱλαρὸν γὰρ δότην ἀγαπᾷ ὁ θεός. 8 δυνατεῖ δὲ ὁ θεὸς πᾶσαν
χάριν περισσεῦσαι εἰς ὑμᾶς, ἵνα ἐν παντὶ πάντοτε πᾶσαν αὐτάρκειαν ἔχοντες
περισσεύητε εἰς πᾶν ἔργον ἀγαθόν· 9 (καθὼς γέγραπται· Ἐσκόρπισεν, ἔδωκεν
τοῖς πένησιν, ἡ δικαιοσύνη αὐτοῦ μένει εἰς τὸν αἰῶνα· 10 ὁ δὲ ἐπιχορηγῶν σπόρον
τῷ σπείροντι καὶ ἄρτον εἰς βρῶσιν χορηγήσει καὶ πληθυνεῖ τὸν σπόρον ὑμῶν καὶ
αὐξήσει τὰ γενήματα τῆς δικαιοσύνης ὑμῶν·) 11 ἐν παντὶ πλουτιζόμενοι εἰς πᾶσαν
ἁπλότητα, ἥτις κατεργάζεται δι' ἡμῶν εὐχαριστίαν τῷ θεῷ.12 ὅτι ἡ διακονία τῆς

169–87, states that Jewish sages, for centuries before Paul's ministration, taught the need and method of charitable giving as an act of fidelity to Jehovah. Thus, Paul's teaching would have fallen well within traditional Jewish theology and, thus, resonated with his Jewish readers. The Apostle did, however, give the deed a decidedly Christian cast by placing individual responsibility on getting directly involved.

67. *NID*, 1:701–9.

68. Seifred, *Second Letter*, 350–51.

69. Guthrie, *Second Corinthians*, 442; Martin, *2 Corinthians*, 465–66.

λειτουργίας ταύτης οὐ μόνον ἐστὶν προσαναπληροῦσα τὰ ὑστερήματα τῶν ἁγίων, ἀλλὰ καὶ περισσεύουσα διὰ πολλῶν εὐχαριστιῶν τῷ θεῷ.
13 διὰ τῆς δοκιμῆς τῆς διακονίας ταύτης δοξάζοντες τὸν θεὸν ἐπὶ τῇ ὑποταγῇ τῆς ὁμολογίας ὑμῶν εἰς τὸ εὐαγγέλιον τοῦ Χριστοῦ καὶ ἁπλότητι τῆς κοινωνίας εἰς αὐτοὺς καὶ εἰς πάντας,
14 καὶ αὐτῶν δεήσει ὑπὲρ ὑμῶν ἐπιποθούντων ὑμᾶς διὰ τὴν ὑπερβάλλουσαν χάριν τοῦ θεοῦ ἐφ' ὑμῖν.
15 χάρις τῷ θεῷ ἐπὶ τῇ ἀνεκδιηγήτῳ αὐτοῦ δωρεᾷ. [SBLGNT]

King James Version

6 But this I say, He which soweth sparingly shall reap also sparingly; and he which soweth bountifully shall reap also bountifully.
7 Every man according as he purposeth in his heart, so let him give; not grudgingly, or of necessity: for God loveth a cheerful giver.
8 And God is able to make all grace abound toward you; that ye, always having all sufficiency in all things, may abound to every good work:
9 (As it is written, He hath dispersed abroad; he hath given to the poor: his righteousness remaineth for ever.
10 Now he that ministereth seed to the sower both minister bread for your food, and multiply your seed sown, and increase the fruits of your righteousness;)
11 Being enriched in every thing to all bountifulness, which causeth through us thanksgiving to God.
12 For the administration of this service not only supplieth the want of the saints, but is abundant also by many thanksgivings unto God;
13 Whiles by the experiment of this ministration they glorify God for your professed subjection unto the gospel of Christ, and for your liberal distribution unto them, and unto all men;
14 And by their prayer for you, which long after you for the exceeding grace of God in you.
15 Thanks be unto God for his unspeakable gift.

New Rendition

6 Now the point is this: one who sows sparingly will also reap sparingly, and one who sows bounteously will also reap bounteously.
7 Each person should give as much as he has decided in his heart, neither reluctantly nor out of compulsion, for God loves a cheerful giver.
8 God can provide you with every grace in abundance so that you will always have enough of everything and ample means for every good work.
9 As it is written, "He distributed; he gave to the poor; his righteousness endures forever" [Ps. 112:9; LXX Ps. 111:9].
10 Now he who provides seed to the sower and bread for food will provide and multiply your seed and increase the harvest of your righteousness.
11 You are enriched in every way, resulting in generosity of every kind that through us produces gratitude to God
12 because the performance of this service is not only fully providing for the needs of the saints but is also overflowing in many expressions of gratitude to God.
13 Because of having experienced this service, they will glorify God for your obedience to the covenant you made in accepting the gospel of Christ and for your generosity in sharing with them and with everyone else.
14 And by their prayers for you they yearn for you because of the surpassing grace of God that rests upon you.
15 Thank God for his indescribable gift!

Translation Notes and Comments

9:6 ***But this I say / Now the point is this:*** The demonstrative pronoun τοῦτο (*touto*), "this," is here used as an adverbial accusative that can be translated as "in respect to this."[70] With the conjunction δέ (*de*), which here expresses a simple continuation of the narrative,[71] the pronoun forms a verbless interjection calling attention to what follows.[72] To better express this in contemporary English, we have rendered the phrase as above.

He which soweth sparingly shall reap also sparingly; and he which soweth bountifully shall reap also bountifully / one who sows sparingly will also reap sparingly, and one who sows bounteously will also reap bounteously: Paul is obviously expressing an aphorism, but one that is not found in any surviving contemporary literature of the New Testament period. It echoes Old Testament agrarian imagery of sowing and reaping grain and expresses the results of doing so either inadequately or abundantly (see, for example, Prov. 11:24).[73] The adverb φειδομένως (*pheidomenōs*) denotes "in a scanty or meager manner, sparingly."[74] The noun εὐλογία (*eulogia*), as noted in 9:5, usually refers to "a gift" or "a benefit" that one bestows upon another.[75] However, the prepositional phrase in which it is found here (ἐπ' εὐλογίαις, *ep' eulogiais*) forces it to take on a different and more abstract nuance.[76] This nuance refers to what is large or abundant and, by extension, generates the adverbial sense of "generously" or, in agricultural terms, "bounteously."[77]

9:7 ***Every man according as he purposeth in his heart, so let him give / Each person should give as much as he has decided in his heart:*** This phrase begins with the adjective ἕκαστος (*hekastos*), "each," acting in the

70. Smyth, *Greek Grammar*, §§1606–11.

71. BDAG, 213.

72. Martin, *2 Corinthians*, 469.

73. LXX Prov. 11:24–25 reads, "Those who sow their own things make them more, and those who gather [their own things] receive less. A soul who blesses is completely sincere, but a violent man is not respectable" (our translation). The Masoretic text has, "A generous soul will prosper [literally "be made fat"]. He who waters deeply, will also be watered deeply" (our translation).

74. It is derived from the verb φείδομαι (*pheidomai*), "to spare." BDAG, 1051.

75. Louw-Nida, §57.105. Louw-Nida, §59.56 translates the idiom as "on the basis of blessings," noting that it refers to a large amount or an abundance.

76. A preposition followed by a noun in the dative case (as here) indicates the manner in which an act is done, in this case with abundance. BDAG, 364.

77. BDAG, 408–9.

Christian is not the act itself but the motivation that stands behind it.[102] Such giving denotes a state of mind that produces a joyous readiness to supply what is needed generated by an "inner freedom of generosity."[103]

9:8–14: These verses make up an extraordinarily complex single sentence in the Greek text that contains some areas of vagueness. Our Rendition breaks it up into several sentences in order to communicate its meaning more clearly in English. In doing so, we have translated a number of participles as verbs.

9:8 ***And God is able to make all grace abound toward you / God can provide you with every grace in abundance:*** The verb δυνατέω (*dynateō*), "to be able, can,"[104] denotes not just capacity but "great ability."[105] It stresses the power that either Deity or an individual has to bring about the indicated result. The noun χάρις (*charis*), "grace,"[106] in this context, refers to a divine benefaction or blessing of a temporal or spiritual nature that God bestows in the present world. The verb περισσεύω (*perisseuō*) means "to cause something to exist in abundance."[107] Paul's phrase emphasizes God's inexorable capacity to richly bless temporally and spiritually those who do his will.

that ye, always having all sufficiency in all things, may abound to every good work / so that you will always have enough of everything and ample means for every good work: The conjunction ἵνα (*hina*), indicating purpose, "so that," points back to the absolute ability God has to provide temporal blessings for those who follow his ways. Paul looks at two categories. He delimits the first by the use of the noun αὐτάρκεια (*autarkeia*), "what is sufficient."[108] The word describes having an adequate or sufficient supply of something. What that is the Apostle identifies with the phrase ἐν παντί (*en panti*), "everything," meaning "temporal goods." The second he does not delimit but refers to with the verb περισσεύω (*perisseuō*), found here as an aorist subjunctive, denoting having a superabundance or an ample amount of whatever is needed.[109] Both apply to doing ἔργον ἀγαθόν (*ergon*

---

102. The proper attitude needed in giving as God would have it done is rooted in the Old Testament and is thoroughly Jewish (Barrett, *Second Epistle,* 236); it was adopted and promulgated by the Christians.

103. Rudolf Bultmann, "ἱλαρός," in *TDNT,* 3:297–300, particularly 299.

104. BDAG, 264; Louw-Nida, §74.5.

105. Walter Grundmann, "δύναμαι," in *TDNT,* 3:284; note *DAG,* s.v. "δύνᾰμις."

106. BDAG, 1079–81.

107. BDAG, 805.

108. Louw-Nida, §75.6; BDAG, 152.

109. BDAG, 805. The word connotes an amount that not only fills up but also overflows. See Translation Notes for 1:5.

agathon), a "good work"—that is, what God wants done. The present context points to the collection for the Judean poor.

There are in this sentence two stylistic devices by which Paul gives emphasis to his appeal. The first is his excellent use of alliteration. Here he uses three different forms of the adjective πᾶν (*pan*), "all, every,"[110] and the related adverb πάντοτε (*pantote*), "always,"[111] as well as repeating the verb περισσεύω (*perisseuō*)—ἐν **π**αντὶ **π**άντοτε **π**ᾶσαν αὐτάρκειαν ἔχοντες **π**ερισσεύητε εἰς **π**ᾶν ἔργον ἀγαθόν (*en **panti pantote pasan** autarkeian echontes **perisseuēte** eis **pan** ergon*). The second is his arrangement of the words in a chiastic form:[112]

God can provide you
A with every grace
  B in abundance,
    C so that you will always have enough of everything
  B′ and have an ample means
A′ for every good work.

Through this arrangement, he emphasizes that God *always* blesses the cheerful giver with whatever he or she needs to do God's work.

9:9 ***As it is written, He hath dispersed abroad; he hath given to the poor: his righteousness remaineth for ever / As it is written, "He distributed; he gave to the poor; his righteousness endures forever":*** To bolster his point, Paul again appeals to scripture. Here he quotes LXX Psalm 111:9 (Ps. 112:9, KJV). The noun "he" does not appear in the Greek text but is inferred by the context and refers to the giver. The verb σκορπίζω (*skorpizō*) means "to cause a group or gathering to go in various directions, scatter, disperse," and also "to distribute."[113] It is the translation of the Hebrew verb פִּזַּר (*pizzar*), which has the sense "to distribute freely, to lavish."[114] On that basis, we have rendered it as above.

The object of the liberal giving is the πένης (*penēs*), "the poor."[115] The noun refers to that class of people who, due to necessity, must do menial work to sustain themselves. It does not generally nuance those reduced to begging.[116]

110. BDAG, 782–84.
111. BDAG, 755.
112. Guthrie, *2 Corinthians*, 451.
113. BDAG, 931.
114. HAL, 921.
115. BDAG, 795.
116. Louw-Nida, §57.50.

The final clause identifies the result of a person's generous giving. The noun δικαιοσύνη (*dikaiosynē*), "righteousness,"[117] when applied to humankind generally, denotes "religious, moral, and compassionate activity."[118] In Judaism, righteousness was equated with and expressed through alms giving. The term, however, connotes an outward token of a person's right relationship with God.[119] Thus some viewed such charitable acts less as expressions of benevolence or kindness and more as signs of a godly nature. The context here, however, looks to a divine state of righteousness. It expresses God's "covenantal rule in fellowship with his people" as exemplified in his generous and continual giving.[120] Thus the giver, in emulating God's ways, takes on a godly attribute. Describing the result, the scripture uses the verb μένω (*menō*), "to stay, remain, persist," with the connotation of continuous existence.[121] Since the English word "endure" means "to continue in the same state," we have chosen that as the best rendering. The noun αἰών (*aiōn*), "forever," denotes the never-ending nature of this remarkable and kindly attribute.[122]

Paul actually repurposes the scripture such that it points not to the generous giver but to God.[123] He uses the phrase to highlight the idea that God will never cease to give because his righteousness as expressed in his volitional giving will last forever. The implication is that God ever blesses those who willingly and generously give to the collection.

9:10 *Now he that ministereth seed to the sower both minister bread for your food / Now he who provides seed to the sower and bread for food:* Paul here paraphrases LXX Isaiah 55:10 (compare Hosea 10:12). This

117. BDAG, 247–48. Louw-Nida in §53.4 defines the noun as "observances or practices required by one's religion," in §88.13 as "the act of doing what God requires," and in §57.111 as the act of charity or alms giving.

118. Martin, *2 Corinthians,* 471 n. 264.

119. Barrett, *Second Epistle,* 238.

120. The Greek term is the translation of the Hebrew צְדָקָה (*ṣĕdākāh*), which looks to the "consistent and normative action of God." Gottlob Schrenk, "δικαιοσύνη," in *TDNT,* 2:195; see generally 2:192–210. For an LDS study, see Marvin K. Gardner, "Righteousness," in *EM,* 3:1235–37.

121. BDAG, 630–31. Louw-Nida, §13.89.

122. BDAG, 32–33.

123. For a study, see David I. Starling, "Meditations on a Slippery Citation: Paul's Use of Psalm 112:9 in 2 Corinthians 9:9," *Journal of Theological Interpretation* 6, n. 2 (2012): 241–55, who concludes that Paul reapplied the scripture as a means of provoking "an enriched understanding of the relationship between divine and human grace and righteousness" through the act of generous giving (241).

sentence begins with a definite article that functions as a demonstrative pronoun, meaning "the one who,"[124] and refers to God.

The verb ἐπιχορηγέω (*epichorēgeō*), "to provide,"[125] found here as a present active participle, connotes the idea of providing necessities at one's own expense and also has connotations in the broader Greco-Roman empire of providing generous public service.[126] We have rendered the participle as the finite verb "provides" for the sake of flow.

The noun σπόρος (*sporos*), "seed," refers to both the process of sowing and to what is sown—namely, kernels of wheat, barley, and other crops. [127]

The verb σπείρω (*speirō*), "to sow,"[128] is found here as a masculine participle and thus means "the one sowing"; we have rendered it as the noun "sower" for flow in English.

The noun ἄρτος (*artos*), "bread," usually refers to any product made from cereal grains but can also designate any type of food.[129]

multiply your seed sown, and increase the fruits of your righteousness / will provide and multiply your seed and increase the harvest of your righteousness: The verb χωρηγέω (*chōrēgeō*) denotes defraying "the expenses of something" and thus "to provide, supply."[130] It is the latter generalized sense that we use in our Rendition.

The verb πληθυνω (*plēthynō*), "to multiply," carries the nuance of causing something to greatly increase in number,[131] while the verb αὐξάνω (*auxanō*), "to grow, to increase,"[132] denotes the idea of becoming greater not only in number but also in quality.[133]

On the noun δικαιοσύνη (*dikaiosynē*), "righteousness," see Translation Notes for 9:9. Here it denotes an uprightness based on divine standards.[134]

---

124. BDAG, 686–89.

125. Louw-Nida, §35.31.

126. BDAG, 386–87.

127. BDAG, 939.

128. BDAG, 936.

129. Louw-Nida, §§5.1, 8; BDAG, 136.

130. The verb originally meant "to pay the expenses for training a chorus" but over time became generalized to defraying another's obligation. BDAG, 1087.

131. BDAG, 826.

132. Louw-Nida, §§23.188; 59.62.

133. BDAG, 151.

134. Louw-Nida, §88.13; BDAG, 247–49. The noun carries the sense of acting in accordance with divine, moral law and, thus, being acceptable to God. For discussion, see Translation Notes for 5:21.

The second noun, λειτουργία (*leitourgia*), "service, help, assistance," found here in the genitive case, would generally denote either regular or formal service, but in the New Testament, it carries a religious connotation along with an "aura of high status" for those who render such service.[147] Thus we have translated the phrases ἡ διακονία (*hē diakonia*) as "the performance," and τῆς λειτουργίας ταύτης (*tēs leitourgias tautēs*) as "of this service," that service being, of course, the charitable contribution for the Judean poor.

The verb προσαναπληρόω (*prosanaplēroō*), "to fill up or replenish besides, supply,"[148] denotes supplying something fully or completely. The emphasis is on the abundance of what is supplied.[149] The verb, as found here as a present active participle and with the verb ἐστίν (*estin*), "is," expresses a periphrastic present tense[150] that corresponds to the English present continuous tense, yielding the rendering "is . . . fully providing."

The phrase looks to the temporal effect that the Achaean gift will have on the receivers—namely, meeting the needs of the Judean Saints. The noun ὑστέρημα (*hysterēma*), "need, want, deficiency," denotes items that are essential needs and not just desired or wanted.[151] As such, the word suggests the depth of the lack that these people are facing and the motivation that pushes the Apostle to work in their behalf.

but is abundant also by many thanksgivings unto God / but is also overflowing in many expressions of gratitude to God: The phrase ἀλλὰ καί (*alla kai*), "but also," points the reader to the second product of the Corinthians' contribution to the Judean collection.

The verb περισσεύω (*perisseuō*) "to abound, be extremely abundant, overflow,"[152] found here as a participle with the verb ἐστίν (*estin*), "is," as noted in the phrase above, expresses a periphrastic present tense[153] that corresponds to the English present continuous tense, yielding the rendition "is . . . overflowing."

---

147. BDAG, 591. Paul's sincere feelings about the deep religious nature of what the Corinthian Saints are doing is evidenced by this use of λειτουργία (*leitourgia*) in Rom. 15:27 to refer to this very contribution.

148. BDAG, 876.

149. Louw-Nida, §35.38.

150. Wallace, *Greek Grammar,* 647–48.

151. Louw-Nida, §57.38; BDAG, 1044.

152. BDAG, 805.

153. Wallace, *Greek Grammar,* 647–48.

The noun εὐχαριστία (*eucharistia*), as noted above, means "gratitude for benefits or blessings."[154] In this case, the effusive expression of gratitude will be from the recipients of the Corinthians' generosity.

The direction of that gratitude, however, is not to the Corinthians, as Paul views it, but to God. For an explanation as to why, see the next phrase.

9:13 ***Whiles by the experiment of this ministration / Because of having experienced this service:*** The preposition διὰ (*dia*), "because," in the genitive case as here, can generally mean "through," indicating agency or means, but in the present context it carries a causal sense pointing to the reason why an action is taken.[155]

The noun δοκιμή (*dokimē*), "experience," refers both to "a testing process" and "the experience of going through a test with special ref[erence] to the result."[156] The phrase carries the idea that the ministry of charitable giving has proven its effectiveness and that this proof has come through the positive experience of those who have been affected by it.[157] Thus the phrase can be rendered literally as either "because of the proof of this service" or "because of the experience of this service." We felt "experience" better captures Paul's idea, and so we rendered it as a participial phrase to better convey the sense in English.

they glorify God / they will glorify God: In this phrase, Paul notes the third product that the generous giving of the Corinthian Saints will have on those in Jerusalem. He expresses it with the verb δοξάζω (*doxazō*) "to praise, honor, glorify,"[158] found here as a present participle used circumstantially with an understood subject being the Holy Land Saints. For clarity and flow, we have translated it as a finite verb in the future tense.

The object of the praise is τὸν θεόν (*ton theon*), "God." The phrase shows that Paul understands that the immediate givers are the Achaean Saints, but the ultimate giver is the One who inspired and enabled the giving. Recognizing this, the Judean Saints give glory to God.

for your professed subjection unto the gospel of Christ / for your obedience to the covenant you made in accepting the gospel of Christ: This and the following phrase present translation difficulties because they house an

---

154. Louw-Nida, §33.349.

155. BDAG, 225.

156. BDAG, 256. The idea that stands behind the word is "that which causes something to be known as true or genuine," thus the sure proof of what it is. Louw-Nida, §72.7.

157. Guthrie, *2 Corinthians,* 458–59.

158. BDAG, 258; Louw-Nida, 87.24.

9:15 ***Thanks be unto God for his unspeakable gift / Thank God for his indescribable gift:*** Once again Paul uses the noun χάρις (*charis*), "grace," but in this context it refers to heart-felt thanksgiving toward God for what he has done for the Corinthians.[172] The noun δωρεά (*dōrea*) denotes "a bounty" or "gift" but carries the nuance of one that is freely given.[173] In the New Testament, *dōrea* always refers not to gifts given by men but to those that come from God.[174] In the present context, as noted in 9:14, *charis* refers to God's bounteous grace that abides upon the Achaean Christians. It points specifically to the enabling power that has assisted these Saints in overcoming the propensities of the "natural man" such that they can make a generous and heartfelt offering.

Paul describes this gift with the adjective ἀνεκδιήγητος (*anekdiēgētos*), the word denoting something so marvelous that it is beyond words, thus "indescribable."[175] This is an apt description for the loving, transforming, and enabling power that flows from both God and Christ to those striving to do their will.

Analysis and Summary

Having explained how he has both urged members of the delegation he is sending and instructed them in how they are to help in collecting funds for the Jerusalem needy, Paul now turns to instructions on the collection itself, beginning with a plea and adding an assurance.

In 9:6, he uses the agricultural imagery to make his point. Though Corinth itself was very urban, its general environment was agrarian, and therefore its inhabitants would have related to rural imagery.[176] This imagery would have been especially relevant to the Jewish Christian community due to references in their wisdom literature.[177] The Apostle's point in using such a metaphor is that those who contribute stingily to the collection are like a farmer who is unwilling to sacrifice his grain in the present and thus gets but a poor harvest. On the other hand, those who contribute fully are like a farmer who willingly sacrifices his grain in the present and thus receives a bounteous harvest in the future.

---

172. Louw-Nida, §33.350.
173. BDAG, 266.
174. Bernard, "Second Epistle," 94.
175. BDAG, 76.
176. Barnett, *Second Epistle,* 436.
177. For example, see LXX Prov. 11:21, 24, 26, 30; 22:8; Job 4:8; Hos. 8:7.

Earlier in the epistle (8:14), Paul identified what constitutes for these Saints the bounteous harvest "of blessings" (ἐπ' εὐλογίαις, *ep' eulogiais*), specifically meeting the temporal needs of their Judean counterparts. However, he pointed out in that chapter that their primary motive in giving should not be getting a reward as much as reaching out to those suffering. Further, he stressed that the amount given was not as important as the care and concern it reflected (8:12). At this point in his epistle (9:6), however, he does focus on the reward that will come to the giving Saints, assuring them that their blessing of others will yield an even greater blessing to themselves.[178]

The passage is quite theocentric since it is God who, as Paul has made clear earlier in this work, grants the heavenly and earthly blessings (3:18; 7:6; 8:1, 16).[179] Thus Paul's imagery points neither to an economic return on an investment resulting from one's ingenuity nor to an act of sheer luck. Rather, "it is the reality of faith, which has its works but which cannot be reduced to them. It [is] a participation in the goodness of God, who supplies both seed and harvest."[180]

In 9:7, the Apostle identifies two feelings that should not accompany the giving. These are internal reluctance (ἐκ λύπης, *ek lypēs*) and external pressure (ἐξ ἀνάγκη, *ex anangkē*). Further, people should give only as much as they determined in their hearts when they initially heard of the opportunity. By placing the seat of motivation in each person's heart, Paul makes the giving an individual choice and thus, ideally, precludes both internal and external impositions.[181] In this way, he guards against their losing the spiritual reward.

Here Paul is in concert with the prophet Moroni, who warned, "A man being evil cannot do that which is good; for if he offereth a gift, or prayeth unto God, except he shall do it with real intent it profiteth him nothing. For behold, it is not counted unto him for righteousness. For behold, if a man being evil giveth a gift, he doeth it grudgingly; wherefore it is counted unto him the same as if he had retained the gift; wherefore he is counted evil before God" (Moro. 7:6–8).

---

178. Martin, *2 Corinthians,* 469–70.

179. Matera, *II Corinthians,* 207–8; Seifred, *Second Letter,* 354.

180. Seifred, *Second Letter,* 354.

181. Guthrie, *2 Corinthians,* 449. The sentiment Paul expresses here strongly echoes Deut. 15:10, which identifies Jehovah's will concerning the attitude of giving that should exist during the "year of release" (Deut. 15:9).

Guarding against this, the Apostle gives no criteria as to the amount that should be given. Each individual must decide for herself or himself but do so in light of the grace that flows from God. Thus giving is to be voluntary (8:3), free (9:5), and generous (9:6); "any legalistic impost [would be] inimical to this principle."[182]

He concludes the verse by paraphrasing a scripture that states, "God blesses a cheerful man and a giver" (LXX Prov. 22:8, our translation).[183] Paul renders it as "God loves a cheerful giver." His rewording is telling. In the Apostle's view, love is God's immediate and active response to those who give cheerfully. Paul's pronouncement does not look to some future relationship with God but to one that is realized through the giving. In the process, the Apostle removes all economic overtones because neither purpose nor amount matter any longer—only the proper attitude. Such giving is the door through which the Christian enters into the broad love and goodness of God.[184] Paul seems to have designed his request as a means of motivating the Saints to examine their own reasons for giving. He is not intimating, however, that God's love is exclusive to willing givers. He intends no warning. Rather, he is encouraging his audience to give liberally, not because they were made to feel badly or spurred on by outside pressures, but because of God's response toward those who do so.[185]

In 9:8, Paul addresses the possible concern of those who might fear that giving would hurt them financially. The Apostle makes a five-fold promissory assertion highlighted by the repeated use of the term "all" (πᾶν, *pan*), which "emphasizes the comprehensiveness and ultimacy of God's goodness."[186] His response centers on God's ability to give the faithful a superabundance (περισσεύω, *perisseuō*) of what they need, the verb suggesting an amount that not only fills up but overflows.[187] What God is able to lavish on cheerful givers is "all kinds of grace" (πᾶσαν χάριν, *pasan charin*), the phrase referring in this case to everything that the Corinthian Saints need so that they can make a generous contribution to the Judean poor. In other words, the gift of grace is God's way of enabling these people to give generously in response to a plea for help. Paul's admonition shows

182. Barnett, *Second Epistle,* 437.

183. The idea is thoroughly Jewish and based on Old Testament requirements. Barrett, *Second Epistle,* 236. See also Martin, *2 Corinthians,* 470 n. 257, for rabbinic sources.

184. Seifred, *Second Letter,* 356.

185. Guthrie, *2 Corinthians,* 450.

186. Seifrid, *Second Letter,* 356.

187. This idea Paul refers to time and time again in this epistle. See 1:5; 3:9; 4:15; 8:2, 7.

that God blesses people so that they can do what they desire. They are not, as Paul warns, to glut themselves on God's gifts but to use the resources he provides to promote "every good work" (πᾶν ἔργον ἀγαθόν, *pan ergon agathon*).[188] In this we see the practical application of the Lord's command that includes a promise: "Seek first [God's] kingdom and his righteousness and all these things shall be given to you" (Matt. 6:33, authors' translation; compare 3 Ne. 13:33).

Lest his readers misunderstand his admonition and expect too much, Paul stresses that what God actually gives is "enough" or "a sufficient amount" (αὐτάρκεια, *autarkeia*[189]) to do the needed work. Two points grow out of Paul's use of this term. First, the emphasis is on sufficiency, but of a specific kind. Both the Stoics and Cynics of the time stressed the virtue of self-sufficiency as a means of obtaining moral superiority. Indeed, the objective was to lose all dependence on others.[190] Paul rejects this idea and replaces it with divine sufficiency, through which the Father provides all the resources that a Saint needs to accomplish the work at hand. Second, this kind of sufficiency is neither self-centered nor consumerist but stresses generous giving to assist others.[191]

Paul's promise, we must stress, is not that of an elaborate lifestyle, but sufficient resources to adequately perform "every good work." Indeed, the larger context of Paul's encouragement that God gives sufficiently in all things and at all times should not be taken to mean that the Apostle believes the Saints will never suffer from want or need. The Apostle has made it very clear that suffering, including the want for temporal goods, comes hand in glove with being a Christian. Undeniably, the Macedonian Saints gave not out of their abundance but out of deficiency. Even so, due to the grace that God bestowed upon them, they were not made temporally poorer through their generous giving, but rather abounded in the richness of the Spirit. The point is that God did compensate the giving but did so in his own way and according to his own timetable. By this means, he promoted (and still promotes) the need for the continual expression of faith, the end blessing of which will not be fully realized until one is made pure and enters into the rest of the Lord (see Alma 12:26; 13:12; 16; and Moro. 7:3).[192]

---

188. Based on the chiastic structure of this phrase, "all kinds of grace" is parallel to and modified by "every good work." Thus, "grace" and "good works" take on the same nuance.

189. Louw-Nida, §75.6; BDAG, 152.

190. Guthrie, *2 Corinthians*, 452–53.

191. Harris, *Second Epistle*, 638.

192. Seifrid, *Second Letter*, 358–59.

Paul's admonition brings out yet another important lesson. God's extending his grace brings its willing participants into a genuine sharing of that grace as they in turn extend it by giving generously to others. Further, in doing so, they thereby open the door through which they will come to receive that grace in its fulness (D&C 93:19–20). In this way, the Christians participate in God's kind of giving (that is, in extending grace) and enhance within themselves this divine quality. By this means, a kind of "deification" takes place that does not replace God but rather confirms God as the enabler and one true Giver who models the way and blesses those who follow it.[193]

To shore up his point, Paul again turns to scripture in 9:9. Likely because it states exactly what he wants, he quotes part of LXX Psalm 111:9 (112:9 in the KJV) verbatim. The whole psalm is an acrostic poem that celebrates the acts of the God-like man who uses his riches in accordance with divine dictates. The poem highlights the person's generosity, noting that he disperses or scatters (σκορπίζω, *skorpizō*) his goods widely. His lavish giving is a disclosure of an inherent righteousness (*hē dikaiosynē*; compare Matt. 6:1–4), a characteristic that, because it is at the heart of the person's being, will remain with him forever and thus ensure his eternal place with God.[194]

As is his wont, Paul repurposes the scripture so that it points not to the deeds and attributes of the righteous man, but to those of God. In 9:10, the Apostle plays off the word found in the scripture (σκορπίζω, *skorpizō*, "to disperse, scatter") to transition to horticultural imagery once again. He notes that God provides both the source (seed) and product (bread) for the faithful sower, suggesting that he will never run out of either.[195] Paul's design is to have his readers focus on the abundant blessings that come to the individual who gives to the poor (πένης, *penēs*). *Penēs* is found only here in the NT, and therefore, its Old Testament nuance helps to determine what Paul has in mind. The term generally refers to those who derive their living neither from having property nor from being highly skilled. Thus the untrained mass of people living in the Greco-Roman world composed "the poor." Jewish society attributed no religious value to being

---

193. Compare Seifrid, *Second Letter,* 358.

194. The verse in the psalm ends with the observation that such a person "shall be exalted with honour" (ὑποθήσεται ἐν δόξῃ, *hypothēsetai en doxē*).

195. Paul's thought strongly echoes Isa. 55:10. The benefactor in that verse is, however, not God but rain. Still, the Divine stands behind all forces of nature and, therefore, to ascribe the blessed outcome to God is but a small reach.

poor, and so these people were not generally viewed as being spiritually inferior.[196] Though in the Masoretic Text the Hebrew word refers to anyone needing assistance,[197] the context in the LXX allows Paul to reference those Jewish Christians who are suffering from lack of material goods.

In this verse (9:10), he assures his readers that God will give them increase, but he does not promise it will be all in material goods; rather it will be in "righteousness." This part of Paul's response strongly echoes Hosea 10:12, where the prophet addressed the results of sowing righteousness—namely, that justice will come to the individual. Exactly what Paul has in mind with this genitive phrase is a bit ambiguous. If he is using "righteousness" as a "genitive of production," then he is referring to a quality resulting from the Saints' generous acts adduced by their moral lives being in harmony with God's ways. Taking the phrase in this way, the thought parallels that of the quality of the life of the righteous giver noted in Paul's quote of LXX Psalm 111:9. As such, the phrase would refer to the relatively high standard of life of the Achaean Saints generally. The phrase, however, can also be read as a "genitive of possession"—that is, as referring to an individual's internal righteousness that is composed of his or her right standing with God. Such a state of righteousness God would bestow upon each Saint in response to his or her generosity.[198] It is also possible that Paul has in mind both the result of their generous acts and God's response thereto by enhancing their righteousness.[199] This more comprehensive interpretation would fit nicely with the general tenor of this section since the Apostle looks at the multifaceted ways the Saints' generous giving positively affects them.

In 9:11, the Apostle transitions away from emphasizing God's vast resources and his bounteous giving that both encourage and supply the Saints' generosity and moves toward that generosity's results. He begins by stating that God will "enrich [the givers] in every way," making it possible for them to give liberally and thus enhance their righteousness. But the benefit to them does not stop there. In 9:11–12, Paul notes that the beneficiaries will experience an overflowing (περισσεύω, *perisseuō*) "gratitude

---

196. *NID*, 3:704–6.

197. The term is found only here in the New Testament and, therefore, its Old Testament echo helps to determine its force. The LXX follows closely the Hebrew meaning of the noun אֶבְיוֹן (*'ebyôn*), which refers generally to anyone in need, but especially to that class that does not have the means of protecting themselves from abuse or oppression and thus must be assisted. BDB, 2.

198. Guthrie, *2 Corinthians*, 455–56.

199. Barnett, *Second Epistle*, 442.

[εὐχαριστία, *eucharistia*] to God." His point is that they should understand that their deed is an expression of their faith in and response to God's power that rests upon them. The result of their understanding of how the process works is deep and heartfelt gratitude.

In 9:13, the Apostle elaborates on this point—because of the Greek Saints' generosity, the Jewish Saints will express their gratitude by giving glory to God. Their praise will be generated for two reasons: first, because the recipients of the gift will recognize it as an expression of the Corinthians' obedience to the covenant that they made when accepting the gospel,[200] and second, because they will recognize the gift, as Paul notes, as an expression of the "surpassing grace of God that rests upon" their fellow Saints.

An element of the Apostle's theology woven into this part of his instructions must not be overlooked. Describing what will happen due to the Corinthian Saints' generosity, he states that Jewish Saints will express gratitude *to God.* Though they will neither forget nor discount the generous gift from their Greek brothers and sisters, they will nonetheless view their fellow travelers as but vehicles of God's work, and therefore they will give all praise appropriately to him. In sum, for the Apostle, it is the gift of God working through the Corinthians that is significant.[201]

In 9:14, Paul identifies another result of the Achaeans' generous giving: the Jerusalem Saints will both pray for and yearn to be connected with their generous benefactors because they wish to partake of the divine grace that sits so fully upon the Achaean Saints. Due to the wonderous and enabling power of this grace and what it brings about, it is little wonder that in 9:15 Paul exclaims, "Thank God for his indescribable gift!"

In sum, a central element in this portion of Paul's supplication centers on a God-given gratitude expressed in thanksgiving. Noteworthy is that the Apostle does not indicate the content of the super-abundant gratitude inspired by the Corinthian Saints' goodness, but he does mark out the virtue "as a basic and lasting element of the Christian life. Indeed, a life based on thanksgiving is the converse of an evil life (Rom 1:21; Eph 5:4)."[202] One reason is that for the "natural man" there is an instinctive love of money driving him to pursue riches and influence, with the expectation that these

200. The thought Paul expresses carries shades of Mosiah 18:8–9, where the qualifications for baptism are listed, among other items, as being "desirous . . . to be called [Christ's] people, and are willing to bear one another's burdens, that they may be light; Yea, and are willing to mourn with those that mourn; yea, and comfort those that stand in need of comfort."

201. Seifred, *Second Letter,* 364–65.

202. *NID,* 2:335.

will yield to a more secure and abundant temporal life. But if a Saint yields "to the enticings of the Holy Spirit" and, by that power, puts off "the natural man and [becomes] a saint through the atonement of Christ the Lord" (Mosiah 3:19), he or she loses trust in the mundane and temporal. Instead, that Saint looks to pleasing God as the seat of his or her security. At that point, as the prophet Jacob states, Saints become "familiar with all and free with [their] substance," using it so that others "may be rich like into [themselves]." However, such a state, as Jacob reminds his hearers, comes initially by both seeking the kingdom of God before all else and receiving "a hope in Christ." Once changed by God's transforming power, the Saint, should he or she seek for wealth, will do it "for the intent to do good—to clothe the naked, and to feed the hungry, and to liberate the captive, and administer relief to the sick and afflicted" (Jacob 2:17–19). A Saint thus becomes, as Elder McConkie notes, "subject to a higher law. Money is no longer his master; it is his servant to do good and work righteousness; he becomes a cheerful giver."[203] Indeed, gratitude for what God has given him on both the temporal and spiritual plain fills his soul for the opportunity and reinforces his desire to do good. Thus, like Paul, he can exclaim, "Thank God for his indescribable gift!"

203. *DNTC,* 2:435.

Chapter 10

Paul Confronts His Detractors

Introduction

As we move into the last section of this rather heavy and polemic epistle, a point made by a very observant scholar seems most relevant. He observed "that 2 Corinthians fills much the same place in the New Testament as does the book of Job in the Old. It is a letter written by one whose heart has been broken by the many intolerable burdens heaped on him: a man struggling with a recalcitrant church and a malignant foe. If in Romans and Galatians we see the apostle *proclaiming* the cross with might and main, in 2 Corinthians we see him *bearing* the cross, and bearing it triumphantly."[1] The final portion of 2 Corinthians especially highlights this point as Paul battles to reclaim some people who do not really wish to be reclaimed.

As noted early in this work, Titus's report to the Apostle consisted of items both reassuring and distressing. The reassurance rested on three positive actions certain Corinthian members had taken: their encouraging response to Paul's harsh letter, the expressed loyalty to the Apostle by many of them, and their willingness to continue to collect for the Judean poor. The distressing portion was that there continued to be active groups hostile to Paul who were undermining not only his teachings and doctrine but also his authority. Their inroads demanded immediate attention, and thus Paul devotes a full third of his letter to vindicating his authority and teachings.[2]

The text allows for three sets of antagonists. These can be detected through the third-person pronouns and other third-person references that Paul sprinkles though chapters 10–13. By using this technique, Paul could

---

1. John E. Wood, "Death at Work in Paul," *Evangelical Quarterly* 54, no. 3 (July–September 1982): 151, italics in original.

2. Bernard, "Second Epistle," 94.

refer to these people in an indirect way and so castigate them while drawing his readers to his side.[3]

The clearest faction is those whom Paul sarcastically calls "super-apostles" (ὑπερλίαν ἀπόστολοι, *hyperlian apostoloi*, 11:5), a group of outsiders who have joined the Corinthian Saints. They accuse Paul of teaching a false gospel (10:12–12:5). These were likely Judaizers—that is, converts who follow the Messiah Jesus not as one who fulfilled the law of Moses but rather as one who showed the way to its true meaning and implementation (2:17–3:1, and probably 5:11–13). Initially, they demanded that Gentile males be circumcised and that all converts follow the demands of the Mosaic law. Due to the policy set down during the Jerusalem Council in AD 49, some may have softened on the issue of circumcision but maintained the importance of living other aspects of the law. They paraded their stricter way of life as proof of a more spiritual and thus God-favored acceptance. Given that some of the Gentile converts could have felt somewhat inferior to Jewish members, the interlopers could have easily won some over to their side. These outsiders arrived with letters of recommendation from their branch of the Church. All these items combined to give them rather high cachet, especially among those who already felt they had cause to oppose Paul. The Apostle castigates the outsiders, calling them "false apostles" (11:13) who preach both another gospel and another Jesus (11:4) and also glory in their own ministry (11:12). He points out to his readers that their seeming high standing came from meeting requirements that they themselves set, not the Lord (10:12).

The other two groups of antagonists appear to be insiders—that is, members living within the city of Corinth itself. The text (10:1–2, 9–10) reveals the focus of the first group's attack, which consists of three alleged flaws. The first was the falseness of Paul's "humility" (ταπεινός, *tapeinos*).[4] They seem to have alleged that he put on a false, even condescending, modesty during this last visit, but as soon as he left, he exposed himself to be an arrogant, insolent man. The second attack focused on the manner of his life that, they insisted, was steeped in worldliness (κατὰ σάρκα, *kata sarka*, 10:2), the antithesis of "spirit" (πνεῦμα, *pneuma*),[5] that divine power that they professed to be upholding in the Corinthian branches (11:4). The final

3. Barnett, *Second Epistle*, 452–54.

4. BDAG, 989.

5. BDAG, 832–36.

focus of attack was on his authority (ἐξουσία, *exousia*)[6] as a Church leader. They insisted that they themselves were "belonging to Christ" (10:7, NR)—that is, following the ways of the Master.

The Apostle's claim to be a "Christ person" (Χιστοῦ εἶναι, *Xristou einai*), they bawled, simply couldn't be true given two factors: first, his bodily weakness (ἀσθενής, *asthenēs*,[7] 10:10), which revealed he was little more than an ill man unable to heal himself, and second, that he lived as a worldly person that fell far below the dignity his office demanded (10:10)[8] and that he did not possess its necessary skills (11:6). The way Paul describes these people in this part of his epistle shows that he saw them as having a self-declared super-spirituality and a lofty sense of self-satisfaction that revealed itself in full-scale self-aggrandizement.

The final group appears to consist of those "who had sinned before and [had] not repented of the impurity and sexual immorality and licentiousness that they have indulged in" (12:21, NR). Some of these were likely members of the group Paul addressed in his former letter who supported a member who had committed incest (1 Cor. 5:1–5), while others were enmeshed in immorality associated with the pagan practices (1 Cor. 6:15–20).

In this letter, Paul warns all of these that when he comes, if he does not find the necessary repentance, he will not spare them from the force of his Christ-ordained authority (2 Cor. 13:2–3).

Chapters 10–13 are marked by Paul's consistent use of the first-person pronoun "I." Its use is deliberate and telling. Through it he accomplishes three main objectives: he defends himself against the attacks of his enemies, he defeats these opponents and puts their pernicious vision right, and he teaches the Corinthians the reality that power and weakness go together. Of these aims, the text suggests that it is the last—that power and weakness go together—that is his primary thrust. The basis of his argument, and a major means by which he appeals to the Saints, is his personal example. For instance, the Apostle takes the situation of "the thorn" in his flesh and Christ's message that, despite Paul's pleas, he will not remove it (12:7–10) and presents them as a model of suffering through which he participates in the experience of the crucified and risen Lord. Paul legitimizes his ministry by describing his participation in the weakness, power, and grace of

6. BDAG, 352–53.

7. BDAG, 142.

8. Martin, *2 Corinthians*, 482.

Christ—realities that are common to all believers. Because of this, his "I" is a model for the congregation as a whole.

Paul is concerned also with a fundamental distortion of the Christian life, which, as he insists, must embody both the power and weakness of the cross. Underlying Paul's intensity is a concern that the congregation misunderstands their union with Christ and the fundamental events of the gospel. His opponents' boasting in the flesh has led the Corinthians to put confidence in human strength and in the absence of weakness. Paul maintains that power and weakness must go together, even though this brings him into conflict with the cultural ideal that says a strong public presence is a fundamental precondition for a leader and teacher. Intended to correct the Corinthians' misconceptions, Paul's "I" language speaks not only about his own leadership but also about the Corinthians' lives in Christ and their embodiment of the gospel. Paul's "I" illustrates that Christian life and leadership are not matters of moving beyond weakness. Experiences of vulnerability are not aberrations from an ideal; they grant access to the grace and power of the Lord. If Paul can win the Corinthians to this truth, then their acceptance of it will authenticate his authority, undermine the boasts of his opponents, and secure the congregation's relationship with Christ and the gospel.[9]

Chapter 10 is Paul's opening salvo against his enemies. It reveals that a fierce and toxic spiritual battle is fully underway. He appeals to his readers insisting that they take action against his detractors so he will not have to. He declares that his critics have misread him and the force of his ministry, misunderstanding that his seeming weakness is actually the strength that follows Christlike—and thus, powerful—meekness. To push his attack, Paul uses the language of warfare, assuring his target audience that the boldness of his letters will be matched by the power of God that he will display upon his arrival. The result will be punitive punishment for the impenitent. His words reveal a harsh indignation and an assertion of authority pushed to the uttermost.[10] To put his seeming threats in their proper context, however, he assures his readers that his boldness, either

9. For a study, see Dustin W. Ellington, "Not Applicable to Believers?: The Aims and Basis of Paul's 'I' in 2 Corinthians 10–13," *Journal of Biblical Literature* 131, no. 2 (2012): 325–40.

10. Martin, *Second Epistle,* 482, quoting A. Plummer, *A Critical and Exegetical Commentary on the Second Epistle of St. Paul to the Corinthians* (1915).

expressed in his letters or in person, is not an attempt at intimidation but an effort to improve their spiritual welfare. Their only proper course of action, he insists, is to submit fully to his leadership.[11]

In his excellent defense (ἀπολογία, *apologia*), Paul answers the charges brought against him with skill, irony, sarcasm, parody, and persuasion. He does this primarily by quoting phrases and catchwords used by his enemies, but he remints them by giving them a novel twist in one of two ways: applying them in a fresh context or modifying their intent through a play on words.[12] His rhetoric is actually shaped by his perception of "God's dealings with human beings in the gospel. Paul must (first) 'tear down' before he can engage in his proper work of 'building up' [10:4, 8; 12:19; 13:10]. He prepares for his third visit in the closing of the letter by addressing the Corinthians with the severity that is necessary to this end. He prefers to do so in this letter, from a distance, so that, if it is at all possible, he may perform his proper work while he is with them (13:10)."[13]

This chapter breaks easily into three parts. In 10:1–6, Paul begs his readers not to force him to use his authority with severity when he arrives among them. In 10:7–12, he promises that if he does not find his antagonists contrite when he arrives, they will feel the full brunt of his authority. In 10:13–18, he focuses on boasting. He acknowledges the claim that boasting can be wrong but insists that some boasting is proper if it is in the Lord and not in oneself.

In sum, he argues that, despite superficial appearances to the contrary, he continues to exercise legitimate and apostolic authority that he will use to bless these people unless they choose otherwise.

---

11. Guthrie, *2 Corinthians,* 465.

12. Examples include his use of λογίζομαι (*logizomai*), "expect," in 10:2b that looks on to 10:2c; λογισμός (*logismos*), "argument" (10:4) relates to 10:7, *λογιζέσθω* (*logizesthō*), "consider"; κατὰ σάρκα (*kata sarka*), "according to worldly standards," in 10:2 he transforms into ἐν σαρκί (*en sarki*), "in the flesh," in 10:3, thus giving it a different nuance. Martin, *2 Corinthians,* 482 with n. 31.

13. Seifrid, *Second Letter,* 372.

Paul's Intent to Use His Apostolic Authority If Necessary (10:1–2)

Greek Text

1 Αὐτὸς δὲ ἐγὼ Παῦλος παρακαλῶ ὑμᾶς διὰ τῆς πραΰτητος καὶ ἐπιεικείας τοῦ Χριστοῦ, ὃς κατὰ πρόσωπον μὲν ταπεινὸς ἐν ὑμῖν, ἀπὼν δὲ θαρρῶ εἰς ὑμᾶς· 2 δέομαι δὲ τὸ μὴ παρὼν θαρρῆσαι τῇ πεποιθήσει ᾗ λογίζομαι τολμῆσαι ἐπί τινας τοὺς λογιζομένους ἡμᾶς ὡς κατὰ σάρκα περιπατοῦντας. [SBLGNT]

King James Version

1 Now I Paul myself beseech you by the meekness and gentleness of Christ, who in presence am base among you, but being absent am bold toward you: 2 But I beseech you, that I may not be bold when I am present with that confidence, wherewith I think to be bold against some, which think of us as if we walked according to the flesh.

New Rendition

1 Now I Paul myself appeal to you by the humility and gentleness of Christ—I who am "humble" when face to face with you but "bold" toward you when I am absent. 2 But I plead with you that when I am present, I will not have to act boldly with the confidence that I consider to be bold enough to use against those who are of the opinion that we conduct our lives according to worldly standards.

Translation Notes and Comments

10:1 *Now I Paul myself beseech you by the meekness and gentleness of Christ / Now I Paul myself appeal to you by the humility and gentleness of Christ:* The conjunction δέ (*de*), "now," signals a change in subject matter and, in this case, a change in tone. The phrase αὐτὸς δὲ ἐγὼ Παῦλος (*autos de ego Paulos*), "Now I Paul, myself," shows that from this point on, the Apostle is speaking for and in behalf of himself.

The verb παρακαλέω (*parakaleō*), "exhort" or "appeal," carries the general meaning of "call[ing] to one's side," usually for the purpose of aid, and therefore it has a uniting affect.[14]

Paul makes his appeal by attaching to himself two virtues associated with the Lord. The first is πραΰτης (*prautēs*), "humility." It denotes the state of not being overly impressed by one's station or accomplishments

14. BDAG, 764–65.

and expresses itself in social virtues and high ideals. Thus, it carries such additional nuances as "courteousness, considerateness, graciousness, and nobleness."[15] The translation of the term as "meekness," as used in the KJV, could work, carrying as it does not only the idea of "the absence of passion or wrath" but also one of "a consistent mildness or gentleness of temper." But because in modern usage it "suggests spiritlessness or undue submissiveness that even when it is employed without derogation these ideas are often connoted," it does not quite capture Paul's point.[16] On the other hand, the rendition "humility" does work because it denotes "lacking all signs of pride, aggressiveness, or self-assertiveness either in spirit our outward show" and marks itself as "the absence of pride in oneself or in one's achievements and, in religious use, a consciousness of one's weakness and a disposition to ascribe to the Supreme Being all credit for whatever one is or does that is meritorious."[17]

The second attribute of Christ that Paul attributes to himself is ἐπιεικεία (*epieikeia*), "gentleness." The noun also carries such nuances as "fairness, and peaceableness."[18] There is another nuance, however, that, given Paul's historical situation, is likely at play here. The noun expresses "the quality of making allowances despite facts that might suggest reason for a different reaction." In this light, such words as "clemency, indulgence, tolerance," and, more importantly, "gracious forbearance" also give a proper cast.[19]

who in presence am base among you / I who am "humble" when face to face with you: This phrase catches one of the charges that Paul's antagonists level against him. The noun ταπεινὸς (*tapeinos*), "humble," in the

15. BDAG, 861; Louw-Nida, §88.59; *NID,* 4:123–26.

16. *Dictionary of Synonyms,* s.v. "humble."

17. *Dictionary of Synonyms,* s.v. "humble." In Greek philosophy, *praus* carried the idea of "gentle friendliness," a virtue highly prized in human relations. The term was used in the Septuagint and Hebrew tradition a major characteristic possessed by the royal hero and led to his being called "the prince of peace." Friedich Hauck and Siegfried Schulz, "πραΰς, πραΰτης," in *TDNT,* 6:645–51.

18. BDAG, 371; *NID,* 2:240–41. Harris, *Second Epistle,* 667, gives the full range of meanings as "'kindness,' 'considerateness,' 'magnanimity,' 'reasonableness,' 'fairness,' 'forbearance,' 'yieldingness,' 'moderation,' 'gentleness,' 'clemency,' 'consideration,' 'patience,' 'self-forgetfulness,' 'great-heartedness,' 'selflessness.'"

19. Louw-Nida, §88.62. See also BDAG, 371; and *NID,* 2:240–41. According to Herbert Preisker, "ἐπιεικεία, ἐπιεικεῆς," in *TDNT,* 2:588–90, in Paul's context the noun "refers to the meekness of Christ as for Paul and the community. Christ is an example as the Revealer of divine and majesty." He goes on to explain that this virtue is something that someone must seek after when trusting in the atonement, and manifests itself in trusting in apostolic authority.

present context does not carry the positive idea of lacking arrogance or haughtiness but denotes a condition of character brought on by "having low and humble status."[20] expressing itself in self-depreciation, subservience, and abjectness.[21] Because these characteristics denote the character of a slave, not the demeanor of a free person, they were highly frowned upon in the face-conscious Greco-Roman world.[22] Paul's enemies, however, were likely putting a nasty spin on the word, suggesting Paul evidenced a mock humility or self-abasement that the Apostle used in an artful, devious way to get what he wanted.[23]

The phrase κατὰ πρόσωπον (*kata prosopon*), literally "according to face," denotes being present in person and is thus rendered "face to face."[24]

but being absent am bold toward you / but "bold" toward you when I am absent: This phrase catches another of the charges Paul's enemies have brought against him. The verb θαρρέω (*tharreō*), "to have courage, to be bold,"[25] denotes certainty leading to a confident or daring manner that best expresses itself during periods of danger or testing.[26] In the present context, however, it carries more negative nuances, such as being "arrogant," "haughty," or "insolent."[27] Here Paul uses the word in an ironic sense to poke fun at his accusers.[28]

The verb ἄπειμι (*apeimi*), "to be absent," or more literally to be "away,"[29] found here as a present participle, denotes being away from those addressed.

10:2 The first phrase of this sentence (reading δέομαι δὲ τὸ μὴ παρὼν θαρρῆσαι, *deomai de to mē parōn tharrēsai,* literally "now I request not being present to be bold") well illustrates the brevity and compactness of the Greek language, since (as the rendition below shows) it requires more than twice as many English words to translate its meaning.

But I beseech you that I may not be bold when I am present / But I plead with you that when I am present, I will not have to act boldly: The verb δέομαι (*deomai*), "to ask, . . . to plead, to beg," carries the nuance of

20. Louw-Nida, §87.61; 88.52.

21. BDAG, 989. Even more negative connotations such as "servility," "obsequiousness," and "sycophancy" may not be out of the question. Martin, *2 Corinthians,* 482.

22. BDAG, 989. For a study, see *NID,* 4:448–54.

23. Martin, *2 Corinthians,* 485 n. 52.

24. Louw-Nida, §83.38.

25. Louw-Nida, §25.156.

26. BDAG, 444.

27. Martin, *2 Corinthians,* 485.

28. Barnett, *Second Epistle,* 458; Seifrid, *Second Letter,* 376.

29. BDAG, 100; Louw-Nida, §85.27.

"urgency, with the implication of presumed need."[30] Paul's use of the term stresses his strong desire that his readers not put him in a position where he must act against them.

The verb θαρρέω (*tharreō*) means "to be confident, courageous, bold,"[31] and is found here in the form of the articular infinitive phrase τὸ μὴ . . . θαρρῆσαι (*to mē . . . tharrēsai*), literally "not to be bold," but rendered as above.

Embedded within the phrase is the present participle of the verb πάρειμι (*pareimi*), "to be present."[32] As a nominative, masculine singular, it refers to its subject "I" (Paul) and is used circumstantially, thus "when I am present."

with that confidence, wherewith I think to be bold / with the confidence that I consider to be bold enough: With this phrase, Paul stresses his determination to use unabashed boldness if he finds it necessary. The noun πεποίθησις (*pepoithēsis*), "confidence,"[33] based on the perfect stem of *peithō,* as used here, expresses a state of certainty since this class of Greek verbs uses the perfect tense to dramatically express experience. In the present context, the noun nuances Paul's confidence in his apostolic authority.[34]

The adverbial phrase τῇ πεποιθήσει (*tē pepoithēsei*), "with the confidence," acts to define τὸ μὴ . . . θαρρῆσαι (*to mē . . . tharrēsai*), "to not . . . be bold," in the previous phrase and "speaks of the manner in which boldness might be exercised: 'to be bold *with confidence.*'"[35] The two can be conflated, thus reading either "confident boldness"[36] or "bold confidence."[37] Either way, Paul's intent is clear: he is fully confident in his apostolic authority and has the boldness to use it if necessary.

The verb τολμάω (*tolmaō*), found here as an aorist infinitive, means "to be bold, resolute, courageous."[38] It refers to an action that takes a certain amount of daring, a willingness to push against a social line. In this case, it shows the Apostle's concern that the Corinthian Saints are pushing him over the limit of gentle Christlike conduct and into an aggressive punitive demeanor. The phrase stresses his intended show of determined strength, if necessary, in the face of his opposition.

---

30. Louw-Nida, §33.170.
31. BDAG, 444.
32. BDAG, 773.
33. Louw-Nida, §31.82.
34. BDAG, 796.
35. Guthrie, *2 Corinthians,* 469–70, italics in original.
36. Barrett, *Second Epistle,* 243.
37. Guthrie, *2 Corinthians,* 470.
38. The infinitive force of the verb carries such additional meanings as "to dare, be brave enough." BDAG, 1010; Guthrie, *2 Corinthians,* 470.

The verb λογίζομαι (*logizomai*), "to believe, think, be of the opinion, consider,"[39] expresses the limit of the Apostle's intended actions—whatever is enough: no less, no more.

against some, which think of us as if we walked according to the flesh / against those who are of the opinion that we conduct our lives according to worldly standards: The preposition ἐπί (*epi*), "against," acts as a marker of hostile opposition when followed by a noun in the accusative case.[40] The adjective τίς (*tis*), found here as a plural and rendered as "those who," points to Paul's antagonists. This is his first direct mention of them.

The verb περιπατέω (*peripateō*), found here as a present plural masculine participle, denotes "to go about, walk around," but here carries a figurative sense meaning "to conduct one's life."[41] Paul's use of the plural form suggests that he is now including his fellow missionaries in the argument and thereby recognizing that they too carry apostolic authority.[42]

The verb λογίζομαι (*logizomai*), as noted above, means literally to count something and, more idiomatically, "to be of the opinion."[43] It governs the phrase that translates literally as "according to the flesh walking around."

In the prepositional phrase ὡς κατὰ σάρκα (*hōs kata sarka*), literally "as according to the flesh," the particle *hōs,* "as," acts as a marker pointing to the perspective from which one person views the activity of another[44] and thus can be translated as "under the (false) assumption that."[45] The phrase *kata sarka,* literally "according to the flesh," carries the figurative sense of acting "according to human standards" or the ordinary desires of the natural man or woman.[46] We have rendered it as above. Paul's point is that his detractors are judging him on the basis of a false standard, one that looks to what is external, showy, and popular and conforms to the standards of the Greek Sophists, not to Christian ideals.[47]

---

39. BDAG, 597–98.

40. BDAG, 363–67.

41. BDAG, 803.

42. The issue at hand addresses who exactly works under authentic apostolic authority and who does not. Paul's use of the plural shows that he recognizes that he is not the only one who carries legitimate authority. Seifrid, *Second Letter,* 387.

43. BDAG, 597–98.

44. BDAG, 1103–6, see specifically 3.c.

45. Guthrie, *2 Corinthians,* 470.

46. BDAG, 914–16.

47. On the Sophists, see Analysis below.

Analysis and Summary

The last section of the epistle (chapters 10–13) begins with such a sharp break with the subject matter, style, and tone of the earlier parts of the epistle that some scholars argue that it was not part of the original letter but added later on (see introduction to this volume). But because earlier portions of the letter clearly indicate that Paul is well aware that he has enemies working among the Corinthian Saints (for example, see 6:14–7:4), it is most likely that we have the letter as he originally dictated it. The question is how to account for the difference in tone and style. It is possible that while Paul was dictating the letter, bitter news came from Corinth that his enemies were gaining ever more support. If so, at this point in his dictation, he may have fully turned his attention to respond to the news and, with an overflowing fervor, dictated his defense in such a way as to give his readers a hard knock, thus bringing them to their senses. It is also possible that Paul deliberately designed the epistle as it stands, thus saving his skillfully developed and biting polemic against his enemies for the last portion of his letter. In doing so, he gives his defense and warning with such a solid punch that it should have brought his readers into sensibility.[48] Either way, there is little doubt but that he realizes his intent.[49]

One of Paul's challenges was to respond to the popular belief of physiognomy in the Greco-Roman world, or the idea that an individual's character could be judged based upon his or her appearance and actions, especially bodily comeliness and physical grace, a belief most notably evident in Seutonius's *Twelve Caesars.* The charge by Paul's critics that he was physically deficient and, as a result, not a proper leader was likely based on this belief system. Those of this party used some physical deformity or persistent medical condition with which he was afflicted as their platform (for discussion, see Translation Notes and associated Analysis for 12:7). For them, his humble demeanor (10:1) was a visible signal of shame and humiliation, while his physical weakness (10:10) signified a morally suspect person.[50] As a result, both Paul's conduct and physical condition hampered his message.

---

48. Guthrie, *2 Corinthians,* 464.

49. Barnett, *Second Epistle,* 450 with n. 1.

50. The general Corinthian attitude would rebut the idea that humility was strength and that the "meek . . . inherit the earth" (Matt 5:5). Rather, they would insist, the meek get plowed under it. Seifrid, *Second Letter,* 371.

Rather than letting these classical stereotypes get in his way, however, the Apostle opted to fill these and similar terms with positive meaning by associating them with Jesus' earthly life and the Apostle's own conformity to Christ and him crucified. His response to his enemies' criticism reveals his perception that the weakness in his own body actually reflects his understanding of the nature of the mortal Jesus, who could also be seen as lacking physiognomic perfection.[51] Thus, he defused his detractors' arguments by teaching a corrected vision of what Christianity, and proper perspective based on it, really is.

He begins this section with a formal introduction, "I Paul, myself." In doing so, he is likely not discounting Timothy as coauthor but rather emphasizing that Paul is now speaking on his own authority—that being apostolic, the major issue in this last section of the epistle.[52]

In 10:1, we obliquely hear the disparaging remarks of Paul's enemies, who accuse him of being two-faced. One face, they say, reveals itself through the letters he writes. These epistles show him to be bold, even arrogant and intimidating. The other reveals itself in his demeanor when he is with them. It shows him to be humble and modest, but, in their estimation, actually pathetic.[53] Indeed, "humility was an attitude suitable to one who was 'base, ignoble or despised,' not the attitude of any self-respecting person." Thus, his deportment made him appear weak.[54]

"These accusations are particularly personal in nature."[55] The Apostle counters these by attributing to himself two virtues associated with the Lord—namely, humility and gracious forbearance. By doing so, Paul turns seeming weaknesses into Christian strengths. The first virtue, according to the Greek Old Testament, carried the strong nuance of submissiveness to divine will, a point the Apostle clearly wants to make.[56] The second virtue suggested a willingness to make allowances even when reason might ask for a different reaction.[57] By appealing to these virtues, Paul clearly takes upon himself not

---

51. For studies, see Stephan J. Joubert, "'Walking the Talk': Paul's Authority in Motion in 2 Corinthians 10–13," *In Die Skriflig* 49 no. 2 (2015), art. #1899, https://doi.org/10.4102/ids.v49i2.1899; and Wenhua Shi, *Paul's Message of the Cross as Body Language* (Tübingen, Ger.: Mohar Siebeck, 2008), 172–86.

52. Martin, *2 Corinthians,* 484.

53. Harris, *Second Epistle,* 699–71.

54. Garland, *2 Corinthians,* 430, quoting Spicq, *Theological Lexicon of the New Testament,* 3:369.

55. Holzapfel and Wayment, *Making Sense,* 375.

56. Garland, *2 Corinthians,* 427.

57. BDAG, 371; Louw-Nida, §88.62; see also *NID,* 2:240–41.

only the attributes of the Master but also his authority.[58] In addition, he shows a high level of goodwill towards his detractors.[59] In essence, Paul is showing that, despite his antagonists' arrogance and disputations, his scorned humility will not allow him to bring this Christlike virtue to bear against them. As one author stated, such humility has its basis in love and "cannot therefore think in terms of harsh punishment even in relation to the disobedient, which Christ exemplified for the community during His life on earth." Hence, the author notes, that it is devoid of the negative Hellenistic overtones and even "enables the Christian to correct the erring brother without arrogance, impatience, or anger."[60] All this clearly plays into Paul's hands by allowing him, properly, to be "the good guy" and strengthens his position against those who have bought into the perspective of the world around them.

Paul Discloses His Battle Plan (10:3–6)

Greek Text

3 ἐν σαρκὶ γὰρ περιπατοῦντες οὐ κατὰ σάρκα στρατευόμεθα— 4 τὰ γὰρ ὅπλα τῆς
στρατείας ἡμῶν οὐ σαρκικὰ ἀλλὰ δυνατὰ τῷ θεῷ πρὸς καθαίρεσιν ὀχυρωμάτων—
λογισμοὺς καθαιροῦντες 5 καὶ πᾶν ὕψωμα ἐπαιρόμενον κατὰ τῆς γνώσεως τοῦ
θεοῦ, καὶ αἰχμαλωτίζοντες πᾶν νόημα εἰς τὴν ὑπακοὴν τοῦ Χριστοῦ, 6 καὶ ἐν ἑτοίμῳ
ἔχοντες ἐκδικῆσαι πᾶσαν παρακοήν, ὅταν πληρωθῇ ὑμῶν ἡ ὑπακοή. [SBLGNT]

King James Version

3 For though we walk in the flesh, we
do not war after the flesh: 4 (For the
weapons of our warfare are not carnal,
but mighty through God to the pulling
down of strong holds;) 5 Casting down
imaginations, and every high thing that
exalteth itself against the knowledge of
God, and bringing into captivity every

New Rendition

3 For although we live in the world, we
do not wage war according to worldly
standards. 4 For the weapons of our
warfare are not worldly but weapons
made powerful by God for the purpose
of destroying fortresses. 5 We demol-
ish sophistries and every arrogant
obstacle that rises up in opposition to

58. *DNTC,* 2:437, notes that "the meek are the godfearing and righteous; the gentle are those who shun strife and contention, who teach the gospel in kindness and patience," attributes Paul emulated.

59. Garland, *2 Corinthians,* 427–28.

60. Hauck and Schulz, "πραΰς," in *TDNT,* 6:650.

thought to the obedience of Christ; 6 And having in a readiness to revenge all disobedience, when your obedience is fulfilled.

the knowledge of God, and we take captive every thought to make it obedient to Christ. 6 And we are ready to punish all disobedience whenever your obedience is complete.

Translation Notes and Comments

10:3–6: In the Greek text, these verses constitute one long sentence that has a single finite verb, στρατευόμεθα (*strateuometha*, "we wage war"), in 10:3. For clarity and flow, we have broken it into discrete sentences by rendering the circumstantial participles therein as finite verbs.

Noteworthy is that the limits of translation sadly have not allowed us to capture the full force and persuasive power of Paul's argument in this section of his epistle. With the hope of somewhat mitigating this deficiency, we here observe that there is a severity in Paul's warning conveyed by (1) the repetitive use of πᾶν (*pan*), "every," continued from 10:5 (where it is used twice); (2) the complex alliterations based on the Greek letters ε (*epsilon*) and π (*pi*);[61] and (3) the inversion of "disobedience" (παρακοή, *parakoē*) and obedience (ὑπακοή, *hypakoē*) in 10:6. The forceful rhetorical phrases and "strong military imagery combine to make vv. 3–6 among the more memorable passages in 2 Corinthians, and indeed within the Pauline writings."[62]

10:3 ***For though we walk in the flesh, we do not war after the flesh / For although we live in the world, we do not wage war according to worldly standards:*** The conjunction γάρ (*gar*), "for," acts as a marker clarifying Paul's rebuttal against those who judge him by external or worldly standards.

The noun σάρξ (*sarx*), literally "flesh," has a broad range of meanings, including a human being or her or his physical body. It can also refer to a people or nation and, more metaphorically, to a human or physical nature, or what Latter-day Saints might understand as the natural man or woman.[63] In the present context, the word takes on two distinct meanings. The first use denotes the mortal sphere (the world) and includes both human nature and the realm of human habitation. The participial phrase ἐν σαρκὶ . . . περιπατοῦντες (*en sarki . . . peripatounetes*), literally "in the flesh walking around," is concessive and is thus rendered as "although we

61. The alliterations can best be conveyed to the English reader by highlighting these features in transliteration thus, *kai en hetoimō echontes ekdikēsai* and ***p**an noēma . . . **p**asan **p**arakoēn . . . hotan **p**lērōthē.*

62. Barnett, *Second Epistle,* 467.

63. For the semantic range, see Louw-Nida, §§8.4, 63; 9:11, 12; 10:1; 58.10.

live in the world." The phrase is Paul's tacit acknowledgement that he is a mortal working in a mortal world with all the challenges and limitations that brings.[64]

The second distinct use refers to "the outward side of life," specifically all that is based on human, not religious, standards.[65] Since the adverb "worldly" denotes that which is "devoted to this world and its pursuits rather than to religion or spiritual affairs,"[66] we have rendered the second use of *sarx* with that nuance as "worldly standards." With this phrase, Paul separates his methods, which he compares to weapons of war (see 10:4), from those used by his enemies, who limit their judgment of his ways according to strictly human standards.

The verb στρατεύω (*strateuō*) means "to wage war"[67]—that is, to engage in a hostile conflict with an enemy. The Romans associated waging war with the principles of great discipline and obedience. In the next few verses, Paul skillfully uses this metaphor to extol the centrality of obedience. Given that Paul is referring to the application of cultural mores that have influenced some in the Church, the term is very strong and tacitly reveals not only how Paul sees the nature of the conflict but also how he views his critics.[68] This connotation also helps explain why the Apostle puts so much energy into his mission and is so hard on his antagonists. With the phrase οὐ κατὰ σάρκα (*ou kata sarka*), literally, "not according to the flesh," he strongly defines his stance: he has not and will not work according to the standards of the world to satisfy his enemies' notions of what is proper.

10:4 ***For the weapons of our warfare are not carnal / For the weapons of our warfare are not worldly:*** The noun ὅπλον (*hoplon*), "weapon of war,"[69] in the figurative sense indicated any "non-material means of fighting."[70] On the noun σάρξ (*sarx*), "flesh," see 10:3 above. With this phrase, Paul rebuts the false worldly standards his opponents use against him.

but mighty through God to the pulling down of strong holds / but weapons made powerful by God for the purpose of destroying fortresses: Paul's idea here reflects Proverbs 21:22. Paul describes his weapons as δυνατὰ τῷ

64. Martin, *2 Corinthians*, 487.

65. BDAG, 914–16, particularly 916.

66. *Collegiate Dictionary*, s.v. "worldly."

67. BDAG, 947.

68. That Paul sees the Christian ministry as a war against worldly ways, see Rom. 13:12–13; 1 Cor. 9:7; Eph. 6:10–17; 1 Thes. 5:8; 1 Tim. 1:18; and 2 Tim. 2:3–4.

69. BDAG, 716.

70. Louw-Nida, §6.29.

θεῷ (*dynata tō theō*), literally "powerful to God." The adjective δυνατός (*dynatos*), "powerful,"[71] denotes not only sufficient power but also special ability to perform a task.[72] The dative case in the phrase τῷ θεῷ (*tō theō*) has three possible nuances. One is a dative of reference, expressing the idea that the weapons are powerful in God's sight.[73] The context, however, suggests, that it is a dative of either means or agency, indicating that the weapons are made powerful *by* God.[74] Thus Paul shows that his weapons rest on divine, not worldly, power.

The preposition πρός (*pros*), "for,"[75] denotes the express purpose of these divinely empowered weapons. That purpose is expressed by the noun καθαίρεσις (*kathairesis*), which means the complete "tearing down" or "demolishing" of something by dismantling it.[76]

The noun ὀχύρωμα (*ochyrōma*), found here as a plural genitive, denotes "fortresses,"[77] but the context suggests Paul has in mind "vaunting reason," referring to the assumptions and logic used by his enemies.[78]

10:5 *Casting down imaginations / We demolish sophistries:* Some early manuscripts have this participial phrase as concluding 10:4 when it properly belongs to 10:5. In our Rendition, we have moved it to the beginning of this verse.

The noun λογισμός (*logismos*) describes "the product of a cognitive process, calculation, reasoning, reflection, thought," or "arguments" and is here found in the plural with a negative nuance. Hence, we have rendered the word as "sophistries,"[79] denoting as the English word does a subtle deception by means of reasoning or argument.

and every high thing that exalteth itself against the knowledge of God / and every arrogant obstacle that rises up in opposition to the knowledge of God: The phrase πᾶν ὕψωμα (*pan hypsōma*), literally "every high thing," denotes anything that postures itself arrogantly or that is exaggerated in

71. BDAG, 264.

72. Louw-Nida, §74.2, 4.

73. Moule, *Idiom Book,* 184.

74. Wallace, *Greek Grammar,* 162–63; Smyth, *Greek Grammar,* §1507–8.

75. BDAG, 873–75.

76. BDAG, 487; Louw-Nida, §20.54.

77. BDAG, 746.

78. The noun is used to describe the tower of Babel and is associated with the hubris and vaunting reason that stood behind its construction. Hans Wolfgang Heidland, "ὀχύρωμα," in *TDNT,* 5:590–91.

79. BDAG, 598; Carl Schneider, "καθαίρεσις," *TDNT,* 3:412–13.

substance or ability by others.[80] The reference likely points to false reasoning and the unsupportable and sad arrogance that grows out of it.

The verb ἐπαίρω (*epairō*), literally to raise against or "to raise up," found here as a present participle, denotes offering resistance to or opposing someone or something.[81] The imagery is that of ramparts that are raised up to make a stronghold or fortress designed to protect an area from its enemies. In a metaphorical sense, as in this case, these ramparts are the false reasoning or sophistries that Paul's opponents use.

The target of the opposition, Paul makes clear is actually not him but τῆς γνώσεως τοῦ θεοῦ (*tēs gnōseōs tou theou*), "the knowledge of God." The phrase is a pointed reference to a proper understanding, even a testimony, of the gospel and the plan of salvation associated with it. His detractors have come preaching a false gospel that he attacks in order to tear it down.

and bringing into captivity every thought to the obedience of Christ / and we take captive every thought to make it obedient to Christ: Here Paul changes his metaphor from that of destroying to that of taking captives. The verb αἰχμαλωτίζω (*aichmalōtizō*) means "to take captive in war" but also carries the nuance of taking control of someone.[82]

Paul identifies what he intends to take captive with the noun νόημα (*noēma*), "thought, intention," or "mind."[83] In its negative connotation, the word refers to "sinful aspirations to human independence (Rom 1:18–23; 7:23; cf. 2 Tim 3:6) [that] are to be curbed and brought into submission to Christ."[84] To keep with Paul's analogy, we have rendered it as "thought."

Paul's taking the mind captive has its upside. Its objective is to bring it into ὑπακοή (*hypakoē*), "obedience."[85] The noun nuances paying attention to what is taught or ordered with the intent of complying with it.[86] The verb phrase "to make it" is not in the Greek text but it is implied by the construction. The Apostle waits until the next verse to state how he will make others conform, but he does make it clear that the obedience is to Christ, likely referring to the doctrines of the Church as Paul teaches them.

---

80. Louw-Nida, §88.207. The noun also designates the domain of transcendent forces and supernatural powers; BDAG, 1046; Louw-Nida, §12.46. Paul's context, however, points to a more terrestrial setting but keeps the idea of a great strength of power alive.

81. BDAG, 357.

82. Louw-Nida, §§37.29; 55.24.

83. BDAG, 675.

84. Martin, *2 Corinthians*, 488.

85. BDAG, 1028.

86. Louw-Nida, §36.15. The noun connotes the obedience that slaves are to give to their masters. BDAG, 1028.

confidence in false and highly worldly values and precepts. On this basis, they have launched their attack against the Apostle. He, however, refuses to justify himself by countering their major objections to him. In short, in this and the following chapters, we do not find a self-defense. The real debate, as he presents his argument, has nothing to do with him personally. It actually centers on the gospel that Paul has already defined as "the word of the cross" (1 Cor. 1:18, English Standard Version).[97] Thus, he furthers this epistle's intent "to remove obstacles to reconciliation between Paul and his people, and so between the Corinthians and the truth of God."[98]

In his attack, Paul builds on Proverbs 21:22, which defines his offensive. It is one of destruction. And the God-empowered weapons he uses are designed expressly for that purpose. The irony is that these powerful weapons achieve their power through seeming weakness as understood by the paradox of the cross. As Paul has previously shown, the Savior's death via the cross and his subsequent Resurrection have demonstrated, for all to see, that God's weakness is manifestly more powerful than human wisdom (1 Cor. 1:25). His ways cannot be stopped, turned, or frustrated—but they can destroy. Thus Paul discloses the fact behind his imagery: "We demolish sophistries," he declares. In so doing, he reveals that his thrust is at human reckoning that regards walking according to "worldly standards," or more literally "the things of the flesh" (κατὰ σάρκα, *kata sarka*), as the sure means of proper judgment. Paul's point is that the Saints, like himself, are to "walk by faith, not by sight" (5:7; compare 5:12). They are, further, to follow the Apostle in no longer knowing "anyone from a human point of view" (5:16, NR)—that is, by strictly external appearance. But looking strictly at the external is precisely what those who oppose him are doing. Here he forcefully makes known that the goal of his fight is to destroy such false judgments.[99]

In 10:5, the Apostle reveals the nature of his attack. It is to utterly destroy everything that rises up in rebellion against the knowledge of God. The imagery is that of ramparts built to withstand a siege against a stronghold. Having secure battlements was essential to survival during a defensive war. Therefore, these walls were designed to withstand strong opposition and worked very well unless the enemy had overwhelming numbers. Context suggest that the imagery looks to arguments and positions taken by the Apostle's detractors.[100] Paul declares that their position, clearly seen, is

97. Seifrid, *Second Letter*, 380.
98. Witherington, *Conflict and Community*, 438.
99. Seifrid, *Second Letter*, 380–81.
100. Guthrie, *2 Corinthians*, 474.

not an attack on the Apostle himself but rather actual rebellion against a correct understanding of God and his plan of salvation that the Apostle has been commissioned and empowered to proclaim.

The image of strong, high, seemingly impregnable ramparts underscores the strength and might of the God-empowered weapons those with God's authority wield. Paul has already made it clear to the Corinthian Saints that his methods were not those used by even the brightest of men but "the convincing proof of the Spirit and of power" (1 Cor. 2:4, NR). The gospel, as he makes clear, has come via revelation, not through reasoned arguments or philosophical enlightenment. Even so, it is not "an irrational system, but one which is beyond the capacity of reason to discover or to fathom to its depths."[101] The message he proclaims, as he has forcefully testified, is one that came to him directly through divine channels (Gal. 1:11–12), thus bypassing tradition or interpretation. As a result, he possessed a certainty which no demonstration of learning, however cogent, could match.[102]

With the divinely empowered weapons of the convincing proof of the Spirit and the might of God, Paul aims at two objectives. The first is the destruction of incorrect reasoning and calculations—that is, the "sophistries" put forth and strongly defended by the gainsayers in Corinth. The second is the pulling down of everything that has been falsely exalted as a means of protecting those incorrect teachings and the ill position such have forced.

His first objective is then to destroy the promulgation of those ideas based upon the thinking of the Sophist. The noun σοφιστής (*sophistēs*) refers to a class of mostly itinerant intellectuals who set up their practice in various towns in the Greco-Roman world, gathering students by teaching courses in various subjects as a means of making a living.[103] For many, gaining not only wealth but also prestige played an important part in their activities, for it was by this means that they attracted and held students. This objective necessitated becoming exceptionally good not only at self-promotion but also at flattering others. A byproduct of this ability was that they set themselves and their methods up as the standard against which others were to be measured. From them, outward show was everything, and that included strength and attractiveness in physical appearance, a forceful demeanor to cow others and stifle agency, and proper fashion. Many sophists did exhibit great expertise, even cleverness,

101. Bernard, "Second Epistle," 96.
102. Bernard, "Second Epistle," 96.
103. *DAG*, s.v. "σοφιστής."

in the use of oratory and other methods in presenting their credentials and ideas.[104]

Some of the more educated Christians brought these standards into the Church and expected their teachers and leaders to conform. This expectation was the root problem between Paul and some of his opponents. This is because the Apostle promoted a blatant anti-sophist agenda. He refused to flatter people (1 Thes. 2:4-5), he would not accept money for his services (1 Thes. 2:9), he refused to use undue skill as a public speaker, and finally, he strove to show not his own power but that of God (see for example, 1 Cor. 2:1–5). Sophists held that excellence could be granted only by them, while Paul, like Socrates before him, encouraged the Saints to conform to the will of God. Paul certainly and deliberately sought to distance himself from the sophist tradition.[105]

That objective meant that he has to do more than counter their falsehoods; he must also destroy those incorrect notions that supported those falsehoods. In 10:4–5, he symbolizes these as fortresses and, less symbolically, as everything raised up, high, or exalted (ὕψωμα, *hypsōma*) in opposition to the true witness of God.

His second objective, then, is to pull down all that protects those false teachings and the position such had forced certain individuals to take. These incorrect ideas would likely have been either the perversion of gospel truths or an attack on the proclaimer of those truths.[106]

The present chapter strongly evidences Paul's stand. Note particularly that according to 10:10, his antagonists focus on his weak bodily appearance and his poor ability at elocution. Since his letters reveal his skill at using balanced clauses, carefully crafted arguments, and a forceful style, it is unlikely that his language skills were in question. His detractors may have accused him of lacking spiritual power,[107] but the context suggests that what really got them was his refusal to exhibit the compelling eloquence or essential charisma many expected of a public orator.[108] But by his own admission, the Apostle does not use the wisdom of oratory

---

104. For a study, see John Dillon and Tania Gergel, *The Greek Sophists* (London: Penguin Books, 2003).

105. For a study, see Bruce W. Winter, "Is Paul among the Sophists?" *Reformed Theological Review* 53, no. 1 (1994): 28–38.

106. Bruce, *1 and 2 Corinthians,* 230.

107. Barnett, *Second Corinthians,* 462; Hafemann, *2 Corinthians,* 392.

108. Garland, *2 Corinthians,* 446; Winter, *Philo and Paul among the Sophists,* 174, 212; Guthrie, *2 Corinthians,* 471.

because he thinks that the message of the cross should speak for itself rather than words or messages being superimposed onto it (1 Cor. 1:17). Unfortunately, like most prophets of all dispensations, he and his message became unpopular.

His objective is to take every thought captive—not to destroy it but to bring it into obedience to Christ. The purpose of the gospel is not to abolish free thinking but to subject it to proper discipline, which was associated with the Roman military in Paul's time, so that it might come to truth. As Elder McConkie noted, "Thoughts are the material from which belief is built, and to be saved men [and women] must believe and therefore think the right things."[109] That right thinking comes by being obedient to God's will (John 7:17).

In 10:5, the Apostle concludes his siege metaphor by declaring what he will do once he has demolished the towering walls and destroyed the errant thinking they protect. The new objective is to take prisoners. In this case, the prisoners are "every mind" that opposes a true knowledge of God. Against such minds he will mete out punishment so as to destroy "every act of disobedience" to the present leadership. He clearly states that his purpose is not to destroy thinking but to bring it into obedience to the Christ, denoting conformance to the gospel as taught by the Apostle.

As 10:6 shows, Paul stands ready to act as soon as he arrives in Corinth. If he has to do so, he will display for all to see the comprehensive nature of his apostolic authority. But he will not unleash his full authority until certain conditions have been met—namely, that his target audience has obeyed his request that they deal with the troublemakers themselves. The point is that the Apostle will act against the recalcitrant only after the Corinthian leaders and others have brought themselves in line and then tried to do the same with the others and failed. Either through self-discipline or via the heavy use of apostolic authority, hopefully the whole Church will be unified and under apostolic direction.[110]

The Apostle clearly sees that the Corinthian Church is suffering from a very real and grievous battle. It is in the midst of spiritual warfare, an inside attack in some ways far more concerning than the occasional physical and

---

109. *DNTC,* 2:438. Because of the critical place thoughts play in the salvation process, they must be governed. The scriptures counsel "let thy thoughts be directed unto the Lord" (Alma 37:36) and "let virtue garnish thy thoughts unceasingly" (D&C 121:45), because, if improper, "our thoughts will also condemn us" (Alma 12:14).

110. Guthrie, *2 Corinthians,* 476.

social outbreaks that these Saints have had to endure. And why? Because of the Church-destroying nature of the clash. False gospels promulgated by false teachers thrive in the absence of an understanding of true doctrine and accurate teachings as declared and administered by proper authority. The Apostle clearly understands what is at stake for the nascent Church as he fights for its very existence.[111]

Paul's Threat to His Detractors (10:7–11)

Greek Text

7 Τὰ κατὰ πρόσωπον βλέπετε. εἴ τις πέποιθεν ἑαυτῷ Χριστοῦ εἶναι, τοῦτο
λογιζέσθω πάλιν ἐφ᾽ ἑαυτοῦ ὅτι καθὼς αὐτὸς Χριστοῦ οὕτως καὶ ἡμεῖς. 8 ἐάν τε
γὰρ περισσότερόν τι καυχήσωμαι περὶ τῆς ἐξουσίας ἡμῶν, ἧς ἔδωκεν ὁ κύριος εἰς
οἰκοδομὴν καὶ οὐκ εἰς καθαίρεσιν ὑμῶν, οὐκ αἰσχυνθήσομαι, 9 ἵνα μὴ δόξω ὡς
ἂν ἐκφοβεῖν ὑμᾶς διὰ τῶν ἐπιστολῶν·10 ὅτι Αἱ ἐπιστολαὶ μέν, φησίν, βαρεῖαι καὶ
ἰσχυραί, ἡ δὲ παρουσία τοῦ σώματος ἀσθενὴς καὶ ὁ λόγος ἐξουθενημένος. 11 τοῦτο
λογιζέσθω ὁ τοιοῦτος, ὅτι οἷοί ἐσμεν τῷ λόγῳ δι᾽ ἐπιστολῶν ἀπόντες, τοιοῦτοι καὶ
παρόντες τῷ ἔργῳ. [SBLGNT]

King James Version

7 Do ye look on things after the outward appearance? If any man trust to himself that he is Christ's, let him of himself think this again, that, as he is Christ's, even so are we Christ's. 8 For though I should boast somewhat more of our authority, which the Lord hath given us for edification, and not for your destruction, I should not be ashamed: 9 That I may not seem as if I would terrify you by letters. 10 For his letters, say they, are weighty and powerful; but his bodily presence is weak, and his speech contemptible. 11 Let such an one think this, that, such as we are in word by letters

New Rendition

7 Look at what is before your eyes! If anyone is convinced in his own mind that he belongs to Christ, he should ponder again concerning himself that just as he belongs to Christ, so do we also. 8 For if I do boast a little too much concerning our authority that the Lord gave us for building you up, not for tearing you down, I will not be ashamed of it 9 so that I will not appear to be frightening you with my letters. 10 Because some say, "His letters are weighty and forceful, but when he is here in person, he appears weak and his speech is of no account"— 11 such a person

111. Guthrie, *2 Corinthians,* 477.

when we are absent, such will we be also in deed when we are present.

should consider that just as we are in word through our letters when we are not present, so we will also be in our actions when we are present.

Translation Notes and Comments

10:7 ***Do ye look on things after the outward appearance? / Look at what is before your eyes!*** The KJV treats this phrase as a question rather than as a command, contrary to our Rendition. The reason for the difference is that in the second-person plural present tense of the verb βλέπω (*blepō*), "to see, look," as here, the indicative and imperative have the same form, so Paul's intended meaning could be either. Given the context, however, we have opted for the imperative as the more likely.[112]

Paul's focus here is on the πρόσωπον (*prosōpon*), literally "face" but symbolically "outer appearance"[113]—that is, what is before one's eyes and therefore evident.[114] With this phrase, Paul pushes the idea that if the Christians will just look at the evidence, they will see that it validates his apostleship.

If any man trust to himself that he is Christ's / If anyone is convinced in his own mind that he belongs to Christ: The conjunction εἰ (*ei*), "if," marks a direct question but indicates that "an actual case is taken as a supposition"[115] and is used here by Paul to make his audience rethink their ideas or positions.

The pronoun τις (*tis*), "anyone,"[116] has an indefinite referent, and therefore it could denote a specific person, but the context suggests it is notational and thus includes all whom Paul addresses, more particularly his antagonists.[117]

The verb πείθω (*peithō*), "to be convinced," found here in the perfect tense since the perfect tense of verbs of knowing are usually translated in the present tense, denotes an abiding deep trust, even certainty in a matter.[118]

The reflexive pronoun ἑαυτός (*heautos*), found here in the dative case with the sense "to/for himself," we have rendered "in his own mind" to

---

112. The NET and NIV treat it as a statement but with a footnote that it could also be imperative; The RSV treats is as an imperative. For discussion, see Barnett, *Second Epistle,* 469–70.

113. Louw-Nida, §§8.18; 24.24; 31.31.

114. Garland, *2 Corinthians,* 440; Barnett, *Second Epistle,* 469.

115. BDAG, 277–79.

116. Louw-Nida, §92.12

117. Barnett, *Second Epistle,* 469 with n. 6.

118. BDAG, 791–92; Louw-Nida, §31.82.

better convey the sense of the Greek.[119] Thus, such a person's confidence comes not through confirmation of the Spirit but is self-generated.[120]

The infinitive phrase Χριστοῦ εἶναι (*Xristou einai*), literally "to be Christ's," denotes a special relationship between subject and object;[121] thus it means "to belong to Christ" in the sense of being fully accepted by him. One's position on this state is critical to what is happening in Corinth. The issue under debate is who actually belongs to Christ—that is, who is the true Christian and therefore is accepted by the Lord and should, because of that relationship, be accepted by the community of Saints?

let him of himself think this again / he should ponder again concerning himself: The verb λογίζομαι (*logizomai*), found here as a third-person singular imperative, commands that careful attention be given to a matter and therefore means "to consider," "count out," or "ponder" a point."[122]

The preposition ἐπί (*epi*) acts as a marker of perspective, meaning "in regard to, concerning," and the object of the preposition, ἑαυτοῦ (*heautou*), refers to "himself."[123] Thus we have translated ἐφ' ἑαυτοῦ (*eph' heautou*) literally as "concerning himself."

The adverb πάλιν (*palin*), "again," asks for a repetition of what has been done before, in this case to carefully rethink the matter at hand.

that, as he is Christ's, even so are we Christ's / that just as he belongs to Christ, so do we also: The conjunction καθώς (*kathōs*), "just as," dictates that a comparison is being made.

The genitive case of the noun Χριστοῦ (*Christou*), "Christ," indicates possession. To belong to Christ means to be fully his—that is, to accept him and to be accepted by him. The phrase shows that Paul is willing to give his adversaries some credit for being Christians on the same level that he is. The underlying point is that they should also give him the same credit as he does them.[124]

10:8 ***For though I should boast somewhat more of our authority / For if I do boast a little too much concerning our authority:*** The conjunction γάρ (*gar*), "for," indicates Paul's reason why he is not ashamed to boast.[125]

---

119. BDAG, 268–69.
120. Seifred, *Second Letter,* 386–87.
121. BDAG, 282–86.
122. BDAG, 597–98.
123. BDAG, 363–67.
124. Barnett, *Second Epistle,* 471.
125. BDAG, 189–90.

In classical Greek, the verb καυχάομαι (*kauchaomai*), "to boast,"[126] carried the negative connotation of exhibiting pridefulness and vainglory, but the Greeks did allow people to have some pride in themselves without this pejorative connotation. In New Testament times, the verb continued to carry a general negative nuance, but it was somewhat mollified by the word's use in the LXX and other Jewish writings, where it denoted an attitude of trust in a person or idea, especially in Jehovah and his ways.[127] By extension, the verb gained the sense of rejoicing and even exalting in someone or something. For a more detailed study, see "Excurses on Self-Praise and Boasting" below.

Within the New Testament, Paul is almost the only writer who uses this word.[128] His position is that his boasting is good because it centers in Christ. Indeed, from the Apostle's point of view, faith in the Lord is a surrender of all self-glorying, making self-praise impossible. This condition also permits Paul's apostolic self-boasting because it pertains to his Christ-given power and authority (ἐξουσία, *exousia*) and what he is able to do through them.[129] The point he stresses is that his boasting does not come from his own efforts but from doing the work of God. Indeed, the success of his work as an expression of his authentic authority is an objective, undeniable fact that he can clearly boast about. In short, Paul's boasting comes from the work that he does for the Lord. As a result, his boasting is in what Christ does and not in what he himself does. By using this forceful means of persuasion, the Apostle is able to somewhat blunt the attacks on his authority.[130]

The nominalized comparative adjective περισσότερος (*perissoteros*) combined with the neuter indefinite pronoun τι (*ti*), literally "something more," has here the sense of "a little too much" and therefore what is excessive.[131]

Though the noun (ἐξουσία, *exousia*), "authority,"[132] in its broadest definition denotes the ability or power to perform an act,[133] it carries heavy overtones of the right to rule, control, or govern as well as the power to

126. Louw-Nida, §33.368.

127. The translators of the LXX used καυχάομαι (*kauchaomai*) to interpret the Hebrew הָלַל (*hālal*) "to praise." BDB, 237–39. For a study, see *NID*, 2:651–55. Compare Louw-Nida, §§25.203, 204; 33.371, 372; and MM, 339.

128. Besides Paul's writings, it is found only in James 3:5; 4:16.

129. Garland, *2 Corinthians*, 442–43.

130. Garland, *2 Corinthians*, 454–55. For a study, see Rudolph Bultmann, "καυχάομαι, καύχημα, καύχησις," in *TDNT*, 3:645–54.

131. BDAG, 805–6.

132. BDAG, 352–53; MM, 225.

133. Louw-Nida, §76.12.

of the group.[149] Others, however, see both the verb and the demonstrative pronoun of the next verse as simply generic.[150]

are weighty and powerful / "His letters are weighty and forceful: With this phrase, we see clearly the scathing charges Paul's enemies make against him. This faction refers to his "letters," the noun ἐπιστολή (*episotlē*) found here as a plural. This suggests that Paul's detractors may have included more than his "sorrowful letter" as the point of their accusations.

On the surface, his critics' description of his letters could be taken as positive. The adjective βαρύς (*barys*), "weighty,"[151] can indicate something of unusual importance or significance. However, it carries the nuance of what is troubling because of the demands it makes. Thus, other translations would be "burdensome, severe, cruel,"[152] and this seems to be the spin here.

The adjective ἰσυχρός (*ischyros*), "strong,"[153] also denotes that which is highly impressive—thus, "powerful, intense"[154]—but here carries the more negative inference of "haughty" (a corollary to 10:1, where this charge is made against him personally). Thus, what might be considered praise is actually biting sarcasm.[155]

but his bodily presence is weak / but when he is here in person, he appears weak: The phrase παρουσία τοῦ σώματος ἀσθενής (*parousia tou sōmatos asthenēs*) means literally "[his] bodily presence is weak"—that is, "when he is present in person, he appears to be weak."[156] The adjective ἀσθενής (*asthenēs*), "weak," denotes some incapacity that prevents one from doing a given task[157] but here suggests being unimpressive.[158]

and his speech contemptible / and his speech is of no account: The noun λόγος (*logos*) refers to speech proper,[159] but, in the current context, it points to oratorical ability.[160] The verb ἐξουθενέω (*exoutheneō*), found here

149. Martin, *2 Corinthians,* 494.

150. Harris, *Second Epistle,* 665–66 n. i, 698. Most translators also treat these as generic, for example, KJV, NIV, New English Translation, and Revised Standard Version.

151. BDAG, 167.

152. Louw-Nida, §§20.7; 22.30; 86.1.

153. BDAG, 483–84.

154. Louw-Nida, §§76.11; 78.16.

155. Barnett, *Second Epistle,* 476.

156. BDAG, 780–81.

157. Louw-Nida, §§74.25; 79.69

158. BDAG, 142–43.

159. Louw-Nida, §33.99.

160. BDAG, 598–601.

as a perfect passive participle, means to be "of no account" or "amounts to nothing."[161]

10:11 ***Let such an one think this / such a person should consider:*** The demonstrative adjective τοιοῦτος (*toioutos*), "such a one,"[162] preceded by a definite article, as here, can refer to either a definite individual with special characteristics or to any bearer of certain definite qualities.[163] As noted above in the comments to the preceding verse, it is more likely that Paul is using it in the latter sense.

The verb λογίζομαι (*logizomai*), "to ponder, count out or consider,"[164] found here as a present imperative, denotes the need to give careful thought to a matter. Paul's use of the verb should force his assailant(s) to take Paul's coming threat seriously.

such as we are in word by letters when we are absent, such will we be also in deed when we are present / that just as we are in word through our letters when we are not present, so we will also be in our actions when we are present: The relative pronoun οἷος (*hoios*) means "such as, of what kind, as, that."[165] It is here used with its correlative compliment τοιοῦτος (*toioutos*) in the second half of this verse, producing the sense "just as . . . so also."[166] Paul assures his readers that when he arrives, he will back up his words with actions, contrary to his accusers' claim that he comes across as "weighty and forceful" in his letters but "appears weak" in person.

Though likely referring only to himself, Paul possibly uses the plural "we" to emphasize the fact that he does not stand alone in his position toward these people. The articular nouns τῷ λόγῳ (*tō logō*), "by word," and τῷ ἔργῳ (*tō ergō*), "by deed," are both instrumental datives indicating means by which an action is carried out.[167]

Analysis and Summary

This section of the Apostle's argument breaks up easily into four primary thoughts, but it takes some unpacking to piece together his logic as he moves from one point to the next. The first point (10:7a) demands that his

161. BDAG, 352; Louw-Nida, §88.195.
162. Louw-Nida, §64.2.
163. BDAG, 1009–10.
164. BDAG, 597–98.
165. *DAG*, s.v. "οἷος"; BDAG, 701.
166. *DAG*, s.v. "τοιοῦτος"; BDAG, 1009–10.
167. Smyth, *Greek Grammar*, §1503.

readers accept what is clearly before their eyes. The second (10:7b) calls for the Apostle's antagonists to consider Paul's relationship to the Savior in a more accurate way. The third (10:8) declares that he will not be ashamed of boasting in the exercise of his apostolic authority in relation to the Corinthian Saints, even if it seems overbearing to some. The fourth (10:11) mirrors the same language as in 10:7, affirming that his actions when he comes among them will match the power and severity of his letters unless conditions dictate otherwise. With the repetition of the verb "ponder" in 10:7 and 10:11, Paul uses what is called an *inclusio,* or bracketed structure, to tie this subsection of chapter 10 together. All four parts affirm one idea: the reality of Paul's apostolic authority.[168]

With 10:7, Paul shifts his argument from his determination to bring all to Christ to a defense of his authority to do so. Though he addresses his argument against "a certain one," the context suggests he is actually referring to a group. These could be either those who compose the local opposition or the interlopers who have come from outside the area. His detractors accuse him of not being a Spirit-empowered minister, insisting, rather, that he is a mere man working in human ways. The difficulty in being precise with just who these people are is that "Paul portrays [them] in terms of what they question in him [10:2, 4], rather than what they claim for themselves or even what he sees them to be. Their primary criticism appears to be in the area of disciplining moral offenders when present face to face (10:1–2; 12:21; 13:2a) [and then writing a scalding letter when absent]. They appear to doubt that Paul will achieve any better result when he makes yet another visit to them (10:2; 12:20) since they question whether Christ is 'speaking through' Paul (13:4)."[169] All this suggests that they could be the local critics. Even so, the possibility that they are the interlopers cannot be ruled out. The text shows that these people had convinced many that they have the right to direct the local Church, based on their presumptive claim that they work by and under Christ's authority. This position fits well with both the flow of the argument and the general theme of the epistle as a whole.[170]

Whichever group this is, it is clear that they have claimed that Paul is not truly "of Christ." The meaning of the phrase is important. It appears to be a

168. Guthrie, *2 Corinthians,* 477–78.

169. Barnett, *Second Epistle,* 471 n. 20.

170. Guthrie, *2 Corinthians,* 478.

catchphrase bantered about by this segment of the Christian community in Corinth who claim special relationship to the Lord. Their stance is clearly that they have either a special relationship with or authority from Jesus.[171]

As he makes his defense, Paul likely does not accept their position, but neither does he deny it. He does, however, insist that they accept his. As if speaking to a "certain one," Paul asks "him" to consider this idea: If he, *within himself,* is confident that he is Christ's, then, on that same basis, so too is Paul, for he considers himself such. In short, as the Apostle accepts that (notational) person's standing with Christ on the basis of that person's belief, so also that person should extend that same recognition to the Apostle on the basis of Paul's belief.[172] Fair is fair.

The Apostle, however, adds yet another reason why he should be accepted as a fellow faithful Saint and empowered Christian leader, which all these people should clearly see if they will but open their eyes: the obvious and undeniable success of the Church, which he himself—albeit through the power of his legitimate apostolic authority—has organized, taught, and led. That alone, he insists, should prove that he does not, as some maintain, walk in worldly ways but uses the power of Christ to build his Church and effect positive change in the lives of the Saints.[173] In this defense, we see the real issue. Whichever party is attacking Paul, they are putting him in a position where he has to defend not his relationship with Christ but his apostolic authority.[174]

It is evident that Paul's greatest fear is that his work in Corinth will come to naught if his competitors win the battle for the Saints' allegiance. "At risk is not only Paul's apostolic credibility but his entire Gentile mission in the Aegean region, with its headquarters at Corinth. If this church is lost to him, his entire work is in jeopardy—as is his prospect for a future mission in the west (Rome, Spain), to say nothing of his task to get the [Gentile] collection to Jerusalem."[175]

---

171. The phrase could refer to one of three groups: Christians in general, one who has been authorized directly by the Lord, or one was authorized through his representatives. See Furnish, *II Corinthians,* 476. The context suggests that the best reference is to those who live in such a way that they have access to the Lord's spirit. See Barnett, *Second Epistle,* 470 nn. 18, 19.

172. Barnett, *Second Epistle,* 471.

173. Barnett, *Second Epistle,* 471–72.

174. Guthrie, *2 Corinthians,* 477–78.

175. Martin, *2 Corinthians,* 492.

were stern, boastful, imperious, and uncompromisingly bold, even widely reckless. Thus their statement was nothing short of damning sarcasm.[186]

His adversaries did not stop there. They went on to contrast the (in their view) extreme boldness of his letters with his personal appearance when he was among them, which they branded as "weak." This pejorative word generally refers to being sickly or infirm, and this element is likely at play here.[187] Absorbing the tenants of the predominate, Hellenistic culture of being well-rounded in every way, including possessing an ideal physical body, some of the Saints bought in to the idea of physiognomy, a belief system that centered on the idea that an individual's character could be judged based upon his or her grace of movement and outward comeliness. Further, "it is likely that the Corinthians were generally influenced by the traditional Greek veneration of gods and heroes, as portrayed by statues emphasizing physical perfection and power."[188] For an orator to be accepted, society insisted that excellence in rhetoric skill had to be balanced with an ideal, physical presence. The orator needed "both the power of his voice and an imposing bearing," thus displaying the characteristic of Latin *gravitas* in the Roman world, to be considered worthy of consideration.[189] In his opponents' view, because Paul lacked both, they concluded, and tried to persuade others, that he was not a true Apostle but rather a fraud (*gons,* "a trickster").[190]

Against such physical perfectionism, Paul could not compete.[191] Further, as will be explored in the next chapter, Paul suffered from what he called

186. Barnett, *Second Epistle,* 476.

187. Jacob Jervell, "The Signs of an Apostle: Paul's Miracles," trans. Roy A. Harrisville, in *The Unknown Paul: Essays on Luke–Acts and Early Christian History* (Minneapolis: Augsburg Publishing, 1984), 94, argues, with others, that it was the position of Paul's detractors that a weak charismatic and a person of divine power was a contradiction in terms.

188. Barnett, *Second Epistle,* 476 n. 47.

189. Barnett, *Second Epistle,* 477 n. 49.

190. Martin, *2 Corinthians,* 494–95.

191. The Latin name "Paulus," by which the Apostle went while in Gentile territory, may give insight on this issue. It was never used by the Romans as a praenomen (that is, a name chosen by parents for a child). BDAG, 789–90. Rather, it was a surname or nickname attached to or by a family. The name means "little," likely referring to one who was short in stature. For a general study, see Christopher Forbes, "Comparison, Self-Praise, and Irony: Paul's Boasting and the Conventions of Hellenistic Rhetoric," *New Testament Studies* 32, no 1 (1986): 1–30. A second-century Christian work, entitled *The Acts of Paul and Thecla,* if it preserves an authentic memory, may contribute. It describes the Apostle as a man of modest height, balding, with bowlegs and protruding knees. His nose was rather long, his eyes dark and his eyebrows touching in the middle. For a

"a thorn in the flesh," which seems to have been a very visible chronic condition that continually sucked energy from him and hampered his work.

The word, however, allows for another aspect to be at play. This pertains to Paul's demeanor. His detractors are likely pointing at the humble, modest, and unpretentious deportment that he exhibited while with them. Indeed, they insist, he lacks the real elements of one who was supposedly filled with the spirit, governing capability (10:8), and "oratorical skill" (10:10). Above all, they say that he lacks "divine power," which was defined as "a dynamic and impressive force to convey powerfully the triumph and effectiveness of his message."[192] As proof of the rightness of their position, they emphasize Paul's total lack of eloquence in putting forth his cause. His presentations, they state, are meritless, being contemptable and worthy of disdain (10:10).[193]

Paul's defense rests upon what these people refuse to see but which is plain to all who will look. Though his recent visit, according to his enemies, revealed his ineffectiveness, they should not overlook the fact that he still retains the loyalty of the majority of the Saints in most of the house churches, even if they could have been more demonstrative in supporting him (2:6; 6:11–13; 7:12).[194]

His defense further rests upon his skillful handling of his detractors' insistence that he fell flat in both appearance and oratorical skill. He begins by insisting that he has been misread on both accounts. Concerning his letters, he assures his readers, he never designed them as tools of terror but rather as a means to highlight the role that God had given him. His point in writing was to clearly explain the nature of his God-given ministry to these

---

translation of this work, see *The Acts of Paul and Thecla,* New Advent, accessed March 9, 2021, https://www.newadvent.org/fathers/0816.htm. Joseph Smith described Paul as "about five foot high; very dark hair; dark complexion; dark skin; large Roman nose; sharp face; small black eyes, penetrating as eternity; round shoulders; a whining voice, except when elevated and then it almost resembles the roaring of a Lion." It is likely he drew on the *Acts of Paul* for this description. For discussion, see Thomas A. Wayment, "Joseph Smith's Description of Paul the Apostle," *Mormon Historical Studies* 13, no. 1–2 (Spring/Fall 2012): 39–53, accessed March 9, 2021, https://ensignpeakfoundation.org/wp-content/uploads/2013/07/Joseph-Smith's-Description-of-Paul-the-Apostle.pdf, quoting Andrew F. Ehat and Lyndon W. Cook, comp. and eds., *The Words of Joseph Smith* (Provo, Utah: Grandin Book, 1991), 59, reported by William Clayton, bolding removed.

192. Martin, *2 Corinthians,* 495.

193. Guthrie, *2 Corinthians,* 482–83. The accusation may have been based on the Sophists/philosopher debate that maintained that a sophist was a trickster who made his living though deception while a philosopher sought only for truth.

194. Barnett, *Second Epistle,* 477–78.

Saints. Concerning his deportment while among them, he insists that it should not be seen as a manifestation of either bodily weakness or a lack of character or presiding authority. In fact, he states, his actions mirror the true nature of Christ (10:1)—who is consistent yet was misunderstood—and, by extension, the true nature of apostolic ministry.[195]

In sum, his critics have greatly underestimated his authority. He will, he assures his readers, correct this misperception upon his arrival when his actions will manifest his full apostolic power. Indeed, his enemies, who have described his letters as "terrifying," will find that the word fully matches his actions once he arrives.[196]

Paul's Mission (10:12–18)

Greek Text

12 Οὐ γὰρ τολμῶμεν ἐγκρῖναι ἢ συγκρῖναι ἑαυτούς τισιν τῶν ἑαυτοὺς συνιστανόν-
των· ἀλλὰ αὐτοὶ ἐν ἑαυτοῖς ἑαυτοὺς μετροῦντες καὶ συγκρίνοντες ἑαυτοὺς ἑαυτοῖς
οὐ συνιᾶσιν. 13 ἡμεῖς δὲ οὐκ εἰς τὰ ἄμετρα καυχησόμεθα, ἀλλὰ κατὰ τὸ μέτρον τοῦ
κανόνος οὗ ἐμέρισεν ἡμῖν ὁ θεὸς μέτρου, ἐφικέσθαι ἄχρι καὶ ὑμῶν— 14 οὐ γὰρ ὡς
μὴ ἐφικνούμενοι εἰς ὑμᾶς ὑπερεκτείνομεν ἑαυτούς, ἄχρι γὰρ καὶ ὑμῶν ἐφθάσαμεν
ἐν τῷ εὐαγγελίῳ τοῦ Χριστοῦ— 15 οὐκ εἰς τὰ ἄμετρα καυχώμενοι ἐν ἀλλοτρίοις
κόποις, ἐλπίδα δὲ ἔχοντες αὐξανομένης τῆς πίστεως ὑμῶν ἐν ὑμῖν μεγαλυνθῆ-
ναι κατὰ τὸν κανόνα ἡμῶν εἰς περισσείαν, 16 εἰς τὰ ὑπερέκεινα ὑμῶν εὐαγγελίσα-
σθαι, οὐκ ἐν ἀλλοτρίῳ κανόνι εἰς τὰ ἕτοιμα καυχήσασθαι. 17 Ὁ δὲ καυχώμενος ἐν
κυρίῳ καυχάσθω· 18 οὐ γὰρ ὁ ἑαυτὸν συνιστάνων, ἐκεῖνός ἐστιν δόκιμος, ἀλλὰ ὃν
ὁ κύριος συνίστησιν. [SBLGNT]

King James Version

12 For we dare not make ourselves of the number, or compare ourselves with some that commend themselves: but they measuring themselves by themselves, and comparing themselves among themselves, are not wise. 13 But

New Rendition

12 For we do not presume to classify or compare ourselves with some who commend themselves. But when they measure themselves by one another and commend themselves with one another, they lack understanding. 13 However,

195. Guthrie, *2 Corinthians,* 484.

196. Anderson, *Understanding Paul,* 141, notes that apostolic power includes the right to excommunicate any transgressor.

we will not boast of things without our
measure, but according to the measure
of the rule which God hath distributed
to us, a measure to reach even unto you.
14 For we stretch not ourselves beyond
our measure, as though we reached not
unto you: for we are come as far as to you
also in preaching the gospel of Christ:
15 Not boasting of things without our
measure, that is, of other men's labours;
but having hope, when your faith is
increased, that we shall be enlarged by
you according to our rule abundantly,
16 To preach the gospel in the regions
beyond you, and not to boast in another
man's line of things made ready to our
hand. 17 But he that glorieth, let him
glory in the Lord. 18 For not he that
commendeth himself is approved, but
whom the Lord commendeth.

we will not boast beyond proper lim-
its but according to the limits of the
assigned area that God has given us to
reach even to you. 14 For we are not
overextending ourselves as if we did
not reach to you, for we were the first
to come to you with the gospel of Christ.
15 We do not boast beyond proper limits
in the labors of others, but we have the
hope that as your faith continues to grow
that, with your help, our assigned area
will be greatly enlarged 16 to preach the
gospel in lands that lie beyond you with-
out boasting about work already done in
someone else's assigned area. 17 Rather,
let one who boasts, boast in the Lord,
18 for it is not the one who commends
himself that is approved but the one
whom the Lord commends.

Translation Notes and Comments

10:12 *For we dare not / For we do not presume:* At this point, the Apostle begins a clarification of the issue at hand, as signaled by his use of the conjunction γάρ (*gar*), "for,"[197] at the beginning of this pericope.

The verb τομάω (*tolmaō*) has the basic sense of showing "boldness or resolution in the face of danger" or opposition but, in the present context, means "to presume,"[198] in the sense of assuming something with confidence.

make ourselves of the number or compare ourselves with some that commend themselves / to classify or compare ourselves with some who commend themselves: Here Paul engages in wordplay through his choice of verbs. The verb ἐγκρίνω (*enkrinō*), "to classify," means "to make a judgment about something, and classify it in a specific group,"[199] while the verb συγκρίνω (*synkrinō*), "to compare," denotes "drawing a conclusion based on comparison."[200] Both verbs share the same root, κρίνω (*krinō*), "to make a selection, judge,"[201]

197. BDAG, 189–90.
198. BDAG, 1010.
199. BDAG, 274.
200. BDAG, 953.
201. BDAG, 567–69.

modified by the prefixes ἐν- (*en-*), "in,"[202] and συν- (*syn-*), "with,"[203] respectively. The doubling of the same idea stresses Paul's disapproval of such behavior.

With his use of the indefinite pronoun τὶς (*tis*), "someone,"[204] found here as a plural and, thus, "some" or "some people," Paul no longer singles out an individual (if he ever did) as the object of his remarks but looks at a specific group. These appear to be the interlopers who have entered Corinth. They have come with impressive credentials that have convinced some of the Saints to follow them and turn against Paul.[205]

The verb συνίστημι (*synistēmi*), "to commend," denotes the public approval of persons with the implication that others adopt their ways due to their merits.[206] Together with the plural pronoun ἑαυτούς (*heautous*), "themselves," the idea is "self-commendation."[207] Thus Paul returns to the issue of what legitimizes a person within a community. The act of self-promotion, as noted in 3:1, was generally viewed negatively,[208] and Paul is playing on this idea as he battles with the interlopers.[209]

but they measuring themselves by themselves, and comparing themselves among themselves / But when they measure themselves by one another and commend themselves with one another: The conjunction ἀλλά (*alla*), "but,"[210] has a strong adversative sense and is important here because it draws negative attention to a situation and begs for additional consideration.[211]

The verb μετρέω (*metreō*), "to measure,"[212] found here as a plural participle, denotes the process of evaluating something. The plural pronoun ἑαυτούς (*heautous*), "themselves," shows that this group is the object of its own evaluation. For the sake of flow, we have rendered the participle as a finite verb.

---

202. Smyth, *Greek Grammar,* §1687.2.

203. Smyth, *Greek Grammar,* §1696.2.

204. Louw-Nida, §92.12.

205. See the introduction to this chapter and Barnett, *Second Epistle,* 452–54, 480–81.

206. Louw-Nida, §33.344. For a study, see Wilhelm Kasch, "συνίστημι," in *TDNT,* 7:896–98.

207. BDAG, 972–73. This suggests the issue's importance to the Apostle—even though the verb is found sixteen times in the New Testament, in Paul's writings it is found thirteen times with nine of them in this epistle (3:1, 4:2; 5:12; 6:4; 7:11;10:12, 10:18, twice; 12:11).

208. BDAG, 972–73.

209. Barnett, *Second Epistle,* 482 with n. 14.

210. Louw-Nida, §§89.125; 91.11.

211. BDAG, 44–45.

212. BDAG, 643.

For συνίστημι (*synistēmi*), "to commend," with the plural pronoun ἑαυτούς (*eautous*), "themselves," see above.

are not wise / they lack understanding: The verb συνίημι (*syniēmi*), "to understand," denotes the ability to evaluate a situation or condition and thereby gain insight into it.[213] The negative particle, οὐ (*ou*), "not," negates that meaning.[214] In this case, the phrase points to the incapacity of Paul's detractors, and likely those who have been won over by them, to see the flaw in how they draw their conclusions about themselves and Paul. His words show that he is less concerned about his detractors' false judgments than he is about the false reasoning that stands behind and propels those judgments.[215] It is this reasoning that needs the most serious attention and correcting.

10:13 ***But we will not boast of things without our measure / However, we will not boast beyond proper limits:*** With the use of the conjunction δέ (*de*) serving as a marker of contrast,[216] thus, "however," Paul further separates his actions from those of his detractors. The adjective ἄμετρος (*ametros*) means "immeasurable"[217] and, with the verb καύχομαι (*kauchaomai*), "to boast,"[218] denotes "boasting illimitably."[219] The phrase is an oblique knock at the self-promoting activities of Paul's enemies.

but according to the measure of the rule which God hath distributed to us / but according to the limits of the assigned area that God has given us: The conjunction ἀλλά (*alla*), "but," here denotes a strong alternative[220] and further separates Paul's actions from those of his enemies.

The noun μέτρον (*metron*), "measure," denotes quantity but here specifies "limits."[221]

Though the noun κανών (*kanōn*) usually refers to a straight rod used for measuring, its extended meanings include "rule, standard," as well as "assignment or formulation for public service."[222] It is in this latter sense

---

213. Louw-Nida, §32.26; BDAG, 972.

214. BDAG, 733–34.

215. Seifred, *Second Letter,* 396.

216. BDAG, 213.

217. BDAG, 53.

218. Louw-Nida, §33.368; BDAG, 536.

219. Louw-Nida, §78.27; BDAG, 53. The phrase τὰ ἄμετρα (*ta ametra*) limits any boasting beyond any unmeasured way. Martin, *2 Corinthians,* 503. See also Moule, *Idiom Book,* 71.

220. BDAG, 44–45.

221. BDAG, 644.

222. BDAG, 507–8. The noun is the basis for the English word "canon" and carries the idea of "a measured length and denotes distance in a linear way. But it also tends

that Paul uses the word, thus referring to the breadth of his assignment or calling as a missionary to the Gentiles, which includes both the breadth of the ministering service and the geographical area.[223] For this reason, we have translated the noun as "assigned area" in our Rendition.

The verb μερίζω (*merizō*), "to divide,"[224] found here in the aorist tense, in the present context means "to assign, apportion," certain responsibilities,[225] and refers to the area of Paul's responsibilities as indicated by the preceding relative pronoun οὗ (*hou*), "which, that."[226]

a measure to reach even unto you / to reach even to you: The verb ἐφικνέομαι (*ephikneomai*), found here as an aorist infinitive, means "come to, reach,"[227] and carries the idea of extent and result.[228] The preposition ἄχρι (*achri*), "as far as," denotes limitation.[229] The adverb καί (*kai*), "even,"[230] is emphatic, stressing the comparative and broad reach of Paul's jurisdiction and therefore the area in which he can have a certain proper pride. Putting the phrase together, Paul's point is that his God-given authority results in and even extends to the Corinthian branches, and therefore he can boast about them without it being improper.

10:14–16: These verses constitute one sentence in the Greek text, and in it, Paul uses linked verbs in the form of participles instead of finite verbs.[231] These present some translation challenges because when rendered literally, they make for neither smooth transitions nor easy comprehension.[232] To render Paul's thinking into flowing English requires breaking the long sentence into shorter ones and, in some cases, adding additional words to a Greek word or phrase.

---

to include the area thus measured: hence it means territory as well as boundary limit." Martin, *2 Corinthians,* 504. The word also denotes "a measured area or a limited domain of service." The idea of "jurisdiction" also works. See Witherington, *Conflict and Community,* 440 n. 46; and MM, 320–21.

223. BDAG, 508.

224. Louw-Nida, §63.23.

225. Louw-Nida, §37.100.

226. Louw-Nida, §92.27.

227. BDAG, 418.

228. BDF, §391.4.

229. BDAG, 160–61.

230. Louw-Nida, §89.93.

231. Though the Society of Biblical Literature Greek New Testament breaks these verses into two sentences, Nestle and others, *Novum Testamentum Graece: Nestle-Aland,* 28th ed., more accurately shows them to be one sentence.

232. Martin, *2 Corinthians,* 506.

10:14 ***For we stretch not ourselves beyond our measure / For we are not overextending ourselves:*** Due to the Apostle's vague diction in the fore part of this sentence, as the rather extensive translation notes that follow indicate, his point takes a bit of unpacking to become clear.

Paul begins this sentence with the negative particle οὐ (*ou*), "not," which modifies the verb ὑπερεκτείνω (*hyperekteinō*), meaning "to stretch out beyond, overextend,"[233] and also stresses the negation of the verb. The explanatory conjunction γάρ (*gar*), "for,"[234] acts here as a marker of clarification, signaling that Paul will now explain why he has not overextended himself.

as though we reached not unto you / as if we did not reach to you: In the Greek text, this clause stands between the first explanatory phrase that introduces the sentence, οὐ γάρ (*ou gar*), "for we are not," and the verb ὑπερεκτείνω (*hyperkteinō*), "go beyond, overextend." In this clause, the subordinate conjunction *hos*, "as," acts as an analogous comparison,[235] and the verb ἐφικνέομαι (*ephikeneomai*), as noted above, means "to come to, reach."[236] Its form here is a present plural masculine participle with the understood subject being "we." The negative particle μή (*mē*), "not," acts to negate any idea that Paul is overreaching. Though the clause reads literally "as not reaching to you," what Paul is saying is that he would be overextending himself only if his ministry did not extend as far as Corinth, but since it does, any claim that he is overreaching is incorrect.[237]

for we are come as far as to you also in preaching the gospel of Christ / for we were the first to come to you with the gospel of Christ: Again, the use of the explanatory conjunction γάρ (*gar*), "for," signals the reader that Paul is clarifying why he is not overreaching. The verb φθάνω (*phthanō*), "to come before, proceed,"[238] found here in the aorist tense, carries the idea of arriving at a place before others[239] and thus is translated as "were the first to come" in our Rendition. For the phrase "the gospel of Christ," see Translation Notes for 4:3–4. Here we have an objective genitive showing that the "gospel," or "good news," is about Christ, suggesting his work as a savior.[240]

---

233. BDAG, 1033.

234. BDAG, 189–90.

235. BDAG, 1103–6; Guthrie, *Second Corinthians,* 493.

236. BDAG, 418.

237. Barnett, *Second Epistle,* 487; Guthrie, *2 Corinthians,* 493.

238. BDAG, 1053.

239. Louw-Nida, §15.141.

240. Barnett, *Second Epistle,* 488 n. 41.

10:15 *Not boasting of things without our measure, that is, of other men's labours / We do not boast beyond proper limits in the labors of others:* This phrase begins by repeating almost verbatim what the Apostle said in 10:13 but goes beyond that to clarify his position. In doing so, Paul states his major problem with the interlopers. See 10:13 for "boasting beyond proper limits."[241] We treat the participle καυχώμενοι (*kauchōmenoi*), "boasting," as a finite verb and thus render it as "we . . . boast." The adjective ἀλλότριος (*allotrios*) designates that which belongs to another.[242] The noun κόπος (*kopos*), "labor, toil," denotes "hard work, implying difficulties and trouble."[243] The Apostle's choice of words emphasizes how wrong it is for others (an oblique reference to the interlopers) to intrude upon an area in which they have neither toiled nor suffered and then have the audacity to claim that they have some authority over it.

but having hope, when your faith is increased / but we have the hope that as your faith continues to grow: The verb ἔχω (*echō*), "to have," is found here as a participle. As we noted above, we translate it as a finite verb, "we have." The noun ἔλπις (*elpis*), "hope, expectation,"[244] evidences the confidence Paul has in his readers because they already have said hope in Christ.[245] The noun πίστις (*pistis*), "faith,"[246] here denotes "a state of believing."[247] The verb αὐξάνω (*auxanō*), found here as a present passive participle, means "to be increased, grow." The participal is used circumstantially with the sense "as your faith continues to grow."

Significantly, this phrase shows that, despite the work of his enemies, Paul actually has a rather positive view of his supporters. His congeniality

---

241. The Greek phrase found here translates literally as "we do not boast in[to] the unmeasured." The phrase likely refers to areas either where Paul has not set up the Church or beyond the field assigned to him at the Jerusalem Council—that is, the Gentiles.

242. BDAG, 47–48.

243. Louw-Nida, §42.47. Paul uses the plural κόποι (*kopoi*), "labors, toils," to describe both his work and that of those associated with him. See, for example, Rom. 16:6; 1 Cor. 3:8; 15:10, 58; Gal. 4:11; and 1 Thes. 5:12. In doing so, he does not underplay the fact that missionary work is hard.

244. BDAG, 319–20.

245. In the New Testament, "good hope" both anticipates and articulates the Saints' confidence in the Father and the Son. For a study, see C. F. D. Moule, *The Meaning of Hope: A Biblical Exposition with Concordance* (Philadelphia: Fortress Press, 1963).

246. The noun is based on the idea of a trust so complete that one is willing to fully rely on, be loyal to, and obedient to the object of that trust. In the New Testament, it denotes one who follows the Savior with an understanding of the content and requirements of his teachings. Louw-Nida, §31.85, 88, 102, 104.

247. BDAG, 818–20.

will again be highlighted in 13:5–14. Together these show that, though Paul can be biting and ironic toward his enemies, he is also well aware of and has hope in those who are on his side.[248]

that we shall be enlarged by you according to our rule abundantly / that, with your help, our assigned area will be greatly enlarged: In the phrase ἐν ὑμῖν (*en hymin*), the preposition ἐν (*en*) is used as a marker of agency and has the sense "with the help of,"[249] and this is reflected in our translation.

See 10:13 for the rendering of κανών (*kanōn*) as "assigned area." The verb μεγαλύνω (*megalynō*) means "to make large."[250] It is modified by the adverbial prepositional phrase εἰς περισσείαν (*eis persseian*), literally "in abundance," but we have rendered it as the adverb "greatly."[251]

This phrase is revealing because it evidences why Paul felt he had to win the battle for the Corinthian Saints' loyalty. He viewed the area as the jumping-off point for his intended work further to the west, and he needed these people to stand behind him and, likely, to support him with their prayers and perhaps in other ways in his efforts to extend his field of operation.

10:16 ***To preach the gospel in the regions beyond you / to preach the gospel in lands that lie beyond you:*** The Greek of this phrase is very compact, consisting of just five words, εἰς τὰ ὑπερέκεινα ὑμῶν εὐαγγελίσασθαι (*eis ta hyperekeina hymōn euangelisasai*). It has no finite verb but rather an aorist middle infinitive of the verb εὐαγγελίζω (*euangelizō*), "to preach the gospel."[252] The preposition εἰς (*eis*), when used with an infinitive, as here, can express purpose.[253]

The adverb ὑπερέκεινα (*hyperekeina*), "beyond," with the definite article τά (*ta*) and modified by the genitive pronoun ὑμῶν (*hymōn*), "of you," designates "the lands that lie beyond you" [254] and refers to Paul's intended missionary activity in Italy and Spain. Thus our resulting English translation.

---

248. Barnett, *Second Epistle,* 490.

249. BDAG, 329.

250. BDAG, 623.

251. BDAG, 804–5.

252. Louw-Nida, §33.215. Paul uses the verb εὐαγγελίζω (*euangelizō*) almost always for the declaration of Christ and his saving work. For examples, see Rom. 1:15; 10:15; 1 Cor. 1:17; 9:16, 18; Gal. 1:8–9, 11, 16, 23; and Eph. 2:17; 3:8.

253. BDAG, 290.

254. BDAG, 1032. The phrase is found only here in the Bible and may have been coined by Paul. It contains an improper use of a genitive preposition (in this case, ἡμῶν, *hymōn*) with an adverb (in this case, ὑπερέκεινα, *hyperekeina*), forcing the latter to be translated

and not to boast in another man's line of things made ready to our hand / without boasting about work already done in someone else's assigned area: Once again, Paul brings up the idea of the impropriety, if not outright wrongness, of taking credit for another's work. This phrase begins with the negative particle οὐκ (*ouk*), "not," which modifies the verb καυχάομαι (*kauchaomai*), "to boast," found here as an aorist infinitive. We have rendered these as "without boasting." By placing the particle first, Paul gives force to his lack of boasting.

The adjective ἕτοιμος (*hetoimos*) means "prepared, ready," and with the neuter definite article τά (*ta*), "the works," it designates "the work already done."[255] The adjective ἀλλότρις (*allotrios*)[256] designates that which belongs to another and is rendered as "someone else's."

Again, as noted in 10:13 and 10:15 above, κανών (*kanōn*) has the sense "assigned area."

10:17 ***But he that glorieth, let him glory in the Lord / Rather, let one who boasts, boast in the Lord:*** The conjunction δέ (*de*), "rather," acts as a marker of contrast with the preceding phrase.[257] Here Paul paraphrases LXX Jer. 9:22–23 (Jer. 9:23–24, KJV), wherein Jehovah states that proper boasting must be based on and in delight of an understanding of his works.[258] The verb καυχάομαι (*kauchaomai*), "to boast," is found here in the imperative mood, thus "let the one boast." With this verse, Paul sets the proper standard for boasting and gives it scriptural authority.

10:18 ***For not he that commendeth himself is approved / for it is not the one who commends himself that is approved:*** The conjunction γάρ (*gar*), "for," acts as a marker of clarification.[259] For συνίστημι (*synistēmi*), "to commend," with the pronoun ἑαυτός (*heautos*), see Translation Notes for 10:12. The adjective δόκιμος (*dokimos*), "approved," denotes what is considered "worthy of high respect" and honor based on being tested and found genuine. [260]

but whom the Lord commendeth / but the one whom the Lord commends: For συνίστημι (*synistēmi*), "to commend," see Translation Notes

---

as a preposition, "beyond." BDF, §184. The phrase appears to refer to a westward trajectory beyond Corinth. Barnett, *Second Epistle,* 490 n. 55.

255. BDAG, 401.

256. BDAG, 47–48.

257. BDAG, 213.

258. Guthrie, *2 Corinthians,* 497.

259. BDAG, 189–90.

260. Louw-Nida, §§73.4; 87.7; BDAG, 256.

for 10:12. The noun κύριος (*kyrios*), "lord,"[261] based on the scripture Paul paraphrased, could refer to Jehovah. Here the noun would refer to the Christ, who continues to direct the ministry through his Apostles (John 14:17; Acts 1:1–2).[262]

Analysis and Summary

In this epistle, Paul has earlier categorically denied that he and his missionary companions have conducted their activities "according to human standards" (10:2–3), which included such activities as boasting. He, however, fully admits that he has used boasting as a means of promoting the gospel. In his case, however, it is fully appropriate because it is based not on his own virtues but on the Christ-given authority he wields and has used to build up the Church of God (10:8). He now turns to the misuse of boasting, of which his critics are guilty (10:12–18). He insists that it is they who work according to human standards, gain legitimization only through self-comparison, and boast most inappropriately. By doing so, the Apostle offers tantalizing insights into the accusations and activities of this intractable group.[263] Given textual evidence, it would appear that his focus is not on native Corinthian Saints but on the interlopers, those who have come from outside the area. He has already noted their arrival (2:17–3:1; compare 5:11–13). At this point he focuses on them at considerable length (chapters 11–12) for the purpose of undermining their damaging influence. However, he does so obliquely, referring to them simply as "some" and, thereby, does not dignify them with a direct reference.[264]

Just in what the interlopers centered their boast is unclear, but it led them to claim superiority over Paul and, therefore, the authority to administer the affairs of the local Church. However, the Apostle shows that they have clearly intruded into an area that does not belong to them and in so doing have greatly overreached any prerogatives they might have.[265] The text suggests that these people have made the claim that the Apostle has no real jurisdiction over the Corinthian Saints, and thus he has no authority over what the people do. Further, he evidences no charismatic powers, and thus God does not appear to be with him. Of themselves, they have brought both the necessary credentials and have the spirit with them.

---

261. BDAG, 576–79.
262. Barnett, *Second Epistle,* 493 n. 68.
263. Guthrie, *2 Corinthians,* 486.
264. Barnett, *Second Epistle,* 480.
265. Barnett, *Second Epistle,* 486–87.

In 10:12, with heavy irony, Paul turns his attention to a defense against them by stressing both the inappropriate nature and subject of the boasting through which they evidence their superiority. Paul notes he would not "presume" or "dare" to put himself in such a self-important position (compare Rom. 1:18 and Jude 1:9). That is not to say he is unwilling to boast. Indeed, he is very willing to use bold confidence against these antagonists (10:2), but he refuses to join in their game of self-promotion. Let them think he is weak, an abysmal public speaker (10:10), and, likely, beneath them in other respects, but he will prove himself more fit than they. Ironically, he agrees he should not go head-to-head with these braggarts. His read on the situation, however, differs radically from theirs and, as he will show, vindicates him in every respect. Because of this, he refuses to enter into the game of comparison.[266]

By way of background, a number of Greek orators were adept at turning the technique of comparison into a vicious smear tactic aimed at denigrating their opponents with the objective of demobilizing them and removing their support base.[267] Indeed, "in the cutthroat competition for plaudits and pupils, one had to advertise oneself publicly with audacious praise while impugning the qualities of other contenders for honor. People were constantly vying with others to attain elusive glory and engaged in a constant game of one-upmanship."[268] These people seem to have believed that the only way to move up in their world was to tear others down by shredding their public image. Paul's opponents seem to be using this technique on him. However, he refuses to get caught up in such worldly competition.[269]

The issue at hand is not whether Paul was a member of the circle of the twelve Apostles, but the nature and breadth of the authority he held. Though the text is clear that the majority of Saints recognized and accepted those who composed the Apostolic quorum as general officers of the Church and knew them by the title of apostles, the Saints did not view them as holding that title exclusively, as is the case today. As noted in the introduction to this volume, the title by itself carried the idea of a fully empowered messenger with nuanced godly authority. In 8:23, Paul calls his fellow missionaries "apostles" and notes they function as envoys to the

---

266. Guthrie, *2 Corinthians,* 487–88.

267. On this rather shameful but accepted conduct in Corinth, see Harry Stansbury, "Corinthian Honor, Corinthian Conflict: A Social History of Early Roman Corinth and Its Pauline Community" (PhD diss., University of California, Irvine, 1990), 276–78.

268. Garland, *2 Corinthians,* 452.

269. Guthrie, *2 Corinthians,* 490.

Churches. The biblical text suggests that, in the broad use of the term, it designated those appointed and sent out by certain branches of the Church to represent them. The primary function of these men was to proclaim the gospel and assist in the founding and administration of the branches of the ever-expanding Church.[270] Most branches seem to have accepted Apostles' authority and were willing to follow their lead. The issue facing the Corinthian Saints was determining just who exercised that authority. Paul's Corinthian detractors denied the Apostle's authority, denigrated his works, and spurned his doctrine, all the while promoting their own authority and teachings. To defend himself, Paul attacks their methods of self-commendation and boasting.

He is, however, walking a fine line here, because he himself resorts to both boasting and commending himself (3:1; 4:2; 5:12; 6:4), but he does so only when it comes to defending himself, his ministry, and his apostolic authority. Further, like them, he also does his own classifying and comparing, both here and later as he builds his defense.[271]

The center of the whole issue is the act of boasting. Paul's critics have accused him of improper boasting. The Apostle takes this attack head on. At the beginning of chapter 10, he admits he has not made a strong public performance, likely due to his manual labor during the months he worked in that city. It seems that these interlopers have used his self-accepted menial station as evidence to criticize Paul's position and authority. They appear to have insisted that his proclaimed power has gone beyond the lowly station his work evinced, thus making him a boaster in the worst sense. In 10:3–6, Paul refutes this charge because he considers his enemies' accusations to be stumbling blocks or obstacles against Christ, which must be destroyed. In 10:8, he clearly states he is not ashamed to boast because his position is based not on worldly status but on God-given objective criteria that show his role as authorized leader is not improper.

In 10:12, he points out that his critics' means of classifying and measuring themselves show ignorance of "what constitutes true Christian ministry" on their part and underscore that they are nothing less than "spiritual dullards."[272] He, on the other hand, evaluates his own ministry and that of his associates based on set standards.

---

270. For a discussion, see Hans Dieter Betz, "Apostle," in *ABD,* 1:309–11; and the Translation Notes and the accompanying Analysis for 8:23.

271. Guthrie, *2 Corinthians,* 488–89.

272. Guthrie, *2 Corinthians,* 490.

In 10:13, the Apostle distinguishes between true and false boasting: The latter goes beyond what is proper and correct while the former rests exactly on these two strictures. Propriety and correctness consist of following the doctrine as declared by Paul and his associates, being faithful to the Lord, and being in accord with apostolic authority. Thus Paul feels justified in openly boasting because, as he notes in 10:13, 15–18, he does so according to the criteria God has set down, which shows that proper boasting rests on commendation from Deity alone. Vitally, what Paul is doing for Corinthian Christianity parallels that which the Lord did for the Judaic community. Both men criticize much of the cultural expectations of their respective societies and reveal a new and better way.[273]

Even so, Paul's words show that he is uncomfortable in having to boast, even though the—at best—lukewarm support of his friends has forced him into this rather painful position (12:11). He is, however, willing to do some bragging because it is fundamentally different from that of his detractors, who use it "only to inflate their pride and bolster their self-praise."[274] Paul, on the other hand, boasts exclusively in the Lord (10:17–18), not in human—including his own—abilities or successes.[275] As he already made clear to the Galatian Saints, he will "never boast except in the cross of our Lord Jesus Christ, through which the world has been crucified to me, and I to the world" (Gal. 6:14, our translation). Thus his boasting is stripped of all self-praise. He does, however, extend his boasting to—that is, his pride in—one other area—namely, to the part that God has assigned him, and that includes the people therein.[276] Thus, he assures his readers, they continue to be the center of his boastful feelings as they evidence their continued faith in the Lord and his true representatives.

Paul builds on his negative assertion in 10:13 by making another in 10:14. In the former case, he insisted that his boasting was not out of bounds. In 10:14, he insists that neither is his sphere of ministry. He had earlier received authority for his claim in two ways, either of which or both could be at play here. The first was the direct assignment from the Lord himself that Paul's area of work would be among the Gentiles (Acts 26:16–18). The second

---

273. For a discussion of the issue of boasting within Paul's framework, see Arthur J. Dewey, "A Matter of Honor: A Social-Historical Analysis of 2 Corinthians 10," *Harvard Theological Review* 78, no. 1–2 (April 1985): 209–17.

274. Martin, *2 Corinthians,* 503.

275. Guthrie, *2 Corinthians,* 489.

276. For a study, see *NID,* 2:651–55.

was the confirmation of this assignment at the conclusion of the Jerusalem Council in AD 49 (Acts 15:10–35; Gal. 2:1–9). To make his point, Paul repeats his position that he is not guilty of overreaching because his sphere of authority extends as far as Corinth. His seat of proof is that he was the first to bring the "gospel of Christ" to these people. Thus his detractors have, without proper authority, moved into his field of ministry and are but "interlopers and usurpers of apostolic prerogative" and further have brought with them heterodox teachings.[277]

Paul likely understood that winning this battle was crucial to his future work. Corinth was ideally located as a home base from which he could take the gospel to the lands beyond—namely, Spain. Thus "more was at risk than just the disaffection of a local congregation; his present and future work 'in the gospel' was in jeopardy by a situation that could develop into a renewed slide away from Paul and his mission on the part of the Corinthian believers."[278]

In 10:15, Paul continues his insistence that he has not boasted beyond proper limits or, better, "unfairly."[279] He emphasizes his point by repeating the phrase he used in 10:13 verbatim but then adding the words "in the work done by others." His argument is that he has never poached on areas of missionary work opened by fellow missionaries. But such poaching is exactly what the interlopers have done by trying to capture his ministry for themselves.[280]

Next Paul expresses his expectation that once the Corinthian Saints' confidence has been restored in him, they will assist him in using their area as a launching pad for his intended mission to points west, where his field of labor, he feels, will be "greatly enlarged" (10:15, NR). As a result, he will continue to be free of boasting—that is, of horning in on areas where others have already worked. The phrase suggests that Paul views prior and original work in a field of labor as rightly determining who has authority over it and that this authority should not be broached by others.[281] Behind that is

277. Martin, *2 Corinthians,* 506; Barnett, *Second Epistle,* 488.

278. Martin, *2 Corinthians,* 506.

279. The phrase can be rendered "in an exaggerated way" or "to an unwarranted degree." However, the idea of unfairness seems to better carry the sense since it appears to be an accusation leveled by Paul's detractors. Martin, *2 Corinthians,* 506.

280. Barnett, *Second Epistle,* 491 n. 59; Martin, *2 Corinthians,* 506.

281. Barnett, *Second Epistle,* 488 n. 39; Martin, *2 Corinthians,* 507.

the idea that the advancement of the work is under apostolic authority as directly assigned by the Lord (Matt. 28:19–20).

Paul states the basis of his support as coming from the ever-increasing faith of these Saints. He has already made it clear that his entire purpose as an Apostle is to further their faith in Christ (1:12). "This faith, which is to bring joy to the Corinthians (1:24), is not merely an outward confession of their lips but the living confession of their lives," [282] which they can now express by helping Paul further the work of Christ as he moves into the lands to the west.

In 10:16, having stated his hope to evangelize the regions beyond Corinth, he immediately returns to his defense. He obliquely marks his opponents' guilt in boasting about what they have not done, saying he will not boast in—that is, take credit for, as he said in 10:15—the work done by others by encroaching on their field of labor. It is worth noting that he is true to this position concerning Rome, where he does not open a field of labor because that work was already going on apace, likely due to the efforts of Peter.[283]

In 10:17, Paul begins to bring the train of thought he began in 10:12 full circle, and as is his wont, he clinches his point with a scriptural citation. The hook word is "commend," and the issue is on what basis can a proper commendation and thereby appropriate boasting be made. The basis of the answer is in defining the proper "assigned area" of influence and its demarcation. Is that sphere determined by human effort, wherein the person should receive the commendation or condemnation for what happens, or is it determined by the Lord, who gives the work validity and who is the only one who can rightly commend the work as "approved"? The scripture Paul paraphrases (LXX Jer. 9:22–23; Jer. 9:23–24, KJV) underscores that all boasting must be grounded in the Lord and in an understanding of his ways. Though Paul could claim the title of "sage," he shows "he will follow Jeremiah's warning and will therefore boast in his foolishness, weakness, and poverty—all of which set him at odds with the way the Corinthians want their leaders to be and to boast."[284] But by this means, as shown in 10:18, he is again able to ridicule his detractors' method of self-commendation based on their own standards, which has resulted in them being, as he states, "clueless" to the purpose and nature of proper boasting. When all is

282. Seifred, *Second Letter,* 395.

283. Barnett, *Second Epistle,* 491.

284. Witherington, *Conflict and Community,* 441.

said and done, ultimate approval does not come from self-commendation but from godly sources. Certainly, true commendation rests only here, and boasting can only be in God.[285] Paul has already affirmed that his labor is driven by the grace of God that continually attends him (1 Cor. 15:10). On that basis, he does not need nor will he engage in self-commendation. "Nor does he need the approval of the Corinthians. The evidence of his calling as an apostle comes from God alone, who works savingly in and through the crucified Christ. Paul's approval therefore appears in a form contrary to all human judgments. It is present in the faith of the Corinthians, even though they are in danger of ignoring it."[286]

---

285. Guthrie, *2 Corinthians*, 498–99.
286. Seifred, *Second Letter*, 398–99.

In Jewish culture of the diaspora,[295] the words nuancing the difference between self-praise and boasting is less clear.[296] This is because the LXX, on which both Jews and Christians were dependent, uses the same words to indicate boasting in the sense of presumption and vainglory (1 Kgs. 20:11; Prov. 25:14; 27:1) and justifiable pride in the sense of praise and glorification (Prov. 16:31; 17:6). Usually, the words carried a very negative connotation, denoting the base characteristic of the foolish and ungodly man who insisted on independence and reliance on what he can do and control (Ps. 52:1; 74:4; 94:3). But there were places in that text where they had a very positive cast denoting trust in God and revealing that true boasting centered on humbly acknowledging the place and power of God in one's life (Ps. 5:11; 32:11; 89:7; 1 Chr. 16:27). That association allowed them to carry the sense of rejoicing and exulting in the Lord.[297]

The positive sense, however, does not carry over in Paul's writings. Indeed, he uses the terms in their most negative sense.[298] For him, the words designate a "self-confidence which seeks glory before God and which relies upon itself."[299] Therefore, it sits opposite faith (*pistis*), which is expressed as trust in Christ.[300]

Paul's Reaction to His Detractor's Accusations

The text of 2 Corinthians shows that Paul's critics accused him of boasting when they were guilty of that very offense. It is clear that some of the Saints, and particularly the interlopers, engaged in the act of boasting and self-adulation in the hope of gaining other Saints' support and acceptance of their doctrine. They may have thought, even insisted, that they were engaged in socially acceptable self-praise and were, therefore, not boasting as they attempted "to excel in the cultural game of honor."[301]

It was the inability of the Christian community within the city to grasp the difference between boasting in themselves and having faith in Christ

295. The noun designated Jews who lived outside the Holy Land.

296. These were the verb καύχομαι (*kauchaomai*), "to boast, brag, take pride in, be proud of," and the nouns καύχμα (*kauchēma*), "taking pride in, boasting," and καύχησις (*kauchēsis*), "boasting, taking pride in." BDAG, 536–37.

297. Bultmann, "καύχομαι," in *TDNT*, 3:646–47.

298. For some clear examples, see 1 Cor. 1:29, 31; 3:21; 5:6; 9:15–16; 15:31; and 2 Cor. 9:2–4; 10:8, 13, 15; 11:16.

299. Bultmann, "καύχομαι," in *TDNT*, 3:649.

300. Bultmann, "καύχομαι," in *TDNT*, 3:649.

301. Donahoe, "From Self-Praise to Self-Boasting," 210.

that led Paul to address the issue. But he did so "as a reluctant and unwelcomed competitor in the field of professional 'sophistry' and . . . he promoted a deliberate collision with its standards of value."[302] His epistles betray, even in the face of his denial, that he was a very good thinker and a highly skilled writer who knew how to present a very convincing argument. His self-defense clearly followed the overarching and basic conventions of rhetorical means skillful ancient rhetors promoted.[303] Even his enemies admitted to the effective force of his letters, objecting only to his weak physical presence and oral performance (10:10). The level of his writing skill suggests the breadth of his education, his family's rather high social standing, and his willingness to glean ideas and skills from Gentiles.[304] Paul put his expertise to work by using his rather barbed but effective pen to critique both the Saints' attitudes and the Greco-Roman cultural values that formed their basis.

> Through irony, self-presentation, imitation, differentiating between theocentric [God-centered] and anthropocentric [human-centered] 'boasting,' and distinguishing between personality and gospel rhetoric, Paul challenges the secular notions of social status, power, wisdom, leadership, and patronage and exhorts the Corinthians to focus their attention on their relationship with the Lord rather than on improving their social status or on increasing their honor.[305]

Though Greco-Roman rhetorical conventions informed Paul's view on boasting, his personal and penetrating experience with divine grace and the power that flowed from the cross of Jesus transformed his understanding. Through his enlightened approach, the Apostle removed the subjective element in judging between self-praise and boasting from the audience, entirely minimizing that role and establishing that of the Divine in the process.[306]

His understanding came from an inspired scriptural insight he found in LXX Jeremiah 9:22–23 (Jer. 9:23–24, KJV). There Jehovah made it very clear just wherein proper boasting lay: "Let not the wise man boast in his wisdom, and let not the strong man boast in his strength, and let not the

302. Judge, "Paul's Boasting in Relation to Contemporary Professional Practice," 67.

303. Witherington, *Conflict and Community,* 436.

304. Forbes, "Comparison, Self-Praise and Irony," 23–24, argues that Paul was highly educated and that speaks to a high social standing in his community. As a result, his willingness to work a menial job to support himself at Corinth belied his station and training.

305. Donahoe, "From Self-Praise to Self-Boasting," ii.

306. Donahoe, "From Self-Praise to Self-Boasting," 210.

he addresses the accusations of those whom he calls "super-apostles," comments on his pattern of ministry, and berates their deceitful character. In the third unit (11:16–21), he repeats themes from the first section as he uncomfortably enters into his "fool's speech," in which he parodies his readers' willingness to put up with the foolish boasting of Paul's critics. In the fourth (11:22–29), he finally begins his own boasting, listing his heritage, sacrifices, and work for the kingdom. In the fifth (11:30–33), he confirms that despite all he has done, the seat of his glorying will be his infirmities. He goes on to testify to the truthfulness of his position. He concludes the unit with a recount of a most embarrassing event that took place shortly after his conversion, when he had to escape arrest by being lowered over a wall in a large net or rope mesh.

Paul's Foolishness (11:1–6)

Greek Text

1 Ὄφελον ἀνείχεσθέ μου μικρόν τι ἀφροσύνης· ἀλλὰ καὶ ἀνέχεσθέ μου. 2 ζηλῶ
γὰρ ὑμᾶς θεοῦ ζήλῳ, ἡρμοσάμην γὰρ ὑμᾶς ἑνὶ ἀνδρὶ παρθένον ἁγνὴν παραστῆσαι
τῷ Χριστῷ· 3 φοβοῦμαι δὲ μή πως, ὡς ὁ ὄφις ἐξηπάτησεν Εὕαν ἐν τῇ πανουργίᾳ
αὐτοῦ, φθαρῇ τὰ νοήματα ὑμῶν ἀπὸ τῆς ἁπλότητος καὶ τῆς ἁγνότητος τῆς εἰς τὸν
Χριστόν. 4 εἰ μὲν γὰρ ὁ ἐρχόμενος ἄλλον Ἰησοῦν κηρύσσει ὃν οὐκ ἐκηρύξαμεν, ἢ
πνεῦμα ἕτερον λαμβάνετε ὃ οὐκ ἐλάβετε, ἢ εὐαγγέλιον ἕτερον ὃ οὐκ ἐδέξασθε,
καλῶς ἀνέχεσθε. 5 λογίζομαι γὰρ μηδὲν ὑστερηκέναι τῶν ὑπερλίαν ἀποστόλων·
6 εἰ δὲ καὶ ἰδιώτης τῷ λόγῳ, ἀλλ' οὐ τῇ γνώσει, ἀλλ' ἐν παντὶ φανερώσαντες ἐν
πᾶσιν εἰς ὑμᾶς. [SBLGNT]

King James Version

1 Would to God ye could bear with me
a little in my folly: and indeed bear with
me. 2 For I am jealous over you with godly
jealousy: for I have espoused you to
one husband, that I may present you
as a chaste virgin to Christ. 3 But I
fear, lest by any means, as the serpent
beguiled Eve through his subtilty, so
your minds should be corrupted from
the simplicity that is in Christ. 4 For
if he that cometh preacheth another

New Rendition

1 I hope you will bear with me in a little
bit of foolishness; indeed, do bear with
me! 2 For I am jealous of you with a
divine jealousy, for I betrothed you to
one husband to present you as a pure
virgin to Christ. 3 But I am afraid that
just as the snake deceived Eve with his
cunning, your minds may be led astray
from sincerity and purity to Christ.
4 For if someone comes and preaches
another Jesus that we did not preach,

Jesus, whom we have not preached, or if ye receive another spirit, which ye have not received, or another gospel, which ye have not accepted, ye might well bear with him. 5 For I suppose I was not a whit behind the very chiefest apostles. 6 But though I be rude in speech, yet not in knowledge; but we have been throughly made manifest among you in all things.

or you receive a different spirit that you did not receive from us or a different gospel that you did not receive from us, you bear it readily enough. 5 For I consider that I am in no way inferior to the super-apostles. 6 But even if I am unskilled in speaking, nevertheless I am not unskilled in knowledge. On the contrary, in every way we have made this clear to you in all things.

Translation Notes and Comments

11:1 ***Would to God ye could bear with me a little in my folly / I hope you will bear with me in a little bit of foolishness:*** The adverbial accusative ὄφελον (*ophelon*) is used to express a wish or hope that some event or condition has taken or will take place.[2] The following verb, ἀνέχω (*anechō*), is in the imperfect tense, showing the condition is present. The translation of the word in the KJV as "would to God" is a bit too strong; thus we have rendered it as "I hope." The verb ἀνέχω (*anechō*) means "to bear with, regard with tolerance, endure."[3]

What Paul wants his audience to bear with is his ἀφροσύνης (*aphrosynē*), "foolishness," the noun denoting "a state that lacks prudence or good judgment"[4] and carries the nuances of senselessness, mindlessness, and a stupidity that can lead to a shameful arrogance.[5] Paul uses the term in an ironic sense, but one that is not too sarcastic and so avoids any sense of cutting or taunting his target audience.[6] However, it is likely that some Corinthians did consider Paul foolish in some ways. His desire not to push overly hard is reinforced by his use of the adjective plus indefinite pronoun μικρόν τι (*mikron ti*), "a little, bit," which carries the nuance of that which is of minor significance or of unimportance.[7]

2. BDAG, 743.

3. BDAG, 78.

4. BDAG, 159.

5. The noun belongs to the same family group as the verb ἄφρων (*aphrōn*). The verb connotes a person who is without reason, lacks mental sanity, or is reckless or inconsiderate in his or her state of mind with the result of lacking common sense. See BDAG, 159; and Louw-Nida, §§32.52, 53. For a study of the word group, see Georg Bertram, "φρήν, ἄφρων, ἀφροσύνη," in *TDNT,* 9:220–235.

6. Guthrie, *2 Corinthians,* 504 n. 1.

7. BDAG, 651.

and indeed bear with me / indeed, do bear with me: The Greek text contains the phrase ἀλλὰ καὶ (*alla kai*), literally "but even," to doubly strengthen the force of a command.[8] Here the two words are rendered as "indeed," emphasizing Paul's strong appeal.[9] The phrase adds an aspect of hope to his wish.

11:2 ***For I am jealous over you with godly jealousy / For I am jealous of you with a divine jealousy:*** The conjunction γάρ (*gar*), "for,"[10] is causal, signaling that Paul will now explain what motivates him in his request. The verb ζηλόω (*zēloō*), "to be jealous," [11] denotes a state of being "positively and intensely interested" in something or someone. It carries the nuance of having one's heart set on another because of deep concern for her or his welfare.[12] The verb lacks any sense of the petty possessiveness that jealousness carries in modern English but rather invokes the intense care, even zeal, that God has for his children[13] and that godly men and women have for their spiritual brothers and sisters.

for I have espoused you to one husband, that I may present you as a chaste virgin to Christ / for I betrothed you to one husband to present you as a pure virgin to Christ: As with the phrase above, the conjunction γάρ (*gar*), "for,"[14] is causal, signaling that Paul will explain further why he is acting as he does.

The verb ἁρμόζω (*harmozō*), found here as an aorist in the middle voice, denotes bringing two objects into close association and, in the context of people, refers to the act of betrothal.[15] This act, in ancient Jewish culture, legally and socially bound a couple together, in a manner far more serious than a modern engagement. They were considered husband and wife with all the privileges of marriage except cohabitation and conjugal intimacy.[16] Therefore, to betray the agreement through sexual impropriety was considered adultery. The act of betrothal originated with neither the future

8. Smyth, *Greek Grammar,* §2881.

9. Bernard, "Second Epistle," 99.

10. BDAG, 189–90.

11. BDAG, 427.

12. Louw-Nida, §§25.46, 76. Harris, *Second Epistle,* 734, notes that the verb carries the idea of a deep concern for the welfare of another.

13. Barnett, *Second Epistle,* 499–500.

14. BDAG, 189–90.

15. BDAG, 132; Louw-Nida, §34.74.

16. Marcus Jastrow and Bernard Drachman, "Betrothal," in *Jewish Encyclopedia* (1906), accessed April 4, 2021, https://jewishencyclopedia.com/articles/3229/.

husband nor the future wife, but rather with their parents. In this verse, the position that Paul sees for himself is ambiguous. He could be viewing himself as either the friend of the bride or groom, among whose duties are to see that all goes well; or as the groomsman or best man, who provides the escorting service; or as the agent of the father of the bride; or as the father himself.[17] That he gives himself credit for doing the betrothing suggests that he sees his role as the father of the bride, zealously guarding her purity for the sake of her husband-to-be.[18]

With the phrase ἑνὶ ἀνδρὶ (*heni andri*), "to one husband,"[19] Paul stresses that he, with fatherly affection, has protected the Church in preparation for unity with a single, specific spouse. His words emphasize that his efforts have not been for himself but for his audience and their relationship with Christ.

The noun παρθένος (*parthenos*), "virgin," can denote either a male or female who is unmarried and connotes the idea of her or his sexual purity.[20] In the present context, it denotes a woman of marriageable age with emphasis on her high moral standing. By modifying the noun with the adjective ἁγνός (*hagnos*), "pure, holy,"[21] Paul stresses the idea of absolute purity that, in this context, covers the whole of a person's life, not just his or her chastity.[22] Since the word also denotes a state of holiness, one of the chief characteristics of the Divine, it also suggests the state a Saint is to achieve and maintain in order to be one with God.

3 ***But I fear, lest by any means, as the serpent beguiled Eve through his subtilty / But I am afraid that just as the snake deceived Eve with his cunning:*** The event noted here is chronicled in Genesis 3:1–6. The verb φοβέομαι (*phobeomai*), to "be afraid,"[23] denotes an apprehensive state but, in this case, nuances more the idea of concern than of dread. The noun ὄφις (*ophis*) refers to a snake or serpent but connotes a dangerous person.[24] Here Paul apparently has the devil in mind.

---

17. Harris, *Second Epistle,* 736–38. Bernard, "Second Epistle," 100, opts for the παρανύφιος (*paranyphios*), the "bridesman." See also *DAG,* s.v. "παρανύφιος."

18. Garland, *2 Corinthians,* 460–61; Seifrid, *Second Epistle,* 402.

19. The noun *anēr* denotes both a man and a husband, the context giving the nuance. BDAG, 79–80. The adjective, εἷς (*heis*), "one," points to a specific person. BDAG, 291–93.

20. Louw-Nida, §§9.33, 39; 34.77.

21. BDAG, 13.

22. Louw-Nida, §88.28.

23. BDAG, 1060–62.

24. BDAG, 744–45.

The verb ἐξαπατάω (*exapataō*) means "to mislead, deceive, cheat," by presenting erroneous ideas as truth.[25] The noun πανουργία (*panourgia*), "craftiness, treachery, evil cunning,"[26] denotes a state of acute discernment combined with willingness to gain one's ends through unscrupulous means. Paul's combination of the verb *exapataō* and the noun *panourgia* provides an excellent description of the major means by which Satan is able to influence people and also of how Paul sees his personal adversaries working—that is, by using cunning deception.

so your minds should be corrupted from the simplicity that is in Christ / your minds may be led astray from sincerity and purity to Christ: The noun νόημα (*noēma*), "mind," refers to "the faculty of processing thought, understanding."[27] The verb φθείρω (*phtheirō*), "destroy, ruin," found here as an aorist passive, means "to be lead astray"[28] but carries the overtone of being corrupted or even spiritually destroyed. It is of note that it is not the thoughts of the Corinthians that Paul is concerned about being corrupted but their very "minds," a metonymy for the persons themselves.[29]

The noun ἁπλότης (*haplotēs*) describes the trait of "personal integrity expressed in word or action," thus "simplicity, sincerity, uprightness."[30] The noun ἁγνότης (*hagnotēs*) denotes "purity."[31] This word is missing in many manuscripts, including the one the KJV is based on. Several early manuscripts, however, do include it, and therefore it appears to be original.[32]

4 ***For if he that cometh preacheth another Jesus, whom we have not preached / For if someone comes and preaches another Jesus that we did not preach:*** As in the two verses above, the explanatory conjunction γάρ (*gar*), "for,"[33] is causal, signaling that Paul will explain why he is as he is. In this case, it indicates his passionate concern that his readers are being deceived and thus led away from truth.

---

25. Louw-Nida, §31.12; BDAG, 345.

26. Louw-Nida, §88.270. The noun means literally "all working" and refers to being able and willing to do anything to get one's way. Otto Bauernfeind, "πανουργία, πανοῦργος," in *TDNT,* 5:722–27.

27. BDAG, 675. The noun carries the idea of plans or conceptions but here refers to mental faculties. Seifrid, *Second Epistle,* 405 n. 280.

28. BDAG, 1054.

29. Seifrid, *Second Epistle,* 405 with n. 282.

30. BDAG, 104.

31. BDAG, 13.

32. Metzger, *Textual Commentary,* 514–15. For discussion, see Seifrid, *Second Epistle,* 406 n. 283; and Martin, *2 Corinthians,* 512 n. c.

33. BDAG, 189–90.

The conjunction εἰ (*ei*), "if," acts as a marker of a condition that is either real or hypothetical.[34] In this case, the condition does exist and demands an immediate response.

The prepositional phrase ὁ ἐρχόμενος (*ho erchomenos*), literally "the coming one,"[35] refers obliquely to a person already present. The Apostle is likely referencing the chief spokesmen for the interlopers, but he could be using the singular to refer to the group as a whole.[36]

The verb κηρύσσω (*kērysso*), "to preach," denotes the public proclamation or pronouncement of "religious truths and principles while urging acceptance."[37] Here the focus of that preaching is about the person of Ἰησοῦς (*Iēsous*) but one modified by the adjective ἄλλος (*allos*), "a different kind, another," the word carrying the connotation of "alien" or "rival,"[38] by which Paul signals that his adversaries are teaching that the Lord is a different type of being than what he taught. The text does not indicate precisely what kind of difference is meant.

or if ye receive another spirit, which ye have not received / or you receive a different spirit that you did not receive from us: The verb λαμβάνω (*lambanō*), "to take, receive," carries the nuance of both experiencing something and accepting it as true.[39]

Though there are instances where the noun πνεῦμα (*pneuma*), "spirit," refers to the Holy Ghost, here it denotes the influence through which the Divine works on, with, and through humankind.[40] Here it is modified by the adjective ἕτερος (*heteros*), "a different, another,"[41] and suggests the interlopers have introduced a false interpretation or understanding of what the spirit is and does. The phrase ὃ οὐκ ἐλάβετε (*ho ouk elabete*) translates literally as "which you did not receive," which is a bit awkward. We have added "from us," which is not in the actual text, to clarify the sense of the passage.

---

34. Louw-Nida, §89.65.

35. The phrase consists of the masculine definite article ὁ (*ho*) functioning as a demonstrative pronoun, thus "the one" (BDAG, 686) coupled with the masculine present particle of the verb ἔρχομαι (*erchomai*), "to come" (BDAG, 393–94).

36. Martin, *2 Corinthians,* 520.

37. Louw-Nida, §33.256. The verb also bears an aura of officiality or authenticity to what is being proclaimed. BDAG, 543–44.

38. Louw-Nida, §§58.36, 37; BDAG, 46–47; Martin, *2 Corinthians,* 521.

39. BDAG, 583–85; Louw-Nida, §§18.1; 57.125; 90.63.

40. BDAG, 832–36.

41. BDAG, 399; Louw-Nida, §§58.36, 37.

or another gospel, which ye have not accepted / or a different gospel that you did not receive from us: The noun εὐαγγέλιον (*euangelion*), "gospel," generally denotes "good news," but in a Christian setting, it refers to both the life and teachings of Jesus.[42] On the adjective ἕτερος (*heteros*), "a different, another," see above.

The verb δέχομαι (*dechomai*), "receive,"[43] carries the nuance of welcoming something, in this case the teachings of the Lord that the interlopers have somehow twisted to meet their false understanding of what the gospel means.

ye might well bear with him / you bear it readily enough: The verb ἀνέχω (*anechō*) means "to put up with, to bear with." The adverb καλῶς (*kalōs*) denotes that which meets a "relatively high standard of excellence or expectation" as well as that which is considered beneficial or acceptable.[44] The word carries the connotations of something "done 'well,' 'beautifully,' 'appropriately,' 'acceptably' or 'commendably'" but can be used in an ironic sense, which is how Paul is using it here to refer to the ease with which the Corinthian Saints accepted the interlopers and their accompanying teachings.[45]

5 ***For I suppose I was not a whit behind the very chiefest apostles / I consider that I am in no way inferior to the super-apostles:*** This sentence is central to Paul's defense, and he uses the causal conjunction γάρ (*gar*), "for,"[46] used to make his point. The verb λογίζομαι (*logizomai*) means "to hold a view, to have an opinion, to consider," in the sense of making a careful calculation.[47] The verb ὑστερέω (*hystereō*) refers to "being less than" or "inferior to" something else.[48] It is modified by the neuter accusative singular of the adjective μηδείς (*mēdeis*), here used adverbially with the sense of "in no way."[49] By its use, Paul asserts he is inferior in nothing—not himself, his teachings, or his activities—when compared to his critics.

At this point, we reach yet another ambiguity. To whom does the phrase τῶν ὑπερλίαν ἀποστόλων (*tōn hyperlian apostolōn*), translated as "chiefest apostles" in the KJV, refer? The adverb ὑπερλίαν (*hyperlian*) denotes what

42. BDAG, 402–3.
43. BDAG, 221.
44. BDAG, 505–6.
45. Guthrie, *2 Corinthians,* 511.
46. BDAG, 189–90.
47. Louw-Nida, §§30.9; 31.1; BDAG, 597–98.
48. BDAG, 1043–44.
49. BDAG, 647.

is "superlative, superior," and "chiefest" in its nature, but it also denotes "considerable excess."[50] The noun ἀπόστολος (*apostolos*), "apostle," refers in general to a "delegate, envoy, messenger,"[51] specifically those who have been literally "sent out" and thereby commissioned by others to represent them. Though the word is often used specifically to refer to the Twelve whom Jesus chose to minister with him, its more general use designates those engaged in officially preaching the gospel to all the world. It is the term that Paul applies to his companions (8:23; Philip. 2:25). Thus Paul could be referring to the Quorum of the Twelve, to those considered to be the head of the apostleship—namely, Peter, John and James—or to a specific group of official ambassadors who have accorded themselves or been accorded the title. There is, however, no question that the title bore with it a certain amount of authority that could be exercised over the various and scattered branches of the Church. The adverb ὑπερλίαν (*hyperlian*) could be helpful in determining who Paul had in mind if it could be interpreted in only one way. Unfortunately, as noted above, it has two meanings. One could be Paul's reference to the very high and holy calling of an Apostle, referencing either the Quorum members or its leadership. The other could be his ironic jab at the extreme view (one that was beyond measure) of the importance of Paul's detractors held either by themselves or by their supporters. In that case, the phrase would evidence Paul's (perhaps) exaggerated reference to the interlopers' perceived station.

Scholars have come down on both sides of the issue, and the Restoration has not shed any light on the subject. Those scholars who see *hyperlian* as referring to the Jerusalem Apostles or to the leadership of that group posit a breach between Paul and Peter and others in the Jerusalem leadership. Some postulate that the primary antagonist, obliquely referred to by Paul, is actually Peter, who, due to misinformation, Paul may have thought was present in Corinth.[52] Others see the eastern Church as having sent and even given letters of recommendation to Paul's antagonist to counter his acceptance among the Corinthian Saints. Still others, less willing to push a

50. Louw-Nida, §78.34. The term has generated a wide range of translations by commentators. These include "superlative," "superlatively great," "famous," "highest ranking," "very special," "(apostles) *par excellence*," "arch- (apostles)," "top," "ultra," "super-extra," "exalted," "eminent," "super- (apostles)," "superfine," "extra-super," "surpassingly superior," "extra-special," and "pre-eminent."

51. BDAG, 122.

52. Margaret E. Thrall, "Super-Apostles, Servants of Christ, and Servants of Satan," *Journal for the Study of the New Testament* 2, no. 6 (1980): 42–57.

breach between Paul and Jerusalem to that extreme, suggest the interlopers took the task upon them.[53] They may have felt, perhaps wrongly, that they represented the leadership in their distrust of him.[54] These scholars see Paul using the phrase either respectfully—pointing to the leadership's superior status—or ironically—exposing the overblown view of that leadership that the interlopers held.[55] A major problem with this view is that it rests heavily on an antagonism between Peter and Paul, an antagonism that the scriptures do not support.[56]

The majority of scholars argue that the reference is to the interlopers themselves. These scholars posit, like some of those noted above, that the interlopers were either misreading the Jerusalem leadership or taking upon themselves a mission to counter Paul. Whichever, they appear to be unabashed in presenting their heretical ideas. That they did so suggests they felt they had authority from somewhere. The scholars who hold this view argue that in this section of his epistle, Paul is rebutting the interlopers' accusations that he was inferior in his ministering skills and authority. Paul meets their challenge by branding them with the ironic title "super-apostles," his derisive term likely highlighting (and perhaps exaggerating for effect) how they viewed themselves or were viewed by others. This assessment is sustained by three primary points. First, the adverb *hyperlian* is loaded with harsh irony, and it seems unlikely that Paul would use it to refer to the Church's leadership, given his acknowledged deep respect for them. Second, if Paul was conceding inferiority to the Twelve, it certainly would not have been in oral skills, for the leadership, especially Peter, were viewed as low on these (Acts 4:13). Third, Paul uses this exact phrase again

---

53. This would not be the first time such occurred. About AD 49, certain Jewish Christians took it upon themselves a mission to Antioch and there promulgated their wrongful position without the support or knowledge of Church leadership. See Bruce, *Acts of the Apostles,* 329–31.

54. For an example of the arguments used by those who hold this view, see Barrett, *Second Epistle,* 278; Martin, *2 Corinthians,* 522–23; and the excellent summary by Thrall, *Critical and Exegetical Commentary,* 2:671–72.

55. There is no doubt that Paul did confront Peter over the potential of unnecessary Jewish practices being imposed on the Gentiles converts in Antioch (Gal. 2:11–14), but nowhere in the text does it suggests that an antagonism endured. In fact, near the end of his ministry, Peter commends Paul to the Saints (2 Pet. 3:15, assuming the epistle is not pseudonymous. Even if it is, it still evidences a known lack of antagonism between the two). Further, Paul "was the most conciliatory of men where no compromise of gospel liberty was at stake" and held no grudges against Peter. Bruce, *Acts of the Apostles,* 331.

56. Witherington, *Conflict and Community,* 446 with n. 25.

in 12:11, where he is definitely referencing and disparaging his antagonists.[57] We as authors cautiously hold with the majority view that the interlopers are the intended subject, feeling it has the greatest weight of evidence to support it.

That being the case, Paul is arguing that, since some Saints have, with exceptional ease, listened to his detractors, and since he feels he is on par with them, his readers should also just as easily listen to him.

11:6 *But though I be rude in speech / But even if I am unskilled in speaking:* That Paul begins this clause with the phrase εἰ δὲ καὶ (*ei de kai*), "but even if," gives a soft nod to the correctness of his detractors' criticism of his oratorical skills. The phrase "I am" is not found in the Greek text, but it is assumed, since forms of the verb "to be" often must be supplied in English translation.

The noun ἰδιώτης (*idiōtēs*), from which the English "idiot" is derived and rendered as a private, "unskilled" person, generally refers to a person who is inexperienced or amateurish.[58] Paul's use of the term is telling. In a pejorative sense, it referred to someone belonging to the uneducated and unqualified lower class. It also pointed to "those trained in rhetoric but who choose not to function as public orators or teachers of rhetoric. Thus 'non-orators' may indeed possess some knowledge or rhetoric, but they have abandoned [fraud or trickery] in their practice of it."[59] This understanding fits well with what we know of Paul's skill in argument. Though the word is a noun, it takes on the cast of an adjective in conjunction with the phrase τῷ λόγῳ (*tō logō*), "in speaking."[60] The noun λόγος (*logos*), in the present context, refers to speech,[61] specifically public speaking. For the sake of the English idiom, we have rendered it as a gerund, "speaking."

---

57. Guthrie, *2 Corinthians,* 516. For others who hold this view and give reasons therefore, see Barnett, *Second Epistle,* 522–23; Garland, *2 Corinthians,* 469; and Witherington, *Conflict and Community,* 446–47.

58. Louw-Nida, §27.26. Though the noun is the etymological source of the English word "idiot," it does not carry the sense of one hampered by severe mental disability. Philo, *On Agriculture* 143, 159–60, shows a clear demarcation between the unskilled common people, the *idiōtēs* or less skilled group, and the *sophistēs* or highly skilled set and notes that the *idiōtēs* included those who had been rhetorically trained. Isacrates, *Antidosis* 201–4, notes that the *idiōtēs* included a group trained in rhetoric that chose not to be orators.

59. Guthrie, *2 Corinthians,* 517. For a study of this issue, see Winter, *Philo and Paul among the Sophists,* 223–28.

60. BDAG, 598–601.

61. Louw-Nida, §33.99.

yet not in knowledge / nevertheless I am not unskilled in knowledge. The conjunction ἀλλά (*alla*), "but, nevertheless," signals that the matter at hand needs to be carefully considered.[62] Here, with the negative particle ου (*ou*), "not," it sets up a strong contrast to the concession made in the first clause. The noun γνῶσις (*gnōsis*), "knowledge," denotes a comprehensive grasp and understanding of certain material.[63] Here the Apostle could be referring to spiritual insight (compare 6:6; 8:7) by which he knows the will of God,[64] or he could be denoting his superior understanding of the gospel in the fullest sense of the word (compare 2:14; 4:6; 10:5).[65] The context suggests that the latter seems the more likely.

but we have been throughly made manifest among you in all things / On the contrary, in every way we have made this clear to you in all things: Paul again uses the contrasting power of the conjunction ἀλλά (*alla*), "on the contrary," to enhance the force of the point he is now making. The adjective πᾶς (*pas*), "all, total,"[66] found here as a neuter singular in the dative case, denotes the totality or the whole of something and, with the preposition ἐν (*en*), "in," points to the means or methods used by Paul and his colleagues.

The verb φανερόω (*phaneroō*), "to make clear," found here as an aorist participle, denotes the process of making something "fully known by revealing [it] clearly and in some detail."[67] The noun "this" is not in the text but is implied and refers to γνῶσις (*gnōsis*), "gospel knowledge," found in the clause above.

It is unclear how the phrase "in every way" should be distinguished from the phrase "in all things," leaving the whole clause vague.[68] "In every way" seems to point to the means by which the Apostle made gospel knowledge clear. "In all things" repeats the use of πᾶς (*pas*), "all," but this time as a plural in the dative case. Since the dative plural of *pas* can be masculine or neuter, there is some ambiguity as to what it refers to. However, the context suggests Paul is referring either to the occasions on which he made the gospel clear or to other means that he used to do so.[69]

---

62. BDAG, 44–45.

63. BDAG, 203–4; Louw-Nida, §§28.17; 32.16.

64. Furnish, *II Corinthians,* 490.

65. Barnett, *Second Epistle,* 507; Guthrie, *2 Corinthians,* 518.

66. Louw-Nida, §§58.28; 59.23; 63.2; 78.44.

67. Louw-Nida, §28.36.

68. Barrett, *Second Epistle,* 280–81.

69. Guthrie, *2 Corinthians,* 518–19.

Though the last clause is unclear, the intent of the sentence is not. The Apostle uses it to emphasize that he has left nothing to chance when it comes to declaring, in both its breadth and depth, his understanding of the Savior's doctrine, nature, mission, and Atonement.

Analysis and Summary

This section of Paul's writing begins with an asyndeton—that is, a sudden break in thought that carries no direct connection with what came before. As a result, the transition between the argument that ends chapter 10 and that which opens chapter 11 is very abrupt.[70] That abruptness, however, serves Paul well, for the moderate jar causes the thoughtful reader and listener to pay attention to what comes next.

In 11:1, Paul uses the pejorative noun "foolishness" (ἀφροσύνη, *aphrosynē*) as a bold self-criticism of what he is about to do. It is in light of the circumstances in which he finds himself, however, that he is forced to set himself up, not on the spiritual plane where he would like to be, but on the carnal, where, as he will show, both his antagonists and his audience reside.[71] Because his audience has been less than supportive of his apostolic office, they have forced him to take on a very foolish posture (12:1, 11). In his efforts, the Apostle comes very close to boasting according to "human standards" (κατὰ σάρκα, *kata sarka*[72]), of which he accuses his enemies. Their guilt lies in a boast that focuses on their accomplishments and fails to give credit to God and Christ in their work (10:12–13; 11:18–19). It seems that Paul senses that if he stoops to their level by boasting, he is acting the fool. On the other hand, if he does not defend himself and his authority, he will likely lose the Corinthian Saints to those whom he considers to be the actual fools.[73] Because of this, Paul allows himself to come close to sharing the interlopers' guilt, but only because he is willing to "fight fire with fire," and boasting is the means. However, his efforts do play to his ends. "By thus playing the fool, the apostle 'models' the utter foolishness of the interlopers' ministry style" and throws light on the silliness of their position and the acceptance it has brought them.[74]

70. Seifrid, *Second Epistle,* 401.
71. Georg Bertram, "ἄφρων, ἀφροσύη," in *TDNT,* 9:230–31.
72. On the translation of the Greek, see Translation Notes for 10:2.
73. Garland, *2 Corinthians,* 458.
74. Guthrie, *2 Corinthians,* 504.

Interestingly, Paul uses the term "foolishness," as it applies to him, in both an ironic and a factual way: ironically because he is actually ridiculing both his detractors and his audience throughout this portion of his epistle and by so doing exposes and parodies their own foolishness,[75] and factually because what he boasts about are very real events and accomplishments about which he does not exaggerate.

In 11:2, Paul states the dual reason why he is acting as he does. The first reason is his strong personal affection for these people. To express that affection, the Apostle uses the verb "to be jealous" (ζηλόω, *zēloō*). The term must be stripped of its modern sense of "the petty possessiveness that mars human relationships" by connecting it to the theme of God's covenantal care for his people (LXX Isa. 9:6; 37:32; 63:15–16).[76] In Paul's sense, the word connotes the intense care, even zeal, that God has for his children[77] and that godly men and women have for their spiritual brothers and sisters.

Such zeal is not foreign to Paul. Rather, it seems to mark the force that motivates much of his life as he seeks to maintain what he views as the purity of life and doctrine that is necessary to keep God's people one with him. Before Paul's conversion, his former zeal "sought to preserve the purity of Israel by violently trying to purge Christians (Gal 1:16–17). His former zeal has now been converted by Christ's love. He no longer resorts to violence, and he zealously strives to preserve purity and devotion to Christ rather than to Jewish tribal traditions."[78]

Paul stresses his work in uniting these people with God. To put his point over, Paul portrays himself as the father of a bride whose purity he is protecting as she prepares herself for marriage.[79] To be absolutely clear, however, Paul identifies the person he wants these people united to as the Lord Jesus Christ. By using this analogy, Paul clears himself of all personal benefit. His total efforts have been and are keeping the Saints sufficiently pure in the conduct of their lives and the purity of their doctrine that they stand united with their Savior.

However, he does not hesitate to chastise them in their pure folly in being so easily, perhaps even anxiously, bewitched by the interlopers. In 11:4, he gives his second reason for the zeal he feels for these Saints. Setting

75. Barnett, *Second Epistle,* 508.

76. Barnett, *Second Epistle,* 499–500.

77. Barnett, *Second Epistle,* 499–500. Harris, *Second Epistle,* 734, notes that the term expresses deep and sincere concern.

78. Garland, *2 Corinthians,* 462.

79. Seifrid, *Second Epistle,* 402.

aside the metaphor of the caring father, he identifies the specific dangers the Corinthians face.[80] These consist of an abandonment of the understanding of Christ, his gospel, and even the workings of the spirit that Paul had taught them. Just what the different and aberrant Christ, gospel, and spirit were the text does not reveal. During this period (and even centuries after), there were various speculations circulating that may have surfaced among the Corinthian Saints. Four are noteworthy: those professed by the Gnostics, Docetists, Ebionites, and Judaizers.

Gnosticism seems to have developed in the area east of the Holy Land and made its way from there into both the Jewish and Christian cultures at some point during the first century. Those among the Christians drawn to its central tenants were a diverse group of thinkers who never united into one organization. Thus their varied belief systems never coalesced into a coherent unified whole. The proponents, however, did share certain beliefs.

The name of this assemblage was derived from the Greek noun γνῶσις (*gnosis*), denoting knowledge. The various assemblages believed that personal spiritual knowledge was the key to salvation and trumped the teachings, traditions, and authority of apostolic leadership. They viewed the material existence as flawed and even evil, one which came into existence through the hubris of certain lesser divine beings who took upon themselves the act of creation. Some taught that the star of the less noble beings was Jehovah, the God of the Old Testament, who was responsible for the creation of the material, corrupt universe. Gnostics taught that the principal element of salvation was revealed knowledge of the supreme god of light. They derived such knowledge through mystical or esoteric insight. They were less concerned with the destructive nature of sin, and therefore they did not see the value of repentance. Instead, they feared illusion and sought for enlightenment. Though some believed that Jesus was the supreme being who came in the flesh, most adamantly denied this idea, insisting that flesh, indeed anything material, was too vile for deity to be associated with. Instead, they saw Jesus as merely human, but one who had obtained enlightenment through gnosis and taught his disciples how to do the same and thus gain unity with the Father of Light.[81]

---

80. Seifrid, *Second Epistle,* 407.

81. For an overview, see Kurt Rudolph, "Gnosticism," in *ABD,* 2:1033–40. For an in-depth study, see David Brakke, *The Gnostics: Myth, Ritual, and Diversity in Early Christianity* (Cambridge, Mass.: Harvard University Press, 2010).

Also moving with some force were the ideas promulgated by the Docetists. The name of this belief system is derived from the Greek verb δοκέω (*dokēō*), meaning "to seem," and is related to the noun δόκησις (*dokēsis*), denoting an apparition or phantom. As with the Gnostics, there was no one united doctrinal system, but two primary concepts vied for top honor. One group promoted the idea that Christ was fully divine and therefore never had any physical component. Rather, he only appeared to have a body that was, in fact, but a phantom. Another group posited the notion that there were two different persons at play. One was Jesus, a mere mortal but a very righteous person, and the other was Christ, a fully divine being. This divine being, in the form of a dove, entered the body of Jesus at baptism, bestowed upon him power to do miracles and to teach true principles and doctrines, and then abandoned him before his suffering on the cross.[82]

Correspondingly moving with some force during this time were ideas taught by the Ebionites. Their name comes from a transliteration of the Greek Ἐβιωναῖοι (*Ebiōnaioi*). The term itself is derived from the Hebrew אֶבְיוֹנִים (*ebyônîm*), denoting "poor ones." The proponents of this belief system spurned wealth and viewed poverty as holy. They taught the need and efficacy of ritual ablutions, rejected the Mosaic system of animal sacrifice, and refused to eat meat. Salvation was obtained through the written law of Moses alone, minus the sacrificial system. Thus they excluded the "oral law" as advanced by the Pharisees. They did, however, have their own scriptures in addition to the Old Testament. They viewed Jesus as a mere mortal, but one whom God chose due to Jesus' righteousness and made the saving Messiah. Even so, they rejected the idea of his virgin birth and insisted there was nothing divine about him. They disallowed the idea that Jesus chose Peter as his successor but rather put forth James the Just, whom they considered the epitome of moral righteousness.[83] They rejected Paul, insisting he was a false Apostle guilty of pulling people away from the true law of God.[84]

Of these heretical systems, it is the Judaizers who come directly into the New Testament spotlight.[85] These were primarily Christian Jews, likely

---

82. For an overview, see B. Studer, "Docetism," in *Encyclopedia of the Early Church,* ed. Angelo Di Berardino, trans. Adrian Walford, 2 vols. (Cambridge, Mass.: James Clarke, 1992), 1:244. Many scholars lump this system with Gnosticism.

83. He was the Lord's brother and rose to prominence after the Savior's death. See Matt. 13:55; Acts 12:17; 15:13; 21:18; 1 Cor. 15:7; and Gal. 1:19.

84. For an overview, see Stephen Goranson, "Ebionites," in *ABD,* 2: 260–61.

85. For background, see Wayment, *From Persecutor to Apostle,* 93–98; and Bruce, *Acts of the Apostles,* 329–31.

converted out of the Pharisaic sect. The group's name is derived from the Greek word Ἰουδαΐζειν (*Ioudaizein*), used by Paul (Gal. 2:14) when he challenged Peter for fear that the Apostle might be persuaded to compel converts to "judaize" (Gal. 2:11–14). Paul was concerned about those who insisted that salvation continued to be gained only by obedience to the Jewish laws and customs as laid down in the works of Moses (Acts 15:1). Though it is unclear exactly how the Judaizers viewed the role of Jesus, the text suggests they regarded him less as the fulfiller of the ancient law and more as a rabbi who taught the proper application of the law in daily life. Such a view either negated the Lord's divinity or lessened it. Paul directly addressed the false ideas of these men in his epistles to the Galatians and Romans.[86] It is unlikely, however, that they were his primary opponents in Corinth, because the defense he used against them in other epistles is not evidenced in his arguments preserved in 2 Corinthians.[87]

Which, if any, of the other systems the interlopers were promulgating cannot be determined. It is clear that their view of Christ was so very radically different from the true one as to be irreconcilable. This alien proclamation "adds up to a wrong-headed preconception of the entire Christian kerygma [that is, doctrine] as Paul understood it. The Christ they proclaimed is κατὰ σάρκα [*kata sarka*], 'from an outward point of view' (5:16), which means that the power on display is visible and self-centered." Their spiritual superiority centers in their assumed authority that "they construed as lordly power which in turn lends itself to a posture" of boasting that has won over some of the Saints.[88]

The Apostle does explicitly identify certain issues that are helpful in determining the major area of conflict. These people are guilty of "peddling the word of God" (2:17; 11:12–15), basing their judgments on valuing appearance, boasting, and making self-comparisons (5:12; 10:12–18; 11:16, 21b; 12:1). They regarded the authority of "Christ as being revealed in power—particularly their own gifts and powers—and not in weakness and suffering. This practical human reasoning, according to Paul, is a violation of the Gospel. It is human reasoning, together with all the judgments that flow from it, that the Gospel overturns."[89]

---

86. For an overview, see James W. Aageson, "Judaizing," in *ABD,* 3:1089. For an extended study, see Michele Murray, *Playing a Jewish Game: Gentile Christian Judaizing in the First and Second Centuries CE* (Waterloo, Can.: Wilfrid Laurier University Press, 2004).

87. Seifrid, *Second Epistle,* 409.

88. Martin, *2 Corinthians,* 526.

89. Seifrid, *Second Epistle,* 409, 410.

Knowing that such false doctrines and bold presumptions were actively being disseminated by some allows us to see why Paul was so alarmed and why he was justified in the forthrightness and even sternness of his defense. At the center of the conflict was the attempted diminishing of the station and person of the Lord. Paul had met the divine Savior—who identified himself as Jesus—and personally experienced his glory, power, and divinity. Any idea that the Savior was less than what he was Paul could not abide.

Further, the Apostle clearly acknowledges evil's cleverness, which not only transcends the Corinthians' capacity to understand and fight it but also Paul's own. For him, Satan is neither a mere metaphor nor the "personification of an impersonal power of evil, but precisely the power of evil, fully personal in nature."[90] And his fear is that somehow, and in a way beyond him, the Evil One will be successful in corrupting the Corinthians; thus Paul must use all his power to try to prevent it.

However, the Corinthians are not assisting him. They have, as he notes in 11:3, forgotten the simplicity of the gospel of Jesus Christ. Then, as now, as Elder McConkie has noted, "the gospel of Jesus Christ is plain, pure, simple, easy to be understood. It is not some hidden mystery beyond man's comprehension. Its doctrines are clear to the understanding; its ordinances are easy to identify; its symbols are not buried in obscurity. Its God stands revealed and is known to the true worshippers. Mystery, complexity, an incomprehensible and unknowable God—these and all such like are born of apostasy."[91]

In 11:5, Paul expresses his second reason he is willing to act as a fool. The first was his zeal for the well-being of these Saints (11:1). The second is to show them that he regards himself as in no way inferior to his detractors despite the support they've gained due to their self-proclaimed expertise and self-adulation.[92] With a phrase dripping with irony, Paul refers to these self-assured, influential, but destructive interlopers as "super-apostles."[93] He uses the adverb ὑπερλίαν (*hyperlian*), "super," to stress their supposed exalted position. The modern colloquial expression "super-duper" catches the force of Paul's satire. His personal self-assurance, on the other hand, rests upon his view of the success of his ministry and reflects his careful

90. Seifrid, *Second Epistle,* 405.
91. *DNTC,* 2:439.
92. Seifrid, *Second Epistle,* 411.
93. For discussion, see Translation Notes for 11:5.

consideration and appreciation of his God-given skills in correctly and powerfully carrying out that ministry.

Paul begins 11:6 with a concession to his detractors that his speaking proficiency is somewhat lacking. The noun he uses (ἰδιώτης, *idiotēs*), rendered here as private and therefore "unskilled," refers to a person who is inexpert or amateurish in a field of knowledge or expertise because it is not often practiced in public.[94] Such a reference could be pejorative when referring to the common or lower class of society since many of these had no formal training or skill. On the other hand, it could be complimentary when it denoted persons who were genuine instead of proverbially trained in the art of rhetoric like Sophists, who proverbially utilized trickery or deception to persuade others, often to seek gain and fame.[95]

Paul's defense, at this point, suggests that he is actually not totally unskilled in public speaking but refuses to show off by using the empty and self-promoting eloquence and disingenuous ornamental style displayed by many contemporary Sophists. His skill in argument, as captured in his letters, clearly evidences a solid knowledge of the art, and therefore his admission is less about an actual lack of skill and more a refusal to yield to the public's demand for and expected use thereof.[96] Thus his humble admission is likely a bit tongue-in-cheek in order to demonstrate his pure motives.[97]

His point is that even if his preaching lacks the eloquence of some, he is in no way guilty before God. Such guilt, however, could rest on any who, no matter how well they spoke, were ignorant of the ways of God and, thereby, did not declare the means of salvation. Paul's point is that he is careful to refrain from using the overblown, self-promoting, ornate, and disgusting methods used by others. Thus it is not eloquence that commends his message but the power it has to save.[98]

---

94. Louw-Nida, §27.26.

95. Guthrie, *2 Corinthians,* 517.

96. Given Paul's apparent status as upper-class and also as a Jew of the diaspora, it is unlikely he would not have had heavy exposure to, if not some actual training in, the art. Winter, *Philo and Paul among the Sophists,* 225–28; Witherington, *Conflict and Community,* 447.

97. Guthrie, *2 Corinthians,* 518.

98. Gerald Bray, ed., *1–2 Corinthians,* vol. 7 of Ancient Christian Commentary on Scripture, New Testament (Downers Grove, Ill.: InterVarsity Press, 1999), 291–92.

Paul's Defense Continued (11:7–15)

Greek Text

7 Ἢ ἁμαρτίαν ἐποίησα ἐμαυτὸν ταπεινῶν ἵνα ὑμεῖς ὑψωθῆτε, ὅτι δωρεὰν τὸ τοῦ
θεοῦ εὐαγγέλιον εὐηγγελισάμην ὑμῖν; 8 ἄλλας ἐκκλησίας ἐσύλησα λαβὼν ὀψώ-
νιον πρὸς τὴν ὑμῶν διακονίαν, 9 καὶ παρὼν πρὸς ὑμᾶς καὶ ὑστερηθεὶς οὐ κατε-
νάρκησα οὐθενός· τὸ γὰρ ὑστέρημά μου προσανεπλήρωσαν οἱ ἀδελφοὶ ἐλθόντες
ἀπὸ Μακεδονίας· καὶ ἐν παντὶ ἀβαρῆ ἐμαυτὸν ὑμῖν ἐτήρησα καὶ τηρήσω. 10 ἔστιν
ἀλήθεια Χριστοῦ ἐν ἐμοὶ ὅτι ἡ καύχησις αὕτη οὐ φραγήσεται εἰς ἐμὲ ἐν τοῖς κλίμασι
τῆς Ἀχαΐας. 11 διὰ τί; ὅτι οὐκ ἀγαπῶ ὑμᾶς; ὁ θεὸς οἶδεν. 12 Ὃ δὲ ποιῶ καὶ ποιήσω,
ἵνα ἐκκόψω τὴν ἀφορμὴν τῶν θελόντων ἀφορμήν, ἵνα ἐν ᾧ καυχῶνται εὑρεθῶ-
σιν καθὼς καὶ ἡμεῖς. 13 οἱ γὰρ τοιοῦτοι ψευδαπόστολοι, ἐργάται δόλιοι, μετα-
σχηματιζόμενοι εἰς ἀποστόλους Χριστοῦ· 14 καὶ οὐ θαῦμα, αὐτὸς γὰρ ὁ Σατανᾶς
μετασχηματίζεται εἰς ἄγγελον φωτός· 15 οὐ μέγα οὖν εἰ καὶ οἱ διάκονοι αὐτοῦ μετα-
σχηματίζονται ὡς διάκονοι δικαιοσύνης, ὧν τὸ τέλος ἔσται κατὰ τὰ ἔργα αὐτῶν.
[SBLGNT]

King James Version

7 Have I committed an offence in abasing
myself that ye might be exalted, because
I have preached to you the gospel of
God freely? 8 I robbed other churches,
taking wages of them, to do you service.
9 And when I was present with you, and
wanted, I was chargeable to no man:
for that which was lacking to me the
brethren which came from Macedonia
supplied: and in all things I have kept
myself from being burdensome unto
you, and so will I keep myself. 10 As the
truth of Christ is in me, no man shall
stop me of this boasting in the regions
of Achaia. 11 Wherefore? because I love
you not? God knoweth. 12 But what
I do, that I will do, that I may cut off
occasion from them which desire occa-
sion; that wherein they glory, they may
be found even as we. 13 For such are
false apostles, deceitful workers, trans-
forming themselves into the apostles

New Rendition

7 Or have I sinned by humbling myself
so that you might be lifted up because
I preached the gospel of God to you
without payment? 8 I robbed other
churches by taking their support to
serve you. 9 And when I was with you
and was in need, I was not a burden to
anyone because the brethren who came
from Macedonia took care of my needs,
and in every way, I kept myself from
being a burden to you and will continue
to do so. 10 As Christ's truth is in me,
as far as I am concerned, this boast of
mine will not be quashed in the regions
of Achaia. 11 Why? Because I do not
love you? God knows that I do. 12 And
what I am doing, I will continue to do
so that I may undercut any opportunity
for those who want an opportunity to
appear to be our equals in the things
they boast about. 13 For such men are
false apostles, deceitful workers, who

of Christ. 14 And no marvel; for Satan himself is transformed into an angel of light. 15 Therefore it is no great thing if his ministers also be transformed as the ministers of righteousness; whose end shall be according to their works.

disguise themselves as apostles of Christ. 14 And no wonder! For Satan disguises himself as an angel of light. 15 Thus it is not surprising that his servants also disguise themselves as servants of righteousness, whose end will be according to their works.

Translation Notes and Comments

11:7 ***Have I committed an offence in abasing myself that ye might be exalted / Or have I sinned by humbling myself so that you might be lifted up:*** The conjunction ἤ (*ē*), "or," often signals a rhetorical question that anticipates a negative response.[99] The verb ποιέω (*poieō*) has the basic meaning of "to do, to make," but it is often used with a noun as a periphrasis for a simple verb.[100] Here it modifies the noun ἁμαρτία (*hamartia*), "sin," giving the literal sense "to do sin," which we have rendered as simply "sinned."[101]

The verb ταπεινόω (*tapeinoō*) means "to lower, degrade, abase, humiliate," but also "to make humble."[102] It is found here as a present participle, thus inferring Paul's continued humble state of working to support himself.

The verb ὑψόω (*hypsoō*), "to exalt, lift up," found here as an aorist passive subjunctive, means "to cause enhancement in honor, fame, position, power, or fortune."[103] Paul's use of this word points to his view of his mission and why he was willing to assume a lowly station.

There is an interesting play in the grammar here. "Humbling" is a present participle and is set in contrast to "lift up" and "preach" (in the clause below), which are in the aorist tense. Thus "debasing" is a process that began when Paul first came to Corinth and took a menial job to support himself in order to preach the gospel to the people "free of charge" (1 Cor. 9:18, NR) and thereby lift them up. While "lifting up" and "preaching" are acts now completed, the humbling still continues. It began with the humiliation he suffered during his second visit and continues to endure due to their present attitudes.[104]

99. BDAG, 432–33.
100. BDAG, 839–42.
101. BDAG, 50–51.
102. BDAG, 990; Louw-Nida, §87.62; 88.56.
103. BDAG, 1045–46.
104. Barnett, *Second Epistle,* 514.

which one person was obliged socially to another"[118] and thus was a burden to a lesser or greater degree. That it is found here in the aorist tense suggests that the period when Paul could have been a burden was short-lived.

The adjective οὐδείς (*oudeis*) means "no," but here it acts as a substantive and thus references "no one,"[119] or as we render it, "not . . . anyone."

Paul's point is that, even in his extremity, he refused to ask for or receive assistance from the Saints. It was through this refusal that he debased, lowered, or humbled himself. The irony is that one would expect that those who stood on their own in determined self-reliance would be admired.

for that which was lacking to me the brethren which came from Macedonia supplied / because the brethren who came from Macedonia took care of my needs: The conjunction γάρ (*gar*), "for,"[120] is causal and explains how Paul's needs were met. The noun ὑστέρημα (*hysterēma*) means "need, want, deficiency." The verb προσαναπληρόω (*prosanaplēroō*) means "to fill up, supply," and denotes providing fully whatever is needed.[121]

The plural noun ἀδελφοὶ (*adelphoi*), "brethren," likely refers to Silas and Timothy, who stayed behind to oversee affairs in Macedonia after Paul had left (based on Acts 18:5; Philip. 4:15).[122]

The verb ἔρχομαι (*erchomai*), "to come,"[123] is found here as an aorist participle. The tense suggests a one-time visit.[124] The noun Μακεδονία (*Makedonia*) refers to the Roman province just north of the province of Achaia. This phrase explains how Paul "robbed" others—that is, by accepting assistance from the northern Saints. Of whatever nature those supplies were, they allowed Paul time to get established and not require any help from the Corinthian Saints.

and in all things I have kept myself from being burdensome unto you, and so will I keep myself / and in every way, I kept myself from being a burden to you and will continue to do so: The phrase ἐν παντὶ (*en panti*), "in all things" or "by whatever means,"[125] points to the measures Paul took, including accepting Macedonian help along with his manual labor, to keep

118. Guthrie, *2 Corinthians,* 522.
119. Louw-Nida, §92.23.
120. BDAG, 189–90.
121. Louw-Nida, §35.34.
122. Bernard, "Second Epistle," 102.
123. BDAG, 393–94.
124. Barnett, *Second Epistle,* 517 n. 28.
125. Barnett, *Second Epistle,* 517.

from burdening the local Saints. The verb τηρέω (*tēreō*), "to guard, keep,"[126] found here in the aorist tense, emphasizes that Paul went to some lengths not to burden these people. The adjective ἀβαρής (*abarēs*), "not burdensome," refers to something of light weight, but it is used here figuratively to denote little to no financial drain.[127] We render it as "from being a burden." Paul ends the sentence by repeating the verb *tēreō*, but this time in the future tense, showing he will continue to be of no financial load, likely referring to the stance he plans to maintain during his upcoming visit.

11:10 ***As the truth of Christ is in me / As Christ's truth is in me:*** To emphasize his point, Paul begins this sentence with an oath formula. Such declarations held a very strong force among his contemporaries for the truthfulness of what is being said. The noun ἀλήθεια (*alētheia*), "truth," denotes what is real and certain and also the content of that reality.[128] The noun Χριστός (*Christos*), "Christ," found here as a subjective genitive, points to the truth that originates with the Lord and looks particularly at the gospel message. Paul's phrasing here perhaps reveals an indignant tone due to charges by his detractors that he intended to use some of the collection for the poor for his own use.[129]

no man shall stop me of this boasting in the regions of Achaia / as far as I am concerned, this boast of mine will not be quashed in the regions of Achaia: With this phrase, Paul turns again to the issue of proper and improper boasting. The parenthetical phrase εἰς ἐμέ (*eis eme*), literally "toward me, with respect to me," carries the idea of "as far as I am concerned" or, in effect, "not if I have anything to do about it."[130]

On the noun καύχησις (*kauchēsis*), "boasting," see Translation Notes for 10:8. The present issue seems to center once again on those who have insinuated themselves into an area of missionary work that had been assigned to him.

The verb φράσσω (*phrassō*) means "to shut, close," and by extension "to silence, or quash,"[131] with the idea of forcefully putting an end to ideas or teachings. Here it refers to Paul's "boast." Context suggests he is referring to his humble action in not accepting assistance for the work that he does.

126. BDAG, 1002.
127. Louw-Nida, §57.225; BDAG, 1.
128. Louw-Nida, §§72.1, 2.
129. Martin, *2 Corinthians*, 533.
130. Guthrie, *2 Corinthians*, 524.
131. BDAG, 1064–65.

The noun κλίμα (*klima*), found here as a plural, denotes a district or region[132] and in this case refers specifically to the areas within the Roman province of Achaia.

11:11–12: The Greek in these sentences is complex and elliptical, thus requiring some flexibility in rendering it into English in order to capture Paul's thought.[133]

11:11 ***Wherefore? because I love you not? God knoweth / Why? Because I do not love you? God knows that I do:*** The phrase διὰ τί (*dia ti*), literally "through this," indicates an indirect question, thus rendered "why."[134] The next phrase suggests Paul has been accused of not loving the people, likely because he refused to accept their offered help. His words may be hiding the actual accusation, "He despises us,"[135] thus his need to assure them of his genuine feelings.

The phrase ὁ θεὸς οἶδεν (*ho theos oiden*), "God knows," is Paul's second use of an oath formula that he uses to stress the truthfulness of the points he is making. For flow in English, the phrase needs an object; thus we supply "that I do" in our Rendition.

11:12 ***But what I do, that I will do / And what I am doing, I will continue to do:*** With this phrase, Paul clearly identifies his stance and states it will not change. The conjunction δέ (*de*), "and," "points to a conclusion now to be stated."[136] Paul uses the verb ποιέω (*poieō*), "to perform, work, do,"[137] twice. The first occurrence is in the present tense and refers to the Apostle's continued practice of ministry. The second occurrence is in the future tense and points to the Apostle's determination to not change his methods even if he must resist forces that demand change.[138]

that I may cut off occasion from them which desire occasion / so that I may undercut any opportunity for those who want an opportunity: In this phrase, Paul explains his purpose in continuing to practice the ministry in his own way. The verb ἐκκόπτω (*ekkoptō*), found here as an aorist subjunctive, means "to cut off, cut down, undercut."[139] By extension, it means "to

132. BDAG, 549.
133. Martin, *2 Corinthians,* 533.
134. BDAG, 223–26.
135. Barnett, *Second Epistle,* 520 n. 42.
136. Barnett, *Second Epistle,* 520 n. 46.
137. Louw-Nida, §§42.7, 41; 90.45.
138. Guthrie, *2 Corinthians,* 525.
139. BDAG, 305.

eliminate" or "do away with" something.[140] Paul's use of the phrase shows his intent to cut off or eliminate the opportunity that his antagonists are seeking.[141]

The verb θέλω (*thelō*), found here as a present participle, means "to have a desire, wish, or want."[142] The noun ἀφορμή (*aphormē*) denotes "an occasion, pretext, opportunity."[143] The word originated as a military term designating the base of operations during a campaign,[144] and its use by Paul reveals that his enemies see themselves as engaged in a battle against him and are seeking a definite opportunity to attack him.[145]

that wherein they glory, they may be found even as we / to appear to be our equals in the things they boast about: In this final phrase, Paul expands on why he will do the undercutting. This phrase begins with the conjunction ἵνα (*hina*), "in order that, that."[146] It modifies the verb εὑρίσκω (*heuriskō*), "to find," found here as a subjunctive aorist passive, and thereby carries the sense of "to be found, appear, be shown to be."[147]

The phrase also includes the relative clause ἐν ᾧ καυχῶνται (*en hō kauchōntai*), literally "in what they boast (about)," and refers to the specific items the interlopers use to show they have authority at least equal to Paul's. For the verb *kauchaomai*, "to glory, boast,"[148] see Translation Notes for 10:8. The sentence ends with the phrase καθὼς καὶ ἡμεῖς (*kathōs kai hēmeis*), "just as we (are)."[149]

In sum, we get "so that, in what they boast about, they might appear to be just as we are." We have chosen to use an infinitive to express the purpose clause to provide a better contemporary English translation.

This phrase suggests that Paul is not referring to the interlopers' boast that they are equal to him in the nature, power, and veracity of their lives and ministry.[150] Since they are claiming equality here, whereas in other places

---

140. Louw-Nida, §13.101.
141. Guthrie, *2 Corinthians,* 525.
142. BDAG, 447–48.
143. BDAG, 158.
144. Hughes, *Second Epistle,* 392 n. 54; Barnett, *Second Epistle,* 521 n. 48.
145. Bernard, "Second Epistle," 103.
146. BDAG, 475–77.
147. BDAG, 411–12.
148. Louw-Nida, §33.368.
149. BDAG, 493–94.
150. BDAG, 411, notes it as their desire to "be found (leading the same kind of life) as we."

drawing an inference from it.[168] The adjective μέγας (*megas*) usually means "great" or "large,"[169] but in this context it becomes a substantive noun, looking back at θαῦμα (*thauma*), "wonder," and carries the meaning of what is "surprising in view of being important."[170] It is negated by the particle οὐ (*ou*), "not," and therefore denotes what is absolutely not surprising.

The conjunction καί (*kai*) in the present context has adverbial force and translates as "likewise,"[171] thereby linking Satan's actions as noted in 11:14 with that of his "servants" here. The noun διάκονος (*diakonos*), "agent, minister, servant," in the present context, denotes one who is an intermediary or an assistant to a higher authority.[172] Thus its association with Satan is particularly barbed.

For the third time, Paul uses the verb μετασχηματίζω (*metaschēmatizō*), "to transform, masquerade, disguise" (see above). It is again found as a present tense of the middle voice, but here it is plural, thus referring to the interlopers. The verb strongly suggests that they knowingly put on an act of being righteous.

The noun δικαιοσύνη (*diakiosunē*), "righteousness," found here in the genitive case, denotes "the quality or characteristic of upright behavior."[173] When modifying the noun διάκονοι (*diakonoi*), "servants, ministers," it could be taken either as an objective genitive denoting "ministers who produce righteousness" or as an attributive genitive denoting "righteous ministers."[174] The former is the more likely sense. The noun captures the image that these people deliberately portray regarding themselves, their status, and mission. They pretend to be in the service of righteousness, boast about deeds that support their interpretation, and claim to be superior to Paul.

---

168. BDAG, 736–37.

169. BDAG, 623–24. The phrase reads literally, "nothing so great." It is actually an understatement used for emphasis. Barnett, *Second Epistle*, 526 n. 16.

170. Louw-Nida, §25.207. The expression οὐ μέγα οὖν εἰ (*ou mega oun ei*) translates literally as "it is therefore no great thing if," but the literal translation gives a false impression because it was a great thing that the interlopers were able to ingratiate themselves among quite a number of the Saints and thereby gain threatening influence. Martin, *2 Corinthians*, 538.

171. BDF, §442.10.

172. BDAG, 230–31; The noun *diakonos*, from which the English word "deacon" is derived, in an ecclesiastical context, denotes a person who had "responsibility to care for the needs of believers." Louw-Nida, §53.67.

173. BDAG, 247–49.

174. Guthrie, *2 Corinthians*, 529.

whose end shall be according to their works / whose end will be according to their works: The noun τέλος (*telos*), "result, end," denotes "the final goal" or "the outcome or destiny" that awaits each soul according to her or his nature.[175] The noun ἔργον (*ergon*), "deed, activity, work," found here as a plural, nuances deeds that are brought about through regular activity "with possible focus on the energy or effort involved."[176] The preposition κατά (*kata*), "according to," marks "the norm to which . . . punishments or rewards are given."[177] The context shows that Paul has punishment in mind because of the effort his detractors have put into their attempt to thwart his authority and teachings.

Analysis and Summary

The central issue of Paul's defense in this pericope is his refusal to accept patronage or other forms of assistance from any of the Corinthian Saints (1 Cor. 9:6–18).[178] "Paul would not take certain kinds of support from the Corinthians because of the elitist, benefactor attitudes and obligations that would come with such support. Such attitudes kept the Corinthians from seeing the gospel as grace and Paul as *their* patron or benefactor."[179] As a result, some insisted that he was not a true Apostle. Their claim was based on the Lord's command that this group was to minister the gospel through the generosity of the people (Matt. 10:8–10; Luke 10:7).

In 11:7, Paul challenges that idea by asking if he is guilty of sinning and thus worthy of punishment just because he acted with humility, even debasement (*tapeinoō*), in refusing payment for his declaration of the gospel. In doing so, he uses bitter irony.[180] We see the force of that irony in his emphasis that it was "God's gospel"—not any teaching or skill arising from his own merits—that he preached freely.

---

175. Louw-Nida, §89.40; BDAG, 998–99.

176. Louw-Nida, §42.11; BDAG, 390–91.

177. BDAG, 511–13.

178. For a study on the of the Greco-Roman idea of patronage, see John K. Chow, *Patronage and Power: A Study of Social Networks in Corinth* (Sheffield, Eng.: JSOT Press, 1992).

179. Witherington, *Conflict and Community,* 448, italics in original.

180. Barrett, *Second Epistle,* 281. Both the Old and New Testaments celebrate those who humble themselves in the Lord's service. See, for example, 1 Sam. 2:7; Job 5:11; Ezek. 17:24; 21:26; Matt. 23:12; Luke 14:11; and James 4:10. It appears that Paul's antagonists, likely due to culturally accepted myopia, had a badly blurred vision of what constituted true greatness. Guthrie, *2 Corinthians,* 519.

Two aspects of the Greco-Roman world are playing in the background. The first is the very public and disdainful attitude of the Greek upper class toward manual work. Many insisted that free citizens should never stoop to physical labor. The second takes root from this idea. It was promulgated by certain Sophists since the fifth century BC. They insisted it was necessary for them to accept payment for their services because anything done for free was worthless. Thus they not only charged for their services but also sought for patrons to support them. Paul violated both of these social mores when he went to work for Aquila and Prisca in their very successful business of making tents, sails, and awnings.[181] Such employment, however, had a major drawback because this occupation involved working with leather—that is, the skin of dead animals—and thus some Jewish Christians may have considered those working in the profession ritually unclean.[182] Because the Apostle was broadly known as their chief leader and teacher, certain Saints expected him to model the role that society dictated. When he stooped to doing manual labor, they felt an acute embarrassment. His actions were "a slap at their public status and dignity."[183]

Paul's refusal to accept assistance and, likely, patronage allowed some, probably abetted by the interlopers, to charge that he did not love, and likely trust, them (11:11; 12:13, 15).[184] They felt that he certainly did not stand up to the status of those whom he called "super-apostles," who fit well into the norms and expectations of the culture and had willingly accepted the Corinthians' support, patronage, and direction. Thus the interlopers had become their men.

Despite the strong feelings of this group, the Apostle could not bow to their desires. The reason? Because they were simply wrong in their understanding of what the gospel meant and how it was to be spread. Paul was not willing to be bound down by the desires of the few through accepting money from them. Instead, he humbled, even debased himself (*tapeinoō*), by becoming the slave "to all people, even the weak, so that he might win as many people as possible (1 Cor. 9:19–22)." In doing so, he demonstrated to the Christian community that proper service is not for self-promotion but for other-exaltation. Such service worked for the promotion of others, allowing them "to move up and move on in their relationship to God. Consequently, the effect of Paul's 'humiliation' is that the Corinthians are exalted."[185]

---

181. Martin, *2 Corinthians,* 529–30.

182. See m. Baba Batra 2.9; Wilhelm Michaelis, "σκηνοποιός," in *TDNT,* 7:393–94.

183. Guthrie, *2 Corinthians,* 519–20.

184. Guthrie, *2 Corinthians,* 519.

185. Guthrie, *2 Corinthians,* 520.

Paul does not hide the fact that, as a servant of the Lord who is preaching full-time, he could legitimately ask for and receive support (1 Cor. 9:4–6, 14). So why did he not? In short, because he did not want anything to hinder the furtherance of the spread of the gospel (1 Cor. 9:12). His writings allow us to see his concerns. First, he could not be bound to the direction, desires, or whims of a patron. Second, he did not want such a financial burden to become an obstacle in people's acceptance of the gospel (1 Cor. 9:12; 2 Cor. 6:3; compare 2 Cor.2:17; 1 Thes. 2:5). Therefore he had to declare it without personal cost to them. Third, he feels that preaching the gospel freely carries its own reward (1 Cor. 9:17), and thus he feels fully compensated for his efforts. Fourth, it allows him to express a Christlike grace that all could see and hopefully be drawn to and imitate (1 Cor. 4:16; 11:1). Finally, he views himself as the slave (δοῦλος, *doulos*) of Christ (Rom. 1:1; Gal. 1:10), and as such he is not to be paid for doing what that status requires.[186]

There is, however, a complication with his scenario. As Paul states in 11:8–9, he readily accepted assistance from the Macedonian Saints. That he refers to that assistance as an act of robbery (συλάω, *sylaō*) reveals the height of his irony and gives a glimpse of his acute frustration with the local Saints. It also sets the nature of his reception of those funds apart from that which the Corinthians might give, thus disallowing a comparison. And he really rubs it in. Though it may be painful, what he did was *for them*—he brought the gospel for them, and he preached it for them, and he sustained it for them, and he did it "free of charge."[187] (He will explain the reason for his policy in 11:10–12.)

But why take from the northern Saints and not the Corinthians? Likely it was for pragmatic reasons. The situation in Corinth was not the same as in, for example, Philippi. Paul was no longer living in that city, and therefore any funds they gave he would not be using for their direct benefit. Even so, they were willing to give in order to support the extension of his missionary efforts beyond their city. Further, he enjoyed a strong bond of fellowship (*koinonia*) with these Saints. Both of these conditions allowed him to accept their support without feeling obligated to them.[188] In contrast, Paul would be returning to Corinth, where he had spent considerable time

186. For a study, see Bengt Holmberg, *Paul and Power: The Structure of Authority in the Primitive Church as Reflected in the Pauline Epistles* (Philadelphia: Fortress Press, 1980), 86–93.

187. Barnett, *Second Epistle,* 516.

188. Holmberg, *Paul and Power,* 91–92; Martin, *2 Corinthians,* 530–31.

but had not established the breadth of the bond of fellowship he enjoyed with the northern branch. Further, the Corinthians would be paying for services that he would render to them instead of extending his missionary service. Finally, given the patron-client attitude that these people held, they would have felt the Apostle was accepting wages that obligated him to them.[189] Even if it hurt their feelings that he preached the gospel "free of charge" (1 Cor. 9:18, NR), Paul could not accept their support. His duty was to offer the gospel as a "gift" rather than as "goods."[190] In doing so, he boldly, but not without opposition, set up a counterculture—one based on eternal principles looking to everlasting life, not mortal perspectives that sought for immediate fulfillment and self-promotion.

In 11:9, Paul does three things: he explains exactly how he lowered or humbled himself, how he "robbed" other churches, and how careful he was not to be a burden to anyone in Corinth. The context he presents suggests that Paul supported himself when his funds ran low. Even so, he went out of his way not to be burdensome (*katanarkeō*) to anyone there. He referred to his stance as "lowering" or "humbling" himself. Fortunately, his needs were met by a party that came from Macedonia, most likely Philippi (Philip. 4:14). Accepting the donation, he notes, is how he "robbed" other churches. The party probably consisted of Silas and Timothy, who joined him early in his Corinth mission (1:1, 19). When Silas and Timothy arrived, bringing money from the Macedonian Saints, Paul was able to give himself to preaching full-time.[191] The funds they brought from the Macedonian Saints allowed Paul the needed time to establish his independence. In that way, he was able to avoid falling into a patron-client relationship and also escape any charge of exploitation.[192] He concludes the sentence by noting that his stance on this issue will not change during his upcoming visit. He will maintain his independence at all cost.

To emphasize his point, he begins the next sentence with a strong oath, testifying that "Christ's truth is in me" (11:10, NR). That truth is undeniably the seat of all that Paul does, including his insistence on depending on no one when it comes to preaching the gospel. That gospel centers on Christ's truth, as given to the Apostle from his first encounter with the Lord on the

189. Matera, *II Corinthians,* 250–51.
190. Witherington, *Conflict and Community,* 448.
191. Guthrie, *2 Corinthians,* 522.
192. Guthrie, *2 Corinthians,* 522.

road to Damascus and persisting through the course of his ministry.[193] The one salient truth is that Christ lives and continues to minister through his chosen leaders. Paul's oath is a firm statement of his "resolute commitment to the truth given by Christ" and acts as "a solid affirmation of the apostle's commitment to the truth, undergirded by his relationship with the truth-giving Christ."[194]

Paul's defense is that he has been reluctantly drawn into the battle of boasting due to the boasting of his antagonists (11:18, 21). His argument contains a rhetorical masterstroke: he begins boasting of his strengths, but then he transitions to boasting about his weaknesses and celebrating them, barely calling attention to the shift. The particular weakness in focus here is his refusal to accept local assistance. His humbling himself, which some have found culturally jarring, has made him enemies. Even so, he declares he will not be turned from his stance. Indeed, nothing will prevent him from continuing to declare—in his own way—the word throughout the entire province of Achaia.[195] That way dictates complete independence from anyone except God and Christ.

In 11:11–12, Paul first heads off a misguided explanation as to why he preaches the gospel free of charge and then explains why he continues to do so. He begins with the rhetorical question "Why? Because I do not love you?" His assurance may have arisen from complaints that he accepted support from Macedonia, thus showing his love for those Saints, while he showed no love for the Corinthian Saints by rejecting assistance from them. Here he reassures them of his genuine care for them. To stress his point, he uses his second oath, "God knows that I do." "The oath itself implicitly expresses the essential matter of the dispute, the question of the presence of Christ in the apostle (13:3)."[196] His appeal is based on God's full knowledge of the hearts and minds of people and, therefore, the Apostle's desires, intents, and motives. No matter what cultural or social appearances may dictate, God knows the true state of Paul's heart.[197] The Apostle now must win over the Corinthians' hearts. His aim is not to "win" at the cost of their "loss" but to have all "win" together in Christ.[198]

193. Harris, *Second Epistle,* 763: Barnett, *Second Epistle,* 519.
194. Guthrie, *2 Corinthians,* 523.
195. Guthrie, *2 Corinthians,* 524.
196. Seifrid, *Second Epistle,* 417.
197. Guthrie, *2 Corinthians,* 524–25.
198. Seifrid, *Second Epistle,* 417.

His actions are based in no way on favoritism but on love. That his accusers (both those local and those who arrived later) would impute a lack of love on Paul's part is quite remarkable given what we know of them. In none of Paul's writings does there appear a notice that these people have shown any love for him or any group beyond their own circle. There is even doubt of their love for one another. Such a case would explain why Paul would have been led to write his wonderful treatise on love in 1 Corinthians 13.[199]

Paul's argument at 11:12–15 reaches its turning point, allowing him to transition from addressing his detractors generally to facing the interlopers themselves, whose self-proclaimed apostolic position he now takes on.[200]

In 11:12, he states the explicit reasons why he will continue to refuse any wages for his ministerial labors, perhaps to deflect any attempt to put pressure on him before he ever arrives. The sentence breaks down into three parts. In the first, Paul declares his stance (I will continue doing as I have done); second, he explains his purpose (that I might undercut the ground from those who seek a basis); and in the third, he expands on why he will do the undercutting (because they seek to boast that they are equal to us). Paul's point appears to be insisting that he will continue to refuse payment for his preaching because it will undercut the claim of those who insist they are his equals.[201] Paul is using the verb figuratively here, explaining that he will not give his enemies (the "false apostles" of the next verse) the "occasion, opportunity" (ἀφορμή, *aphormē*),[202] to claim that they have accomplished the same thing he and his companions have.

The point of the long phrase is simply that the interlopers are seeking to become Paul's equals. In sum, they are claiming that they minister in the same way he does, but with greater effect (compare 10:10). By not taking pay, Paul draws the stark line between his methods and intents of ministry and theirs. The Apostle clearly sets off his position from his opposers and thereby emphasizes a total lack of equality.[203]

Apparently, the interlopers are boasting that they preach their brand of the gospel, which they insist is the authentic one, on the same basis of authority that Paul does. But by accepting wages, they claim they are acting

199. Barnett, *Second Epistle,* 520.
200. Seifrid, *Second Epistle,* 418.
201. Barnett, *Second Epistle,* 520–21.
202. BDAG, 158.
203. Guthrie, *2 Corinthians,* 526.

as true apostles and that, by rejecting them, Paul not only undercuts his insistence that he is a true apostle but also shows his lack of love for the Corinthian Saints. He will attack their position in the next paragraph. But at this point, it is important to understand the basis of Paul's position. The Lord, at his first encounter with the future Apostle, made it clear that Paul's ministry would be to the Gentiles (Acts 26:16–18; Gal. 1:15–16; Rom. 1:5; 15:14–16). Paul's badge of apostleship therefore necessitated suffering the humiliation of manual labor so he could spread the gospel "free of charge" (11:7, NIV; compare 1 Cor. 9:18), which he felt was at the core of the Lord's call to him. It assured that he would be obliged to no one but Deity himself. As such he could proudly wear the badge "Apostle to the Gentiles," which his opponents, because they received wages, could not do. Thus he undercut their insistence on equality in preaching to the Gentiles.[204]

Of note is Paul's teaching to the Thessalonian Saints just a few years before he brought the gospel to the Corinthians. He had warned those Saints of the impending apostasy, noting that both letters and individuals were already circulating false doctrine. As of yet, he noted, a restraining power operated, but when it left, lawlessness would be revealed, and for those who did not love the truth, deception followed by condemnation would come (2 Thes. 2:3–12). A few years after his visit to Corinth, he will tell the Christian leadership in the province of Asia that, not long after he leaves, "among your own selves, men shall arise teaching falsehoods, to draw away disciples after them. As a consequence, be alert, remembering that for three years I did not cease night and day to admonish every one with tears" (Acts 20:29–31, our translation).

Sandwiched between those two warnings was his work among the Corinthians. And what do we find there? His first letter "reveals a community racked with divisions (1 Cor. 1:10–17; 3:1–4), thankless for Paul's ministry (4:8–15), internally litigious (6:1–6), thoughtless about the new convert (8:1–13), culturally insensitive toward the unsaved (10:23–11:1), selfish at the communal meal (11:17–22), and proudly displaying the [spiritual gifts] at their meetings (14:1–4)."[205] Paul's second letter reveals that the same willful individualism continued unabated. Some of these people were very willing to write of Paul as "tepid, vacillating, and defeated" (6:11–13)[206] and at the same time gladly welcomed and gave comfort to outsiders who

204. Barnett, *Second Epistle,* 522.
205. Barnett, *Second Epistle,* 520 n. 44.
206. Barnett, *Second Epistle,* 520 n. 44.

intruded into the Apostle's field of labor (10:12–17). They were blind to the fact that these interlopers were taking full advantage of the people financially.[207] Thus the Church at Corinth, with its fractious environment and willingness to dismiss genuine authority and accept spurious doctrines along with those who disseminated them, is a case study in how the apostasy began and advanced. As one scholar noted, the "speedy appearance of false teachers was one of the most remarkable features of the Apostolic age."[208] Apostasy seems to have been all too widespread in Corinth.

Paul's statement in 11:13 gives his reason for refusing to allow the interlopers an opportunity to meet their claim that their ministry is on an equal footing with his own.[209] He clearly focuses on the debate about authority—who has the right to administer in the area and set the doctrine. He bluntly rejects their claim to both by describing them by two very strong epithets. The first is "false apostles" (ψευδαπόστολοι, *pseudapostoloi*). The disparaging term is found only here in the New Testament and appears to be coined by Paul. In his view, they are "false" because they lack the proper authorization of Christ (compare 1:1), preach a "different gospel," promote a "different spirit," proclaim "another Jesus" (11:4, NR), and trespass into the Gentile mission field without authorization in order to usurp Jesus' command to preach the gospel in all the earth. In sum, they are without proper authority and "carriers of an alien message."[210] He next calls them "deceitful workers" (ἐργάται δόλιοι, *ergatai dolioi*), the term denoting a lack of allegiance to the Christian way and connoting a certain treacherousness in what they do,[211] because they present a hidden danger.

The text suggests that they are neither Gnostics nor Judaizers, "since the point of distinction between them and Paul is Christology, not speculation, and not the Torah or circumcision or sabbath rites; all these latter items are conspicuous by their absence from 2 Corinthians."[212] The interlopers do, however, claim to live a superior and more acceptable quality of life that gives evidence to the authenticity of their authority and teaching. Paul castigates their stand, insisting they not only are false but also know it. He states they willfully "disguise" or "masquerade" themselves (*metaschēmatizō*) as apostles of Christ when they are, in reality, emissaries of Satan.

---

207. Barnett, *Second Epistle,* 520 n. 44.

208. Bernard, "Second Epistle," 103.

209. Guthrie, *2 Corinthians,* 526.

210. Martin, *2 Corinthians,* 536.

211. BDAG, 256; Louw-Nida, §88.155.

212. Martin, *2 Corinthians,* 536.

In 11:14, Paul explains how this masquerade has and continues to go on. He introduces his point with the striking and irony-filled statement "and no wonder!" The phrase "serves as a strident call to be alert."[213] Alert to what? That the interlopers are following the pattern of their true master, Satan, who, when it serves his purpose, disguises himself as an "angel of light."[214] These men, as Paul insists in 11:15, are the devil's ministers (*diakononoi autou*) masquerading as "servants of righteousness."[215] Paul's charges against them are clear: promoting false doctrine, distorting the nature and work of Christ (11:4), attacking God's true Apostle, bearing false witness against that Apostle (10:12; 11:18–20), and intruding into his area of missionary work (10:13–16).[216] Looking ahead to 11:22–23, we see on what base they lay their claim: they have the proper lineage, being Hebrews through Abraham's line and the house of Israel. Further, they have given themselves fully as "ministers of Christ," having suffered and sacrificed for the kingdom. Since this is their claim for both legitimacy and support, Paul puts his own credentials up against theirs in 11:22 through 12:5 (see below) and in doing so outclasses them in every way.

Paul closes this section (11:15) by giving a stiff warning to his readers about the fate of these people: "Their end," he says simply, "will be the result of their deeds." The implication is that God's judgment upon them will be very severe due to their dissembling. It is unlikely Paul's readers would have missed his point: "to align themselves with such people constitutes more than a preference for one minister over another; it involves an entanglement in the work of Satan and a destiny of destruction."[217]

It is of note that Paul never identifies his antagonists, either by name or by origin, possibly to demonstrate their insignificance. He does state that they are self-recommenders (10:12, 18) and preach their own brand of doctrine (11:4), but he leaves much unsaid, likely deliberately. By using this indirect means, the Apostle is able to denigrate the claims and behavior of his detractors and compare them unfavorably with the exemplary life he has lived while also keeping the form of his argument and pointing out the sophistic dangers of apostasy, all without ever losing dignity.[218]

---

213. Martin, *2 Corinthians,* 537.

214. For details on this phrase, see Translation Notes for 11:14.

215. Barrett, *Second Epistle,* 287.

216. Guthrie, *2 Corinthians,* 529. See also Holzapfel and Wayment, *Making Sense,* 377.

217. Guthrie, *2 Corinthians,* 529.

218. For a study, see Peter Marshall, "Invective: Paul's Enemies in Corinth," in *Perspectives on Language and Text,* ed. Edger W. Conrad and Edward G. Newing (Winona Lake, Ind.: Eisenbrauns, 1987), 359–73, particularly 366–70.

Paul's Suffering as an Apostle (11:16–27)

Greek Text

16 Πάλιν λέγω, μή τίς με δόξῃ ἄφρονα εἶναι—εἰ δὲ μή γε, κἂν ὡς ἄφρονα δέξασθέ
με, ἵνα κἀγὼ μικρόν τι καυχήσωμαι· 17 ὃ λαλῶ οὐ κατὰ κύριον λαλῶ, ἀλλ' ὡς
ἐν ἀφροσύνῃ, ἐν ταύτῃ τῇ ὑποστάσει τῆς καυχήσεως. 18 ἐπεὶ πολλοὶ καυχῶνται
κατὰ σάρκα, κἀγὼ καυχήσομαι. 19 ἡδέως γὰρ ἀνέχεσθε τῶν ἀφρόνων φρόνιμοι
ὄντες· 20 ἀνέχεσθε γὰρ εἴ τις ὑμᾶς καταδουλοῖ, εἴ τις κατεσθίει, εἴ τις λαμβάνει, εἴ
τις ἐπαίρεται, εἴ τις εἰς πρόσωπον ὑμᾶς δέρει. 21 κατὰ ἀτιμίαν λέγω, ὡς ὅτι ἡμεῖς
ἠσθενήκαμεν· ἐν ᾧ δ' ἄν τις τολμᾷ, ἐν ἀφροσύνῃ λέγω, τολμῶ κἀγώ. 22 Ἑβραῖοί
εἰσιν; κἀγώ. Ἰσραηλῖταί εἰσιν; κἀγώ. σπέρμα Ἀβραάμ εἰσιν; κἀγώ. 23 διάκονοι
Χριστοῦ εἰσιν; παραφρονῶν λαλῶ, ὑπὲρ ἐγώ· ἐν κόποις περισσοτέρως, ἐν φυλα-
καῖς περισσοτέρως, ἐν πληγαῖς ὑπερβαλλόντως, ἐν θανάτοις πολλάκις· 24 ὑπὸ
Ἰουδαίων πεντάκις τεσσεράκοντα παρὰ μίαν ἔλαβον, 25 τρὶς ἐραβδίσθην, ἅπαξ
ἐλιθάσθην, τρὶς ἐναυάγησα, νυχθήμερον ἐν τῷ βυθῷ πεποίηκα· 26 ὁδοιπορίαις πολ-
λάκις, κινδύνοις ποταμῶν, κινδύνοις λῃστῶν, κινδύνοις ἐκ γένους, κινδύνοις ἐξ
ἐθνῶν, κινδύνοις ἐν πόλει, κινδύνοις ἐν ἐρημίᾳ, κινδύνοις ἐν θαλάσσῃ, κινδύνοις
ἐν ψευδαδέλφοις, 27 κόπῳ καὶ μόχθῳ, ἐν ἀγρυπνίαις πολλάκις, ἐν λιμῷ καὶ δίψει,
ἐν νηστείαις πολλάκις, ἐν ψύχει καὶ γυμνότητι· [SBLGNT]

King James Version

16 I say again, Let no man think me a fool;
if otherwise, yet as a fool receive me, that
I may boast myself a little. 17 That which
I speak, I speak it not after the Lord, but
as it were foolishly, in this confidence of
boasting. 18 Seeing that many glory after
the flesh, I will glory also. 19 For ye suf-
fer fools gladly, seeing ye yourselves are
wise. 20 For ye suffer, if a man bring you
into bondage, if a man devour you, if a
man take of you, if a man exalt himself,
if a man smite you on the face. 21 I speak
as concerning reproach, as though we
had been weak. Howbeit whereinsoever
any is bold, (I speak foolishly,) I am bold
also. 22 Are they Hebrews? so am I. Are
they Israelites? so am I. Are they the
seed of Abraham? so am I. 23 Are they
ministers of Christ? (I speak as a fool)

New Rendition

16 Again I say, let no one consider me
a fool, but if you indeed think other-
wise, at least put up with me as a fool
so that I that can boast a little. 17 What
I say, I say not according to the Lord
but as a fool in undertaking this boast-
ing. 18 Since many are boasting accord-
ing to human standards, I too will boast.
19 For you gladly endure fools since you
yourselves are wise. 20 For you endure
if someone enslaves you, if someone
exploits you, if someone takes you cap-
tive, if someone is arrogant with you, if
someone slaps you on the face. 21 To
my shame, I say we were too weak for
that. But whatever anyone dares (I am
speaking foolishly), I also dare. 22 Are
they Hebrews? So am I. Are they Isra-
elites? So am I. Are they descendants

I am more; in labours more abundant, in stripes above measure, in prisons more frequent, in deaths oft. 24 Of the Jews five times received I forty stripes save one. 25 Thrice was I beaten with rods, once was I stoned, thrice I suffered shipwreck, a night and a day I have been in the deep; 26 In journeyings often, in perils of waters, in perils of robbers, in perils by mine own countrymen, in perils by the heathen, in perils in the city, in perils in the wilderness, in perils in the sea, in perils among false brethren; 27 In weariness and painfulness, in watchings often, in hunger and thirst, in fastings often, in cold and nakedness.

of Abraham? So am I. 23 Are they ministers of Christ? (I am speaking irrationally.) I am even more. With much greater labors, with far more imprisonments, with severe beatings, often in danger of death. 24 Five times I received forty lashes minus one from the Jews, 25 three times I was beaten with a rod, once I was stoned, three times I was shipwrecked, a night and a day I spent adrift in the sea. 26 On frequent journeys, I have been in dangers from rivers, in dangers from thieves, in dangers from my own countrymen, in dangers from foreigners, in dangers in the city, in dangers in the wilderness, in dangers at sea, in dangers from false brethren, 27 with hard work and toil, frequently with lack of sleep, with hunger and thirst, frequently with fasting, with cold and lack of clothing.

Translation Notes and Comments

11:16 ***I say again, Let no man think me a fool / Again I say, let no one consider me to be a fool:*** Paul's opening remark πάλιν λέγω (*palin legō*), "again, I say," refers back to 11:1, where he asks his readers to bear with him in that bit of foolishness that he is being forced to engage in.

The phrase μή τίς (*mē tis*), "no one," with the verb δοκέω (*dokeō*), "to think, consider,"[219] found here in the aorist subjunctive mood, makes a strong request. The masculine singular adjective τίς (*tis*), "a certain one," could refer to a single person, and thus the leader of the opposition party, or to the group itself. By using such an indefinite reference, Paul skillfully avoids giving them the dignity of being referred to by name and thus stunts the alleged authority they are attempting to usurp.[220]

The adjective ἄφρων (*aphrōn*), "foolish,"[221] in the present context, is used as a substantive and thus is rendered "a fool." The term refers to a person

219. BDAG, 254–55.
220. Guthrie, *2 Corinthians*, 539.
221. BDAG, 159.

who lacks intelligence or good judgment[222] and suggests blindness to the consequences of an action that a thinking person would easily recognize.

if otherwise, yet as a fool receive me / but if you indeed think otherwise, at least put up with me as a fool: Paul introduces his next request with the phrase εἰ δὲ μή γε (*ei de mē ge*), literally "but if indeed not," where the conjunction δέ (*de*), "but," is mildly contrastive but intensified by the particle γέ (*ge*), "indeed." There is an ellipsis of a verb after εἰ that is to be supplied from the context—that is, "but if indeed you (think) otherwise)"—which we have supplied in the translation. The adverb κἄν (*kan*), literally "and if," acts here as "an emphatic marker of concession,"[223] thus rendered as "at least."[224] The verb δέχομαι (*dechomai*), found here as an aorist plural imperative, means "to receive, tolerate, put up with"[225] and references Paul's audience. The whole phrase then carries the sense of "if this is not to be" (that is, if my request is to be denied because my detractors refuse the request, then, at least, I request that you also put up with me acting like a fool).[226] In the next phrase, Paul explains why he makes the request.

that I may boast myself a little / so that I too can boast a little: The conjunction ἵνα (*hina*), "so that," marks Paul's purpose[227]—namely, so that he can give way to boasting. For the verb καύχομαι (*kauchaomai*), "to glory, boast,"[228] see Translation Notes for 10:8. His use of the crasis κἀγώ (*kagō*), derived from καί (*kai*) and ἐγω (*egō*), "I, too,"[229] reveals that his opponents have been and likely continue to be engaged in this practice. With the phrase μικρόν τι (*mikron ti*), literally "a little something" or more colloquially "a little bit," he signals his readers that he plans only to skim the surface of his accomplishments and credentials.[230]

11:17 ***That which I speak, I speak it not after the Lord / What I say, I say not according to the Lord:*** The verb λαλέω (*laleō*), "to speak or talk,"[231] in the present context does not refer to Paul's usual means of verbal communication but to the particular form he must use here—namely, boasting. Just what he means by the phrase οὐ κατὰ κύριον (*ou kata kyrion*), "not

---

222. BDAG, 159; Louw-Nida, §32.52.
223. Louw-Nida, §89.73.
224. BDAG, 507.
225. BDAG, 221.
226. Guthrie, *2 Corinthians,* 534–35.
227. BDAG, 475–76.
228. Louw-Nida, §33.368.
229. BDAG, 487.
230. Guthrie, *2 Corinthians,* 535.
231. Louw-Nida, §33.70; Guthrie, *2 Corinthians,* 535–36.

according to the Lord," is unclear, for he could be referring to something the Lord would not condone or inspire or what would not be properly done using the Lord's authority.[232] What the Apostle makes clear, however, is that such an activity steps way beyond anything that God would condone.

but as it were foolishly / but as a fool: The conjunction ὡς (*hōs*), "as it were, as," acts as a marker denoting the perspective from which an activity is taken or understood,[233] and as such, in the present context, it emphasizes the inappropriate nature of what Paul is about to do. The noun ἀφροσύνη (*aphrosynē*) denotes a state that lacks "prudence or good judgment" in both a "moral and intellectual" sense, "foolishness."[234] It is governed by the preposition ἐν (*en*), "marker of a state or condition, in,"[235] and so the entire phrase is literally "but as it were in foolishness." We have rendered the entire phrase "but as a fool" to better catch the sense in contemporary English. The entire phrase carries a very pejorative cast.[236] Paul considers anyone who engages in this activity to be so silly and senseless that they should not be taken seriously. In this way, he highlights his embarrassment in being forced to point out this ironic situation.

in this confidence of boasting / in undertaking this boasting: The noun ὑπόστασις (*hypostasis*), "plan, project, undertaking,"[237] can also denote an intention or stratagem. Since the noun "undertaking" carries the idea of engaging in an activity, it works well here.

11:18 *Seeing that many glory after the flesh, I will glory also / Since many are boasting according to human standards, I too will boast:* The conjunction ἐπεί (*epei*), "since,"[238] acts as a marker of cause and points to Paul's reason for boasting. On the verb καυχάομαι *(kauchaomai)*, "to boast," see Translation Notes for 10:8.

232. See Harris, *Second Epistle,* 780–81.

233. BDAG, 1103–6.

234. BDAG, 159.

235. BDAG, 327, italics in original.

236. In 1 Corinthians, Paul repeatedly uses the adjective μωρός (*mōros*), "foolish, stupid," and the noun μωρία (*mōria*), "foolishness," to describe some of the ideas being put forth. Though the idea is present, the word group is missing in 2 Corinthians and replaced by the adjective ἄφρων (*aphrōn*), "foolish, ignorant," and the noun ἀφροσύνη (*aphrosynē*), "foolishness." The change suggests these words were currently being used as a criticism of the Apostle. Barnett, *Second Epistle,* 529 n. 1.

237. BDAG, 1040–41. Scholars no longer give the translation of the word as "confidence," as in the KJV, any credit because there is no evidence it carried such a meaning during the first century. On other legitimate possibilities, see Matera, *II Corinthians,* 255; Thrall, *Critical and Exegetical Commentary,* 2:714; and Harris, *Second Epistle,* 781.

238. BDAG, 360.

The adjective πολύς (*polys*), "many,"[239] found here as a plural, suggests that quite a number of Paul's detractors could be engaging in this practice, but it could also be a stylistic method Paul uses in a derogatory manner as "a further way of seeking to diminish their stature in the eyes of the Corinthians."[240]

For the rendering of the phrase κατὰ σάρκα (*kata sarka*), literally "according to the flesh" as "according to human standards," see the Translation Notes for 10:2. The phrase carries with it a "decisive distinction, in moral terms, between humankind and God," with the noun σάρξ (*sarx*), "flesh," connoting that which constitutes the "human frailty that concurs in sin's appeal and powerful attack, leading men and women to live independently of God,"[241] or what Latter-day Saints might refer to as "the natural man" (Mosiah 3:19).

11:19 ***For ye suffer fools gladly, seeing ye yourselves are wise / For you gladly endure fools since you yourselves are wise:*** The conjunction γάρ (*gar*), "for," "introduces the basis—delayed by some verses—on which [the Apostle] has made the original statement," requesting that his readers put up with him as a fool (11:16).[242] The reason he is forced to engage in this activity is the fault of his readers. The verb ἀνέχω (*anechō*) means "to bear with, endure" others with tolerance.[243] It is modified by the adverb ἡδέως (*hēdeōs*), "gladly," which the Greek text has as the first word in the sentence, thus giving it emphasis. Its position and use suggest how willingly Paul's audience accepted those whom he branded with the nominalized plural adjective ἀφρόνων (*aphronōn*), "fools."[244]

He explains the reason for their almost joyful willingness to follow these men with the short phrase φρόνιμοι ὄντες (*phronimoi ontes*), consisting of the adjective φρόνιμος (*phronimos*) "sensible, wise,"[245] followed by a present plural participle of the verb εἰμί (*eimi*) "to be,"[246] thus forming a circumstantial participial phrase with a causative sense,[247] "since you are wise." Thus Paul is certainly using this in a very strong ironic sense.

---

239. Louw-Nida, §59.1.
240. Furnish, *II Corinthians,* 511.
241. Martin, *2 Corinthians,* 550.
242. Barnett, *Second Epistle,* 531.
243. BDAG, 78.
244. BDAG, 159.
245. BDAG, 1066.
246. BDAG, 282–86.
247. Smyth, *Greek Grammar,* §2064.

11:20: There is an important grammatical point encased in Paul's following statements. Each clause begins with the phrase εἴ τις (*ei tis*), "if someone," followed by an indicative verb in the present tense. The arrangement of *ei* with this verb form marks a real condition. Thus Paul is referring to actual, not hypothetical, events that are presently going on within the branches of the Corinthian Church. As noted in 11:16, Paul's use of the indefinite pronoun *tis,* "a certain one, someone," is derogatory, denying his enemies the dignity of naming them.[248]

For ye suffer / For you endure: The conjunction γάρ (*gar*), "for," is causal, pointing to the reason why these people are unwise. The Apostle repeats the verb ἀνέχω (*anechō*), "to bear with, endure," from the verse above to connect the act with the charge he now brings.

if a man bring you into bondage / if someone enslaves you: The verb καταδουλόω (*katadouloō*) means "to enslave."[249] Here its use is more figurative, denoting a person who is persuaded to place herself or himself in the service of another.[250] Even so, it carries heavy negative overtones readily apparent in the common practice of routinely enslaving powerless people or even kidnapping free individuals for the human trafficking that abounded in the Greco-Roman world.

if a man devour you / if someone exploits you: The verb κατεσθίω (*katesthiō*) means literally "to eat up, devour,"[251] but in this context "to exploit."[252] It refers to taking unfair advantage of another. The verb connotes the idea that the exploitation leads to complete and utter destruction of those exploited.[253]

if a man take of you / if someone takes you captive: The verb λαμβάνω (*lambanō*), "to take, receive, capture,"[254] has a wide range of semantic meanings, some of which have strong negative overtones such as taking control by force, as seems to be the situation here.[255] Thus the translation "takes you captive" seems best.[256] The construction shows that it is certain Saints who

248. Guthrie, *2 Corinthians,* 539.

249. BDAG, 516.

250. See MM, 326.

251. Louw-Nida, §23.11.

252. BDAG, 531–32.

253. Louw-Nida, §§20.45; 57.150; 88.145.

254. BDAG, 583–85.

255. See Louw-Nida page 2:150 for examples. The word is used for snaring an animal or catching a fish. Barnett, *Second Epistle,* 532–33.

256. This translation follows both Guthrie, *2 Corinthians,* 540–41; and Bernard, "Second Epistle," 104.

are being forcefully taken captive by the interlopers, likely to keep them from following Paul and his associates.

if a man exalt himself / if someone is arrogant with you: The verb ἐπαίρω (*epairō*) means "to raise up" and by extension, in middle voice, "to raise oneself up, to exalt oneself, be presumptuous or arrogant."[257] The interlopers have apparently convinced some that they have superior ecclesiastical rank and demanded due benevolence.

if a man smite you on the face / if someone slaps you on the face: The verb δέρω (*derō*), "to strike or slap,"[258] coupled with the noun πρόσωπον (*prosōpon*), "face," suggests an act of humiliation. Such a practice was foreign among the Greeks, but among the Jews, to strike one on the right cheek with the back of the hand was deeply insulting, even suggesting one was a heretic.[259] Further, Jewish leaders also had the power (as will be explored below) to inflict beatings upon recalcitrant members of their congregation.[260] Given this background, it is possible that some of the Christians may have been duped into believing that such behavior was an acceptable practice.

11:21 ***I speak as concerning reproach, as though we had been weak / To my shame, I say we were too weak for that:*** The noun ἀτιμία (*atimia*), "dishonor, humiliation, shame," connotes a condition that would be disastrous in Greco-Roman society due to the high premium that the society placed on honor (τιμή, *timē*).[261] Here Paul's self-deprecation drips with irony.

The verb ἀσθενέω (*astheneō*), "to be weak," found here as a perfect plural, usually denotes to "be sick" or "experience some personal incapacity or limitation."[262] This appears to be a parenthetical and ironic reference to Paul's weakness, or perhaps even sickness, during his stay with the Corinthians. With quite a gibe, he blames this for his failure to mistreat the Saints.

---

257. BDAG, 357. The verb carries some very strong implications, such as hitting or punching another repeatedly and also lifting the foot for a kick, expressing contempt. Joachim Jeremias, "αἰρω, ἐπαίρω," in *TDNT,* 1:185–86.

258. BDAG, 218–19; Louw-Nida, §19.2.

259. W. F. Albright and C. S. Mann, *Matthew,* Anchor Bible, (New York: Doubleday, 1971), 68–69. See also Donald A. Hagner, *World Bible Commentary: Matthew 1–13,* vol. 33a (Dallas, Texas: World Book, 1993), 131.

260. Guthrie, *2 Corinthians,* 541. Both Jesus and Paul were slapped while answering charges of the Sanhedrin (Mark 14:65; Acts 23:2). That such practices had crept into the Church was likely the background for Paul's insistence that bishops should not be violent (1 Tim. 3:3; Titus 1:7).

261. BDAG, 149.

262. BDAG, 142; Louw-Nida, §74.26.

For the whole phrase to make sense in English, an object must be supplied; thus we have added "for that," referring to the outrageous behavior of the interlopers described in the previous verse. The plural pronoun ἡμεῖς (*hēmeis*), "we," is emphatic and used to contrast Paul's stand with that of the false apostles.[263]

Paul's use of the perfect tense is important, having as it does a stative aspect, meaning that it looks at a state the Apostle acquired in the past that has continued with him into the present.[264] That state is one of "weakness." Thus Paul's use of the tense shows that his ministry is still permeated with it and that it continues to limit what he does and how he does it.

Howbeit whereinsoever any is bold, (I speak foolishly), I am bold also / But whatever anyone dares (I am speaking foolishly), I also dare: The conjunction δέ (*de*), "but," expresses contrast in reference to the "weakness" Paul mentioned above. The verb τολμάω (*tolmaō*) means "to dare"[265]—that is, have the courage to do a deed—and here indicates that, despite the supposed strength of his adversaries, he is willing to go head-to-head with them. The phrase ἐν ᾧ δ' ἄν τις (*en hō d' an tis*), "whatever,"[266] refers to the content of the interlopers' boast, which Paul, in the next few verses, dismantles point by point.

11:22–32: In these verses Paul contrasts himself with the "false apostles" by cataloging all that he has suffered for the sake of those he has ministered to during his tenure as the Lord's appointed Apostle.

11:22 ***Are they Hebrews? so am I / Are they Hebrews? So am I:*** The noun Ἑβραῖος (*Hebraios*), "Hebrews," can be taken in two ways. First it can be used to distinguish Jews from other people or, in other words, look to "the outer identity or ethic character" of the group. Second, it can be a linguistic label for those who speak Hebrew/Aramaic rather than Greek as their primary tongue.[267] The latter position is the weakest since the interlopers evidence solid skill in speaking Greek.[268]

---

263. Barnett, *Second Epistle,* 533 n. 24.

264. Wallace, *Greek Grammar,* 572–73.

265. BDAG, 1010.

266. A relative pronoun combined with the modal particle ἄν (*an*) and the indefinite pronoun τις (*tis*) followed by a verb in the subjunctive mood produces an indefinite relative clause. See Wallace, *Greek Grammar,* 478–79.

267. Witherington, *Conflict and Community,* 452; BDAG, 269–70. Acts 6:1 suggests that even among the Saints in Jerusalem, there was a noted distinction and perhaps even division between members who spoke Hebrew/Aramaic and those who spoke Greek.

268. Guthrie, *2 Corinthians,* 551–52.

of times Paul was beaten. In his account, he only references the beatings he received from the Jews (see below), but there were more (see, for example, Acts 16:22–23). The adverb he uses suggests that he feels these punishments were excessive, but they appear to be in line with what the Jews considered appropriate for false teaching, likely the charge brought against the Apostle.

Corporal punishment, when administered under Jewish law, consisted of being held to the floor and struck with a rod or whip up to but not more than forty times.[287] This punishment could be administered with a supple cane (Prov. 10:13; 19:29; 26:3) or a leather whip. Such a whip consisting of a number of straps. Though this punishment was rather severe, it paled in comparison to that of the Romans. They used whips with bone and/or bronze pieces braided into the whip's cords, often with hooks on the end of each braid. So brutal was such a whipping that many victims died either not long after or even before it was finished.[288]

in prisons more frequent / with far more imprisonments: The noun φυλακή (*phylakē*) denotes a prison, whether large or small, that served the needs of either the community or the state.[289] The phrase ἐν φυλακαῖς περισσοτέρως (*en phylakais perissoterōs*) literally means "in prisons far more," which we have translated "with far more imprisonments" to better express the sense in English.

Paul again uses the adverb περισσοτέρως (*perissoterōs*), "far more" (see above), thus stressing that his being placed in prisons multiple times was excessive. His use of the adverb suggests his confinements were more acts of harassment against him than due to actual misdeeds against either civil or religious authority on his part. The one example the scriptures preserve is Paul's incarceration with Silas during their stay in Philippi (Acts 16:19–40).[290]

In the Roman world, prisons had little resemblance to modern penitentiaries. Though both removed felons from society, the ancient prison had no interest in reformation. Rather, it had but two major purposes: to

---

287. According to Deut. 25:1–3, the most blows that could be administered was forty. However, the judges could command fewer if they felt that the offense did not deserve the maximum amount. To make certain not to go over that proscribed limit, the actual count was thirty-nine. Any crime that demanded more than forty blows was considered capital, and the person was remanded over to death.

288. James M. Freeman, *Manners and Customs of the Bible* (Plainfield, N.J.: Logos International, 1972), §§656, 724.

289. BDAG, 1067–68.

290. Others are hinted at in Rom. 16:3–4; 1 Cor. 15:32; and 2 Cor. 1:8–10.

hold prisoners until their trial (which sometimes took years) and, when it was deemed necessary, to extract confession from them by torture. Once convicted, such persons did not receive a jail sentence. Instead they were enslaved by the state, fined, beaten, banished (sometimes in combination), or executed. The other purpose of prisons was to serve as a deterrent to crime. For that reason, prisons were deliberately designed to be most unpleasant. To this end, prisons were filthy, stinking, dark, often underground, and either too hot or too cold. They did not have individual cells but an inner and outer keep, the former being the more secure and also the more unpleasant. Prisoners were usually chained by groups in the corners of the keeps. Often the prison provided little food or other means of sustenance or comfort. As a result, the prisoners had to rely on the care of family members, friends, or the graciousness of kind people. So successful were these designs that many people felt that being sent to jail was a sentence worse than death. Christians became known for their willingness to help people suffering in such deplorable conditions.[291]

in deaths oft / often in danger of death: The adverb πολλάκις (*pollakis*), "often,"[292] refers to either the number of times an event occurs or its frequency. Here the context demands the latter. The noun θάνατος (*thanatos*) denotes "death."[293] The word is found here in the plural, but English prefers the singular, and so we have rendered it that way. Since in none of his harrowing experiences did Paul actually suffer death, we have added the phrase "in danger of." The fear Paul felt in the instances where his life was threatened, either by perilous circumstances or angry people, can only be imagined.

11:24 *Of the Jews five times received I forty stripes save one / Five times I received forty lashes minus one from the Jews:* The Greek text does not have the noun "lashes," but the sentence's use of the cardinal adjective τεσσεράκοντα (*tesserakonta*), "forty,"[294] requires an object, and "lashes" is the obvious one. According to Deuteronomy 25:2–3, the maximum number of blows a person could receive was forty. To safeguard against a person being beaten over that amount, the Mishnah prescribed thirty-nine.[295]

---

291. For biblical practice, see Raymond Westbrook, "Punishments and Crimes," in *ABD,* 5:546–56. For a general study, see Craig S. Wansink, *Chained in Christ: The Experience and Rhetoric of Paul's Imprisonments* (Sheffield, Eng.: Sheffield Academic Press, 1996).

292. BDAG, 846.

293. BDAG, 442–43.

294. BDAG, 1000.

295. *M. Makkot* 3:10.

Such punishments were the prerogative of each synagogue. As the בֵּית הַדִּין (*bêt hadîn*), "house of judgment," those appointed as its judges could determine and enforce punishment upon its members for offenses against the law of Moses.[296] That various counsels determined that Paul receive the full weight of punishment suggests the severity of his offense in their eyes. Among others, false teaching demanded no less, and it is likely, given Paul's proclamation of salvation in Christ alone, that this was the charge. "Paul could have claimed Roman citizenship and escaped the scourging but that would have meant excommunication and being cut off from the synagogues—and that is his missionary approach. He willingly submitted to the shameful punishment in order to continue teaching his own people."[297] Since the book of Acts records no such beatings, it is likely that they took place during the fourteen years between Paul's conversion and his call as an apostolate missionary.[298]

11:25 ***Thrice was I beaten with rods / three times I was beaten with a rod:*** In Paul's time, the verb ῥαβδίζω (*rabdizō*), "to beat [someone] with a rod,"[299] had a technical nuance denoting an official punishment imposed by Roman magistrates and executed by lictors (ῥαβδοῦχοι, *rabdouchoi*, literally "rod bearers").[300] Paul's Roman citizenship should have protected him from the pain and associated humiliation that went with such chastisements. However, as the beating he and Silas took in Philippi shows (Acts 16:16–24; 1 Thes. 2:2), being Roman citizens did not help them specifically because the magistrate never bothered to ask about their citizenship status. That may also be the root cause in the other two unrecorded beatings.[301] Even if one was a citizen, there were exceptions to the rule, particularly if a Roman flagrantly broke certain laws.[302]

once was I stoned: The verb λιθάζω (*lithazō*) means to cast stones for the purpose of killing someone. The passive, as here, points to the object of the stoning, in this case Paul himself. Among the Jews, stoning was a means of capital punishment for major breaches of the Mosaic law, such as blasphemy, apostasy, and adultery (Deut. 17:5; 22:22–24).[303] The case Paul

296. See *m. Makkot* 3:1–9, where the offenses are listed.

297. Ogden and Skinner, *Verse by Verse,* 157.

298. Compare Robert E. Osborne, "St. Paul's Silent Years," *Journal of Biblical Studies* 84, no. 1 (1965): 59–65.

299. BDAG, 902.

300. For a study, see Thrall, *Critical and Exegetical Commentary,* 2:739–42.

301. Martin, *2 Corinthians,* 565–66.

302. Thrall, *Critical and Exegetical Commentary,* 2:740.

303. See also *m. Sanhedrin* 7.56–60 for a list of offences as understood by the rabbis.

refers to took place in the Galatian city of Lystra (in central Turkey today) and was not an act resulting from Jewish judicial procedures. Though it did happen as a consequence of Jewish agitation, the stoning itself was due to mob action (see Acts 14:5, 19).

thrice I suffered shipwreck / three times I was shipwrecked: The verb ναυαγέω (*nauageō*) means "to suffer shipwreck."[304] The history in Acts records only one, that which happened near the island of Malta (Acts 27:27–44). Since, however, that wreckage happened some years after Paul wrote to the Corinthians, the three mentioned here happened some time before that. However, no record exists. Acts does record about eight trips by sea, but none of them ended in shipwreck.[305] Paul traveled a great deal by sea. Though an easy and relatively fast means of travel, it was also perilous.[306] That Paul braved sea travel despite multiple shipwrecks highlights his courage and devotion to the cause of Christ.

a night and a day I have been in the deep / a night and a day I spent adrift in the sea: The noun νυχθήμερον (*nychthēmeron*), found here as an accusative of time, denotes a period of twenty-four hours, thus a night and a day.[307] The verb ποιέω (*poieō*) here means "to spend time."[308] It is found here in the perfect tense, which usually describes an event that took place in the past with its effect continuing into the present.[309] That tense is technically grammatically incorrect here, but Paul may have used it either for dramatic effect or more likely because that horrifying experience continued to be very vivid for him.[310] The noun βυθός (*bythos*) refers to depth of something, in this case the wide Mediterranean sea.[311]

To spend such an egregious amount of time clinging to little more than broken boards and hope must have been most harrowing for the Apostle. That this very dramatic event is nowhere found in Luke's history of Paul suggests just how abbreviated and selective that history is.

---

304. BDAG, 666.

305. See Barrett, *Second Epistle,* 298, for the list.

306. For a general study, see Lionel Casson, *Travel in the Ancient World* (Toronto: Hakkert, 1974), 149–57. For the theme in Greek literature, see Wilfred L. Knox, *Some Hellenistic Elements in Primitive Christianity* (London: Oxford University Press, 1944), 13.

307. BDAG, 683.

308. BDAG, 839–42.

309. Wallace, *Greek Grammar,* 573–74.

310. Martin, *2 Corinthians,* 566.

311. Louw-Nida, §1.73.

11:26 ***In journeyings often / On frequent journeys:*** The noun ὁδοιπορία (*hodoiporia*), found here in the dative case, denotes a journey usually but not exclusively by foot.[312] The dative could connote time, thus "during my journeys," or place, thus "in my journeys."[313] The adverb πολλάκις (*pollakis*) means "often, frequently."[314] The phrase sets the stage for the perils Paul now lists. Such were, unfortunately, all too common among travelers in those days.

in perils / I have been in dangers: The clause that composes 11:26 actually continues the thought in 11:25, but for flow we have rendered it as a new sentence, adding the words "I have been." The noun κίνδυνος (*kindynos*) denotes "risk, danger,"[315] and connotes anything that threatens a person with serious bodily injury or death.

of waters / from rivers: The noun ποταμός (*potamos*) refers to any moving body of water, from a small stream (as long as it ran year-round) to a large river.[316] In the wilderness, such bodies of water were bridgeless and therefore had to be forded. Flash floods and uncertain currents made such passages perilous. Paul's double crossing of the Taurus Mountains, as he traveled from the province of Cilicia to that of Galatia (see Acts 13:14; 14:24; 15:41–16:6), would have forced him to make a number of such crossings. The region was known for its cascading and unpredictable rivers.[317]

of robbers / from thieves: The noun ληστής (*lēstēs*) refers to "a robber, highwayman, bandit."[318] Though the Roman army greatly reduced the number of brigands who roamed the backcountry waiting for unwary travelers or ill-protected caravans, it did not get them all.[319] As a result, the wilds remained dangerous places.

by mine own countrymen / from my own countrymen: The noun γένος (*genos*) refers to those related by ancestral stock.[320] In this case, it refers specifically to the Jews. The record in Acts gives ample reason why Paul felt threatened by some of his own people. As he noted in this very epistle (11:24), he received five lashings from them. Some conspired to kill him

312. BDAG, 690.
313. Wallace, *Greek Grammar,* 153–57.
314. BDAG, 846.
315. BDAG, 544–45.
316. Louw-Nida, §1.76.
317. Harris, *Second Epistle,* 806.
318. BDAG, 594.
319. Guthrie, *2 Corinthians,* 560.
320. BDAG, 194–95.

(Acts 9:20–25). Quite a number went so far as to poison the minds of both Jews and Gentiles against him (Acts 14:2) and even instigated mob violence, resulting in his being stoned (Acts 14:5, 19).

by the heathen / from foreigners: The noun ἔθνος (*ethnos*), "foreigner, Gentile," referred to those who were, from a Jewish standpoint, non-Jews or, from a Jewish Christian standpoint, non-Israelite Christians.[321] Paul is here referring to both non-Jews and non-Christians. That he was illegally beaten three times by Roman authorities (11:25; an example is preserved in Acts 16:16–24) and his very life endangered in Ephesus (Acts 19:21–41) suggests how dangerous it was to live among these people. But in Paul's eyes they are neither better nor worse than any of the Jews.[322]

in the city, . . . wilderness, . . . at sea: Taken together, these three show that there was no place where the Apostle felt free from life-threatening situations. The noun πόλις (*polis*) designates any inhabited place, from a small village to a thriving metropolis,[323] while ἐρημία (*erēmia*), "wilderness," denotes all uninhabited areas. Together they constitute all land areas. In contrast, the noun θάλασσα (*thalassa*), "lake, sea,"[324] denotes large bodies of water. Here Paul uses it to refer to the Mediterranean Sea, where, as he has already noted (11:25), he suffered shipwreck three times.[325]

among false brethren / from false brethren: Paul likely saved this reference for last to emphasize the greatest danger he faced. The noun ψευδάδελφος (*pseudadelphos*), "false brethren," denotes "one who pretends to be a fellow-believer, but whose claim is belied by conduct" and/or false teachings.[326] In the New Testament, the noun is used only by Paul (see also Gal. 2:4). Its damning nuance is best seen when juxtaposed with the noun ἀδελφός (*adelphos*), "brother." Among the Saints, that warm and gentle term, though referring to one's immediate siblings, took on special and broader meaning. The Lord referred to his disciples as his dear "brethren" and coaxed them to see each other in the same light (Matt. 23:8; Luke 22:32). His disciples did so (see Rom. 8:29 and Heb. 2:11–18). The strong bond that developed between them resulting from this admonition was love (1 John 2:8–11), a giving one to another as need required. Manifesting

321. BDAG, 276–77.

322. For a study, see Kathy Ehrensperger, "Paul, His People, and Racial Terminology," *Journal of Early Christian History* 3, no. 1 (2013): 17–32.

323. BDAG, 844–45.

324. Louw-Nida, §§1.69, 70.

325. He would suffer one more harrowing experience by sea. See Acts 27:13–44.

326. BDAG, 1096.

from this bond was the title of endearment that they used for one another—namely, ἀγαπητός (*agapētos*), "beloved," (see, for example, Rom. 1:7; 12:19; 1 Cor. 4:17; Col. 4:7; James 1:16; 1 Pet. 2:11; and 1 John 3:2).[327] It was this love, this attribute of care and selflessness, that the "false brethren" lacked. As a result, they did not give but took. In doing so, they undermined the very heart of the gospel of Christ and replaced it with "another gospel," even that of the natural man (1 Cor. 2:14; compare Mosiah 3:19).

11:27 ***In weariness and painfulness / with hard work and toil:*** In this verse, Paul switches his focus from specific trials to the general circumstances he labored in. The noun κόπος (*kopos*), "hard work, trouble,"[328] nuances that which is difficult, even burdensome,[329] while the noun μόχθος (*mochthos*), "hard work, labor, toil,"[330] implies "unusual exertion of energy and effort."[331] Though the nuances between the two are slight, *kopos* looks more at the effort or work that is done, while *mochthos* emphasizes the resultant stage—namely, fatigue.[332] Together they reinforce the idea of the extreme effort that Paul's circumstances continually require of him, most of which derives from his ministry.[333]

in watchings often / frequently with lack of sleep: The noun ἀγρυπνία (*agrypnia*), "sleeplessness," denotes an inability to go to sleep, often due to anxiety or outside pressure.[334] Paul could be referencing either the demands of the ministry that forced him to work long hours or his state of anxiety that disallowed sleep or both.

With the addition of the adverb πολλάκις (*pollakis*),[335] "often," Paul shows that such a state was not uncommon with him. Much of it seems due to worry over the state of the various branches of the Church.[336]

in hunger and thirst / with hunger and thirst: The noun λιμός (*limos*) denotes physical "hunger," and the noun δίψος (*dipsos*) denotes "physical thirst."[337] The connotation of both combined is that of an involuntary lack

327. For a study, see Hans Freiherr von Soden, "ἀδελφός," in *TDNT,* 1:144–46.

328. Louw-Nida, §42.47.

329. BDAG, 558–59.

330. BDAG, 660.

331. Louw-Nida, §42.48.

332. Friedrich Hauk, "κόπος, κοπιάω," in *TDNT,* 3:827–30.

333. On a number of occasions, Paul uses *kopos* specifically to refer to his efforts in Christ's service. See 1 Cor. 3:8; 15:58; 2 Cor. 10:15: 11:23; and 1 Thes. 1:3; 2:9; 3:5.

334. Louw-Nida, §23.73.

335. BDAG, 846.

336. Guthrie, *2 Corinthians,* 564.

337. BDAG, 596, 253.

of food or water. This condition would have most naturally occurred during Paul's travels. The distance between towns and villages in some locals was quite long, forcing travelers to take provisions and even water with them. Unforeseen delays could easily lead to using up food or water before replenishment was available.

in fastings often / frequently with fasting: The noun νηστεία (*nēsteia*), "fasting," denotes voluntarily giving up food for religious purposes,[338] often to seek Deity's help during periods of need or stress. Again, Paul uses the adverb πολλάκις (*pollakis*), "often, frequently" (see 11:26), to highlight his near-constant use of and need for this practice.

in cold / with cold: The noun ψῦχος (*psychos*) refers to cold conditions, due to either climate or elevation.[339] Paul would have met such conditions crossing the Taurus Mountains or traveling anywhere during the winter months. That it happened during his imprisonments cannot be ruled out. Greco-Roman prisons were notorious for being either too hot or too cold.

and nakedness / and lack of clothing:[340] The noun γυμνότης (*gymnotēs*) denotes "nakedness" but also an inadequacy of clothing.[341] The latter is likely the meaning here. Again, the problem probably arose due to travels when weather changed dramatically, leaving those on the road ill prepared for the changed conditions.

Analysis and Summary

After a rather extensive delay, Paul finally begins to make his boast. Its focus consists of comparing himself with the interlopers and showing how much worse, in all aspects, his suffering was than theirs. In 11:16, he again asks his readers not to take him for a fool but admits to his willingness to be considered such if it will help his cause. Interestingly, his audience would likely never have considered his defense an act of foolishness if he had not so forcefully insisted that it was. Of course, from his point of view, he is acting the fool because a true Apostle cannot be judged by human standards (1 Cor. 2:7–16), but that is the seat of boasting.[342] Thus what he is being forced to do borders on a display of near idiocy.

---

338. BDAG, 671–72; Harris, *Second Epistle,* 809–10.

339. BDAG, 1100.

340. This phrase could be read as a hendiadys, thus, "in cold due to a lack of adequate clothing," but the tempo of the piece supports the usual translation.

341. BDAG, 208.

342. Seifrid, *Second Epistle,* 420.

In 11:16–18, the deep embarrassment that he feels because he has been put in this position clearly comes through. The Apostle shows that he is being forced into the absurd and worldly behavior of boasting because his audience glories in that which is worldly and showy and smacks of shamelessness. He hints at surprise that they are willing to follow those who flaunt these vices, but he knows why. The "clever" Corinthians, as he calls them, being fools themselves, "have submitted to the reckless claims of [other] fools."[343] In order to reclaim these Saints, he must apologetically stoop to the level of these other fools. He will, he insists, surpass them in speaking with human folly by cataloging his suffering and sacrifices for the Church. Of note is that, once again, his ironic statements are not actually foolishness but the truth.

That he refers to the scope of the boasting he will undertake as "but a little bit," when juxtaposed by the length of his report that follows (11:21–12:10), suggests and even underscores (though partially veils) the magnitude of what the Apostle has been enduring and continues to go through for the Lord's kingdom. His sacrifices become the means of shaming his accusers.

By assuming the role of the fool, the Apostle puts himself in a position to accomplish two objectives: The first is to provide himself, as noted above, with the platform from which he can coax, perhaps even cajole, his audience into greater support for him and the gospel he proclaims. The second is to provide him with the means of lampooning his opponents by using their methods. Cleverly, he actually turns their ploy on its head by boasting not of his strengths but of his weakness.[344] His use of this tactic is brilliant because it gives him the means of pushing his objective of centering everything not on himself but on the Lord, while still stressing his own authority as Jesus' Apostle.

In 11:17–18, Paul makes it blatantly clear that what he is about to do—boast—violates the way of God and has nothing divine behind it. He takes this position because boasting's focus is not, as it should be, on the Lord (10:7; Jer. 9:23–24) but on the individual who puts himself and his work before that of God to bolster his place before the Saints.[345] These people manifest

343. Georg Bertram, "ἄφρων," in *TDNT,* 9:231.

344. Guthrie, *2 Corinthians*, 535. For a study, see David Alan Black, *Paul, Apostle of Weakness: Astheneia and Its Cognates in the Pauline Literature* (New York: Peter Lang, 1984).

345. Paul sees boasting as working according to human standards, not according to the Lord's (10:2–3; 11:18), and thus antithetical to God's ways and purposes.

themselves in a "trust in outward display and demonstrations of spirit, their reliance on 'sight' . . . , and their glorying in 'the outward.'"[346] Thus the activity is according to inappropriate and ungodly human standards. In sum, it is nothing less than foolishness. Paul notes that quite a number have engaged in this practice. Due to their success, he too will do what they do, but his not-so-hidden stratagem is to expose and undo their hubris.[347]

Given his vocabulary of tolerance, in which he emphasizes "acceptance" and "putting up with" or "bearing with" him and others, the issue does not seem to be a clash of personalities but rather one that focuses on the "legitimacy of mission and the evidence of genuine apostolicity" that Paul uses to open the door to the "discussion of his trials, weaknesses, and credentials."[348] These, in turn, allow him to again emphasize that true boasting must center on the Lord.

In 11:19, with sustained and acute irony, Paul continues to give his reason for stooping to the practice of boasting. It is because his readers gladly put up with people who engage in this practice and have made it nearly into an art form. And why do the Saints do this? (Here Paul's words nearly drip with sarcasm.) Because they are φρόνιμοι (*phronimoi*), "wise." Though the term usually refers to proper insight and understanding and therefore to what is prudent or sensible,[349] the Apostle uses it as a synonym for such foolish thinking that it borders on idiocy. Had these people not been willing to accept the claims of the interlopers, their efforts would have fallen flat,[350] and therefore the Saints must share in the blame of pushing the Apostle into doing the absurd.

Having established why he is forced into this humiliating position, the Apostle exposes just how ridiculous the rather docile stand taken by the Corinthian Saints really is. In 11:20, using a driving repetitive rhythm composed into four conditional clauses, the Apostle details four ways his detractors have abused the local congregations. First, they have reduced certain members to the status of slaves, such that these Saints unquestioningly do the interlopers' bidding. Second, they have exploited or taken unfair advantage of the Saints. The verb Paul uses (κατεσθίω, *katesthiō*) means to devour and therefore exposes the interlopers' veracious appetite, through which they unconscionably eat

346. Martin, *2 Corinthians,* 550.
347. Barnett, *Second Epistle,* 530.
348. Martin, *2 Corinthians,* 547.
349. BDAG, 1066.
350. Guthrie, *2 Corinthians,* 538.

up the resources of the Saints, likely feeling and teaching that it was their due.[351] Third, they have taken some people captive and in the process pulled them away from the freedom of the gospel and its true ministers.[352] Fourth, they have treated the Saints with arrogance, even going so far as to physically abuse some of them by slapping their faces, an act of major humiliation.

From a modern perspective, Paul's charges smack of sheer exaggeration. However, given the times, he likely was not. The interlopers seem to have convinced many of the Saints that their supposed high position granted them rights to be taken care of and to demean and even punish those who opposed them.

Two conditions played on the willingness of some of the Saints to put up with or, as Paul says, "gladly accept" such treatment. The first is that the majority of the converts were not fully informed as to how Christian leaders were supposed to behave, and thus they looked to their social world as a model. There, great deference was given to the higher classes. Second, most were converts from the lower classes and were used to being ill treated and not only accepted it but also assumed it was their lot.[353] Thus many took the abuse admirably, but Paul shows that what had been going on was "blatantly shameful."[354] And further, it stood in strong opposition to the model Paul and his associates had given these very people during the months that they had worked among them. Any self-exaltation stood in strong contrast to Paul's demeanor, ministering to these people with the "humility and gentleness of Christ" (10:1, NR). He never abused any but worked "by patience, by kindness, by the Holy Spirit, [and] by genuine love" (6:6, NR). But rather than seeing these early missionaries as modeling the proper way, (as Paul ironically says) the Corinthians were so "wise" that they would not look past their social norms and thus not only missed understanding how proper leadership was to be done but also accepted un-Christian abuse.

Concern with the misuse of prophecy and the prophetic office for worldly gain continued throughout the first century. One document in particular, the *Didachē* ("The Teachings"), addresses the problem and offers solutions.[355] It shows that some self-proclaimed prophets abused the generosity

351. Guthrie, *2 Corinthians,* 540.

352. Guthrie, *2 Corinthians,* 542.

353. For a study, see Meeks, *First Urban Christians,* especially pp. 51–73.

354. Guthrie, *2 Corinthians,* 542.

355. This document, written in the later first century, was also known as "The Lord's Teaching through the Twelve Apostles to the Nations" (Διδαχὴ Κυρίου διὰ τῶν δώδεκα

of the Saints by insisting that they get money or a good meal.[356] The *Didachē* teaches that true prophets labor for their own needs and do not act like merchants "trading on Christ."[357] The true prophet will focus on what is best for the community and what promotes the love of God, Christ, and one another. He will further teach the importance of prayer, fasting, baptism, and proper sacramental worship.[358] Such prophets are to be welcomed and given every hospitality the Saints can offer.[359]

The text also states how to tell true prophets from false ones: simply compare their teachings with their lifestyles. "Any prophet who teaches the truth but does not practice what he advocates is a false prophet."[360] Thus compliance to the gospel standard becomes the litmus test of authenticity. There is, however, a caveat. If the Saints test him and find his teachings accord with the gospel, they should put up with him even if he seems a bit rough around the edges or is not living up to all that he preaches, for such were the prophets of old, and they will be judged by God, not humankind. The prophet must, however, never advocate that anyone follow in his weakness.[361]

The document suggests that the Christian or Christians who composed it were aware of Paul's writings and took up his cause. It may be that the parallel positions gave the *Didachē* a certain cachet that made it acceptable as scripture by quite a number of the early Christian congregations. The work eventually lost favor because it did not meet the requirements necessary for placement in the canon of the New Testament.[362] Even so, it

---

ἀποστόλων τοῖς ἔθνεσιν). For the text of the document itself, see Michael W. Holmes, ed., *The Apostolic Fathers: Greek Texts and English Translations,* 3rd ed. (Grand Rapids, Mich.: Baker Academic, 2007), 344–69.

356. *Didachē,* 11.3–12.

357. *Didachē,* 12.5.

358. *Didachē,* 1–10.

359. *Didachē,* 11.4; 13.1–7.

360. *Didachē,* 11.10, authors' translation.

361. *Didachē,* 11.11–12. On this subject, see also Erik Odin Yingling, "Worship and Ritual Practices in the New Testament," in *New Testament History, Culture, and Society: A Background to the Texts of the New Testament,* ed. Lincoln H. Blumell (Provo, Utah: Religious Studies Center, Brigham Young University; Salt Lake City: Deseret Book, 2019), 894–95.

362. For a brief analysis of the background and content of the *Didachē,* see Robert K. Draft, "Didache," in *ABD,* 2:197–98. For an extensive study, see Aaron Milavec, *The Didache: Text, Translation, Analysis, and Commentary* (Collegeville, Minn.: Liturgical Press, 2003).

presents an interesting and insightful picture of early Christian concerns and responses thereto that are similar to the problems Paul faced.

Paul ends this section of his argument with a mock "confession" (11:21a), wherein his irony "reaches its most biting expression."[363] In it, he acknowledges the shameful state of weakness in which he continually lives, one that has prevented him, unlike the interlopers, from abusing the Corinthian Saints. But Paul's confession is in reality a brilliant transition into his "fool's speech," for in it he quickly passes through his heritage (11:22) to what he has endured during the course of his decades-old ministry (11:30). In doing so, he forces his audience to see clearly his counterculture "boasting" that focuses on the validating "weaknesses." In doing so, Paul shows that the antics of his detractors are nothing short of bullying "strength" evidenced in destructive abuse. In this way, he highlights the stark contrast between the interlopers' harsh and arrogant ways and the kind and loving ways used by him and his companions. His ministry, though modeled on that of the Savior, has been filled with not only patient sacrifice and suffering but also periods of dread and even alarm—all for the sake of Christ Jesus. In this way, "he has turned the cultural values of 'strength' (which would accord with honor) and 'weakness' (which would accord with shame) on their heads by trumpeting 'weakness' as the defining characteristic of his ministry." Of course, when he confesses to acting "according to weakness," he means nothing of the kind. Indeed, his ministry and mission have been filled with examples of strong but gentle leadership that authenticates and models Christ and his gospel of love and vividly exposes the absolute wrongheadedness of the cultural norms that drive pagan society.[364]

To emphasize his recognition of the inanity of what he is about to do, Paul admits in 11:21, albeit as a careful aside, that he is taking on the role of a complete fool. Whatever anyone else dares to do, he boasts, he dares to do. Considering that he has admitted to a position of "weakness" vis-à-vis the "strength" of his opponents, going head-to-head with them would certainly be an act of sheer folly, but Paul knows exactly what he is doing. With biting irony, he admits to the condition his opponents ascribe to him—namely, "weakness"—but a weakness, he says, that expresses itself in being unable to engage in the outrageous behavior displayed by the interlopers against the Saints.[365] Thus his admission is actually a condemnation of both

363. Barnett, *Second Epistle*, 533.
364. Guthrie, *2 Corinthians*, 542.
365. Barnett, *Second Epistle*, 533.

the shameful actions of the interlopers and the willingness of some of the Saints to put up with them.

With this admission, Paul skillfully introduces the central theme of the "fool's speech" that he will now launch into—namely, "power-in-weakness" (12:7–10). To keep his thesis ever before his audience, he will continually build on the vocabulary of weakness (12:13), but at the same time, he "changes his tone from irony to direct and masterful assertion, and in the splendid passage which follows he makes the 'boast' which he has been leading up to with such prolonged explanations."[366] Through all of this, the modern reader must keep in mind that Paul's purpose is to win these Saints, heart and soul, to his side.[367]

He begins his "boast" (11:22–23b) with four "identity" questions, followed by an answer for each. These appear to be rejoinders to certain claims made by either the interlopers or their supporters (3:1) and may reflect the qualifications they have foisted off on a gullible audience to substantiate their status as authentic missionaries and leaders.

The first three questions deal with ethnic identity and seem designed to address the issue of proper breeding. Paul orders them by ethnic label, from general to specific.[368] The first label, "Hebrews," distinguishes Jews from other people and shows that this distinction and separateness go back millennia. The second, "Israelites," refers to the descendants of Jacob and looks more specifically at the founder of a distinct people with which the Jews highly identified, for they were the "men of Israel." The third, "descendants of Abraham," echoes the covenants made to the great patriarch, through which both he and his descendants became the chosen people of God. The three together emphasize "genuine Jewishness"[369] and more particularly "sum up what it means to be a religiously devoted Jew."[370]

In the mindset of the Greco-Roman world, "good breeding" meant much, and here the focus seems to be on who comes from "good Jewish stock."[371] Paul has already made it clear that basing one's position within

366. Bernard, "Second Epistle," 105.

367. Seifrid, *Second Epistle,* 423.

368. Martin, *2 Corinthians,* 557.

369. Barnett, *Second Epistle,* 537 n. 9. Witherington, *Conflict and Community,* 452, posits that the term "Hebrew" referred to either one who spoke that language or the ethnic identity of the person, while "Israelite" referred to "one's spiritual allegiance," and "seed of Abraham" referred to "one's ancestry."

370. Guthrie, *2 Corinthians,* 552.

371. Furnish, *II Corinthians,* 534.

In 11:25, he notes dangers he experienced on the sea when three times the ships he sailed on sank. Fortunately, he was rescued rather quickly after two of these wrecks. There was, however, one very harrowing time when he was adrift through a night and much of a day before rescuers found him.

In 11:26, he lists eight dangers he faced while in the service of the Lord. The first two relate to those arising from having to move through open country—namely, being swept away by torrents when trying to cross rivers where there were no bridges and being attacked by bandits. The next two note dangers that came from two sets of people—namely, the Jews and the Gentiles. The next three were places in which he faced danger—namely, in the city, the wilderness, and the sea.[381] In sum, no matter where he traveled or where he was at or among whom he dwelt, danger was ever present.

He saves the most worrisome and grievous danger till last: the threat he faced from "false brethren." His reference is likely to more than the interlopers he is now confronting, though they are definitely included. For years he had known of and is now seeing the fulfillment of prophecy as apostasy gains force over much of the area.[382] This rebellion or mutiny within God's kingdom will eventually succeed in pulling the entire Church away from the fulness of the gospel, leaving in its wake the loss of priesthood authority and truths both plain and precious (2 Thes. 2:1–3; 2 Ne. 13:21–26).[383] Its leadership will be composed of false brethren. Thus Paul's enemies within the Corinthian branches "constituted the most insidious danger of all. Whereas all the other dangers in this subset of Paul's hardships were external forces brought to bear against him personally, the

---

381. Some scholars see the last set as composed of four items; thus, they include betrayal by false brothers. See Martin, *2 Corinthians,* 568. Others separate out the latter, making it its own piece. See Thrall, *Critical and Exegetical Commentary,* 2:742; and Guthrie, *2 Corinthians,* 559–60.

382. The Savior had warned his Apostles that false prophets and teachers would swarm the Church and deception would catch many unawares (Matt. 24:5, 11). This idea was well-known to Paul. He first warning came in AD 53 when he informed the Thessalonian Saints of the coming apostasy. The KJV translates the Greek word ἀποστασία (*apostasia*) as "falling away," but it denotes a rebellion against established authority. BDAG, 120.

383. Though his warnings have been largely lost, from AD 54 on the coming apostasy was one of Paul's major themes. See Acts 20:31. After his visit to Corinth, Paul again raised his warning voice, this time to the Saints in the province of Asia. See Acts 20:28–30, where he warns the leadership that danger will arise from among themselves by those seeking a following. In addition, certain individuals will secret themselves into the various branches, appearing as fellow believers (wolves masquerading as sheep) with the intent to ravage the goods of the people.

'dangers among false brothers' . . . would also involve infiltration of the churches (cf. 2 Cor. 11:28–29). The local churches were in danger of being compromised by false teaching, which could work as a cancer from within, even while it was disguised as Christian 'ministry.'"[384] The result would be the destruction of all that Paul suffered, sacrificed, and lived for.

Next (11:27), Paul lists a general characterization of the hardships he experienced that resulted from challenges arising during daily living or the tasks of the ministry. Most of these hardships were due to a lack of resources. He notes the hard, burdensome, and unrelenting physical work his mission demanded, forcing him to toil to the point of exhausting. However, even though beat down with weariness, his anxiety for the welfare of the branches of the Church often prevented him from getting restful sleep. His work also forced him to travel long distances. During some of these journeys, when villages or towns were far between, he and his fellow travelers ran out of water and food. Thus they were forced to forge on with empty stomachs and thirsty mouths. The ministry itself also required him to go without food and drink as he fasted in behalf of the Church. He also knew biting cold when he was forced to travel in the winter, over high mountain passes, or as he sat shivering being confined by a prison's chilly shackles. During such times he felt the full misery that came with a lack of proper clothing. In sum, his rapid list of hardships emphasizes that his ministry bore tremendous personal cost. Such was neither for the faint of heart nor for those given to comfort and leisure. The force of his message in these few verses gave a figurative slap in the face to his detractors, who sought for the soft and easy life that their demands upon the Church provided.

The Apostle's Major Burden (11:28–29)

Greek Text

28 χωρὶς τῶν παρεκτὸς ἡ ἐπίστασίς μοι ἡ καθ' ἡμέραν, ἡ μέριμνα πασῶν τῶν ἐκκλησιῶν. 29 τίς ἀσθενεῖ, καὶ οὐκ ἀσθενῶ; τίς σκανδαλίζεται καὶ οὐκ ἐγὼ πυροῦμαι; [SBLGNT]

384. Guthrie, *2 Corinthians*, 562.

King James Version	New Rendition
28 Beside those things that are without, that which cometh upon me daily, the care of all the churches. 29 Who is weak, and I am not weak? who is offended, and I burn not?	28 In addition to those external things, I feel the daily pressure of my concern for all the churches. 29 Who is weak, and I am not weak? Who is offended, and I do not burn with indignation?

Translation Notes and Comment

11:28 ***Beside those things that are without, that which cometh upon me daily, the care of all the churches / In addition to those external things, I feel the daily pressure of my concern for all the churches:*** The preposition χωρίς (*chōris*) means "beside, apart from, in addition to."[385] Paul's use of the word signals he is about to switch his focus. The adverb παρεκτός (*parectos*) denotes that which is external to oneself and refers to the suffering Paul listed above.[386] The phrase καθ' ἡμέραν (*kath hēmeran*) means "daily."[387] The noun ἐπίστασις (*epistasis*) describes a feeling of "responsibility for a matter, pressure, care."[388] The dative pronoun μοι (*moi*), "to me," expresses a dative of reference, more specifically of disadvantage; thus we have translated the phrase ἡ ἐπίστασίς μοι ἡ καθ' ἡμέραν (*hē episasis moi hē kath' hēmeran*), literally "the daily pressure to me," as "I feel the daily pressure." The Apostle's use of the term emphasizes the ongoing and unrelenting nature of the suffering he endures for the sake of the churches. The noun μέριμνα (*merimna*) means "anxiety, worry, care."[389] The source of great pressure that Paul feels is his great concern regarding the welfare of the members of the church.

11:29 ***Who is weak, and I am not weak? / Who is weak, and I am not weak?:*** In this verse, Paul states the source of his great anxiety for the Church. The verb ἀσθενέω (*astheneō*), "weak," denotes limited physical capacity and faintheartedness and timidity. More specific to the Corinthian context, it refers to one who is frail in the faith.[390] Because Paul's faith was never weak, he likely had another nuance in mind, that of being "powerless."

---

385. BDAG, 1095.

386. BDAG, 774. The adverb "pertains 'to being different and in addition to something else.'" Guthrie, *2 Corinthians,* 565.

387. BDAG, 436–38.

388. BDAG, 380–81.

389. BDAG, 632.

390. BDAG, 142. In 1 Cor. 8:8–13, Paul warned more established members to be careful not to be a stumbling block to those weak in the faith.

Those in the lowest orders of society bore this burden continually. They were ever vulnerable to being preyed upon or abused.[391] Paul's statement shows that he relates to the problems and difficulties that the humblest members face.

who is offended, and I burn not? / Who is offended, and I do not burn with indignation?: The verb πυρόω (*pyroō*) means literally "to heat, to make fiery hot,"[392] but figuratively "to be enflamed, indignant, livid,"[393] due to egregious circumstances. To capture the tone of the idea, we have rendered it forcefully above.

The verb σκανδαλίζω (*skandalizō*) can be taken in two ways depending on how the verb is understood. It means both to "cause to sin" and "to give offense."[394] It is found here as a present passive. Thus the phrase could be translated as to "be led into sin"[395] or "to be offended, hurt, shocked." [396] If Paul's intent is the former, then he is saying, "Who is led into sin, and I am not livid?"[397] If it is the second, he is saying, "Who is offended, and I am not indignant?" This latter sense is the more likely, and it is the one we have used in our rendition.

The JST changes this verse to read, "Who is weak, and I am not weak? Who is offended and I am not angry?" thus showing that the KJV's translation, "I burn not," refers to Paul's righteous indignation.

Given the circumstances the Apostle is facing, either translation works. Paul's detractors, as he emphasizes, were causing people to fall into sin by substituting false doctrines in place of true. On the other hand, many of his followers, especially those in the lower orders of society, were hurt by being unrecognized, disrespected, or in other ways treated poorly. That Paul suffered these very things suggests that this nuance is what he has in mind.

---

391. For a study, see Gustav Stählin, "ἀσθενέω," in *TDNT,* 1:490–93.

392. Louw-Nida, §79.72.

393. BDAG, 899; Guthrie, *2 Corinthians,* 567–68.

394. BDAG, 926. Among the early Greeks, the noun form of the word denoted a snare or trap, and the verb meant "to snare" or "entrap." Over time, the noun took on the meaning of something that causes a person to fall, more particularly a stumbling stone. The verb took on two nuances. One was "to sin," or "to be led into sin," but carried the idea of falling away or apostatizing from the truth. The second was "to take offense" at something said or done, resulting in being either blinded to or led away from the gospel. Over time, the latter became the more predominate idea. For a study, see *NID,* 4:296–300.

395. BDAG, 926.

396. Louw-Nida, §25.179.

397. Guthrie, *2 Corinthians,* 567.

I will glory of the things which concern mine infirmities / I will glory in my weakness: For the verb καυχάομαι (*kauchaomai*), "to boast, brag, glory," see Notes for 10:8. It is found here in the future tense and points to the reason why Paul is willing to act like a fool. The noun "weakness" again takes the cast of "powerlessness" (see 11:29), rather than that of "feebleness" or "frailty." [404] Indeed, Paul's "weakness" is not just physical. "It is Paul's entire bearing as an unimpressive figure and an outwardly non-powerful presence in Corinth."[405] Having set the stage for the theme of boasting in his weakness, Paul will now build his case.

11:31 ***The God and Father of our Lord Jesus Christ, which is blessed for evermore / God, even the Father of our Lord Jesus, who is blessed forever:*** This verse constitutes an oath, this phrase being the first part. In it, Paul speaks as both a fervent Jew and devout Christian. As the former, he praises God, with the adjective εὐλογητός (*eulogētos*), "blessed,"[406] denoting a being worthy of acclaim and trust. In the scriptures, the appellation is used exclusively in relation to the Father.[407] As the latter, Paul bears witness to the station of Jesus as God's Son as well as his title as Lord. The noun κύριος (*kyrios*), "lord,"[408] connotes, ideally, an appointed governor who took into his considerations the good and well-being of those over whom he exercised authority.[409]

knoweth that I lie not / knows that I do not lie: This part of the oath testifies as to its purpose—to verify the truthfulness of Paul's stated position that he glories in his weakness. The root of the oath is based on God's omniscience, through which he knows the truthfulness or falseness of all things. The verb οἶδα (*oida*), "to know,"[410] carries the idea of knowing through perceiving, experiencing, and seeing, or, in God's case, foreseeing, that which is, thus knowing what is real, authentic, true.[411] That the verb is found here in the perfect tense looks to God's continuous understanding of the fulness of reality. The verb ψεύδομαι (*pseudomai*), "to lie,

---

404. BDAG, 142.

405. Martin, *2 Corinthians,* 571.

406. BDAG, 408.

407. Hermann W. Beyer, "εὐλογητός," in *TDNT,* 2:764–65.

408. Louw-Nida, §37.51.

409. For a study, see Werner Foester and Gottfried Quell, "κύριος," in *TDNT,* 3:1039–98.

410. BDAG, 693–94.

411. For a study, see *NID,* 3:460–62.

tell a falsehood,"[412] nuances a deliberate intent to deceive.[413] Paul's use of the term strongly echoes his charge against his detractors that they are ψευδαπόστολοι (*pseudapostoloi*), "false apostles," who are sent by Satan and serve him.[414]

11:32–33: These verses reference events recorded in Acts 9:23–25.

11:32 *In Damascus the governor under Aretas the king kept the city of the Damascenes with a garrison / In Damascus the governor under Aretas the king was guarding the city of the Damascenes:* Damascus was the capitol of the Roman province of Syria and was governed by Herod Antipas from 4 BC to AD 39. It was about one hundred and thirty-five miles north of Jerusalem. Why Paul, having noted the name of the city, makes the observation that it was "the city of the Damascenes" is not clear, but it could have been a pleonasm (the use of more words than necessary to make a point) that Paul used to stress the location of his harrowing experience.[415]

Aretas IV Philopatris was an Arab king ruling the Nabatean nation between 9 BC and AD 40. His capital was at Petra, over one hundred and sixty miles south of Jerusalem. The noun ἐθνάρχης (*ethnarchēs*), "governor," denotes a king's appointee, usually over a specific area or region,[416] but it also connotes someone who has authority over a specific group of people living in a more localized zone.[417] The verb φρουρέω (*phroureō*), "to guard against, to keep under watch,"[418] is wrongly translated as "kept . . . a garrison" in the KJV. The verb is found here in the imperfect tense, suggesting that the watch was posted over a considerable, indefinite period of time. Paul's context implies that, on a rotating basis, these men were placed within each of the city's gates twenty-four hours a day to control who went out, not who came in.[419]

Paul's account has caused some debate. Rome clearly controlled Syria during the entire time Paul ministered there, assigning its governance initially to Herod Antipas. That being the case, the question becomes why and how Aretas had a governor there. The possibility exists that the king

412. BDAG, 1096–97.
413. Louw-Nida, §33.253.
414. Martin, *2 Corinthians,* 573.
415. Martin, *2 Corinthians,* 575.
416. BDAG, 276.
417. Barnett, *Second Epistle,* 554 n. 62.
418. Louw-Nida, §37.119.
419. BDAG, 1066–67.

did have control of the city for some months during Paul's stay. From the beginning of Herod's reign, he had an antagonistic relationship with Aretas, likely over an endemic border dispute.[420] They initially settled the problem with the marriage of Aretas's daughter to Herod, but the marriage did not last. Herod became infatuated with his brother Philip's wife, Herodias, and both divorced their spouses and remarried (see Matt. 14:3–4). Aretas sought revenge for the slight and was rewarded when his army soundly defeated Herod's in AD 36. It is likely that during that time Aretas was able to take control of Damascus and appoint his own ethnarch to govern the city. When Tiberius Caesar learned of the war, he sided with Herod and set one of his generals to help the Jewish ruler. As a result, Aretas retreated back to his desert stronghold in Petra, and Herod regained Damascus.[421]

desirous to apprehend me / in order to arrest me: The verb πιάζω (*piazō*), "to seize, arrest," carries the nuance of taking someone by force.[422] But why would the Arabian governor have any interest in detaining Paul? According to Acts 9:23–24, it was certain Jews who were on the lookout for the Apostle. It may be that they conspired with the Nabateans in order to presume some governmental authority to arrest Paul. Again, the question is why the Nabateans would want to become involved. We do know that Paul spent some time in Arabia not long after his conversion (Gal. 1:17) and then went back to Damascus, where he preached until he was forced to flee.[423] It is possible that while he preached in Arabia, he upset some powerful individuals with his zealousness for the sake of Christ,[424] and as a result, the Nabatean representative was willing to work with the Jews in seeking the Apostle's life.[425]

11:33 ***And through a window in a basket was I let down by the wall / and I was let down in a basket through a window in the wall:*** The verb χαλάω (*chalaō*), "to let down," found here as an aorist passive, thus "to be let down," is a fishing term describing putting netting into the water.[426] The

420. Barnett, *Second Epistle,* 554 n. 61.

421. See Josephus, *Antiquities of the Jews* 18.109–26.

422. BDAG, 812.

423. For a discussion on the known facts about Nabataea during this time, see Eckhard J. Schnabel, *Early Christian Mission,* vol. 2, *Paul and the Early Church* (Downers Grove, Ill.: InterVarsity Press; Leicester, Eng.: Apollos, 2004), 1032–45.

424. Wayment, *From Persecutor to Apostle,* 51–52.

425. For analyses, see Guthrie, *2 Corinthians,* 575; and Barnett, *Second Epistle,* 554–55.

426. BDAG, 1075.

noun σαργάνη (*sarganē*) denotes a sturdy basket made of twine or ropes, usually for catching fish but also for moving hay, straw, or wool.[427]

The noun θυρίς (*thyris*) denotes "a window," but not one covered by shutters or other closures. These were usually used for letting in light and air.[428] The noun τεῖχος (*teichos*) denotes a city wall.[429] Together they show Paul was lowered through an opening in the city wall, not over its top. It emphasizes that the Apostle left in a very inconspicuous way.

and escaped his hands: The verb ἐκφεύγω (*ekpheugō*) means "to flee" in order to escape danger.[430] The noun χείρ (*cheir*) refers literally to the hand but figuratively to the power of a person. Here that person is the *ethnach* governor of Damascus.[431] Paul's phrasing suggests a rather cowardly act of seizing unlawful power over another person.

Analysis and Summary

The Apostle ends this portion of his defense by briefly relating a very notable tale, one that seems, at first reading, rather odd given the point he has been making. Where before, he has focused on the suffering that he has endured for both Christ and the Lord's community, here he relates an act driven by fear and leading to flight. Rather than being apprehended by the governor of Damascus, he chose, with the help of friends, to flee by being lowered in a net through an opening in the city walls. He had good reason to flee. According to Acts, Paul preached in the synagogues at Damascus with such force and persuasion that he "confounded the Jews" (Acts 9:22). So incensed were some of his hearers that they decided to he had to die. Fortunately for them the city's governor was also after the Apostle, according to Paul's statement in 11:32. Since the governor had influence and resources that the Jews did not, forming a league with him made sense. Thus the Jews cooperated with this political authority by setting a twenty-four-hour watch at all the gates of the city with the hope of apprehending the Apostle, thus forcing his harrowing escape.[432]

Scholars have wrestled with the question of why Paul included this tale. Some argue that, as one of his first acts as a crusader for Christ, it left an

427. Louw-Nida, §6.148; Guthrie, *2 Corinthians*, 575; Martin, *2 Corinthians*, 576.

428. Louw-Nida, §7.47.

429. BDAG, 994.

430. Louw-Nida, §15.63.

431. BDAG, 1082–83.

432. Seifrid, *Second Letter*, 433 n. 370.

Chapter 12

Paul's Vision and Its Aftermath

Introduction

For the general setting on which this chapter rests, see the introduction to chapter 10. In this chapter, Paul brings to a close his "fool's speech" and its highly polemical pitch. His tone softens as he reaches out to his audience to bring to repentance all who need it before he arrives in the city.

The center of the chapter focuses on a powerful, informative, and attitude-changing revelation that the Apostle to the Gentiles received much earlier in his ministry, one that profoundly affected his theological understanding of the gospel and gave him, as he says, a cause about which to boast. One would expect that revelation's focus to center on the remarkable Christological, life-changing, and converting vision that he received as he traveled resolutely toward Damascus. It does not. Nor does it focus on two other powerful revelations that he received, during which he learned things that, due to their sacred and holy character, "are not proper for a person to speak" (12:4, NR). Even so, they informed *him* and gave *him* an appreciation of the ways of God and Christ and a deeper, fuller understanding of how the gospel works.

Based on that, he now shares with his audience the essence and importance of his clearer vision for them and the revelation from which it resulted. With somber insight, he draws the attention of his audience to his "thorn in the flesh," a condition so severe that he calls it "a messenger from Satan" that continually torments him (12:7). Though he struggled against it and even cried to God that it might be removed, he received only a humbling but very informative answer: God gave this weakness to him so that he would not "become overly proud," and so it would not be removed. Paul came to see that God had granted him weaknesses, along with other troubles, to a magnificent end: that Christ's power might be ever present in him. This was the message that provided the ground for his current unabashed boasting. He could glory that "whenever I am weak, then I am strong," that weakness revealed that God's grace was upon him, carrying him through and bringing him success. Thus he can reassure the Corinthian Saints that "I delight in weakness" (12:10, NR). For that reason, no matter how much pressure to the contrary, he will not turn away from affirming the doctrine's importance and insisting that all understand, accept, and embrace it.

Much was at stake here. That too many of the Corinthians were unwilling to support and commend him allowed the interlopers to spread their false gospel over the entire area. This dangerous situation was a threat not only to his present position as leader among these people but also to his future missionary activities (Rom. 15:18–29), for if he lost Corinth, his base of operation in the entire region would also be gone. Thus he had to get these people to wholeheartedly buy into his theological understanding of "weakness-as-strength" (12:5–10; 13:4), one based on the "shame" of the cross and authenticated by his apostolic authority.[1]

The first four verses of the chapter have caused more debate among scholars than any other passage in the entire corpus of Pauline literature. The questions debated include the following: Why does Paul, in a treatise dealing with weakness, introduce it with a reference to visions/revelations that would put its recipient in a position of strength? Were the visions he mentions his or someone else's? If they were his, why does he not say so directly? Further, were the revelations *about* or *from* the Lord? Can anything be determined about their content? What does he mean by the terms "third heaven" and "paradise"? Finally, what was the "thorn in the flesh" that caused him such misery?[2] Some, though not all, of the more important of these questions have been answered through the Restoration.

The chapter breaks down into four units. The first (12:1–10) brings the "fool's speech" to a close and includes an explanation as to why Paul boasts about weakness. He relates the condition (the "thorn in the flesh" [12:7]), his prayer with its answer, and his understanding that grew therefrom.[3] The second (12:11–13) contains an apology for the embarrassment Paul feels

1. Martin, *2 Corinthians,* 627.

2. Guthrie, *2 Corinthians,* 576.

3. Scholars have devoted a lot of time and effort in trying to puzzle out of the items in these verses. For a review and analysis, see Daniel L. Akin, "Triumphalism, Suffering, and Spiritual Maturity: An Exposition of 2 Corinthians 12:1–10 in Its Literary, Theological, and Historical Context," *Criswell Theological Review* 4, no. 1 (1989): 119–44.

for having to boast. However, he lays the blame on some of the Corinthians and the interlopers because neither would support him. In the third (12:14–18), he assures his audience of his love for them and repeats his intent to visit them again. He informs them that, like a good parent, he will continue to take care of them, not they of him. In the final section (12:19–21), he declares that all he has done is for their edification, and his sincere hope is that when he arrives, he will find them as he wishes them to be. He ends with a stern pronouncement that if he finds some yet unrepentant, he will take action.

Visions and Revelations (12:1–10)

Greek Text

1 Καυχᾶσθαι δεῖ· οὐ συμφέρον μέν, ἐλεύσομαι δὲ εἰς ὀπτασίας καὶ ἀποκαλύψεις
κυρίου. 2 οἶδα ἄνθρωπον ἐν Χριστῷ πρὸ ἐτῶν δεκατεσσάρων—εἴτε ἐν σώματι οὐκ
οἶδα, εἴτε ἐκτὸς τοῦ σώματος οὐκ οἶδα, ὁ θεὸς οἶδεν—ἁρπαγέντα τὸν τοιοῦτον
ἕως τρίτου οὐρανοῦ. 3 καὶ οἶδα τὸν τοιοῦτον ἄνθρωπον—εἴτε ἐν σώματι εἴτε χωρὶς
τοῦ σώματος οὐκ οἶδα, ὁ θεὸς οἶδεν— 4 ὅτι ἡρπάγη εἰς τὸν παράδεισον καὶ ἤκου-
σεν ἄρρητα ῥήματα ἃ οὐκ ἐξὸν ἀνθρώπῳ λαλῆσαι. 5 ὑπὲρ τοῦ τοιούτου καυχήσο-
μαι, ὑπὲρ δὲ ἐμαυτοῦ οὐ καυχήσομαι εἰ μὴ ἐν ταῖς ἀσθενείαις. 6 ἐὰν γὰρ θελήσω
καυχήσασθαι, οὐκ ἔσομαι ἄφρων, ἀλήθειαν γὰρ ἐρῶ· φείδομαι δέ, μή τις εἰς ἐμὲ
λογίσηται ὑπὲρ ὃ βλέπει με ἢ ἀκούει τι ἐξ ἐμοῦ, 7 καὶ τῇ ὑπερβολῇ τῶν ἀποκα-
λύψεων. διὸ ἵνα μὴ ὑπεραίρωμαι, ἐδόθη μοι σκόλοψ τῇ σαρκί, ἄγγελος Σατανᾶ,
ἵνα με κολαφίζῃ, ἵνα μὴ ὑπεραίρωμαι. 8 ὑπὲρ τούτου τρὶς τὸν κύριον παρεκάλεσα
ἵνα ἀποστῇ ἀπ' ἐμοῦ· 9 καὶ εἴρηκέν μοι· Ἀρκεῖ σοι ἡ χάρις μου· ἡ γὰρ δύναμις ἐν
ἀσθενείᾳ τελεῖται. ἥδιστα οὖν μᾶλλον καυχήσομαι ἐν ταῖς ἀσθενείαις μου, ἵνα ἐπι-
σκηνώσῃ ἐπ' ἐμὲ ἡ δύναμις τοῦ Χριστοῦ. 10 διὸ εὐδοκῶ ἐν ἀσθενείαις, ἐν ὕβρεσιν,
ἐν ἀνάγκαις, ἐν διωγμοῖς καὶ στενοχωρίαις, ὑπὲρ Χριστοῦ· ὅταν γὰρ ἀσθενῶ, τότε
δυνατός εἰμι. [SBLGNT]

King James Version

1 It is not expedient for me doubtless to
glory. I will come to visions and reve-
lations of the Lord. 2 I knew a man
in Christ above fourteen years ago,
(whether in the body, I cannot tell; or
whether out of the body, I cannot tell:
God knoweth;) such an one caught up

New Rendition

1 It is necessary to boast. Although
there is nothing to be gained by it, nev-
ertheless I will go on to visions and
revelations from the Lord. 2 I know a
person in Christ, fourteen years ago—
whether in the body or out of the body,
I do not know, God knows—who was

to the third heaven. 3 And I knew such a man, (whether in the body, or out of the body, I cannot tell: God knoweth;) 4 How that he was caught up into paradise, and heard unspeakable words, which it is not lawful for a man to utter. 5 Of such an one will I glory: yet of myself I will not glory, but in mine infirmities. 6 For though I would desire to glory, I shall not be a fool; for I will say the truth: but now I forbear, lest any man should think of me above that which he seeth me to be, or that he heareth of me. 7 And lest I should be exalted above measure through the abundance of the revelations, there was given to me a thorn in the flesh, the messenger of Satan to buffet me, lest I should be exalted above measure. 8 For this thing I besought the Lord thrice, that it might depart from me. 9 And he said unto me, My grace is sufficient for thee: for my strength is made perfect in weakness. Most gladly therefore will I rather glory in my infirmities, that the power of Christ may rest upon me. 10 Therefore I take pleasure in infirmities, in reproaches, in necessities, in persecutions, in distresses for Christ's sake: for when I am weak, then am I strong.

taken up to the third heaven. 3 And I know this person—whether in the body I do not know, or out of the body, I do not know, God knows— 4 that he was taken up into paradise, and he heard inexpressible words that are not proper for a person to speak. 5 I will boast about this person, but about myself I will not boast except in my weaknesses. 6 For even if I wanted to boast, I will not be a fool, for I will speak the truth. But I will refrain from boasting so that no one will consider me more than what he sees me to be or hears from me 7 because of the extraordinary nature of the revelations. Therefore, so that I would not become overly proud, I was given a thorn in the flesh, a messenger of Satan, to torment me so that I would not become overly proud. 8 Concerning this, I pleaded with the Lord three times that it would leave me. 9 And he said to me, "My grace is sufficient for you, for my power is brought to perfection in weakness." Therefore, I will most gladly boast in my weaknesses so that the power of Christ may dwell within me. 10 Therefore, I delight in weaknesses, in mistreatments, in calamities, in persecutions and troubles for Christ's sake. For whenever I am weak, then I am strong.

Translation Notes and Comments

12:1 *It is not expedient for me doubtless to glory / It is necessary to boast:* In this new segment, Paul continues giving reasons for his boasting. Though there is a variant reading to this phrase, the earliest and best texts have καυχᾶσθαι δεῖ (*kauchasthai dei*), "It is necessary to boast."[4] The verb δεῖ

4. Metzger, *Textual Commentary,* 516. The KJV follows the very late Textus Receptus, which has καῦχασθαι δή οὐ συμφέρει μοι (*kauchasthai dē ou sympherei moi*), "it is indeed not expedient for me to boast."

(*dei*), "it is necessary," when combined with an infinitive, as here, carries the idea of both need and compulsion. [5] It governs the verb καυχάομαι (*kauchaomai*), "to boast,"[6] found here as a present infinitive. Its use alerts his audience that Paul will continue the theme of boasting.[7] The thought can be taken in two ways. First, it could express his feelings. In that case, though the Apostle does not state here why he feels it necessary to take up such an imprudent task, the implication is clearly that his enemies have driven him to it.[8] Second, it could express a watchword used by his detractors expressing the reason they feel comfortable in boasting. Given Paul's clearly stated objection to boasting, the latter seems the best choice.[9]

— / Although there is nothing to be gained by it: As noted above, the translators of the KJV were relying on the late Textus Receptus, in which this verse had been badly corrupted.[10] The phrase reads οὐ συμφέρον μέν (*ou sympheron men*). The verb συμφέρω (*sympherō*) means "to be advantageous, help, confer a benefit, be profitable/useful."[11] It is found here as a present participle used circumstantially with a concessive sense. The particle μέν (*men*) introduces a concessive clause, which is then followed by a second clause with an adversative sense.[12] Thus our translation renders the phrase as "although there is nothing to be gained by it."

I will come to visions and revelations of the Lord / nevertheless I will go on to visions and revelations from the Lord: The particle δε (*de*), translated here as "nevertheless," introduces the adversative clause following the concessive clause described above that was introduced by the particle μέν (*men*).[13] Paul is explaining that even though boasting may not be advantageous, it does not prevent him from receiving communications from the Lord.

The verb ἔρχομαι (*erchomai*) means "to come," and in this case it refers to a writer of a letter coming to or dealing with a new subject.[14]

---

5. BDAG, 213–14.
6. See Translation Notes for 10:8.
7. Martin, *2 Corinthians,* 586.
8. Bernard, "Second Epistle," 108.
9. Barrett, *Second Epistle,* 306–7.
10. Metzger, *Textual Commentary,* 516. Martin, *2 Corinthians,* 587.
11. BDAG, 960; Louw-Nida, §65.44.
12. BDAG, 629–30.
13. BDAG, 213, 629–30.
14. BDAG, 393–95.

The noun ὀπτασία (*optasia*), "vision, trance," denotes "an event of a transcendent character that impresses itself vividly on the mind,"[15] while the noun ἀποκάλυψις (*apocalypsis*), "revelation," refers to a divine action that discloses God's will or intent to a person.[16] However, the difference between the two terms was hardly distinguishable in common use.[17]

The noun κύριος (*kyrios*), "Lord," refers to Jesus. It is found here in the genitive case, which we have taken as objective rather than subjective.[18] Thus the heavenly manifestations do not disclose the Savior but rather flow from him.

12:2 ***And I knew a man in Christ / I know a person in Christ:*** The verb οἶδα (*oida*), found here in the perfect tense (literally "I have known"), is present in meaning and is thus rendered "I know."[19] Here the tense emphasizes the reality and vividness of the Paul's experience even though years have passed since the visions.

Paul uses the noun ἄνθρωπος (*anthrōpos*), which can describe a person of either sex, thus a "human being,"[20] rather than ἀνήρ (*anēr*), "a man," which only refers to "an adult human male."[21] Hence we have rendered it as "person." Verses 6–7 make it clear that the Apostle is, in fact, referring to himself.

The phrase ἐν Χριστῷ (*en Christō*), "in Christ," denotes "more than simply a reference to being 'a Christian.' It is Paul's way of showing that he was in Christ's power that the following vision and revelations took place."[22]

above fourteen years ago / fourteen years ago: The preposition πρό (*pro*), in its temporal nuance, usually means "earlier than, before," but in calculating a date usually denotes an exact time.[23]

(whether in the body, I cannot tell; or whether out of the body, I cannot tell: God knoweth) / —whether in the body or out of the body, I do not know, God knows—: The noun σῶμα (*sōma*) refers to the mortal or physical body.[24] The first references to the body in both this verse and 12:3 do not

15. BDAG, 717.

16. BDAG, 112.

17. Barrett, *Second Epistle,* 307.

18. Barrett, *Second Epistle,* 307; Guthrie, *2 Corinthians,* 578, with n. 10.

19. BDAG, 693; Bernard, "Second Epistle," 109.

20. BDAG, 81.

21. BDAG, 79.

22. Martin, *2 Corinthians,* 591, states that Paul had access to the Savior's power because of the relationship they had.

23. Wallace, *Greek Grammar,* 379; BDAG, 864; BDF, §213.

24. BDAG, 983–84. The first reference to the body does not have a definite article.

have a definite article, reading literally "in body"; however, a noun that is the object of a preposition can be definite (that is, translated with a definite article in English) even if it lacks a definite article in Greek.[25] Thus we have added a definite article in our translation both here and with the following preposition ἐκτός (*ektos*) that denotes "outside of" or "independent of"[26] and refers to the spirit alone experiencing the rapture.

Though but a parenthetical note, this phrase plays an important part in Paul's intent. On the one hand, the Apostle does not view the body as depraved or evil. Salvation for him includes the body (see 5:1–10). His view ran counter to some of the religious and philosophical views at the time. Their teachings insisted that any divine manifestation, to be valid, had to happen outside or apart from the body. Paul's earlier stated position shows that he rejects this idea. On the other hand, he likely did not want to invalidate the idea that one could have an out-of-body spiritual experience. In this phrase, Paul retains a neutral tone, likely because he really did not know whether he was bodily transported into the divine realm or experienced it only though his spirit. The expression does show that Paul clearly believes that the soul has a conscious existence outside the body,[27] but here he leaves the answer to God alone.[28] In doing so, he does not prejudice his account with whatever position members of his audience may take.[29]

---

25. Wallace, *Greek Grammar,* 247.

26. Louw-Nida, §§83.20; 89.121.

27. Hughes, *Second Epistle,* 431.

28. Martin, *2 Corinthians,* 593–94.

29. Paul is not alone in his uncertainty of the part the body plays in these rapturous experiences. Others have had similar experiences and were left unsure as to what role the body played. For example, according to the Book of Mormon, "the heavens were opened" to the Nephite Twelve, "and they were caught up into heaven, and saw and heard unspeakable things. And it was forbidden them that they should utter; neither was it given unto them power that they could utter the things which they saw and heard; And whether they were in the body or out of the body, they could not tell; for it did seem unto them like a transfiguration of them, that they were changed from this body of flesh into an immortal state, that they could behold the things of God" (3 Ne. 28:11–15). This account shows that such ecstasy so surpasses anything mortals normally experience that they are left confused as to how much the body was involved. Some of the historical accounts of Joseph Smith's experiences with heavenly visions show that he was definitely in the body each time. See JS–H 1:16–17, 30 and D&C sections 76 and 110. In each of these instances, however, the heavenly visitor came to the Prophet. In one where he seems to have been caught up, he was left confused about the role his body played, saying, "I beheld the celestial kingdom of God, and the glory thereof, whether in the body or out I cannot tell" (D&C 137:1).

such an one caught up to the third heaven / who was taken up to the third heaven: The verb ἁρπάζω (*harpazō*), found here as a passive aorist participle, means "to grab or seize suddenly so as to remove or gain control, snatch/take away," with emphasis on the forcefulness of the act.[30] Paul's use of the participle suggests how powerful the experience was. The preposition ἕως (*heōs*), "up to," "to the point of," denotes reaching the top or upper limit in a series of levels,[31] in this case the divisions of heaven.[32]

12:3 ***And I knew such a man / And I know this person:*** On "I knew" and "I know," see Translation Notes on 12:2.

whether in the body, or out of the body, I cannot tell: God knoweth / whether in the body I do not know, or out of the body, I do not know, God knows: This phrase follows the same thought as that in 12:2 and has the same purpose. The Apostle does change the preposition from ἐκτός (*ektos*), "outside of" or "independent of,"[33] to χωρίς (*chōris*), "separate from, without,"[34] but the difference is so slight that it does not change the meaning of what Paul has already said.

12:4 ***How that he was caught up into paradise / that he was taken up into paradise:*** Paul again uses the verb ἁρπάζω (*harpazō*), "snatch/take away,"[35] to describe his experience. This time it does not take the form of a passive participle, but an aorist passive. There is no significant difference in nuance. The stress is really on the passive voice, for it shows that Paul had no active role in what happened. It was done according to God's will, not the Apostle's.

The preposition εἰς (*eis*), "into,"[36] shows that Paul actually entered into paradise. The noun παράδεισος (*paradeisos*), "paradise," was a Persian loan word that referred to an enclosed, nicely kept plot of ground but came to denote "a transcendent place of blessedness."[37]

---

30. BDAG, 134; Louw-Nida, §§18.4; 37.28.

31. BDAG, 424; Louw-Nida, §§78.51; 84.19.

32. In a few instances, Paul referred to the divine realm in the singular, "heaven," but most often he used the plural "heavens," which is not surprising given his understanding of the nature of the divine realm. Anderson, *Understanding Paul,* 143.

33. Louw-Nida, §§83.20; 89.121.

34. Louw-Nida, §§63.31; 89.120.

35. BDAG, 134; Louw-Nida, §§18.4; 37.28.

36. BDAG, 288–91. There is some debate among scholars as to the relationship between the "third heaven" and "paradise," with some believing they reference the same place. See Martin, *2 Corinthians,* 598. Insights from the Restoration make it clear that they are separate places. See *DNTC,* 2:447.

37. BDAG, 761; Louw-Nida, §1.14.

and heard unspeakable words which it is not lawful for a man to utter / and he heard inexpressible words that are not proper for a person to speak: The adjective ἄρρητος (*arrētos*), "inexpressible," has two denotations. First, it refers to material "that cannot be expressed, since it is beyond human power," and second to material "that must not be expressed, since it is holy."[38] Thus the phrase ἄρρητα ῥήματα (*arrēta rēmata*), "inexpressible words," could refer either to ideas that cannot be translated into an earthly language or shared because of their deep sacredness.

The verb ἔξεστιν (*exestin*), "it is right, is authorized, is permitted, is proper," found here as a present participle, denotes authorization to do something, thus what is right, permitted, lawful. It also denotes what is possible.[39] It is modified by the particle οὐκ (*ouk*), "not," that negates the idea carried in its object. Hence the phrase can mean either "it is not possible" or "it is not lawful." We have translated it as "not proper . . . to speak," assuming the latter interpretation.[40] However, recorded parallel experience by others suggests such is not the case. See Analysis below.[41]

12:5 ***Of such an one will I glory / I will boast about this person:*** On the verb καύχομαι (*kauchaomai*), "to boast," see Translation Notes for 10:8. Though the word is found here in the future tense, it does not indicate that Paul intends to boast about this person sometime in the future. The tense indicates a gnomic idea[42]—that is, an idea that is generic, meaning it could take place in the future but may not. It is best expressed in English as "I am willing to boast, but I will not do so."[43]

---

38. BDAG, 134.

39. BDAG, 348–49.

40. Martin, *2 Corinthians,* 599–600.

41. Though not caught up in vision, others have experienced hearing and thus learning divine truths that they, too, could not put into words. During the time when the Savior visited the people of the Americas, he "knelt upon the earth; and behold he prayed unto the Father, and the things which he prayed cannot be written, and the multitude did bear record who heard him. And after this manner do they bear record: The eye hath never seen, neither hath the ear heard, before, so great and marvelous things as we saw and heard Jesus speak unto the Father; And no tongue can speak, neither can there be written by any man, neither can the hearts of men conceive so great and marvelous things as we both saw and heard Jesus speak; and no one can conceive of the joy which filled our souls at the time we heard him pray for us unto the Father" (3 Ne. 17:15–17). It is of note that though the multitude could understand every word the Lord said and also remember them afterward, their feeble mortal language simply could not capture his thoughts on any level. All they could do was leave their impressions.

42. On the rare use of the gnomic future of a verb, see Wallace, *Greek Grammar,* 571.

43. Guthrie, *2 Corinthians,* 584.

We have rendered the masculine genitive phrase τοῦ τοιούτου (*tou toioutou*), literally "of such a one," as "about this person," thereby retaining the ambiguity as to the gender of the person found in 12:2 and 3.

yet of myself I will not glory / but about myself I will not boast: The conjunction δέ (*de*), "but," sets up a strong contrast between what the Apostle will and will not boast about: the mortal versus the spiritual.

Once again, we see Paul's use of irony as a means of setting himself apart from his opponents. He readily admits that boasting of the one who had seen such visions as he has recounted would be in order. However, he refrains from doing so because there is, in his context, only one condition to boast about. He indicates what this is in the next phrase.

but in mine infirmities / except in my weaknesses: The phrase εἰ μή (*ei mē*), "except," is a marker of contrast.[44] With it, Paul admits a willingness to boast, but only if it is of the right quality. In the present context, he defines that quality with the noun ἀσθένεια (*astheneia*), "weakness," found here as a plural. The word refers to that which lacks strength from being ill, incapacitated, limited, or powerless.[45] The plural suggests that Paul may have more than one of these characteristics in mind. Thus he insists his boasting will be in the nonspectacular weaknesses that he continually feels and exhibits.

12:6 ***For though I would desire to glory / For even if I wanted to boast:*** The verb θέλω (*thelō*) denotes "wish to have, desire, want."[46] It is found here as an aorist subjunctive. The conjunction ἐάν (*ean*), "if," when used

---

44. Louw-Nida, §89.131.

45. BDAG, 142–43. The word group of which it is a part usually refers to bodily weakness, but also includes frailty of human life, poverty, lack of influence, and, more metaphorically, weakness of character, lack of conviction, lack of self-control. For a study, see Stahlin, "ἀσθενής, ἀσθένεια, ἀσθενέω, ἀσθένημα," in *TDNT,* 1:490–93. In Paul's writings, though the word group clearly refers to physical ailments or limitations (see, for example, 1 Cor. 11:30; Gal. 4:13; Philip. 2:26–27; 1 Tim. 5:23; and 2 Tim. 4:20), it often refers to weakness arising from being mortal or spiritually immature. In his writings to the Corinthians, however, he gives it a positive quality, showing that humble weakness opens the door to divine strength. To make his case, he presents two examples. The first is the suffering and death of Christ that God overcame through the power of the Resurrection. The second is the hardships, physical trials, and sacrifices of Paul himself, the once Christian-persecutor, whom God has now infused with the apostolic power. Thus, Paul's very life reveals that in the suffering of Christ's followers, God's life-giving power is made manifest. It is in this way that "Paul arrives at the paradoxical statement that he would rather boast about his weaknesses (2 Cor 11:29–30; 12:5, 9–10; 13:9), for God's 'power is made perfect in weakness.'" *NID,* 1:422.

46. BDAG, 447–48.

with a subjunctive verb, denotes an action that is expected to occur if certain conditions are met[47] and carries an element of deliberate choice.[48] Paul knows that the conditions will not be met because they are under his control and he chooses not to meet them.

I shall not be a fool / I will not be a fool: The noun ἄφρων (*aphrōn*), "fool," denotes a person who is without reason for want of mental sanity. It connotes such negative attributes as recklessness, lack of common sense, and an inability to see the reality of things either natural or spiritual. In a religious sense, it refers to an imprudent ordering of a person's life that leads them away from God.[49] This statement links to the one before, showing that if Paul had chosen to boast, it would not end in his playing the fool. He gives the reason in the next phrase.

for I will say the truth / for I will speak the truth: The noun ἀλήθεια (*alētheia*), "truth," has both objective and subjective nuances at play here. Objectively the noun denotes what is in accordance with fact or reality.[50] Subjectively it refers to views that stem from the inner qualities of sincerity and integrity of character[51] Since a fool does not have the capacity to understand and execute either of these states, Paul's ability to so speak the truth proves he is not a fool.

In this, with the phrase above, there is the suggestion that Paul will not be a fool because, unlike his detractors, he will make no false claims, as they seem to have been caught foolishly doing.[52]

but now I forbear / But I will refrain from boasting: The verb φείδομαι (*pheidomai*) means both to spare another from loss or discomfort and to abstain from doing something.[53] Both nuances work here but the idea of refraining better fits the context. Paul's point seems to be that he will not push the issue as to who is telling the truth and who is not.

lest any man should think of me above that which he seeth me to be / so that no one will consider me more than what he sees me to be: The phrase μή τις (*mē tis*), "so that not anyone," is inclusive and therefore comprises both Paul's friends and enemies.

---

47. BDAG, 267–68.

48. Barrett, *Second Epistle,* 312.

49. Georg Bertram, "ἄφρων, ἀφροσύνη," in *TDNT,* 9:230–32.

50. BDAG, 42–43.

51. Rudolph Bultmann, Gottfried Quell, and Gerhard Kittle, "ἀλήθεια," in *TDNT,* 1:232–47.

52. Barrett, *Second Epistle,* 312; Martin, *2 Corinthians,* 602–3.

53. BDAG, 1051.

The noun σκόλοψ (*skolops*) denotes a "'stake,' . . . thorn, splinter."[73] All produce a good deal of discomfort, with the splinter being the least painful and the stake the most egregious. The noun σάρξ (*sarx*), literally "flesh," refers in the present context to the human body and carries the nuance of the physical limitations imposed by mortality.[74] The whole phrase points to that "which causes serious trouble and difficulty," thus "trouble, woe, suffering, serious inconvenience."[75]

the messenger of Satan / a messenger of Satan: The noun ἄγγελος (*angelos*), though often referring to an angel or divine being, in this case refers to an envoy or messenger commissioned to deliver information. The noun σατανᾶς (*satanas*), "adversary, slanderer, accuser," though initially a title, came to designate Lucifer, the "Son of the Morning" who rebelled against God and with his followers was cast out of heaven.[76] For Paul, Satan is neither a mere metaphor nor the "personification of an impersonal power of evil, but precisely the power of evil, fully personal in nature."[77] Paul's intent with the phrase "a messenger of Satan," however, is unclear. Some scholars take it literally as denoting a supernatural evil being who tormented Paul, while others take it metaphorically as denoting the painful and stressful nature of the affliction Paul continually suffered. The theories about the phrase are so varied as to be beyond the scope of this study.[78] Given that

73. BDAG, 930–31.

74. BDAG, 914–16. Usually, this noun has negative connotations, while the noun σῶμα (*sōma*), "body," is positive. However, Paul seems to use them interchangeably in 4:10–11 to highlight the weaknesses associated with mortality. See Barnett, *Second Epistle,* 237 n. 53.

75. Louw-Nida, §22.20.

76. *NID,* 4:264–68; Chauncey C. Riddle, "Devils," in *EM,* 1:379–82.

77. Seifrid, *Second Epistle,* 405. The extent to which the adversary can afflict a soul in an attempt to impede God's work is clearly seen in the full and vicious attack he made on the young Joseph Smith. See JS–H 1:15–16.

78. The following will give those interested in the topic a place to begin. In the commentaries, see the extensive discussions and bibliography in Thrall, *Critical and Exegetical Commentary,* 2:809–18; Furnish, *II Corinthians,* 547–50; Hughes, *Second Epistle,* 442–46; and Martin, *2 Corinthians,* 577–79, 605–11. For journal articles dedicated to the subject, see David Abernathy, "Paul's Thorn in the Flesh: A Messenger of Satan?," *Neotestamentica* 35, no. 1–2 (2001): 69–79; M. L. Barré, "Qumran and the 'Weakness' of Paul," *Catholic Biblical Quarterly* 42, no. 2 (April 1980): 216–27; D. Landsborough, "St Paul and Temporal Lobe Epilepsy," *Journal of Neurology, Neurosurgery, and Psychiatry* 50 (1987): 659–64; T. J. Leary, "'A Thorn in the Flesh'—2 Corinthians 12: 7," *Journal of Theological Studies,* n.s., 43, no. 2 (October 1992): 520–22; Jerry W. McCant, "Paul's Thorn of Rejected Apostleship," *New Testament Studies* 34, no. 4 (1988): 550–72; Peter Marshall, "A Metaphor of Social Shame: θριαμβεύειν in 2 Cor. 2:14," *Novum Testamentum* 25, no. 4 (1983): 302–17; Terence Y. Mullins, "Paul's Thorn in the Flesh," *Journal of Biblical*

the condition is of a divine source and that it is constant as opposed to sporadic, we believe the metaphorical nuance has the better weight. Whatever the case, the phrase underscores the heavy, even hellish, burden that the condition imposed on the Apostle.

To buffet me / to torment me: The verb κολαφίζω (*kolaphizō*), found here as a present subjunctive, means to "strike with the fist, beat," or otherwise "torment."[79] The mood suggests the probable reason for the action,[80] while the tense suggests that the suffering was ongoing, and thus, Paul was never relieved of it.[81]

lest I should be exalted above measure / so that I would not become overly proud: Paul has already used this phrase at the beginning of the verse (see above) and likely repeats it here so that his audience would not miss his point.

12:8 ***For this thing I besought the Lord thrice / Concerning this, I pleaded with the Lord three times:*** The phrase ὑπὲρ τούτου (*hyper touto*), "concerning this," is ambiguous, since the demonstrative pronoun could refer to either the "thorn" (σκολοψ, *skolops*) or to the "messenger of Satan" (ἄγγελος Σατανᾶ, *angelos Satana*). The majority of translations and commentaries take it as referring to the thorn, although at least one commentary argues it refers to the "angel."[82] But since the "thorn" and the "messenger of Satan" both refer to the same affliction that Paul is experiencing, the point is that Paul had pled with the Lord to remove the affliction, whatever it was.

The verb παρακαλέω (*parakaleō*), "request, implore, entreat," found here in the aorist tense, carries the warm but urgent and earnest sense of calling someone to one's side, usually for assistance.[83]

The adverb τρίς (*tris*) denotes "three times"[84] and likely should be taken literally. It suggests that the condition vacillated between bad and worse

---

Literature 76, no. 4 (1957): 299–303; Patricia Nisbet, "The Thorn in the Flesh," *Expository Times* 80 (1969): 126; David M. Park, "Paul's ΣΚΟΛΟΨ ΤΗ ΣΑΡΚΙ: Thorn or Stake? (2 Cor. XII 7)," *Novum Testamentum* 22, no. 2 (1980): 179–83; R. M. Price, "Punished in Paradise (An Exegetical Theory on II Corinthians 12:1–10)," *Journal of the Study of the New Testament* 2, no. 7 (1980): 33–40; and Neil Gregor Smith, "The Thorn That Stayed: An Exposition of II Corinthians 12:7–9," *Interpretation: A Journal of Bible and Theology* 13, no. 4 (1959): 409–16.

79. BDAG, 555.

80. Wallace, *Greek Grammar,* 461–63.

81. Martin, *2 Corinthians,* 610 n. 896.

82. Martin, *2 Corinthians,* 611; Barrett, *Second Epistle,* 316.

83. BDAG, 764–65.

84. Louw-Nida, §60.71.

and that the Apostle prayed when the suffering became especially heavy. The figure, however, was also used to indicate something done a number of times and thus leaves the door open to repeated prayers on Paul's part.[85]

That it might depart from me / that it would leave me: The verb ἀφίστημι (*aphistēmi*), describes an "action that results in the distancing of person or thing from person, thing, place, or condition."[86] It can be used figuratively to describe the departure or withdrawal of "conditions and moral qualities."[87] The subject of the verb could be either the "thorn" or "the messenger of Satan." But as noted above, since the "thorn" and the "messenger of Satan" both describe the same affliction that Paul is suffering, it is the removal of this affliction that Paul had been pleading for.

12:9 ***And he said unto me, My grace is sufficient for thee / And he said to me, "My grace is sufficient for you:*** The verb λέγω (*legō*), "to tell, say,"[88] found here in the perfect tense, looks at the content of what is said more than the means by which it comes. Whether by inspiration, full voice, or theophany, the message was expressly clear. Further, that Paul uses the perfect tense suggests the intent of the message, though spoken some time before, continues to resonate fully within him.[89]

With the phrase ἡ χάρις μου (*hē charis mou*), "my grace," God's explanation focuses on *his* grace, the preposition μου (*mou*), "my," being a genitive of source.[90]

The verb ἀρκέω (*arkeō*), found here in the present tense, denotes what is to "be enough, sufficient, adequate,"[91] and looks to what is adequate to fulfill a particular purpose, notably one that leads to eventual satisfaction.[92] It gives a particular cast to the noun χάρις (*charis*), "grace."[93] Usually the word denotes God's love for his children as expressed in the ministry of Jesus. In this instance, however, it looks to its enabling power, by which sufficient help comes upon the individual. By its means, no trial, no matter its nature (Rom. 8:38–39), will overpower those who come under the Lord's grace.[94]

---

85. Barrett, *Second Epistle,* 316.

86. BDAG, 157.

87. BDAG, 158.

88. Louw-Nida, §33.69.

89. Moule, *Idiom Book,* 15, notes that this verse contains "a fair example of the true Greek Perfect."

90. Guthrie, *2 Corinthians,* 593 n. 57.

91. BDAG, 131–32.

92. Louw-Nida, §59.46; Gerhard Kittle, "ἀρκέω, ἀρκετός," in *TDNT,* 1:464–67.

93. BDAG, 1079–81.

94. Martin, *2 Corinthians,* 614.

for my strength is made perfect in weakness / for my power is brought to perfection in weakness": The conjunction γάρ (*gar*), "for,"[95] acts here as a marker of clarification explaining why God's grace is sufficient for Paul to do God's work. The pronoun "my" is not found in the Greek text that reads ἡ . . . δύναμις (*hē . . . dynamis*), literally "the power," but the context clearly shows that God is referring to his power, so we have added "my" for clarity. Further, the noun, in the present context, is equated with ἡ χάρις μου (*hē charis mou*), "my grace," referred to above, thus revealing how God's grace makes itself manifest.

The verb τελέω (*teleō*), "to bring to completion, perfection,"[96] is found here in the passive voice, thus rendered "is brought to perfection." Here the idea is that God's power/grace finds its consummation, reaches its completion, or fulfills its purpose when his faithful children properly and successfully use weakness as God intended it—that is, as a means to build an ever-stronger relationship with him that ultimately results in their Christlike perfection.[97]

For the noun ἀσθένεια (*astheneia*), "weakness," see Translation Notes for 12:5.

Most gladly therefore will I rather glory in my infirmities / Therefore, I will most gladly boast in my weaknesses: The conjunction οὖν (*oun*), "therefore,"[98] acts inferentially, signaling Paul's audience that he will now draw a conclusion from his related experience. The adverb ἡδέως (*hēdeōs*), "happily, gladly,"[99] refers to a task one would be pleased to do. It is found here in the form of a superlative, thus rendered "most gladly."[100]

For the verb καυχάομαι (*kauchaomai*), "to boast," found here in the future tense, see Translation Notes for 10:8. The adverb μᾶλλον (*mallon*) associated with it often marks an alternative and is thus translated as "rather."[101] In this case, however, it refers to something being done to a very great degree[102] and, consequently, emphasizes the force of Paul's boasting.

On the noun ἀσθένεια (*astheneia*), "weakness," found here as a plural, see Translation Notes for 12:5. The plural shows that Paul's problems and

95. BDAG, 189–90.

96. Louw-Nida, §68.22; see also 68.23; Gerhard Delling, "τελέω," in *TDNT*, 8:57–61; BDAG, 997–98.

97. Compare Ether 12:27.

98. BDAG, 736–37.

99. Louw-Nida, §25.129.

100. Barrett, *Second Epistle*, 317.

101. BDAG, 613–14.

102. Louw-Nida, §78.28.

challenges include more than the "thorn," and likely the noun refers to the aggregate of all the challenges and mishaps he has been through.

that the power of Christ may rest upon me / so that the power of Christ may dwell within me: The conjunction ἵνα (*hina*), "in order that," acts as a marker denoting purpose.[103] The phrase ἡ δύναμις τοῦ Χριστοῦ (*hē dynamis tou Christou*), "the power of Christ," clearly refers to the enabling grace/power that Paul has mentioned above.

The verb ἐπισκηνόω (*episkēnoō*), "take up quarters,"[104] carries the nuance of taking up an abode and thereby suggests that the Savior's grace/power would be immediately accessible, being ever present in the soul.

Of note is that Paul now readily boasts despite his reluctance to do so. His explanation as to why could suggest that the Apostle sees boasting as the means to open the door to the divine downflow of power. It is not the act of boasting, however, that brings the blessing. It is his weaknesses. This is because they provide not only the necessity but also the demand that the power of the Divine dwells within him. The reason is that it is only by access to divine power—an enabling force—that he is able to do God's work. This is the message he wants to get across to his audience so that they too will understand that Christ works through weakness and thereby yield to the humility and meekness the Savior demands. If they will but accept and live this ideal, they too will be filled with enabling power.

12:10 ***Therefore I take pleasure in infirmities / Therefore, I delight in weaknesses:*** The conjunction διό (*dio*), "therefore, for this reason," acts inferentially, introducing a result.[105] Paul expresses that result with the verb εὐδοκέω (*eudokeō*), "be well pleased, take delight," denoting what brings pleasure or satisfaction.[106] He next lists all the conditions in which he delights.

On the noun ἀσθένεια (*astheneia*), "weakness," found here as a plural, see Translation Notes for 12:5, 9.

---

103. BDAG, 475–77.

104. BDAG, 378; Louw-Nida, §85.75. The verb denotes spreading a tent or a covering over something and thus to dwell or abide with another. This is the only place the word is found in the New Testament, but it is related to the common noun σκήνη (*skēnē*) that, besides referencing a common tent, also referred to the Old Testament Tabernacle. This reference may be the nuance Paul has in mind, for it was there that Jehovah took up residence among his people. Guthrie, *2 Corinthians,* 594–95.

105. BDAG, 250.

106. BDAG, 404. Among the gospel writers, the term has a deeply theological nuance. It is used to refer to the Father's feelings toward the Son (Matt. 3:17; 17:5), of his pleasure in revealing his Son though Paul's work (Gal. 1:15–16), and in saving the lost (1 Cor. 1:21).

in reproaches / in mistreatments: The noun ὕβρις (*hybris*), found here as a plural, denotes "shame, insult, mistreatment"—that is, the result of experiencing others' insolence. It also denotes "hardship, disaster"—that is, the result of damage caused by force.[107] These all work, but given Paul's overall experiences, the idea of ill-treatment dominates.

in necessities / in calamities: The noun ἀνάγκη (*anankē*), found here as a plural, denotes a state of suffering or trouble, thus "distress, calamity, pressure."[108] Given Paul's often difficult and sudden distress or hardships, "calamity" works well.

in persecutions: The noun διωγμός (*diōgmos*), found here as a plural, denotes "persecution," a program deliberately "designed to harass and oppress someone."[109]

in distresses / and troubles: The noun στενοχωρία (*stenochōria*), found here as a plural, denotes "distress, difficulty, anguish," but the idea of varied afflictions, thus "troubles," seems to carry the idea in the present context best.[110]

for Christ's sake: The preposition ὑπέρ (*hyper*) carries two important nuances here. The first is that of cause or reason, thus "because of, in view of," and looks to that which is beneficial.[111] The second is that of benefaction, thus "on behalf of," and looks to a person "who is benefited by an event or on whose behalf an event takes place."[112] That the preposition is in the genitive case shows that the latter is likely what is meant here.[113] Paul has suffered all he has for the benefit of his Lord.

for when I am weak, then am I strong / For whenever I am weak, then I am strong: The conjunction γάρ (*gar*), "for," acts as a marker of clarification concerning what has been previously said.[114] Here it indicates that Paul is stating his conclusion and making his summary statement.

The conjunction ὅταν (*hotan*), "whenever," introduces the idea of the indefinite. At any point in time, not just at one moment, when the conditions are met, the result will occur.[115]

---

107. BDAG, 1022.
108. BDAG, 60–61.
109. BDAG, 253.
110. BDAG, 943.
111. Louw-Nida, §89.28.
112. Louw-Nida, §90.36.
113. BDAG, 1030–31.
114. BDAG, 189–90.
115. BDAG, 730.

On the verb ἀσθενέω (*astheneō*), "to be weak," see Translation Notes for 12:5.

The adjective δυνατός (*dynatos*), "strong," refers not to being physically or mentally robust but to "being capable or competent."[116] In this case, it refers to the strengthening power found in Christ.

Analysis and Summary

At this point, Paul begins his next argument. He starts with the statement "It is necessary to boast." Given his obvious reluctance to engage in such an activity, this statement seems out of character. It is likely, however, that he is not expressing his sentiment but rather quoting a watchword used by the Corinthians. The phrase actually embodies a widely accepted principle followed by many, including, apparently, some of Paul's opponents.[117] But if Paul himself sees boasting as having no advantage, why then does he engage in it? This pericope suggests he does so as a polemical device to thwart the position of his enemies who use this very technique to further their cause. For him, boasting is the best way to overcome the mounting opposition. Further, by using their watchword, he undercuts its value while revitalizing his own position, as he immediately refers to having his own visions and revelations.[118] Noteworthy is how skillfully Paul adopts this methodology while twisting it to make his point: proper boasting leads not to personal glory but to the glory of God. Thus the practice does have an efficacious value, but only if it focuses on Deity. What we must stress here is that, by deflecting praise and glory from himself, Paul turned the Corinthian mindset on its head.[119] Garnering glory for oneself or family was the name of the game that many in most classes played. To deflect that glory to another was unthinkable. But Paul well understood that self-glory can and often does result in a false sense of pride that offends the Spirit and blocks the person from its purifying and empowering influence.

In 12:2–4, Paul relates very briefly and indirectly two highly spiritual and informative visionary experiences that he had had, in which God not only opened to him the divine realm but also gave him valuable instructions and understandings. Paul likely related these experiences because he "realized that with the experientially oriented Corinthians it was not just

116. BDAG, 264.

117. Barrett, *Second Epistle*, 306–7.

118. Francis T. Fallon, *2 Corinthians* (Wilmington, Del.: Michael Glazier, 1980), 105.

119. Martin, *2 Corinthians*, 588.

the authenticity of his ministry that was on trial but also the very authenticity of his experience of God."[120]

However, he does not state directly that he was the one who had such marvelous manifestations. Instead, he obliquely states that "I knew a man" who had them. Just why Paul refers to himself in the third person is unclear. That he did so has led some to feel he was not actually talking about himself. One view holds that he was referencing a missionary companion whose experience Paul admired because the Apostle himself was more prone to revelations than to such high and esoteric visions. Another view was that the Apostle was using parody on the claimed visionary experiences of his detractors. He did so because during this time period a number of people claimed they had been caught up in some kind of ecstatic phenomenon, a group that likely included Paul's detractors.[121]

Most scholars reject both ideas and insist that Paul was referring to himself, but expressing it in such a way in order to distance himself from the event and not draw undue attention to its importance. This position has the best footing for two reasons. The first is that it fits the context wherein Paul admits that though he does not see it as beneficial, he "will go on to visions and revelations from the Lord" (12:1, NR). Second, it serves the purpose of introducing the central subject and the very personal matter of this section, the "thorn in the flesh" (12:7; see below).[122]

But why be so oblique? Often Sophists and others used this technique rhetorically to reduce the offense of boasting about oneself. By using it, the Apostle gives his enemies little ammunition to use against him while making a very strong case. Further, both he and his audience were well aware of the great historical exemplars of faith, such as Moses and Ezekiel, who experienced such grand visions. Paul does not seem to want to openly claim a place among them.[123] His approach also allows him to keep focus on the Lord rather than himself. In this way, he is able to talk about these visions "in a way that makes clear he is not inappropriately boasting about one of the most amazing spiritual experiences of his life."[124]

---

120. Witherington, *Conflict and Community,* 459 n. 80.

121. Witherington, *Conflict and Community,* 459. For discussion, see Andrew T. Lincoln, "'Paul the Visionary': The Setting and Significance of the Rapture to Paradise in II Corinthians XII. 1–10," *New Testament Studies* 25, no. 2 (1979): 204–20; and C. K. Barrett, "New Testament Eschatology," *Scottish Journal of Theology* 6, no. 2 (1953): 238–39.

122. Guthrie, *2 Corinthians,* 579–80.

123. Garland, *2 Corinthians,* 511.

124. Guthrie, *2 Corinthians,* 581.

Clearly, he is reacting to the social situation of the day. The Sophists expounded for money and acclaim, not unlike some of Paul's antagonists. But some Greeks, who considered themselves "true philosophers," used irony, often playing "the fool," to vindicate their own position that promoted self-restraint and even poverty. In some of these cases, the philosophers referred to themselves in the third person to downplay their own accomplishments and thus emphasize and help their position. Further, they insisted that one could indulge in self-praise when, to protect oneself from false accusations, the truth had to be told. It is highly unlikely that Paul was influenced directly by any of the philosophical schools since there is no evidence of such in his writings.[125] Even so, it is probable that he is reflecting the unwritten cultural norms influenced by them.[126] It is more likely that, at the least, the Apostle's use of the third person reflects his ongoing embarrassment in having to use such a senseless exercise as boasting, and this is a way for him to distance himself from it.[127]

It is of note that the leaders of the New Testament era understood that the heavens were again open, and revelations and visions were the result, accordingly, of fulfilling Old Testament promises (Joel 2:28–29; Acts 2:17–18).[128] One dramatic and far-reaching vision given to Peter showed how God had prepared a way for Gentiles to come under the covenant (see Acts 10:10–16, 34–35; 11:1–18). Paul, by direct assignment of the Lord, became the instrument of the realization of that vision (Acts 9:12–15; Gal. 2:9). Visions were opened to him to provide him with the necessary understanding to do such work. Thus he could proclaim that he received the gospel not through human agents but "through the revelation from Jesus Christ" (Gal. 1:12, our translation). It is this knowledge that he declared (1 Cor. 11:23; 15:3). Further, he stated that the most far-reaching aspect of the gospel "was made known unto me by revelation," a revelation "that was not made known to the sons of men in other generations as it has now been revealed to his holy Apostles and prophets by the Spirit; that is, how Gentiles are fellow heirs, members of the same body, and partakers of the promise of Christ Jesus through the gospel" (Eph. 3:3–6, our translation).

---

125. Martin, *2 Corinthians,* 591.

126. Barnett, *Second Epistle,* 578 n. 4.

127. Martin, *2 Corinthians,* 591.

128. Such are the hallmark of the Church in any age. Those who have these constitute "the people of God." *DNTC,* 2:443–44.

As the verses under review indicate, in addition to understanding how missionary work would proceed during the New Testament era, the Apostle also learned about the heavenly realm through two visions that had taken place fourteen years before. That Paul still knew the very year these events occurred shows the impact they had on him. His precision helps date the experience. Since he wrote 2 Corinthians about AD 57, the marvelous manifestations took place around AD 42 or 43, or about ten years after his conversion in AD 32 or 33.[129] At the time he was yet living in Tarsus. It would be about three years before Barnabas recruited him as an assistant to oversee the affairs of the Church in Antioch, around AD 46.[130] Thus the wonders that the Apostle to the Gentiles experienced took place sometime before he became a full-time missionary for Christ.[131]

Reporting on these visions, he states simply that in one he was taken up into the "third heaven" and in the other into "paradise." Due to the ambiguity of the phrase "third heaven" and lack of Restoration insights, scholars have speculated throughout history on just what Paul was referring to. From the Jewish standpoint of Paul's day, because the Hebrew noun שָׁמַיִם (*šāmayim*), "heavens," is plural,[132] many Jewish scholars accepted the idea that there was more than one. The Old Testament supports a threefold "heavenly" division (see Neh. 9:6; 1 Kgs. 8:27–28; 2 Chr. 2:6; and Ps. 148:4). In this view, there is "the atmospheric heaven, a stellar heaven (or firmament), and the limitless, or spiritual, heaven, where God is located."[133] On this basis, the idea of three heavens was popular. Despite this, there was no consensus as to the number.[134] Even though the Apostle advanced the idea that the afterlife

---

129. This dating assumes that the death of Jesus took place about AD 30 or 31.

130. On the chronology, see Wayment, *From Persecutor to Apostle,* viii–ix.

131. For a study, see Robert E. Osborne, "St. Paul's Silent Years," *Journal of Biblical Studies* 84, no. 1 (1965): 59–65. Martin, *2 Corinthians,* 592–93, concludes that these manifestations were separate from any of those recorded in Acts or the Epistles.

132. E. Kautzsch, ed., *Gesenius' Hebrew Grammar* (London: Oxford University Press, 1910), §88d; HAL, 1560.

133. Martin, *2 Corinthians,* 595; see also Hughes, *Second Epistle,* 432–34. For a study, see Lincoln, "Paul, the Visionary," 204–20.

134. Later literature supported such numbers as three, five, seven, and ten. See Barrett, *Second Epistle,* 309–10; Martin, *2 Corinthians,* 596. At the time, a seven-division heaven was gaining popularity. Martin, *2 Corinthians,* 596. According to Jewish apocryphal work *2 Enoch,* paradise was located in the third of seven heavens (*2 En.* 8:1). This ancient document is also known as *The Secrets of Enoch* as well as *The Slavonic Enoch* because its only complete text comes from a midlevel copy in that language. The original appears to have been written in Greek during the early first century. For background, see Michael E. Stone, "Apocalyptic Literature," in *Jewish Writings of the Second Temple*

had three divisions, which he compared to the sun, moon, and stars (1 Cor. 15:41), there is no evidence that any Jewish or Greco-Roman notions of the divine realm influenced Paul. On the other hand, some in his audience may have found the idea of heavenly ascent acceptable because they were aware that others reported such revelatory incidences.[135]

Paul's view, however, focuses on the heavenly realm itself. In his description, he uses the preposition ἕως (*heōs*), "as far as, to," that denotes reaching the top or upper limit of an object.[136] In this case, that upper limit was the highest degree or celestial realm of heaven.[137] Joseph Smith supported this view: "'Paul ascended into the third Heavens and he could understand the three principle rounds of Jacob's Ladder,[138] the Telestial, the Terrestrial and the Celestial glories or Kingdoms, where Paul saw and heard things which were not lawful for him to utter.'"[139] It is also important to note that declaring that he had reached the zenith of glory gave the Apostle cachet with his audience, thus allowing him to retain full credibility.[140]

In addition to being raised into "the third heaven," God also raised Paul into paradise. The noun is a Persian loan word that referred to an enclosed, nicely kept plot or garden. It is in this light that the celestial garden located eastward in Eden became associated with paradise. Over time, this Edenic state became allied with the spirit world. Thus Jesus could say to the thief with whom he was crucified, "Today you will be with me in paradise" (Luke 23:43, NIV). Among the Jews, it also came to denote "a place of

---

Period: Apocrypha, Pseudepigrapha, Qumran Sectarian Writings, Philo, Josephus, ed. Michael E. Stone (Assen, Neth.: Van Gorcum; Philadelphia: Fortress Press, 1984), 406–8. For a translation of this work in English with copious notes, see James H. Charlesworth, ed., *The Old Testament Pseudepigrapha,* vol. 1, *Apocalyptic Literature and Testaments* (Garden City, N.Y.: Doubleday, 1983), 102–213, specifically 115. For a study, see Paula R. Gooder, *Only the Third Heaven: 2 Corinthians 12.1–10 and Heavenly Ascent* (London: T & T Clark, 2006), who views Paul's reference as an admission that he only ascended to the third heaven and thus was halted at the time in his progression.

135. For a study, see James Buchanan Wallace, *Snatched into Paradise (2 Cor. 12:1–10): Paul's Heavenly Journey in the Context of Early Christian Experience* (Berlin: De Gruyter, 2011), who argues that there was no ancient model that influenced Paul. For the Apostle, such extraordinary experiences enable self-transcending love for God and neighbors.

136. BDAG, 423–24; Louw-Nida, §§78.51; 84.19.

137. Holzapfel and Wayment, *Making Sense,* 377.

138. The reference is to Gen. 28:10–15.

139. "History, 1838–1856, Volume D-1 [1 August 1842–1 July 1843]," 1556, Joseph Smith Papers, accessed September 27, 2022, https://www.josephsmithpapers.org/paper-summary/history-1838-1856-volume-d-1-1-august-1842-1-july-1843/199.

140. Martin, *2 Corinthians,* 596.

transcendent blessedness," where the righteous dead resided.[141] In Revelation 2:7, it is associated with the abode of God or, in LDS terminology, the celestial kingdom.

Though some scholars opine that Paul had but one vision, thus combining the third heaven and paradise,[142] the Restoration perspective is that paradise is a subset of the spirit world, which also includes Hades and the spirit prison.[143] Joseph Smith declared that they "are all one, it is a world of Spirits. The righteous and the wicked all go to the same world of Spirits."[144] Even so, the scriptures are clear that there is a division called "a gulf" between the places (Luke 16:22–26; 1 Ne. 15:28–29). One of the Savior's activities between his death and Resurrection was to visit the souls in prison and bridge the gulf that separated the righteous from the wicked by instituting missionary work there (1 Pet. 3:19; 4:6; D&C 138).

In sum, paradise is the temporary abode where reside those who made and kept sacred covenants with God during mortality or accepted him fully and received the temple ordinances performed in their behalf while in spirit prison. All these rest from their labors in a state of peace and happiness, waiting for the time when they will receive their full blessing of entering into the celestial world (2 Ne. 9:13; Alma 40:12; D&C 76:50–70; 137:7–9; 138:31–34).[145]

About his heavenly experiences, Paul adds an aside that, when they happened, he did not know whether he was in or out of his body. Both the pagan mystery religions and Jewish rabbinical writings use this language to describe personal reactions to experiencing esoteric phenomenon.[146] Though but a parenthetical note, this phrase plays an important part in Paul's intent and reveals where he stood on certain issues. On the one hand, the Apostle does not view the body as depraved or evil, and salvation for him also included the physical element (see 5:1–10). Therefore, it could be involved in a revelatory experience. His view ran counter to some of the religious and philosophical views at the time. These assessments

141. BDAG, 761.

142. See, for example, Guthrie, *2 Corinthians,* 582 n. 27; and Barrett, *Second Epistle,* 310.

143. *DNTC,* 2:447.

144. For Joseph Smith's teachings on the subject, see "History, 1838–1856, Volume D-1," 1573–75; quote on 1574.

145. M. Catherine Thomas, "Paradise," in *EM,* 3:1062–63; see also Walter D. Bowen, "Spirit World," in *EM,* 4:1408–9.

146. Martin, *2 Corinthians,* 599, with n. 804. This type of revelation is also known in the Bible (Isa. 8:16; Dan. 12:2–4; Rev. 14:3) and in the Book of Mormon (3 Ne. 28:12–14).

insisted that any divine manifestation, to be valid, had to happen outside or apart from the body. Paul's earlier stated position, however, shows that he rejects this idea. Even so, he likely did not want to invalidate the idea that one could have an out-of-body spiritual experience. In this phrase, Paul retains a neutral tone, likely because he really did not know if he was bodily transported into the divine realm or experienced it only though his spirit. Paul clearly believes that the soul has a conscious existence outside the body,[147] but here he leaves the answer to God alone.[148] In doing so, he does not prejudice his account against whatever position members of his audience may take.[149] We must emphasize, however, that Paul's raptures were "so outside the realm of normal experience, Paul could not be sure exactly what happened to him." To say that the experience overwhelmed him does not come close to describing what happened. It simply left him at a loss of words to explain not only what he saw but also what he heard. Only God knew.[150]

Concerning what happened during these deeply revelatory and informative events, the Apostle states only that he "heard inexpressible words that are not proper for a person to speak" (12:4, NR).

Paul's phrase leaves it unclear whether the reason he will not share what he learned is because it was beyond his language skills or whether he has been specifically forbidden to do so.[151] The Book of Mormon is helpful on this issue. It preserves an account of certain individuals who were also "caught up into heaven, and saw and heard unspeakable things. And it was forbidden them that they should utter; neither was it given unto them power that they could utter the things which they saw and heard." After the vision, "they did again minister upon the face of the earth; nevertheless, they did not minister of the things which they had heard and seen, because of the commandment which was given them in heaven" (3 Ne. 28:14–16). The scripture shows that these men plainly understood the vision's contents at the time and clearly remembered what they had learned long afterward. However, they could not relate them, first because it was forbidden

147. Hughes, *Second Epistle,* 431.

148. Martin, *2 Corinthians,* 593–94.

149. See discussion in note 29.

150. Guthrie, *2 Corinthians,* 583.

151. The phrase ἄρρητα ῥήματα (*arrēta rhēmata*), "unspeakable words," could refer to ideas that cannot be translated into an earthly language or shared because of their deep sacredness. See Louw-Nida, §33.95.

them to even try, and second because they simply did not have the means.[152] The double prohibition is interesting in that it suggests that some portion of what they learned could have been shared. However, they, like Paul, were true to their charge.

But if Paul could not share the information, what value did the communication have? One point is clear—the revelation was for Paul alone. Its intent appears to have been twofold: first to strengthen him in facing the immense spiritual and physical suffering he would have to endure by providing him with an understanding as to why,[153] and second to give him a cosmological perspective of the gospel and God's plans for it that allowed Paul to view his own work from a more complete perspective. As a result, he could put emphasis where it belonged.

In sum, these visions gave him an incalculable boost in preparation for his apostolic career, providing him with not only knowledge of the divine will and workings but also the strength to persevere through disappointment, opposition, hardships, and sacrifices. More, the knowledge and strength did not end with him alone but outflowed to bless not only his generation but that of all the faithful who followed.[154] It appears, however, that Paul mentioned these two supernal visions not because his spiritual experiences were few but because these were exceptional.[155]

In 12:5, Paul states that he is most willing to boast about "such a one" who had such wonderful experiences, but, he says, he is not willing to boast about himself. In doing so, he seems to present a bit of an enigma. If he is the highly blessed individual who has had these unspeakable and perhaps even unimaginable spiritual experiences, how then can he say he is not willing to boast about himself? The Apostle is not actually being contradictory but setting up a contrast to emphasize what he is willing to boast about and what he is not.

We again see Paul's deep irony as he uses the third-person pronoun that allows him to distance himself from the visionary man when it is clearly him. By this means, however, he sets himself apart from his opponents

---

152. In D&C 76:114–19, Joseph Smith states that what he was shown surpasses "all understanding." Some of what he saw, as he states, he was forbidden to share with others, but he also states, "Neither is man capable to make them known, for they are seen and understood by the power of the Holy Spirit."

153. According to his record, the visions Joseph Smith received strengthened him in the face of opposition and persecution. See, for example, JS–H 1:15–20.

154. Hughes, *Second Epistle,* 439.

155. Witherington, *Conflict and Community,* 460.

who seem to readily take bragging rights for their spiritual experiences. Thus Paul admits to the worthiness of boasting about such a person but refuses to take the limelight directly. There is good reason: the only proper boast about himself, he insists, is in his nonspectacular weaknesses and their results, which he feels continually.[156] His objective, however, is not "an attempt to gain pity; rather, it is to show that God works through this man. He is the legitimate apostle, and the Lord has appeared to him in a unique vision."[157]

In sum, his objective does not permit him to use his heavenly ascent as the focal point of his boasting, but it does allow him to use the experience to introduce the singular weakness of his life: the "thorn in the flesh."[158]

By placing his visionary experience between his humiliating escape from Damascus (11:32–33) and the necessity of the "thorn in his flesh" (12:7)—both signs of weakness—"Paul has left no room for the objection that he was no true apostle of God. At one extreme, Paul has placed before his critics the true sign of apostleship, namely, weakness. At the other extreme, Paul has been in the presence of the [heavenly] world, with possibly an experience no one else could share. But Paul was still vulnerable to any detractor who did not accept his understanding of [his position on weakness]. This verse therefore places side by side the two ideas of personal relationship to God and apostolic service in Paul's life."[159]

In 12:6, we see that his boasting about his weaknesses also served another purpose. As he says, it was so that "no one will consider me more than what he sees me to be or hears from me" (12:6, NR). He admits, however, that if he did choose to boast, it would not make him a fool. And why? Because, as he says, "I will speak the truth." Some members, given the conditions in Corinth with which they concurred, would have expected and likely appreciated it if the Apostle did boast about his strengths and accomplishments. He would have been on solid ground to do so, and he admits the point because, as he states, he could do it in truth. His wording is interesting in that it implies that others had boasted and been found to have misrepresented the truth. Given the weight of the honor/shame mentality of Corinthian society, to be caught in either a lie or a gross exaggeration would bring shame upon the individual and prove to be an act of utter foolishness.

---

156. Barrett, *Second Epistle,* 312. In 6:4–10 and 11:23–30, Paul has taught this point.
157. Martin, *2 Corinthians,* 601.
158. Guthrie, *2 Corinthians,* 584–85.
159. Martin, *2 Corinthians,* 602.

Paul's truthfulness shielded him from such a tarnishing situation. Thus, his revelatory involvements, even though only briefly mentioned, topped anything his critics could claim.[160] Given the context, Paul's mention of revelations consisted not only of the rapturous visions he briefly alluded to but also other divine manifestations that he had experienced. In addition to these, there was also his track record of sacrificing for the Church's sake. All these experiences, however, remain unmentioned because to enumerate them, in Paul's view, would also be acting the fool because it would be yielding, as he says, to base "human standards" (κατὰ σάρκα, *kata sarka*[161]). He, however, chose another course; he will boast mainly about God (10:17–18), but in his context that includes his weaknesses. By means of this argument, as he lays it out, the Apostle has brilliantly nullified any accusations of his critics. They can neither repudiate nor match the height of his visions, nor can they "deny the veracity of the stripes he has suffered for the gospel, nor can they overlook that he was the one who founded the church at Corinth. They may evaluate Paul's sufferings incorrectly, but what he is should be evident to all. He is a weak servant of God, chosen by him to be an apostle, which is what he is to the Corinthians."[162]

Further, Paul may have been worried that some of those in his audience would consider him an exceptional person. After all, he did have at least some loyal followers all along (1 Cor. 1:12) and had, according to Titus's report, also won a majority back by this time (2 Cor. 7:8–16). Their feelings of undue reverence may have been exacerbated if he had expanded on his supernal visions or spoke of other unmentioned revelations such as the one he had while among them (see Acts 18:9–10). Paul could not afford to be to be placed on a pedestal if his message and example were to stand.

The Apostle's point is that he wants to be evaluated only on what his audience has seen and known about him personally. If they do, then the inference is that they should judge the interlopers by the same standard, and if they do that, they should clearly recognize that the aggressive, overbearing, and self-centeredness of these men exposes them for what they are: false apostles. By this means, he forces his audience to see God's hand in his life and thereby understand that divine ways are not known by "the precepts of men" (κατὰ σάρκα, *kata sarka*) but "according to the Lord" (κατὰ κύριον, *kata kyrion*), as he states in 11:17–18.[163]

---

160. Barrett, *Second Epistle,* 312.

161. On this rendering of the Greek, see Translation Notes for 10:2.

162. Martin, *2 Corinthians,* 603.

163. Barrett, *Second Epistle,* 313.

In this verse (12:6), we see the essence of Paul's thinking with respect to his apostolic authority. "Paul will support his apostleship only by boasting of his weakness (11:30; 12:5, 9b–10): while he is willing to record this one instance of a private religious experience, he is quite unwilling to claim it as an apostolic credential. . . . Paul does not want to be known as a 'visionary,' but only as a weak and suffering apostle . . . , through whom God's incomparable power is disclosed (4:7–15)."[164] In short, Paul insists that "his apostleship cannot be demonstrated by a recitation of his other worldly experiences, but only by the effectiveness of his this-worldly service as an apostle."[165]

He, therefore, insists that they should judge him on what they see and hear. The way Paul joins the two words "see" and "hear" suggests he is not referring to his general daily activities while among these people but to his overall weakness and humility as seen by them and expressed by himself.[166] The latter evidences that he is an ambassador for Christ while the former evidences that the power of Christ works through him.[167] Thus Paul's polemic nicely transitions from reasons he could boast about himself to reasons why he should not—that is, because he is weak. But rather than leave it there, he makes his weaknesses the center of his boast about himself.[168]

Though the Apostle was not, nor would he become, conceited or proud because of the remarkable spiritual experiences he had had, he still feels the need to deflect any unintended acclaim and, therefore, now explains to the Saints how God helps keep him humble.[169] In 12:7, he admits that "the extraordinary nature of the revelations" (NR) he had received could have opened the door to his becoming "overly proud" (NR). To guard

---

164. Furnish, *II Corinthians,* 544. For a study, see Russell P. Spittler, "The Limits of Ecstasy: An Exegesis of 2 Corinthians 12:1–10," in *Current Issues of Biblical and Patristic Interpretation: Studies in Honor of Merrill C. Tenney Presented by His Former Students,* ed. Gerald F. Hawthorne (Grand Rapids, Mich.: William B. Eerdmans, 1975), 259–66, who argues that for Paul, revelations of the heavenly realm prove neither apostolic superiority nor even legitimacy. What does is persevering service never dominated by nor hindered due to weakness. Such service, Paul insists, must be the seat of boasting. Through the use of his autobiographical report, Paul rejects not only apostolic accreditation based on visions and revelations but also any ecstatic conception of Jesus produced by such a view.

165. Furnish, *II Corinthians,* 546.

166. The conjunction ἤ (*ē*), "and, or," is copulative, thus joining the two activities as one event. See BDF, §446.

167. Martin, *2 Corinthians,* 604.

168. Martin, *2 Corinthians,* 584.

169. Martin, *2 Corinthians,* 605.

against this, in deep humility, he admits that God gave him "a thorn in the flesh, a messenger of Satan" (NR) that continues to torment him.

Just what he references is unclear. One of the problems is that the word Paul uses to describe his ailment, σκόλοψ (*skolops*), can refer to a stake, a splinter, or a thorn.[170] However, based on the words used in the LXX, "thorn" is the better translation. Even so, the idea of something incessantly painful or vexing dominates the imagery.[171] His language describing the problem as a messenger from Satan suggests its cruel and punishing nature. The visualization exposes the trouble as more than a mere annoyance. Rather, it is a chronic burden, but one that falls short of a major incapacitating illness or obstructive condition that could stop the work. Even so, its torment is frequent, if not constant.

Due to the Apostle's lack of elaboration about his "thorn in the flesh," scholars have generated a number of theories as to Paul's intent. These theories include "stuttering, epilepsy, a shrewish wife, an eye affliction, malaria, some mortal antagonist, or some spiritual weakness,"[172] and to the list can be added direct satanic opposition.[173] Some of these positions are more compelling than others, but none are conclusive. For that reason, a study of all these theories is beyond the scope of this commentary.[174]

Even so, the points Paul makes and several of their consequences can be clearly seen. First, whatever the condition was, it seems to have been obvious enough that the Corinthians knew about it. There is, however, a slight possibility that it was not widely known. If that is the case, then Paul is deliberately making the imagery obscure so that it does not interfere with his point or the lesson he wants his audience to get from it. However, this view is not strongly endorsed. Second, there was nothing good about the "thorn" itself—it was inherently evil. It constantly tormented the Apostle and was the cause of consternation and suffering. Third, and most important, being from God, it served a good and useful purpose. Indeed, Paul's statement that the "thorn" was divinely given places his trial on a theological plane and underscores the need for the revelation that followed his thrice-fold requests that the object be taken from him (12:8).[175]

---

170. BDAG, 930.

171. Guthrie, *2 Corinthians,* 587.

172. Ogden and Skinner, *Verse by Verse,* 157. For a review, see Seifrid, *Second Letter,* 447–48.

173. Witherington, *Conflict and Community,* 460–61.

174. See note 78.

175. Martin, *2 Corinthians,* 611. His petitions were likely spread over a period of time and made when the "thorn" became particularly vexing.

That deeply spiritual, if less-than-satisfactory, disclosure forced him and now his audience to view the issue from the perspective of divine grace. It was this that enabled the Apostle to succeed. Though the "thorn" humbled and likely humiliated him, his ability to not only overcome its potential enervating effects but also push forward the cause of his Savior evidenced the continual power of God in his ministry.[176] Thus Paul's unending trials gave God an opportunity to demonstrate his sustaining power while allowing mortal experience to take its course. Therefore, through the Apostle's weakness and its attendant humility, he became a powerful and public witness of God's grace in action.

In 12:9, the Apostle reports that God did eventually respond to his heartfelt pleadings. His words did not promise relief but rather gave understanding. "My grace is sufficient for you," the Lord assured him, "for my power is brought to perfection in weakness." The answer appears to have come through oracular means and thereby was related clearly and forcefully. The answer was not what Paul wanted, but it was what he needed.[177] The perfect tense in which he chose to cast the words "he said" (εἴρηκεν, *eirēken*) underscores that the answer reverberated within him continually.

The godly response gave him two insights. The first explained how Paul would be able to manage the stress of the "thorn." God would enable him to deal with it. Divine grace would be "sufficient, enough" (*arkeō*).[178] As unlikely as it seemed, the "thorn" would be the means by which Paul would continually receive God's grace. Through that grace, as he came to understand it, the malady would not keep him from successfully serving the Lord but actually help him do it.[179] The reason? The condition yielded power and comfort.[180] And once the answer came, Paul fought against neither the godly decision and the reception of divine grace it disclosed nor its understood obligatory requirements.

The summit of Paul's epistle is found here, for "from this vantage-point the entire range of Paul's apostleship is seen in focus."[181] No matter how much the "thorn" might torment him, he would prevail. Further, this "messenger" serves a divine purpose—it is the means by which Paul, and for that

---

176. Martin, *2 Corinthians,* 611.
177. Martin, *2 Corinthians,* 613.
178. Guthrie, *2 Corinthians,* 593.
179. Martin, *2 Corinthians,* 613.
180. Martin, *2 Corinthians,* 613.
181. Hughes, *Second Epistle,* 451.

matter any Saint, becomes the kind of Christian that the Savior is.[182] As the Lord himself stated, when people "come unto me I will show unto them their weakness. I give unto [them] weakness that they may be humble; and my grace is sufficient for all [people] that humble themselves before me; for if they humble themselves before me, and have faith in me, then will I make weak things become strong unto them" (Ether 12:27).[183]

The second insight that the revelation gave the Apostle was an understanding of why he had to endure the torment: the power of God was "brought to perfection in weakness"—that is, its intended effect or fulfillment came in the context of weaknesses experienced in trials and persecutions. This view apparently played against the position of the interlopers, who seem to have emphasized their above-average skills, their supposed superior spirituality, their glorious revelations, and their blessed lives over Paul's trials and hardships. The Apostle's revelatory understanding from God himself proclaimed and thus established that authentic ministry "does not work from a power orientation, but rather from the position of weakness."[184] To this day, the Lord continues to use the same model. On more than one occasion he has declared that he uses the weak to do his mighty works, thus proving he is the master behind them (D&C 1:19, 23; 50:16; 124:1; 133:58–59).

Paul makes his point by tacitly asking his adversaries, as well as his champions, that if he is as weak as he is made out to be—and readily admits to—how can he have experienced both the heavy trials he has been through and the successes he has had? Many would likely admit that these two things would take great strength. Thus the answer that he forces out of these people is that his strength must come from somewhere outside of himself. If that is the case, then what or who? Paul supplies the answer: it comes from Christ Jesus. Thus weaknesses make him "most translucent so that [others] can see the source of the real power and light."[185]

---

182. Barrett, *Second Epistle,* 316.

183. The use of the phrase "my grace is sufficient for you" in the D&C is telling. The first time it is used (D&C 17:8), the Lord uses it to assure certain brethren that they have the power to do the task the Lord has given them with the promise that the gates of hell will not prevail against them. The second time (D&C 18:31), the Lord uses it to assure the Twelve that, through him, they have what it takes to succeed. Consequently, both point to God's grace being an enabling power.

184. Guthrie, *2 Corinthians,* 594.

185. Witherington, *Conflict and Community,* 463.

The point is that through the Savior's grace/power, weakness becomes a means to divine ends in one of two ways: either by allowing the weakness to continue but, with the Savior's help, act as a refining force or by replacing or changing the weakness, through the Lord's transforming enablement, into a strength.

The Lord's primary response to weakness is not usually the immediate bestowal of strength but rather an ever-increasing giving of ability. Why so? As the scriptures explain, it is so that people "may know that it is by [the Savior's] grace, and his great condescensions unto the children of men, that [they] have power to do" his will (Jacob 4:7). As a result, those who "come unto Christ" are "perfected in him" because "his grace [is] sufficient for [them]." Indeed, "by [God's] grace [they are made] perfect in Christ;" and as a result they "can in nowise deny the power of God." And "if [they are], by the grace of God [made] perfect in Christ, and deny not his power, then are [they] sanctified in Christ by the grace of God, through the shedding of the blood of Christ" (Moro. 10:32–33).

These scriptures verify Paul's thesis that godly strength can be displayed through mortal weakness. We must stress, however, that "God's power becomes more evident in weakness, not more real."[186] Further, the weakness Paul refers to manifests itself not as sin but as recognized inability. God's grace/power overcomes mortal weakness and, thus, is made complete by enabling the humble soul to carry out God's will.[187] The depth of the weakness compared with the height of success manifests the magnitude of the grace/power. Weakness can, therefore, play an important part in God's plan for the growth of his children and in his ability to display his divine power.

This thesis works for the Apostle because his focus is on the right thing—that is, his acknowledged weakness and the humility it generates, to which the Lord responds by giving Paul his grace/power.[188] Because he understands this, Paul can exclaim, "I will most gladly boast in my weaknesses." And why? Because he now understands that they are the door that

---

186. Martin, *2 Corinthians,* 617.

187. Doubtless, God's transforming and enabling power assists an individual as she or he strives to overcome sin (Heb. 4:16). That aspect, however, is not what Paul focuses on.

188. See Martin, *2 Corinthians,* 616–17. Weakness, with its accompanying humility, is clearly the door through which the power of Christ comes. The Book of Mormon answers the question as to whether weakness is a means of revealing power that Paul already possesses or the door through which the power descends and rests upon him.

opens to "the power of Christ" that can now "rest upon" or "dwell in" him (ἐπισκηνόω, *episkēnoō*).[189]

In 12:10, he brings this pericope to a close with a sharp rebuke against his detractors. He is able to do so with a statement of paradox: "When I am weak, I am strong." And how is that? Because, as Paul clearly declares, weaknesses provide God with an opportunity to manifest his strength in the success of the humble person's life (10:17).[190]

Paul's standard of true apostleship is grounded on suffering both for the gospel and through the misery of the flesh.[191] Such is the center of his boast because he has paid and continues to pay the price. In so doing, he sets up the distance between him and his opponents, who can match him in neither the grandness of his visions nor the suffering he continually endures. For those reasons, he insists, they are not fit to claim apostleship.[192]

Throughout this epistle, the Apostle has stressed that *the* key aspect of true ministry rests on motive. Paul's total efforts have not been directed by personal profit; he desires "to advance the kingdom of Christ and God, not his own kingdom. Only such a posture could undergird the endurance depicted in the Fool's Speech. But God's divine proclamation concerning the purpose of his 'thorn' (12:9) has also helped Paul keep his hardships in perspective."[193] Further, he does not see strength through weakness as peculiar to himself. Though his focus is self-directed, his point allows for broad application. His teaching shows that "whenever God's servants humble themselves and acknowledge their weakness, then the power of Christ

189. The verb means "to reside, dwell" and carries the nuance of taking up an abode. The imagery could refer to the *shekinah* (the manifestation of divine glory as light; see Ex. 16:10; 24:17; 40:34) that bequeaths divine power and protection. Witherington, *Conflict and Community,* 463.

190. Martin, *2 Corinthians,* 585.

191. Suffering "for Christ's sake," or better, "on behalf of Christ," runs counter to the kind of self-inflicted suffering that pervaded Christianity from the second century on. Those who sought righteousness through austerity, denial, and self-administered woundings missed Paul's point. They were guilty of reaching for salvation through merit, not through faith and its accompanying grace. Self-imposed suffering on its own behalf does not result in the acquisition of divine power. Such self-bravado cannot produce rewards except for the foolish or the morbidly fanatic. The result is a joyless insecurity that demands continued suffering. Rather, Paul proclaims "a joyful walk with God," who, through his grace, empowers the individual to work with or overcome hardship, adversity, and suffering. "So deep seated is Paul's delight that what he has endured does not compare to what he is in Christ." Martin, *2 Corinthians,* 618.

192. Martin, *2 Corinthians,* 586.

193. Guthrie, *2 Corinthians,* 597.

can flow through them. This is the justification of 'my grace is sufficient for you.' [For Paul,] God has more than compensated for the fact that the thorn was not removed" through the bestowal of comfort, divine power, direction, and success. Thus God taught Paul that opposition—even as punishing and humiliating as a "thorn in the flesh"—can and does build a relationship with the Divine.[194]

Proof of Apostleship (12:11–13)

Greek Text

11 Γέγονα ἄφρων· ὑμεῖς με ἠναγκάσατε· ἐγὼ γὰρ ὤφειλον ὑφ' ὑμῶν συνίστασθαι.
οὐδὲν γὰρ ὑστέρησα τῶν ὑπερλίαν ἀποστόλων, εἰ καὶ οὐδέν εἰμι· 12 τὰ μὲν σημεῖα
τοῦ ἀποστόλου κατειργάσθη ἐν ὑμῖν ἐν πάσῃ ὑπομονῇ, σημείοις τε καὶ τέρασιν καὶ
δυνάμεσιν. 13 τί γάρ ἐστιν ὃ ἡσσώθητε ὑπὲρ τὰς λοιπὰς ἐκκλησίας, εἰ μὴ ὅτι αὐτὸς
ἐγὼ οὐ κατενάρκησα ὑμῶν; χαρίσασθέ μοι τὴν ἀδικίαν ταύτην. [SBLGNT]

King James Version

11 I am become a fool in glorying; ye
have compelled me: for I ought to have
been commended of you: for in nothing
am I behind the very chiefest apostles,
though I be nothing. 12 Truly the signs
of an apostle were wrought among
you in all patience, in signs, and won-
ders, and mighty deeds. 13 For what is
it wherein ye were inferior to other
churches, except it be that I myself was
not burdensome to you? forgive me
this wrong.

New Rendition

11 I have become foolish. You your-
selves forced me to do it for I ought to
have been commended by you; for I am
in no way inferior to the super-apostles
even though I am nothing. 12 Indeed,
the signs of an apostle were performed
among you in all patience with signs
and wonders and deeds of power. 13 In
what respect, then, were you made
to feel less important than the other
churches except that I myself was not
a burden to you? Forgive me for this
injustice!

Translation Notes and Comments

12:11 ***I am become a fool in glorying / I have become foolish:*** The adjective ἄφρων (*aphrōn*), "foolish," describes one who has a "lack of prudence or

194. Martin, *2 Corinthians*, 619.

good judgment" and as a result is unwise.[195] Paul is using the word ironically. The verb γίνομαι (*ginomai*) means to "become something."[196] It is found here in the perfect tense showing that the state of Paul's self-proclaimed foolishness began sometime in the past and continues into the present.

The phrase "in glorying" is not found in the Greek manuscripts and is, therefore, left out of our Rendition.

ye have compelled me / You yourselves forced me to do it: That Paul places the pronoun ὑμεῖς (*hymeis*), "you," found here as a plural, first in the phrase makes it emphatic.[197] To catch that force, we have added the reflexive pronoun "yourselves."

The verb ἀναγκάζω (*anankazō*), "compel, force,"[198] is found here in the aorist tense, thus showing that the deed was done in the past. The tense leaves open whether or not the effect continues into the present. The infinitive phrase "to do it" is not found in the Greek text, but it is implied.

for I ought to have been commended of you / for I ought to have been commended by you: The conjunction γάρ (*gar*), "for,"[199] signals that a reason will be given for the statement that came before, in this case why Paul was forced to take an action he considered foolish. The verb ὀφείλω (*opheilō*) denotes being constrained by circumstances, thus, "have to, ought."[200] It carries the nuance of complying to a debt owed and serves as a tacit reminder to Paul's audience of their debt to him.[201] It is found here in the imperfect tense, showing what they should have done but did not do.[202] The verb συνίστημι (*synistēmi*) means "to recommend, commend," a person because of approval.[203]

for in nothing am I behind the very chiefest apostles / for I am in no way inferior to the super-apostles: Once again, the conjunction γάρ (*gar*), "for,"[204] signals that Paul will give a reason for his statement in the previous phrase, notably why the Saints should have commended him. The verb ὑστερέω (*hystereō*) here has the sense of "to be lower in status, to be

195. BDAG, 159.
196. BDAG, 198.
197. Barnett, *Second Epistle*, 578; Martin, *2 Corinthians*, 626.
198. BDAG, 60.
199. BDAG, 189–90.
200. Louw-Nida, §§71.25, 35; BDAG, 743.
201. Louw-Nida, §57.219.
202. The imperfect tense without the particle ἄν (*an*) (which shows contingency) stresses "necessity, obligation, duty." BDF, §358.1.
203. Louw-Nida, §33.343.
204. BDAG, 189–90.

inferior to someone."[205] The neuter adjective οὐδέν (*ouden*) in this context means "in no respect, in no way"[206] and emphasizes no lack on Paul's part. That the verb is found in the aorist tense suggests that he is referring to the time he sojourned in Corinth.[207] The force of his argument, however, advocates that the former condition—that is, his lack of inferiority to the "super-apostles"—remains, and therefore we have rendered the verb in the present tense.

On the phrase ὑπερλίαν ἀποστόλων (*hyperlian apostolōn*), "super-apostles," see Translation Notes and the accompanying Analysis for 11:5. The phrase constitutes Paul's ironic jab at these "false apostles" (11:13) for their decidedly self-promoting stance.

though I be nothing / even though I am nothing: The neuter adjective οὐδέν (*ouden*), "nothing," [208] here used nominally, in this context is emphatic, thus stressing his nothingness. The word when dealing with people denotes a nonentity—that is, a person of little consequence or significance. The phrase εἰ καί (*ei kai*), "even if, even though," marks a concession."[209] The clause is a rather pejorative reference to Paul, and his applying it to himself shows his sincere humility as evidenced in his understanding that God did the work (3:4–6). The whole sentence puts his detractors in a very bad light, for despite their boasting otherwise, if the Apostle is in no way inferior to them, then then they too must be "nothing."

12:12 ***Truly the signs of an apostle were wrought among you in all patience / Indeed, the signs of an apostle were performed among you in all patience:*** This phrase continues Paul's argument as to why the Corinthians should have defended him. When the particle μέν (*men*) introduces a clause and is not followed by another clause with the adversative particle δέ (*de*), "the antithetical clause is to be supplied in thought,"[210] something like "but you refused to acknowledge them."

The affirmative particle μέν (*men*) acts as a marker of emphasis, thus rendered "indeed."[211] The noun σημεῖον (*sēmeion*), "sign, token, indication,"[212] denotes a distinguishing act or object by which something is made known

205. BDAG, 1043.
206. BDAG, 735. It is an accusative of respect. Smyth, *Greek Grammar,* §1601.b.
207. Barnett, *Second Epistle,* 578.
208. Louw-Nida, §92.23.
209. BDAG, 278; Guthrie, 2 *Corinthians,* 603.
210. Smyth, *Greek Grammar,* §2896; BDAG, 629–30.
211. Louw-Nida, §91.6.
212. BDAG, 920–21.

or confirmed, but also "points to a reality with even greater significance" than the act or object itself.[213] Thus it can also refer to the activity of the divine expressed as in signs such as "portents, omens, and miracles."[214] The sense of the word in this phrase seems to be that of a "token"—that is, an outward manifestation and distinguishing feature that evidences authenticity.[215] The noun is found here in the plural and linked with the noun "apostle" (for an analysis of ἀπόστολος, *apostolos,* see Translation Notes for 11:5). The latter generally refers to one who has been duly commissioned and empowered to carry out a work, and that seems to be the proper nuance here. The noun is in the genitive case, thus expressing attributes or characteristics.[216] As such, the "tokens of an apostle" are characteristic of, exhibit, and authenticate the legitimacy of the person properly bearing that office.[217]

The verb κατεργάζομαι (*katergozomai),* "to bring about, produce," found here as an aorist passive, denotes the causation of an event or condition.[218] That condition, in this case, is "signs." The passive tacitly denotes divine activity.[219] With the phrase ἐν ὑμῖν (*en hymin*), "among you," the clause shows that Paul's audience had seen the spiritually generated evidence of his apostleship.

The noun ὑπομονή (*hypomonē*), "patience, endurance, fortitude," denotes the virtue of holding out or bearing up under difficult circumstances, a condition that grows according to the increasing depth of the trial one faces.[220] Thus, it is more active than passive in that it expresses itself in effort.[221] In the present context, the phrase ἐν πάσῃ ὑπομονῇ (*en pasē hypomonē*), "in all

---

213. Louw-Nida, §33.477.

214. K. H. Rengstorf, "σημεῖον," in *TDNT,* 7:258–60, notes this kind of "sign" points to God as its author.

215. *Collegiate Dictionary,* s.v. "token." For a study, see *NID,* 4:283–90.

216. Guthrie, *2 Corinthians,* 604 n. 12.

217. Furnish, *II Corinthians,* 553, renders the phrase as "the apostolic signs" and in this way stresses the authenticating force of these divinely produced and highly spiritual activities.

218. BDAG, 531.

219. Wallace, *Greek Grammar,* 437–38.

220. BDAG, 1039–40.

221. It stands in contrast to its near synonym μακροθυμία (*makrothymia*) that also denotes "endurance, steadfastness, patience." While ὑπομονή (*hypomonē*) denotes a temperament that resists succumbing under suffering, μακροθυμία (*makrothymia*) denotes self-restraint against retaliating against a wrong. *Hypomonē* opposes despondence while *markrothymia* opposes wrath or revenge. For a study, see F. Hauk, "ὑπομονή," in *TDNT,* 4:581–89.

patience," shows that the authenticating signs wrought by Paul were done within the context of his gospel ministry (1:19) and thus in "weakness" (11:23–24; 12:9–10). The reaction thereto by some caused the Apostle great affliction of soul that, with great effort, he had to bear.

in signs, and wonders, and mighty deeds / with signs and wonders and deeds of power: This phrase lists the authenticating tokens of Paul's apostleship.[222] The noun σημεῖον (*sēmeion*), "signs," in the present context, refers to validating deeds in which divine elements are clearly evident. The noun τέρας (*teras*), "portent, omen, wonder," denotes a condition or event that astounds one because of its transcendence.[223] The noun δύναμις (*dynamis*), though normally denoting the exertion of force to perform a function, thus "power,"[224] in this context refers to "a deed manifesting great power" that displays supernatural activity.[225] Note that all three performances look not to the events themselves but to the source behind them—namely, God.

12:13 ***For what is it wherein ye were inferior to other churches / In what respect, then, were you made to feel less important than the other churches:*** The conjunction γάρ (*gar*), "then," acts here as a marker of inference,[226] referring back to the manifold spiritual authenticating deeds done through Paul. The phrase τί . . . ἐστιν ὃ (*ti . . . estin ho*), translates literally as "what is it with reference to which . . . ?"[227] We have rendered the phrase as the smoother "in what respect."

The verb ἑσσόομαι (*hessoomai*), "to be inferior,"[228] is found here as a second-person aorist plural, the tense suggesting that the condition has now been resolved.

The adjective λοιπός (*loipos*), "other, rest of,"[229] in connection with the noun ἐκκλησία (*ekklēsia*), "assembly, congregation, church,"[230] found here as a plural, refers to those branches of the Church, likely in Macedonia, that had been so helpful in providing for Paul's needs in the past.

---

222. The way the phase is cast suggests that Paul sees these not as defining his office but rather the idea of "accompaniment." See Moule, *Idiom Book,* 45.

223. BDAG, 999.

224. Louw-Nida, §76.1.

225. Louw-Nida, §76.7.

226. BDAG, 189–90.

227. Guthrie, *2 Corinthians,* 605 n. 14. Moule, *Idiom Book,* 131, treats this phrase as an accusative of respect.

228. BDAG, 440; ἡσσάομαι LSJ, 779.

229. BDAG, 602–3.

230. Louw-Nida, §§11.32, 33, 78.

except it be that I myself was not burdensome to you? / except that I myself was not a burden to you?: The phrase εἰ μή (*ei mē*) means "except"[231] and introduces a possible reason why the Corinthian Saints may have taken umbrage with Paul. The reflexive pronoun αὐτός (*autos*), "myself," emphasizes that the doer of the possible misdeed was the Apostle and he owns it.

The verb καταναρκάω (*katanarkaō*) means to "be a burden."[232] It is a rather harsh term implying a deliberate idleness on the part of one person used to take advantage of others.[233] That it is found here in the aorist tense points back to the period when Paul ministered among them. With the use of the negative particle οὐ (*ou*), "not,"[234] Paul distances himself from any taint that he had burdened them.

forgive me this wrong / Forgive me for this injustice: The verb χαρίζομαι (*charizomai*), "to forgive," denotes a gracious pardoning for a wrongdoing.[235] It is found here as a plural imperative, thus referring to an act to be performed by the offended Corinthian Saints.

The noun ἀδικία (*adikia*), "injustice,"[236] in a religious context usually carries the nuance of a deliberate wicked or unrighteous act, but in this setting the idea is more that of an act that results in undeserved hurt, especially an unfair one.[237] To call Paul's loving, sacrificial service *adikia* was "tacitly ridiculous," and that is exactly the Apostle's point.[238] This sentence clearly shows, once again, Paul's biting use of satire, for he feels he has neither done anything wrong nor deliberately hurt anyone. A colloquial English phrase that catches Paul's thrust might be "Well, excuse me!"

Analysis and Summary

At this point, Paul concludes his "fool's speech" begun in 11:1. He does so with an acknowledgement that he has lowered himself by playing the fool. But, he goes onto explain, there was a good reason why: he was forced to

---

231. Louw-Nida, §89.131.

232. BDAG, 522.

233. Hughes, *Second Epistle,* 387, notes the idea is that of a "dead weight." For analysis, see Translation Notes for 11:9.

234. BDAG, 733–34.

235. BDAG, 1078. The word carries no theological nuance; it refers to "forgiveness between two parties." Martin, *2 Corinthians,* 635.

236. BDAG, 20–21; Louw-Nida, §88.21.

237. *Collegiate Dictionary,* s.v. "injustice." The verb denotes a condition of not being right with either God or humankind, according to whose standards are at play. G. Schrenk, "ἀδικία," in *TDNT,* 1:153–57.

238. Guthrie, *2 Corinthians,* 606.

do it. This is because he was caught in a dilemma. On the one hand, only by boasting would he get the attention and accreditation he needed. Indeed, many saw boasting as the mark of apostleship, and thus if he refused to do so, he was tacitly admitting to lacking such authority. On the other, by boasting he engaged in a practice he detested. Thus it was a "necessary evil" forced upon him by the exigencies of the condition rampant among the Saints in Corinth and more especially by his "rhetorically trained opponents for the support of his rhetorically fastidious converts."[239]

He lays the blame squarely on the shoulders of the Corinthians Saints themselves, for they had every reason to commend him, in the sense of defending him by holding up his credentials, but they did not. As he has made clear (1 Cor. 4:3; 2 Cor. 5:12–16), their commendation of him, however, was not and is not the basis of his apostleship. God is (Gal. 1:1). As stressed in chapter 5, their lack of support did not interfere with his insistence that he was a true Apostle of the Lord. Even so, these people themselves evidenced the seal of his apostleship (1 Cor. 9:2) and remain the validation of his work (2 Cor. 3:2–3). Therefore, their commendation means much to him. And this, he insists, they should have given because they owed it to him: he was the one who united them with Christ (1 Cor. 4:15; 2 Cor. 11:2). Unfortunately, some either forgot, undervalued, or ignored this fact. Thus when they compared him with his polished, self-promoting, and domineering rivals, they could not bring themselves to defend their less-than-powerful orator and humble self-employed minister.[240]

There were two more reasons why they should have defended him, and these make their refusal even worse. First, he had suffered much for the sake of Christ, including the pain these people had caused him over the years (11:28), and yet he still loved them (2:4; 12:15).[241] What they had done was, in essence, forget, ignore, or, worse, disrespect his love. Second, he was not in any way supporting those whom he insisted were promoting a false gospel and whom he again brands with the disparaging title "super-apostles."

To emphasize his point, he quickly adds a humble disclaimer: he is, in reality, "nothing" (οὐδείς, *oudeis*). The term refers to a person who, on his own, is of little consequence or significance.[242] He makes no claim to

239. Judge, "Paul's Boasting in Relation to Contemporary Professional Practice," 68.

240. Barrett, *Second Epistle,* 319–20.

241. Martin, *2 Corinthians,* 627.

242. It is possible the tone here could be ironic, but even so there is sincerity behind it. See Martin, *2 Corinthians,* 629; and Bultmann, *Second Letter,* 231.

personal adequacy. The only way he can boast, therefore, is "in the Lord" (10:17–18). He clarifies this position in the next verse, where he shows himself, under God, to be everything and thus, in reality, superior to all. Here he is using the force of understatement to help make his point. Through this oblique disclaimer, he posits that he is actually, to these people, everything so far as their salvation is concerned. The reason is, as he has clearly stated (10:1), that "it is God, not he, who validates his ministry because God is the source of what he does."[243] Thus "he is nothing that Christ may be seen to be everything."[244]

It is to support this point that Paul makes his statement in 12:12. He appeals to the signs (σημεῖα, *semeia*—that is, the divine outward manifestation that evidenced his authority[245]) that God made manifest among the Corinthian Saints during the time the Apostle sojourned among them. Paul states these marvels were produced through the exercise of "extreme patience" (*pasē hypomonce*), the phrase likely referring to the effort required of the Apostle in dealing with these people.[246]

On just what these signs, wonders, and powerful deeds were, biblical history is blank,[247] but Paul's statements in 1 Corinthians 12 and 14 suggest that through his administration the people came to possess remarkable gifts of the Spirit, such as speaking in and interpreting tongues, healing the sick, discerning spirits, prophesying, and casting out devils. He himself seems to have led out in some of these (for example, see 1 Cor. 14:18). It is noteworthy that he does not suggest that these define the apostolic office but rather that they are attributes that accompany it.[248] What does define the office, as he has made clear in chapters 11 and 13, is the power of God that enables these deeds to be done. Even so, Paul's "signs" helped establish his position as a spiritual leader with broad power.[249]

---

243. Barnett, *Second Epistle*, 578–79.

244. Martin, *2 Corinthians*, 629.

245. *NID*, 4:283–90.

246. Guthrie, *2 Corinthians*, 605.

247. However, some have suggested all three look to Paul's known healing abilities. See Martin, *2 Corinthians*, 633.

248. Moule, *Idiom Book*, 45.

249. Paul's statement shows that he performed and that many in his audience saw a number of his miracles. The scriptures, however, record none for his various ministries at Corinth. The scriptures preserve accounts of miracles that Paul performed in Paphos (Acts 13:6–12), Lystra (Acts 14:8–10), Ephesus (Acts 19:11–12), Troas (Acts 20:9–12), and Melita (Acts 28:3–5). That he makes this almost gratuitous statement to a group that housed some of his worst antagonists gives strong support that such really did occur, otherwise he would

What the Apostle is doing here, however, "is pleading with the Corinthians to dispense of the secondary criteria (signs, wonders, mighty works) and judge the would-be apostles by the yardstick of the primary criterion, namely, . . . 'apostolic signs,' of the crucified Jesus (13:1–4)."[250] If these Saints would use these standards, then they would see Paul not as inferior to these "super" but false apostles but as the true, authorized servant of the Lord. Until that happens, it is likely that some would continue to see him as little more than second-rate when compared to the interlopers.[251] The result would be ecclesiastically threating and spiritually dangerous, for it would give the false teachers a home in which to live and a place from which to promulgate their false doctrine.

In 12:13, Paul ends this portion of his treatise. He does so by addressing the major problem that stuck in the craw of some of the Corinthian Saints. As noted in the introduction to this volume and elsewhere, the problem stemmed from the practice of patronage and its associated social reciprocity that permeated every level of society in Paul's day.[252] This custom some of the Saints still clung to. As a result, it influenced how they interpreted the Apostle's actions. As Paul knew (1 Cor. 9:14), Christian practice allowed missionaries to accept financial aid while preaching the gospel. As the Corinthians saw it, rather than accept the help they willingly offered (and the obligation it entailed), he stooped to menial labor. As a result, these converts felt that his act was akin to a socially demeaning slap in the face.[253] What added to their gall was that he gladly received financial help from the Macedonian Saints (Philip. 4:15–17).

To forcibly get his audience to understand that his former actions should in no way be interpreted as a disgrace to them, he continues to put his very barbed pen to good use with a question and then a demand. His question is designed to force them to see that in matters that really counted—namely, the reception and participation in wondrous spiritual manifestations during Paul's administration—they had not missed out on a single blessing.[254]

---

have been called on his claim. Barnett, *Second Epistle,* 580 n. 16. For a study, see Holmberg, *Paul and Power,* 75–77, where he examines the breadth of Paul's "wonders." Holmberg makes the point that in the early Church, its leaders continuously reinstitutionalized charismatic authority through the people and institutions they directed.

250. Martin, *2 Corinthians,* 633.

251. Martin, *2 Corinthian,* 633.

252. See the material in the introduction of this volume under the heading "Challenges the Social Conditions Made for the Church."

253. Guthrie, *2 Corinthians,* 605–6.

254. Bruce, *1 and 2 Corinthians,* 250.

In sum, they were not one whit behind other Churches and, as a result, should feel good about themselves.

The only rub, then, had to be Paul's unwillingness to burden them with meeting his needs. The silliness of their position Paul discloses with his less-than-sincere demand: "Please forgive me this injustice!" His point is that they were in no way actually mistreated.[255] What they do not seem to have seen is that Paul's seemingly ungracious response was his attempt to create a new, Christian attitude toward receiving and giving. It primarily focused on the nature of benefactions with the obligations they demanded. This attitude replaced reciprocation between persons with reciprocation between the Saints and Christ,[256] and though it came with demands, it also came with the highest of recompences.

Promise to Not Be a Burden (12:14–18)

Greek Text

14 Ἰδοὺ τρίτον τοῦτο ἑτοίμως ἔχω ἐλθεῖν πρὸς ὑμᾶς, καὶ οὐ καταναρκήσω· οὐ γὰρ ζητῶ τὰ ὑμῶν ἀλλὰ ὑμᾶς, οὐ γὰρ ὀφείλει τὰ τέκνα τοῖς γονεῦσιν θησαυρίζειν, ἀλλὰ οἱ γονεῖς τοῖς τέκνοις. 15 ἐγὼ δὲ ἥδιστα δαπανήσω καὶ ἐκδαπανηθήσομαι ὑπὲρ τῶν ψυχῶν ὑμῶν. εἰ περισσοτέρως ὑμᾶς ἀγαπῶν, ἧσσον ἀγαπῶμαι; 16 ἔστω δέ, ἐγὼ οὐ κατεβάρησα ὑμᾶς· ἀλλὰ ὑπάρχων πανοῦργος δόλῳ ὑμᾶς ἔλαβον. 17 μή τινα ὧν ἀπέσταλκα πρὸς ὑμᾶς, δι' αὐτοῦ ἐπλεονέκτησα ὑμᾶς; 18 παρεκάλεσα Τίτον καὶ συναπέστειλα τὸν ἀδελφόν· μήτι ἐπλεονέκτησεν ὑμᾶς Τίτος; οὐ τῷ αὐτῷ πνεύματι περιεπατήσαμεν; οὐ τοῖς αὐτοῖς ἴχνεσιν; [SBLGNT]

King James Version

14 Behold, the third time I am ready to come to you; and I will not be burdensome to you: for I seek not yours, but you: for the children ought not to lay up for the parents, but the parents for the children. 15 And I will very gladly spend and be spent for you; though the

New Rendition

14 Look, for the third time I am ready to come to you, and I will not be a burden to you for I do not want your possessions but you yourselves. Children should not save up for their parents but parents for their children. 15 And I will be most happy to spend and be spent

255. Guthrie, *2 Corinthians,* 605–6.

256. For studies, see Schmidt, *Relational Grace*; and G. W. Peterman, *Paul's Gift from Philippi: Conventions of Gift Exchange and Christian Giving* (Cambridge: Cambridge University Press, 1997).

more abundantly I love you, the less I be loved. 16 But be it so, I did not burden you: nevertheless, being crafty, I caught you with guile. 17 Did I make a gain of you by any of them whom I sent unto you? 18 I desired Titus, and with him I sent a brother. Did Titus make a gain of you? walked we not in the same spirit? walked we not in the same steps?

for your souls. If I love you so very much more, should I be loved even less? 16 But be that as it may, I have not been a burden to you; however, being the crafty fellow that I am, I caught you by deceit. 17 Have I taken advantage of you by any of those whom I sent to you? 18 I urged Titus to go to you and sent the brother with him. Did Titus take advantage of you? Didn't we conduct ourselves with the same spirit? Did we not walk in the same footsteps?

Translation Notes and Comments

12:14 ***Behold, the third time I am ready to come to you / Look, for the third time I am ready to come to you:*** The particle ἰδού (*idou*), "behold, look,"[257] signals the reader to pay attention to what comes next. The phrase τρίτον τοῦτο (*triton touto*), "this third," is an example of an accusative of reference with the noun "time" understood, thus "for the third time."[258] The adverb ἑτοίμως (*hetoimōs*) denotes being willing or ready to do something.[259] Used with the verb ἔχω (*echō*), it is the equivalent of the verb εἶναι (*einai*), "to be," with an adjective and is thus translated "I am ready."[260] It is followed by the aorist infinitive of the verb ἔρχομαι (*erchomai*), "to come."

This sentence, due to word order, is grammatically ambiguous. The placing of ἑτοίμως ἔχω (*hetoimōs echō,* "I am ready") between τρίτον τοῦτο (*triton touto,* "a third time") and the infinitive ἐλθεῖν (*elthein,* "to come") allows for two interpretations. If *triton touto* is taken with *hetoimōs echo,* then Paul is saying, "For the third time I am preparing to visit you." The implication is that he tried twice before and failed. If that is the case, then his arrival will be but his second time visiting these Saints. On the other hand, if the phrase is taken with *elthein,* then Paul is telling his readers that this will be his third visit. The latter is the best alternative based on 13:1, which clearly states that his coming will mark his third visit.[261]

---

257. BDAG, 468.
258. BDAG, 1016; BDF, §154.
259. BDAG, 401.
260. Smyth, *Greek Grammar,* §1438.
261. Martin, *2 Corinthians,* 635.

and I will not be burdensome to you / and I will not be a burden to you: With this sentence, Paul tacitly declares that, despite all that has happened, he has not changed his position one whit. On the verb καταναρκάω (*katanarkaō*), "be a burden,"[262] see Translation Notes for 12:13.

for I seek not yours, but you / for I do not want your possessions but you yourselves: The conjunction γάρ (*gar*), "for,"[263] signals that Paul will give a reason for his last statement. The verb ζητέω (*zēteō*), "seek, look for,"[264] also carries the nuance of desiring to have something.[265] We have rendered it as "want," which in English also denotes a desire.[266] The phrase τὰ ὑμῶν (*ta hymōn*), literally "the (things) of you," denotes their possessions. The reflexive pronoun "yourselves" is not in the Greek text but is used here to help stress the force of the Greek: only the Saints and nothing else are the object of Paul's desire.

for the children ought not to lay up for the parents, but the parents for the children / Children should not save up for their parents but parents for their children: In the Greek text, this material is actually the last part of one long sentence that constitutes 12:14. In that work, it begins with the conjunction γάρ (*gar*), "for," again signaling that a reason will be given for the statement that came before. For ease of reading, we have dropped it and captured the idea with a new sentence.

The noun τέκνον (*teknon*), "child,"[267] found here as a neuter plural, thus denoting children in general, carries an endearing nuance.[268] The verb ὀφείλω (*opheilō*), "owe, be indebted," denotes being indebted to someone due to financial, social, moral, or other constraints.[269]

The verb θησαυρίζω (*thēsaurizō*), "store up," denotes storing up something for future needs,[270] in this case those of one's children. The idea looks to the future when children, having reached maturity, must step out on their own. Having an inheritance, as it were, helps them make their way.[271]

---

262. BDAG, 522.

263. BDAG, 189–90.

264. BDAG, 428.

265. Louw-Nida, §§25.9.

266. *Collegiate Dictionary,* s.v. "want."

267. BDAG, 994.

268. Louw-Nida, §§9.46; 10.36.

269. BDAG, 743.

270. BDAG, 456. The verb is based on the noun θησαυρός (*thēsauros*), "treasure," and denotes keeping something safe by storing it away in case it is needed. Louw-Nida, §65.10. Figuratively, it means to cause something of a more extensive nature to happen in the future, thus "to make [something] even greater." Louw-Nida, §13.135.

271. Seifrid, *Second Letter,* 462–63.

12:15 ***And I will very gladly spend and be spent for you / And I will be most happy to spend and be spent for your souls:*** The conjunction δέ (*de*), "and," draws attention to and connects with Paul's statement in 12:14, dealing with his parental relationship with these people, to the point he makes here.[272] The adverb ἡδέως (*hēdeōs*), "gladly, happily," here found as a superlative, expresses delight based on the pleasure a person anticipates deriving from an act.[273] To emphasize that aspect as expressed in Paul's context, we have rendered the adverb as "most happy."

The verb δαπανάω (*dapanaō*), "spend, spend freely,"[274] found here in the future tense, generally refers to the expenditure of funds for the sake of obtaining certain benefits.[275] It also carries a more figurative nuance of expending great effort to accomplish some goal.[276] Hence, Paul could be indicating his willingness to do anything he can, even up to using all his resources in behalf of these people.

The verb ἐκδαπανάω (*ekdapanaō*), found here as a future passive, denotes "to spend completely, use up."[277] It carries the general meaning of using up all of one's resources, but figuratively, as here, of spending one's life in service to others.[278] Paul is telling these people there is no end to the effort he is willing to give or to the time he will spend "in order to secure their affection and allegiance."[279]

That he refers to what he is willing to give so much for as ὑπὲρ τῶν ψυχῶν ὑμῶν (*hyper tōn psychōn hymōn*), "for your souls," is telling. The noun ψυχή (*psychē*) denotes the "whole person viewed in terms of one's animating inward life"[280] as well as the "seat and center of life that transcends the earthly."[281] Because it is that portion of the self that can partake of the divine, it must have precedence over physical and other demands. It is, on an eternal scale, invaluable.[282] It is therefore well worth the Apostle's time and efforts to exhaust himself in its behalf.

---

272. Guthrie, *2 Corinthians,* 611 n. 8.

273. Louw-Nida, §25.129.

274. BDAG, 212.

275. Louw-Nida, §57.146.

276. Louw-Nida, §42.27.

277. BDAG, 300; DAG, s.v. "ἐκδαπανάω."

278. Louw-Nida, §42.28.

279. Bruce, *1 and 2 Corinthians,* 250, opines that δαπανάω (*dapanaō*) refers to the sending of means while ἐκδαπανάω (*ekdapanaō*) refers to the spending of time and effort.

280. Seifrid, *Second Letter,* 463.

281. BDAG, 1098–1100.

282. For a study, see *NID,* 4:725–34.

though the more abundantly I love you, the less I be loved / If I love you so very much more, should I be loved even less?: The conjunction εἰ (*ei*), "if," introduces a question that expects a "no" answer. The very rich verb ἀγαπάω (*agapaō*), "to love,"[283] expresses the warm and inclusive love peculiar to Christianity.[284] The second time Paul uses the word, he puts it in the present passive, thus giving the phrase an imperfect aspect hinting at a continual declining relationship with some of these people.[285]

The adverb περισσοτέρως (*perissoterōs*), "(even) more" or "far greater," expresses a degree of something that is well beyond a standard.[286] Here it is the highly warm regard that Paul has for these people.

The adverb ἧσσον (*hēssōn*), "lesser," expresses a degree of something well below a standard.[287] Paul is asking if his great love for these people, as expressed in his fatherly caring and willingness to work in their behalf, should generate less love toward him on their part.[288]

There is a textual variant here that plays on Paul's intent. Some manuscripts, such as the Textus Receptus (followed by the KJV), have the phrase ending with a period. Taken in this way, the statement forms a rather blunt condemnation of Paul's audience. Other variants have it end in a question. Taken in this way, Paul is leaving the door open for the Corinthians to return his love. Context gives the latter the better support, and thus we follow it in our Rendition.[289]

12:16 *But be it so, I did not burden you / But be that as it may, I have not been a burden to you:* The beginning phrase, ἔστω δέ (*estō de*), literally "so be it," expresses "a point on which writer and readers are in at least provisional agreement," and thus we have rendered it as above.[290] Using it allows Paul to move on to his next point without conceding his previous one.

Here he emphatically repeats his statement from 12:13–14 that he never troubled anyone with his upkeep. The verb he uses, καταβαρέω (*katabareō*), means "to burden" through the imposition of undue hardship.[291] It emphasizes the weight of the demand that results from an active imposition of a heavy load on others.[292]

---

283. BDAG, 5–6.

284. For a study, see *NID,* 1:103–15.

285. Guthrie, *2 Corinthians,* 612 n. 14.

286. BDAG, 806.

287. BDAG, 440.

288. Louw-Nida, §78.38.

289. Martin, *2 Corinthians,* 621 nn. H–i, 641.

290. Barnett, *Second Corinthians,* 586 n. 16.

291. BDAG, 514; Louw-Nida, §22.26.

292. Louw-Nida, §22.26. Hughes, *Second Epistle,* 387, notes the idea is that of a "dead weight." For analysis, see Translation Notes for 11:9.

being crafty, I caught you with guile / however, being the crafty fellow that I am, I caught you by deceit: Once again, Paul makes his point using irony. The conjunction ἀλλά (*alla*), "but, yet, rather,"[293] plays an important role here in setting up a contrast between Paul not being a burden and yet doing something rather sly. The verb ὑπάρχω (*hyparchō*), "to be," found here as a present participle used causally, thus rendered "being," denotes full submersion in a state or circumstance.[294]

Paul describes that state by using the adjective πανοῦργος (*panourgos*), literally "readiness to do anything," with the idea of being unscrupulous. It is used in the New Testament only in the unfavorable sense of being "clever, crafty, sly."[295] With the participle ὑπάρχων (*hyparchōn*), it carries a very ironic and extended meaning of being, in one's very constitution, a cunning or crafty person.[296]

The verb λαμβάνω (*lambanō*), "take, acquire, . . . receive,"[297] has a wide range of semantic meanings, including some very negative ones, such as snaring an animal or catching a fish by using bait,[298] which is likely the sense here.

The noun δόλος (*dolos*), "deceit, cunning, treachery," denotes "taking advantage through craft or underhanded methods."[299] Its correlation with the adjective πανοῦργος (*panourgos*) emphasizes the depth of Paul's supposed guile.

It is likely that Paul is deliberately painting this very negative picture of his doings because it echoes, if not actually restates, the attack his detractors are using against him.

12:17 ***Did I make a gain of you by any of them whom I sent unto you? / Have I taken advantage of you by any of those whom I sent to you?:*** The construction of this question in Greek is not as smooth as our rendering suggests. The lack of clarity is due to an anacoluthon (an unexpected discontinuity in the expression of an idea), in which, for a moment, Paul loses track of how he was going to make his point.[300]

---

293. BDAG, 44–45.

294. Moule, *Idiom Book,* 103; BDAG, 1029–30.

295. BDAG, 754.

296. Hughes, *Second Epistle,* 464.

297. BDAG, 583–85.

298. See Louw-Nida page 2:150 for examples. See also Barnett, *Second Epistle,* 532–33.

299. BDAG, 256; Louw-Nida, §88.154.

300. The awkward construction may have resulted from the emotion Paul was feeling at the time. Strong feelings often led to anacolutha during that era. See BDF, §467.

In the Greek text, the first word is the negative particle μή (*mē*), "no" (untranslated), that clues Paul's audience that he hopes for a "no" answer to his question.[301]

The verb πλεονεκτέω (*pleonekteō*), found here in the aorist tense, denotes taking advantage of or exploiting another through deception or fraud due to greed.[302] The tense looks back to the time when the delegation Paul sent was working among these people.

The masculine plural genitive relative pronoun ὧν (*hōn*),[303] means literally "of whom," but since in Greek a demonstrative pronoun is often concealed within a relative pronoun, this can be translated as "of those whom," as we have done here.[304] The reference is to the delegation headed by Titus.

The verb ἀποστέλλω (*apostellō*), "to send," found here in the perfect tense, carries the nuance of dispatching someone with authority to carry out a particular assignment.[305] The tense indicates that the authority is still in operation. It also forces Paul's audience to see if they can come up with a single instance when his delegates violated that authority by taking advantage of the Saints.[306]

12:18 ***I desired Titus, and with him I sent a brother / I urged Titus to go to you and sent the brother with him:*** On Titus, see Translation Notes for 2:13 with related Analysis. The role he played at this time is important because he was known as having considerable stature among the Saints.[307]

The verb παρακαλέω (*parakaleō*), "implore, entreat," denotes a strong request that something be done.[308] The phrase "to go to you" is not in the Greek text, but it is implied.

The verb συναποστέλλω (*synapostellō*), "to send someone together with someone else,"[309] carries the same nuance as the related verb ἀποστέλλω (*apostellō*), "to send a message, presumably by someone."[310]

---

301. BDAG, 644–46.

302. BDAG, 824. In LXX Hab. 2:9 and LXX Ezek. 22:27, the idea of greed and unjust material gain come through.

303. BDAG, 725–27.

304. BDAG, 725–27.

305. BDAG, 120–21. The Greeks applied the word especially to envoys who were empowered to transact business in the name of their master. Over time the word took on a religious nuance that gave it even more cachet. For a study, see *NID,* 1:365–76.

306. Martin, *2 Corinthians,* 643.

307. Barnett, *Second Corinthians,* 589.

308. BDAG, 764–65.

309. BDAG, 966.

310. Louw-Nida, §15.67, 69.

On τὸν ἀδελφόν (*ton adelphon*), "the brother," see Translation Notes for 8:18 with related Analysis.

Did Titus make a gain of you? / Did Titus take advantage of you?: The question is blunt. It begins with the interrogative particle μήτι (*mēti,* untranslated), an emphatic marker that invites a negative response.[311] On the verb πλεονεκτέω (*pleonekteō*), "to take advantage of another," see 12:17 above.

walked we not in the same spirit? / Did we not conduct ourselves with the same spirit?: The sentence begins with the negative particle οὐ (*ou*), "not," which signals that an affirmative answer to a question is expected and is rendered "Did . . . not."[312]

The verb περιπατέω (*peripateō*), "to conduct one's life," in its general sense means to "go about, walk around." In its secondary sense, it means to "comport oneself, behave, live," and refers to the conduct of one's life.[313] Here is it is found as an aorist plural, the latter bringing Paul into the picture. Accordingly, the focus is no longer on Titus and "the brother" alone but now includes the Apostle.

The phrase τῷ αὐτῷ πνεύματι (*tō autō pneumati*), "with the same spirit," is somewhat ambiguous but important to Paul's point and therefore deserves some attention. Earlier, he has pointed out that the "super-apostles" had brought with them "a different spirit" than the spirit under which he, and initially the Corinthian Saints, had operated (11:4). Here he reminds his audience that he himself continues in the same spirit that he initially brought with him. But exactly what does he mean? He could be referring to the spiritual dimension of his own life. He notes in the next question (see below) that he and others walk in the same footsteps, which supports the idea that he has a personal spiritual state in mind. This idea is further supported by the fact that he has used this aspect several times in this letter (see 2:13; 4:13; 7:1, 13).

However, the idea that he is actually referring to the Holy Spirit has strong support. In some of his other epistles, he has written of walking by that Spirit (Rom. 8:4; Gal. 5:16) or being influenced thereby (1 Cor. 1:9). In this very epistle, he has clearly referred to the workings of the Holy Spirit in the ministry (3:3, 6, 8, 17–18; 5:5). Thus his reference in 12:18 to walking in the footsteps of another does not necessarily refer to walking according to a spiritual state. Rather, it more likely refers to the mutual inspiration that directs both

311. BDAG, 649.
312. BDAG, 733–34.
313. BDAG, 803.

the Apostle's efforts and those of his companions. All are influenced and facilitated by the power of this divine influence.[314]

walked we not in the same steps? / Did we not walk in the same footsteps?: To stress his point, Paul askes the same question but this time with a metaphor. Again, he begins the question with the negative particle οὐ (*ou*), "not," rendered "Did we not," which anticipates a positive response to the question.

The noun ἴχνος (*ichnos*) figuratively denotes walking in another's footsteps with the nuance of exceptional performance in behaving in the same manner as the other.[315] Thus the imagery stresses how closely Paul and his companions followed the same course of behavior as dictated by the Holy Spirit.

Analysis and Summary

Paul signals his transition from the "fool's speech" to his new subject with the interjection "look" (ἰδου, *idou*). The word tells his readers to pay attention to what he is going to say next and think about its implication. He then informs them that, for the third time, he is about to make an appearance. His first was his months-long stay when he established the Church among them (see Acts 18), and the second, his short, very painful visit during his ministry in Ephesus (2 Cor. 2:1). His purpose in writing this portion of his epistle is not just to inform them that he is coming but to stress the need to be ready to receive him properly. Though much of the former portion of the letter addresses this same matter, the implication here looks to a possible collision with his detractors.

His major focus in 12:14–18 addresses the Corinthians' concerns about him. He addresses his concerns about them in the next section, 12:19–21.[316] In both, Paul's focus is no longer on his detractors, be they interlopers or locals, but on the low spiritual condition that exists broadly among the Saints, albeit a condition that has not extinguished his love for them. Even so, "apostolic love is not divorced from apostolic authority. It is this authority that has been the matter of contention between Paul and the Corinthians. Paul now threatens, as he has already done [10:2, 11], to bring the contention to a decisive conclusion by virtue of the power of Christ, who is present in him."[317]

---

314. Gordon D. Fee, *God's Empowering Presence: The Holy Spirt in the Letters of Paul* (Peabody, Mass.: Hendrickson Publishers, 1994), 357–59.

315. BDAG, 485; Louw-Nida, §41.47.

316. Seifrid, *Second Letter,* 460.

317. Seifrid, *Second Letter,* 459–60.

This portion of his letter is "deeply interpersonal and, indeed, animated (1) with references to 'I . . . you' in every verse, (2) the emphatic 'I' appearing in vv. 15–16, and (3) no less than five rhetorical questions (vv. 15, 17, 18 [twice], 19)."[318]

With his statement in 12:14 that "I will not be a burden to you" (NR), Paul makes very clear an important aspect of his visit: he fully plans to take care of his own upkeep. In so saying, he affirms, tacitly, that in spite of the pressure he has received to reverse his stand, he has not budged a bit from his former position. The implication is that all had better be ready to accept that fact. With the next two phrases, he gives two reasons for his position and in doing so, again undercuts the activities, teachings, and, hopefully, the influence of his enemies. In the first phrase, he notes his objective: though he is not in the least interested in their possessions, he is highly interested in something of far greater value, they themselves. Considering that there were those who insinuated that Paul planned to use some of the funds gathered for the poor in the Holy Land for himself,[319] his statement puts a damper on their position. With the second phrase, he explains why he has taken the position that he has. It is the responsibility of parents, he insists, to take care of their children, not the other way around. Since he was the one who, parent-like, brought the Corinthians into a new life in the gospel, he must keep up the duty of a loving parent. The metaphor of father/child is for the Apostle neither arbitrary nor changeable. In his earlier letter, he introduced the imagery and there elaborated on its theology, stating, "For though you may have countless guardians in Christ, you do not have many fathers, because I became your father in Christ Jesus through the gospel" (1 Cor. 4:15, NR). As Paul sees it (and so should the Saints), life through the gospel is the binding force between Apostle and Church. By recognizing him as "father," these Saints should also recognize his authority as the source through which spiritual life came and thereby honor him in that role.[320]

The sincerity of his feelings exposes the compassion he yet has for these people.[321]

His desire to lead the Corinthians is based neither on a wish to rule over them forever nor to gain personal satisfaction in having them follow him.

318. Barnett, *Second Epistle,* 583, ellipses and brackets in original.
319. Barnett, *Second Epistle,* 586.
320. Seifrid, *Second Letter,* 461–62.
321. Martin, *2 Corinthians,* 636–37.

On the contrary, he sees his duty as returning them to their espoused mate, Christ Jesus (11:2). Admittedly, he also desires to have them accept and validate his apostleship. This desire shows how much he values their assessment of him. Thus, that he is writing with a rather barbed quill should not mask the genuine care he has for these people (see 6:11–13; 7:2–4).[322] Indeed, it is his tender heart that drives him to be so tough on them.

We see this in 12:15 where his quill, though no less strident, becomes less barbed. This allows for the personal disappointment and hurt that these people have caused him to come clearly through. Even so, their uncalled-for actions have not quelled his love for them (see 2:4; 8:7; 11:11). As a result, he can declare his continued willingness to not only spend (δαπανάω, *dapanaō*) his means but also to exhaust (ἐκδαπανάω, *ekdapanaō*) his life to work for the salvation of their souls. The force of his chosen verbs emphasizes his willingness to expend great effort in their behalf.[323] But the verb "to spend" carries another nuance that is also at play here, that of paying out various assets in order to obtain benefits.[324] With this nuance, we hear the strong echo of two major issues that have brought the current crises to a head. The first is the unfounded accusations that Paul's efforts to collect funds for the Jerusalem needy are but a way for him to milk the Saints for money.[325] The second is Paul's menial labor during his ministry among them to support himself and not be supported by them. The irony of his position is that on the one hand he is unwilling to receive resources as from a patron, but on the other, he is very willing "to spend and be spent" in their service as a father would.[326]

In an attempt to push them to see the purity of his motive, he assures them that his willingness to do menial labor, though demanding, time-consuming, and perhaps even distasteful to some, actually demonstrated his very deep love for them.[327] Thus they should interpret his actions that way. Given that, he asks why his hard yet loving labor has caused him to be loved less by some. In no way was he attempting to demean them or spurn their offering. Thus, he points out, any withdrawal of their love and respect for him was and is uncalled for.

---

322. Hughes, *Second Epistle*, 462.

323. The two related verbs he uses, δαπανάω (*dapanaō*) and ἐκδαπανάω (*ekdapanaō*) carry the nuance of pushing something to the limit. BDAG, 212, 300; Louw-Nida, §42.27, 28.

324. Louw-Nida, §57.146.

325. Barnett, *Second Epistle*, 586.

326. Guthrie, *2 Corinthians*, 611.

327. Martin, *2 Corinthians*, 639.

What Paul is trying to do in 12:14–15 is get the Saints to change the way they think about their relationship with him. "He is not dependent on them; they are dependent on him. Let them think in child-parent—not patron-client—terms. Self-support, making the gospel free of charge, is an insignia of his apostleship."[328] Therefore, as he insists, he is very willing to spend his strength "for your souls" (ὑπὲρ τῶμ ψυχῶν ὑμῶν, *hyper tōn psychōn hymōn*). The preposition is important, showing that what he does, he does *for* them—that is, in their behalf. He has already called upon them to be "reconciled to God" (5:20), and to this end, he works even though it forces him to minister through his weaknesses. Thus "in his ministry Paul replicates the sufferings of Christ as he gives himself for the people. Paul makes no hint that he saves people, as Christ does; nonetheless, his sufferings, though not propitiatory, are in continuity with those of Christ. Such sufferings, indeed, validate his labor in the ministry of Christ, as opposed to that of the triumphalist 'superlative' apostles," who minister for themselves.[329] The result, as he sees it, should be an increase, not a decrease, in the love these Saints have for him.

In 12:16–18, the Apostle clarifies his mission.[330] To do so, he changes tactic in the second half of 12:16. His focus shifts away from those hurt or upset by his seeming rejection of them through his scrupulous independence. Even his most vociferous enemies had to admit he received no local help. It may well be that some of the Saints, given Paul's defense, began to question why the interlopers demanded pay or or at the very least so much pay (insinuated in 11:20).

Thus the Apostle addresses charges brought against him that he has in fact taken advantage of the local Saints, but through a cunning artifice.[331] And what artifice is that? He supplies the answer in 12:17–18. The text suggests that at one time, the interlopers had their greedy eye on the growing collection of funds that Paul had initiated for the Jerusalem poor. Since, however, it was designated strictly for helping these people, the interlopers had no way of accessing it. It was but an easy step for them to project their greed on Paul.[332] They seem to have put forth the idea that though Paul personally maintained the appearance of righteous independence, he actually had Corinthian money siphoned to him by Titus and

---

328. Barnett, *Second Epistle,* 585–86.
329. Barnett, *Second Epistle,* 586.
330. Guthrie, *2 Corinthians,* 607.
331. Hughes, *Second Epistle,* 464; Martin, *2 Corinthians,* 640.
332. Hughes, *Second Epistle,* 465.

his companions. In short, he was guilty of positioning his delegates such that they could take advantage of the kindness and generosity of the Saints to his financial benefit.[333] The final clause in 12:16, dripping with irony, is Paul's blunt insistence that he has acted in all matters with complete integrity.[334]

In 12:17, the Apostle presses the Saints to come up with concrete examples of instances when he or his delegates have acted with deviousness. In 8:16–24, he noted that he specifically tasked his delegates to make sure that the collection for the Jerusalem poor was administered properly. He now asks anyone in his audience, having examined carefully what has happened and is happening through his representatives, to step forward if they have detected any malfeasance. His tacit point is that some of his detractors have been hiding behind generalizations that cannot be proved or disproved.[335] He now demands that, on the basis of specifics, his accusers either prove their accusations or drop the case. To push his innocence, in 12:18 he reiterates his interaction with Titus. This well-recognized and respected Christian minister had made frequent trips to Corinth as the Apostle's envoy and was therefore well-known to the people.[336] Paul makes it clear not only that he was responsible for initiating Titus's visit to the city (8:16–17) but also that he was the one who sent another brother along with Titus. The point of the latter seems to be that the addition of another minister guarded against collusion. Thus Paul can ask his audience if they have found any misappropriation of the funds by his delegates. Ingeniously, he phrases the question such that the answer demands the admission that his delegates, and therefore he himself, have acted with complete integrity.[337] In this way he successfully rebuts the false accusations against him.[338]

---

333. Barnett, *Second Epistle,* 587.

334. Paul has stressed that he has worked continually among these people with a clear conscience (1:12; 4:2; 5:11) as he serves them in God-given sincerity (1:12). Guthrie, *2 Corinthians,* 614.

335. Barrett, *Second Epistle,* 325.

336. Barnett, *Second Epistle,* 590.

337. Guthrie, *2 Corinthians,* 615.

338. Barnett, *Second Epistle,* 590.

Fears about the Corinthians' State (12:19–21)

Greek Text

19 Πάλαι δοκεῖτε ὅτι ὑμῖν ἀπολογούμεθα; κατέναντι θεοῦ ἐν Χριστῷ λαλοῦμεν. τὰ
δὲ πάντα, ἀγαπητοί, ὑπὲρ τῆς ὑμῶν οἰκοδομῆς, 20 φοβοῦμαι γὰρ μή πως ἐλθὼν
οὐχ οἵους θέλω εὕρω ὑμᾶς, κἀγὼ εὑρεθῶ ὑμῖν οἷον οὐ θέλετε, μή πως ἔρις, ζῆλος,
θυμοί, ἐριθεῖαι, καταλαλιαί, ψιθυρισμοί, φυσιώσεις, ἀκαταστασίαι· 21 μὴ πάλιν
ἐλθόντος μου ταπεινώσῃ με ὁ θεός μου πρὸς ὑμᾶς, καὶ πενθήσω πολλοὺς τῶν προ-
ημαρτηκότων καὶ μὴ μετανοησάντων ἐπὶ τῇ ἀκαθαρσίᾳ καὶ πορνείᾳ καὶ ἀσελγείᾳ
ᾗ ἔπραξαν. [SBLGNT]

King James Version

19 Again, think ye that we excuse our-
selves unto you? we speak before God
in Christ: but we do all things, dearly
beloved, for your edifying. 20 For I
fear, lest, when I come, I shall not find
you such as I would, and that I shall be
found unto you such as ye would not:
lest there be debates, envyings, wraths,
strifes, backbitings, whisperings, swell-
ings, tumults: 21 And lest, when I come
again, my God will humble me among
you, and that I shall bewail many which
have sinned already, and have not
repented of the uncleanness and for-
nication and lasciviousness which they
have committed.

New Rendition

19 Have you been thinking all this time
that we have been defending our-
selves to you? We speak before God
in Christ, and everything, dear broth-
ers and sisters, is for your edification.
20 For I am afraid that perhaps when I
come, I may not find you to be the kind
of people I want you to be, and I may
not be found by you to be the kind of
person you want me to be. I also fear
that perhaps there will be contention,
jealousy, anger, selfishness, speaking
ill of each other, gossiping, pride, dis-
order. 21 So that when I come again,
God may humble me before you, and
that I shall grieve over many of those
who have sinned previously and have
not repented of the impurity and sexual
immorality and licentiousness that they
have indulged in.

Translation Notes and Comments

12:19 ***Again, think ye that we excuse ourselves unto you? / Have you been thinking all this time that we have been defending ourselves to you?:*** At this point, Paul softens his polemic to address a misconception some in his audience may have been laboring under.

Paul's construction of this sentence leaves it vague. It could be translated as a statement or a question. The context gives slight preference to a question, and thus we have rendered it that way.[339]

The adverb πάλαι (*palai*) denotes a "continuous extent of time in the past"[340] and translates as "all this time." It refers to some earlier point at which Titus read Paul's harsh epistle to those who were gathered to hear and continues forward into the present.[341]

The verb δοκέω (*dokeō*), "think, believe, suppose,"[342] refers to the subjective opinion or understanding.

The verb ἀπολογέομαι (*apologeomai*), "defend oneself," found here as a present plural, means "to speak in own's own defense against charges presumed to be false."[343] Though the verb is plural and can therefore include Titus and his companion, the major focus is on the Apostle himself.[344]

The plural dative pronoun ὑμῖν (*hymin*), "to you," shows that the object of the supposed defense is the Corinthian Saints.[345] At first blush, it seems odd, after reading the material, especially in chapters 10 through 12, that Paul would deny he is arguing in self-defense. However, his denial is technically correct. A defense "is a self-regarding composition, designed to further the writer's own interests and to commend him to the person who appears to be in a position to pass judgment."[346] Note that Paul's epistle fails to be a defense in two ways. First, Paul is not furthering his own interests but those of God and Christ. Second, the Corinthian members hold no jurisdiction over the Apostle and therefore have no authority to pass judgment on him.

---

339. The adverb πάλαι (*palai*) with the present progressive aorist is the equivalent of an English perfect but yields to a question form. Barrett, *Second Epistle,* 327–28; Barnett, *Second Epistle,* 590 n. 47.

340. Louw-Nida, §67.141.

341. It should be kept in mind that the vast majority of people, during this time, were illiterate. Part of Church worship, therefore, consisted of reading materials, including epistles, to the congregation. See 1 Thes. 5:27; Col. 4:16; and Rev. 1:3. For studies, see Bernard M. W. Knox, "Silent Reading in Antiquity," *Greek, Roman, and Byzantine Studies* 9, no. 4 (1968): 421–35; and Frank D. Gilliard, "More Silent Reading in Antiquity: *Non Omne Verbum Sonabat,*" *Journal of Biblical Literature* 112, no. 4 (1993): 689–94.

342. BDAG, 254–55.

343. BDAG, 116–17.

344. Martin, *2 Corinthians,* 655, with n. 1180.

345. BDAG, 949–50.

346. Barrett, *Second Epistle,* 328.

we speak before God in Christ / We speak before God in Christ: With this sentence, Paul points to the actual parties that he and his associates are answerable to. The verb λαλέω (*laleō*) means to "speak, express oneself,"[347] while the adverb κατέναντι (*katenanti*), "before," denotes "a position relative to someone who is viewed as having jurisdiction."[348] Paul cannot allow his audience, especially his detractors, to view themselves as having jurisdiction over him or his associates. Rather, the authority before whom he speaks is God "in Christ." This phrase is a mild but potent oath.[349] "He is speaking in the presence of God as a Christian believer. The omniscient God is witness to the truth of the words that he has written to [these Saints]. Paul is conscious that all that he has done will be revealed in the presence of Christ, his judge (see on 5:10)."[350]

but we do all things, dearly beloved, for your edifying / and everything, dear brothers and sisters, is for your edification: With this clause, Paul reveals his actual intent in writing to them. The nominal adjective ἀγαπητοί (*agapētoi*), "beloved ones," is masculine in gender but applies to both men and women,[351] so for clarity we have translated it as "dear brothers and sisters."

The plural phrase τὰ δὲ πάντα (*ta de panta*) denotes "everything," nothing being left out.[352] Here Paul uses it to describe the total of his words, admonitions, and teachings in the whole of this letter and likely that of his entire ministry among these people.[353]

His use of the preposition ὑπέρ (*hyper*) is telling. It denotes doing something "in behalf of" or "for the good of" another.[354]

The noun οἰκοδομή (*oikodomē*) has reference to "building, construction," but in a spiritual sense it refers to "edification, building up."[355] This metaphor Paul had already used in his former letter (1 Cor. 3:9; 8:1, 10; 10:23; 14:3, 4, 5, 12, 17, 26), and therefore it was well-known to his audience.[356]

---

347. BDAG, 582–83.
348. BDAG, 530–31.
349. Barnett, *Second Epistle,* 591.
350. Barnett, *Second Epistle,* 591–92.
351. BDAG, 7.
352. Louw-Nida, §§59.23; 78.44.
353. Guthrie, *2 Corinthians,* 618.
354. Louw-Nida, §90.36.
355. BDAG, 696–97.
356. Schütz, *Paul and the Anatomy of Apostolic Authority,* 224–25 (on 1 Cor. 3:10–15), 260.

12:20 ***For I fear, lest, when I come / For I am afraid that perhaps when I come:*** The conjunction γάρ (*gar*), "for,"[357] looks back at the idea of edification and signals a transition from the general concept to specific examples, since the need for understanding is particularly great.[358] Though all the Apostle does is for the Saints' edification, this time it may take the form of housecleaning.

The verb φοβέω (*phobeō*), "to fear," found here as a first-person passive singular, thus "to be afraid," is quite strong, carrying the nuances of "terror."[359] By placing the verb as the first word in the sentence with its implied "I," the Apostle places himself and his authority at center stage. In this way, he signals to all that they will definitely not find him as they have known him in the past.[360] This time, humility and weakness will stand behind strength and authority.

The adverb πως (*pōs*) often means "somehow,"[361] but with the negative particle μή (*mē*), "not," it expresses "negative purpose, often with the implication of apprehension" or misgiving,[362] thus rendered as "perhaps."[363]

The verb ἔρχομαι (*erchomai*), "to come,"[364] though found here as an aorist participle, is used relatively and thus points to the future, not the past.[365] For that reason, it is rendered "when I come."

I shall not find you such as I would / I may not find you to be the kind of people I want you to be: The verb εὑρίσκω (*heuriskō*), "to find,"[366] is found here in the subjective mood, not the indicative as one would expect. Paul's choice of mood indicates a degree of uncertainty and likely suggests to his readers that his threatened discipline (see below) is not a foregone conclusion, thus giving them motivation and, likely, time to repent.[367] Even so, the verb's modification by the negative particle *ou*, "not," indicates that the Apostle's concern is genuine.

---

357. BDAG, 189–90.
358. Guthrie, *2 Corinthians*, 619.
359. BDAG, 1060–62.
360. Martin, *2 Corinthians*, 649–50.
361. BDAG, 901.
362. Louw-Nida, §89.62; BDF, §428.6; Moule, *Idiom Book*, 139.
363. Guthrie, *2 Corinthians*, 619.
364. BDAG, 393–95.
365. Wallace, *Greek Grammar*, 614.
366. BDAG, 411–12.
367. Guthrie, *2 Corinthians*, 620; Martin, *2 Corinthians*, 658.

The relative pronoun οἷος (*hoios*), "such as," in this context, has the sense of "the sort of person who."[368]

The verb θέλω (*thelō*), "wish, desire," is rather strong, expressing as it does something that one sincerely wants or plans to take pleasure in.[369]

and that I shall be found unto you such as ye would not / and I may not be found by you to be the kind of person you want me to be: That Paul begins this clause with the crasis κἀγώ (*kagō*), "and I," is meaningful. It places the pronoun in emphatic position, again putting the Apostle and his authority at center stage.

On the verb εὑρίσκω (*heuriskō*), "to find," see above. Here the verb is found as a passive subjunctive. The mood again suggests a degree of uncertainty, showing that how his audience will find Paul is not a foregone conclusion, and therefore they have a choice in the outcome.[370]

On the relative pronoun οἷος (*hoios*), "the kind of person," and the verb θέλω (*thelō*) "desire, want," see above.

lest there be debates / I also fear that perhaps there will be contention: The phrase "I also fear" is not in the Greek text, which actually lacks a verb. Because the Greek text does imply the idea, and a verbal phrase is necessary for flow in English, we have added one.[371]

On the phrase μή πως (*mē pōs*), "lest, perhaps," see above.

The noun ἔρις (*eris*), "strife, discord, contention," denotes a rivalry arising from people taking different sides on a matter. It carries the nuance of antagonism and even hostility.[372]

envying / jealousy: The noun ζῆλος (*zēlos*), "jealousy, envy," denotes "intense negative feelings over another's achievements or success."[373] The emphasis here is on the depth of the feelings that can reach even to fierceness.[374]

wraths / anger: The noun θυμός (*thymos*), "anger, wrath, rage, indignation," denotes a "state of intense displeasure" and the potential "of passionate outbursts."[375]

---

368. LSJ, 1209; BDAG, 701.

369. Louw-Nida, §§25.1, 102.

370. Guthrie, *2 Corinthians,* 620; Martin, *2 Corinthians,* 659.

371. Barrett, *Second Epistle,* 329.

372. Louw-Nida, §§33.447; 39.22; BDAG, 392.

373. BDAG, 427.

374. Louw-Nida, §§78.25; 88.162.

375. BDAG, 461–62; Louw-Nida, §88.178.

strifes / selfishness: the noun ἐριθεία (*eritheia*), "hostility, selfish ambition, selfishness," denotes "a feeling of resentfulness based upon jealousy and implying rivalry." It carries the nuance of not only an unwillingness to give what one owns but also a desire to be better than someone else.[376]

backbitings / speaking ill of each other: The noun καταλαλιά (*katalalia*), "evil speech, slander, defamation," denotes specifically speaking ill of another.[377]

whisperings / gossiping: The noun ψιθυρισμός (*psithyrismos*), "slander, gossip," denotes passing on harmful information about another "with the implication that such information is not widely known and therefore should presumably be kept secret."[378]

swellings / pride: The noun φυσίωσις (*physiōsis*), "pride, conceit," denotes an inflated or bloated ego based on a false view of one's importance.[379]

tumults / disorder: The noun ἀκαταστασία (*akatastasia*), "disorder, unruliness," is very strong, denoting as it does an "opposition to established order," with the nuance of an open rebellion against established authority that can result in mob action.[380]

12:21 ***And lest, when I come again / So that when I come again:*** This phrase begins with the conjunction μή (*mē*), "so that,"[381] which likely points to Paul's worry that the humbling he anticipates (see below) has the full potential of being realized.[382]

The verb ἔρχομαι (*erchomai*), "to come," is found here as an aorist participle but one taken in a relative or subsequent aspect, and thus rather than looking at the past, it looks to the future.[383] In that light, the adverb πάλιν (*palin*), "again," references his upcoming trips.[384]

---

376. Louw-Nida, §§39.7; 88.162. There is some uncertainty about the exact nuance of this noun. It is found in only one place in Greek literature before New Testament times (Aristotle, *Politics* 5.3), where it designates a person seeking political office through unscrupulous means. See BDAG, 392.

377. BDAG, 519; Louw-Nida, §33.387.

378. Louw-Nida, §33.404.

379. Louw-Nida, §88.215.

380. BDAG, 35; Louw-Nida, §§39.34, 36.

381. BDAG, 644–46; BDF, §370; Smyth, *Greek Grammar,* §2221.

382. Harris, *Second Epistle,* 901. This force stands in contrast to the use of μὴ πως (*mē pōs*), "perhaps," in the previous verse that suggests more uncertainty.

383. Wallace, *Greek Grammar,* 614–15.

384. There is some disagreement as to what the adverb *palin,* "again," refers. It is possible that it refers to the Apostle being humbled again before these people. The first time

my God will humble me among you / God may humble me before you: The verb ταπεινόω (*tapienoō*), to "humble, humiliate, abase," found here in the subjunctive mood, emphasizes the act of embarrassing or shaming someone.[385] The mood suggests that God's humbling act need not take place.[386]

The preposition πρός (*pros*), "before, in relation to," though generally marking proximity, in the present context could refer to a relationship between parties, either hostile or friendly.[387] Paul's point does not seem to be that he will be humiliated "before" these Saints, meaning that they will see God's work in humbling him. Rather it would appear that he is concerned that his relationship with them in their unrighteous state will bring God's judgment upon him because he is responsible for them.[388]

and that I shall bewail many which have sinned already and have not repented / and that I shall grieve over many of those who have sinned previously and have not repented: The verb πενθέω (*pentheō*), "to grieve," found here in the future tense, denotes a heavy sorrow due to the depressing circumstances or condition of a person or people.[389] Here it specifically points to the potentially low spiritual state of the Corinthian branches.

The adjective πολύς (*polys*), "many," denotes a large number but not necessarily a majority.[390] Paul's use of the word does suggest that, though the dissention was widespread, there were many souls who refused to be a part of it.

The verb προαμαρτάνω (*proamartanō*), "to sin previously,"[391] is found here as a perfect genitive participle. The mood emphasizes the antecedent nature of the act and is rendered by the perfect tense, "have sinned."

The verb μετανοέω (*metanoeō*), "to repent,"[392] is found here as an aorist genitive participle, suggesting that the effects of a past action remain in the present. It is negated by the particle μή (*mē*), "not," showing that

---

would have been during his quick visit to the area. However, the force of the grammar gives emphasis to the adverb referring to Paul's visits, not to his humbling. For discussion, see Harris, *Second Epistle,* 901; Hughes, *Second Epistle,* 472 n. 166.

385. BDAG, 990; Louw-Nida, §§25.198; 87.62; 88.56.

386. Wallace, *Greek Grammar,* 463.

387. BDAG, 873–75.

388. Guthrie, *2 Corinthians,* 623 with n. 45.

389. Louw-Nida, §25.142. BDAG, 795, gives it the nuance of mourning for one who is dead.

390. BDAG, 847–50.

391. Louw-Nida, §88.293.

392. BDAG, 640.

repentance has not yet taken place.[393] The Greek idea of repentance denotes a changing of the mind, the seat of moral reflection, and in the New Testament the change is always for the better. It carries the nuance that, based on new or reinforced knowledge, there is regret for former actions and a determination to follow the new way. However, "though in English a focal component of repent is the sorrow or contrition that a person experiences because of sin, the emphasis in μετανοέω (*metanoeō*) ["to repent"] and μετάνοια (*metanoia*) ["repentance"] seems to be more specifically the total change, both in thought and behavior, with respect to how one should both think and act."[394]

of the uncleanness / of the impurity: The noun ἀκαθαρσία (*akatharsia*), "vileness, impurity," denotes anything that is filthy either physically or spiritually.[395] In the latter case, it points to moral corruption and, more specifically, sexual immorality. The word is also associated with both sensuality and the evil doctrine that promotes it.[396]

and fornication / and sexual immorality: The noun πορνεία (*porneia*), "fornication, sexual immorality,"[397] denoted all acts of sexual intercourse outside proper marriage, including prostitution, participation in prohibited degrees of marriage, and, with a transcendent nuance, idol worship.[398]

and lasciviousness / and licentiousness: The noun ἀσέλγεια (*aselgeia*), "licentiousness,"[399] denoted a "lack of self-constraint which involves one in conduct that violates all bounds of what is socially acceptable," and connotes a willful self-abandonment.[400]

which they have committed / that they have indulged in: The verb πράσσω (*prassō*), "to behave, commit,"[401] found here as an aorist, denotes an act performed repeatedly or habitually.[402] Given, however, the context

393. The force of the aorist participle suggests that those indulging in the sins noted, despite Paul's visit and sorrowful letter, refused to repent. Hughes, *Second Epistle,* 472–73; Guthrie, *2 Corinthians,* 624 n. 49.

394. Louw-Nida, §41.52. For a study, see *NID,* 3:290–93.

395. Louw-Nida, §§79.54; 88.261.

396. BDAG, 34. For a study, see F. Hauk, "ἀκαθαρσία," in *TDNT,* 3:427–29.

397. Louw-Nida, §88.271.

398. BDAG, 854.

399. Louw-Nida, §88.272.

400. BDAG, 141.

401. BDAG, 860–61.

402. The nuance of the verb is very broad, including the collection of dues or faring well in life. Its force is best seen in contrast to the verb ποιέω (*poieō*), "to do," which stresses

in which Paul uses the word, "indulge," referring as it does to taking unrestrained pleasure in something (here moral depravity), seems to best capture the idea.[403]

Analysis and Summary

In 12:19, the Apostle clarifies the purpose of his writing. He explains to his audience that his ministry is being "carried out before God, in relationship with Christ." In that regard, it has but one purpose: the edifying of the Saints.[404] The purpose of his focus is to get those in need of repentance to do so before he arrives and to do so quickly. That his visit lasted only a couple of months (Acts 20:2–3) suggests some success.[405]

With his reference to his audience as "my beloved brothers and sisters," we see a definite softening of tone. Noteworthy is that the first verse in this new portion acts as an interim conclusion, not only for the section but also for the entire epistle. The Apostle has not and is not writing strictly or only in self-defense, as would a contemporary apologist, but, as he insists, he is writing "before God" and for the purpose of edifying them. Emphasizing this point is his statement in 13:10 that he is writing harshly so that "I may not have to deal with you severely according to the authority the Lord has given me."

No matter what the perceptions, the reality is that it has not been the Corinthians who have been sitting in judgment of Paul, but rather he of them. Some of these people may have supposed that his legitimation rests with them, specifically with their judgment of his authority and comportment. He now sets the record straight, showing that his legitimation does not come *from them* but rests *in them*—that is, in their faith in Christ and the quality of life it has brought.[406]

In the past, he has willingly exposed his weaknesses, even though doing so has brought him ridicule and rejection by some. They simply refused to see that his self-deprecation was never "due to a lack of, but rather a demonstration of, strength."[407] Now he will fully come in that strength (12:19–13:10). Indeed, he will come fully prepared to bring severe consequences

---

accomplishment and points to the result of an action. The verb πράσσω (*prassō*) stresses the process leading up to the accomplishment and points to the character and scope of the result. For a study, see C. Maurer, "πράσσω," in *TDNT,* 6:632–44.

403. *Collegiate Dictionary,* s.v. "indulge."

404. Guthrie, *2 Corinthians,* 607.

405. Martin, *2 Corinthians,* 649.

406. Seifrid, *Second Letter,* 466.

407. Martin, *2 Corinthians,* 657.

against any found out of the way (10:2, 6, 11). If that means they all face another painful visit, so be it. He will not withhold his wrath. On the other hand, if they repent of their errant ways, he will instead express his unbounded love for them. They get to choose which they want.[408]

Thus in Paul, as in his Master, Christ, strength and weakness combine to bring forth the will of God (1 Cor. 1:25). The point is that Paul does not have his heart set on disciplining those out of the way, but they must show they have repented. His position is driven by his ministering spirit that unites him with the suffering of the Saints (2 Cor. 11:28–29) and propels the vulnerable love he has for them even at the cost of revealing his native weaknesses. These, however, he will not allow to excuse him from the burden of ministry (12:10), but rather he will use them to express his persistent love for the Saints (12:15). It is to let the people feel his care—whether expressed in kind caring or strict disciplining—that is behind the whole epistle. His hope is that his caring will continue the course set by his earlier "severe letter" and bring full reconciliation between him and these beloved people and allow him to more fully build them up.[409]

It is Paul's sincere oath—in speaking "before God in Christ" in behalf of these people—that will act to mediate the "building up" of these Saints. He has already assured them that "we speak in Christ before God as men of pure motive, as men of God" (2:17, NR). The Apostle indicates to his readers that he is well aware everything he says is under God's scrutiny. Indeed, this letter reveals the feeling of the gravity that he has for his position, one that leads him to a profound sense of responsibility to his God, whose call and commission he carries continually (4:2; 8:21). Thus he speaks neither to impress others nor to build himself up but to please his God.[410] He also speaks "in Christ," the phrase suggesting he is looking at his personal relationship with the Lord. His words to these Saints are in no way arbitrary. They do not originate in him "but are given him by Another." His speech, he assures them, comes from beyond their judgment and therefore is not subject to them. "Quite the contrary, it judges them."[411] On that basis, "he not only preaches by the authority of Christ; he also preaches grounded in a profound relationship *with Christ.*"[412]

---

408. Martin, *2 Corinthians,* 656.
409. Martin, *2 Corinthians,* 652–53.
410. Guthrie, *2 Corinthians,* 617.
411. Seifrid, *Second Letter,* 467–68.
412. Guthrie, *2 Corinthians,* 618, italics in the original.

Here, he shows that what he "speaks" is in the content of this letter. Indeed, every point has not been solely for his defense but also expressly for the edification and strengthening of these people, "whether (1) explaining his actions and movements (1:1–2:13; 7:5–16), (2) describing the new covenant ministry (2:14–7:4), (3) appealing for the completion of the collection (chaps 8–9), or (4) admonishing the Corinthians for, on the one hand, welcoming false apostles (10:12–12:13) and, on the other, continuing in immorality (12:20–13:4). At every point in the letter Paul has provided some theological and pastoral teaching for 'upbuilding' the spiritual and moral lives of the believers."[413]

There is, however, another dimension of his message centered on him. It is located in those brief but intimate glimpses that the Apostle gives of himself and his motives. These set him apart from the "super-apostles" with their superior attitude that has beguiled too many of the local Saints. These glimpses focus on Paul's servant-like work in their behalf (for example, see 4:1–15; 6:3–13). Though his detractors claimed that his actions were slave-like, servile, and demeaning, Paul insists that all he did was for the building up of the Church and in behalf of these people.[414] More importantly, it was based on his sincere love for them.[415] He has shown that, despite God's reverencing him with unusual and telling visions and revelations, not to mention the miracles wrought through him,[416] he has had to lean on divine grace and power to support him at every turn due to his "weaknesses." That support has never failed him and will not fail the Corinthians if they will but follow his humble way.[417]

In 12:20–21, he expresses his fears. The first is that he and these Saints will be quite disappointed in one another. The second is that the seriousness of certain sins among these people has not been properly addressed.

---

413. Barnett, *Second Epistle,* 592.

414. The preposition *hyper,* "in behalf of, for the sake of," Paul has consistently used to describe his work for these people (see, for example, 1:6; 5:20; 12:10, 15). That he also uses it to describe the Savior's suffering for others gives it a vicarious shading and joins the work of the Lord with his own. Louw-Nida, §§90.36; 89.28; Barnett, *Second Epistle,* 592 nn. 56, 58.

415. Schütz, *Paul and the Anatomy of Apostolic Authority,* 260, shows that Paul's point is that love is the sole criterion that determines what builds up.

416. Though there is no specific mention of Pauline miracles occurring at Corinth, they did occur in Ephesus. Even so, Paul's first epistle to the Corinthians shows that these people were not unfamiliar with the wide-ranging gifts of the Spirit and Paul's role therein. For a study, see Jervell, "Signs of an Apostle: Paul's Miracles," 77–95.

417. Barnett, *Second Epistle,* 592.

On this latter matter, Paul stresses his position is not defensive but rather offensive, because he will hold accountable all those who have either committed or supported division or immorality.[418] This is an important transition moment in the letter, for here the Apostle turns the tables on his audience by stressing that his letter is not about them testing him to see if Christ speaks in him; it is a test to see if Christ lives in them. The center of the test rests here because they can proclaim themselves Christians only if he is what he says he is, because he founded the gospel among and *in* them. "If he is not a genuine *apostolos,* then neither have they genuinely been converted, since they came to faith through his preaching! On the other hand, if they are genuine Christians then they ought to be his letter of recommendation (3:2) and ought to defend him against his opponents."[419]

In 12:20–21, the Apostle lists vices that he fears he will find among the people. The list in 12:20 differs in content from that in 12:21. The list in verse 20 is composed of items that reveal a divided Church. The vices Paul names are a natural and shameful outgrowth of the effects of factions competing one with another. The central concern that the list reveals is that the Church is in turmoil. Indeed, the depth of hostility that possibly exists among these people, if left unchecked, could destroy the local Church.[420] For that very important reason, there must be a remedial aspect to the Apostle's visit. In this, we see that "Paul understands his labor with the Corinthians as something 'suffered' rather than accomplished," and thus he "does not live a purpose-driven life, but a God-driven life. His own goals remain secondary to the larger work of God that is being worked in him."[421]

The list in verse 21 is composed of items that reveal the conditions of individuals beset by immorality. These vices taken together reflect the condition of those who never left their pagan ways (6:14) and continue in that dissolute lifestyle.[422] The center of concern here is less with the destruction of the Church and more with the destruction of the individual soul.

---

418. Guthrie, *2 Corinthians,* 607.

419. Witherington, *Conflict and Community,* 466; italics in original.

420. Paul's list could suggest that developments in Corinth were exceptional and certainly explain how that area could be a locus for the ever-approaching apostasy. Unfortunately, it is not the only place where there were deep problems. See Ralph P. Martin, *Philippians,* New Century Bible Commentary (Grand Rapids, Mich.: Wm. B. Eerdmans; London: Marshal, Morgan, and Scott Publishers, 1980), 22–23, 31–34. Holzapfel and Wayment, *Making Sense,* 379, posit that Paul is concerned that his visit and letter will not turn the tide of apostasy.

421. Seifrid, *Second Letter,* 471.

422. Martin, *2 Corinthians,* 659.

Taken together, the lists indicate that both parties, unfortunately, remain untouched by the gospel of reconciliation he continually promotes (5:20; 6:14). It may be that the Apostle is expressing his stand that whether the people are guilty of communal strife or immorality or both, all the unrepentant will most definitely feel the full brunt of his wrath. It is, however, possible that Paul is actually separating the two in order to isolate and thereby more powerfully drive home his warning to each—namely, they will come under censure to the degree their actions and recalcitrance demand.[423]

He fears that, should he arrive and find that many of these people have continued to be embroiled in strife and immorality, he will suffer deep shame from God. How so? Paul's divinely assigned task was twofold. The first was to bring these people as a pure bride to Christ (11:2). The second was to build them up through teaching and example (12:19). Failure to accomplish these tasks would result in deep shaming by the God who entrusted him with the task.[424]

Nonetheless, the Apostle recognizes that even his shaming would be done according to God's will. "Rival apostles and superior Corinthians might feel free to crow over a defeated Paul, but they could do nothing that was not permitted and indeed willed by God. It might be God's will that this should happen."[425] After all, it was God's will that Paul continue his ministry with a thorn in his flesh (12:8–9) and also bear the marks of the crucified Lord (4:10). Therefore, Paul's shaming, if done at all, will bring about God's purposes.

In the present case, the Apostle's divinely induced shaming will inspire wholehearted determination to restore his reputation with his God. That determination will express itself in harsh but justifiable measures against those who "sinned before." This likely refers to the period especially after Paul's second visit and his harsh letter. These people simply refuse to heed Paul's teachings to "be reconciled to God" (5:20) and live as Christians should (6:14–7:1). Thus they have forced him into a position in which he must take action.[426]

He is, however, not a bit thrilled about that, and as he says in 12:21, he will grieve over them. His words reveal that he remains pastorally and emotionally invested in these people, and his desire to build them up—that is,

423. Martin, *2 Corinthians,* 659, 666.

424. Guthrie, *2 Corinthians,* 623.

425. Barrett, *Second Epistle,* 330–31.

426. Martin, *2 Corinthians,* 665.

to edify them—remains his primary motivation.[427] It is telling that the verb in the phrase "my God will humble me" (ταπεινώσῃ, *tapeinōsē*) is in the subjunctive mood. It suggests that Paul holds out a strong hope that God will not have to humble him because these people will heed the Apostle's warning and will take proper action.[428] Even so, it is clear that Paul blames the possible Corinthian failure and his cause for deep grief not primarily on his detractors but with the Saints themselves. Thus the repentance he demands has very wide application.[429]

The three words he uses in 12:21 to describe the sins that these people have indulged in and likely continue to indulge in all have sexual ties. The first (ἀκαθαρσία, *akatharsia*) points to vile and moral corruption expressing itself in unnamed but unusually obscene sexual acts. It also hints at the base ideas that support them.[430] The second (πορνεία, *porneia*) refers broadly to any immoral sexual act.[431] The final one (ἀσέλγεια, *aselgeia*) denotes conduct that is so vile it exceeds any acceptability. The result of such a total lack of self-restraint gives way to full indulgence and debauchery.[432] The strength of these words gives a shocking view of the conduct of some who called themselves Christians even while yielding to their lusts. These seem to have never abandoned the sexual depravity for which Corinth was known. Such rank promiscuity distressed Paul and demanded that he take stern action. Of this he warns them in the final chapter of his epistle.

---

427. Martin, *2 Corinthians,* 664.

428. Martin, *2 Corinthians,* 664.

429. Seifrid, *Second Letter,* 474.

430. Louw-Nida, §§79.54; 88.261.

431. Louw-Nida, §88.271.

432. BDAG, 141. Martin, *Philippians,* 143–44, posits that even in that remarkable branch, there were those who denied the doctrine of the cross and with it the Resurrection. The consequences led to the abandonment of the ethical and moral demands of the gospel just as it did in Corinth.

Chapter 13

Final Warnings and Conclusion

Introduction

For the general setting on which this chapter rests, see the introduction to chapter 10. In this chapter, Paul brings his epistle to a close. In the first portion, he continues his warning that he fully intends to use his apostolic power against any he finds yet unrepentant when he arrives. Since the recalcitrant Saints want proof that Christ speaks through him, he assures them that his actions will prove his apostolic authority. He therefore bids them to do a self-examination to make sure they themselves are yet in the faith. In the process, he states they will discover that Paul and his associates do have that spirit. He assures them, however, that it is his hope that they will find themselves in possession of the spirit even if he should hypothetically be found not to, for the truth of the matter must prevail. Therefore, even if he should be found weak, he is thrilled with their strength, and his prayer is for their further development in this area. It is for this latter reason, he assures them, that he is motivated to write. He really does not want to have to use harsh measures against them because, ultimately, the Lord gave him the assignment with its accompanying authority not to tear down but to build up. In the closing verses, the Apostle admonishes his audience to leave in peace so that God's love may have place in them and then closes with his benediction.

The chapter clearly "communicates a resounding note of accountability"[1] but with an undertone of care and concern. The Apostle sincerely does not want to deal with these people harshly. Even so, his heavenly assigned mission demands that he build them up even if he must tear some down to do so. He assures his audience that he will not hesitate to fulfill his divine mandate one way or another. It is their choice.

1. Guthrie, *2 Corinthians*, 628.

Warning of Impending Discipline (13:1–4)

Greek Text

1 Τρίτον τοῦτο ἔρχομαι πρὸς ὑμᾶς· ἐπὶ στόματος δύο μαρτύρων καὶ τριῶν σταθή-
σεται πᾶν ῥῆμα. 2 προείρηκα καὶ προλέγω ὡς παρὼν τὸ δεύτερον καὶ ἀπὼν νῦν,
τοῖς προημαρτηκόσιν καὶ τοῖς λοιποῖς πᾶσιν, ὅτι ἐὰν ἔλθω εἰς τὸ πάλιν οὐ φείσομαι,
3 ἐπεὶ δοκιμὴν ζητεῖτε τοῦ ἐν ἐμοὶ λαλοῦντος Χριστοῦ· ὃς εἰς ὑμᾶς οὐκ ἀσθενεῖ ἀλλὰ
δυνατεῖ ἐν ὑμῖν, 4 καὶ γὰρ ἐσταυρώθη ἐξ ἀσθενείας, ἀλλὰ ζῇ ἐκ δυνάμεως θεοῦ. καὶ
γὰρ ἡμεῖς ἀσθενοῦμεν ἐν αὐτῷ, ἀλλὰ ζήσομεν σὺν αὐτῷ ἐκ δυνάμεως θεοῦ εἰς ὑμᾶς.
[SBLGNT]

King James Version

1 This is the third time I am coming to
you. In the mouth of two or three wit-
nesses shall every word be established.
2 I told you before, and foretell you,
as if I were present, the second time;
and being absent now I write to them
which heretofore have sinned, and to
all other, that, if I come again, I will not
spare: 3 Since ye seek a proof of Christ
speaking in me, which to you-ward is
not weak, but is mighty in you. 4 For
though he was crucified through weak-
ness, yet he liveth by the power of God.
For we also are weak in him, but we
shall live with him by the power of God
toward you.

New Rendition

1 This is the third time I will come to you.
"By the mouth of two or three witnesses
every matter will be established" [Deut.
19:15]. 2 I have warned those who sinned
before as well as all the others, like I did
when I was present on my second visit
and I am now warning them when I am
not present, that if I come again, I will
not spare anyone 3 since you demand
proof of Christ speaking in me, who
is not weak in dealing with you but is
powerful among you. 4 For indeed, he
was crucified because of weakness, and
yet he lives because of the power of God.
For indeed we are weak in him, but we
shall live together with him because of
the power of God toward you.

Translation Notes and Comments

13:1 *This is the third time I am coming to you / This is the third time I will come to you:* Paul repeats his intent to come to Corinth (12:14). He does so as a means of introducing the next segment of his address.[2] His first visit was his months-long stay when he brought the gospel to them. The second appears to have been his quick trip made during his work in Ephesus that resulted in his sending them the severe letter.

2. Guthrie, *2 Corinthians*, 629.

The verb ἔρχομαι (*erchomai*), "to come," though in the present tense, has a future cast and therefore is rendered "will come."[3] This usage stresses the idea that the anticipated event, in this case Paul's visit, will be realized shortly and with certainty.[4] The Apostle's statement should be seen less as one of intent and more as one of exasperation.

In the mouth of two or three witnesses shall every word be established / "By the mouth of two or three witnesses every matter will be established": Paul quotes from the Old Testament scripture Deuteronomy 19:15. Doing so enables him to focus specifically on the point he wants to make. The verse stands as the basis of Old Testament distillery action. It establishes the procedure that such action requires more than one witness. Though no fewer than two are demanded, more can be brought to the case, the use of the numeral "three" not limiting the number of witnesses.[5]

Paul uses the quote without the usual introduction, "It is written." He likely feels he does not need to because his audience will recognize that, through the paraphrase, he is indicating the second reason for his upcoming visit.[6] It will focus on disciplinary action of some kind.

But who or what are the witnesses, and about what do they witness? One idea is that Paul is referring to a justification some of his enemies are using to bring formal charges against him. If that is the case, he is signaling that he is well aware of their planned action. Another is that he is referring to his own warnings against his adversaries, two of which have already been given during his first and second visits among them, and the third is about to be executed.[7] In this case, he is signaling that his disciplinary actions will be unilateral. Another is that he plans to hold a formal inquiry, one that will follow all necessary regulations, including the use of witnesses to sustain charges.[8] Based on Restoration practice, even during the

3. BDAG, 393–95.

4. On a futuristic present, see Wallace, *Greek Grammar,* 535–37.

5. For a study, see Hendrick van Vliet, *No Single Testimony: A Study on the Adoption of the Law of Deut. 19:15 Par. into the New Testament* (Utrecht, Neth.: Kemink en Zoon, 1958).

6. Guthrie, *2 Corinthians,* 529–30.

7. Harris, *Second Epistle,* 907–8.

8. For points of view, see Bernard, "Second Epistle," 115; Barnett, *Second Epistle,* 598; Martin, *2 Corinthians,* 667; and Garland, *2 Corinthians,* 540–41. For a study, see Laurence L. Welborn, "'By the Mouth of Two or Three Witnesses': Paul's Invocation of a Deuteronomic Statute," *Novum Testamentum* 52 (2010): 207–20. The opinion of Barrett, *Second Epistle,* 333, may be right, suggesting as he does that Paul is using the scripture in a more general way to let the Corinthians Saints know they have had ample warning and he plans to act but does not commit himself to actually how.

early period of Church history, a disciplinary counsel rather than the sole and independent action of the Apostle himself, though not certain, seems more in order.

13:2 ***I told you before, and foretell you, as if I were present, the second time; and being absent now I write to them which heretofore have sinned, and to all other / I have warned those who sinned before as well as all the others, like I did when I was present on my second visit and I am now warning them when I am not present:*** This is a rather complicated clause in Greek and takes some parsing to get at its sense. The aorist verb προεῖπον (*proeipon*) means "to tell beforehand," often connoting a warning.[9] It is here found in the first person singular of the perfect tense and can be rendered as both "I have told beforehand" and "I have warned." The verb προλέγω (*prolegō*) also means "to tell beforehand."[10] Thus we render the phrase προείρηκα καὶ προλέγω (*proeirēka kai prolegō*) as "I have warned and am warning."

The next phrase is introduced by the conjunction ὡς (*hōs*), "as, like"[11] (with an understood "I did"). The conjunction modifies the verb πάρειμι (*pareimi*), "to be present,"[12] found here as a present participle used circumstantially in a temporal sense, thus rendered "when I was present." The articular neuter adjective τὸ δεύτερον (*to deuteron*) is used adverbially with the sense "the second time,"[13] referring to his second visit to the area.

Next phrase is introduced by the conjunction καί (*kai*), "and," followed by the verb ἄπειμι (*apeimi*), "to be absent,"[14] also as a present participle used circumstantially in a temporal sense, thus meaning "when I am not present." The adverb νῦν (*nyn*), "now,"[15] reinforces the temporal sense of the participle. The phrase "I am warning them" is not in the Greek but is inferred by context, and we have added it in our translation for clarity.

The verb προαμαρτάνω (*proamartanō*) means "to sin previously."[16] It is found here as a plural participle in the perfect tense and with its modifying definite article τοῖς (*tois*), "those who," refers to all who had sinned before Paul's second visit and were warned by him at that time. The perfect tense

---

9. BDAG, 867–68.
10. BDAG, 872.
11. BDAG, 1103–6.
12. BDAG, 773–74.
13. BDAG, 220–21.
14. BDAG, 100.
15. BDAG, 681–82.
16. Louw-Nida, §88.293.

suggests these people had not taken his warning seriously and, therefore, refused to repent.

The adjective λοιπός (*loipos*), "that which remains,"[17] found here as a plural, together with its adjective πᾶσιν (*pasin*), "all,"[18] refers to "all the others," but just who Paul has in mind is ambiguous. It could include those who had fallen into sin since Paul's last visit, those who had sinned before then but whom he had not personally confronted, or those under the influence of the interlopers. Whatever the case, Paul's point is that he will not overlook improper behavior on the part of anyone this time.

that, if I come again, I will not spare / that if I come again, I will not spare anyone: The conditional conjunction ἐάν (*ean*), "if," with the aorist subjunctive refers to a condition that is "uncertain of fulfillment, but still likely"[19]—namely, Paul's upcoming visit.[20] Here Paul combines the conjunction with the aorist subjunctive form of the verb ἔρχομαι (*erchomai*), "to come," thus connoting that Paul thinks it is likely that the confrontation will take place.[21]

The future form of the verb φείδομαι (*pheidomai*), "to spare," means to "save from loss or discomfort."[22] The negative particle, οὐ (*ou*), "not," indicates that no such leniency will be taken.

13:3 ***Since ye seek a proof of Christ speaking in me / since you demand proof of Christ speaking in me:*** This phrase does not begin a new thought, as in the KJV, but concludes the previous one. The conjunction ἐπεί (*epei*), "since," marks a reason or cause[23] and signals why Paul will not spare any who continue to resist his warnings.

The verb ζητέω (*zēteō*) usually means "to seek,"[24] but in this instance, context suggests a stronger rendering, thus "demand."[25] The noun δοκιμή (*dokimē*) usually refers both to a testing process and also the results of that process, "proof."[26]

---

17. BDAG, 602–3.

18. BDAG, 782–83.

19. Wallace, *Greek Grammar,* 696; italics removed. This form is also known as the "future more vivid." Smyth, *Greek Grammar,* §2323.

20. For discussion, see Harris, *Second Epistle,* 909–10.

21. Wallace, *Greek Grammar,* 696.

22. BDAG, 1051; Louw-Nida, §22.28.

23. Louw-Nida, §89.32.

24. BDAG, 428.

25. BDAG, 428; Guthrie, *2 Corinthians,* 633 n. 15.

26. BDAG, 256.

The preposition ἐν (*en*), "in," denotes not the place but the agent of the action.[27] The verb λαλέω (*laleō*), found here as a present participle, usually means "to speak or talk,"[28] but in this context, it nuances the Savior's delegated authority. What Paul is saying is that those resisting him "have challenged his Apostolic authority"[29] and, by this means, forced his hand.

which to you-ward is not weak / who is not weak in dealing with you: The relative pronoun ὃς (*hos*), "who,"[30] refers to Jesus, not Paul. This and the next phrase make up a short digression in which the Apostle emphasizes the present reality of how Christ continues to deal with the Saints. In this phrase, Paul's emphasis is on the Savior's manifest strength as experienced by Paul's audience.

The verb ἀσθενέω (*astheneō*), "to be weak," refers to that which lacks strength either from being ill, incapacitated, limited, or powerless[31] but nuances ineffectiveness or impotence.[32] Paul negates these limitations with the use of the particle οὐ (*ou*), "not," and thereby tacitly emphasizes the unlimited capacity and power of the Lord.

In the prepositional phrase εἰς ὑμᾶς (*eis hymas*), the preposition can denote a reference to something, thus "in respect to you,"[33] or it can denote a special aspect, thus "toward" or "in dealing with you." The latter seems better since it hints at an interpersonal relationship with the Lord.[34]

but is mighty in you / but is powerful among you: The conjunction ἀλλά (*alla*), "but,"[35] marks an emphatic contrast with the weakness mentioned above and thus emphasizes the power of God. The verb δυνατέω (*dynateō*), "be effective," denotes a display of capability.[36] Since its cognates are δύναμις (*dymamis*) and δυνατός (*dynatos*), both referring to what is powerful and mighty, we have rendered the word as "powerful" with the idea that it is by the display of God's power that God is effective among the Saints. This is likely a reference to the displays of power that began at the time Paul introduced the gospel to these people and continued after he left (1 Cor. 12:4–11).

---

27. Guthrie, *2 Corinthians,* 633.
28. Louw-Nida, §33.70.
29. Bernard, "Second Epistle," 115.
30. BDAG, 725.
31. BDAG, 142–43.
32. Guthrie, *2 Corinthians,* 635.
33. BDAG, 289–91.
34. Guthrie, *2 Corinthians,* 635.
35. Louw-Nida, §89.125.
36. BDAG, 264.

In the prepositional phase ἐν ὑμῖν (*en hymin*), the preposition "in you" could mean that Christlike power is exercised "in" or "through" each individual or that it is exercised "among" them—that is, as a body.[37] Given Paul's treatment of spiritual gifts in 1 Corinthians 12 and 14, the latter seems the better choice.

13:4 ***For though he was crucified through weakness / For indeed, he was crucified because of weakness:*** The sentence begins with the phrase καὶ γάρ (*kai gar*), "for indeed,"[38] a phrase that Paul uses to stress a point; in this case it focuses on the Lord's ἀσθενεία (*astheneia*), "weakness." For the range of meanings, see above. The preposition ἐκ (*ek*), "because of,"[39] points to an ultimate condition, in this case the Lord's self-assumed powerlessness, that allowed this event to happen.[40]

It was this state that allowed the crucifixion to happen. In a theological sense, the noun referred to those self-imposed conditions that made it possible for Christ to suffer and die.[41] These were a result of his condescension, by which he came into mortality and took upon himself "the image" or "form of man" (Mosiah 7:27; 13:34) and suffered as mortals do. It was the "weakness" that his mission imposed that both allowed and forced him to suffer "temptation, and pain of body, hunger, thirst, and fatigue" (Mosiah 3:7) and required him to yield when his enemies considered him to be but "a man, and say that he [had] a devil and [to] scourge him, and [to] crucify him" (Mosiah 3:9).

yet he liveth by the power of God / and yet he lives because of the power of God: The conjunction ἀλλά (*alla*), "and, yet," denotes a slightly adversative condition.[42] It plays off the notion of weakness, thus enhancing the idea of power.

The verb ζάω (*zaō*), "to live," does not, in the present context, denote mortal life but rather the transcendent condition of the Divine, one that can be partially realized by the righteous during mortality.[43]

---

37. Guthrie, *2 Corinthians,* 635.
38. BDAG, 189. The translation as "also" or "indeed" takes καί (*kai*) as an adverb.
39. BDAG, 295–98.
40. Bernard, "Second Epistle," 116.
41. For a study, see *NID,* 1:420–24.
42. Louw-Nida, §91.2.
43. BDAG, 424–25.

As above, the preposition ἐκ (*ek*), "because of,"[44] points to the ultimate condition that leads to an event. In this case, it is God's strength as displayed in the Resurrection.[45] The noun δύναμις (*dynamis*), "power, might, strength," also carries the nuance of working wonders.[46] The phrase stresses the idea that the Savior's weakness, which allowed for his death, did not stop God's power from bringing him back to life.

For we also are weak in him / For indeed we are weak in him: On the meaning and thrust of the phrase καὶ γάρ (*kai gar*), see above. On the verb ἀσθενέω (*astheneō*), "weak," see Translation Notes for 13:3.

There is an important manuscript variation with this verse. Some manuscripts have ἐν αὐτῷ (*en autō*), "in him," while others have σύν αὐτῷ (*syn autō*), "with him." The two textual variants are both possible, and support for each is nearly equally divided.[47] With the first variant, the preposition ἐν (*en*), "in," denotes a "close association within a limit" and points to a very personal association between two parties displayed by the controlling influence of one over the other.[48] In this case, it would indicate that Paul and his associates carry the same self-imposed weakness as did the Lord; that is, they are deliberately humble and, thus, not willing to push themselves on the Corinthian Saints as they work with and among them. With the second variant, the preposition σύν (*syn*), "with," denotes an association with another under some condition.[49] In this case, it would indicate that the missionaries, as viewed by some of the Corinthians Saints, are weak in the same way that the world saw Jesus—that is, lacking influence, station, and power.[50] The context gives slight preference to the first nuance.

but we shall live with him by the power of God toward you / but we shall live together with him because of the power of God toward you: The conjunction ἀλλά (*alla*), signals the expression of a contrast;[51] here it is weakness with power.

44. BDAG, 295–98.
45. Bernard, "Second Epistle," 116.
46. BDAG, 262–63.
47. Metzger, *Textual Commentary*, 518.
48. BDAG, 326–30.
49. BDAG, 961–62.
50. Bernard, "Second Epistle," 116.
51. BDAG, 44–45.

On the verb ζάω (*zaō*), "to live," see above. It is likely that the nuance here looks less at resurrection and more at the high spiritual quality of life the righteous can have during mortality.[52] The preposition σύν (*syn*), "with, together with," denotes, in the present context, being in association with another[53] and suggests a harmonious relationship with the Lord.

The phrase ἐκ δυνάμεως θεός (*ek dynameōs theou*), "the power of God," again looks less at the resurrective power of God and more at the authority carried by Paul and his associates.

The preposition εἰς (*eis*), "for, to, with respect to,"[54] marks a point of reference, here specifically to the Corinthian branch as a whole. Though it can carry a sense of benefaction,[55] context suggests that it sounds a note of warning to these people.[56] Thus the phrase εἰς ὑμᾶς (*eis hymas*), "toward you, in reference to you," signals that Paul's godly power will manifest itself though the apostolic display of sanctions his authority will impose on the Church.[57]

Analysis and Summary

This chapter begins with Paul's note that this will be his third visit to these people. The tone carries a suggestion of exasperation that such is necessary. Like other branches, they should have been well on their way to self-governance in the discipline of the gospel. They are not, even though he has visited them twice alread,y each serving as a witness to his position. By referring to Deuteronomy 19:15, he stresses that the law of witnesses has been fulfilled, and if he arrives and finds them yet unrepentant, it will not result in sorrow like he had when he wrote his earlier harsh letter. This time he will meet unrepentant sinners with unmitigated severity.[58] There is no doubt that he plans to hold a formal inquiry conforming to the strictest requirements of ecclesiastical procedure.[59] He will spare none from his scrutiny (13:2).

---

52. BDAG, 424–26.
53. BDAG, 961–62.
54. BDAG, 291; Louw-Nida, §§83.9; 90.23, 41.
55. Louw-Nida, §90.41.
56. Barnett, *Second Epistle,* 603 n. 60.
57. Bernard, "Second Epistle," 116.
58. Seifrid, *Second Letter,* 476. Paul's language here reflects his warning in 1 Cor. 4:18–21.
59. Bernard, "Second Epistle," 115.

Noteworthy is Paul's change of pronouns from the third-person plural "we" to the first-person singular pronoun "I." No longer are his references to his work in association with his fellow missionaries. He now focuses on what he personally intends to do and in doing so brings his apostolic authority to center stage. Of course, he has no authority or power other than his word, but that "word" is not of human origin. His word is that of the Lord, for as he has informed these Saints already, "the kingdom of God is not demonstrated by mere [human] words, but by power" (1 Cor. 4:20, NR).[60]

He informs his audience that he has delayed his visit thus far in the hope that such an action will not be necessary (compare 1:23). He then explains why he will take strict action if he does find it necessary: some have challenged his apostolic authority, demanding that he show some sign that Christ speaks through him (13:3). Using his sense of irony, he assures them that his proof will be the opposite of what they likely expect: stern judgment rather than obsequious allowance. His detractors may have based their position on Paul's actions when he visited them the second time. He apparently had used "the meekness and gentleness of Christ" (10:1), but to no avail. As a result, conditions forced him to withdraw for a time to let matters settle (1:23; 2:1). He then sent them the "severe letter," an ultimatum as it were, in an attempt to restore his position. This act seems to have worked, as Titus reported, among a large segment of the Saints (7:7, 9–11, 13–16)—likely because such an action fit better with the culture in which the Church sat. These people were accustomed to more callous modes of treatment, especially when being disciplined, not only by both Roman magistrates and local officials but also by members of the upper crust toward those of the lower. That such unkind behavior should not be the case within the Christian community does not seem to have registered with some. Hence, some felt no compunction in yielding to the interlopers' mistreatment of them (11:20).[61]

It is on this basis that these Saints would view Paul's threatened disciplinary action as proof that he does carry the authority of the Lord. Though Paul does not say so, it would appear his judgment could go so far as excommunications if necessary.[62] There is good reason why Paul must use such

60. Seifrid, *Second Letter,* 477. The same idea is expressed in D&C 1:38; 21:4–5.

61. Barnett, *Second Epistle,* 595 n. 7.

62. Harris, *Second Epistle,* 911; Martin, *2 Corinthians,* 652.

rather harsh measures. The sinners certainly need to be held accountable for their recalcitrance for the sake of spiritual welfare of the Church as a whole, but their spiritual health also depends on their relationship with God's true Apostle. That requires not only that they move into a moral life but also reject false teachings and those who promulgate them, most notably the false apostles.[63]

Paul's mention of the Lord leads him into a short digression. In it, he plays on his paradoxical theme of strength through weakness. He tells his audience that the one who commissioned Paul, even in the Apostle's weakness, is not himself weak but has displayed his power among the Saints in two ways: through the majesty of the Resurrection by which the Lord overmastered death, and through his empowering of the Saints in discharging their duties.[64] Paul admits that Jesus was crucified through weakness (ἀσθένεια, *astheneia*; compare Philip. 2:8 and 1 Pet. 3:18), but that weakness was self-assumed. Even so, he now lives in might through God's power. By that same power, the Apostle assures his audience, they, too, shall live with Christ.

The force of 13:2 reveals Paul's desire that his strong language will have the same effect his "severe letter" did in bringing repentance and humility, but to a larger group. Hence, his focus changes from fear that he will be forced to use severe discipline to a much more optimistic hope that the Corinthians will see that an outward lack of power such as the Lord demonstrated is actually not a sign of real weakness and that this is true of Paul as well. Godly power, he insists, will allow all to live with the Lord. Its result would be further reconciliation, allowing the Apostle to fulfill his God-given mission to "build up" the kingdom, rather than tearing down these people. This is possible, Paul's language reveals, because the power of Christ is yet active among them.[65]

In 13:4, the Apostle draws a parallel. Christ was crucified because of weakness. Admittedly, he only assumed that weakness temporarily, for he always had access to divine power, but he became weak so that God's will could be accomplished through him. This point is important because the "weakness" of the Lord is often taken to refer exclusively to his human frailty

63. Guthrie, *2 Corinthians*, 633.

64. Bernard, "Second Epistle," 115. Paul understood that the power that raised Christ from the dead could also dwell in the souls of the Saints (Rom. 8:11) and enlighten their understanding of the hope of Christ's calling and of his power toward the believers (Eph. 1:17–19).

65. Martin, *2 Corinthians*, 653.

and apparent defenselessness before both Jewish and Roman authorities. Rather, the phrase seems more pointed toward the Savior's *posture* of non-retaliation due to his willingness to follow his determined obedience even into the most torturous of deaths (Philip. 2:5–8).[66]

In much the same way, Paul and his associates are "weak in him," or in the imposition they have placed on themselves to properly carry out his work. By virtue of their relationship with the Savior they must be "weak" in the same way he was—that is, by "choosing a posture of humble obedience before God rather than a power posture that exerts control through power (10:1)."[67] Paul, especially, refuses to dominate by imposing on their faith and generosity.

Paul's point, however, is that the Savior's display of weakness did not stop God from giving the Son eternal life. In the same way, weakness will not stop the Father from working in and through the Apostle and his fellow missionaries. Indeed, Paul will display that very power toward these Saints as he uses his authority to purge the Church, if necessary, of the unrepentant and defiant.

With great expertise, Paul beautifully and skillfully makes his argument. In the last two verses, he adeptly

> ties the authenticity of his apostolic ministry not to a power inherent in himself, but ultimately to the power of God, which was preeminently demonstrated in the resurrection of Christ. Thus, when we consider the relational quadrangle and flow of power through these relationships, we find that God's power underlies all that Paul proclaims here. God's power was manifested in the resurrection of Christ in the past, will be manifested in Paul's resurrection in the future, and presently manifests itself in Paul's christocentric ministry to the Corinthians at present. Paul, in relationship with Christ, manifests the power of the living God in the church. There can be no greater authentication of Paul's ministry.[68]

---

66. Harris, *Second Epistle,* 914–15.
67. Guthrie, *2 Corinthians,* 636.
68. Guthrie, *2 Corinthians,* 637.

A Plea for Self-Examination (13:5–10)

Greek Text

5 Ἑαυτοὺς πειράζετε εἰ ἐστὲ ἐν τῇ πίστει, ἑαυτοὺς δοκιμάζετε· ἢ οὐκ ἐπιγινώ-
σκετε ἑαυτοὺς ὅτι Ἰησοῦς Χριστὸς ἐν ὑμῖν; εἰ μήτι ἀδόκιμοί ἐστε. 6 ἐλπίζω δὲ ὅτι
γνώσεσθε ὅτι ἡμεῖς οὐκ ἐσμὲν ἀδόκιμοι. 7 εὐχόμεθα δὲ πρὸς τὸν θεὸν μὴ ποιῆσαι
ὑμᾶς κακὸν μηδέν, οὐχ ἵνα ἡμεῖς δόκιμοι φανῶμεν, ἀλλ᾽ ἵνα ὑμεῖς τὸ καλὸν ποιῆτε,
ἡμεῖς δὲ ὡς ἀδόκιμοι ὦμεν. 8 οὐ γὰρ δυνάμεθά τι κατὰ τῆς ἀληθείας, ἀλλὰ ὑπὲρ
τῆς ἀληθείας. 9 χαίρομεν γὰρ ὅταν ἡμεῖς ἀσθενῶμεν, ὑμεῖς δὲ δυνατοὶ ἦτε· τοῦτο
καὶ εὐχόμεθα, τὴν ὑμῶν κατάρτισιν. 10 διὰ τοῦτο ταῦτα ἀπὼν γράφω, ἵνα παρὼν
μὴ ἀποτόμως χρήσωμαι κατὰ τὴν ἐξουσίαν ἣν ὁ κύριος ἔδωκέν μοι, εἰς οἰκοδομὴν
καὶ οὐκ εἰς καθαίρεσιν. [SBLGNT]

King James Version

5 Examine yourselves, whether ye be
in the faith; prove your own selves.
Know ye not your own selves, how
that Jesus Christ is in you, except ye
be reprobates? 6 But I trust that ye
shall know that we are not reprobates.
7 Now I pray to God that ye do no evil;
not that we should appear approved,
but that ye should do that which is
honest, though we be as reprobates.
8 For we can do nothing against the
truth, but for the truth. 9 For we
are glad, when we are weak, and
ye are strong: and this also we wish,
even your perfection. 10 Therefore I
write these things being absent, lest
being present I should use sharpness,
according to the power which the
Lord hath given me to edification, and
not to destruction.

New Rendition

5 Test yourselves to see if you are in
the faith! Examine yourselves! Or
don't you realize that Jesus Christ is
in you?—unless, of course, you fail the
test. 6 Now I hope you will understand
that we have not failed the test. 7 And
we pray to God that you will not do
anything wrong, not so that we will
appear to have passed the test, but so
that you will do what is right even if
we seem to have failed the test. 8 For
we cannot do anything against the
truth but for the sake of truth. 9 For
we rejoice when we are weak, but you
are strong. Indeed, this is what we pray
for: your inner strength. 10 Therefore,
I write these things when I am absent
so that when I am present, I may not
have to deal with you severely accord-
ing to the authority the Lord has given
me for the purpose of building up and
not for tearing down.

Translation Notes and Comments

13:5 ***Examine yourselves, whether ye be in the faith / Test yourselves to see if you are in the faith:*** Though the verb πειράζω (*peirazō*), found here as an imperative, can be translated as "to tempt," here it has the sense of "to endeavor to discover the nature or character of something by testing," thus "try, make trial of, put to the test."[69] The plural reflexive pronoun ἑαυτούς (*heautous*), "[your]selves," points to the direction the test should take. Paul's point is that it is not he but they who need to be proved.

The phrase ἐν τῇ πίστει (*en tē pistei*), "in the faith," refers both to membership in the community of the faithful (compare 1 Cor. 16:13) and also to their personal relationship with the Lord.

prove your own selves / Examine yourselves: The verb δοκιμάζω (*dokimazō*), "examine," found here as an imperative, has a similar meaning as πειράζω (*peirazō*, see above) but carries the additional nuance of making "a critical examination of something to determine genuineness."[70] Again, the plural reflexive pronoun ἑαυτούς (*heautous*), "[your]selves," shows the direction the examination needs to take.

Know ye not your own selves, how that Jesus Christ is in you / Or don't you realize that Jesus Christ is in you?: The conjunction ἤ (*ē*), "or," marks an alternative.[71] Here it refers to that which is necessary for the Saints to properly test themselves.

The verb ἐπιγινώσκω (*epiginōskō*), "to recognize," "to know," "to come to understand,"[72] in the present context, leans more toward "realize," meaning to be fully aware of something.[73]

The phrase ἐν ὑμῖν (*en hymin*) could mean "among you," but the twice repeated "yourselves" shows that it refers to the power of the Savior that should be dwelling "in" these people.[74]

except ye be reprobates / unless, of course, you fail the test: The phrase εἰ μήτι (*ei mēti*), "if surely not," can also be translated as "except, lest, unless." Its use indicates that a negative response to a question is expected and is more emphatic than a simple μή (*mē*), hence our use of the phrase "of course" to express this nuance.[75]

---

69. BDAG, 792.
70. BDAG, 255.
71. BDAG, 432.
72. Louw-Nida, §§27.61; 28.2; 32.16.
73. Guthrie, *2 Corinthians,* 640.
74. Barnett, *Second Epistle,* 608 n. 6.
75. BDAG, 649.

The adjective ἀδόκιμος (*adokimos*)[76] is formed by adding the negative prefix ἀ- (*a*-), "not,"[77] to the adjective δόκιμος (*dokimos*), denoting something "pertaining to being genuine on the basis of testing."[78] The resultant meaning is "not approved (by test)."[79]

13:6 ***But I trust that ye shall know that we are not reprobates / Now I hope you will understand that we have not failed the test:*** The conjunction δέ (*de*), "but, and, now,"[80] links this statement to the one before and suggests that, given the above information, Paul hopes that these people will realize its implications—namely, that he and his companions have not failed the test.

The verb ἐλπίζω (*elpizō*), "to hope," denotes a view that looks forward to something, fully believing that it will be realized.[81]

The verb γινώσκω (*ginōskō*), "to know," "understand,"[82] found here in the future tense, also carries the nuance of both grasping the significance of and acknowledging something.[83] The tense looks to Paul's hope for this outcome during his upcoming visit.[84]

13:7 ***Now I pray to God that ye do no evil / And we pray to God that you will not do anything wrong:*** The verb εὔχομαι (*euchomai*), "to pray,"[85] is found here as a present plural, and by this means, Paul brings his fellow missionaries back into the picture. The verb, though in the present tense, has an imperfective aspect, thus suggesting that Paul is either presently praying for them or that his prayer has been ongoing for some time.[86] By placing the

---

76. The word usually refers to either that which is proven worthless (Louw-Nida, §65.13) or failed to be in accordance to what is right or proper (Louw-Nida, §88.111). All together it emphasizes not meeting the standards of the test. BDAG, 21.

77. Smyth, *Greek Grammar,* §885.1.

78. BDAG, 256.

79. In the archaic English of the KJV, the term "reprobate" referred to something that could not pass a test and was considered, therefore, worthless. *Collegiate Dictionary,* s.v. "reprobate."

80. BDAG, 213.

81. BDAG, 319.

82. Louw-Nida, §28.1; 32.16.

83. BDAG, 199–201; Louw-Nida, §31.27. The verb ἐπιγινώσκω (*epiginōskō*) that Paul used in 13:5 often carries the idea of the sureness of what is known, while the verb γινώσκω (*ginōskō*) carries more of the nuance of knowing about something. In the present usage, however, it appears that there is no real difference between the meanings of the word. Martin, *2 Corinthians,* 676–77.

84. Barnett, *Second Epistle,* 609.

85. BDAG, 417.

86. Guthrie, *2 Corinthians,* 641 n. 30.

word first in the sentence, Paul makes his action of caring emphatic, thus emphasizing the hope that moves from him and his companions (in 13:6) to his audience.[87]

The substantive adjective κακός (*kakos*) has a broad range of meanings, all denoting what is bad but pointing more specifically to anything that hurts a person's soul and separates him or her from God. Its primary nuances are "evil, harm, wrong."[88] Context (12:20–21) suggests the "wrong" Paul has in mind is any refusal to see to it that repentance is carried out.[89]

not that we should appear approved / not so that we will appear to have passed the test: The conjunction ἵνα (*hina*), "so that,"[90] denotes the purpose of something[91] but with the addition of the particle οὐ (*ou*), "not," emphasizes what is not the objective of an act, in this case Paul's prayer.

The verb φαίνω (*phainō*), "to appear,"[92] found here as an aorist subjunctive passive, denotes that which makes an appearance or impression on the mind. On the adjective δόκιμος (*dokimos*), "approved (by test)," see 13:5 above.

With this phrase, Paul states that the prayers of him and his fellow workers are not intended to validate their own position at the expense of the Corinthian Saints.

but that ye should do that which is honest / but so that you will do what is right: The conjunction ἀλλά (*alla*), "but," points back to the content or purpose of the missionaries' prayer. As in the phrase above, the conjunction ἵνα (*hina*), "so that," marks purpose.

The substantive adjective καλός (*kalos*), "good,"[93] like its antonym κακός (*kakos*), has a wide range of meanings, but basically all point to those attributes that bring one in line with God and his salvation. Its primary nuances are "good, proper, moral, right."[94] Here it likely refers to following Paul's demands that they purge the evil that is among them before he arrives.

With this phrase, Paul clarifies the essence of the heartfelt prayer of these missionaries.

87. Barnett, *Second Epistle,* 609 n. 9.
88. BDAG, 501. For a study, see *NID,* 2:597–601.
89. Martin, *2 Corinthians,* 679.
90. Louw-Nida, §90.22.
91. BDAG, 475–77.
92. BDAG, 1046–47.
93. BDAG, 504–5.
94. BDAG, 504–5. For a study, see *NID,* 2:607–11.

though we be as reprobates / even if we seem to have failed the test: The conjunction δέ (*de*), "but,"[95] marks a contrast. It points to the difference between what the missionaries want for their audience (doing right) and how they themselves might, hypothetically, be found (having failed). The verb εἰμί (*eimi*), "to be," is found here as a present subjunctive, the mood suggesting mere possibility as something indefinite and together with the comparative particle ὡς (*hōs*), "as, like, as if,"[96] is thus rendered "as if we seem to have,"[97] referring to the spiritual test. In this instance, however, the probability of this happening is unlikely. On the adjective ἀδόκιμος (*adokimos*), "not approved (by test)," see 13:5 above.

In this phrase, Paul again assures his audience of the purity of his prayer. He assures them that all he and his companions want is to do right, even if it should prove that he does not measure up in the eyes of some.

This sentence is very complex and thus can lead to some difficulty in understanding Paul's point. The Apostle uses a four-part structure wherein parts one and three contain his antithetical prayer for these people ("not to do evil," "to do good") and parts two and four focus on him and his companions. The first portion of his prayer (that they do no evil) is negatively juxtaposed with part two, his status ("not that we may appear to pass the test"). Likewise, the second part of his prayer (that they do good) is negatively juxtaposed with part four, his concession against him and his fellow workers (that they, especially he, seem not to have passed the test). His point is that the moral welfare for the Saints is more important to him than his being seen as passing the test.

13:8 ***For we can do nothing against the truth / For we cannot do anything against the truth:*** The conjunction γάρ (*gar*), "because, for,"[98] signals that the reason for an action will be given. The verb δύναμαι (*dynamai*) means "to be able."[99] The particle οὐ (*ou*), "not," negates the ability.

The preposition κατά (*kata*) can denote opposition, thus "against,"[100] but in the present context it carries more of the idea of hurting something—namely, "the truth"—which the Apostle cannot do no matter the consequences.

95. BDAG, 213.

96. BDAG, 1103–6.

97. Though the subjunctive mood usually nuances probability, in some instances, as here, it points to hypothetical possibility. Wallace, *Greek Grammar,* 462.

98. BDAG, 189–90.

99. BDAG, 261–62.

100. Louw-Nida, §90.31.

The object of the preposition is ἀλήθεια (*alētheia*), "truth." The noun denotes reality[101] and refers to "the quality of being in accord with what is true."[102] The phrase stresses the accuracy, reliability, and inspiration behind what the missionaries speak. In the present context, however, Paul is likely, if obliquely, referring to his own power and authority bestowed upon him by the Savior.[103]

but for the truth / but for the sake of truth: The preposition ὑπέρ (*hyper*), "for the sake of,"[104] denotes the cause, end, or purpose for some state, belief, or action. In this case, it is "the truth." As noted above, the noun "truth" is most likely a somewhat-veiled reference to the Christ-invested authority that Paul holds and his willingness to use it.

13:9 ***For we are glad, when we are weak, / For we rejoice when we are weak:*** The conjunction γάρ (*gar*) marks a cause or reason for an action.[105] The verb χαίρω (*chairō*), "rejoice," denotes a state of happiness or well-being.[106]

For the verb ἀσθενέω (*astheneō*), "weak," see Translation Notes for 13:3 above. Here it references Paul's decorum of humility and graciousness, in imitation of that of the Savior (see 13:4), which he has used and hopes again to use in dealing with these people.

and ye are strong / but you are strong: The conjunction δέ (*de*), "but," marks a contrast between weakness and strength.[107] The adjective δύνατός (*dynatos*), "strong," refers to capability, competence, strength,[108] and here, conformance to gospel standards.

and this also we wish, even your perfection / Indeed, this is what we pray for: your inner strength: The demonstrative pronoun αὐτπός (*autos*), "certainly, indeed," acts as an intensive marker emphasizing its object.[109] The verb εὐχομαι (*euchomai*) can mean "to desire, to wish,"[110] though in the present context it is better understood as "to pray for."

---

101. BDAG, 42–43.
102. BDAG, 42.
103. Guthrie, *2 Corinthians,* 643.
104. BDAG, 1030–31.
105. BDAG, 189–90.
106. Louw-Nida, §25.125.
107. Louw-Nida, §89.124.
108. Louw-Nida, §§74.2, 4; BDAG, 264.
109. BDAG, 152–54.
110. Louw-Nida, §§25.6; 33.178; BDAG, 417.

The noun κατάρτισις (*katartisis*), "maturity, restoration, inner strength,"[111] denotes making something or someone "completely adequate or sufficient."[112] Context suggests that Paul is referring to the outcome of restoring the Corinthian Saints' relationship with him and Christ through excising iniquity from among them. The result of this exercise will be the inner strengthening of both the community and the individual as they mature as Christians.[113]

13:10 ***Therefore I write these things being absent / Therefore, I write these things when I am absent:*** The phrase διὰ τοῦτο (*dia touto*), "therefore," marks the reason or cause for an action stated in a previous section.[114] In this case, it refers to Paul's hope for the Saints' spiritual strength. The plural neuter adjective ταῦτα (*tauta*), "these things," refers to the harsh words Paul is writing to them.[115]

The verb ἄπειμι (*apeimi*), "be absent/away," [116] is found here as a circumstantial present participle with a temporal sense: "when I am away."

lest being present I should use sharpness / so that when I am present, I may not have to deal with you severely: The conjunction ἵνα (*hina*), "so that," marks the reason why an action is done. The verb πάρειμι (*pareimi*), "to be present," found here as a participle, is also used circumstantially in a temporal sense: "when I am present."

The verb χράομαι (*chraomai*), "to make use of, employ,"[117] is found here as an aorist subjunctive, the mood suggesting possibility only. The particle μή (*mē*), "not," negates the force of the verb and thus is rendered "may not have to deal with."

The adverb ἀποτόμως (*apotomōs*) means "severely, rigorously"[118] and looks to the kind of action Paul hopes not to have to take.

---

111. Only here in the corpus of the scriptures does this word appear. As a result, its exact nuance, as understood by Paul, is unclear. Even so, we can get close. The word group to which this noun belongs denotes such things as "to prepare, finish, complete, restore, perfect" and is used "related to Christian growth, whether in the context of problems that needed to be remedied, or in connection with training for service, or more generally to encourage spiritual maturity." *NID,* 1:410. For a study, see Gerhard Delling, "ἄρτιος, κατάρτισις," in *TDNT,* 1:475–76.

112. Louw-Nida, §75.5.

113. Delling, "ἄρτιος," *TDNT,* 1:476.

114. Wallace, *Greek Grammar,* 333.

115. Barrett, *Second Epistle,* 340; Furnish, *II Corinthians,* 574.

116. BDAG, 100.

117. BDAG, 1087–88.

118. BDAG, 124.

according to the power which the Lord hath given me to edification / according to the authority the Lord has given me for the purpose of building up: The preposition κατά (*kata*), in the present context, means "in accordance with"[119] and points specifically to the obligation that Jesus placed on Paul.

The noun ἐξουσία (*exousia*), "power, authority," can have a forensic force, denoting a judicial power that must be obeyed. This kind of authority can be delegated and in being so gives the receiver the right to rule and to judge.[120] In a religious context, it denotes divine power, whether expressed by Deity or an agent.[121]

On the noun οἰκοδομή (*oikodomē*), "construction," "edification, building up," see Translation Notes for 12:19.[122] Here we need note only that in a religious context it denotes spiritual edification and strengthening.[123] The preposition εἰς (*eis*), "to, toward," here has the sense of "for the purpose of."[124] As Paul noted in the previous chapter, his Christ-given charge and authority lie in building up the kingdom among the Gentiles.

and not to destruction / and not for tearing down: The noun καθαίρεσις (*kathairesis*) means "destruction by tearing down."[125] The particle οὐκ (*ouk*), "not," negates the act. Though Paul rightly held the power to correct, rebuke, and straiten the branches of the Church, that was not the primary mission the Lord assigned him, and therefore he is pleased if he does not have to do so.

Analysis and Summary

At this point (13:5), Paul turns the tables on his audience. Where some demanded he prove that Christ "speaks in him," he now demands—twice!—that the congregation examine themselves (πειράζω, *peirazō*). The object of that self-examination is to see if they are "in the faith." The articular noun shows that, in this context, faith is not a mere human response to or disposition of belief. Often, "for Paul, faith not only takes its orientation from the content of the Gospel, it is born of it. Indeed, faith's origin in the proclaimed word is of fundamental importance for Paul."[126] Here the Apostle

119. Louw-Nida, §89.8.
120. Louw-Nida, §§30.122; 37.35
121. Louw-Nida, §12.44. For a study, see Werner Foerster, "ἐξουσία," in *TDNT,* 2:562–74.
122. BDAG, 696–97.
123. BDAG, 696–97.
124. BDAG, 288–91.
125. BDAG, 487.
126. Seifrid, *Second Letter,* 480–81.

aligns with the Book of Mormon, wherein faith is a response to what one hears and is willing to act on by making and keeping covenants. Through that action, confirmation comes, and faith is rewarded (Alma 32:26–43). In the present context, however, Paul looks at the content of faith or, in other words, the system of belief held by (or that should be held by) the Christian community at large.[127]

To push his point, he asks a rhetorical question requiring a positive answer, "Or don't you realize [ἐπιγινώσκω, *epiginōskō*] that Jesus Christ is in you?" (13:5, NR). In no way could the members of his audience deny the reality of the living Spirit that had operated and continues to operate both among and in them. But Paul includes an ironic barb, "unless, of course, you fail the test." Such could happen only if they could not detect any action of the Spirit in their lives. Even though they lived in a less-than-ideal harmonious condition, through the grace of God they still enjoyed the amazing and palpable impact of the Spirit personally.[128] Indeed, it continually manifested itself in both public and private ways. To deny that such is the case is, for them, unthinkable. That being a fact, there is only one conclusion they can draw, as Paul notes in 13:6: the Apostle himself must also possess that same spirit. And why? Because it was he who initially brought the gospel with its attendant spiritual gifts to the Corinthians. Thus the positive result of the Corinthians' self-examination is proof of God's endorsement of Paul and his companions. As he notes in 13:6, he fully anticipates that such will be fully proven during his upcoming visit.

Though the apostle's expressed view of some of these people has been rather harsh, we see that he is actually motivated by his love for them. He can be patient with them because of his perspective on how evil works. From his point of view, evil rules in the unrejuvenated human soul and causes a person to do wrong even when it is not his or her deliberate intent (see Rom. 7:15–21; compare 2 Ne. 4:16–35). It expresses itself in malevolent acts, with the result that the sinner not only is separated from God but also comes under his severe judgment. In doing so, she or he experiences spiritual death rather than eternal life. Overcoming this evil nature by human desire or will alone is impossible (compare Mosiah 16:4–5; Alma 22:14; 34:9; 42:7–15). For that reason, the solution to the human problem

---

127. Paul never loses sight of faith as "belief in Christ" and the resurrection he wrought (1 Cor. 15:14, 17), but he does emphasize from time to time, as here, the corporate nature of faith, that is, the beliefs held by the Christian community at large.

128. Barnett, *Second Epistle*, 608.

cannot be found in human effort, no matter how hard one struggles. Paul witnesses that it can only be accomplished through Christ's victorious conquest of evil through the power of the cross and the Resurrection (Rom. 7:25; compare 2 Ne. 9:10; Mosiah 3:19; Alma 22:14; Hel. 14:15–17). Paul's admonitions to shun or lay aside evil must be seen in this context (Rom. 12:17, 21; 16:19; 1 Cor. 10:6; Col. 3:5; compare 1 Pet. 3:11). Human victory is possible only because Christ has stripped evil of its power. It is ultimately only through the force of justification and sanctification that evil is rooted out of the human breast, allowing goodness to reign (compare Mosiah 14:11; D&C 20:30–31; Moses 6:60). Thus "the one who is justified is in the sphere of influence" of the Redeemer, who has "conquered evil and gives the Spirit. Hence believers do not face the powers of evil without strength (Rom. 13:10; 1 Cor. 13:5; 2 Cor. 13:7)."[129]

In this light, it is easy to see why in 13:7 Paul opens his heart to the Corinthians, noting his sincere prayer in their behalf and why he makes it. His prayer "that you will do what is right" is balanced by his prayer "that you will do nothing wrong" (NR). Together they suggest that the rightness he hopes for is that they will accept his demands to expunge the evil from among them before he arrives.[130] He also assures them that there is nothing self-centered in his motive. He has no desire to prove he and his companions have passed the test of authenticity at the expense of his audience, even if it appears that the missionaries seem to fail the test.

But how would they appear to have failed the test (ἀδόκιμος, *adokimos*)? Some of his detractors have demanded proof that Christ speaks through the Apostle or, in other words, that he carries authentic apostolic authority. Paul assures them that his use of that authority against the recalcitrant will be the proof they demand (13:1–3). Even though he is most willing to make a very public and undeniable display of that power, he prefers that these people repent, even though it would mean he would not exhibit his authority, and hence he would appear to have failed that test. Though his enemies might view his lack of force as showing weakness, the true Saints will understand that in reality he is powerful. But Paul's ultimate concern is not with their perception of him but with the spiritual welfare of the branch as a whole as well as that of each individual.[131] As he has made clear in 12:19, the goal driving all he does is to build these people up.

---

129. *NID,* 2:600.

130. Martin, *2 Corinthians,* 680.

131. Martin, *2 Corinthians,* 679–80.

Thus in 13:8 he can proclaim that his whole motivation rests upon one thing: the truth. The former portion of this letter has made clear that his purpose is to openly proclaim the truth (4:2), which he had done throughout this ministry (6:7; 7:14; 12:6). By this means he has shown that the "truth of Christ" is in him (11:10) or, in other words, that what he teaches he has received from the Savior himself. His whole work, as he notes earlier in this letter, is to manifest the truth "by the open proclamation" through which "we commend ourselves to everyone's conscience in the sight of God" (4:2, NR). Indeed, truthful speech, as he notes, "is essential to his commendation as an apostle and agent of God (6:7)."[132] His words reveal his understanding that truth is found exclusively in the gospel of Christ Jesus. In it, when properly viewed, the Saint can see the saving response of the Father to human blindness, a blindness often caused by deception, either human or demonic (4:3–4; 11:3, 12–15).[133]

For this reason, all that Paul does is in support or to reinforce the end purposes of the gospel. So strong is his conviction of the truth that he cannot fight against it.[134] Even so, in the present context, "the truth" seems to point in but one direction: Paul's Christ-given authority and his ability to use it. Thus this sentence, though mild, stands as the Apostle's warning that he will not forsake his use of power if he finds it necessary.

However, as he notes in 13:9, it is not his use of power that will cause both him and his companions to rejoice. On the contrary, it is that they might appear to some to be weak. This causes him such delight because it means he will not have to negatively display his apostolic power. This is because these people have, as he asked, gotten rid of the evil among them either through repentance or expungement.[135] His words stress that his concern for their spiritual welfare outweighs by far any anxiety he might have over his personal reputation.[136] He highlights the degree to which this is true as he shares with them another item for which he prays: their spiritual strength (κατάρτισις, *katartisis*). "He wants them to move beyond the spiritual muddle caused by the interloping and false teachers and the Corinthians' bad, immoral choices. Then their community will be put in order and restored to a healthy progress in faith."[137]

---

132. Seifrid, *Second Letter,* 485.
133. Seifrid, *Second Letter,* 485.
134. Guthrie, *2 Corinthians,* 643.
135. Hughes, *Second Epistle,* 483.
136. Guthrie, *2 Corinthians,* 642.
137. Guthrie, *2 Corinthians,* 644.

In 13:10, Paul states clearly why he has spoken so harshly to these people (chaps. 10–13)—to clearly let them know his goal is to promote both repentance and spiritual strengthening. But behind his goal, he is offering them a chance to restore their relationship with him. If that happens, then his epistolary efforts will have been as effective as he desires, for he will not have to exercise the degree of harshness his letter both carries and threatens. Instead, he will be able to use his apostolic powers for the primary reason Christ gave them to him: to edify, build up, and strengthen the branches of the Church, not to tear down the people.[138]

Conclusion (13:11–13)

Greek Text

11 Λοιπόν, ἀδελφοί, χαίρετε, καταρτίζεσθε, παρακαλεῖσθε, τὸ αὐτὸ φρονεῖτε, εἰρηνεύετε, καὶ ὁ θεὸς τῆς ἀγάπης καὶ εἰρήνης ἔσται μεθ' ὑμῶν. 12 ἀσπάσασθε ἀλλήλους ἐν ἁγίῳ φιλήματι. ἀσπάζονται ὑμᾶς οἱ ἅγιοι πάντες. 13 ἡ χάρις τοῦ κυρίου Ἰησοῦ Χριστοῦ καὶ ἡ ἀγάπη τοῦ θεοῦ καὶ ἡ κοινωνία τοῦ ἁγίου πνεύματος μετὰ πάντων ὑμῶν. [SBLGNT]

King James Version

11 Finally, brethren, farewell. Be perfect, be of good comfort, be of one mind, live in peace; and the God of love and peace shall be with you. 12 Greet one another with an holy kiss. 13 All the saints salute you. 14 The grace of the Lord Jesus Christ, and the love of God, and the communion of the Holy Ghost, be with you all. Amen.

New Rendition

11 Finally, brothers and sisters, rejoice, mend your ways, be comforted, agree with one another, live in peace, and the God of love and peace will be with you. 12 Greet each other with a holy kiss. All the saints greet you. 13 May the grace of the Lord Jesus Christ and the love of God the Father and the companionship of the Holy Spirit be with all of you.

Translation Notes and Comments

13:11 ***Finally, brethren, farewell / Finally, brothers and sisters, rejoice:*** The adverb λοιπόν (*loipon*), "finally," signals that the conclusion of a subject is coming, but in this instance it carries the nuance of "otherwise" or

138. Martin, *2 Corinthians,* 683–85.

"beyond these matters."[139] On the plural noun ἀδελφοι (*adelphoi*), rendered "brothers and sisters," see Translation Notes for 1:8.

The verb χαίρω (*chairō*), found here as an imperative, means to "rejoice, be glad."[140] Though it is often used in the imperative mood as a simple warm greeting,[141] that is not the case here. Context gives two reasons: first, because in 13:9 Paul clearly uses it in the fuller sense of rejoicing; and second, because it is followed by four additional imperatives. In the present context, it carries the idea of taking great delight in something, but Paul does not say what.

Be perfect / mend your ways: The verb καταρτίζω (*katartizō*) means primarily to "put in order, . . . restore to a former condition, put to rights,"[142] with stress on the fullness of the job done. Thus the KJV translates it as "be perfect" in the sense of reaching not flawlessness but completeness. The verb, however, is found here as an imperative passive. As such, the voice forces it to take on the nuance of "complete" or "restore yourselves," or as we have rendered it, "mend your ways."[143]

be of good comfort / be comforted: The verb παρακαλέω (*parakaleō*) normally means "to urge strongly," thus to "exhort, encourage."[144] It is found here, however, as an imperative passive, the voice giving it the force of finding comfort either through a favorable change in circumstances or through positive words.[145]

be of one mind / agree with one another: The verb φρονέω (*phroneō*), to "think, form/hold an opinion," denotes the exercising of the mind, resulting in developing a position, attitude, or an opinion on a given matter.[146] It is found here as a plural imperative, thus imposing on these people the need to have the same mind—that is, to agree with one another.

live in peace: The verb εἰρηνεύω (*eirēneuō*), whether in the active voice or, as here, in the passive, means to "live in peace."[147] That it is in the imperative mood makes the sentence an admonition.

---

139. Seifrid, *Second Letter,* 487.

140. BDAG, 1074; Barnett, *Second Epistle,* 615.

141. Louw-Nida, §33.22, translates it as "hail, greetings," while BDAG, 1074, has the more broad "good day, welcome," and "glad to see you."

142. BDAG, 526.

143. BDAG, 526; Guthrie, *2 Corinthians,* 650.

144. BDAG, 764–65.

145. BDAG, 764–65.

146. BDAG, 1065–66; Louw-Nida, §§26.16; 31:1.

147. BDAG, 287.

and the God of love and peace shall be with you / and the God of love and peace will be with you: The conjunction καί (*kai*), "and," in this instance does not signal the last piece in a series but rather the result of responding to what has come before, in this case obedience to Paul's admonitions.[148]

In his promise, the Apostle focuses on two attributes of God. The noun ἀγάπη (*agapē*), "love," denotes a very deep, warm, and accepting affection[149] and more specifically looks to the motivational feelings of the Divine that causes God to act in behalf of his children. Noteworthy is that this is the only place in the Bible where the phrase "God of love" is found.[150]

The noun εἰρήνη (*eirēnē*), "peace," denotes not just a state of personal tranquility and well-being but also one of concord and harmony with others.[151] The word also hints at messianic salvation.

The verb εἰμί (*eimi*), "to be,"[152] is found here in the future tense (thus rendered "will be") and thereby marks a promise.

It is noteworthy that not these attributes but the One who possesses these attributes will be with these people. The reason such is the case is because, once they have purged out the iniquity among them, they will be in accord with the Father, the Son, and their Apostle.

13:12–14: The KJV and Greek texts differ in versification at this point. The Greek text combines 13:12 with 13:13 while the KJV separates them. As a result, KJV 13:14 is 13:13 in the Greek text, and we have followed this versification in the NR.

13:12 ***Greet one another with an holy kiss / Greet each other with a holy kiss:*** The verb ἀσπάζομαι (*aspozomai*), "to greet," denotes a warm exchange of welcome between parties.[153] The noun φίλημα (*philēma*) means "a kiss." It is modified by the adjective ἅγιος (*hagios*), "holy," thus guaranteeing its use as not only a sign of affection but also one of solemnity. It also assures all that the act does not nuance any impropriety.[154] The JST changes the word "kiss" to "salutation," thus making Paul's request conform more to western and modern practices.[155]

---

148. BDAG, 494–96.

149. BDAG, 6–7. For a study, see *NID,* 1:103–15.

150. In 1 John 4:8, 16, that Apostle notes that "God is love," thus, defining more the nature of his being that an attribute he has.

151. BDAG, 287–88.

152. Louw-Nida, §§13.1, 69.

153. BDAG, 144.

154. For a study, see Yingling, "Worship and Ritual Practices," 592–94.

155. Ogden and Skinner, *Verse by Verse,* 148, notes that the kiss was, among the ancient Jews, a form of salutation. Holzapfel and Wayment, *Making Sense,* 366, notes that it was

KJV 13:13; NR 13:12 *All the saints salute you / All the saints greet you:* The reference is likely to those in the branches of Macedonia from where the Apostle was writing.

KJV 13:14; NR 13:13 *The grace of the Lord Jesus Christ / May the grace of the Lord Jesus Christ:* Paul's desire again turns to a bright thread that runs through the tapestry of the whole epistle, the χάρις (*charis*), "grace of the Lord." Through this benediction, as is his wont, the Apostle again subtly reminds his audience of the place the Messiah, his Atonement, and his resultant power play in their salvation.

and the love of God: With this phrase, Paul mentions another bright thread that runs though his work. The noun ἀγάπη (*agapē*), "love," connected with God the Father, denotes that pure motivational force that stands behind all that he does in behalf of his children. The genitive case in which the noun "God" is found can be taken in one of two ways. It could be subjective, indicating the love given by God, or objective, meaning one's love for God. Given the context, the former seems to be the case because the Apostle is wishing them a gift from God.[156]

and the communion of the Holy Ghost, be with you all. Amen / and the companionship of the Holy Spirit be with all of you: The noun κοινωνία (*koinōnia*), "communion, fellowship," denotes a shared association of mutual interest.[157] The genitive case in which the noun "Holy Spirit" is found can be taken in two ways. As an objective generative, it points to the Saints' relationship with the Holy Ghost, and as a subjective genitive, it refers to having the presence of the Spirit dwell among and in them. Context suggests the latter.[158] The grammar makes an important if subtle theological point here. That a person can have a relationship with "the Holy Spirit" shows that the Spirit is not a "force" or "influence" but an actual person.[159]

The word "amen" is not in the Greek text but was added by the KJV translators.

---

more of an eastern Mediterranean custom, the West preferring the handshake. See also William Klassen, "The Sacred Kiss in the New Testament: An Example of Social Boundary Lines," *New Testament Studies* 39 (1993): 122–35.

The JST change of the Greek from "holy kiss" to "holy salutation" suggests that such a greeting could convey a special bond between participants. For an example, see D&C 88:119–20, 133–36.

156. Guthrie, *2 Corinthians,* 654.

157. BDAG, 552–53.

158. Guthrie, *2 Corinthians,* 654.

159. Barnett, *Second Epistle,* 619.

Analysis and Summary

Having expressed clearly in the previous section of his epistle his intent and purpose in writing, the Apostle now (13:11) brings the whole to a close. He does so, as he has done in other letters, by admonishing his audience to carry on in a certain way with a promise of what will happen if they do (1 Thes. 5:14–23; Philip. 4:4–7). His words suggest that he discernibly directed his comments to the particular circumstances of the church addressed.[160] That is certainly the case here.

He heads his list with the admonition to "rejoice" (χαίρω, *chairō*). Though his ministry has been plagued by suffering, rejection, and both mental and physical hardships, nonetheless he has experienced the joy that comes through the strength and grace that the gospel of Christ gives (1:24; 2:3; 6:10; 7:4, 13). He wants the Saints, who have suffered and still do suffer, to feel the same.[161]

Second, he admonishes them to "mend their ways" (καταρτίζω, *katartizō*). They desperately need to repair the damage that has been done to their relationship with God, Christ, Paul, and one another and restore the order demanded by a Christian community. Only in this way can they heal the breach between them, recover their spiritual, theological, and practical bearings, and find that unity in Christ that the Savior demands of his people.[162]

Third, he admonishes them to "be comforted" or "encouraged" (παρακαλέω, *parakaleō*). The reference is to what he has taught and admonished them though the course of this letter. His words suggest that he feels that they are fully capable of meeting the conditions he has set down and can therefore be heartened rather than discouraged by what he has said. Though he has been forced to use harsh words to get these people to move against the unrighteous among them, Paul's desired effect for his letter overall is that of comfort. Reading just chapters 10–13 most certainly would have left some, if not most, of his readers in distress, but taking the epistle as a whole, as Paul wishes, the Saints should realize that God is yet with them and that it is the Apostle's intent to let them know that, because of this, all can be regained.

---

160. For a study, see Jeffrey A. D. Weima, *Neglected Endings: The Significance of the Pauline Letter Closings,* Journal for the Study of the New Testament Supplement Series 101 (Sheffield, Eng.: JSOT Press, 1994).

161. Barnett, *Second Epistle,* 615–16.

162. Barnett, *Second Epistle,* 616.

Fourth, he admonishes them agree with one another (φρονέω, *phroneō*). The focus of his comment does not rule out individual opinion in matters of little consequence to the faith, but he does want them to be agreed on matters concerning faith and their expression of it. Paul's letter clearly shows areas of division where there should have been none. Examples include definitions of what constitutes spirituality (10:2–7), the nature of apostolic authority (11:1–12:14), the degree to which God's old covenant is overtaken by the new (3:3–18), and the improperness of continuing in a gentile lifestyle (6:16–7:1). In these matters there should have been no division, for as his letter has pointed out, the correct position on all such matters is clear and nonnegotiable.

Fifth, he admonishes them to live in peace (εἰρήνη, *eirēnē*). This admonition is closely related to and grows out of the one above. Doctrinal and policy disputes have ravaged the unity of the branches (12:20–13:2), but if they will just find unity in what they believe and their expressions of faith, they will also find accord in their dealings with one another.

On the basis of following these admonitions, the Apostle can assure them that "the God of love and peace" will be with them (13:11). The implications is that if they will but yield to Paul's demands, God will bestow upon them these heavenly attributes, and thus they will enjoy peace and warm association with both him and one another.

In 13:12–14, Paul closes his letter using the valedictory formula followed within both the Christian and larger Greco-Roman communities, but with some variance. The command to "greet" others is common. It denotes the extension of a warm welcome and recognition. Paul, however, denotes just how such a greeting was to be given: with a holy kiss. There is little known about this greeting ritual, which is a bit surprising since it seems to have been a central practice among various branches of the Church and endorsed by Paul (1 Cor. 16:20; 1 Thes. 5:26). Though it is not certain, it is likely that such a kiss was not mouth to mouth but mouth to cheek. The gesture was a show of respect and honor, often used by disciples to honor their teachers,[163] and was also designed to, ideally, quell contention and bring unity among the members. Further, in a society rife with the potentially harsh social hierarchies of the patron/client relationship, this Christian act of love, properly motivated, could transcend these social boundaries and work toward establishing a family of equals.[164]

---

163. Gustav Stälin, "The Kiss in the New Testament," in *TDNT,* 9:138–41. The hypocrisy of Judas's kiss of the Lord is clearly evident.

164. Yingling, "Worship and Ritual," 592–94.

The Apostle closes with a heartfelt prayer that, though brief, is very theologically profound and imposing.[165] It reflects the experience that being a Saint allows on both the individual and collective levels. It is on these levels that the grace of Christ acts to lift, purify, and enable.[166] By apprehending this grace, Saints feel and enjoy the love of God (8:9; Rom. 5:5). Being the "God of love" (11:13), he is also the one who loves his children (compare Rom. 9:25) and provides mercy, comfort, and resurrected life (1:3; 9–10). By further apprehending this grace, Saints gain the companionship of the Holy Ghost with all its powers, gifts, and blessings.[167]

Significantly, the benediction shows Paul's understanding of the Godhead as composed of three distinct individuals. There is the "God of love and peace," who is also the Father of his Son, the Lord Jesus Christ from whom mercy flows. Finally, there is the Holy Spirit, with whom fellowship can be achieved, thus showing that such is neither a "force" nor an "influence" but an actual personage.[168]

Noteworthy is that here, at end of his epistle, Paul once again enjoins grace and peace. His wont is to open his epistles with the apostolic pronouncement of "grace and peace" and often to close with the inverted echo "peace and grace" of that desire. Here he follows his admonition that his audience live in peace with a reference to the "grace of Christ." In this way, he "envelops the letter within the Gospel, signaling that all that he has said to the church in addressing its particular needs is nothing other than an expression of the Gospel."[169] As he has made clear, his life reflects that of his Lord, who, though he took upon himself the weakness of humanity, overcame it through the power of God.[170] Paul is doing the same and asks the Saints to follow suit, for therein lies the power that grows out of weakness, if they will let it.

It would be nice to know how effective Paul's letter turned out to be. History, unfortunately, has not left anything but vague hints that it was successful, leading to a pleasant and fruitful visit. These hints are based

---

165. See Furnish, *II Corinthians,* 587; and Fee, *God's Empowering Presence,* 363.

166. This part of Paul's benediction is not unique. For example, see 1 Cor. 16:23; Gal. 6:18; and 1 Thes. 5:28.

167. Barnett, *Second Epistle,* 618.

168. Barnett, *Second Epistle,* 619.

169. Seifrid, *Second Letter,* 490.

170. On one occasion, Joseph Smith noted that "none ever were perfect but Jesus; and why was he perfect? because he was the son of God, and had the fullness of the Spirit, and greater power than any man." "To those of our readers who reside at remote distances . . . ," *Times and Seasons* 2 (June 1, 1841): 429–30.

on the assumption that the apostle stayed in Corinth during the three-month period he was in Greece (Acts 20:2–3) and there wrote his epistle to the Romans. That work gives evidence that the collection from the area for the Jerusalem poor had been completed (Rom. 15:26–27), a task Paul would have finalized before going back to the east. If that is the case, then his comments in Romans 15:30–31 apply. Though he expresses some apprehension in these verses, it is not for the present but the future. His personal circumstances seem to be okay at the time as he writes from Corinth. Further, he tells his Roman readers that he plans to visit them before pushing on westward to Spain (Rom. 15:24, 28). Such a move seems unreasonable if the Church in Corinth were still in disarray, since it would no longer serve as his western anchor.[171] Unfortunately, these hints are not conclusive. We must note, however, that at some point the Corinthian church definitely turned away from Paul, reverting back to its old ways.[172]

The force of the epistle can, however, warn others of the danger of disunity, engaging in the ways of the world, discounting Church doctrine, and leaving behind apostolic authority. It can also reinforce the idea that power comes through unity, following priesthood authority, and ascribing to and living Church doctrine. By these means, the way is opened for the powers of the three members of the Godhead to flow into one's life, as Paul declares, to lift, empower, bless, and save.

171. Harris, *Second Epistle,* 404–5.

172. This is clearly seen in the writing of Clement, Bishop of Rome, who wrote to the unruly branch in AD 96. See his epistle *1 Clement,* NTS Library, accessed November 27, 2021, http://ntslibrary.com/PDF%20Books/First%20Epistle%20of%20Clement%20to%20the%20Corinthians.pdf.

Selected Bibliography

Abernathy, David. "Paul's Thorn in the Flesh: A Messenger of Satan?" *Neotestamentica* 35, nos. 1–2 (2001): 69–79.

Aland, Kurt, and Barbara Aland. *The Text of the New Testament: An Introduction to the Critical Editions and to the Theory and Practice of Modern Textual Criticism.* 2nd ed. Trans. Erroll F. Rhodes. Grand Rapids, Mich.: Eerdmans; Leiden, Neth.: E. J. Brill, 1995.

Andersen, Neil L. "It's a Miracle." *Ensign* 43, no. 5 (May 2013): 77–80.

Anderson, Richard Lloyd. *Understanding Paul.* Salt Lake City: Deseret Book, 1983.

Andrus, Hyrum L. *God, Man, and the Universe.* Salt Lake City: Deseret Book, 1968.

Ascough, Richard S. "The Completion of a Religious Duty: The Background to 2 Corinthians 8.1–15." *New Testament Studies* 42, no. 4 (1996): 584–99.

Baird, William. "Letters of Recommendation: A Study of II Cor 3 1–3." *Journal of Biblical Literature* 80, no. 2 (June 1961): 166–72.

Baker, William R. "Did the Glory of Moses' Face Fade?: A Reexamination of καταργέω in 2 Corinthians 3:7–18." *Bulletin for Biblical Research* 10, no. 1 (2000): 1–15.

Banks, Robert. *Paul's Idea of Community: The Early House Churches in Their Historical Setting.* Peabody, Mass.: Hendrickson, 1994.

Barclay, John M. G. "Paul, Philemon, and the Dilemma of Christian Slave-Ownership." *New Testament Studies* 37, no. 2 (1991): 161–86.

Barnett, Paul. *The Second Epistle to the Corinthians.* Grand Rapids, Mich.: William B. Eerdmans, 1997.

Barré, M. L. "Qumran and the 'Weakness' of Paul." *Catholic Biblical Quarterly* 42, no. 2 (April 1980): 216–27.

Barrett, C. K. *A Commentary on the Second Epistle to the Corinthians.* London: Adam and Charles Black, 1973.

———. *Essays on Paul.* Philadelphia: Westminster Press, 1982.

———. "New Testament Eschatology." *Scottish Journal of Theology* 6, no. 2 (1953): 225–43.

Barrett, Matthew. "What Is So New about the New Covenant?: Exploring the Contours of Paul's New Covenant Theology in 2 Corinthians 3." *Southern Baptist Journal of Theology* 19, no. 3 (Fall 2015): 61–96.

Bauckham, Richard. *God Crucified: Monotheism and Christology in the New Testament.* Grand Rapids, Mich.: William B. Eerdmans, 1999.

———. *Jesus and the God of Israel:* God Crucified *and Other Studies on the New Testament's Christology of Divine Identity.* Grand Rapids, Mich.: William B. Eerdmans, 2009.

Beale, G. K. "The Old Testament Background of Reconciliation in 2 Corinthians 5–7 and Its Bearing on the Literary Problems of 2 Corinthians 6:14–7:1." *New Testament Studies* 35, no. 4 (1989): 550–81.

Bednar, David A. "Converted unto the Lord." *Ensign* 42, no. 11 (November 2012): 106–9.

———. "Exceeding Great and Precious Promises." *Ensign* 47, no. 11 (November 2017): 90–93.

———. "Ye Must Be Born Again." *Ensign* 37, no. 5 (May 2007): 19–22.

Belleville, Linda L. "A Letter of Apologetic Self-Commendation: 2 Corinthians 1:8–7:16." *Novum Testamentum* 31, no. 2 (1989):142–63.

Benson, Ezra Taft. In *Annual Conference of The Church of Jesus Christ of Latter-day Saints,* 109–14. Salt Lake City: The Church of Jesus Christ of Latter-day Saints, 1963.

———. "Prepare Yourselves for the Great Day of the Lord." Devotional, Brigham Young University, April 14, 1981. Provo, Utah. Audio recording and transcript. https://speeches.byu.edu/talks/ezra-taft-benson/prepare-great-day-lord/.

Benz, Ernst W. "Imago Dei: Man in the Image of God." In *Reflections on Mormonism: Judeo-Christian Parallels,* ed. Truman G. Madsen, 201–21. Provo, Utah: Religious Studies Center, Brigham Young University, 1978.

Bernard, J. H. "The Second Epistle to the Corinthians." In *The Expositors Greek Testament.* Ed. W. Robertson Nicoll. Grand Rapids, Mich.: Wm. B. Eerdmans, 1980.

Berrett, William E. *Blessed Are They Who Come unto Me.* Provo, Utah: Ensign, 1979.

Betz, Hans Dieter. *2 Corinthians 8 and 9: A Commentary on Two Administrative Letters of the Apostle Paul.* Ed. George W. MacRae. Hermenia. Philadelphia: Fortress Press, 1985.

Bieringer, Reimund, and Jan Lambrecht. *Studies on 2 Corinthians.* Brussels: Louven University Press, 1994.

Black, David Alan. *Paul, Apostle of Weakness: Astheneia and Its Cognates in the Pauline Literature.* New York: Peter Lang, 1984.

Blass, F., and A. Debrunner. *A Grammar of the New Testament and Other Early Christian Literature.* Trans. and ed. Robert W. Funk. Chicago: University of Chicago Press, 1961. Cited as BDF.

Blomberg, Craig. "The Structure of 2 Corinthians 1–7." *Criswell Theological Review* 4, no. 1 (1989): 3–20.

Botterweck, G. Johannes, Helmer Ringgren, and Heinz-Josef Fabry, eds. *Theological Dictionary of the Old Testament.* Trans. David E. Green. 15 vols. Grand Rapids, Mich.: Wm. B. Eerdmans, 2006.

Bowens, Lisa M. "Investigating the Apocalyptic Texture of Paul's Martial Imagery in 2 Corinthians 4–6." *Journal for the Study of the New Testament* 39, no. 1 (September 2016): 3–15.

Brakke, David. *The Gnostics: Myth, Ritual, and Diversity in Early Christianity.* Cambridge, Mass.: Harvard University Press, 2010.

Bray, Gerald, ed. *1–2 Corinthians.* Vol. 7 of Ancient Christian Commentary on Scripture, New Testament. Downers Grove, Ill.: InterVarsity Press, 1999.

Brink, Laurie. "From Wrongdoer to New Creation: Reconciliation in 2 Corinthians." *Interpretation: A Journal of Bible and Theology* 71, no. 3 (2017): 298–309.

———. "A General's Exhortation to His Troops: Paul's Military Rhetoric in 2 Cor 10:1–11 [Part 1]." *Biblische Zeitschrift* 49, no. 2 (2005): 191–201.

Briones, David. "Mutual Brokers of Grace: A Study in 2 Corinthians 1.3–11." *New Testament Studies* 56, no. 4 (October 2010): 536–56.

Brown, Colin. *Dictionary of New International Theology.* 4 vols. Grand Rapids, Mich.: Zondervan, 1986.

Brown, Francis, S. R. Driver, and Charles A. Briggs. *A Hebrew and English Lexicon of the Old Testament.* Corrected ed. Oxford: Clarendon Press, 1976. Cited as BDB.

Brown, Victor L. In *Official Report of the One Hundred Thirty-Sixth Annual General Conference of The Church of Jesus Christ of Latter-day Saints,* 21–23. Salt Lake City: The Church of Jesus Christ of Latter-day Saints, 1966.

Bruce, F. F. *The Acts of the Apostles: Greek Text with Introduction and Commentary.* 3rd rev. ed. Grand Rapids, Mich.: William B. Eerdmans, 1990.

———. *1 and 2 Corinthians.* Grand Rapids, Mich.: Wm. B. Eerdmans, 1971.

———. *New International Biblical Commentary: Philippians.* Peabody, Mass.: Hendrickson Publishers, 1989.

Buchanan, George Wesley. "Jesus and the Upper Class." *Novum Testamentum* 7, no. 3 (1964–65): 195–209.

Budge, E. A. "Paul's Boasting in Relation to Contemporary Professional Practice." *Australian Biblical Review* 16 (1968): 37–50.

Bultmann, Rudolf. *The Second Letter to the Corinthians.* Minneapolis: Augsburg, 1985.

Callister, Tad R. "The Book of Mormon—a Book from God." *Ensign* 41, no. 11 (November 2011): 74–76.

Carlson, Stephen C. "On Paul's Second Visit to Corinth: Πάλιν, Parsing, and Presupposition in 2 Corinthians 2:1." *Journal of Biblical Literature* 135, no. 3 (2016): 597–615.

Casson, Lionel. *Travel in the Ancient World.* Toronto: Hakkert, 1974.

Choi, Sungho. *The Messianic Kingship of Jesus: A Study of Christology and Redemptive History in Matthew's Gospel with Special Reference to the Royal-Enthronement Psalms.* Eugene, Ore.: Wipf and Stock, 2011.

Chow, John K. *Patronage and Power: A Study of Social Networks in Corinth.* Sheffield, Eng.: JSOT Press 1992.

Christofferson, D. Todd. "The Power of Covenants." *Ensign* 39, no. 5 (May 2009): 19–23.

Clark, J. Reuben. *Behold the Lamb of God.* Salt Lake City: Deseret Book, 1962.

Cockerill, Garth Lee. *The Epistle to the Hebrews.* Grand Rapids, Mich.: William B. Eerdmans, 2012.

Collins, John N. *Diakonia: Re-interpreting the Ancient Sources.* New York: Oxford University Press, 1990.

Cover, Michael. *Lifting the Veil: 2 Corinthians 3:7–18 in Light of Jewish Homiletic and Commentary Traditions.* Berlin: de Gruyter, 2015.

Craddock, Fred B. "The Poverty of Christ: An Investigation of II Corinthians 8:9." *Interpretation* 22, no. 2 (January 1968): 158–70.

Cullmann, Oscar. *Christ and Time: The Primitive Christian Conception of Time and History.* Trans. Floyd V. Filson. Philadelphia: Westminster Press, 1950.

———. *Immortality of the Soul or Resurrection of the Dead?: A Witness of the New Testament.* London: Epworth Press, 1964. Reprint, Eugene, Oreg.: Wipf and Stock, 2000.

Cunningham, Lawrence S. *The Meaning of Saints.* San Francisco: Harper and Row, 1980.

Dahl, Larry E., and Charles D. Tate Jr., eds. *The Lectures on Faith in Historical Perspective.* Salt Lake City: Deseret Book, 1990. Reprint, 2014.

Danker, Frederick William, ed. *A Greek-English Lexicon of the New Testament and Other Early Christian Literature.* 3rd ed. Chicago: University of Chicago Press, 2000. Cited as BDAG.

Deissmann, G. Adolf. *Bible Studies: Contributions Chiefly from Papyri and Inscriptions to the History of the Language, the Literature, and the Religion of Hellenistic Judaism and Primitive Christianity.* Trans. Alexander Grieve. Peabody, Mass.: Hendrickson, 1988.

———. *Light from the Ancient Near East: The New Testament Illustrated by Recently Discovered Texts of the Graeco-Roman World.* Trans. Lionel R. M. Strachan. Grand Rapids, Mich.: Baker Book House, 1978.

Derrett, J. D. M. "2 Corinthians 6:14ff: A Midrash on Deuteronomy 22:10." *Biblica* 52, no. 2 (1978): 231–50.

Derrick, Royden G. "The Beatitudes and Our Perfection." *Ensign* 7, no. 5 (May 1977): 58.

Dewey, Arthur J. "A Matter of Honor: A Social-Historical Analysis of 2 Corinthians 10." *Harvard Theological Review* 78, nos. 1–2 (April 1985): 209–17.

Dillon, John, and Tania Gergel. *Greek Sophists.* New York: Penguin Classics, 2003.

Donahoe, Kate C. "From Self-Praise to Self-Boasting: Paul's Unmasking of the Conflicting Rhetorico-linguistic Phenomena in 1 Corinthians." PhD thesis, University of St Andrews, 2007. http://hdl.handle.net/10023/493.

Douglas, Mary. *Thinking in Circles: An Essay on Ring Composition.* New Haven, Conn.: Yale University Press, 2007.

Downs, David J. *The Offering of the Gentiles: Paul's Collection for Jerusalem in Its Chronological, Cultural, and Cultic Contexts.* Tübingen: Mohr Siebeck, 2008.

Draper, Richard D. "The Earliest New Testament." In *The New Testament and How It Came to Be.* Ed. Kent P. Jackson and Frank F. Judd Jr. The 35th Annual Sidney B. Sperry Symposium. Salt Lake City: Deseret Book, 2006.

———. "Light, Truth, and Grace: Three Themes of Salvation." In *Sperry Symposium Classics: The Doctrine and Covenants,* ed. Craig K. Manscill, 234–47. Provo, Utah: Religious Studies Center, Brigham Young University, 2004.

Draper, Richard D., and Michael D. Rhodes. *Epistle to the Hebrews.* BYU New Testament Commentary. Provo, Utah: BYU Studies, 2019.

———. *Paul's First Letter to the Corinthians.* BYU New Testament Commentary. Provo, Utah: BYU Studies, 2017.

Duff, Paul Brooks. "Metaphor, Motif, and Meaning: The Rhetorical Strategy behind the Image 'Led in Triumph' in 2 Corinthians 2:14." *Catholic Biblical Quarterly* 53, no. 1 (1991): 79–92.

Dumbrell, William J. "The Newness of the New Covenant: The Logic of the Argument in 2 Corinthians 3." *Reformed Theological Review* 61, no. 2 (August 2002): 61–84.

Dunn, James D. G. "'The Letter Kills, but the Spirit Gives Life' (2 Cor. 3:6)." *Pneuma* 35, no. 2 (2013): 163–79.

Ehrensperger, Kathy. "Paul, His People, and Racial Terminology." *Journal of Early Christian History* 3, no. 1 (2013): 17–32.

Ellis, E. Earle. *Paul's Use of the Old Testament.* Grand Rapids, Mich.: Wm. B. Eerdmans, 1957. Reprint, Eugene, Ore.: Wipf and Stock, 2003.

———. *Prophecy and Hermeneutic in Earl Christianity: New Testament Essays.* Tübingen, Ger.: J. C. B. Mohr (Paul Siebeck), 1978.

Engberg-Pedersen, Troels. "The Unity of 2 Corinthians as Reflected in the Account of Paul's and Titus' Travels between Ephesus, Macedonia, and Corinth and the Theology of 2:14–7:4." Paper presented at the Society of Biblical Literature Annual Meeting, San Francisco, California, November 19, 2011.

Engels, Donald W. *Roman Corinth: An Alternative Model for the Classical City.* Chicago: University of Chicago, 1990.

Eubank, Nathan. "Justice Endures Forever: Paul's Grammar of Generosity." *Journal for the Study of Paul and His Letters* 5, no. 2 (Fall 2015): 169–87.

Eyring, Henry B. "Finding Safety in Counsel." *Ensign* 27, no. 5 (May 1997): 25.

Fallon, Francis T. *2 Corinthians.* Wilmington, Del.: Michael Glazier, 1980.

Faulring, Scott H., Kent P. Jackson, and Robert J. Matthews, eds. *Joseph Smith's New Translation of the Bible: Original Manuscripts.* Provo, Utah: Religious Studies Center, Brigham Young University, 2004.

Faust, James E. "The Great Imitator." *Ensign* 17, no. 11 (November 1987): 33–36.

———. "Standing in Holy Places." *Ensign* 35, no. 5 (May 2005): 62–68.

———. "The Weightier Matters of the Law: Judgment, Mercy, and Faith." *Ensign* 27, no. 11 (November 1997): 53–54, 59.

Fee, Gordon D. "*Χαρίσ* in II Corinthians 1:15: Apostolic Parousia and Paul-Corinthian Chronology." *New Testament Studies* 24 (1978): 533–38.

———. *The First Epistle to the Corinthians.* The New International Commentary on the New Testament. Grand Rapids, Mich.: Wm B. Eerdmans, 1987.

———. *God's Empowering Presence: The Holy Spirt in the Letters of Paul.* Peabody, Mass.: Hendrickson, 1994.

———. "II Corinthians VI.14–VII.1 and Food Offered to Idols." *New Testament Studies* 23 (1977): 140–61.

Fitzgerald, John T. *Cracks in an Earthen Vessel: An Examination of the Catalogues of Hardships in the Corinthian Correspondence.* Atlanta: Scholars Press, 1988.

Fitzmyer, Joseph A. *First Corinthians: A New Translation with Introduction and Commentary.* Anchor Yale Bible. New Haven, Conn.: Yale University Press, 2008.

Forbes, Christopher. "Comparison, Self-Praise, and Irony: Paul's Boasting and the Conventions of Hellenistic Rhetoric." *New Testament Studies* 32, no. 1 (1986): 1–30.

Ford, David F. "The Economy of God: Exploring a Metaphor." In *Meaning and Truth in 2 Corinthians,* ed. Frances Young and David F. Ford, 166–85. London: SPCK, 1987.

Frederick, Nicolas J., and Frank F. Judd Jr. "The Revelation of Jesus Christ to Paul: Presenting a Deeper, Full Christology." In *Thou Art the Christ, the Son of the Living God: The Person and Work of Jesus in the New Testament,* ed. Eric D. Huntsman, Lincoln H. Blumell, and Tyler J. Griffin, 216–43. Provo, Utah: Religious Studies Center, Brigham Young University; Salt Lake City: Deseret Book, 2018.

Freedman, David Noel, ed. *The Anchor Bible Dictionary.* 6 vols. New York: Doubleday, 1992. Cited as *ABD.*

Freeman, James M. *Manners and Customs of the Bible.* Plainfield, N.J.: Logos International, 1972.

Fuller, R. M. "Rewards." In *Dictionary of Paul and His Letters,* ed. Gerald F. Hawthorne, Ralph P. Martin, and Daniel G. Reid, 819–20. Downers Grove, Ill.: InterVarsity Press, 1993.

Furnish, Victor Paul. "Corinth in Paul's Time: What Can Archeology Tell Us?" *Biblical Archeological Review* 14, no. 3 (May–June 1988): 14–27.

———. *II Corinthians.* Vol. 32A of Anchor Bible. Garden City, N.Y.: Doubleday, 1984.

Garland, David E. *2 Corinthians.* Vol. 29 of New American Commentary. Nashville: Broadman and Holman, 1999.

Georgi, Dieter. *Remembering the Poor: The History of Paul's Collection for Jerusalem.* Nashville: Abingdon Press, 1992.

Gignilliat, Mark. "2 Corinthians 6:2: Paul's Eschatological 'Now' and Hermeneutical Investigation." *Westminster Theological Journal* 67, no. 1 (2005): 147–61.

Gillman, John. "A Thematic Comparison: 1 Corinthians 15:50–57 and 2 Corinthians 5:1–5." *Journal of Biblical Studies* 107 (1988): 439–54.

Greenwood, David. "The Lord Is the Spirit: Some Considerations of 2 Cor 3: 17." *Catholic Biblical Quarterly* 34, no. 4 (October 1972): 467–72.

Grey, Matthew J. "'A Slave of Christ Jesus': Ancient Slavery as a Biblical Metaphor for Salvation." In *Selections from the Religious Education Student Symposium 2003,* 81–100. Provo, Utah: Religious Studies Center, Brigham Young University, 2003.

Griffin, Bruce W. "The Paleographical Dating of P-46." Paper delivered at the Society of Biblical Literature conference, New Orleans, November 1996. http://biblical-data.org/P-46%20Oct%201997.pdf.

Griffith, Gary Webster. "Abounding in Generosity: A Study of *Chari*s in 2 Corinthians 8–9." PhD diss., Durham University, 2005. http://etheses.dur.ac.uk/1760/1/1760.pdf.

Guthrie, George H. "Καταργέω and the People of the Shining Face (2 Corinthians 3:7–18)." *Southern Baptist Journal of Theology* 19, no. 3 (Fall 2015): 41–60.

———. "Paul's Triumphal Procession Imagery (2 Cor 2.14–16a): Neglected Points of Background." *New Testament Studies* 61, no. 1 (2015): 79–91.

———. *2 Corinthians.* Grand Rapids, Mich.: Baker Academic, 2015.

Hafemann, Scott J. *Paul, Moses, and the History of Israel: The Letter/Spirit Contrast and the Argument from Scripture in 2 Corinthians 3.* Eugene, Oreg.: Wipf and Stock, 2008.

———. *2 Corinthians.* NIV Application Commentary. Grand Rapids, Mich.: Zondervan, 2000.

———. "'Self-Commendation' and Apostolic Legitimacy in 2 Corinthians: A Pauline Dialectic?" *New Testament Studies* 36, no. 1 (January 1990): 66–88.

———. *Suffering and Ministry in the Spirit: Paul's Defense of His Ministry in II Corinthians 2:14–3:3.* Grand Rapids, Mich.: William B. Eerdmans, 1990.

Hales, Robert D. "Preserving Agency, Protecting Religious Freedom." *Ensign* 45, no. 5 (May 2015): 111–13.

Hall, David R. *The Unity of the Corinthian Correspondence.* London: T&T Clark, 2003.

Hamilton, James M., Jr. *God's Glory in Salvation through Judgment: A Biblical Theology.* Wheaton, Ill.: Crossway, 2010.

Hanson, Anthony Tyrrell. *Jesus Christ in the Old Testament.* London: SPCK, 1965.

Hardy, C. Brian. "Paul: Personal Disclosures through His Epistles." In *A Symposium on the New Testament: August 14, 15, 16, 1980, Brigham Young University, Provo, Utah,* 88–90. Salt Lake City: The Church of Jesus Christ of Latter-day Saints, [1980].

Harris, Murray J. *The Second Epistle to the Corinthians: A Commentary on the Greek Text.* Grand Rapids, Mich.: William B. Eerdmans, 2005.

Harrison, James R. *Paul's Language of Grace in Its Graeco-Roman Context.* Tübingen, Ger.: Mohr Siebeck, 2003.

Hatch, Gary Layne. "Paul among the Rhetoricians: A Model for Proclaiming Christ." In *The Apostle Paul, His Life and His Testimony: The 1994 Sperry Symposium on the New Testament,* ed. Paul Y. Hoskisson, 62–78. Salt Lake City: Deseret Book, 1994.

Hay, David M. "The Shaping of Theology in 2 Corinthians: Convictions, Doubts, Warrants." *Society of Biblical Literature 1990 Seminar Papers,* ed. D. J. Lull, 257–72. Atlanta: Scholars Press, 1990.

Hays, Richard B. *Echoes in Scripture in the Letters of Paul.* New Haven, Conn.: Yale University Press, 1989.

Hemer, C. J. "A Note on 2 Corinthians 1:9." *Tyndale Bulletin* 23 (1972): 103–7.

Hendry, G. S. "ἡ γὰρ ἀγάπη τοῦ Χριστοῦ συνέχει ἡμᾶς—2 Corinthians v. 14." *Expository Times* 59, no. 3 (December 1947): 82.

Hinkley, Gordon B. "Mormon Should Mean 'More Good.'" *Ensign* 20, no. 11 (November 1990): 51–54.

———. "To Men of the Priesthood." *Ensign* 32, no. 11 (November 2002): 56–59.

"History, 1838–1856, Volume B-1 [1 September 1834–2 November 1838]." Joseph Smith Papers. Accessed November 17, 2022. https://www.josephsmithpapers.org/paper-summary/history-1838-1856-volume-b-1-1-september-1834-2-november-1838/.

"History, 1838–1856, Volume C-1 [2 November 1838–31 July 1842]." Joseph Smith Papers. Accessed November 17, 2022. https://www.josephsmithpapers.org/paper-summary/history-1838-1856-volume-c-1-2-november-1838-31-july-1842/.

"History, 1838–1856, Volume D-1 [1 August 1842–1 July 1843]." Joseph Smith Papers. Accessed November 17, 2022. http://www.josephsmithpapers.org/paper-summary/history-1838-1856-volume-d-1-1-august-1842-1-july-1843/.

Hoad, John. "Some New Testament References to Isaiah 53." *Expository Times* 68, no. 8 (May 1957): 254–55.

Holmberg, Bengt. *Paul and Power: The Structure of Authority in the Primitive Church as Reflected in the Pauline Epistles.* Philadelphia: Fortress Press, 1980.

Holzapfel, Richard Neitzel, and Thomas A. Wayment. *Making Sense of the New Testament: Timely Insights and Timeless Messages.* Salt Lake City: Deseret Book, 2010.

Hopkins, Keith. *Conquerors and Slaves.* Vol. 1 of Sociological Studies in Roman History. Cambridge: Cambridge University Press, 1978.

Horrell, David. "Paul's Collection: Resources for a Materialist Theology." *Epworth Review* 22, no. 2 (1995): 74–83.

Hubbard, Moyer V. "Was Paul Out of His Mind?: Re-reading 2 Corinthians 5:13." *Journal for the Study of the New Testament* 70 (1998): 39–64.

Hughes, Philip Edgcumbe. *Paul's Second Epistle to the Corinthians: The English Text with Introduction and Notes.* Grand Rapids, Mich.: Wm. B. Eerdmans, 1962.

Huntsman, Eric D. "The Occasional Nature, Composition, and Structure of Paul's Letters." In *How the New Testament Came to Be: The 35th Annual Sidney B. Sperry Symposium,* ed. Kent P. Jackson and Frank F. Judd Jr., 190–207. Provo, Utah: Religious Studies Center, Brigham Young University; Salt Lake City: Deseret Book, 2006.

Hurtado, Larry W. *One God, One Lord: Early Christian Devotion and Ancient Jewish Monothesim.* 2nd ed. Edinburgh: T&T Clark, 1998.

Instone-Brewer, David. "The Eighteen Benedictions and the *Minim* before 70 CE." *Journal of Theological Studies* 54 (April 2003): 25–44.

Jervell, Jacob. "The Signs of an Apostle: Paul's Miracles." Trans. Roy A. Harrisville. In *The Unknown Paul: Essays on Luke-Acts and Early Christian History,* 77–95. Minneapolis: Augsburg Publishing, 1984.

Jewett, Robert. *Paul's Anthropological Terms: A Study of Their Use in Conflict Settings.* Leiden, Neth.: E. J. Brill, 1971.

Johnson, Luke Timothy. *Hebrews: A Commentary.* Louisville: Westminster John Knox Press, 2006.

Jones, Ivor H. *The Contemporary Cross: A Study for Passiontide—a Theme and Four Biblical Variations.* London: Epworth, 1973.

Jordaan, Gert J. C. "A Hypothesis for the Composition History of Paul's Second Letter to the Corinthians." *In die Skriflig* 48, no. 2 (2014): 1–9.

Joubert, Stephan J. "Behind the Mask of Rhetoric: 2 Corinthians 8 and the Inter-textual Relations between Paul and the Corinthians." *Neotestamentica* 26, no. 1 (1992): 101–12.

———. "Χαρισ in Paul: An Investigation into the Apostle's "Performative" Application of the Language of *Grace* within the Framework of His

Theological Reflection on the Event/Process of Salvation." In *Salvation in the New Testament: Perspectives on Soteriology,* ed. Jan G. van der Watt, 187–211. Leiden, Neth.: Brill, 2005.

———. "'Walking the Talk': Paul's Authority in Motion in 2 Corinthians 10–13." *In die Skriflig* 49, no. 2 (2015): art. #1899. https://doi.org/10.4102/ids.v49i2.1899.

Journal of Discourses. 26 vols. London: Latter-day Saints Book Depot, 1854–86.

Judge, E. A. "Paul's Boasting in Relation to Contemporary Professional Practice." *Australian Biblical Review* 16 (1968): 37–50. Reprinted in *Social Distinctives of the Christians in the First Century: Pivotal Essays by E. A. Judge,* ed. David M. Scholer, 57–71. Peabody, Mass.: Hendrickson Publishers, 2008.

———. "The Social Identity of the First Christians: A Question of Method in Religious History." *Journal of Religious History* 11, no. 2 (1980): 201–17.

Kang, Bo Young. *Heralds and Community: An Enquiry into Paul's Concept of Mission and Its Indebtedness to the Jesus-Tradition.* Carlisle, U.K.: Langham Monographs, 2016.

Kaplan, Jonathan. "Comfort, O Comfort, Corinth: Grief and Comfort in 2 Corinthians 7:5–13a." *Harvard Theological Review* 104, no. 4 (2011): 433–45.

Kautzsch, E., ed. *Gesenius' Hebrew Grammar.* 2nd ed. London: Oxford University Press, 1910.

Keck, L. E. "The Poor among the Saints in the New Testament." *Zeitschrift für die neutestamentliche Wissenschaft und die Kunde der älteren Kirche* 56 (1965): 100–129.

Keddie, Anthony G. "Paul's Freedom and Moses' Veil: Moral Freedom and the Mosaic Law in 2 Corinthians 3.1–4.6 in Light of Philo." *Journal for the Study of the New Testament* 37, no. 3 (Fall 2015): 267–89.

Kim, Seyoon. "2 Corinthians 5:11–21 and the Origin of Paul's Concept of Reconciliation." *Novum Testamentum* 39 (1997): 360–84.

Kimball, Spencer W. "It Becometh Every Man." *Ensign* 7, no. 10 (October 1977): 5.

———. In *One Hundred Thirty-Fourth Semi-annual Conference of The Church of Jesus Christ of Latter-day Saints,* 24–29. Salt Lake City: The Church of Jesus Christ of Latter-day Saints, 1964.

Kittel, Gerhard, ed. *Theological Dictionary of the New Testament.* Trans. Gerhard Friedrich and Geoffrey William Bromiley. 10 vols. Grand Rapids, Mich.: Wm. B. Eerdmans, 1976. Cited as *TDNT.*

Klassen, William. "The Sacred Kiss in the New Testament: An Example of Social Boundary Life." *New Testament Studies* 39 (1993): 130–33.

Klauck, Hans-Josef. *Ancient Letters and the New Testament: A Guide to Context and Exegesis.* Trans. Daniel P. Bailey. Waco, Texas: Baylor University Press, 2006.

Knox, Wilfred L. *Some Hellenistic Elements in Primitive Christianity.* London: Oxford University Press, 1944.

Köhler, L., W. Baumgartner, and J. J. Stamm. *The Hebrew and Aramaic Lexicon of the Old Testament.* Trans. and ed. M. E. J. Richardson. 5 vols. Leiden: E. J. Brill, 1994–2000. Cited as *HAL.*

Kwon, Yon-Gyong. "Ἀρραβών as Pledge in Second Corinthians." *New Testament Studies* 54, no. 4 (2008): 525–41.

Lambrecht, Jan. "Paul's Boasting about the Corinthians: A Study of 2 Corinthians 8:24–9:5." *Novum Testamentum* 40 (1998): 352–68.

Lampe, G. W. H. "Church Discipline and the Interpretation of the Epistles to the Corinthians." In *Christian History and Interpretation: Studies Presented to John Knox,* ed. W. R. Farmer, C. F. D. Moule, and R. R. Niebuhr, 337–61. Cambridge: Cambridge University Press, 1967.

———. *The Seal of the Spirit: A Study in the Doctrine of Baptism and Confirmation in the New Testament and the Fathers.* 2nd ed. London: SPCK, 1976.

Landsborough, D. "St Paul and Temporal Lobe Epilepsy." *Journal of Neurology, Neurosurgery, and Psychiatry* 50 (1987): 659–64.

Lane, Jennifer C. "Jews and Greeks: The Broader Context for the Writings of the New Testament." In *How the New Testament Came to Be,* ed. Kent P. Jackson and Frank F. Judd Jr., 62–77. *35th Annual Brigham Young University Sidney B. Sperry Symposium.* Provo, Utah: Religious Studies Center, Brigham Young University; Salt Lake City: Deseret Book, 2006.

Lane, Jennifer C., and Keith H. Lane. "God Incarnate: The Word Made Flesh." In *Thou Art the Christ, the Son of the Living God: The Person and Work of Jesus in the New Testament,* ed. Eric D. Huntsman, Lincoln H. Blumell, and Tyler J. Griffin, 136–52. 47th Annual Brigham Young University Sidney Sperry Symposium. Provo, Utah: Religious Studies Center, Brigham Young University; Salt Lake City: Deseret Book, 2018.

Largey, Dennis L, ed. *Book of Mormon Reference Companion.* Salt Lake City: Deseret Book, 2003.

Leary, Timothy J. "'A Thorn in the Flesh'—2 Corinthians 12: 7." *Journal of Theological Studies,* n.s., 43, no. 2 (October 1992): 520–22.

Lee, Harold B. In *One Hundred Twentieth Semi-annual Conference of The Church of Jesus Christ of Latter-day Saints,* 54–59. Salt Lake City: The Church of Jesus Christ of Latter-day Saints, 1949.

———. "The Place of the Living Prophet, Seer, and Revelator." Address to seminary and Institutes of Religion Faculty, BYU, July 8, 1968, L. Tom Perry Special Collections, Harold B. Lee Library, Brigham Young University, Provo, Utah.

Liddell, Henry G., and Robert Scott, comp. *Greek English Lexicon.* Rev. and aug. Henry Stuart Jones. Oxford: Clarendon Press, 1968. Cited as LSJ.

Lim, Kar Yong. "Generosity from Pauline Perspective: Insights from Paul's Letters to the Corinthians." *Evangelical Review of Theology* 37, no. 1 (2013): 20–33.

Lincoln, Andrew T. "'Paul the Visionary': The Setting and Significance of the Rapture to Paradise in II Corinthians XII. 1–10." *New Testament Studies* 25, no. 2 (1979): 204–20.

Lindgård, Fredrik. *Paul's Line of Thought in 2 Corinthians 4:16–5:10.* Tübingen, Ger.: Mohr Siebeck, 2005.

Louw, Johannes P., and Eugene A. Nida. *Greek-English Lexicon of the New Testament Based on Semantic Domains.* 2nd ed. 2 vols. New York: United Bible Societies, 1989.

Ludlow, Daniel H., ed. *Encyclopedia of Mormonism.* 4 vols. New York: Macmillan, 1992. Cited as *EM.*

MacMullen, Ramsay. *Roman Social Relations, 50 BC to AD 284.* New Haven, Conn.: Yale University Press, 1974.

Magness, Lee. "The Significance of Paul's Addition of 'and Daughters' in 2 Corinthians 6:18." *Priscilla Papers* 29, no. 2 (2015): 3–5.

Marshall, Peter. *Enmity in Corinth: Social Conventions in Paul's Relations with the Corinthians.* Tübingen, Ger.: J. C. B. Mohr (Paul Siebeck), 1987.

———. "Invective: Paul's Enemies in Corinth." In *Perspectives on Language and Text,* ed. Edger W. Conrad and Edward G. Newing, 359–73. Winona Lake, Ind.: Eisenbrauns, 1987.

——— "A Metaphor of Social Shame: θριαμβεύειν in 2 Cor. 2:14." *Novum Testamentum* 25, no. 4 (1983): 302–17.

Martin, Ralph P. "The Opponents of Paul in 2 Corinthians: An Old Issue Revisited." In *Traditions and Interpretations in the New Testament: Essays in Honor of E. Earle Ellis for His 60th Birthday,* ed. Gerald F. Hawthorne and Otto Betz, 279–89. Grand Rapids, Mich.: Wm. B. Eerdmans Publishers, 1987.

———. *Reconciliation: A Study of Paul's Theology.* 2nd ed. Grand Rapids, Mich.: Academie Books, 1989. Reprint, Eugene Ore.: Wipf and Stock, 1997.

———. *2 Corinthians.* 2nd ed. Vol. 40 of Word Biblical Commentary. Grand Rapids, Mich.: Zondervan, 2014.

Matera, Frank J. *II Corinthians: A Commentary.* Louisville: Westminster John Knox Press, 2003.

Matthews, Robert J. *A Bible! A Bible!* Salt Lake City: Bookcraft, 1990.

———. *"A Plainer Translation": Joseph Smith's Translation of the Bible—a History and Commentary.* Provo, Utah: Brigham Young University Press, 1975.

Maxwell, Neal A. "Answer Me." *Ensign* 18, no. 11 (November 1988): 31–33.

———. "Brightness of Hope." *Ensign* 24, no. 11 (November 1994): 34–36.

McCant, Jerry W. "Paul's Thorn of Rejected Apostleship." *New Testament Studies* 34, no. 4 (1988): 550–72.

McConkie, Bruce R. *Doctrinal New Testament Commentary.* 3 vols. Salt Lake City: Bookcraft, 1973. Cited as *DNTC.*

———. *The Millennial Messiah.* Salt Lake City: Deseret Book, 1982.

———. In *One Hundred Thirty-Fourth Semi-annual Conference of The Church of Jesus Christ of Latter-day Saints,* 36–38. Salt Lake City: The Church of Jesus Christ of Latter-day Saints, 1964.

Mealand, David L. "As Having Nothing and yet Possessing Everything: 2 Kor 6:10c." *Zeitschrift für de newtestamentliche Wissenshaft und de Kunde de ältern Kirche* 67 (1976): 277–79.

Meeks, Wayne A. *The First Urban Christians: The Social World of the Apostle Paul.* 2nd ed. New Haven, Conn.: Yale University Press, 2003.

Merriam-Webster's Collegiate Dictionary. Springfield, Mass.: Merriam-Webster, 2003.

Merriam-Webster's Dictionary of Synonyms. Springfield, Mass.: Merriam-Webster, 1984.

Metzger, Bruce M. *A Textual Commentary on the Greek New Testament, Second Edition: A Companion Volume to the United Bible Societies' Greek New Testament (Fourth Revised Edition).* Stuttgart, Ger.: Deutsche Bibelgesellschaft/United Bible Societies, 1994.

Millet, Robert L. *Selected Writings of Robert L. Millet.* Salt Lake City: Deseret Book, 2000.

———. *What Happened to the Cross?: Distinctive LDS Teachings.* Salt Lake City: Deseret Book, 2007.

Millis, Benjamin W. "The Social and Ethnic Origins of the Colonists in Early Roman Corinth." In *Corinth in Context: Comparative Studies on Religion and Society,* ed. Steven J. Friesen, Daniel N. Schowalter, and James C. Walters, 13–35. Leiden: Brill, 2010.

Mitchell, Margaret M. "New Testament Envoys in the Context of Greco-Roman Diplomatic and Epistolary Conventions: An Example of Timothy and Titus." *Journal of Biblical Literature* 111, no. 4 (1992): 641–62.

Moffitt, David M. "The Interpretation of Scripture in the Epistle to the Hebrews," *Reading the Epistle to the Hebrews: A Resource for Students,* ed. Eric F. Mason and Patrick B. McCruden, 77–98. Atlanta: Society of Biblical Literature, 2011.

Monson, Thomas S. "The Spirit Giveth Life." *Ensign* 15, no. 5 (May 1985): 68.

Montanari, Franco. *The Brill Dictionary of Ancient Greek.* Ed. Madeleine Goh and Chad Schroeder. Leiden: Brill, 2015. Cited as DAG.

Moo, Douglas J. *We Still Don't Get It: Evangelicals and Biblical Translation Fifty Years after James Barr.* Grand Rapids, Mich.: Zondervan, 2014.

Mott, Stephen Charles. "The Power of Giving and Receiving: Reciprocity in Hellenistic Benevolence." In *Current Issues in Biblical and Patristic Interpretation: Studies in Honor of Merrill C. Tenney Presented by His Former Students,* ed. Gerald F. Hawthorne, 60–72. Grand Rapids, Mich.: William B. Eerdmans, 1975.

Moule, C. F. D. *An Idiom Book of New Testament Greek.* 2nd ed. London: Cambridge University Press, 1960.

———. *The Meaning of Hope: A Biblical Exposition with Concordance.* Philadelphia: Fortress Press, 1963.

Moulton, James H., and George Milligan. *The Vocabulary of the Greek Testament: Illustrations from the Papyri and Other Non-literary Sources.* 1930. Reprint, Grand Rapids, Mich.: William B. Eerdmans, 1985.

Moxnes, Halvor. "Honor, Shame, and the Outside World in Paul's Letter to the Romans." In *The Social World of Formative Christianity and Judaism: Essays in Tribute to Howard Clarke Kee,* ed. Jacob Neusner, Ernest S. Frerichs, Peder Borgan, and Richard Horsley, 207–18. Philadelphia: Fortress Press, 1988.

Mullins, Terence Y. "Benediction as a New Testament Form." *Andrews University Seminary Studies* 15 (1977): 59–64.

———. "Paul's Thorn in the Flesh." *Journal of Biblical Literature* 76, no. 4 (1957): 299–303.

Muraoka, Takamitsu. "The Use of ΩΣ in the Greek Bible." *Novum Testamentum* 7 (1964): 51–72.

Murphy, Frederick J. *Early Judaism: The Exile to the Time of Jesus.* Peabody, Mass.: Hendrickson Publishers, 2002.

Murphy-O'Connor, Jerome. "Being at Home in the Body We Are in Exile from the Lord (2 Cor. 5:6b)." *Revue Biblique* 93, no. 2 (1986): 214–21.

———. *Paul on Preaching.* New York: Sheed and Ward, 1963.

———. "Truth: Paul and Qumran." In *Paul and Qumran: Studies in New Testament Exegesis,* ed. Jerome Murphy-O'Connor, 179–230. Chicago: Priory Press, 1968.

Murray, Michele. *Playing a Jewish Game: Gentile Christian Judaizing in the First and Second Centuries CE.* Waterloo, Can.: Wilfrid Laurier University Press, 2004.

Mutie, Jeremiah. *Death in Second-Century Christian Thought: The Meaning of Death in Earliest Christianity.* Eugene, Oreg.: Pickwick, 2015.

Nathan, Emmanuel, and Thomas A. Vollmer. "Paul's Reference to the Macedonians in 2 Cor 8:1–5: A Test-case to Introduce Reputation Theory." *Australian Biblical Review* 63 (2015): 42–51.

Nelson, Russell M. "Living by Scriptural Guidance." *Ensign* 30, no. 11 (November 2000): 18.

Nibley, Hugh. *The Ancient State: The Rulers and the Ruled.* Ed. Donald W. Parry and Stephen D. Ricks. Vol. 10 of The Collected Works of Hugh Nibley. Salt Lake City: Deseret Book; Provo, Utah: Foundation for Ancient Research and Mormon Studies, 1991.

Nickle, Keith F. *The Collection: A Study in Paul's Strategy.* London: SCM Press, 1966.

Nicolson, Adam. *God's Secretaries: The Making of the King James Bible.* New York: HarperCollins, 2003.

Nisbet, Patricia. "The Thorn in the Flesh." *Expository Times* 80 (1969): 126.

Novick, Tzvi, "Peddling Scents: Merchandise and Meaning in 2 Corinthians 2:14–17." *Journal of Biblical Studies* 130 (2011): 543–49.

Oaks, Dallin H. "Apostasy and Restoration." *Ensign* 25, no. 5 (May 1995): 86.

———. "Weightier Matters." *Ensign* 31, no. 1 (January 2001): 13.

Ogden, D. Kelly. *Where Jesus Walked: The Land and Culture of New Testament Times.* Salt Lake City: Deseret Book, 1991.

Ogden, D. Kelly, and Andrew C. Skinner. *Verse by Verse, Acts through Revelation.* Salt Lake City: Deseret Book, 1998.

Ogereau, Julien M. "The Jerusalem Collection as Κοινωνία: Paul's Global Politics of Socio-economic Equality and Solidarity." *New Testament Studies* 58, no. 3 (2012): 360–78.

O'Mahony, Kieran J. *Pauline Persuasion: A Sounding of 2 Corinthians 8–9.* Vol. 199 of Journal for the Study of the New Testament Supplement Series. Sheffield, Eng.: Sheffield Academic Press, 2000.

Oropeza, B. J. *Exploring Second Corinthians: Death and Life, Hardship and Rivalry.* Atlanta: SBL Press, 2016.

Osborne, Robert E. "St. Paul's Silent Years." *Journal of Biblical Literature* 84, no. 1 (1965): 59–65.

Park, David M. "Paul's ΣΚΟΛΟΨ ΤΗ ΣΑΡΚΙ: Thorne or Stake? (2 Cor. XXI 7)." *Novum Testamentum* 22, no. 2 (1980): 179–83.

Parry, Jay, and Donald Parry. *Understanding the Book of Revelation.* Salt Lake City: Deseret Book, 1998.

Perrimann, A. C. "Paul and the Parousia: 1 Corinthians 15:50–57 and 2 Corinthians 5:1–5." *New Testament Studies* 35, no. 4 (October 1989): 512–21.

Peterman, G. W. *Paul's Gift from Philippi: Conventions of Gift Exchange and Christian Giving.* Cambridge: Cambridge University Press, 1997.

Petersen, Mark E. "Signs of the True Church." *Ensign* 9, no. 5 (May 1979): 22.

Peterson, Brian K. "Conquest, Control, and the Cross: Paul's Self-Portrayal in 2 Corinthians 10–13." *Interpretation: A Journal of Bible and Theology* 52, no. 3 (1998): 258–70.

———. *Eloquence and the Proclamation of the Gospel in Corinth.* Vol. 163 of Society of Biblical Literature Dissertation Series. Atlanta: Scholars Press, 1998.

Pingree, Anne C. "Charity: One Family, One Home at a Time." *Ensign* 32, no. 11 (November 2002): 108–10.

Price, R. M. "Punished in Paradise (An Exegetical Theory on II Corinthians 12:1–10)." *Journal of the Study of the New Testament* 2, no. 7 (1980): 33–40.

Rensberger, David. "2 Corinthians 6:14–7:1—a Fresh Examination," *Studia Biblica et Theologica* 8 (1978): 25–49.

Richard, Earl J. "Polemics, Old Testament, and Theology: A Study of II Cor., III, 1–IV. 6." *Revue Biblique* 88, no. 3 (July 1981): 340–67.

Richards, LeGrand. In *One Hundred Sixteenth Annual Conference of The Church of Jesus Christ of Latter-day Saints,* 81–85. Salt Lake City: The Church of Jesus Christ of Latter-day Saints, 1946.

Richards, Steven L. In *One Hundred Twenty-Fourth Annual Conference of The Church of Jesus Christ of Latter-day Saints,* 10–13. Salt Lake City: The Church of Jesus Christ of Latter-day Saints, 1954.

Riesner, Rainer. *Paul's Early Period: Chronology, Mission Strategy, Theology.* Trans. Doug Stott. Grand Rapids, Mich.: Wm. B. Eerdmans, 1988.

Robinson, Henry S. *Corinth: A Brief History of the City and a Guide to the Excavations.* Athens: The American School of Classical Studies in Athens, 1972.

Robinson, Stephen E., and H. Dean Garrett. *A Commentary on the Doctrine and Covenants.* 4 vols. Salt Lake City: Deseret Book, 2000–2005.

Rollins, Wayne G. "Greco-Roman Slave Terminology and Pauline Metaphors." In *Society of Biblical Literature Seminar Papers*, ed. Kent Harold Richards, 100–110. Atlanta: Scholars Press, 1987.

Sabin, Gary B. "Stand Up Inside and Be All In." *Ensign* 47, no. 5 (May 2017): 52–55.

Sanders, E. P. *Paul and Palestinian Judaism: A Comparison of Patters of Religion.* London: SCM, 1977. Reprint, 40th Anniversary Edition. Minneapolis: Fortress Press, 2017.

Savage, Timothy B. *Power through Weakness: Paul's Understanding of the Christian Ministry in 2 Corinthians.* Vol. 86 of Society for New Testament Studies Monograph Series. Cambridge: Cambridge University Press, 1996.

Schaelling, Philip. "How Paul Used the Old Testament as a Witness for Christ." In *The Third Annual Church Educational System Symposium*, 260–66. Salt Lake City: The Church of Jesus Christ of Latter-day Saints, 1979.

Schmeller, Thomas. "No Bridge over Troubled Water?: The Gap between 2 Corinthians 1–9 and 10–13 Revisited." *Journal for the Study of the New Testament* 36 (2013): 73–84.

Schmidt, Brent J. *Relational Faith: The Transformation and Restoration of* Pistis *as Knowledge, Trust, Confidence, and Covenantal Faithfulness.* Provo, Utah: BYU Studies, 2022.

———. *Relational Grace: The Reciprocal and Binding Covenant of* Charis. Provo, Utah: BYU Studies, 2015.

Schmithals, Walter. *Gnosticism in Corinth.* Nashville: Abingdon Press, 1971.

Schnabel, Eckhard J. *Early Christian Mission,* vol. 2, *Paul and the Early Church.* Downers Grove, Ill.: InterVarsity Press; Leicester, Eng.: Apollos, 2004.

Schütz, John Howard. *Paul and the Anatomy of Apostolic Authority.* Cambridge: Cambridge University Press, 1975. Reprint, Louisville: Westminster John Knox Press, 2007.

Scott, James M. *2 Corinthians.* Peabody, Mass.: Hendrickson Publishers, 1998.

———. "The Triumph of God in 2 Corinthians 2:14: Additional Evidence of Merkabah Mysticism in Paul." *New Testament Studies* 42 (1996): 260–81.

Scott, Richard G. "To Be Healed." *Ensign* 24, no. 5 (May 1994): 7–9.

Scrivener, Frederick H. A., and Edward Miller. *A Plain Introduction of the New Testament for Use of Biblical Students.* Cambridge, Eng.: George Bell and Sons, 1894.

Seifrid, Mark A. *The Second Letter to the Corinthians.* Grand Rapids, Mich.: William B. Eerdmans, 2014.

Serrano, Andrés García. "The Pauline Sense of the Expression 'Now the Lord Is the Spirit' (2 Cor. 3:17a)." *Expository Times* 127, no. 10 (2016): 479–87.

Shi, Wenhua. *Paul's Message of the Cross as Body Language.* Tübingen, Ger.: Mohr Siebeck, 2008.

Silva, Moisés. *New International Dictionary of New Testament Theology and Exegesis.* 5 vols. Grand Rapids, Mich.: Zondervan: 2014. Cited as *NID.*

Smith, Joseph. "Baptism for the Dead," 759. *Times and Seasons,* 15 April 1842.

———. "To the Editor of the Times & Seasons." *Times and Seasons* 4 (May 15, 1843): 194.

Smith, Joseph F. In *One Hundred Fifteenth Semi-annual Conference of The Church of Jesus Christ of Latter-day Saints,* 109–13. Salt Lake City: The Church of Jesus Christ of Latter-day Saints, 1944.

Smith, Joseph Fielding. *Answers to Gospel Questions.* Vol. 1. Salt Lake City: Deseret Book, 1957.

———. *Doctrines of Salvation: Sermons and Writings of Joseph Fielding Smith,* ed. Bruce R. McConkie, 3 vols. in one. 1954–56. Reprint, Salt Lake City: Bookcraft, 1999.

Smith, Neil Gregor. "The Thorne That Stayed: An Exposition of II Corinthians 12:7–9." *Interpretation: A Journal of Bible and Theology* 13, no. 4 (1959): 409–16.

Smyth, Herbert Weir. *Greek Grammar.* Revised by Gordon M. Messing. Cambridge, Mass.: Harvard University Press, 1963.

Sperry, Sidney B. *Paul's Life and Letters.* Salt Lake City: Bookcraft, 1955.

Spicq, Ceslaus. *Agape in the New Testament.* 3 vols. Eugene, Ore.: Wipf and Stock, 2006.

———. *Theological Lexicon of the New Testament.* Trans. James D. Ernest. 3 vols. Peabody, Md.: Hendrickson, 1994.

Spittler, Russell P. "The Limits of Ecstasy: An Exegesis of 2 Corinthians 12:1–10." In *Current Issues of Biblical and Patristic Interpretation: Studies in*

Honor of Merrill C. Tenney Presented by His Former Students, ed. Gerald F. Hawthorne, 259–66. Grand Rapids, Mich.: William B. Eerdmans, 1975.

Stansbury, Harry. "Corinthian Honor, Corinthian Conflict: A Social History of Early Roman Corinth and Its Pauline Community." PhD diss., University of California, Irvine, 1990.

Stapley, Delbert L. "Easter Thoughts." *Ensign* 6, no. 5 (May 1976): 76.

Starling, David. "Meditations on a Slippery Citation: Paul's Use of Psalm 112:9 in 2 Corinthians 9:9." *Journal of Theological Interpretation* 6, no. 2 (2012): 241–55.

———. "'We Do Not Want You to Be Unaware . . .': Disclosure, Concealment and Suffering in 2 Cor 1–7." *New Testament Studies* 60, no. 2 (2014): 266–79.

Stegman, Thomas D. "Reading ἔγραψα in 2 Corinthians 2:9 as an Epistolary Aorist." *Novum Testamentum* 54, no. 1 (2012): 50–67.

Sumney, Jerry L. *Identifying Paul's Opponents: The Question of Method in 2 Corinthians.* Sheffield, Eng.: JSOT Press, 1990.

———. "Paul's 'Weakness': An Integral Part of His Conception of Apostleship," *Journal of New Testament Studies* 52 (1993): 71–91.

Talbert, Charles H. "Money Management in Early Mediterranean Christianity: 2 Corinthians 8–9." *Review and Expositor* 86, no. 3 (1989): 359–70.

Talmage, James E. *The Vitality of Mormonism.* Salt Lake City: Deseret Book, 1919.

Tasker, R. V. G. *The Second Epistle of Paul to the Corinthians: An Introduction and Commentary.* Grand Rapids, Mich.: Wm. B. Eerdmans, 1958.

Tenney, Merril C., and Steven Barabas, eds. *The Zondervan Pictorial Encyclopedia of the Bible.* 5 vols. Grand Rapids, Mich.: Zondervan, 1975–76.

Thayer, Joseph. *Thayer's Greek-English Lexicon of the New Testament.* Rev. ed. Peabody, Mass.: Hendrickson Publishers, 1995.

Thiselton, Anthony C. *First Epistle to the Corinthians: A Commentary on the Greek Text.* Grand Rapids, Mich.: Wm. B. Eerdmans; Carlisle, U.K.: Paternoster, 2000.

Thomas, John Christopher. "'An Angel from Satan': Paul's Thorn in the Flesh (2 Corinthians 12.7–10)." *Journal of Pentecostal Theology* 9 (October 1996): 39–52.

Thrall, Margaret E. *A Critical and Exegetical Commentary on the Second Epistle to the Corinthians.* 2 vols. London: T&T Clark, 1994–2000.

———. *Greek Particles in the New Testament Linguistic and Exegetical Studies.* Leiden: Brill, 1962.

———. "Salvation Proclaimed, V. 2 Corinthians 5:18–21: Reconciliation with God." *Expository Times* 93 (1981–82): 227–32.

———. "Super-Apostles, Servants of Christ, and Servants of Satan." *Journal for the Study of the New Testament* 2, no. 6 (1980): 42–57.

Tomson, Peter J. *Paul and the Jewish Law: Halakha in the Letters of the Apostle to the Gentiles.* Assen/Maastricht, Neth: Van Gorcum; Minneapolis: Fortress Press, 1990.

Turner, Nigel. *Grammatical Insights into the New Testament.* Edinburgh: T&T Clark, 1965.

———. *Syntax.* Vol. 3 of *A Grammar of New Testament Greek.* Ed. James Hope Moulton. Edinburgh: T. & T. Clark, 1963.

Uchtdorf, Dieter F. "Lord, Is It I?" *Ensign* 44, no. 11 (November 2014): 56–59.

———. "You Can Do It Now!" *Ensign* 42, no. 10 (October 2013): 55–57.

Vander Broek, Lyle D. *Breaking Barriers: The Possibilities of Christian Community in a Lonely World.* Grand Rapids, Mich.: Brazos, 2002.

van Vliet, Hendrick. *No Single Testimony: A Study on the Adoption of the Law of Deut. 19:15 Par. into the New Testament.* Utrecht, Neth.: Kemink en Zoon, 1958.

Versnel, H. S. *Triamphus: An Inquiry into the Origin, Development, and Meaning of the Roman Triumph.* Leiden: Brill, 1970.

Walker, William O., Jr. "Apollos and Timothy as the Unnamed 'Brothers' in 2 Corinthians 8:18–24." *Catholic Biblical Quarterly* 73, no. 2 (2011): 318–38.

Wallace, Daniel B. *Greek Grammar beyond the Basics: An Exegetical Syntax of the New Testament.* Grand Rapids, Mich.: Zondervan, 1996.

Wallace, James Buchanan. *Snatched into Paradise (2 Cor. 12:1–10): Paul's Heavenly Journey in the Context of Early Christian Experience.* Berlin: De Gruyter, 2011.

Wansink, Craig S. *Chained in Christ: The Experience and Rhetoric of Paul's Imprisonments.* Sheffield, Eng.: Sheffield Academic Press, 1996.

Ward, R. F. "Pauline Voice and Presence as Strategic Communication." *Semeia* 65 (1994): 102–4.

Watson, Deborah Elaine. "Paul's Collection in Light of the Motivations and Mechanisms for Aid to the Poor in the First-Century World." PhD diss., University of Durham, 2006.

Wayment, Thomas A. *From Persecutor to Apostle: A Biography of Paul.* Salt Lake City: Deseret Book, 2006.

Welborn, Laurence L. "'By the Mouth of Two or Three Witnesses': Paul's Invocation of a Deuteronomic Statute." *Novum Testamentum* 52 (2010): 207–20.

———. "Paul and Pain: Paul's Emotional Therapy in 2 Corinthians 1.1–2.13; 7.5–16 in the Context of Ancient Psychagogic Literature." *New Testament Studies* 57, no. 4 (2011): 547–70.

———. "'That There May Be Equality': The Contexts and Consequences of a Pauline Ideal." *New Testament Studies* 59, no. 1 (2013): 73–90.

Welch, John W. "Modern Revelation: A Guide to Research about Apostasy," in *Early Christians in Disarray: Contemporary LDS Perspectives on the Apostasy,* ed. Noel R. Reynolds. Provo, Utah: Brigham Young University Press, 2005.

———. "Sherem's Accusation Against Jacob." *FARMS Update* 74 (January 1991).

Wenham, David. "2 Corinthians 1:17, 18: Echo of the Dominical Legion." *Novum Testamentum* 28, no. 3 (1986), 271–79.

Wenkel, David H. "*Gezerah Shawah* as Analogy in Hebrews." *Biblical Theological Bulletin: Journal of Biblical Culture* 37, no. 2 (May 2007): 62–68.

Winter, Bruce W. *After Paul Left Corinth: The Influence of Secular Ethics and Social Change.* 2nd ed. Grand Rapids, Mich.: Wm. B. Eerdmans, 2001.

———. "Are Philo and Paul among the Sophists?: A Hellenistic Jewish and a Christian Response to a First Century Movement." PhD diss., MacQuarrie University, 1988.

———. *Philo and Paul among the Sophists: Alexandrian and Corinthians Responses to a Julio-Claudian Movement.* 2nd ed. Grand Rapids, Mich.: William B. Eerdmans, 2002.

Wirthlin, Joseph B. "Valued Companions." *Ensign* 27, no. 11 (November 1997): 34.

Witherington, Ben, III. *Conflict and Community in Corinth: A Socio-rhetorical Commentary on 1 and 2 Corinthians.* Grand Rapids, Mich.: William B. Eerdmans; Carlisle, U.K.: Paternoster Press, 1995.

———. *Jesus, Paul, and the End of the World.* Downers Grove, Ill.: InterVarsity Press, 1992.

Wood, John E. "Death at Work in Paul." *Evangelical Quarterly* 54, no. 3 (July–September 1982): 151–56.

Wright, N. T. "Israel's Scriptures in Paul's Narrative Theology." *Theology* 115, no. 5 (2012): 32–29.

———. *The Resurrection of the Son of God.* Philadelphia: Fortress Press, 2003.

Wu, J. L. "Liturgical Elements." In *Dictionary of Paul and His Letters,* ed. Gerald F. Hawthorne, Ralph P. Martin, and Daniel G. Reid, 557–59. Downers Grove, Ill.: InterVarsity Press, 1993.

Yingling, Erik Odin. "Worship and Ritual Practices in the New Testament." In *New Testament History, Culture, and Society: A Background to the Texts of the New Testament,* ed. Lincoln H. Blumell, 586–602. Provo, Utah: Religious Studies Center, Brigham Young University; Salt Lake City: Deseret Book, 2019.

Yoon, David I. "Ancient Letters of Recommendation and 2 Corinthians 3.1–3: A Literary Analysis." *Journal of Greco-Roman Christianity and Judaism* 12 (2016): 45–72.

Scripture Index

This index is ordered by book under Old Testament, New Testament, Book of Mormon, Other Ancient Sources, Pearl of Great Price, and Doctrine and Covenants.

Old Testament

2 Corinthians

Numbers in ***bold italics*** indicate the main discussion of the scriptural passage.

Galatians

Ephesians

Subject Index

C

E

F

M

T